P9-ARP-753

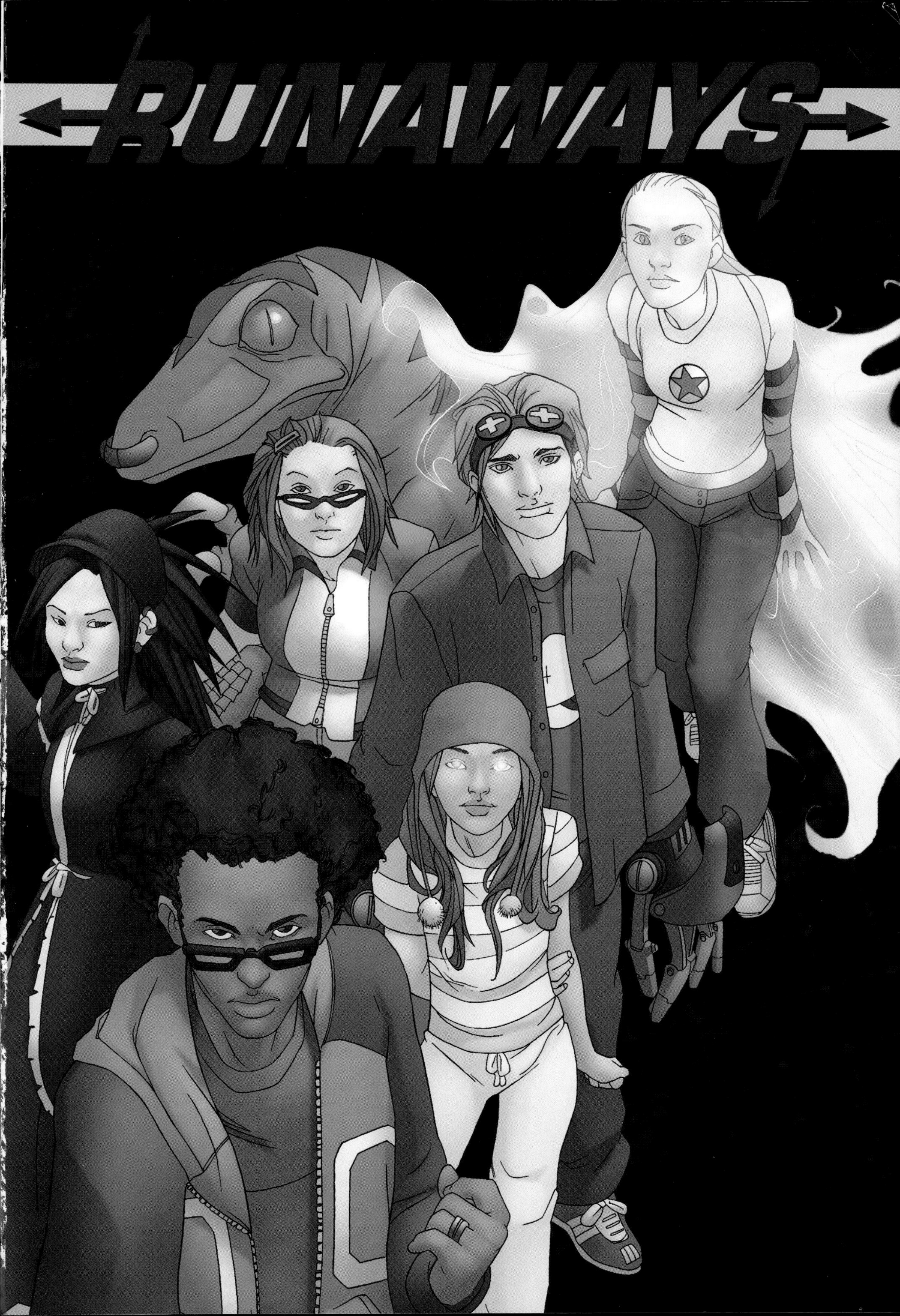
RUNAWAYS

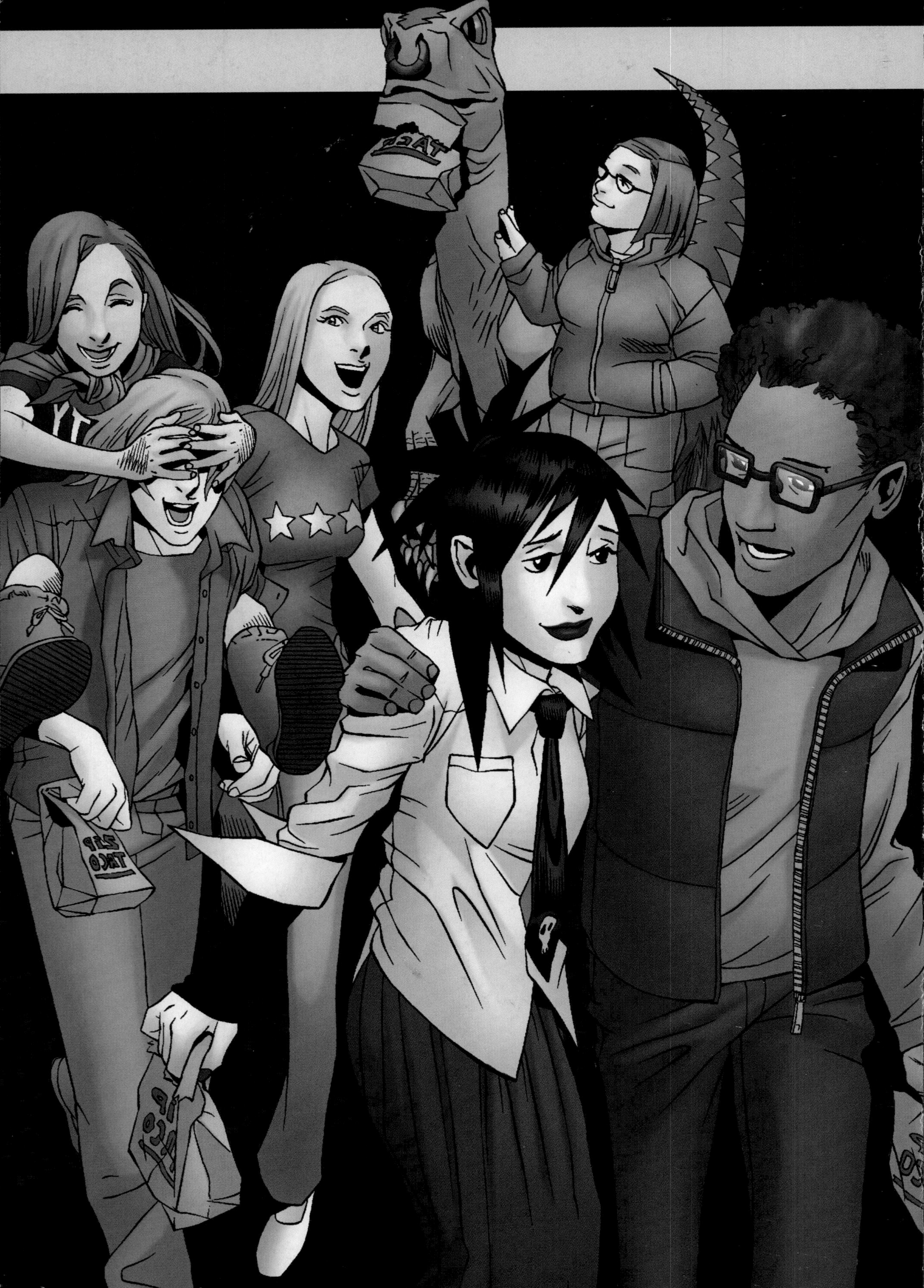
ZIP TACO

RUNAWAYS

Writer: **Brian K. Vaughan**

Pencils: **Adrian Alphona with Takeshi Miyazawa (Issues #11 & 12)**

Inks: **Craig Yeung and David Newbold**

Colors: **Christina Strain and Brian Reber**

Covers: **Jo Chen with Joshua Middleton (Issues #11 & 12)**

Book Cover: **Adrian Alphona**

Letters: **Virtual Calligraphy's Randy Gentile and Chris Eliopoulos with Paul Tutrone**

Assistant Editors: **MacKenzie Cadenhead with Stephanie Moore**

Editor: **C.B. Cebulski**

Runaways created by **Brian K. Vaughan & Adrian Alphona**

Collection Editor: **Jennifer Grünwald**

Senior Editor, Special Projects: **Jeff Youngquist**

Director of Sales: **David Gabriel**

Book Designer: **Meghan Kerns**

Creative Director: **Tom Marvelli**

Editor in Chief: **Joe Quesada**

Publisher: **Dan Buckley**

First of all, I don't hate my parents.

Yes, I did name Alex Wilder's evil mom and dad after my folks, but I swear that Catherine and Geoffrey Vaughan are delightful human beings who never beat me, threw away my comic collection and/or killed young girls in sacrificial rituals.

(My kid sister, Molly Hayes Vaughan, however, is just as adorable and powerful as her namesake.)

Still, I always thought that there was something slightly suspicious about the way adult comic writers had protagonists like Spider-Man and Batman revere their guardians. I mean, if Uncle Ben or Dr. and Mrs. Wayne had lived to see their children turn seventeen, Peter and Bruce probably would have ended up hating them, the way so many kids grow apart from their parents around that age. To me, it felt like grown-up comic creators were subtly suggesting to their young readers that true heroes always respect their elders and blindly follow their teachings.

(On the other hand, maybe the real message was that the only good parent is a dead one?)

Anyway, despite my severe lack of hair, I'm still a fairly young dude who thinks that it's always important to question authority and challenge the status quo established by the previous generation.

Thankfully, the decidedly non-evil adults at Marvel (including the always supportive Joe Quesada, Dan Buckley and Bill Jemas) were either too cool or too busy to stop me from turning my subversive agenda into an all-ages book filled with decoder rings, secret hideouts and everything I loved about comics as a kid.

If I'm the Runaways' mommy dearest, artist Adrian Alphona is definitely our kids' big daddy. Back when he was a relative newcomer to the medium, Adrian sent in a few sketches that immediately brought my two-dimensional character descriptions to life. Along with being a great storyteller, Adrian is also the undisputed king of fashion in comics. I defy you to find another "teen book" on the market where the teenagers look as true as they do in Adrian's panels. Even when he's drawing a telepathic dinosaur from the 87th century (whose facial expressions Adrian bases on his pet dog), my partner-in-crime always makes the fantastic feel absolutely real.

Obviously, Adrian and I couldn't have brought our baby into the world without a lot of help from countless collaborators, including powerhouse penciler Takeshi Miyazawa, incredible inkers David Newbold and Craig Yeung, courageous colorists Brian Reber and UDON's Christina Strain, laudable letterers like Virtual Calligraphy's Randy Gentile and David Sharpe, and especially ever-excellent editors C.B. Cebulski and MacKenzie Cadenhead. And we all owe a tremendous debt of gratitude to Stan "The Man" Lee, whose work at the House of Ideas helped inspire not only our book's classical high concept, but also my own off-putting obsession with alliteration.

In addition, I have to thank every kid who wasn't mean to me from kindergarten through senior year at NYU, since each of the Runaways is a composite of so many of you, my friends. And maximum respect to my brilliant wife Ruth McKee, who told me that the book should simply be called "Runaways" way back when I stupidly thought it should have a title like "SuperKrunk6" to appeal to the hipster kids of today.

(Sorry, I may not be an adult yet, but I'm not cool either.)

Finally, I'd be remiss not to recognize the amazing work of one of the best artists in the medium, Ms. Jo Chen, who painted almost every cover of our initial run (with the exception of the Cloak and

Dagger two-parter, which was handled by the equally sensational Joshua Middleton). I have it on good authority that it was the come-hither look Jo gave Nico on her unforgettable first cover that inspired Buffy the Vampire creator/my personal hero/dirty old man Joss Whedon to pick up our book, and he's been one of our most loyal backers ever since.

Speaking of our devoted readership, this series probably would have been cancelled three issues in if it weren't for the tireless support of people like you. I know I sound like a bad PBS pledge drive, but really, new books starring all-new characters are just not supposed to survive in today's crowded marketplace. The conventional wisdom is that comic fans only want to read about old characters, but Honorary Runaways like Mindy Owens (dedicated webmistress of www.runawaysthecomic.com) fought long and hard to help get our book into the hands of a whole new audience.

Not too long ago, we were all pretty sure that the eighteen issues you hold in your hands were going to be the last we'd ever see of the Runaways, but because of you, our heroes are back, and I look forward to writing their ongoing adventures until the day I die... or at least until the day I finally succumb to adulthood, at which point, I hope that one of you young writers reading this now will rightfully take my place.

For now, thank you all from the bottom of my Hostel for loving these characters as much as I do. Enjoy this special collection, and remember that under the bed is the first place evil parents usually check for contraband, so be sure to hide your copy in that special spot in your neighbor's backyard!

Keep running,
BKV

A Secret Location
2005

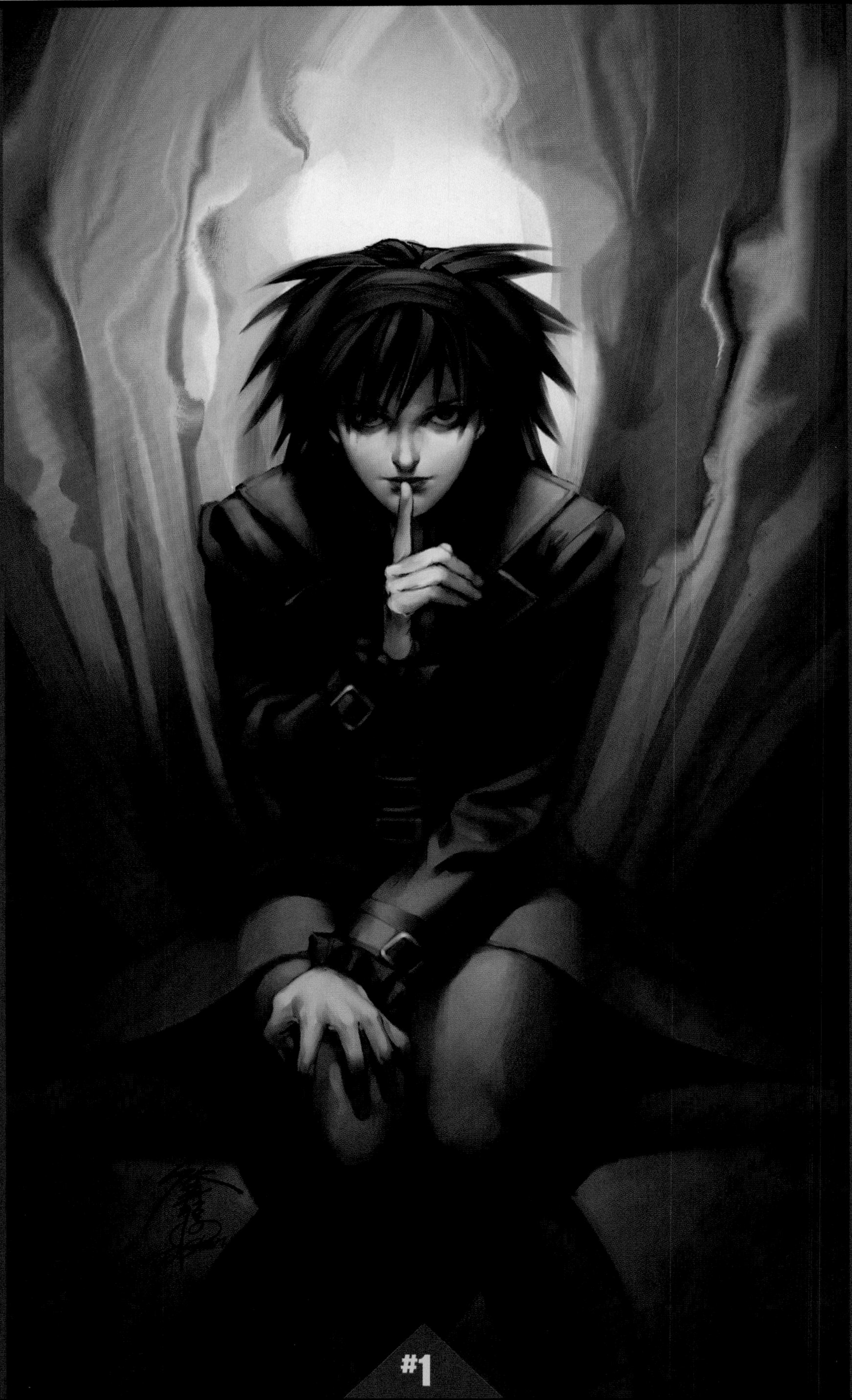
#1

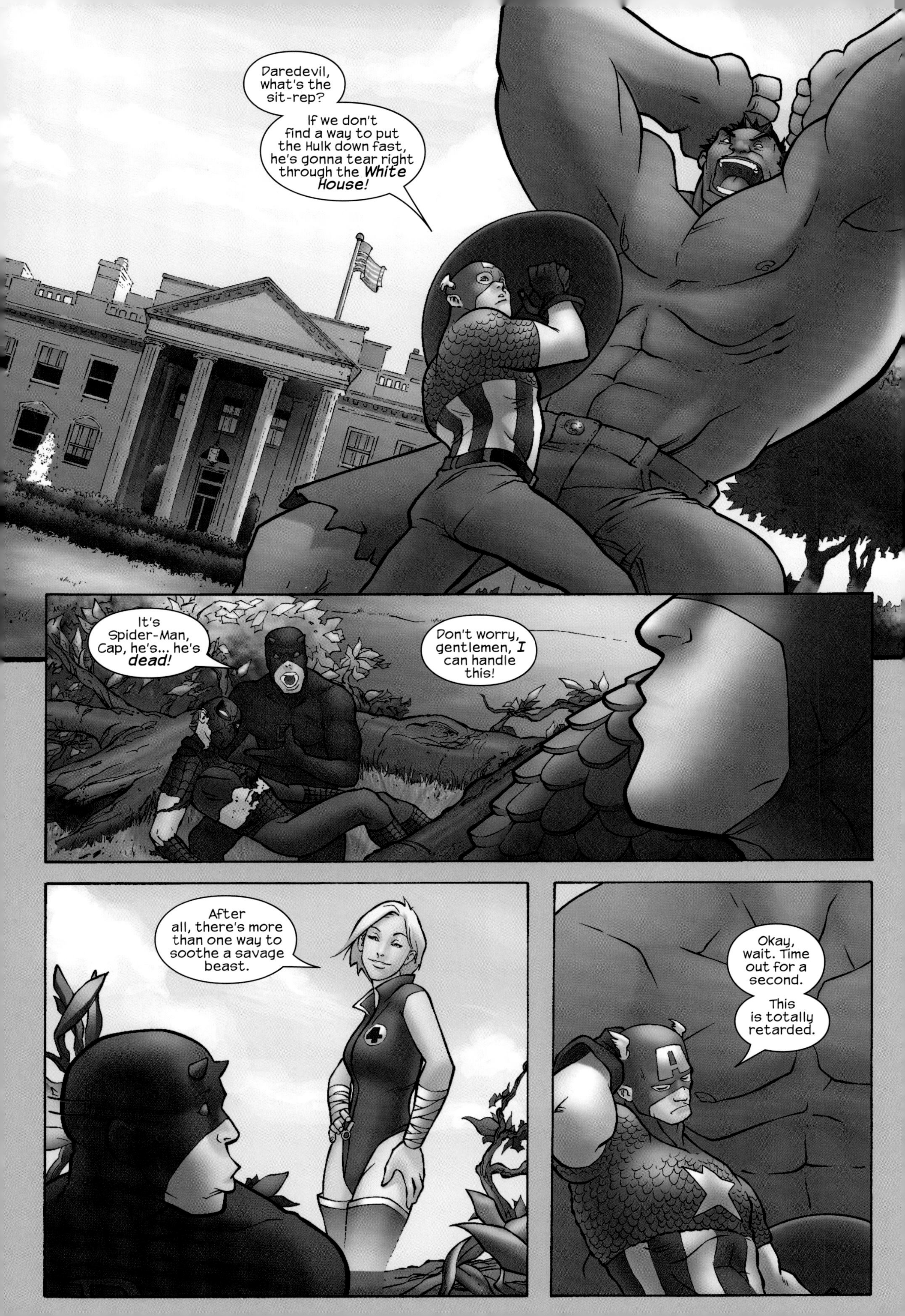
Daredevil, what's the sit-rep?
If we don't find a way to put the Hulk down fast, he's gonna tear right through the *White House!*
It's Spider-Man, Cap, he's... he's *dead!*
Don't worry, gentlemen, *I* can handle this!
After all, there's more than one way to soothe a savage beast.
Okay, wait. Time out for a second.
This is totally retarded.

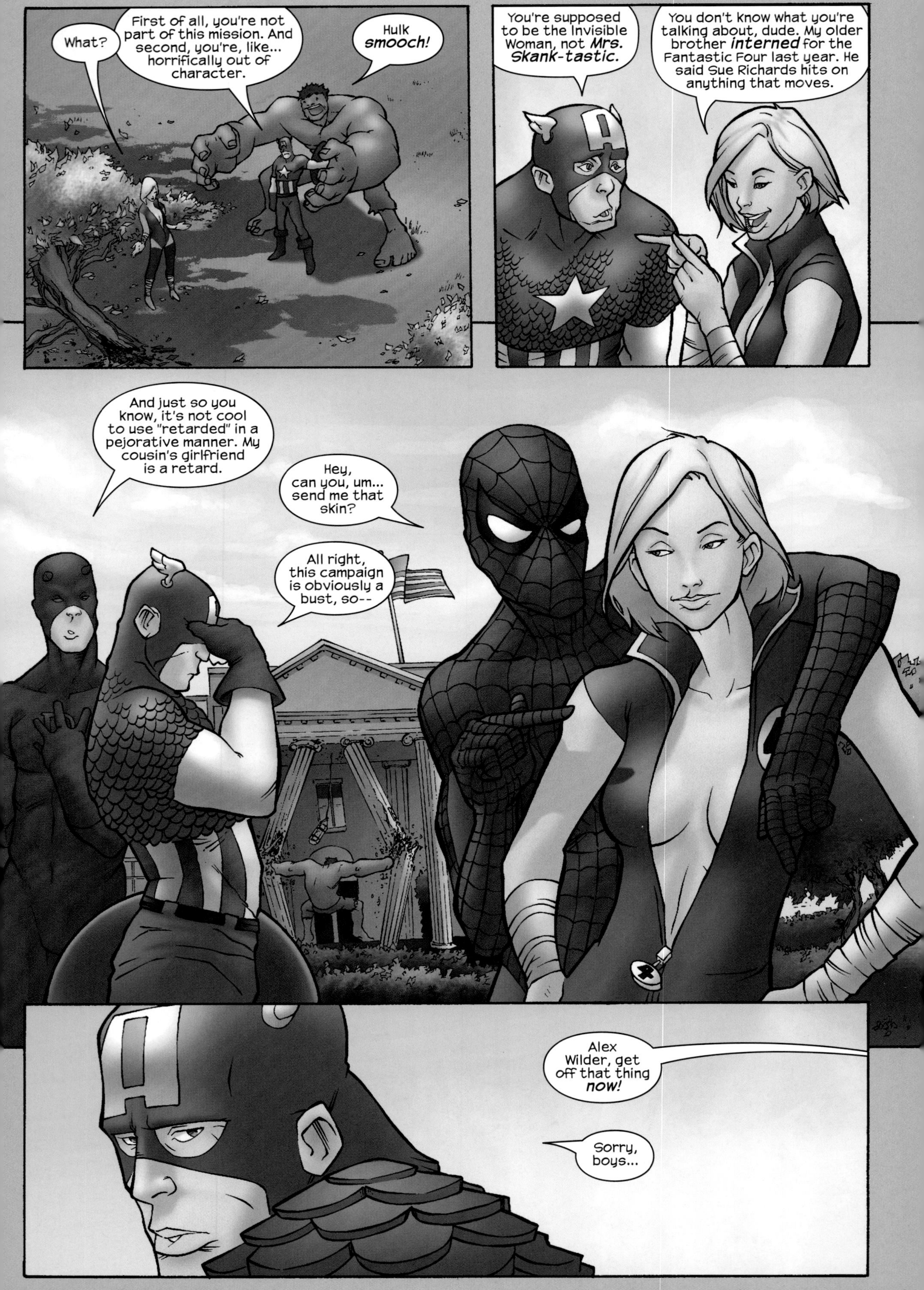
What?
First of all, you're not part of this mission. And second, you're, like... horrifically out of character.
Hulk *smooch!*
You're supposed to be the Invisible Woman, not *Mrs. Skank-tastic.*
You don't know what you're talking about, dude. My older brother *interned* for the Fantastic Four last year. He said Sue Richards hits on anything that moves.
And just so you know, it's not cool to use "retarded" in a pejorative manner. My cousin's girlfriend is a retard.
Hey, can you, um... send me that skin?
All right, this campaign is obviously a bust, so--
Alex Wilder, get off that thing *now!*
Sorry, boys...

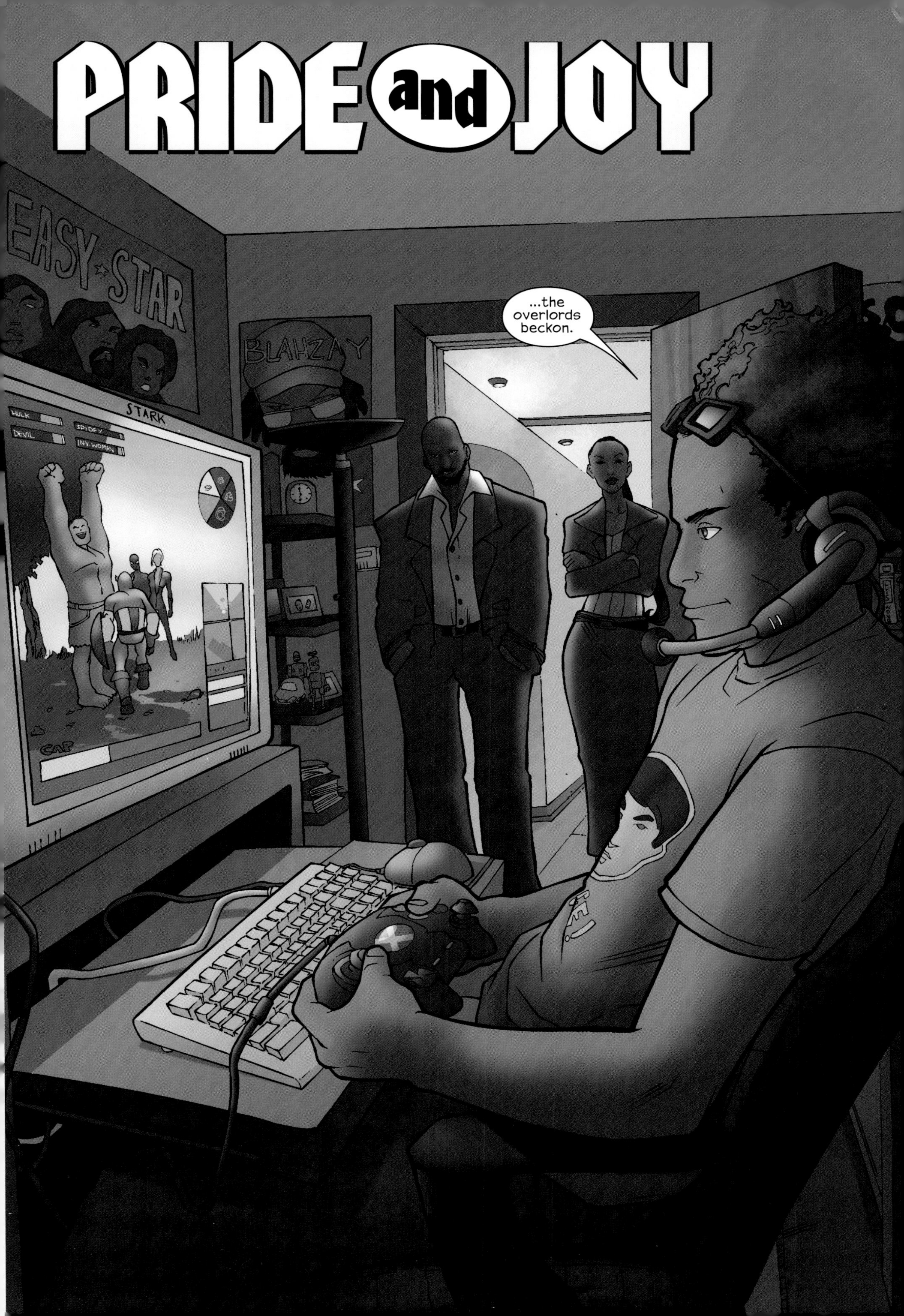
PRIDE and JOY
EASY ★ STAR
BLAHZAY
STARK
HULK
SPIDEY
DEVIL
INV. WOMAN
CAP
...the overlords beckon.

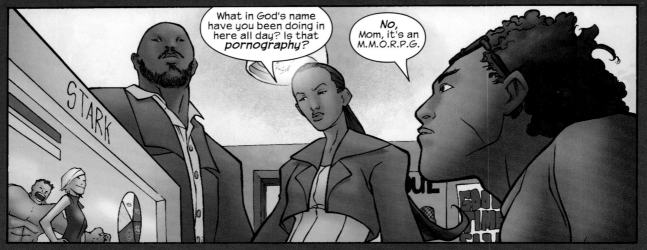

What in God's name have you been doing in here all day? Is that *pornography*?

NO, Mom, it's an M.M.O.R.P.G.

What the hell is that?

A massively multi-player...

¿sigh? It's a game, *Dad*. Like *Scrabble*, but for the computer, you know?

Does it cost me money?

Well, yeah, but you got it for me as a birthday gift!

You turned sixteen *months* ago, Alex. I wasn't paying for a lifetime subscription.

But it's the only place I can hang out with my friends!

Besides, we live in *Malibu!*

What difference does a few dollars make?

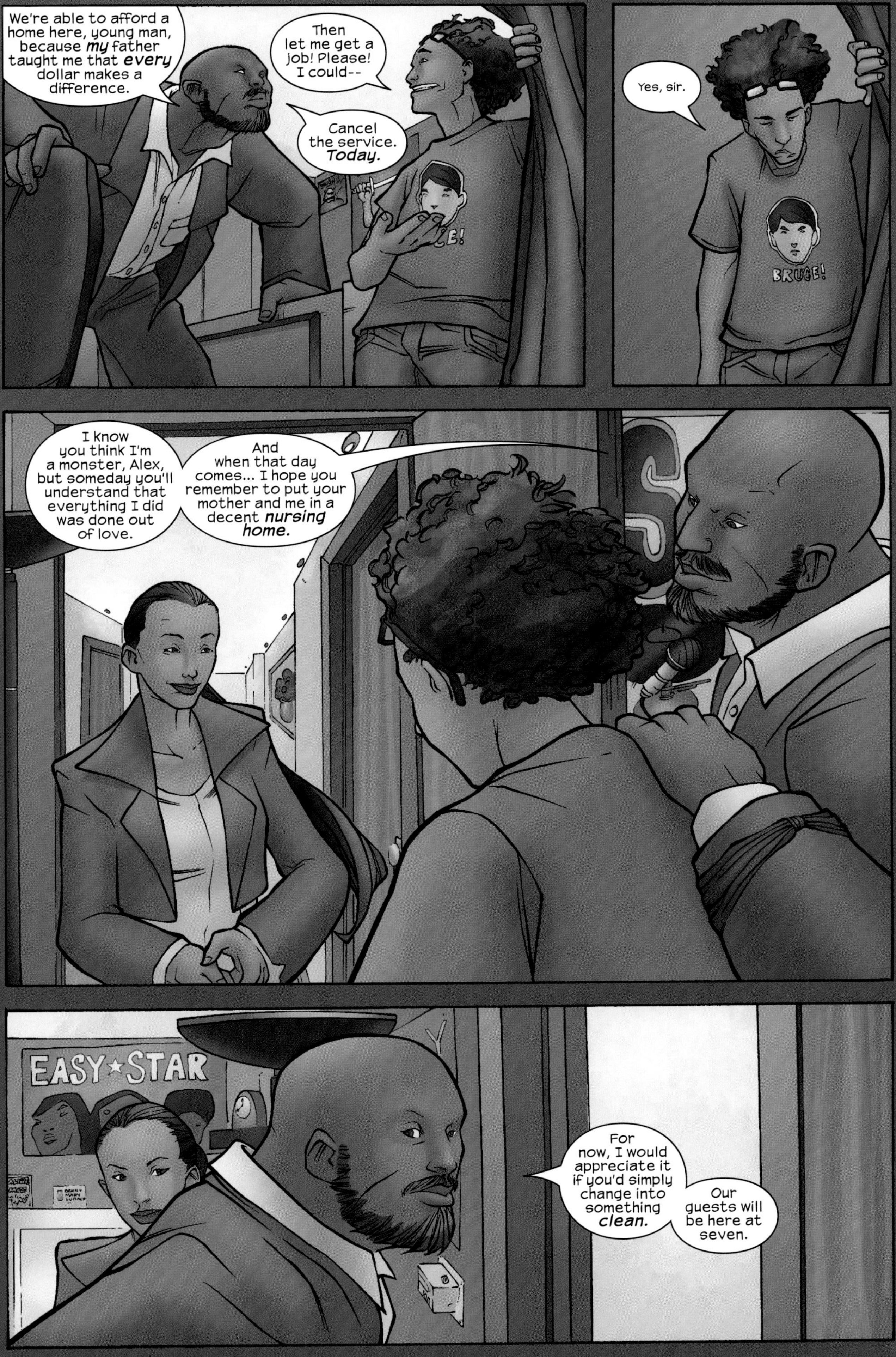
We're able to afford a home here, young man, because *my* father taught me that *every* dollar makes a difference.
Then let me get a job! Please! I could--
Cancel the service. ***Today.***
Yes, sir.
BRUCE!
I know you think I'm a monster, Alex, but someday you'll understand that everything I did was done out of love.
And when that day comes... I hope you remember to put your mother and me in a decent ***nursing home.***
EASY★STAR
For now, I would appreciate it if you'd simply change into something ***clean.***
Our guests will be here at seven.

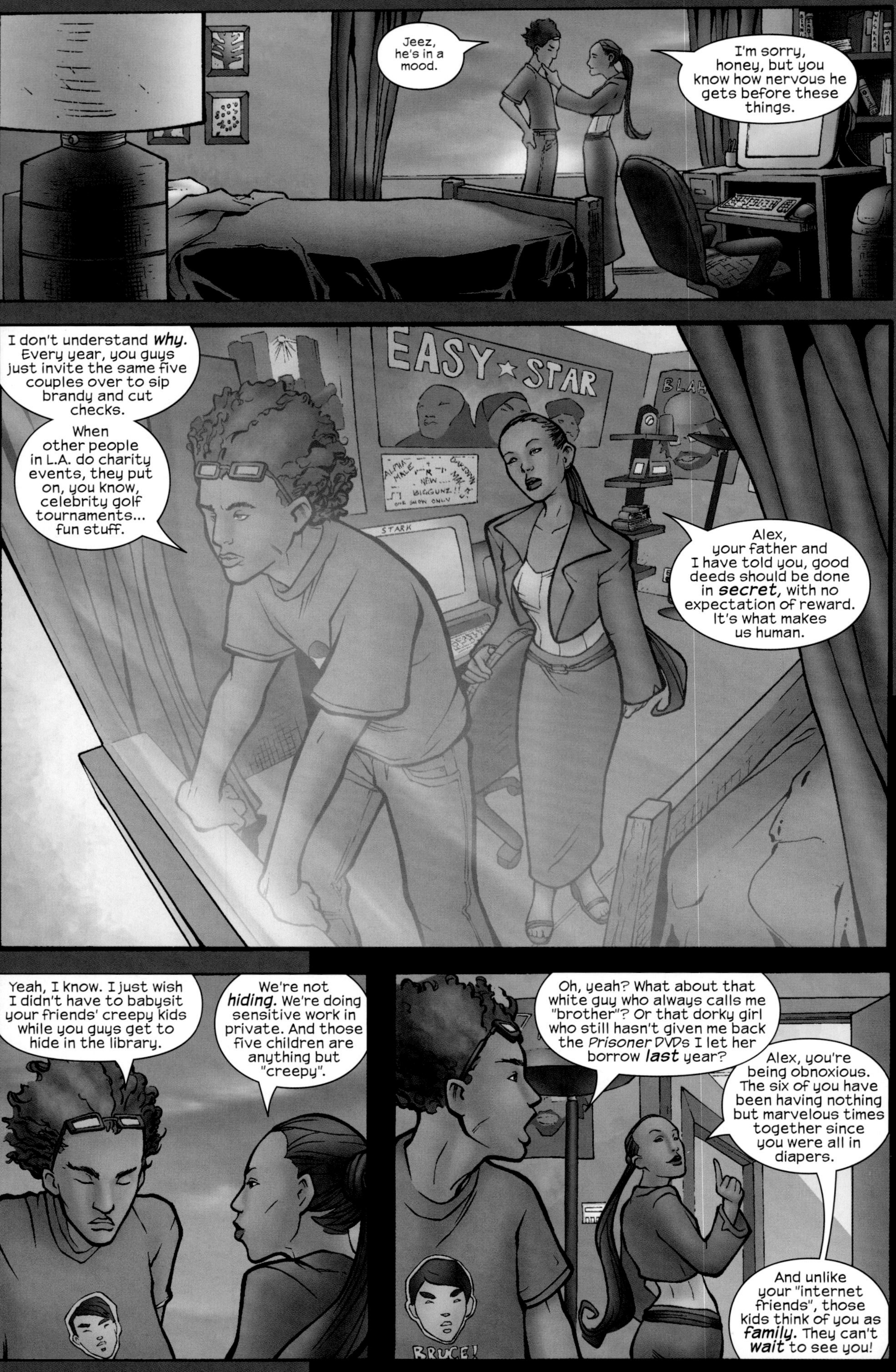
Jeez, he's in a mood.
I'm sorry, honey, but you know how nervous he gets before these things.
EASY ★ STAR
BLAH
STARK
I don't understand *why.* Every year, you guys just invite the same five couples over to sip brandy and cut checks.
When other people in L.A. do charity events, they put on, you know, celebrity golf tournaments... fun stuff.
Alex, your father and I have told you, good deeds should be done in ***secret,*** with no expectation of reward. It's what makes us human.
Yeah, I know. I just wish I didn't have to babysit your friends' creepy kids while you guys get to hide in the library.
We're not ***hiding.*** We're doing sensitive work in private. And those five children are anything but "creepy".
Oh, yeah? What about that white guy who always calls me "brother"? Or that dorky girl who still hasn't given me back the *Prisoner* DVDs I let her borrow ***last*** year?
Alex, you're being obnoxious. The six of you have been having nothing but marvelous times together since you were all in diapers.
And unlike your "internet friends", those kids think of you as ***family.*** They can't ***wait*** to see you!
BRUCE!

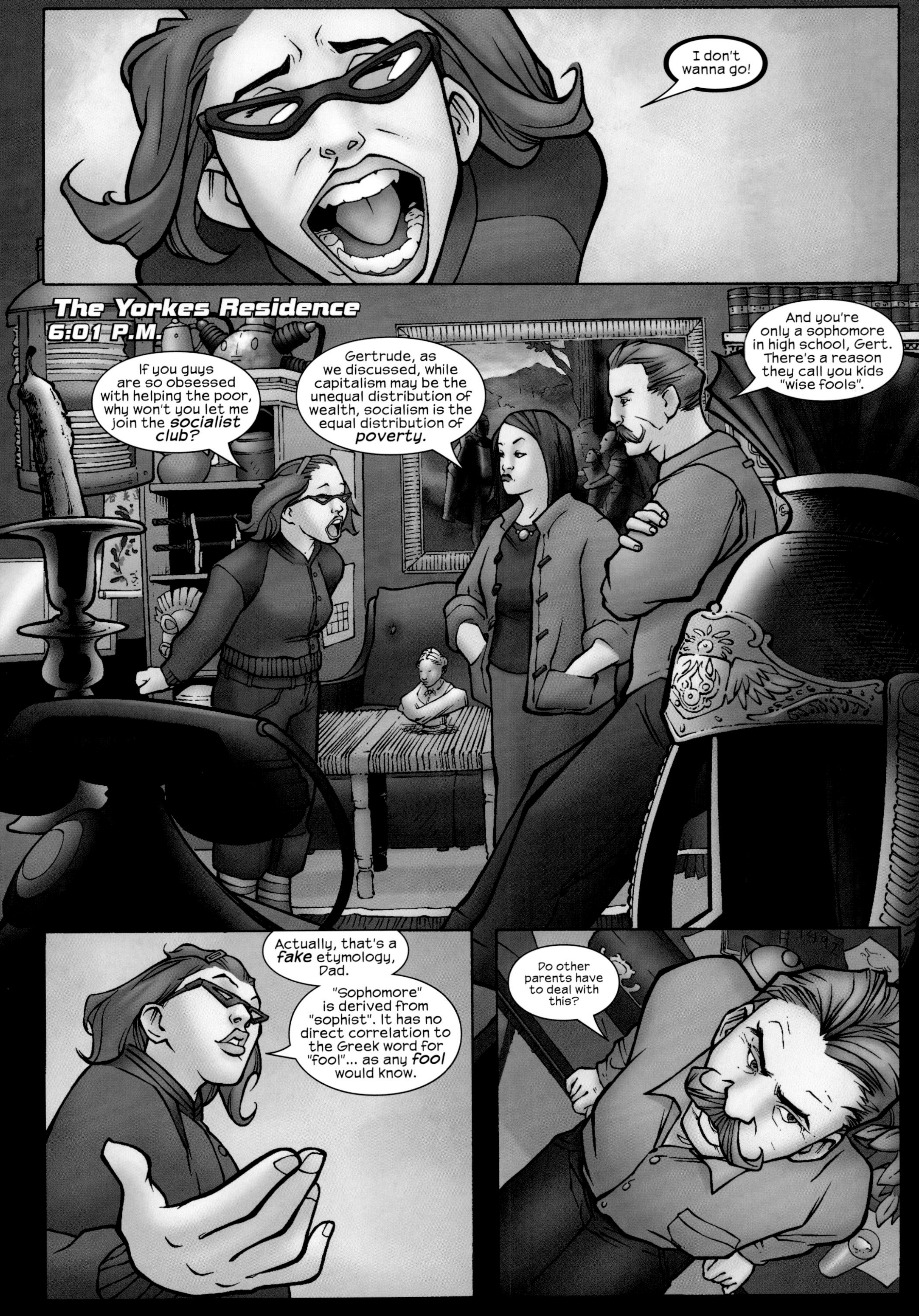
I don't wanna go!
The Yorkes Residence 6:01 P.M.
If you guys are so obsessed with helping the poor, why won't you let me join the socialist club?
Gertrude, as we discussed, while capitalism may be the unequal distribution of wealth, socialism is the equal distribution of poverty.
And you're only a sophomore in high school, Gert. There's a reason they call you kids "wise fools".
Actually, that's a fake etymology, Dad.
"Sophomore" is derived from "sophist". It has no direct correlation to the Greek word for "fool"... as any fool would know.
Do other parents have to deal with this?

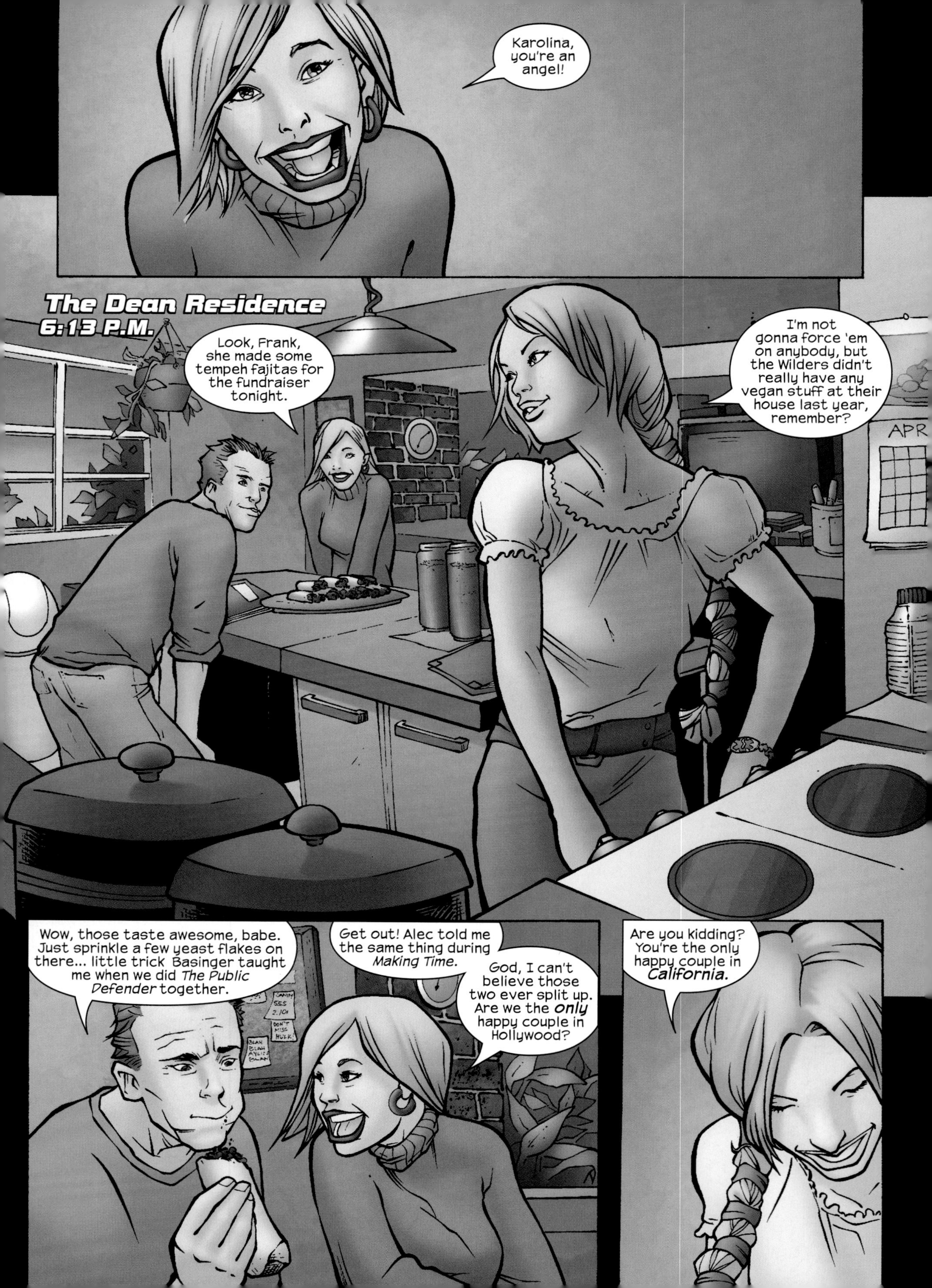
Karolina, you're an angel!
The Dean Residence 6:13 P.M.
Look, Frank, she made some tempeh fajitas for the fundraiser tonight.
I'm not gonna force 'em on anybody, but the Wilders didn't really have any vegan stuff at their house last year, remember?
APR
Wow, those taste awesome, babe. Just sprinkle a few yeast flakes on there... little trick Basinger taught me when we did The Public Defender together.
Get out! Alec told me the same thing during Making Time.
God, I can't believe those two ever split up. Are we the only happy couple in Hollywood?
Are you kidding? You're the only happy couple in California.

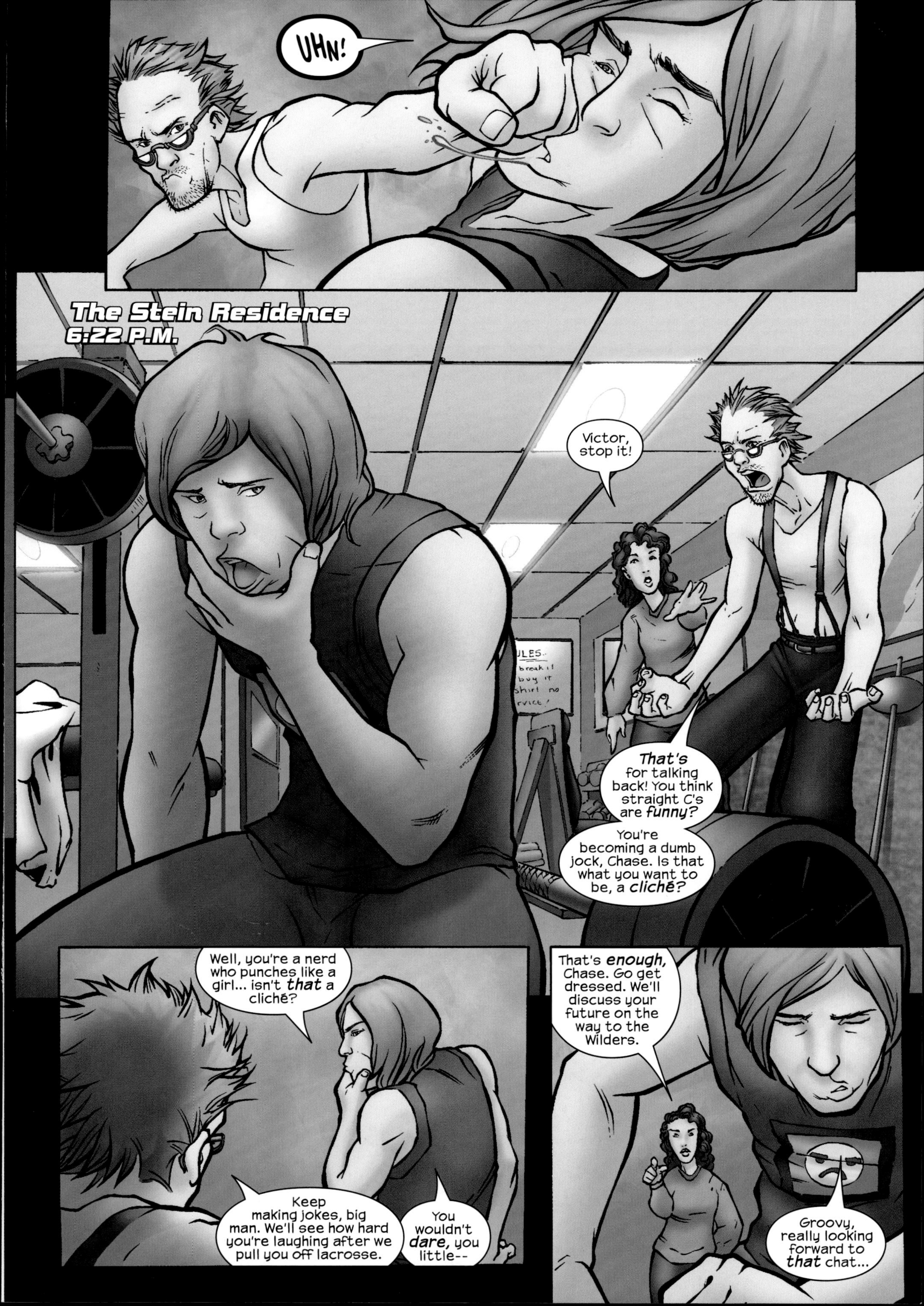
UHN!
The Stein Residence
6:22 P.M.
Victor, stop it!
That's for talking back! You think straight C's are funny?
You're becoming a dumb jock, Chase. Is that what you want to be, a cliché?
Well, you're a nerd who punches like a girl... isn't that a cliché?
Keep making jokes, big man. We'll see how hard you're laughing after we pull you off lacrosse.
You wouldn't dare, you little--
That's enough, Chase. Go get dressed. We'll discuss your future on the way to the Wilders.
Groovy, really looking forward to that chat...

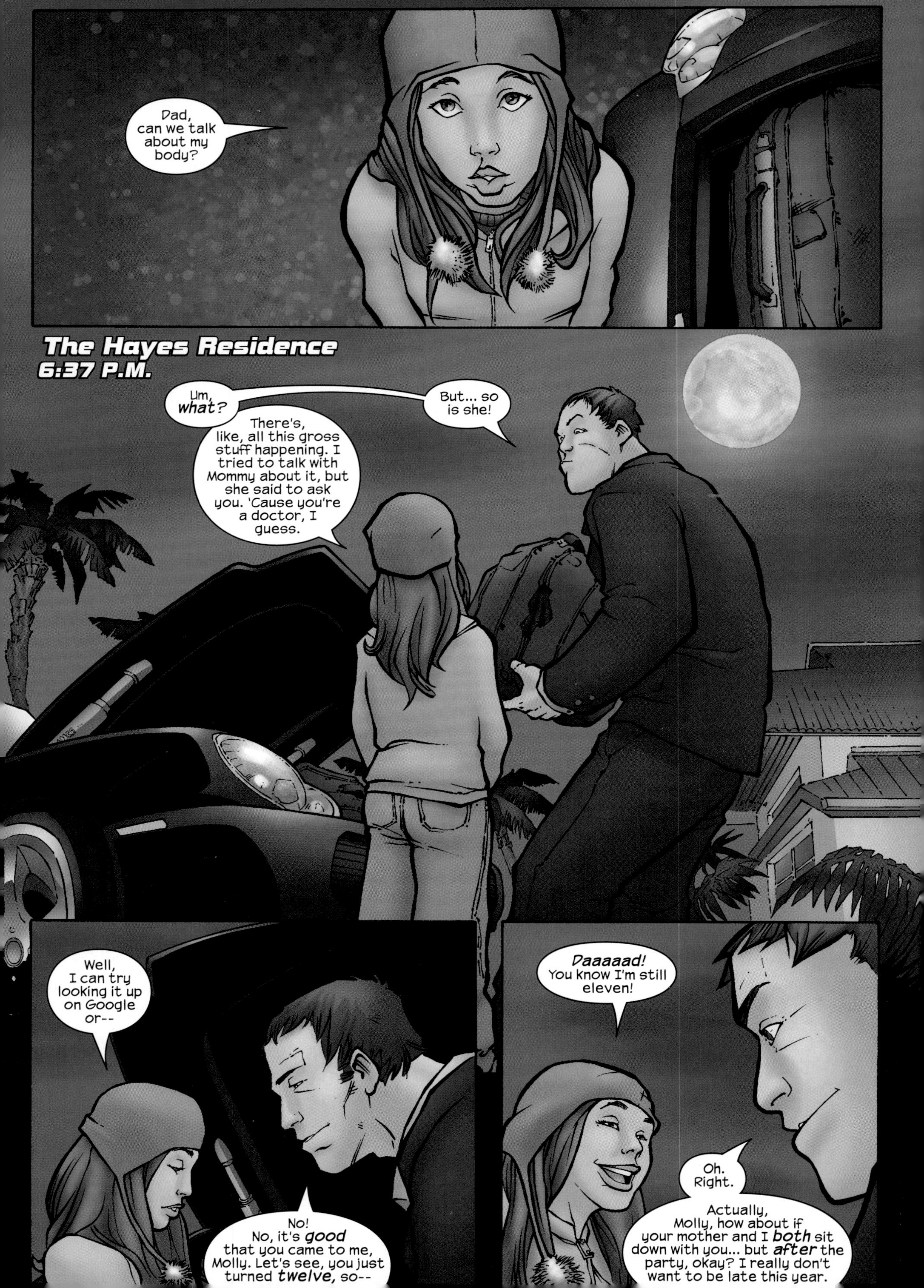
Dad, can we talk about my body?
The Hayes Residence
6:37 P.M.
Um, *what?*
But... so is she!
There's, like, all this gross stuff happening. I tried to talk with Mommy about it, but she said to ask you. 'Cause you're a doctor, I guess.
Well, I can try looking it up on Google or--
No! No, it's *good* that you came to me, Molly. Let's see, you just turned *twelve,* so--
Daaaaad! You know I'm still eleven!
Oh. Right.
Actually, Molly, how about if your mother and I *both* sit down with you... but *after* the party, okay? I really don't want to be late this year.

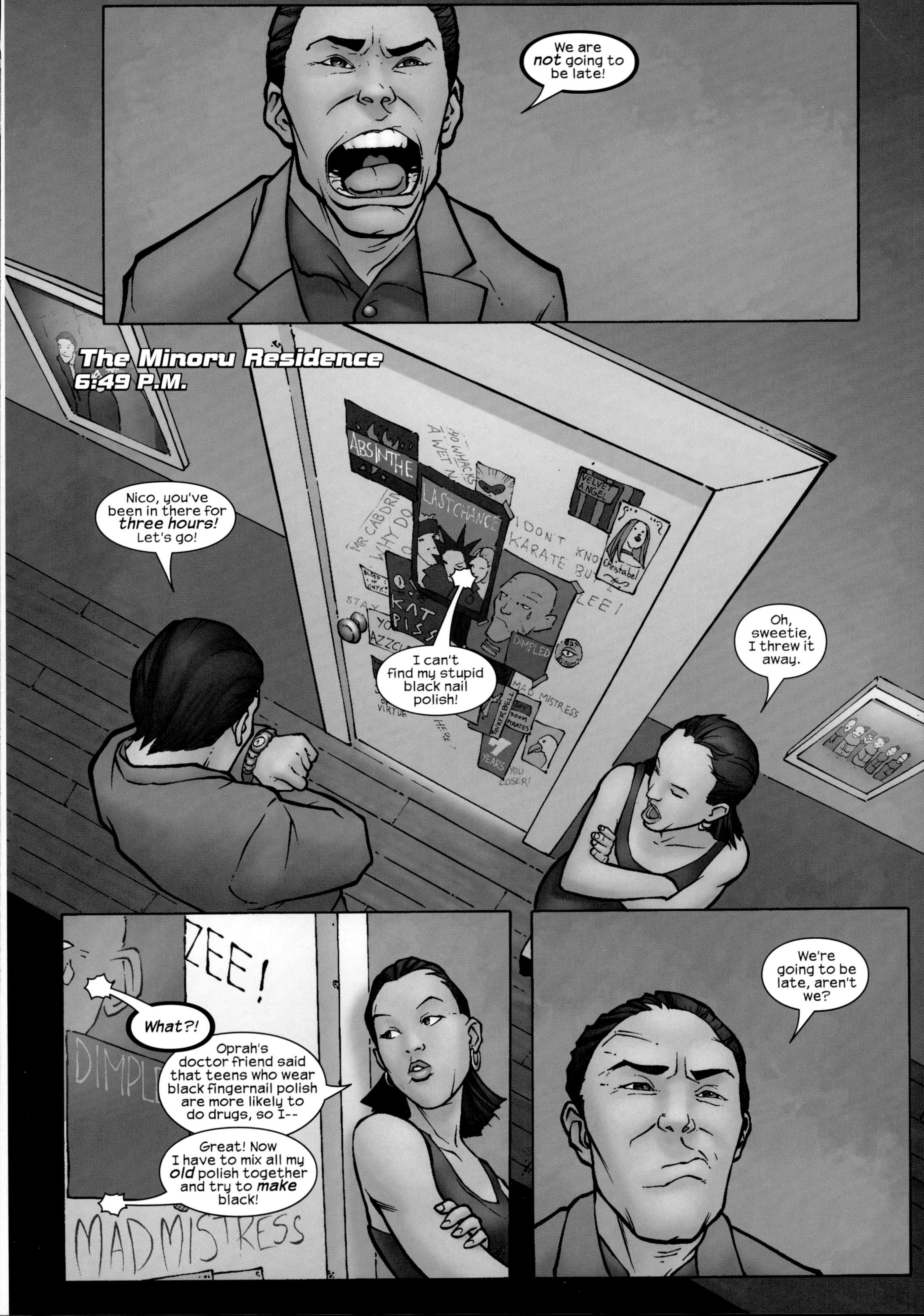
We are *not* going to be late!
The Minoru Residence 6:49 P.M.
Nico, you've been in there for *three hours!* Let's go!
I can't find my stupid black nail polish!
Oh, sweetie, I threw it away.
What?!
Oprah's doctor friend said that teens who wear black fingernail polish are more likely to do drugs, so I--
Great! Now I have to mix all my *old* polish together and try to *make* black!
We're going to be late, aren't we?

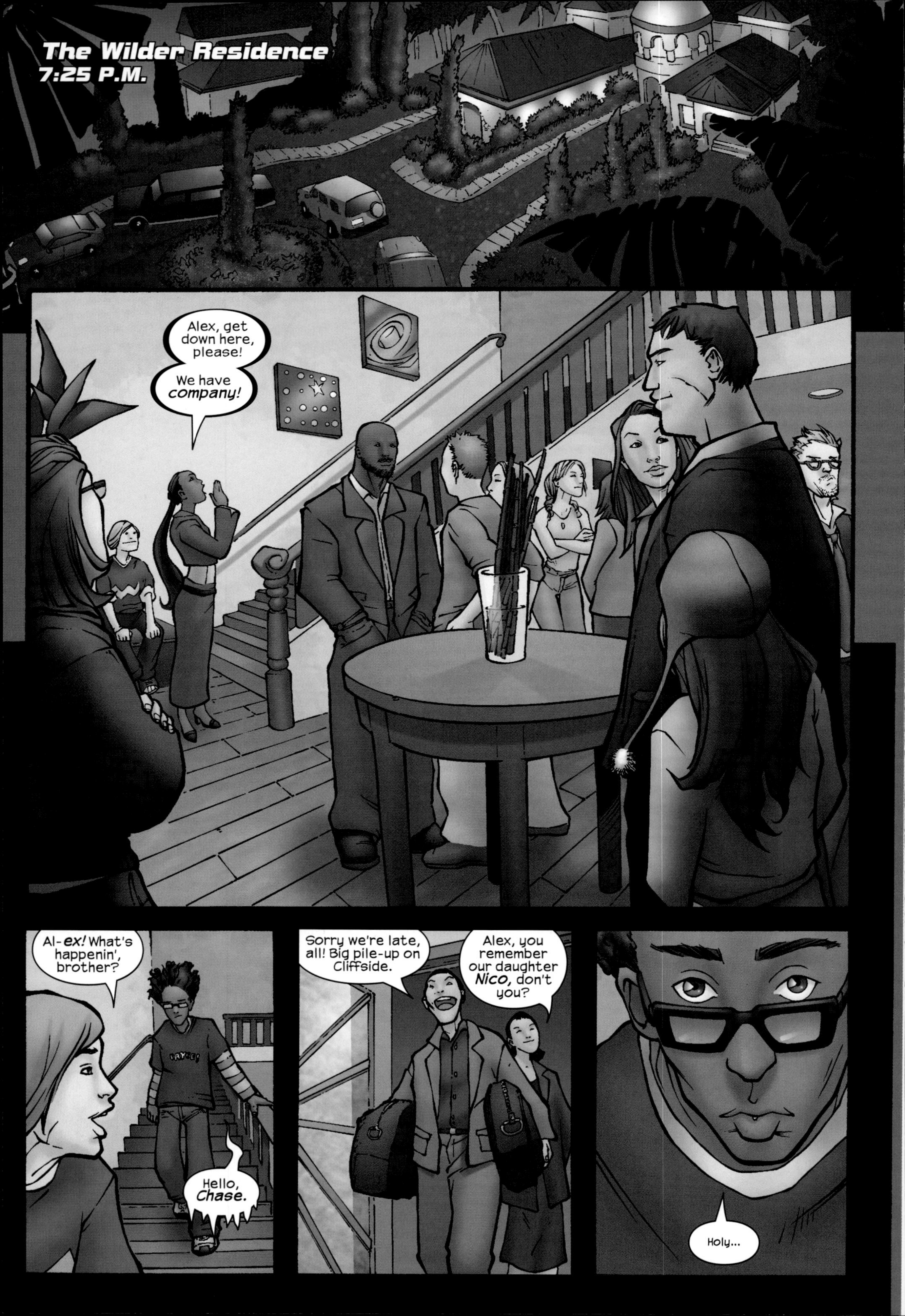
The Wilder Residence
7:25 P.M.
Alex, get down here, please!
We have company!
Al-ex! What's happenin', brother?
Hello, Chase.
Sorry we're late, all! Big pile-up on Cliffside.
Alex, you remember our daughter Nico, don't you?
Holy...

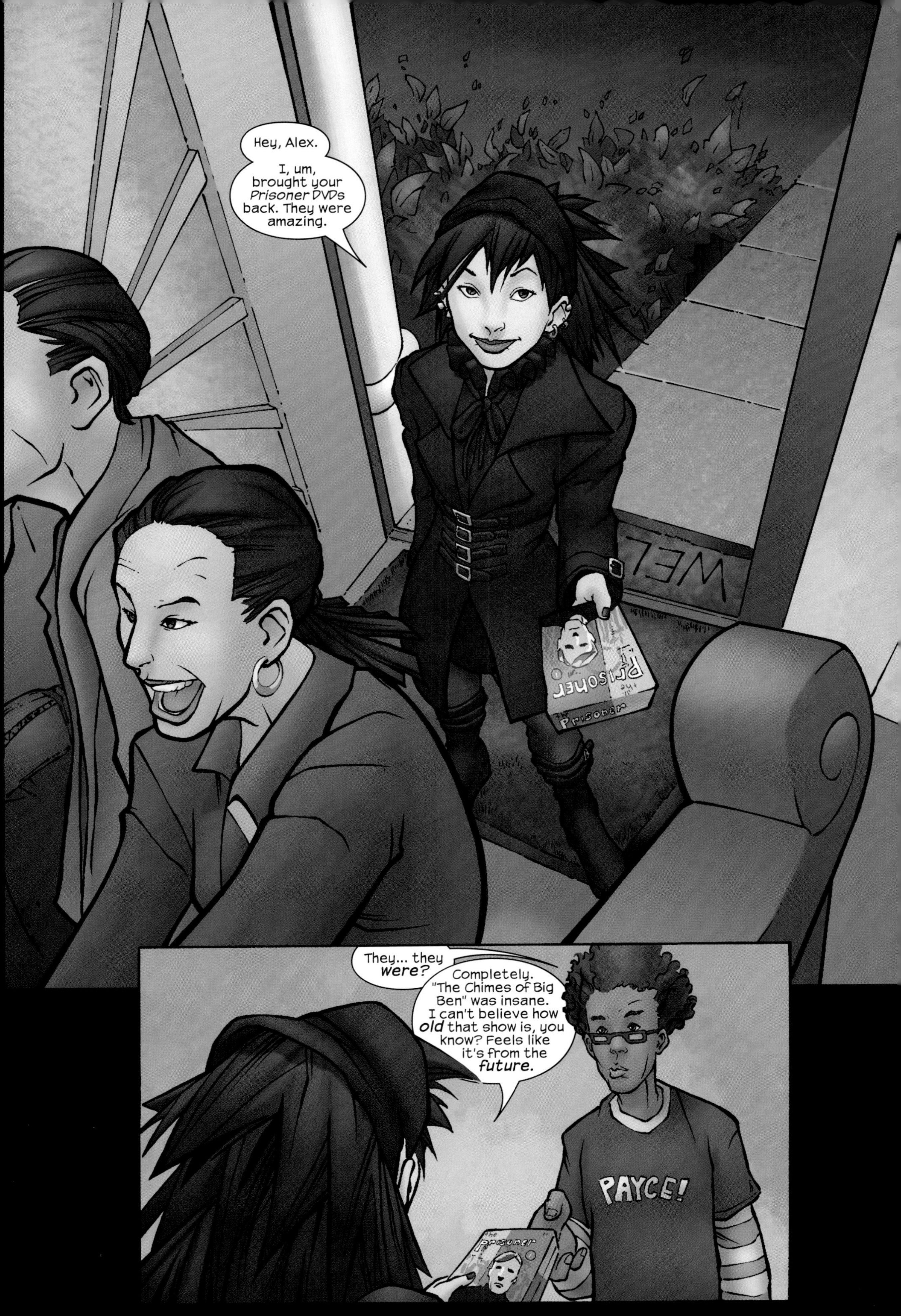
Hey, Alex.
I, um, brought your *Prisoner* DVDs back. They were amazing.
WEL
the Prisoner
They... they *were*?
Completely. "The Chimes of Big Ben" was insane. I can't believe how *old* that show is, you know? Feels like it's from the *future*.
PAYCE!

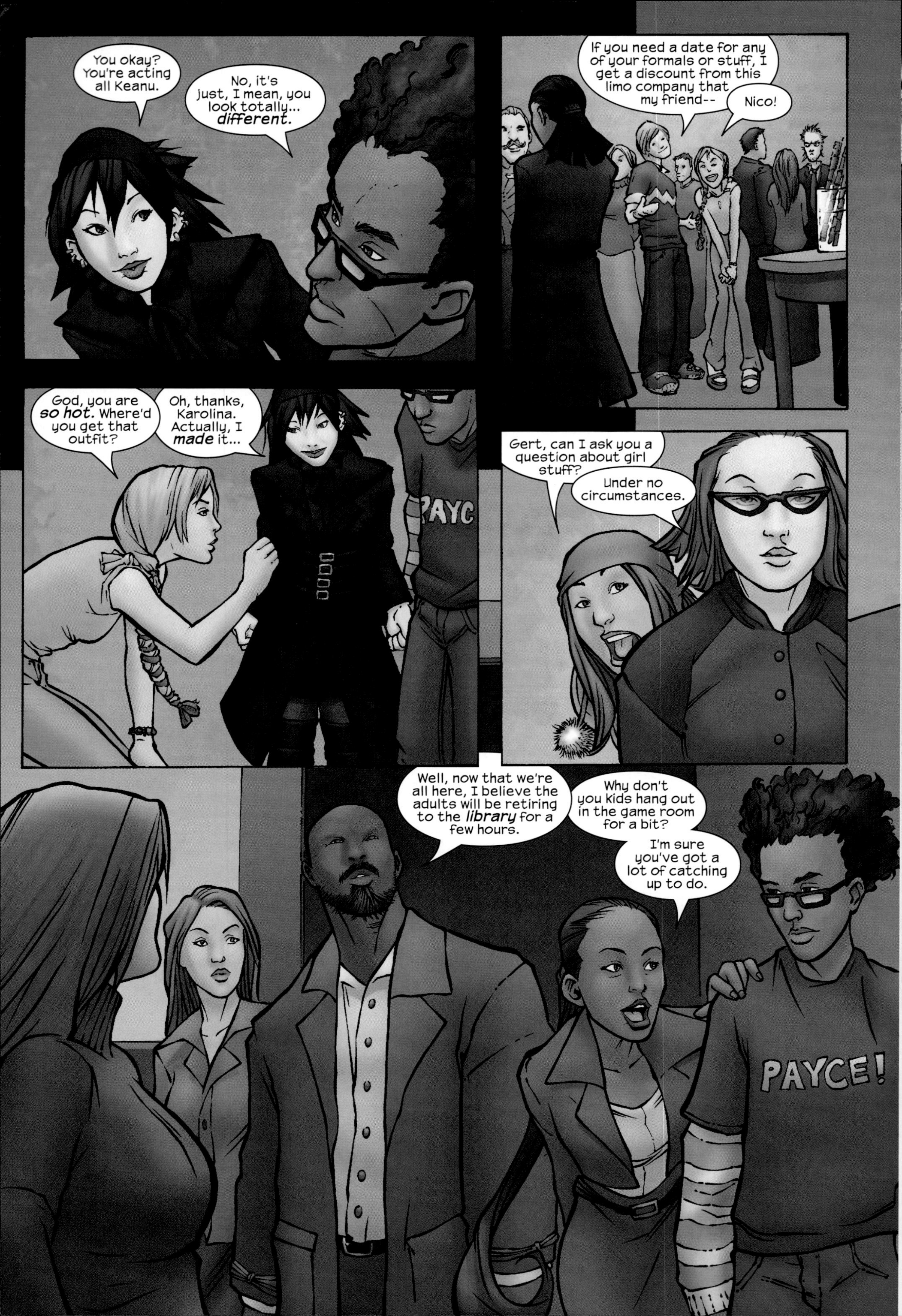

You okay? You're acting all Keanu.
No, it's just, I mean, you look totally... *different.*
If you need a date for any of your formals or stuff, I get a discount from this limo company that my friend--
Nico!
God, you are *so hot.* Where'd you get that outfit?
Oh, thanks, Karolina. Actually, I *made* it...
AYC
Gert, can I ask you a question about girl stuff?
Under no circumstances.
Well, now that we're all here, I believe the adults will be retiring to the *library* for a few hours.
Why don't you kids hang out in the game room for a bit?
I'm sure you've got a lot of catching up to do.
PAYCE!

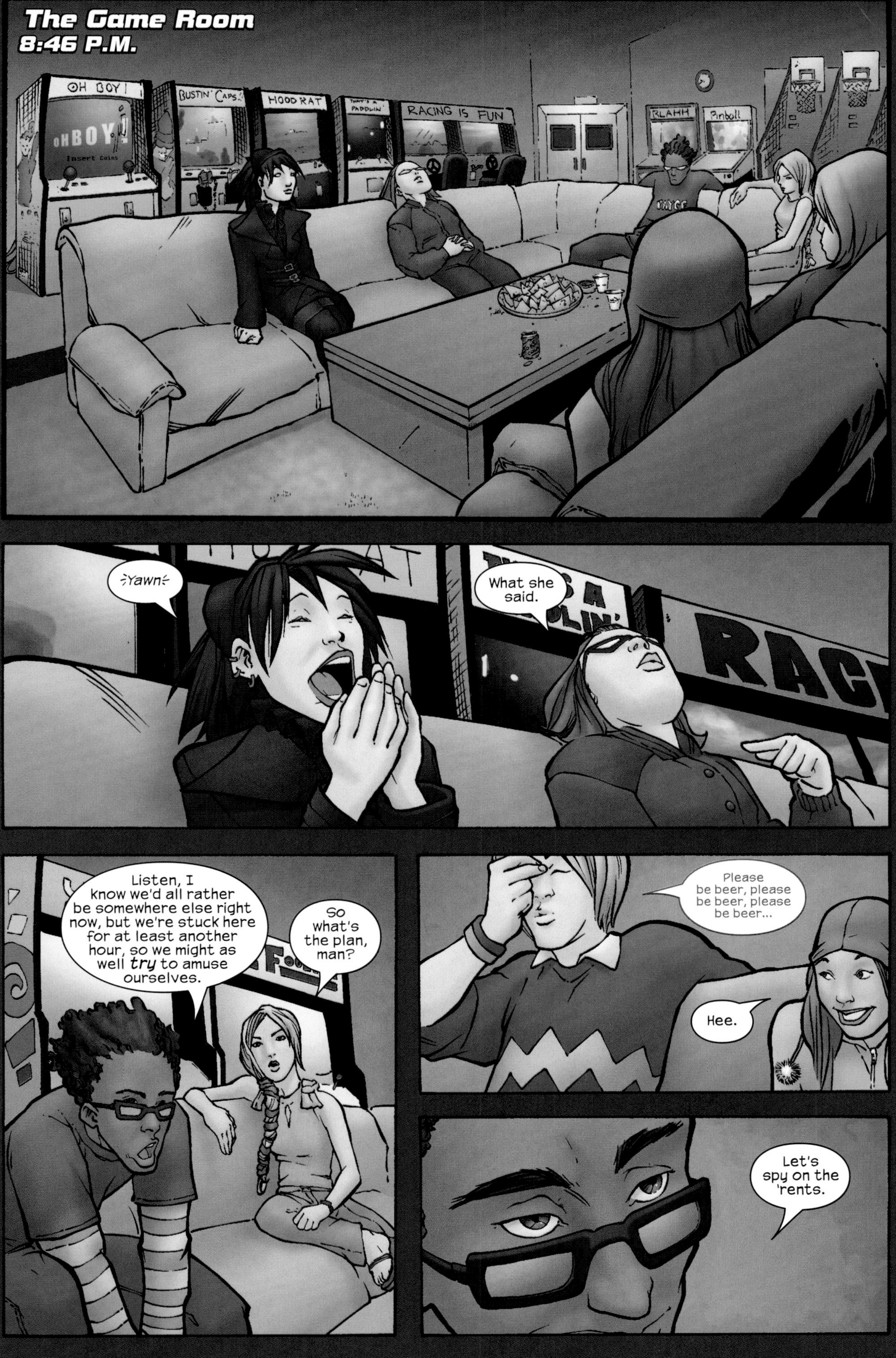
The Game Room
8:46 P.M.
OH BOY!
BUSTIN' CAPS
HOOD RAT
RACING IS FUN
Pinball
ɜYawnɛ
What she said.
Listen, I know we'd all rather be somewhere else right now, but we're stuck here for at least another hour, so we might as well *try* to amuse ourselves.
So what's the plan, man?
Please be beer, please be beer, please be beer...
Hee.
Let's spy on the 'rents.

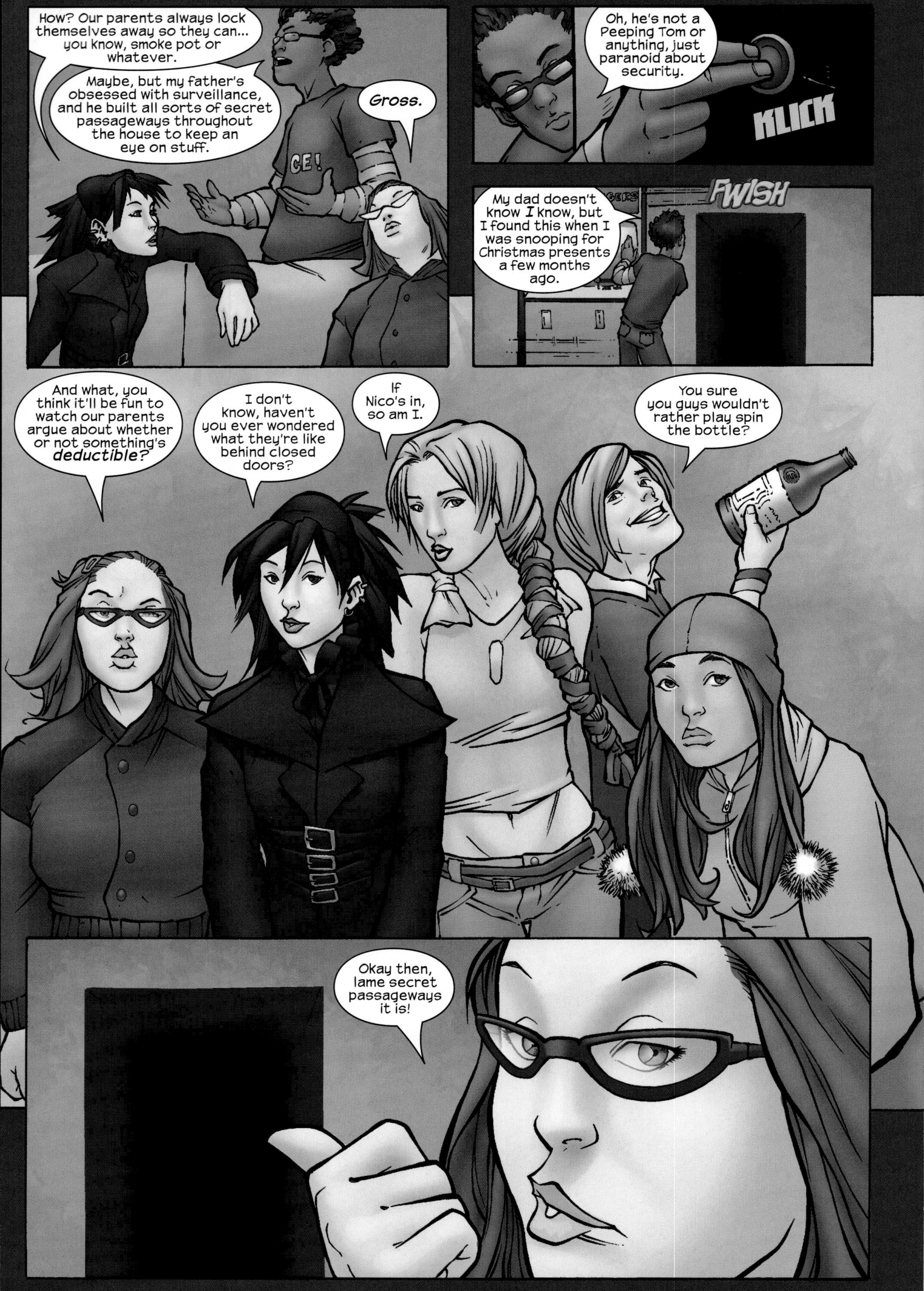
How? Our parents always lock themselves away so they can... you know, smoke pot or whatever.
Maybe, but my father's obsessed with surveillance, and he built all sorts of secret passageways throughout the house to keep an eye on stuff.
Gross.
CE!
Oh, he's not a Peeping Tom or anything, just paranoid about security.
KLICK
FWISH
My dad doesn't know *I* know, but I found this when I was snooping for Christmas presents a few months ago.
And what, you think it'll be fun to watch our parents argue about whether or not something's ***deductible***?
I don't know, haven't you ever wondered what they're like behind closed doors?
If Nico's in, so am I.
You sure you guys wouldn't rather play spin the bottle?
Okay then, lame secret passageways it is!

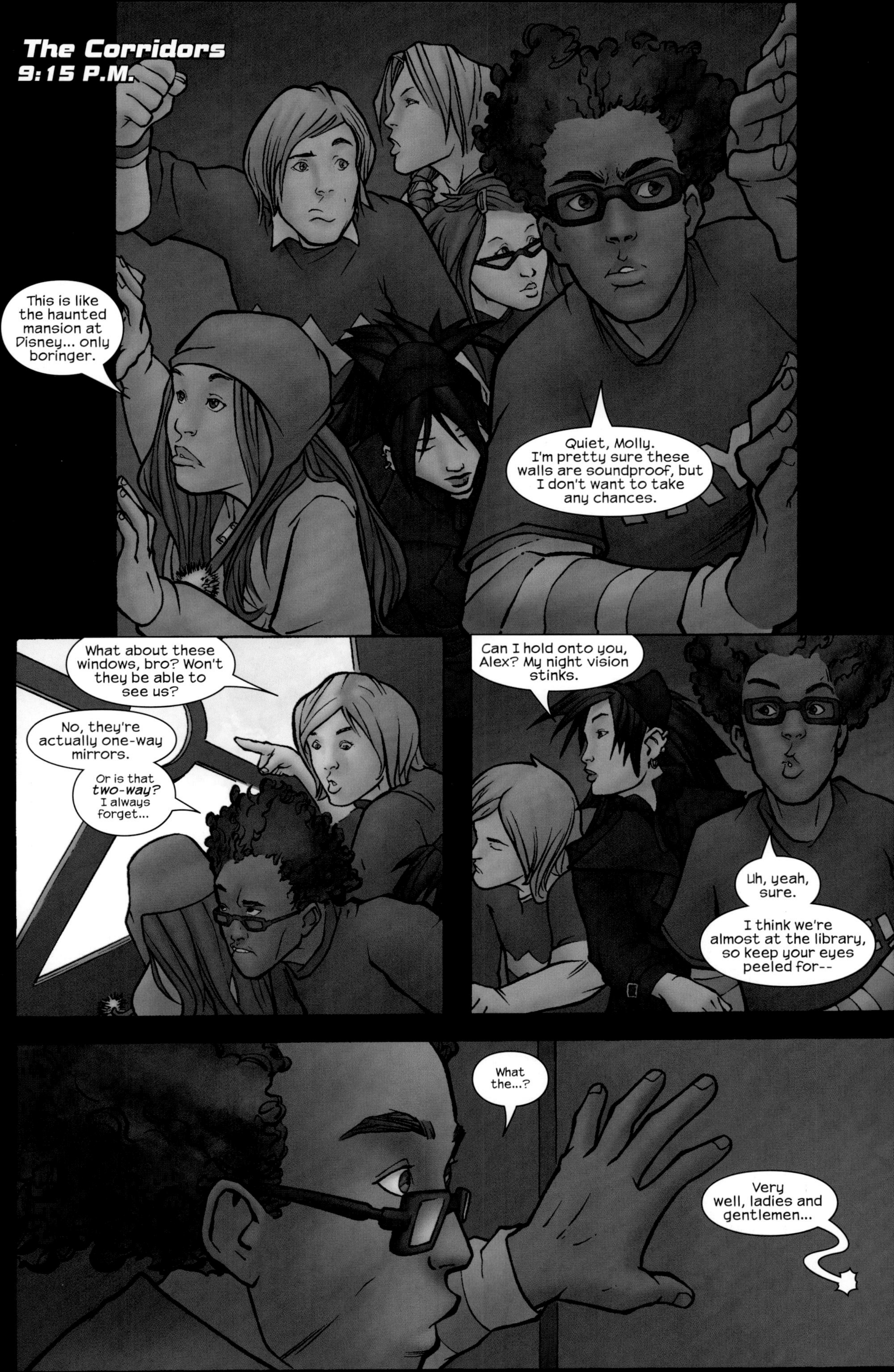

The Corridors
9:15 P.M.
This is like the haunted mansion at Disney... only boringer.
Quiet, Molly. I'm pretty sure these walls are soundproof, but I don't want to take any chances.
What about these windows, bro? Won't they be able to see us?
No, they're actually one-way mirrors.
Or is that two-way? I always forget...
Can I hold onto you, Alex? My night vision stinks.
Uh, yeah, sure.
I think we're almost at the library, so keep your eyes peeled for--
What the...?
Very well, ladies and gentlemen...

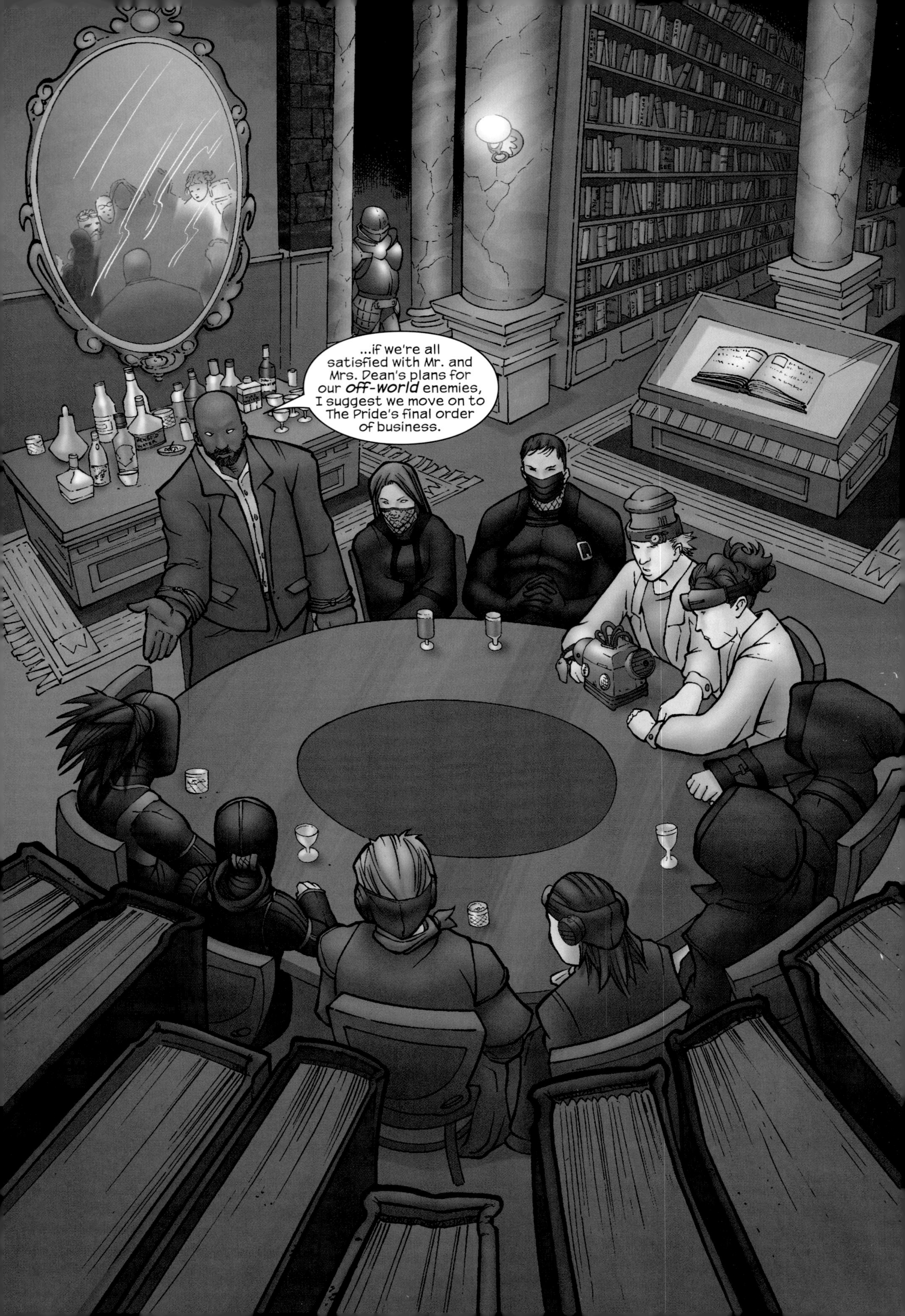
...if we're all satisfied with Mr. and Mrs. Dean's plans for our off-world enemies, I suggest we move on to The Pride's final order of business.

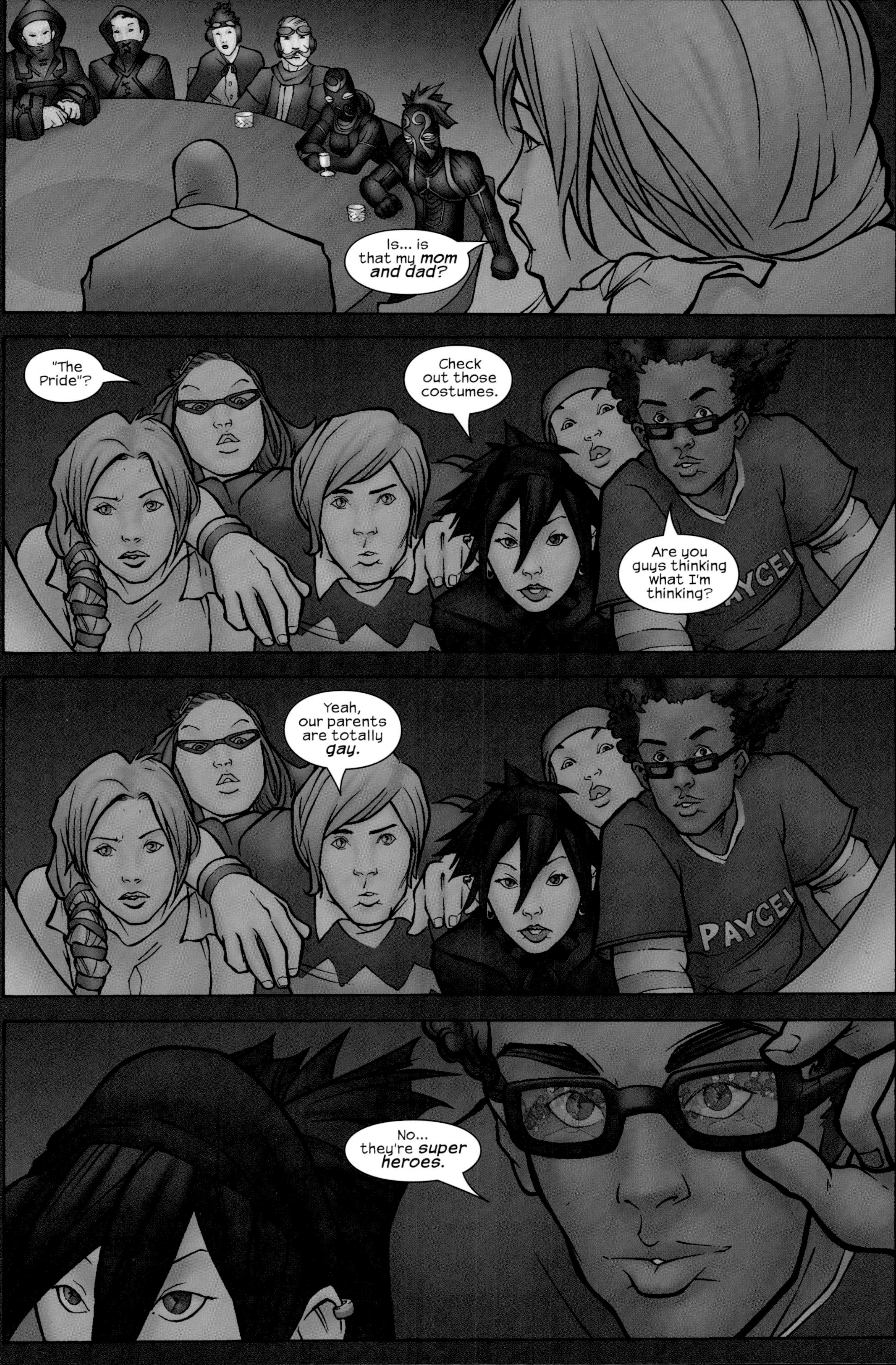

Is... is that my *mom and dad?*
"The Pride"?
Check out those costumes.
Are you guys thinking what I'm thinking?
PAYCE
Yeah, our parents are totally *gay.*
PAYCE
No... they're *super heroes.*

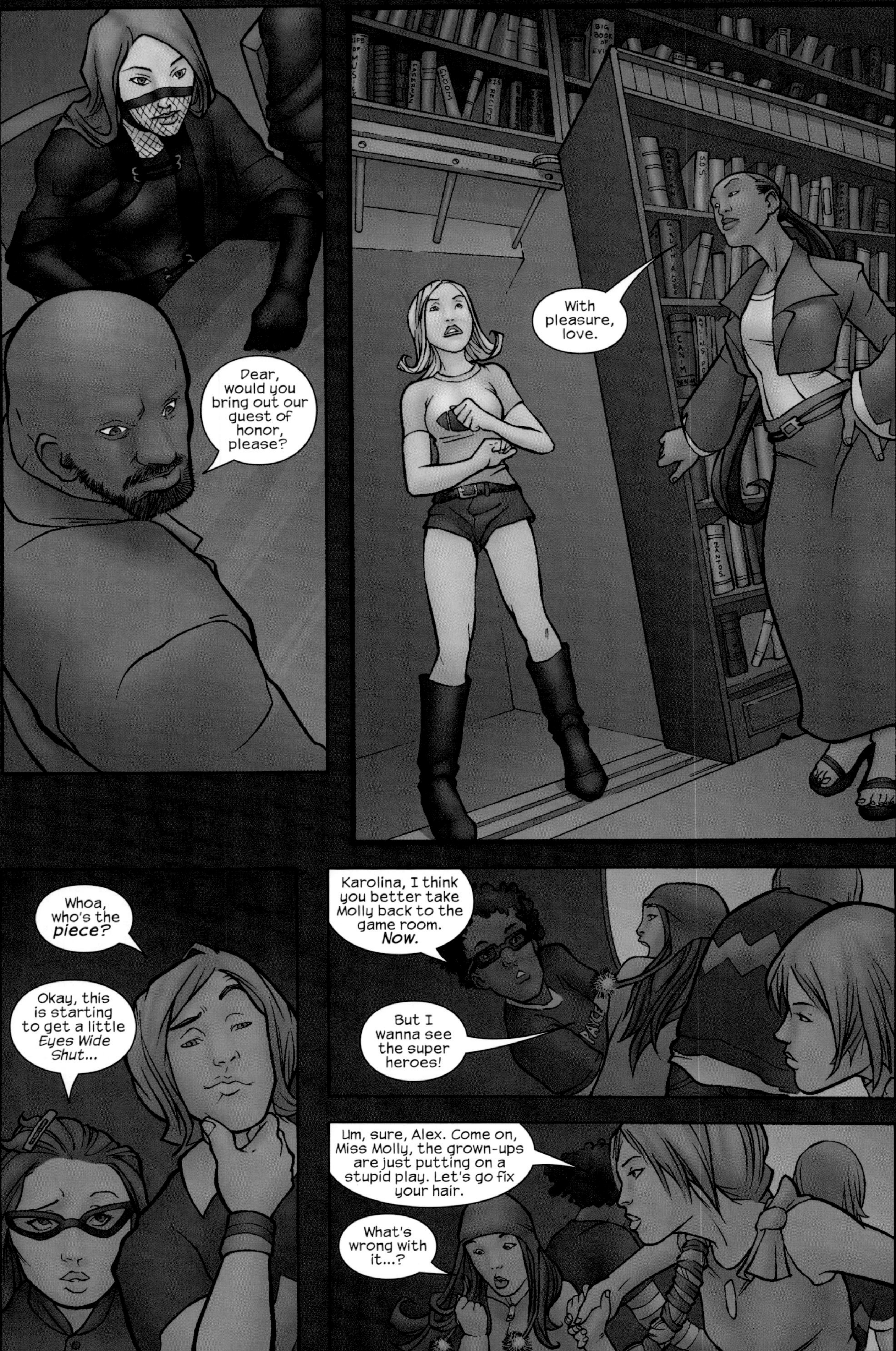

Dear, would you bring out our guest of honor, please?
With pleasure, love.
Whoa, who's the *piece*?
Okay, this is starting to get a little *Eyes Wide Shut*...
Karolina, I think you better take Molly back to the game room. ***Now.***
But I wanna see the super heroes!
Um, sure, Alex. Come on, Miss Molly, the grown-ups are just putting on a stupid play. Let's go fix your hair.
What's wrong with it...?

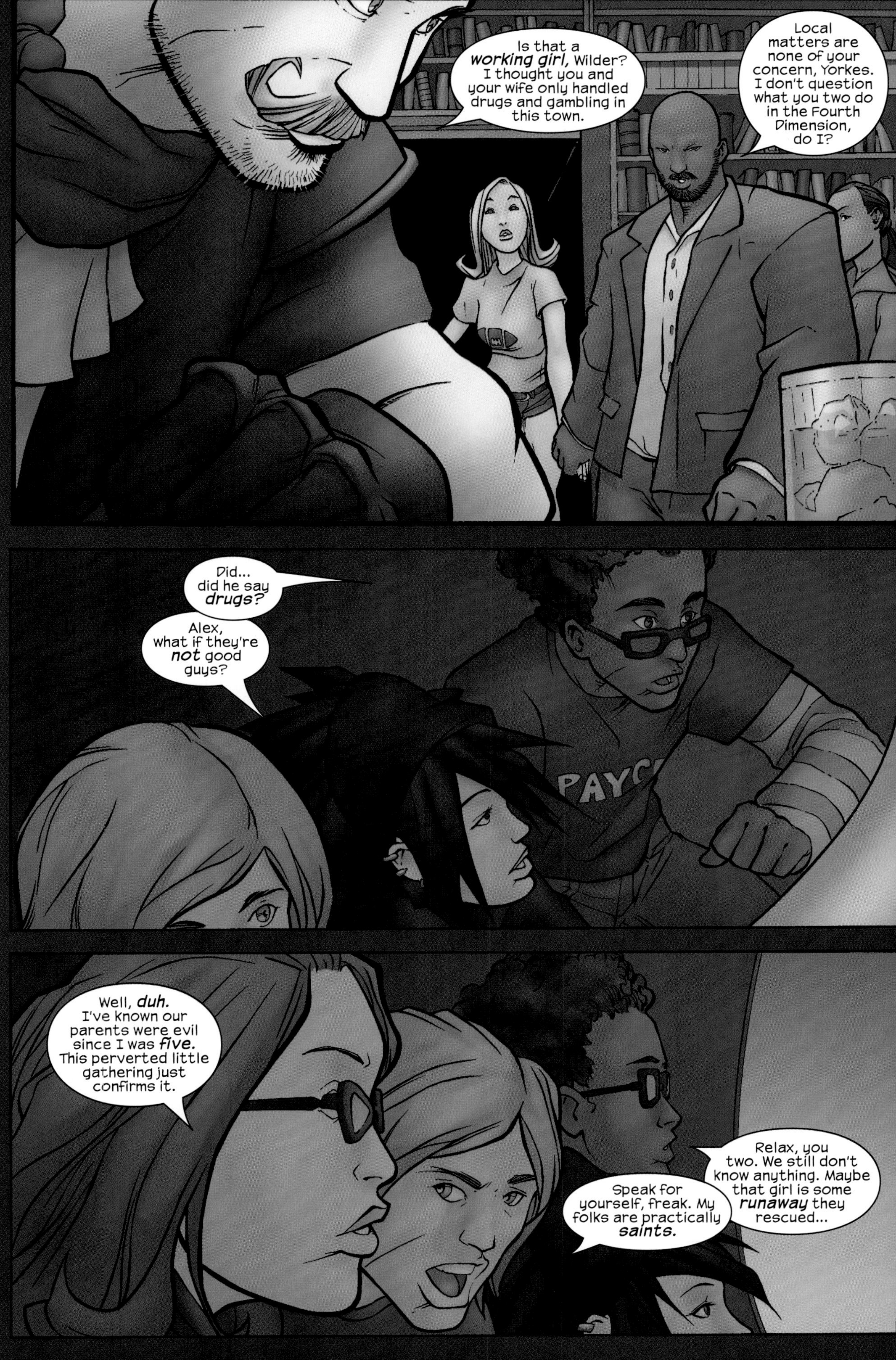

Is that a *working girl,* Wilder? I thought you and your wife only handled drugs and gambling in this town.
Local matters are none of your concern, Yorkes. I don't question what you two do in the Fourth Dimension, do I?
Did... did he say *drugs?*
Alex, what if they're *not* good guys?
Well, *duh.* I've known our parents were evil since I was *five.* This perverted little gathering just confirms it.
Speak for yourself, freak. My folks are practically *saints.*
Relax, you two. We still don't know anything. Maybe that girl is some *runaway* they rescued...

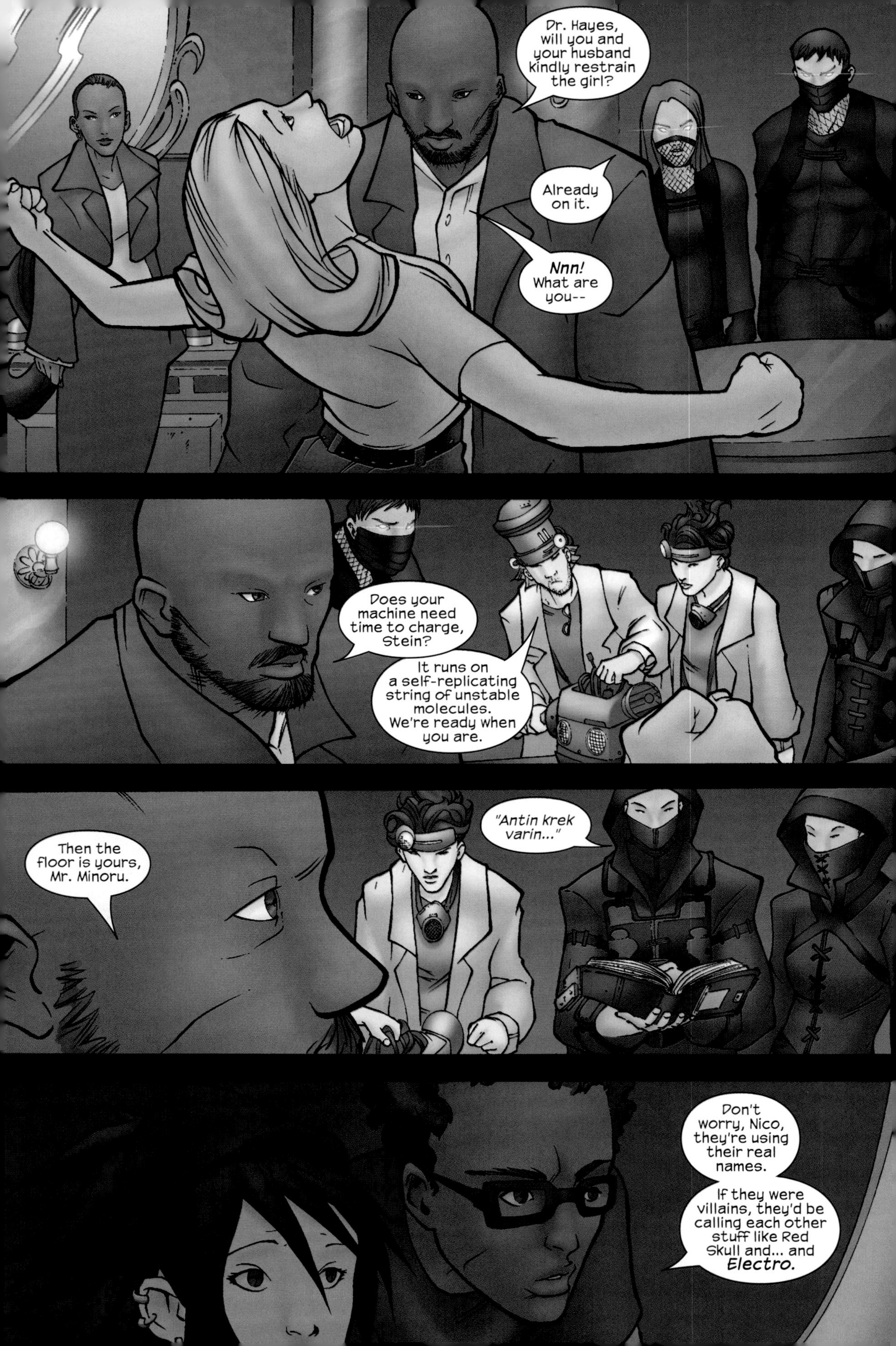
Dr. Hayes, will you and your husband kindly restrain the girl?
Already on it.
Nnn! What are you--
Does your machine need time to charge, Stein?
It runs on a self-replicating string of unstable molecules. We're ready when you are.
Then the floor is yours, Mr. Minoru.
"Antin krek varin..."
Don't worry, Nico, they're using their real names.
If they were villains, they'd be calling each other stuff like Red Skull and... and ***Electro.***

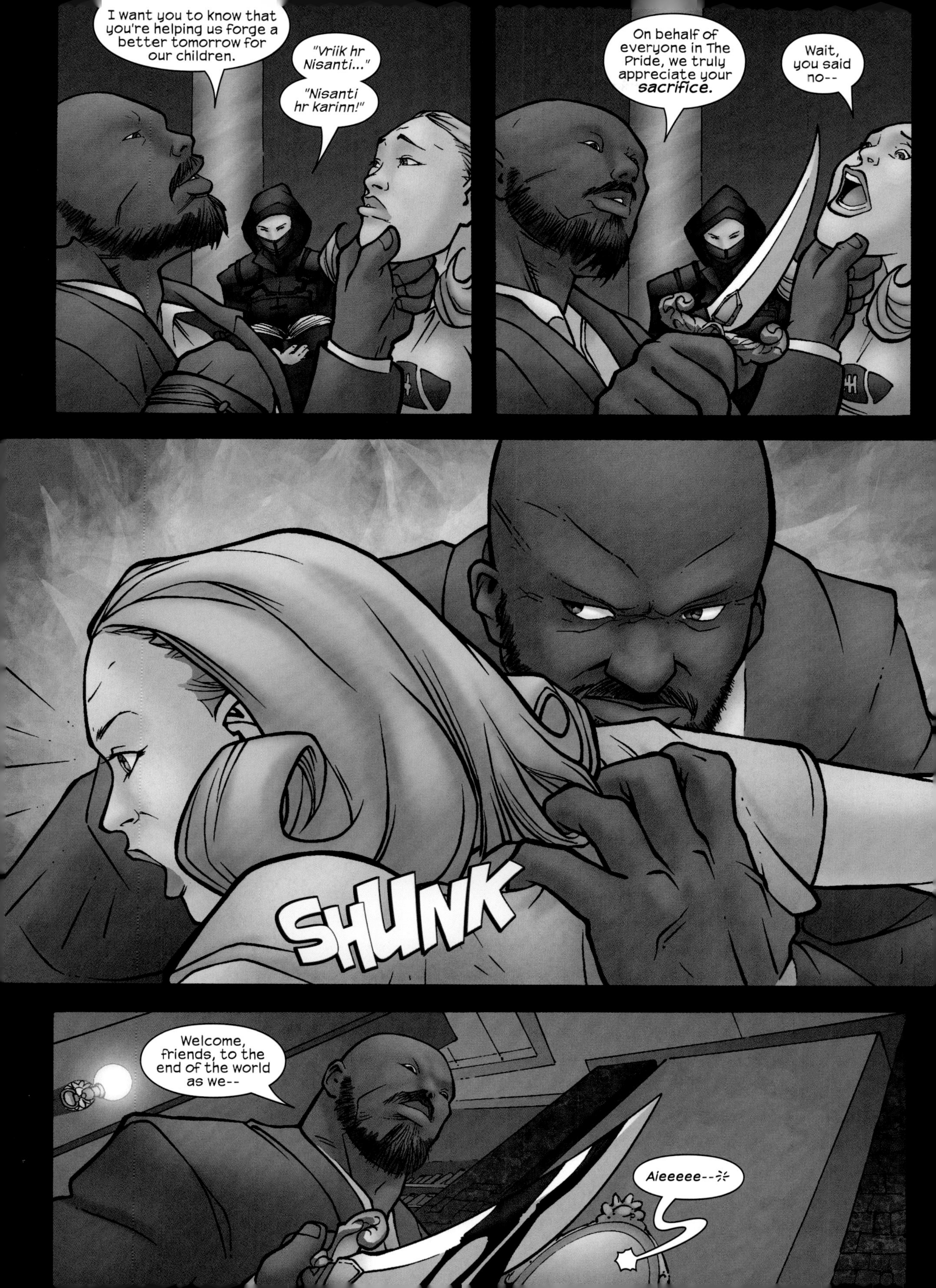
I want you to know that you're helping us forge a better tomorrow for our children.
"Vriik hr Nisanti..."
"Nisanti hr karinn!"
On behalf of everyone in The Pride, we truly appreciate your sacrifice.
Wait, you said no--
SHUNK
Welcome, friends, to the end of the world as we--
Aieeeee--

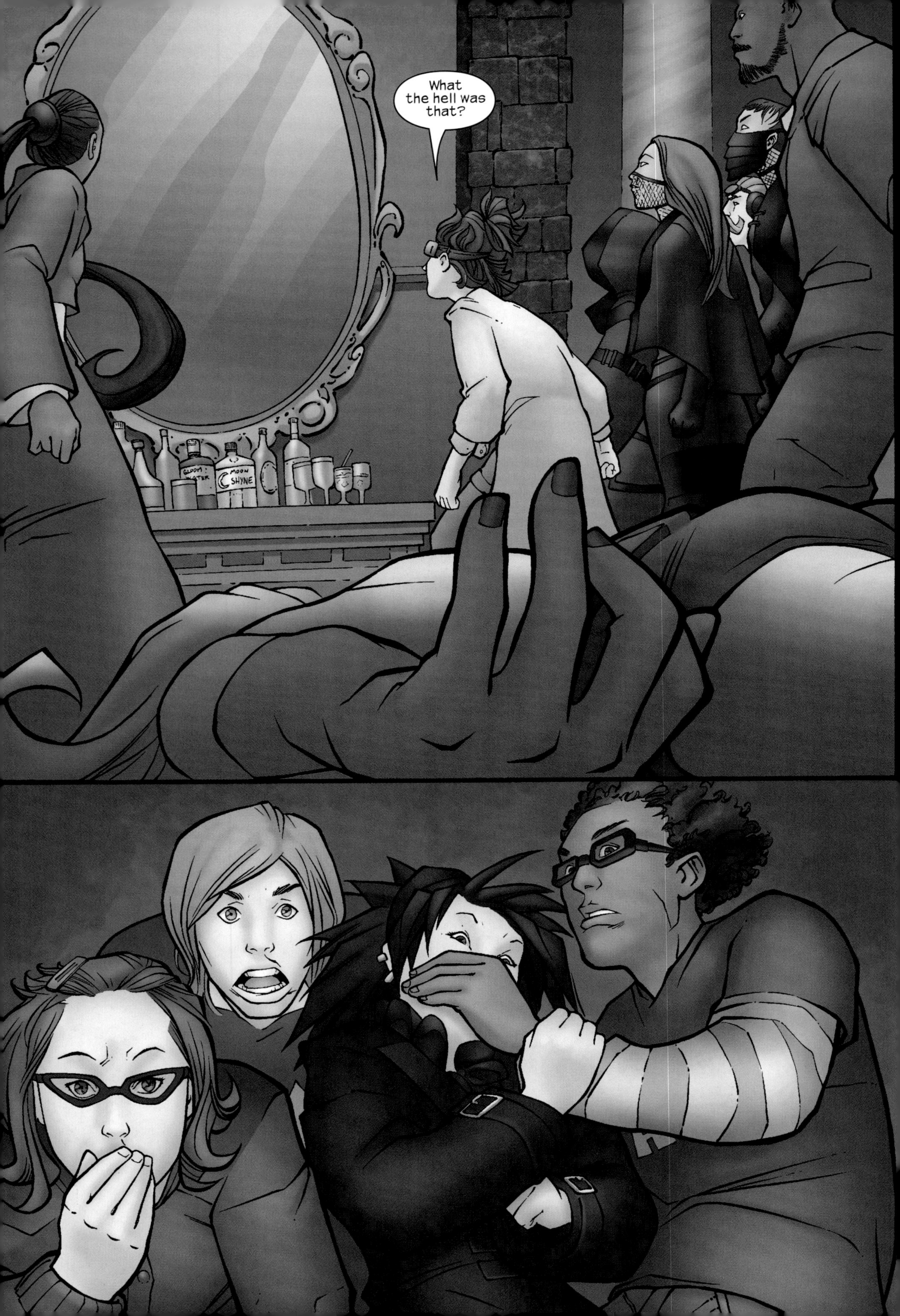
What the hell was that?
GLOOM WATER
MOON SHYNE

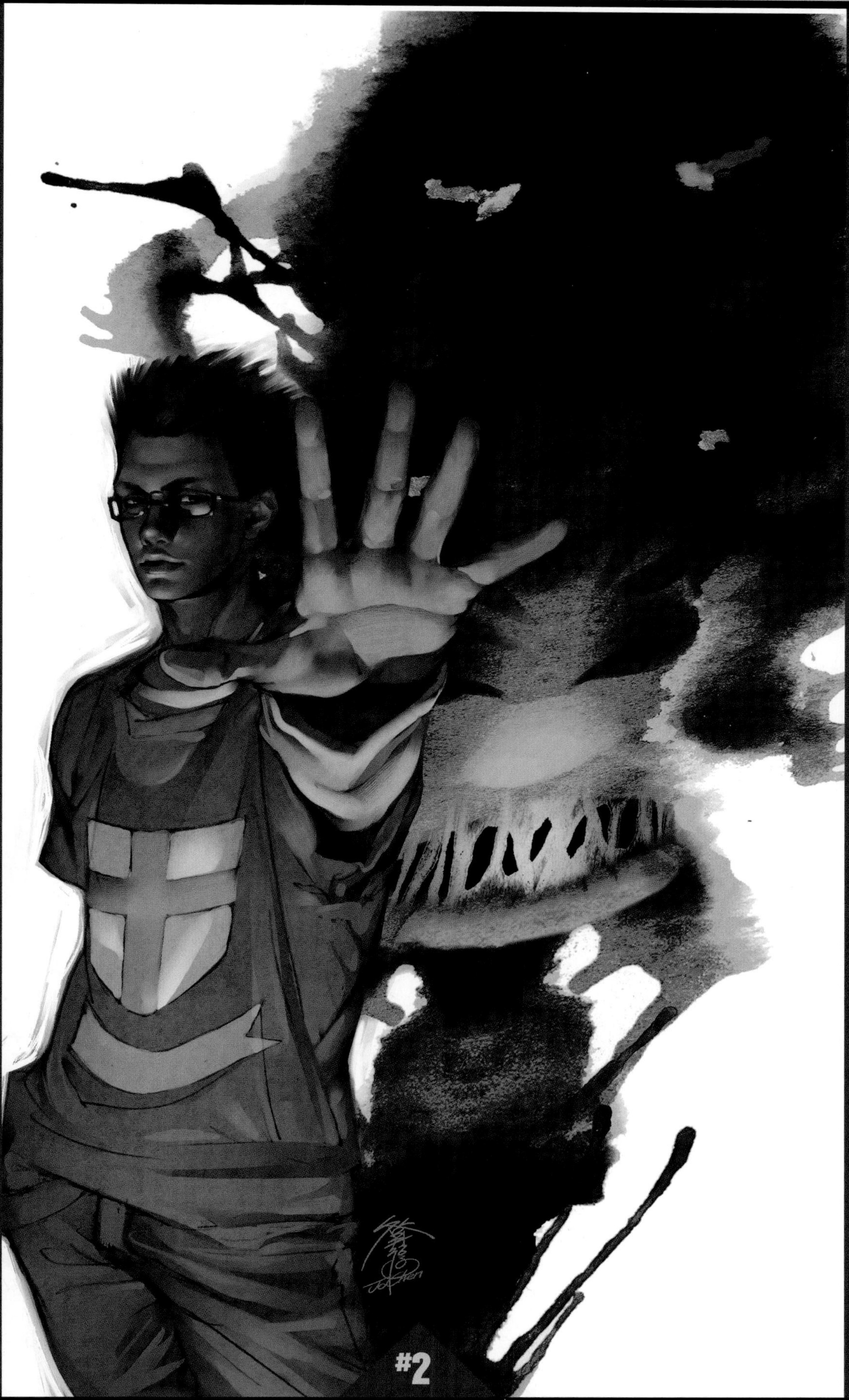
#2

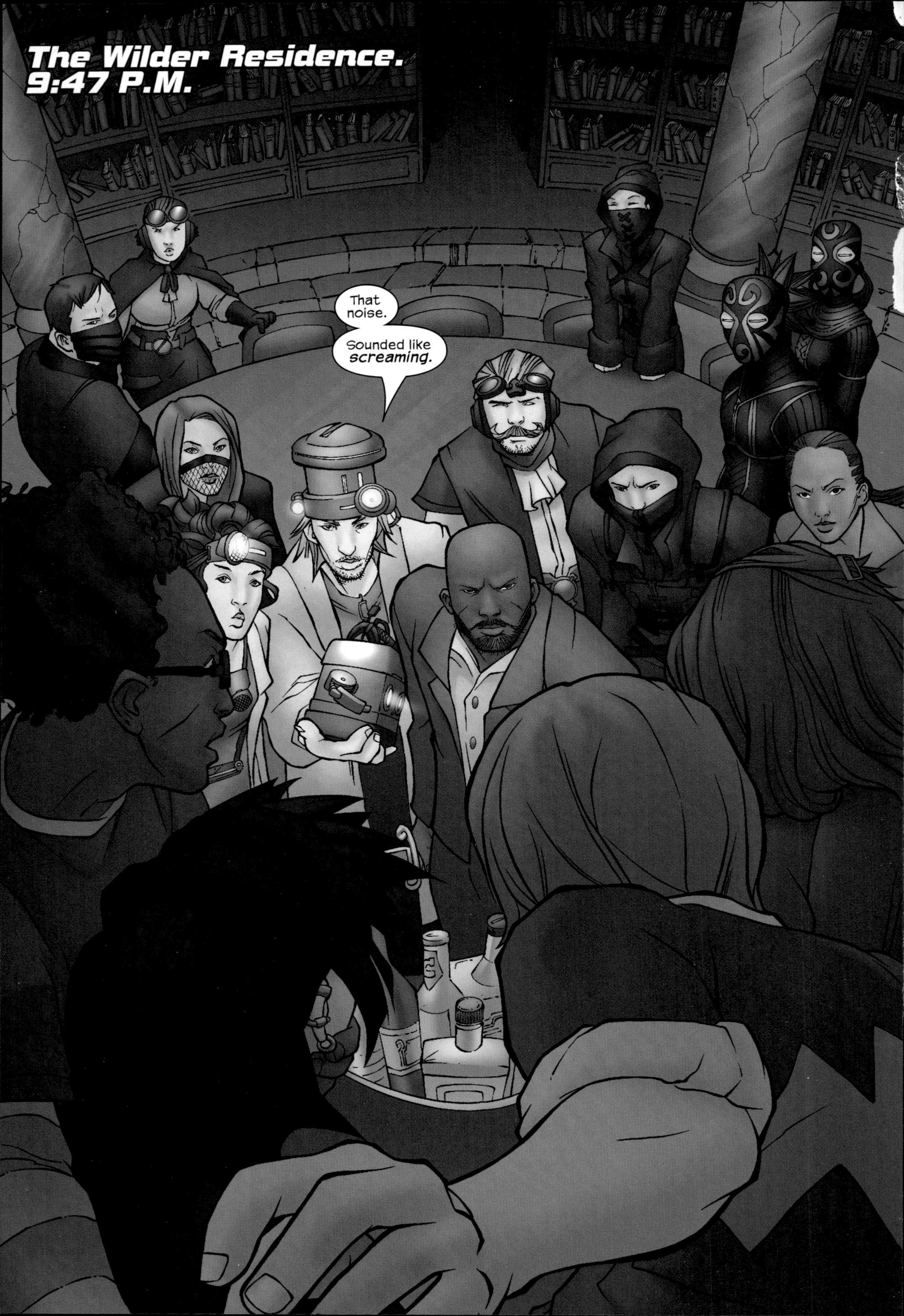
The Wilder Residence.
9:47 P.M.
That noise.
Sounded like *screaming.*

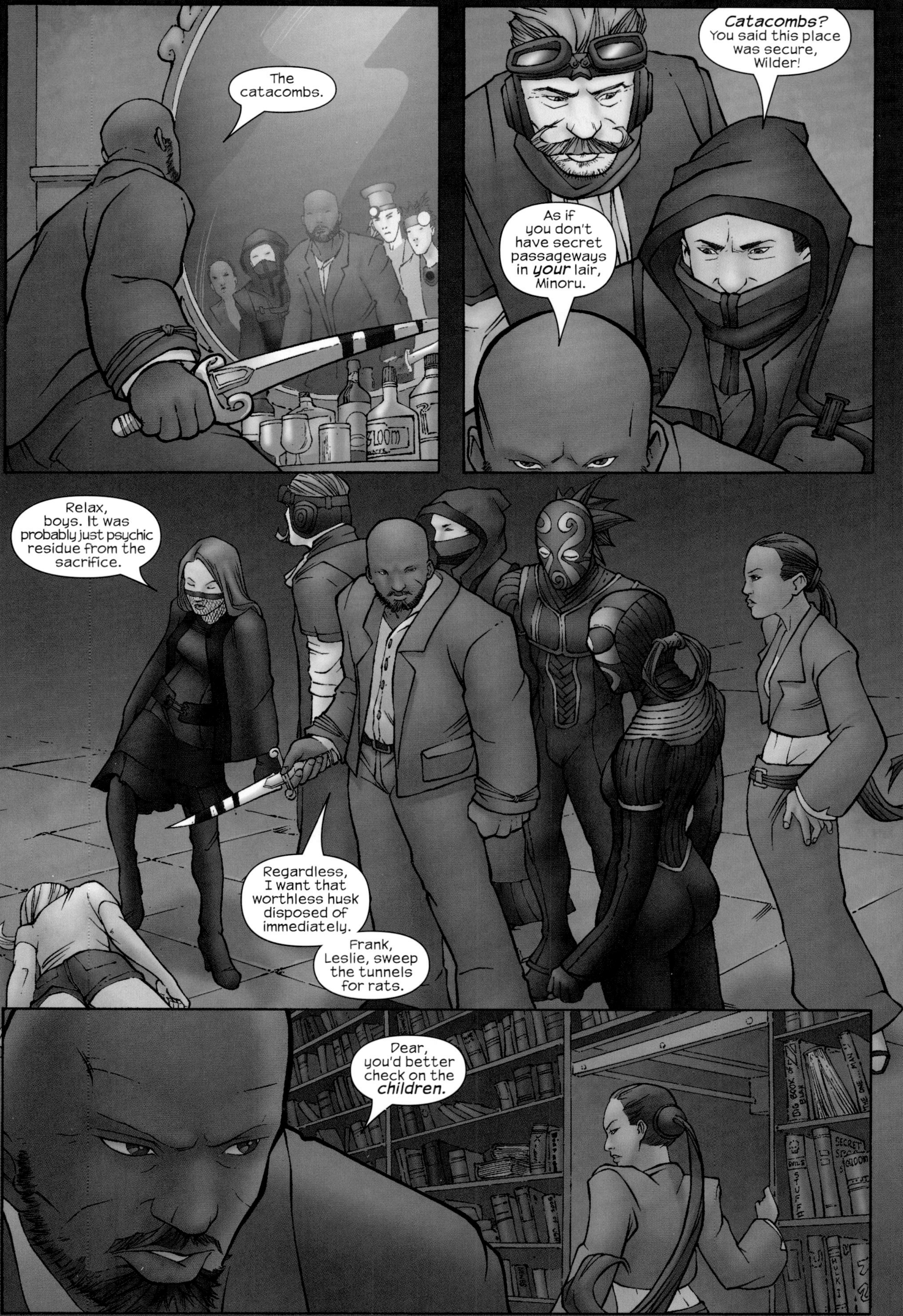
The catacombs.
Catacombs? You said this place was secure, Wilder!
As if you don't have secret passageways in your lair, Minoru.
Relax, boys. It was probably just psychic residue from the sacrifice.
Regardless, I want that worthless husk disposed of immediately.
Frank, Leslie, sweep the tunnels for rats.
Dear, you'd better check on the children.

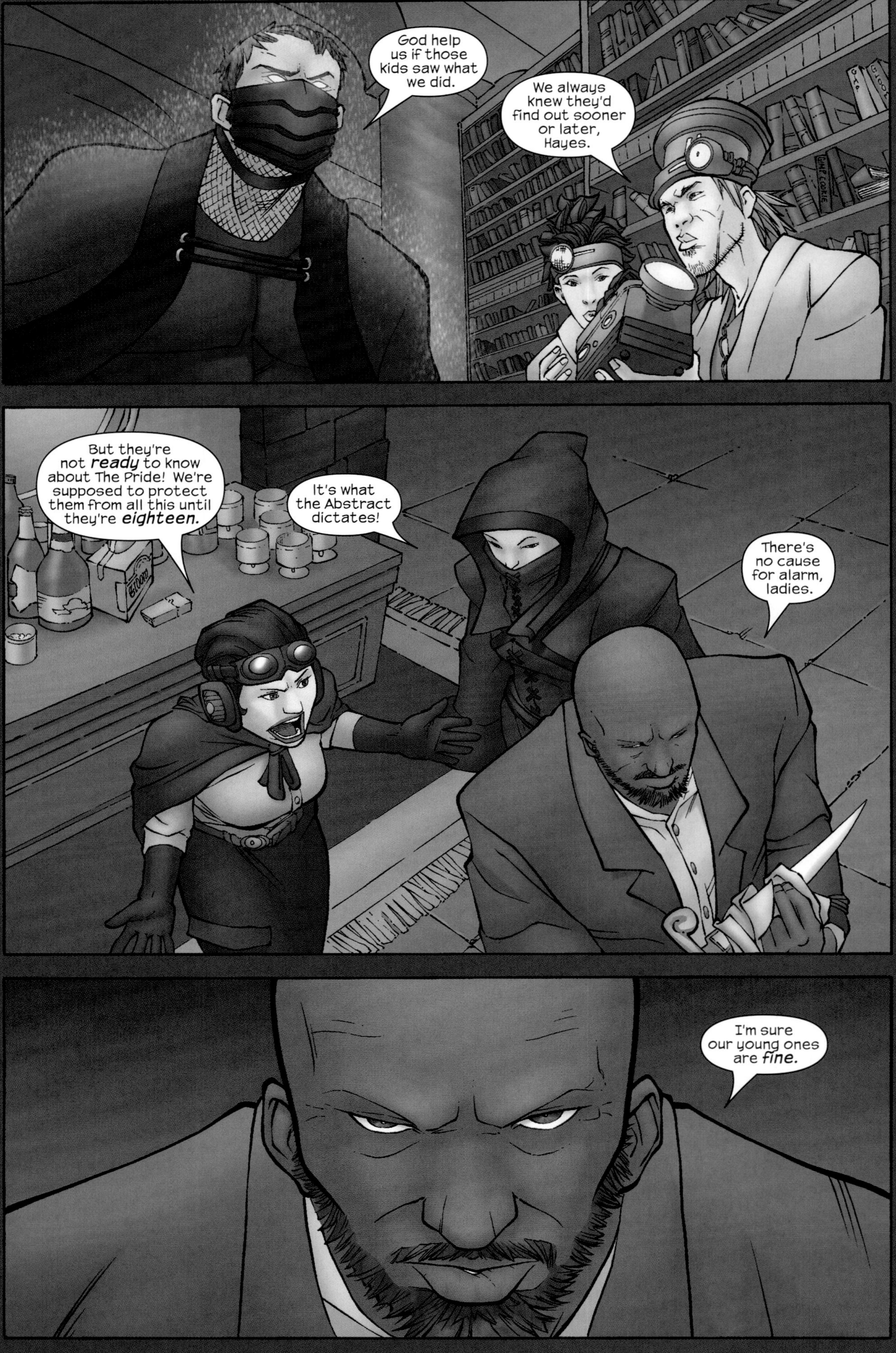
God help us if those kids saw what we did.
We always knew they'd find out sooner or later, Hayes.
But they're not *ready* to know about The Pride! We're supposed to protect them from all this until they're *eighteen.*
It's what the Abstract dictates!
There's no cause for alarm, ladies.
I'm sure our young ones are *fine.*

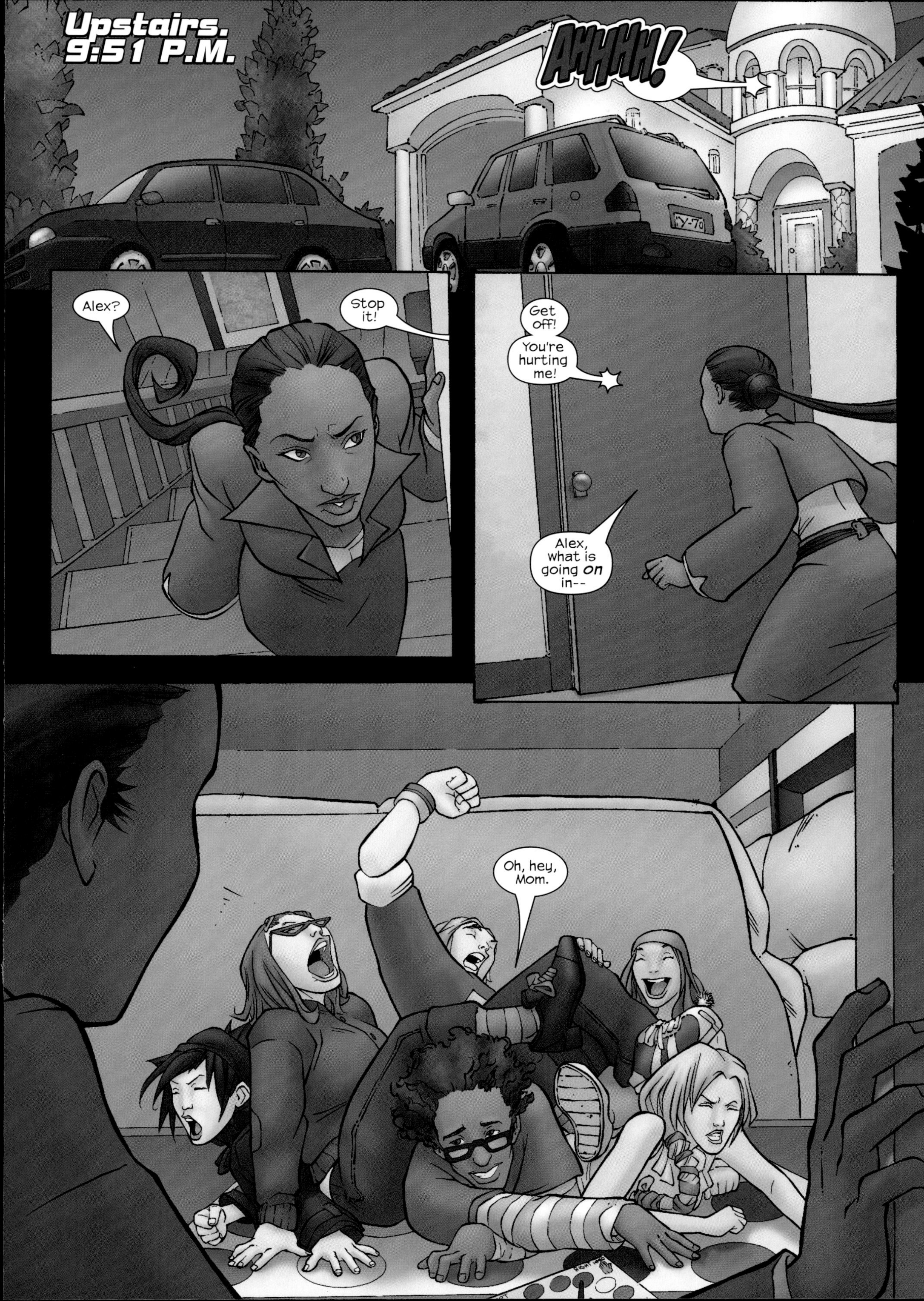
Upstairs.
9:51 P.M.
AHHHH!
Alex?
Stop it!
Get off!
You're hurting me!
Alex, what is going *on* in--
Oh, hey, Mom.

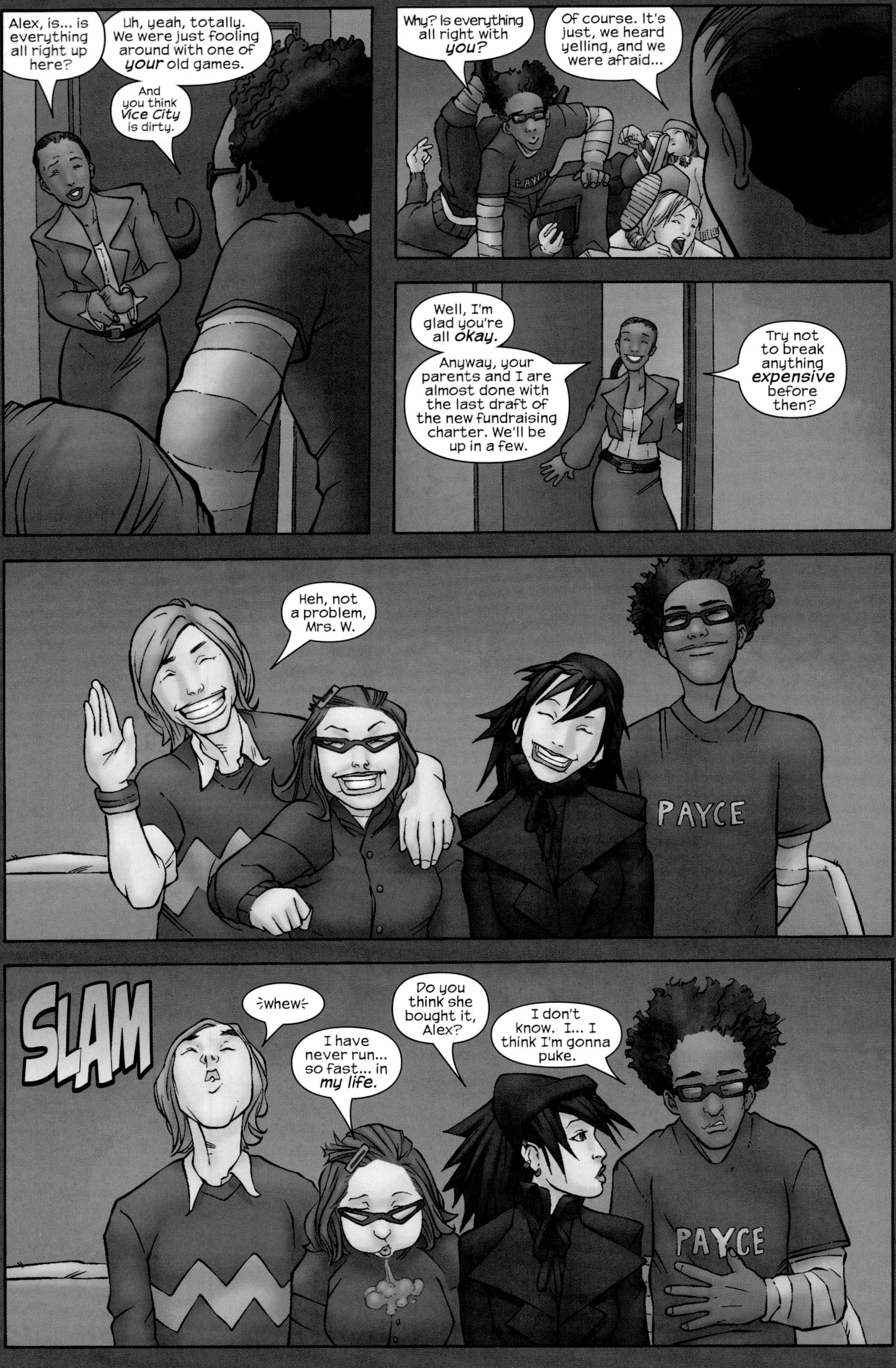
Alex, is... is everything all right up here?
Uh, yeah, totally. We were just fooling around with one of *your* old games.
And you think *Vice City* is dirty.
Why? Is everything all right with *you?*
Of course. It's just, we heard yelling, and we were afraid...
Well, I'm glad you're all *okay.*
Anyway, your parents and I are almost done with the last draft of the new fundraising charter. We'll be up in a few.
Try not to break anything *expensive* before then?
Heh, not a problem, Mrs. W.
PAYCE
SLAM
whew
I have never run... so fast... in *my life.*
Do you think she bought it, Alex?
I don't know. I... I think I'm gonna puke.
PAYCE

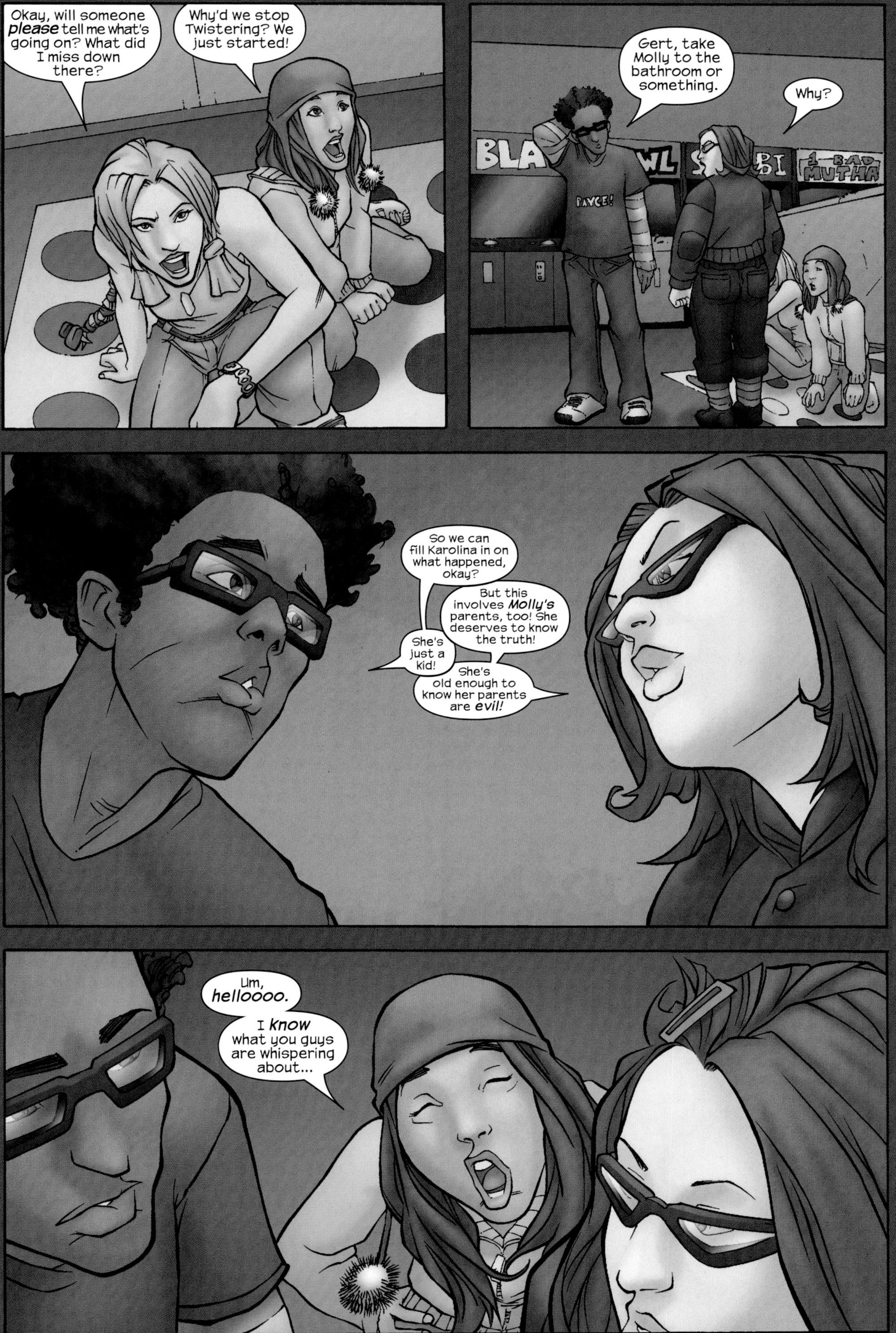
Okay, will someone *please* tell me what's going on? What did I miss down there?
Why'd we stop Twistering? We just started!
Gert, take Molly to the bathroom or something.
Why?
So we can fill Karolina in on what happened, okay?
But this involves *Molly's* parents, too! She deserves to know the truth!
She's just a kid!
She's old enough to know her parents are *evil!*
Um, *helloooo.*
I *know* what you guys are whispering about...

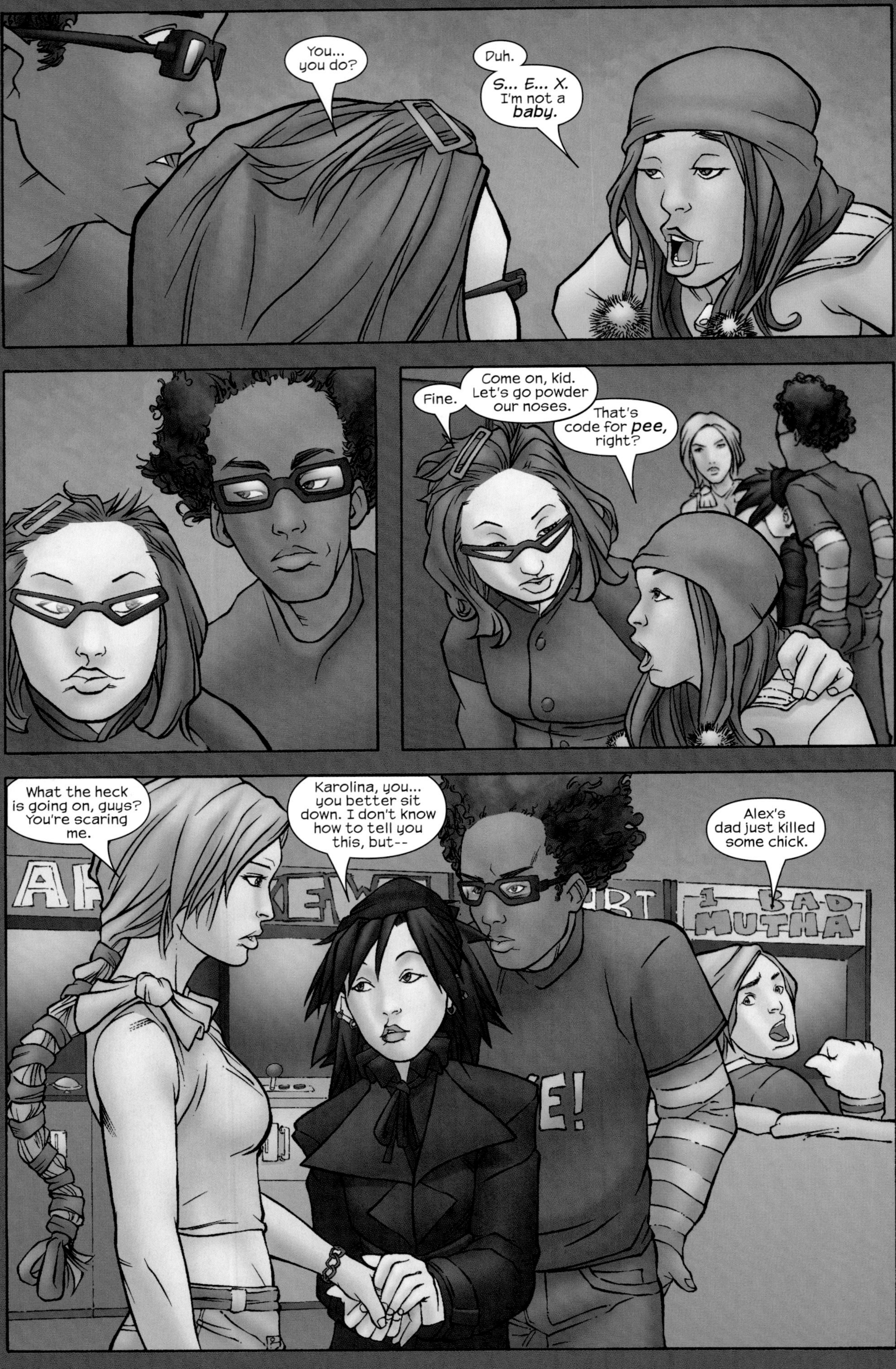
You... you do?
Duh.
S... E... X. I'm not a baby.
Fine.
Come on, kid. Let's go powder our noses.
That's code for pee, right?
What the heck is going on, guys? You're scaring me.
Karolina, you... you better sit down. I don't know how to tell you this, but--
Alex's dad just killed some chick.
1 BAD MUTHA

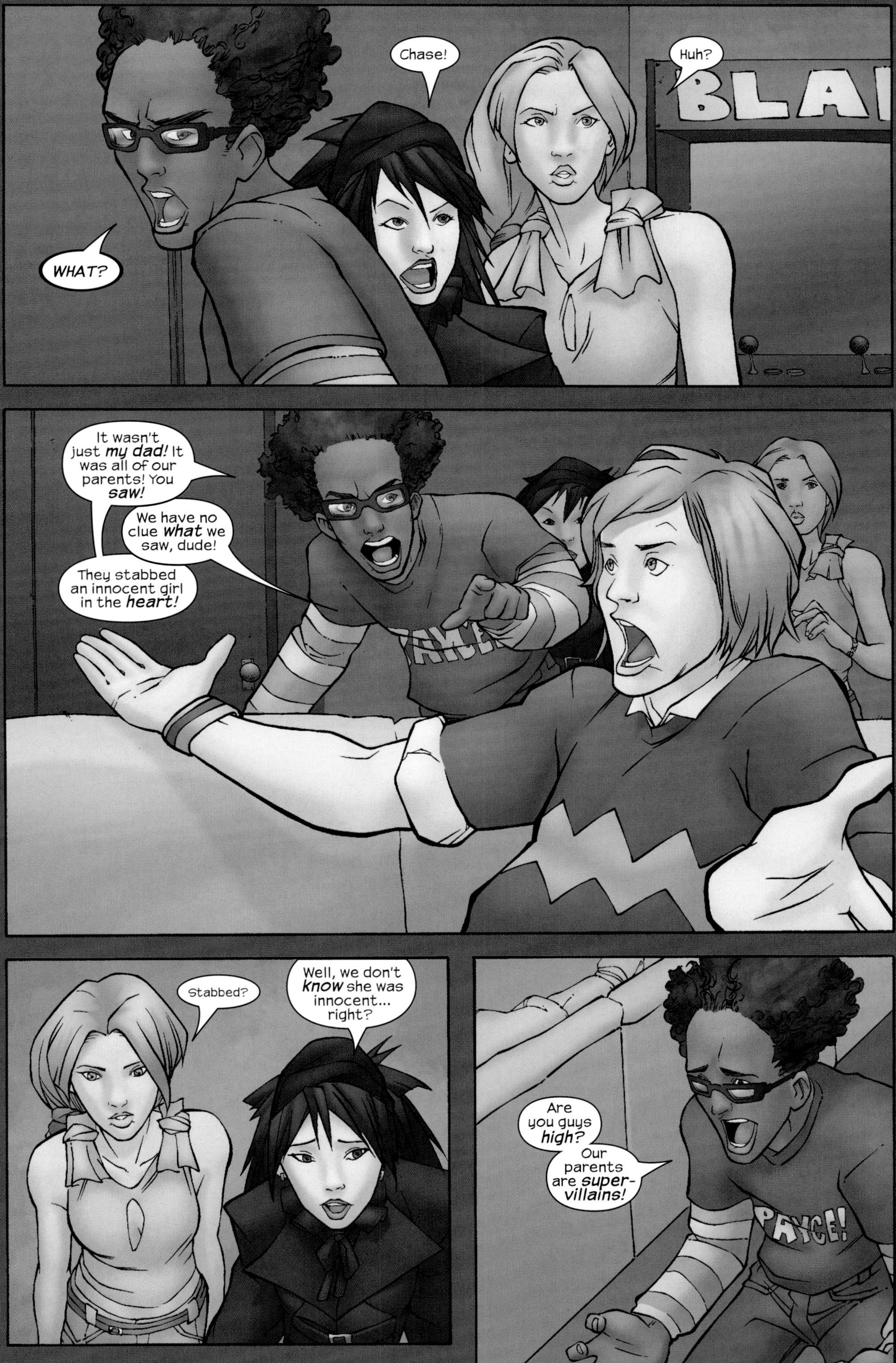
WHAT?
Chase!
Huh?
BLA
It wasn't just my dad! It was all of our parents! You saw!
We have no clue what we saw, dude!
They stabbed an innocent girl in the heart!
Stabbed?
Well, we don't know she was innocent... right?
Are you guys high?
Our parents are super-villains!
PAYCE!

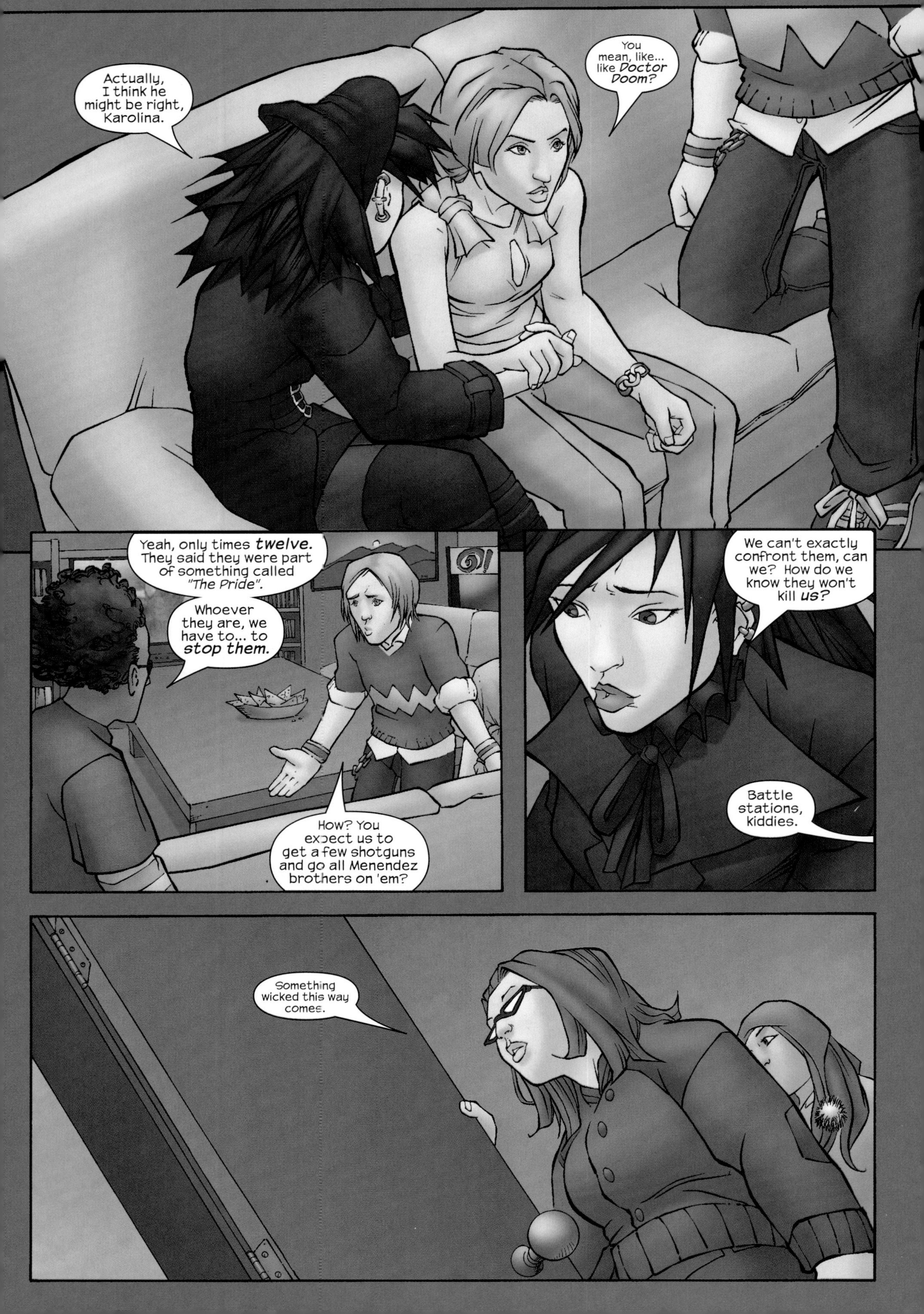
Actually, I think he might be right, Karolina.
You mean, like... like *Doctor Doom*?
Yeah, only times **twelve.** They said they were part of something called *"The Pride"*.
Whoever they are, we have to... to ***stop them.***
How? You expect us to get a few shotguns and go all Menendez brothers on 'em?
We can't exactly confront them, can we? How do we know they won't kill ***us?***
Battle stations, kiddies.
Something wicked this way comes.

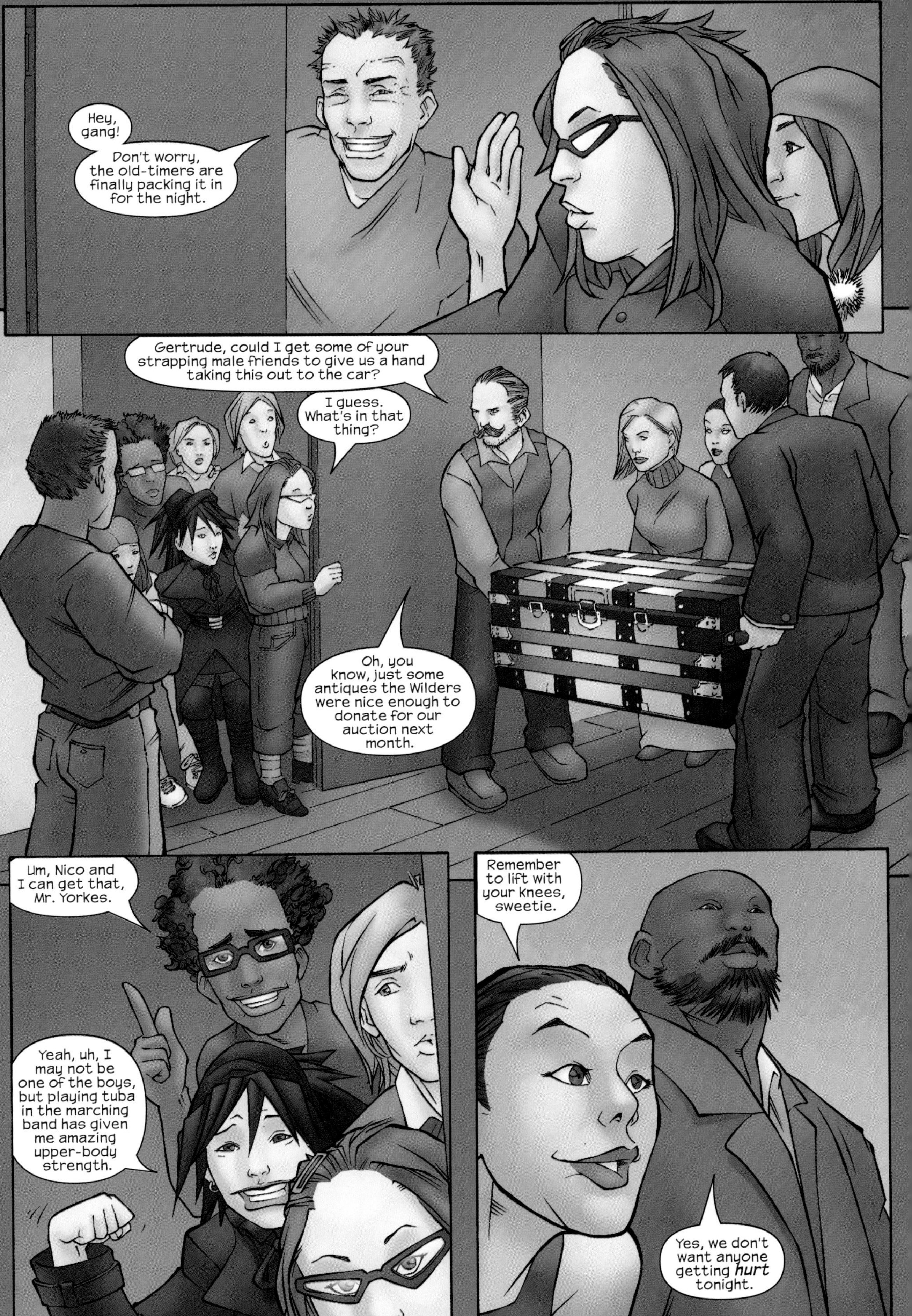
Hey, gang!
Don't worry, the old-timers are finally packing it in for the night.
Gertrude, could I get some of your strapping male friends to give us a hand taking this out to the car?
I guess. What's in that thing?
Oh, you know, just some antiques the Wilders were nice enough to donate for our auction next month.
Um, Nico and I can get that, Mr. Yorkes.
Yeah, uh, I may not be one of the boys, but playing tuba in the marching band has given me amazing upper-body strength.
Remember to lift with your knees, sweetie.
Yes, we don't want anyone getting *hurt* tonight.

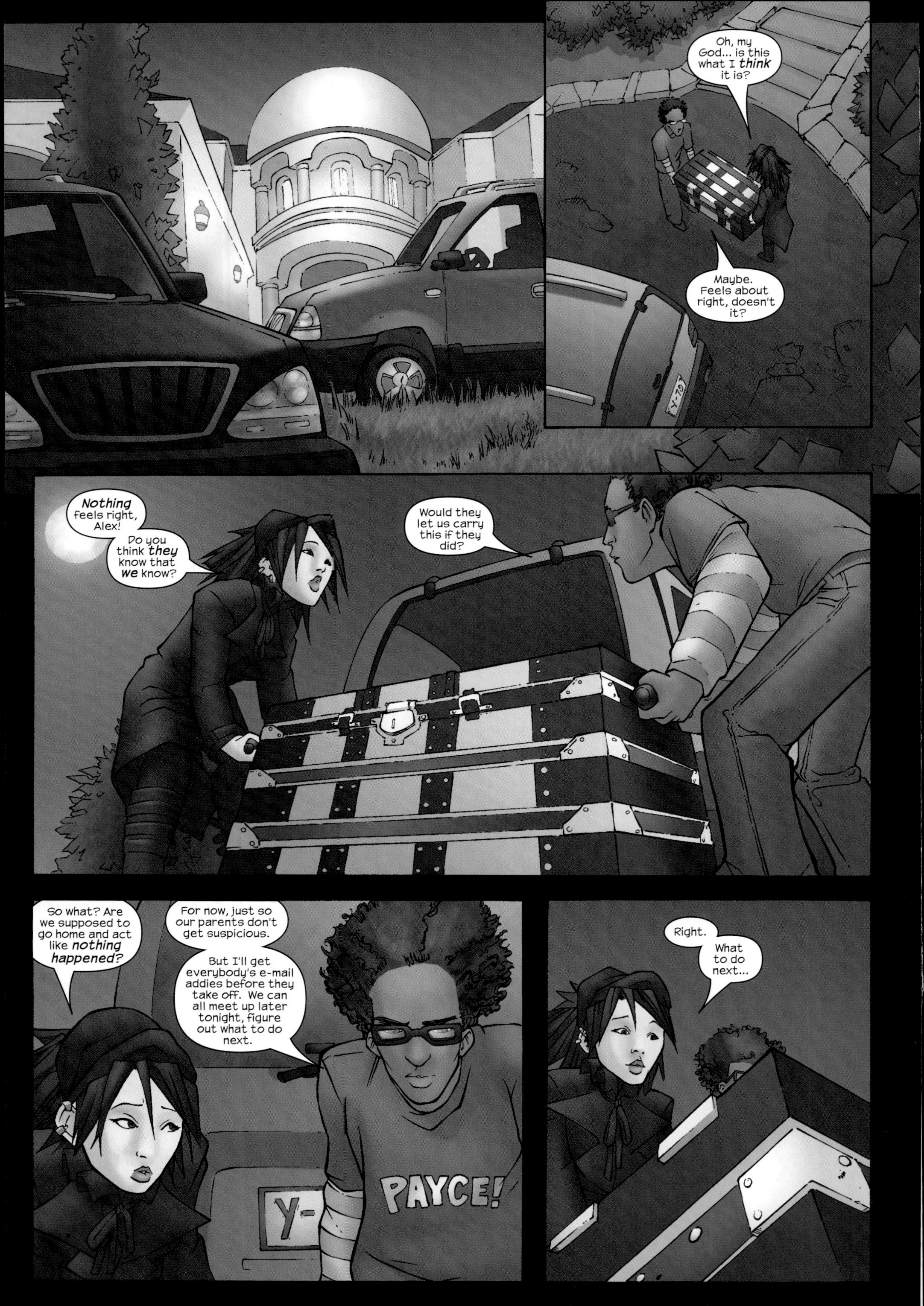
Oh, my God... is this what I *think* it is?
Maybe. Feels about right, doesn't it?
Nothing feels right, Alex!
Do you think *they* know that *we* know?
Would they let us carry this if they did?
So what? Are we supposed to go home and act like *nothing happened?*
For now, just so our parents don't get suspicious.
But I'll get everybody's e-mail addies before they take off. We can all meet up later tonight, figure out what to do next.
PAYCE!
Right.
What to do next...

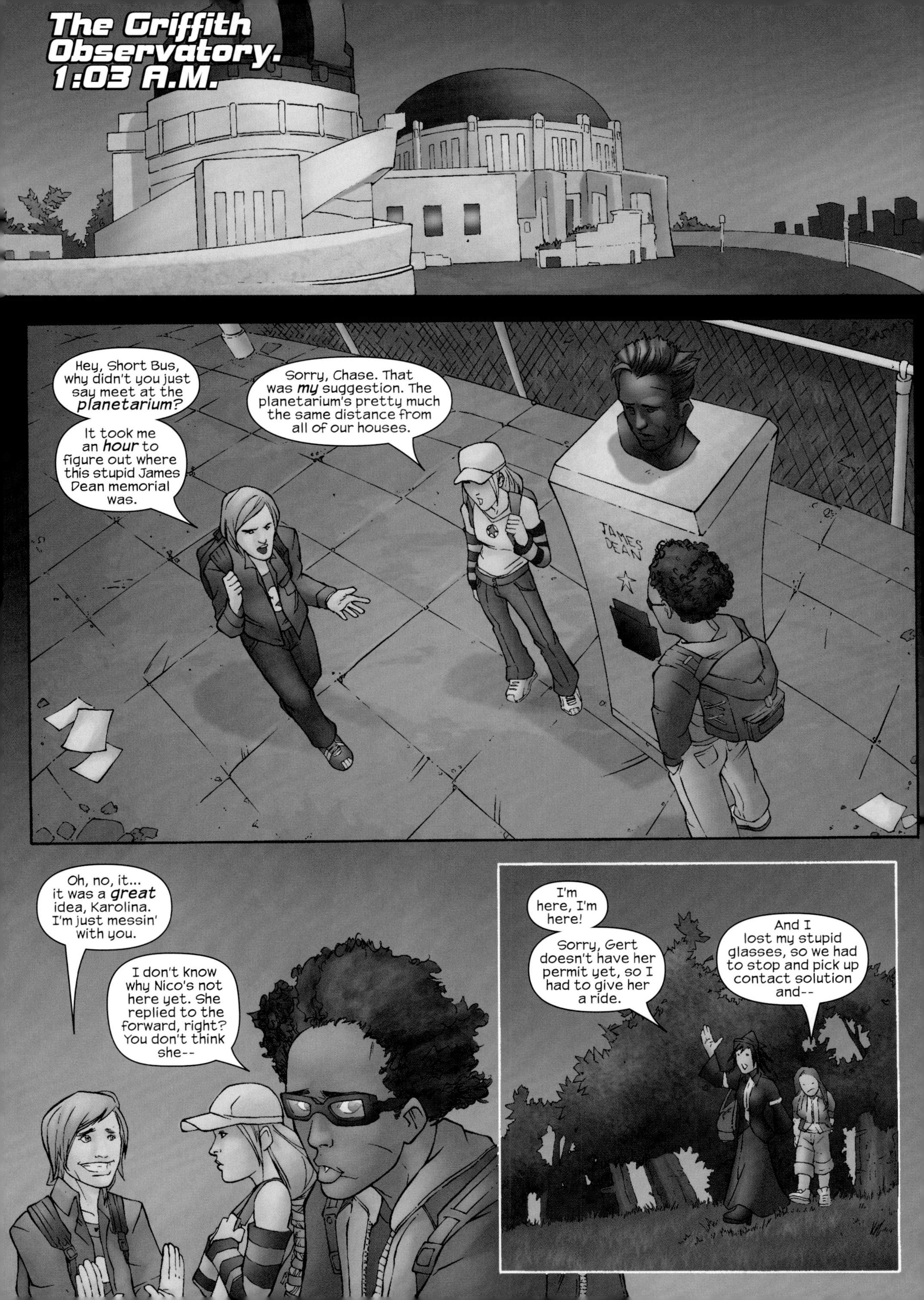
The Griffith Observatory. 1:03 A.M.
Hey, Short Bus, why didn't you just say meet at the planetarium?
It took me an hour to figure out where this stupid James Dean memorial was.
Sorry, Chase. That was my suggestion. The planetarium's pretty much the same distance from all of our houses.
JAMES DEAN
Oh, no, it... it was a great idea, Karolina. I'm just messin' with you.
I don't know why Nico's not here yet. She replied to the forward, right? You don't think she--
I'm here, I'm here!
Sorry, Gert doesn't have her permit yet, so I had to give her a ride.
And I lost my stupid glasses, so we had to stop and pick up contact solution and--

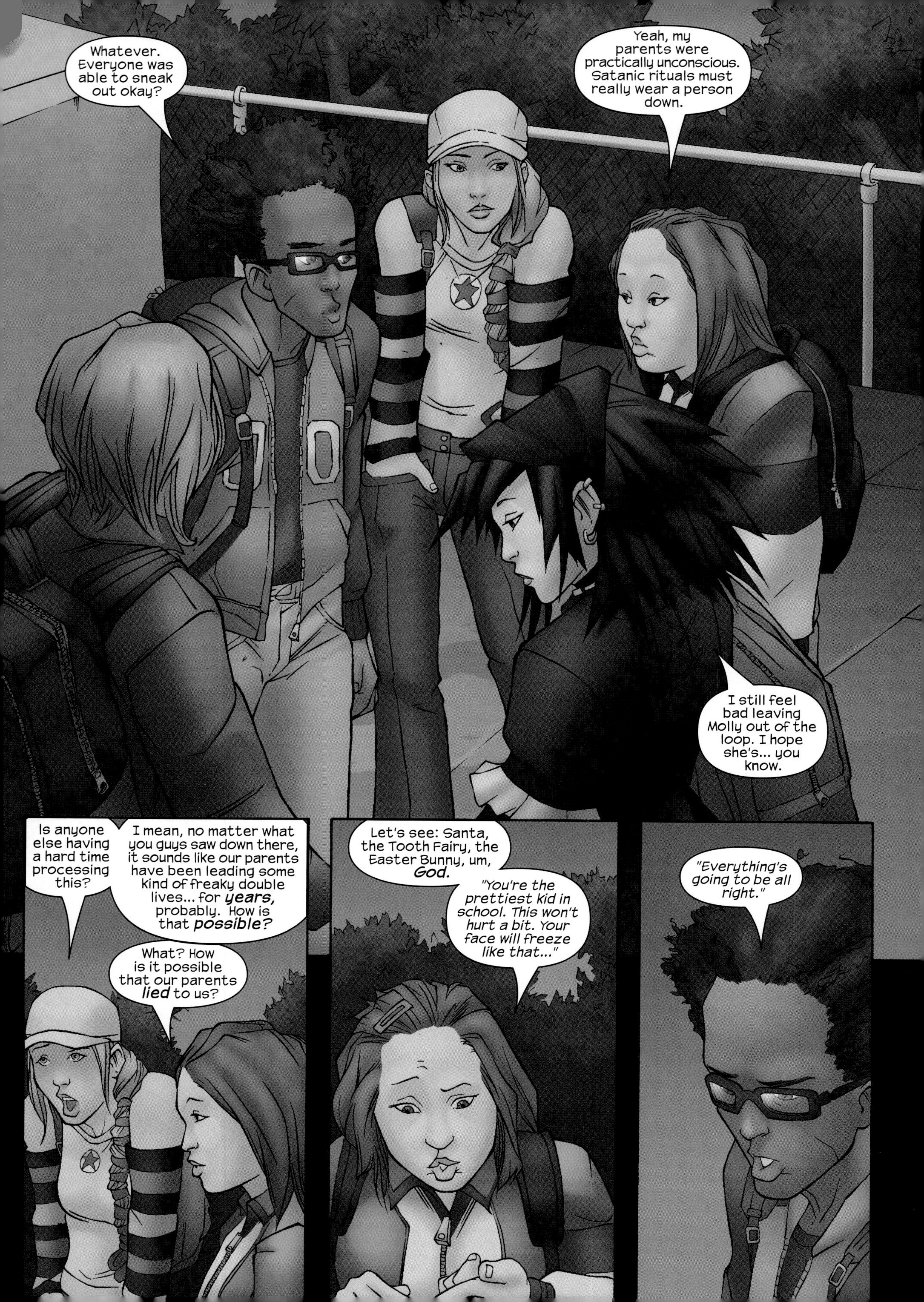
Whatever. Everyone was able to sneak out okay?
Yeah, my parents were practically unconscious. Satanic rituals must really wear a person down.
I still feel bad leaving Molly out of the loop. I hope she's... you know.
Is anyone else having a hard time processing this?
I mean, no matter what you guys saw down there, it sounds like our parents have been leading some kind of freaky double lives... for *years,* probably. How is that *possible?*
What? How is it possible that our parents *lied* to us?
Let's see: Santa, the Tooth Fairy, the Easter Bunny, um, *God.*
"You're the prettiest kid in school. This won't hurt a bit. Your face will freeze like that..."
"Everything's going to be all right."

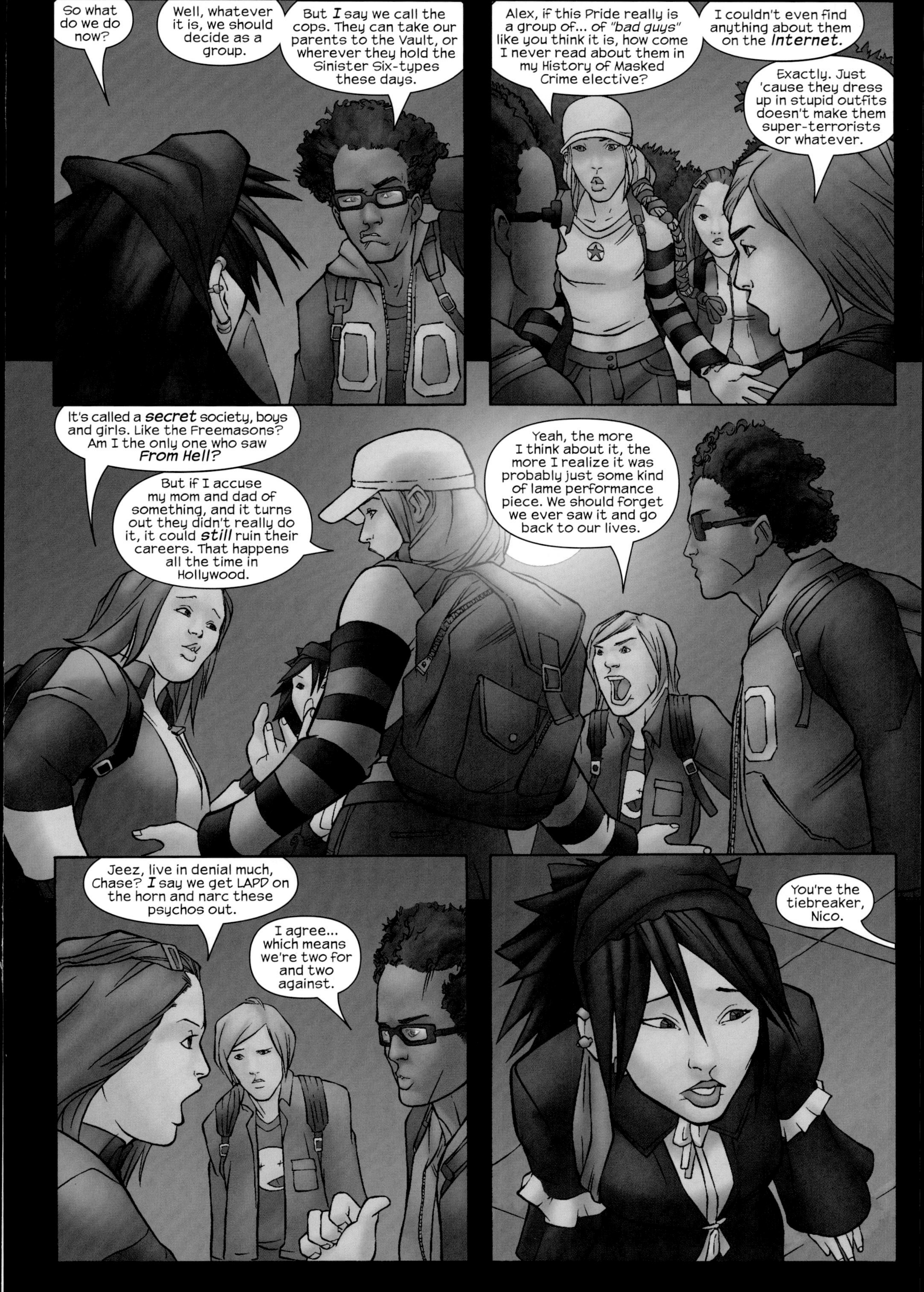
So what do we do now?
Well, whatever it is, we should decide as a group.
But *I* say we call the cops. They can take our parents to the Vault, or wherever they hold the Sinister Six-types these days.
Alex, if this Pride really is a group of... of *"bad guys"* like you think it is, how come I never read about them in my History of Masked Crime elective?
I couldn't even find anything about them on the *Internet.*
Exactly. Just 'cause they dress up in stupid outfits doesn't make them super-terrorists or whatever.
It's called a *secret* society, boys and girls. Like the Freemasons? Am I the only one who saw *From Hell?*
But if I accuse my mom and dad of something, and it turns out they didn't really do it, it could *still* ruin their careers. That happens all the time in Hollywood.
Yeah, the more I think about it, the more I realize it was probably just some kind of lame performance piece. We should forget we ever saw it and go back to our lives.
Jeez, live in denial much, Chase? *I* say we get LAPD on the horn and narc these psychos out.
I agree... which means we're two for and two against.
You're the tiebreaker, Nico.

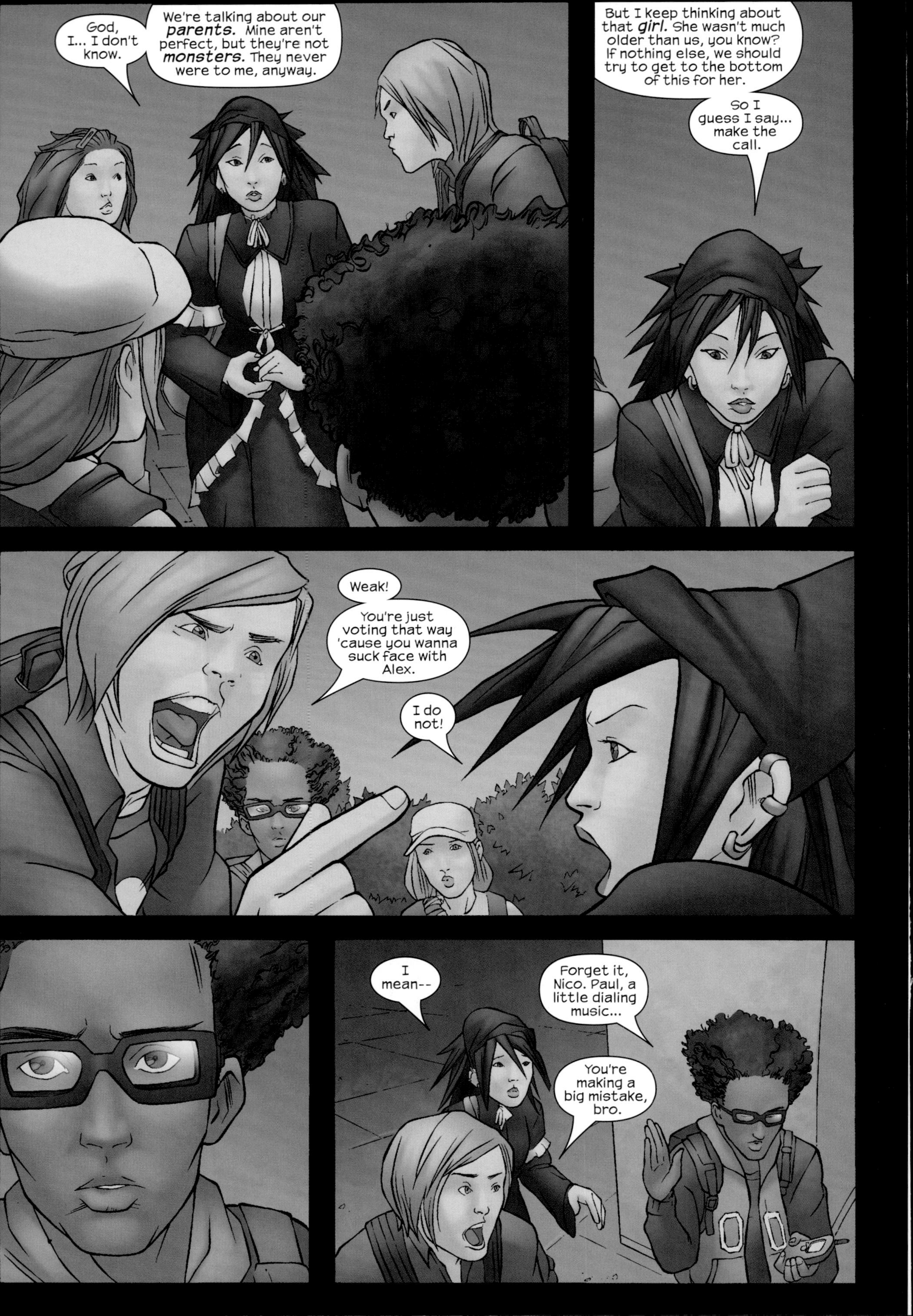
God, I... I don't know.
We're talking about our *parents.* Mine aren't perfect, but they're not *monsters.* They never were to me, anyway.
But I keep thinking about that *girl.* She wasn't much older than us, you know? If nothing else, we should try to get to the bottom of this for her.
So I guess I say... make the call.
Weak!
You're just voting that way 'cause you wanna suck face with Alex.
I do not!
I mean--
Forget it, Nico. Paul, a little dialing music...
You're making a big mistake, bro.

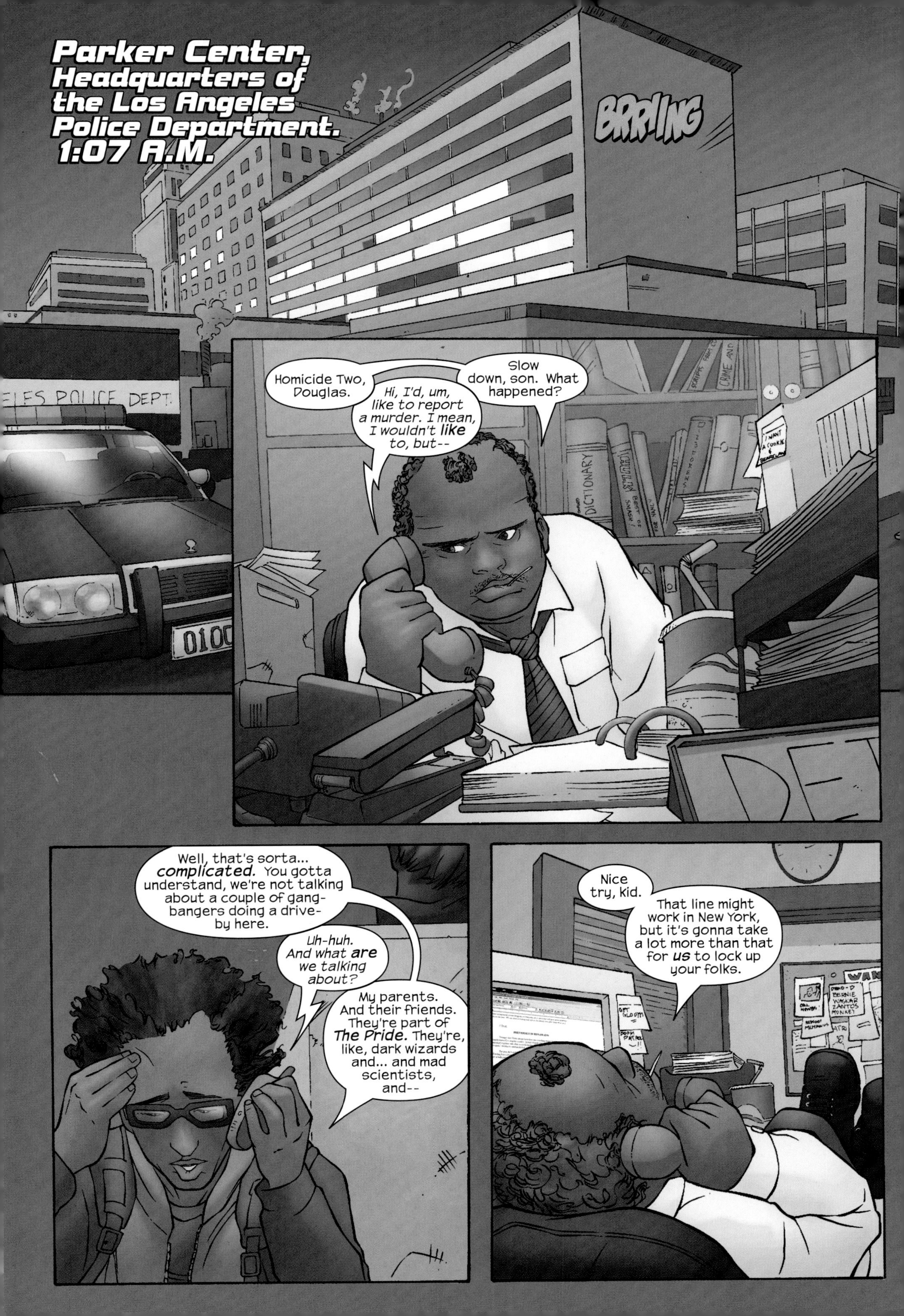
Parker Center, Headquarters of the Los Angeles Police Department. 1:07 A.M.
BRRIING
Homicide Two, Douglas.
Hi, I'd, um, like to report a murder. I mean, I wouldn't like to, but--
Slow down, son. What happened?
DICTIONARY
Well, that's sorta... complicated. You gotta understand, we're not talking about a couple of gang-bangers doing a drive-by here.
Uh-huh. And what are we talking about?
My parents. And their friends. They're part of The Pride. They're, like, dark wizards and... and mad scientists, and--
Nice try, kid.
That line might work in New York, but it's gonna take a lot more than that for us to lock up your folks.

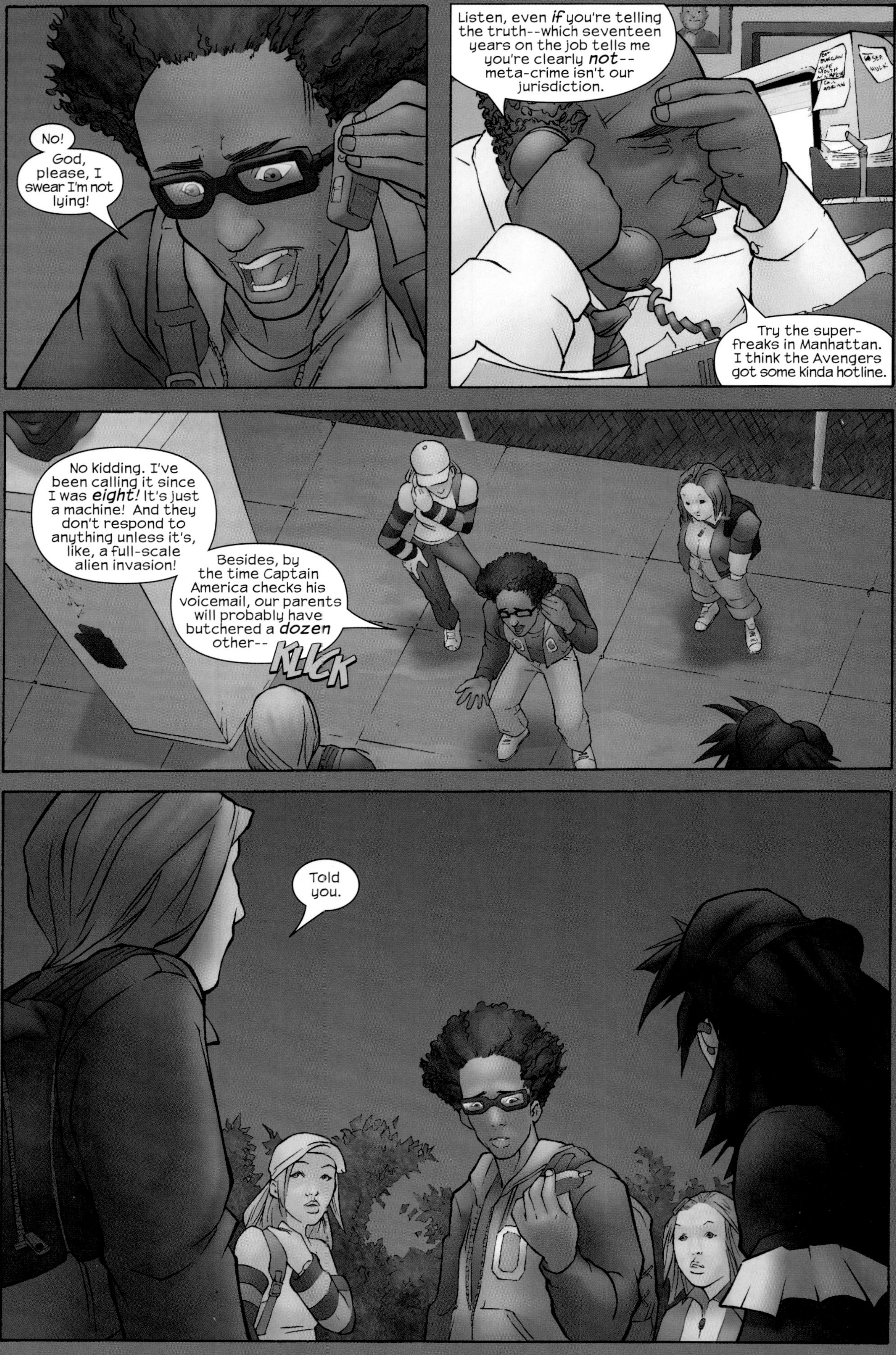
No! God, please, I swear I'm not lying!
Listen, even *if* you're telling the truth--which seventeen years on the job tells me you're clearly *not*--meta-crime isn't our jurisdiction.
Try the super-freaks in Manhattan. I think the Avengers got some kinda hotline.
No kidding. I've been calling it since I was *eight!* It's just a machine! And they don't respond to anything unless it's, like, a full-scale alien invasion!
Besides, by the time Captain America checks his voicemail, our parents will probably have butchered a *dozen* other--
KLICK
Told you.

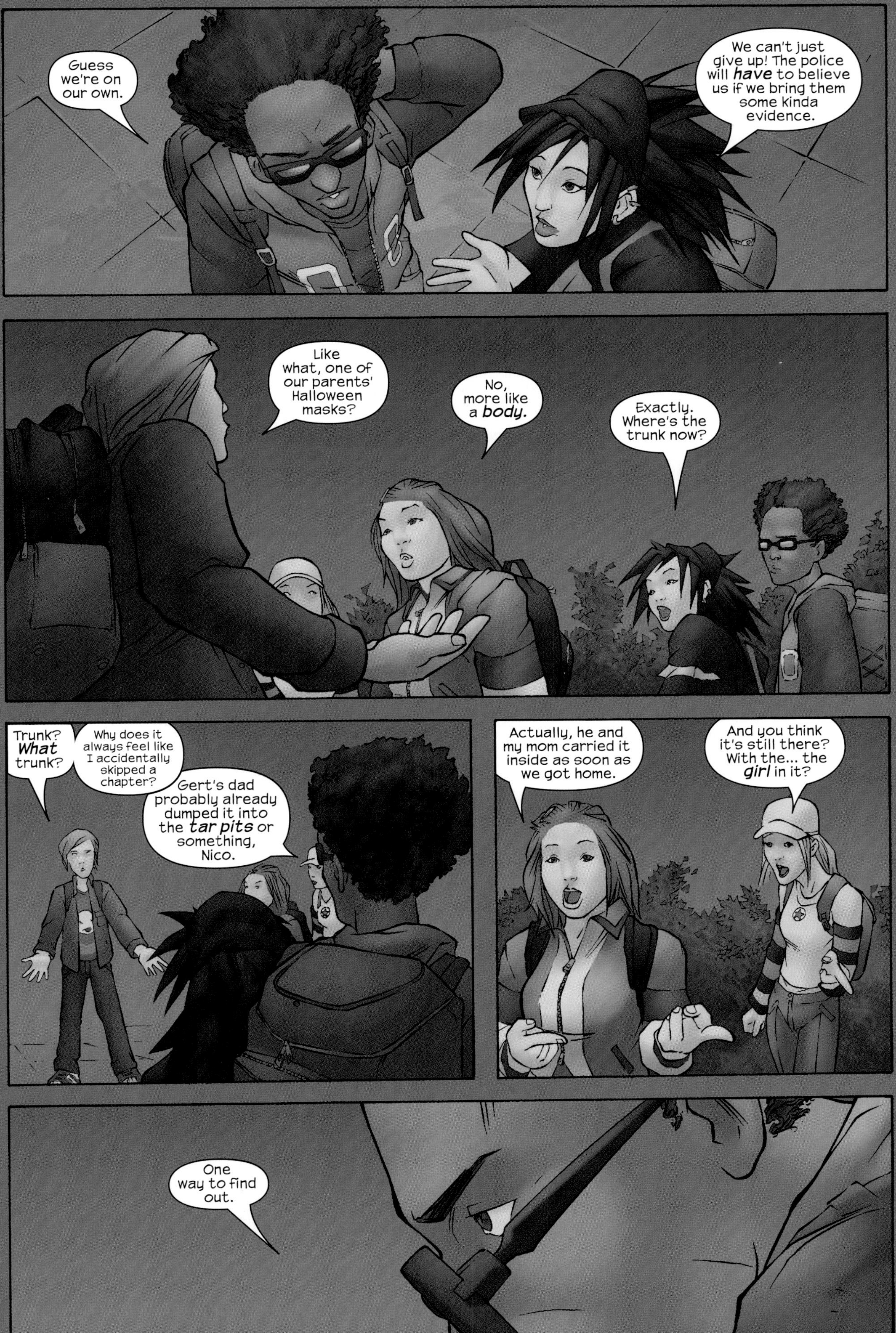
Guess we're on our own.
We can't just give up! The police will *have* to believe us if we bring them some kinda evidence.
Like what, one of our parents' Halloween masks?
No, more like a *body.*
Exactly. Where's the trunk now?
Trunk? *What* trunk?
Why does it always feel like I accidentally skipped a chapter?
Gert's dad probably already dumped it into the *tar pits* or something, Nico.
Actually, he and my mom carried it inside as soon as we got home.
And you think it's still there? With the... the *girl* in it?
One way to find out.

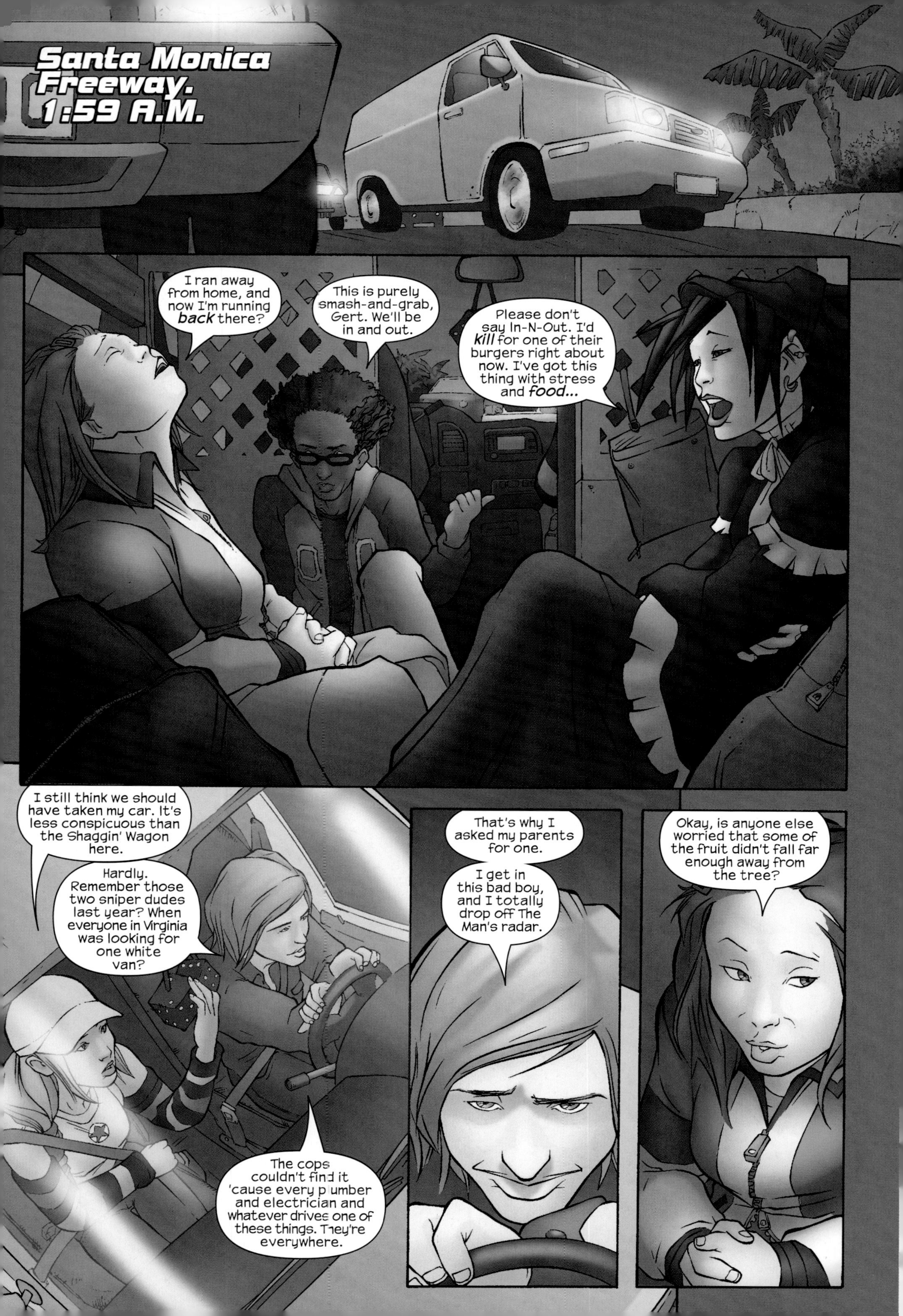
Santa Monica Freeway. 1:59 A.M.
I ran away from home, and now I'm running back there?
This is purely smash-and-grab, Gert. We'll be in and out.
Please don't say In-N-Out. I'd kill for one of their burgers right about now. I've got this thing with stress and food...
I still think we should have taken my car. It's less conspicuous than the Shaggin' Wagon here.
Hardly. Remember those two sniper dudes last year? When everyone in Virginia was looking for one white van?
The cops couldn't find it 'cause every plumber and electrician and whatever drives one of these things. They're everywhere.
That's why I asked my parents for one.
I get in this bad boy, and I totally drop off The Man's radar.
Okay, is anyone else worried that some of the fruit didn't fall far enough away from the tree?

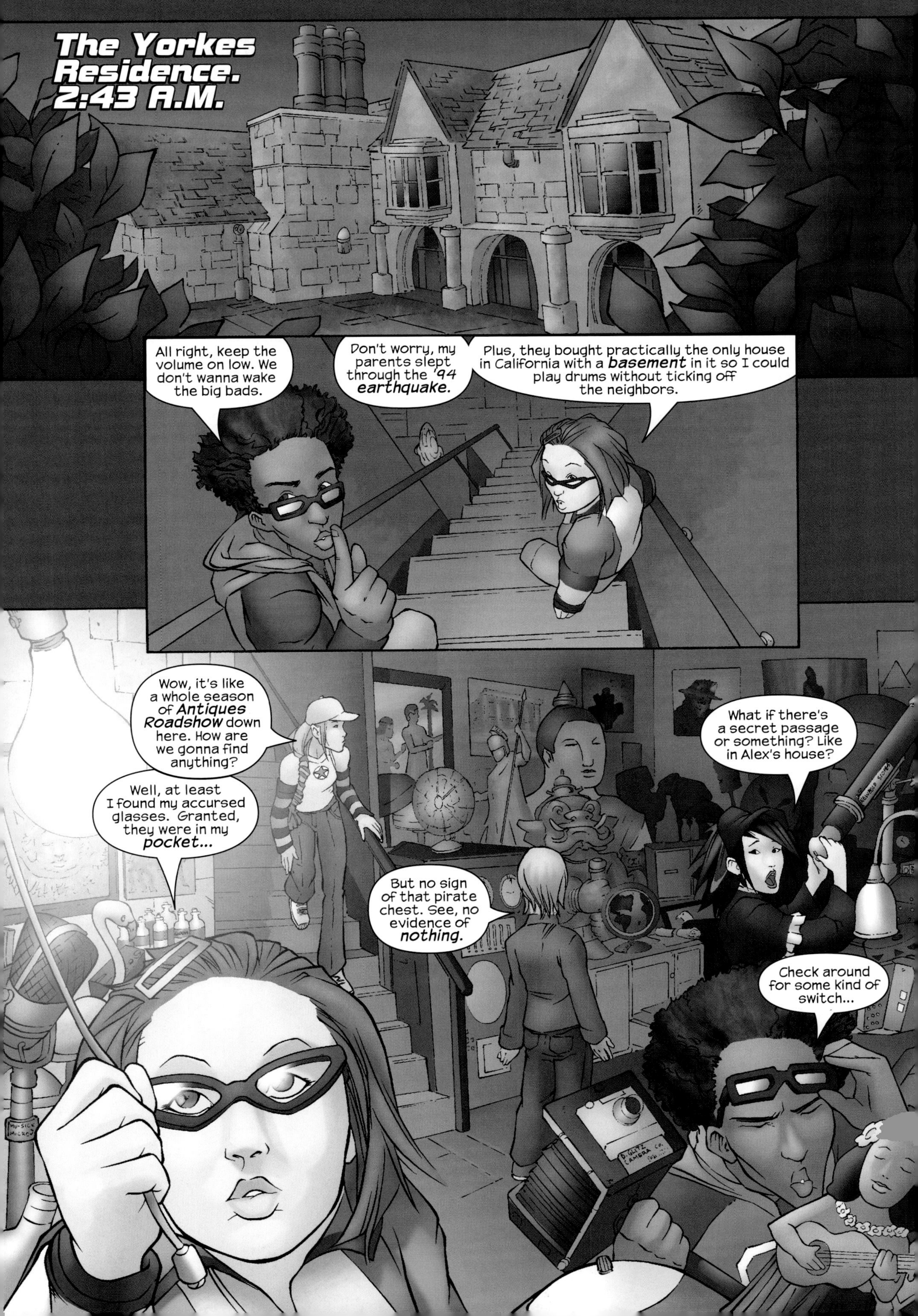
The Yorkes Residence. 2:43 A.M.
All right, keep the volume on low. We don't wanna wake the big bads.
Don't worry, my parents slept through the '94 *earthquake.*
Plus, they bought practically the only house in California with a *basement* in it so I could play drums without ticking off the neighbors.
Wow, it's like a whole season of *Antiques Roadshow* down here. How are we gonna find anything?
Well, at least I found my accursed glasses. Granted, they were in my *pocket...*
But no sign of that pirate chest. See, no evidence of *nothing.*
What if there's a secret passage or something? Like in Alex's house?
Check around for some kind of switch...

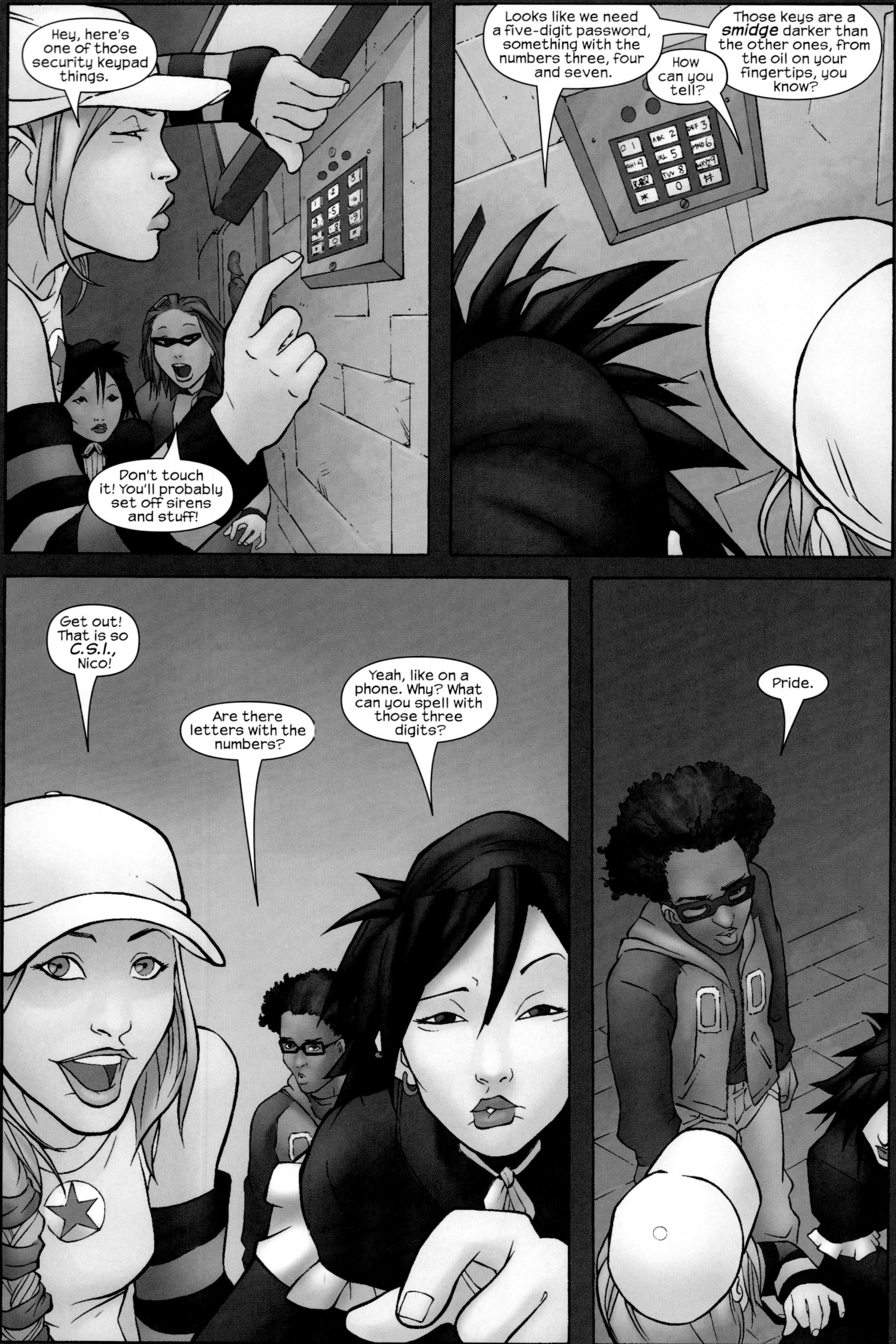
Hey, here's one of those security keypad things.
Don't touch it! You'll probably set off sirens and stuff!
Looks like we need a five-digit password, something with the numbers three, four and seven.
How can you tell?
Those keys are a *smidge* darker than the other ones, from the oil on your fingertips, you know?
Get out! That is so *C.S.I.*, Nico!
Are there letters with the numbers?
Yeah, like on a phone. Why? What can you spell with those three digits?
Pride.

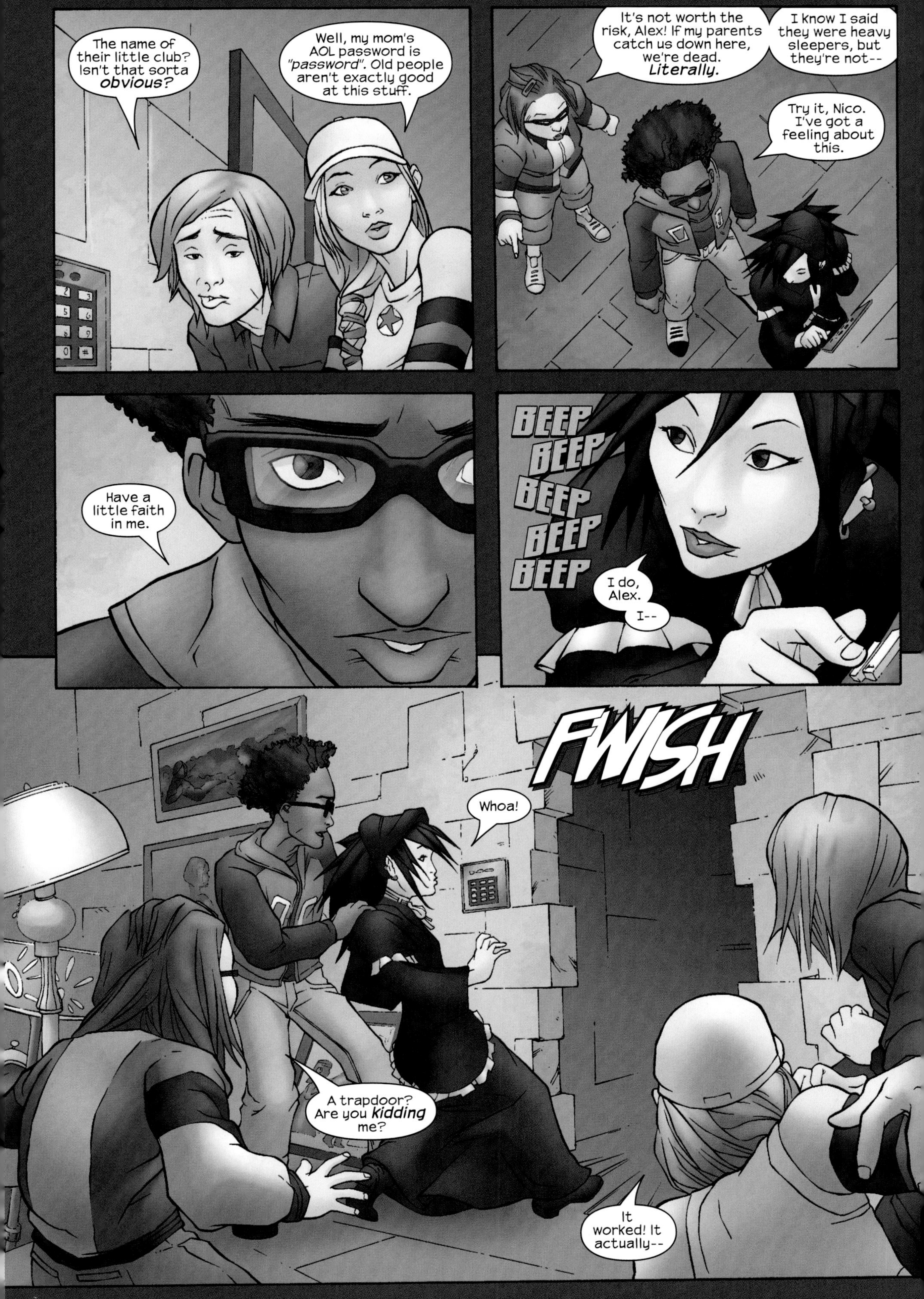
The name of their little club? Isn't that sorta *obvious?*
Well, my mom's AOL password is *"password"*. Old people aren't exactly good at this stuff.
It's not worth the risk, Alex! If my parents catch us down here, we're dead. ***Literally.***
I know I said they were heavy sleepers, but they're not--
Try it, Nico. I've got a feeling about this.
Have a little faith in me.
BEEP BEEP BEEP BEEP BEEP
I do, Alex.
I--
FWISH
Whoa!
A trapdoor? Are you *kidding* me?
It worked! It actually--

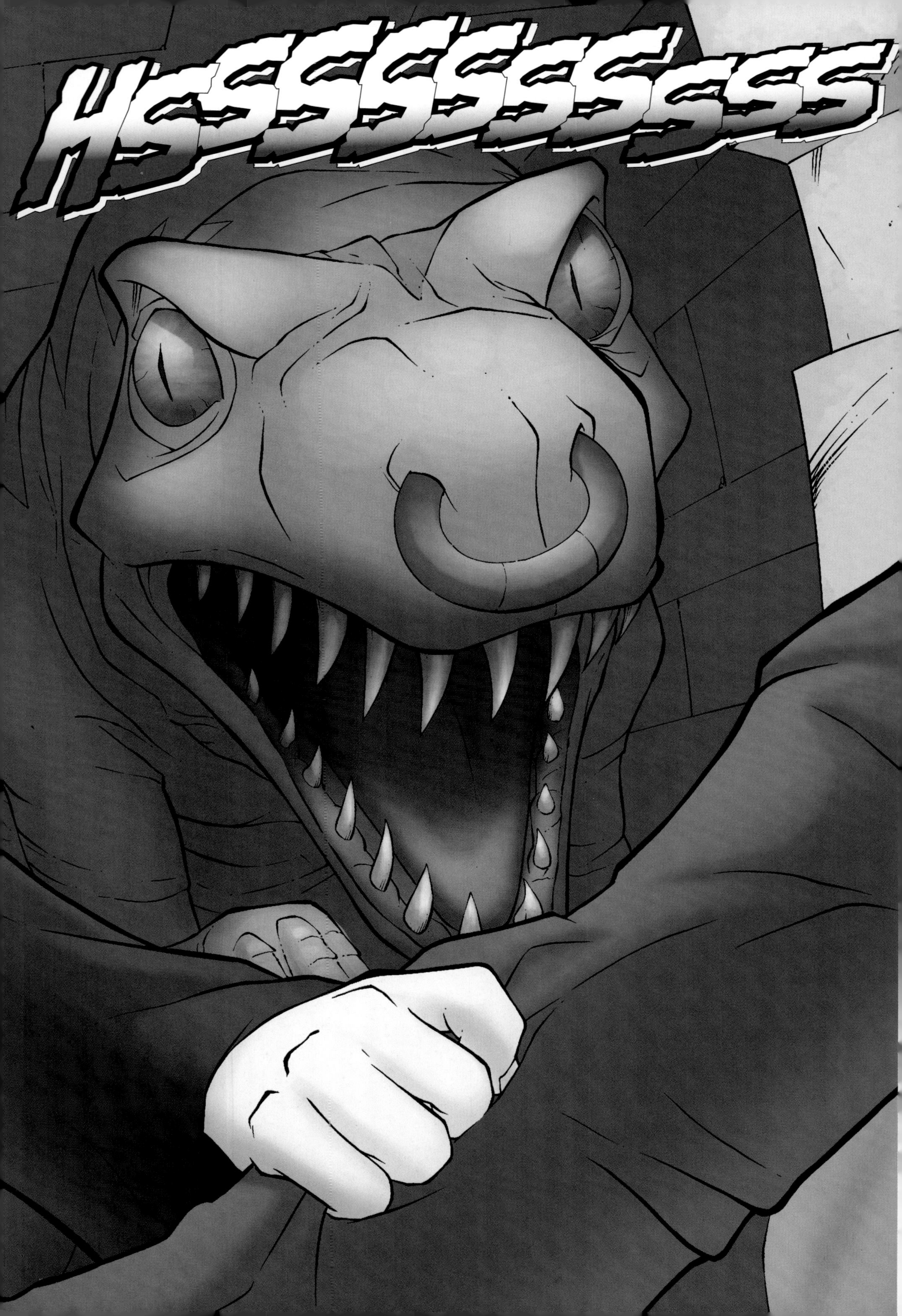
HSSSSSSSsss

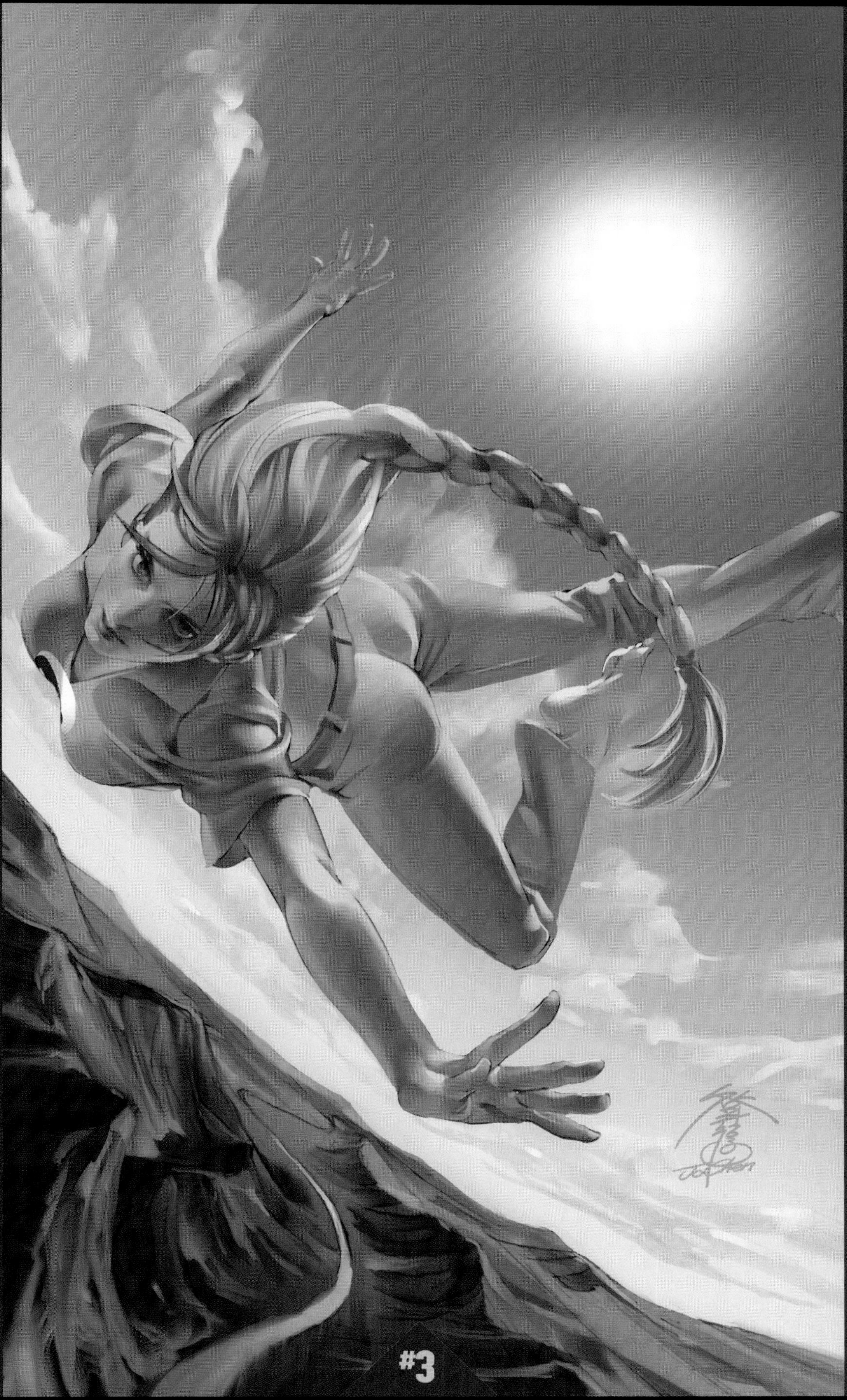

#3

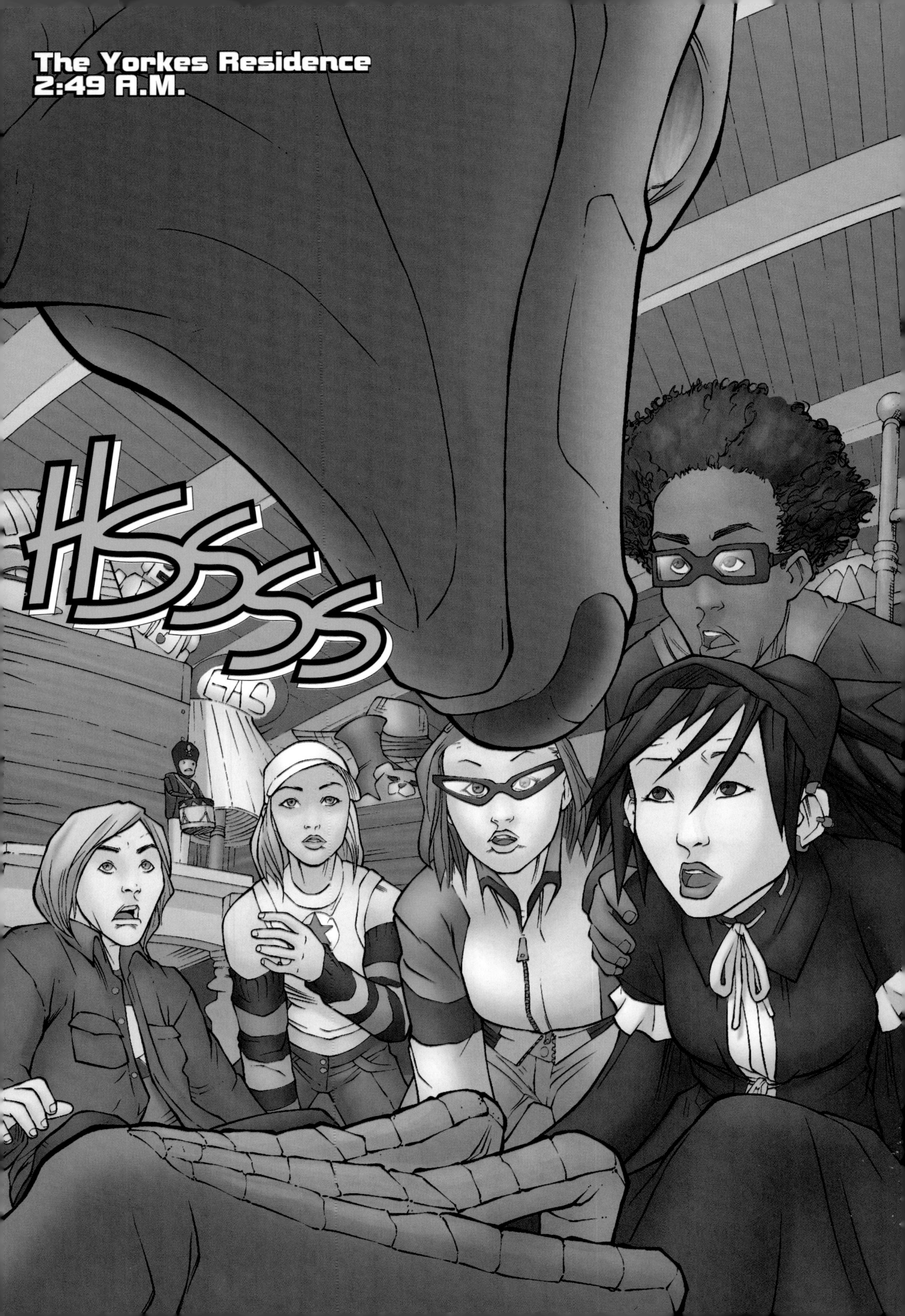
The Yorkes Residence
2:49 A.M.
HSSS

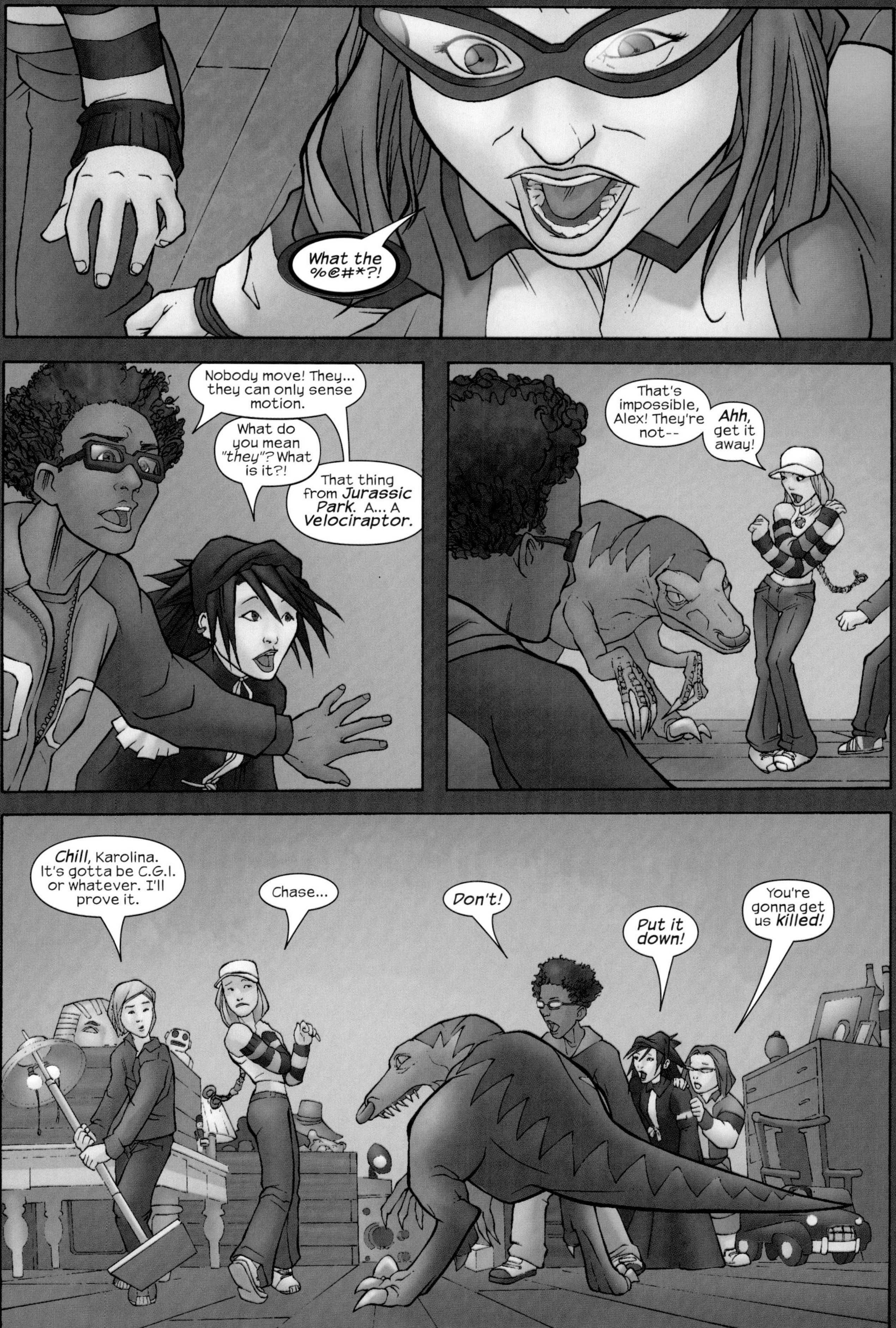
What the %@#*?!
Nobody move! They... they can only sense motion.
What do you mean "they"? What is it?!
That thing from Jurassic Park. A... A Velociraptor.
That's impossible, Alex! They're not--
Ahh, get it away!
Chill, Karolina. It's gotta be C.G.I. or whatever. I'll prove it.
Chase...
Don't!
Put it down!
You're gonna get us killed!

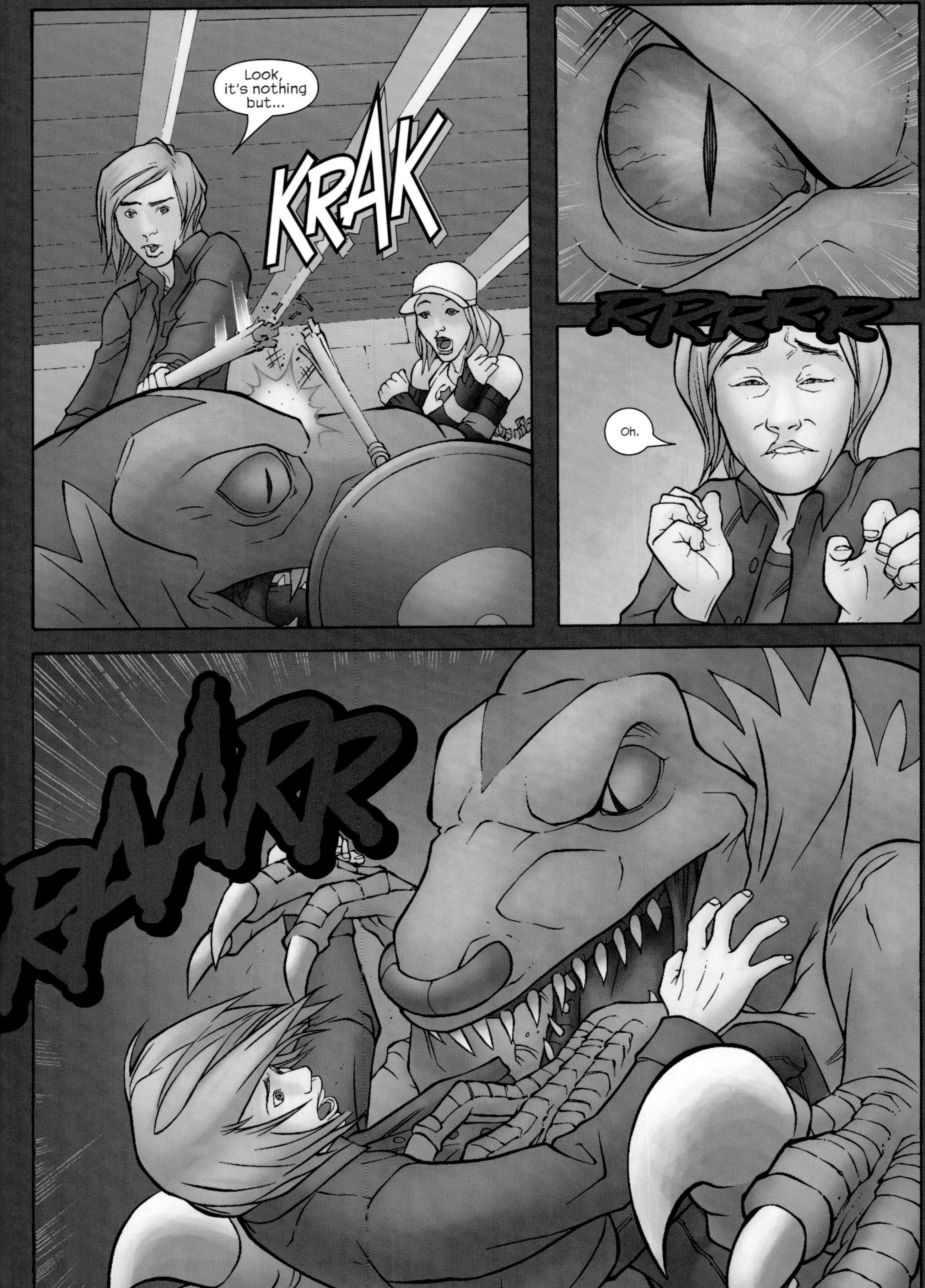
Look, it's nothing but...
KRAK
RRRRRR
Oh.
RRAARR

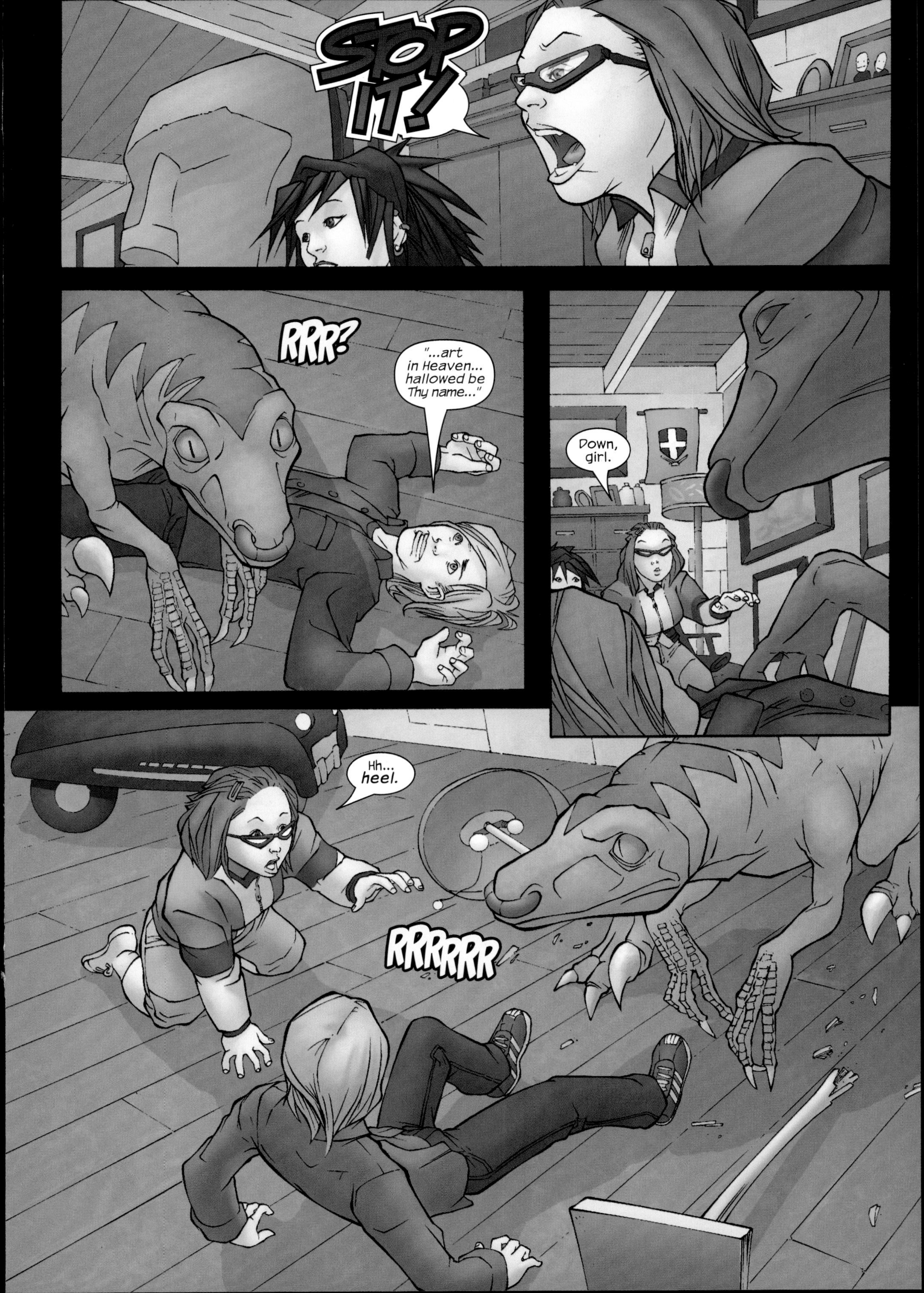
STOP IT!
RRR?
"...art in Heaven... hallowed be Thy name..."
Down, girl.
Hh... heel.
RRRRRR

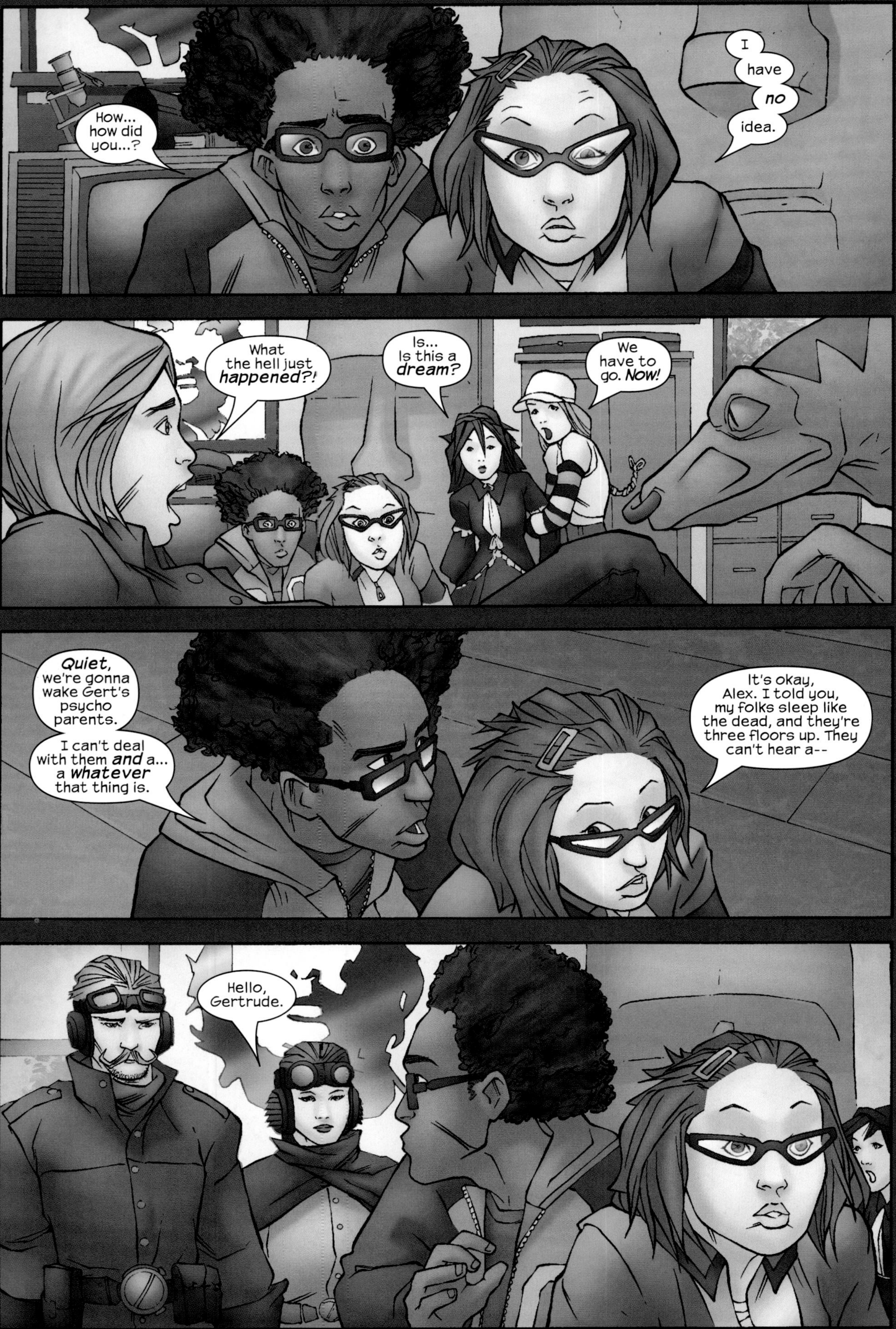
How... how did you...?
I have *no* idea.
What the hell just *happened*?!
Is... Is this a *dream*?
We have to go. *NOW!*
Quiet, we're gonna wake Gert's psycho parents.
I can't deal with them *and* a... a *whatever* that thing is.
It's okay, Alex. I told you, my folks sleep like the dead, and they're three floors up. They can't hear a--
Hello, Gertrude.

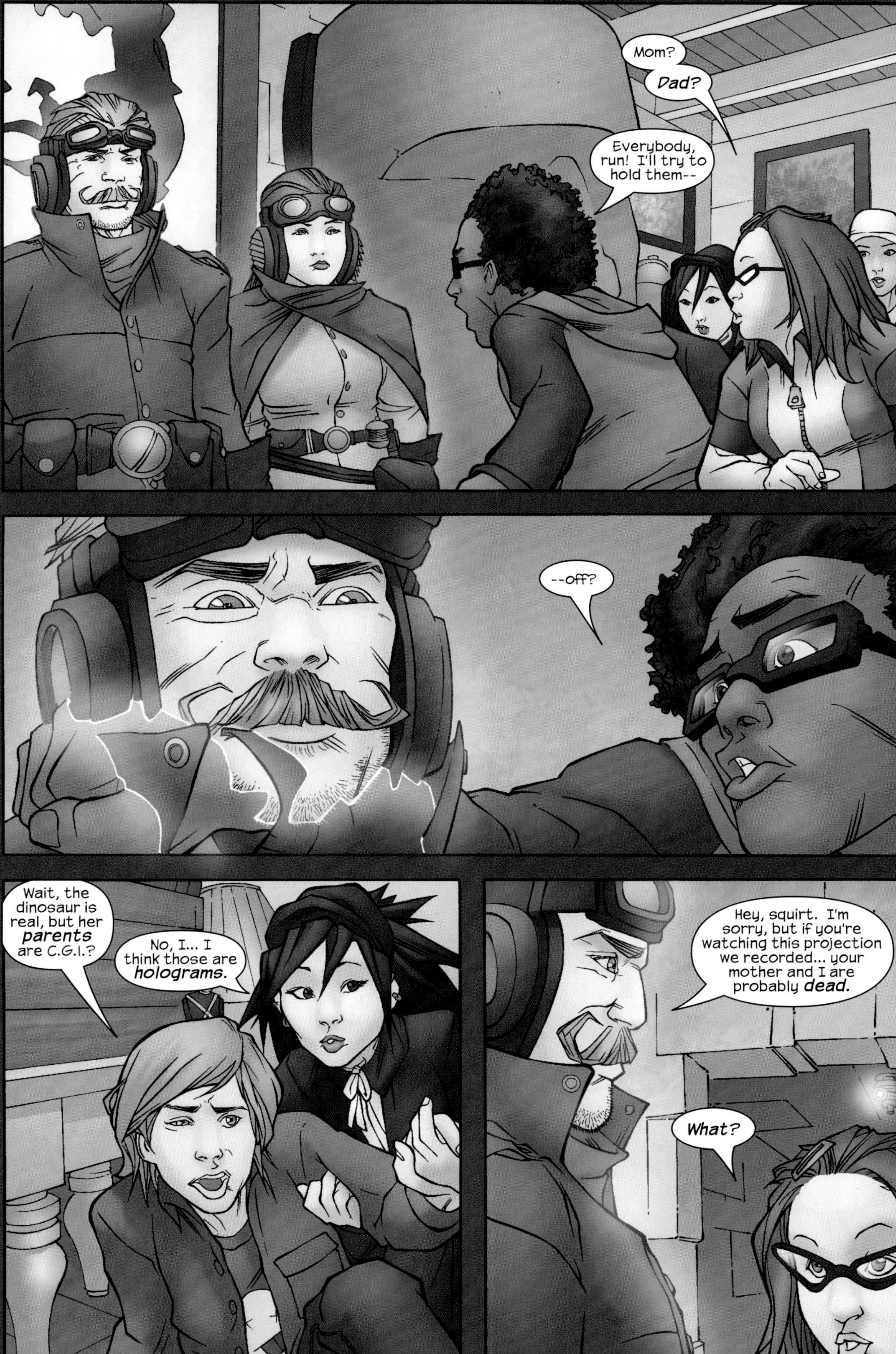

Mom?
Dad?
Everybody, run! I'll try to hold them--
--off?
Wait, the dinosaur is real, but her *parents* are C.G.I.?
No, I... I think those are *holograms.*
Hey, squirt. I'm sorry, but if you're watching this projection we recorded... your mother and I are probably *dead.*
What?

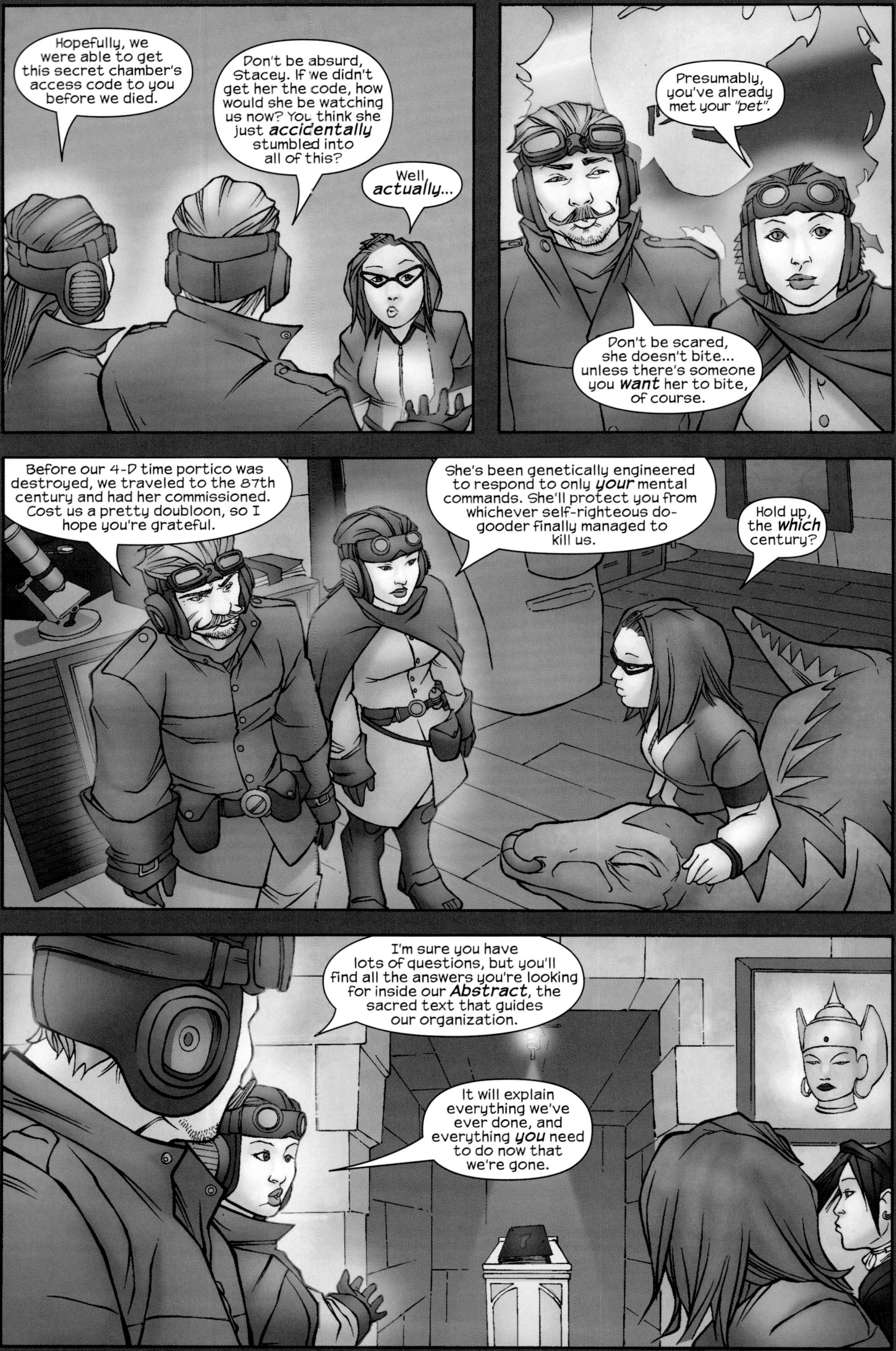
Hopefully, we were able to get this secret chamber's access code to you before we died.
Don't be absurd, Stacey. If we didn't get her the code, how would she be watching us now? You think she just *accidentally* stumbled into all of this?
Well, *actually*...
Presumably, you've already met your "*pet*".
Don't be scared, she doesn't bite... unless there's someone you *want* her to bite, of course.
Before our 4-D time portico was destroyed, we traveled to the 87th century and had her commissioned. Cost us a pretty doubloon, so I hope you're grateful.
She's been genetically engineered to respond to only *your* mental commands. She'll protect you from whichever self-righteous do-gooder finally managed to kill us.
Hold up, the *which* century?
I'm sure you have lots of questions, but you'll find all the answers you're looking for inside our *Abstract*, the sacred text that guides our organization.
It will explain everything we've ever done, and everything *you* need to do now that we're gone.

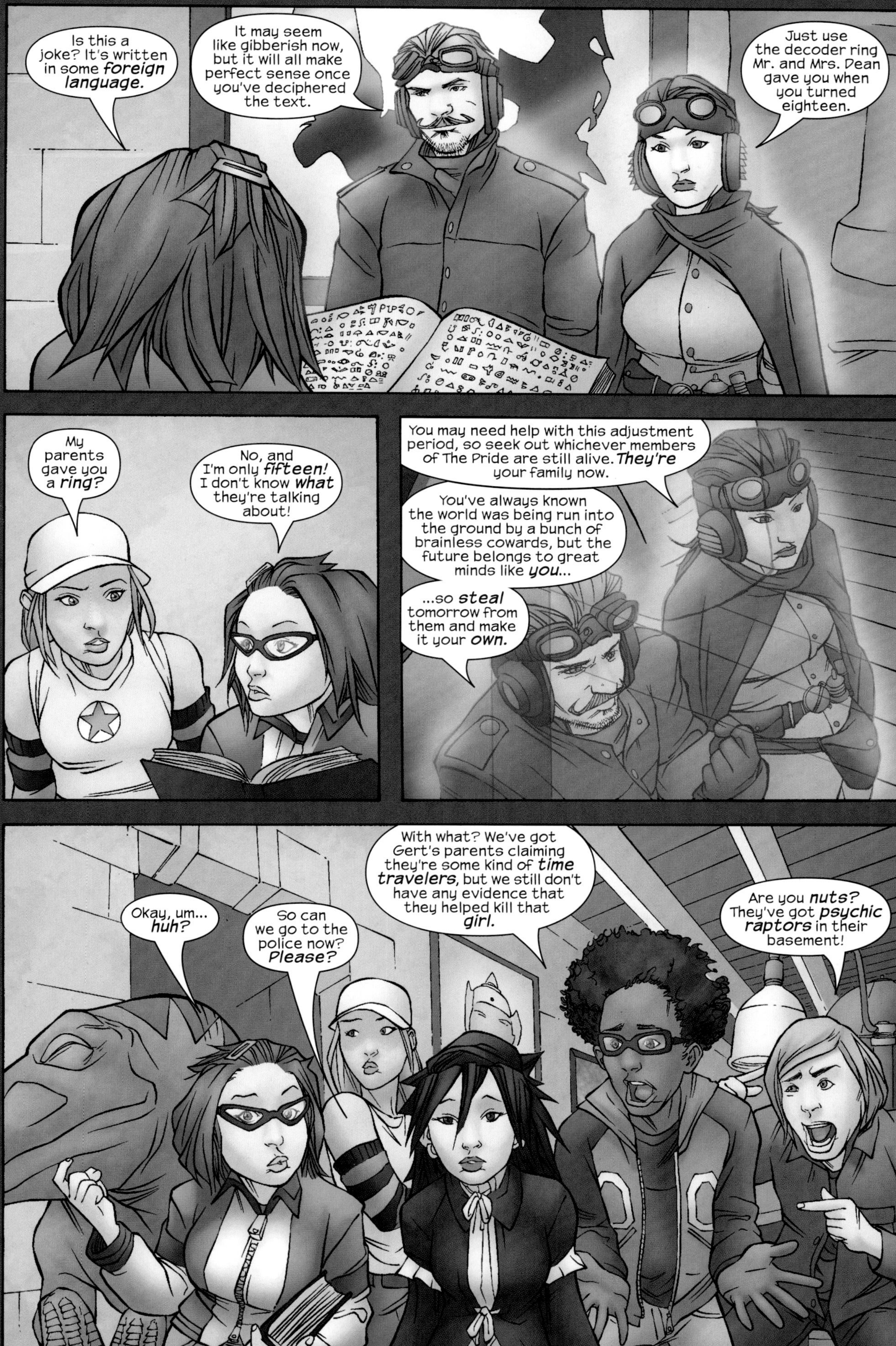

Is this a joke? It's written in some *foreign language.*
It may seem like gibberish now, but it will all make perfect sense once you've deciphered the text.
Just use the decoder ring Mr. and Mrs. Dean gave you when you turned eighteen.
My parents gave you a *ring?*
No, and I'm only *fifteen!* I don't know *what* they're talking about!
You may need help with this adjustment period, so seek out whichever members of The Pride are still alive. *They're* your family now.
You've always known the world was being run into the ground by a bunch of brainless cowards, but the future belongs to great minds like *you*...
...so *steal* tomorrow from them and make it your *own.*
Okay, um... *huh?*
So can we go to the police now? *Please?*
With what? We've got Gert's parents claiming they're some kind of *time travelers*, but we still don't have any evidence that they helped kill that *girl.*
Are you *nuts?* They've got *psychic raptors* in their basement!

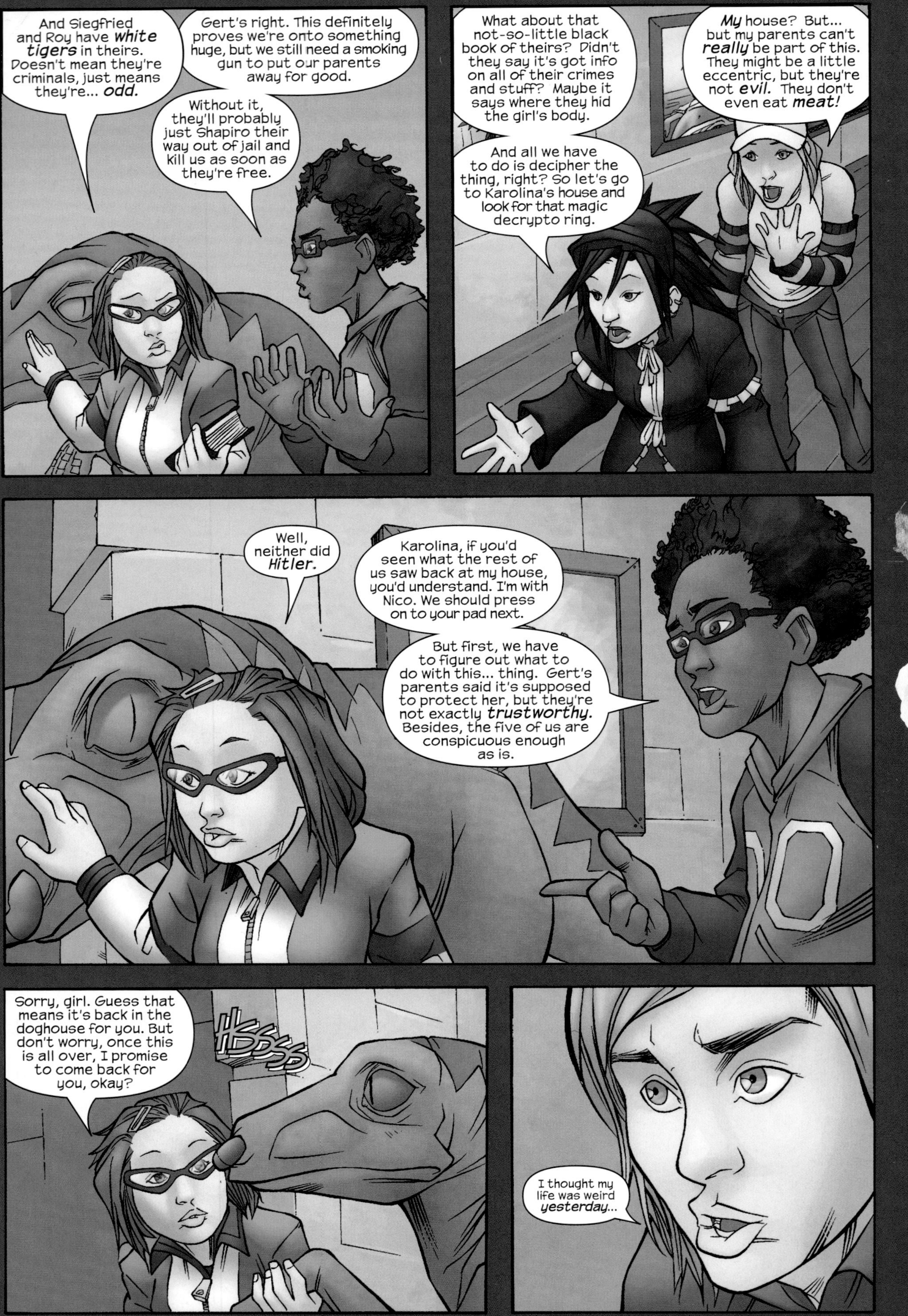
And Siegfried and Roy have *white tigers* in theirs. Doesn't mean they're criminals, just means they're... *odd.*
Gert's right. This definitely proves we're onto something huge, but we still need a smoking gun to put our parents away for good.
Without it, they'll probably just Shapiro their way out of jail and kill us as soon as they're free.
What about that not-so-little black book of theirs? Didn't they say it's got info on all of their crimes and stuff? Maybe it says where they hid the girl's body.
And all we have to do is decipher the thing, right? So let's go to Karolina's house and look for that magic decrypto ring.
My house? But... but my parents can't *really* be part of this. They might be a little eccentric, but they're not *evil.* They don't even eat *meat!*
Well, neither did *Hitler.*
Karolina, if you'd seen what the rest of us saw back at my house, you'd understand. I'm with Nico. We should press on to your pad next.
But first, we have to figure out what to do with this... thing. Gert's parents said it's supposed to protect her, but they're not exactly *trustworthy.* Besides, the five of us are conspicuous enough as is.
Sorry, girl. Guess that means it's back in the doghouse for you. But don't worry, once this is all over, I promise to come back for you, okay?
HSSSS
I thought my life was weird *yesterday*...

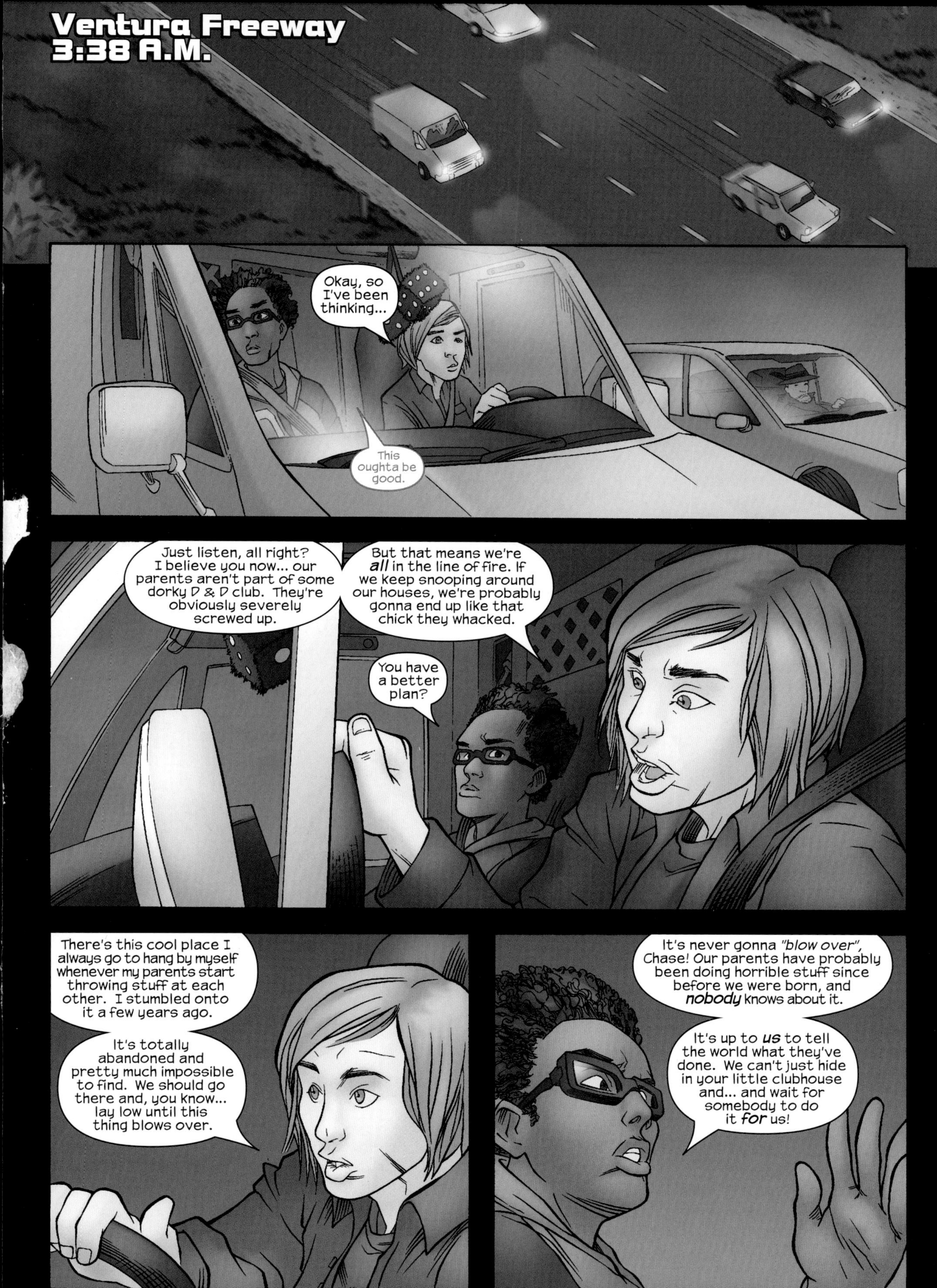
Ventura Freeway
3:38 A.M.
Okay, so I've been thinking...
This oughta be good.
Just listen, all right? I believe you now... our parents aren't part of some dorky D & D club. They're obviously severely screwed up.
But that means we're all in the line of fire. If we keep snooping around our houses, we're probably gonna end up like that chick they whacked.
You have a better plan?
There's this cool place I always go to hang by myself whenever my parents start throwing stuff at each other. I stumbled onto it a few years ago.
It's totally abandoned and pretty much impossible to find. We should go there and, you know... lay low until this thing blows over.
It's never gonna "blow over", Chase! Our parents have probably been doing horrible stuff since before we were born, and nobody knows about it.
It's up to us to tell the world what they've done. We can't just hide in your little clubhouse and... and wait for somebody to do it for us!

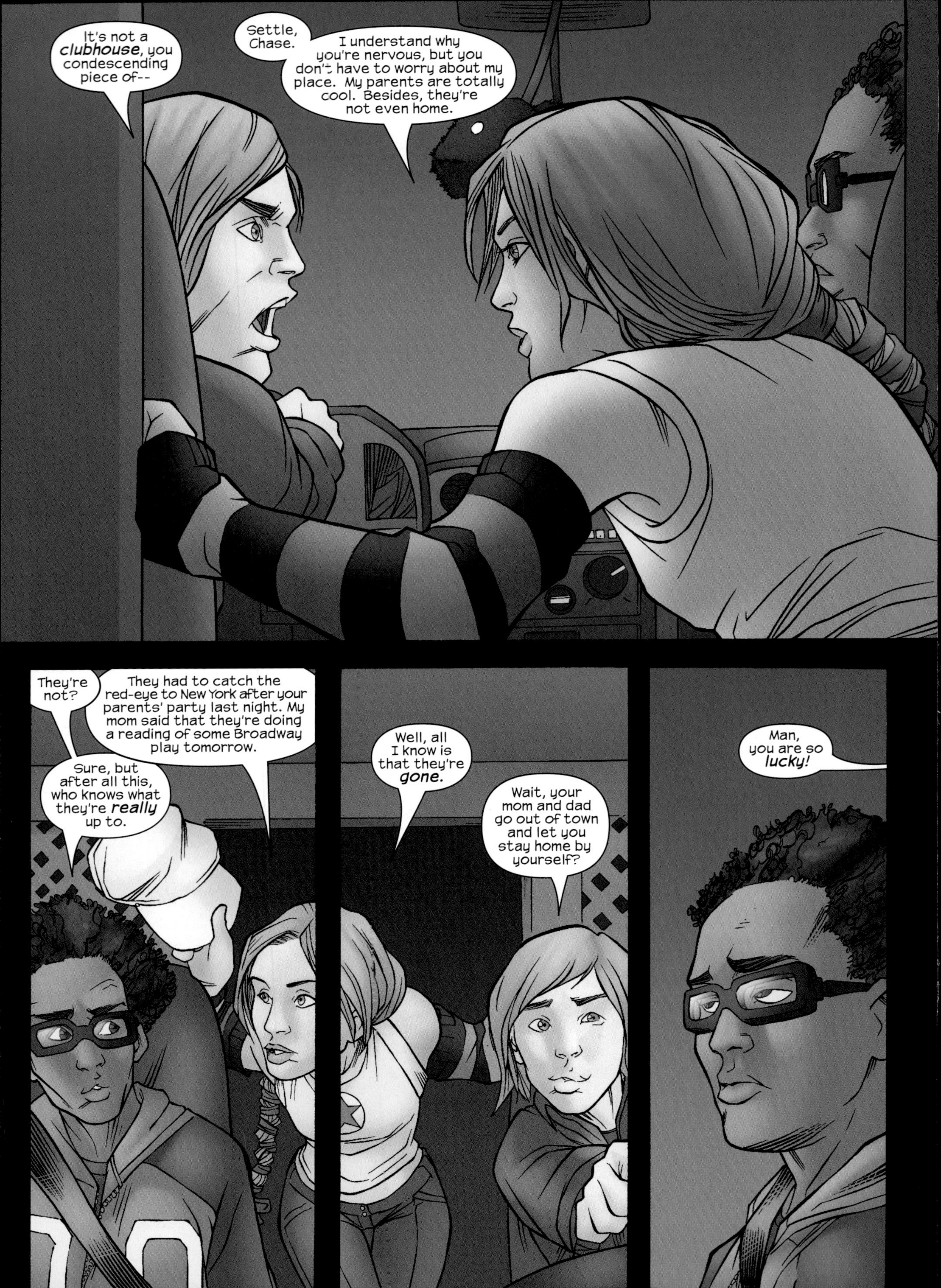
It's not a ***clubhouse***, you condescending piece of--
Settle, Chase.
I understand why you're nervous, but you don't have to worry about my place. My parents are totally cool. Besides, they're not even home.
They're not?
They had to catch the red-eye to New York after your parents' party last night. My mom said that they're doing a reading of some Broadway play tomorrow.
Sure, but after all this, who knows what they're ***really*** up to.
Well, all I know is that they're ***gone.***
Wait, your mom and dad go out of town and let you stay home by yourself?
Man, you are so ***lucky!***

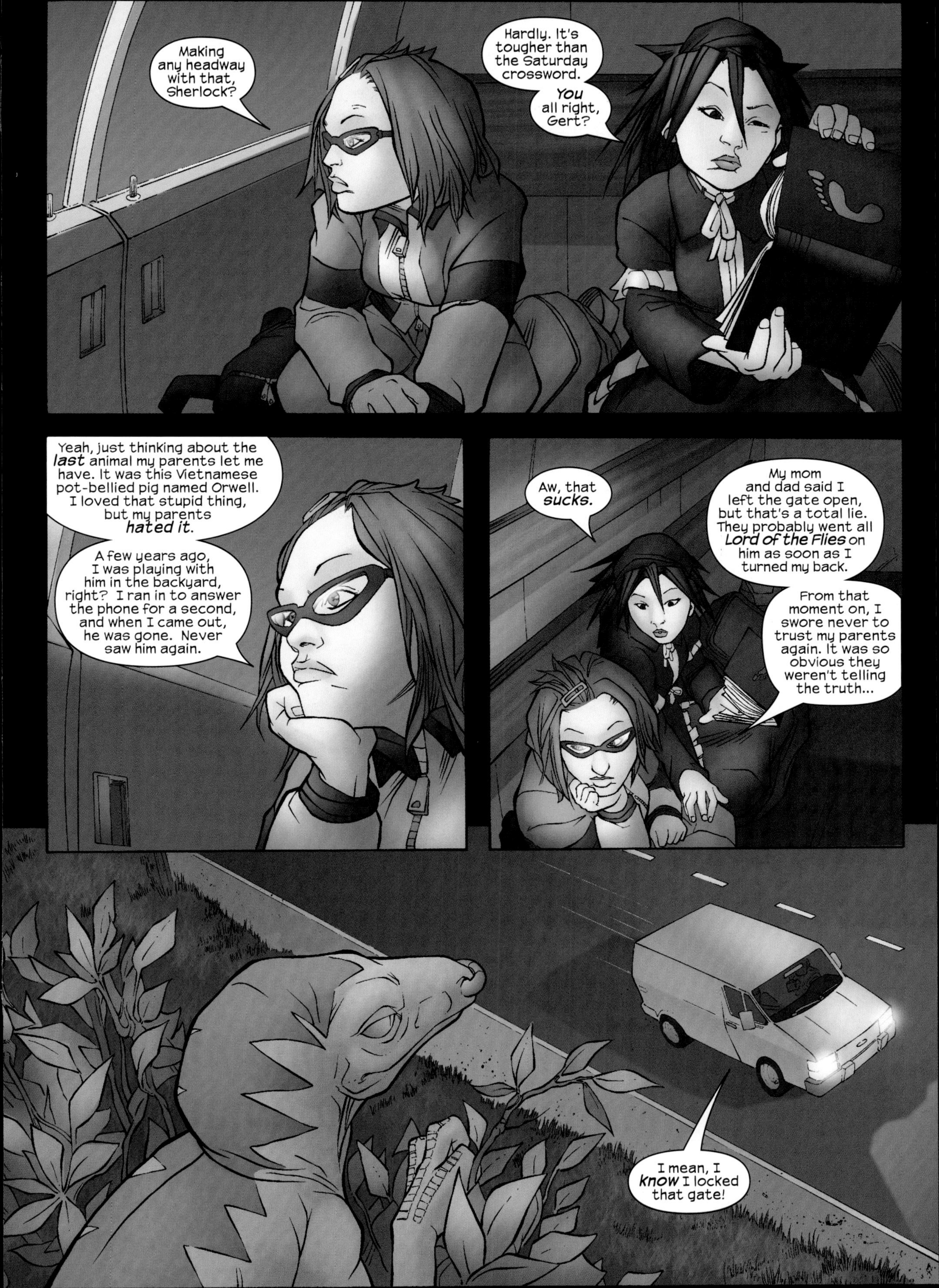

Making any headway with that, Sherlock?
Hardly. It's tougher than the Saturday crossword.
You all right, Gert?
Yeah, just thinking about the last animal my parents let me have. It was this Vietnamese pot-bellied pig named Orwell. I loved that stupid thing, but my parents hated it.
A few years ago, I was playing with him in the backyard, right? I ran in to answer the phone for a second, and when I came out, he was gone. Never saw him again.
Aw, that sucks.
My mom and dad said I left the gate open, but that's a total lie. They probably went all Lord of the Flies on him as soon as I turned my back.
From that moment on, I swore never to trust my parents again. It was so obvious they weren't telling the truth...
I mean, I know I locked that gate!

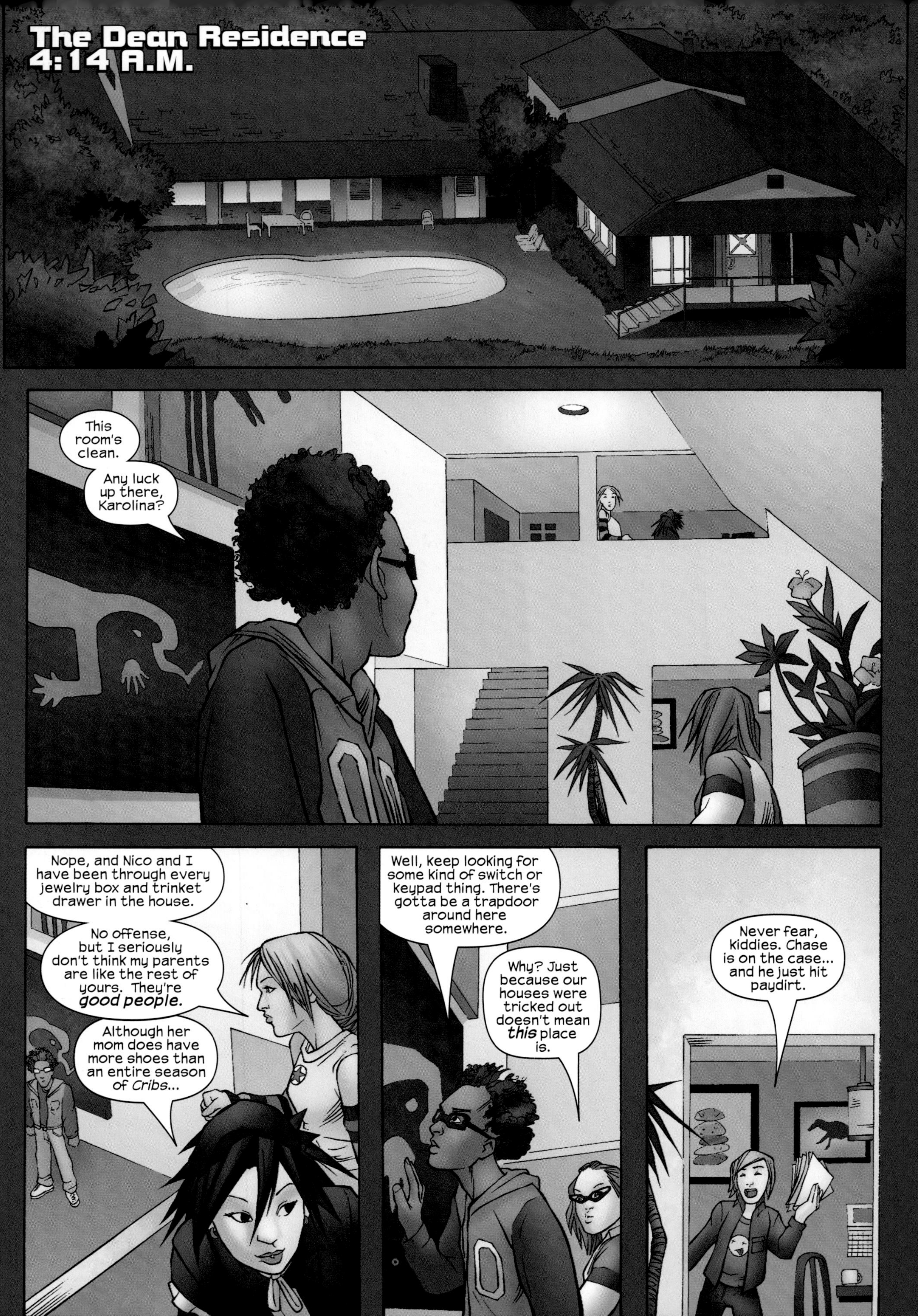
The Dean Residence 4:14 A.M.
This room's clean.
Any luck up there, Karolina?
Nope, and Nico and I have been through every jewelry box and trinket drawer in the house.
No offense, but I seriously don't think my parents are like the rest of yours. They're *good people.*
Although her mom does have more shoes than an entire season of *Cribs*...
Well, keep looking for some kind of switch or keypad thing. There's gotta be a trapdoor around here somewhere.
Why? Just because our houses were tricked out doesn't mean *this* place is.
Never fear, kiddies. Chase is on the case... and he just hit paydirt.

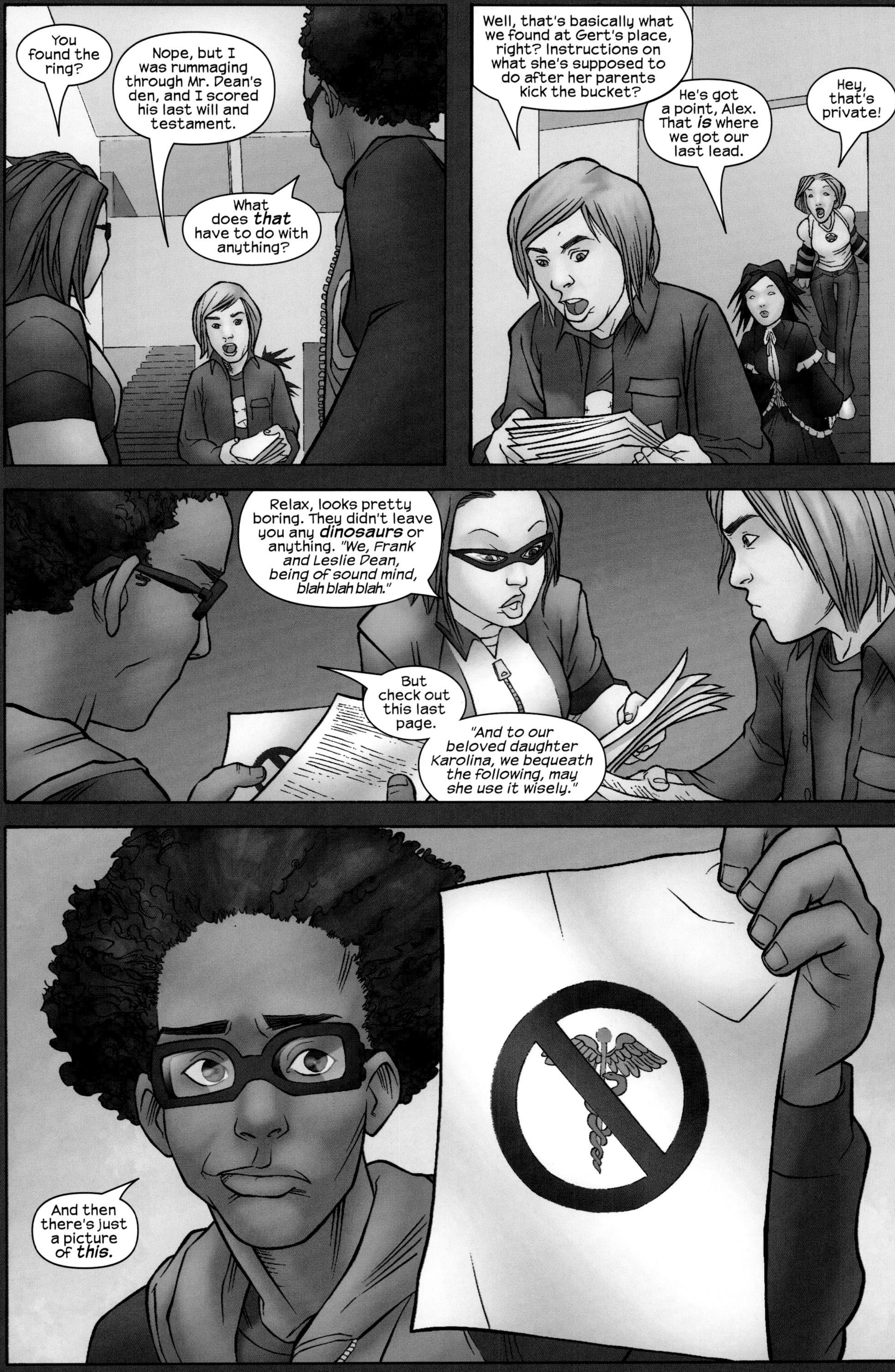
You found the ring?
Nope, but I was rummaging through Mr. Dean's den, and I scored his last will and testament.
What does *that* have to do with anything?
Well, that's basically what we found at Gert's place, right? Instructions on what she's supposed to do after her parents kick the bucket?
He's got a point, Alex. That *is* where we got our last lead.
Hey, that's private!
Relax, looks pretty boring. They didn't leave you any *dinosaurs* or anything. *"We, Frank and Leslie Dean, being of sound mind, blah blah blah."*
But check out this last page.
"And to our beloved daughter Karolina, we bequeath the following, may she use it wisely."
And then there's just a picture of *this.*

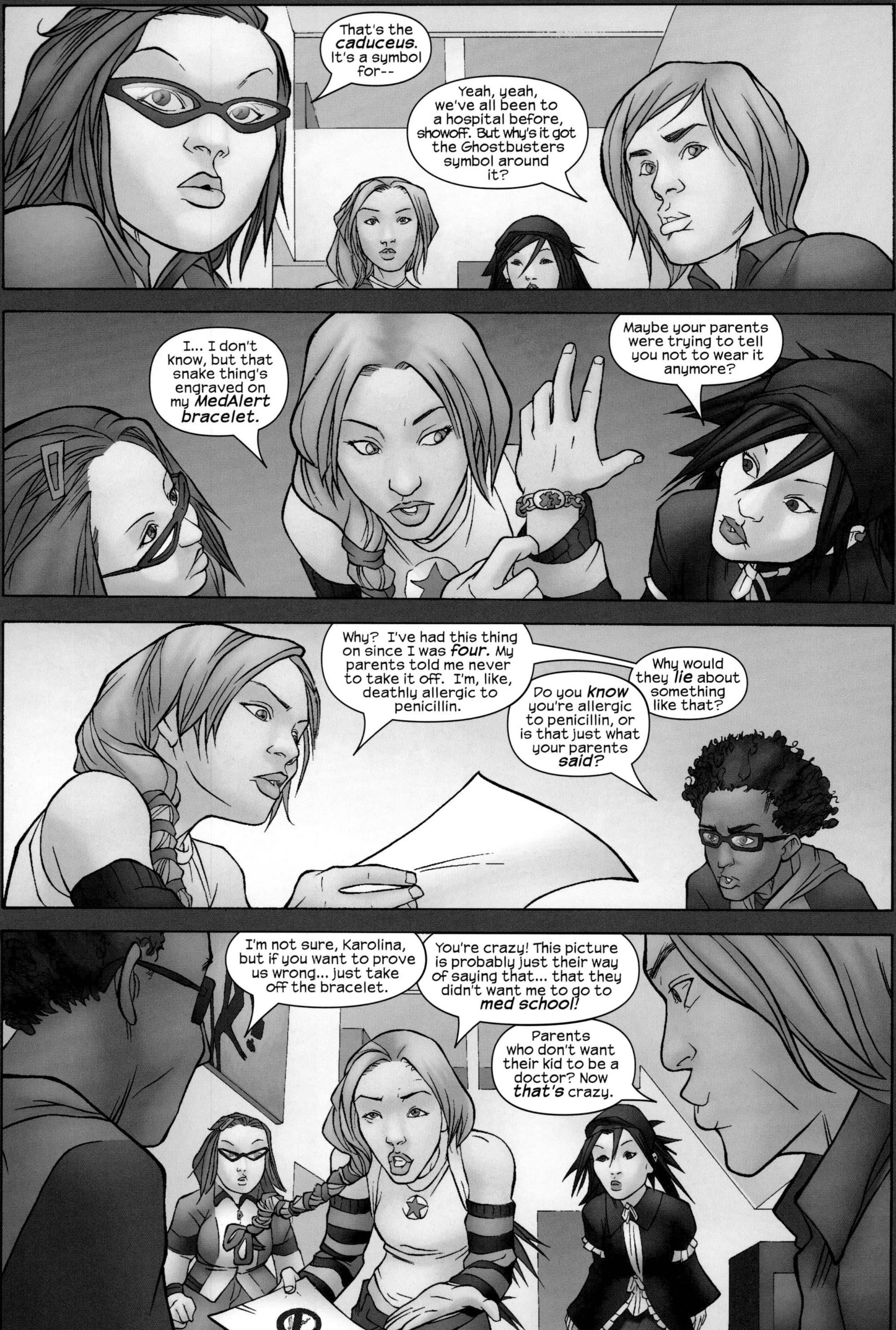

That's the caduceus. It's a symbol for--
Yeah, yeah, we've all been to a hospital before, showoff. But why's it got the Ghostbusters symbol around it?
I... I don't know, but that snake thing's engraved on my MedAlert bracelet.
Maybe your parents were trying to tell you not to wear it anymore?
Why? I've had this thing on since I was four. My parents told me never to take it off. I'm, like, deathly allergic to penicillin.
Why would they lie about something like that?
Do you know you're allergic to penicillin, or is that just what your parents said?
I'm not sure, Karolina, but if you want to prove us wrong... just take off the bracelet.
You're crazy! This picture is probably just their way of saying that... that they didn't want me to go to med school!
Parents who don't want their kid to be a doctor? Now that's crazy.

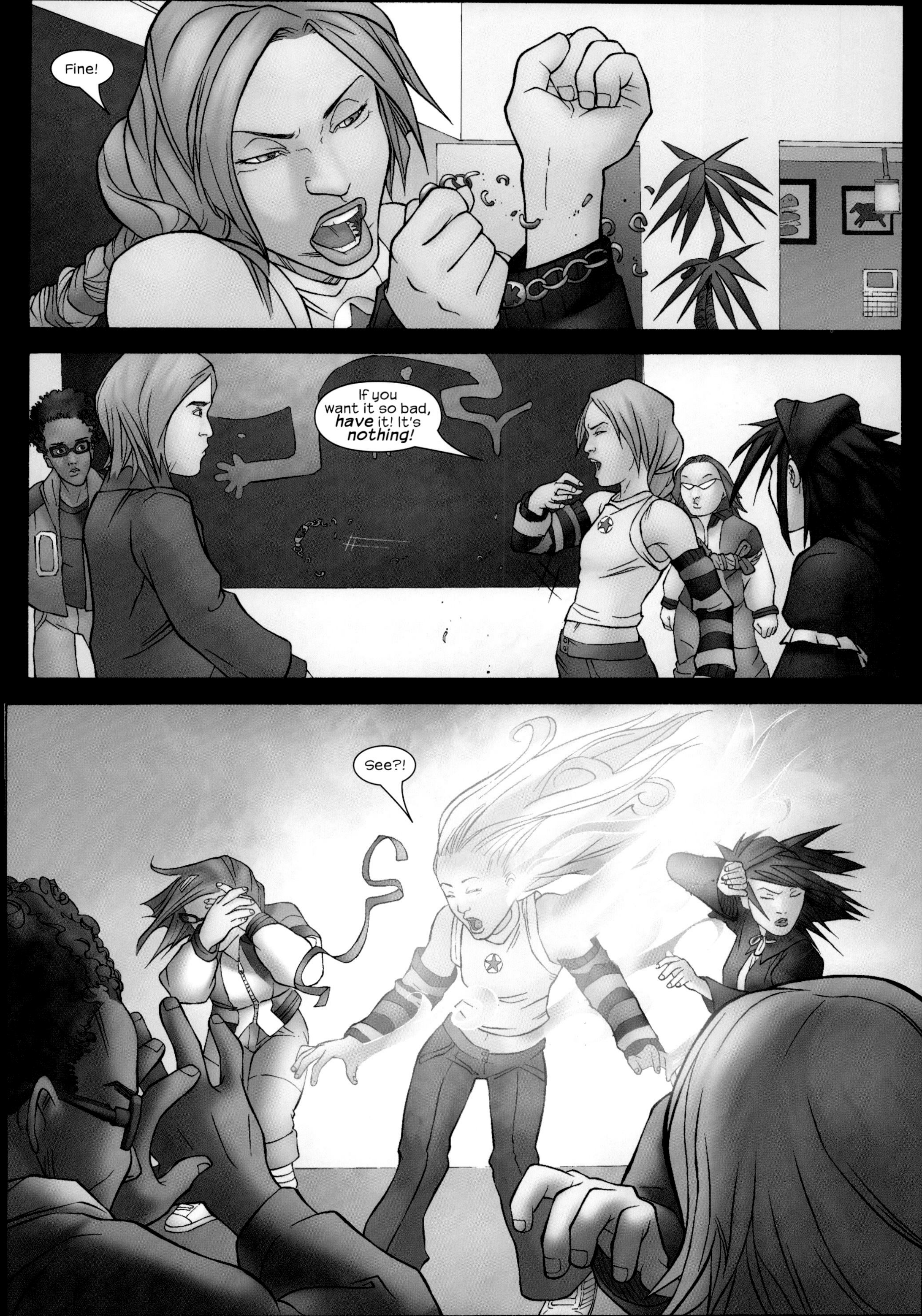

Fine!
If you want it so bad, **have** it! It's ***nothing!***
See?!

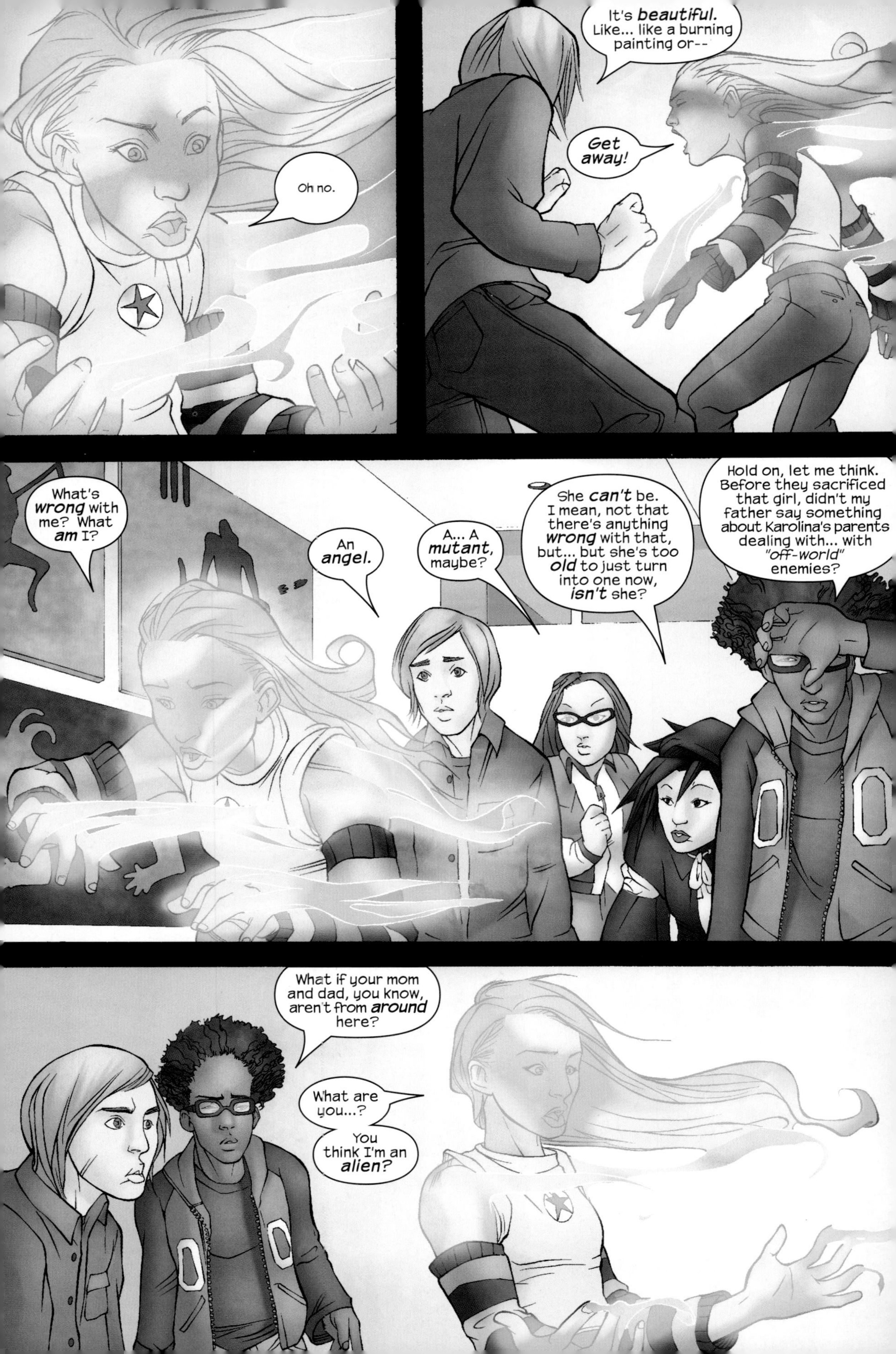

Oh no.
It's beautiful. Like... like a burning painting or--
Get away!
What's wrong with me? What am I?
An angel.
A... A mutant, maybe?
She can't be. I mean, not that there's anything wrong with that, but... but she's too old to just turn into one now, isn't she?
Hold on, let me think. Before they sacrificed that girl, didn't my father say something about Karolina's parents dealing with... with "off-world" enemies?
What if your mom and dad, you know, aren't from around here?
What are you...?
You think I'm an alien?

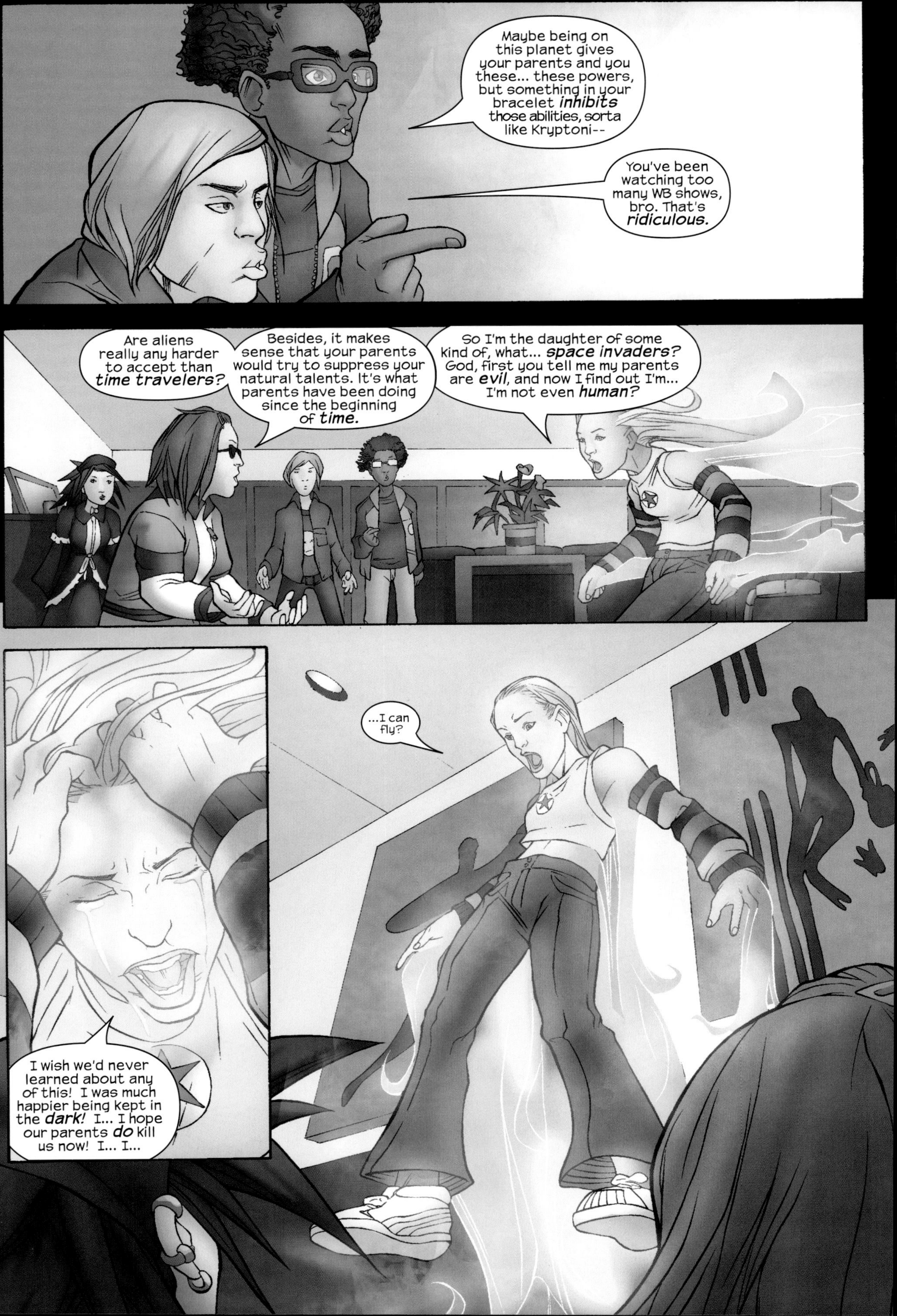

Maybe being on this planet gives your parents and you these... these powers, but something in your bracelet inhibits those abilities, sorta like Kryptoni--
You've been watching too many WB shows, bro. That's ridiculous.
Are aliens really any harder to accept than time travelers?
Besides, it makes sense that your parents would try to suppress your natural talents. It's what parents have been doing since the beginning of time.
So I'm the daughter of some kind of, what... space invaders? God, first you tell me my parents are evil, and now I find out I'm... I'm not even human?
I wish we'd never learned about any of this! I was much happier being kept in the dark! I... I hope our parents do kill us now! I... I...
...I can fly?

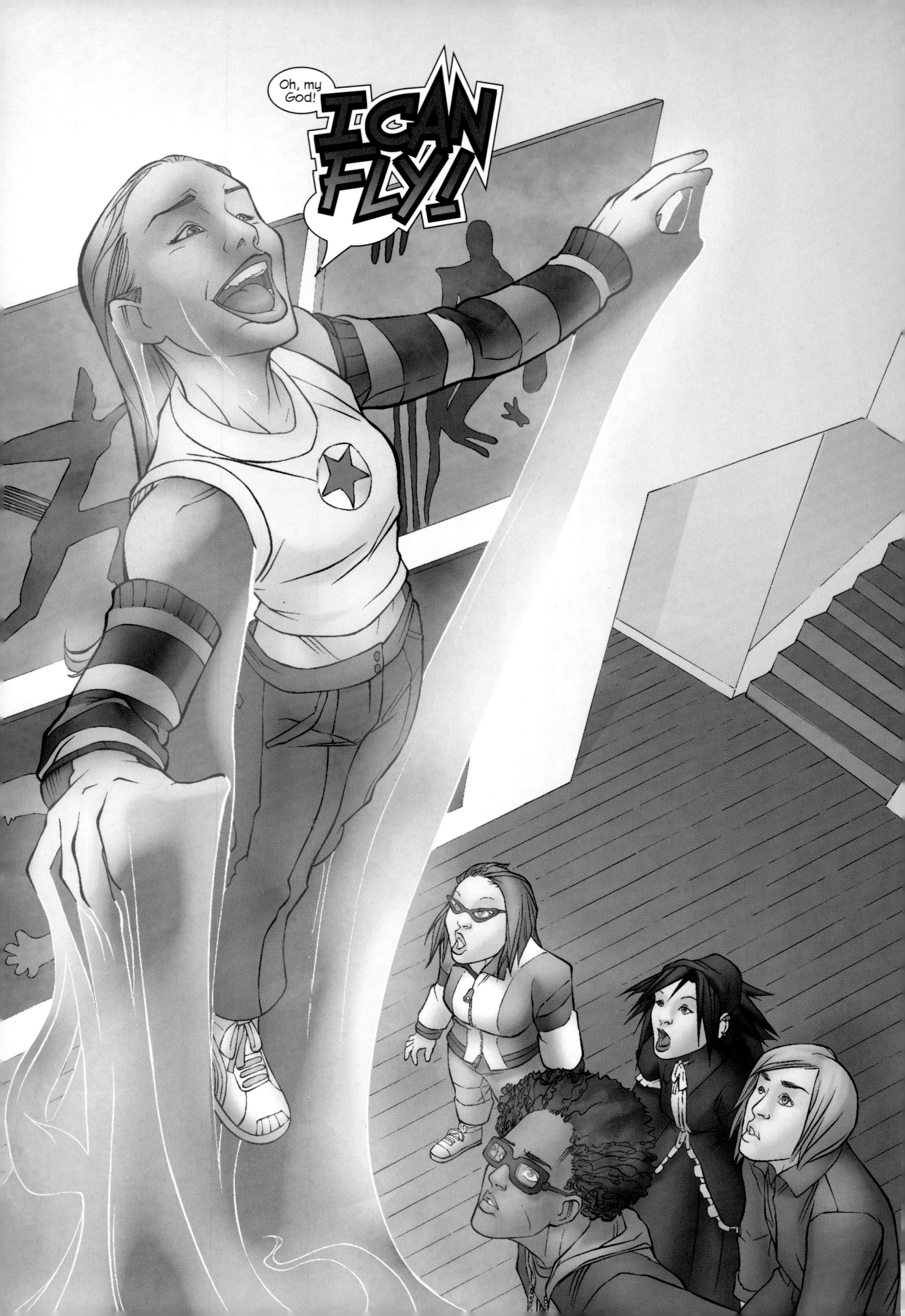
Oh, my God!
I CAN FLY!

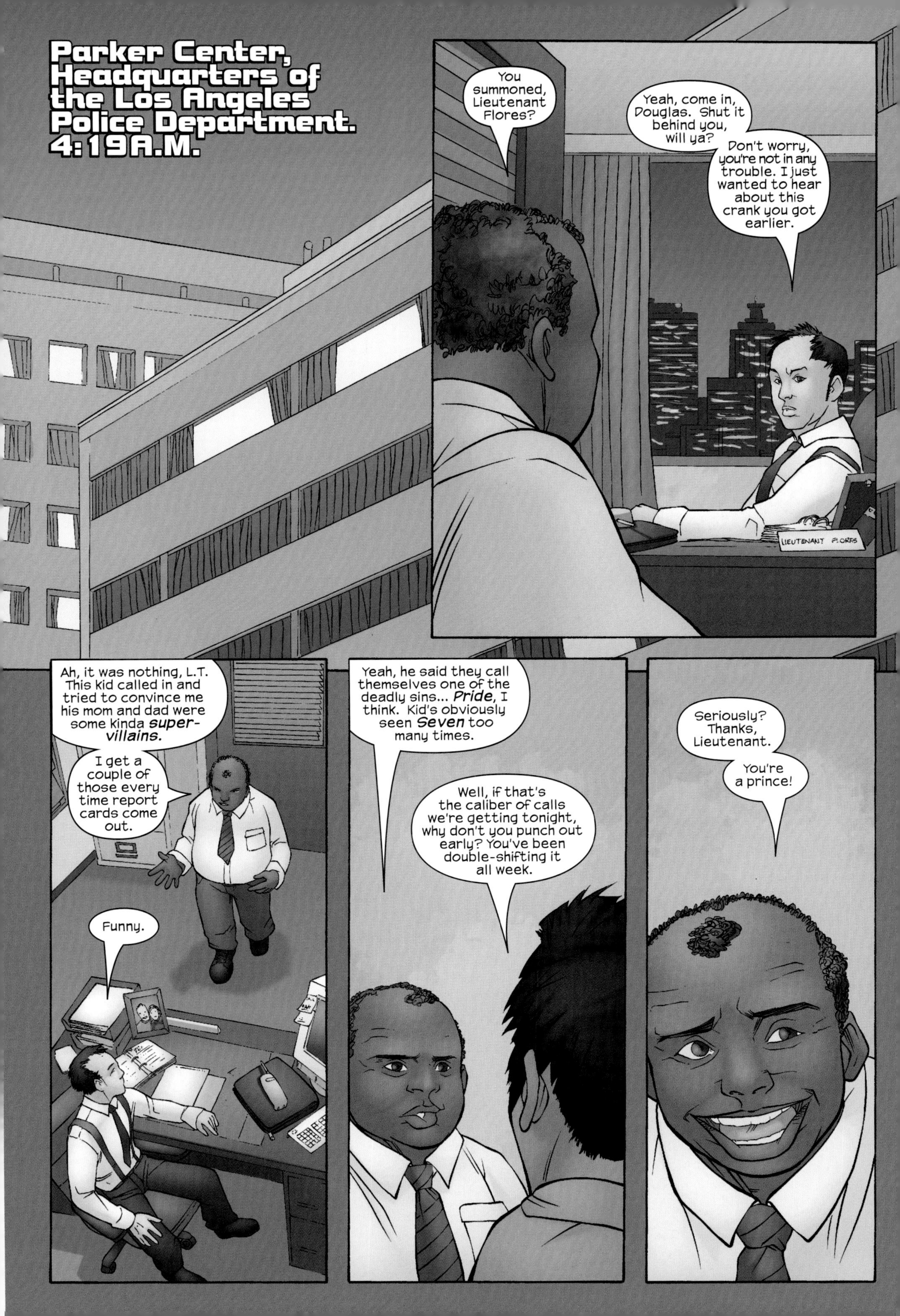
Parker Center, Headquarters of the Los Angeles Police Department. 4:19A.M.
You summoned, Lieutenant Flores?
Yeah, come in, Douglas. Shut it behind you, will ya?
Don't worry, you're not in any trouble. I just wanted to hear about this crank you got earlier.
LIEUTENANT FLORES
Ah, it was nothing, L.T. This kid called in and tried to convince me his mom and dad were some kinda *super-villains.*
I get a couple of those every time report cards come out.
Funny.
Yeah, he said they call themselves one of the deadly sins... *Pride*, I think. Kid's obviously seen *Seven* too many times.
Well, if that's the caliber of calls we're getting tonight, why don't you punch out early? You've been double-shifting it all week.
Seriously? Thanks, Lieutenant.
You're a prince!

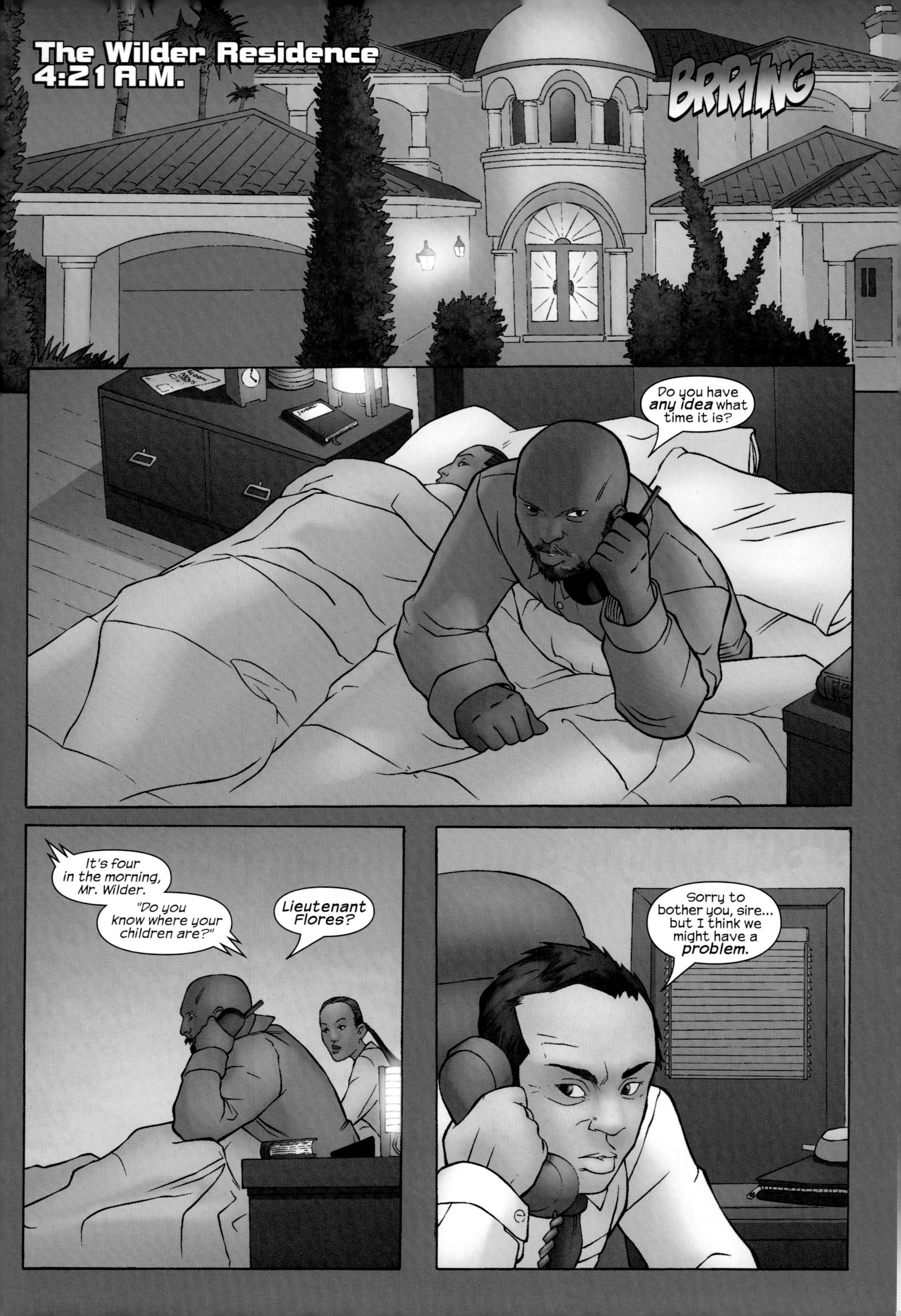
The Wilder Residence
4:21 A.M.
BRRING
Do you have any idea what time it is?
It's four in the morning, Mr. Wilder.
"Do you know where your children are?"
Lieutenant Flores?
Sorry to bother you, sire... but I think we might have a problem.

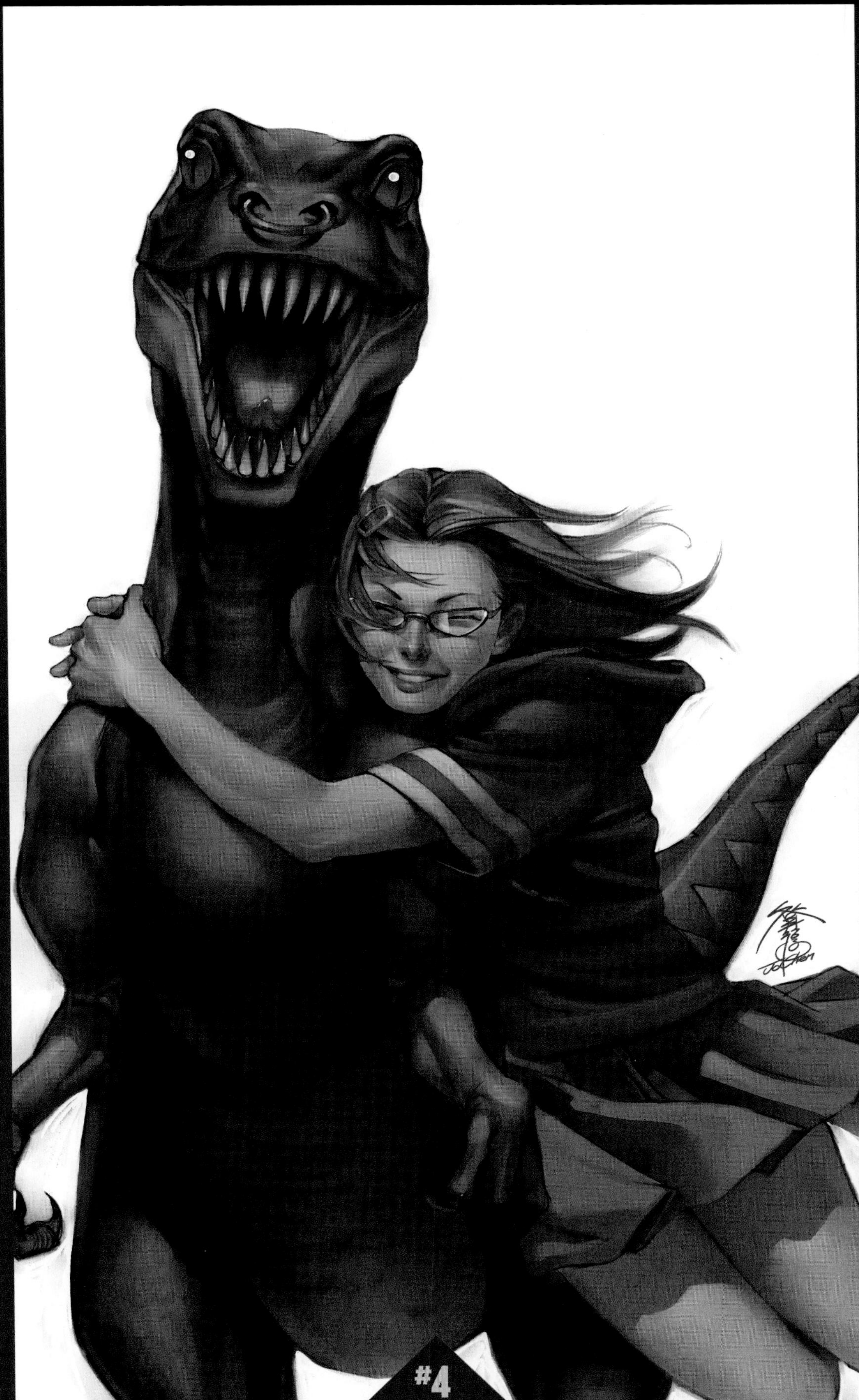
#4

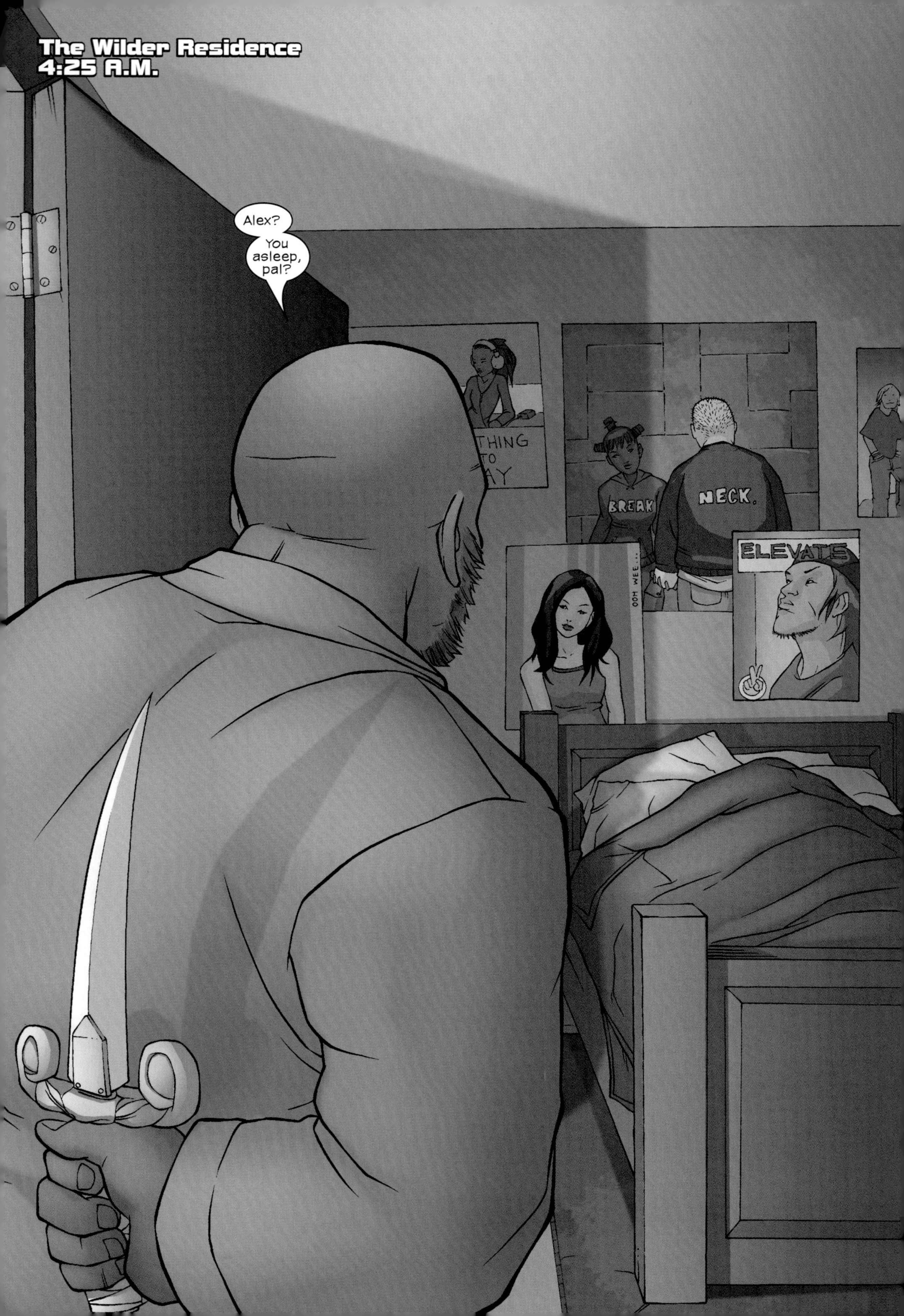
The Wilder Residence
4:25 A.M.
Alex?
You asleep, pal?
THING TO AY
BREAK
NECK.
OOH WEE...
ELEVATE

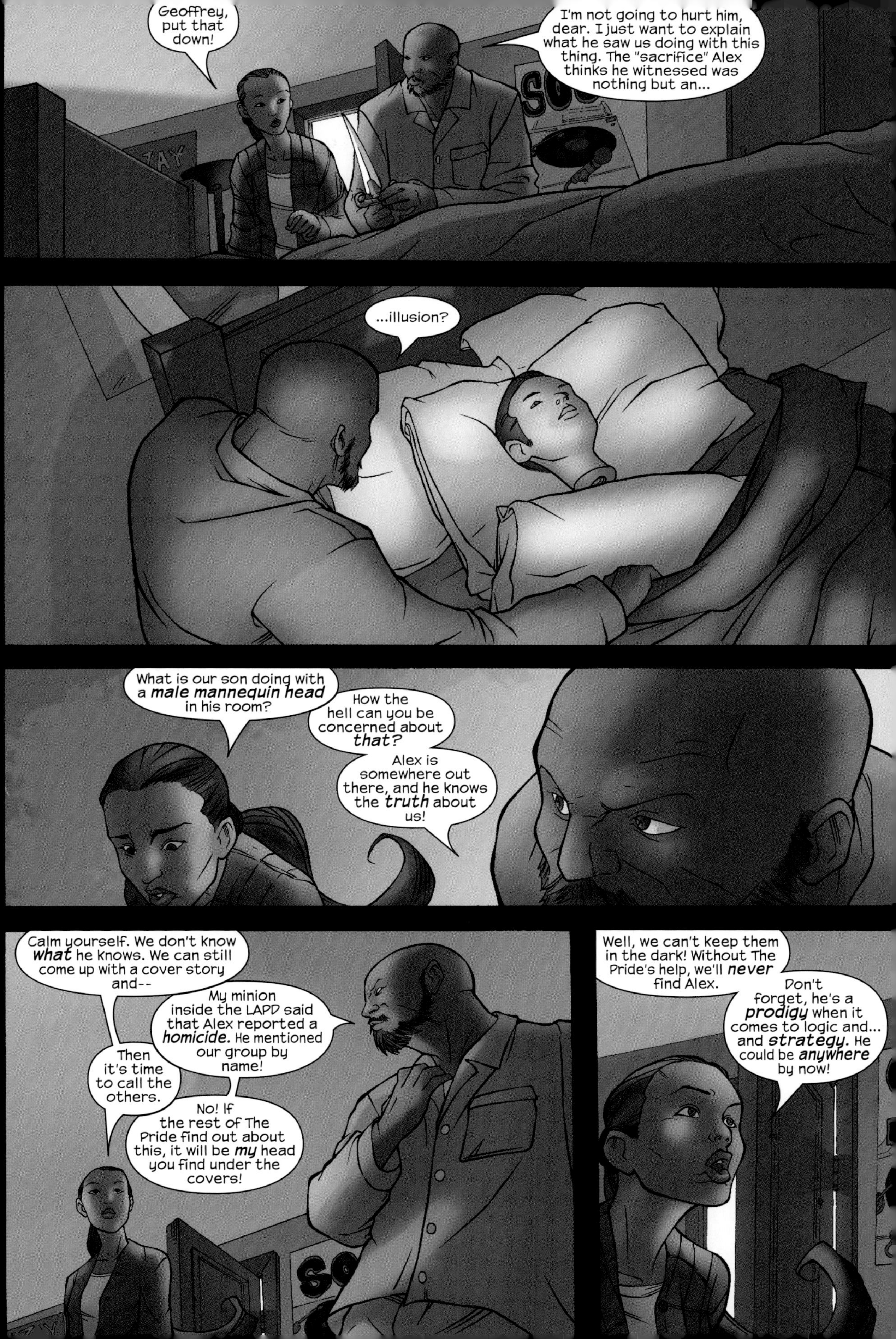
Geoffrey, put that down!
I'm not going to hurt him, dear. I just want to explain what he saw us doing with this thing. The "sacrifice" Alex thinks he witnessed was nothing but an...
...illusion?
What is our son doing with a male mannequin head in his room?
How the hell can you be concerned about that?
Alex is somewhere out there, and he knows the truth about us!
Calm yourself. We don't know what he knows. We can still come up with a cover story and--
My minion inside the LAPD said that Alex reported a homicide. He mentioned our group by name!
Then it's time to call the others.
No! If the rest of The Pride find out about this, it will be my head you find under the covers!
Well, we can't keep them in the dark! Without The Pride's help, we'll never find Alex.
Don't forget, he's a prodigy when it comes to logic and... and strategy. He could be anywhere by now!

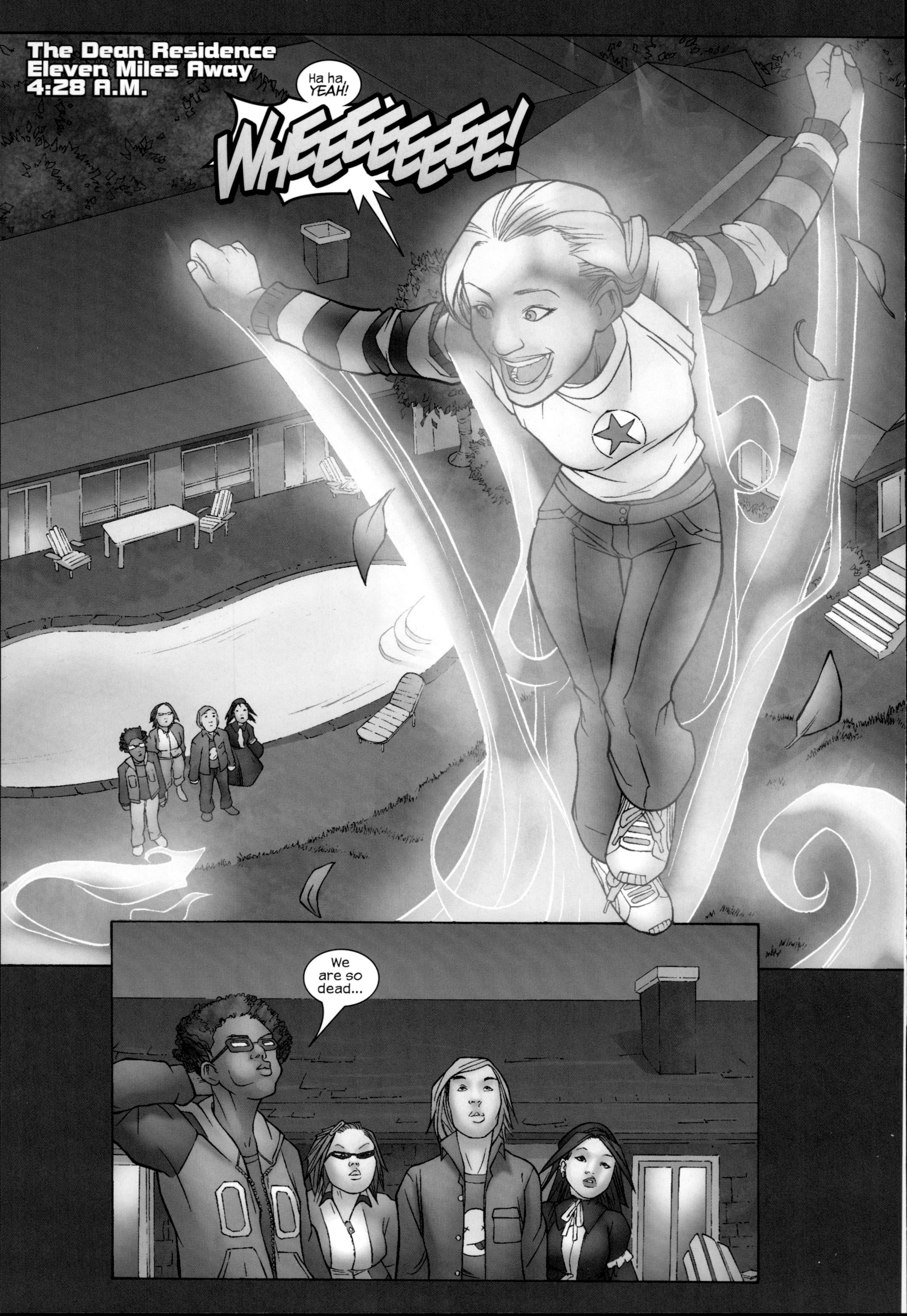
The Dean Residence
Eleven Miles Away
4:28 A.M.
Ha ha, YEAH!
WHEEEEEEEE!
We are so dead...

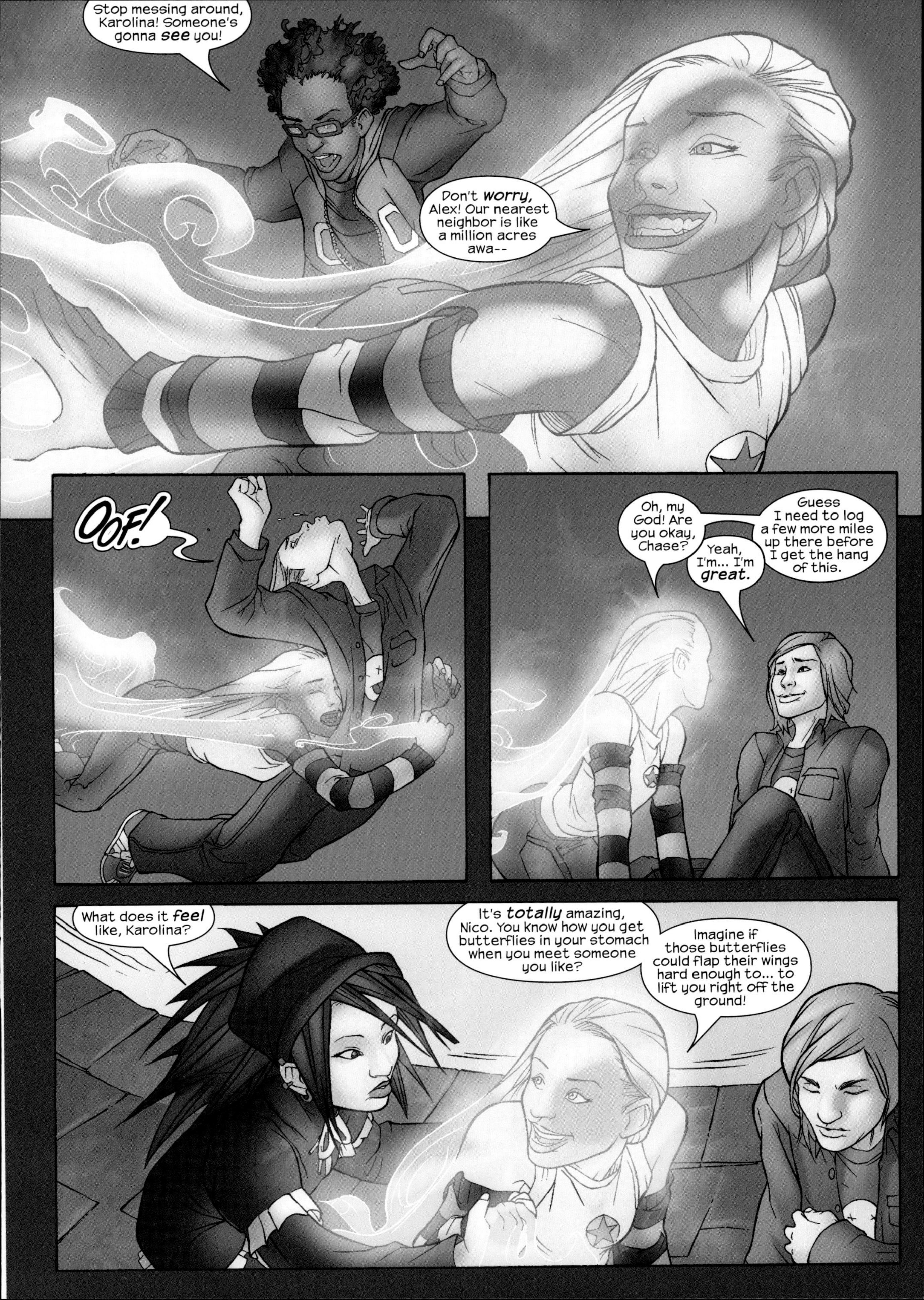
Stop messing around, Karolina! Someone's gonna see you!
Don't worry, Alex! Our nearest neighbor is like a million acres awa--
OOF!
Oh, my God! Are you okay, Chase?
Guess I need to log a few more miles up there before I get the hang of this.
Yeah, I'm... I'm great.
What does it feel like, Karolina?
It's totally amazing, Nico. You know how you get butterflies in your stomach when you meet someone you like?
Imagine if those butterflies could flap their wings hard enough to... to lift you right off the ground!

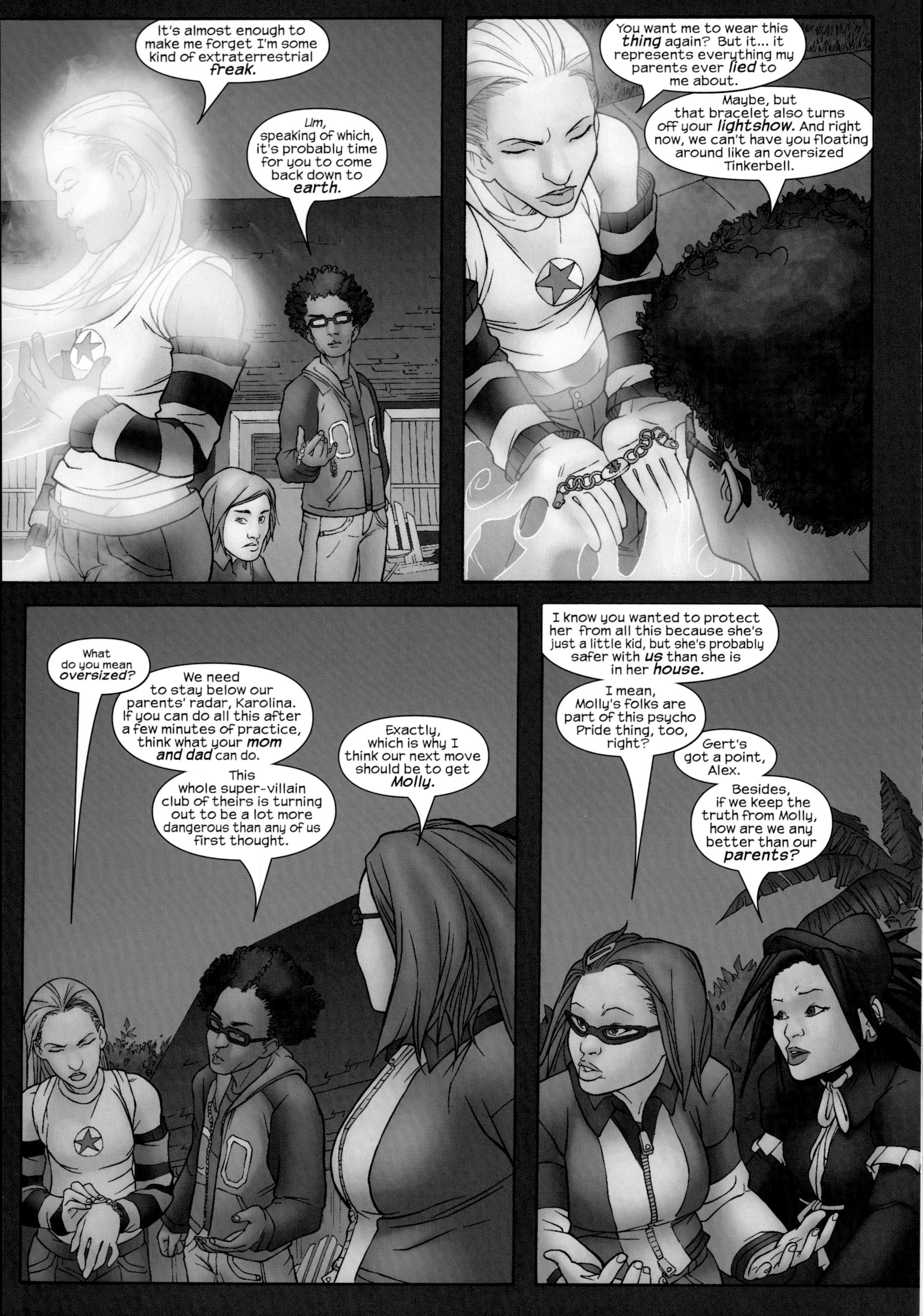
It's almost enough to make me forget I'm some kind of extraterrestrial *freak.*
Um, speaking of which, it's probably time for you to come back down to *earth.*
You want me to wear this *thing* again? But it... it represents everything my parents ever *lied* to me about.
Maybe, but that bracelet also turns off your *lightshow.* And right now, we can't have you floating around like an oversized Tinkerbell.
What do you mean *oversized?*
We need to stay below our parents' radar, Karolina. If you can do all this after a few minutes of practice, think what your *mom and dad* can do.
This whole super-villain club of theirs is turning out to be a lot more dangerous than any of us first thought.
Exactly, which is why I think our next move should be to get *Molly.*
I know you wanted to protect her from all this because she's just a little kid, but she's probably safer with *us* than she is in her *house.*
I mean, Molly's folks are part of this psycho Pride thing, too, right?
Gert's got a point, Alex.
Besides, if we keep the truth from Molly, how are we any better than our *parents?*

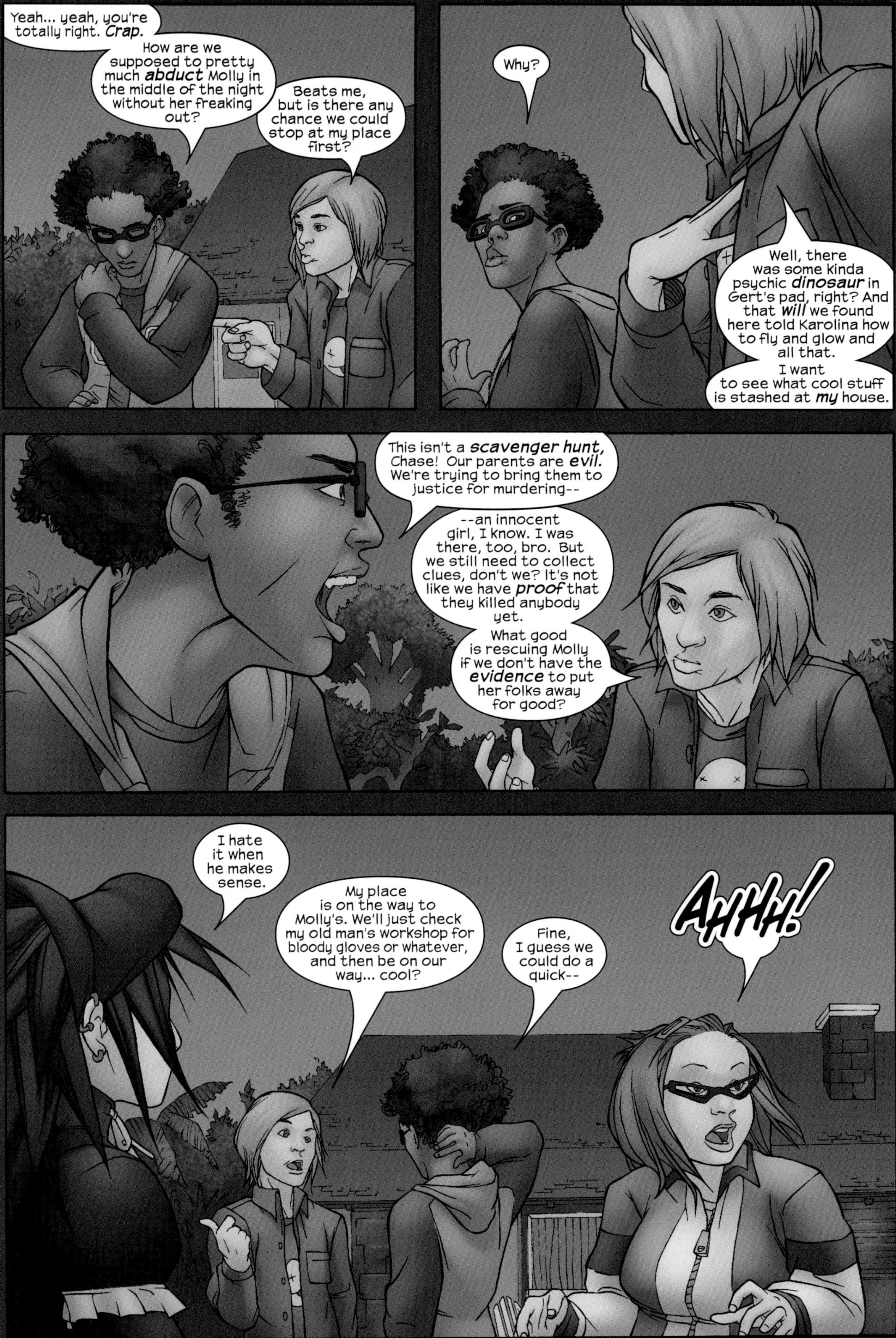
Yeah... yeah, you're totally right. Crap.
How are we supposed to pretty much abduct Molly in the middle of the night without her freaking out?
Beats me, but is there any chance we could stop at my place first?
Why?
Well, there was some kinda psychic dinosaur in Gert's pad, right? And that will we found here told Karolina how to fly and glow and all that.
I want to see what cool stuff is stashed at my house.
This isn't a scavenger hunt, Chase! Our parents are evil. We're trying to bring them to justice for murdering--
--an innocent girl, I know. I was there, too, bro. But we still need to collect clues, don't we? It's not like we have proof that they killed anybody yet.
What good is rescuing Molly if we don't have the evidence to put her folks away for good?
I hate it when he makes sense.
My place is on the way to Molly's. We'll just check my old man's workshop for bloody gloves or whatever, and then be on our way... cool?
Fine, I guess we could do a quick--
AHHH!

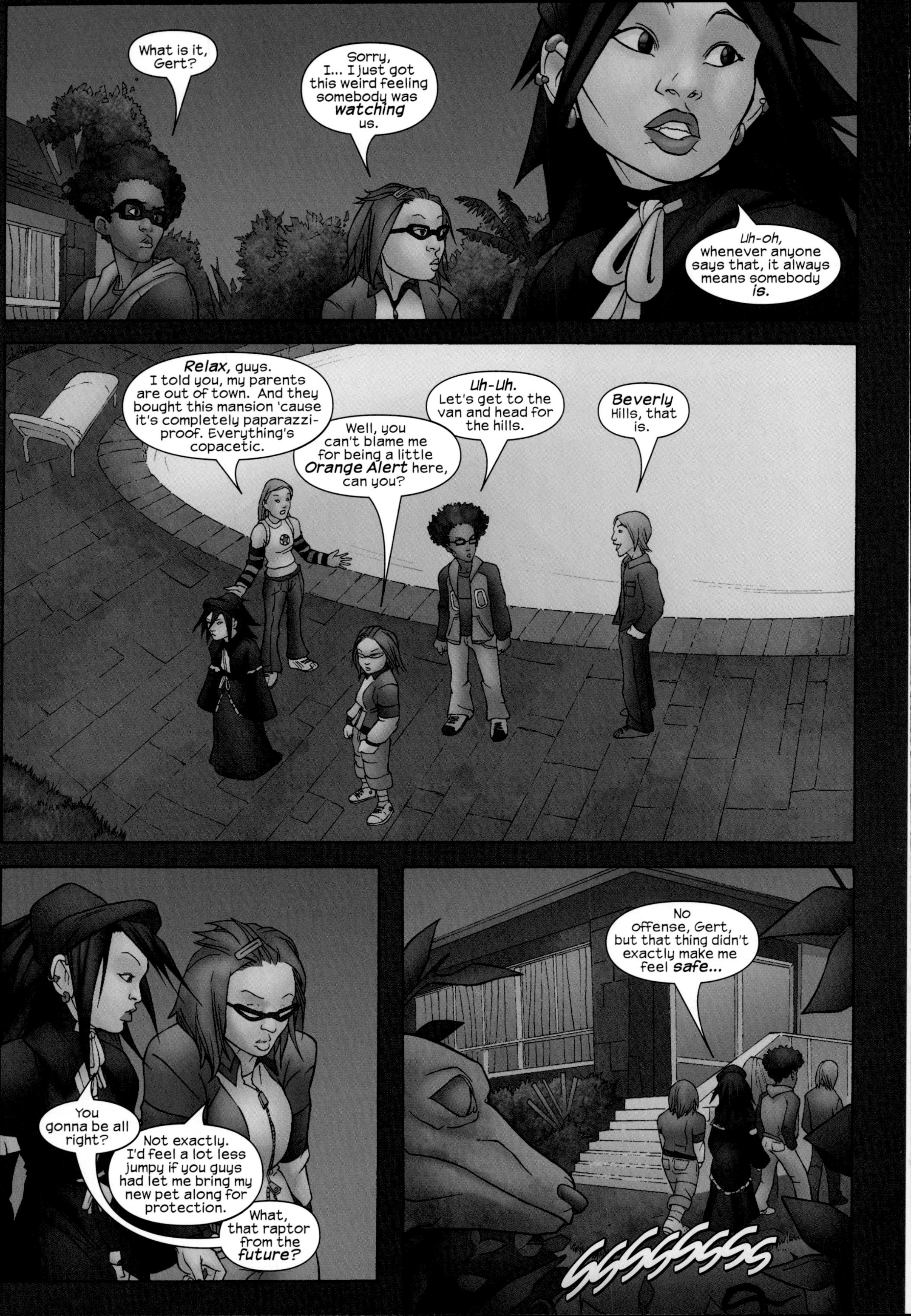
What is it, Gert?
Sorry, I... I just got this weird feeling somebody was watching us.
Uh-oh, whenever anyone says that, it always means somebody is.
Relax, guys. I told you, my parents are out of town. And they bought this mansion 'cause it's completely paparazzi-proof. Everything's copacetic.
Well, you can't blame me for being a little Orange Alert here, can you?
Uh-uh. Let's get to the van and head for the hills.
Beverly Hills, that is.
You gonna be all right?
Not exactly. I'd feel a lot less jumpy if you guys had let me bring my new pet along for protection.
What, that raptor from the future?
No offense, Gert, but that thing didn't exactly make me feel safe...
GGGSSSSS

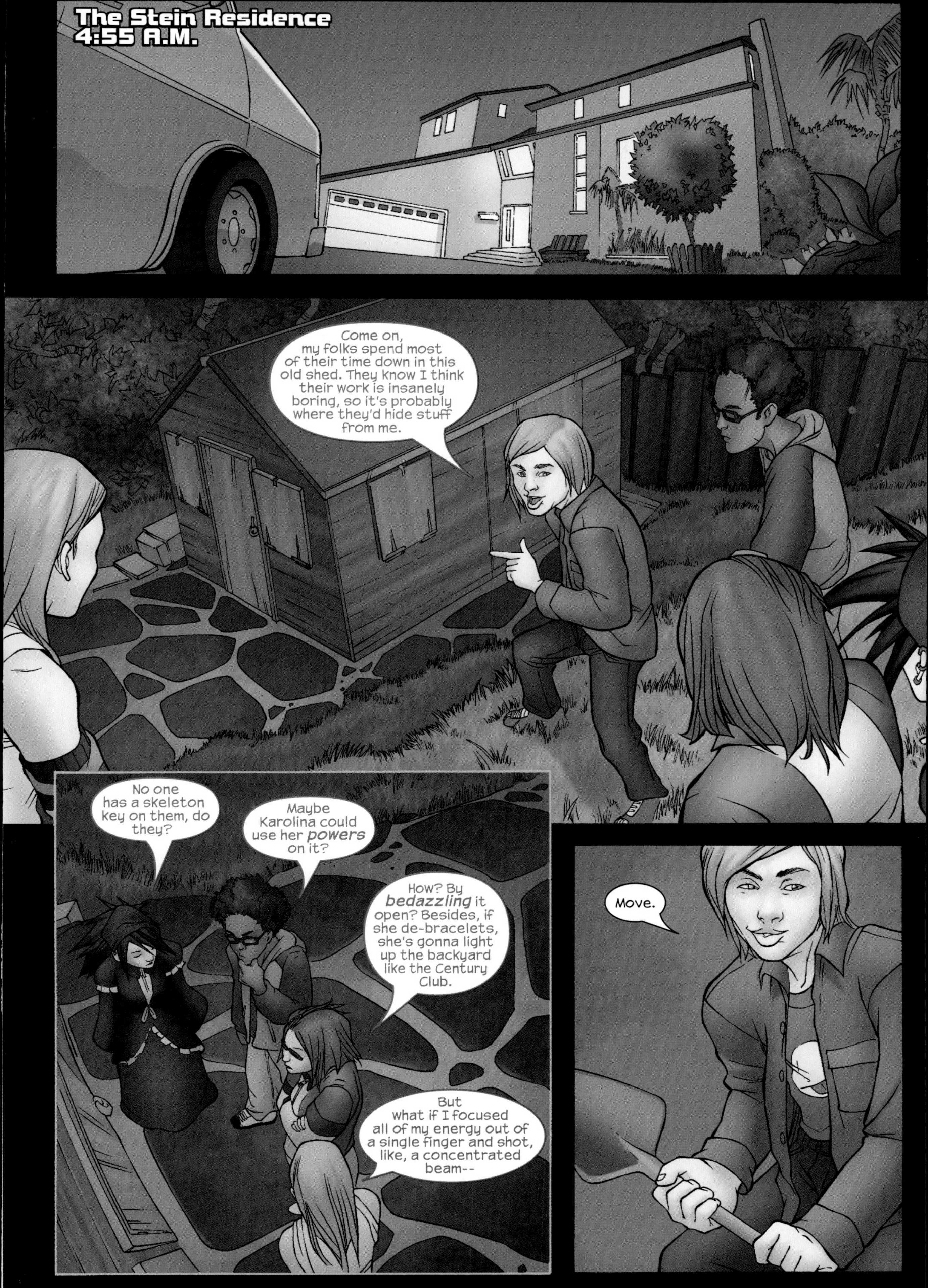
The Stein Residence
4:55 A.M.
Come on, my folks spend most of their time down in this old shed. They know I think their work is insanely boring, so it's probably where they'd hide stuff from me.
No one has a skeleton key on them, do they?
Maybe Karolina could use her *powers* on it?
How? By ***bedazzling*** it open? Besides, if she de-bracelets, she's gonna light up the backyard like the Century Club.
But what if I focused all of my energy out of a single finger and shot, like, a concentrated beam--
Move.

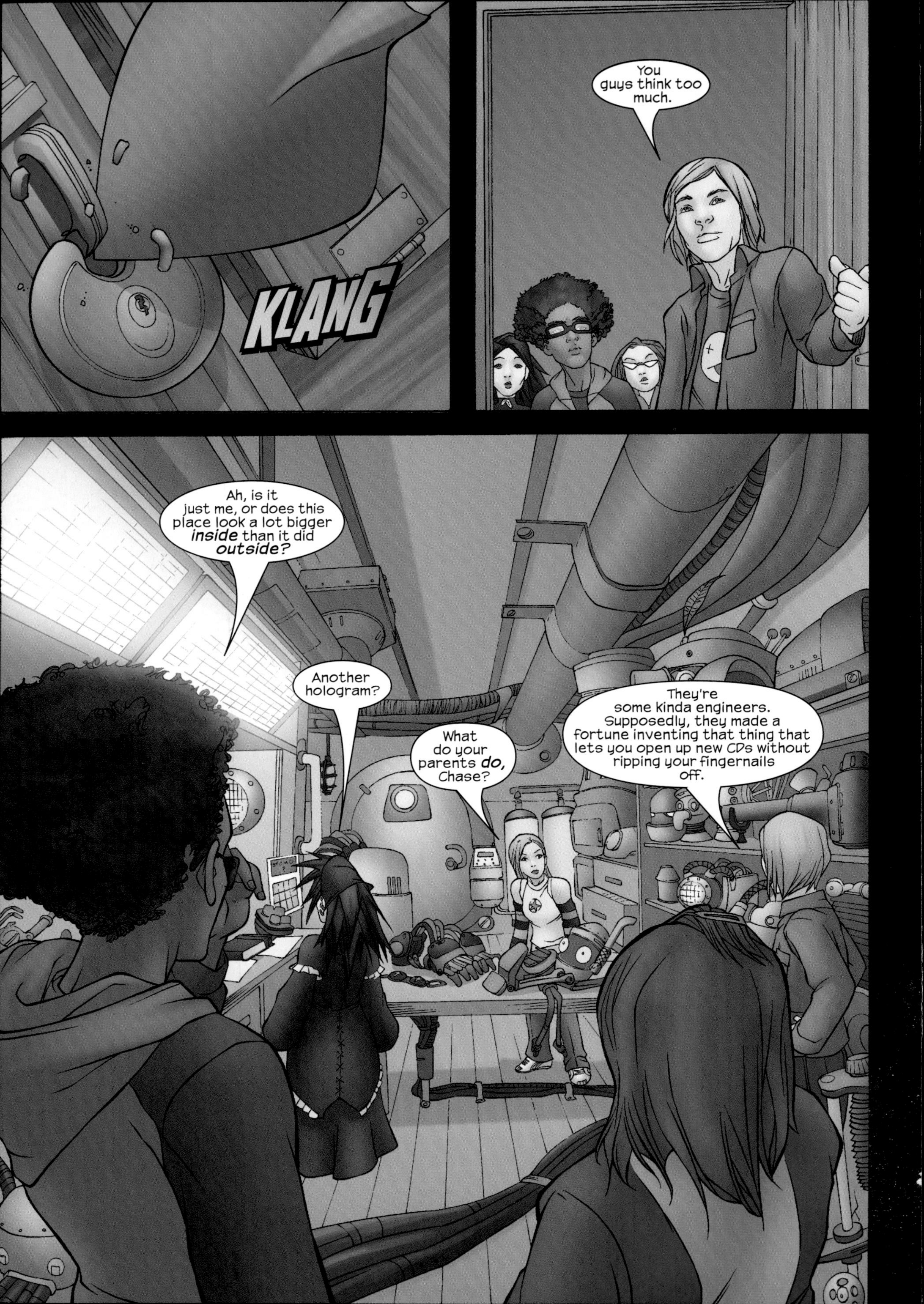
KLANG
You guys think too much.
Ah, is it just me, or does this place look a lot bigger *inside* than it did *outside*?
Another hologram?
What do your parents *do*, Chase?
They're some kinda engineers. Supposedly, they made a fortune inventing that thing that lets you open up new CDs without ripping your fingernails off.

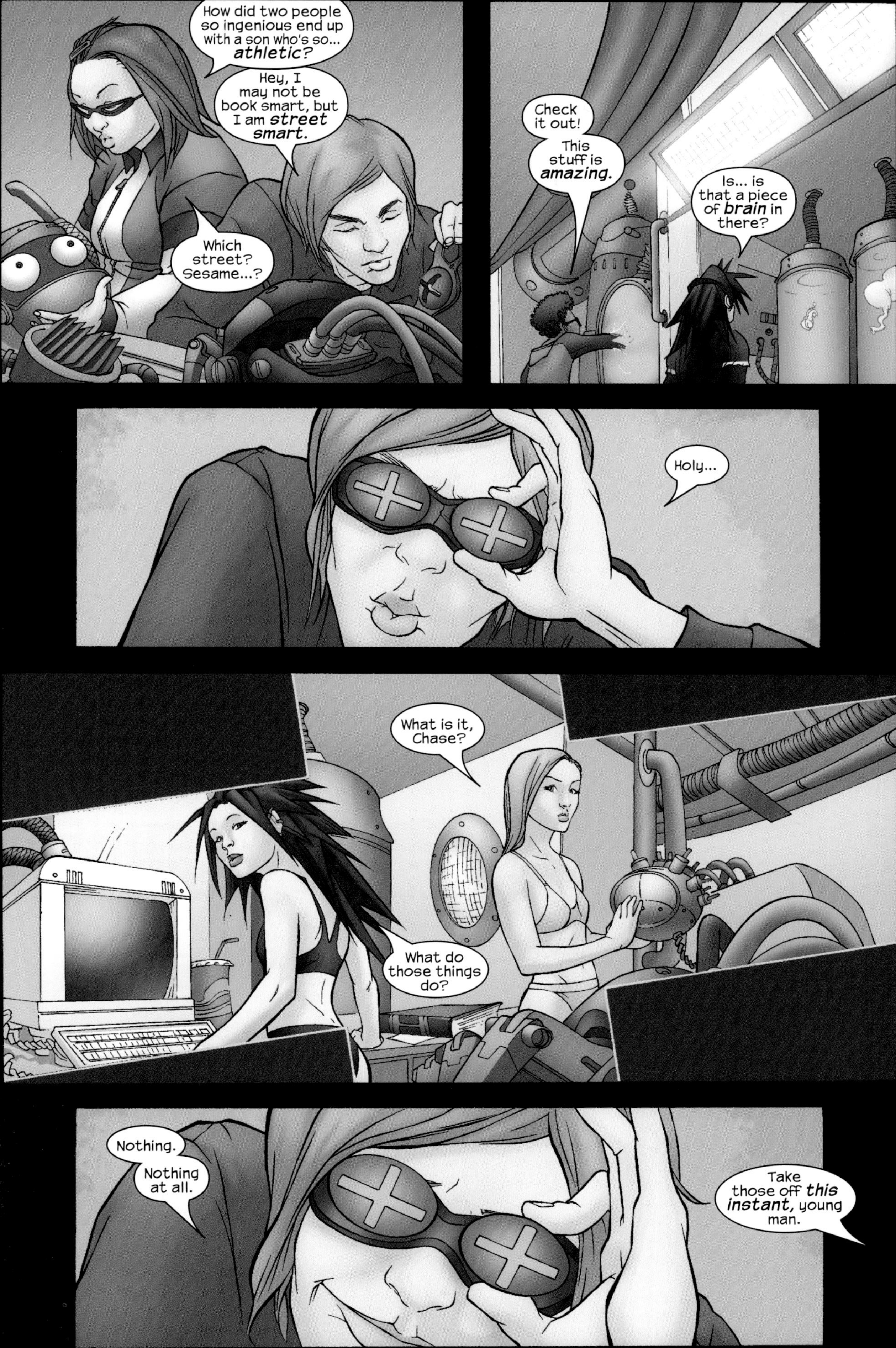
How did two people so ingenious end up with a son who's so... *athletic?*
Hey, I may not be book smart, but I am *street smart.*
Which street? Sesame...?
Check it out!
This stuff is *amazing.*
Is... is that a piece of *brain* in there?
Holy...
What is it, Chase?
What do those things do?
Nothing.
Nothing at all.
Take those off *this instant,* young man.

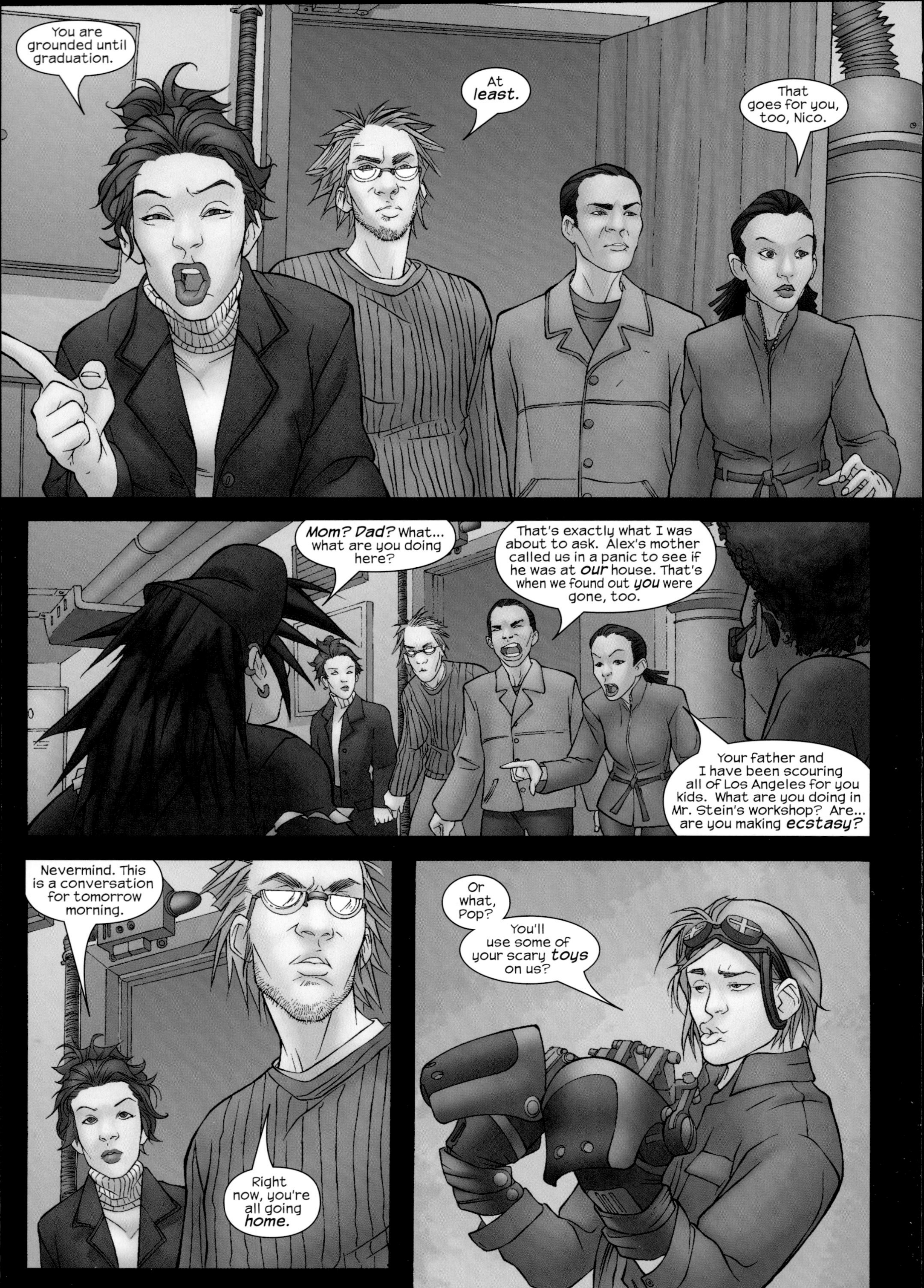

You are grounded until graduation.
At least.
That goes for you, too, Nico.
Mom? Dad? What... what are you doing here?
That's exactly what I was about to ask. Alex's mother called us in a panic to see if he was at our house. That's when we found out you were gone, too.
Your father and I have been scouring all of Los Angeles for you kids. What are you doing in Mr. Stein's workshop? Are... are you making ecstasy?
Nevermind. This is a conversation for tomorrow morning.
Right now, you're all going home.
Or what, Pop?
You'll use some of your scary toys on us?

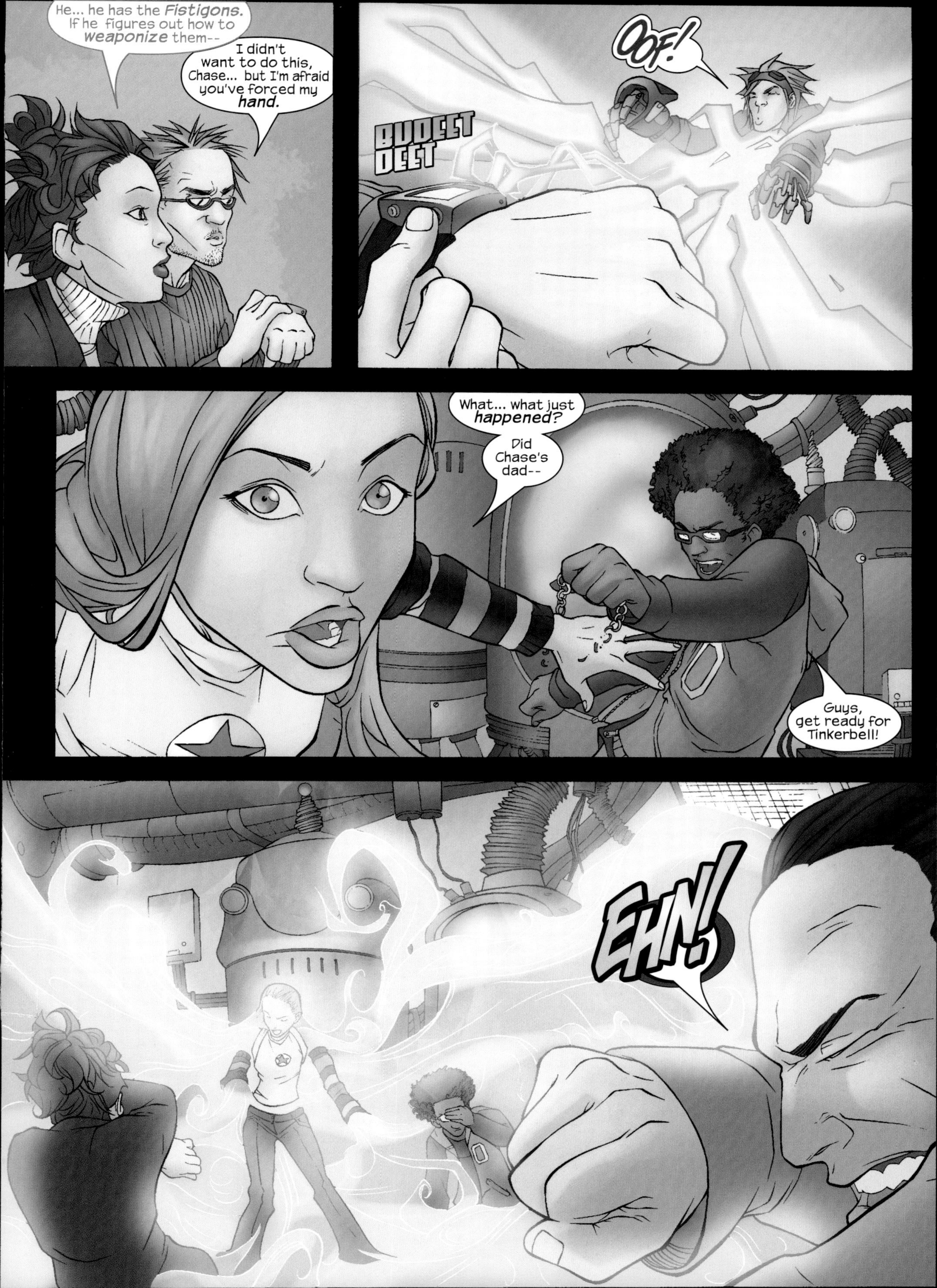
He... he has the Fistigons. If he figures out how to weaponize them--
I didn't want to do this, Chase... but I'm afraid you've forced my hand.
OOF!
BUDEET DEET
What... what just happened?
Did Chase's dad--
Guys, get ready for Tinkerbell!
EHN!

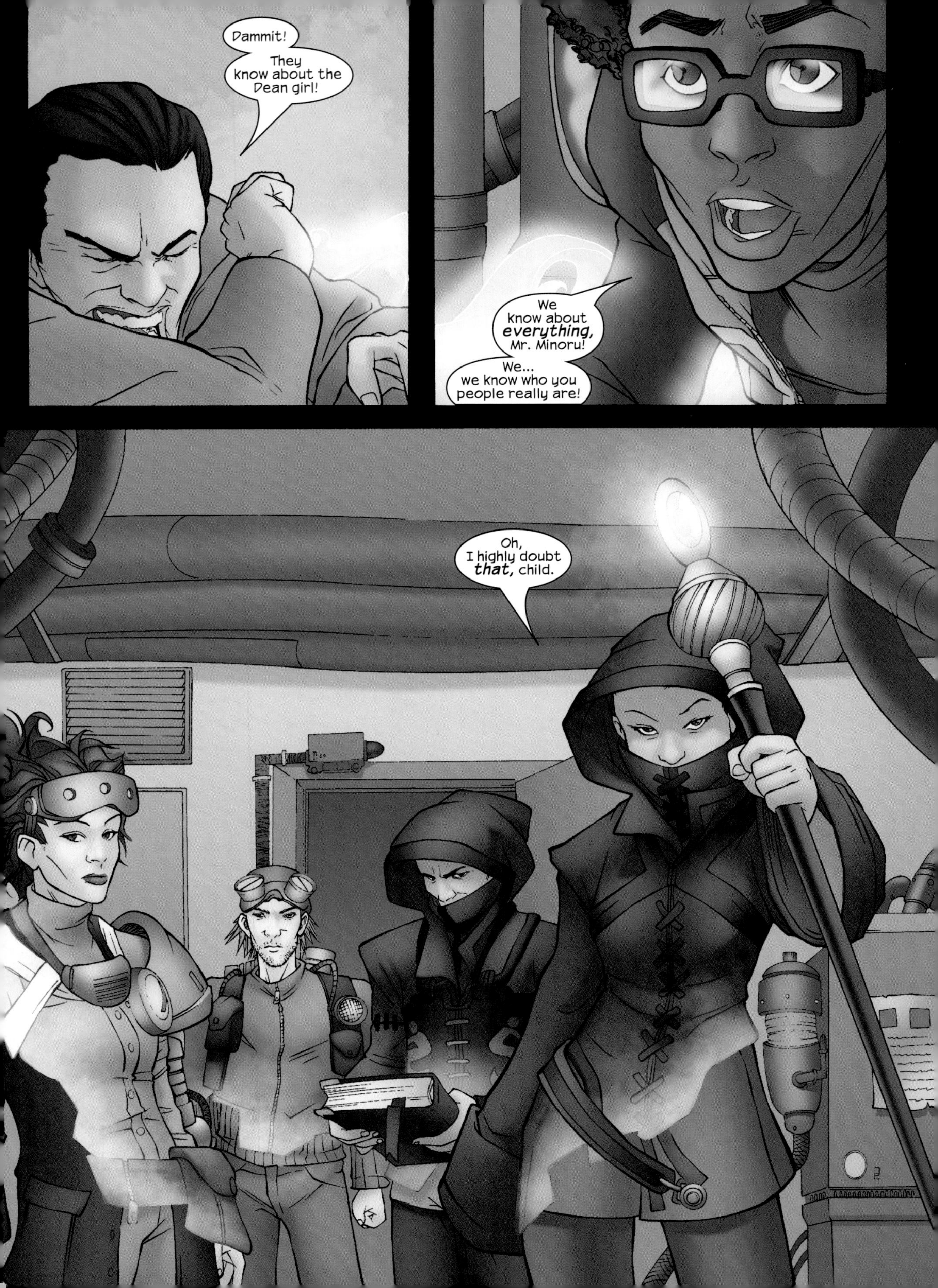
Dammit!
They know about the Dean girl!
We know about *everything,* Mr. Minoru!
We... we know who you people really are!
Oh, I highly doubt *that,* child.

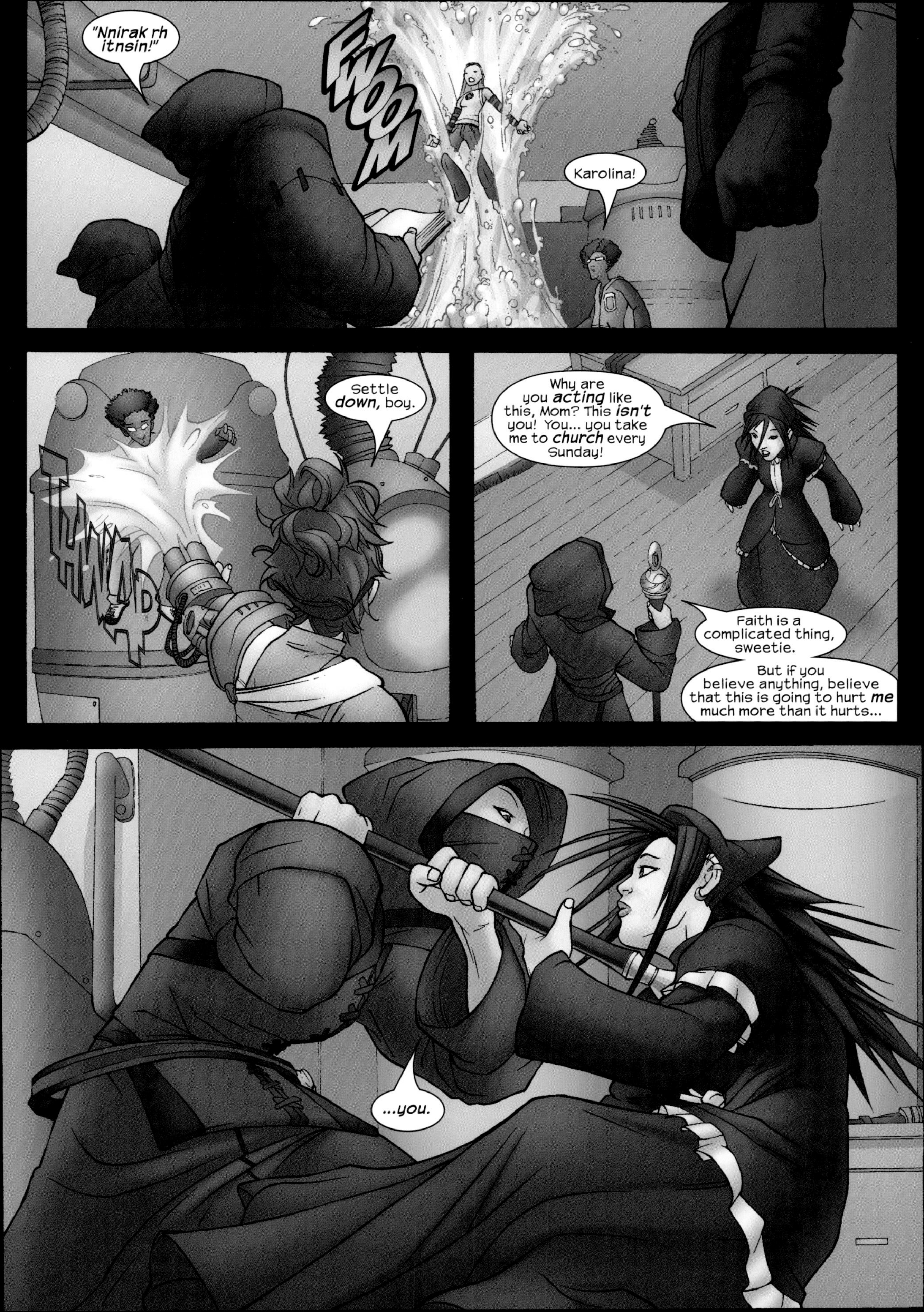

"Nnirak rh itnsin!"
FWOOM
Karolina!
Settle down, boy.
THWAP
Why are you acting like this, Mom? This isn't you! You... you take me to church every Sunday!
Faith is a complicated thing, sweetie.
But if you believe anything, believe that this is going to hurt me much more than it hurts...
...you.

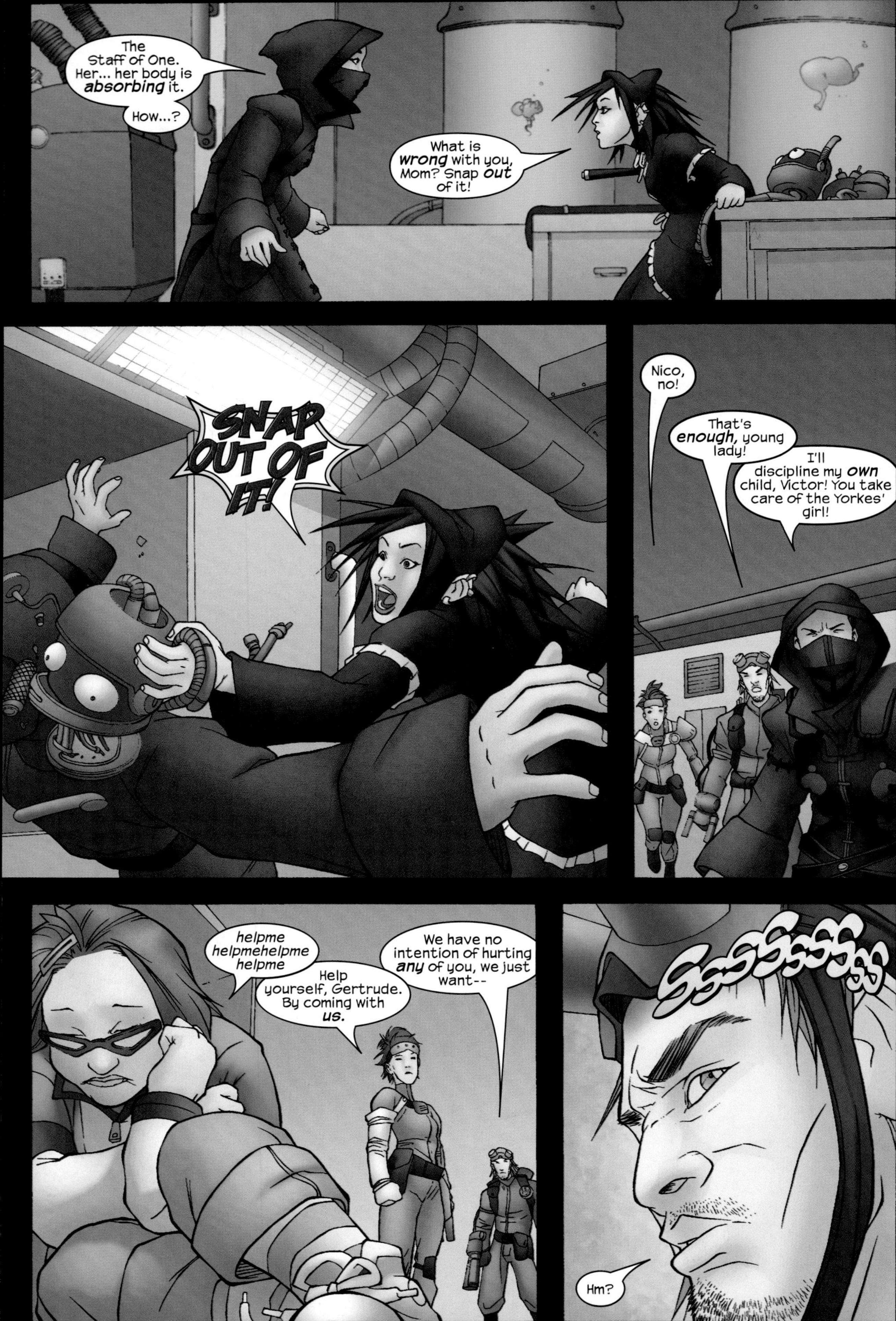
The Staff of One. Her... her body is absorbing it.
How...?
What is wrong with you, Mom? Snap out of it!
SNAP OUT OF IT!
Nico, no!
That's enough, young lady!
I'll discipline my own child, Victor! You take care of the Yorkes' girl!
helpme helpmehelpme helpme
Help yourself, Gertrude. By coming with us.
We have no intention of hurting any of you, we just want--
SSSSSSSSSSS
Hm?

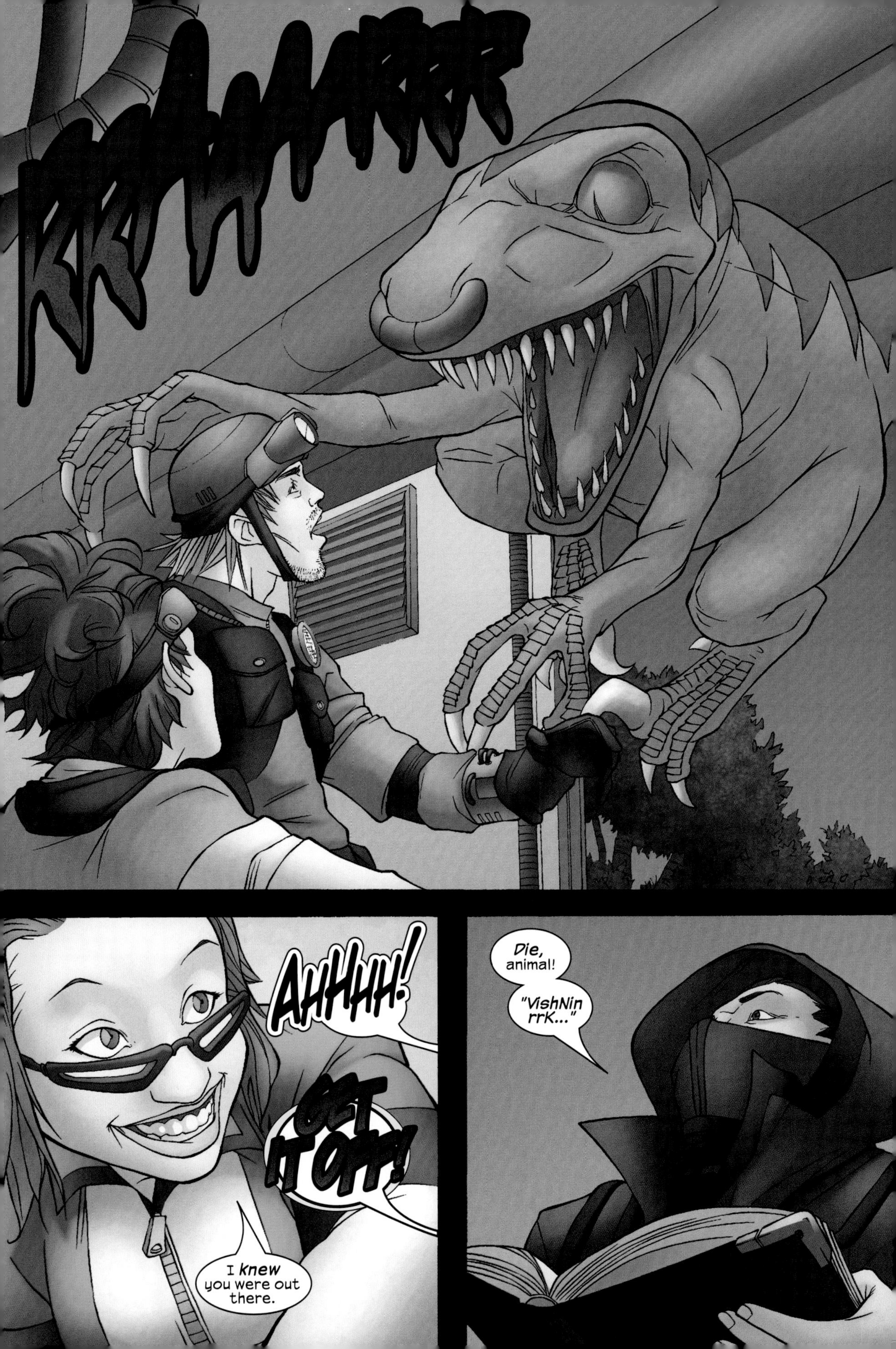
RRAAAARRR
AHHHH!
GET IT OFF!
I knew you were out there.
Die, animal!
"VishNin rrK..."

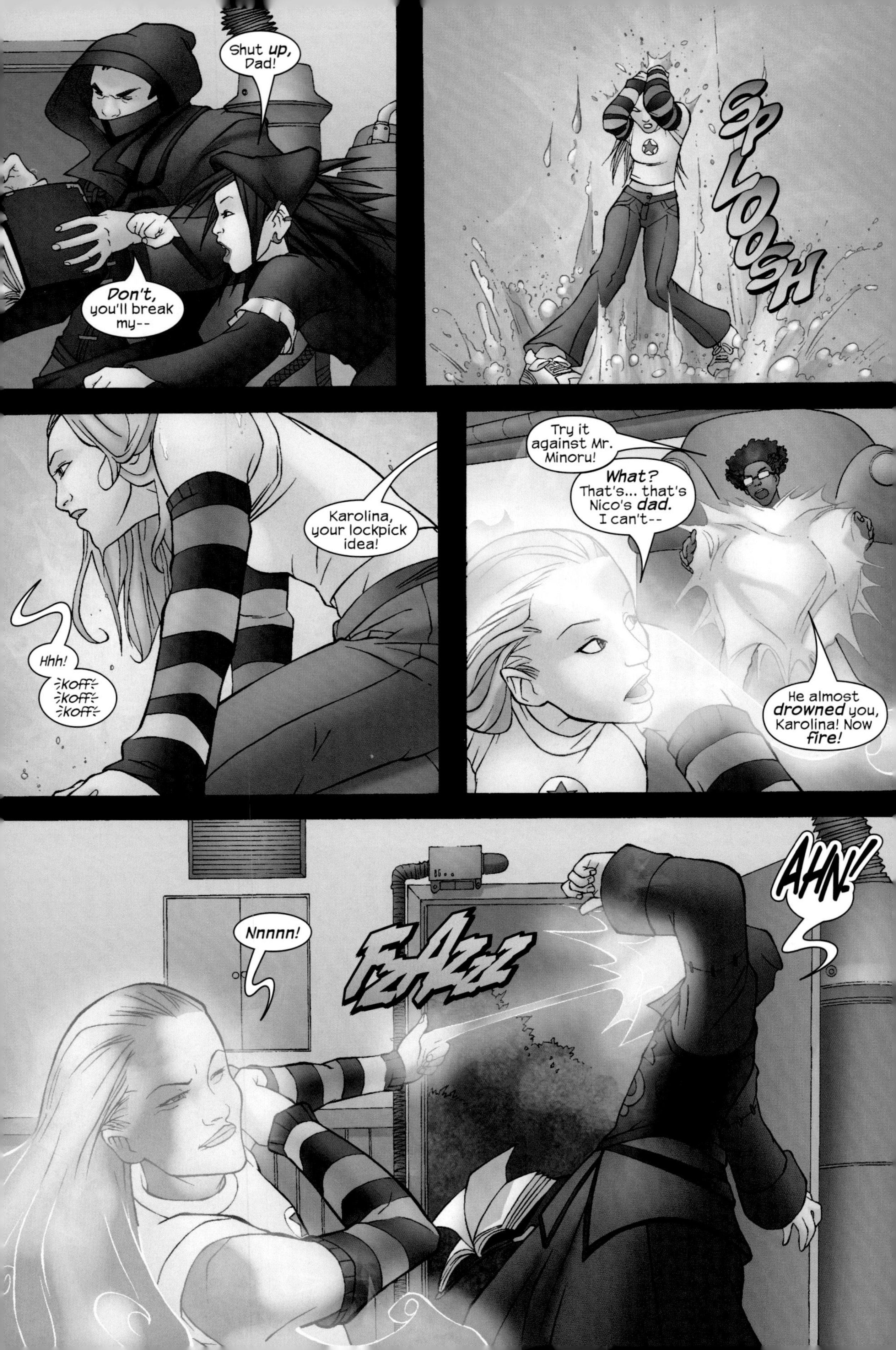

Shut *up,* Dad!
Don't, you'll break my--
SPLOOSH
Karolina, your lockpick idea!
Hhh!
koff *koff* *koff*
Try it against Mr. Minoru!
What? That's... that's Nico's ***dad.*** I can't--
He almost ***drowned*** you, Karolina! Now ***fire!***
Nnnnn!
FZAZZ
AHN!

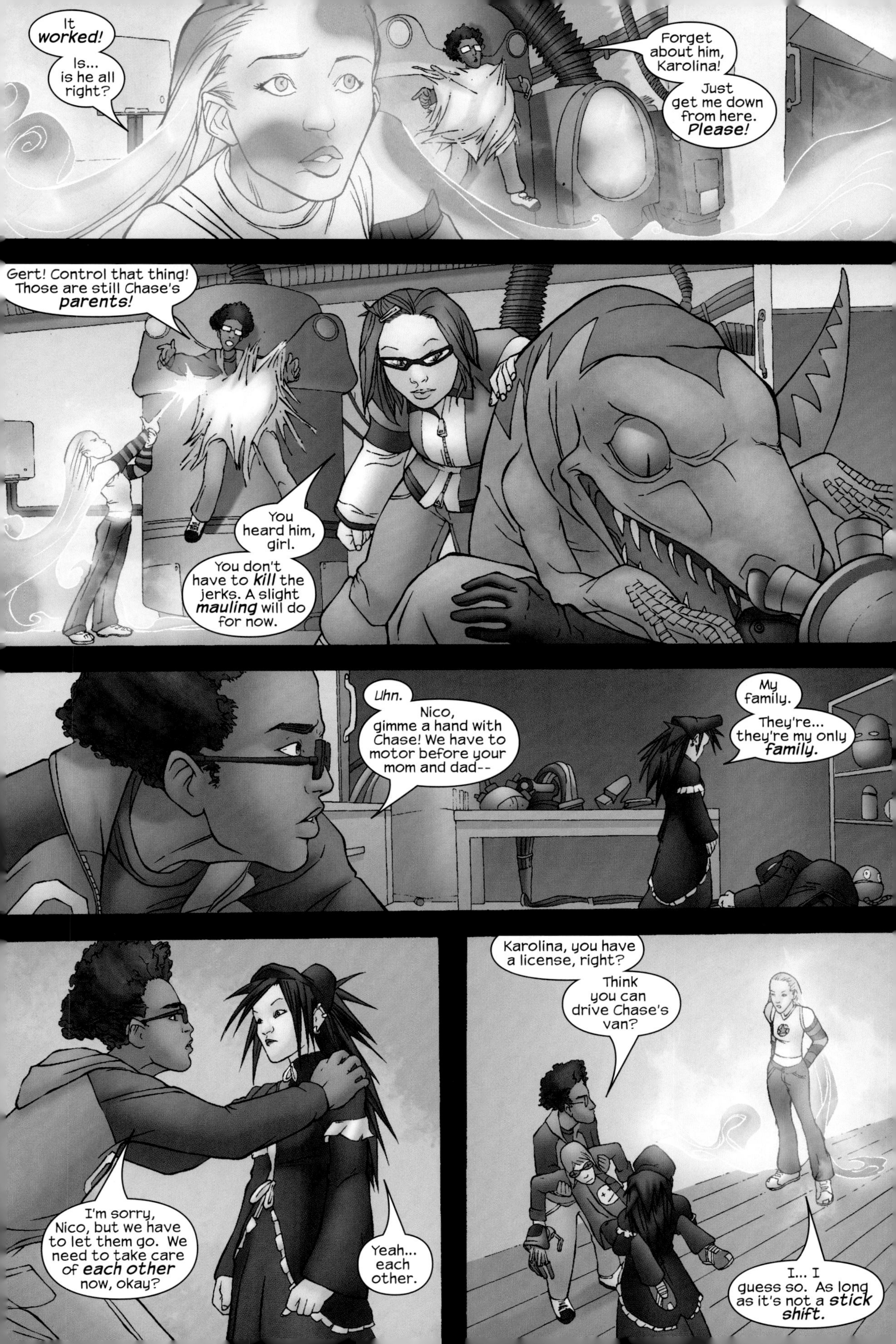
It worked! Is... is he all right?
Forget about him, Karolina!
Just get me down from here. Please!
Gert! Control that thing! Those are still Chase's parents!
You heard him, girl.
You don't have to kill the jerks. A slight mauling will do for now.
Uhn.
Nico, gimme a hand with Chase! We have to motor before your mom and dad--
My family.
They're... they're my only family.
I'm sorry, Nico, but we have to let them go. We need to take care of each other now, okay?
Yeah... each other.
Karolina, you have a license, right?
Think you can drive Chase's van?
I... I guess so. As long as it's not a stick shift.

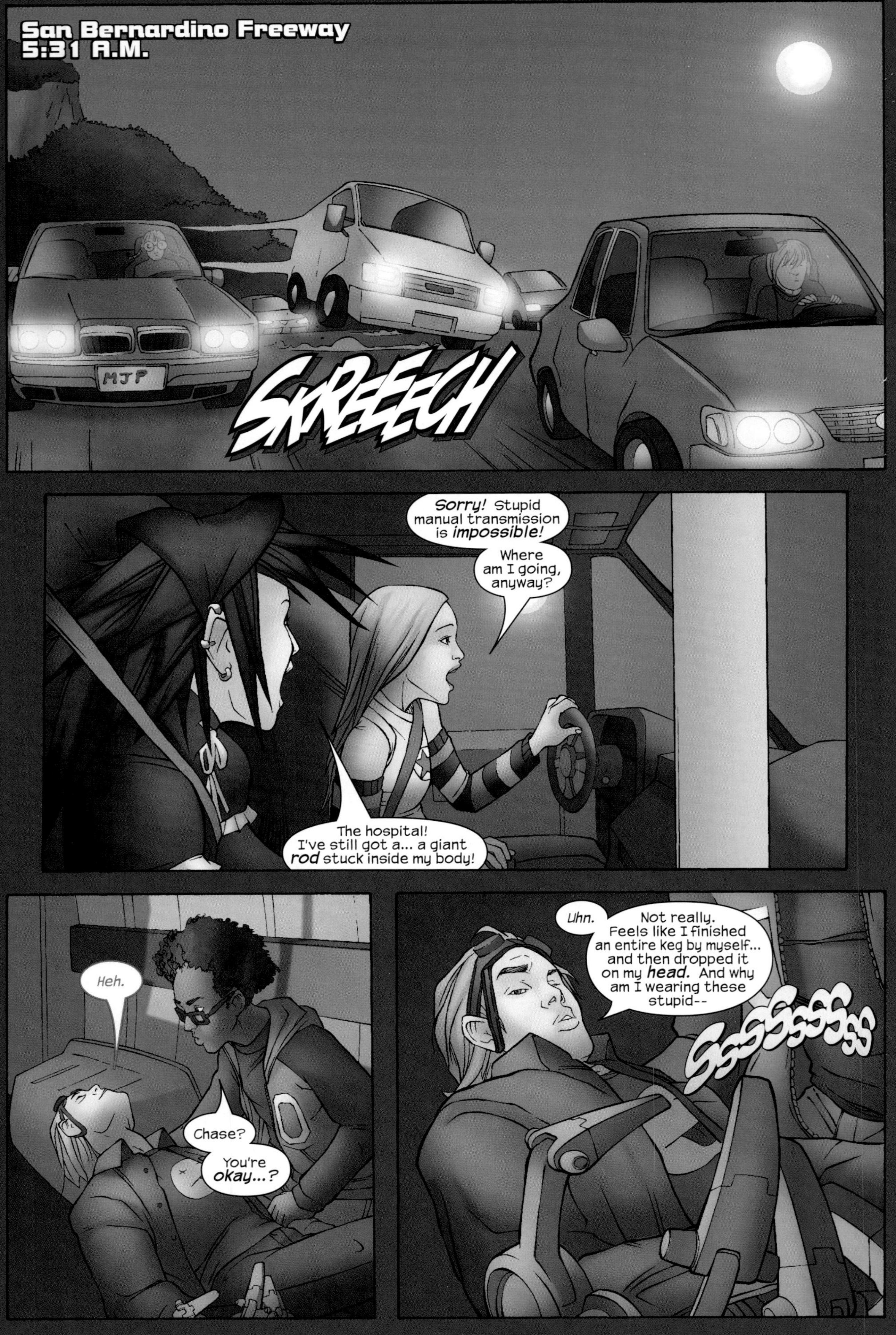
San Bernardino Freeway
5:31 A.M.
MJP
SKREEECH
Sorry! Stupid manual transmission is impossible!
Where am I going, anyway?
The hospital! I've still got a... a giant rod stuck inside my body!
Heh.
Chase?
You're okay...?
Uhn.
Not really. Feels like I finished an entire keg by myself... and then dropped it on my head. And why am I wearing these stupid--
SSSSSSSSS

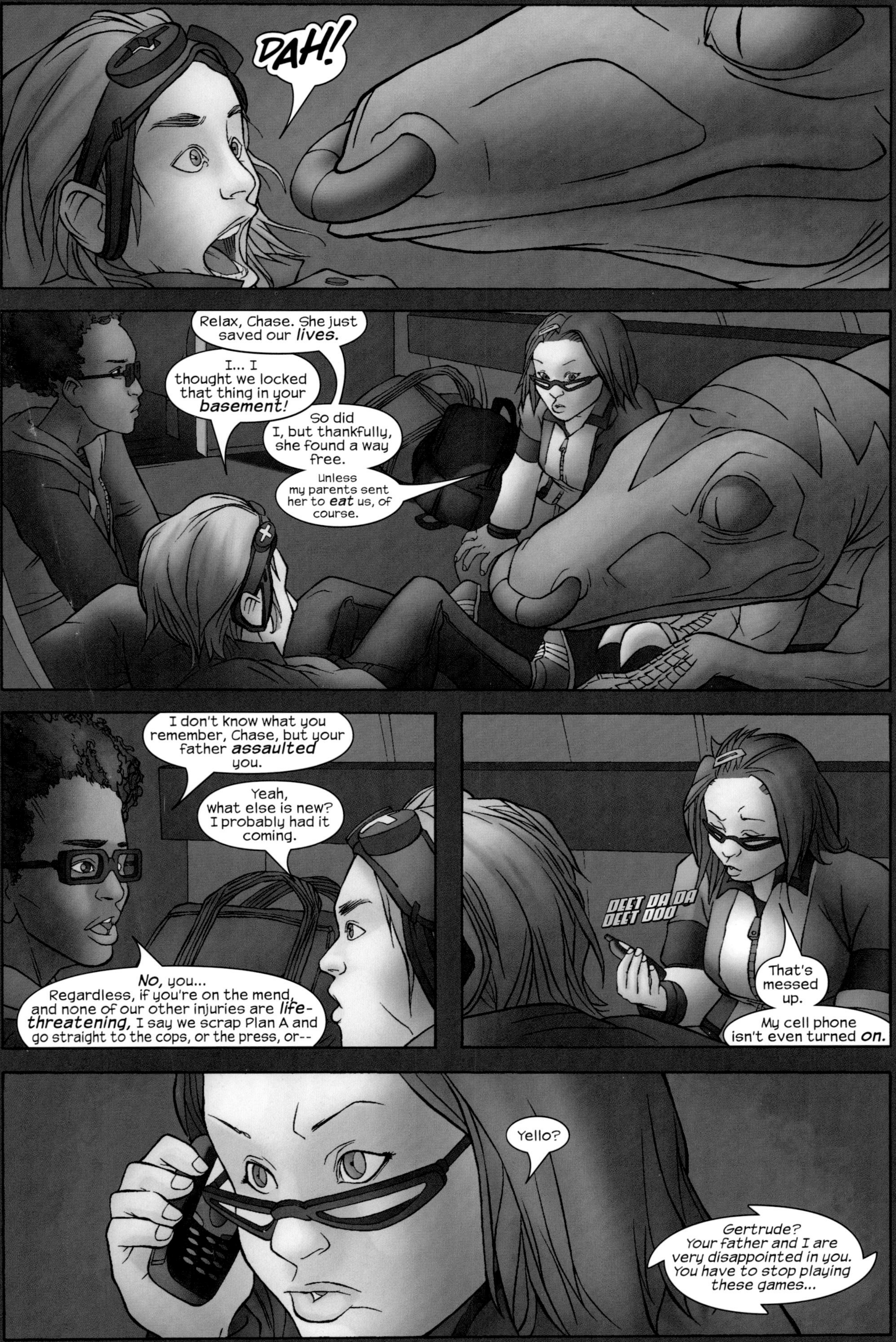
DAH!
Relax, Chase. She just saved our *lives.*
I... I thought we locked that thing in your *basement!*
So did I, but thankfully, she found a way free.
Unless my parents sent her to *eat* us, of course.
I don't know what you remember, Chase, but your father *assaulted* you.
Yeah, what else is new? I probably had it coming.
No, you... Regardless, if you're on the mend, and none of our other injuries are *life-threatening,* I say we scrap Plan A and go straight to the cops, or the press, or--
DEET DA DA DEET DOO
That's messed up.
My cell phone isn't even turned *on.*
Yello?
Gertrude? Your father and I are very disappointed in you. You have to stop playing these games...

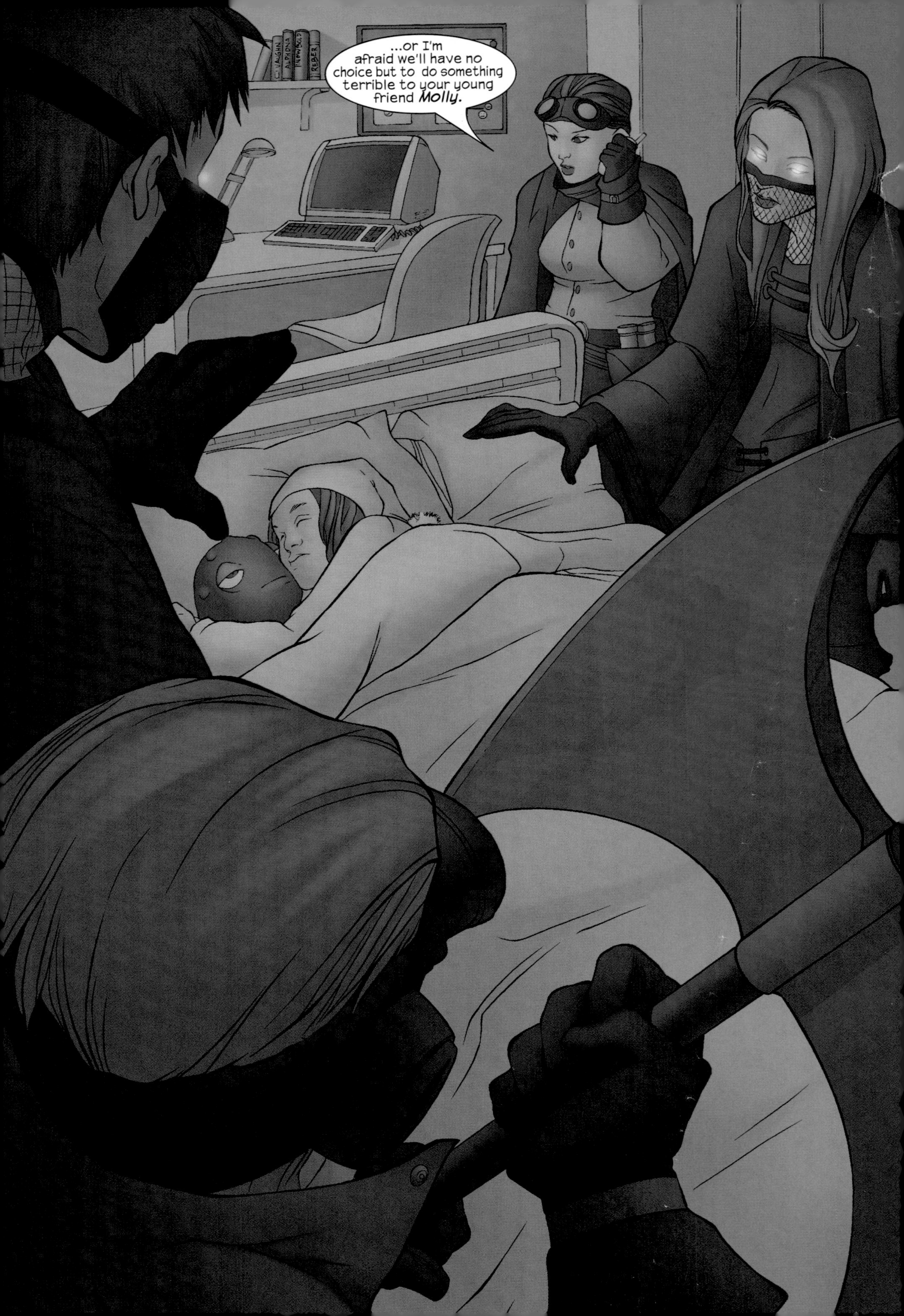
...or I'm afraid we'll have no choice but to do something terrible to your young friend Molly.
VAUGHN
ALPHONA
NEWBOLD
REBER

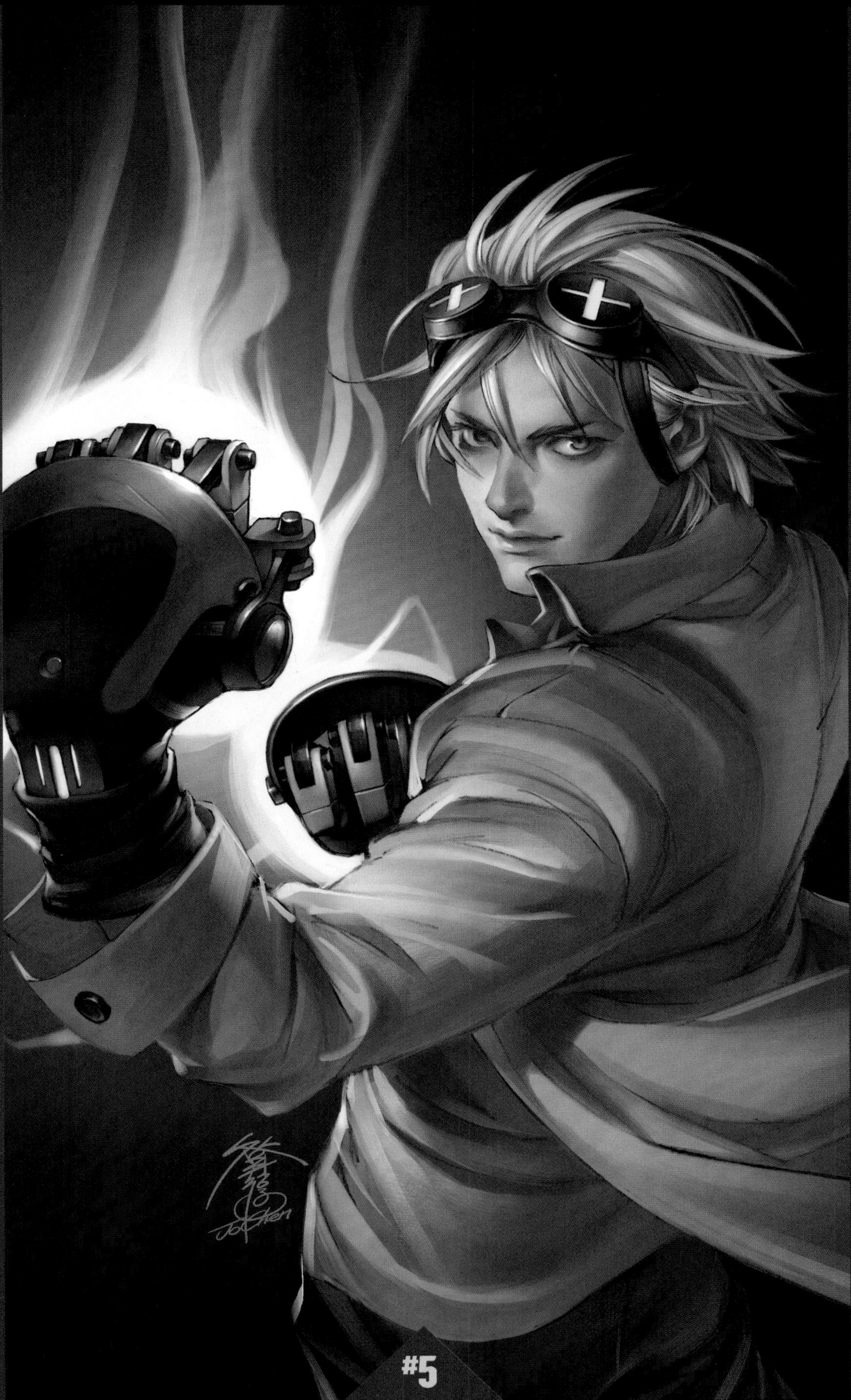

#5

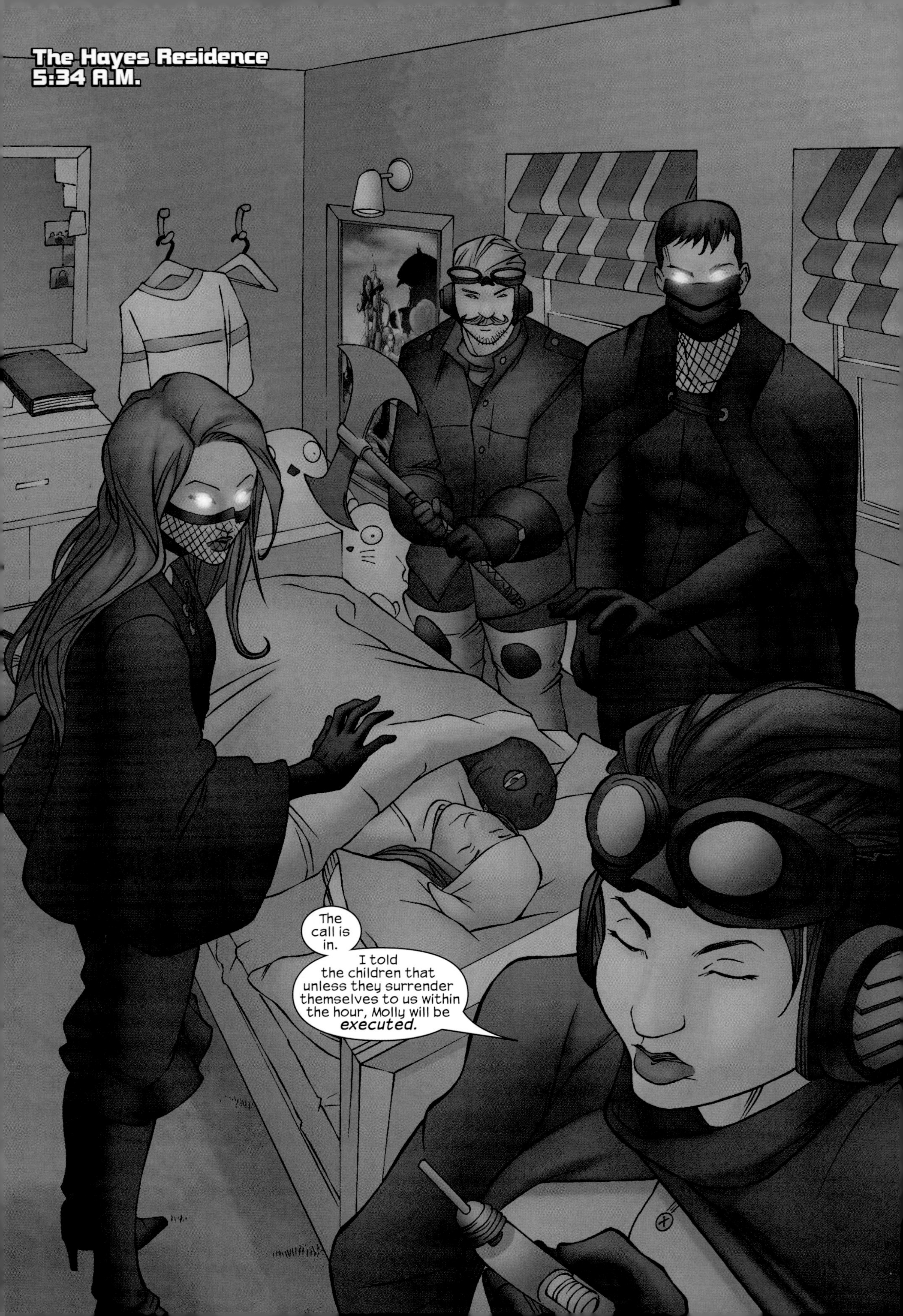
The Hayes Residence
5:34 A.M.
The call is in.
I told the children that unless they surrender themselves to us within the hour, Molly will be *executed.*

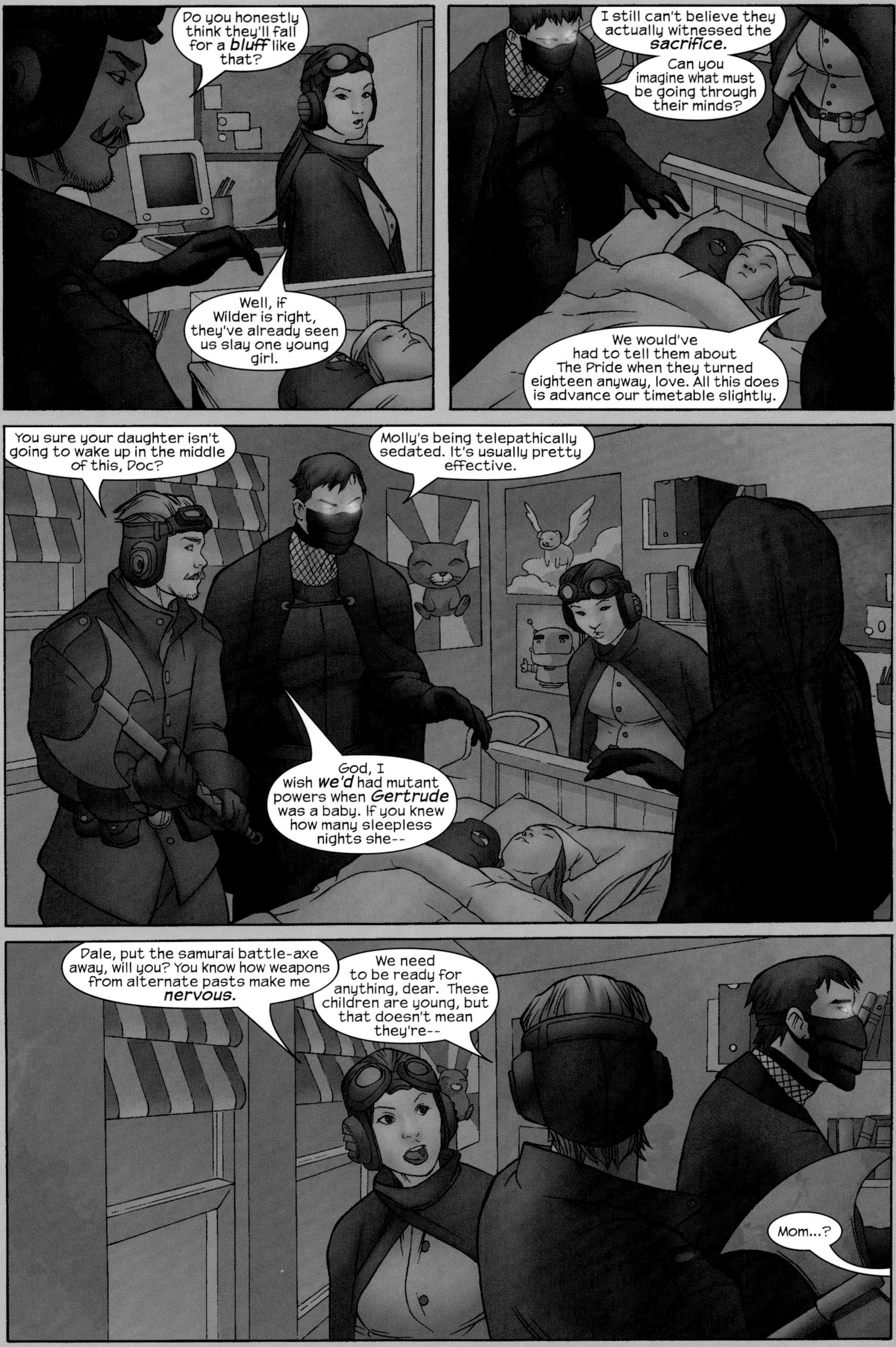

Do you honestly think they'll fall for a **bluff** like that?
Well, if Wilder is right, they've already seen us slay one young girl.
I still can't believe they actually witnessed the ***sacrifice.***
Can you imagine what must be going through their minds?
We would've had to tell them about The Pride when they turned eighteen anyway, love. All this does is advance our timetable slightly.
You sure your daughter isn't going to wake up in the middle of this, Doc?
Molly's being telepathically sedated. It's usually pretty effective.
God, I wish ***we'd*** had mutant powers when ***Gertrude*** was a baby. If you knew how many sleepless nights she--
Dale, put the samurai battle-axe away, will you? You know how weapons from alternate pasts make me ***nervous.***
We need to be ready for anything, dear. These children are young, but that doesn't mean they're--
Mom...?

Mommy...?

Dammit, she's slipping out of the trance.

Everyone get out. *I'll* handle this.

I'm right here, Molly. You were talking in your sleep.

Bad dream?

My... my stomach is all hurtie.

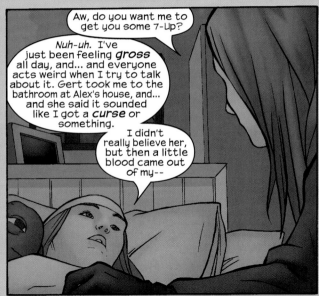

Aw, do you want me to get you some 7-Up?

Nuh-uh. I've just been feeling *gross* all day, and... and everyone acts weird when I try to talk about it. Gert took me to the bathroom at Alex's house, and... and she said it sounded like I got a *curse* or something.

I didn't really believe her, but then a little blood came out of my--

Um, why don't you just try to go back to sleep, precious?

I know this can be a scary time in a young woman's life...

...but right now, Mommy has *other* things to worry about.

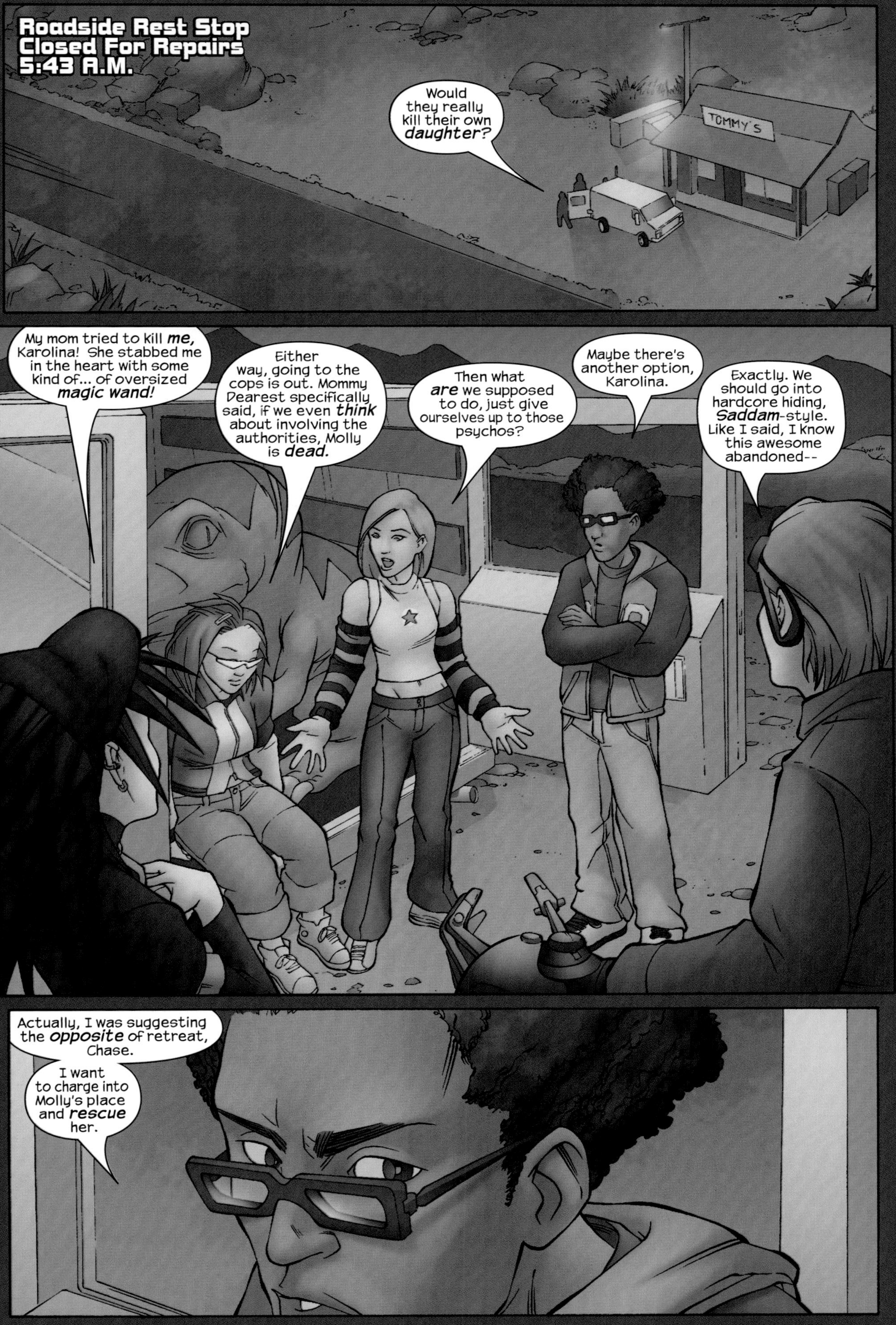
Roadside Rest Stop
Closed For Repairs
5:43 A.M.
Would they really kill their own daughter?
TOMMY'S
My mom tried to kill me, Karolina! She stabbed me in the heart with some kind of... of oversized magic wand!
Either way, going to the cops is out. Mommy Dearest specifically said, if we even think about involving the authorities, Molly is dead.
Then what are we supposed to do, just give ourselves up to those psychos?
Maybe there's another option, Karolina.
Exactly. We should go into hardcore hiding, Saddam-style. Like I said, I know this awesome abandoned--
Actually, I was suggesting the opposite of retreat, Chase.
I want to charge into Molly's place and rescue her.

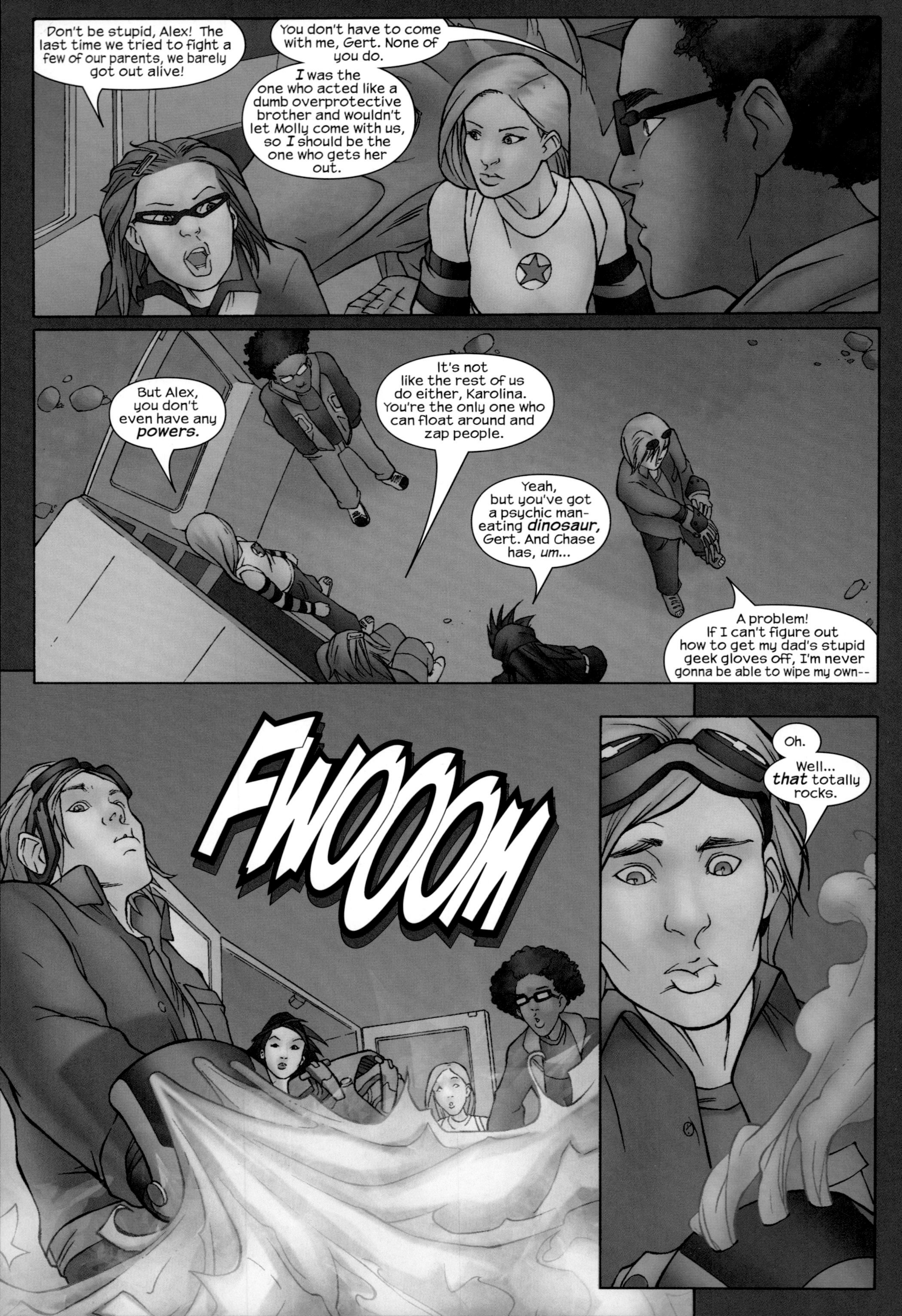
Don't be stupid, Alex! The last time we tried to fight a few of our parents, we barely got out alive!
You don't have to come with me, Gert. None of you do.
I was the one who acted like a dumb overprotective brother and wouldn't let Molly come with us, so I should be the one who gets her out.
But Alex, you don't even have any powers.
It's not like the rest of us do either, Karolina. You're the only one who can float around and zap people.
Yeah, but you've got a psychic man-eating dinosaur, Gert. And Chase has, um...
A problem! If I can't figure out how to get my dad's stupid geek gloves off, I'm never gonna be able to wipe my own--
FWOOOM
Oh.
Well... that totally rocks.

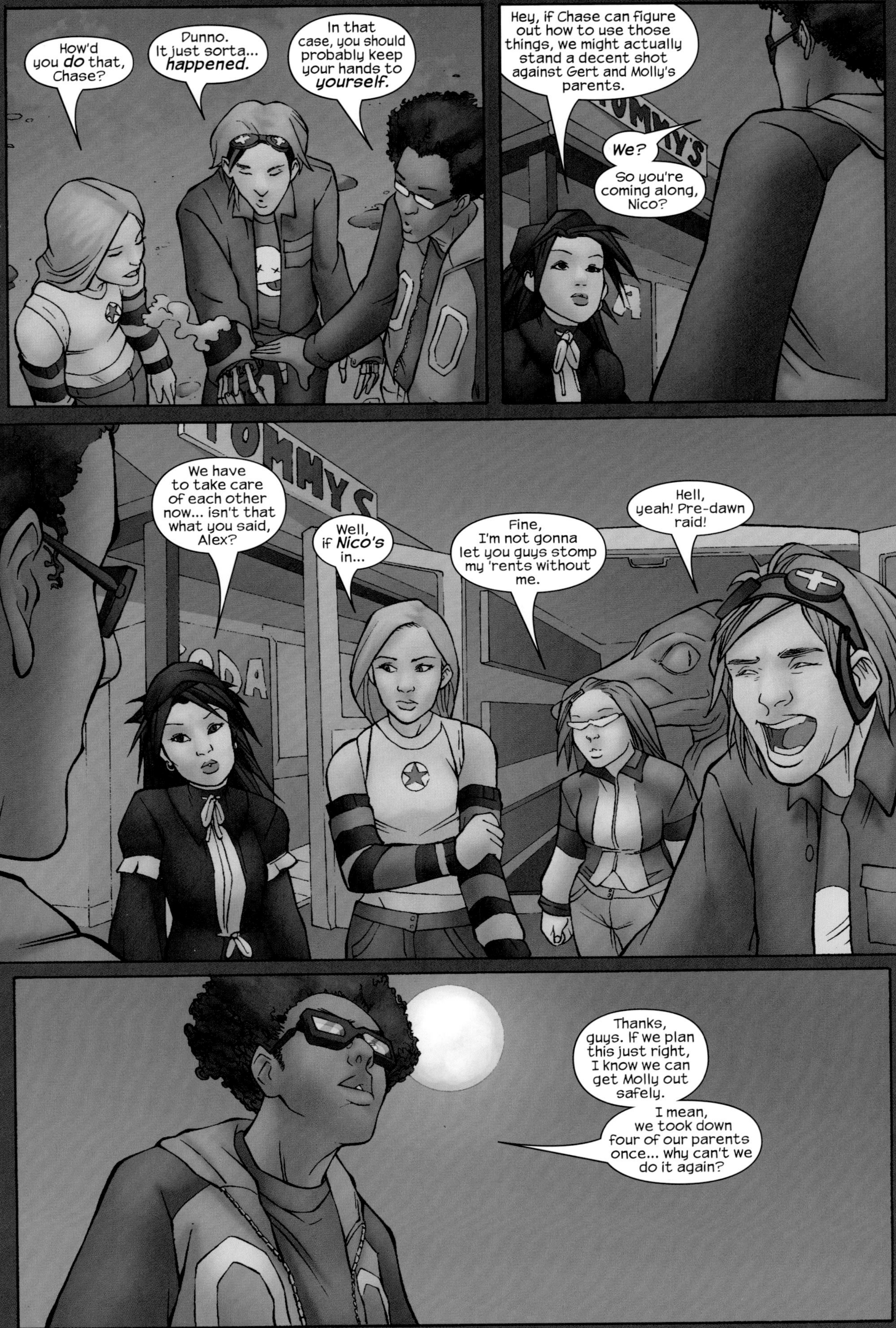
How'd you **do** that, Chase?
Dunno. It just sorta... ***happened.***
In that case, you should probably keep your hands to ***yourself.***
Hey, if Chase can figure out how to use those things, we might actually stand a decent shot against Gert and Molly's parents.
TOMMY'S
We?
So you're coming along, Nico?
TOMMYS
We have to take care of each other now... isn't that what you said, Alex?
Well, if ***Nico's*** in...
Fine, I'm not gonna let you guys stomp my 'rents without me.
Hell, yeah! Pre-dawn raid!
Thanks, guys. If we plan this just right, I know we can get Molly out safely.
I mean, we took down four of our parents once... why can't we do it again?

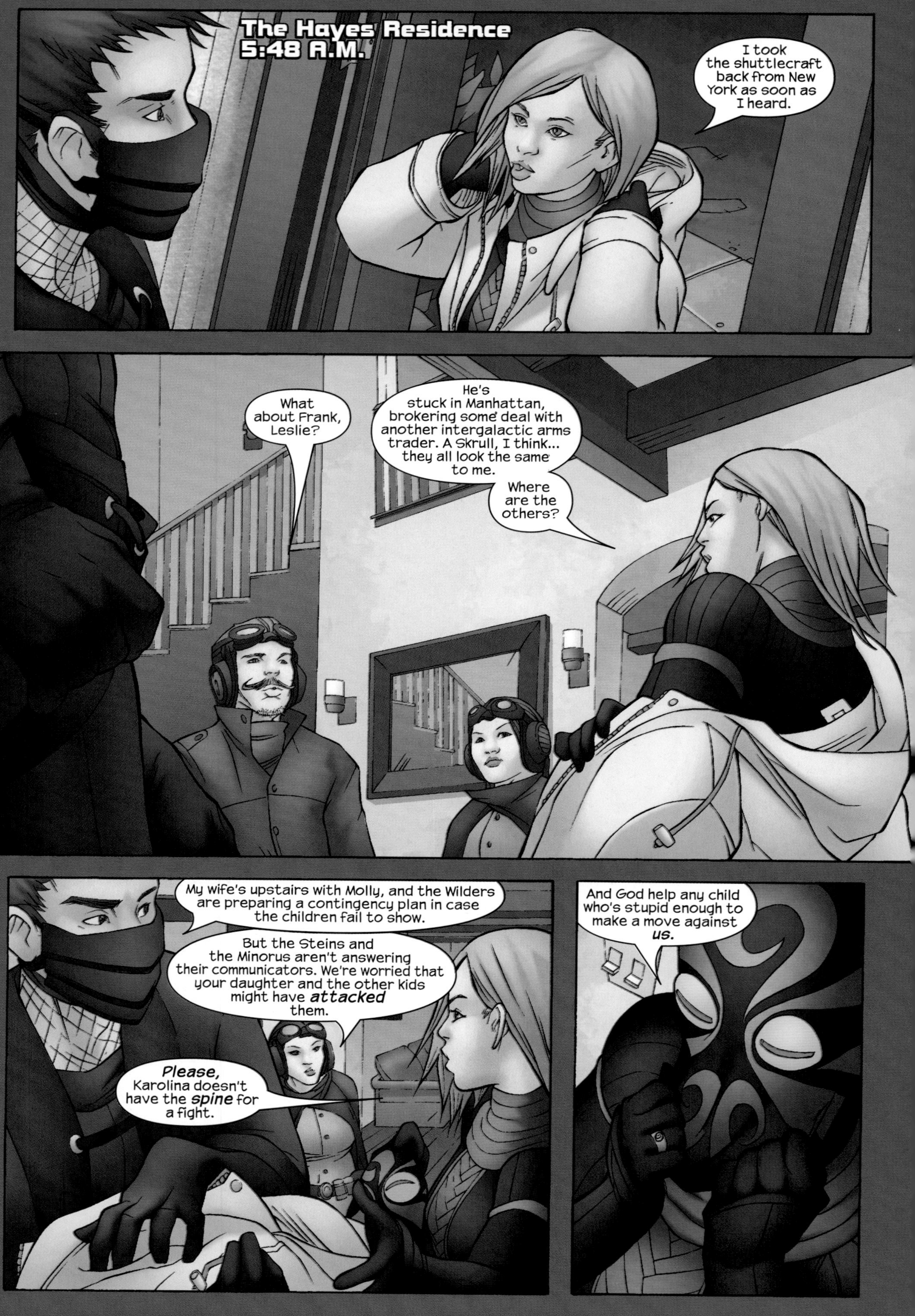
The Hayes Residence 5:48 A.M.
I took the shuttlecraft back from New York as soon as I heard.
What about Frank, Leslie?
He's stuck in Manhattan, brokering some deal with another intergalactic arms trader. A Skrull, I think... they all look the same to me.
Where are the others?
My wife's upstairs with Molly, and the Wilders are preparing a contingency plan in case the children fail to show.
But the Steins and the Minorus aren't answering their communicators. We're worried that your daughter and the other kids might have *attacked* them.
Please, Karolina doesn't have the *spine* for a fight.
And God help any child who's stupid enough to make a move against *us.*

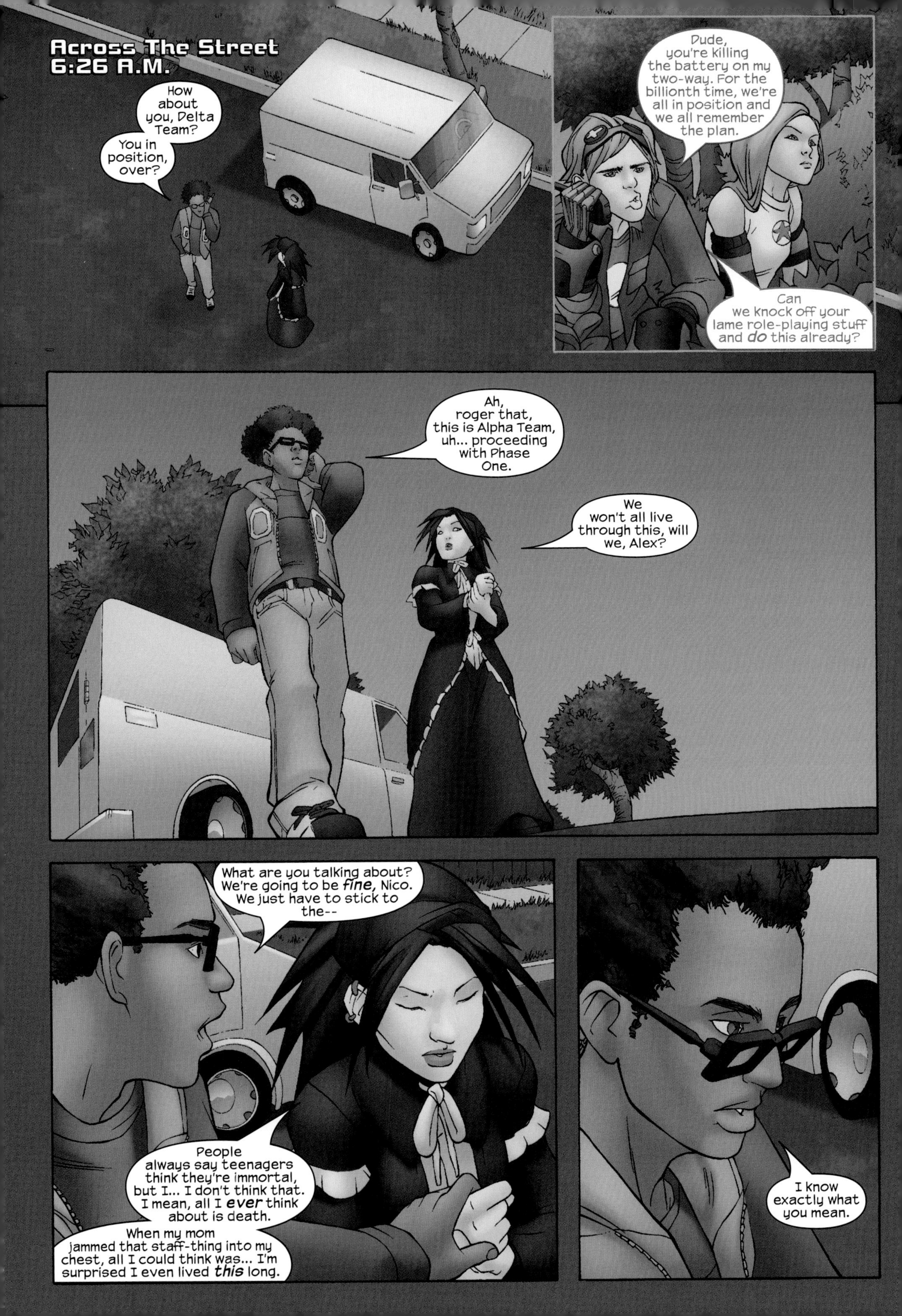
Across The Street
6:26 A.M.
How about you, Delta Team?
You in position, over?
Dude, you're killing the battery on my two-way. For the billionth time, we're all in position and we all remember the plan.
Can we knock off your lame role-playing stuff and do this already?
Ah, roger that, this is Alpha Team, uh... proceeding with Phase One.
We won't all live through this, will we, Alex?
What are you talking about? We're going to be fine, Nico. We just have to stick to the--
People always say teenagers think they're immortal, but I... I don't think that. I mean, all I ever think about is death.
When my mom jammed that staff-thing into my chest, all I could think was... I'm surprised I even lived this long.
I know exactly what you mean.

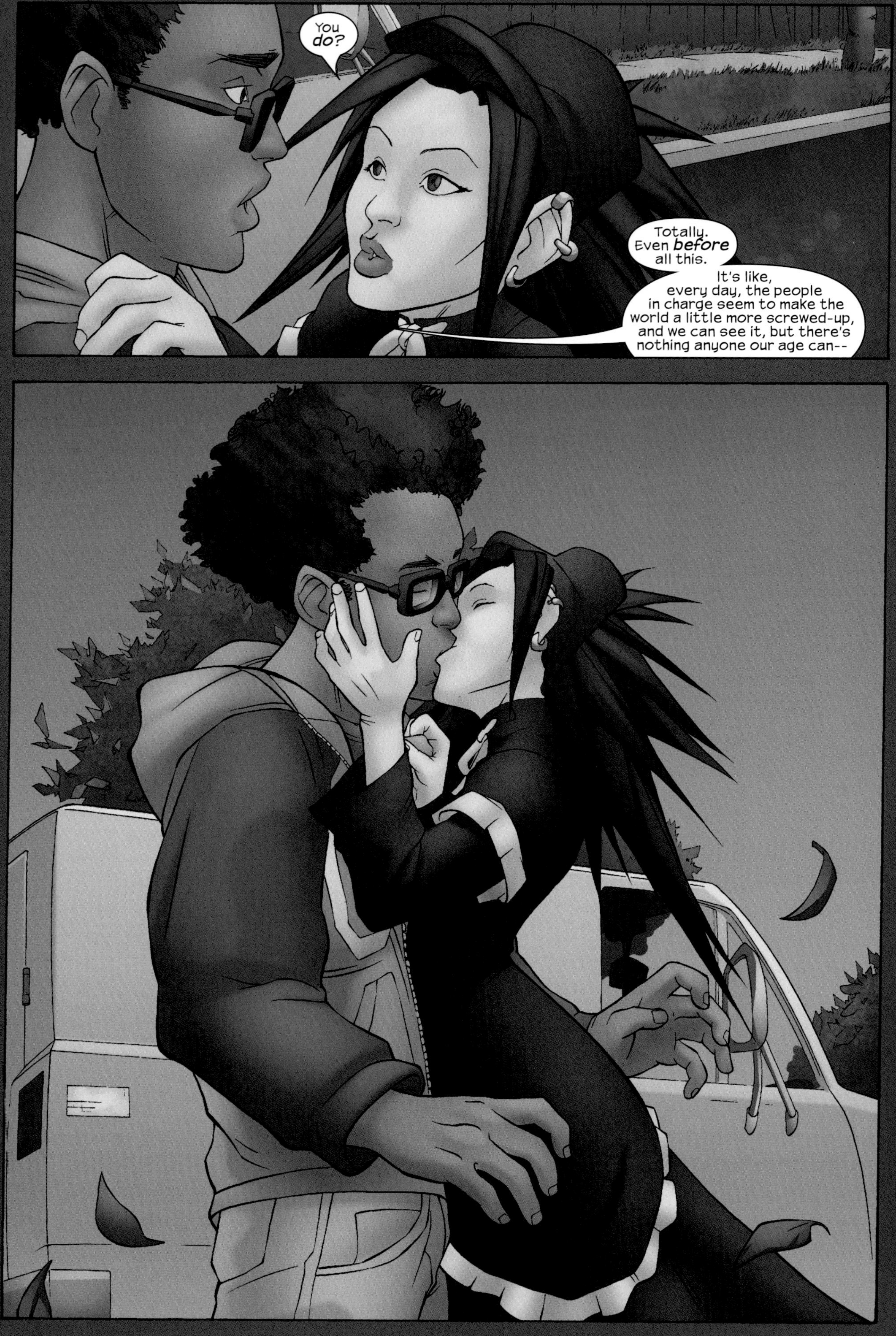

You do?
Totally. Even before all this.
It's like, every day, the people in charge seem to make the world a little more screwed-up, and we can see it, but there's nothing anyone our age can--

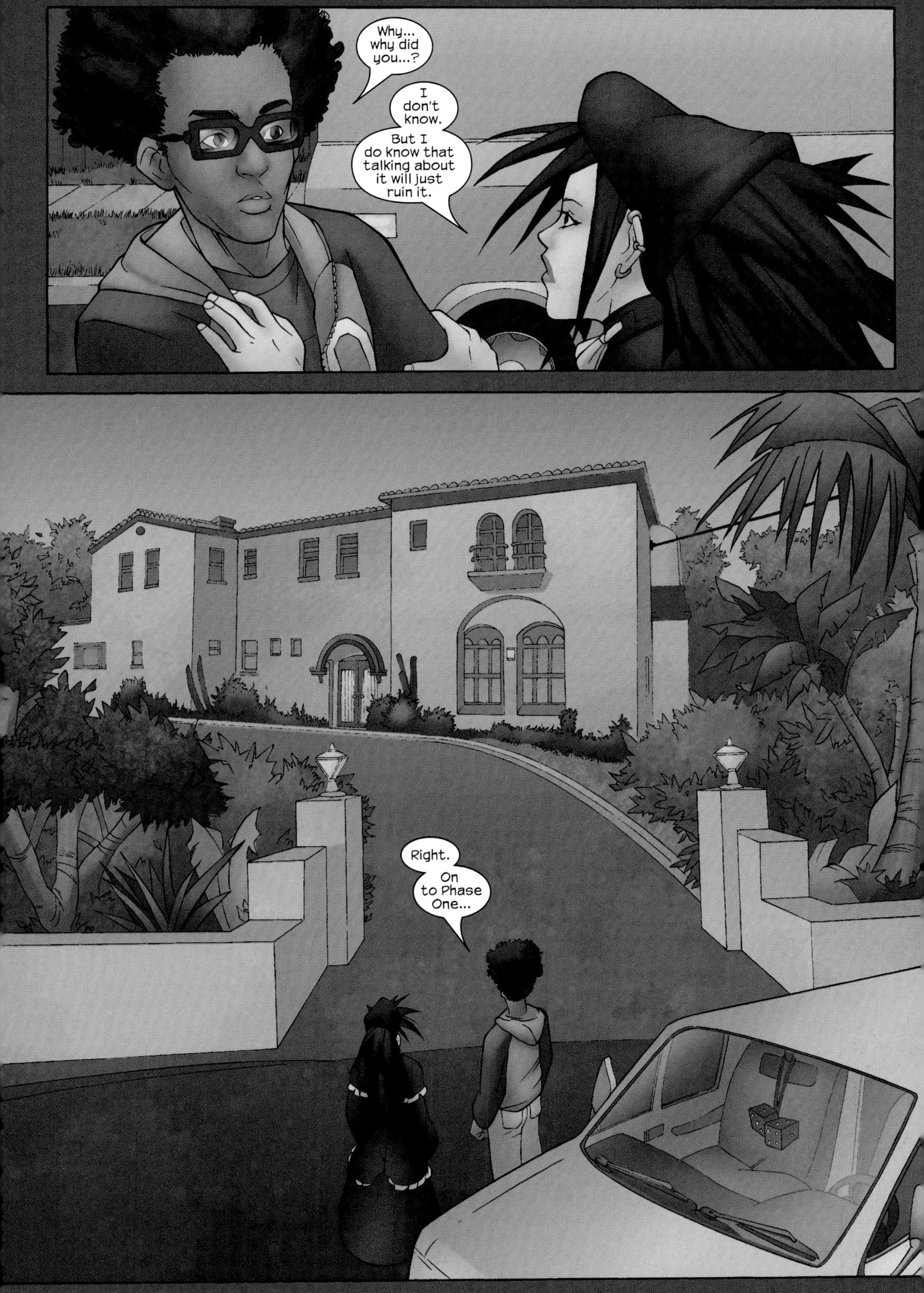
Why... why did you...?
I don't know.
But I do know that talking about it will just ruin it.
Right.
On to Phase One...

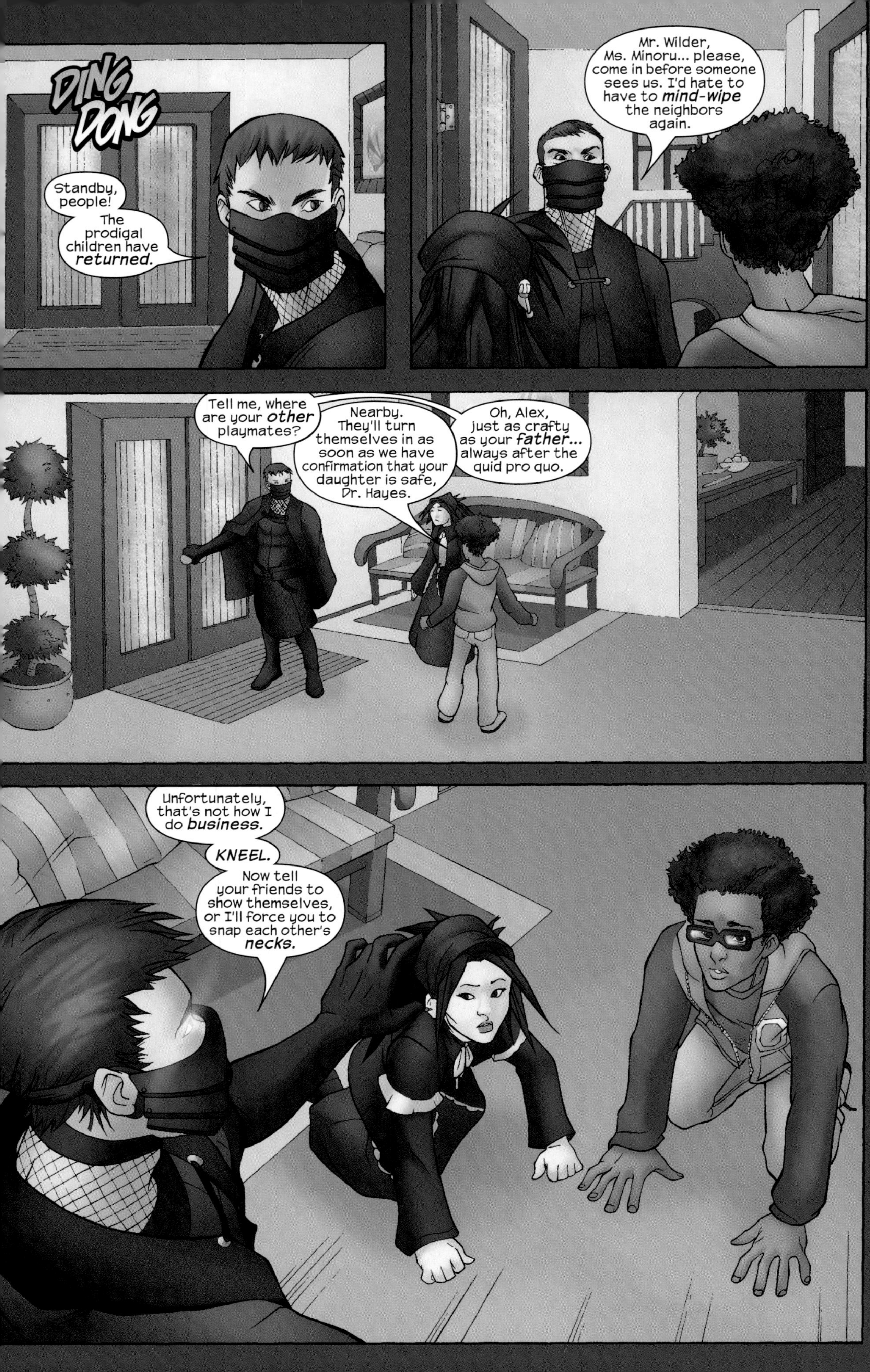
DING DONG
Standby, people!
The prodigal children have returned.
Mr. Wilder, Ms. Minoru... please, come in before someone sees us. I'd hate to have to mind-wipe the neighbors again.
Tell me, where are your other playmates?
Nearby. They'll turn themselves in as soon as we have confirmation that your daughter is safe, Dr. Hayes.
Oh, Alex, just as crafty as your father... always after the quid pro quo.
Unfortunately, that's not how I do business.
KNEEL.
Now tell your friends to show themselves, or I'll force you to snap each other's necks.

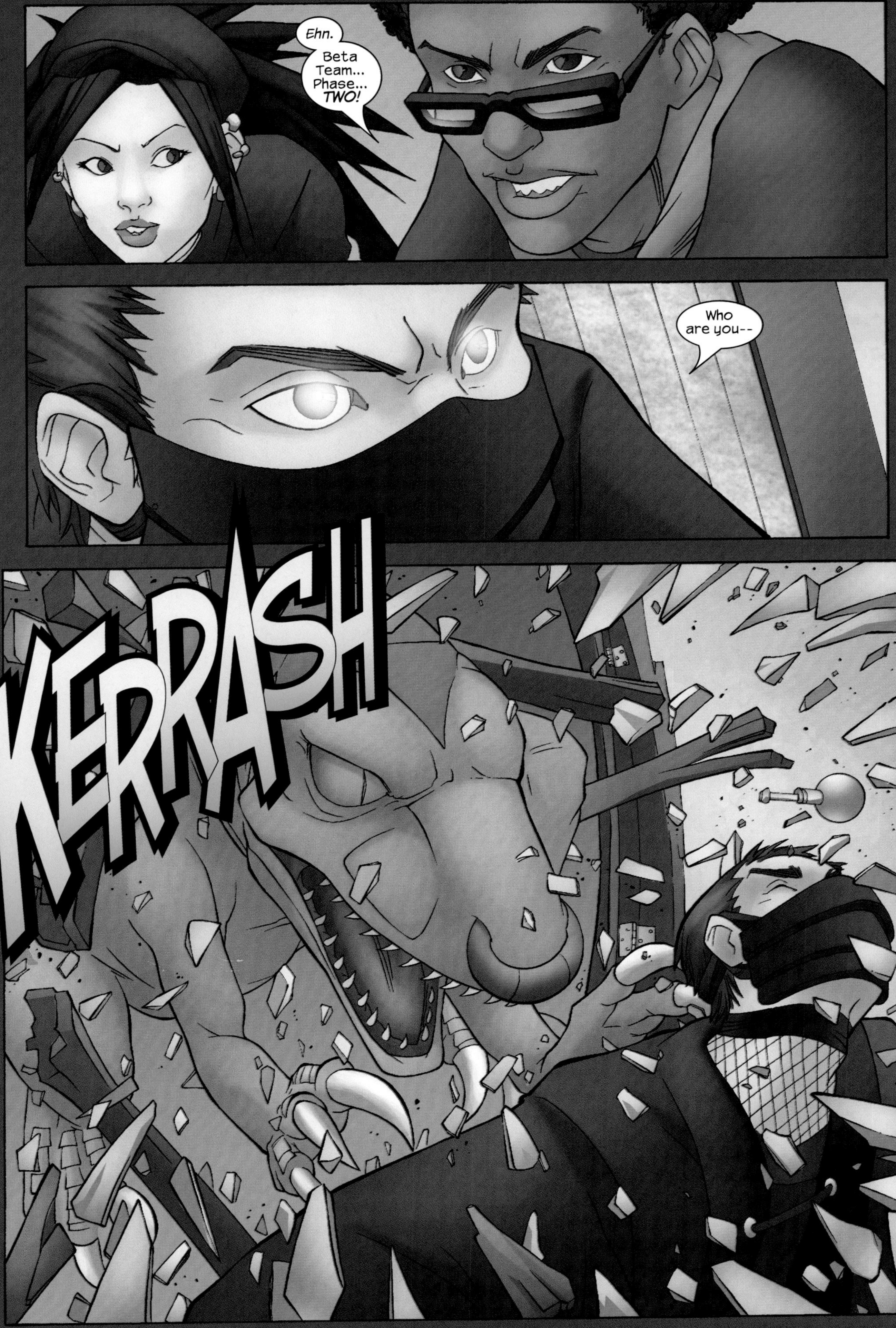
Ehn.
Beta Team... Phase... TWO!
Who are you--
KERRASH

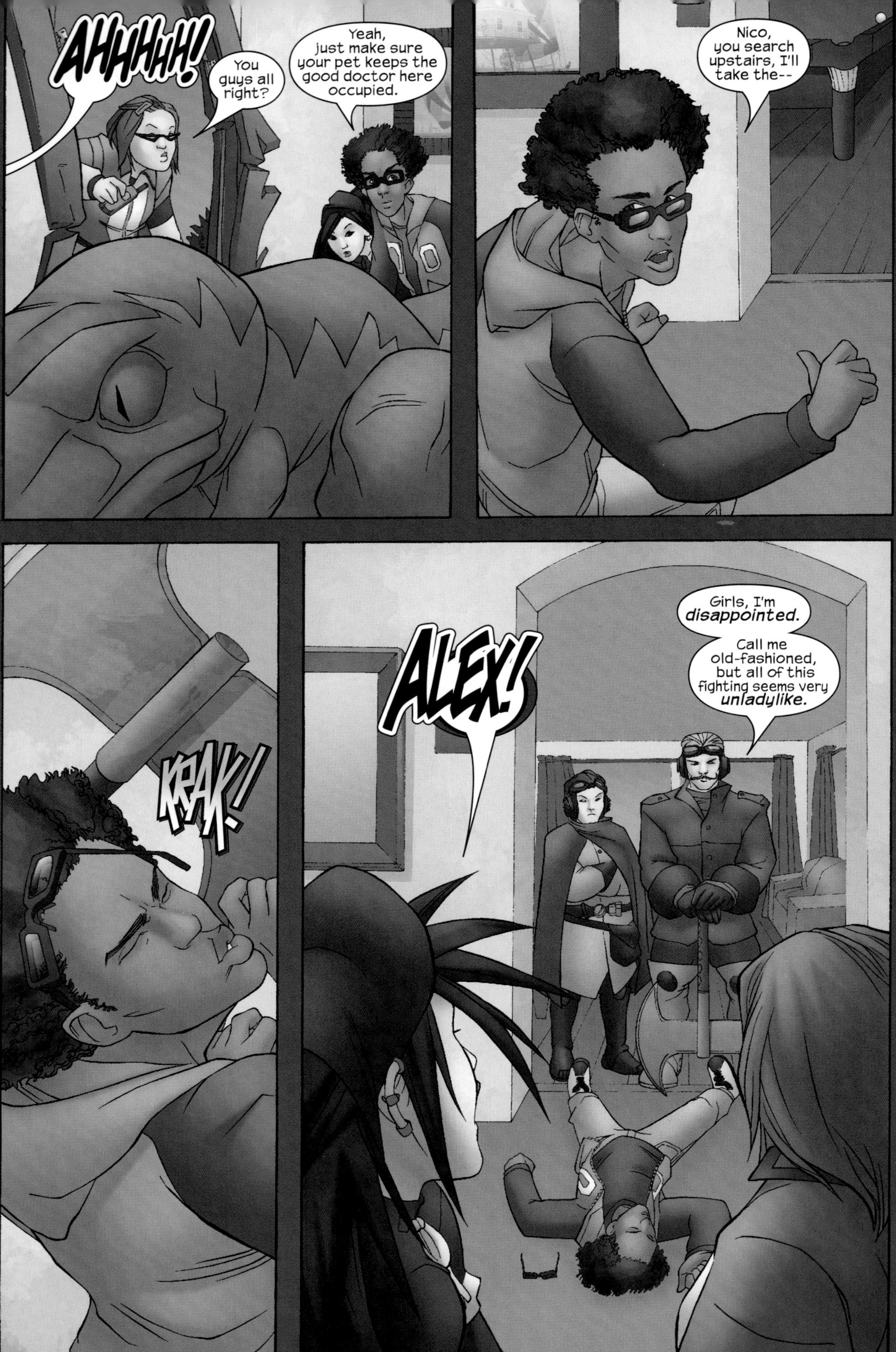
AHHHHH!
You guys all right?
Yeah, just make sure your pet keeps the good doctor here occupied.
Nico, you search upstairs, I'll take the--
KRAK!
ALEX!
Girls, I'm disappointed.
Call me old-fashioned, but all of this fighting seems very unladylike.

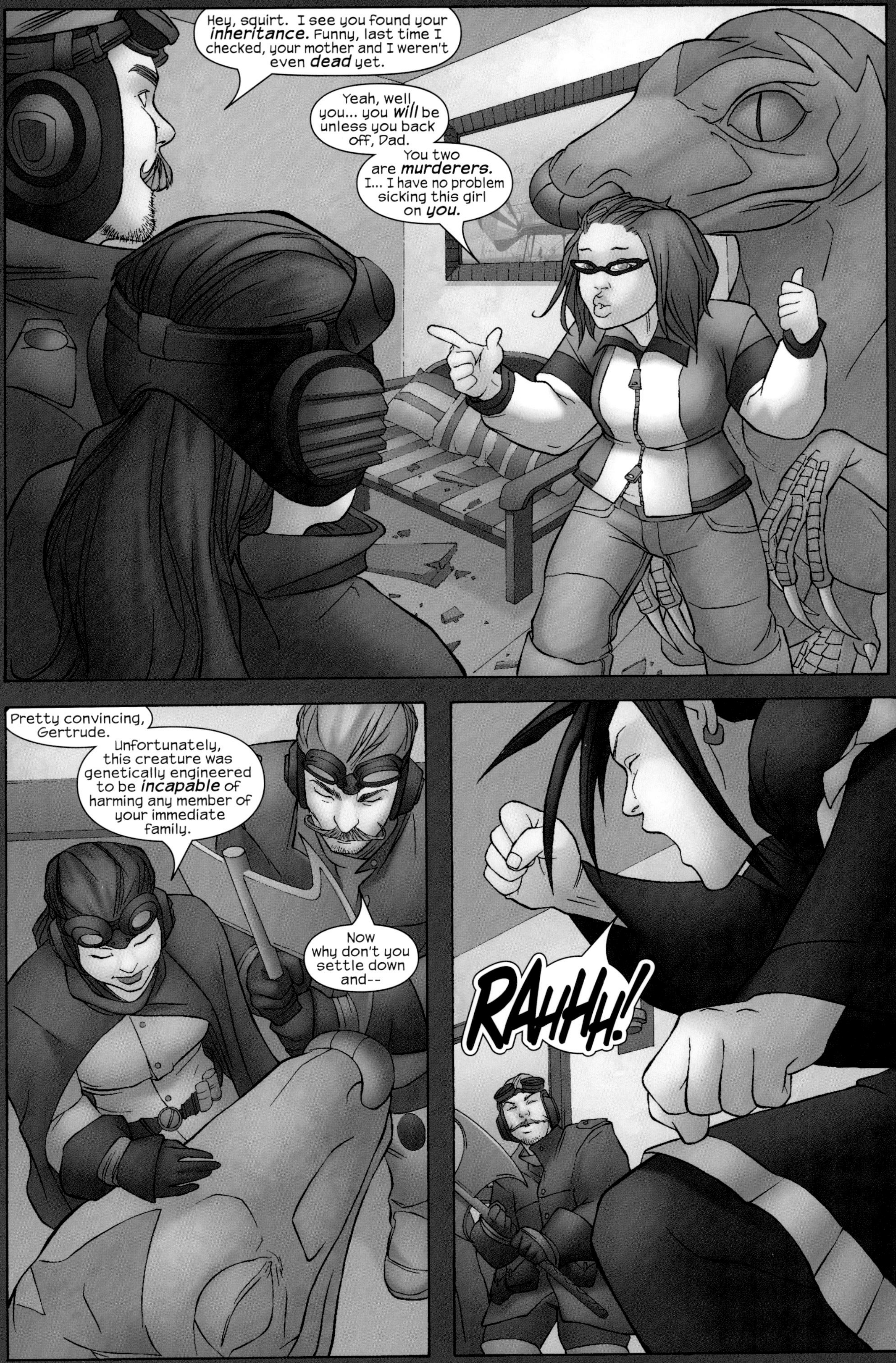
Hey, squirt. I see you found your inheritance. Funny, last time I checked, your mother and I weren't even dead yet.
Yeah, well, you... you will be unless you back off, Dad.
You two are murderers. I... I have no problem sicking this girl on you.
Pretty convincing, Gertrude.
Unfortunately, this creature was genetically engineered to be incapable of harming any member of your immediate family.
Now why don't you settle down and--
RAHHH!

No!

AHN!

What did you *do*?

It... it was *instinct!* I didn't mean--

WHEN BLOOD IS SHED... LET THE STAFF OF ONE EMERGE--

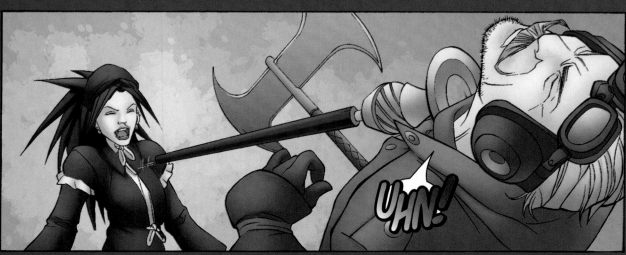

UHN!

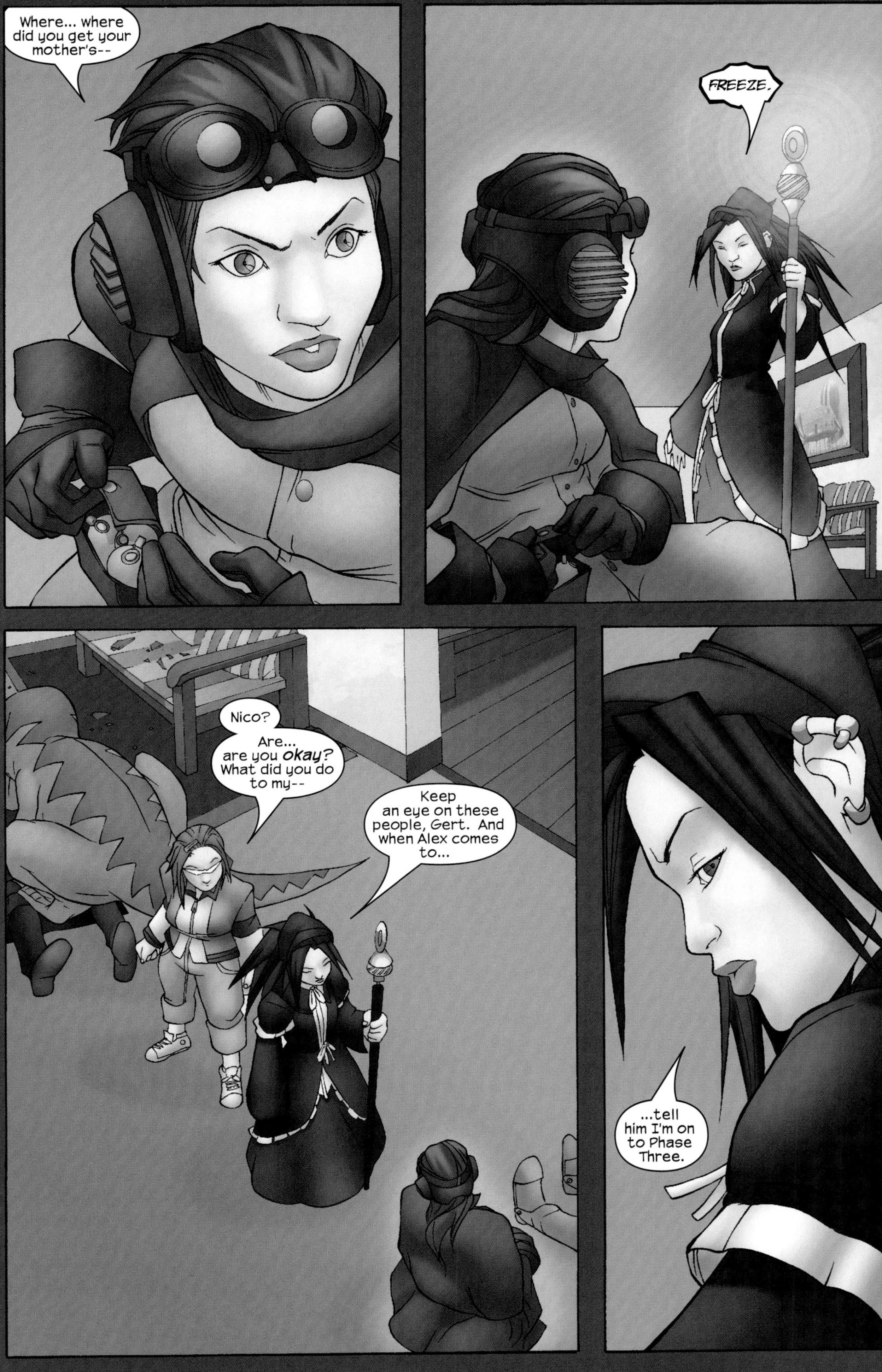
Where... where did you get your mother's--
FREEZE.
Nico? Are... are you okay? What did you do to my--
Keep an eye on these people, Gert. And when Alex comes to...
...tell him I'm on to Phase Three.

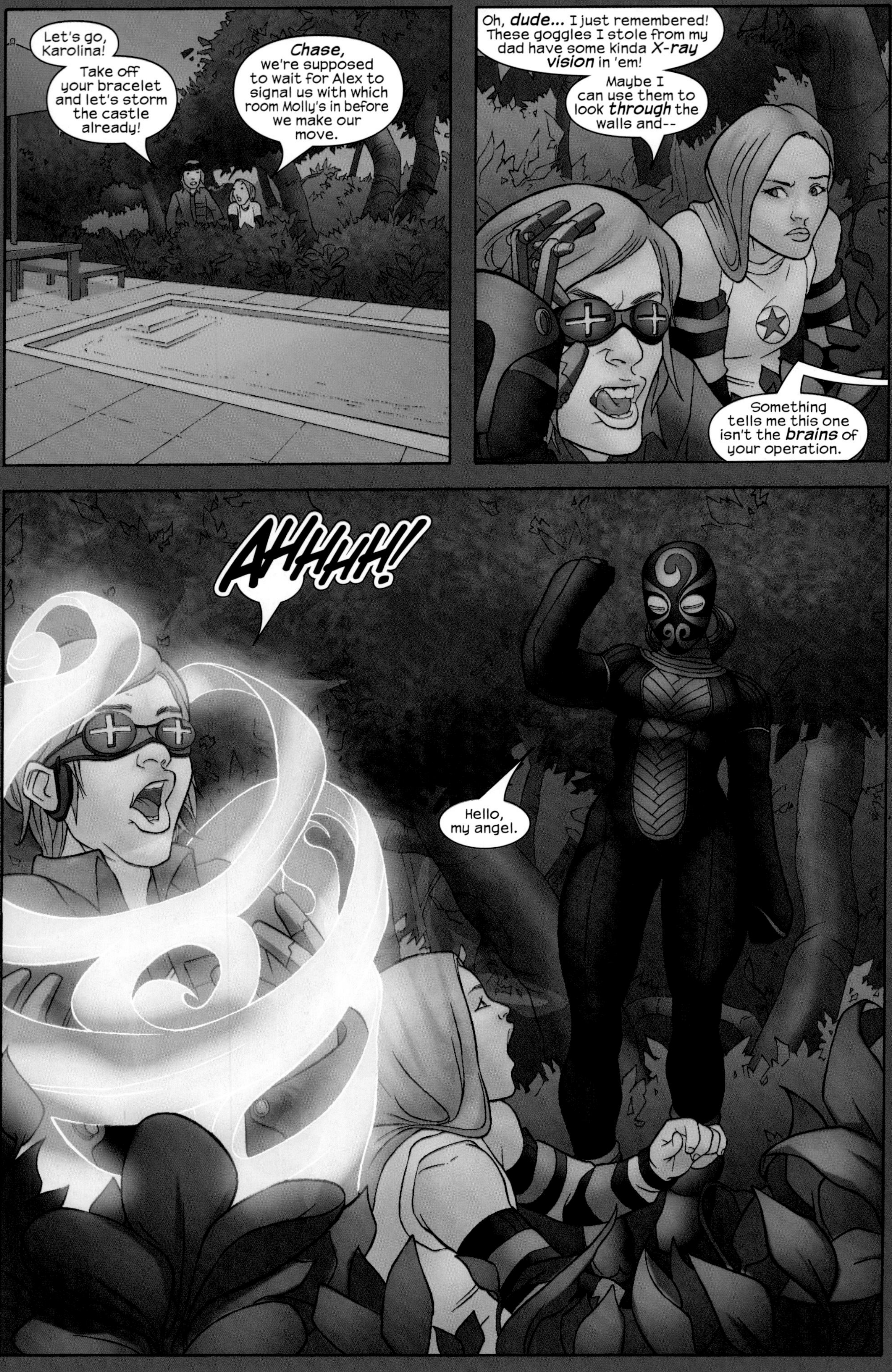
Let's go, Karolina!
Take off your bracelet and let's storm the castle already!
Chase, we're supposed to wait for Alex to signal us with which room Molly's in before we make our move.
Oh, dude... I just remembered! These goggles I stole from my dad have some kinda X-ray vision in 'em!
Maybe I can use them to look through the walls and--
Something tells me this one isn't the brains of your operation.
AHHHH!
Hello, my angel.

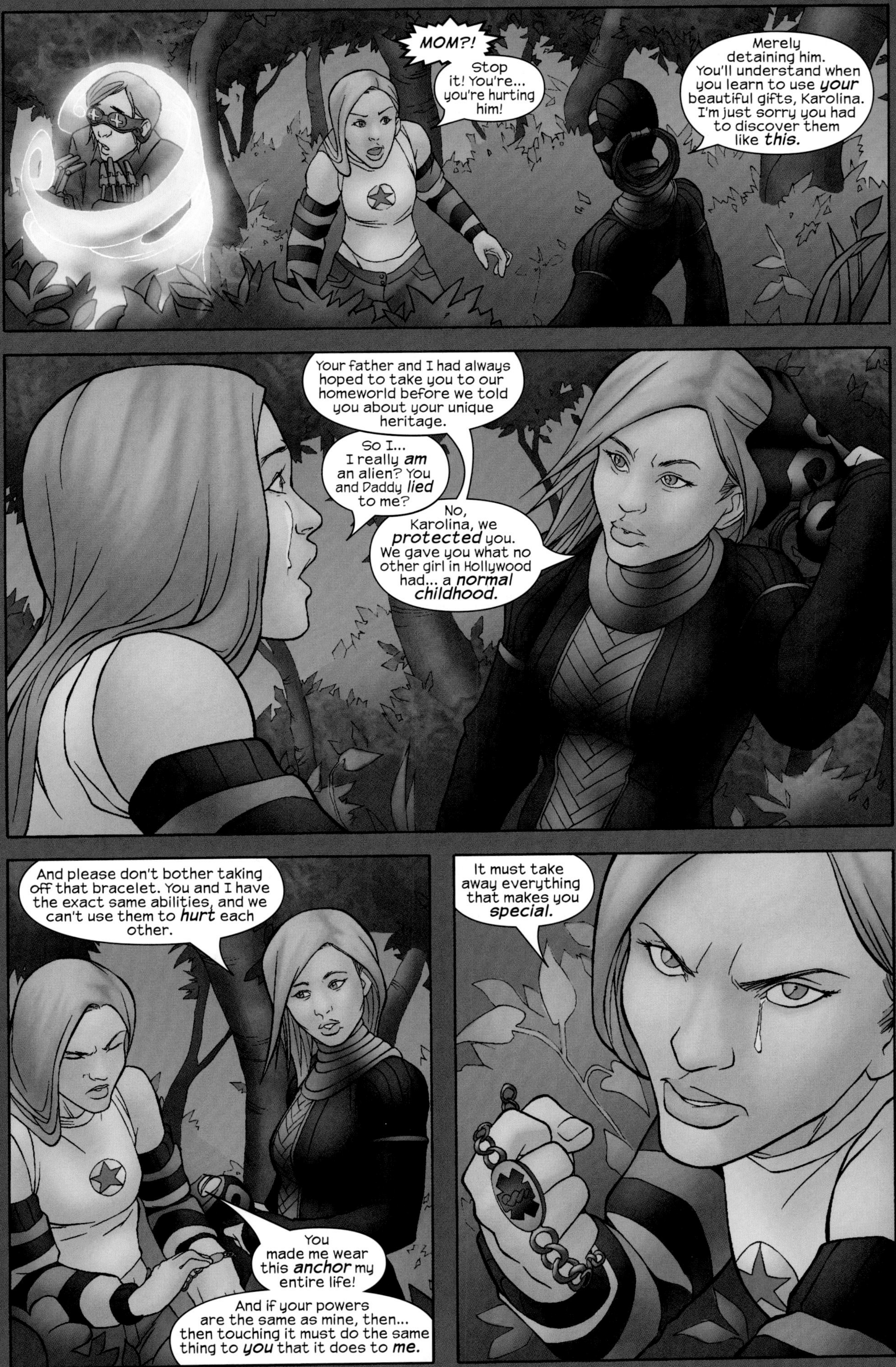

MOM?!
Stop it! You're... you're hurting him!
Merely detaining him. You'll understand when you learn to use **your** beautiful gifts, Karolina. I'm just sorry you had to discover them like **this.**
Your father and I had always hoped to take you to our homeworld before we told you about your unique heritage.
So I... I really **am** an alien? You and Daddy **lied** to me?
No, Karolina, we **protected** you. We gave you what no other girl in Hollywood had... a **normal childhood.**
And please don't bother taking off that bracelet. You and I have the exact same abilities, and we can't use them to **hurt** each other.
You made me wear this **anchor** my entire life!
And if your powers are the same as mine, then... then touching it must do the same thing to **you** that it does to **me.**
It must take away everything that makes you **special.**

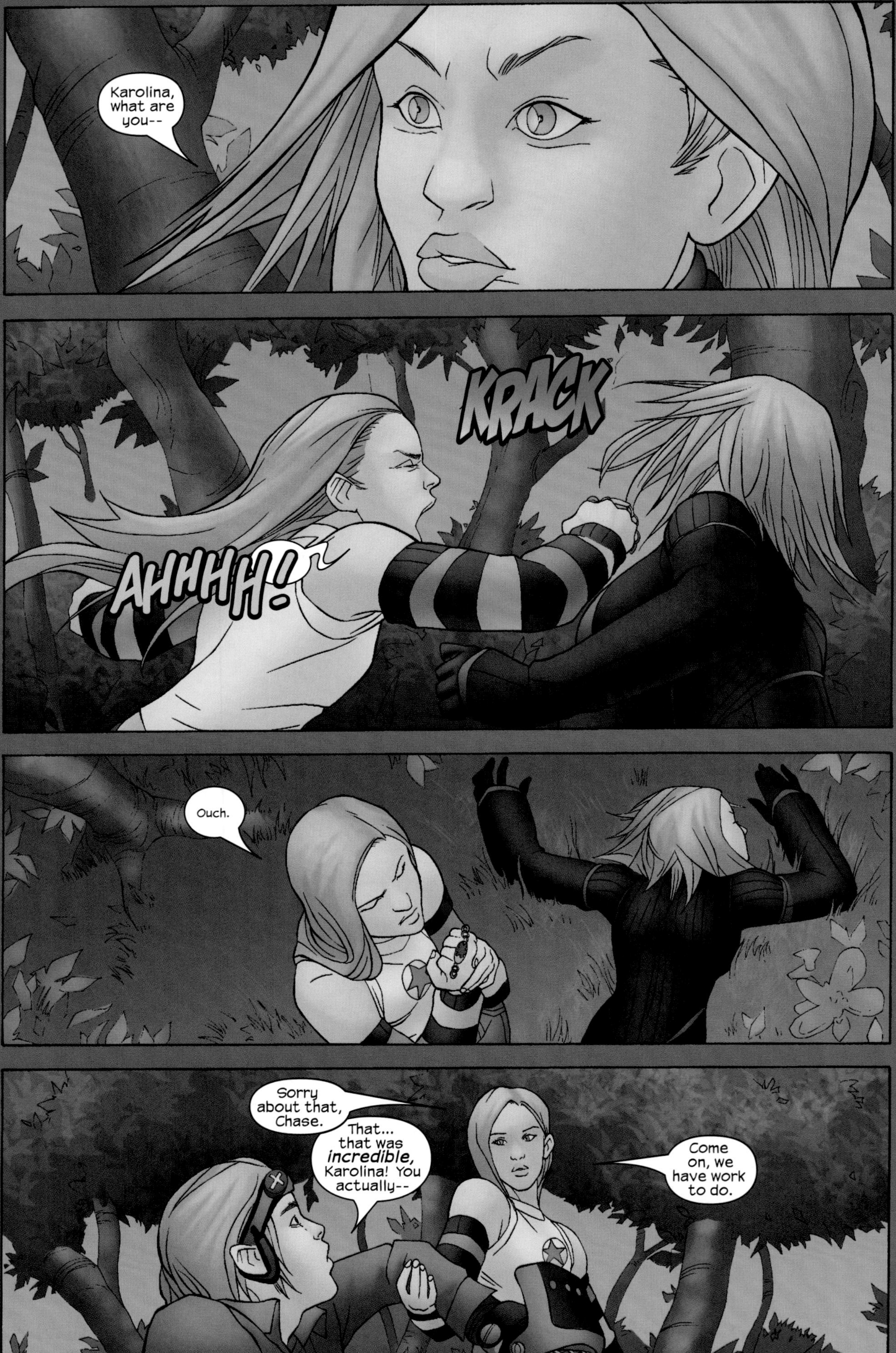
Karolina, what are you--
KRACK
AHHHH!
Ouch.
Sorry about that, Chase.
That... that was *incredible,* Karolina! You actually--
Come on, we have work to do.

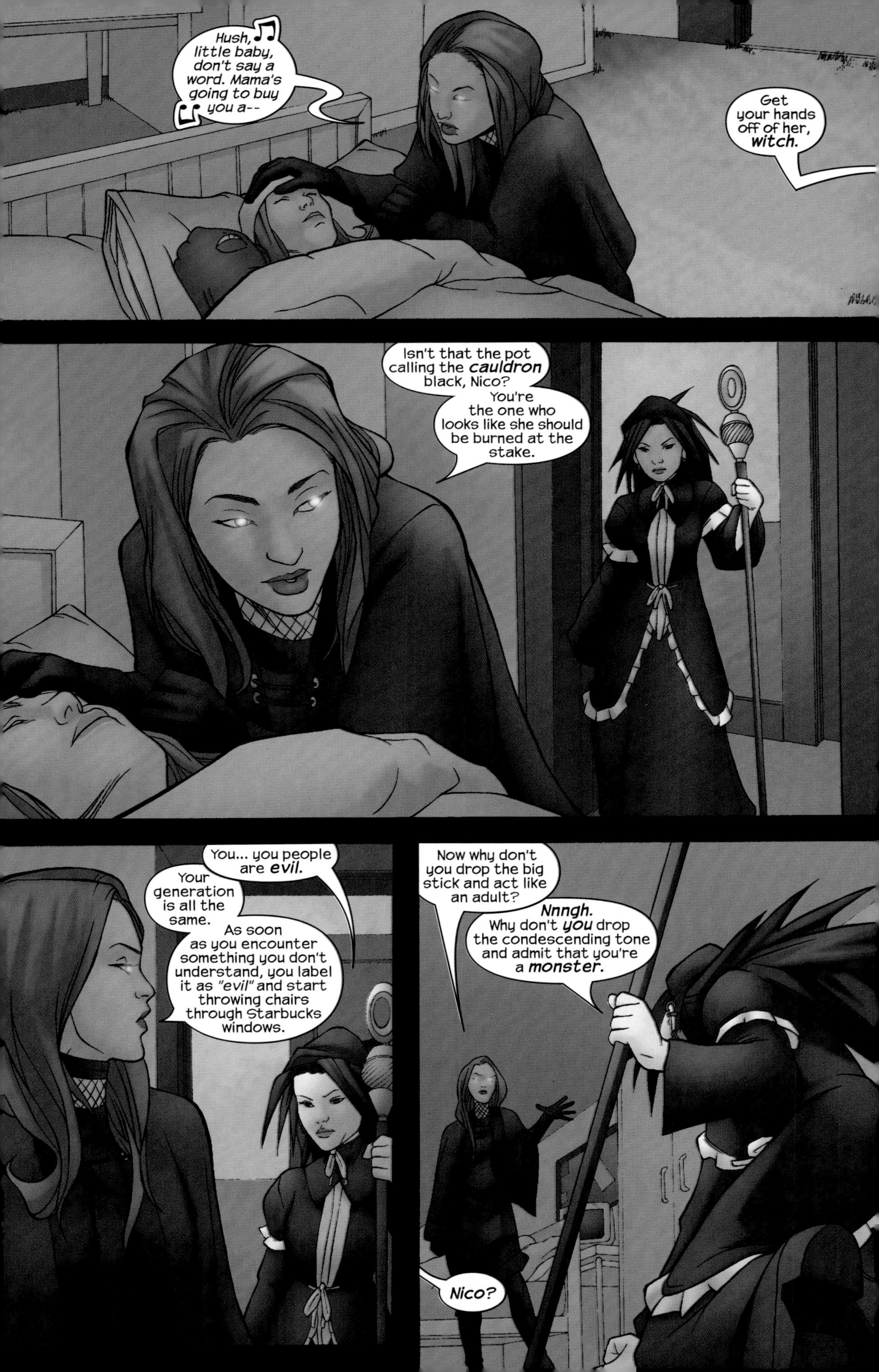
Hush, little baby, don't say a word. Mama's going to buy you a--
Get your hands off of her, witch.
Isn't that the pot calling the cauldron black, Nico?
You're the one who looks like she should be burned at the stake.
You... you people are evil.
Your generation is all the same.
As soon as you encounter something you don't understand, you label it as "evil" and start throwing chairs through Starbucks windows.
Now why don't you drop the big stick and act like an adult?
Nnngh.
Why don't you drop the condescending tone and admit that you're a monster.
Nico?

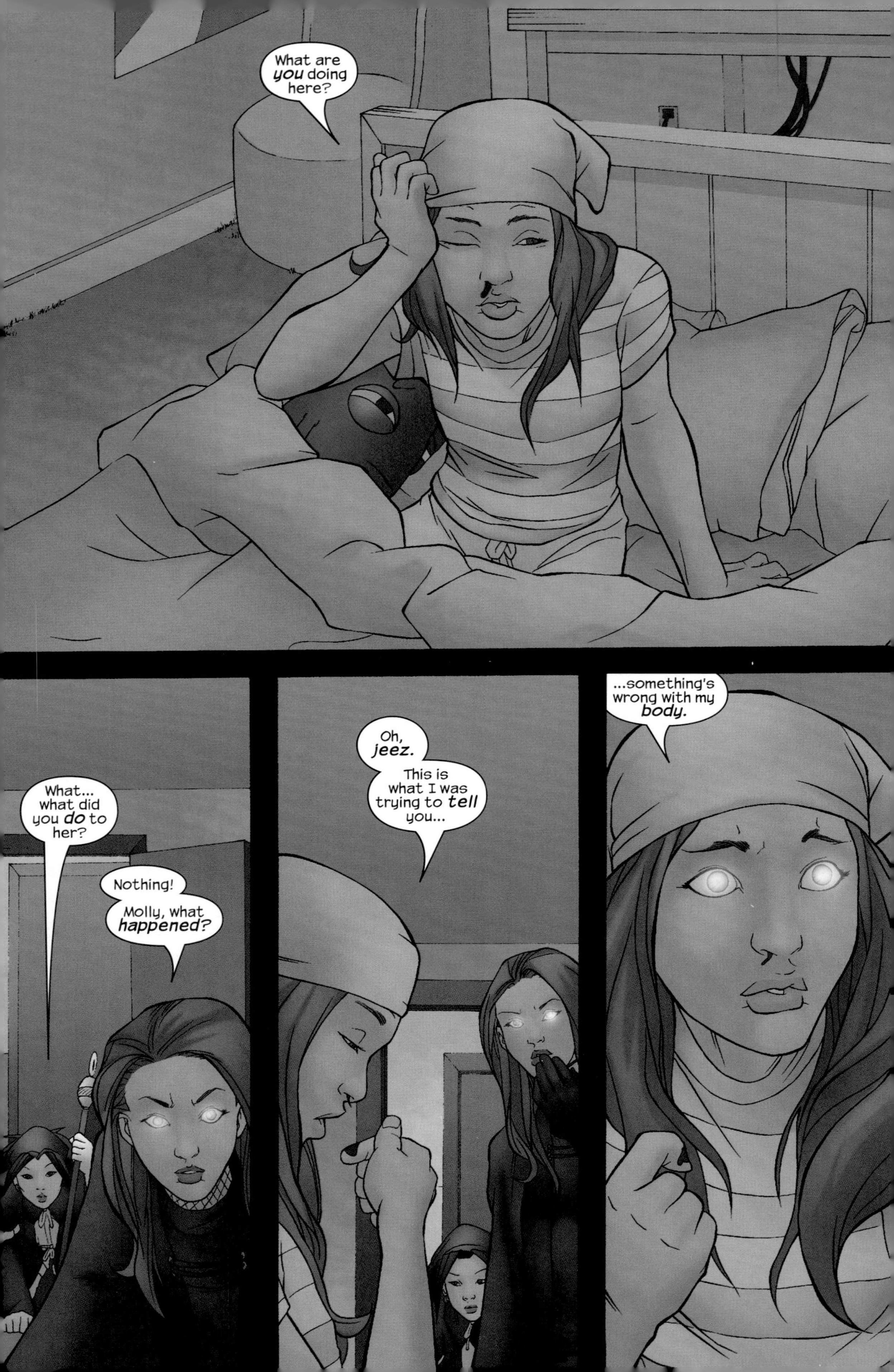
What are *you* doing here?
What... what did you *do* to her?
Nothing!
Molly, what *happened*?
Oh, *jeez.*
This is what I was trying to *tell* you...
...something's wrong with my *body.*

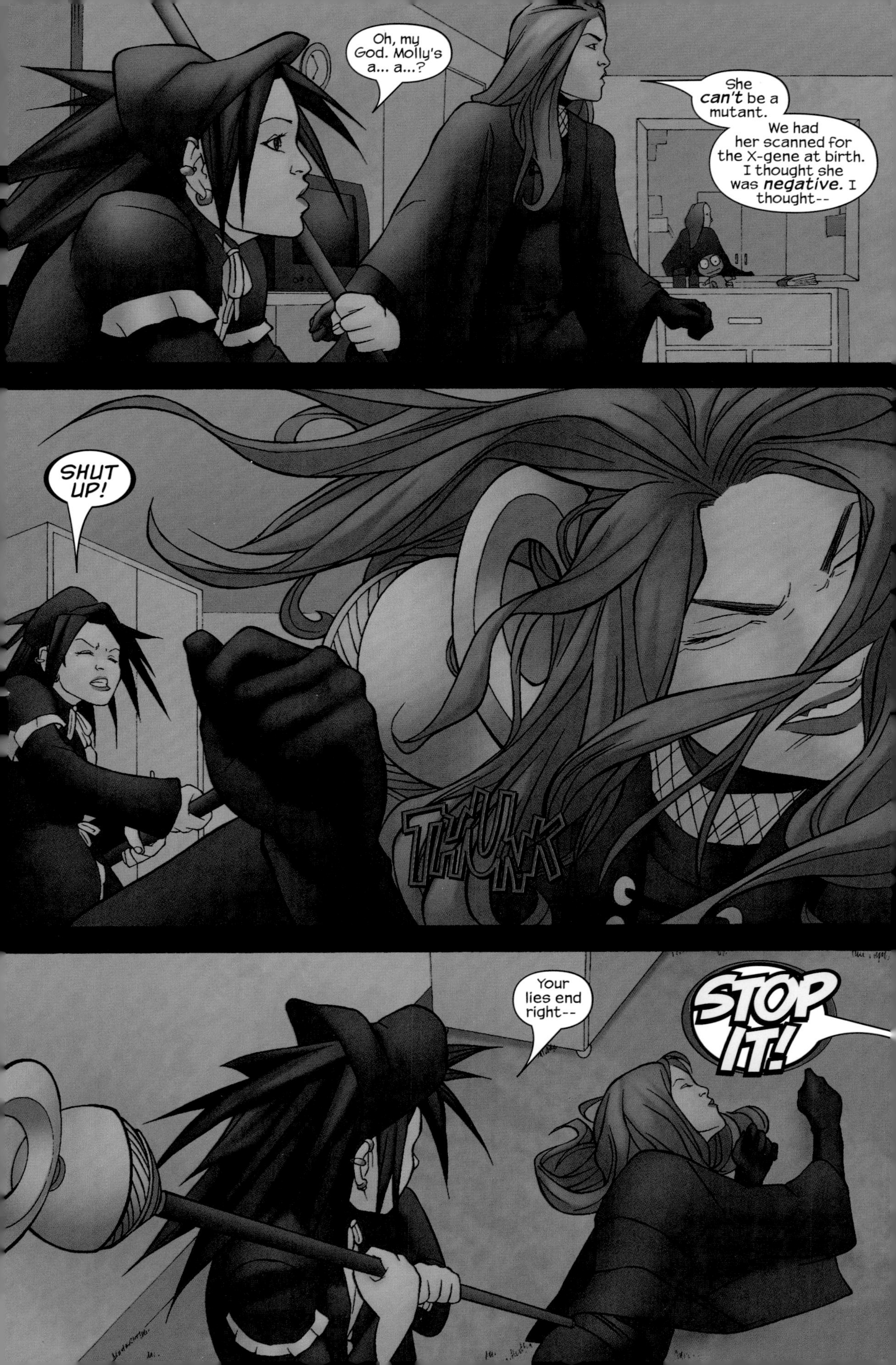
Oh, my God. Molly's a... a...?
She *can't* be a mutant.
We had her scanned for the X-gene at birth. I thought she was *negative.* I thought--
SHUT UP!
THUNK
Your lies end right--
STOP IT!

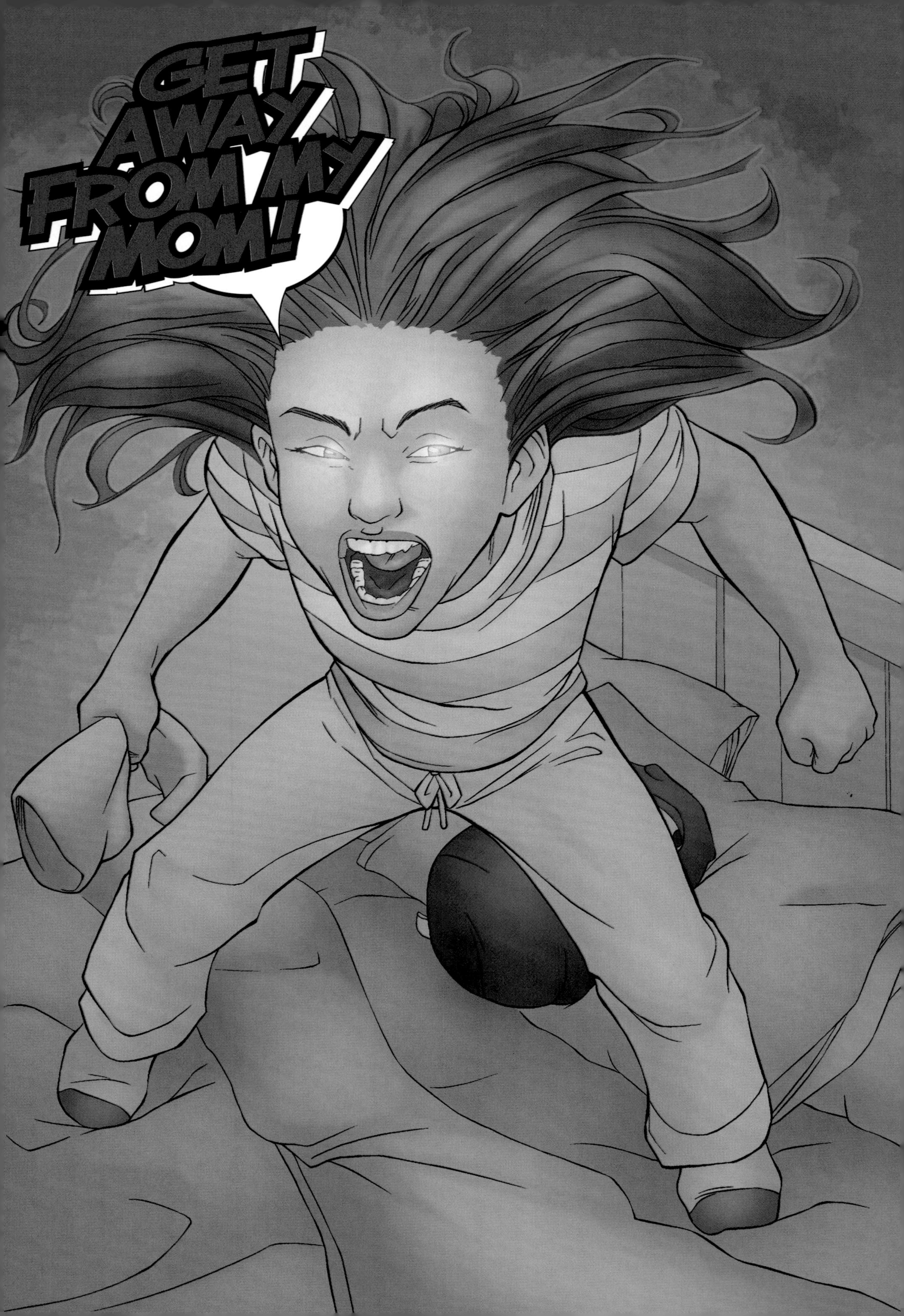
GET AWAY FROM MY MOM!

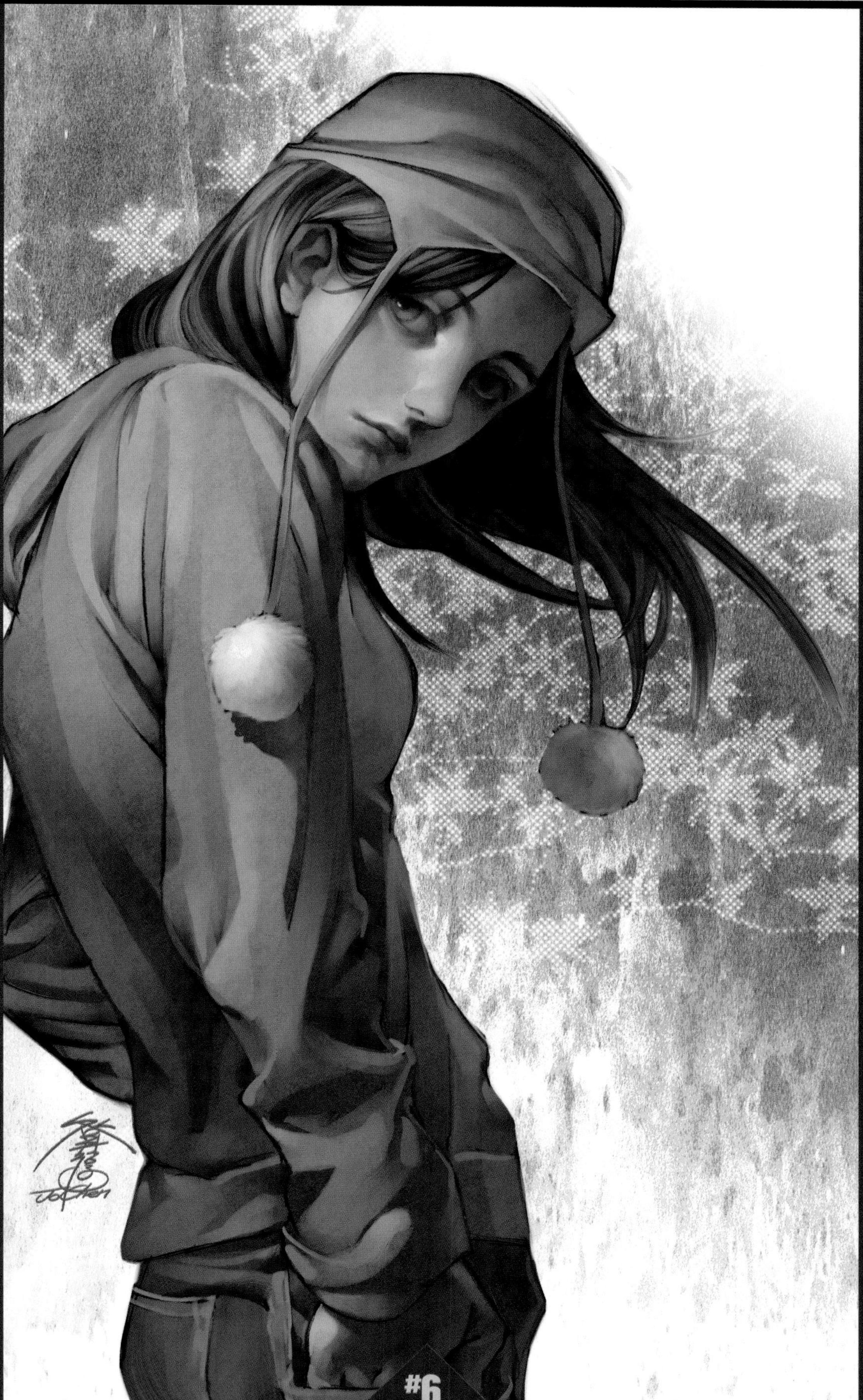
#6

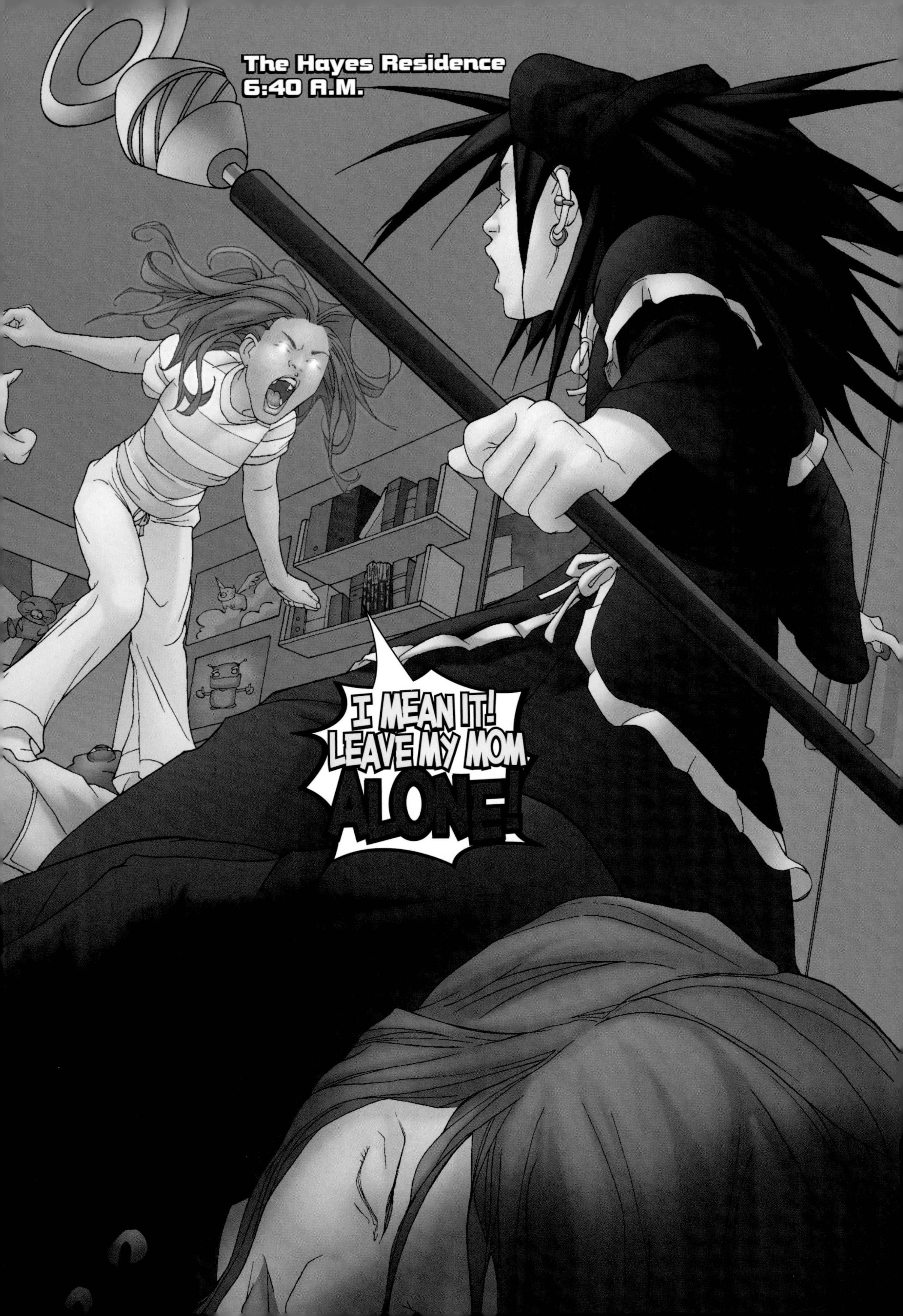
The Hayes Residence
6:40 A.M.
I MEAN IT! LEAVE MY MOM ALONE!

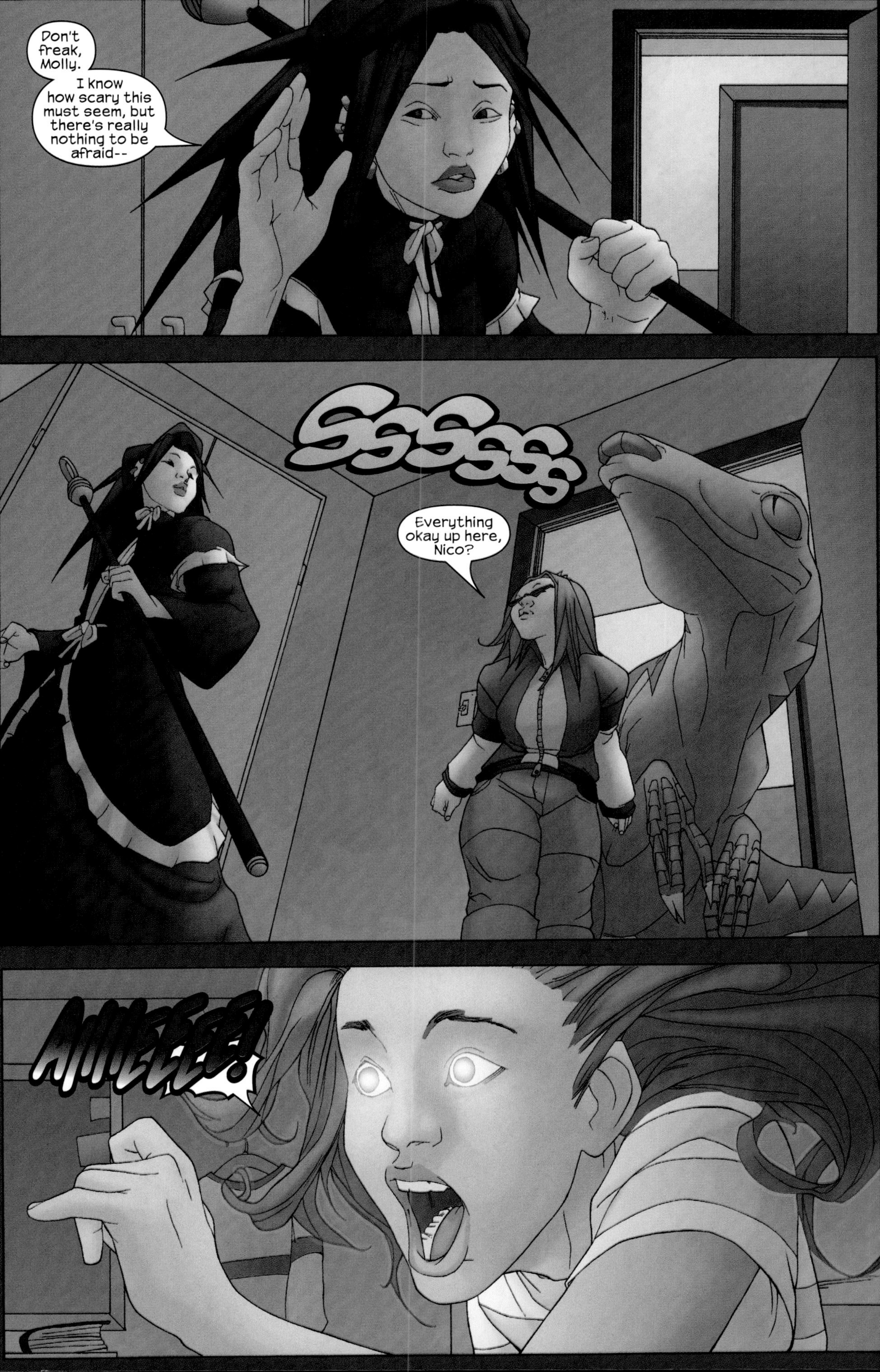
Don't freak, Molly.
I know how scary this must seem, but there's really nothing to be afraid--
SSSSS
Everything okay up here, Nico?
AIIIEEEE!

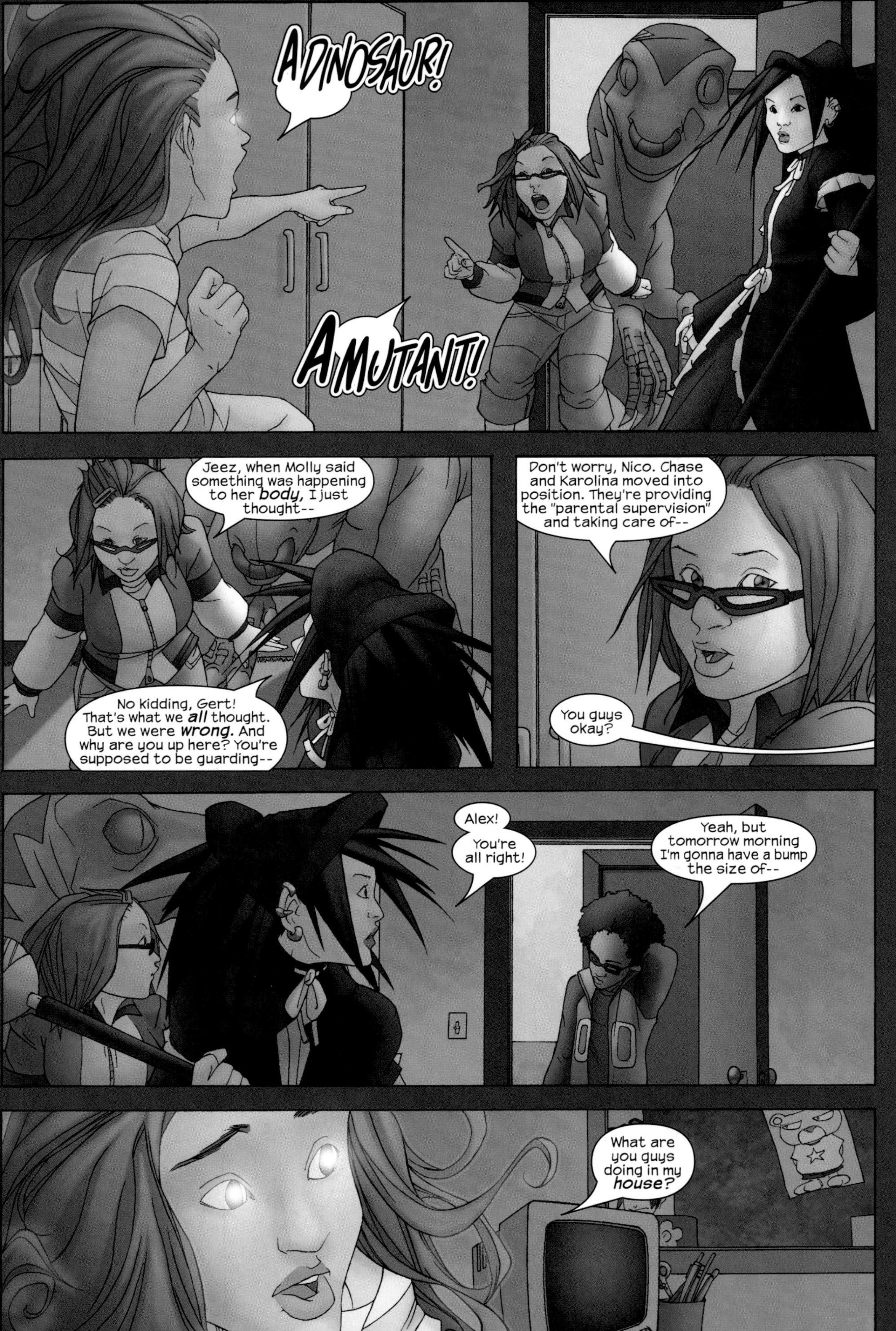
A DINOSAUR!
A MUTANT!
Jeez, when Molly said something was happening to her *body*, I just thought--
No kidding, Gert! That's what we *all* thought. But we were *wrong*. And why are you up here? You're supposed to be guarding--
Don't worry, Nico. Chase and Karolina moved into position. They're providing the "parental supervision" and taking care of--
You guys okay?
Alex!
You're all right!
Yeah, but tomorrow morning I'm gonna have a bump the size of--
What are you guys doing in my *house?*

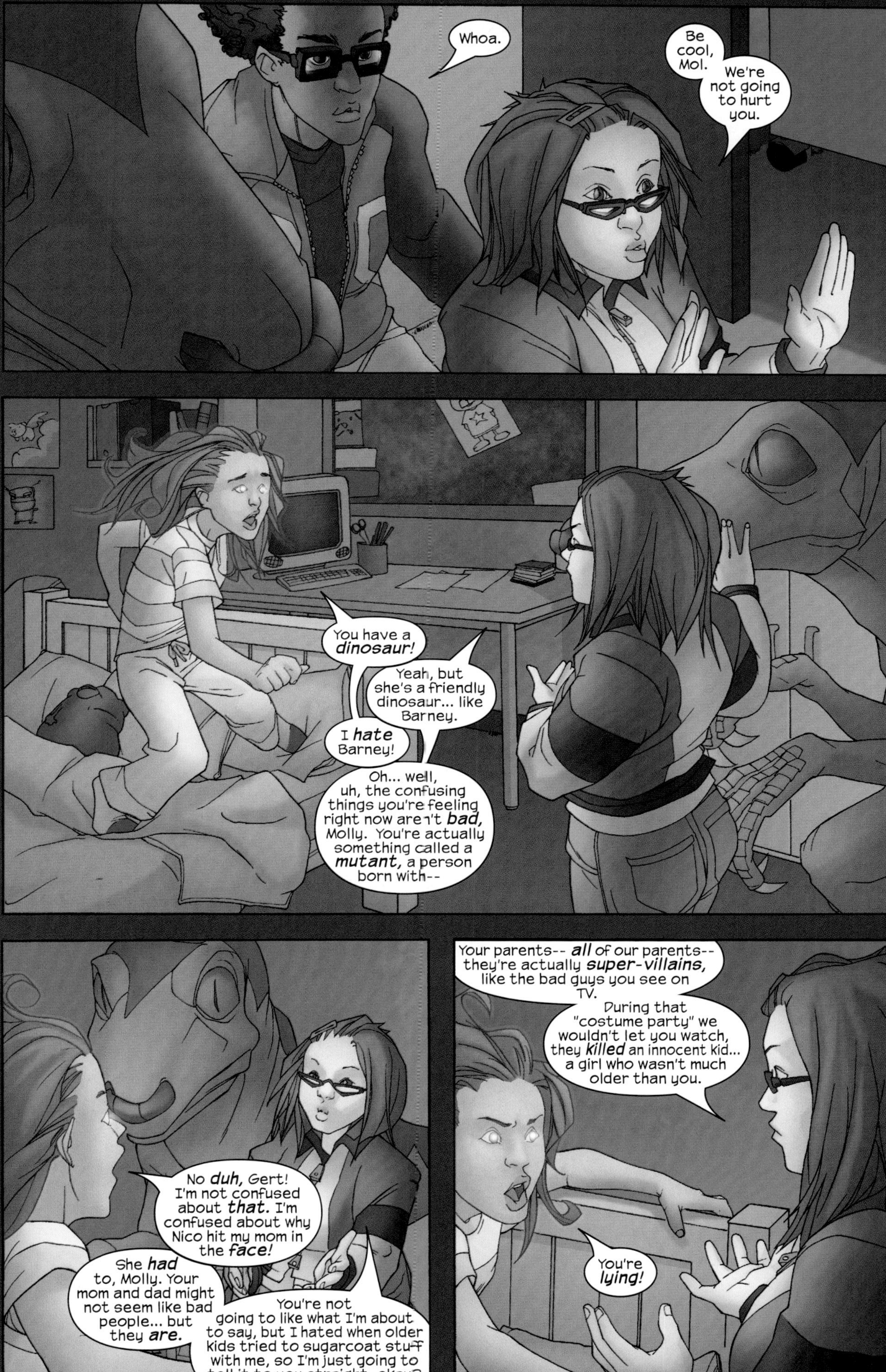
Whoa.
Be cool, Mol.
We're not going to hurt you.
You have a dinosaur!
Yeah, but she's a friendly dinosaur... like Barney.
I hate Barney!
Oh... well, uh, the confusing things you're feeling right now aren't bad, Molly. You're actually something called a mutant, a person born with--
No duh, Gert! I'm not confused about that. I'm confused about why Nico hit my mom in the face!
She had to, Molly. Your mom and dad might not seem like bad people... but they are.
You're not going to like what I'm about to say, but I hated when older kids tried to sugarcoat stuff with me, so I'm just going to tell it to you straight, okay?
Your parents-- all of our parents-- they're actually super-villains, like the bad guys you see on TV.
During that "costume party" we wouldn't let you watch, they killed an innocent kid... a girl who wasn't much older than you.
You're lying!

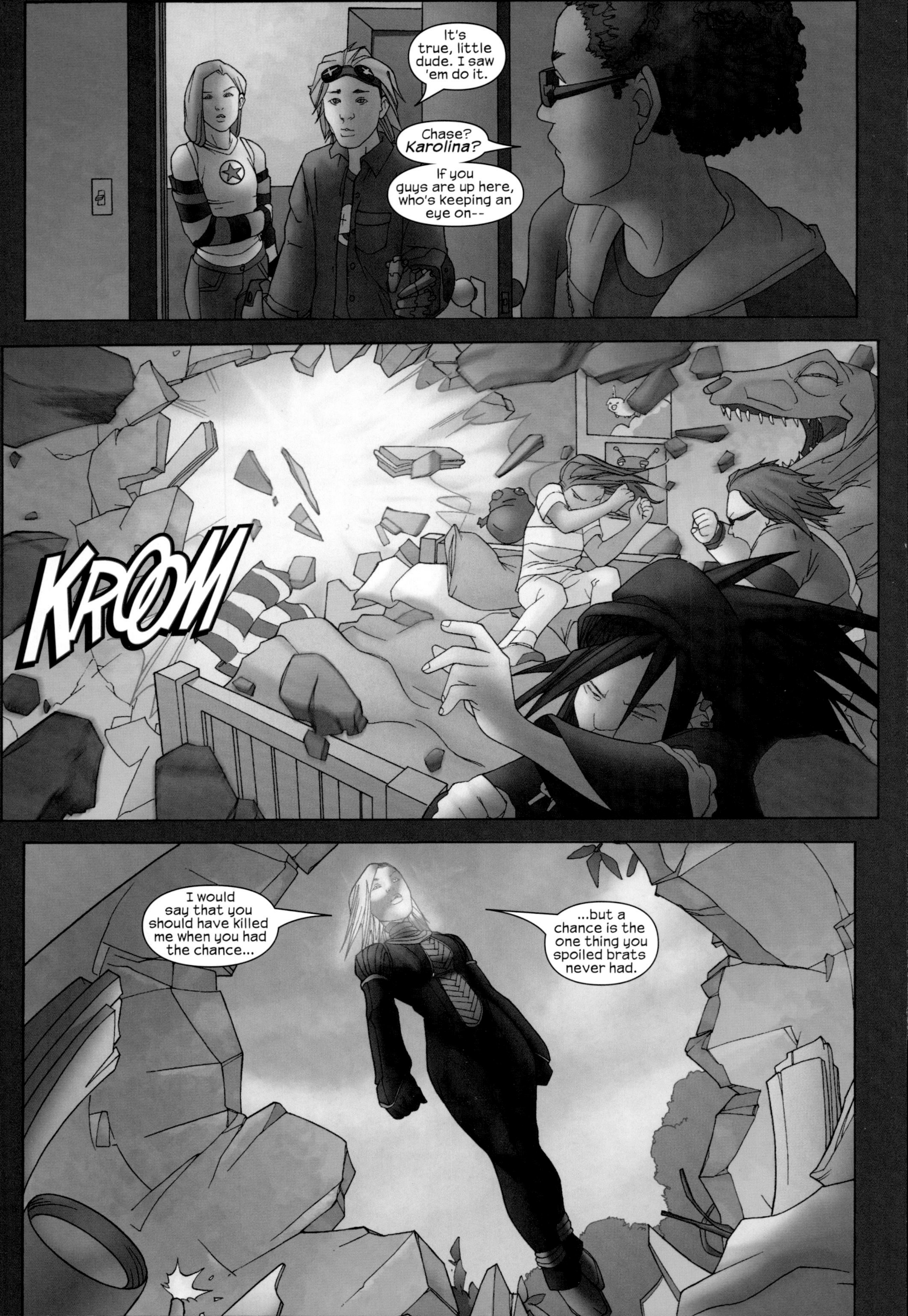
It's true, little dude. I saw 'em do it.
Chase? *Karolina?*
If you guys are up here, who's keeping an eye on--
KROOM
I would say that you should have killed me when you had the chance...
...but a chance is the one thing you spoiled brats never had.

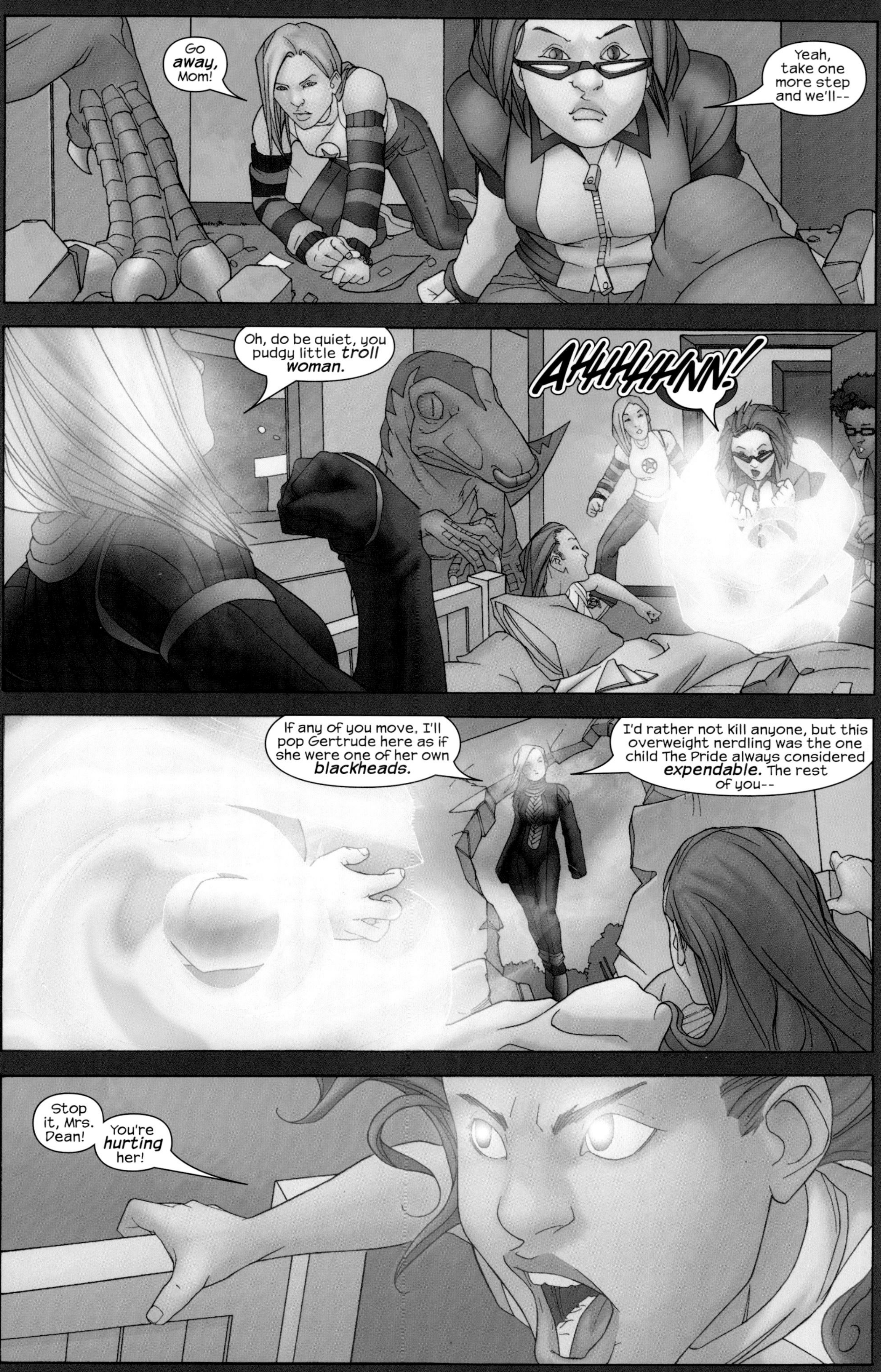
Go away, Mom!
Yeah, take one more step and we'll--
Oh, do be quiet, you pudgy little troll woman.
AHHHHHNN!
If any of you move, I'll pop Gertrude here as if she were one of her own blackheads.
I'd rather not kill anyone, but this overweight nerdling was the one child The Pride always considered expendable. The rest of you--
Stop it, Mrs. Dean!
You're hurting her!

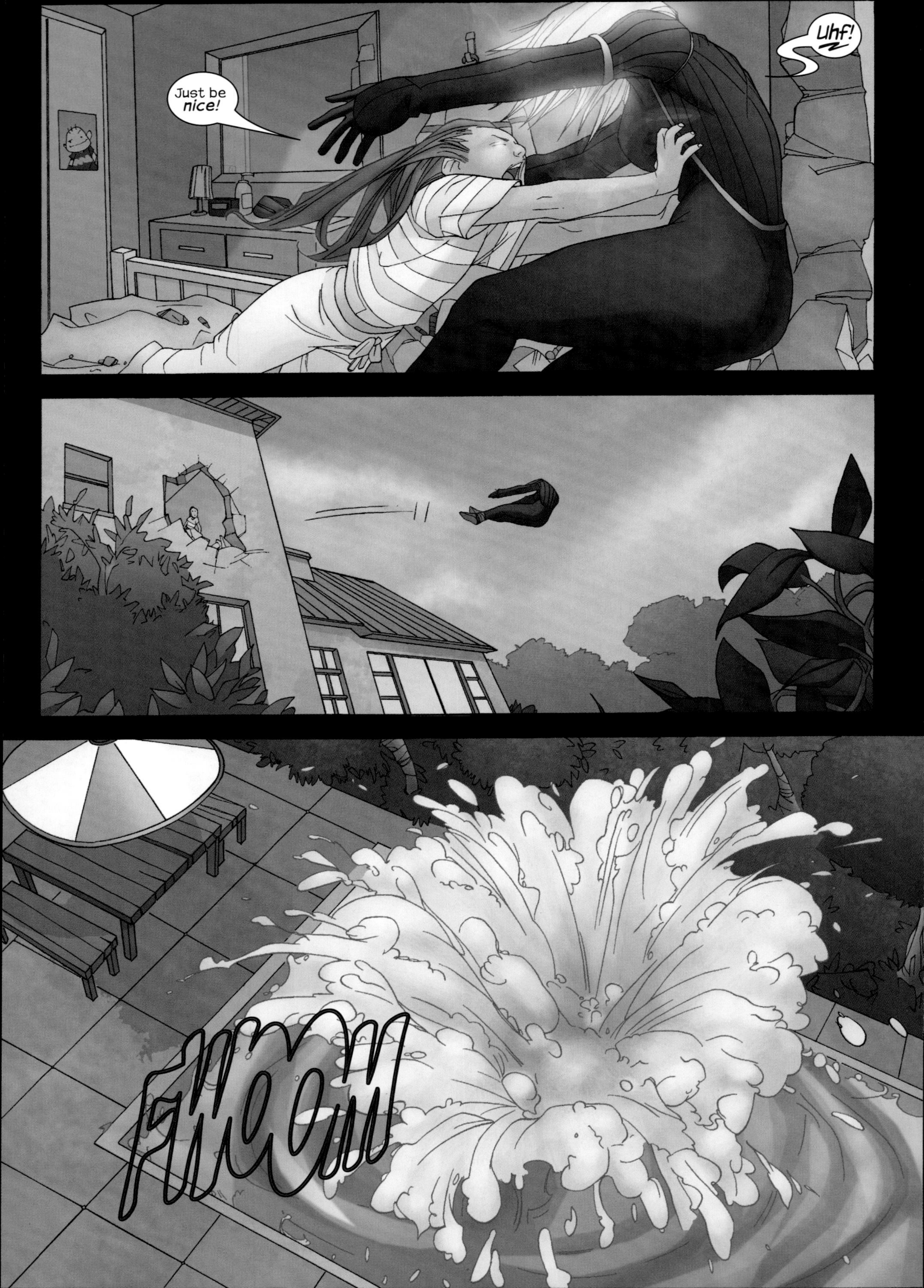
Just be *nice!*
Uhf!

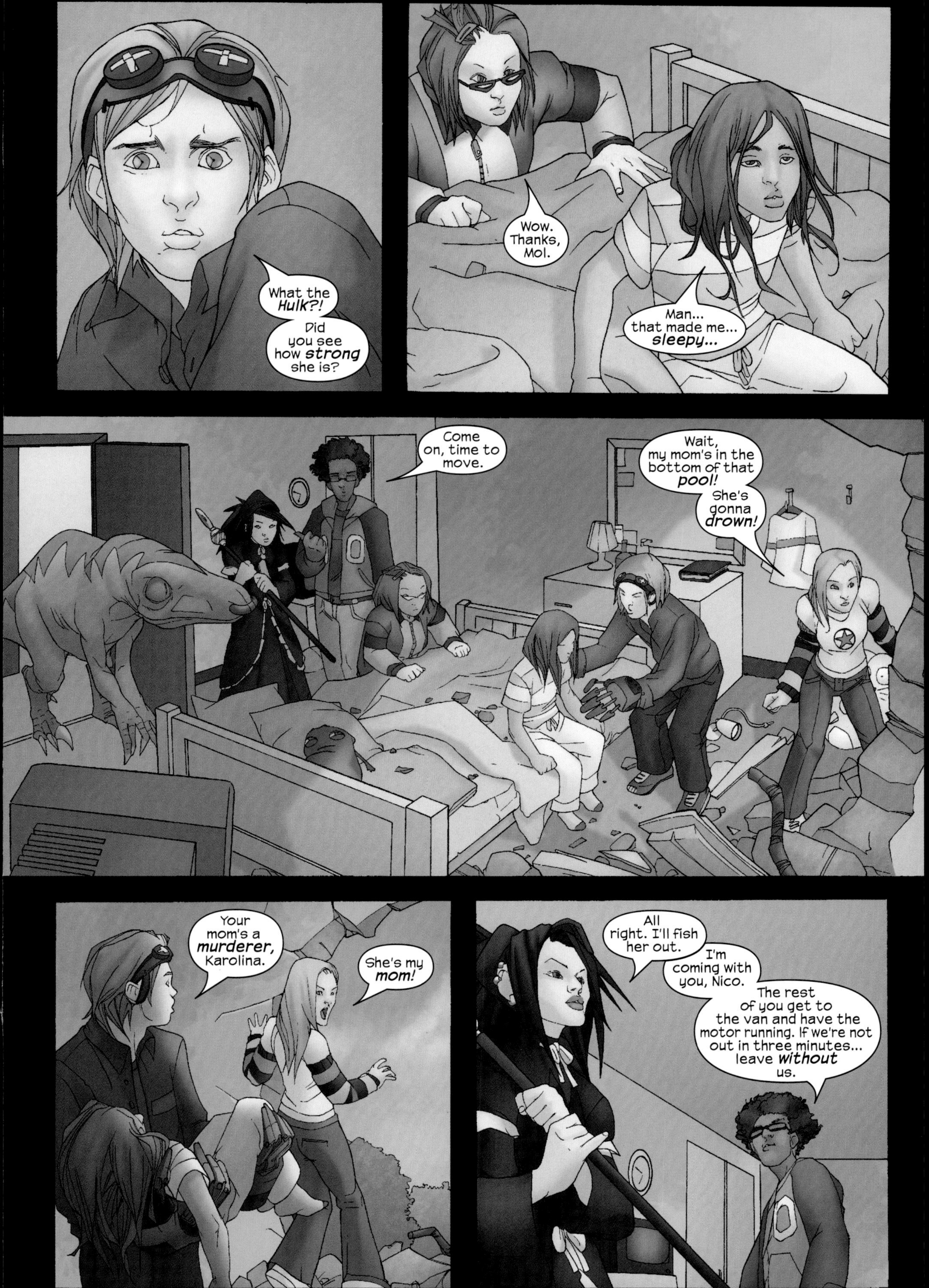
What the *Hulk?!*
Did you see how *strong* she is?
Wow. Thanks, Mol.
Man... that made me... *sleepy...*
Come on, time to move.
Wait, my mom's in the bottom of that *pool!*
She's gonna *drown!*
Your mom's a *murderer,* Karolina.
She's my *mom!*
All right. I'll fish her out.
I'm coming with you, Nico.
The rest of you get to the van and have the motor running. If we're not out in three minutes... leave *without* us.

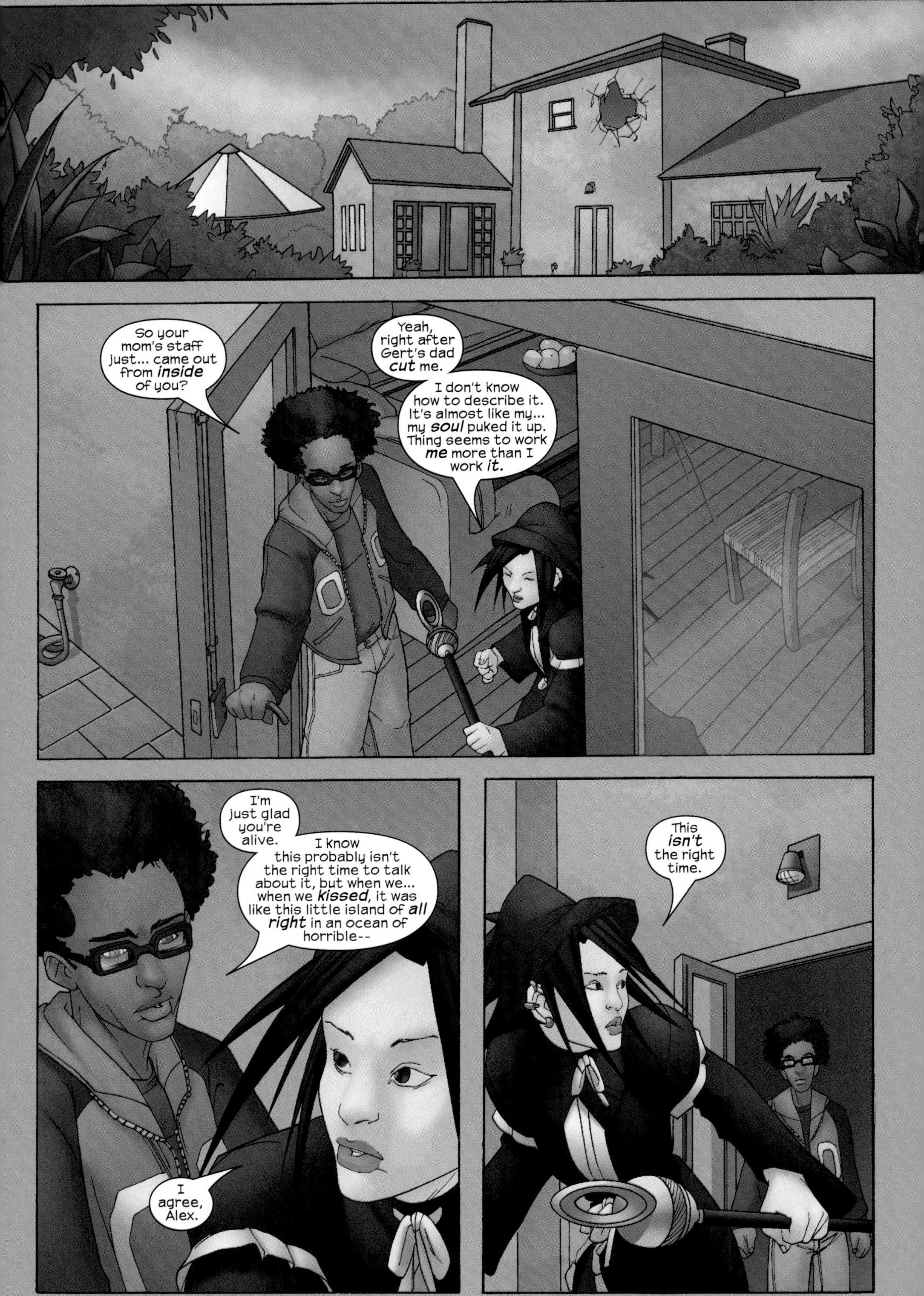

So your mom's staff just... came out from *inside* of you?
Yeah, right after Gert's dad *cut* me.
I don't know how to describe it. It's almost like my... my *soul* puked it up. Thing seems to work *me* more than I work *it.*
I'm just glad you're alive.
I know this probably isn't the right time to talk about it, but when we... when we *kissed*, it was like this little island of *all right* in an ocean of horrible--
I agree, Alex.
This *isn't* the right time.

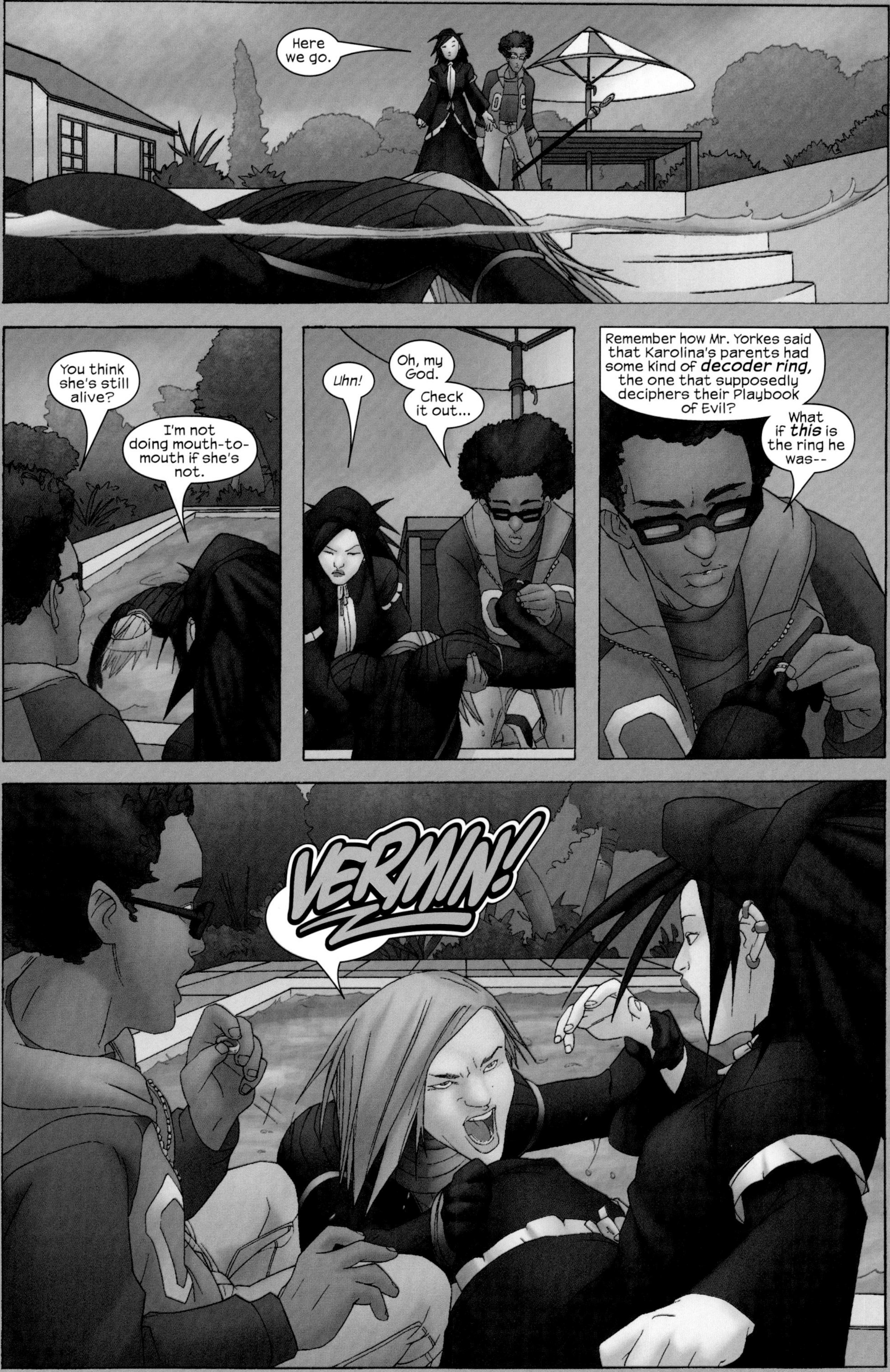
Here we go.
You think she's still alive?
I'm not doing mouth-to-mouth if she's not.
Uhn!
Oh, my God.
Check it out...
Remember how Mr. Yorkes said that Karolina's parents had some kind of decoder ring, the one that supposedly deciphers their Playbook of Evil?
What if this is the ring he was--
VERMIN!

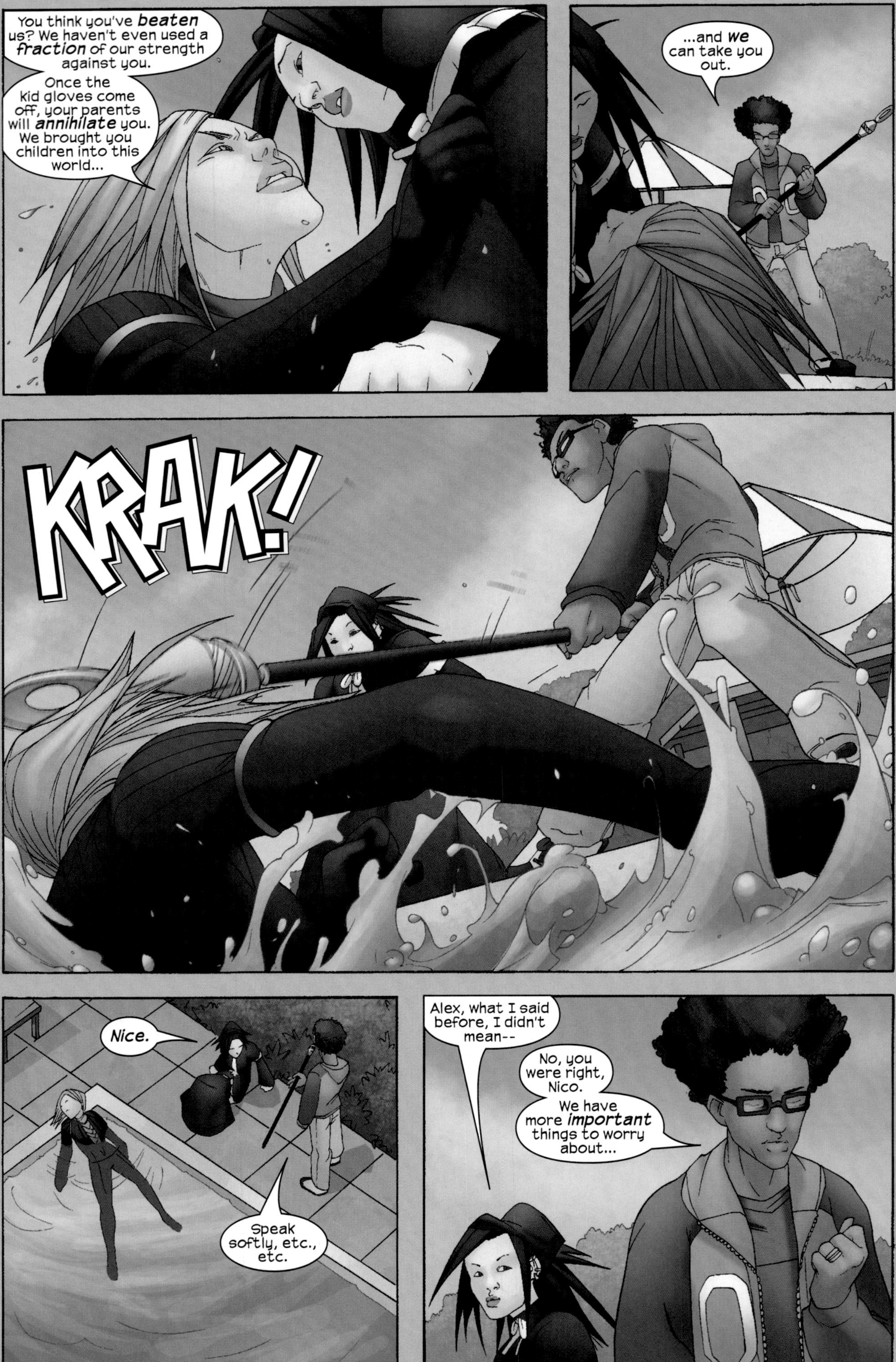
You think you've *beaten* us? We haven't even used a *fraction* of our strength against you.
Once the kid gloves come off, your parents will *annihilate* you. We brought you children into this world...
...and *we* can take you out.
KRAK!
Nice.
Speak softly, etc., etc.
Alex, what I said before, I didn't mean--
No, you were right, Nico.
We have more *important* things to worry about...

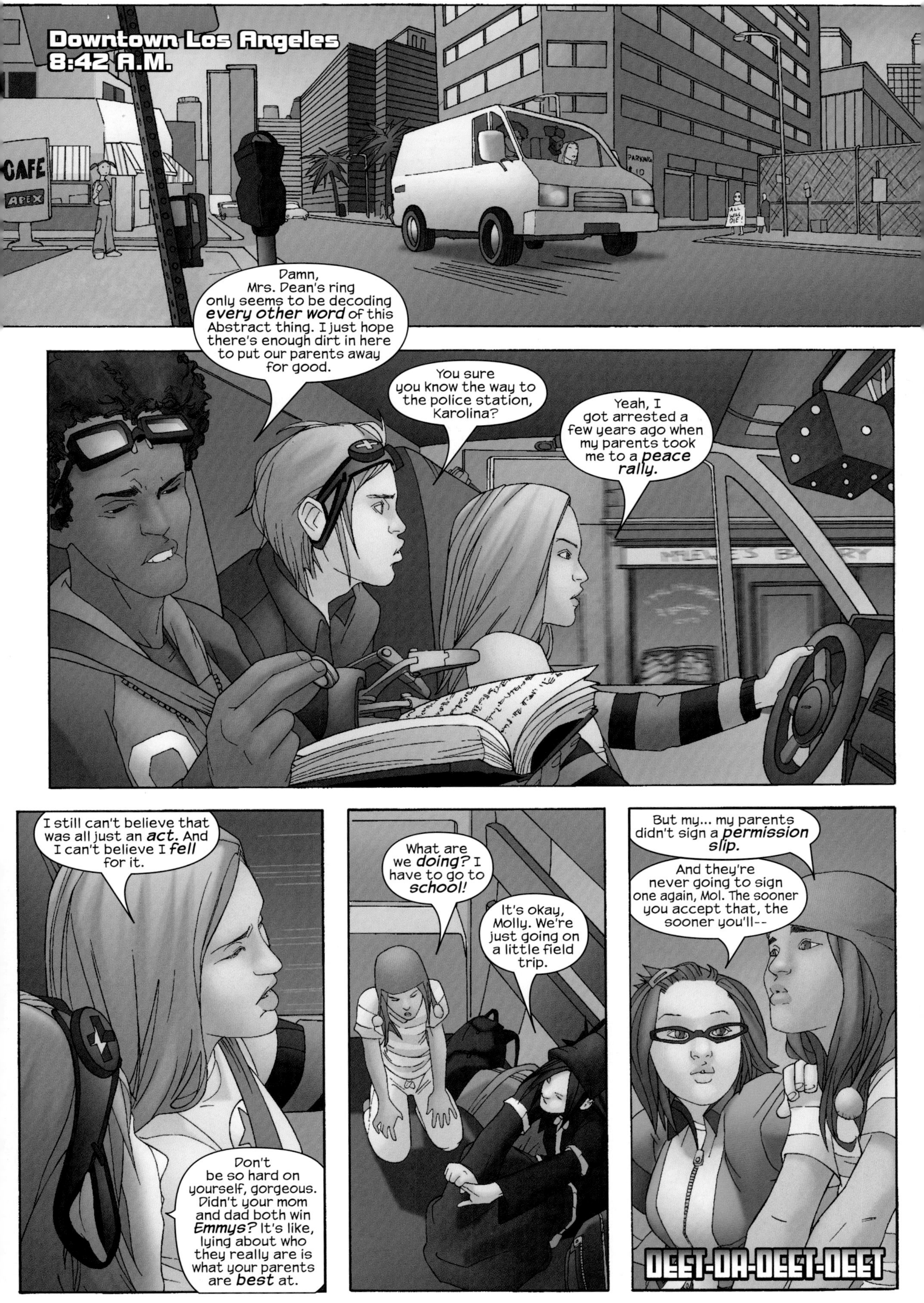
Downtown Los Angeles
8:42 A.M.
CAFE
APEX
PARKING
ALL WILL DIE!
Damn, Mrs. Dean's ring only seems to be decoding *every other word* of this Abstract thing. I just hope there's enough dirt in here to put our parents away for good.
You sure you know the way to the police station, Karolina?
Yeah, I got arrested a few years ago when my parents took me to a *peace rally.*
I still can't believe that was all just an *act.* And I can't believe I *fell* for it.
Don't be so hard on yourself, gorgeous. Didn't your mom and dad both win *Emmys?* It's like, lying about who they really are is what your parents are *best* at.
What are we *doing?* I have to go to *school!*
It's okay, Molly. We're just going on a little field trip.
But my... my parents didn't sign a *permission slip.*
And they're never going to sign one again, Mol. The sooner you accept that, the sooner you'll--
DEET-DA-DEET-DEET

Oh, no.

That's my *father's* ring tone.

Hello?

Well, young man, I would say that this little misadventure violates the *curfew* we agreed upon, wouldn't you?

Save it, Dad. We're on our way to the cops now.

Really? Why don't you turn to AM 1070 in... five... four... three...

Police are still searching for sixteen-year-old *Alex Wilder*, wanted in connection with yesterday's murder in Malibu.

What?

Alex, look!

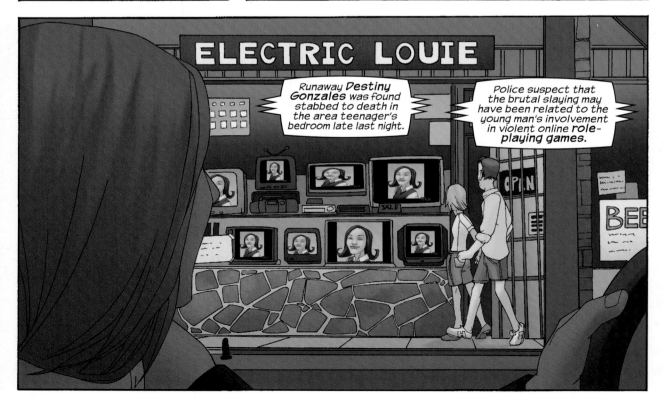

ELECTRIC LOUIE

Runaway *Destiny Gonzales* was found stabbed to death in the area teenager's bedroom late last night.

Police suspect that the brutal slaying may have been related to the young man's involvement in violent online *role-playing games*.

OPEN

BEE

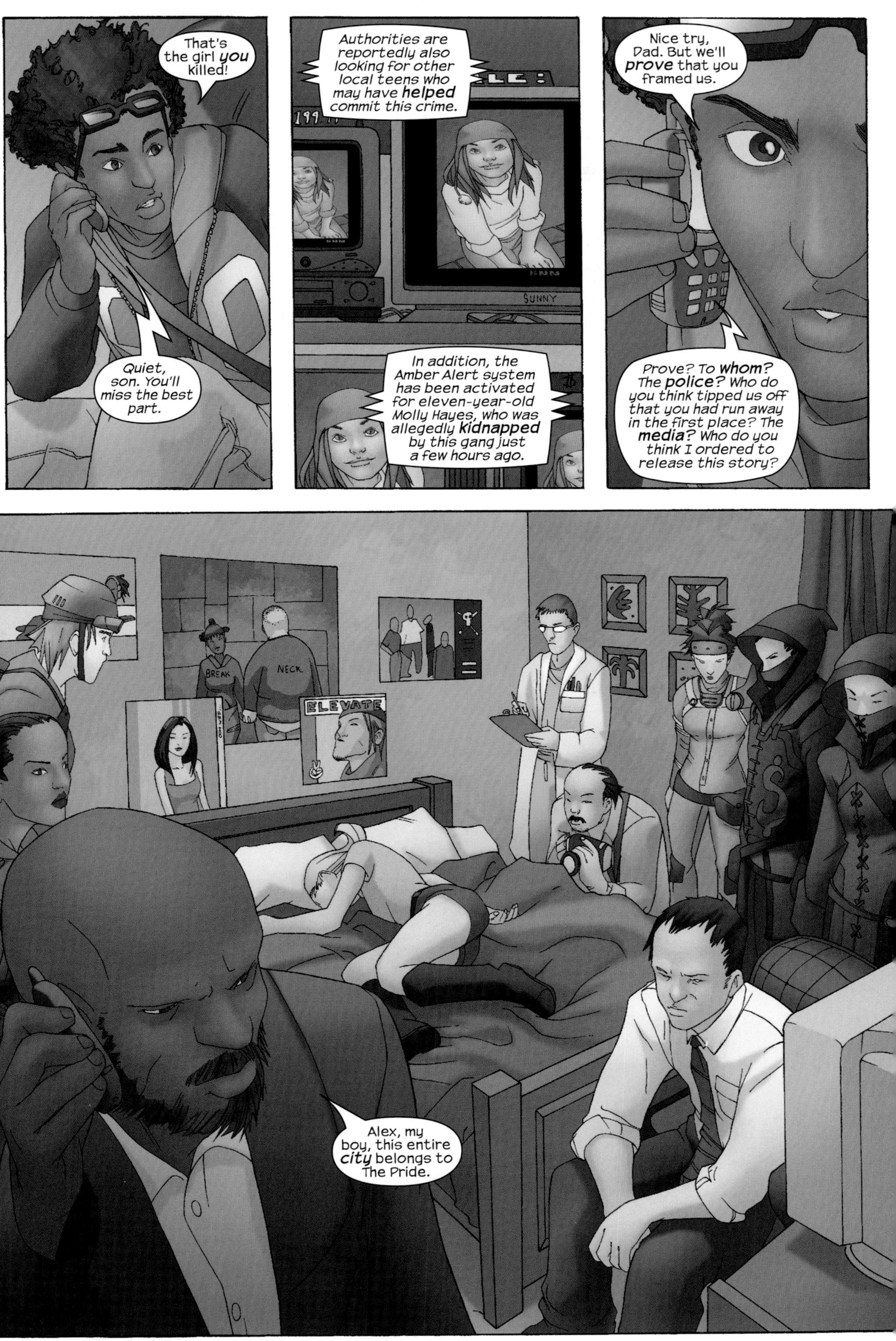

That's the girl *you* killed!
Quiet, son. You'll miss the best part.
Authorities are reportedly also looking for other local teens who may have **helped** commit this crime.
SUNNY
In addition, the Amber Alert system has been activated for eleven-year-old Molly Hayes, who was allegedly **kidnapped** by this gang just a few hours ago.
Nice try, Dad. But we'll **prove** that you framed us.
Prove? To **whom**? The **police**? Who do you think tipped us off that you had run away in the first place? The **media**? Who do you think I ordered to release this story?
BREAK
NECK.
ELEVATE
Alex, my boy, this entire *city* belongs to The Pride.

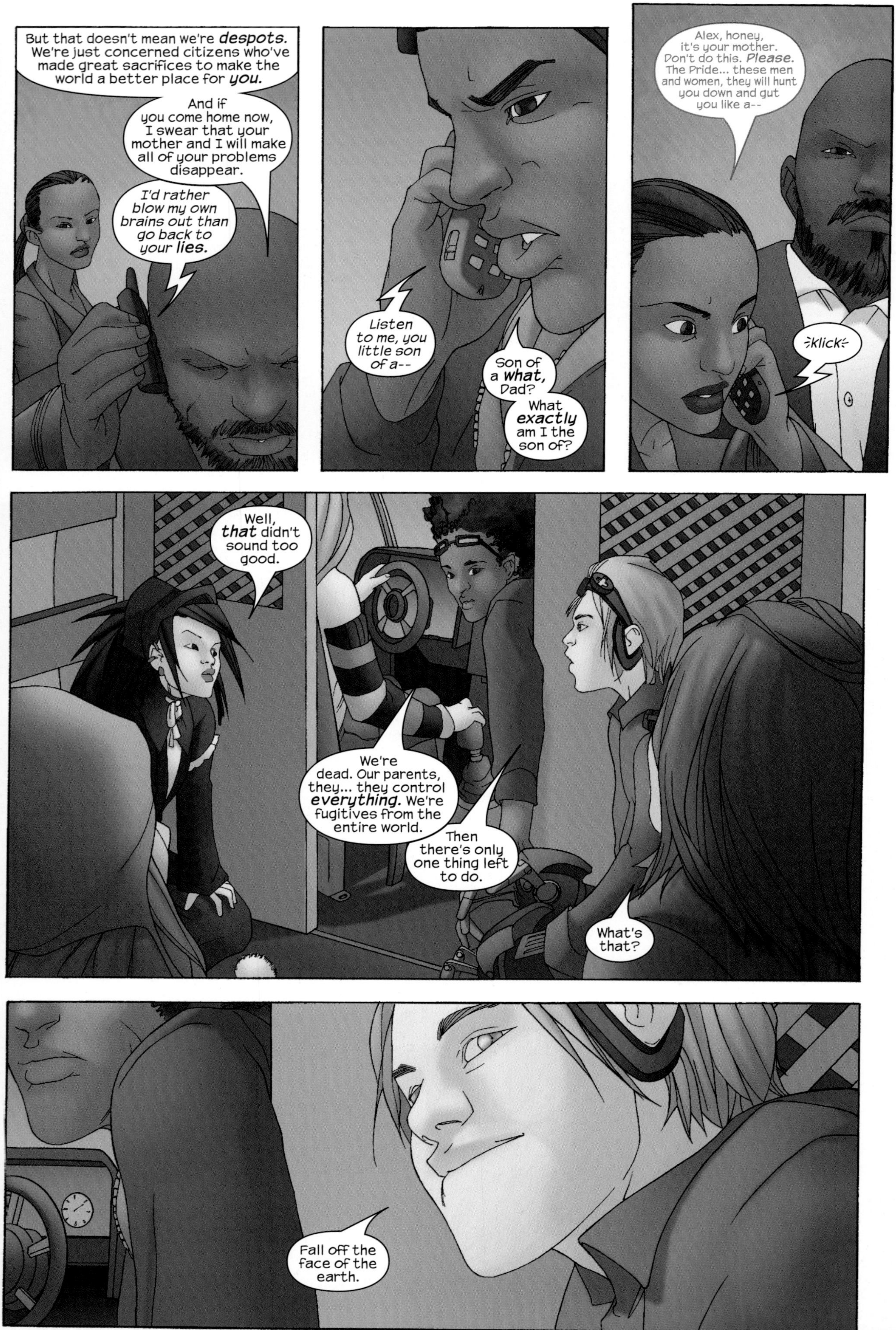
But that doesn't mean we're **despots.** We're just concerned citizens who've made great sacrifices to make the world a better place for **you.**
And if you come home now, I swear that your mother and I will make all of your problems disappear.
I'd rather blow my own brains out than go back to your ***lies.***
Listen to me, you little son of a--
Son of a **what,** Dad?
What **exactly** am I the son of?
Alex, honey, it's your mother. Don't do this. *Please.* The Pride... these men and women, they will hunt you down and gut you like a--
klick
Well, **that** didn't sound too good.
We're dead. Our parents, they... they control **everything.** We're fugitives from the entire world.
Then there's only one thing left to do.
What's that?
Fall off the face of the earth.

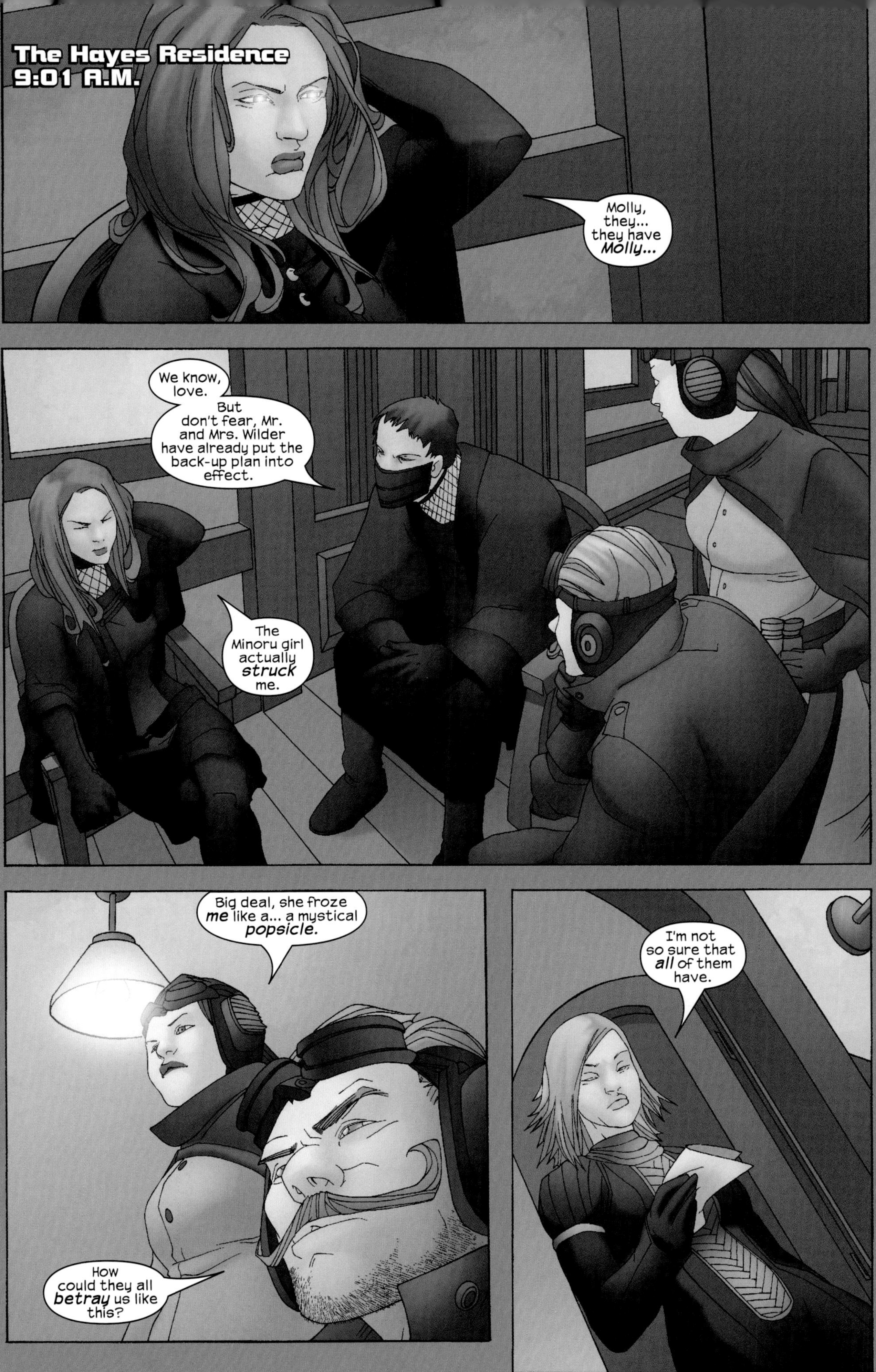

The Hayes Residence
9:01 A.M.
Molly, they... they have *Molly*...
We know, love.
But don't fear, Mr. and Mrs. Wilder have already put the back-up plan into effect.
The Minoru girl actually *struck* me.
Big deal, she froze *me* like a... a mystical *popsicle*.
How could they all *betray* us like this?
I'm not so sure that *all* of them have.

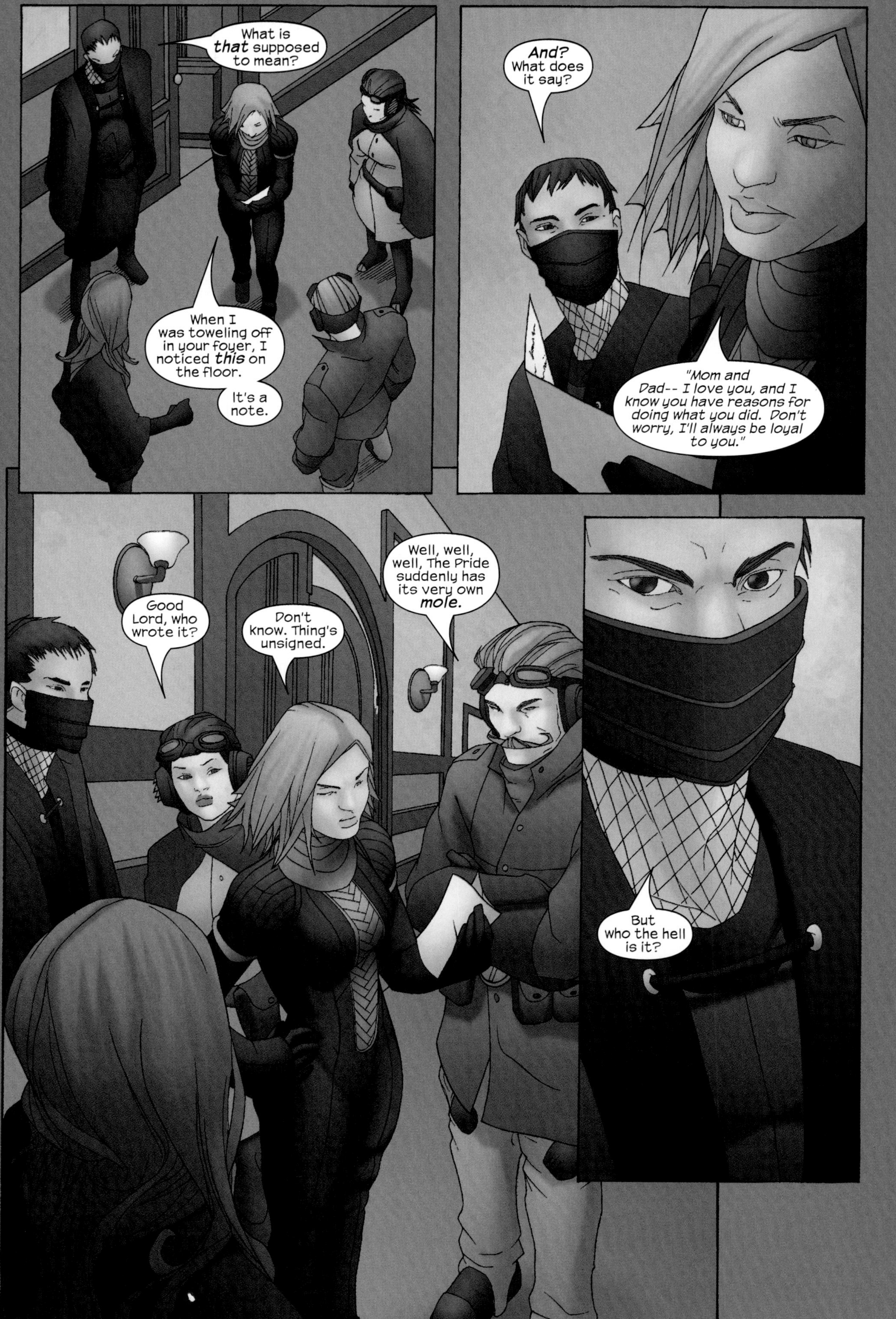

What is *that* supposed to mean?
When I was toweling off in your foyer, I noticed *this* on the floor.
It's a note.
And? What does it say?
"Mom and Dad-- I love you, and I know you have reasons for doing what you did. Don't worry, I'll always be loyal to you."
Good Lord, who wrote it?
Don't know. Thing's unsigned.
Well, well, well, The Pride suddenly has its very own *mole.*
But who the hell is it?

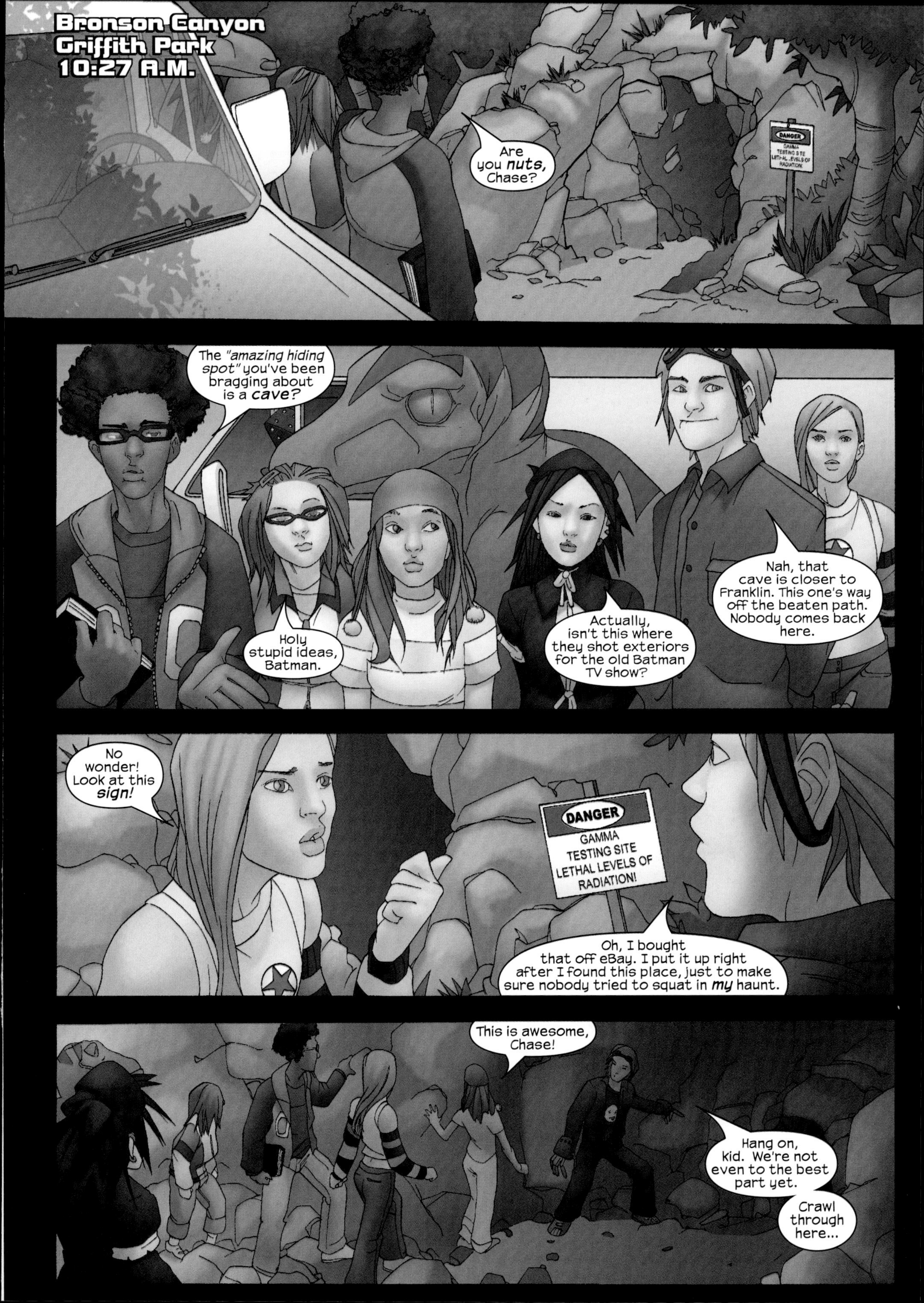

Bronson Canyon
Griffith Park
10:27 A.M.
Are you *nuts,* Chase?
DANGER
GAMMA TESTING SITE LETHAL LEVELS OF RADIATION
The *"amazing hiding spot"* you've been bragging about is a *cave?*
Holy stupid ideas, Batman.
Actually, isn't this where they shot exteriors for the old Batman TV show?
Nah, that cave is closer to Franklin. This one's way off the beaten path. Nobody comes back here.
No wonder! Look at this *sign!*
DANGER
GAMMA TESTING SITE LETHAL LEVELS OF RADIATION!
Oh, I bought that off eBay. I put it up right after I found this place, just to make sure nobody tried to squat in *my* haunt.
This is awesome, Chase!
Hang on, kid. We're not even to the best part yet.
Crawl through here...

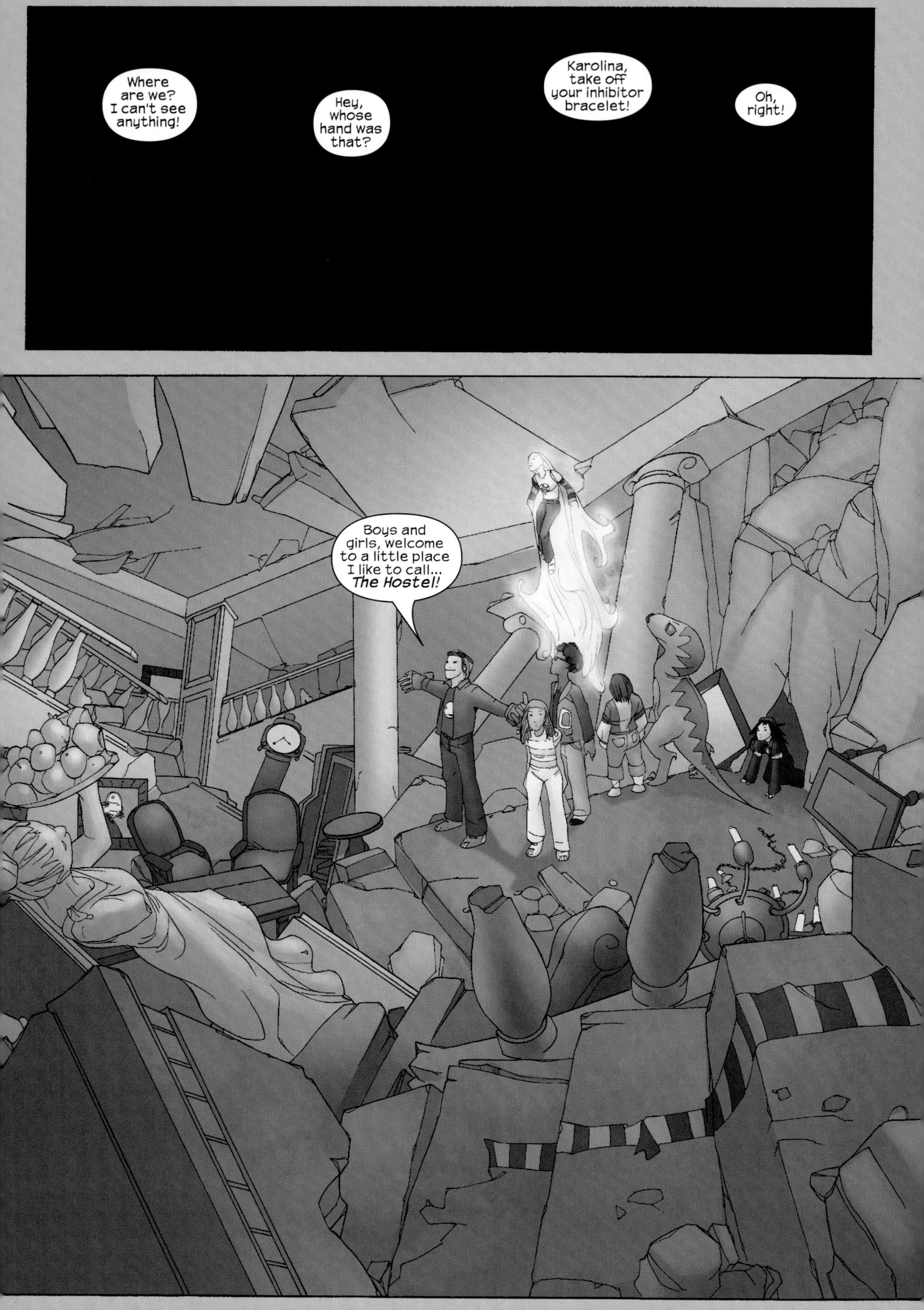

Where are we? I can't see anything!
Hey, whose hand was that?
Karolina, take off your inhibitor bracelet!
Oh, right!
Boys and girls, welcome to a little place I like to call... *The Hostel!*

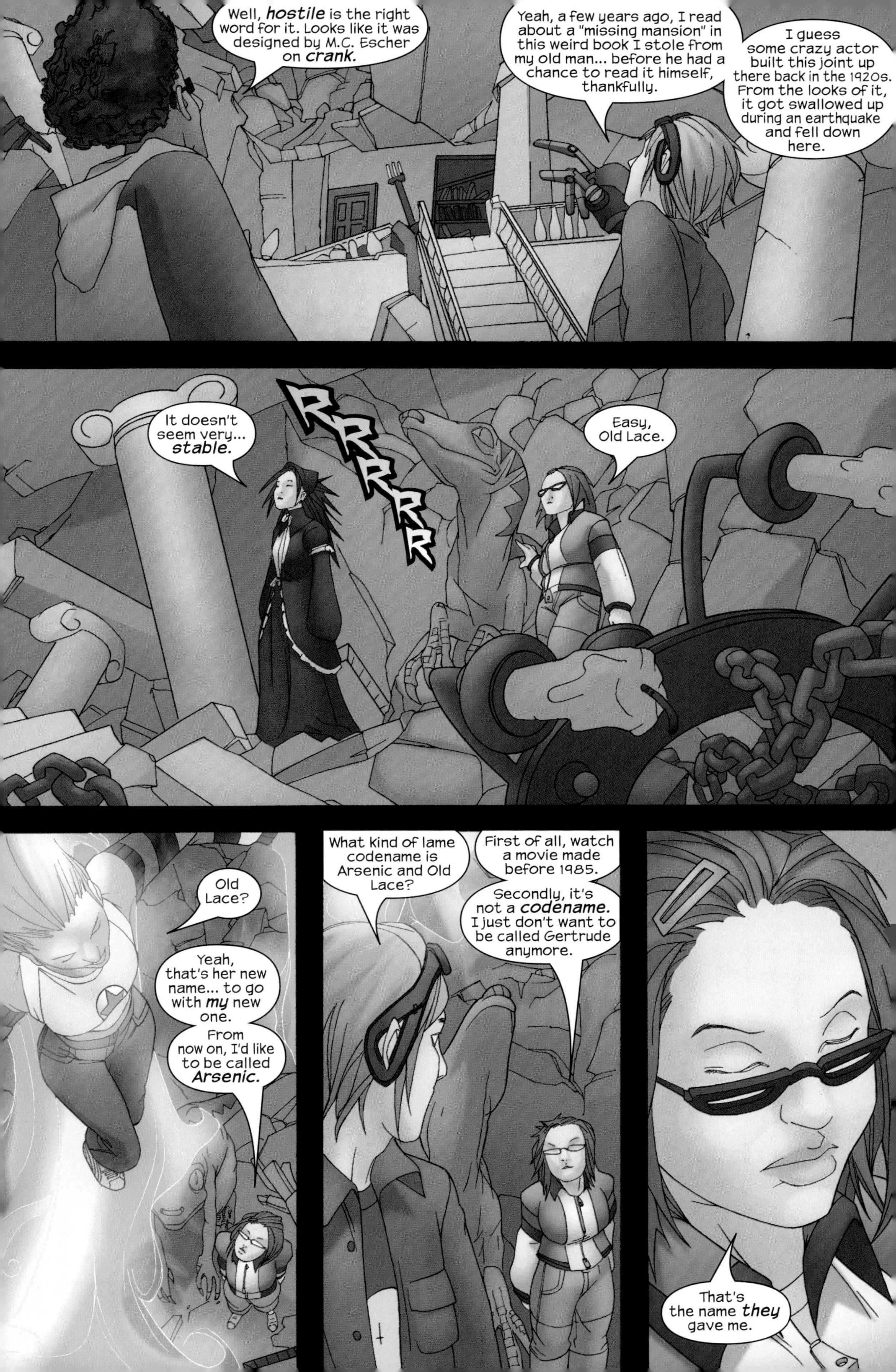
Well, *hostile* is the right word for it. Looks like it was designed by M.C. Escher on *crank.*
Yeah, a few years ago, I read about a "missing mansion" in this weird book I stole from my old man... before he had a chance to read it himself, thankfully.
I guess some crazy actor built this joint up there back in the 1920s. From the looks of it, it got swallowed up during an earthquake and fell down here.
It doesn't seem very... *stable.*
RRRRRR
Easy, Old Lace.
Old Lace?
Yeah, that's her new name... to go with *my* new one.
From now on, I'd like to be called *Arsenic.*
What kind of lame codename is Arsenic and Old Lace?
First of all, watch a movie made before 1985.
Secondly, it's not a *codename.* I just don't want to be called Gertrude anymore.
That's the name *they* gave me.

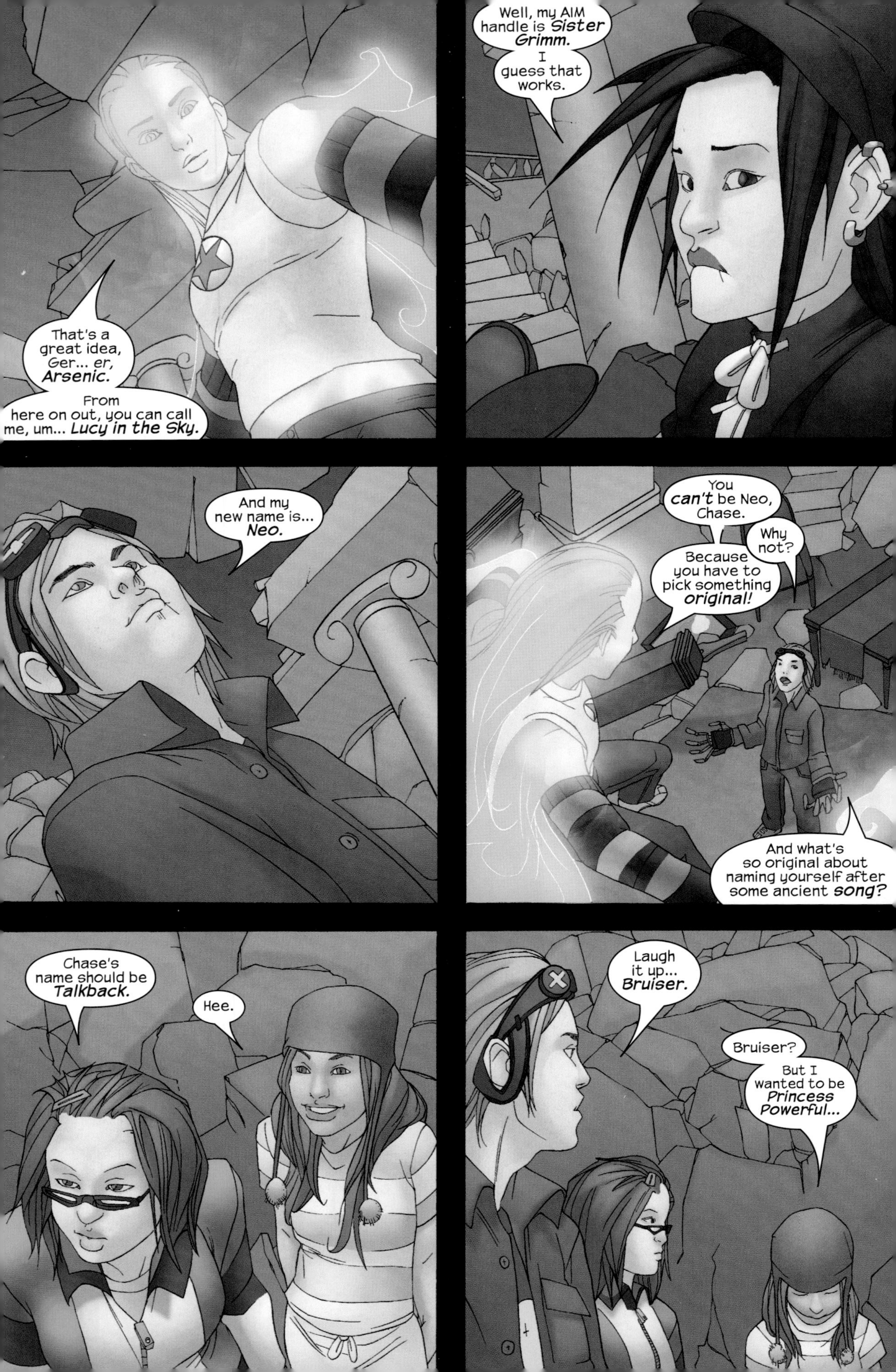
That's a great idea, Ger... er, Arsenic.
From here on out, you can call me, um... Lucy in the Sky.
Well, my AIM handle is Sister Grimm.
I guess that works.
And my new name is... Neo.
You can't be Neo, Chase.
Why not?
Because you have to pick something original!
And what's so original about naming yourself after some ancient song?
Chase's name should be Talkback.
Hee.
Laugh it up... Bruiser.
Bruiser?
But I wanted to be Princess Powerful...

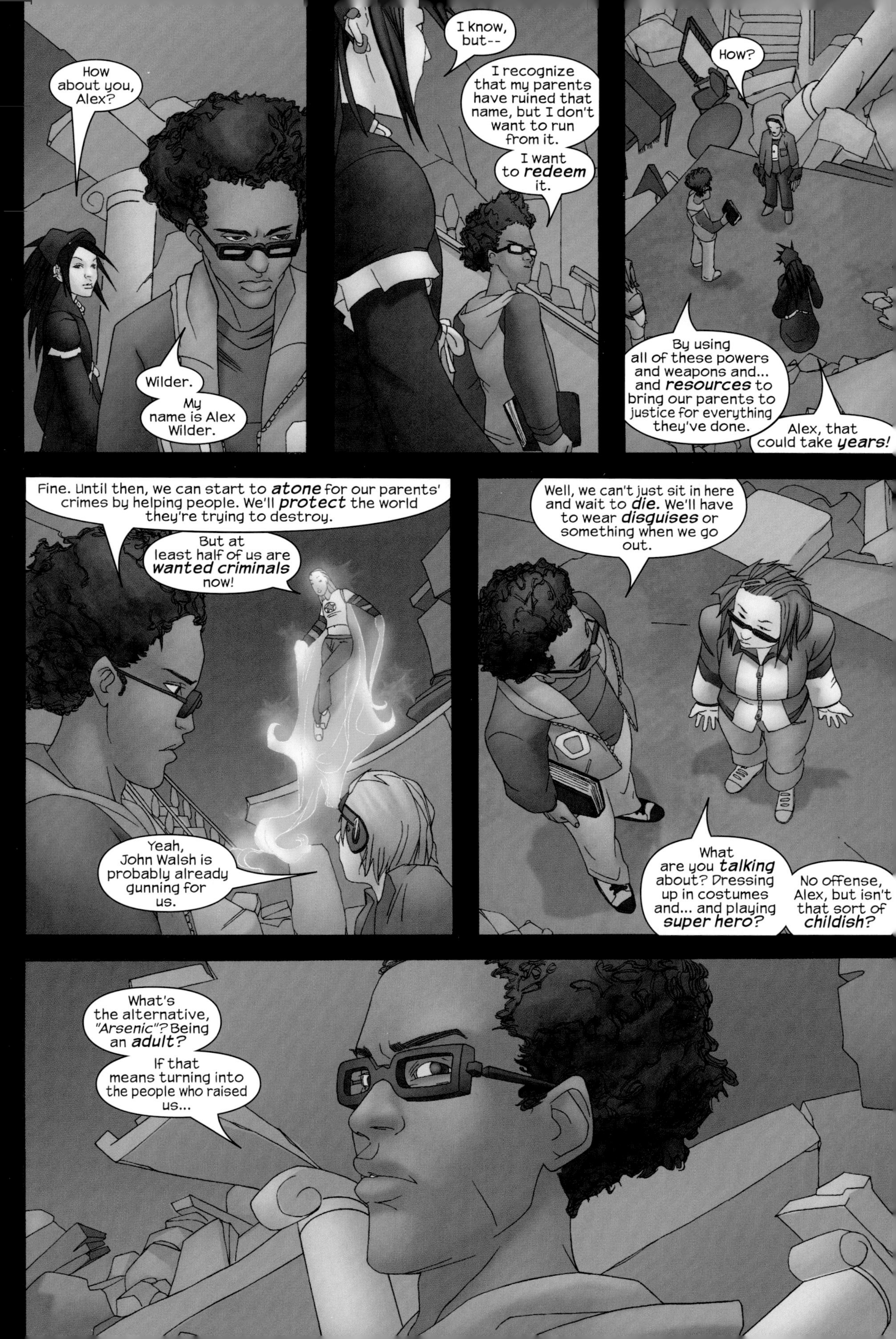

How about you, Alex?
Wilder.
My name is Alex Wilder.
I know, but--
I recognize that my parents have ruined that name, but I don't want to run from it.
I want to redeem it.
How?
By using all of these powers and weapons and... and resources to bring our parents to justice for everything they've done.
Alex, that could take years!
Fine. Until then, we can start to atone for our parents' crimes by helping people. We'll protect the world they're trying to destroy.
But at least half of us are wanted criminals now!
Yeah, John Walsh is probably already gunning for us.
Well, we can't just sit in here and wait to die. We'll have to wear disguises or something when we go out.
What are you talking about? Dressing up in costumes and... and playing super hero?
No offense, Alex, but isn't that sort of childish?
What's the alternative, "Arsenic"? Being an adult?
If that means turning into the people who raised us...

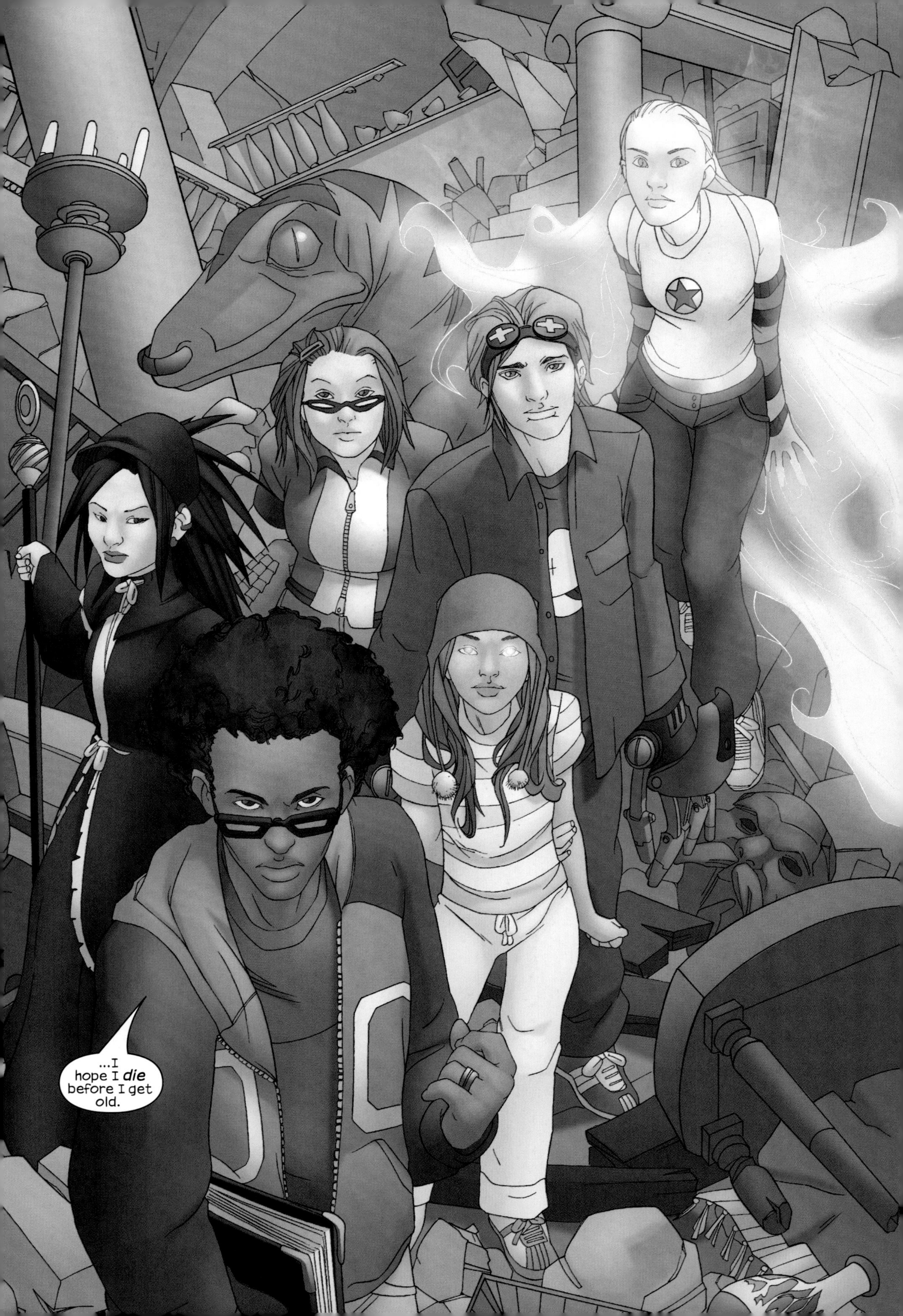
...I hope I *die* before I get old.

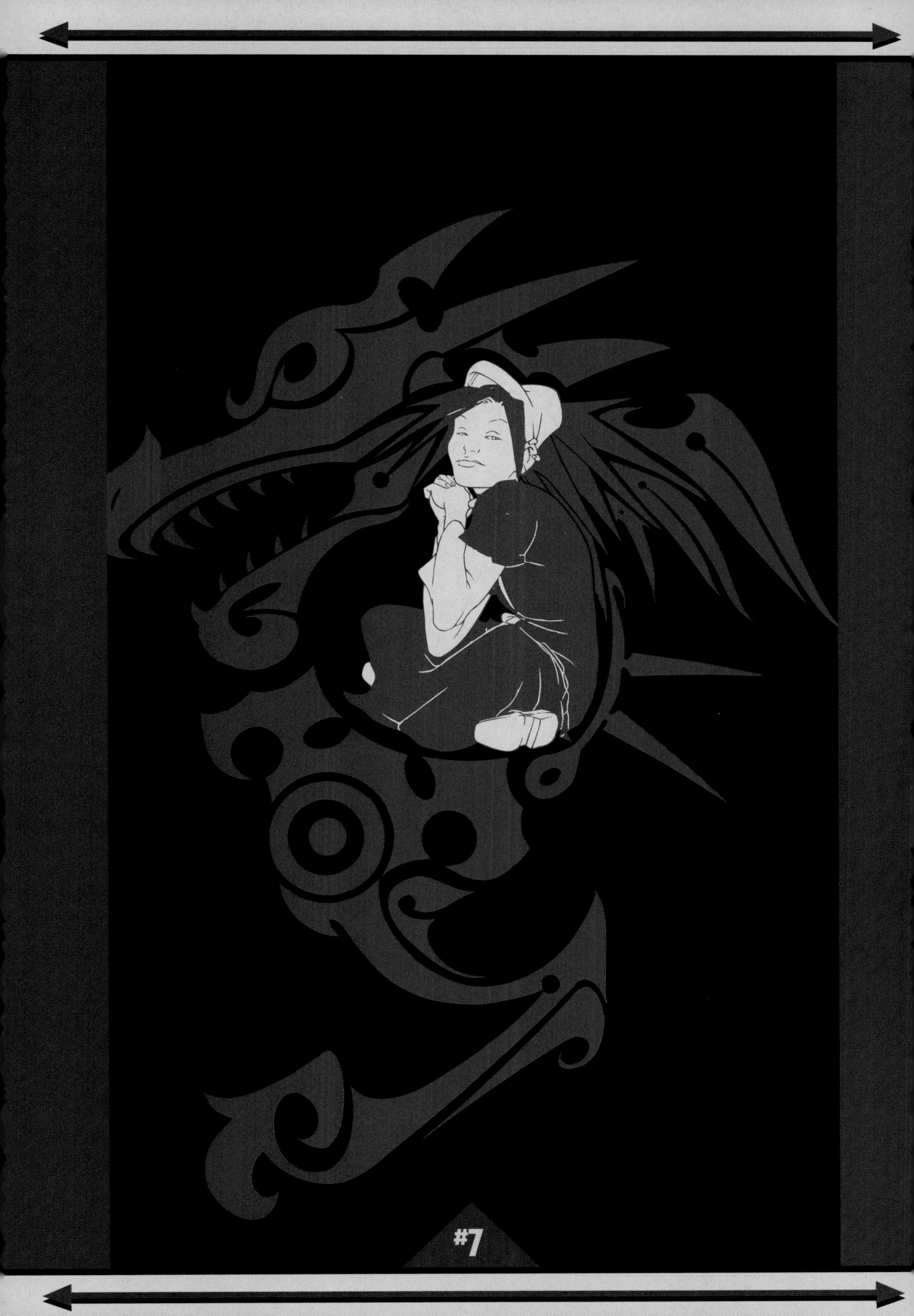
#7

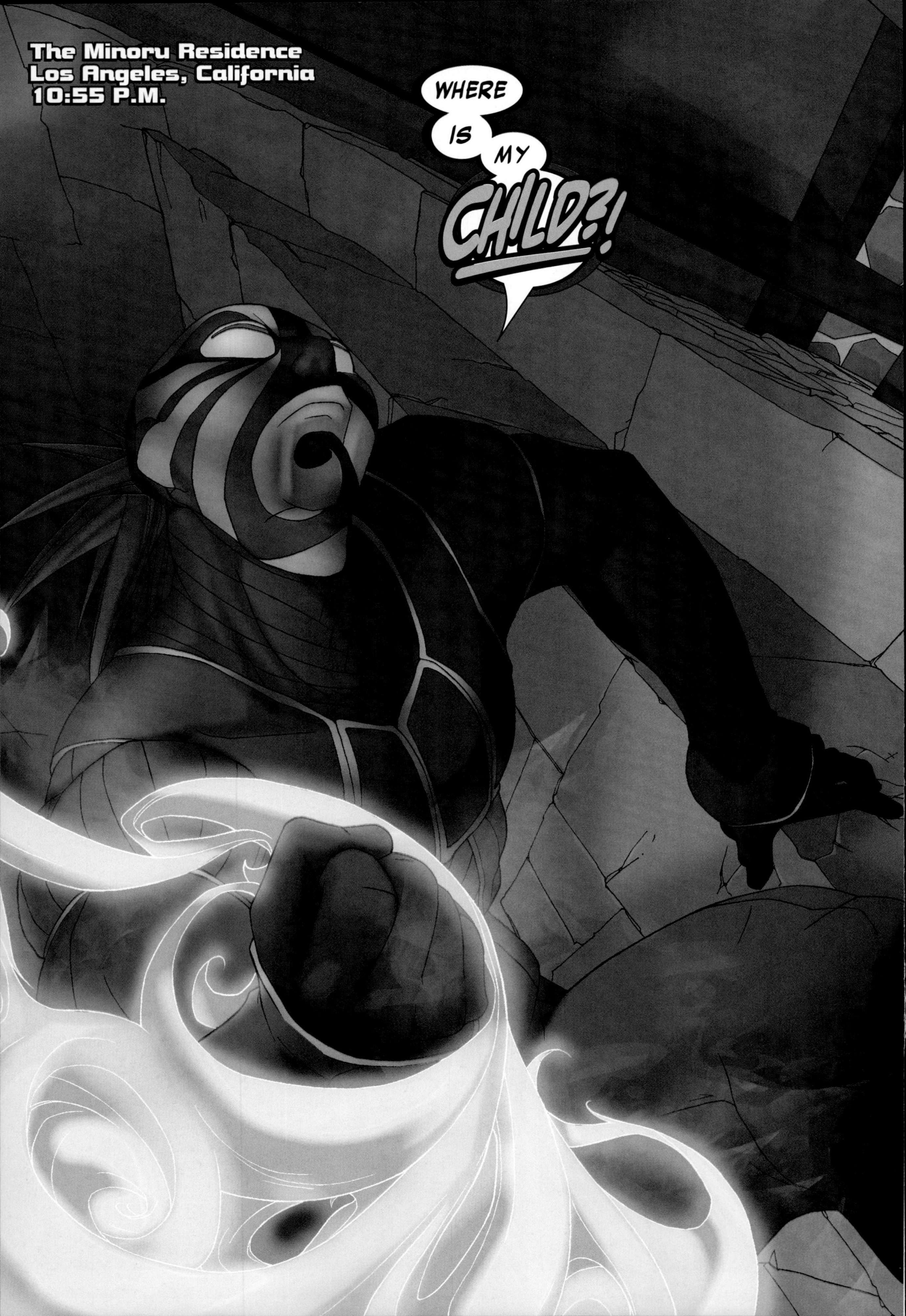
The Minoru Residence
Los Angeles, California
10:55 P.M.
WHERE IS MY CHILD?!

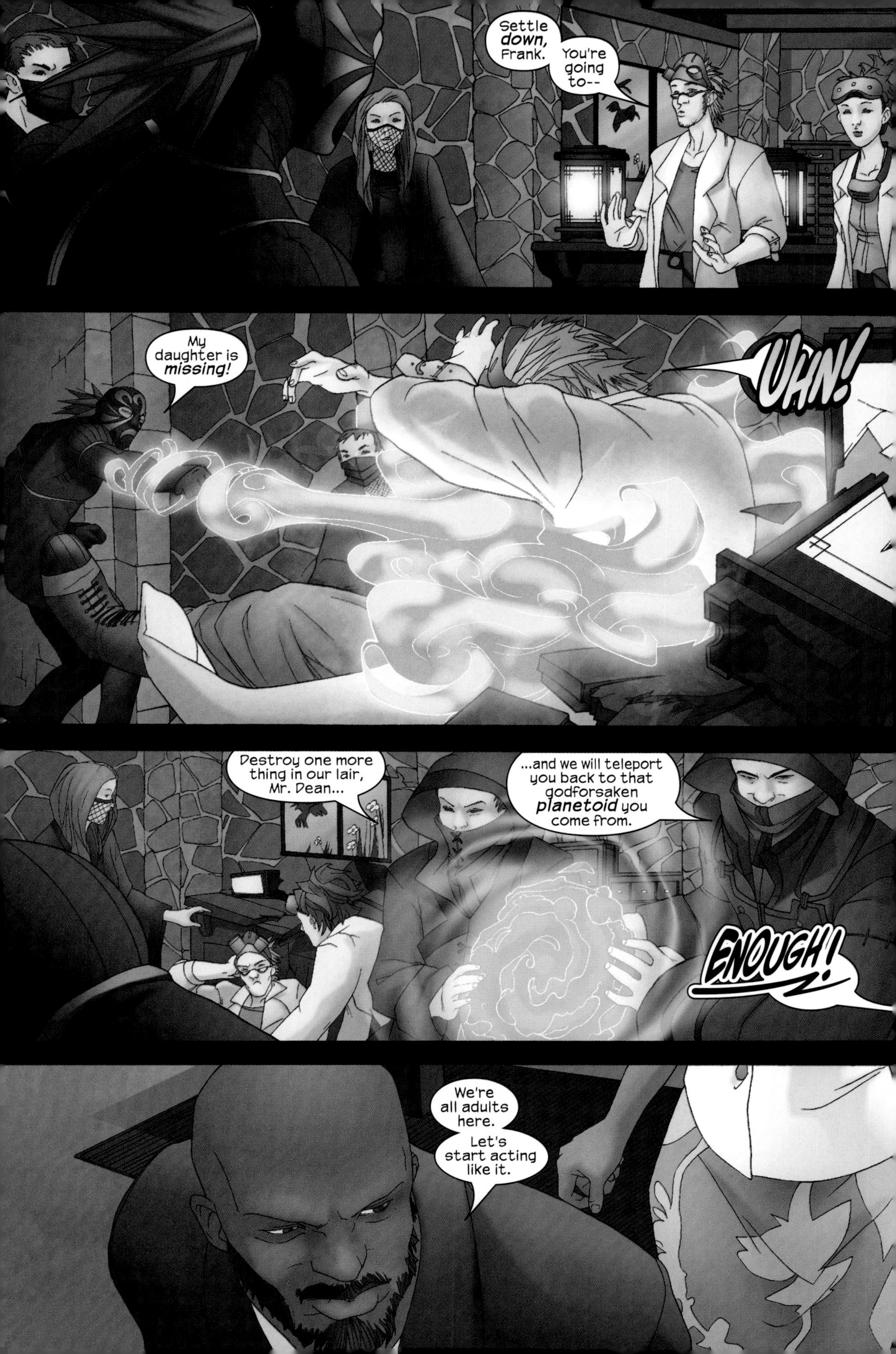
Settle *down,* Frank.
You're going to--
My daughter is *missing!*
UHN!
Destroy one more thing in our lair, Mr. Dean...
...and we will teleport you back to that godforsaken *planetoid* you come from.
ENOUGH!
We're all adults here.
Let's start acting like it.

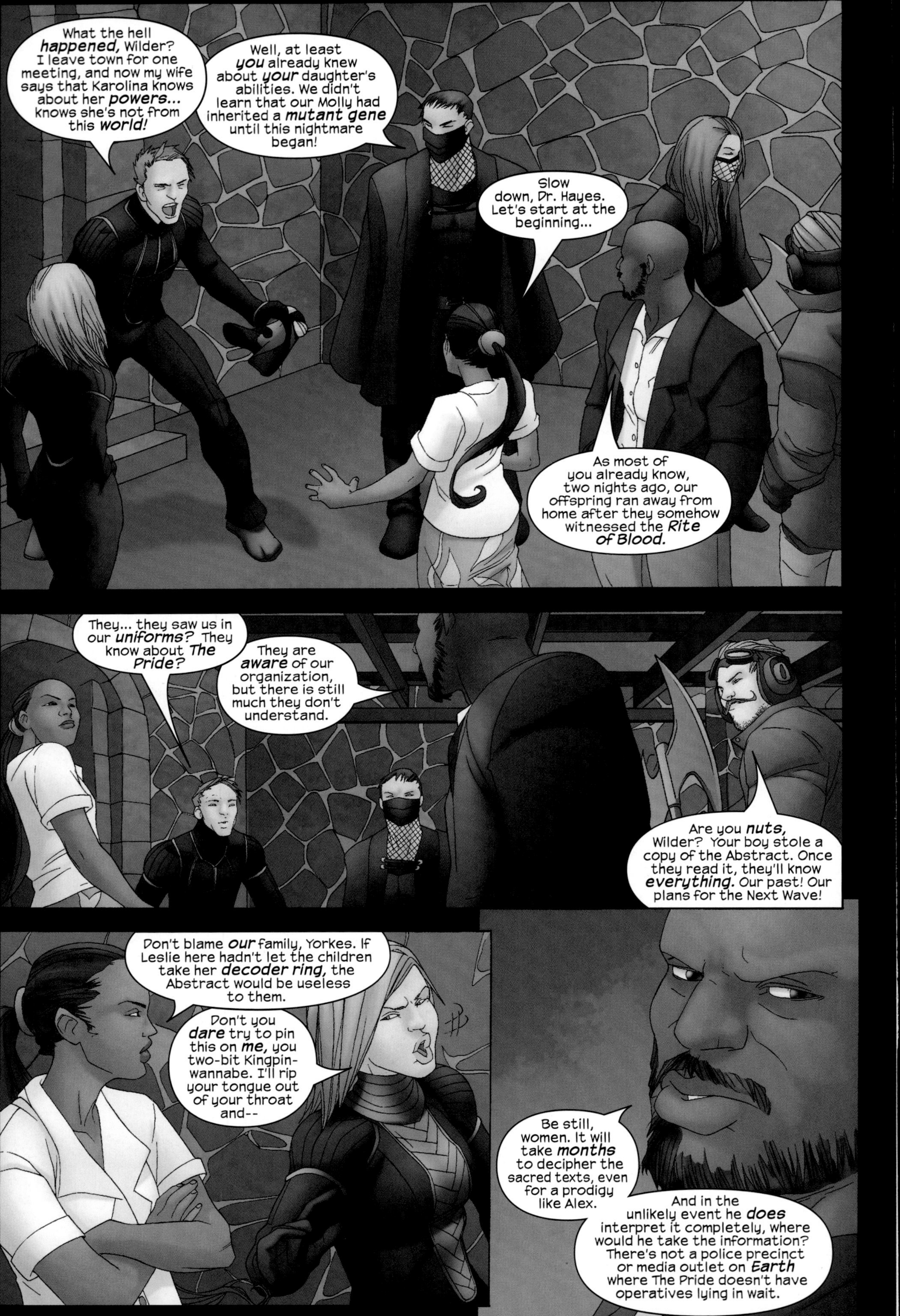

What the hell happened, Wilder? I leave town for one meeting, and now my wife says that Karolina knows about her powers... knows she's not from this world!
Well, at least you already knew about your daughter's abilities. We didn't learn that our Molly had inherited a mutant gene until this nightmare began!
Slow down, Dr. Hayes. Let's start at the beginning...
As most of you already know, two nights ago, our offspring ran away from home after they somehow witnessed the Rite of Blood.
They... they saw us in our uniforms? They know about The Pride?
They are aware of our organization, but there is still much they don't understand.
Are you nuts, Wilder? Your boy stole a copy of the Abstract. Once they read it, they'll know everything. Our past! Our plans for the Next Wave!
Don't blame our family, Yorkes. If Leslie here hadn't let the children take her decoder ring, the Abstract would be useless to them.
Don't you dare try to pin this on me, you two-bit Kingpin-wannabe. I'll rip your tongue out of your throat and--
Be still, women. It will take months to decipher the sacred texts, even for a prodigy like Alex.
And in the unlikely event he does interpret it completely, where would he take the information? There's not a police precinct or media outlet on Earth where The Pride doesn't have operatives lying in wait.

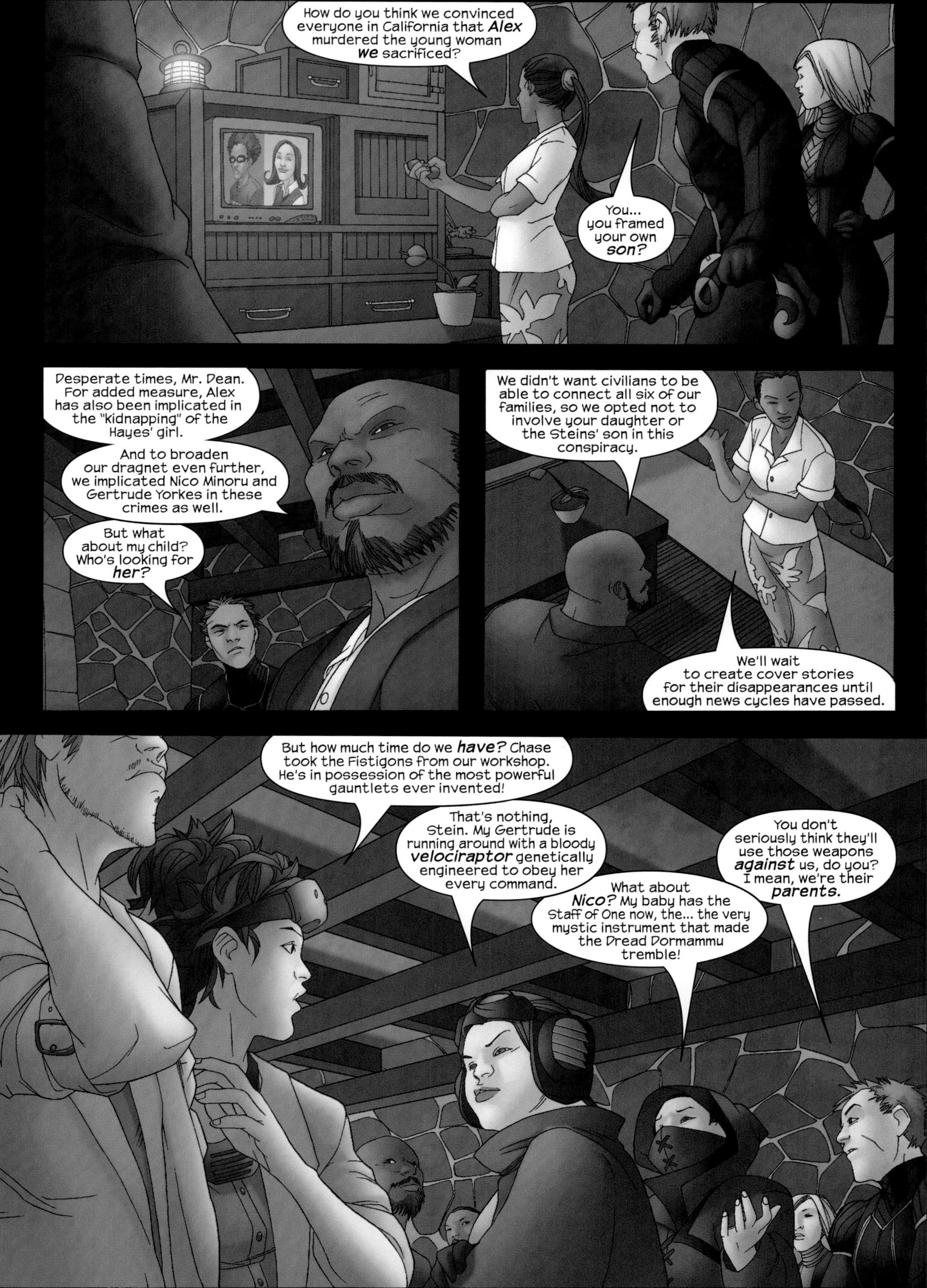
How do you think we convinced everyone in California that Alex murdered the young woman we sacrificed?
You... you framed your own son?
Desperate times, Mr. Dean. For added measure, Alex has also been implicated in the "kidnapping" of the Hayes' girl.
And to broaden our dragnet even further, we implicated Nico Minoru and Gertrude Yorkes in these crimes as well.
But what about my child? Who's looking for her?
We didn't want civilians to be able to connect all six of our families, so we opted not to involve your daughter or the Steins' son in this conspiracy.
We'll wait to create cover stories for their disappearances until enough news cycles have passed.
But how much time do we have? Chase took the Fistigons from our workshop. He's in possession of the most powerful gauntlets ever invented!
That's nothing, Stein. My Gertrude is running around with a bloody velociraptor genetically engineered to obey her every command.
What about Nico? My baby has the Staff of One now, the... the very mystic instrument that made the Dread Dormammu tremble!
You don't seriously think they'll use those weapons against us, do you? I mean, we're their parents.

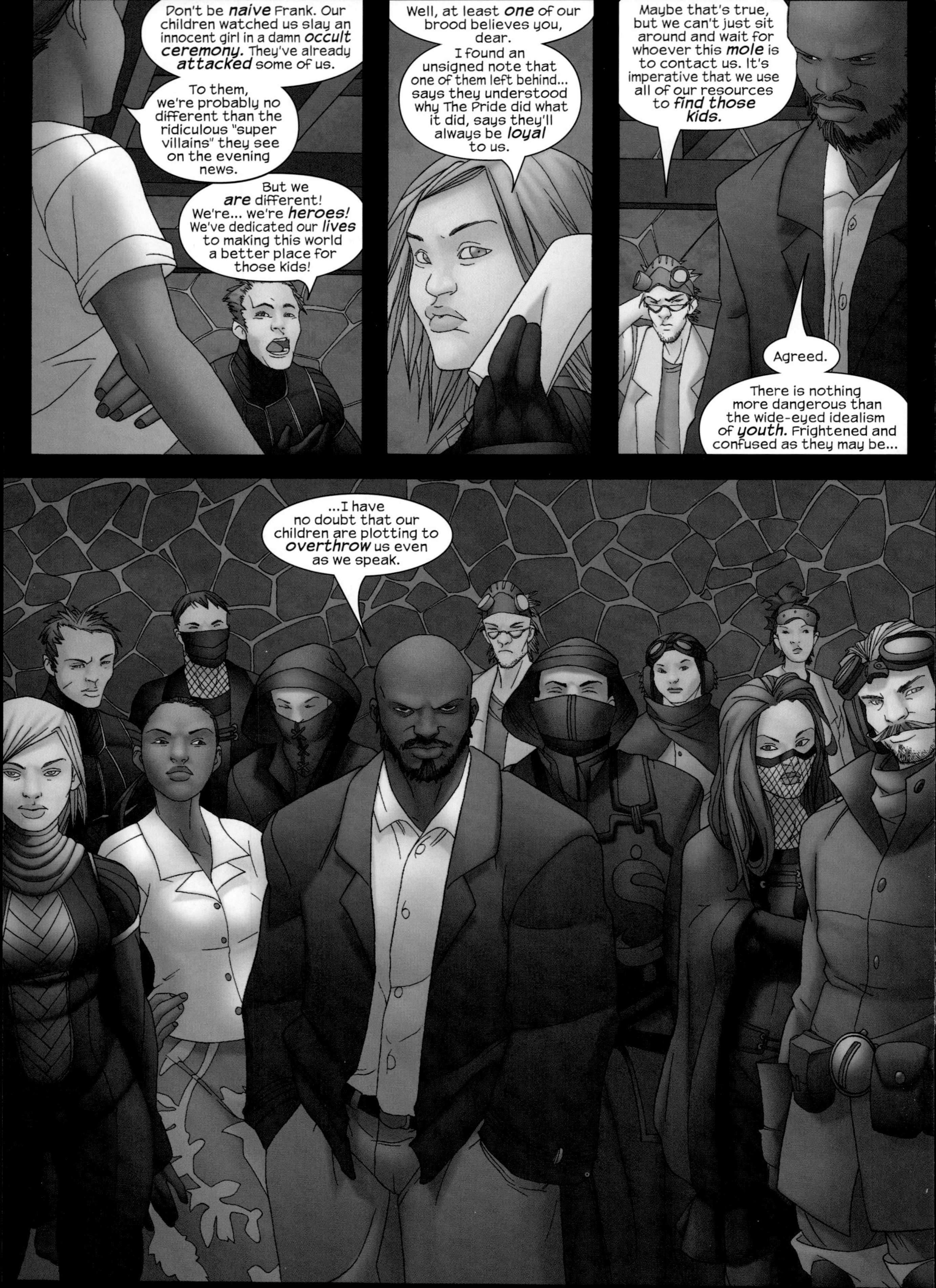

Don't be naive Frank. Our children watched us slay an innocent girl in a damn occult ceremony. They've already attacked some of us.
To them, we're probably no different than the ridiculous "super villains" they see on the evening news.
But we are different! We're... we're heroes! We've dedicated our lives to making this world a better place for those kids!
Well, at least one of our brood believes you, dear.
I found an unsigned note that one of them left behind... says they understood why The Pride did what it did, says they'll always be loyal to us.
Maybe that's true, but we can't just sit around and wait for whoever this mole is to contact us. It's imperative that we use all of our resources to find those kids.
Agreed.
There is nothing more dangerous than the wide-eyed idealism of youth. Frightened and confused as they may be...
...I have no doubt that our children are plotting to overthrow us even as we speak.

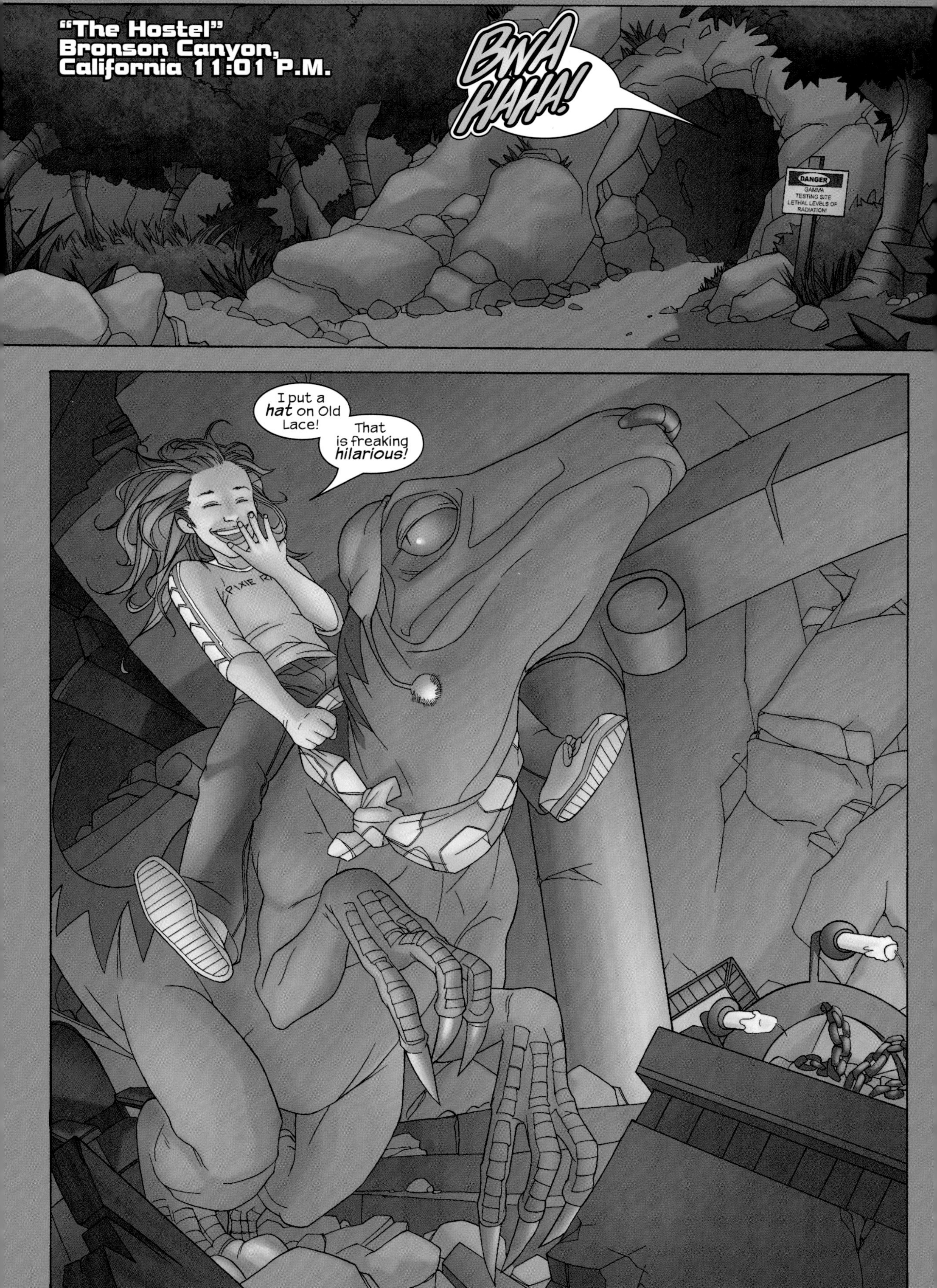
"The Hostel"
Bronson Canyon, California 11:01 P.M.
BWA HAHA!
DANGER
GAMMA TESTING SITE
LETHAL LEVELS OF RADIATION!
I put a *hat* on Old Lace!
That is freaking *hilarious!*

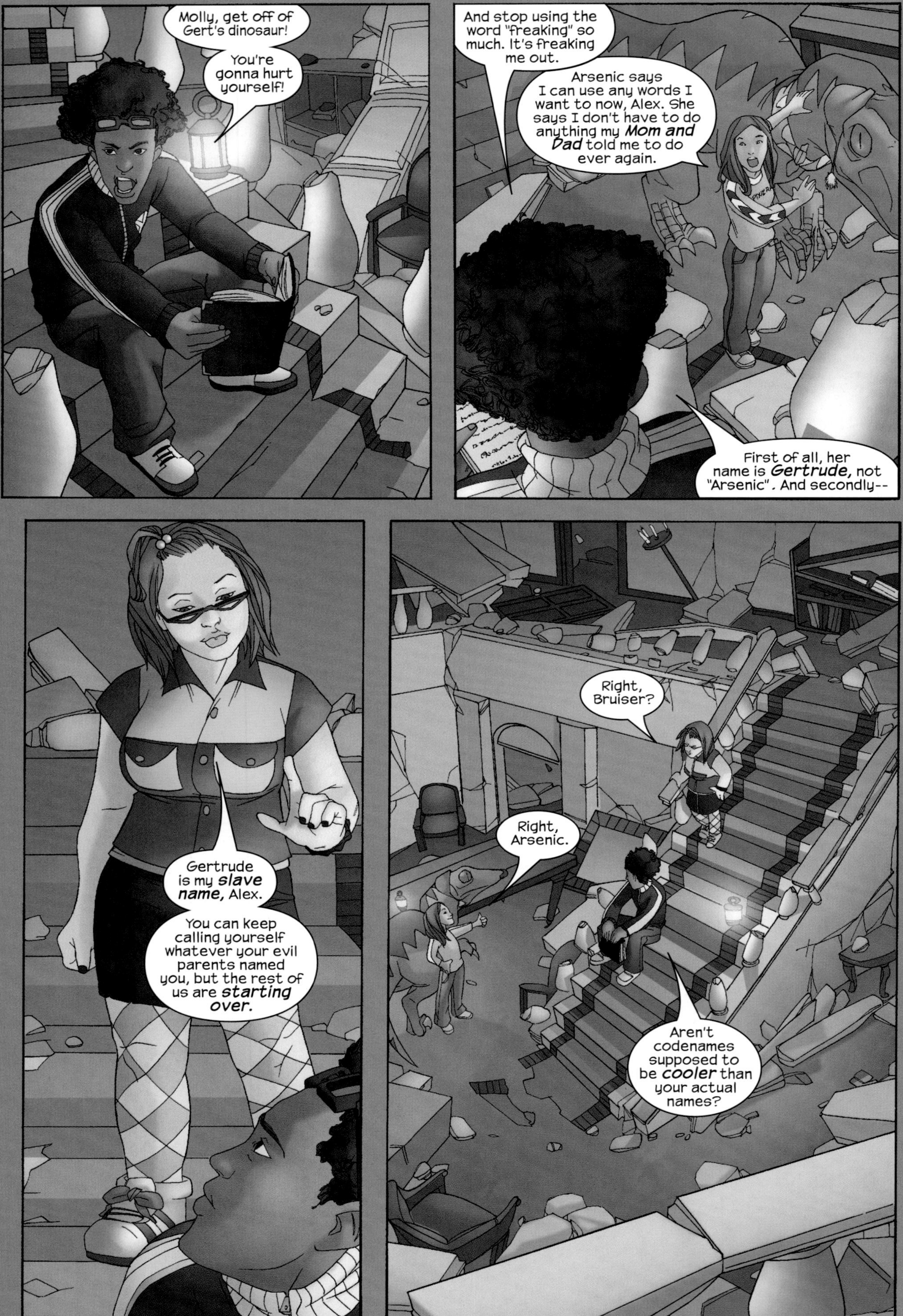

Molly, get off of Gert's dinosaur!
You're gonna hurt yourself!
And stop using the word "freaking" so much. It's freaking me out.
Arsenic says I can use any words I want to now, Alex. She says I don't have to do anything my *Mom and Dad* told me to do ever again.
First of all, her name is *Gertrude,* not "Arsenic". And secondly--
Gertrude is my *slave name,* Alex.
You can keep calling yourself whatever your evil parents named you, but the rest of us are *starting over.*
Right, Bruiser?
Right, Arsenic.
Aren't codenames supposed to be *cooler* than your actual names?

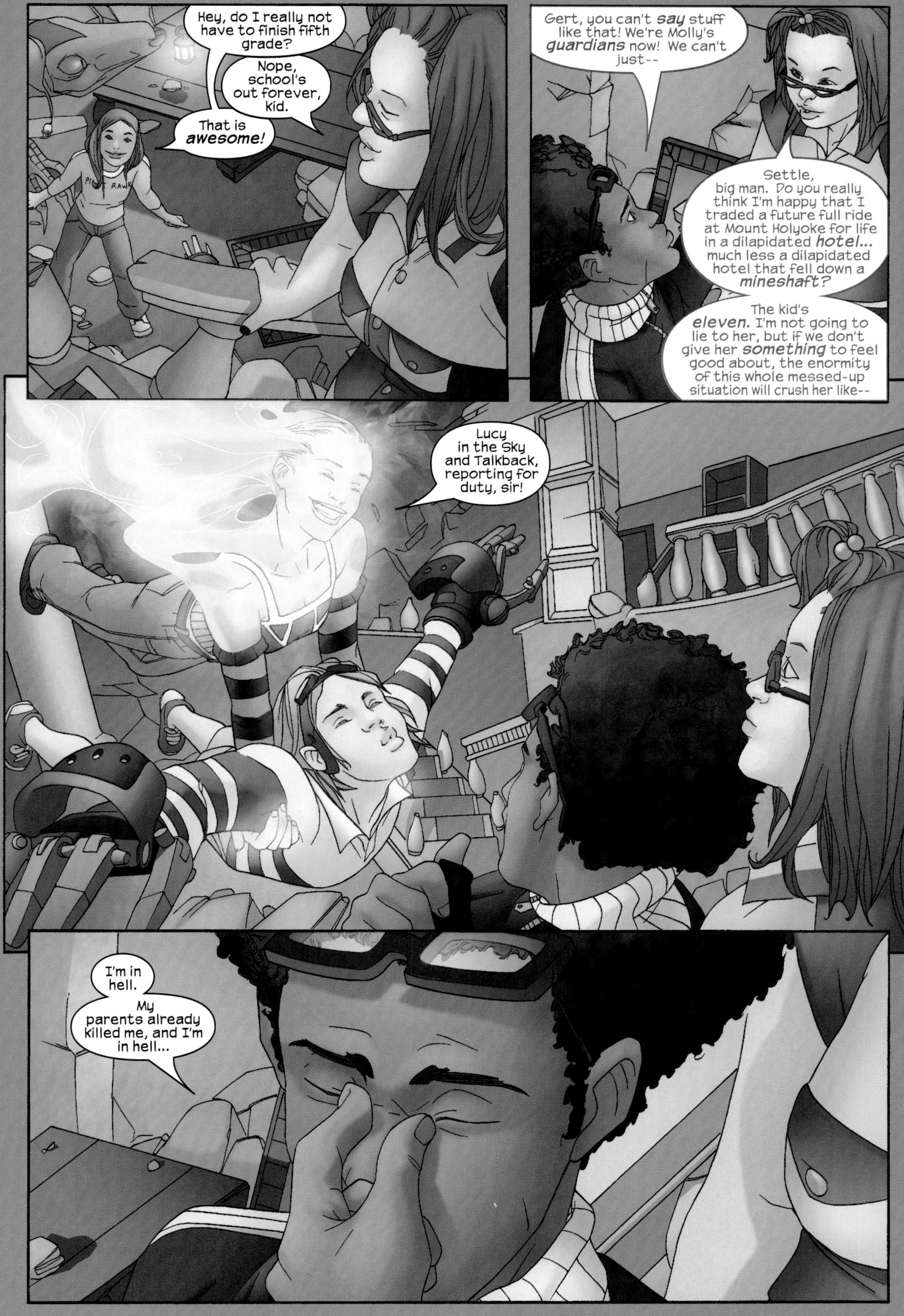
Hey, do I really not have to finish fifth grade?
Nope, school's out forever, kid.
That is ***awesome!***
Gert, you can't ***say*** stuff like that! We're Molly's ***guardians*** now! We can't just--
Settle, big man. Do you really think I'm happy that I traded a future full ride at Mount Holyoke for life in a dilapidated ***hotel...*** much less a dilapidated hotel that fell down a ***mineshaft?***
The kid's ***eleven.*** I'm not going to lie to her, but if we don't give her ***something*** to feel good about, the enormity of this whole messed-up situation will crush her like--
Lucy in the Sky and Talkback, reporting for duty, sir!
I'm in hell.
My parents already killed me, and I'm in hell...

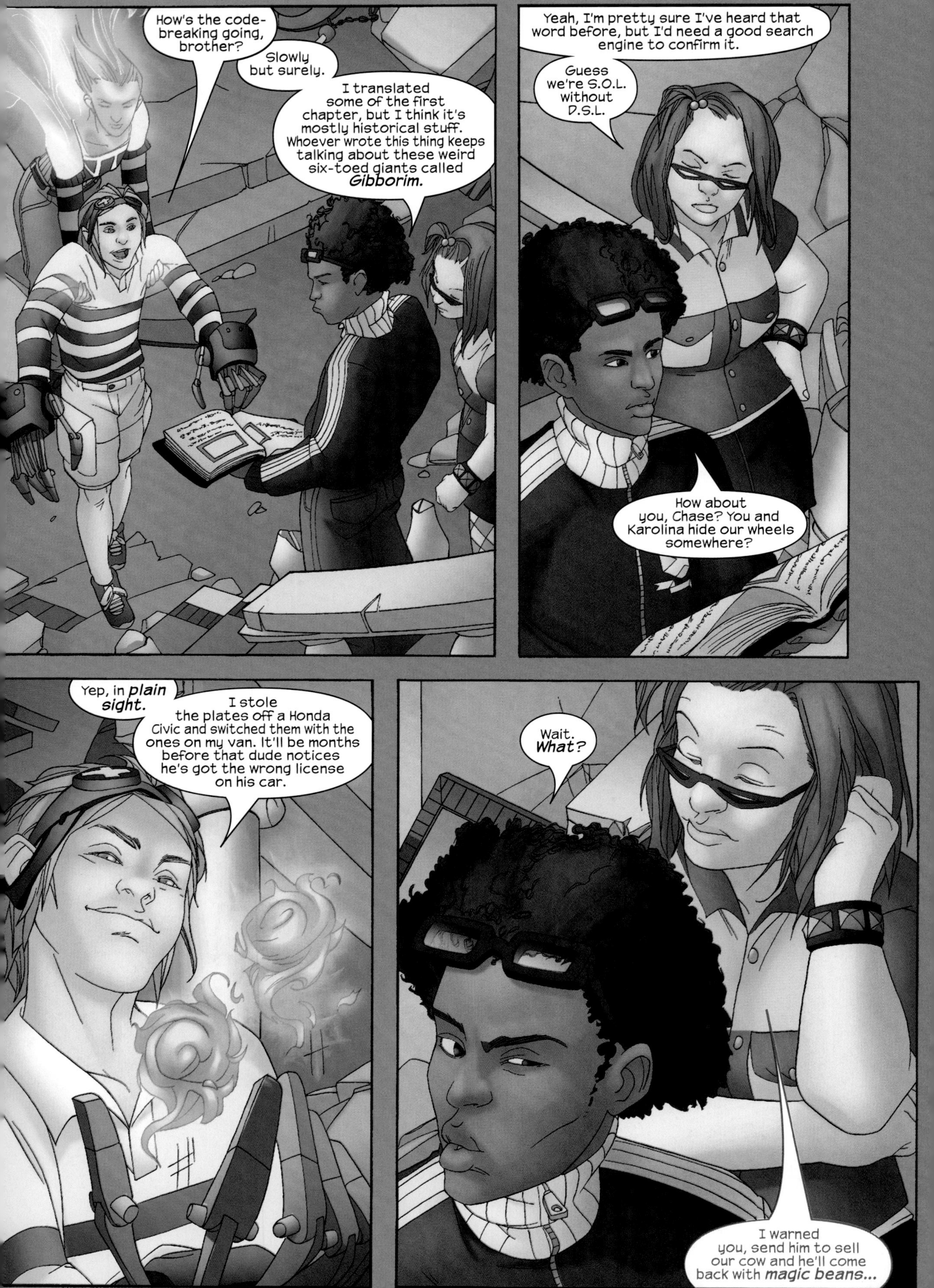
How's the code-breaking going, brother?
Slowly but surely.
I translated some of the first chapter, but I think it's mostly historical stuff. Whoever wrote this thing keeps talking about these weird six-toed giants called *Gibborim.*
Yeah, I'm pretty sure I've heard that word before, but I'd need a good search engine to confirm it.
Guess we're S.O.L. without D.S.L.
How about you, Chase? You and Karolina hide our wheels somewhere?
Yep, in *plain sight.*
I stole the plates off a Honda Civic and switched them with the ones on my van. It'll be months before that dude notices he's got the wrong license on his car.
Wait. *What?*
I warned you, send him to sell our cow and he'll come back with *magic beans...*

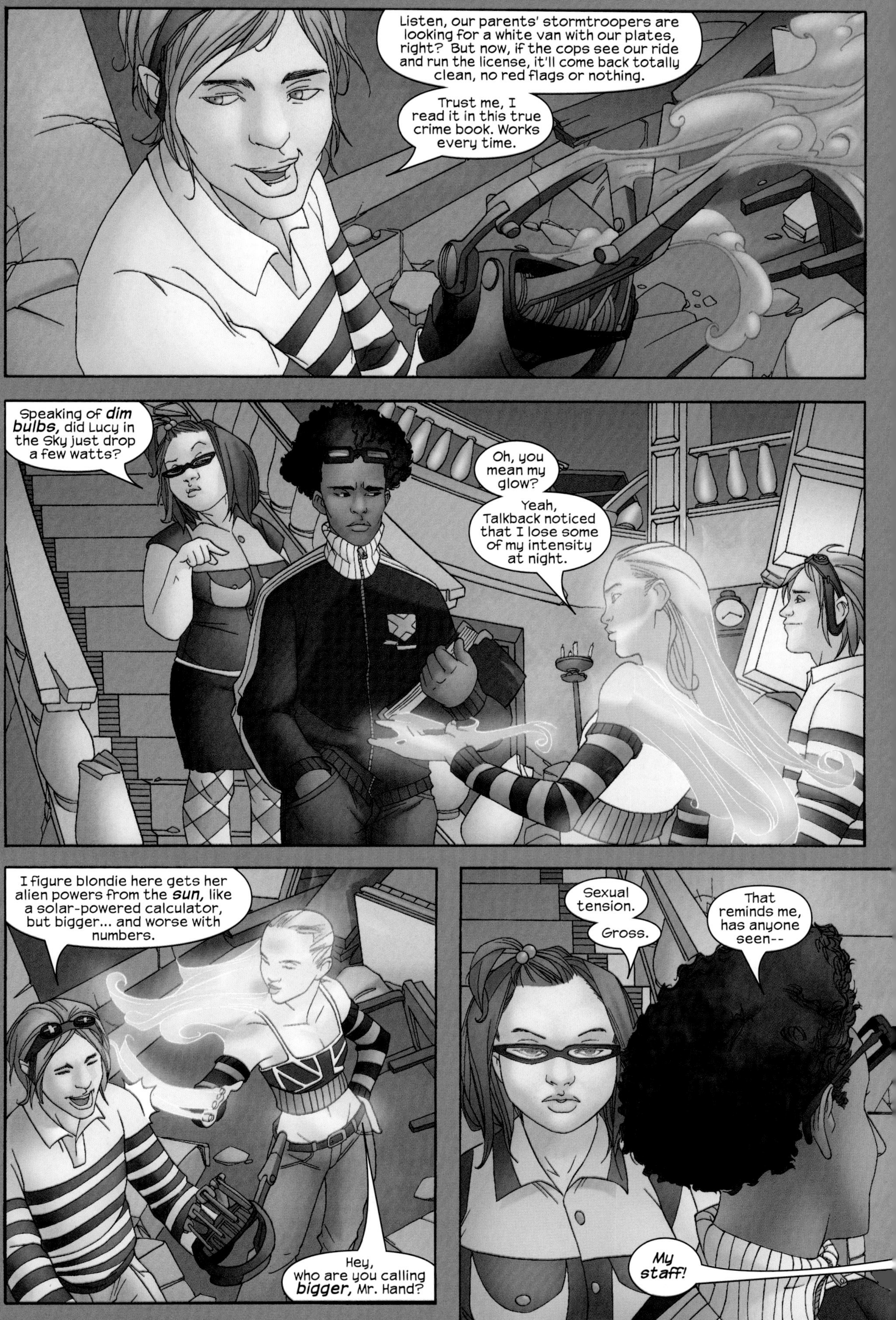

Listen, our parents' stormtroopers are looking for a white van with our plates, right? But now, if the cops see our ride and run the license, it'll come back totally clean, no red flags or nothing.
Trust me, I read it in this true crime book. Works every time.
Speaking of **dim bulbs,** did Lucy in the Sky just drop a few watts?
Oh, you mean my glow?
Yeah, Talkback noticed that I lose some of my intensity at night.
I figure blondie here gets her alien powers from the **sun,** like a solar-powered calculator, but bigger... and worse with numbers.
Hey, who are you calling **bigger,** Mr. Hand?
Sexual tension.
Gross.
That reminds me, has anyone seen--
My staff!

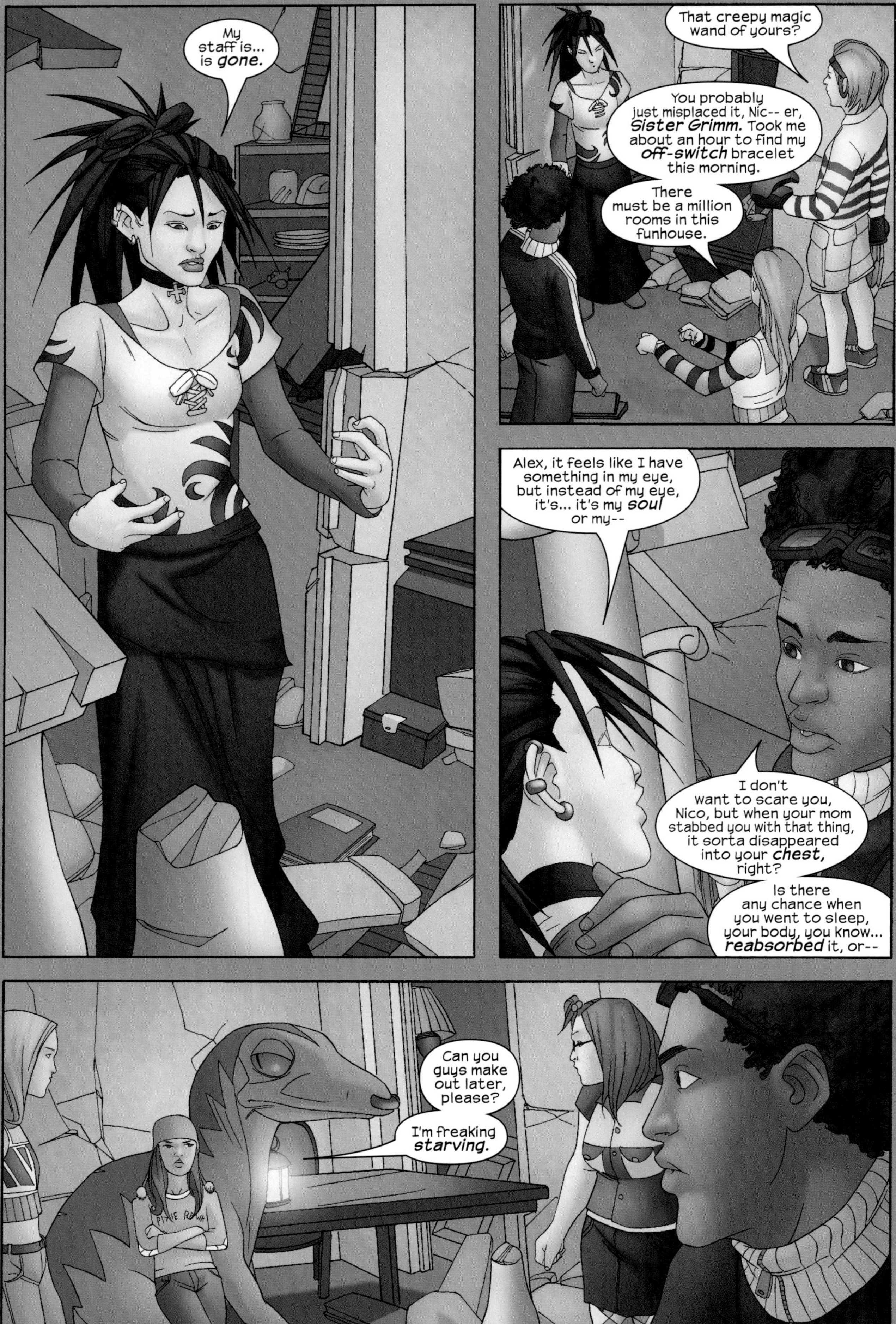
My staff is... is *gone.*
That creepy magic wand of yours?
You probably just misplaced it, Nic-- er, ***Sister Grimm.*** Took me about an hour to find my ***off-switch*** bracelet this morning.
There must be a million rooms in this funhouse.
Alex, it feels like I have something in my eye, but instead of my eye, it's... it's my ***soul*** or my--
I don't want to scare you, Nico, but when your mom stabbed you with that thing, it sorta disappeared into your ***chest,*** right?
Is there any chance when you went to sleep, your body, you know... ***reabsorbed*** it, or--
Can you guys make out later, please?
I'm freaking ***starving.***

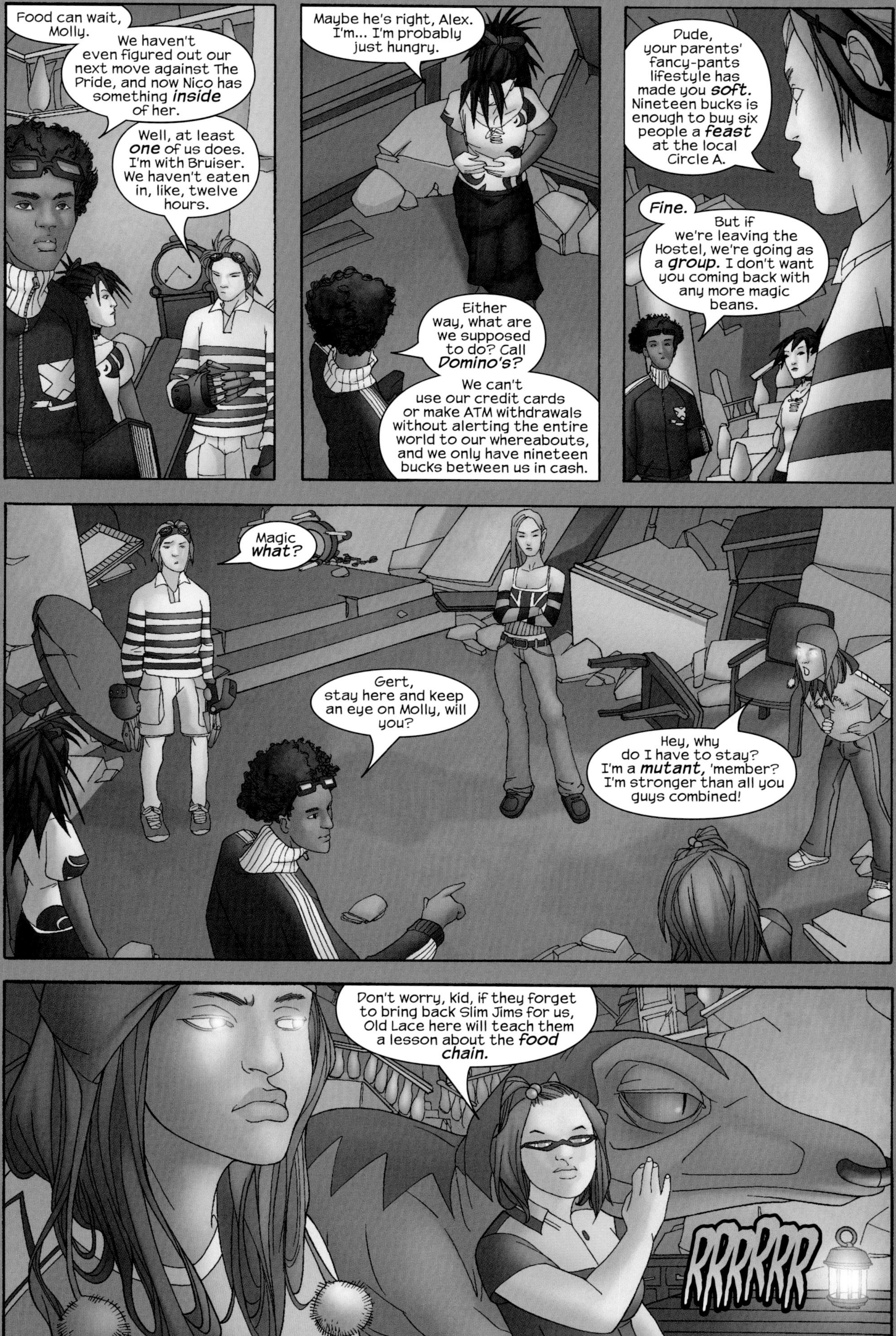
Food can wait, Molly.
We haven't even figured out our next move against The Pride, and now Nico has something *inside* of her.
Well, at least *one* of us does. I'm with Bruiser. We haven't eaten in, like, twelve hours.
Maybe he's right, Alex. I'm... I'm probably just hungry.
Either way, what are we supposed to do? Call *Domino's?*
We can't use our credit cards or make ATM withdrawals without alerting the entire world to our whereabouts, and we only have nineteen bucks between us in cash.
Dude, your parents' fancy-pants lifestyle has made you *soft.* Nineteen bucks is enough to buy six people a *feast* at the local Circle A.
Fine.
But if we're leaving the Hostel, we're going as a *group.* I don't want you coming back with any more magic beans.
Magic *what?*
Gert, stay here and keep an eye on Molly, will you?
Hey, why do I have to stay? I'm a *mutant,* 'member? I'm stronger than all you guys combined!
Don't worry, kid, if they forget to bring back Slim Jims for us, Old Lace here will teach them a lesson about the *food chain.*
RRRRRR

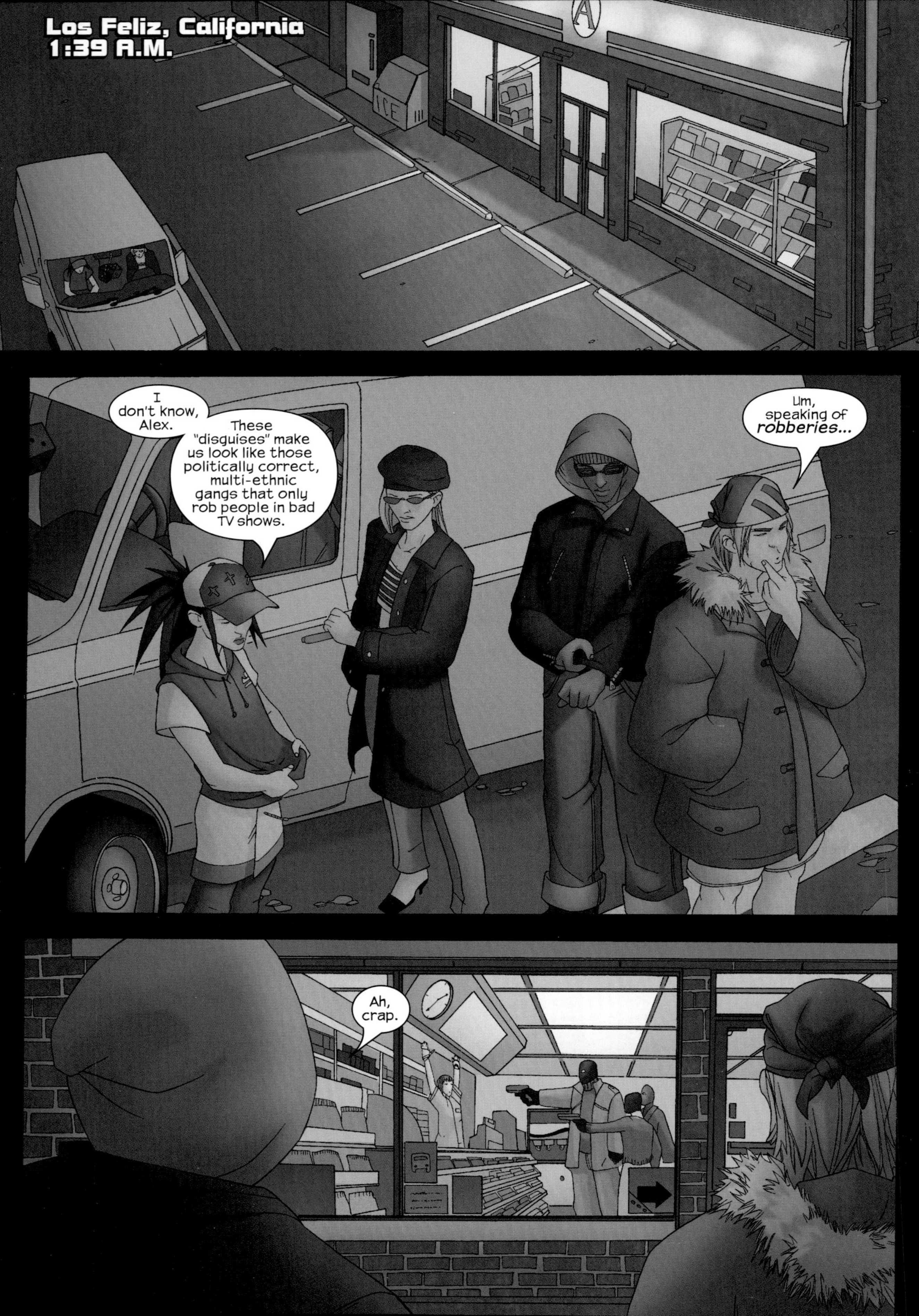
Los Feliz, California 1:39 A.M.
ICE
I don't know, Alex.
These "disguises" make us look like those politically correct, multi-ethnic gangs that only rob people in bad TV shows.
Um, speaking of robberies...
Ah, crap.

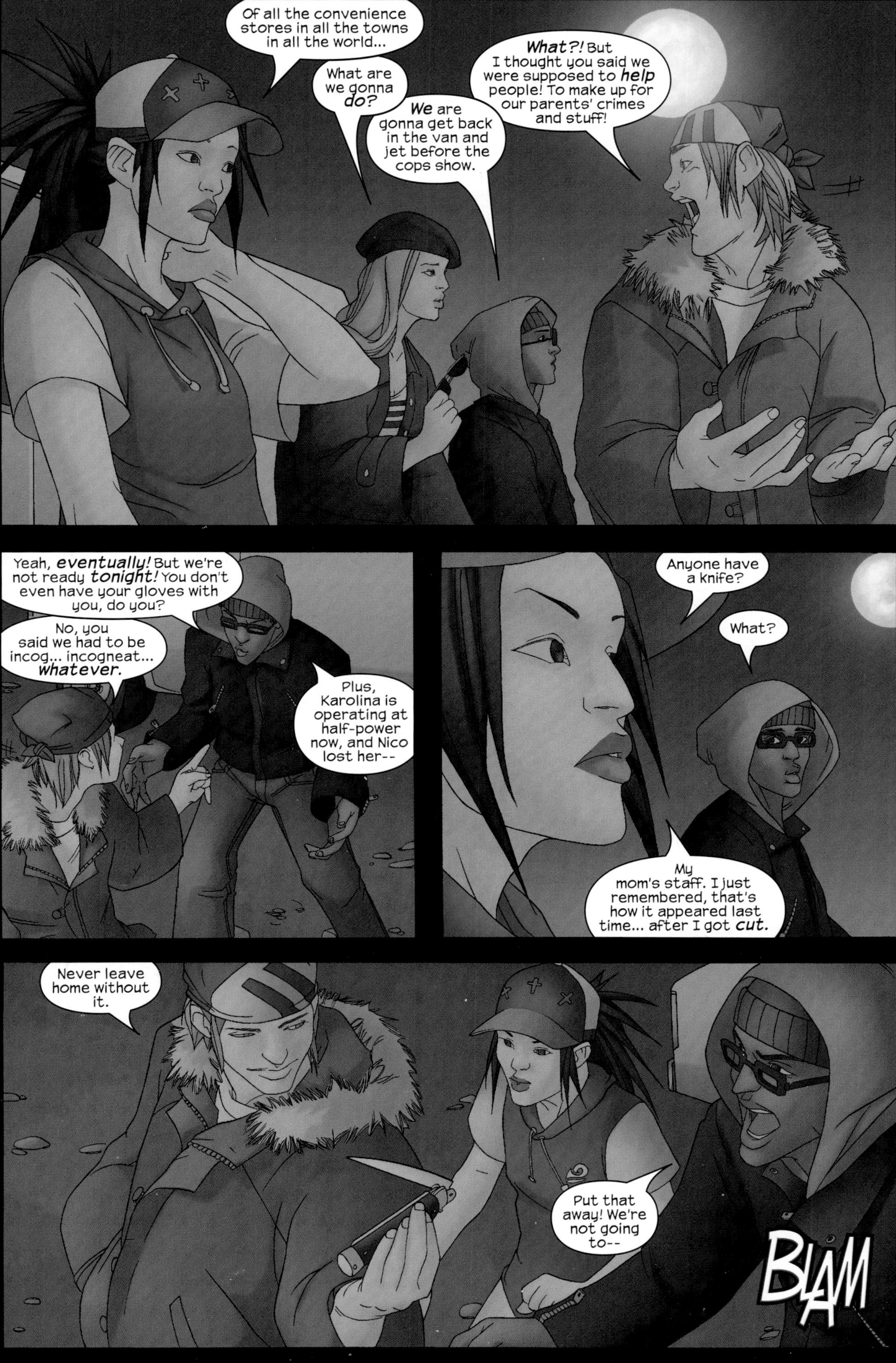

Of all the convenience stores in all the towns in all the world...
What are we gonna *do?*
We are gonna get back in the van and jet before the cops show.
What?! But I thought you said we were supposed to *help* people! To make up for our parents' crimes and stuff!
Yeah, *eventually!* But we're not ready *tonight!* You don't even have your gloves with you, do you?
No, you said we had to be incog... incogneat... *whatever.*
Plus, Karolina is operating at half-power now, and Nico lost her--
Anyone have a knife?
What?
My mom's staff. I just remembered, that's how it appeared last time... after I got *cut.*
Never leave home without it.
Put that away! We're not going to--
BLAM

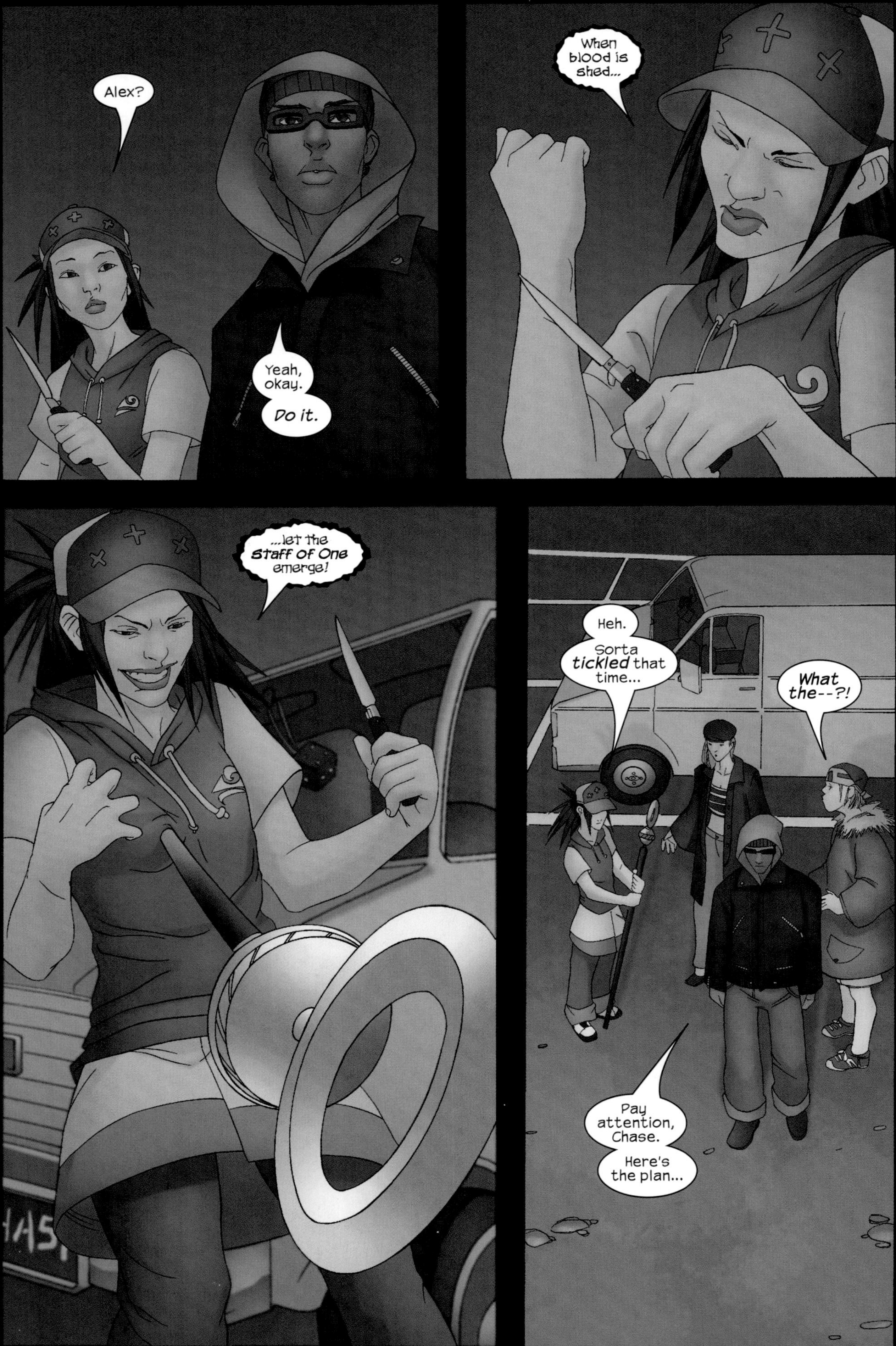
Alex?
Yeah, okay.
Do it.
When blood is shed...
...let the Staff of One emerge!
Heh. Sorta tickled that time...
What the--?!
Pay attention, Chase.
Here's the plan...

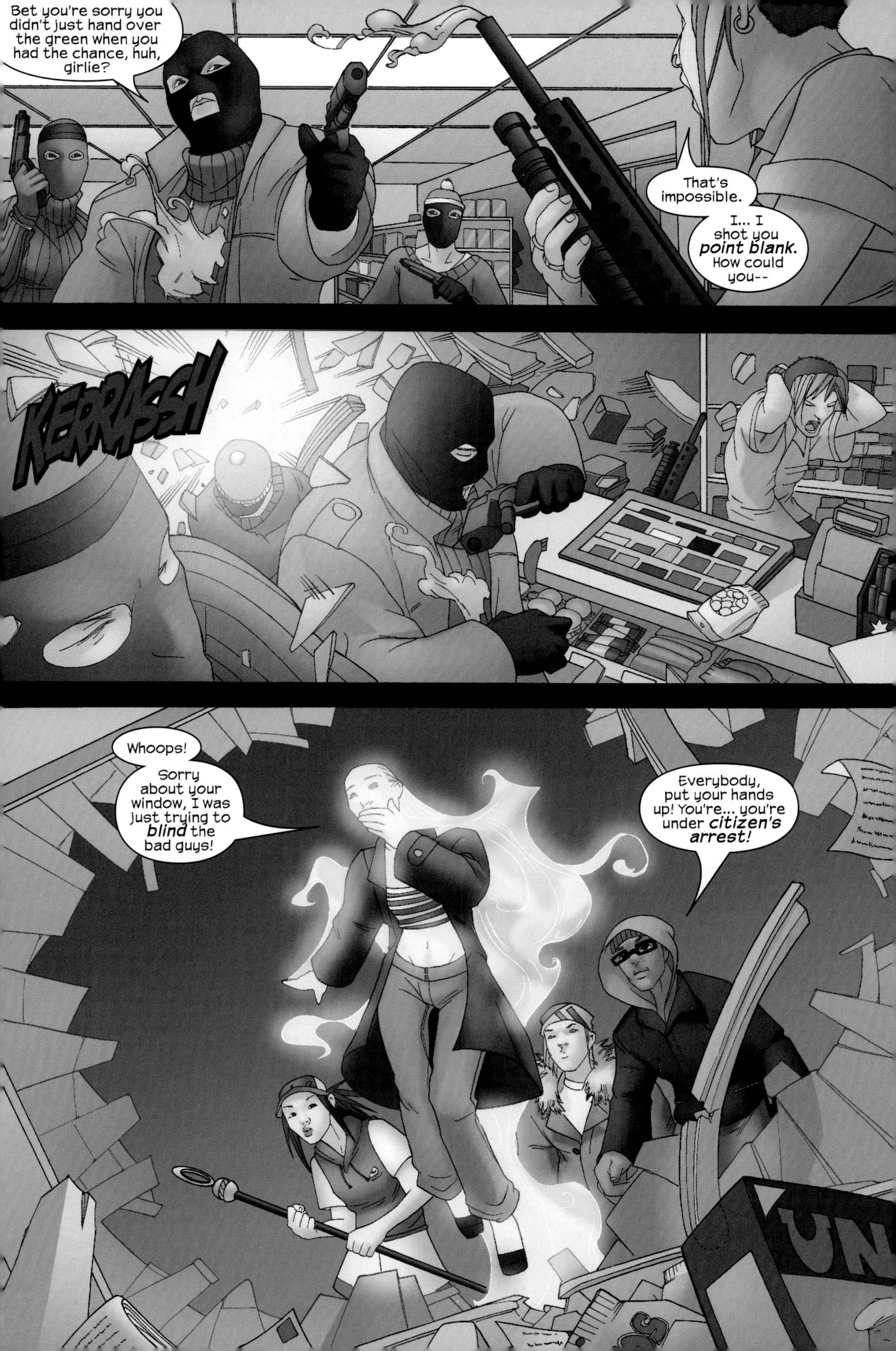

Bet you're sorry you didn't just hand over the green when you had the chance, huh, girlie?
That's impossible.
I... I shot you point blank. How could you--
KERRASSH
Whoops!
Sorry about your window, I was just trying to blind the bad guys!
Everybody, put your hands up! You're... you're under citizen's arrest!

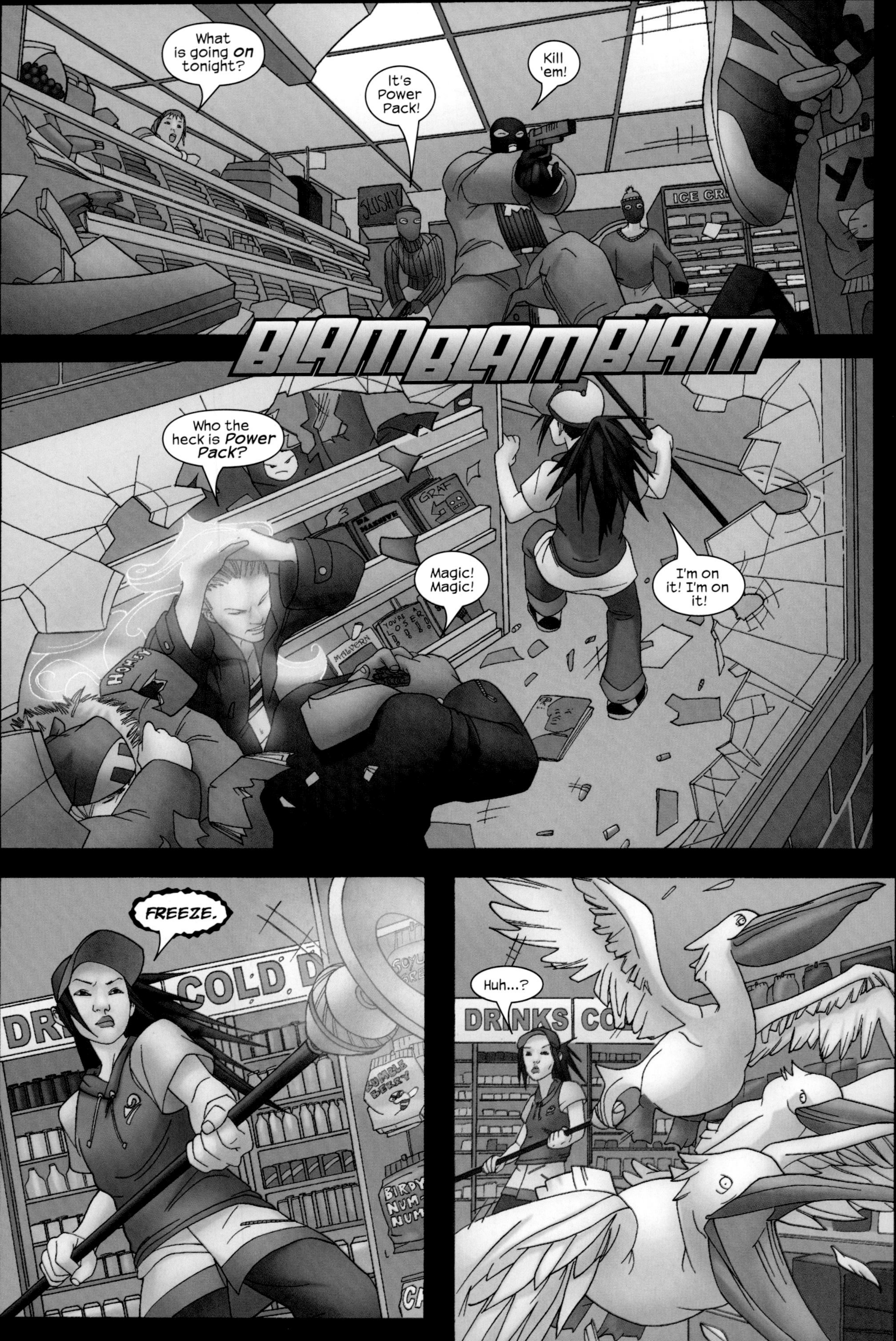
What is going *on* tonight?
It's Power Pack!
Kill 'em!
SLUSHY
ICE CR
BLAMBLAMBLAM
Who the heck is *Power Pack?*
GRAF
Magic! Magic!
I'm on it! I'm on it!
HONEY
FREEZE.
COLD D
DR
BIRDY NUM-NUM
Huh...?
DRNKS CO

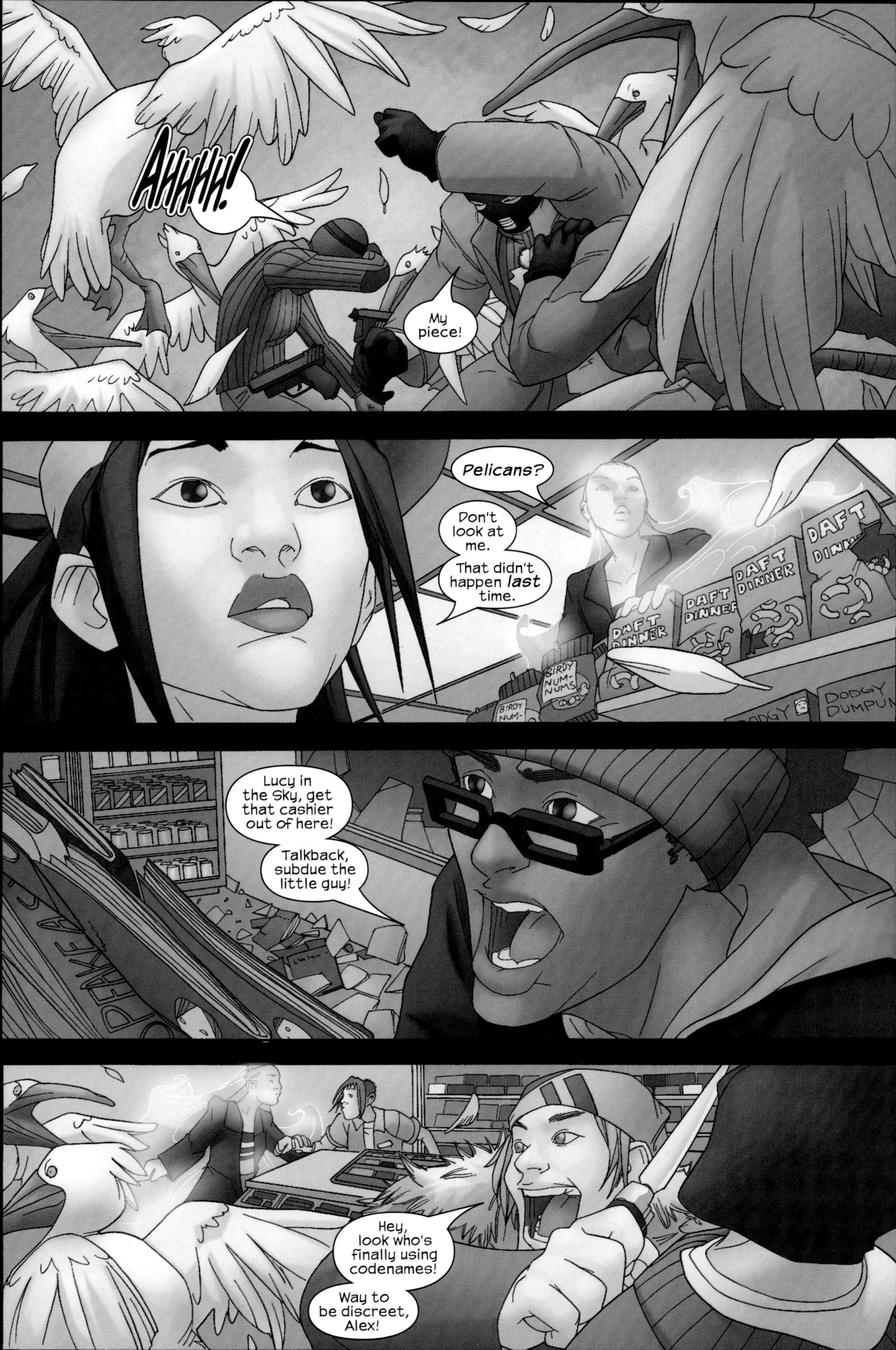
AHHHH!
My piece!
Pelicans?
Don't look at me.
That didn't happen *last* time.
DAFT DINNER
BIRDY NUM-NUMS
DODGY DUMPUM
Lucy in the Sky, get that cashier out of here!
Talkback, subdue the little guy!
Hey, look who's finally using codenames!
Way to be discreet, Alex!

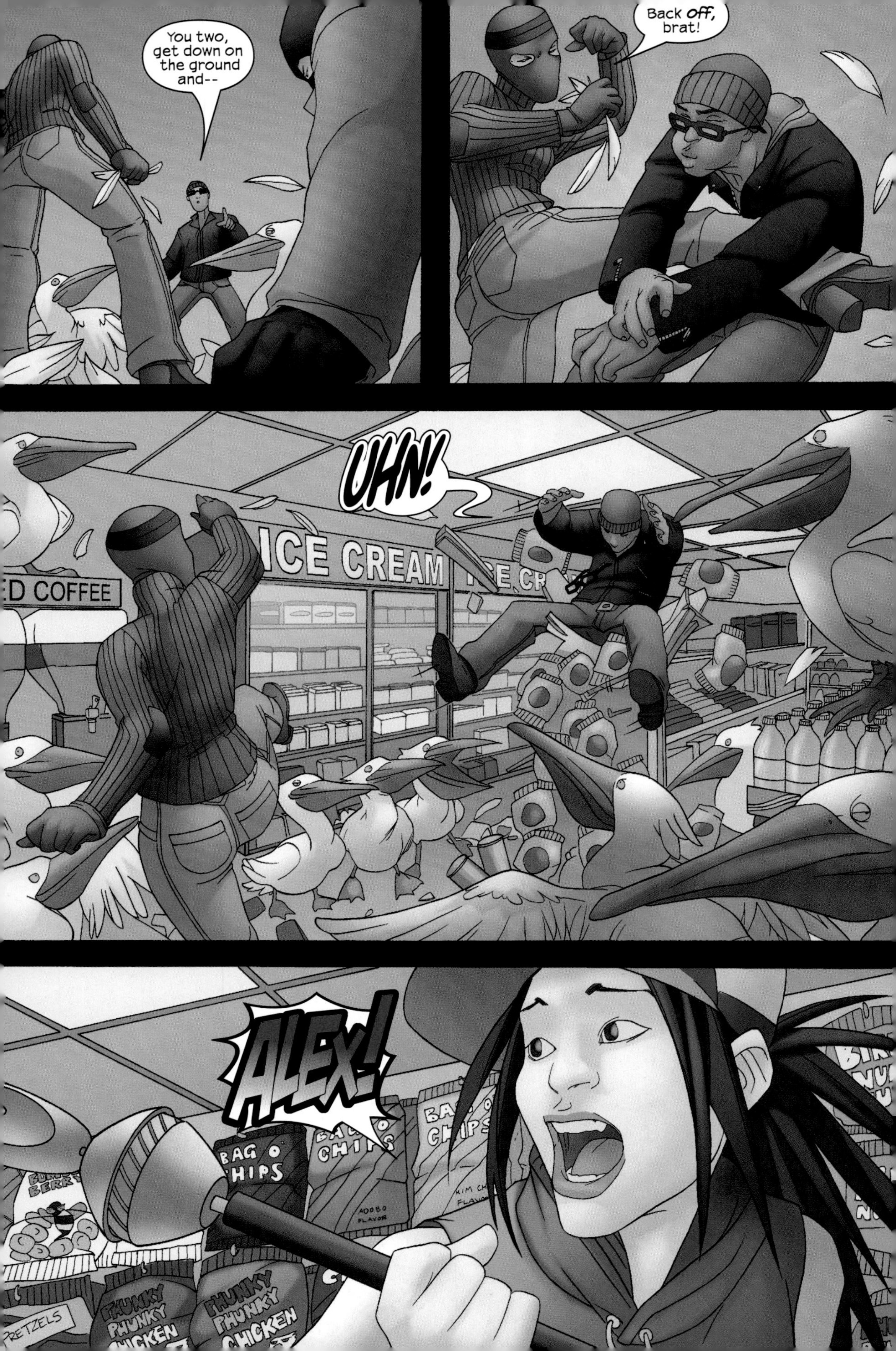
You two, get down on the ground and--
Back off, brat!
UHN!
ICE CREAM
ED COFFEE
ALEX!
BAG O' CHIPS
ADOBO FLAVOR
KIM CHI FLAVOR
CHUNKY PHUNKY CHICKEN
PRETZELS

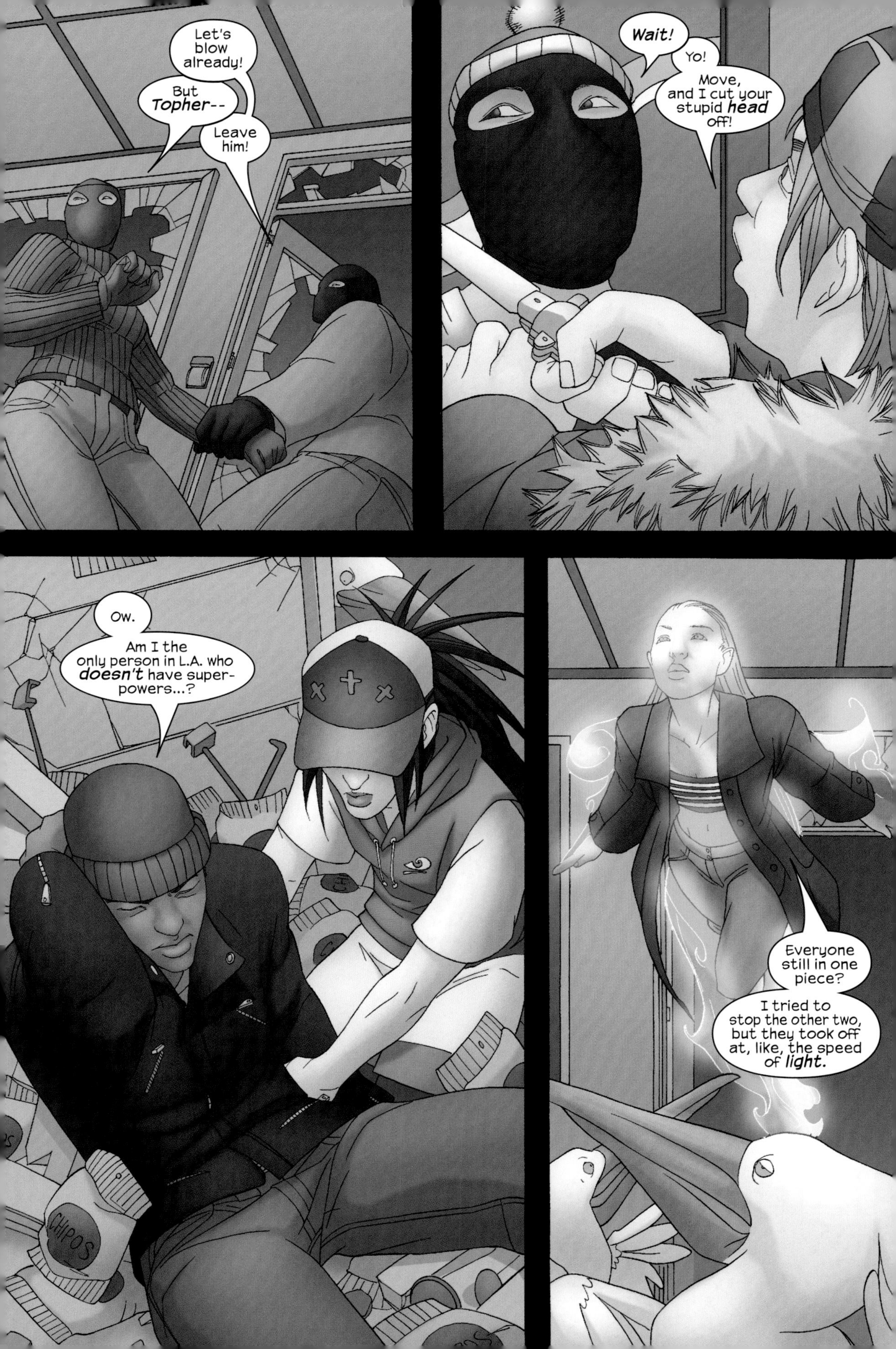
Let's blow already!
But Topher--
Leave him!
Wait!
Yo!
Move, and I cut your stupid head off!
Ow.
Am I the only person in L.A. who doesn't have super-powers...?
Everyone still in one piece?
I tried to stop the other two, but they took off at, like, the speed of light.
CHIPOS

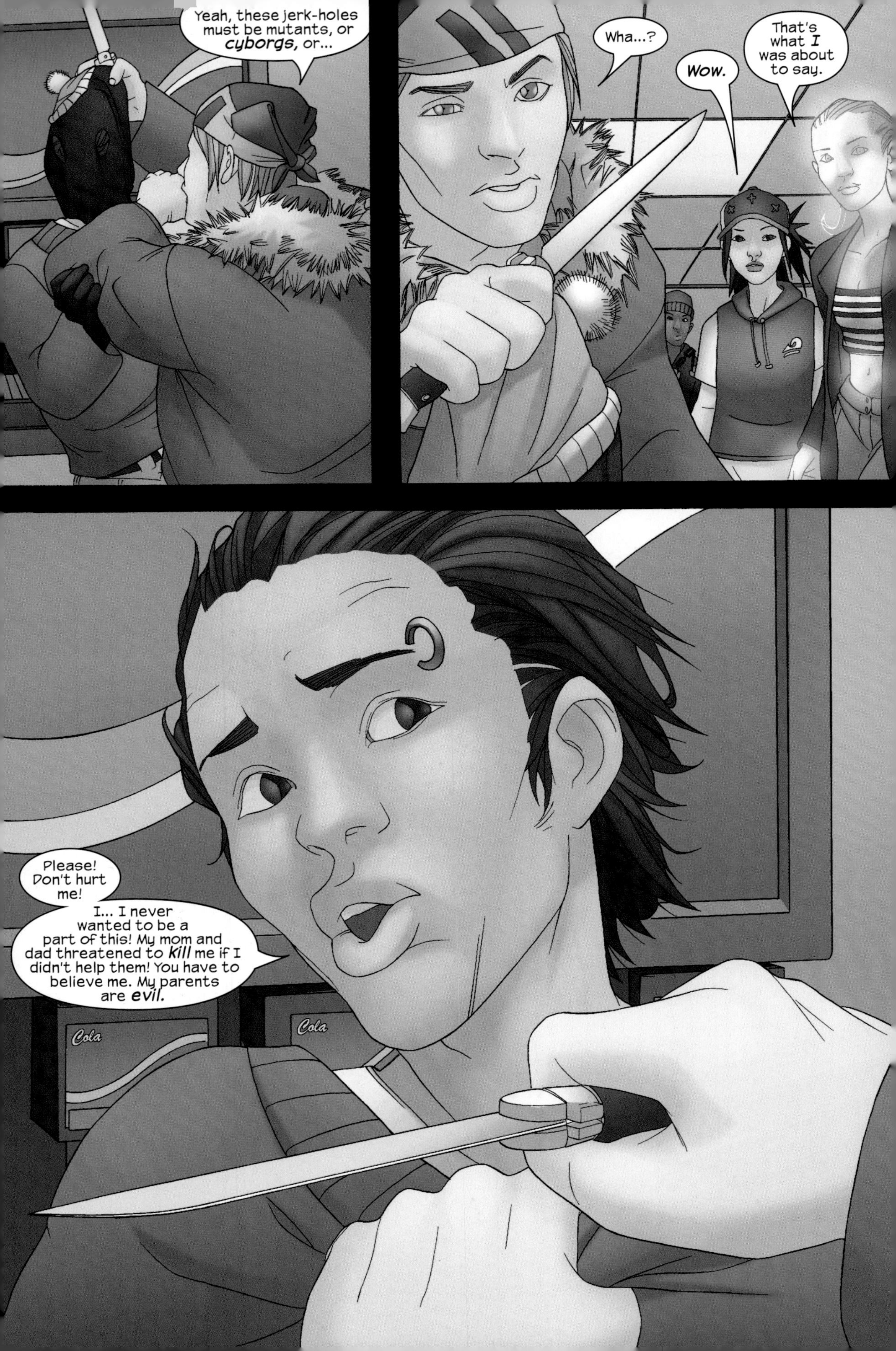
Yeah, these jerk-holes must be mutants, or *cyborgs,* or...
Wha...?
Wow.
That's what *I* was about to say.
Please! Don't hurt me!
I... I never wanted to be a part of this! My mom and dad threatened to *kill* me if I didn't help them! You have to believe me. My parents are *evil.*
Cola
Cola

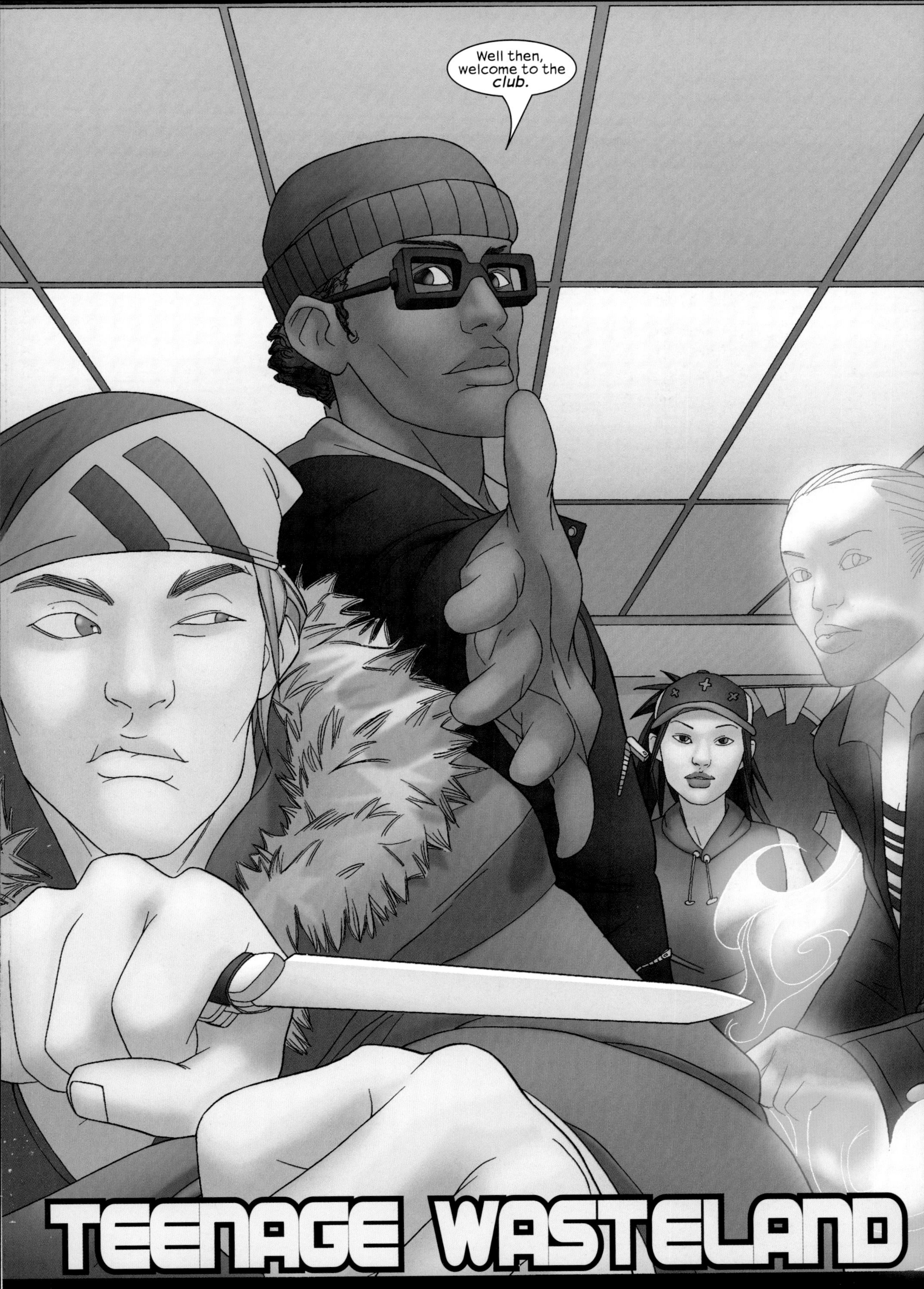
Well then, welcome to the *club.*
TEENAGE WASTELAND

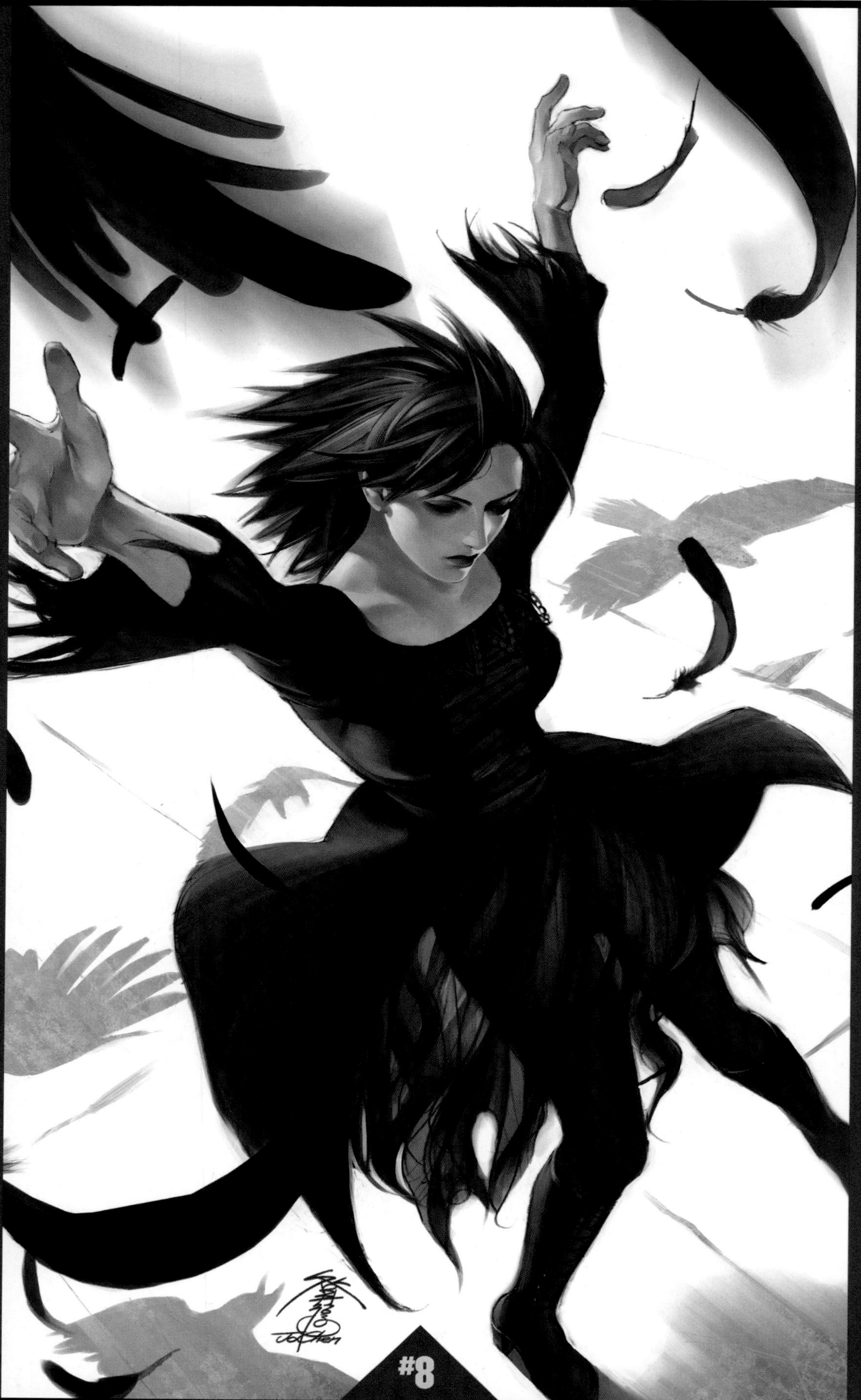
#8

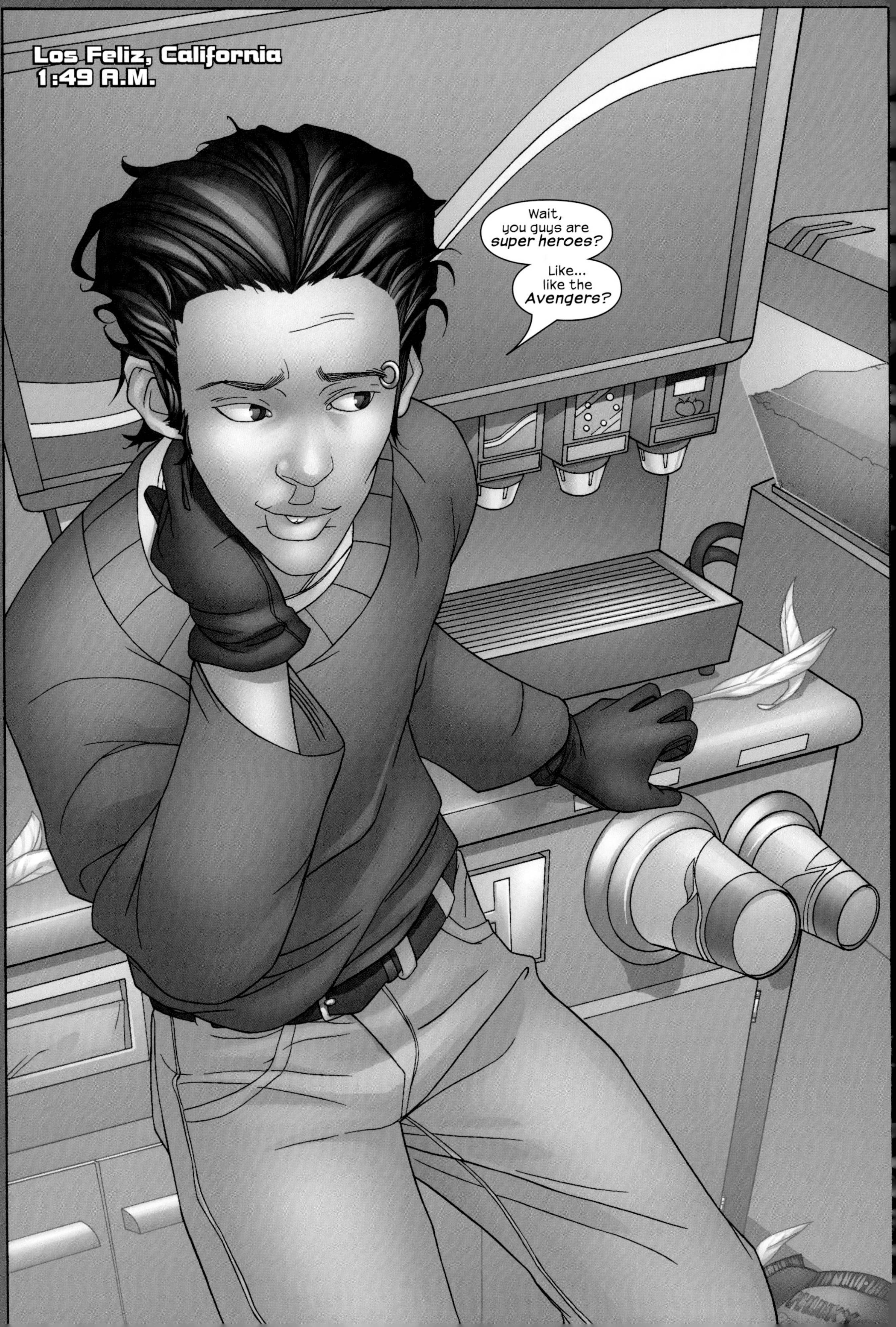
Los Feliz, California
1:49 A.M.
Wait, you guys are super heroes?
Like... like the Avengers?

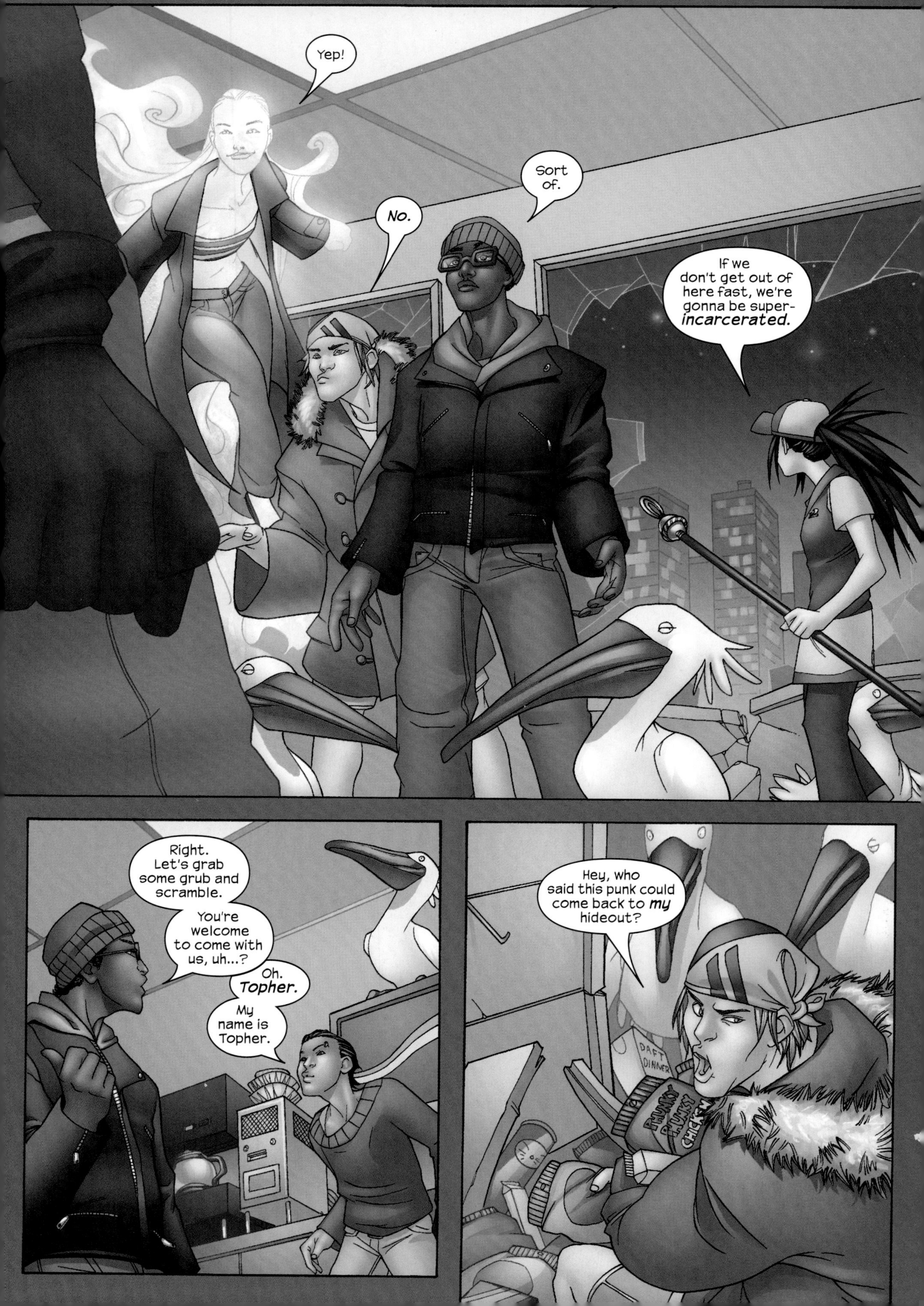
Yep!
No.
Sort of.
If we don't get out of here fast, we're gonna be super-*incarcerated.*
Right. Let's grab some grub and scramble.
You're welcome to come with us, uh...?
Oh. *Topher.*
My name is Topher.
Hey, who said this punk could come back to *my* hideout?
DAFT DINNER
PHUNKY PHUNKY CHICK-N

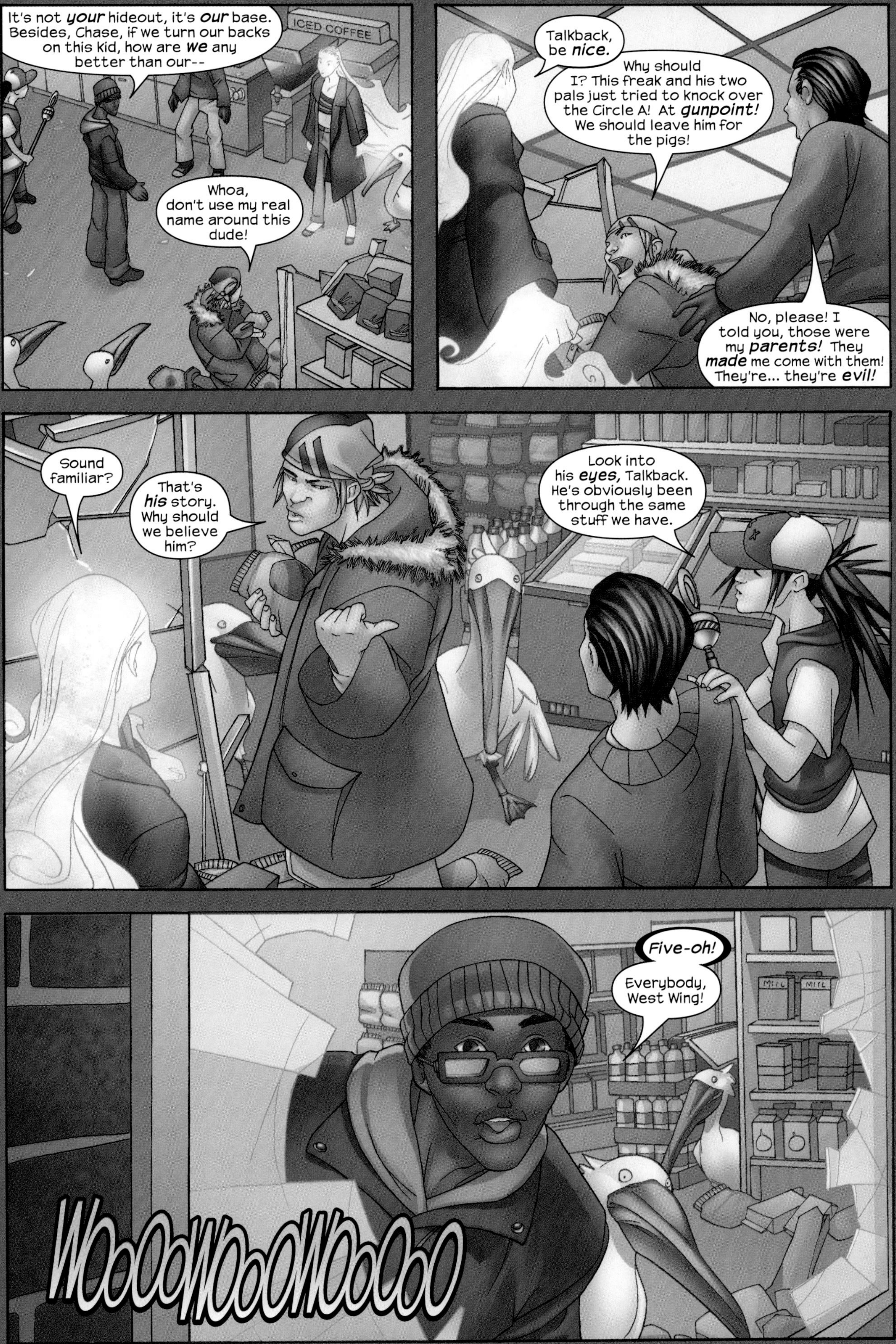
It's not your hideout, it's our base. Besides, Chase, if we turn our backs on this kid, how are we any better than our--
Whoa, don't use my real name around this dude!
Talkback, be nice.
Why should I? This freak and his two pals just tried to knock over the Circle A! At gunpoint! We should leave him for the pigs!
No, please! I told you, those were my parents! They made me come with them! They're... they're evil!
ICED COFFEE
Sound familiar?
That's his story. Why should we believe him?
Look into his eyes, Talkback. He's obviously been through the same stuff we have.
Five-oh!
Everybody, West Wing!
WOoOoWOoOWOoOoO

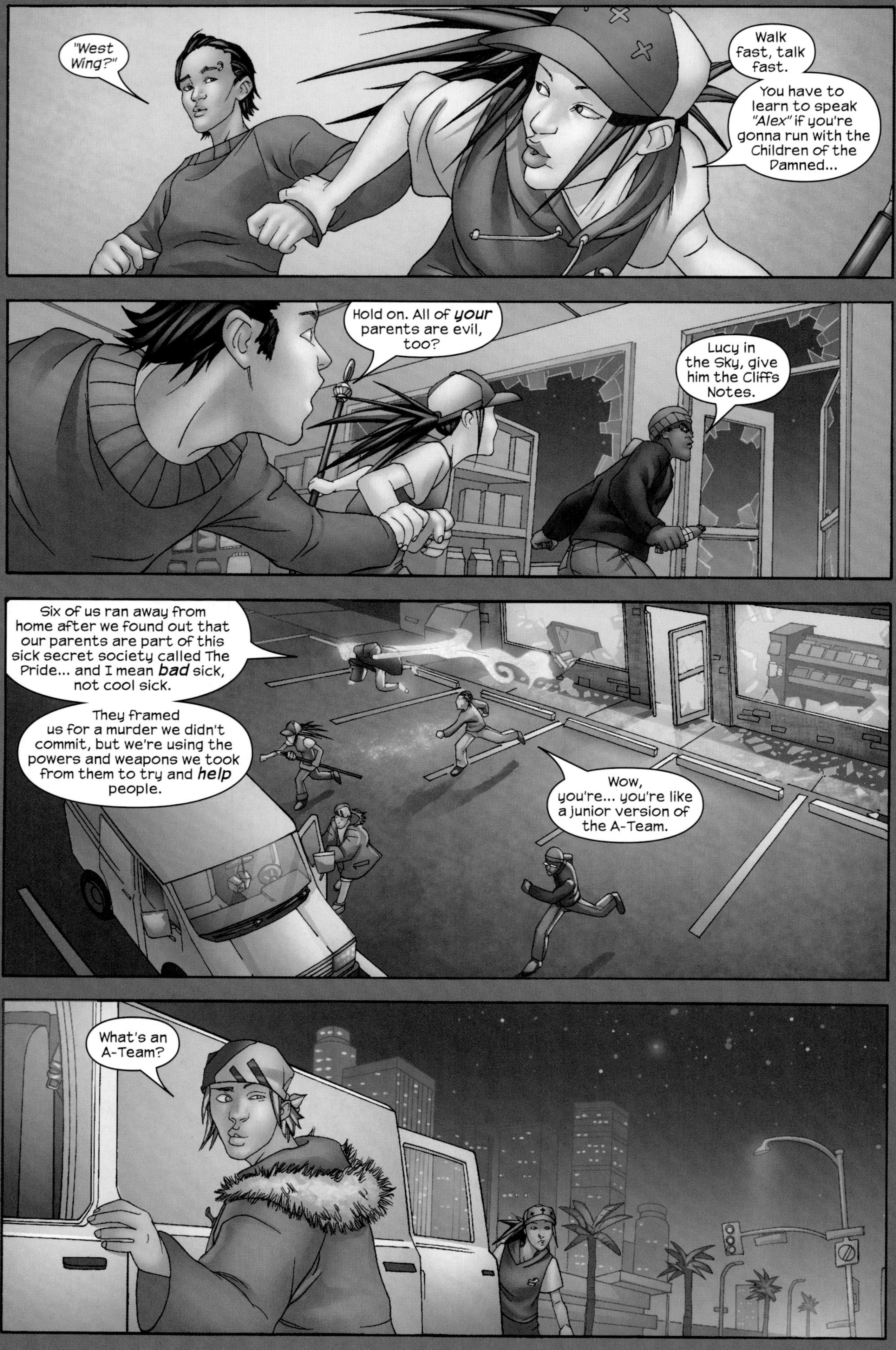
"West Wing?"
Walk fast, talk fast.
You have to learn to speak "Alex" if you're gonna run with the Children of the Damned...
Hold on. All of *your* parents are evil, too?
Lucy in the Sky, give him the Cliffs Notes.
Six of us ran away from home after we found out that our parents are part of this sick secret society called The Pride... and I mean ***bad*** sick, not cool sick.
They framed us for a murder we didn't commit, but we're using the powers and weapons we took from them to try and ***help*** people.
Wow, you're... you're like a junior version of the A-Team.
What's an A-Team?

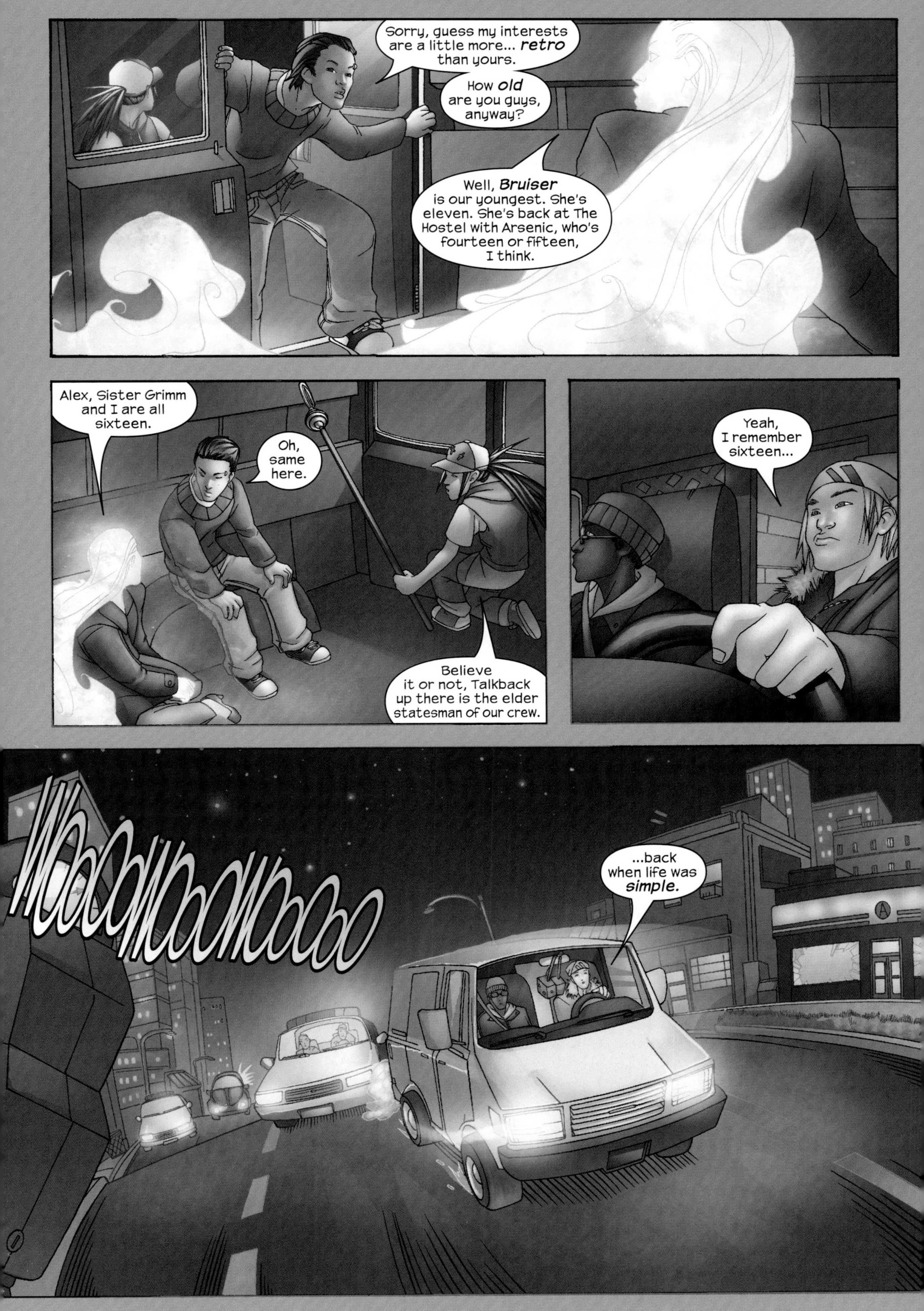
Sorry, guess my interests are a little more... retro than yours.
How old are you guys, anyway?
Well, Bruiser is our youngest. She's eleven. She's back at The Hostel with Arsenic, who's fourteen or fifteen, I think.
Alex, Sister Grimm and I are all sixteen.
Oh, same here.
Believe it or not, Talkback up there is the elder statesman of our crew.
Yeah, I remember sixteen...
WOOOWOOOWOOOOO
...back when life was simple.

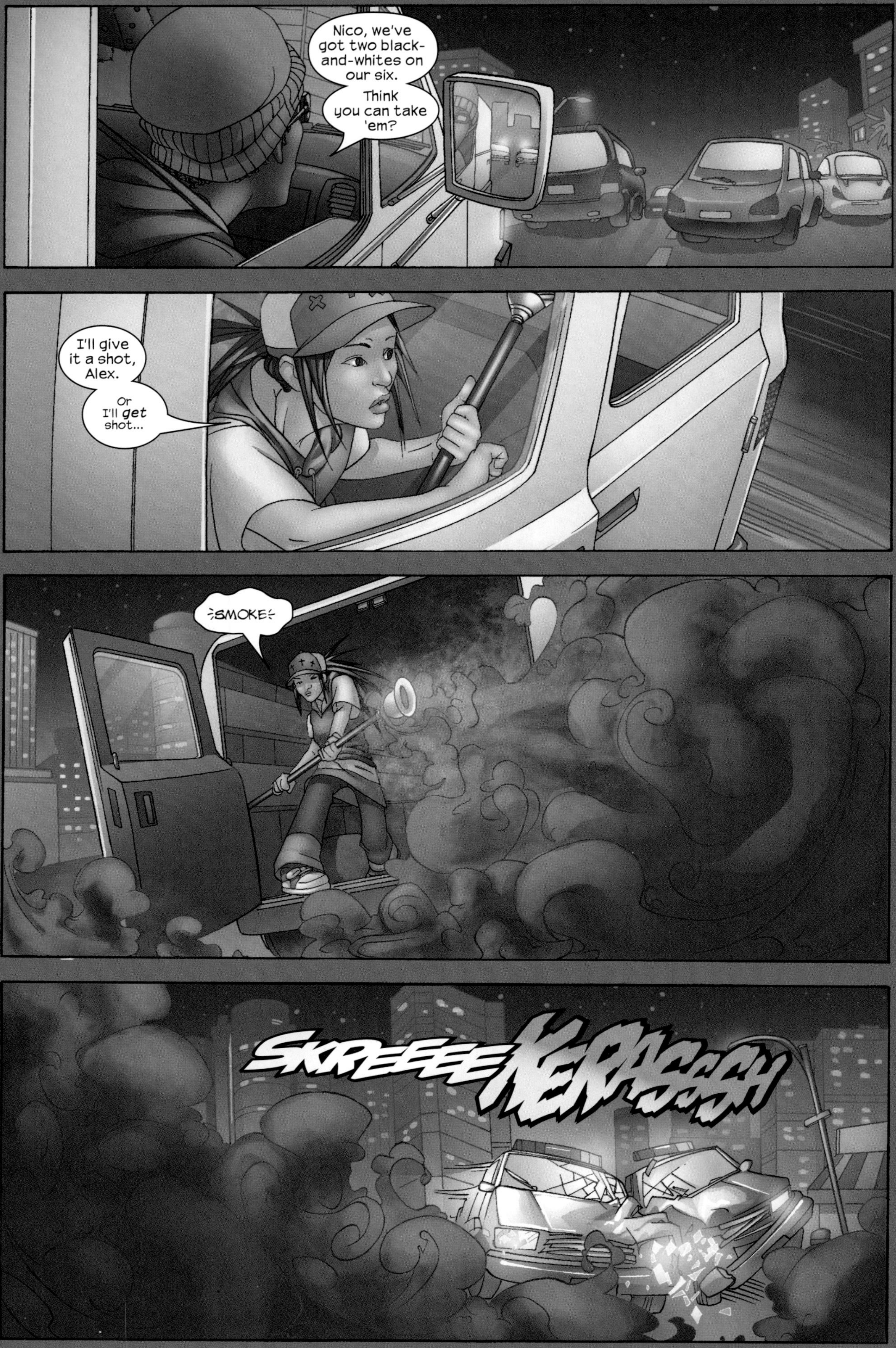
Nico, we've got two black-and-whites on our six.
Think you can take 'em?
I'll give it a shot, Alex.
Or I'll *get* shot...
SMOKE
SKREEEEE KERASSSH

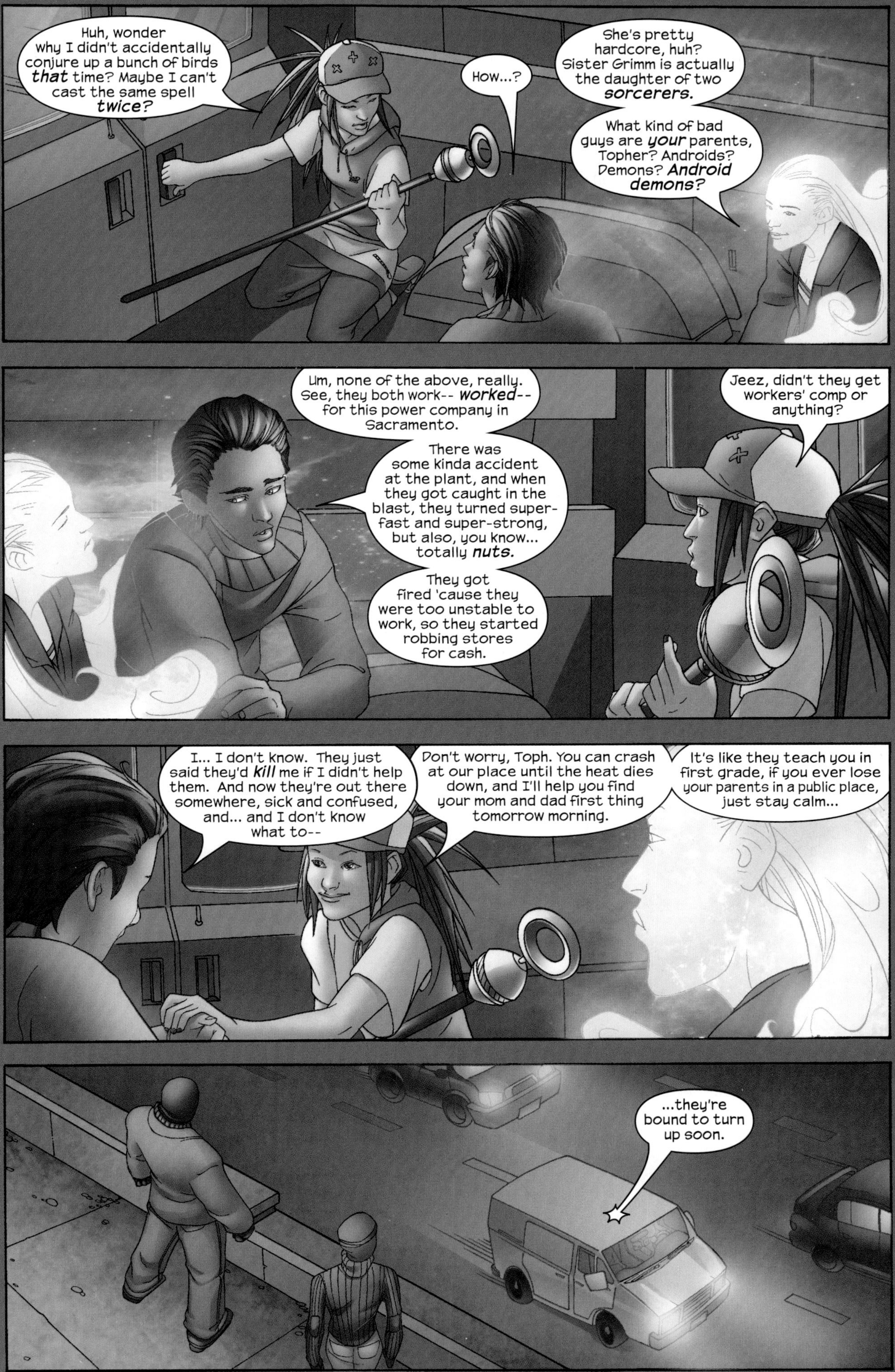
Huh, wonder why I didn't accidentally conjure up a bunch of birds that time? Maybe I can't cast the same spell twice?
How...?
She's pretty hardcore, huh? Sister Grimm is actually the daughter of two sorcerers.
What kind of bad guys are your parents, Topher? Androids? Demons? Android demons?
Um, none of the above, really. See, they both work-- worked-- for this power company in Sacramento.
There was some kinda accident at the plant, and when they got caught in the blast, they turned super-fast and super-strong, but also, you know... totally nuts.
They got fired 'cause they were too unstable to work, so they started robbing stores for cash.
Jeez, didn't they get workers' comp or anything?
I... I don't know. They just said they'd kill me if I didn't help them. And now they're out there somewhere, sick and confused, and... and I don't know what to--
Don't worry, Toph. You can crash at our place until the heat dies down, and I'll help you find your mom and dad first thing tomorrow morning.
It's like they teach you in first grade, if you ever lose your parents in a public place, just stay calm...
...they're bound to turn up soon.

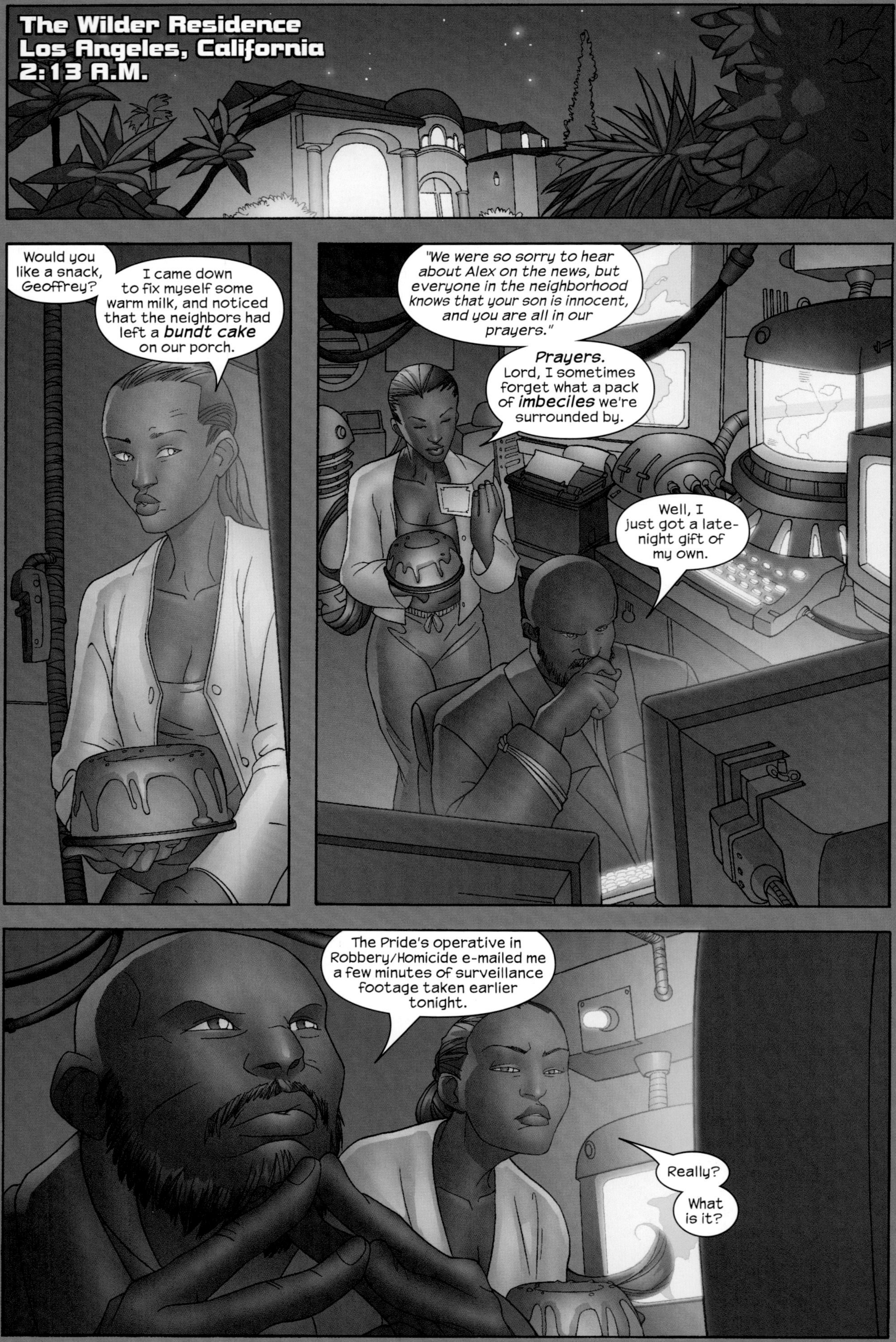
The Wilder Residence
Los Angeles, California
2:13 A.M.
Would you like a snack, Geoffrey?
I came down to fix myself some warm milk, and noticed that the neighbors had left a **bundt cake** on our porch.
"We were so sorry to hear about Alex on the news, but everyone in the neighborhood knows that your son is innocent, and you are all in our prayers."
Prayers. Lord, I sometimes forget what a pack of **imbeciles** we're surrounded by.
Well, I just got a late-night gift of my own.
The Pride's operative in Robbery/Homicide e-mailed me a few minutes of surveillance footage taken earlier tonight.
Really?
What is it?

An answer to our prayers.

That's Alex! Where... where was this taken?

A convenience store in Los Feliz.

The kids are still in *California*? I thought they'd be halfway to *Canada* by now!

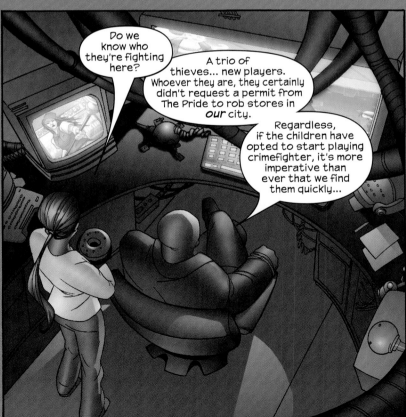

Do we know who they're fighting here?

A trio of thieves... new players. Whoever they are, they certainly didn't request a permit from The Pride to rob stores in *our* city.

Regardless, if the children have opted to start playing crimefighter, it's more imperative than ever that we find them quickly...

...before some two-bit hood makes an *example* out of them.

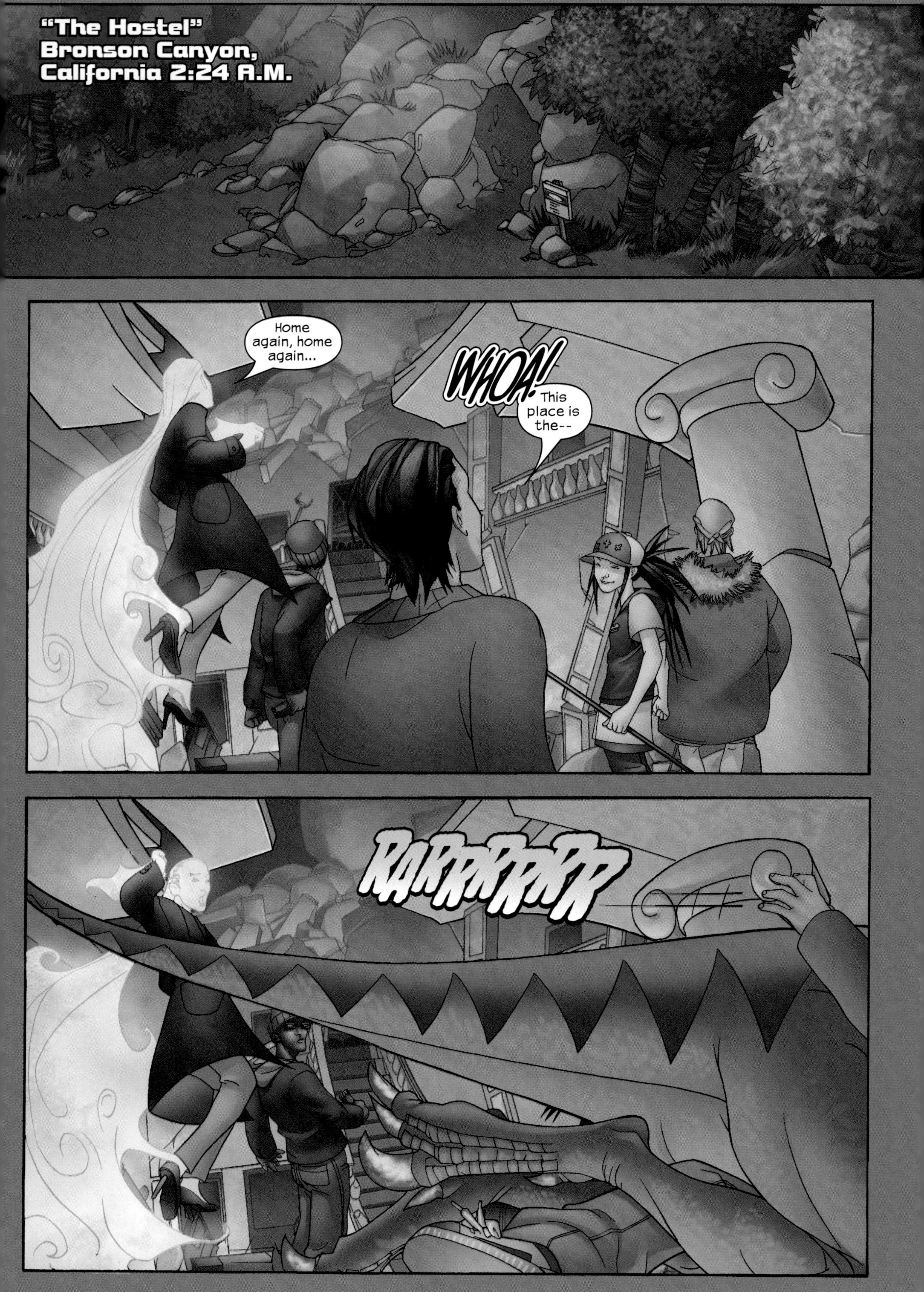
"The Hostel"
Bronson Canyon,
California 2:24 A.M.
Home again, home again...
WHOA!
This place is the--
RARRRRRRR

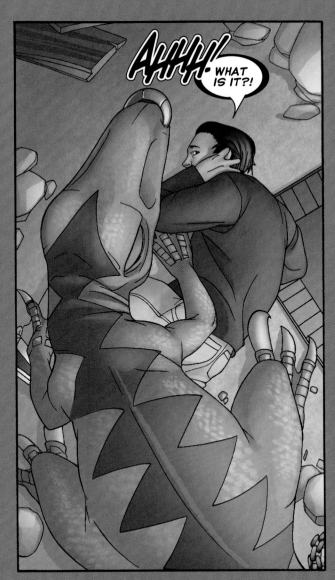

AHHH! WHAT IS IT?!

Oh, my God!

Where's Arsenic?!

HELP ME!

I'm here! I'm here!

Gert, call off your raptor!

I'm trying! Old Lace... she's not listening to my thoughts!

Then think harder, *Arse!* She's, uhh, too heavy to budge!

Says you, wimpster...

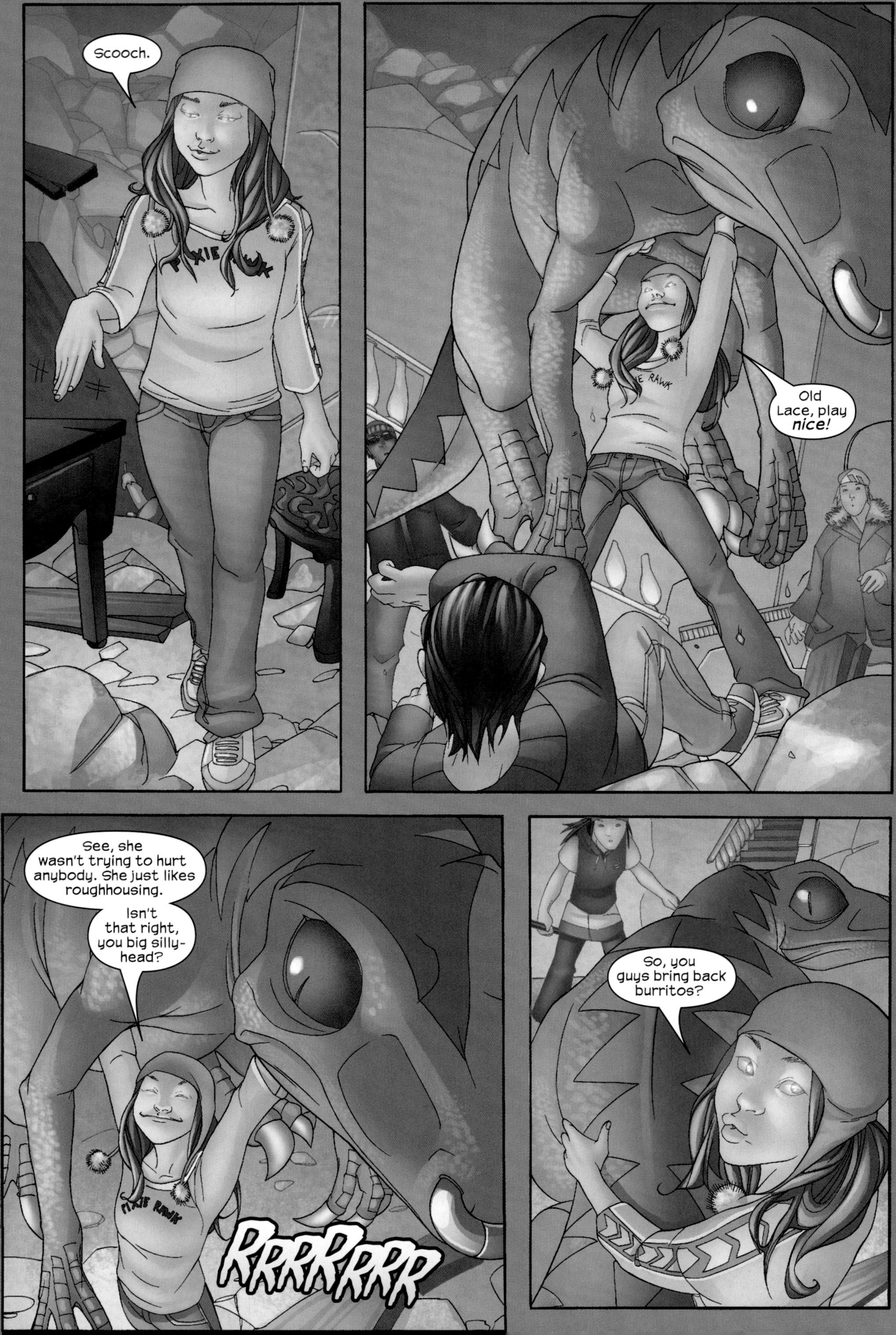
Scooch.
Old Lace, play *nice!*
See, she wasn't trying to hurt anybody. She just likes roughhousing.
Isn't that right, you big silly-head?
RRRRRRRR
So, you guys bring back burritos?

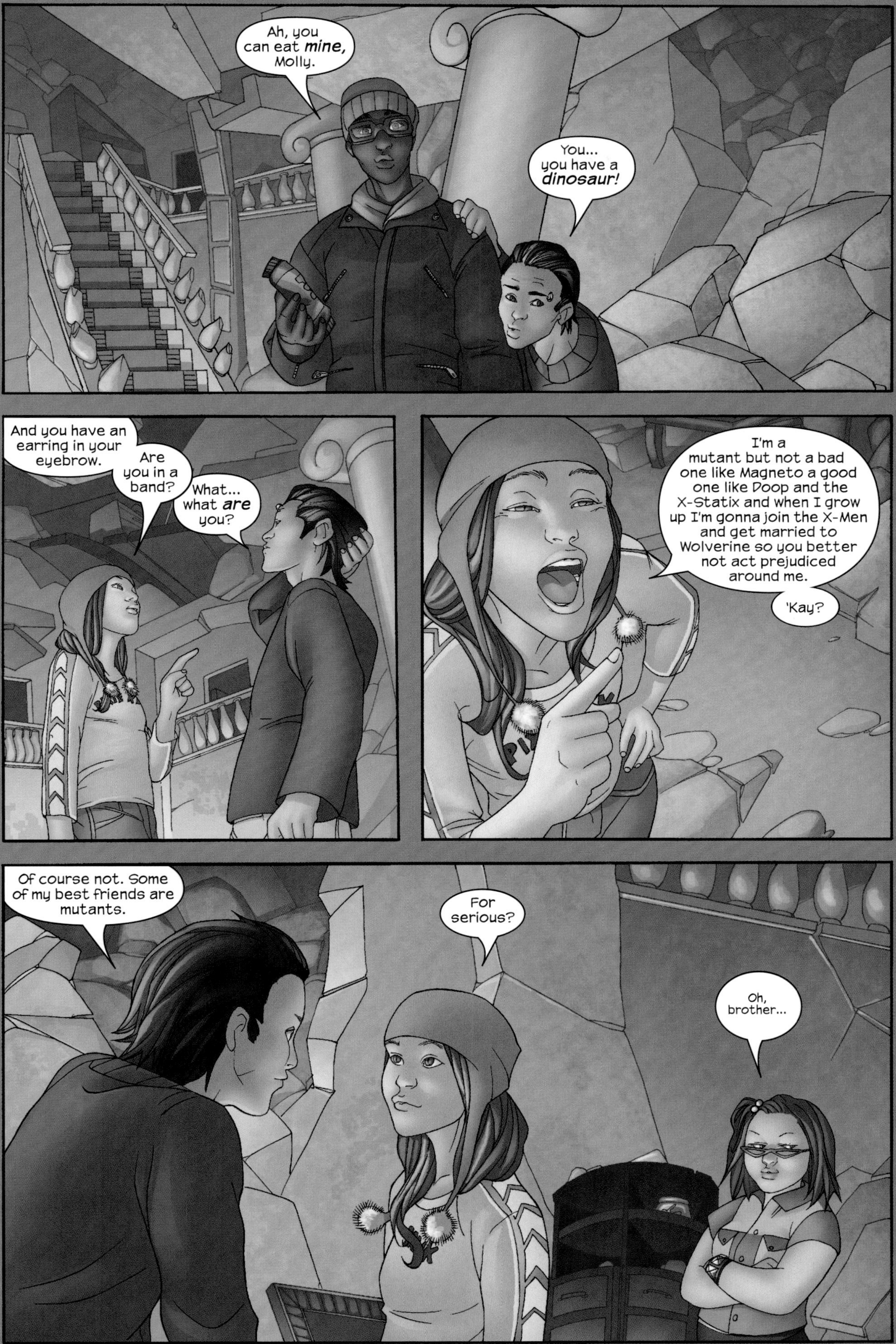
Ah, you can eat *mine,* Molly.
You... you have a *dinosaur!*
And you have an earring in your eyebrow.
Are you in a band?
What... what *are* you?
I'm a mutant but not a bad one like Magneto a good one like Doop and the X-Statix and when I grow up I'm gonna join the X-Men and get married to Wolverine so you better not act prejudiced around me.
'Kay?
Of course not. Some of my best friends are mutants.
For serious?
Oh, brother...

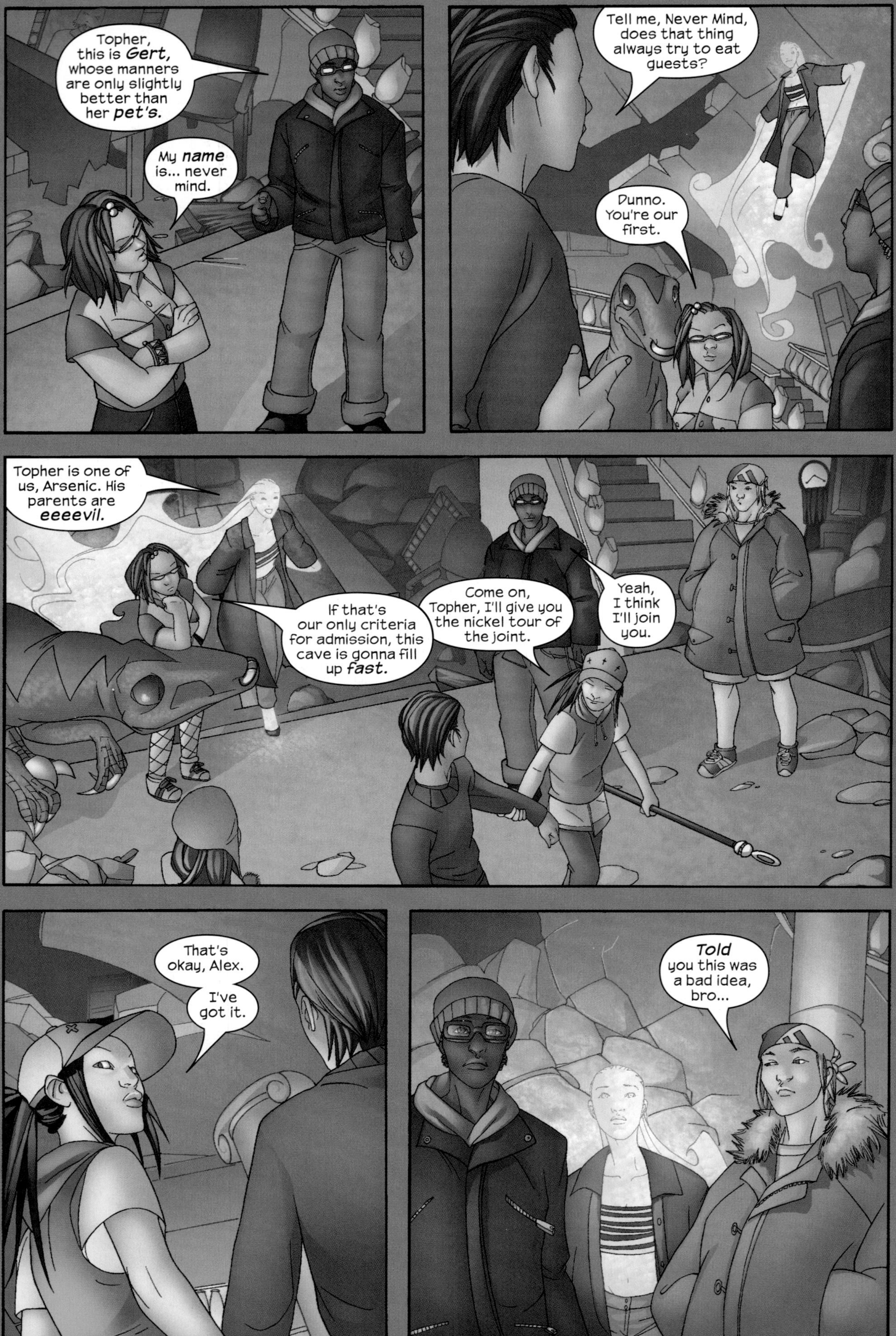

Topher, this is *Gert,* whose manners are only slightly better than her *pet's.*
My *name* is... never mind.
Tell me, Never Mind, does that thing always try to eat guests?
Dunno. You're our first.
Topher is one of us, Arsenic. His parents are *eeeevil.*
If that's our only criteria for admission, this cave is gonna fill up *fast.*
Come on, Topher, I'll give you the nickel tour of the joint.
Yeah, I think I'll join you.
That's okay, Alex.
I've got it.
Told you this was a bad idea, bro...

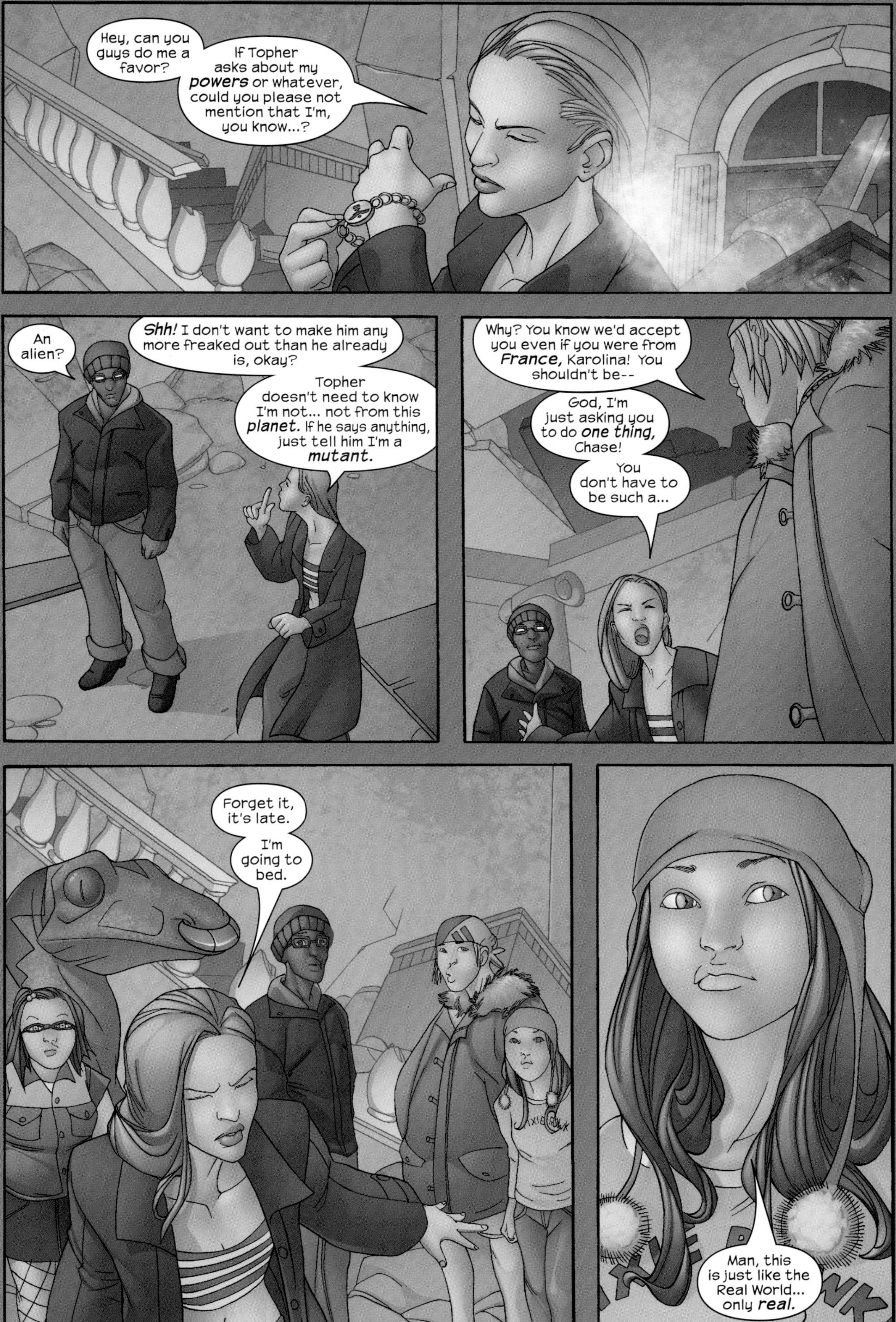
Hey, can you guys do me a favor?
If Topher asks about my **powers** or whatever, could you please not mention that I'm, you know...?
An alien?
Shh! I don't want to make him any more freaked out than he already is, okay?
Topher doesn't need to know I'm not... not from this *planet.* If he says anything, just tell him I'm a ***mutant.***
Why? You know we'd accept you even if you were from *France,* Karolina! You shouldn't be--
God, I'm just asking you to do *one thing,* Chase!
You don't have to be such a...
Forget it, it's late.
I'm going to bed.
Man, this is just like the Real World... only ***real.***

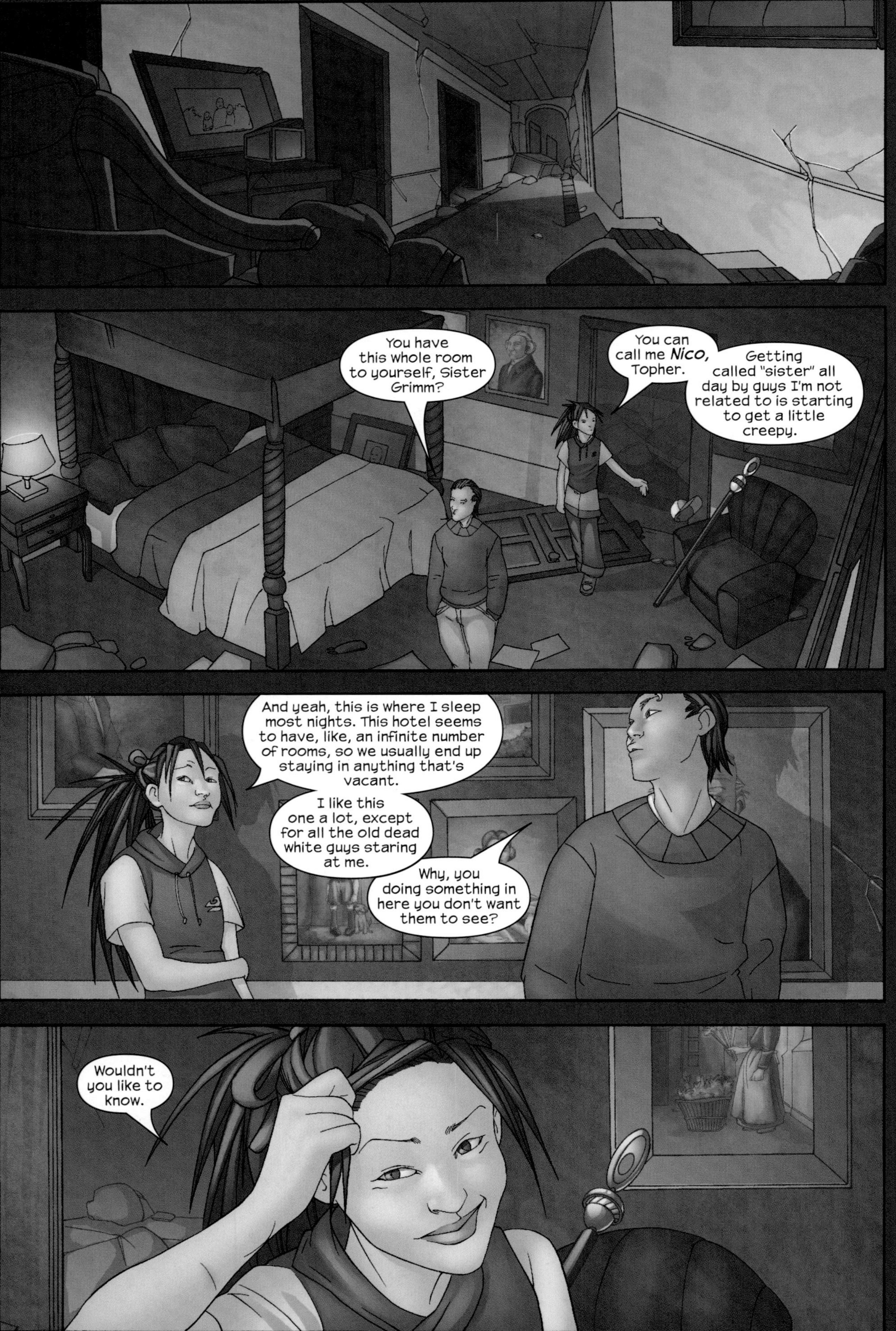
You have this whole room to yourself, Sister Grimm?
You can call me Nico, Topher.
Getting called "sister" all day by guys I'm not related to is starting to get a little creepy.
And yeah, this is where I sleep most nights. This hotel seems to have, like, an infinite number of rooms, so we usually end up staying in anything that's vacant.
I like this one a lot, except for all the old dead white guys staring at me.
Why, you doing something in here you don't want them to see?
Wouldn't you like to know.

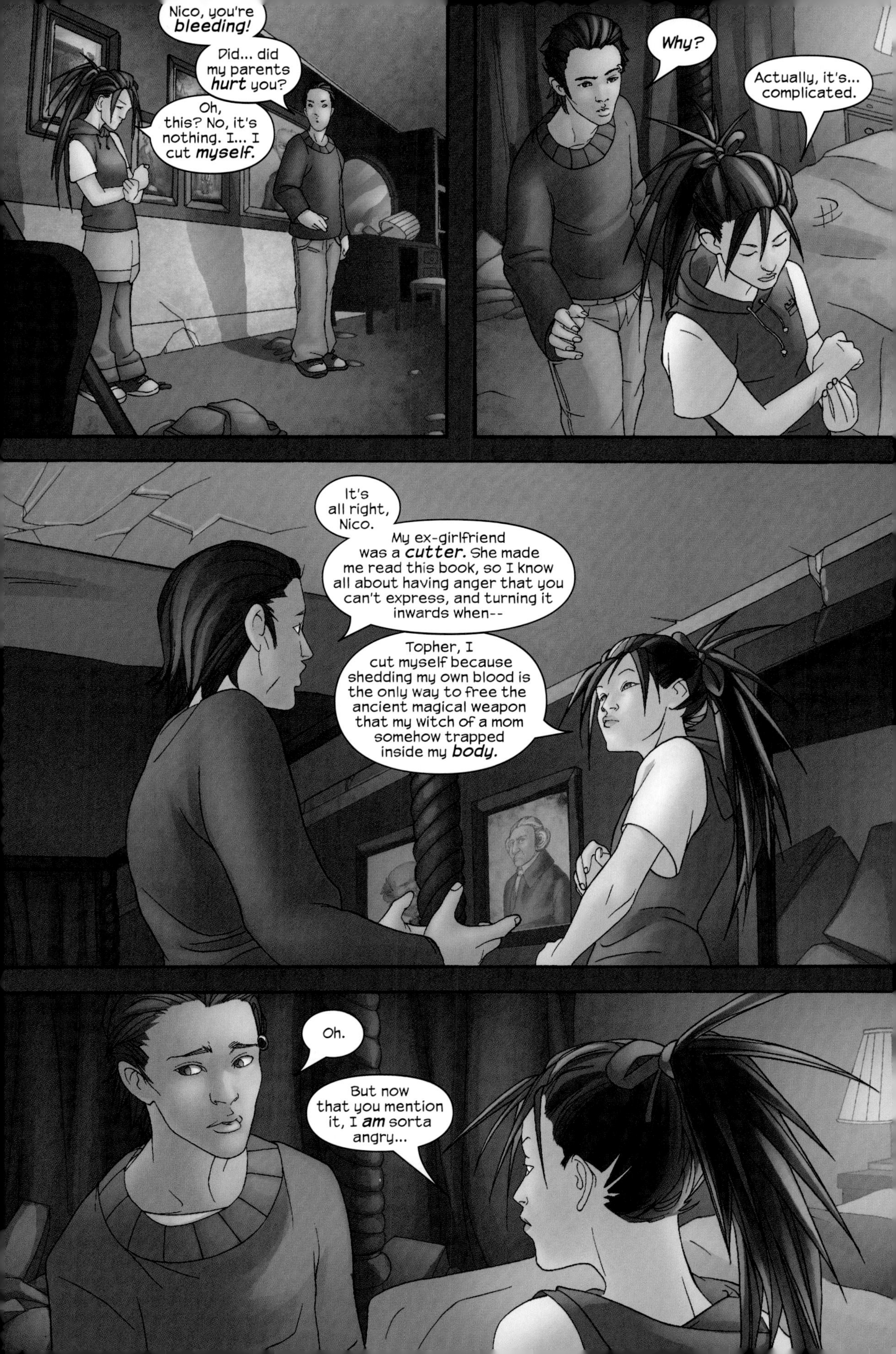

Nico, you're *bleeding!*
Did... did my parents *hurt* you?
Oh, this? No, it's nothing. I... I cut *myself.*
Why?
Actually, it's... complicated.
It's all right, Nico.
My ex-girlfriend was a *cutter.* She made me read this book, so I know all about having anger that you can't express, and turning it inwards when--
Topher, I cut myself because shedding my own blood is the only way to free the ancient magical weapon that my witch of a mom somehow trapped inside my *body.*
Oh.
But now that you mention it, I *am* sorta angry...

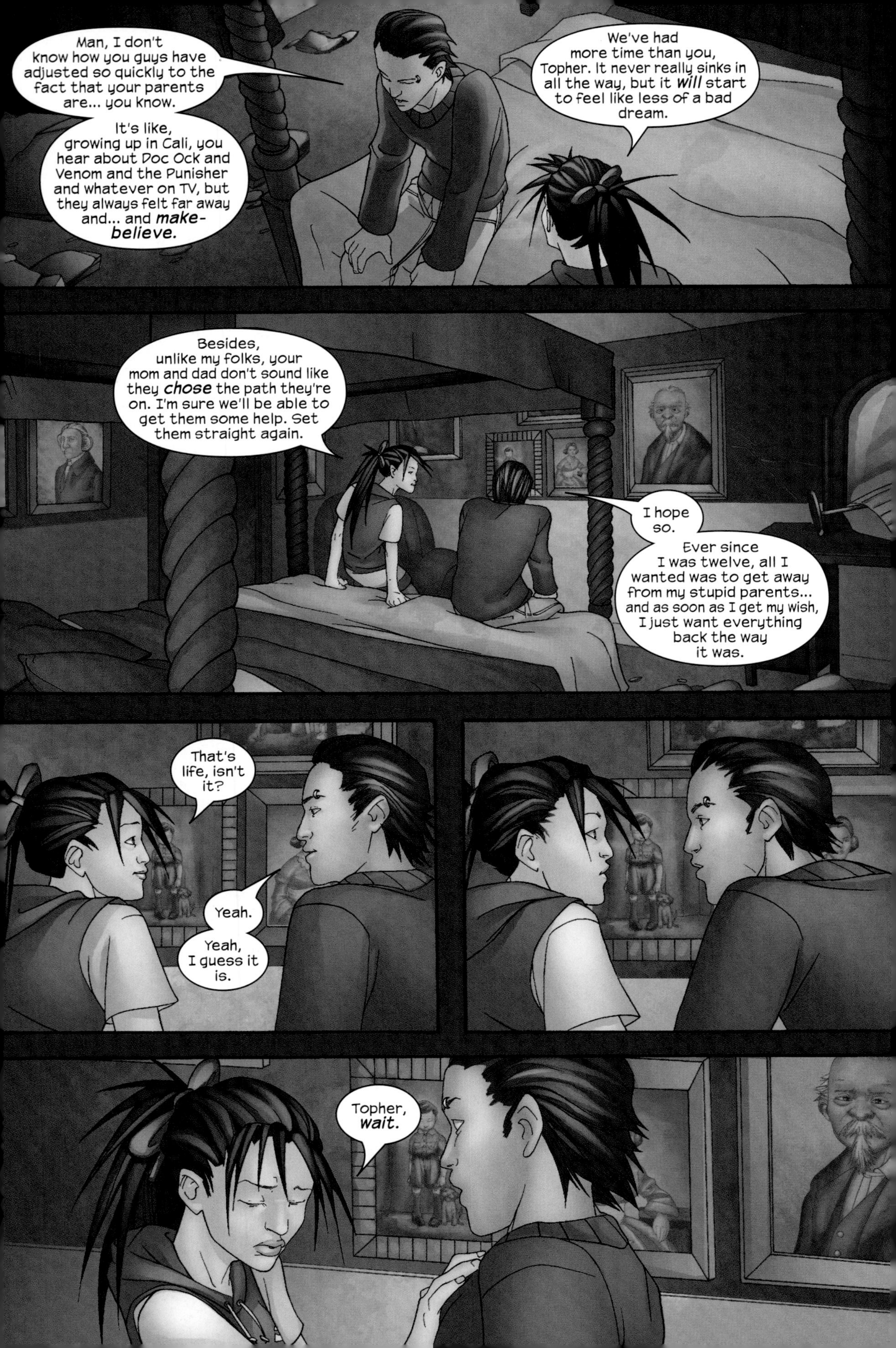

Man, I don't know how you guys have adjusted so quickly to the fact that your parents are... you know.
It's like, growing up in Cali, you hear about Doc Ock and Venom and the Punisher and whatever on TV, but they always felt far away and... and *make-believe.*
We've had more time than you, Topher. It never really sinks in all the way, but it *will* start to feel like less of a bad dream.
Besides, unlike my folks, your mom and dad don't sound like they *chose* the path they're on. I'm sure we'll be able to get them some help. Set them straight again.
I hope so.
Ever since I was twelve, all I wanted was to get away from my stupid parents... and as soon as I get my wish, I just want everything back the way it was.
That's life, isn't it?
Yeah.
Yeah, I guess it is.
Topher, *wait.*

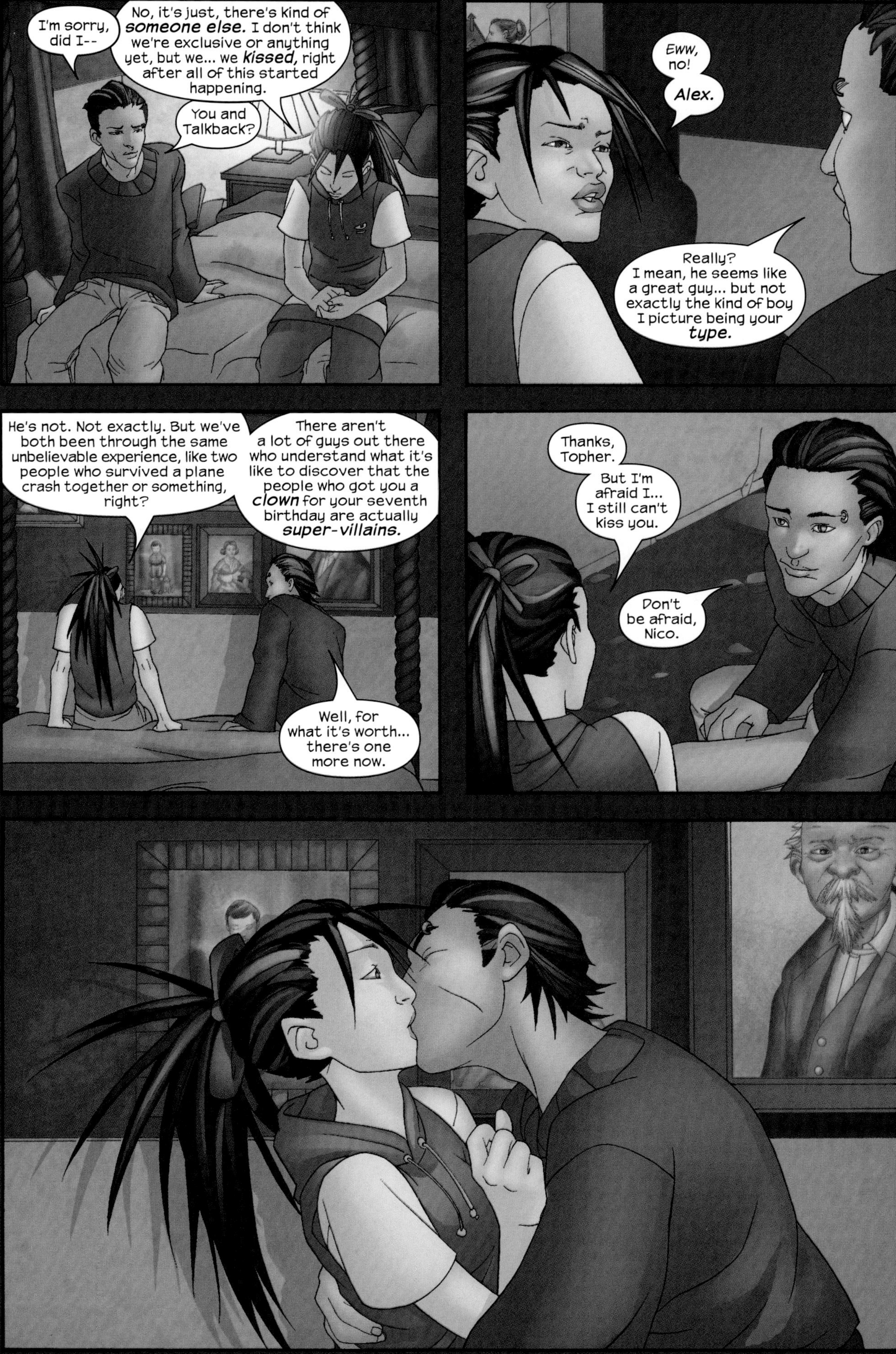
I'm sorry, did I--
No, it's just, there's kind of someone else. I don't think we're exclusive or anything yet, but we... we kissed, right after all of this started happening.
You and Talkback?
Eww, no!
Alex.
Really? I mean, he seems like a great guy... but not exactly the kind of boy I picture being your type.
He's not. Not exactly. But we've both been through the same unbelievable experience, like two people who survived a plane crash together or something, right?
There aren't a lot of guys out there who understand what it's like to discover that the people who got you a clown for your seventh birthday are actually super-villains.
Well, for what it's worth... there's one more now.
Thanks, Topher.
But I'm afraid I... I still can't kiss you.
Don't be afraid, Nico.

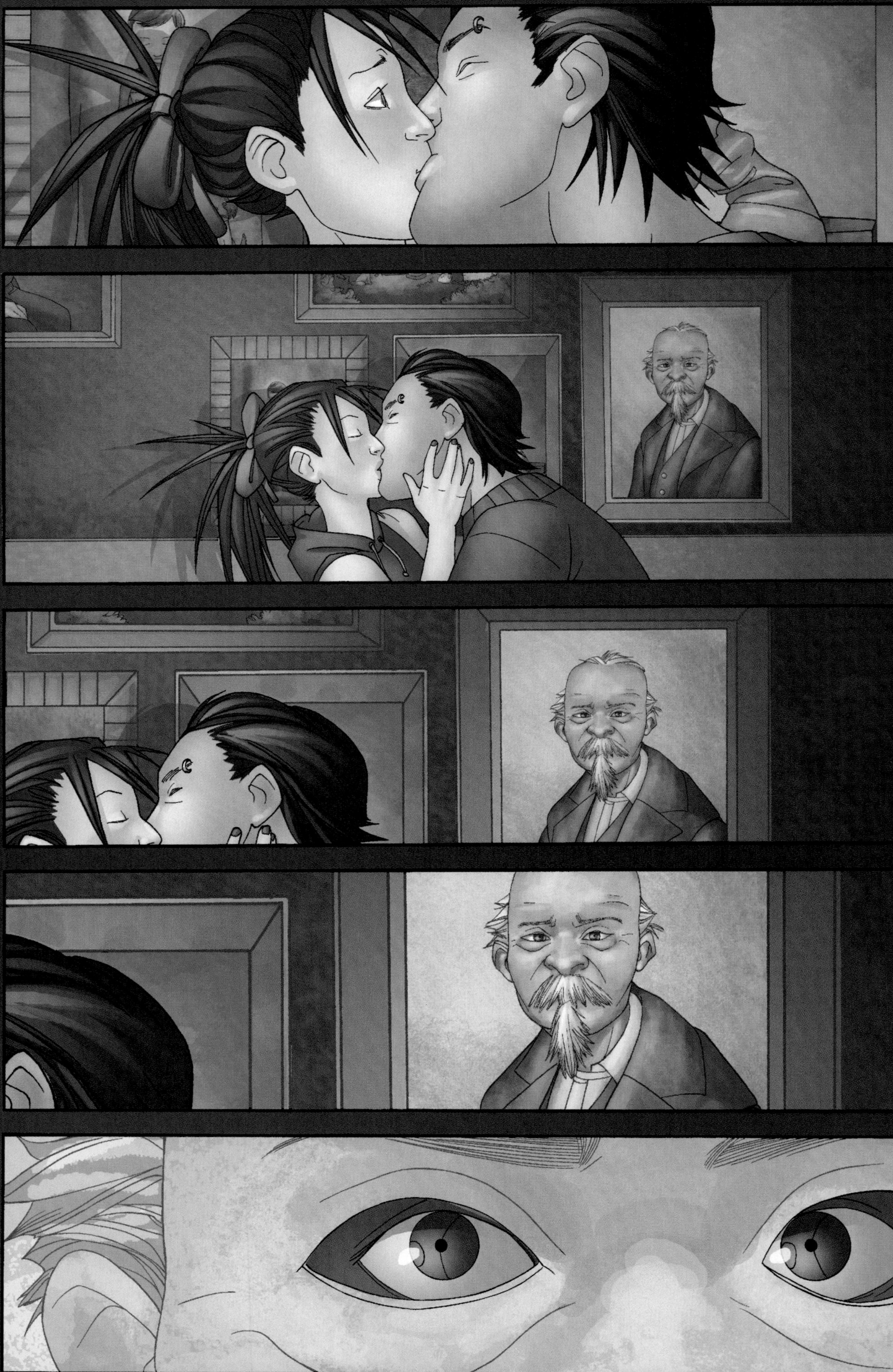

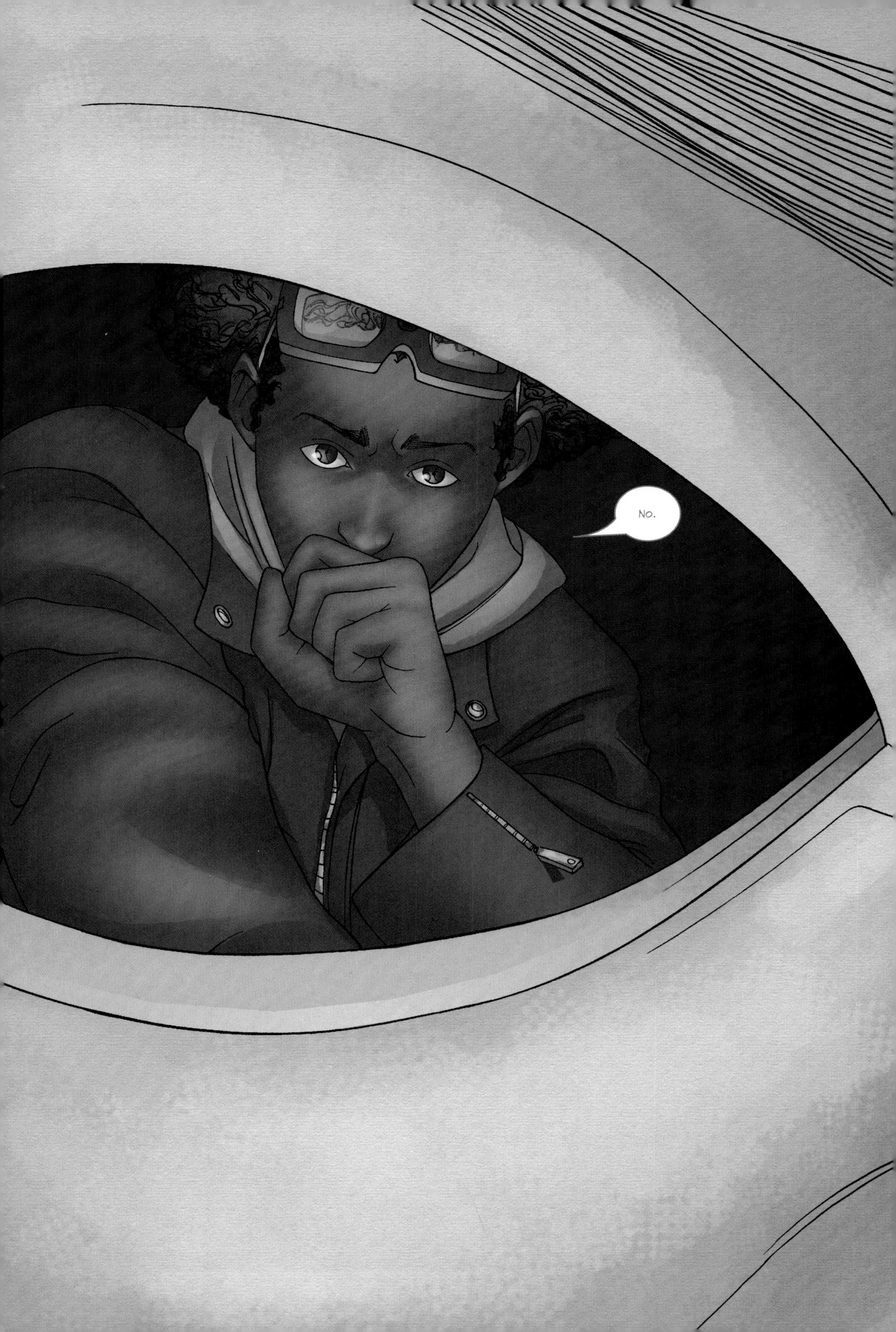
No.

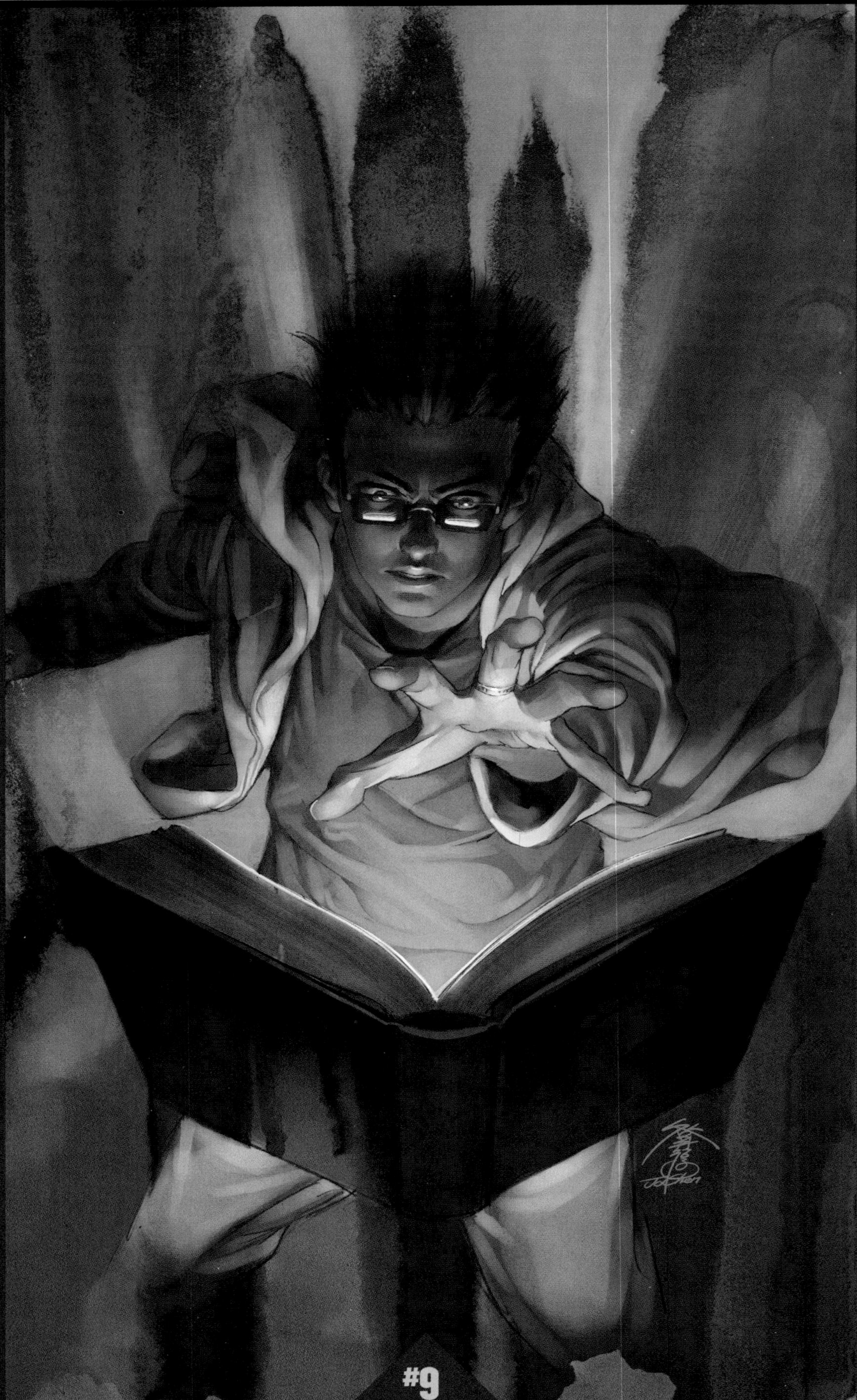
#9

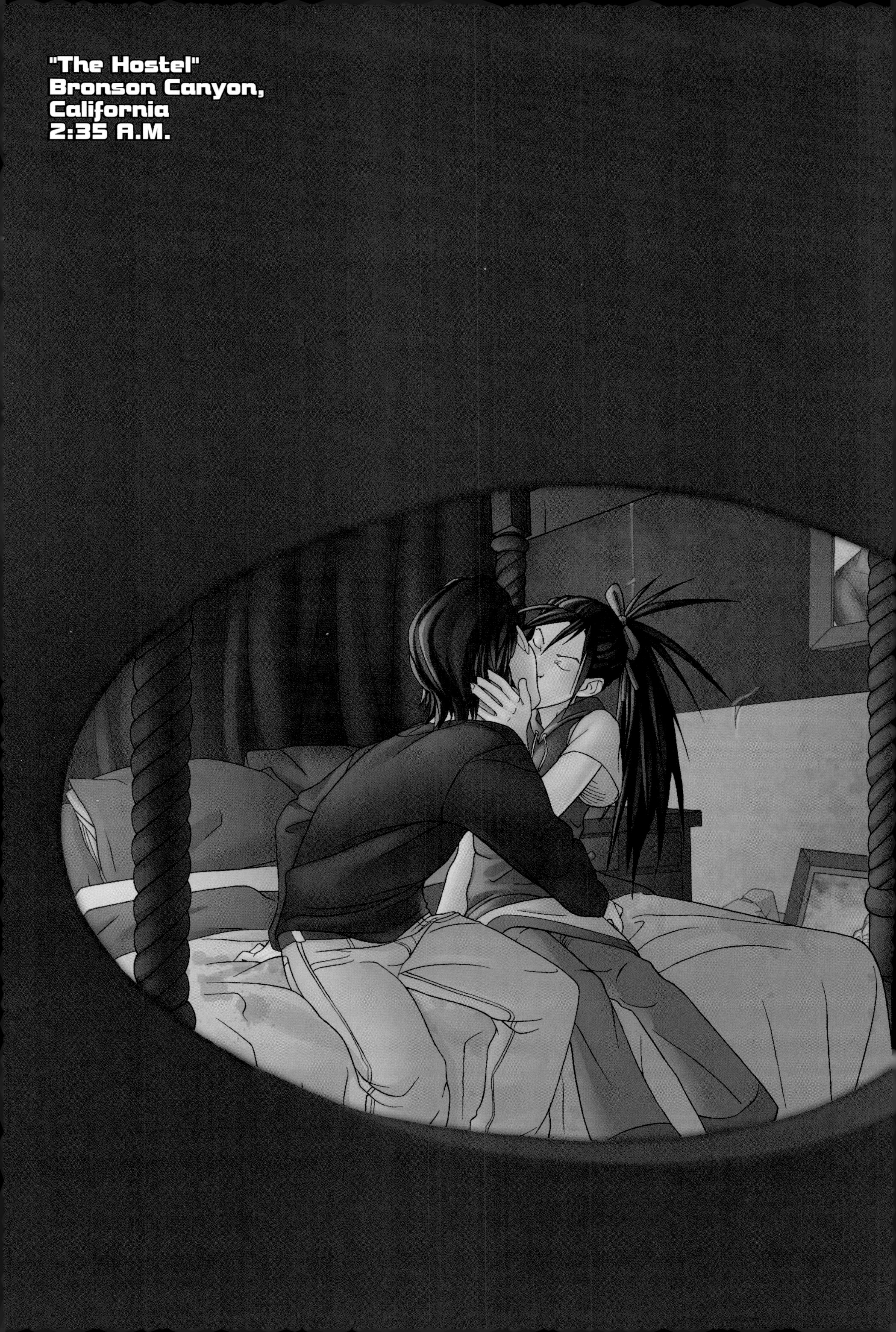
"The Hostel"
Bronson Canyon,
California
2:35 A.M.

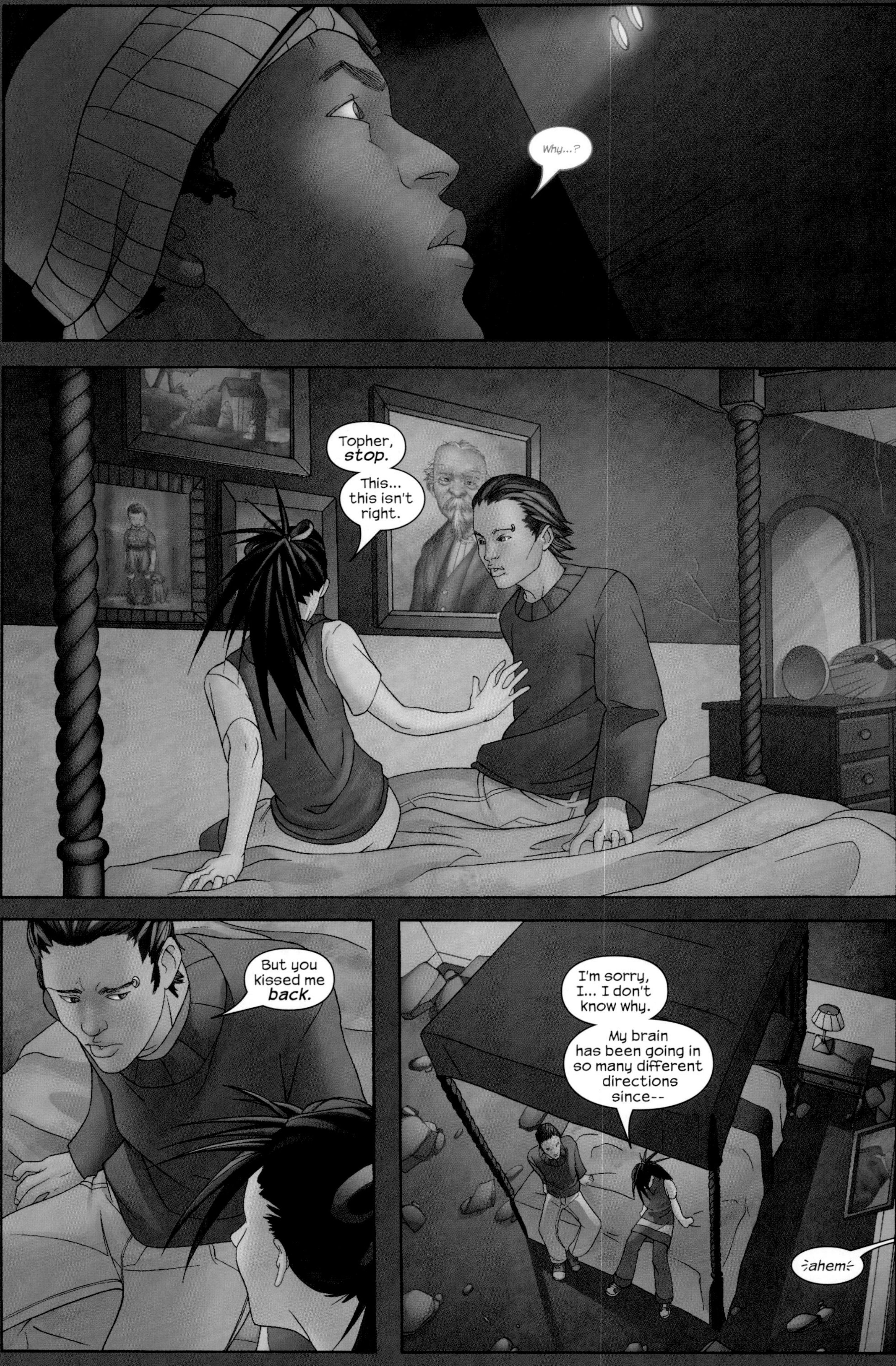
Why...?
Topher, stop.
This... this isn't right.
But you kissed me back.
I'm sorry, I... I don't know why.
My brain has been going in so many different directions since--
ahem

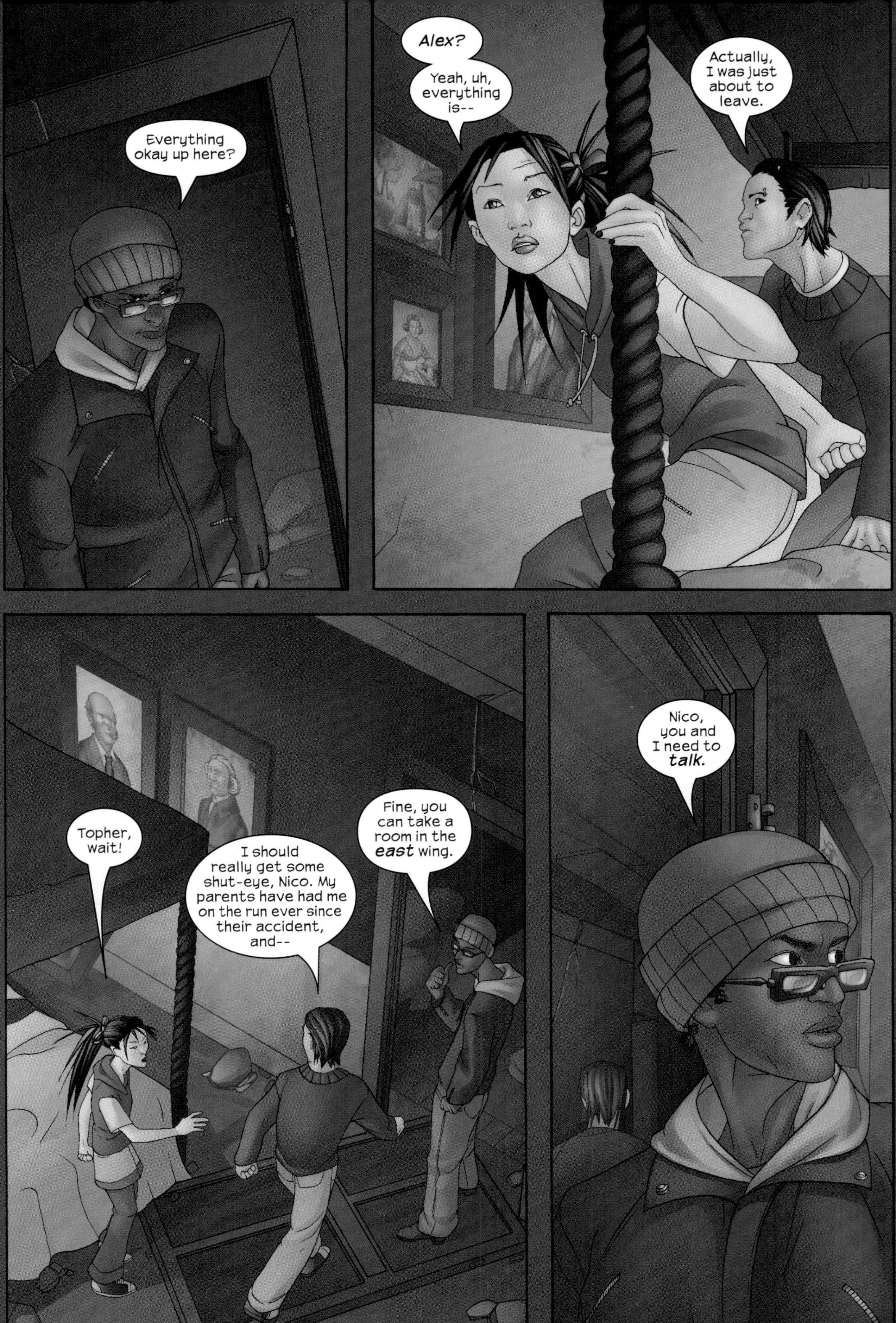

Everything okay up here?
Alex?
Yeah, uh, everything is--
Actually, I was just about to leave.
Topher, wait!
I should really get some shut-eye, Nico. My parents have had me on the run ever since their accident, and--
Fine, you can take a room in the *east* wing.
Nico, you and I need to *talk.*

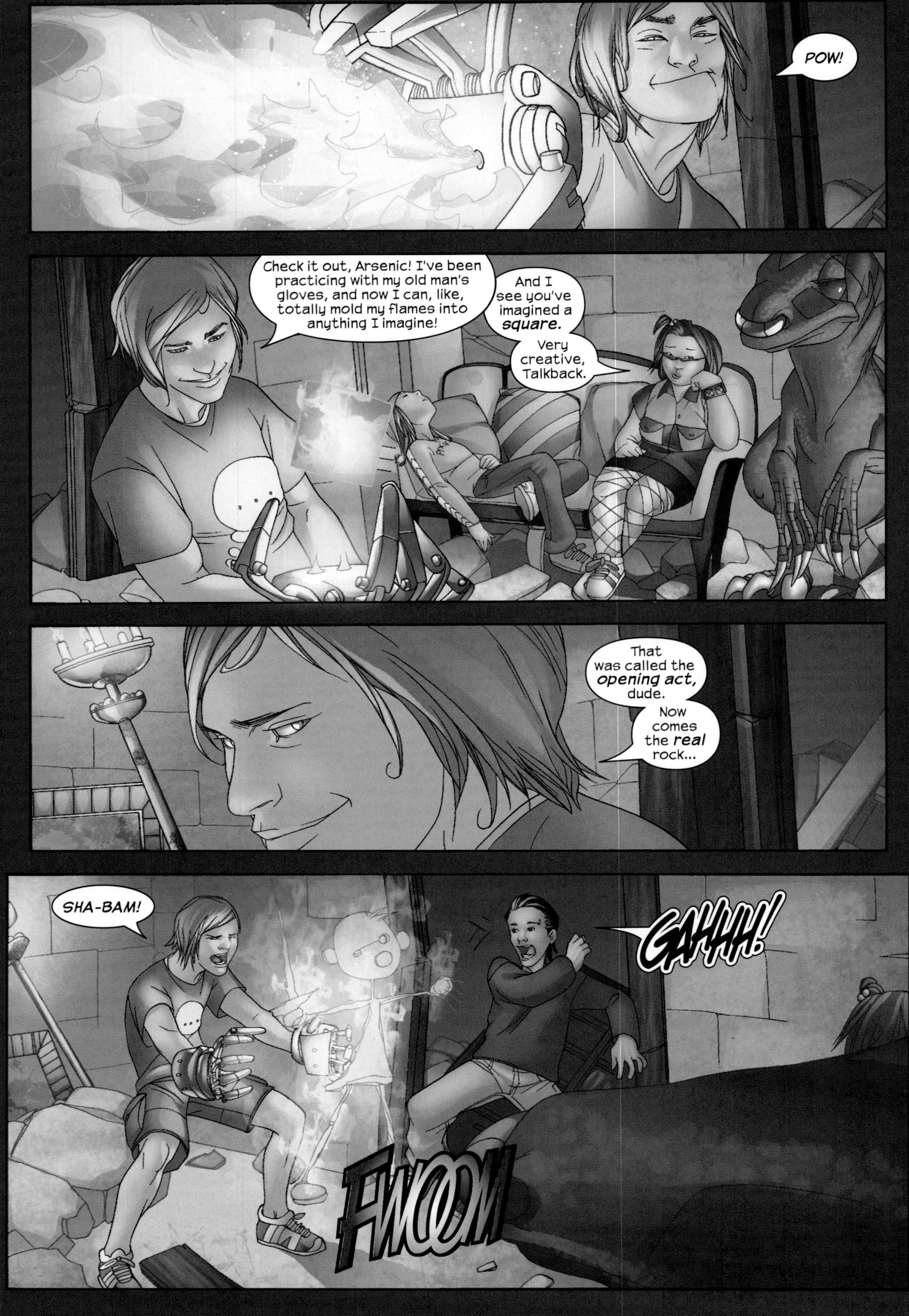
POW!
Check it out, Arsenic! I've been practicing with my old man's gloves, and now I can, like, totally mold my flames into anything I imagine!
And I see you've imagined a square.
Very creative, Talkback.
That was called the opening act, dude.
Now comes the real rock...
SHA-BAM!
GAHHH!
FWOOM

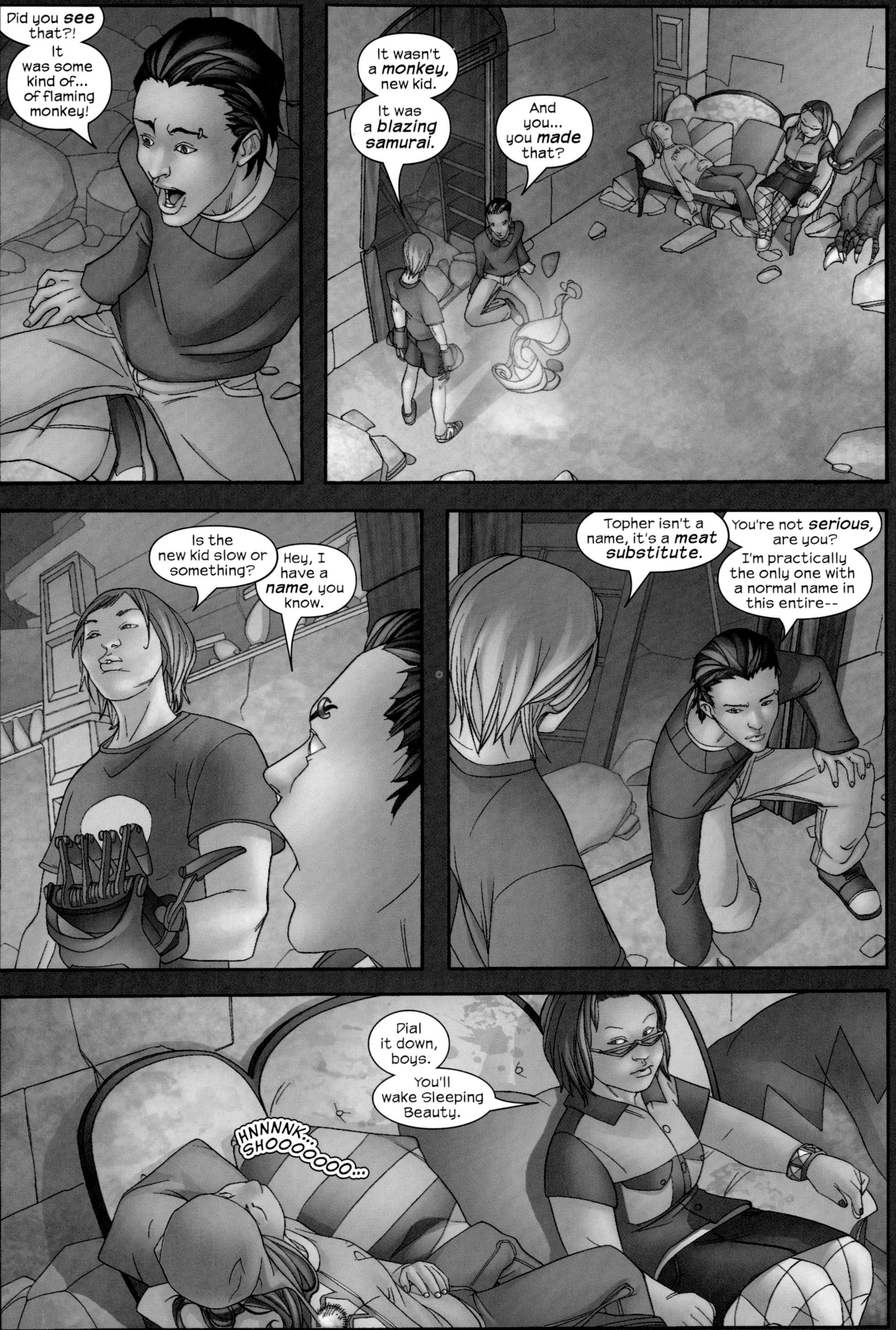
Did you *see* that?! It was some kind of... of flaming monkey!
It wasn't a *monkey,* new kid.
It was a *blazing samurai.*
And you... you *made* that?
Is the new kid slow or something?
Hey, I have a *name,* you know.
Topher isn't a name, it's a *meat substitute.*
You're not *serious,* are you?
I'm practically the only one with a normal name in this entire--
Dial it down, boys.
You'll wake Sleeping Beauty.
HNNNNK... SHOOOOOOOO...

Good luck. The last time Bruiser used her mutant mojo, she sawed logs like that for *hours*.

Speaking of which, it's almost three in the morning. When do the *rest* of you... rest?

I saw my parents kill a girl, and then I found a dinosaur in my basement.

I haven't slept in *four days*.

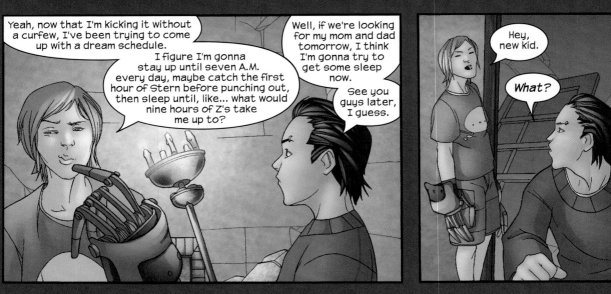

Yeah, now that I'm kicking it without a curfew, I've been trying to come up with a dream schedule.

I figure I'm gonna stay up until seven A.M. every day, maybe catch the first hour of Stern before punching out, then sleep until, like... what would nine hours of Z's take me up to?

Well, if we're looking for my mom and dad tomorrow, I think I'm gonna try to get some sleep now.

See you guys later, I guess.

Hey, new kid.

What?

Don't worry about your folks.

We'll find 'em. I promise.

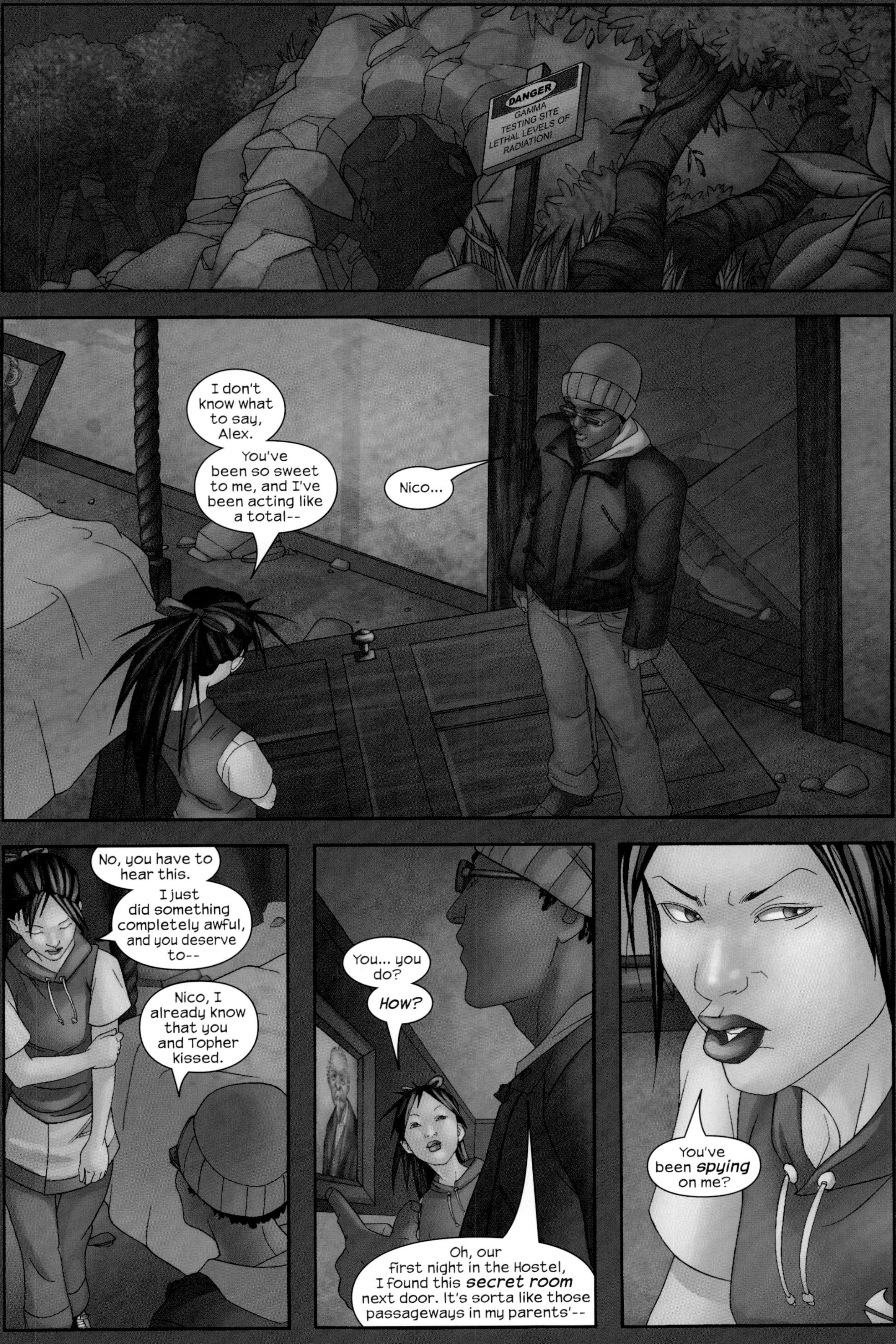
DANGER
GAMMA TESTING SITE LETHAL LEVELS OF RADIATION!
I don't know what to say, Alex.
You've been so sweet to me, and I've been acting like a total--
Nico...
No, you have to hear this.
I just did something completely awful, and you deserve to--
Nico, I already know that you and Topher kissed.
You... you do?
HOW?
Oh, our first night in the Hostel, I found this secret room next door. It's sorta like those passageways in my parents'--
You've been spying on me?

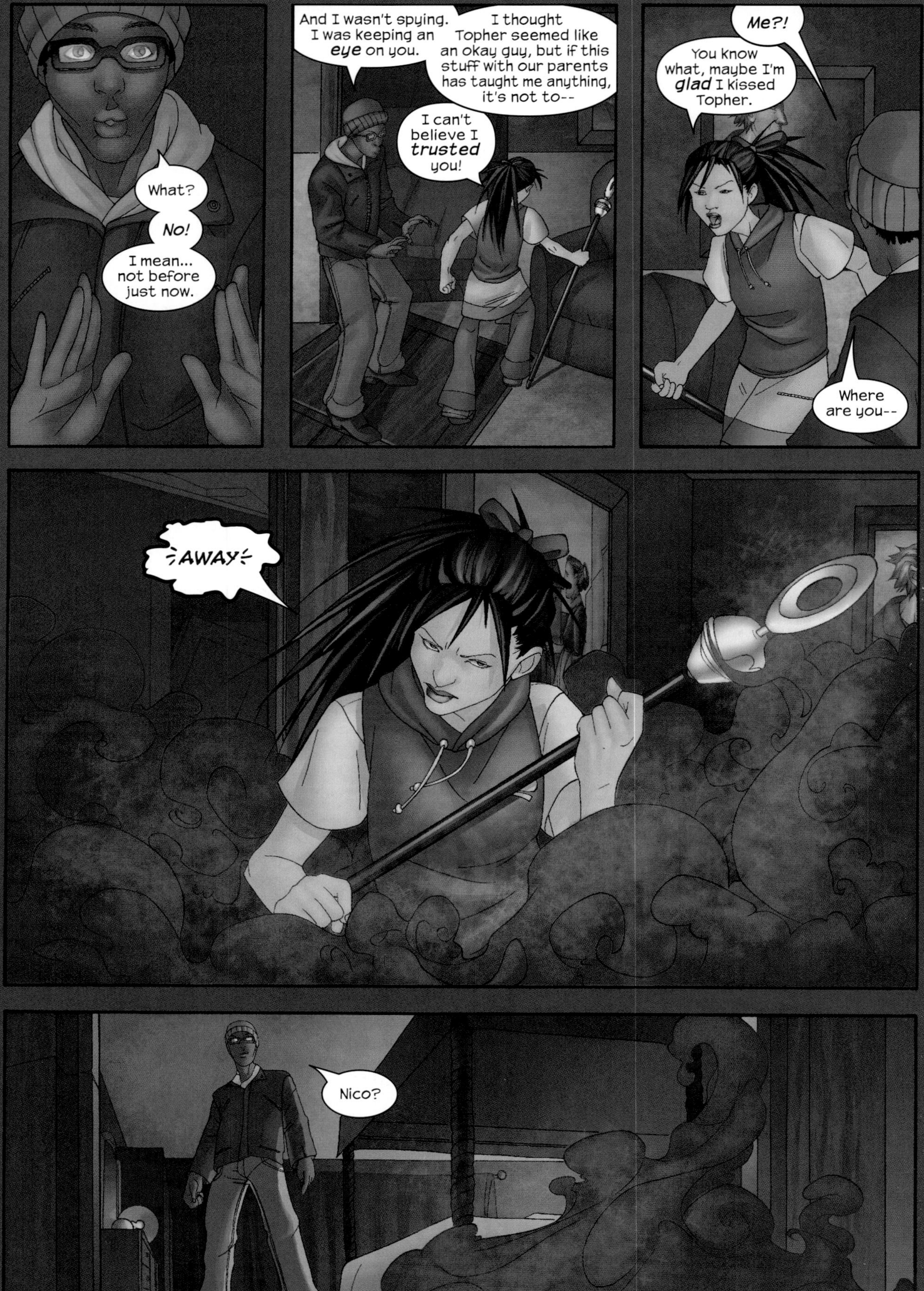
What?
No!
I mean... not before just now.
And I wasn't spying. I was keeping an eye on you.
I thought Topher seemed like an okay guy, but if this stuff with our parents has taught me anything, it's not to--
I can't believe I trusted you!
Me?!
You know what, maybe I'm glad I kissed Topher.
Where are you--
AWAY
Nico?

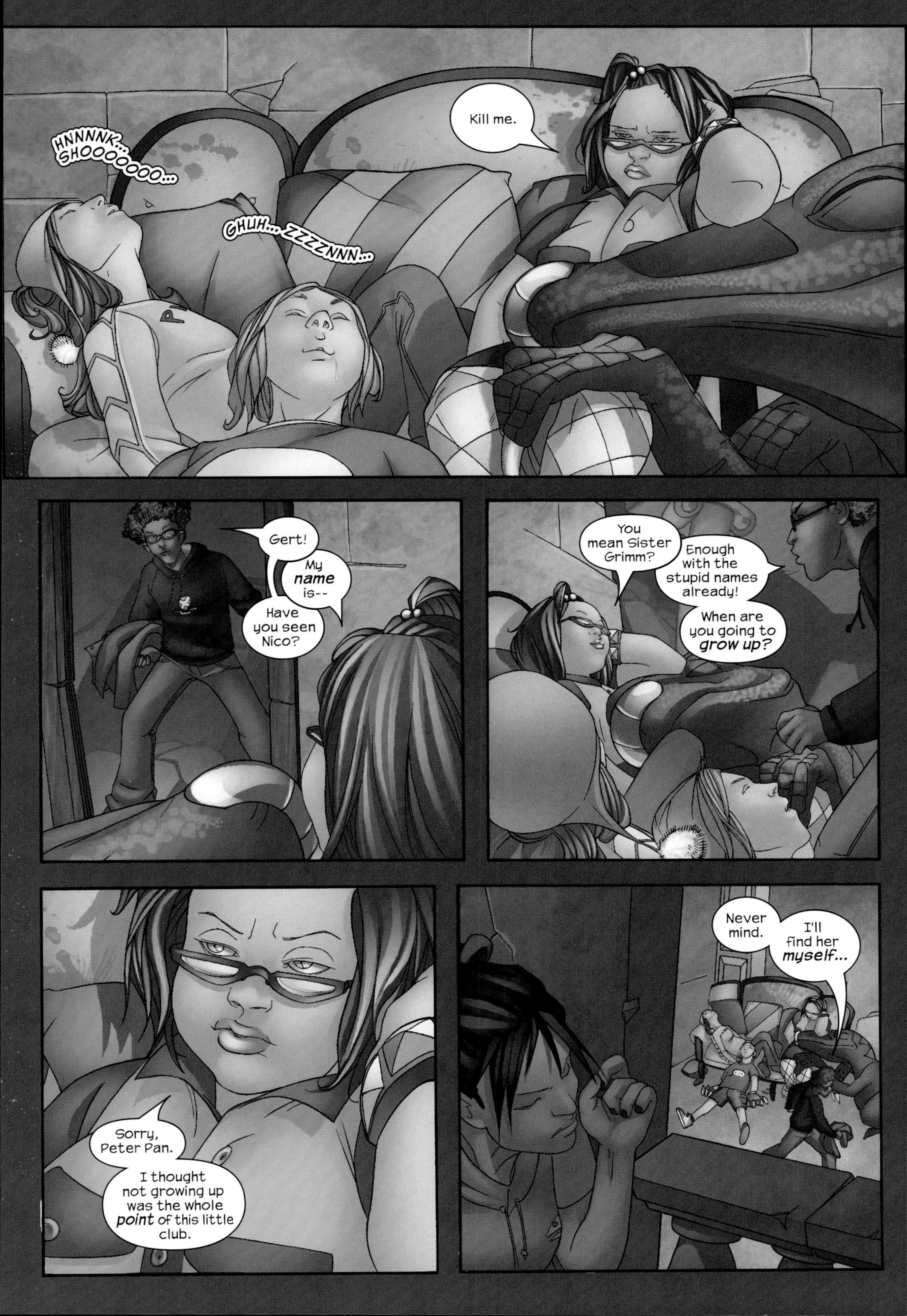
HNNNNK... SHOOOOOOOO...
GHUH... ZZZZZNNN...
Kill me.
Gert!
My **name** is--
Have you seen Nico?
You mean Sister Grimm?
Enough with the stupid names already!
When are you going to ***grow up?***
Sorry, Peter Pan.
I thought not growing up was the whole ***point*** of this little club.
Never mind.
I'll find her ***myself...***

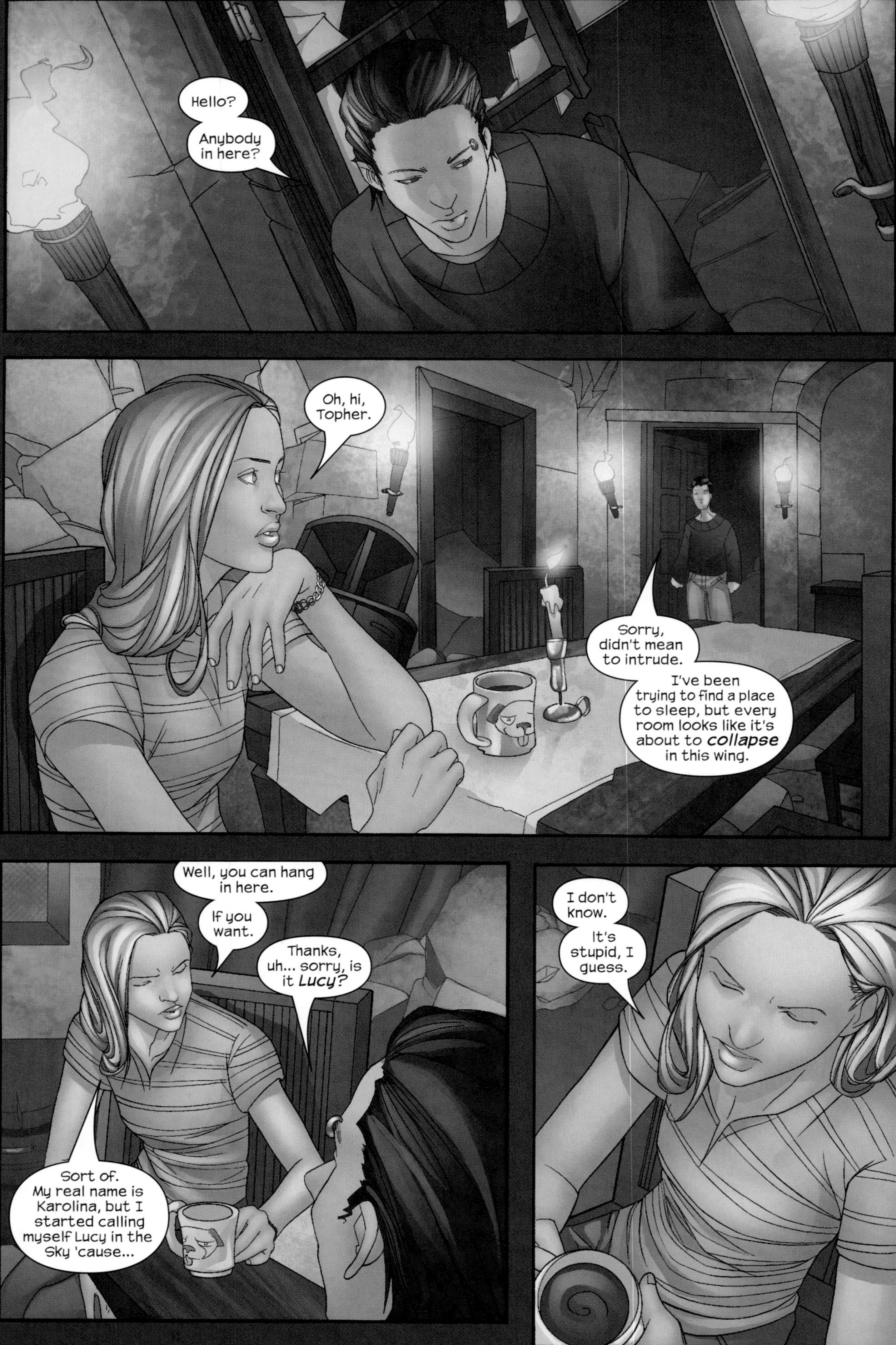
Hello?
Anybody in here?
Oh, hi, Topher.
Sorry, didn't mean to intrude.
I've been trying to find a place to sleep, but every room looks like it's about to *collapse* in this wing.
Well, you can hang in here.
If you want.
Thanks, uh... sorry, is it *Lucy?*
Sort of. My real name is Karolina, but I started calling myself Lucy in the Sky 'cause...
I don't know.
It's stupid, I guess.

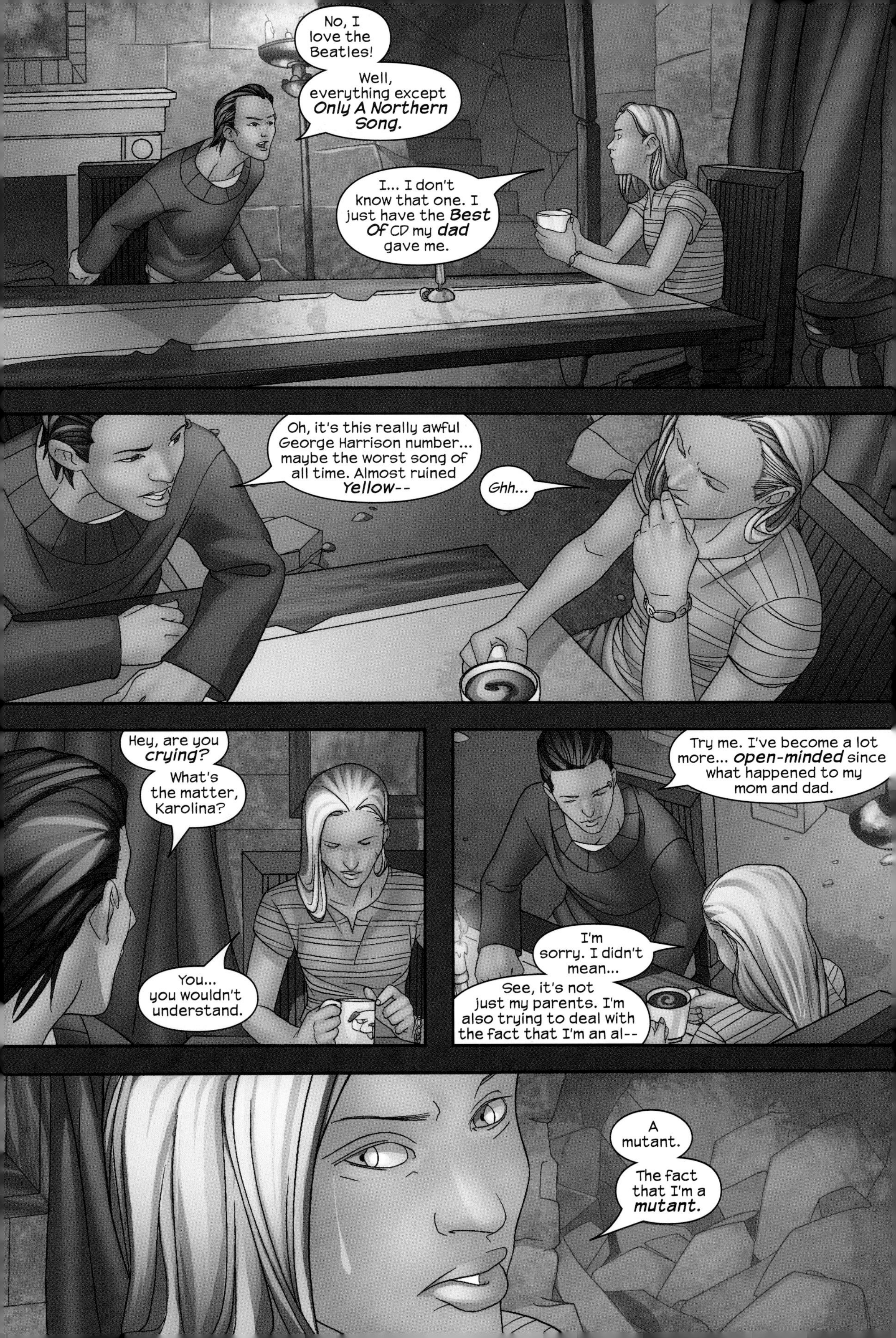
No, I love the Beatles!
Well, everything except Only A Northern Song.
I... I don't know that one. I just have the Best Of CD my dad gave me.
Oh, it's this really awful George Harrison number... maybe the worst song of all time. Almost ruined Yellow--
Ghh...
Hey, are you crying?
What's the matter, Karolina?
You... you wouldn't understand.
Try me. I've become a lot more... open-minded since what happened to my mom and dad.
I'm sorry. I didn't mean...
See, it's not just my parents. I'm also trying to deal with the fact that I'm an al--
A mutant.
The fact that I'm a mutant.

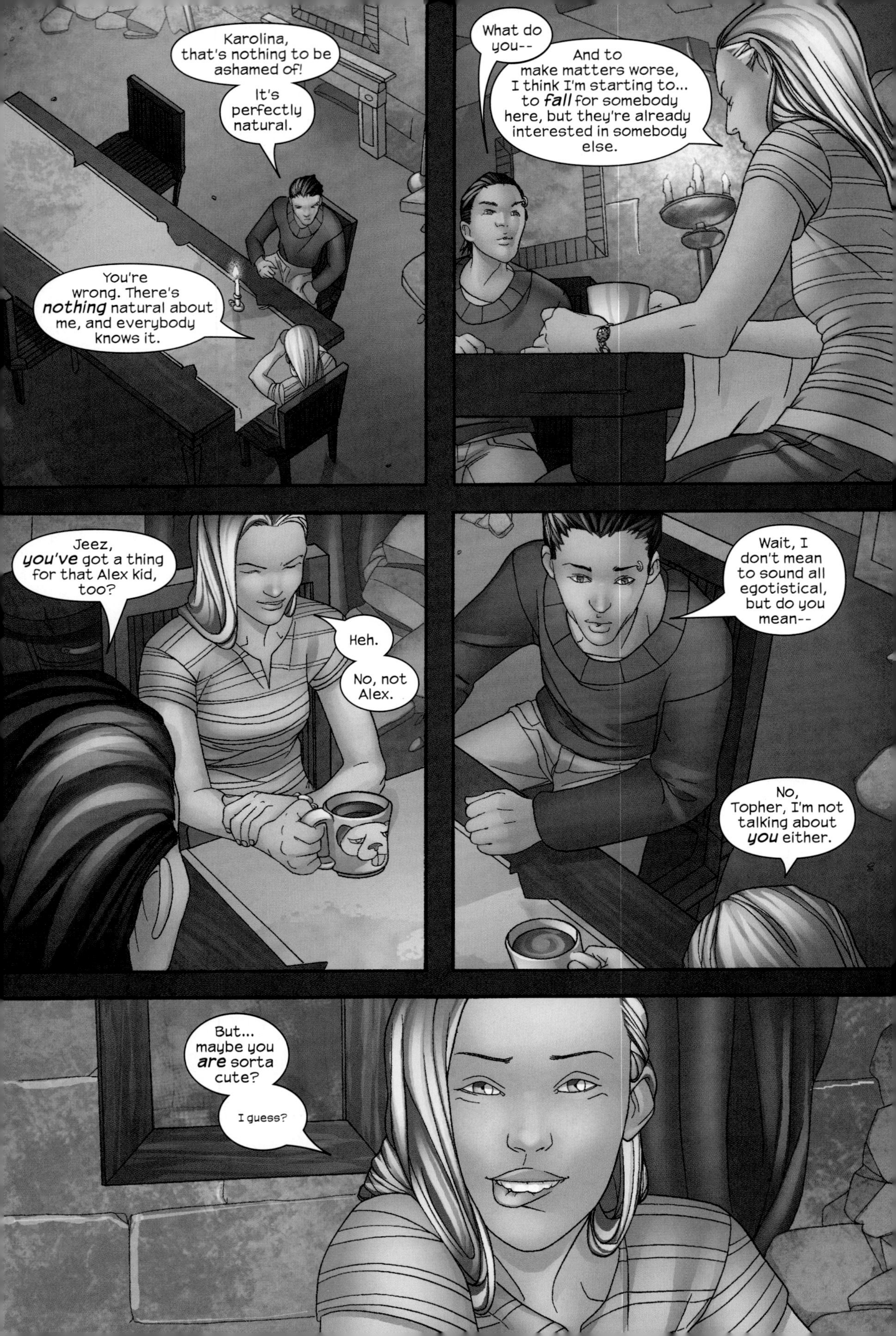
Karolina, that's nothing to be ashamed of!
It's perfectly natural.
You're wrong. There's *nothing* natural about me, and everybody knows it.
What do you--
And to make matters worse, I think I'm starting to... to *fall* for somebody here, but they're already interested in somebody else.
Jeez, *you've* got a thing for that Alex kid, too?
Heh.
No, not Alex.
Wait, I don't mean to sound all egotistical, but do you mean--
No, Topher, I'm not talking about *you* either.
But... maybe you *are* sorta cute?
I guess?

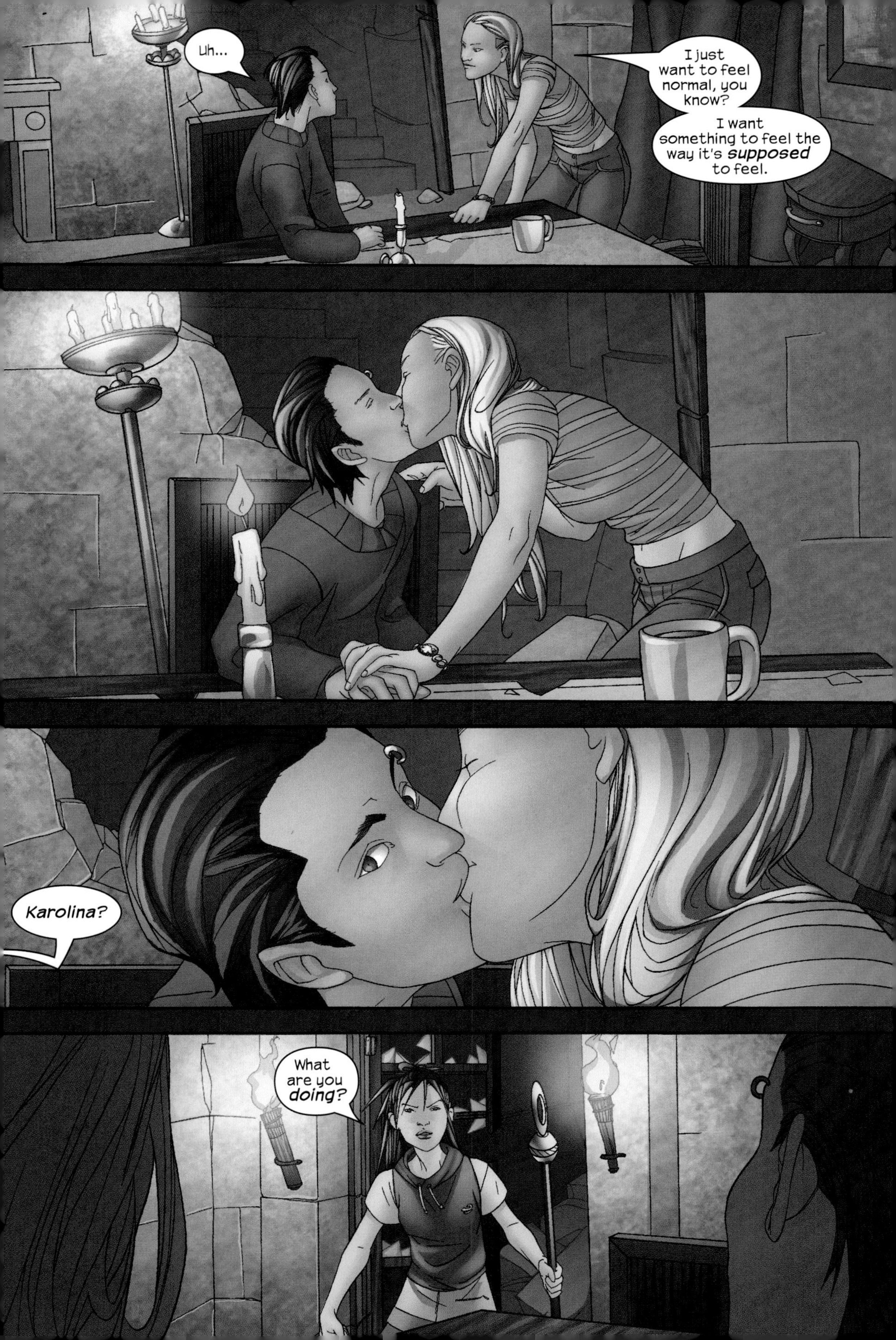
Uh...
I just want to feel normal, you know?
I want something to feel the way it's ***supposed*** to feel.
Karolina?
What are you ***doing?***

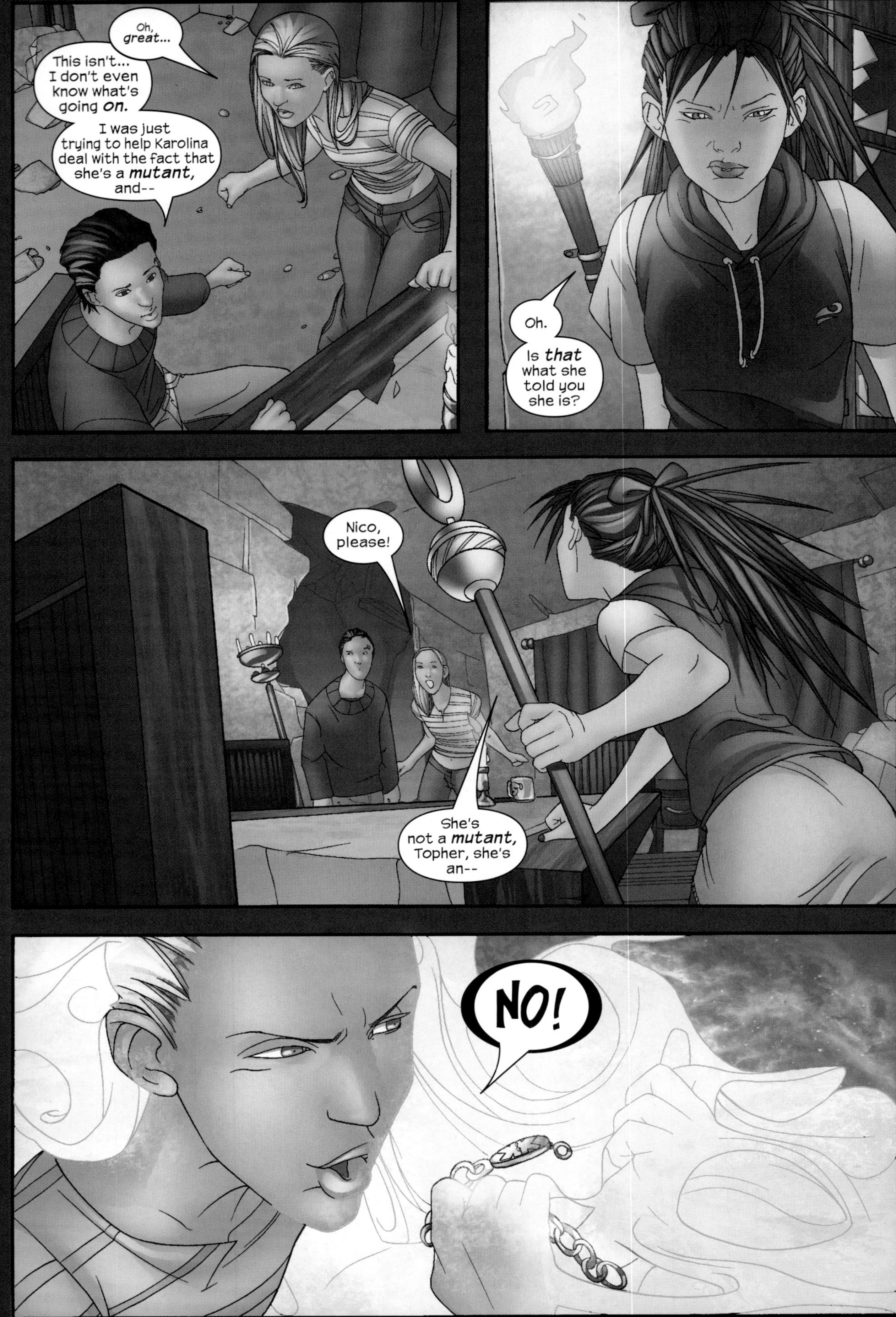

Oh, great...
This isn't... I don't even know what's going on.
I was just trying to help Karolina deal with the fact that she's a mutant, and--
Oh.
Is that what she told you she is?
Nico, please!
She's not a mutant, Topher, she's an--
NO!

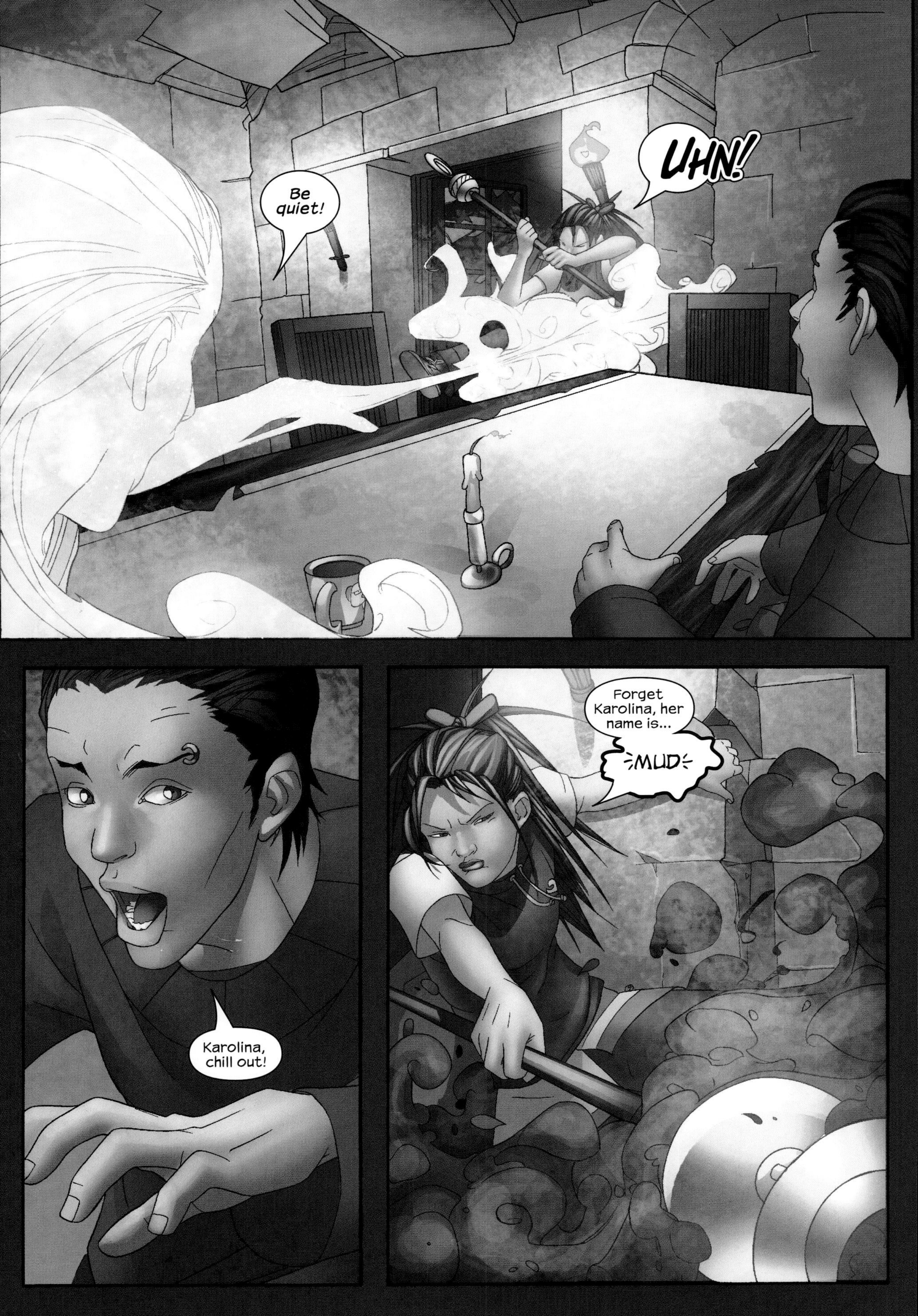
Be quiet!
UHN!
Karolina, chill out!
Forget Karolina, her name is...
MUD

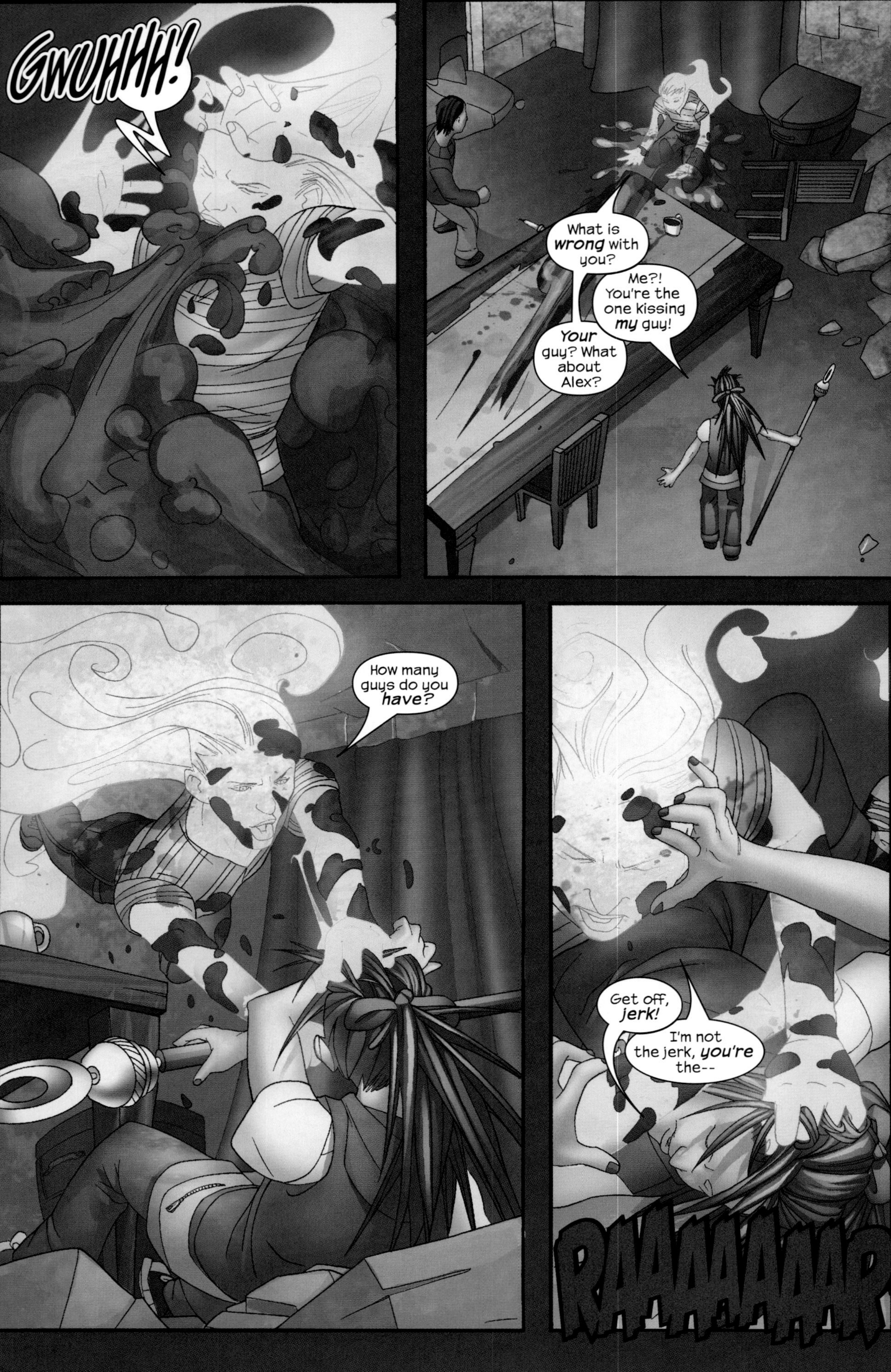
GWUHHH!
What is *wrong* with you?
Me?! You're the one kissing *my* guy!
Your guy? What about Alex?
How many guys do you *have?*
Get off, *jerk!*
I'm not the jerk, *you're* the--
RAAAAAAR

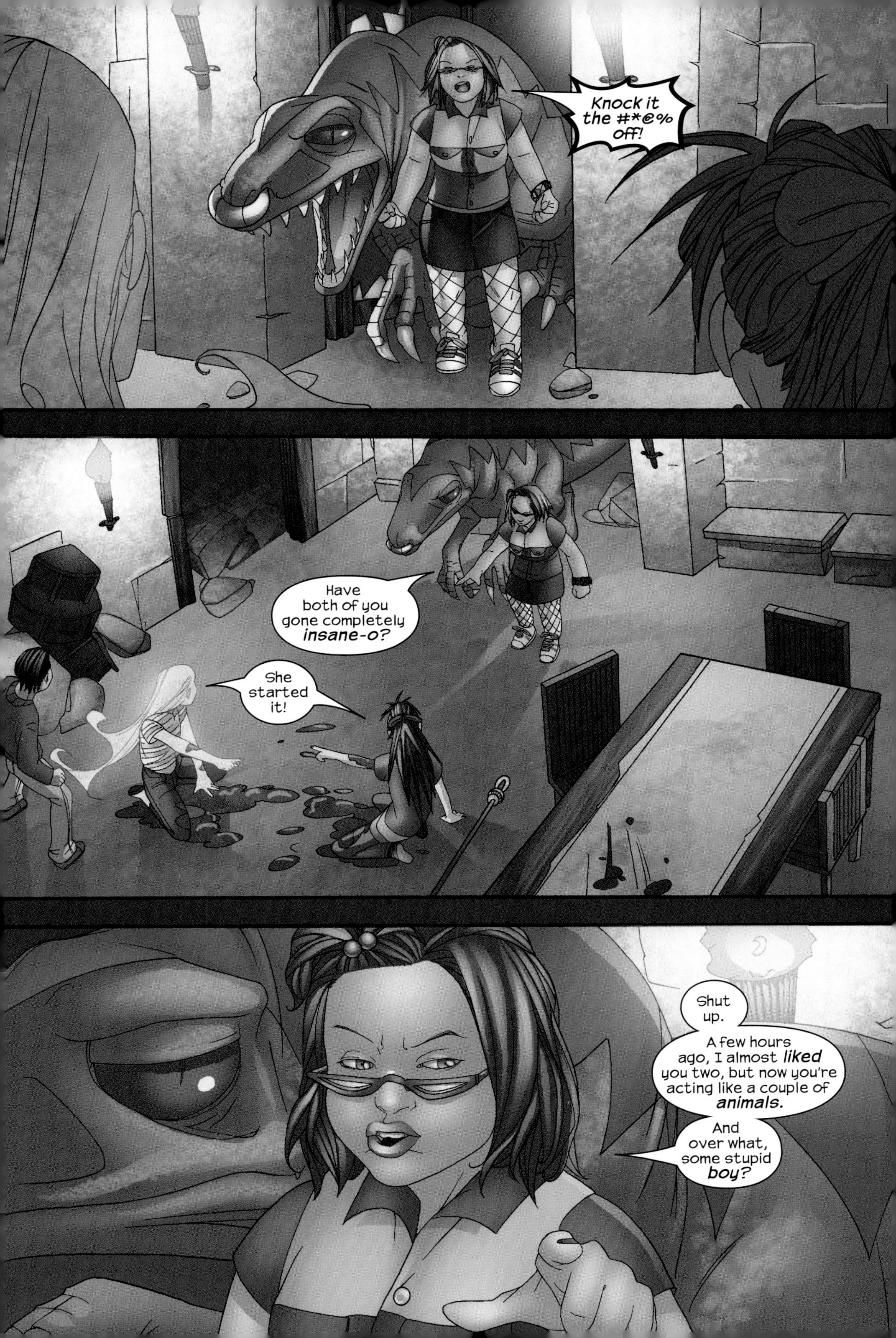
Knock it the #*@% off!
Have both of you gone completely *insane-o?*
She started it!
Shut up.
A few hours ago, I almost *liked* you two, but now you're acting like a couple of *animals.*
And over what, some stupid *boy?*

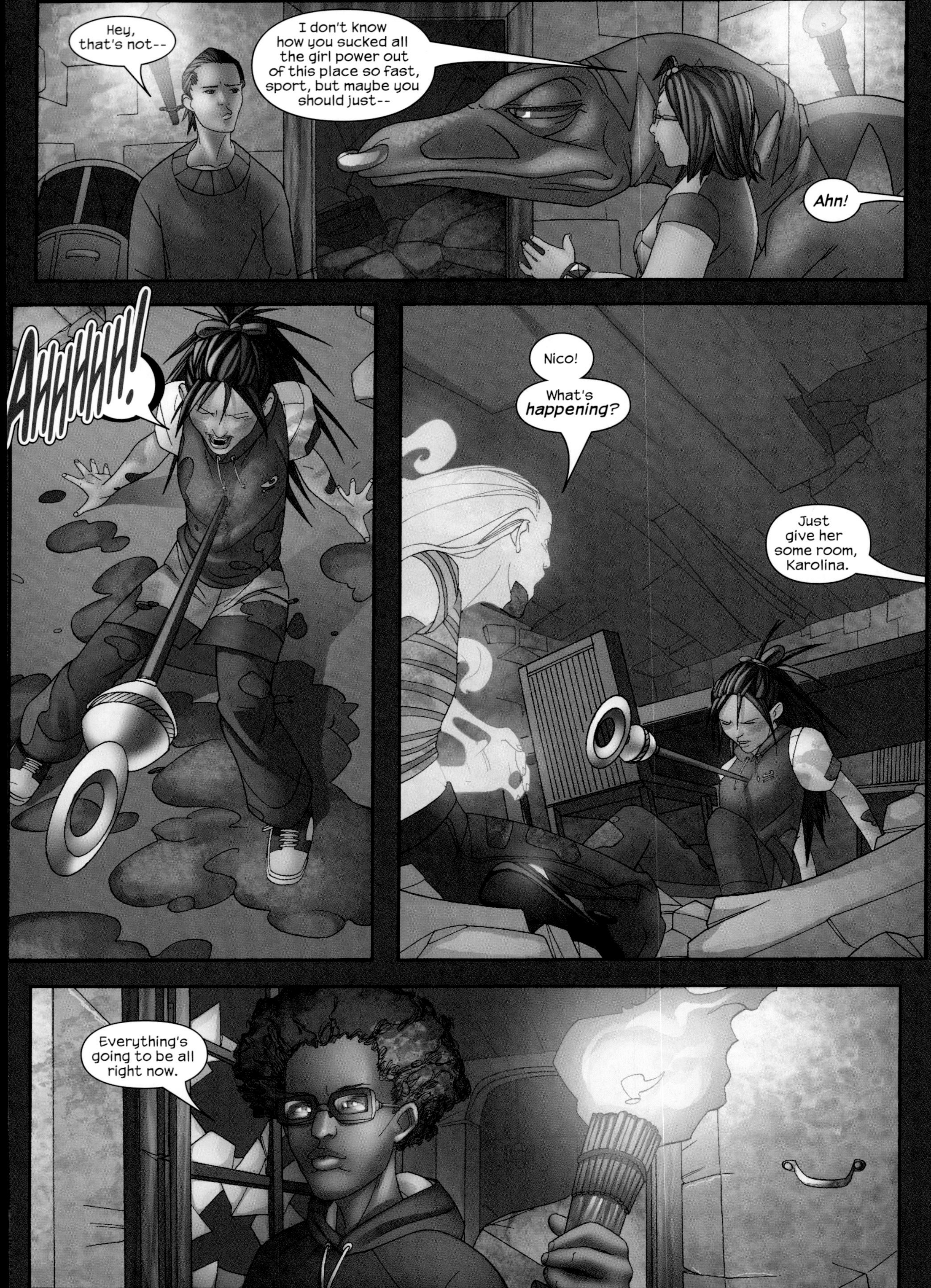

Hey, that's not--
I don't know how you sucked all the girl power out of this place so fast, sport, but maybe you should just--
Ahn!
AHHHHH!
Nico!
What's happening?
Just give her some room, Karolina.
Everything's going to be all right now.

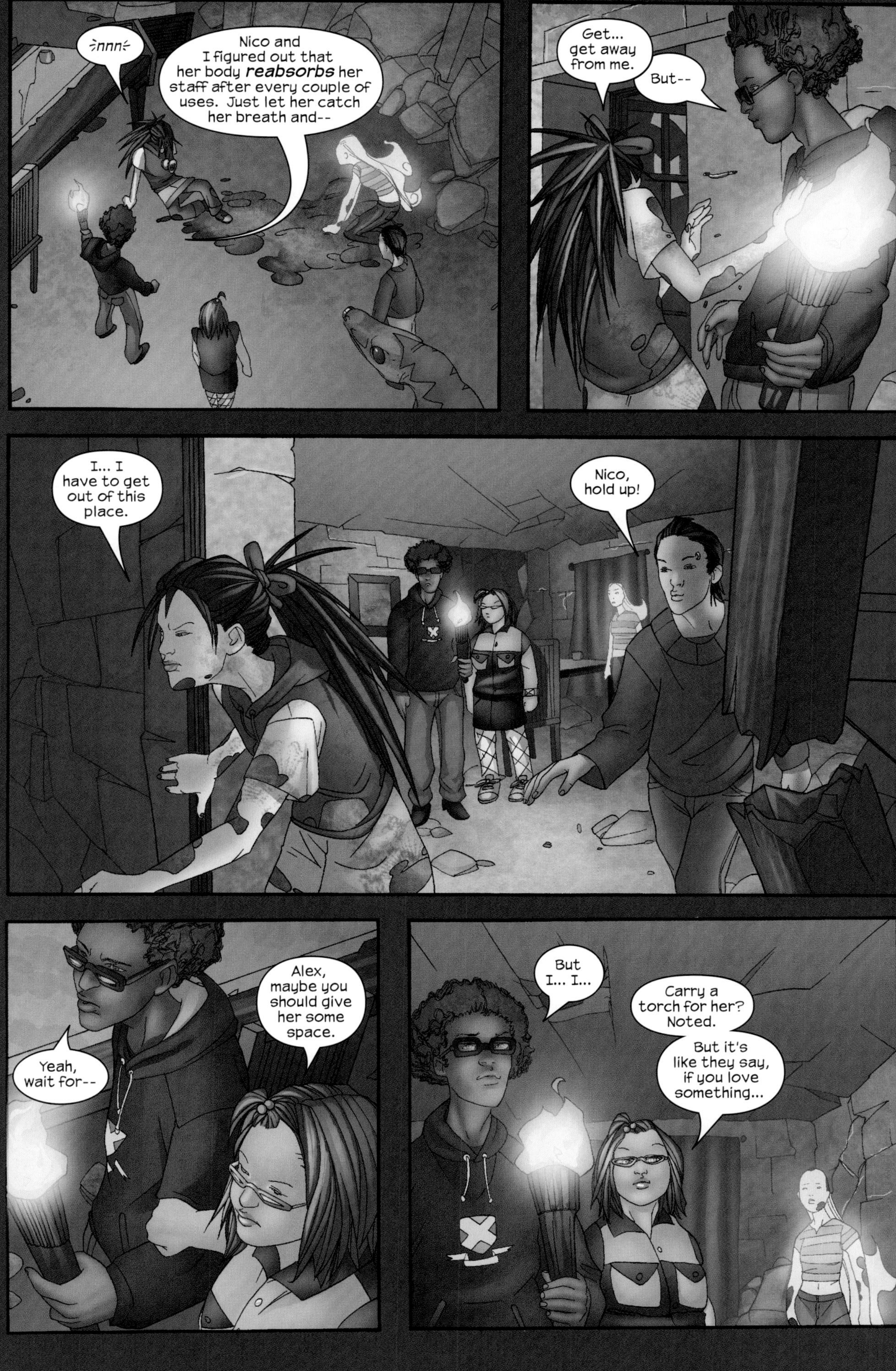

nnn
Nico and I figured out that her body **reabsorbs** her staff after every couple of uses. Just let her catch her breath and--
Get... get away from me.
But--
I... I have to get out of this place.
Nico, hold up!
Yeah, wait for--
Alex, maybe you should give her some space.
But I... I...
Carry a torch for her? Noted.
But it's like they say, if you love something...

"...set it free."

Any progress, dear?

Some.

The rest of The Pride and I have been attempting to identify the three unregistered rogues who attacked our children.

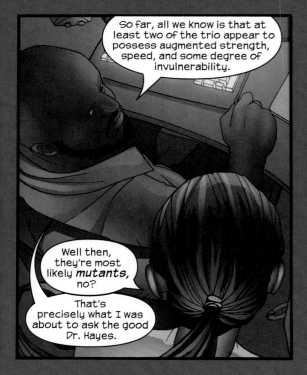

So far, all we know is that at least two of the trio appear to possess augmented strength, speed, and some degree of invulnerability.

Well then, they're most likely *mutants*, no?

That's precisely what I was about to ask the good Dr. Hayes.

It's possible, Wilder, but not likely.

My pureblood union notwithstanding, it's extremely rare to encounter more than one mutant with the exact same power.

These lowlifes probably just stumbled onto a cursed artifact or... or *radioactive meteorite*. You know, the usual.

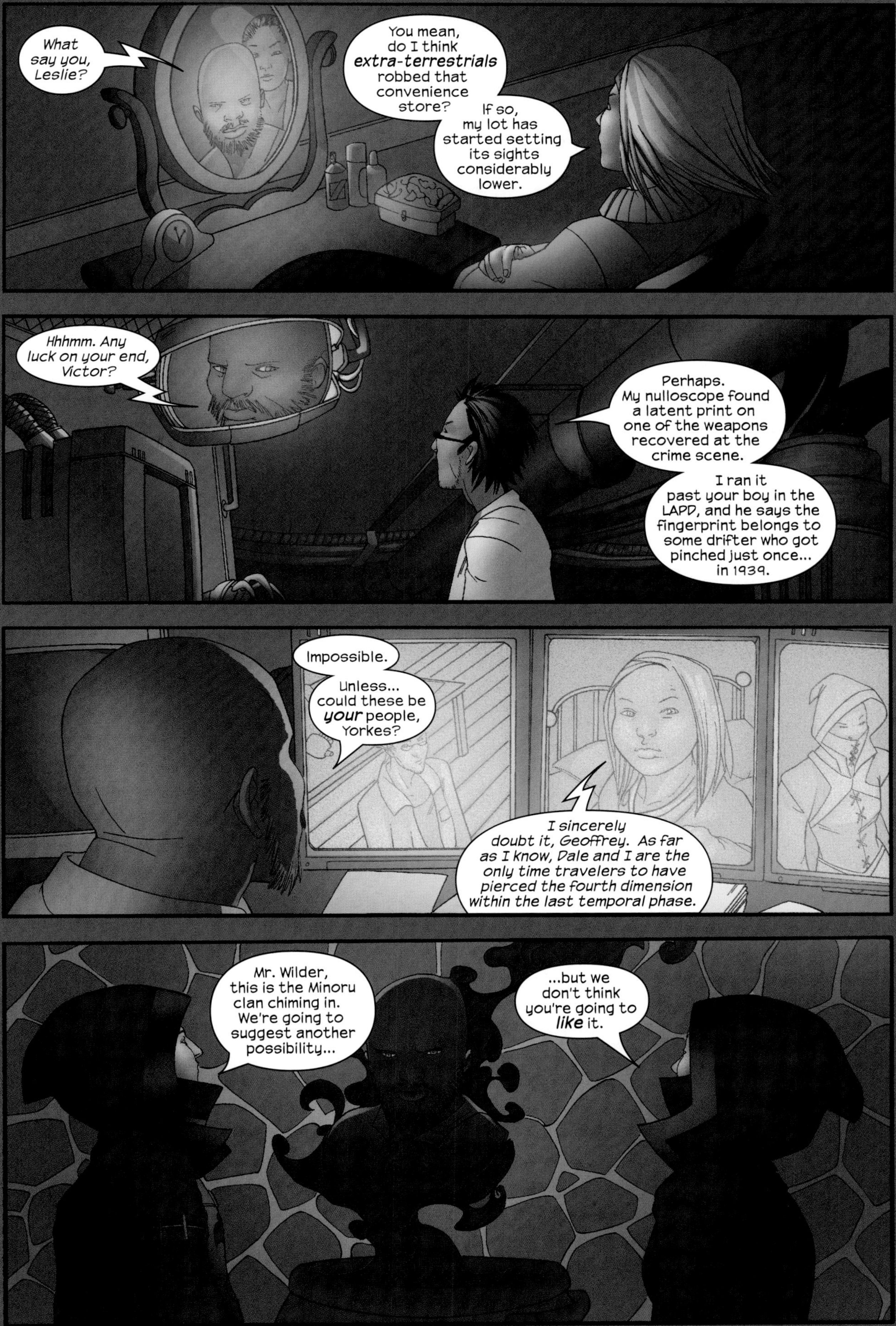
What say you, Leslie?
You mean, do I think extra-terrestrials robbed that convenience store?
If so, my lot has started setting its sights considerably lower.
Hhhmm. Any luck on your end, Victor?
Perhaps. My nulloscope found a latent print on one of the weapons recovered at the crime scene.
I ran it past your boy in the LAPD, and he says the fingerprint belongs to some drifter who got pinched just once... in 1939.
Impossible.
Unless... could these be your people, Yorkes?
I sincerely doubt it, Geoffrey. As far as I know, Dale and I are the only time travelers to have pierced the fourth dimension within the last temporal phase.
Mr. Wilder, this is the Minoru clan chiming in. We're going to suggest another possibility...
...but we don't think you're going to like it.

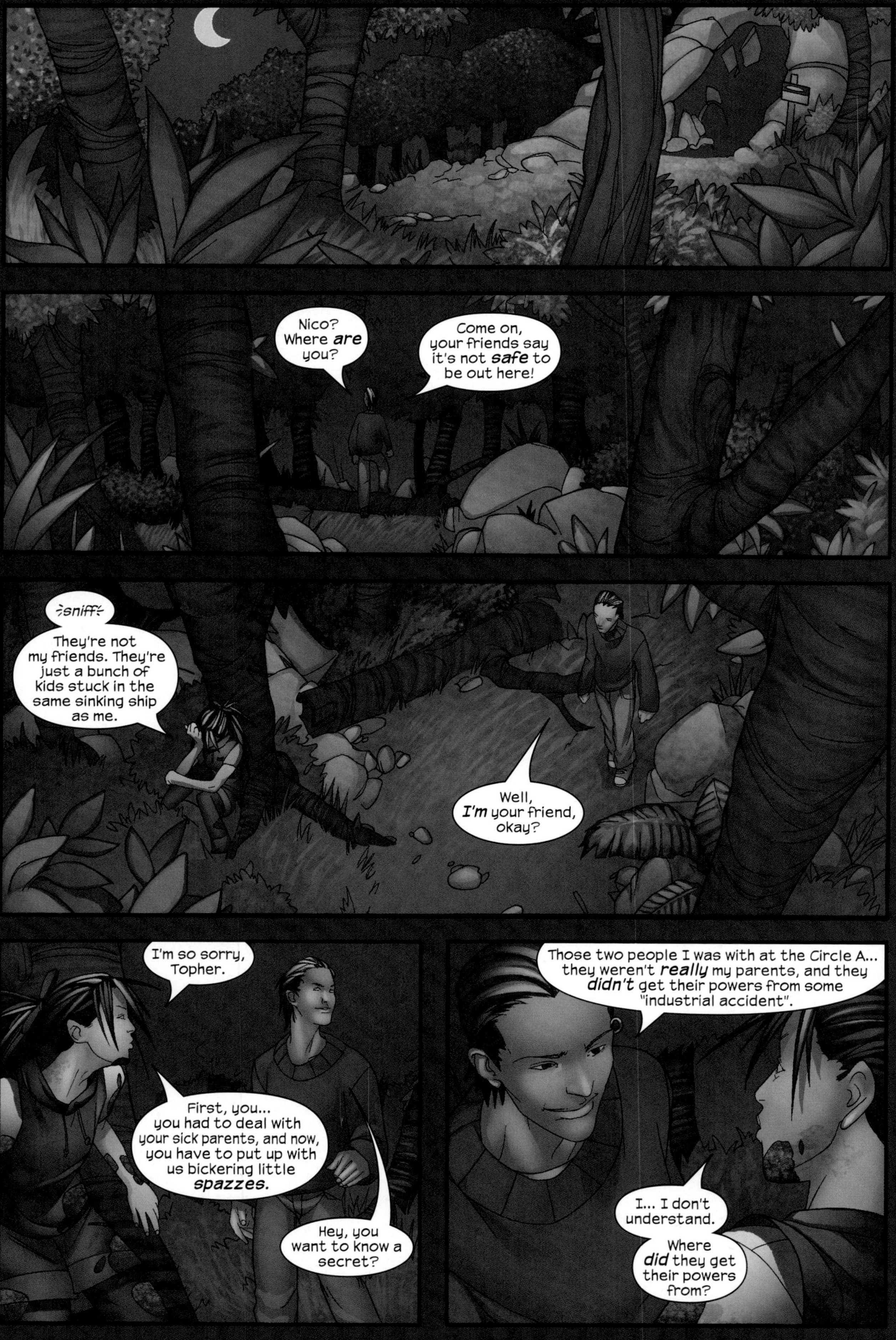

Nico? Where are you?
Come on, your friends say it's not safe to be out here!
sniff
They're not my friends. They're just a bunch of kids stuck in the same sinking ship as me.
Well, I'm your friend, okay?
I'm so sorry, Topher.
First, you... you had to deal with your sick parents, and now, you have to put up with us bickering little spazzes.
Hey, you want to know a secret?
Those two people I was with at the Circle A... they weren't really my parents, and they didn't get their powers from some "industrial accident".
I... I don't understand.
Where did they get their powers from?

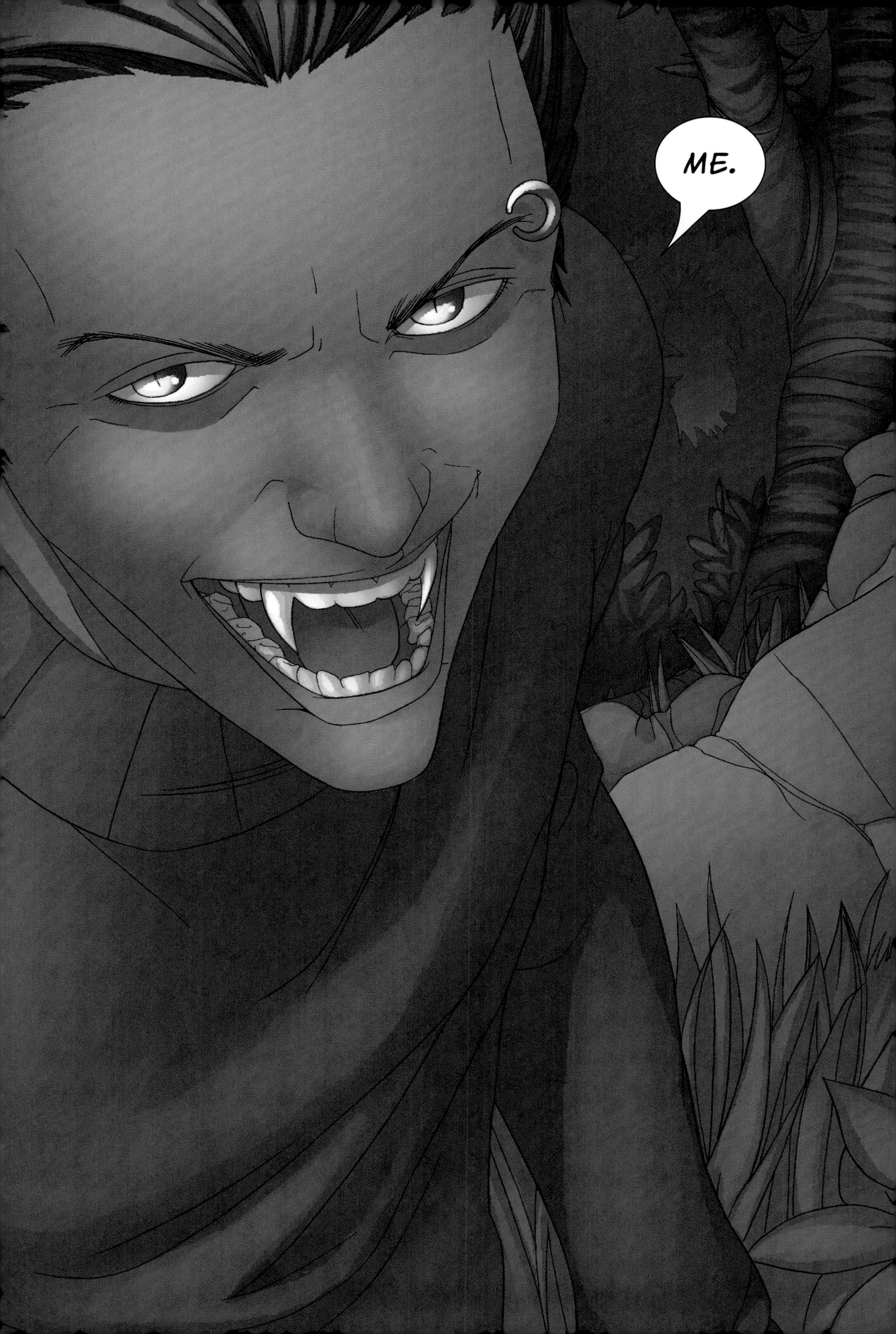
ME.

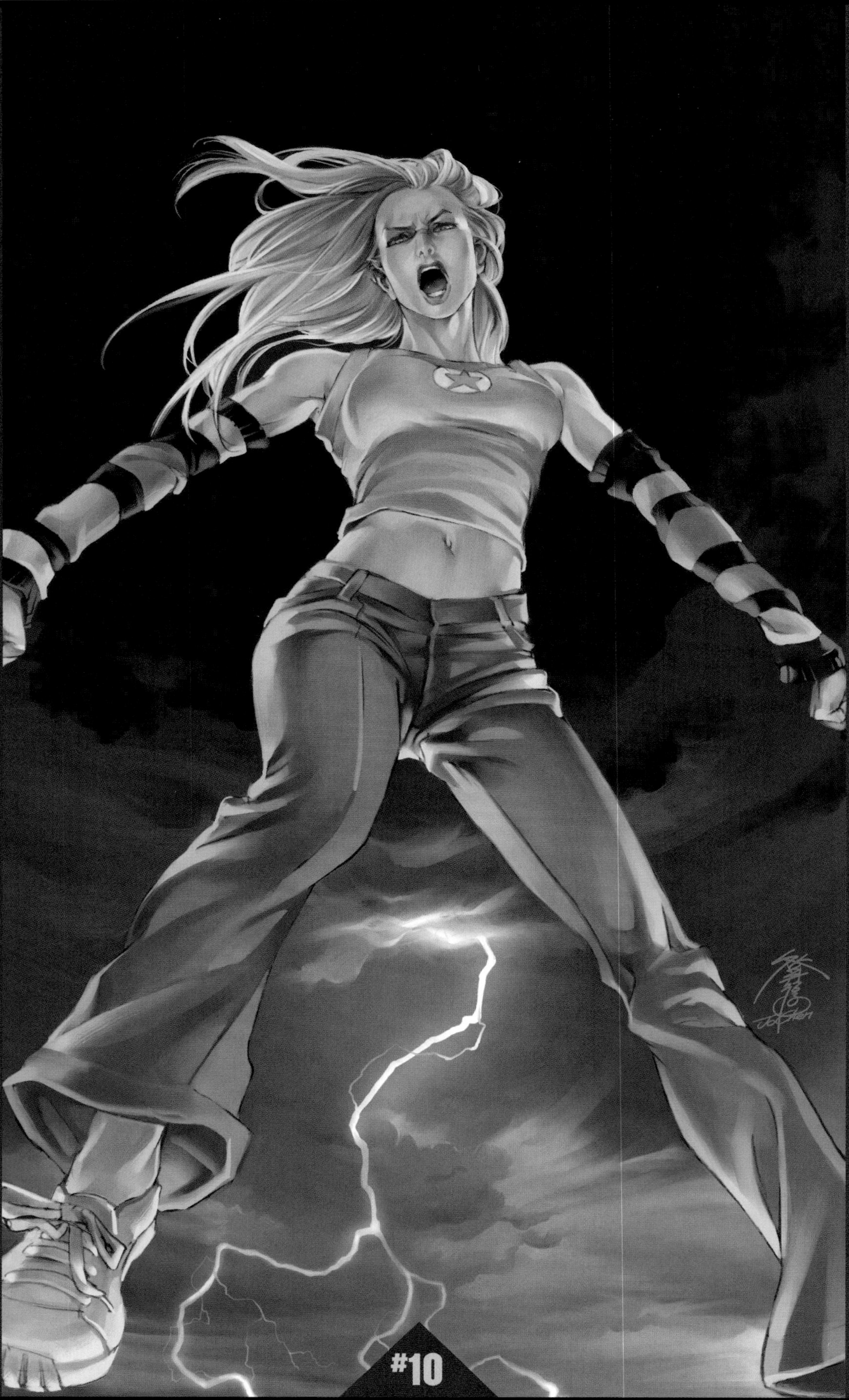
#10

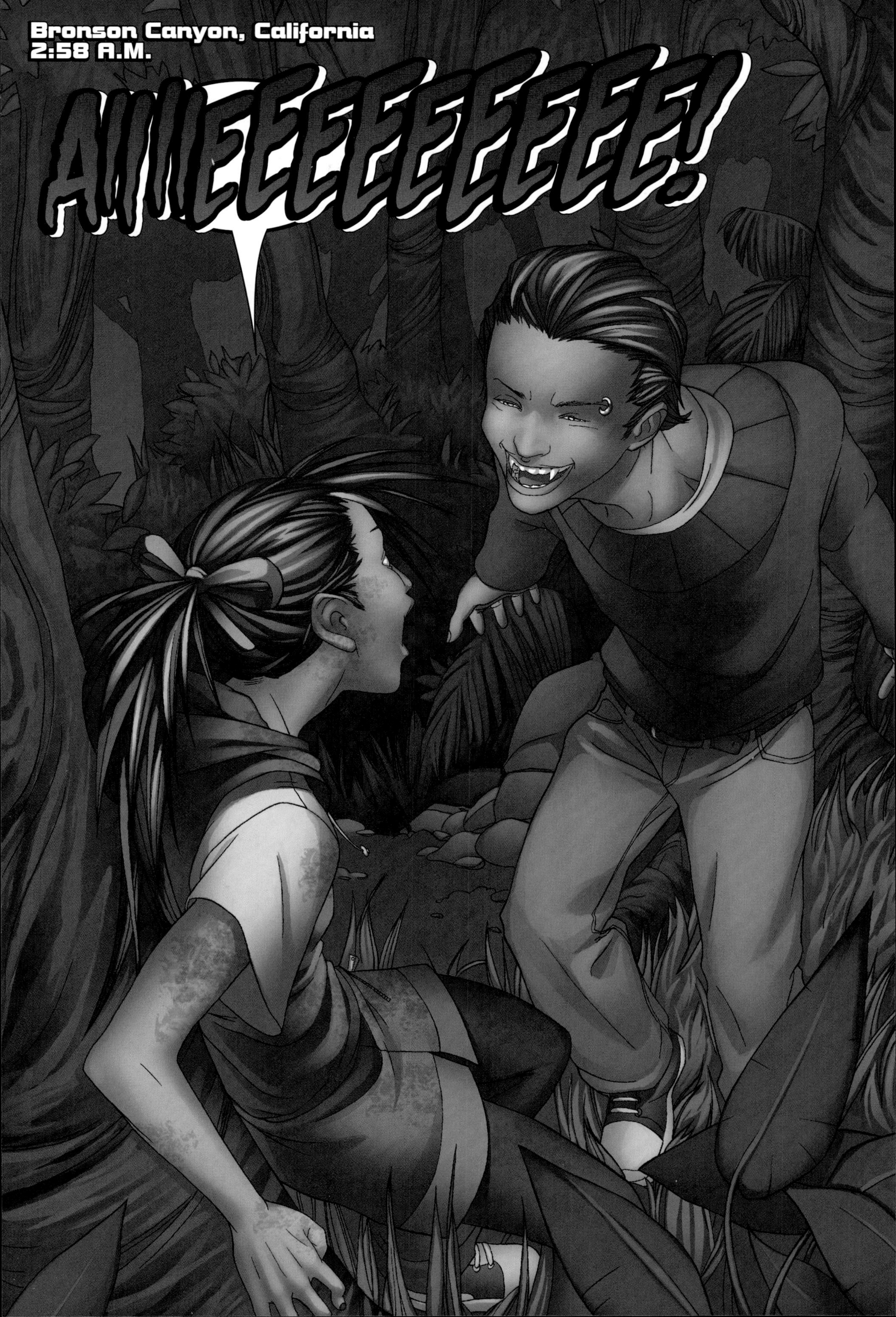
Bronson Canyon, California
2:58 A.M.
AIIIEEEEEEEEEE!

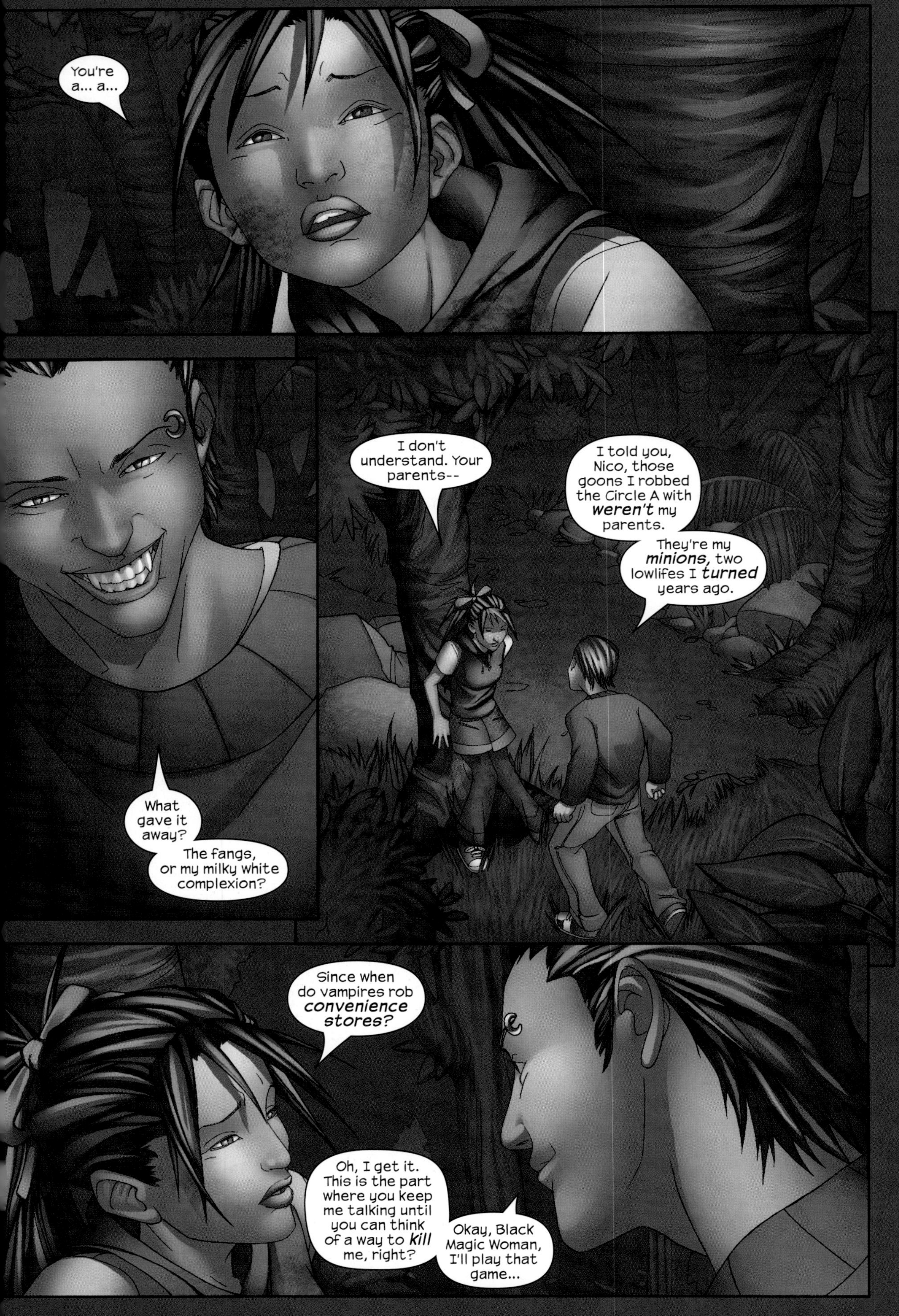
You're a... a...
What gave it away?
The fangs, or my milky white complexion?
I don't understand. Your parents--
I told you, Nico, those goons I robbed the Circle A with weren't my parents.
They're my minions, two lowlifes I turned years ago.
Since when do vampires rob convenience stores?
Oh, I get it. This is the part where you keep me talking until you can think of a way to kill me, right?
Okay, Black Magic Woman, I'll play that game...

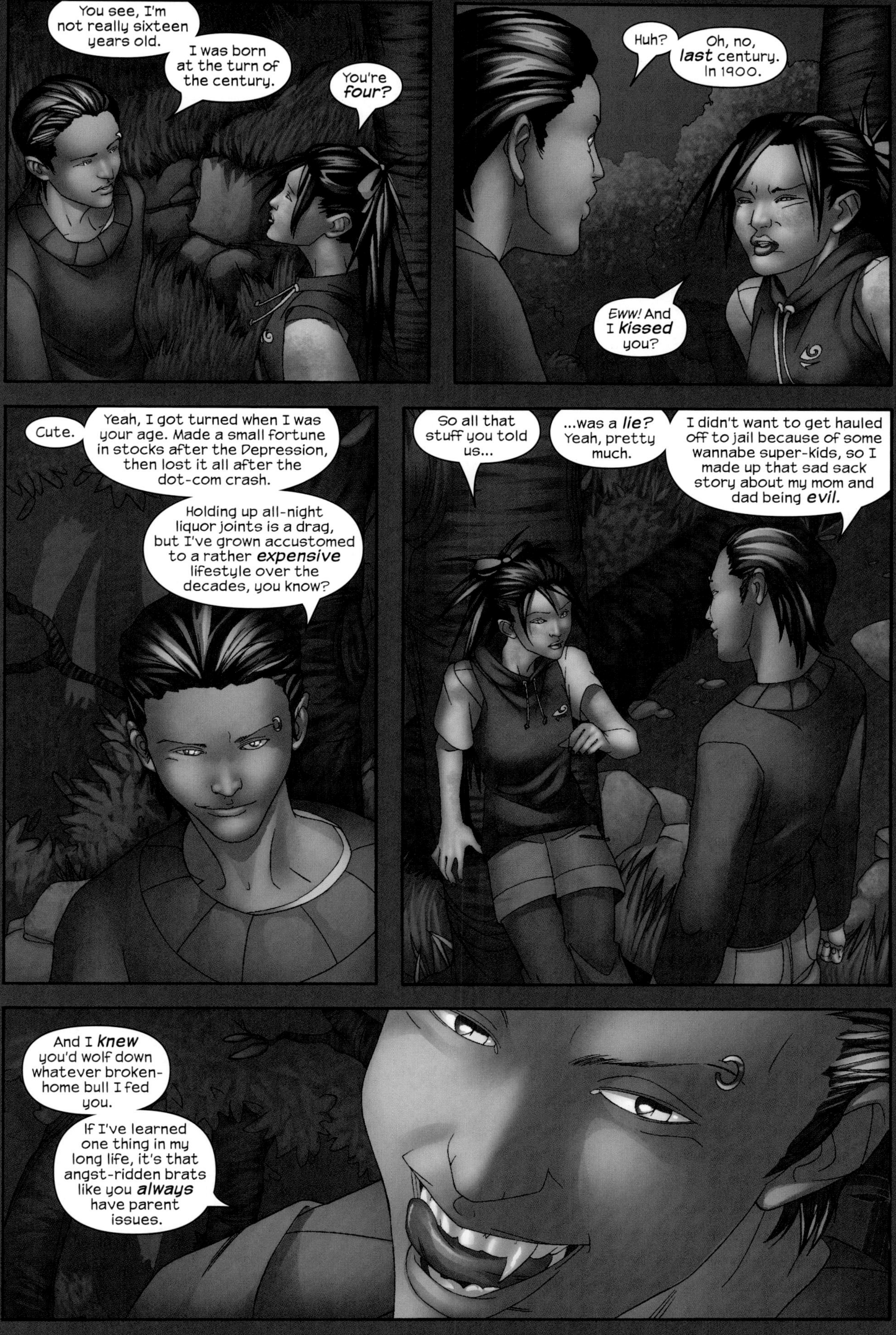
You see, I'm not really sixteen years old.
I was born at the turn of the century.
You're *four?*
Huh?
Oh, no, *last* century. In 1900.
Eww! And I *kissed* you?
Cute.
Yeah, I got turned when I was your age. Made a small fortune in stocks after the Depression, then lost it all after the dot-com crash.
Holding up all-night liquor joints is a drag, but I've grown accustomed to a rather *expensive* lifestyle over the decades, you know?
So all that stuff you told us...
...was a *lie?* Yeah, pretty much.
I didn't want to get hauled off to jail because of some wannabe super-kids, so I made up that sad sack story about my mom and dad being *evil.*
And I *knew* you'd wolf down whatever broken-home bull I fed you.
If I've learned one thing in my long life, it's that angst-ridden brats like you *always* have parent issues.

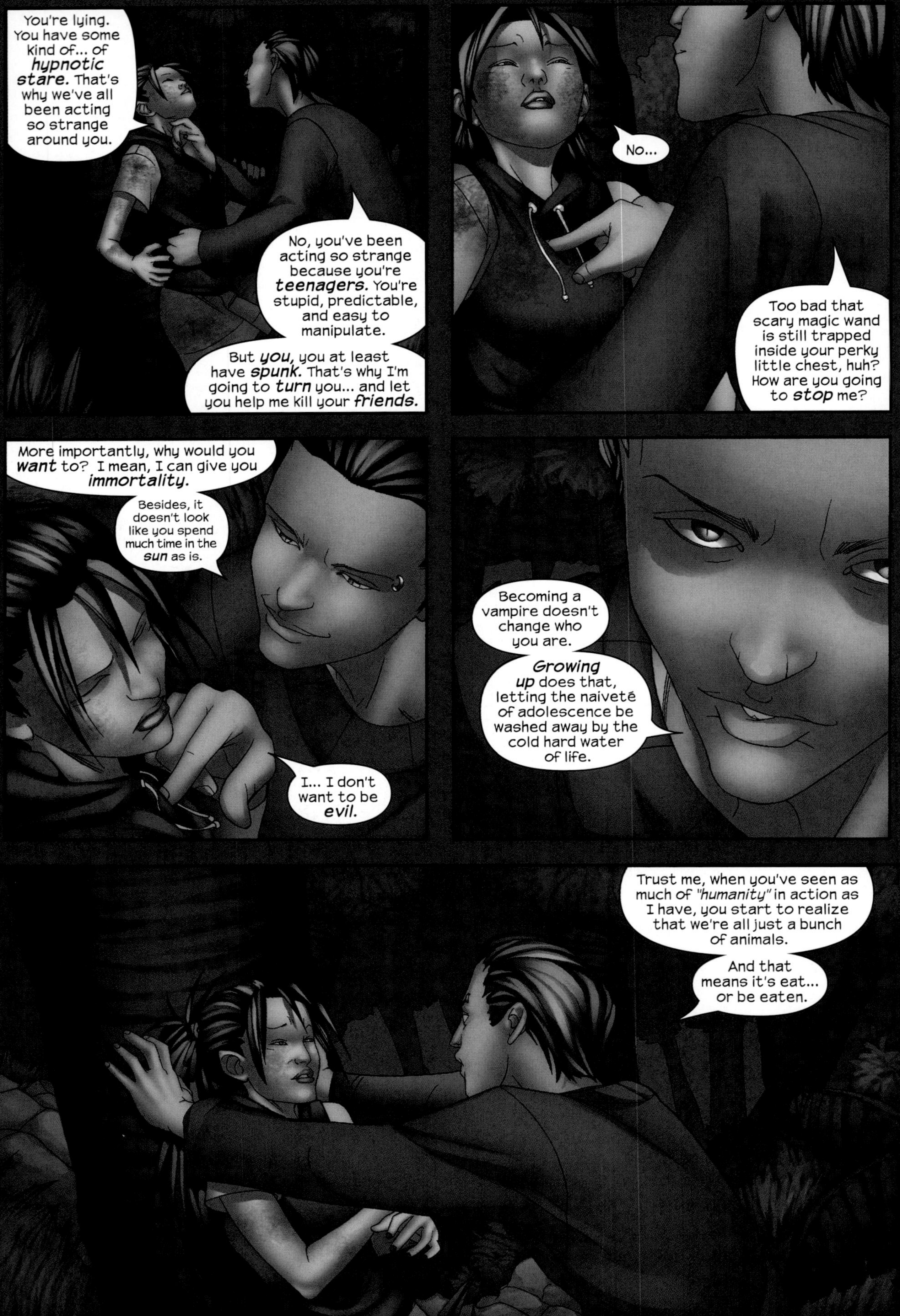

You're lying. You have some kind of... of *hypnotic stare.* That's why we've all been acting so strange around you.
No, you've been acting so strange because you're *teenagers.* You're stupid, predictable, and easy to manipulate.
But *you,* you at least have *spunk.* That's why I'm going to *turn* you... and let you help me kill your *friends.*
No...
Too bad that scary magic wand is still trapped inside your perky little chest, huh? How are you going to *stop* me?
More importantly, why would you *want* to? I mean, I can give you *immortality.*
Besides, it doesn't look like you spend much time in the *sun* as is.
I... I don't want to be *evil.*
Becoming a vampire doesn't change who you are.
Growing up does that, letting the naiveté of adolescence be washed away by the cold hard water of life.
Trust me, when you've seen as much of *"humanity"* in action as I have, you start to realize that we're all just a bunch of animals.
And that means it's eat... or be eaten.

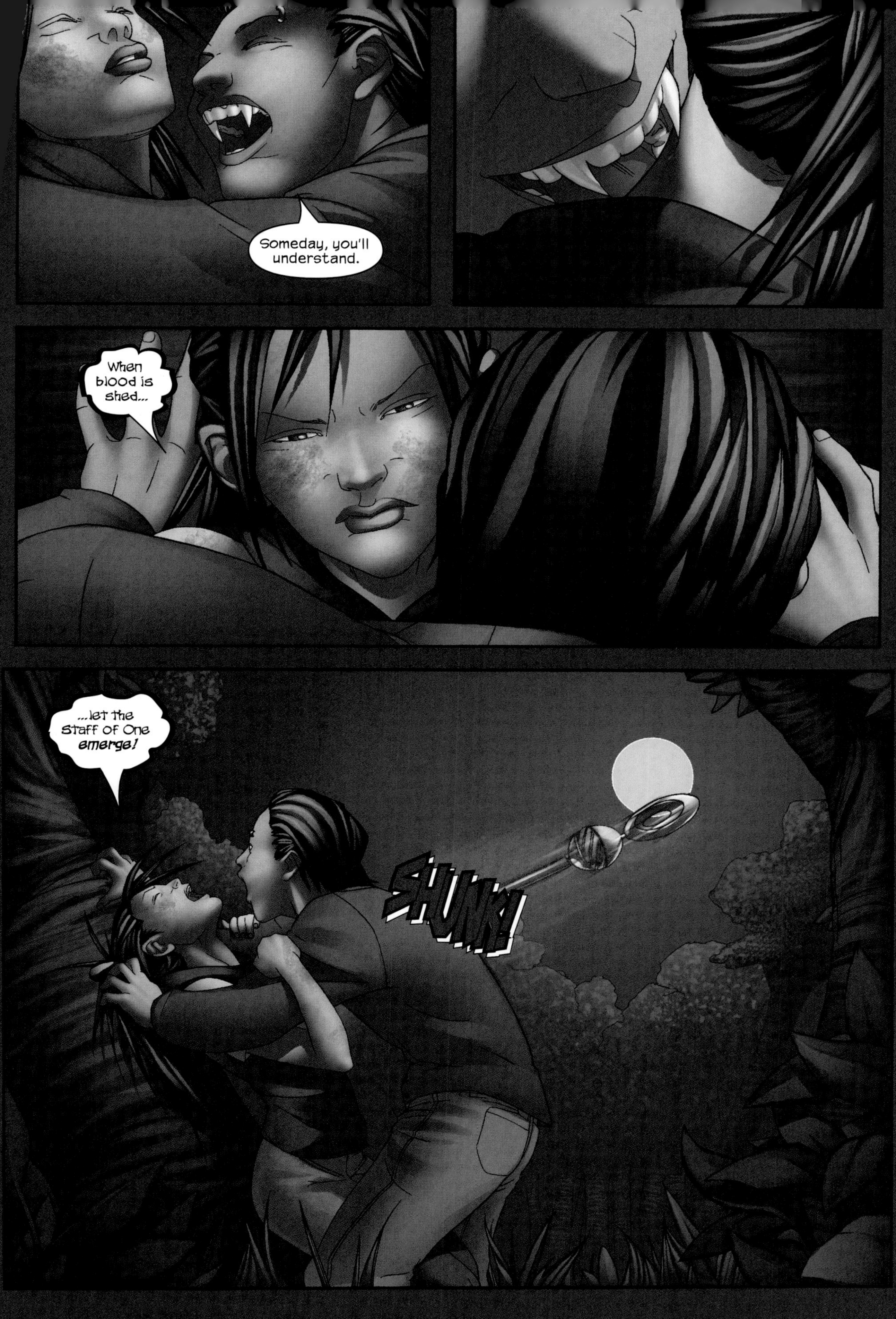
Someday, you'll understand.
When blood is shed...
...let the Staff of One emerge!
SHUNK!

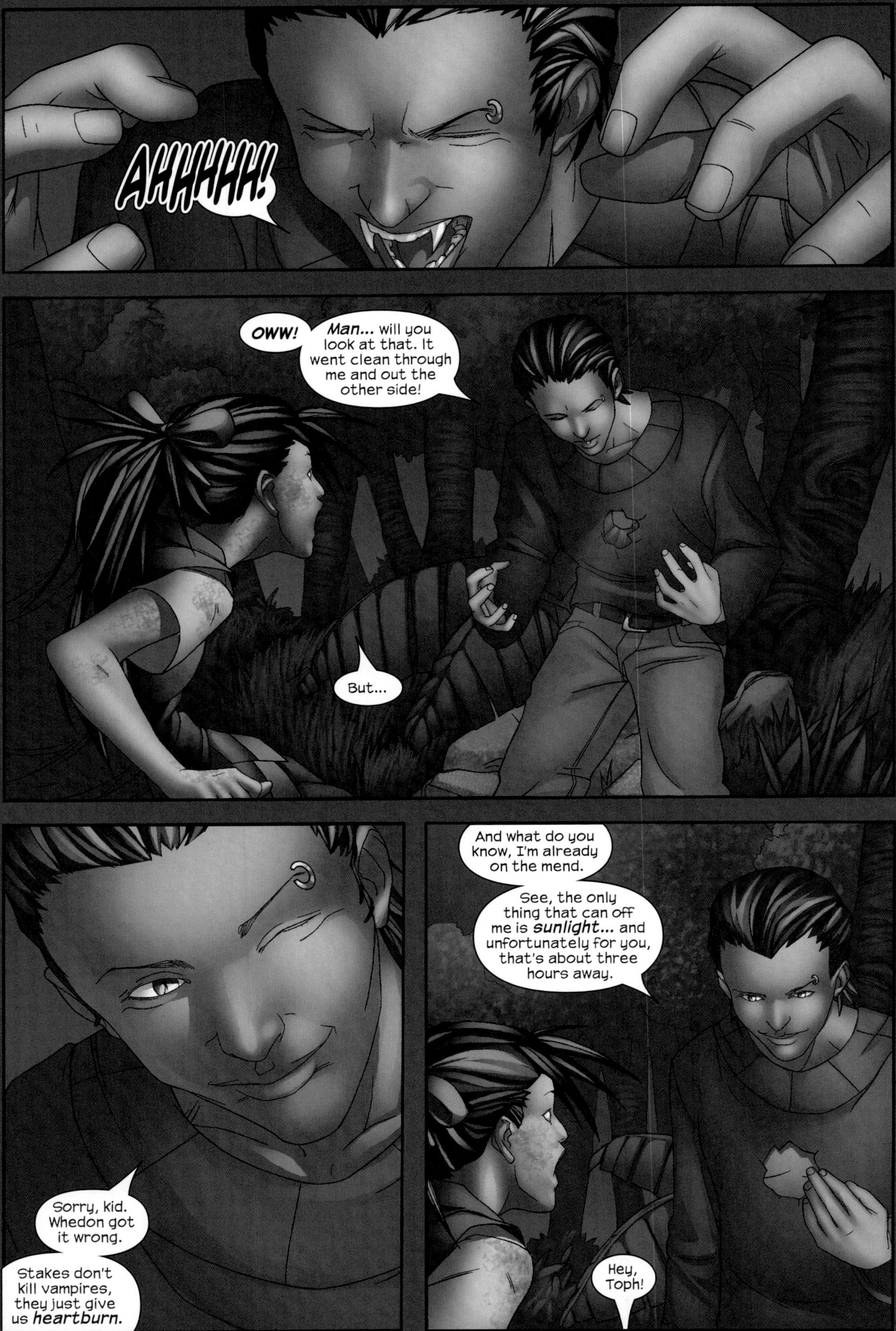
AHHHHH!
OWW!
Man... will you look at that. It went clean through me and out the other side!
But...
Sorry, kid. Whedon got it wrong.
Stakes don't kill vampires, they just give us heartburn.
And what do you know, I'm already on the mend.
See, the only thing that can off me is sunlight... and unfortunately for you, that's about three hours away.
Hey, Toph!

You're off the team.

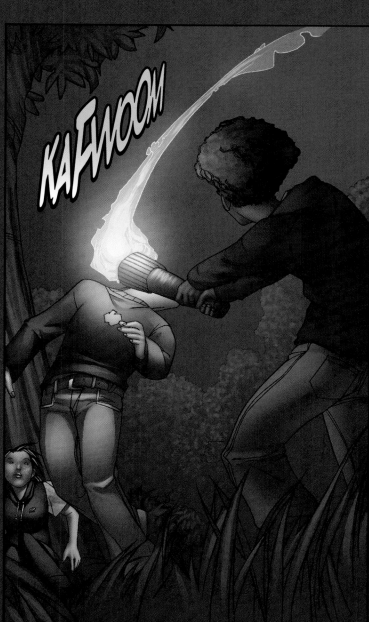

KAFWOOM

Alex!

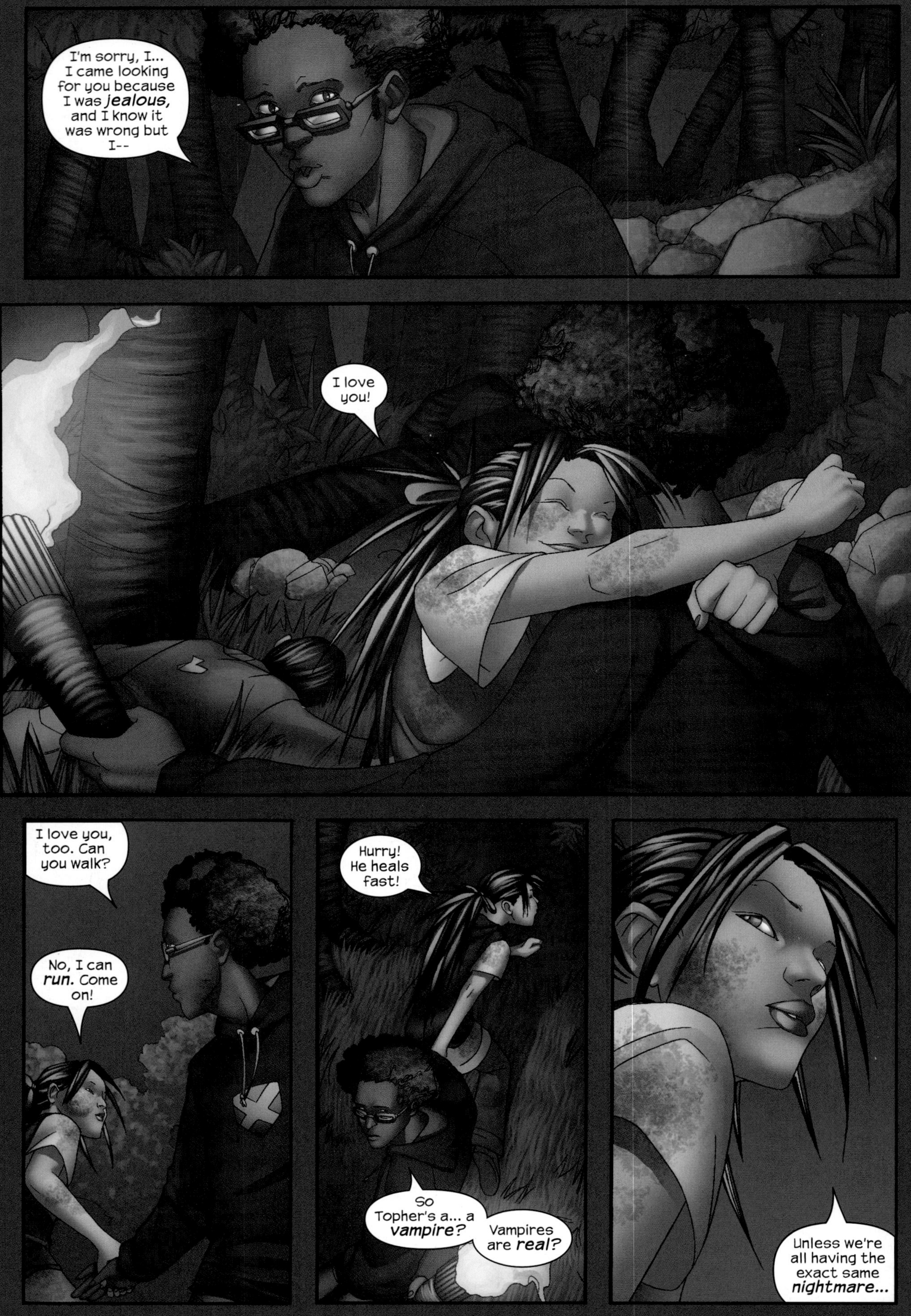
I'm sorry, I... I came looking for you because I was *jealous,* and I know it was wrong but I--
I love you!
I love you, too. Can you walk?
No, I can *run.* Come on!
Hurry! He heals fast!
So Topher's a... a *vampire?*
Vampires are *real?*
Unless we're all having the exact same *nightmare...*

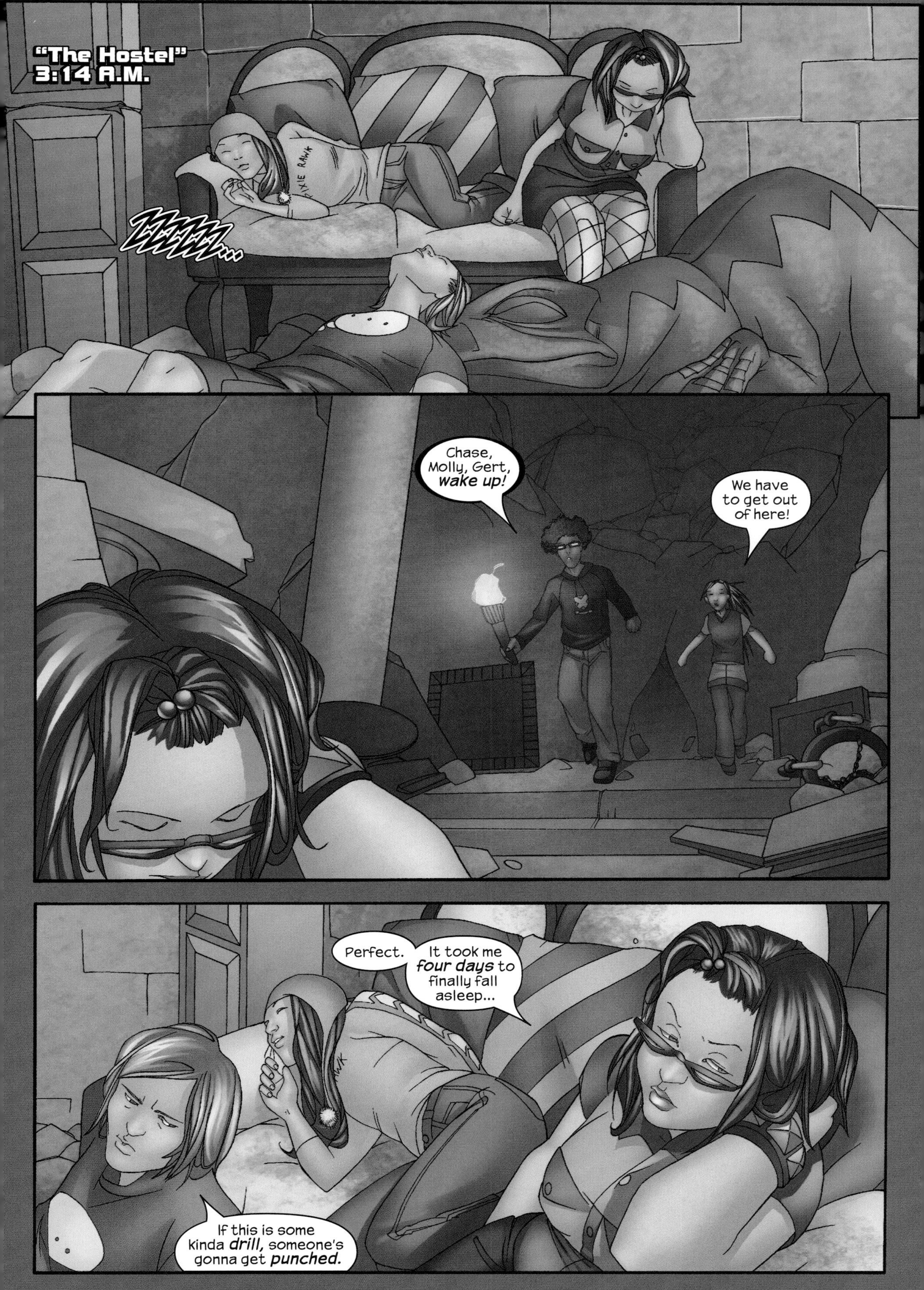
"The Hostel"
3:14 A.M.
PIXIE RAWK
ZZZZZ...
Chase, Molly, Gert, *wake up!*
We have to get out of here!
Perfect.
It took me *four days* to finally fall asleep...
If this is some kinda *drill,* someone's gonna get *punched.*

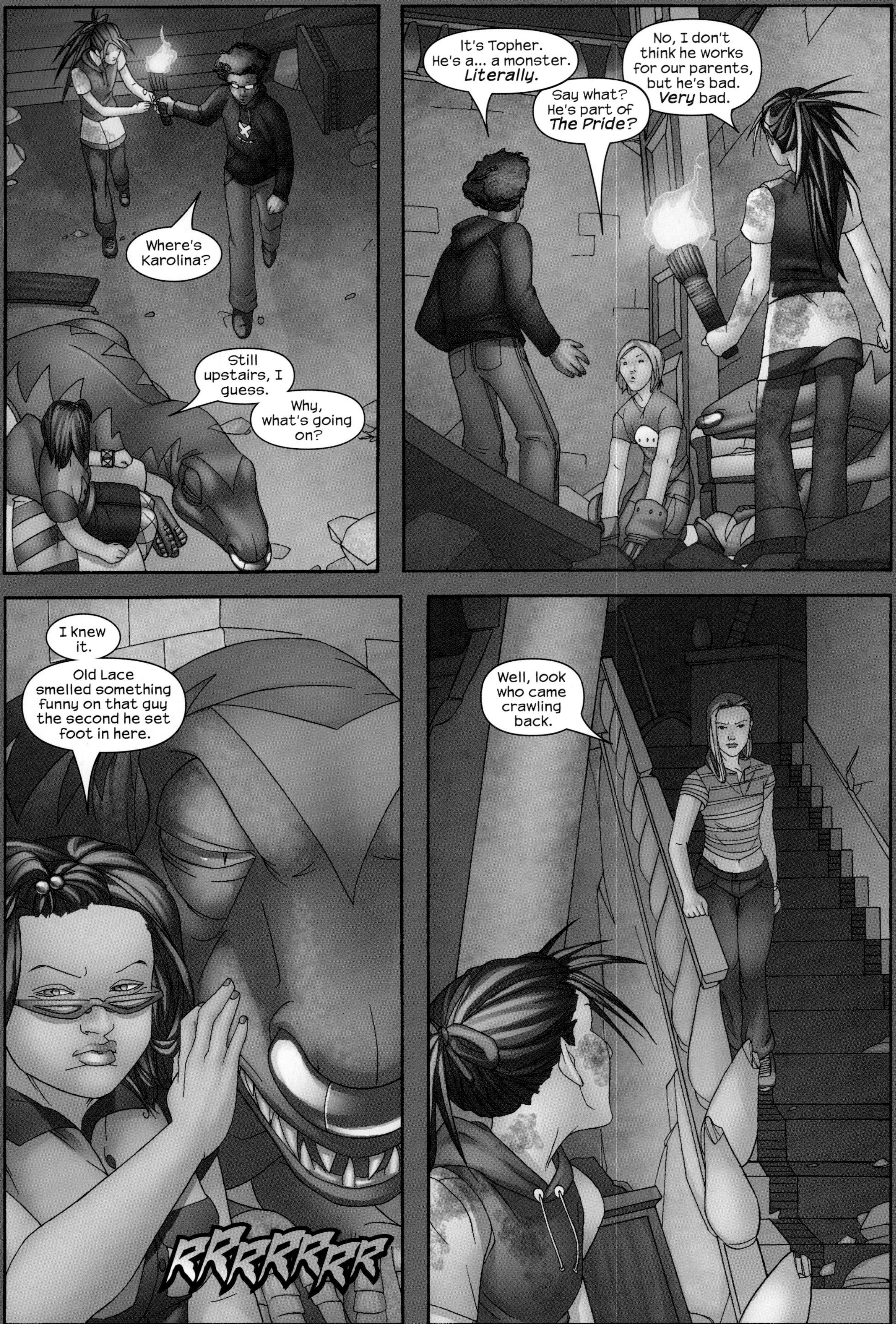
Where's Karolina?
Still upstairs, I guess.
Why, what's going on?
It's Topher. He's a... a monster. *Literally.*
Say what? He's part of *The Pride?*
No, I don't think he works for our parents, but he's bad. *Very* bad.
I knew it.
Old Lace smelled something funny on that guy the second he set foot in here.
RRRRRRR
Well, look who came crawling back.

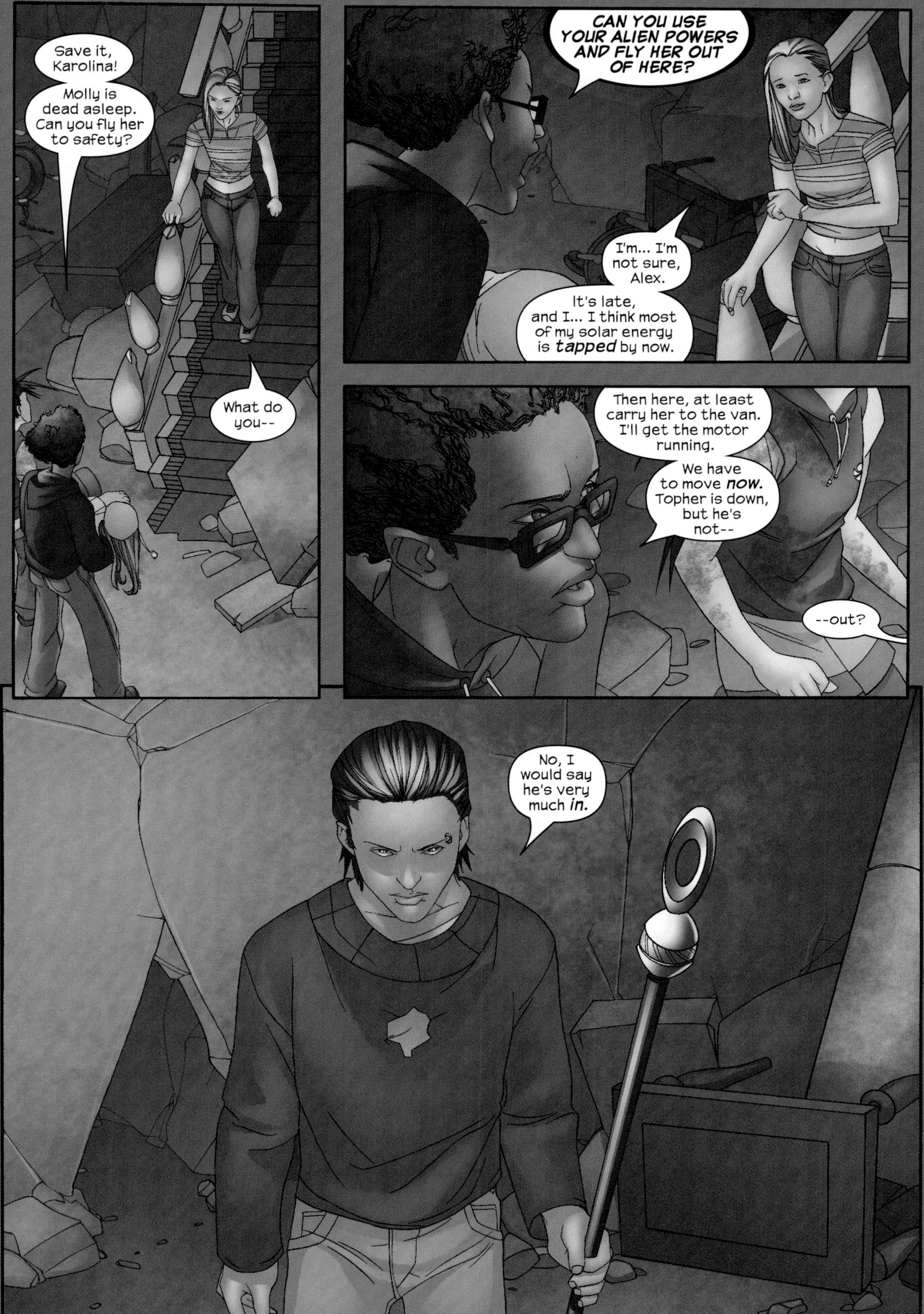
Save it, Karolina!
Molly is dead asleep. Can you fly her to safety?
What do you--
CAN YOU USE YOUR ALIEN POWERS AND FLY HER OUT OF HERE?
I'm... I'm not sure, Alex.
It's late, and I... I think most of my solar energy is *tapped* by now.
Then here, at least carry her to the van. I'll get the motor running.
We have to move **now.** Topher is down, but he's not--
--out?
No, I would say he's very much ***in.***

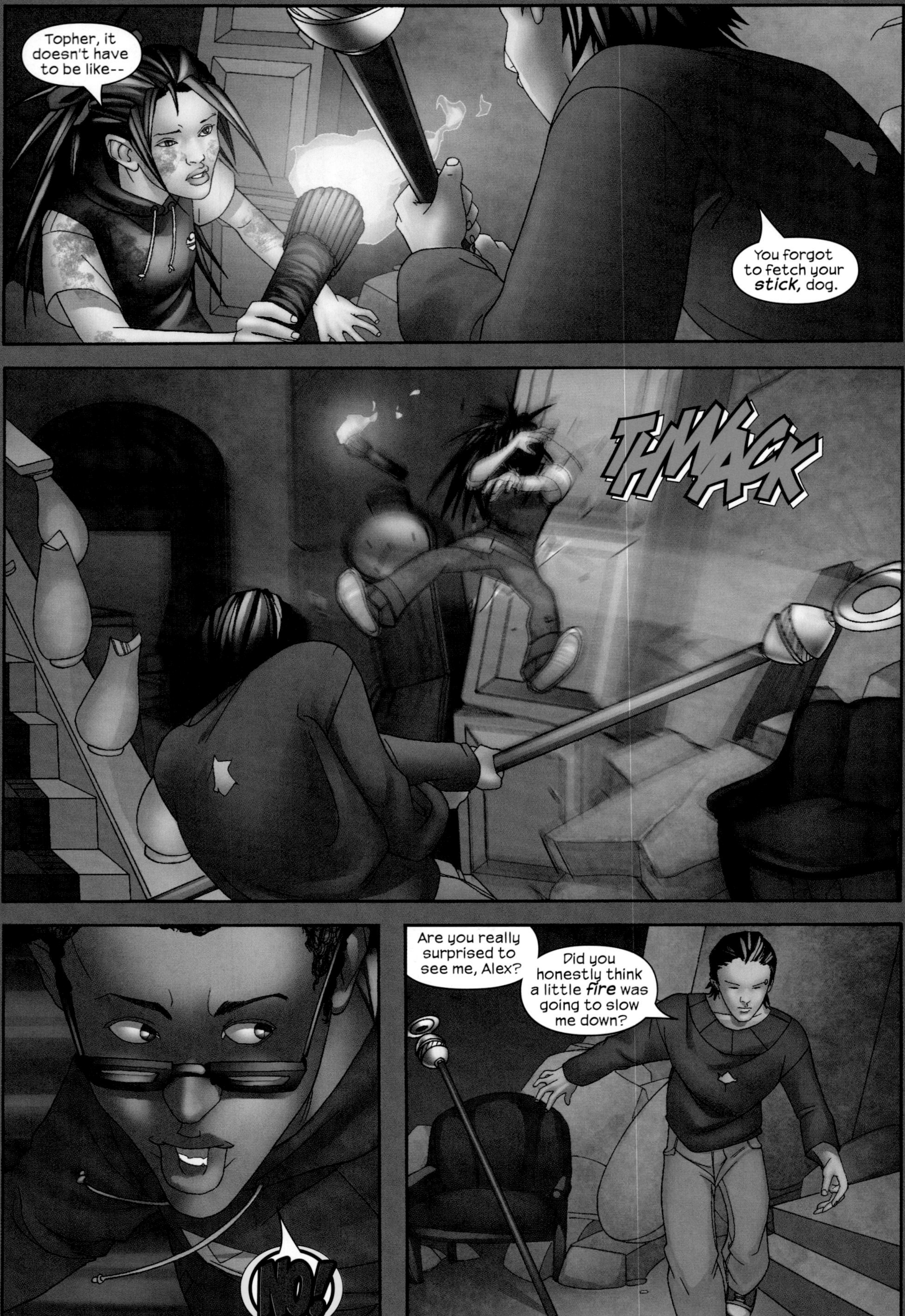
Topher, it doesn't have to be like--
You forgot to fetch your *stick*, dog.
THWACK
NO!
Are you really surprised to see me, Alex?
Did you honestly think a little *fire* was going to slow me down?

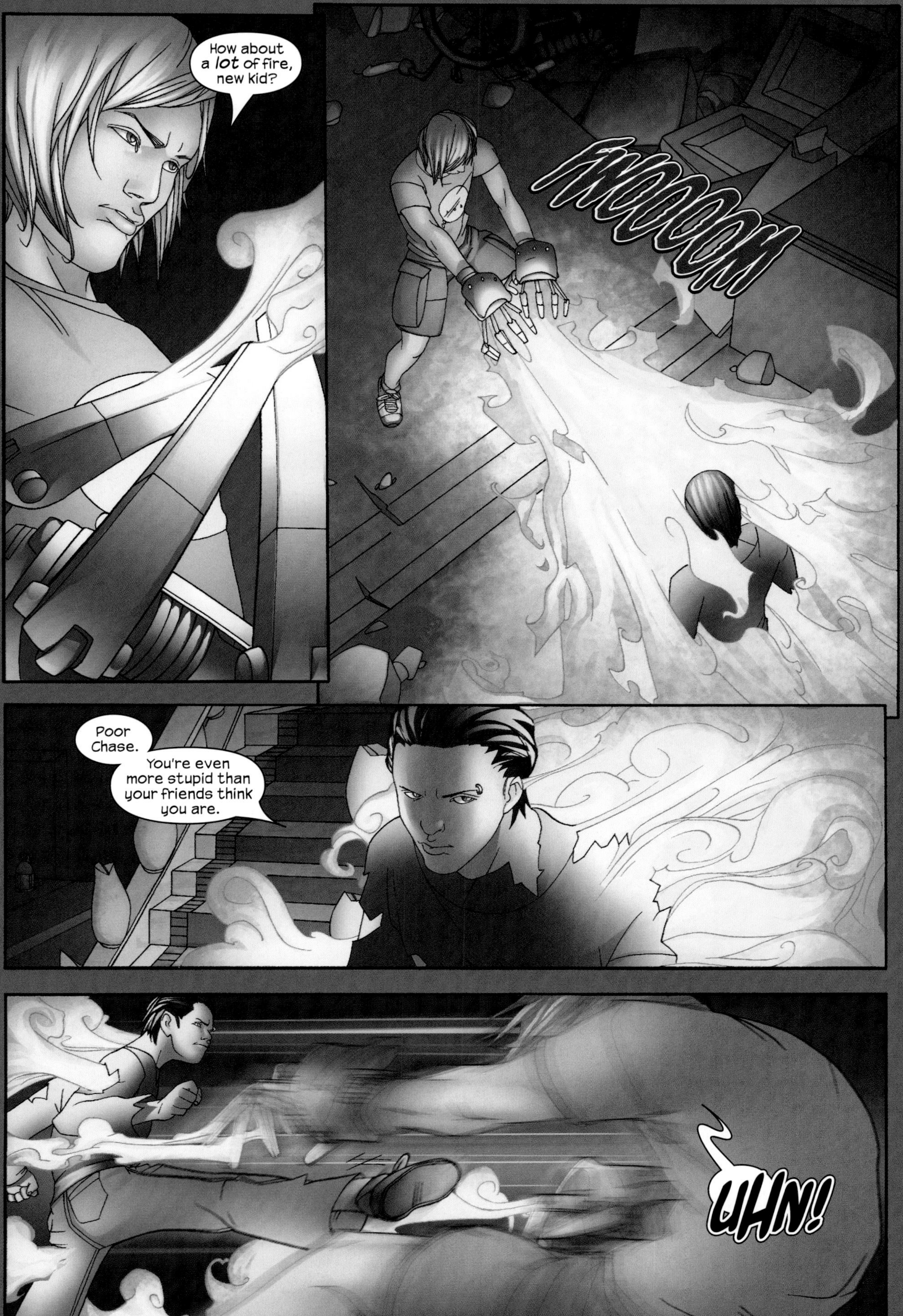
How about a *lot* of fire, new kid?
FWOOOOOM
Poor Chase.
You're even more stupid than your friends think you are.
UHN!

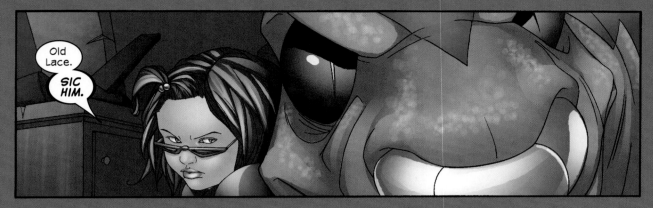

Old Lace.

SIC HIM.

No need to play possum with this thing anymore, huh?

I've already learned all of your *weaknesses*.

Hup!

Uhf!

Hey, Gert? Do you know what really killed all the dinosaurs?

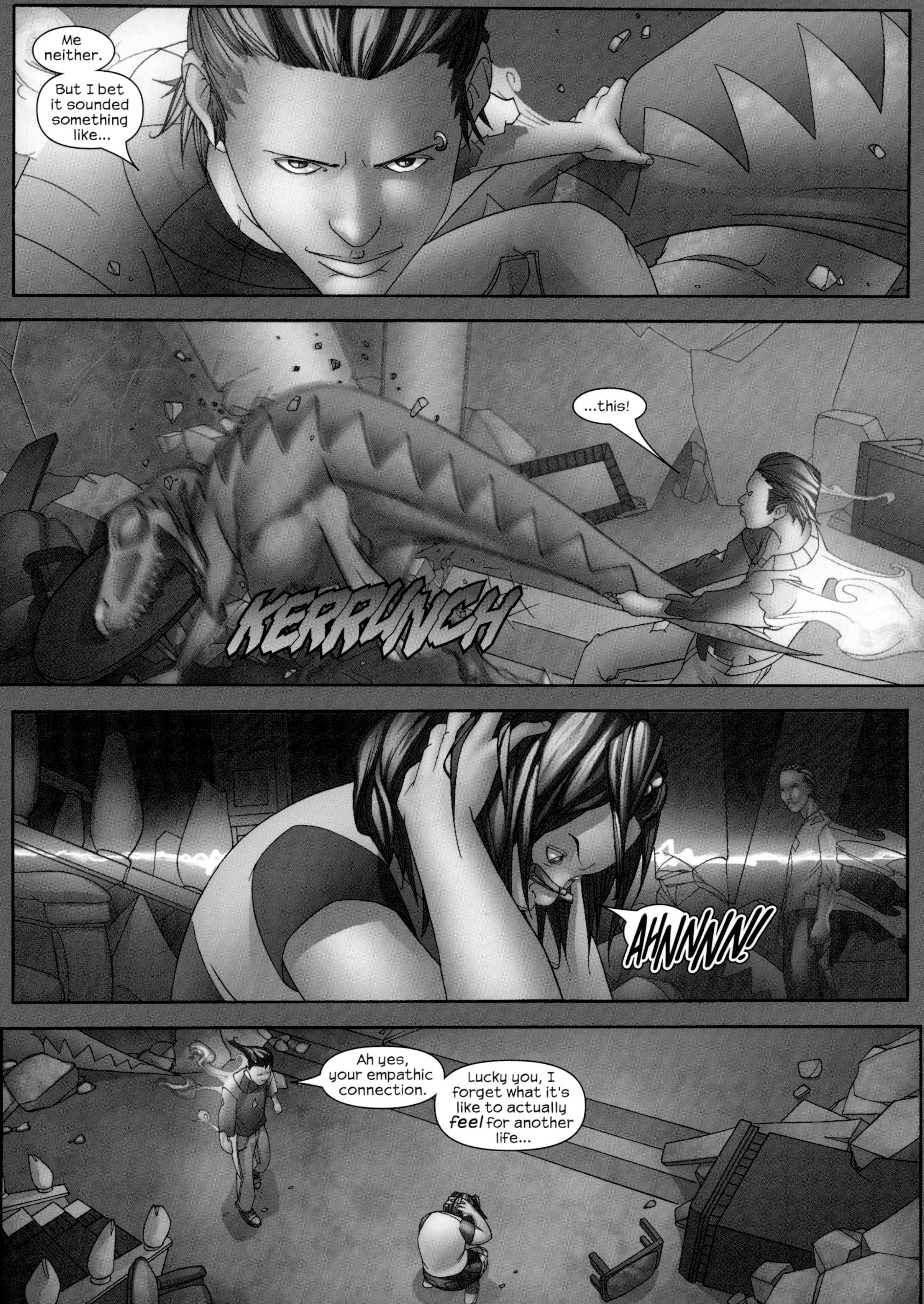
Me neither.
But I bet it sounded something like...
...this!
KERRUNCH
AHNNNN!!
Ah yes, your empathic connection.
Lucky you, I forget what it's like to actually *feel* for another life...

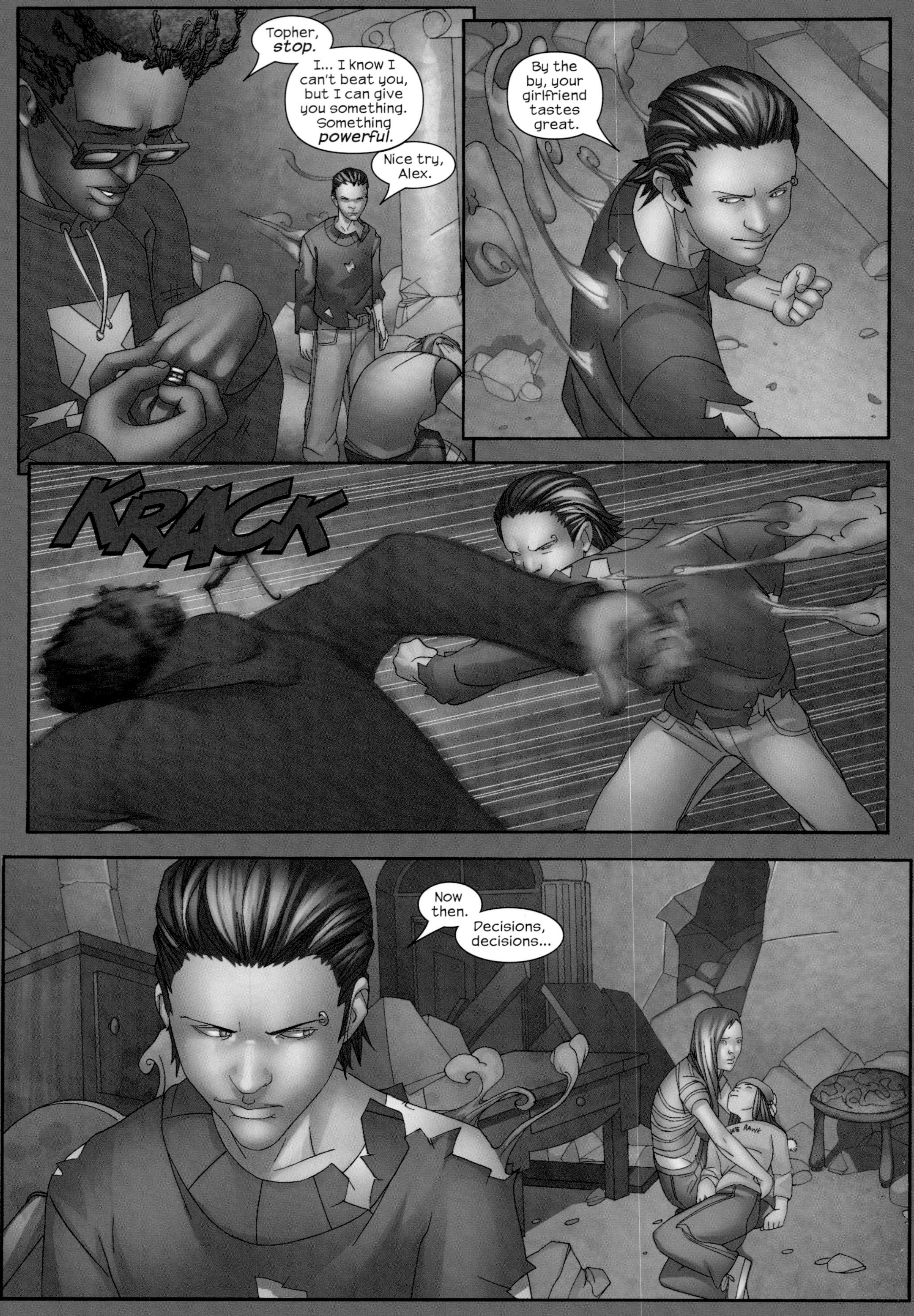
Topher, *stop.*
I... I know I can't beat you, but I can give you something. Something *powerful.*
Nice try, Alex.
By the by, your girlfriend tastes great.
KRACK
Now then.
Decisions, decisions...

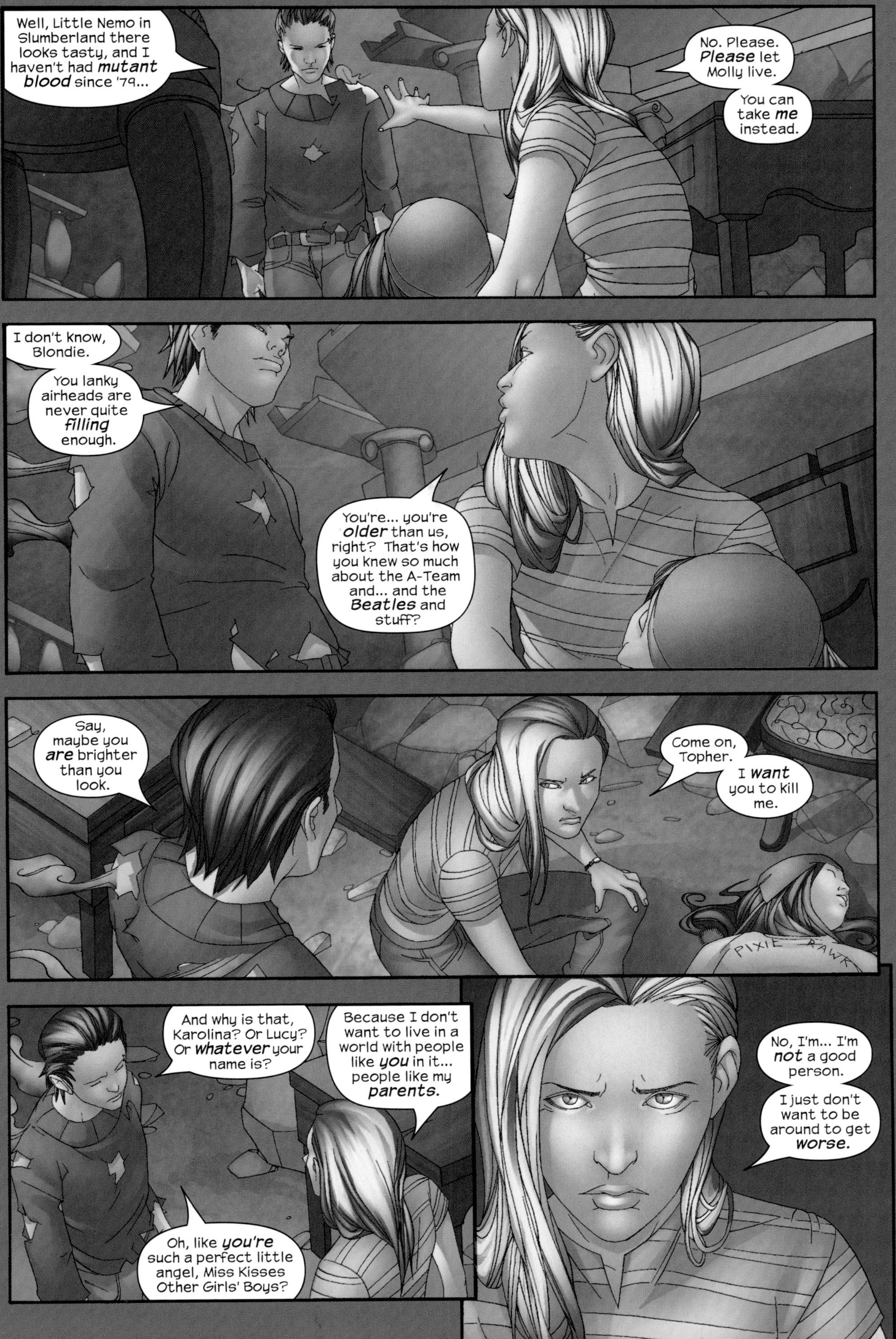

Well, Little Nemo in Slumberland there looks tasty, and I haven't had *mutant blood* since '79...
No. Please. *Please* let Molly live.
You can take *me* instead.
I don't know, Blondie.
You lanky airheads are never quite *filling* enough.
You're... you're *older* than us, right? That's how you knew so much about the A-Team and... and the *Beatles* and stuff?
Say, maybe you *are* brighter than you look.
Come on, Topher.
I *want* you to kill me.
PIXIE RAWK
And why is that, Karolina? Or Lucy? Or *whatever* your name is?
Because I don't want to live in a world with people like *you* in it... people like my *parents.*
Oh, like *you're* such a perfect little angel, Miss Kisses Other Girls' Boys?
No, I'm... I'm *not* a good person.
I just don't want to be around to get *worse.*

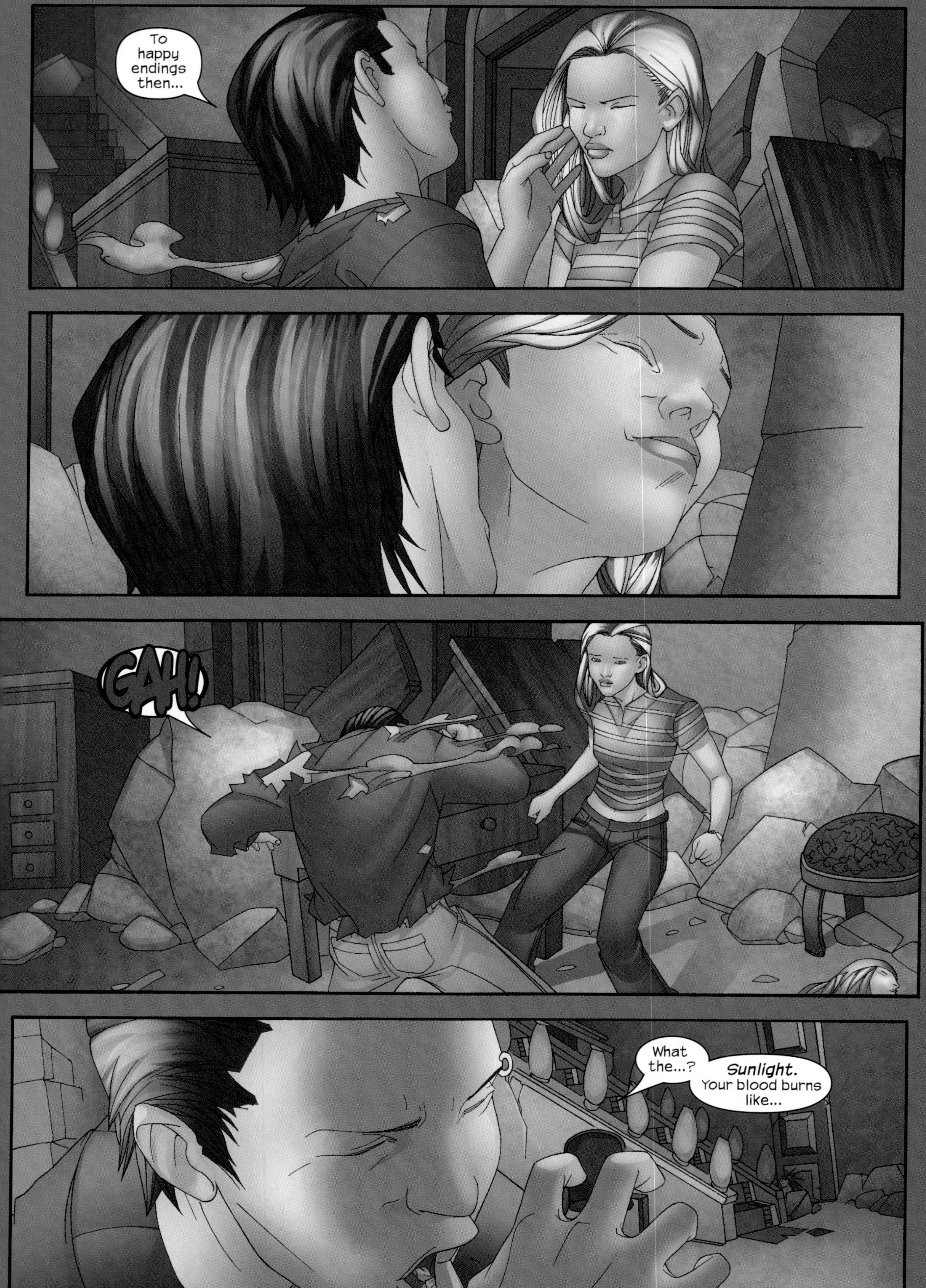

To happy endings then...
GAH!
What the...?
Sunlight. Your blood burns like...

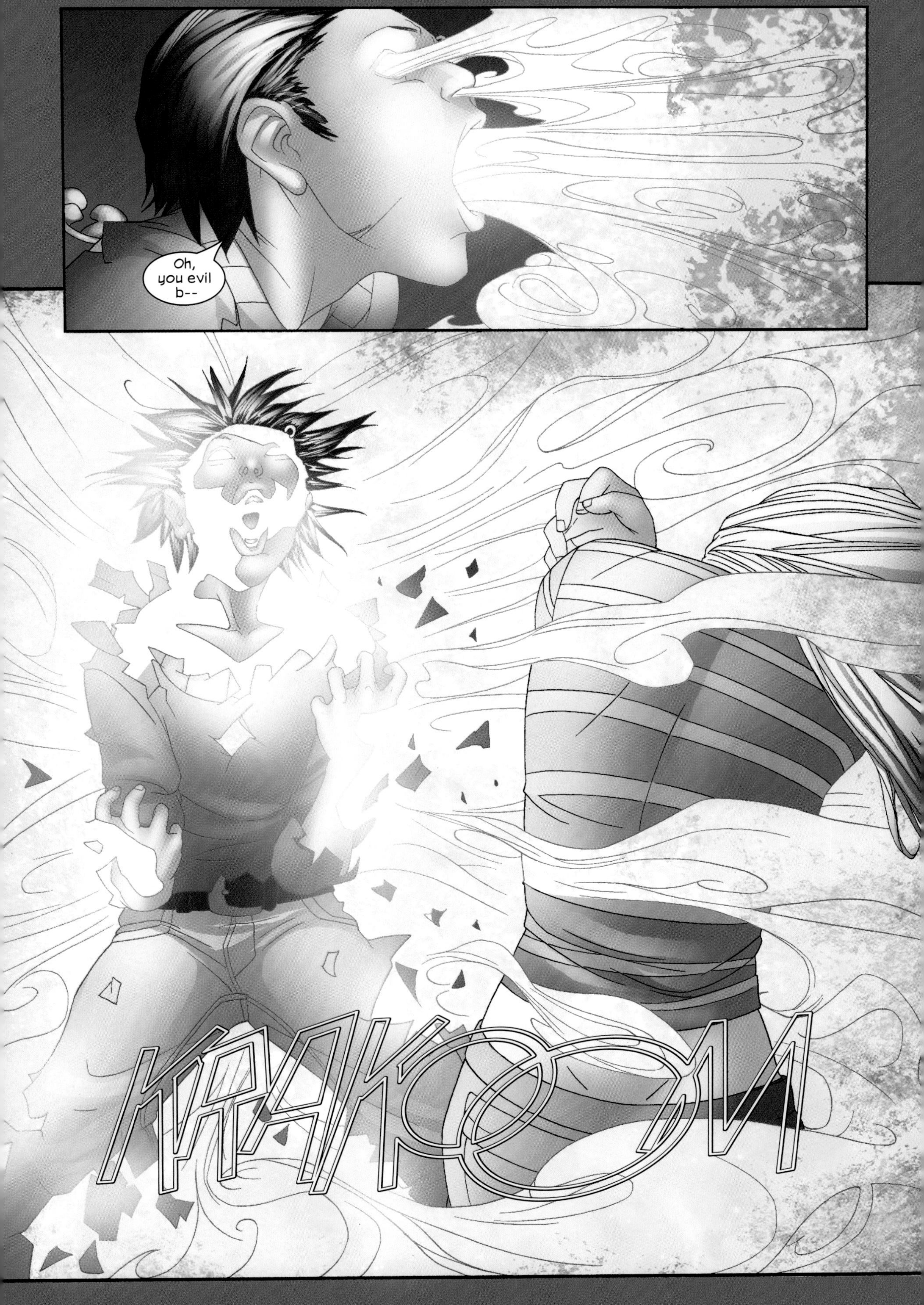
Oh, you evil b--
KRAKOOM

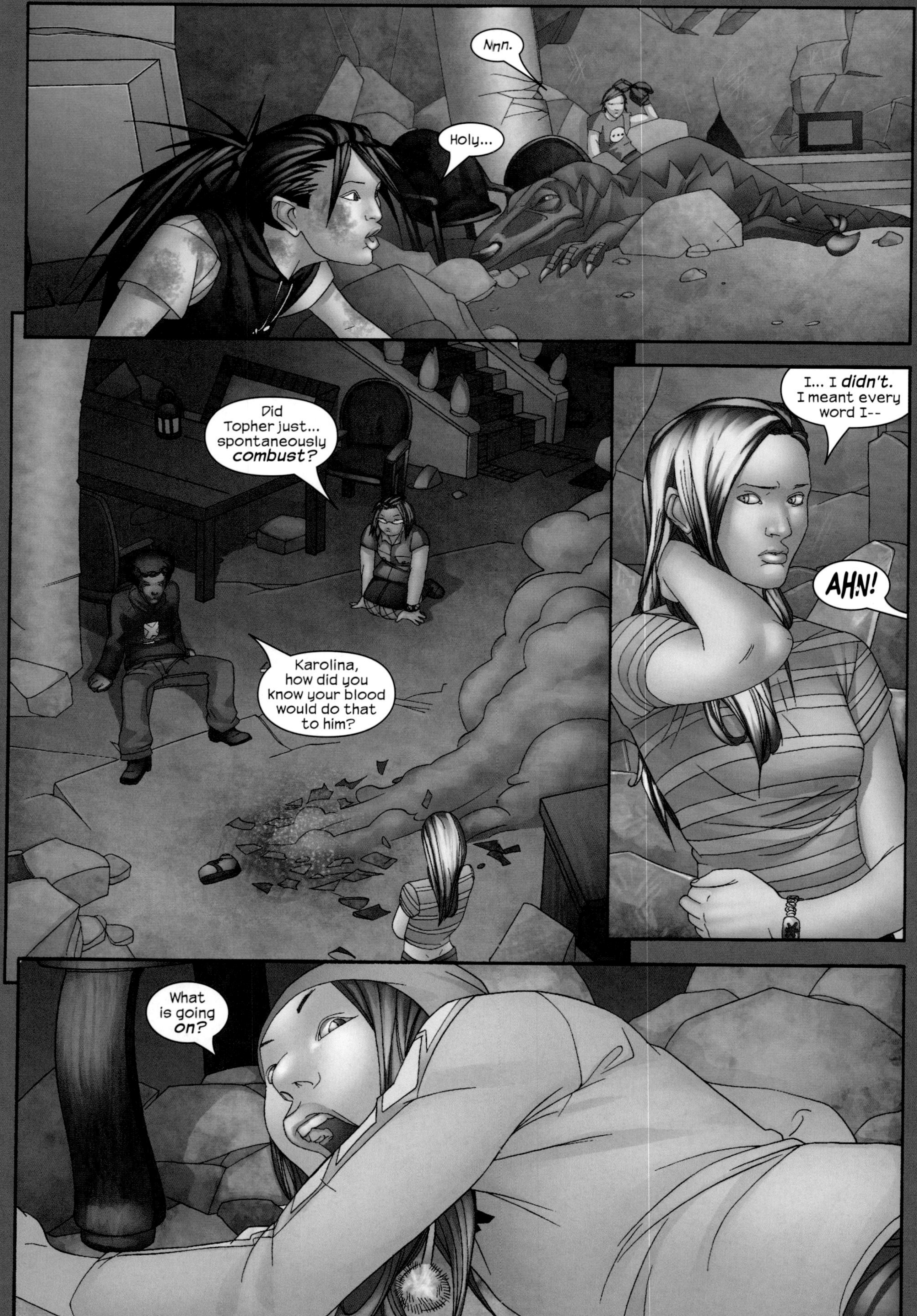
Nnn.
Holy...
Did Topher just... spontaneously *combust?*
Karolina, how did you know your blood would do that to him?
I... I *didn't.* I meant every word I--
AHN!
What is going *on?*

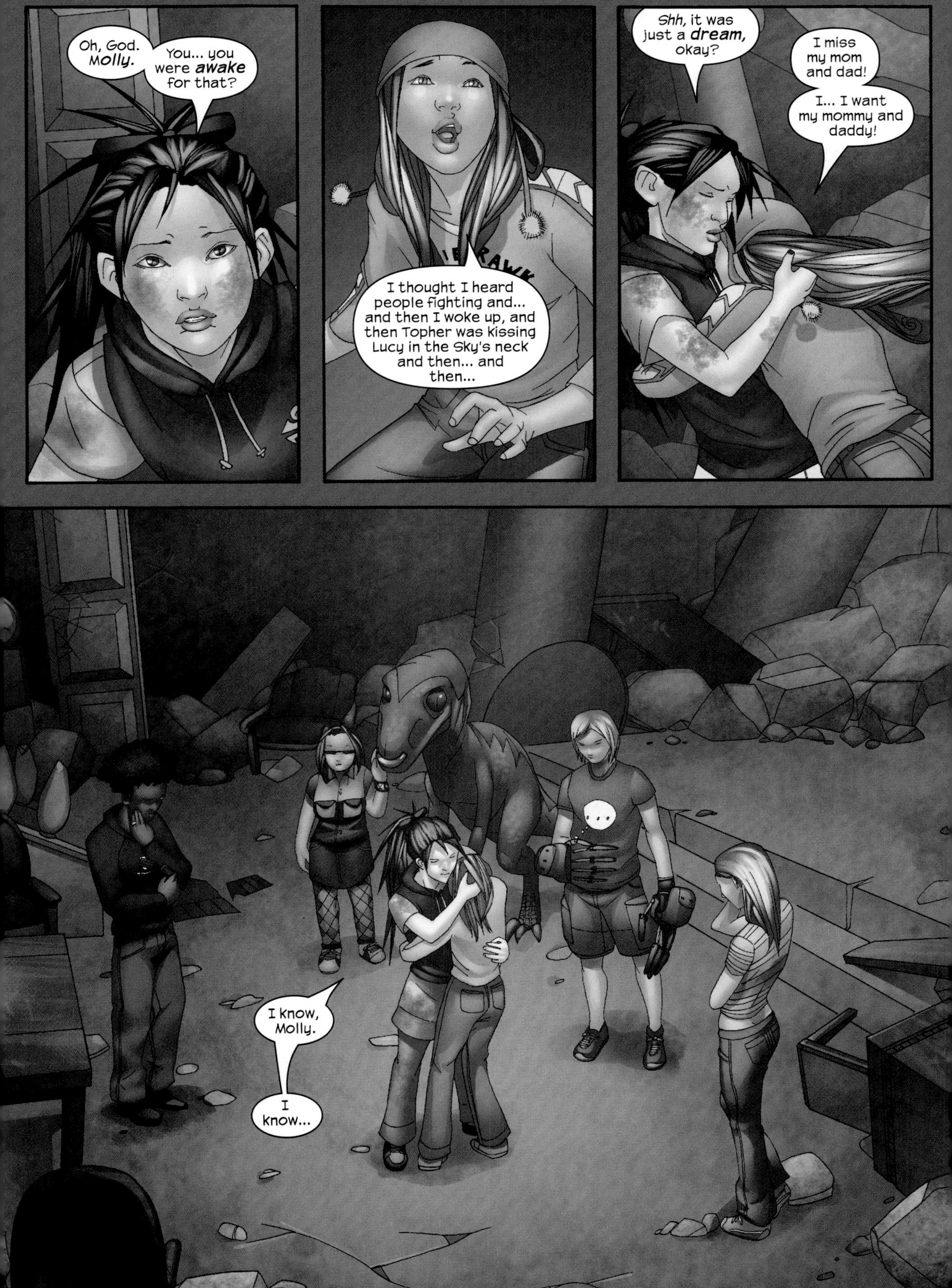
Oh, God. Molly.
You... you were awake for that?
I thought I heard people fighting and... and then I woke up, and then Topher was kissing Lucy in the Sky's neck and then... and then...
Shh, it was just a dream, okay?
I miss my mom and dad!
I... I want my mommy and daddy!
I know, Molly.
I know...

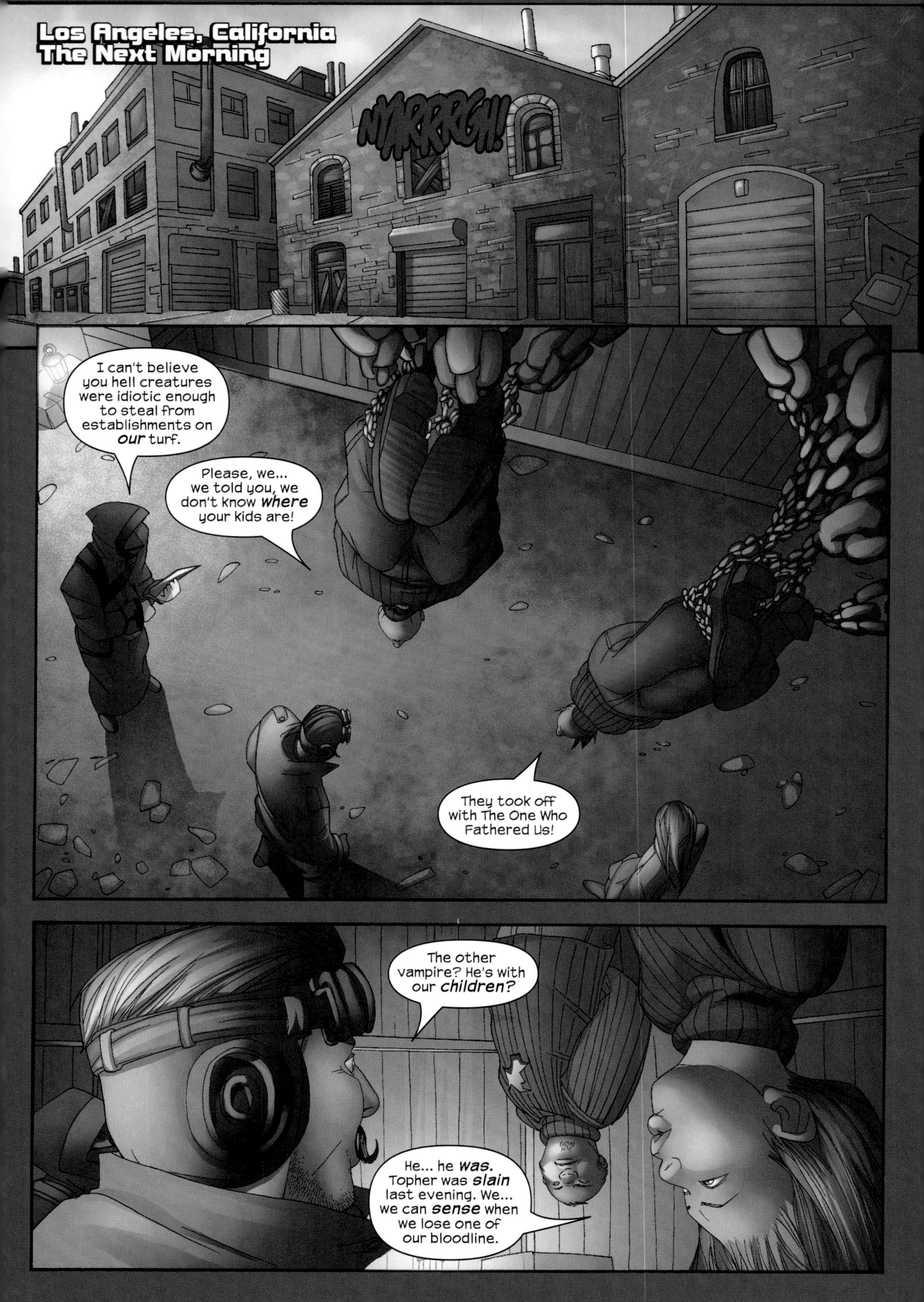
Los Angeles, California
The Next Morning
NYARRRGH!
I can't believe you hell creatures were idiotic enough to steal from establishments on our turf.
Please, we... we told you, we don't know where your kids are!
They took off with The One Who Fathered Us!
The other vampire? He's with our children?
He... he was. Topher was slain last evening. We... we can sense when we lose one of our bloodline.

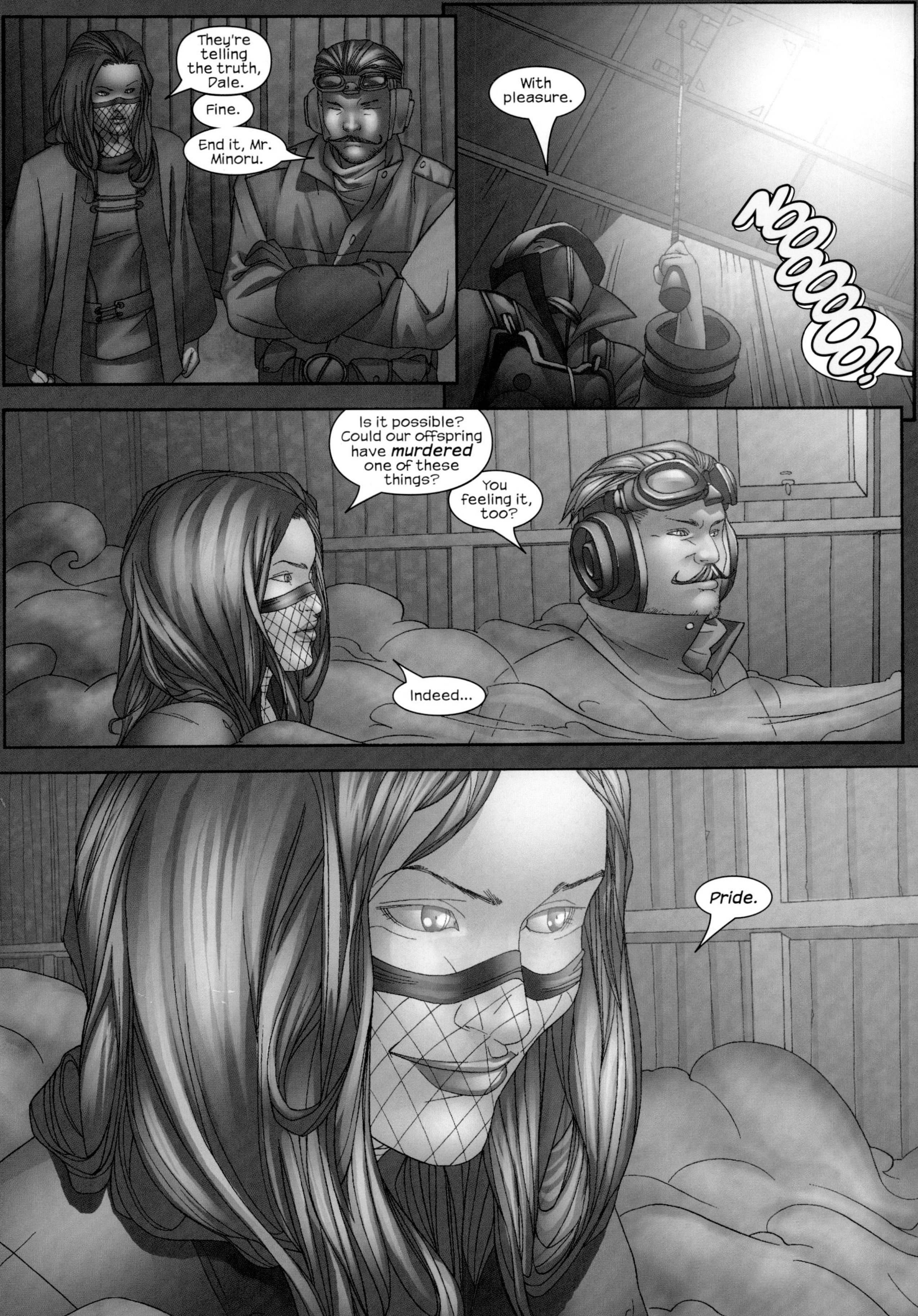

They're telling the truth, Dale.
Fine.
End it, Mr. Minoru.
With pleasure.
NOOOOOOO!
Is it possible? Could our offspring have ***murdered*** one of these things?
You feeling it, too?
Indeed...
Pride.

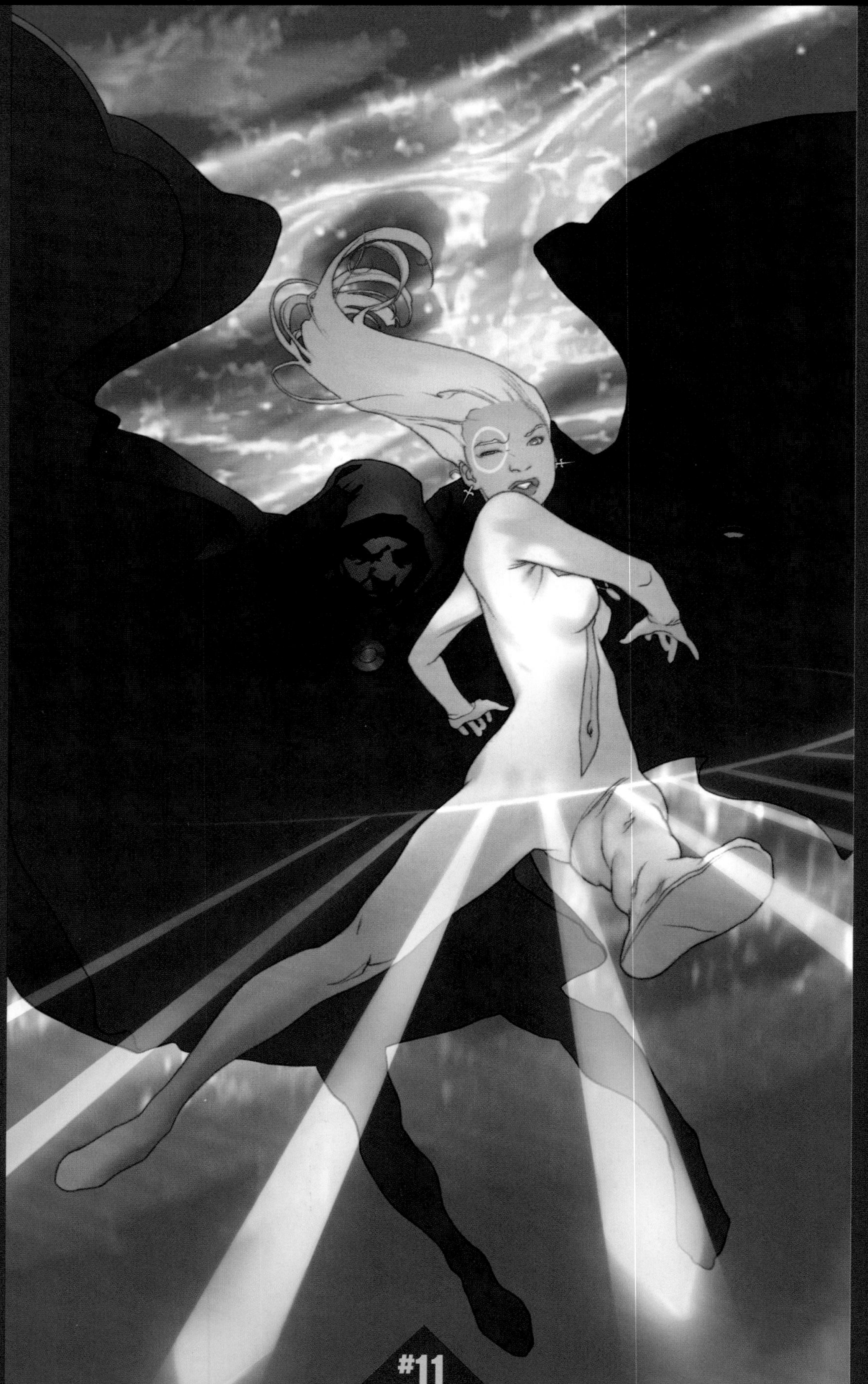
#11

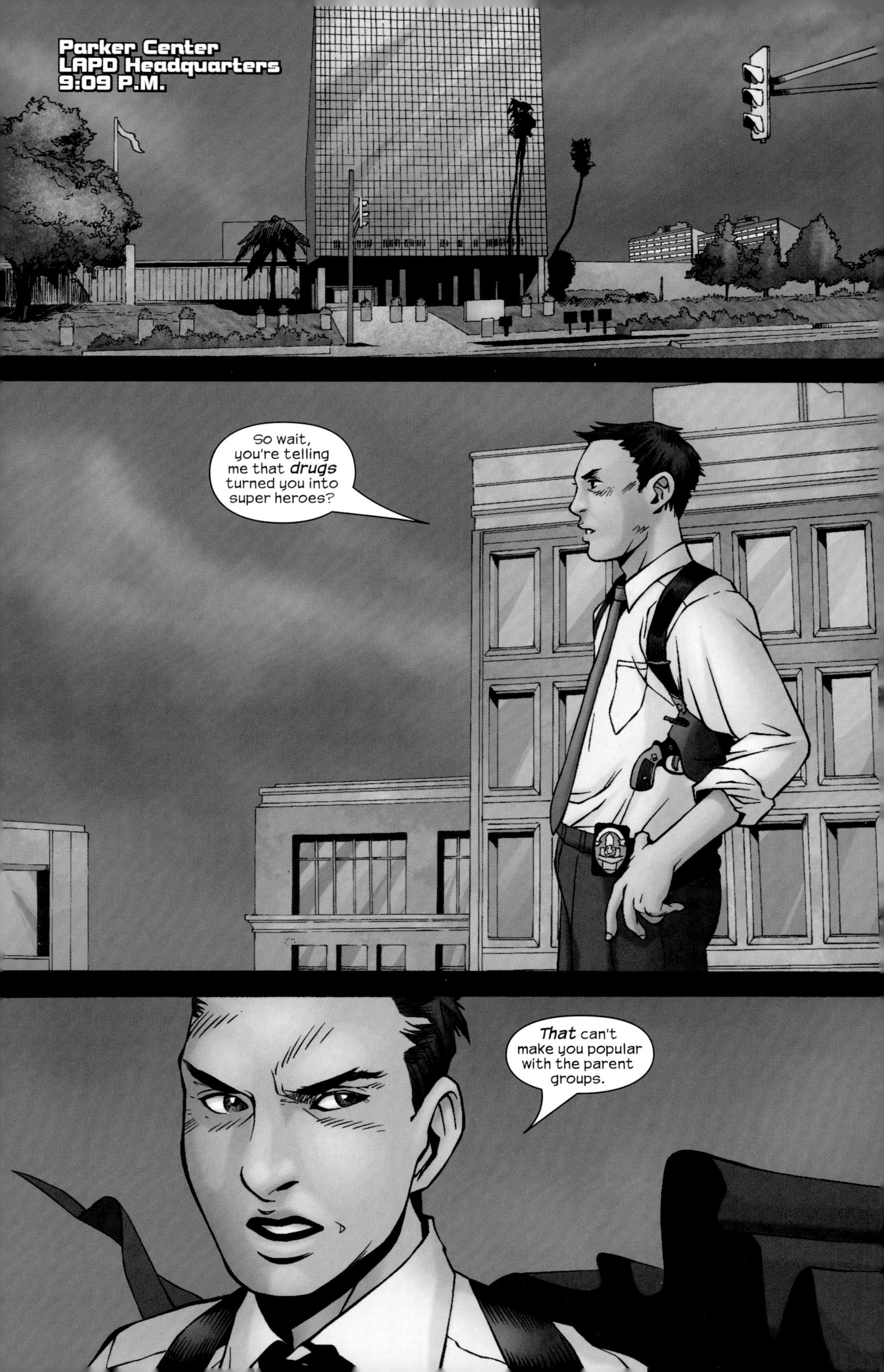
Parker Center
LAPD Headquarters
9:09 P.M.
So wait, you're telling me that *drugs* turned you into super heroes?
That can't make you popular with the parent groups.

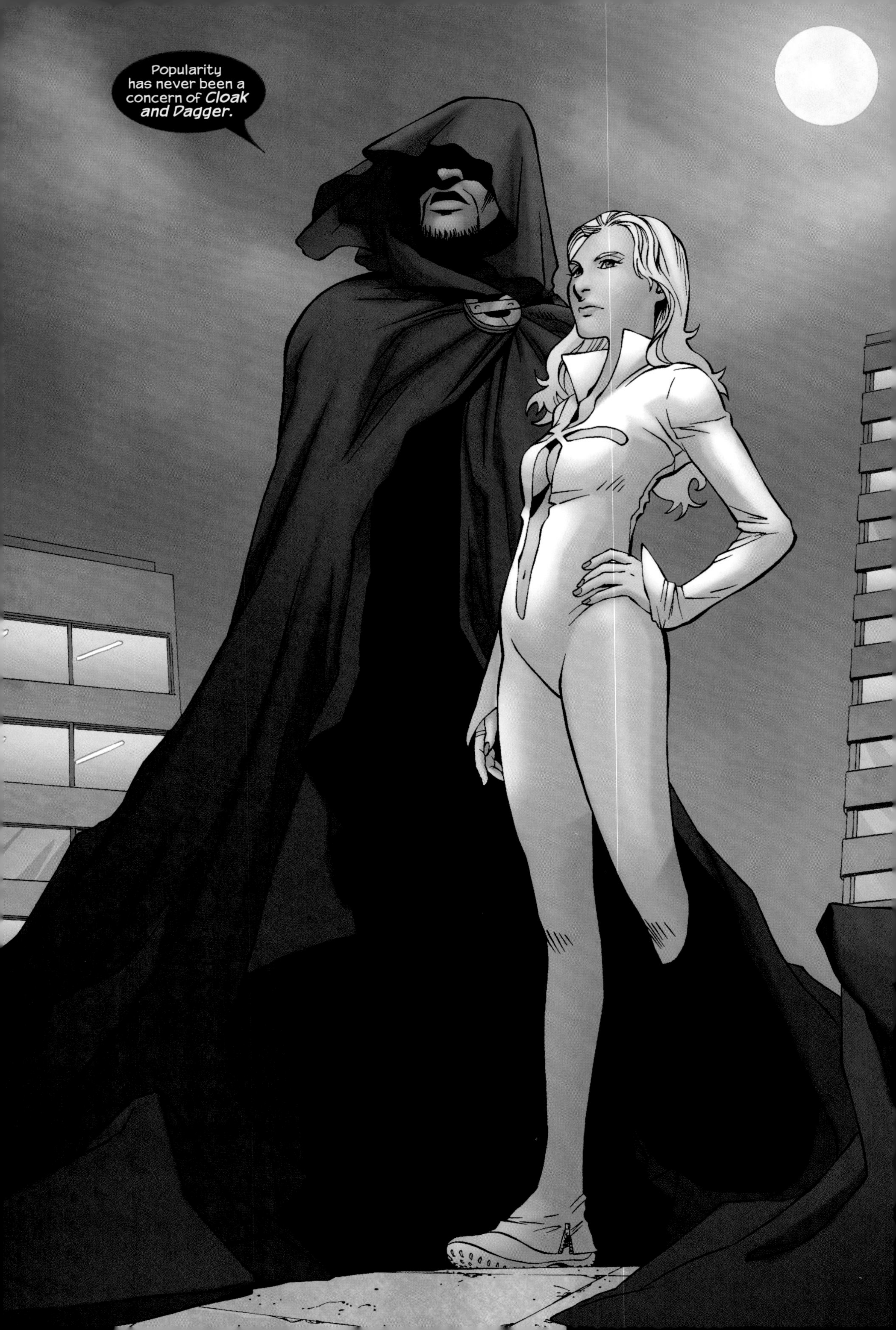
Popularity has never been a concern of *Cloak and Dagger*.

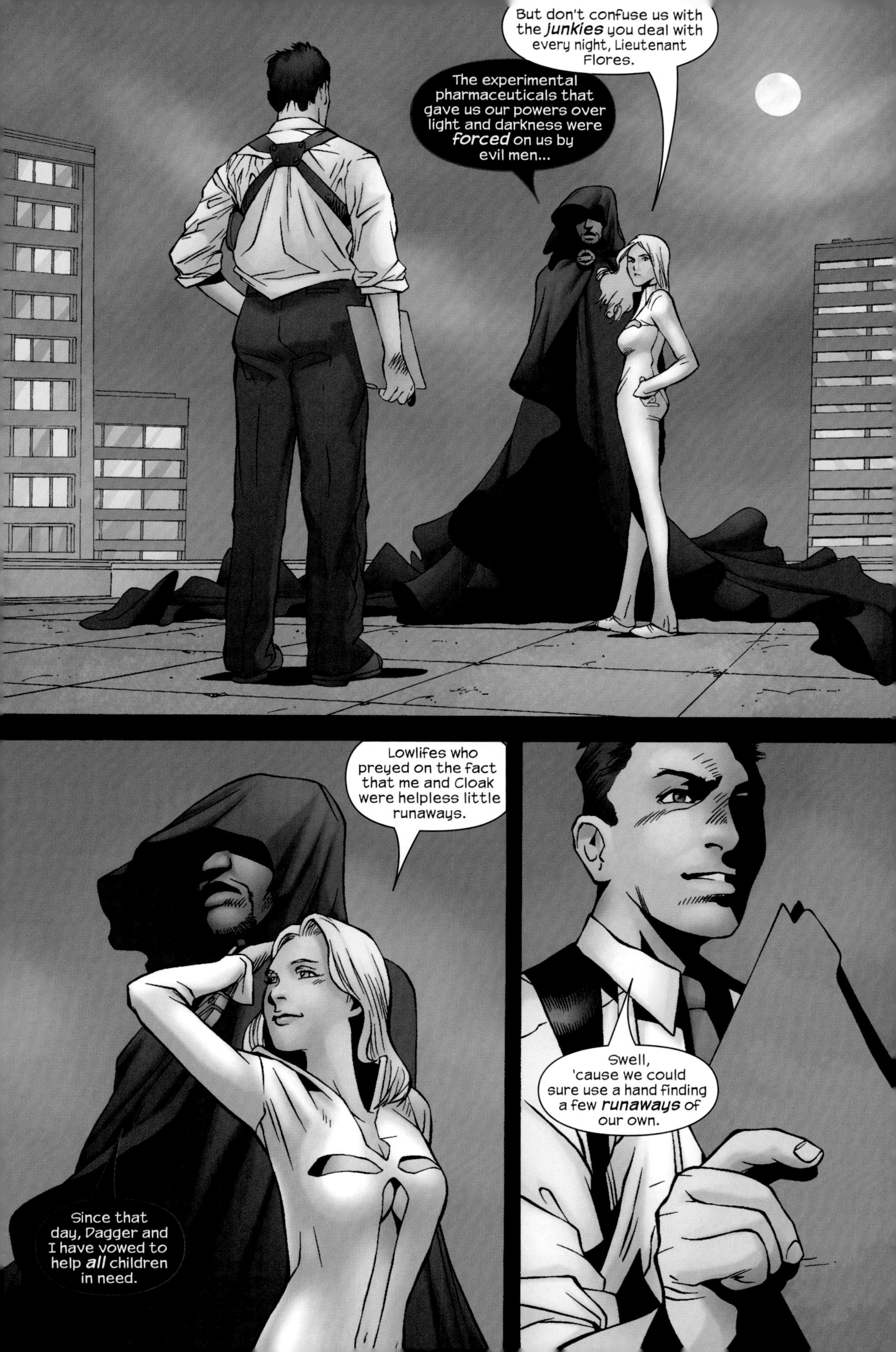
The experimental pharmaceuticals that gave us our powers over light and darkness were *forced* on us by evil men...
But don't confuse us with the *junkies* you deal with every night, Lieutenant Flores.
Lowlifes who preyed on the fact that me and Cloak were helpless little runaways.
Since that day, Dagger and I have vowed to help *all* children in need.
Swell, 'cause we could sure use a hand finding a few *runaways* of our own.

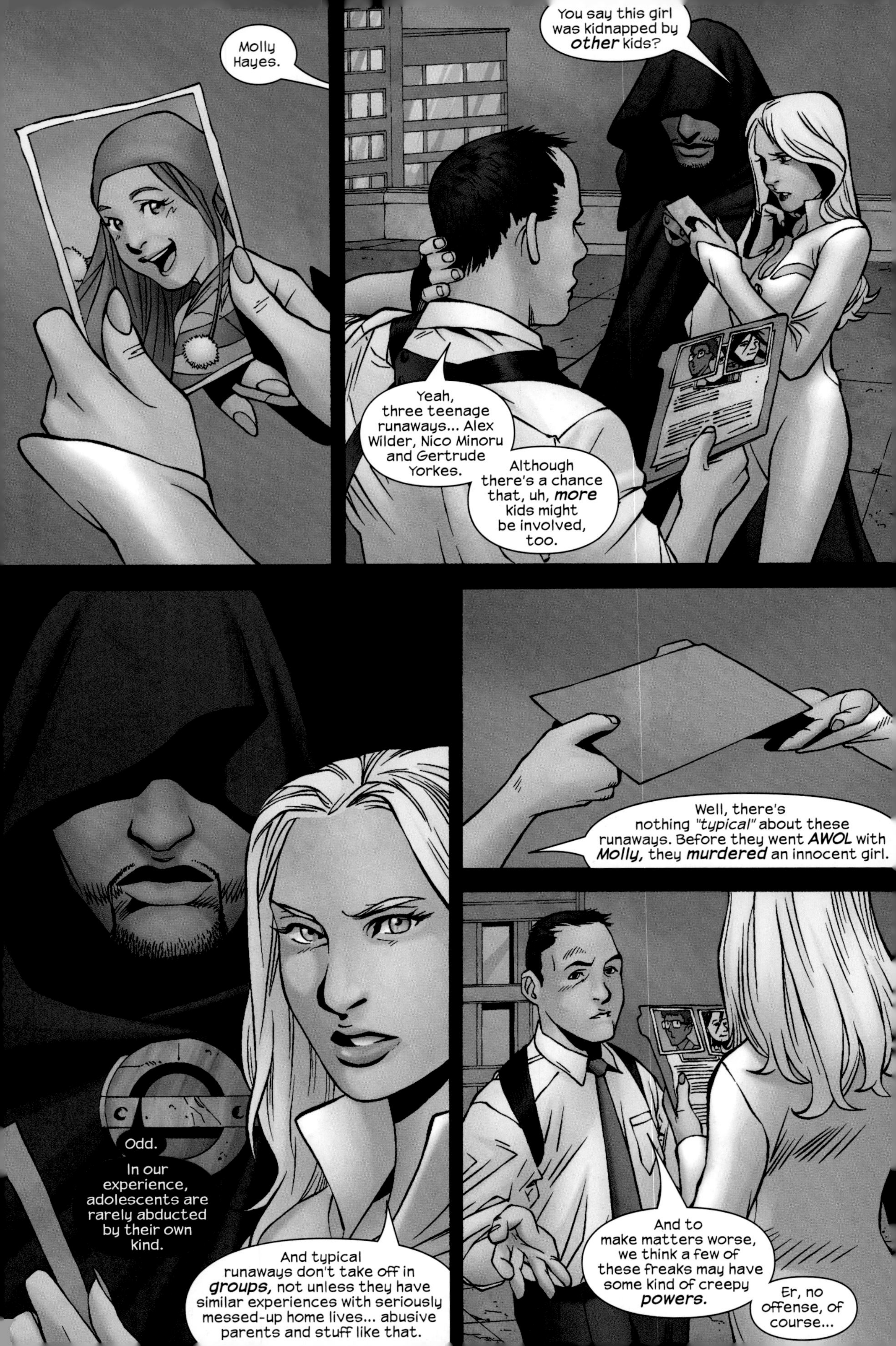
Molly Hayes.
You say this girl was kidnapped by other kids?
Yeah, three teenage runaways... Alex Wilder, Nico Minoru and Gertrude Yorkes.
Although there's a chance that, uh, more kids might be involved, too.
Odd.
In our experience, adolescents are rarely abducted by their own kind.
And typical runaways don't take off in groups, not unless they have similar experiences with seriously messed-up home lives... abusive parents and stuff like that.
Well, there's nothing "typical" about these runaways. Before they went AWOL with Molly, they murdered an innocent girl.
And to make matters worse, we think a few of these freaks may have some kind of creepy powers.
Er, no offense, of course...

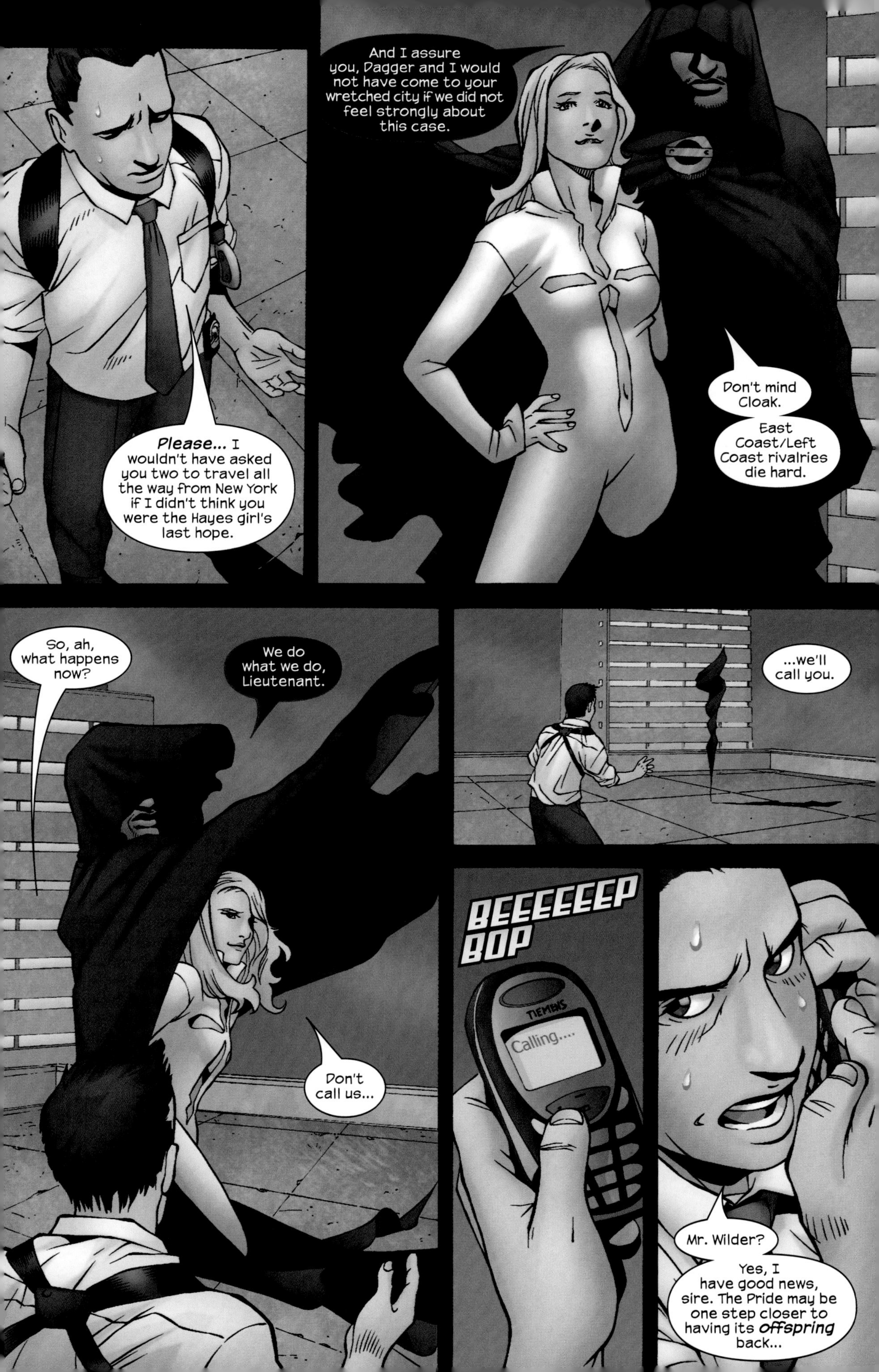
And I assure you, Dagger and I would not have come to your wretched city if we did not feel strongly about this case.
Please... I wouldn't have asked you two to travel all the way from New York if I didn't think you were the Hayes girl's last hope.
Don't mind Cloak.
East Coast/Left Coast rivalries die hard.
So, ah, what happens now?
We do what we do, Lieutenant.
Don't call us...
...we'll call you.
BEEEEEEP BOP
TIEMENS
Calling....
Mr. Wilder?
Yes, I have good news, sire. The Pride may be one step closer to having its offspring back...

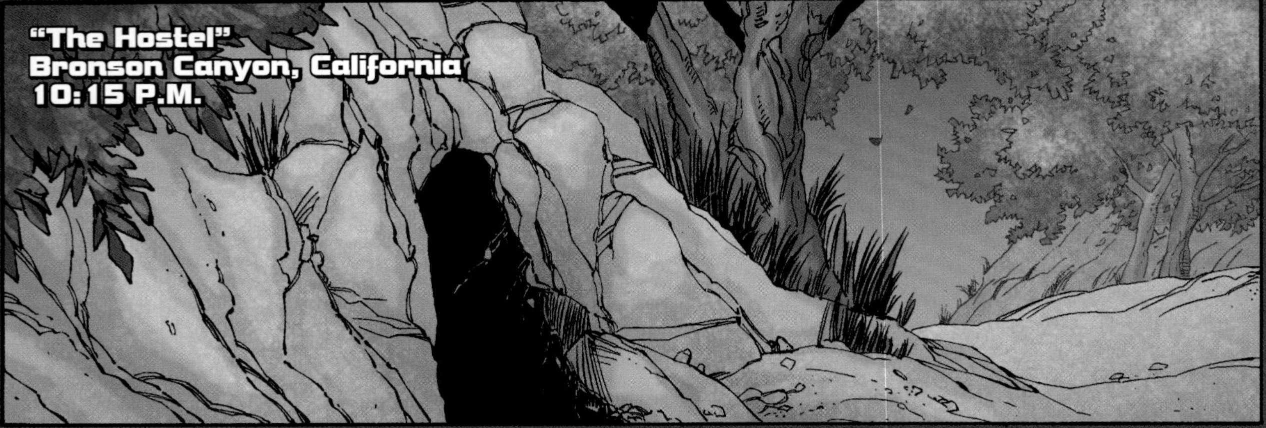
"The Hostel"
Bronson Canyon, California
10:15 P.M.

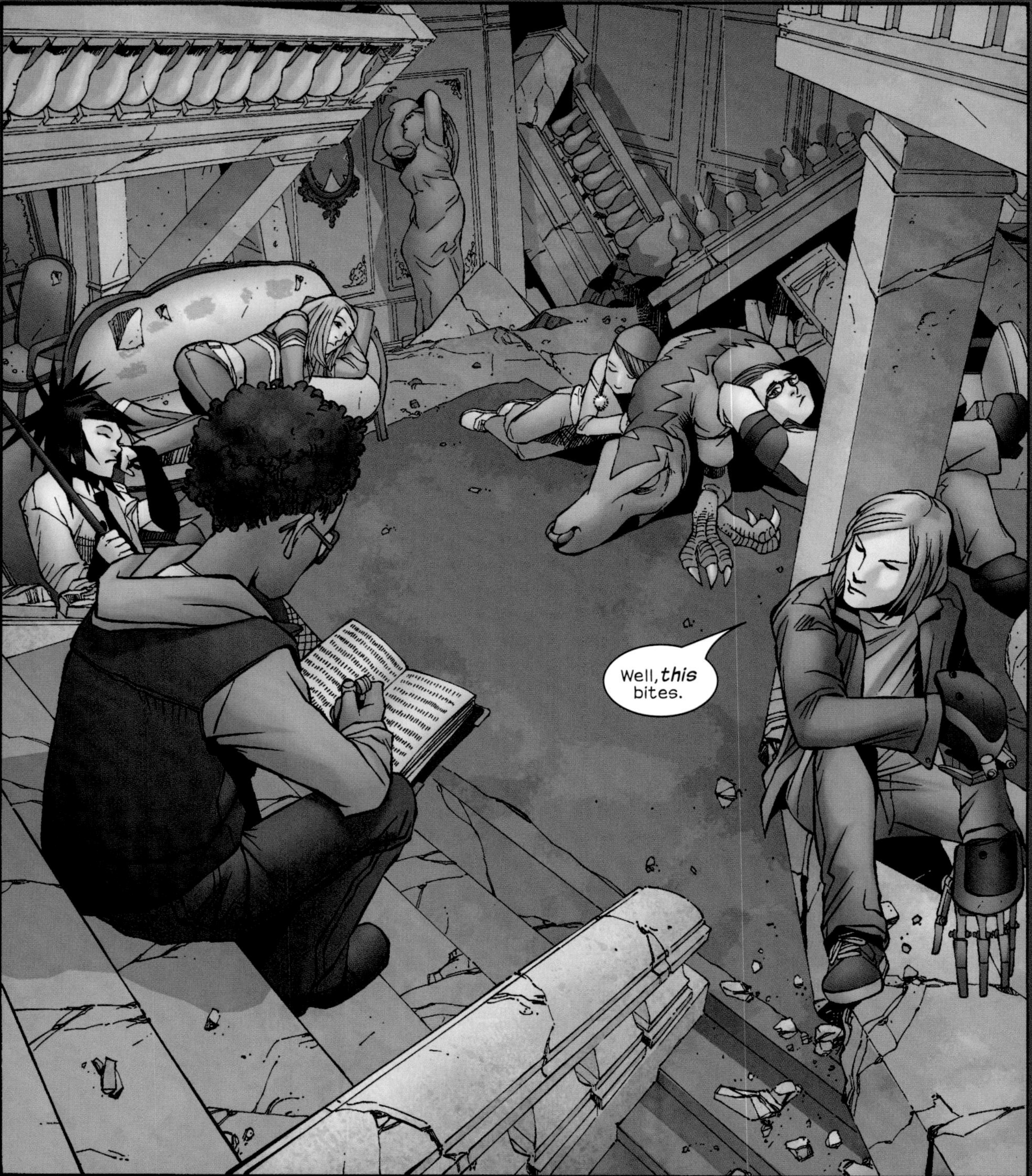
Well, *this* bites.

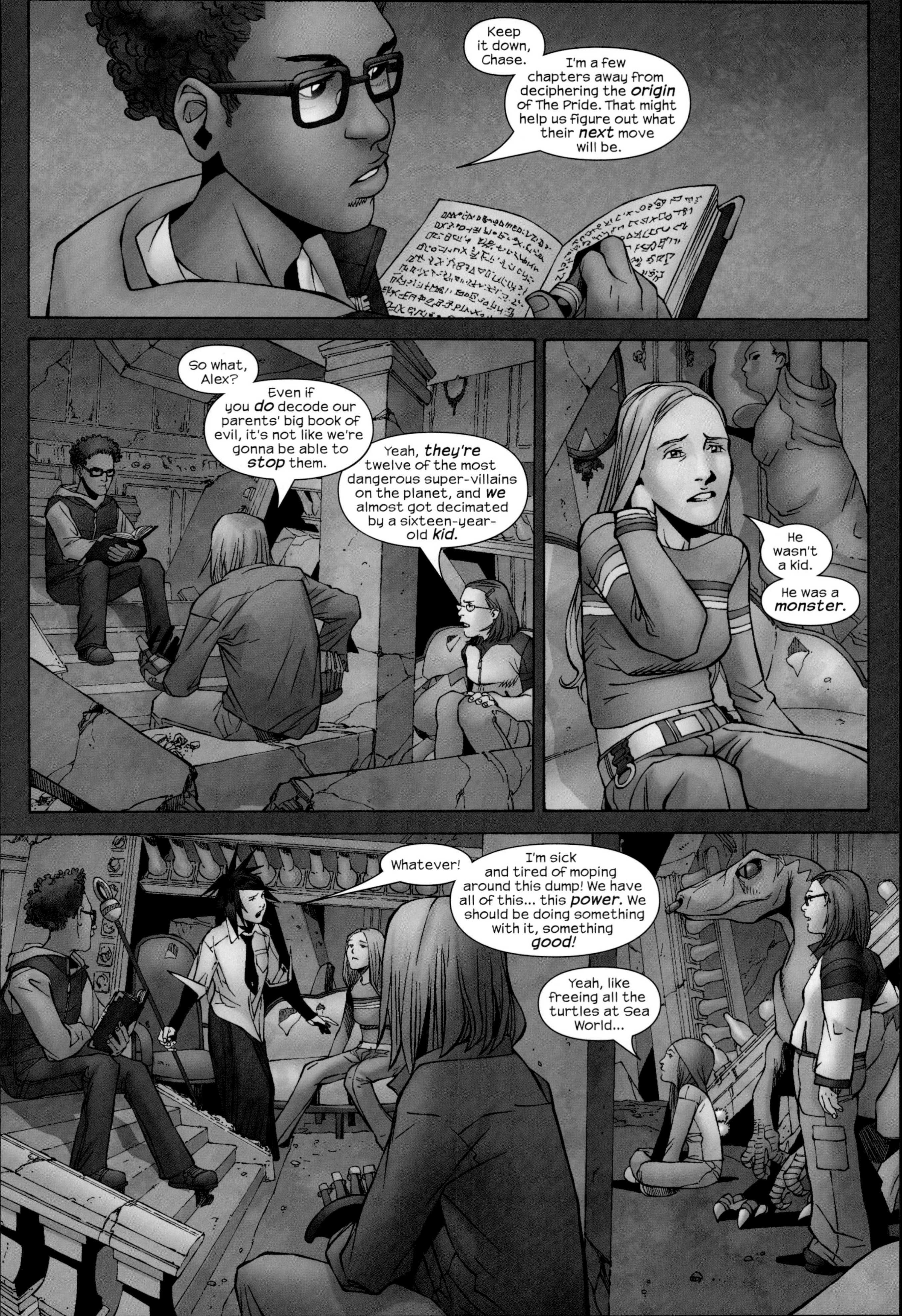
Keep it down, Chase.
I'm a few chapters away from deciphering the *origin* of The Pride. That might help us figure out what their *next* move will be.
So what, Alex?
Even if you *do* decode our parents' big book of evil, it's not like we're gonna be able to *stop* them.
Yeah, *they're* twelve of the most dangerous super-villains on the planet, and *we* almost got decimated by a sixteen-year-old *kid.*
He wasn't a kid.
He was a *monster.*
Whatever!
I'm sick and tired of moping around this dump! We have all of this... this *power.* We should be doing something with it, something *good!*
Yeah, like freeing all the turtles at Sea World...

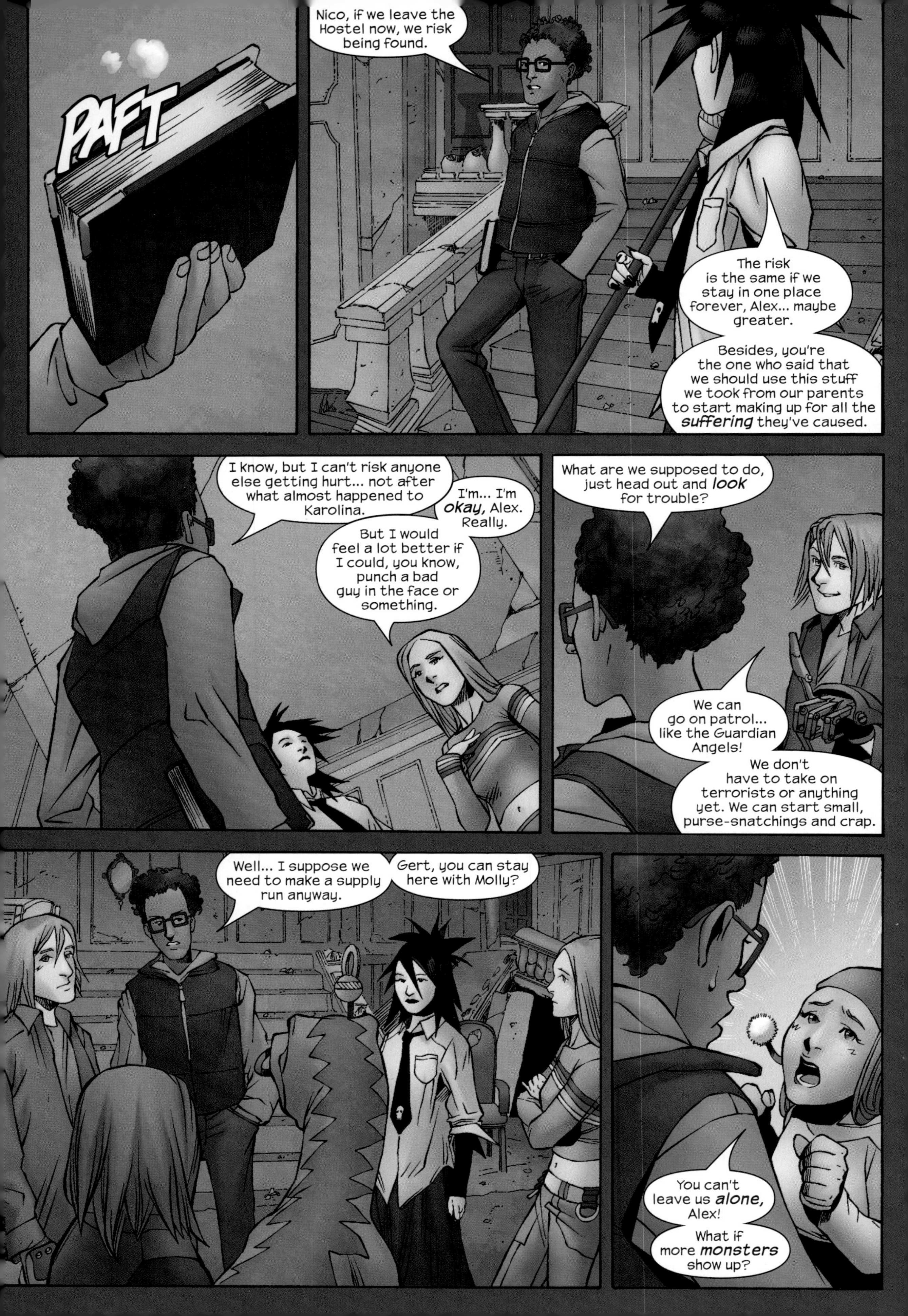
PAFT
Nico, if we leave the Hostel now, we risk being found.
The risk is the same if we stay in one place forever, Alex... maybe greater.
Besides, you're the one who said that we should use this stuff we took from our parents to start making up for all the *suffering* they've caused.
I know, but I can't risk anyone else getting hurt... not after what almost happened to Karolina.
I'm... I'm *okay,* Alex. Really.
But I would feel a lot better if I could, you know, punch a bad guy in the face or something.
What are we supposed to do, just head out and *look* for trouble?
We can go on patrol... like the Guardian Angels!
We don't have to take on terrorists or anything yet. We can start small, purse-snatchings and crap.
Well... I suppose we need to make a supply run anyway.
Gert, you can stay here with Molly?
You can't leave us *alone,* Alex!
What if more *monsters* show up?

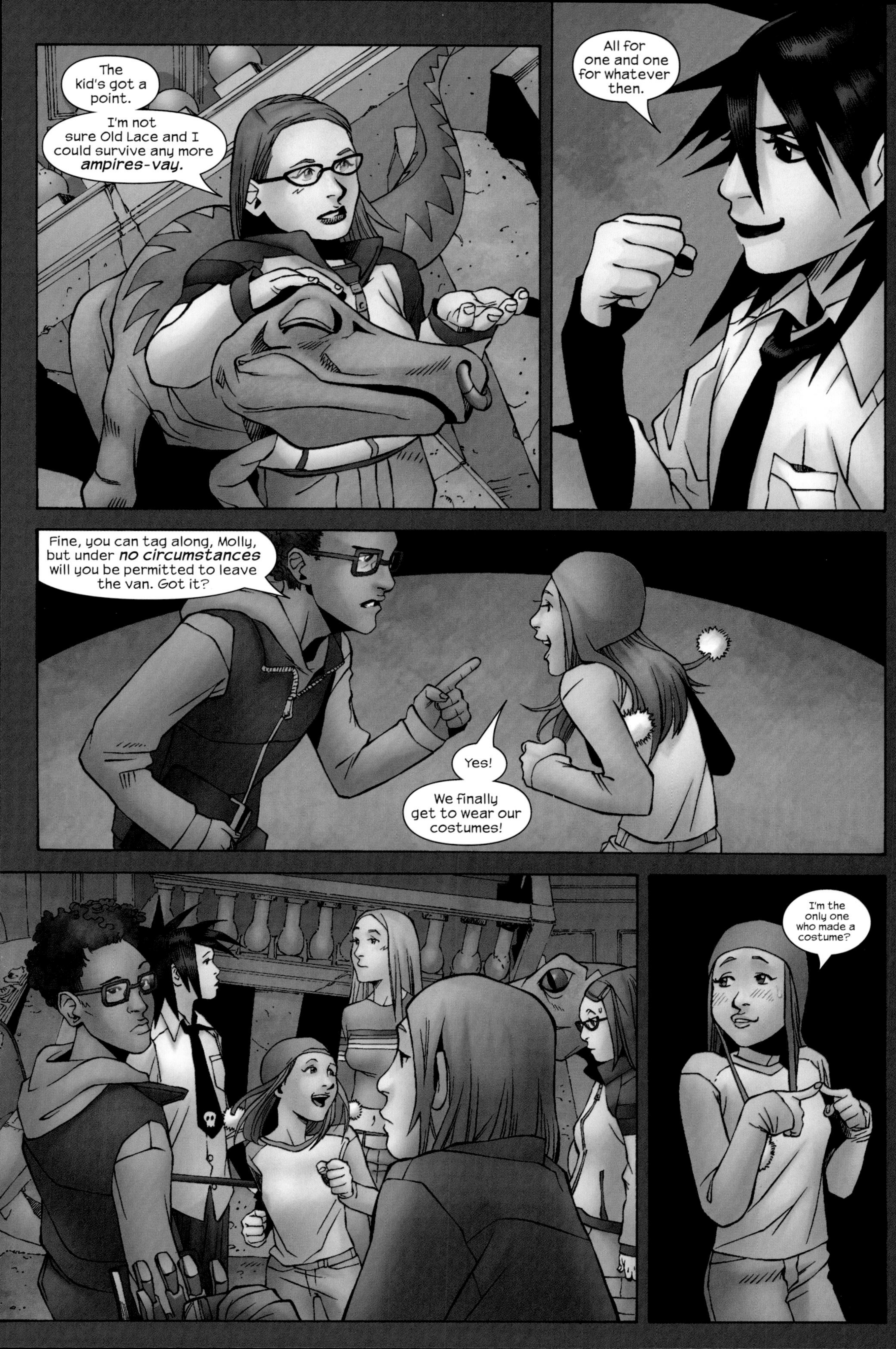
The kid's got a point.
I'm not sure Old Lace and I could survive any more *ampires-vay.*
All for one and one for whatever then.
Fine, you can tag along, Molly, but under *no circumstances* will you be permitted to leave the van. Got it?
Yes!
We finally get to wear our costumes!
I'm the only one who made a costume?

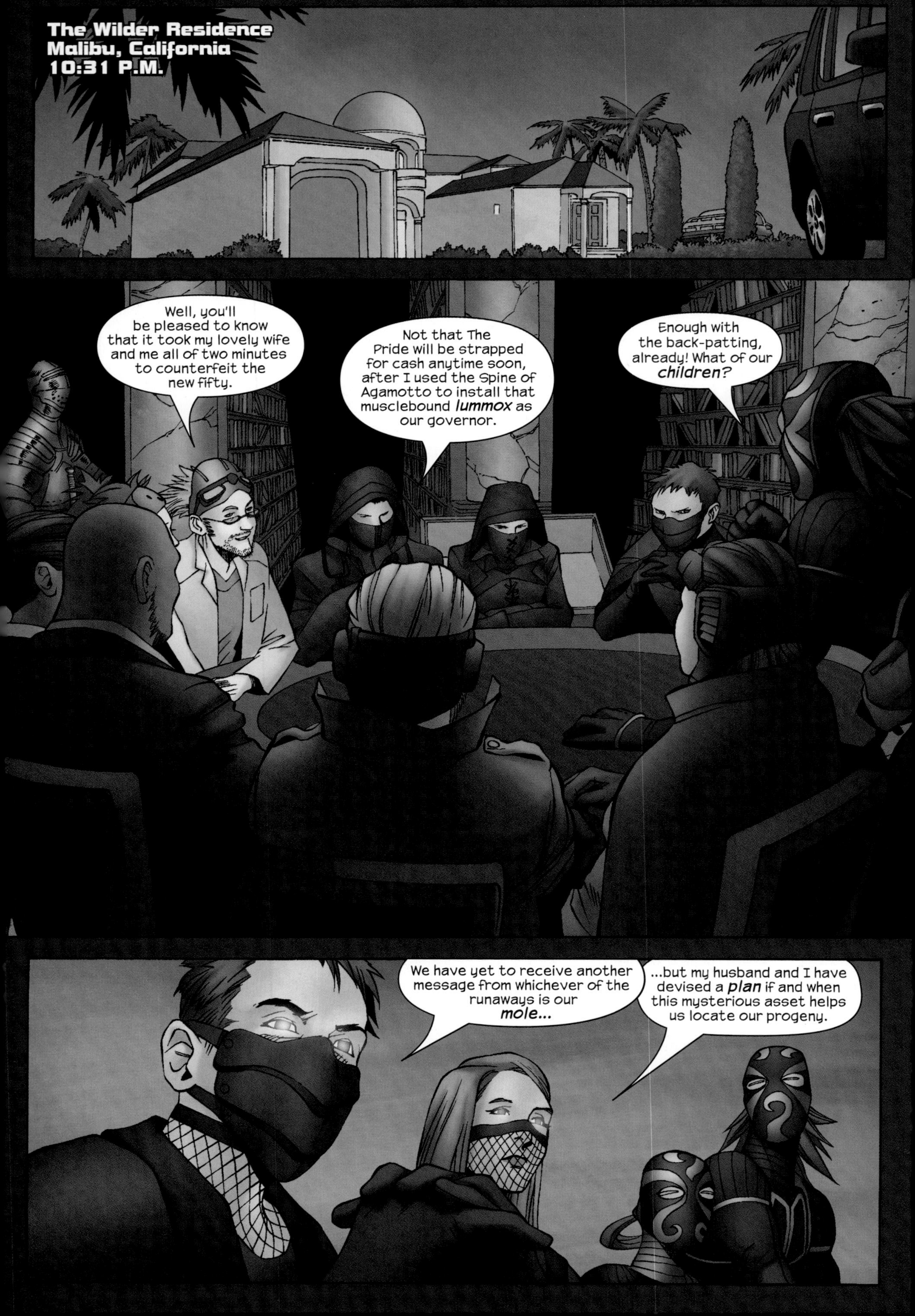
The Wilder Residence
Malibu, California
10:31 P.M.
Well, you'll be pleased to know that it took my lovely wife and me all of two minutes to counterfeit the new fifty.
Not that The Pride will be strapped for cash anytime soon, after I used the Spine of Agamotto to install that musclebound lummox as our governor.
Enough with the back-patting, already! What of our children?
We have yet to receive another message from whichever of the runaways is our mole...
...but my husband and I have devised a plan if and when this mysterious asset helps us locate our progeny.

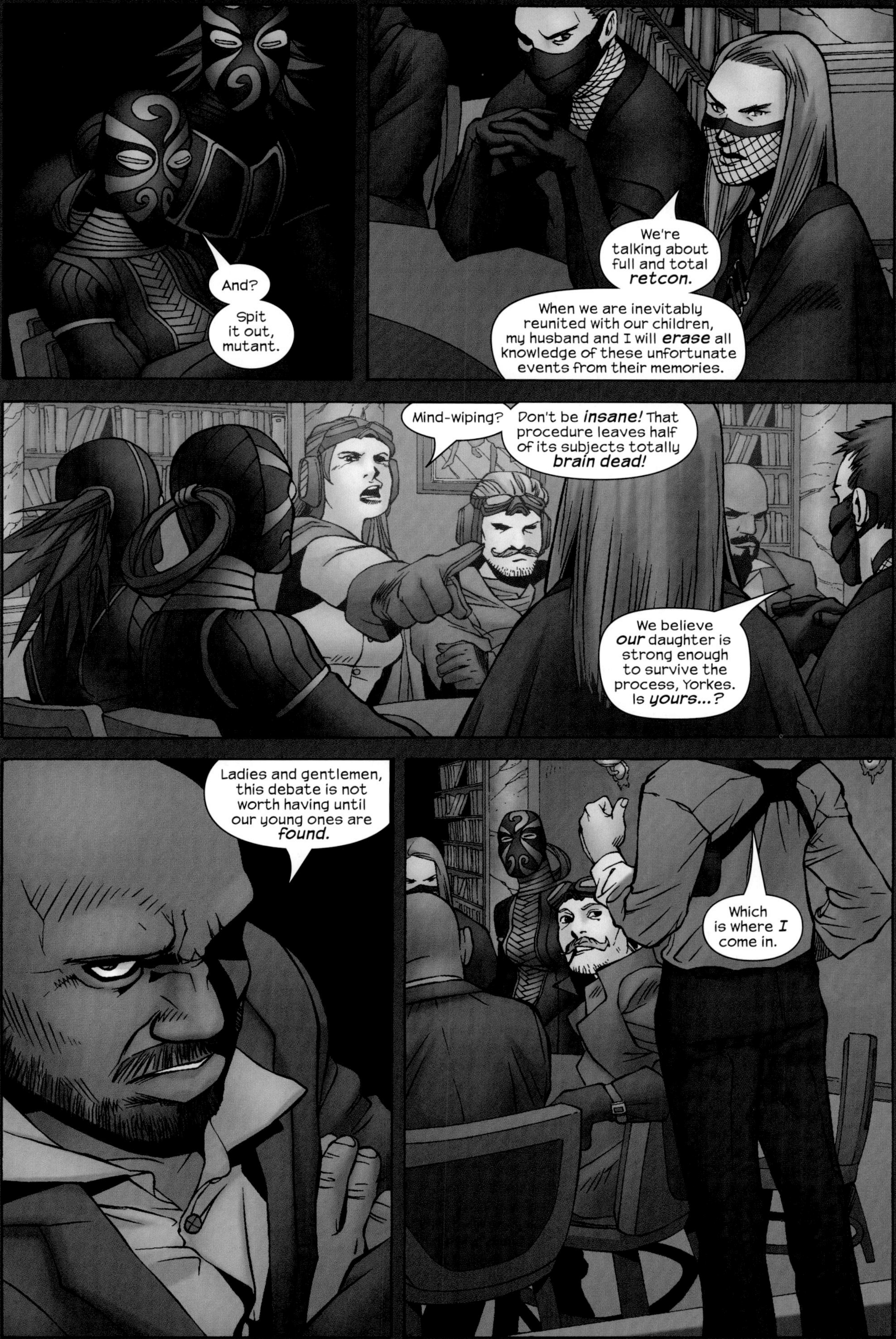

And?
Spit it out, mutant.
We're talking about full and total *retcon.*
When we are inevitably reunited with our children, my husband and I will ***erase*** all knowledge of these unfortunate events from their memories.
Mind-wiping?
Don't be ***insane!*** That procedure leaves half of its subjects totally ***brain dead!***
We believe ***our*** daughter is strong enough to survive the process, Yorkes. Is ***yours...?***
Ladies and gentlemen, this debate is not worth having until our young ones are *found.*
Which is where *I* come in.

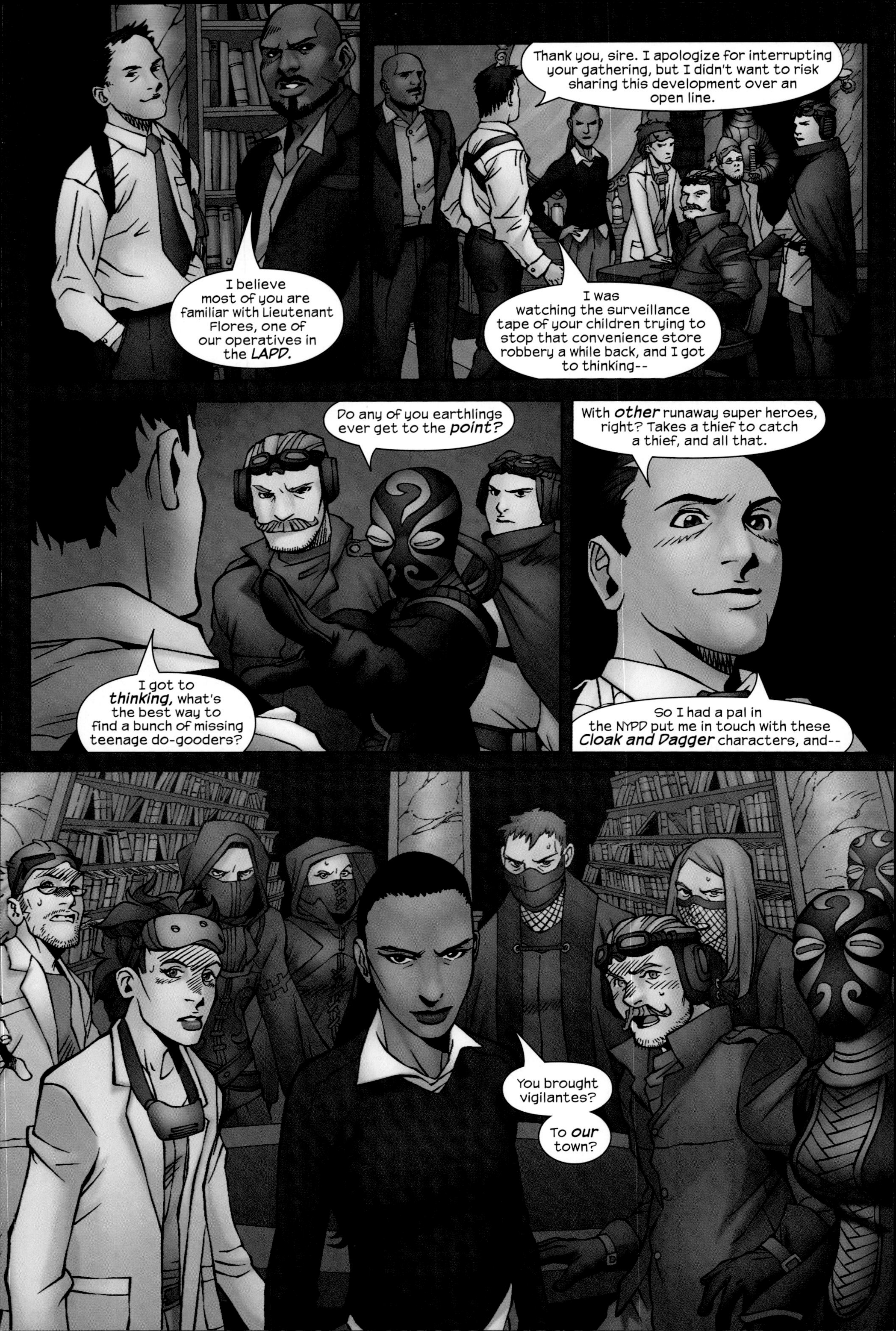
I believe most of you are familiar with Lieutenant Flores, one of our operatives in the LAPD.
Thank you, sire. I apologize for interrupting your gathering, but I didn't want to risk sharing this development over an open line.
I was watching the surveillance tape of your children trying to stop that convenience store robbery a while back, and I got to thinking--
Do any of you earthlings ever get to the point?
I got to thinking, what's the best way to find a bunch of missing teenage do-gooders?
With other runaway super heroes, right? Takes a thief to catch a thief, and all that.
So I had a pal in the NYPD put me in touch with these Cloak and Dagger characters, and--
You brought vigilantes?
To our town?

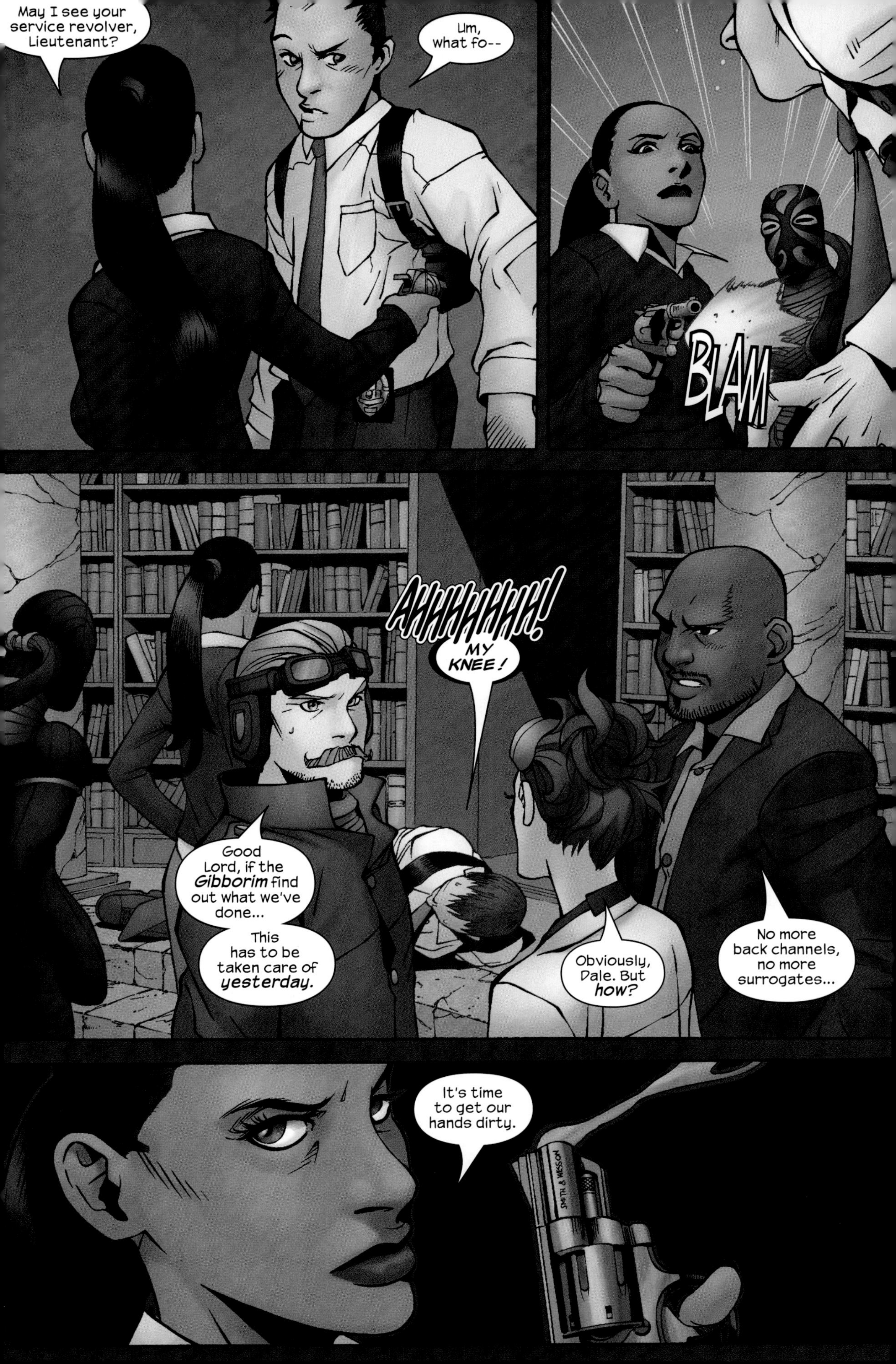
May I see your service revolver, Lieutenant?
Um, what fo--
BLAM
AHHHHHHH! MY KNEE!
Good Lord, if the Gibborim find out what we've done...
This has to be taken care of yesterday.
Obviously, Dale. But how?
No more back channels, no more surrogates...
It's time to get our hands dirty.
SMITH & WESSON

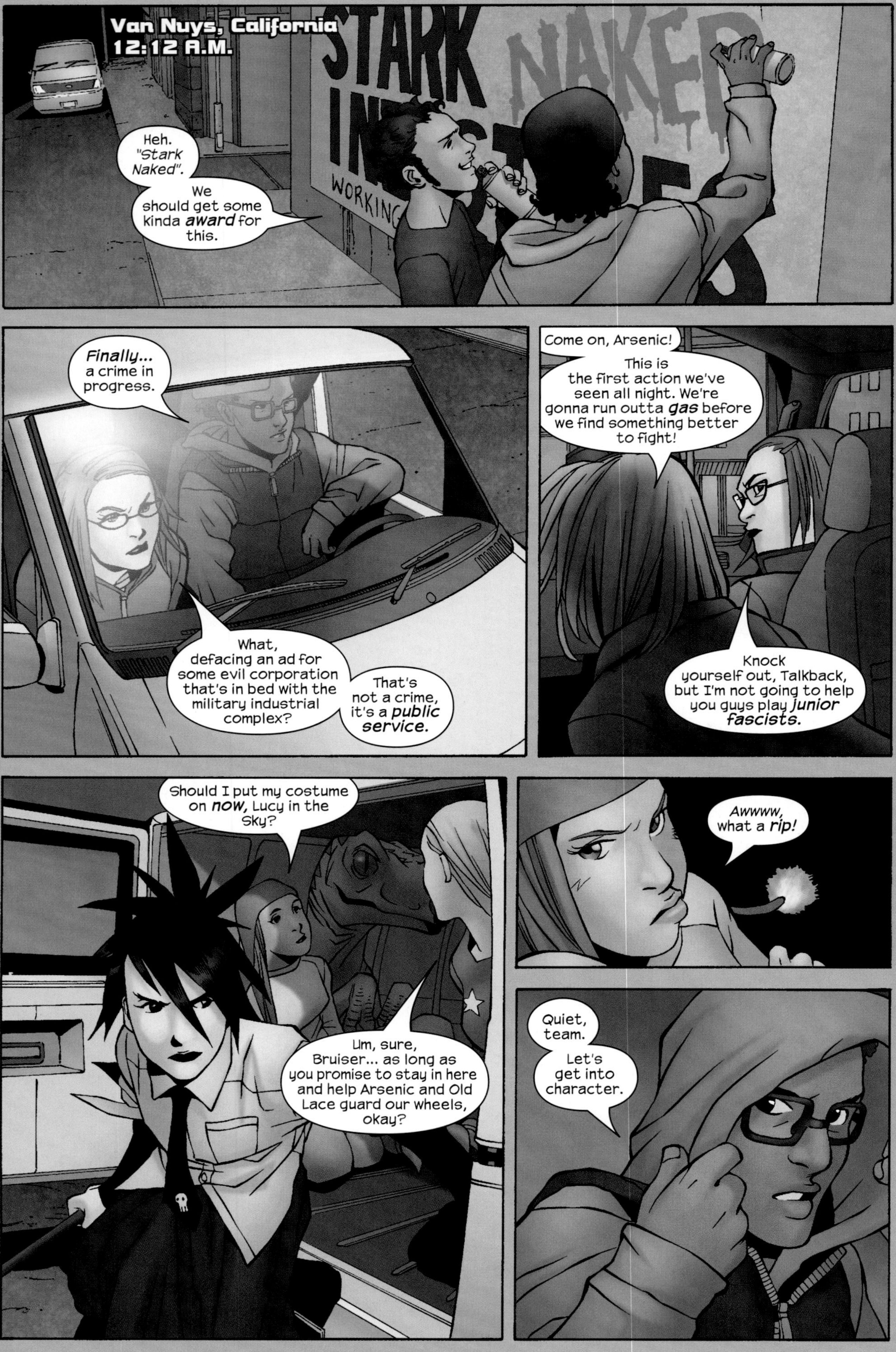
Van Nuys, California
12:12 A.M.
STARK NAKED
IN
WORKING
Heh. "Stark Naked".
We should get some kinda *award* for this.
Finally... a crime in progress.
What, defacing an ad for some evil corporation that's in bed with the military industrial complex?
That's not a crime, it's a *public service.*
Come on, Arsenic!
This is the first action we've seen all night. We're gonna run outta *gas* before we find something better to fight!
Knock yourself out, Talkback, but I'm not going to help you guys play *junior fascists.*
Should I put my costume on *now,* Lucy in the Sky?
Um, sure, Bruiser... as long as you promise to stay in here and help Arsenic and Old Lace guard our wheels, okay?
Awwww, what a *rip!*
Quiet, team.
Let's get into character.

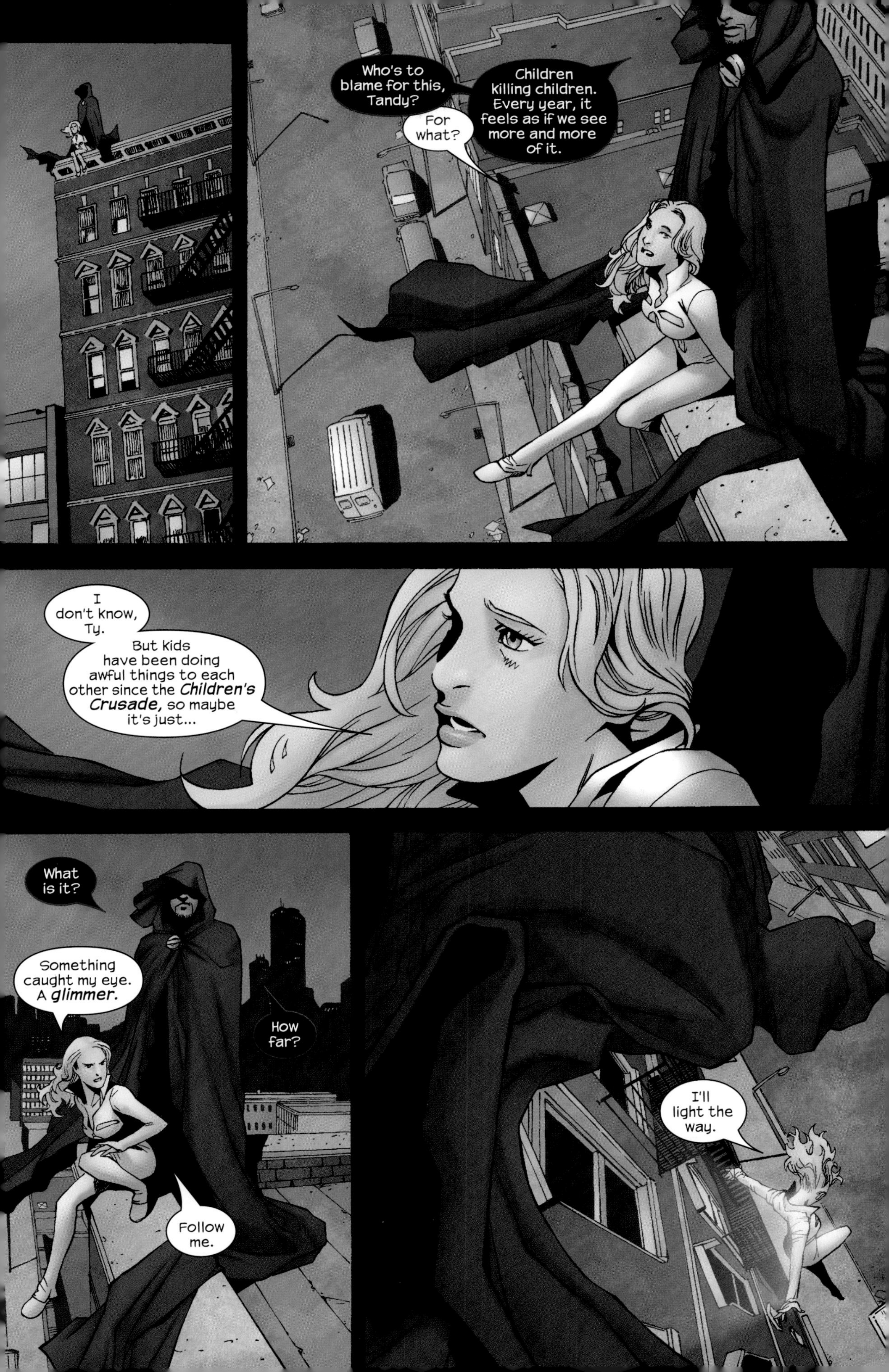
Who's to blame for this, Tandy?
For what?
Children killing children. Every year, it feels as if we see more and more of it.
I don't know, Ty.
But kids have been doing awful things to each other since the *Children's Crusade,* so maybe it's just...
What is it?
Something caught my eye. A *glimmer.*
How far?
Follow me.
I'll light the way.

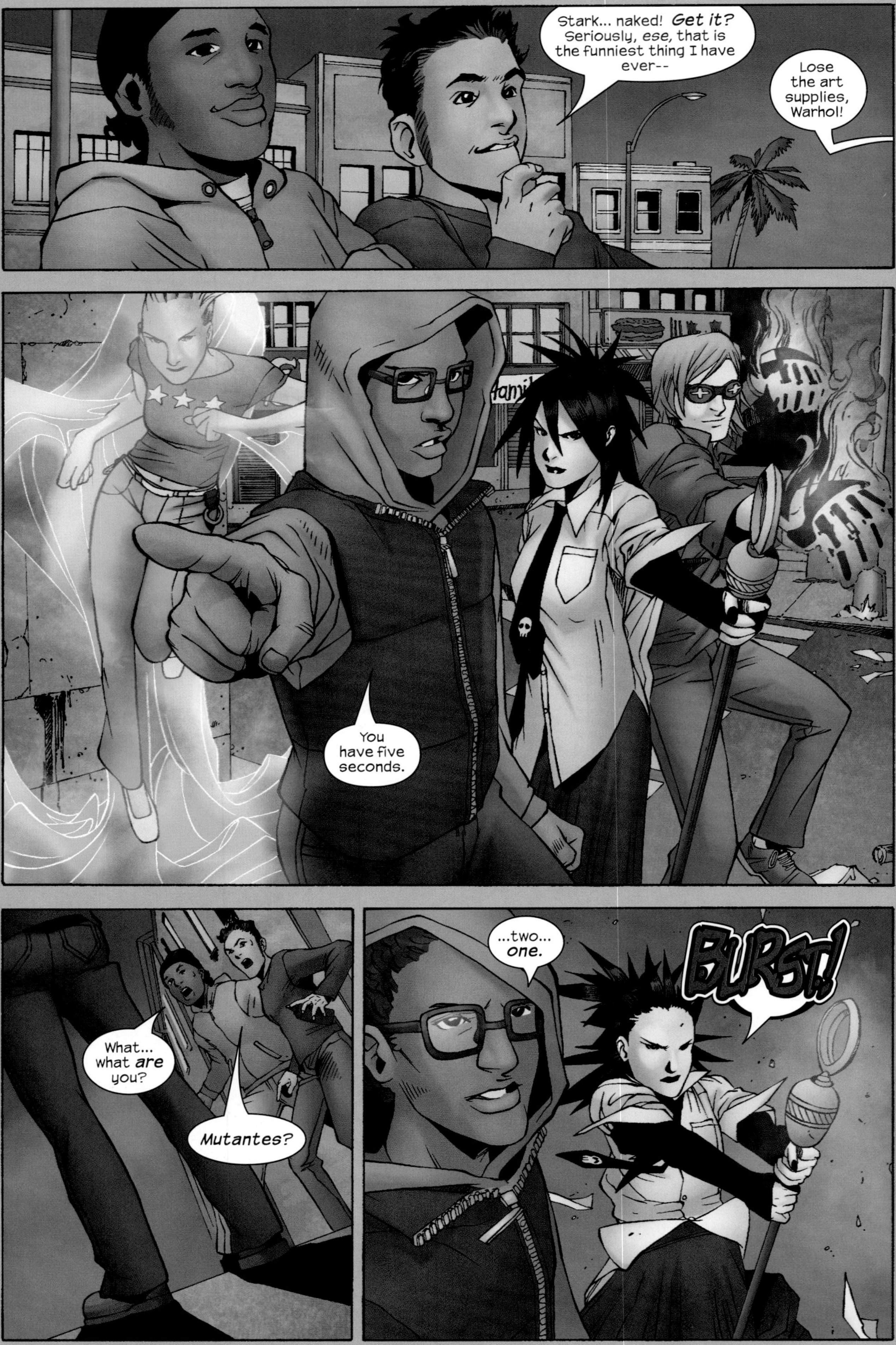

Stark... naked! Get it? Seriously, ese, that is the funniest thing I have ever--
Lose the art supplies, Warhol!
You have five seconds.
What... what are you?
Mutantes?
...two... one.
BURST!

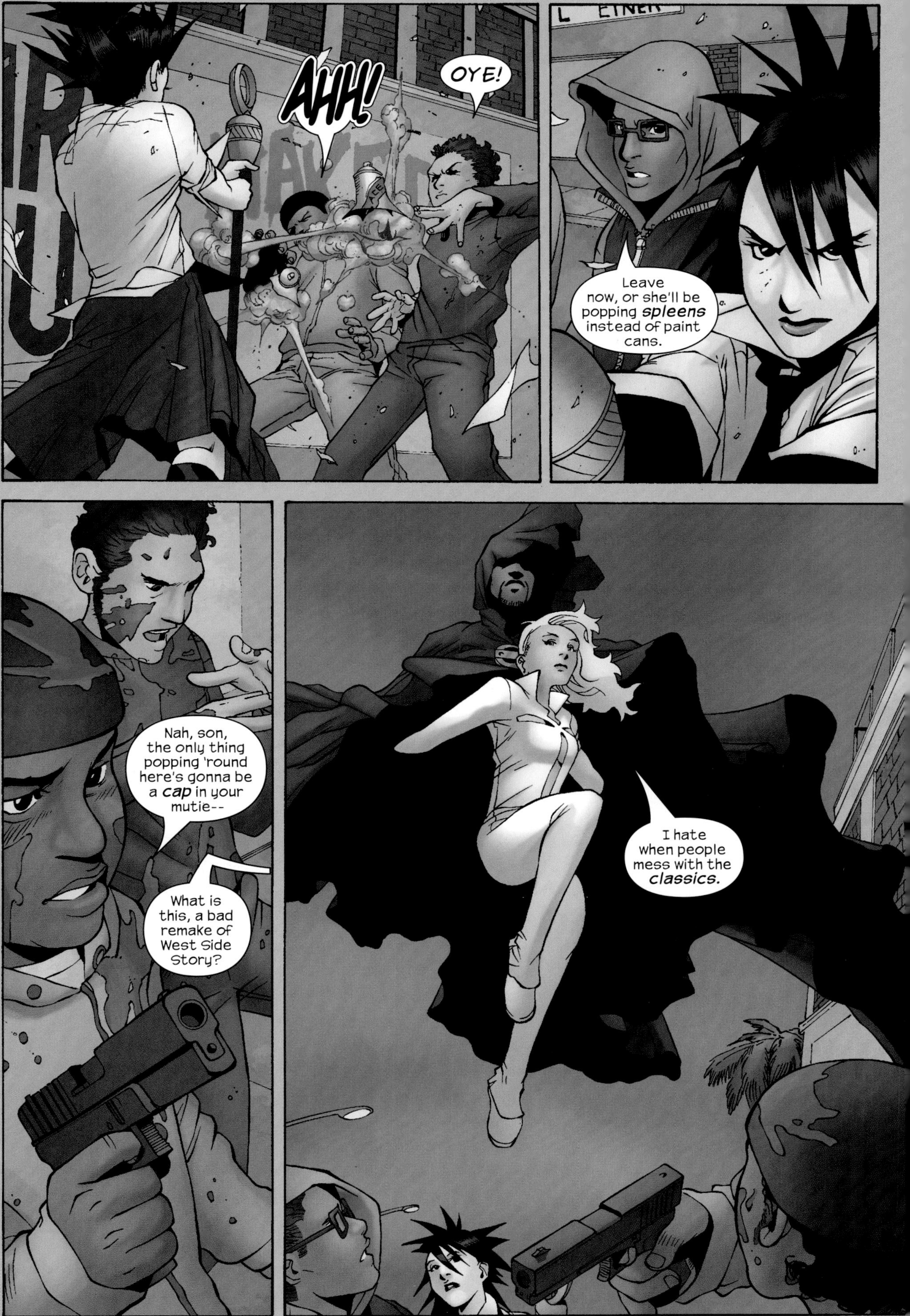
AHH!
OYE!
L ETNER
Leave now, or she'll be popping *spleens* instead of paint cans.
Nah, son, the only thing popping 'round here's gonna be a *cap* in your mutie--
What is this, a bad remake of West Side Story?
I hate when people mess with the *classics.*

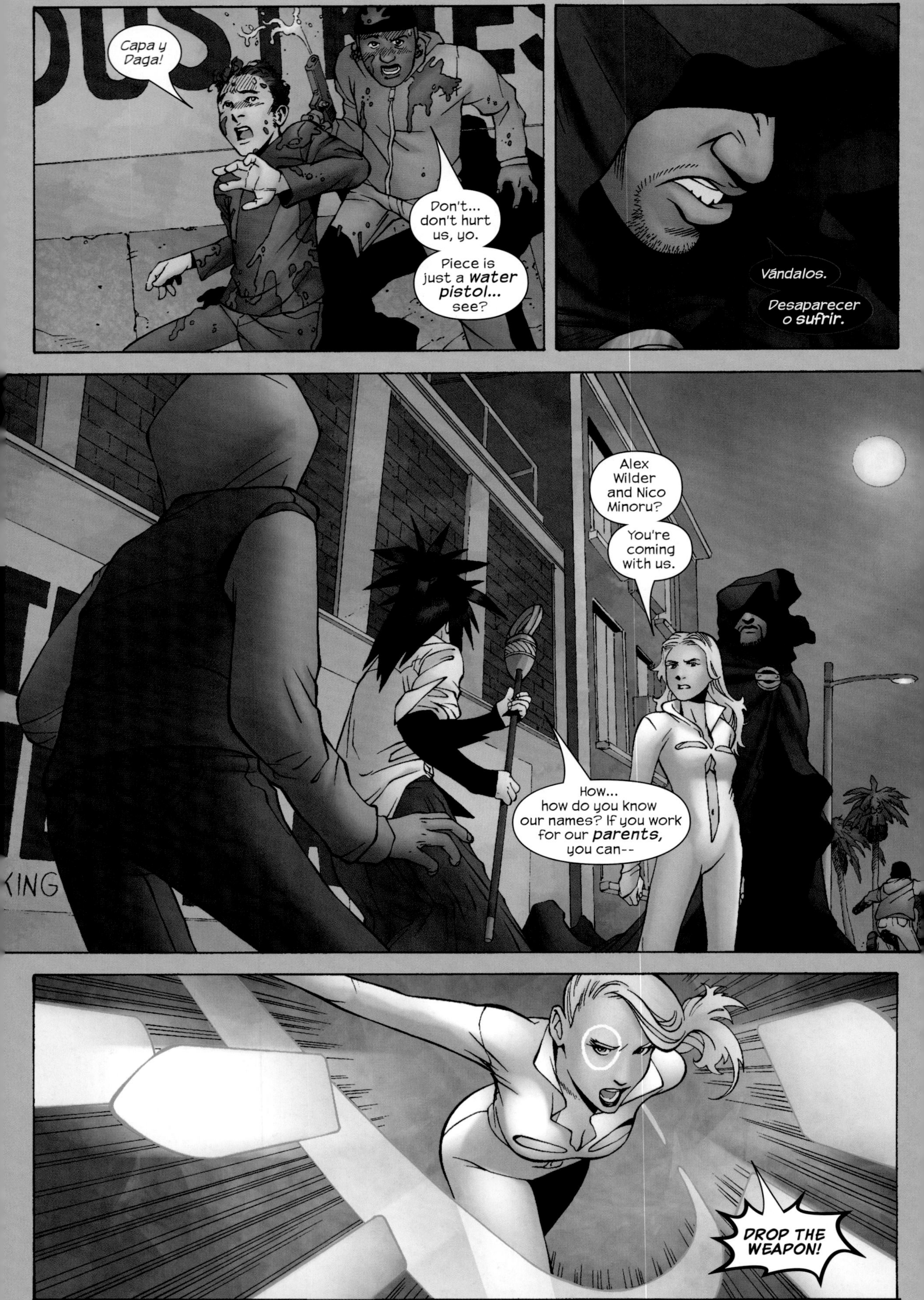

Capa y Daga!
Don't... don't hurt us, yo.
Piece is just a water pistol... see?
Vándalos.
Desaparecer o sufrir.
Alex Wilder and Nico Minoru?
You're coming with us.
How... how do you know our names? If you work for our parents, you can--
DROP THE WEAPON!

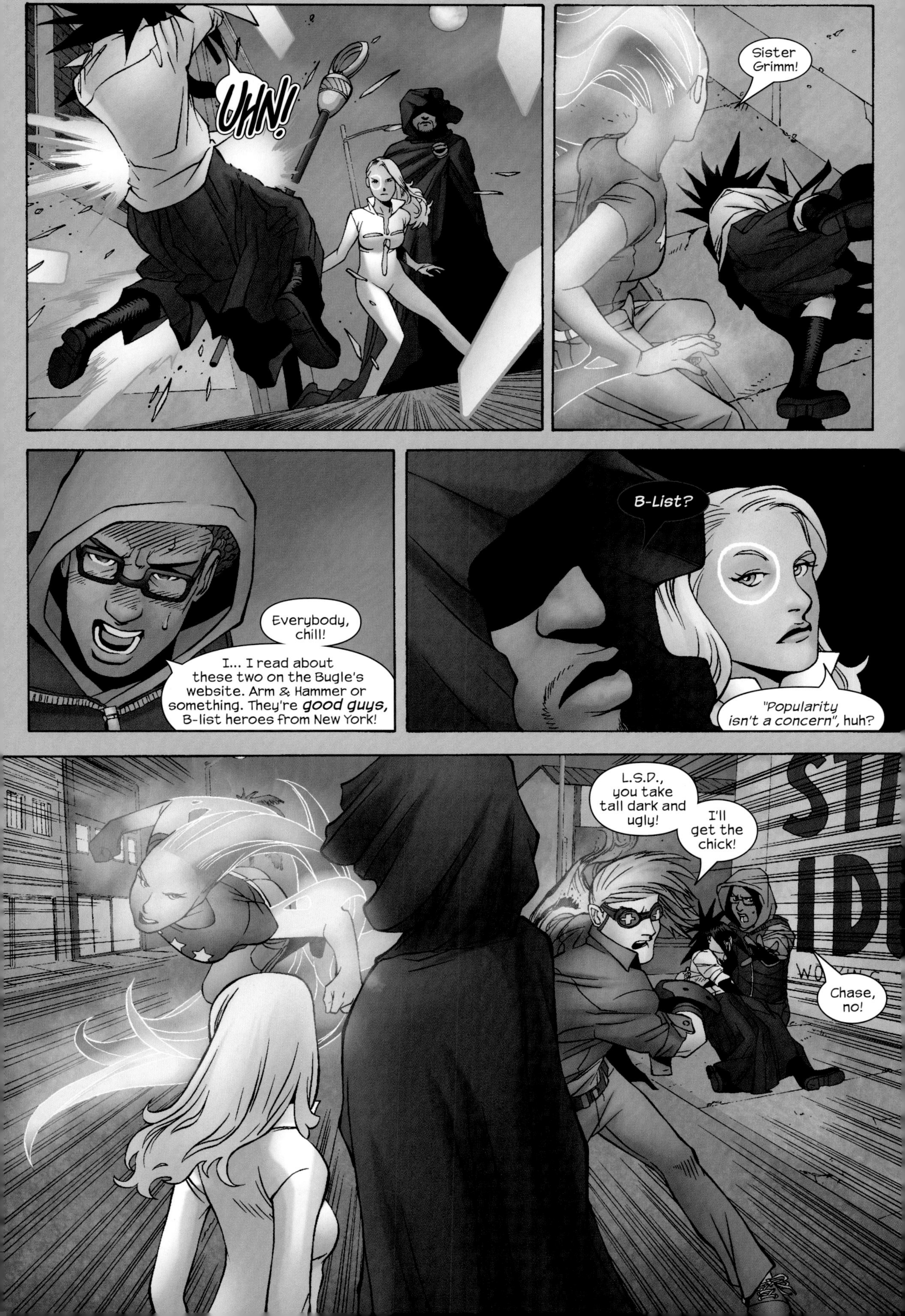
UHN!
Sister Grimm!
Everybody, chill!
I... I read about these two on the Bugle's website. Arm & Hammer or something. They're **good guys,** B-list heroes from New York!
B-List?
"Popularity isn't a concern", huh?
L.S.D., you take tall dark and ugly!
I'll get the chick!
Chase, no!

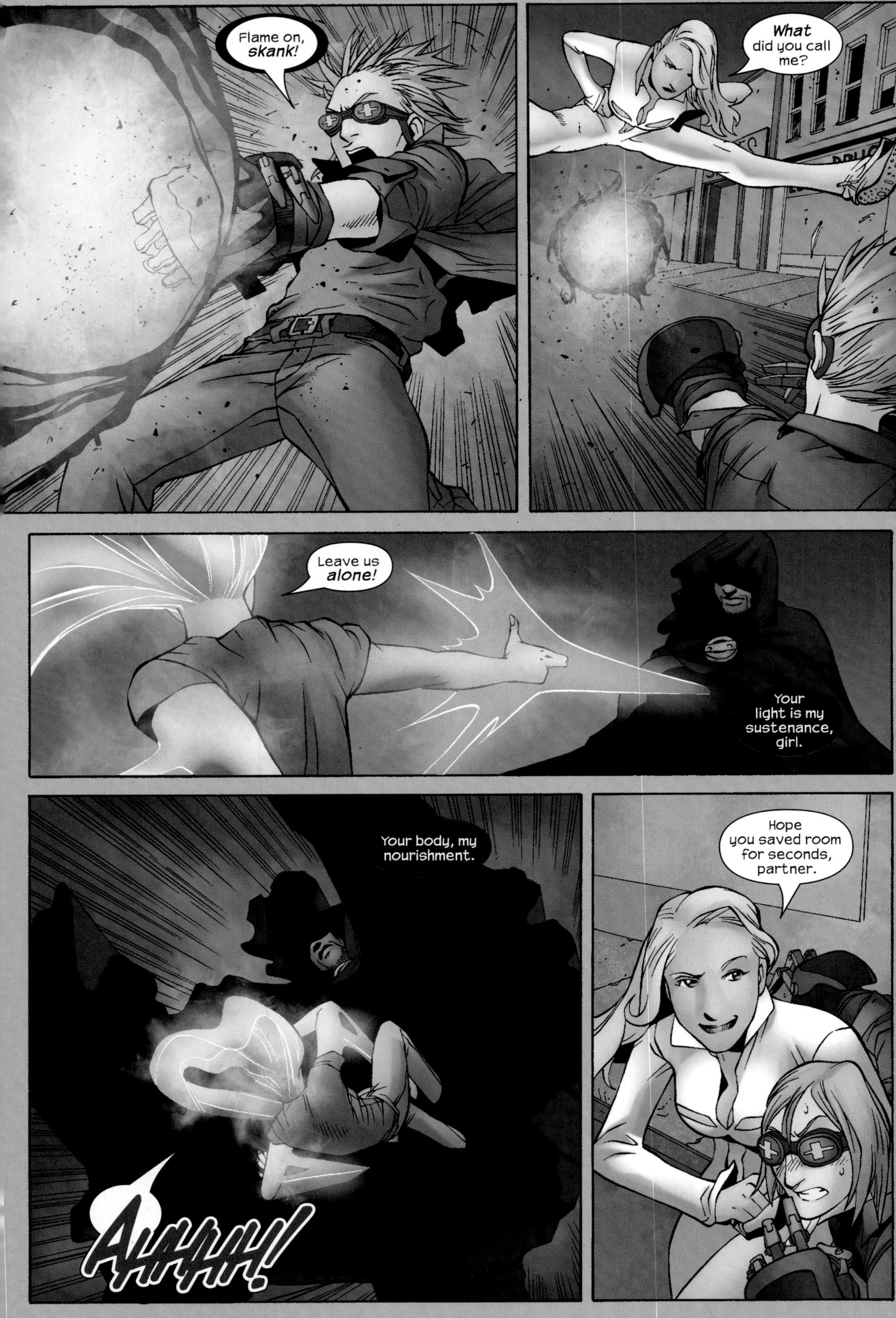
Flame on, skank!
What did you call me?
Leave us alone!
Your light is my sustenance, girl.
Your body, my nourishment.
AHHHH!
Hope you saved room for seconds, partner.

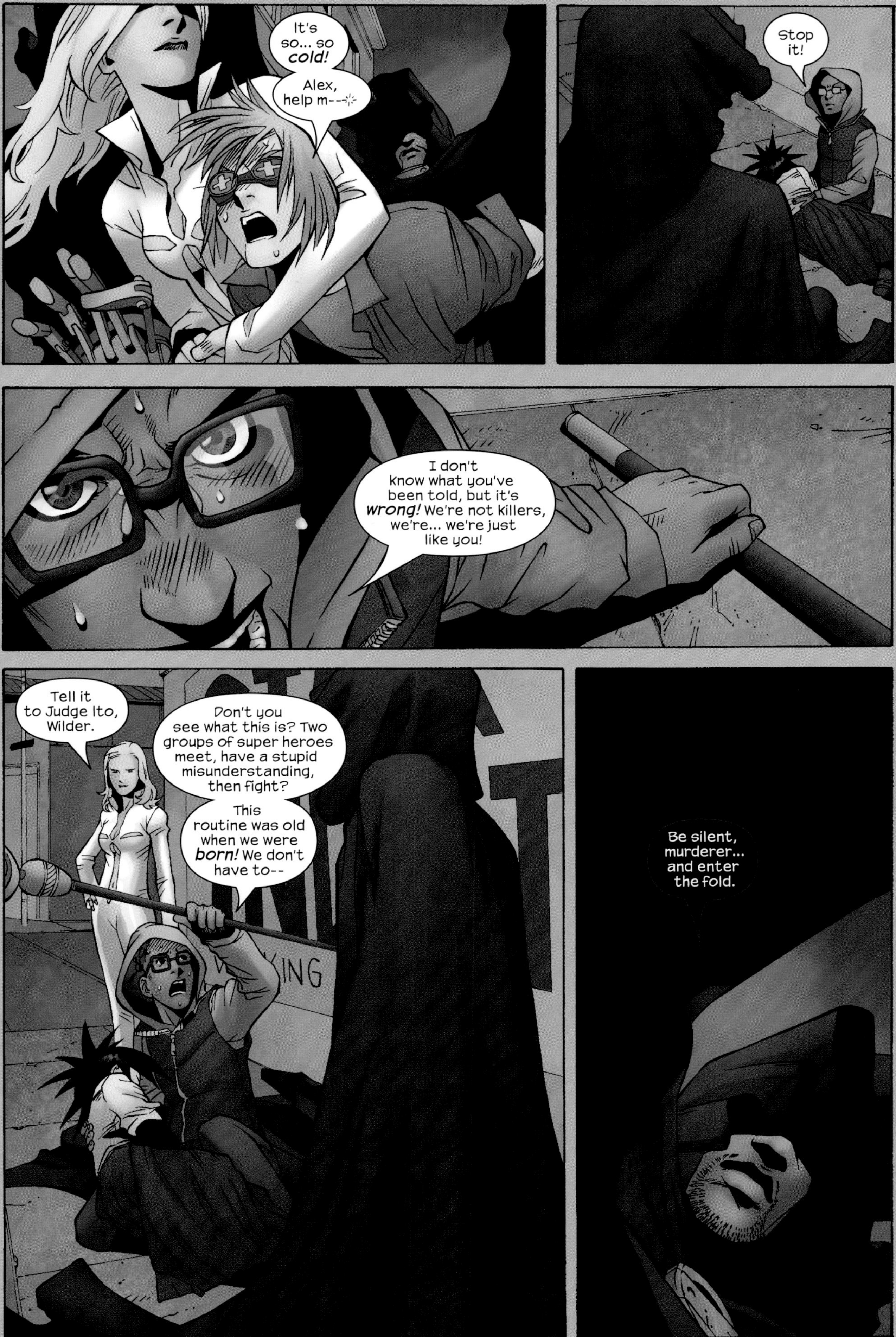
It's so... so cold!
Alex, help m--
Stop it!
I don't know what you've been told, but it's wrong! We're not killers, we're... we're just like you!
Tell it to Judge Ito, Wilder.
Don't you see what this is? Two groups of super heroes meet, have a stupid misunderstanding, then fight?
This routine was old when we were born! We don't have to--
Be silent, murderer... and enter the fold.

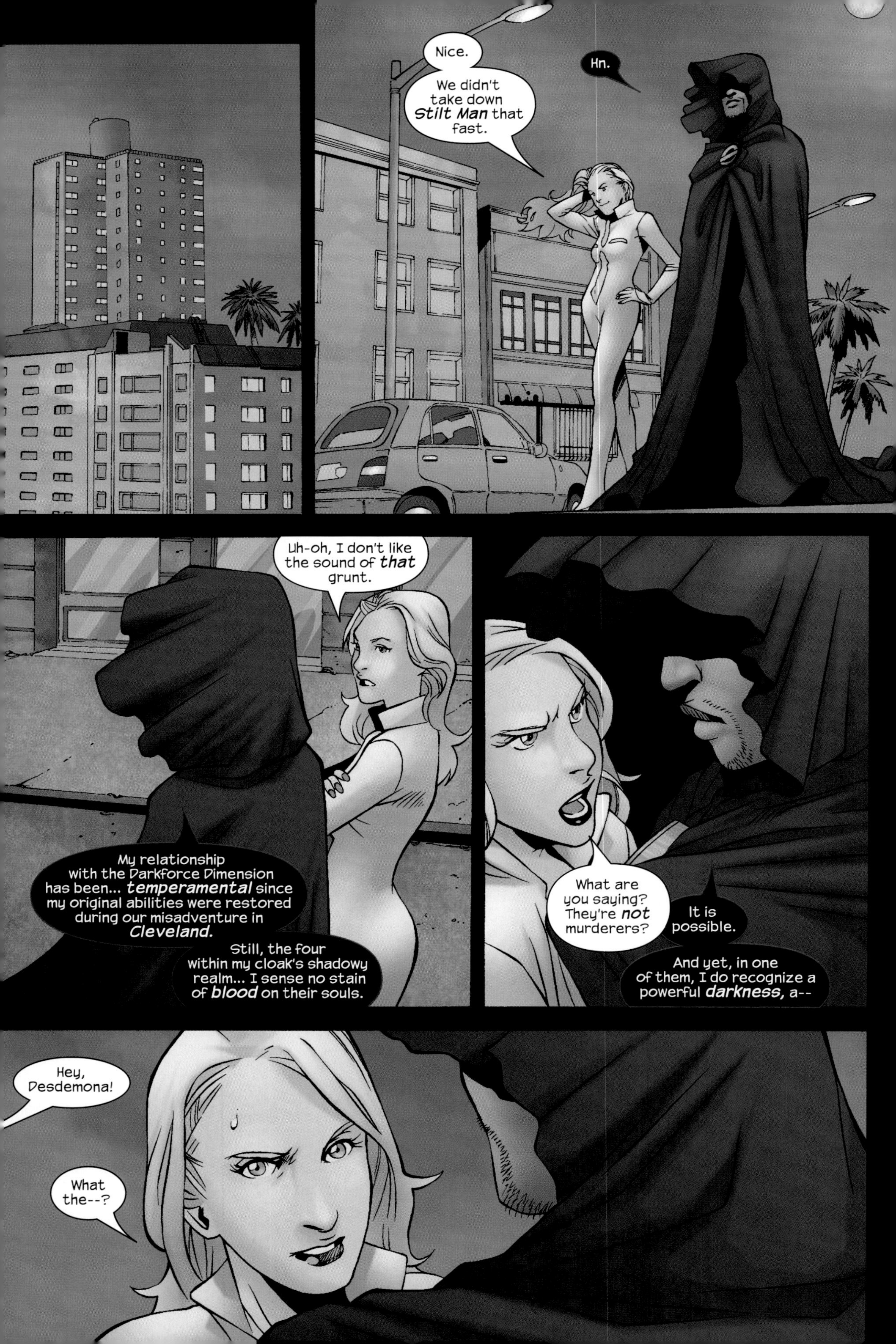
Nice.
We didn't take down Stilt Man that fast.
Hn.
Uh-oh, I don't like the sound of that grunt.
My relationship with the Darkforce Dimension has been... temperamental since my original abilities were restored during our misadventure in Cleveland.
Still, the four within my cloak's shadowy realm... I sense no stain of blood on their souls.
What are you saying? They're not murderers?
It is possible.
And yet, in one of them, I do recognize a powerful darkness, a--
Hey, Desdemona!
What the--?

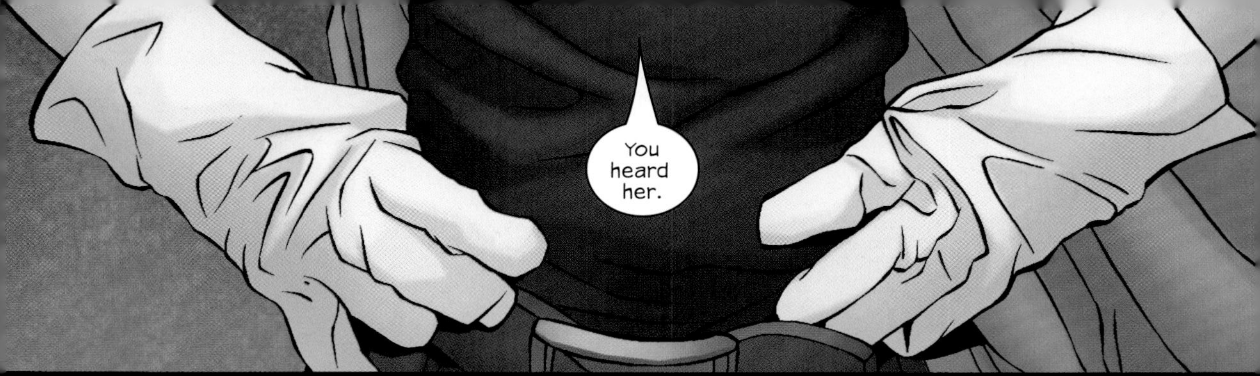
You heard her.

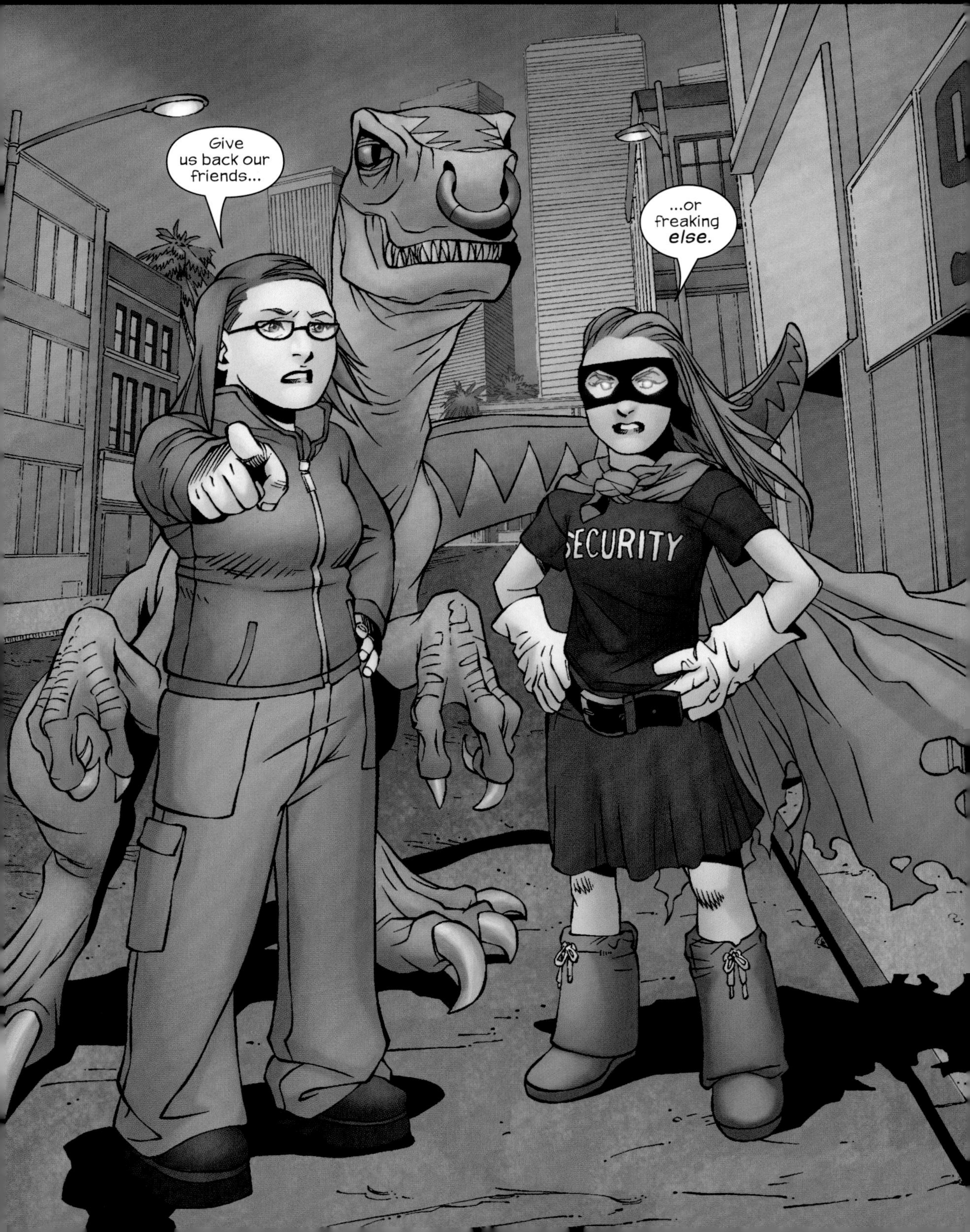
Give us back our friends...
...or freaking *else.*
SECURITY

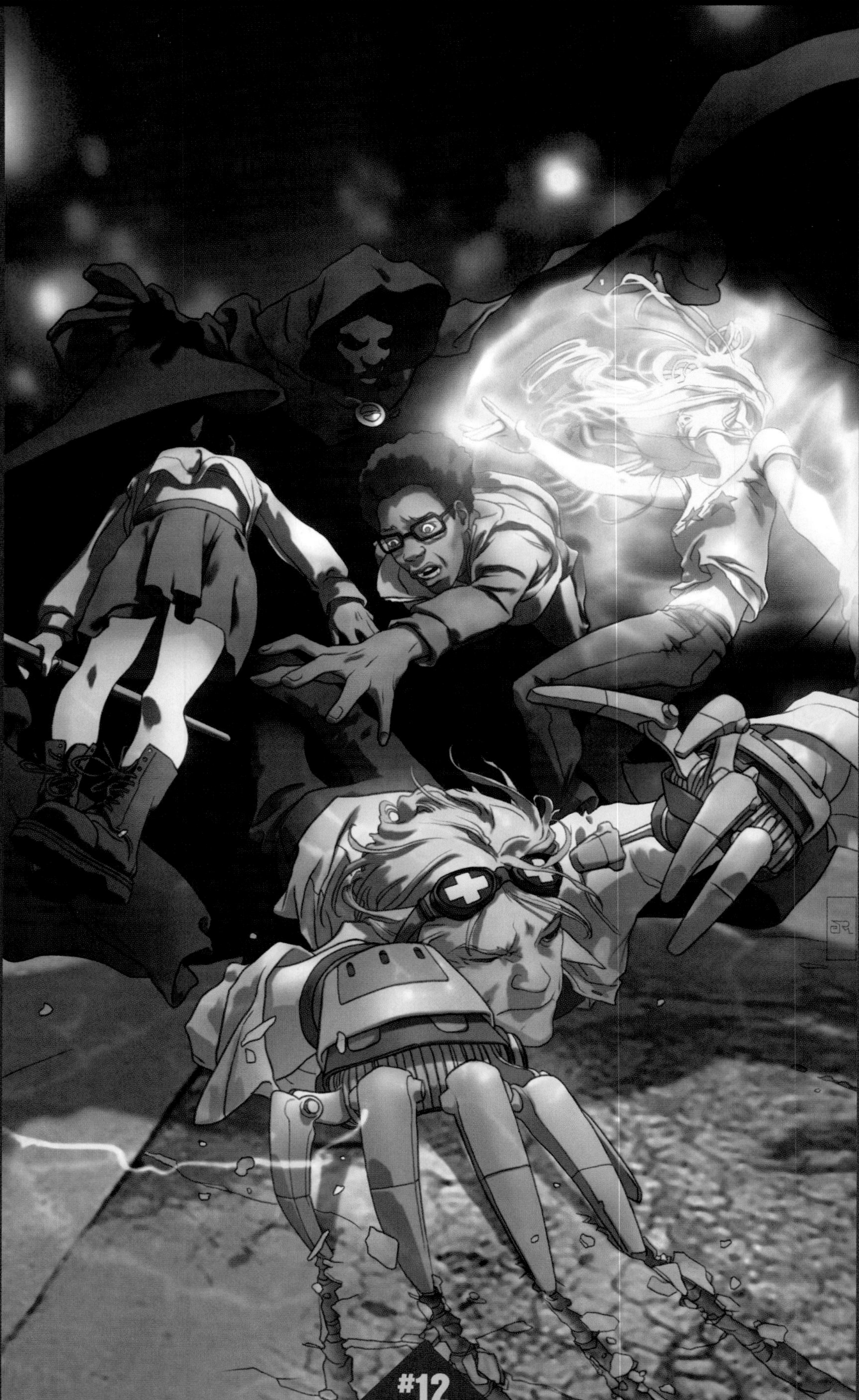
#12

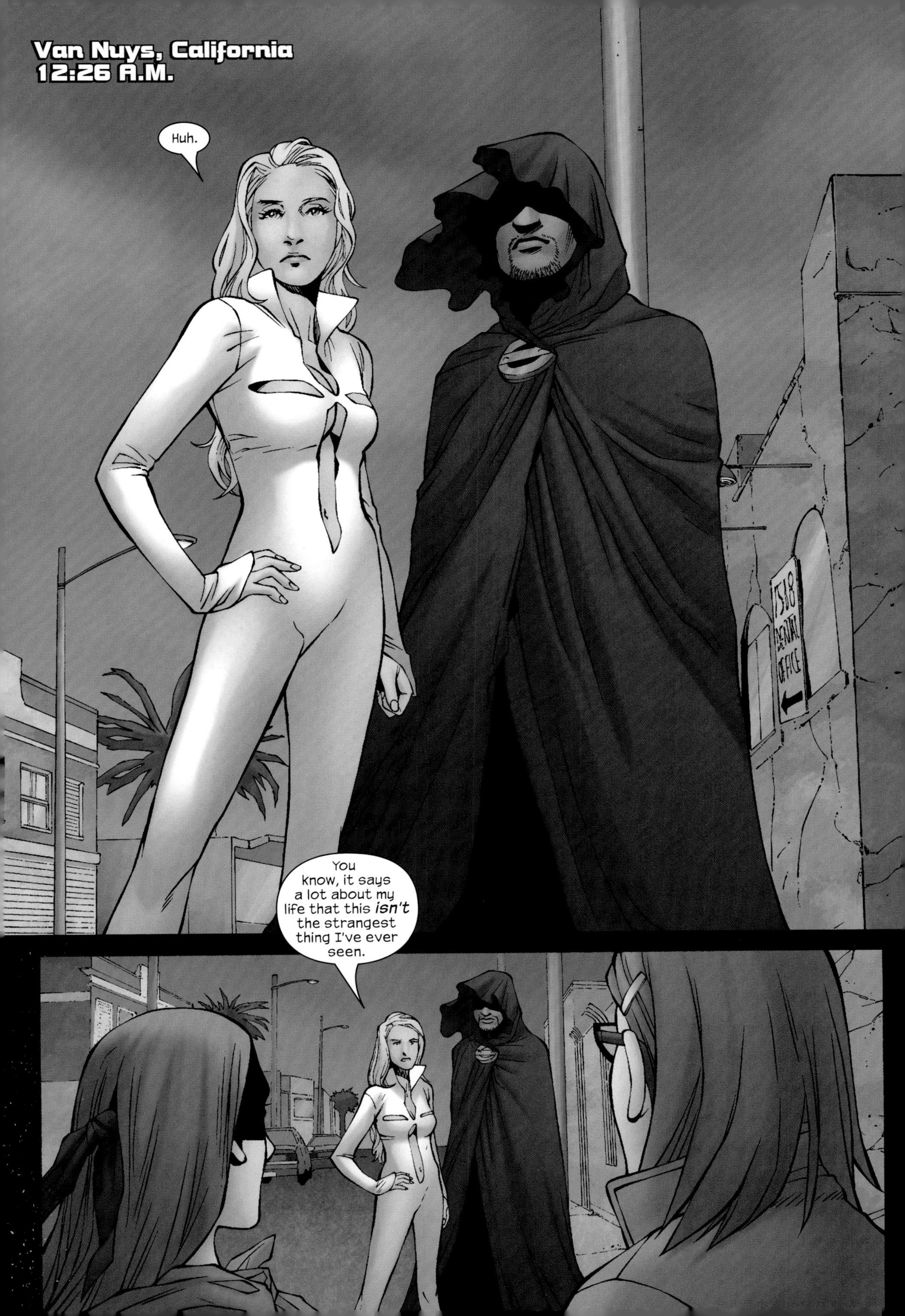

Van Nuys, California 12:26 A.M.
Huh.
1518 DENTAL OFFICE
You know, it says a lot about my life that this *isn't* the strangest thing I've ever seen.

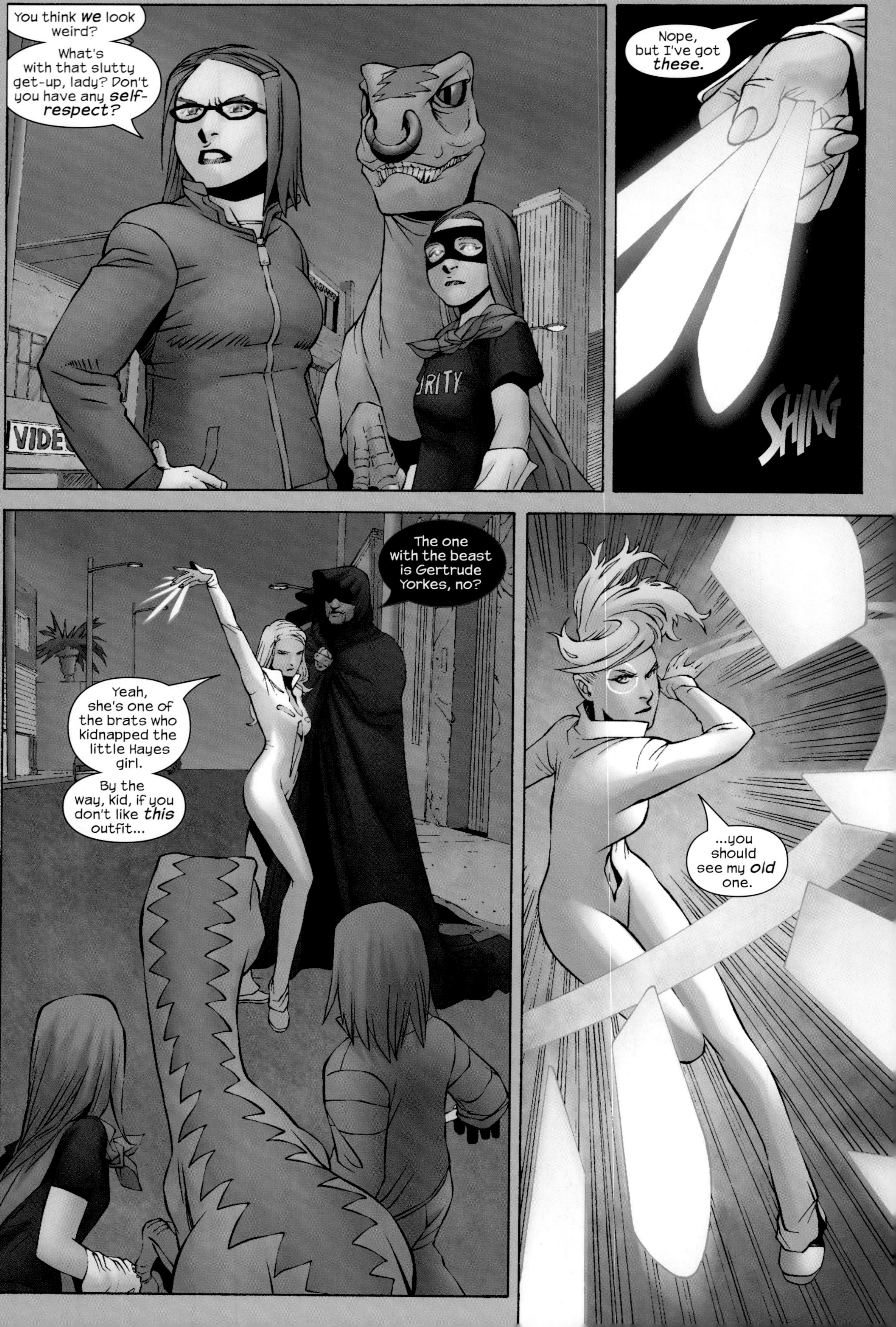
You think we look weird?
What's with that slutty get-up, lady? Don't you have any self-respect?
Nope, but I've got these.
SHING
The one with the beast is Gertrude Yorkes, no?
Yeah, she's one of the brats who kidnapped the little Hayes girl.
By the way, kid, if you don't like this outfit...
...you should see my old one.

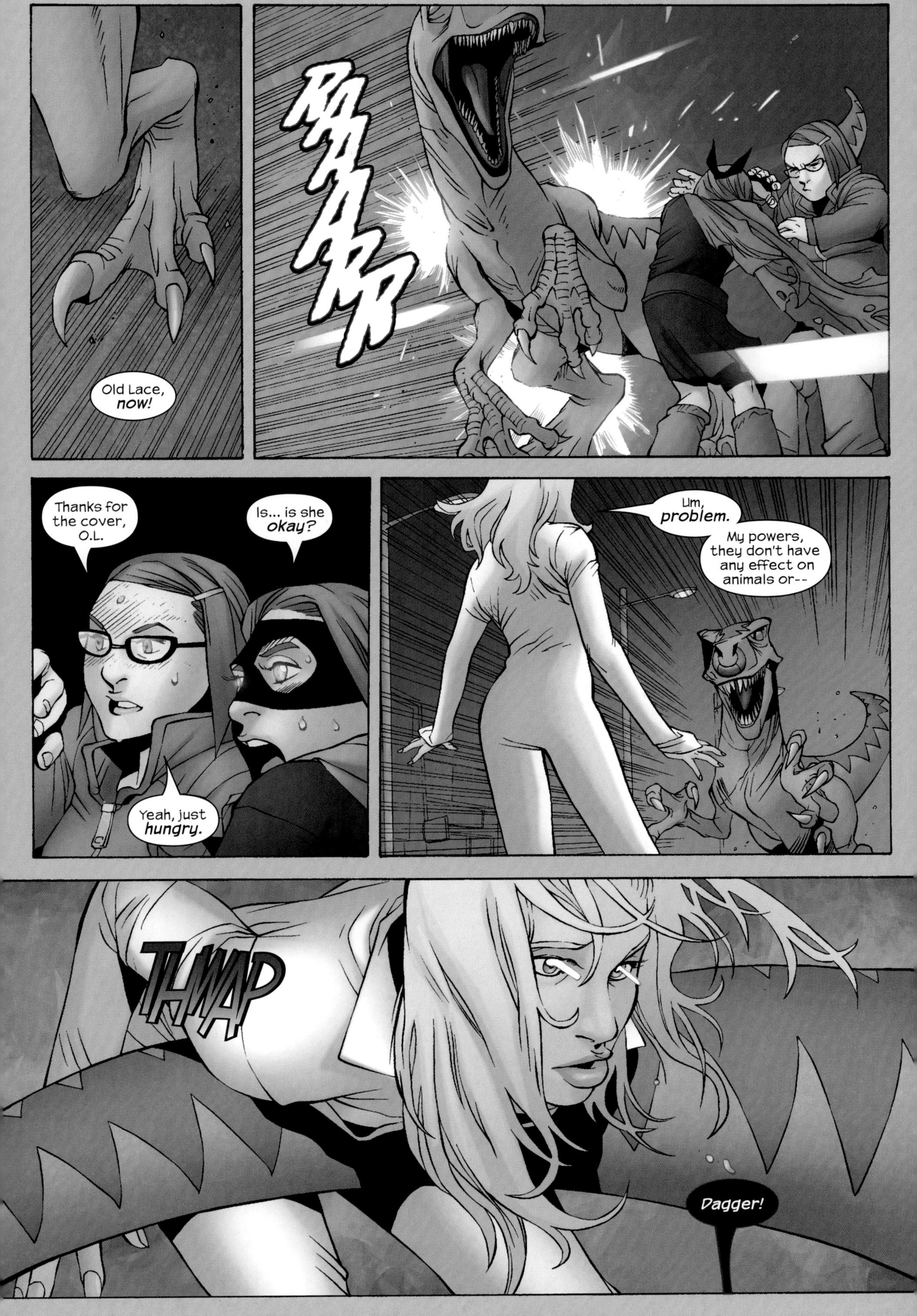
Old Lace, *now!*
RAAARR
Thanks for the cover, O.L.
Is... is she *okay?*
Yeah, just *hungry.*
Um, *problem.*
My powers, they don't have any effect on animals or--
THWAP
Dagger!

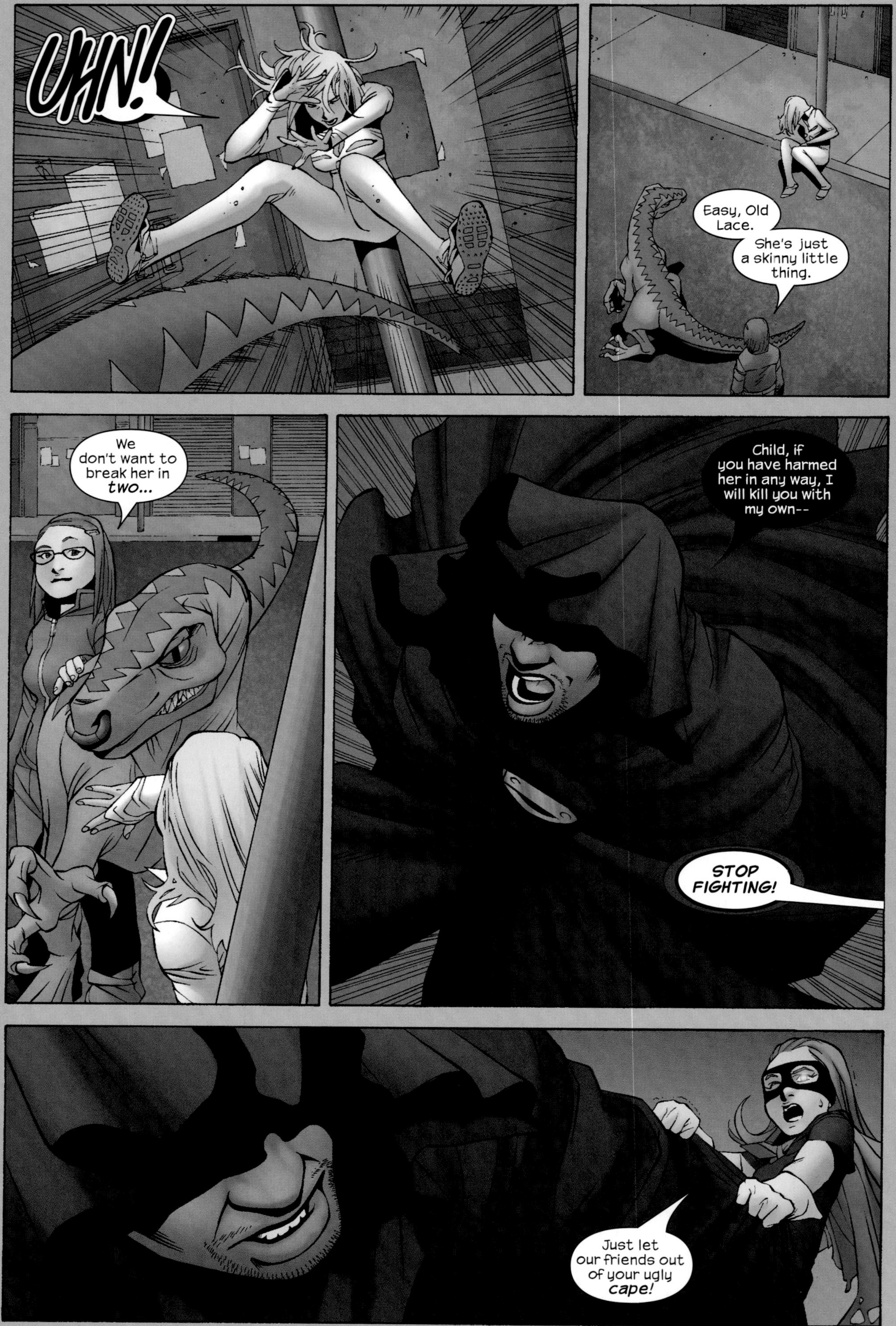
UHN!
Easy, Old Lace.
She's just a skinny little thing.
We don't want to break her in two...
Child, if you have harmed her in any way, I will kill you with my own--
STOP FIGHTING!
Just let our friends out of your ugly cape!

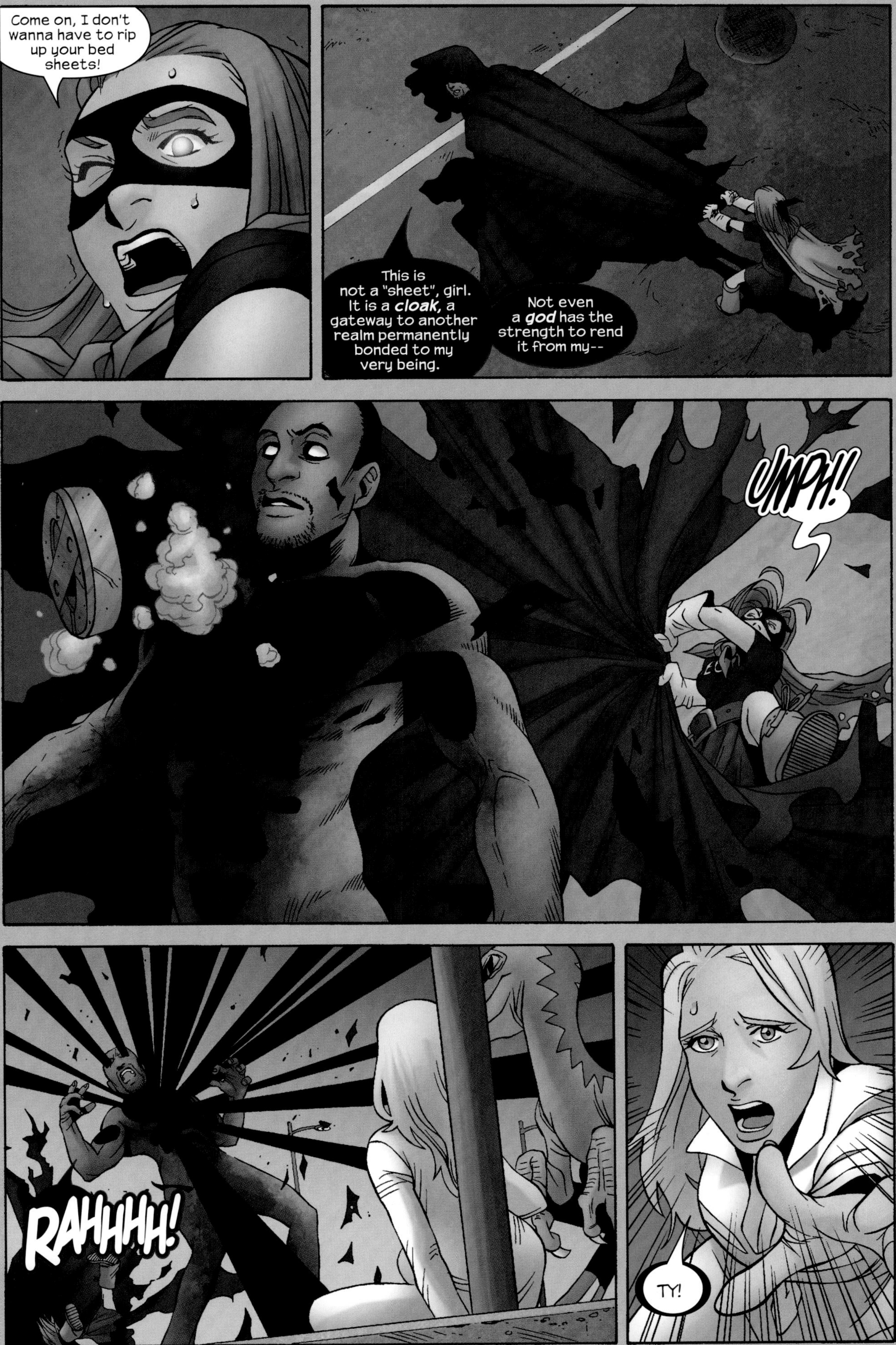
Come on, I don't wanna have to rip up your bed sheets!
This is not a "sheet", girl. It is a *cloak*, a gateway to another realm permanently bonded to my very being.
Not even a *god* has the strength to rend it from my--
UMPH!
RAHHHH!
TY!

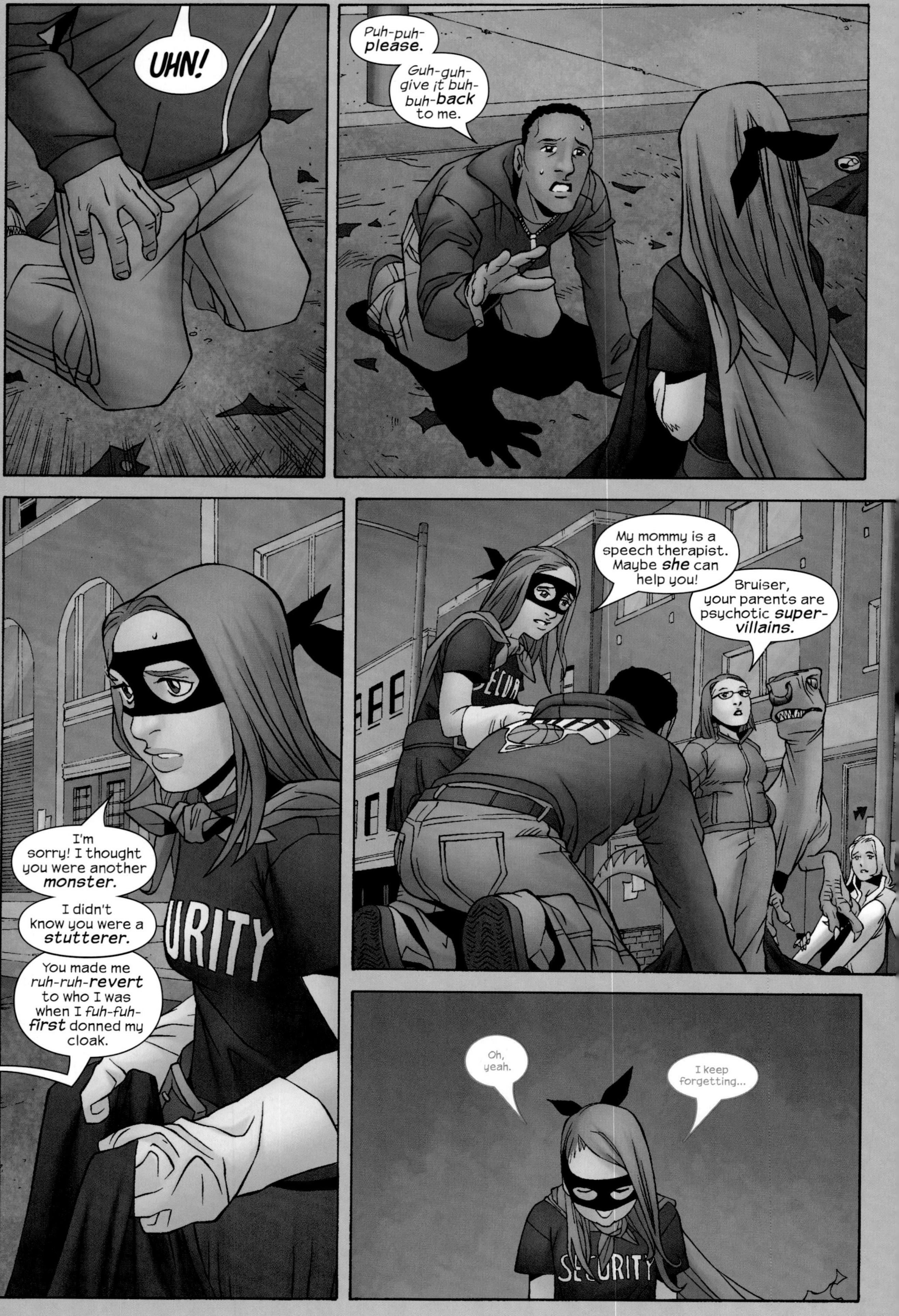
UHN!
Puh-puh-please.
Guh-guh-give it buh-buh-back to me.
I'm sorry! I thought you were another monster.
I didn't know you were a stutterer.
You made me ruh-ruh-revert to who I was when I fuh-fuh-first donned my cloak.
My mommy is a speech therapist. Maybe she can help you!
Bruiser, your parents are psychotic super-villains.
Oh, yeah.
I keep forgetting...

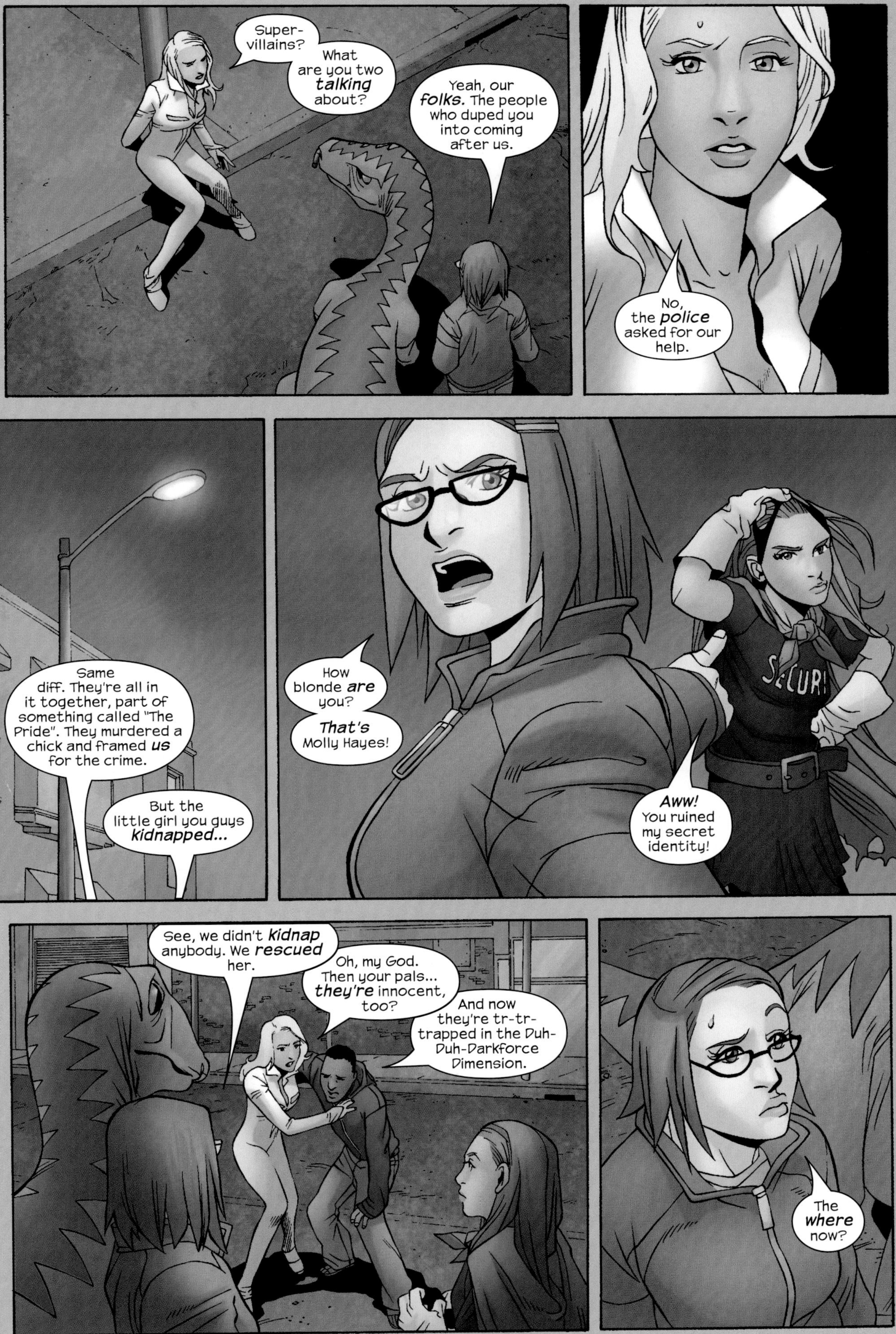
Super-villains? What are you two *talking* about?
Yeah, our *folks.* The people who duped you into coming after us.
No, the *police* asked for our help.
Same diff. They're all in it together, part of something called "The Pride". They murdered a chick and framed *us* for the crime.
But the little girl you guys *kidnapped...*
How blonde *are* you?
That's Molly Hayes!
Aww! You ruined my secret identity!
SECURI
See, we didn't *kidnap* anybody. We *rescued* her.
Oh, my God. Then your pals... *they're* innocent, too?
And now they're tr-tr-trapped in the Duh-Duh-Darkforce Dimension.
The *where* now?

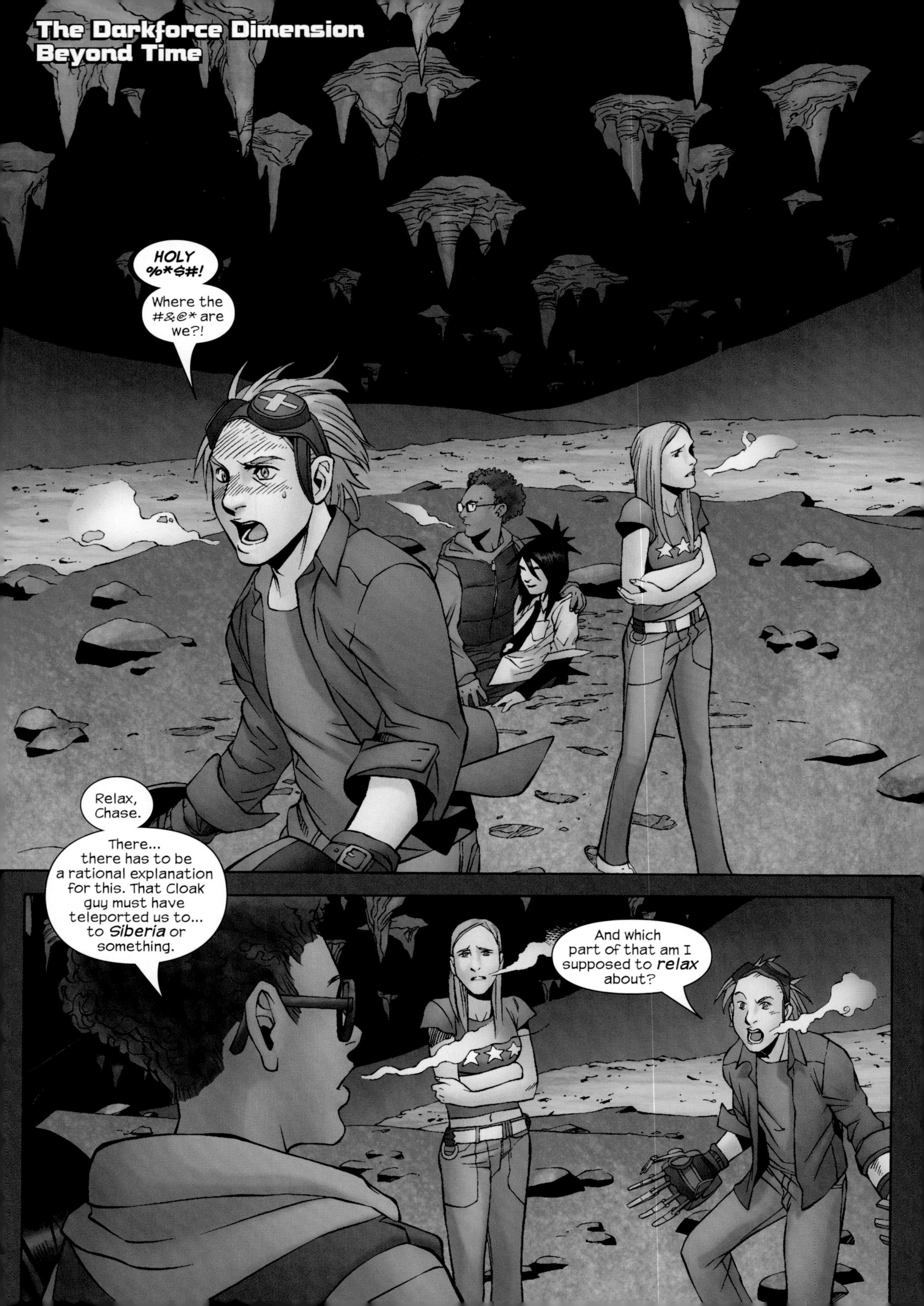

The Darkforce Dimension
Beyond Time
HOLY %*$#!
Where the #&@* are we?!
Relax, Chase.
There... there has to be a rational explanation for this. That Cloak guy must have teleported us to... to *Siberia* or something.
And which part of that am I supposed to *relax* about?

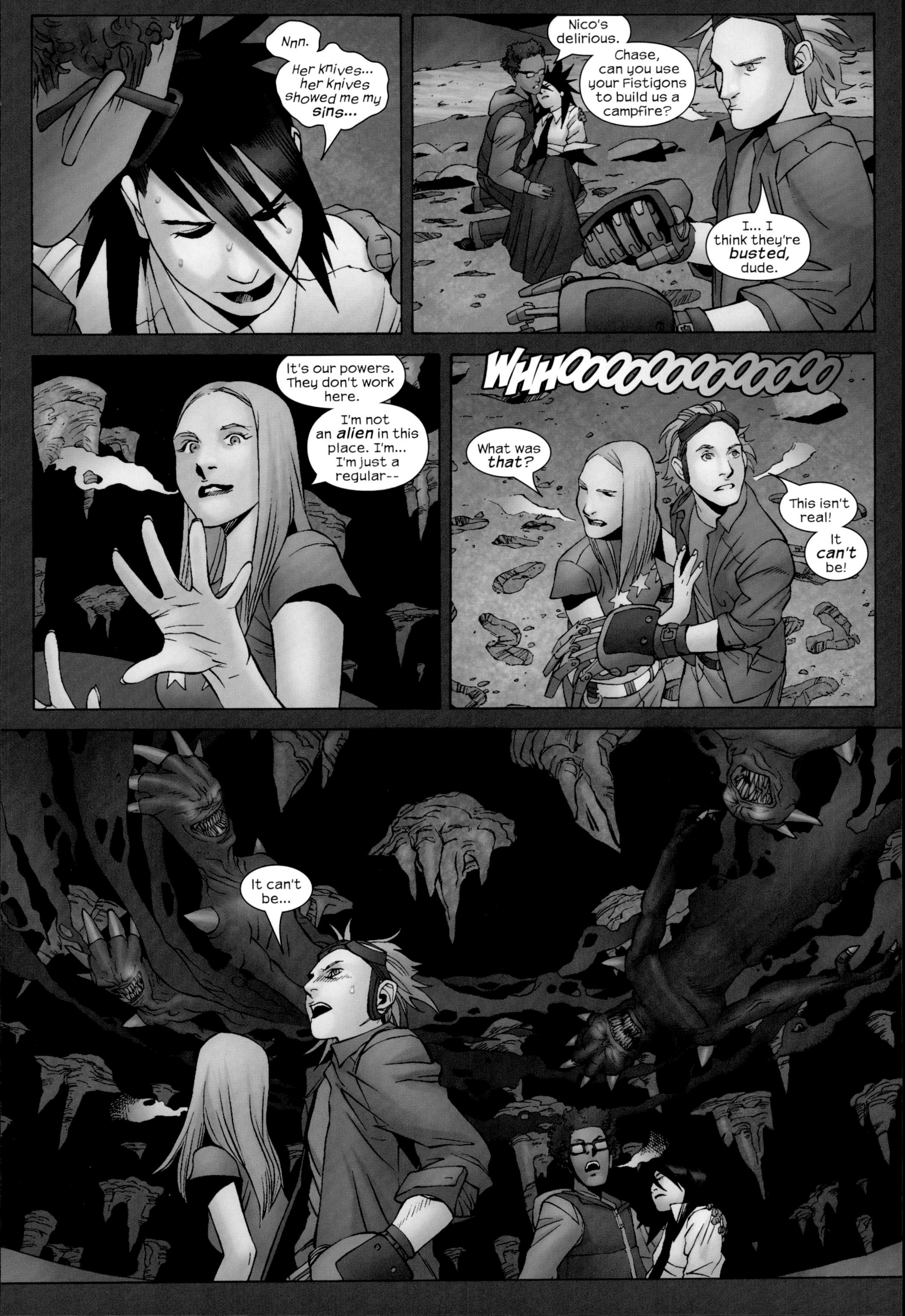
Nnn.
Her knives... her knives showed me my *sins...*
Nico's delirious.
Chase, can you use your Fistigons to build us a campfire?
I... I think they're *busted,* dude.
It's our powers. They don't work here.
I'm not an *alien* in this place. I'm... I'm just a regular--
WHHOOOOOOOOOOOOOO
What was *that?*
This isn't real!
It *can't* be!
It can't be...

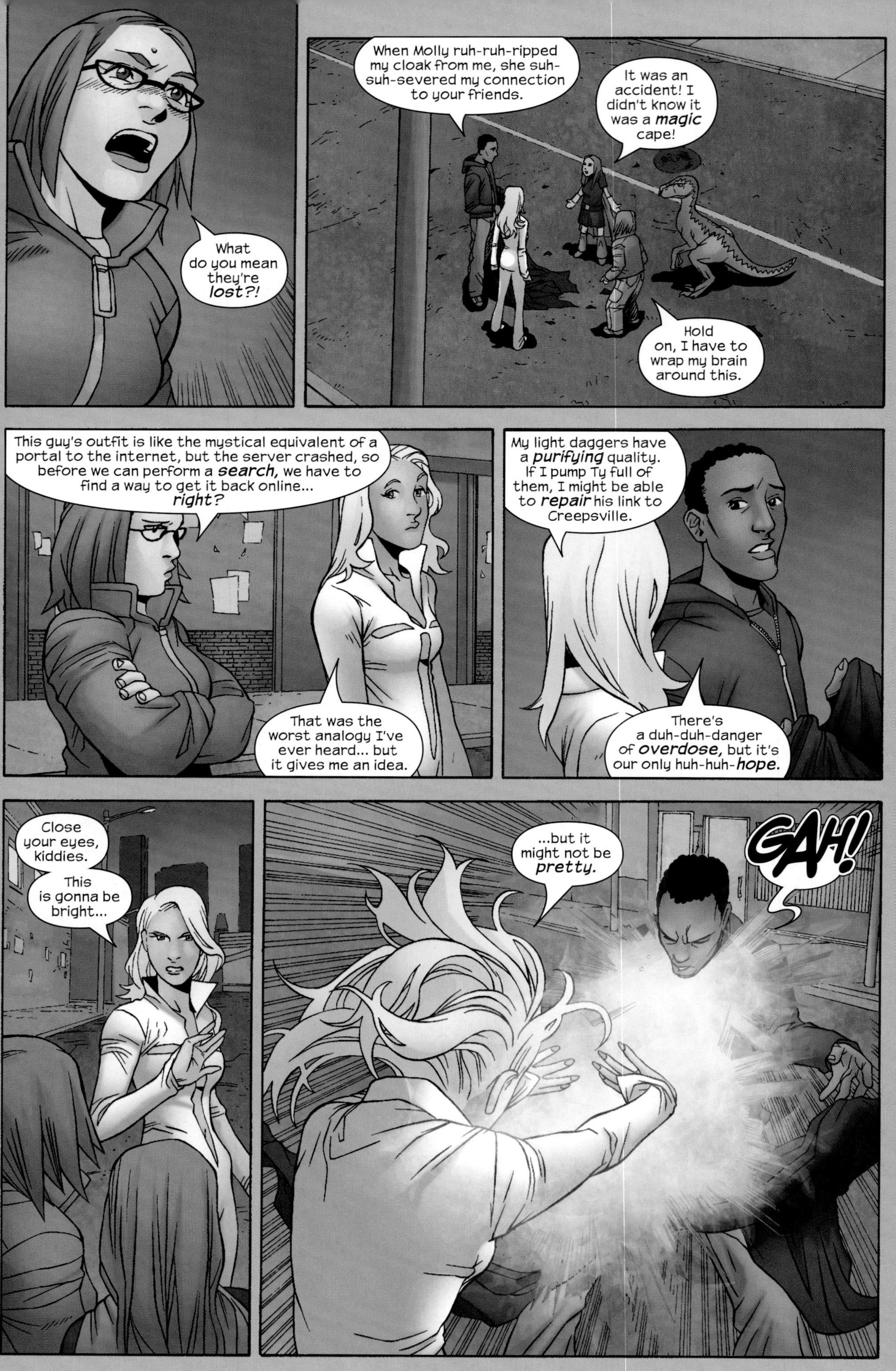
What do you mean they're *lost?!*
When Molly ruh-ruh-ripped my cloak from me, she suh-suh-severed my connection to your friends.
It was an accident! I didn't know it was a *magic* cape!
Hold on, I have to wrap my brain around this.
This guy's outfit is like the mystical equivalent of a portal to the internet, but the server crashed, so before we can perform a *search,* we have to find a way to get it back online... *right?*
That was the worst analogy I've ever heard... but it gives me an idea.
My light daggers have a *purifying* quality. If I pump Ty full of them, I might be able to *repair* his link to Creepsville.
There's a duh-duh-danger of *overdose,* but it's our only huh-huh-*hope.*
Close your eyes, kiddies.
This is gonna be bright...
...but it might not be *pretty.*
GAH!

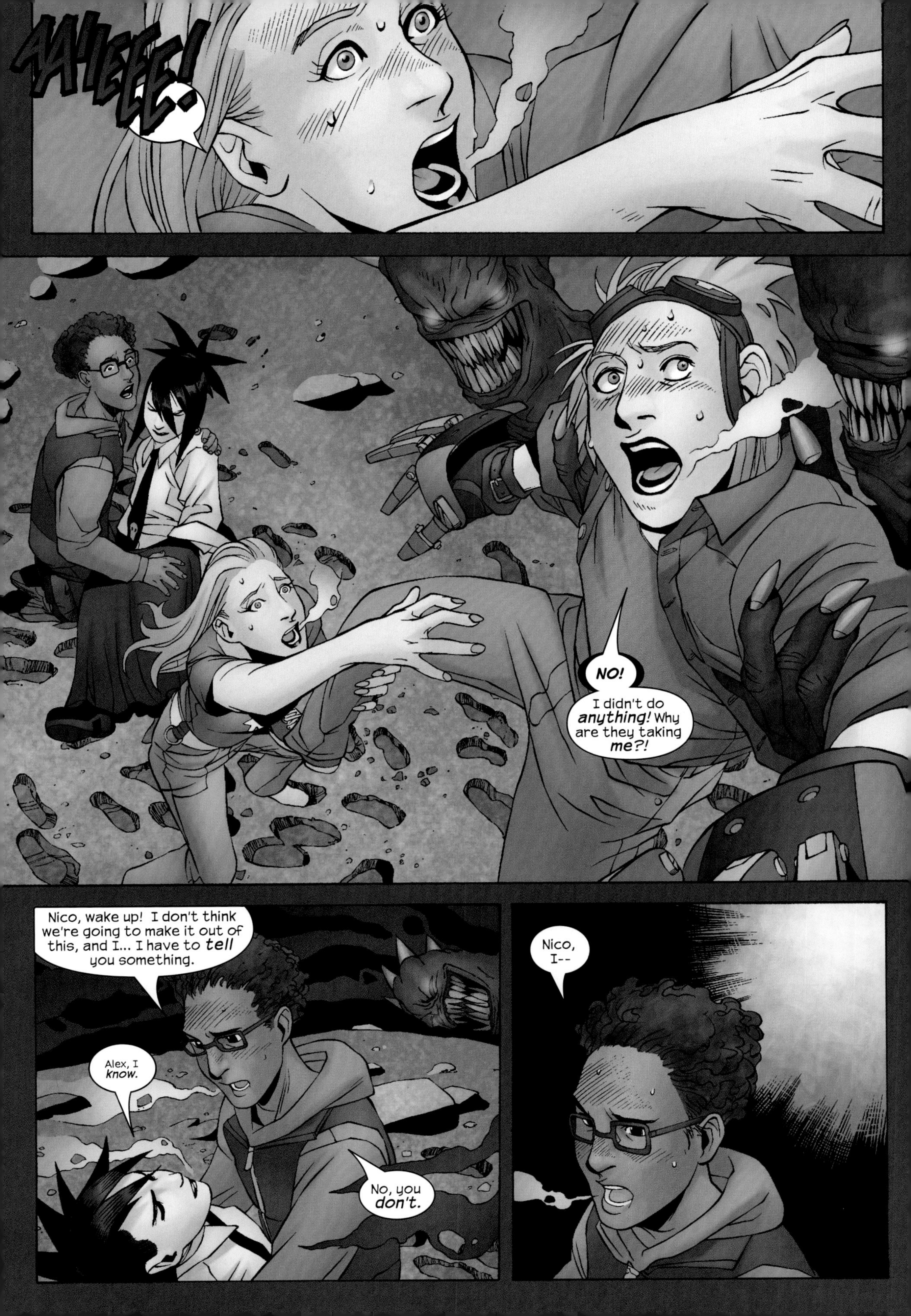
AAHEEE!
NO!
I didn't do anything! Why are they taking me?!
Nico, wake up! I don't think we're going to make it out of this, and I... I have to tell you something.
Alex, I know.
No, you don't.
Nico, I--

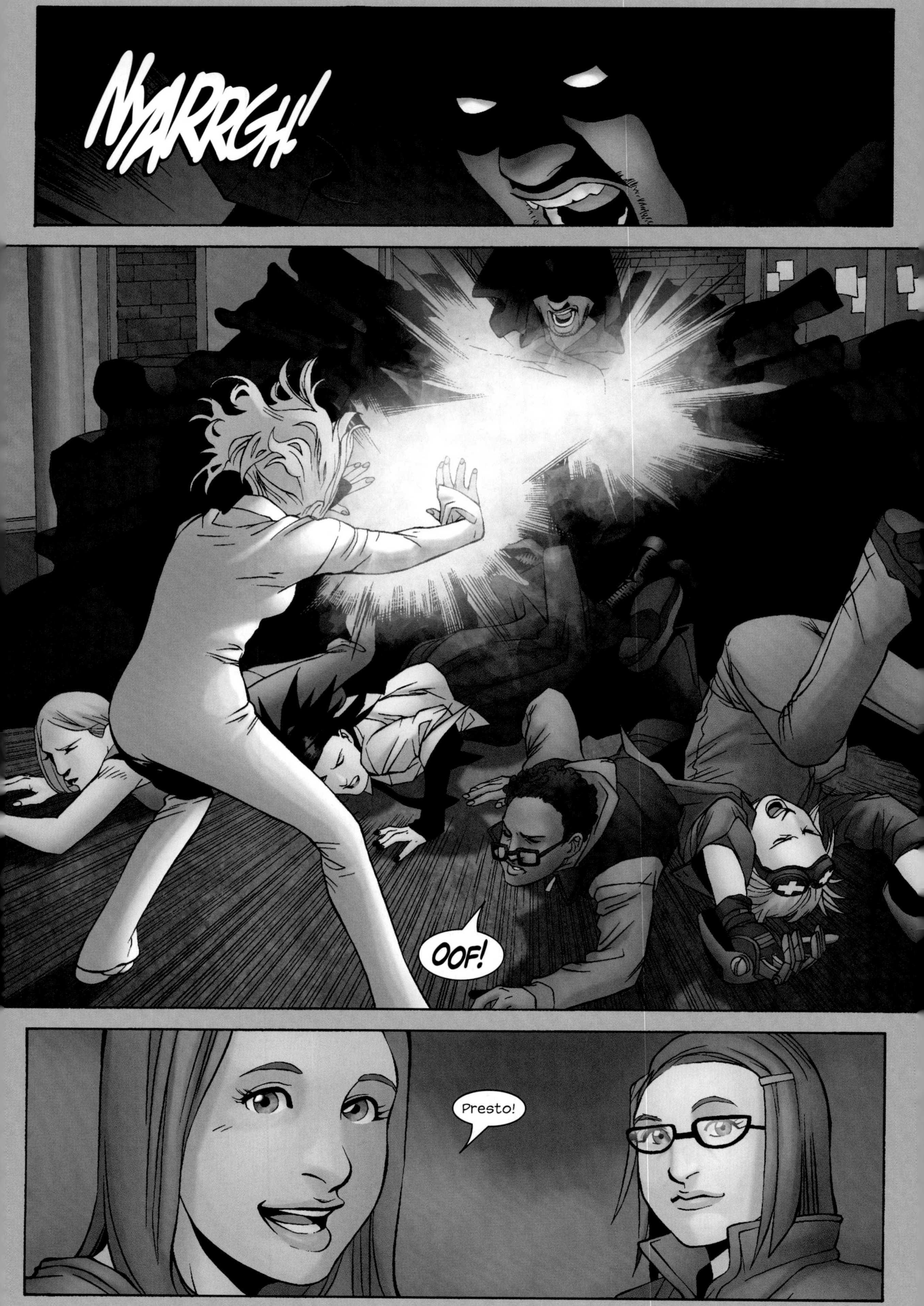

NYARRGH!
OOF!
Presto!

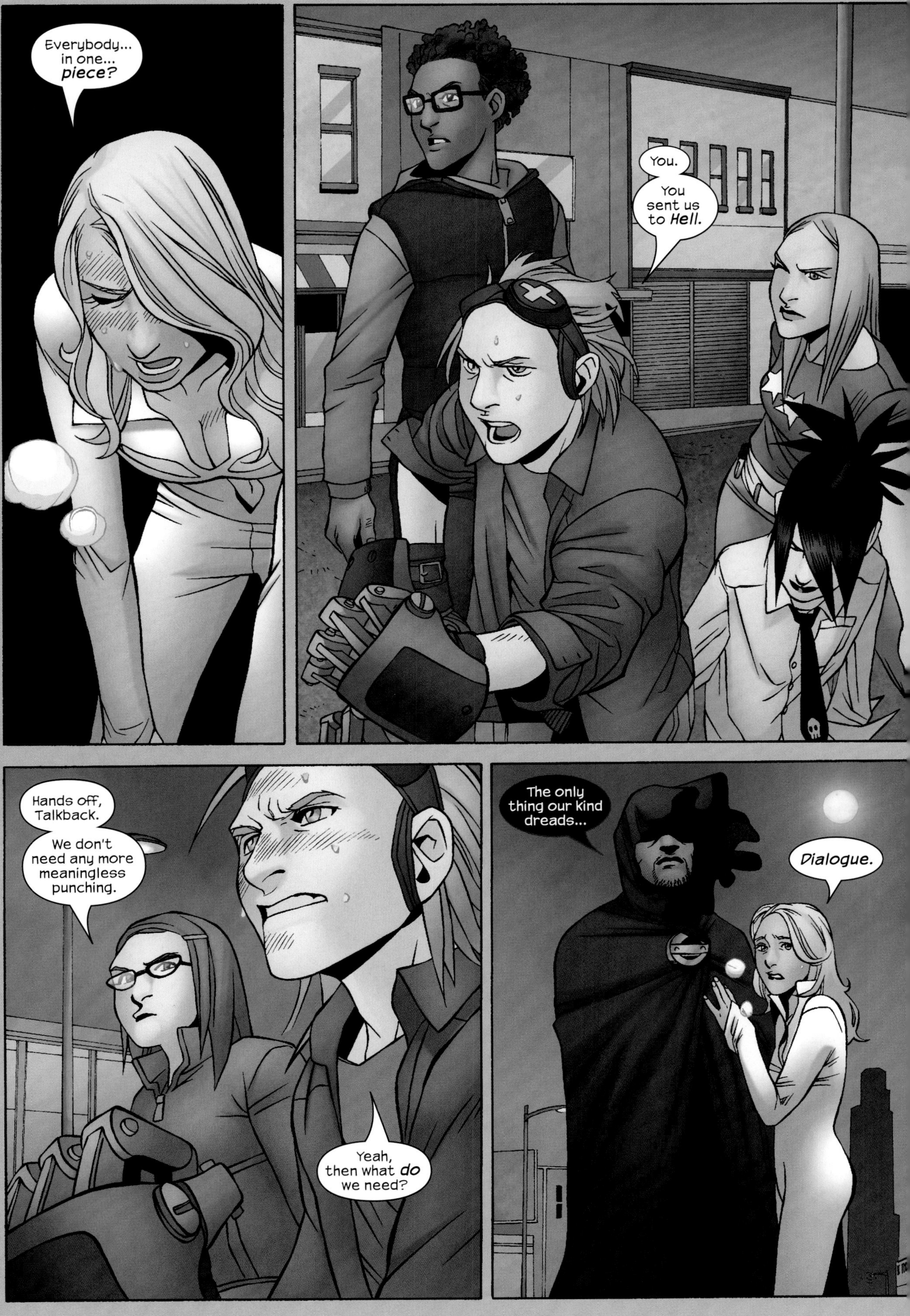

Everybody... in one... *piece?*
You.
You sent us to *Hell.*
Hands off, Talkback.
We don't need any more meaningless punching.
Yeah, then what *do* we need?
The only thing our kind dreads...
Dialogue.

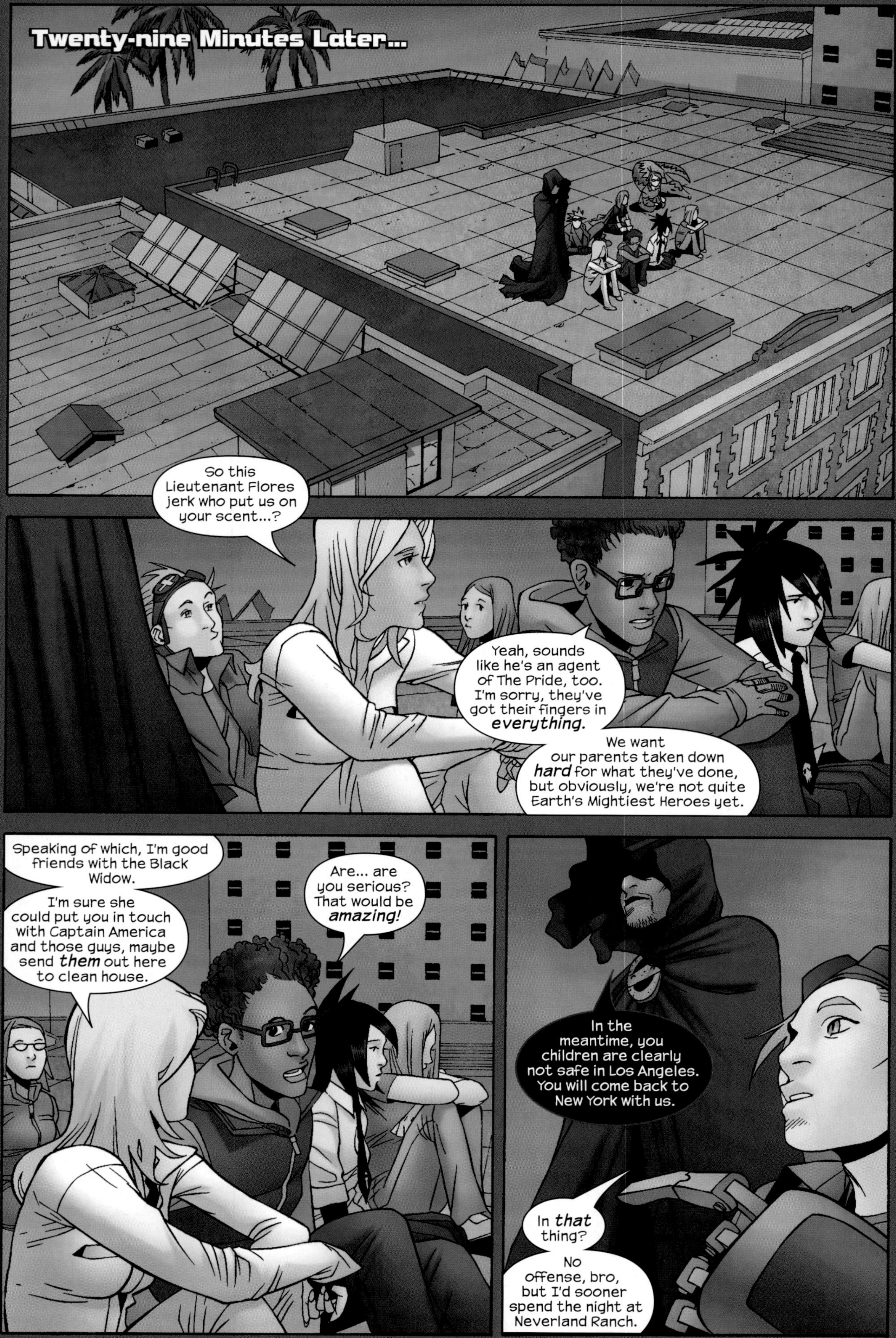
Twenty-nine Minutes Later...
So this Lieutenant Flores jerk who put us on your scent...?
Yeah, sounds like he's an agent of The Pride, too. I'm sorry, they've got their fingers in *everything.*
We want our parents taken down ***hard*** for what they've done, but obviously, we're not quite Earth's Mightiest Heroes yet.
Speaking of which, I'm good friends with the Black Widow.
I'm sure she could put you in touch with Captain America and those guys, maybe send ***them*** out here to clean house.
Are... are you serious? That would be ***amazing!***
In the meantime, you children are clearly not safe in Los Angeles. You will come back to New York with us.
In ***that*** thing?
No offense, bro, but I'd sooner spend the night at Neverland Ranch.

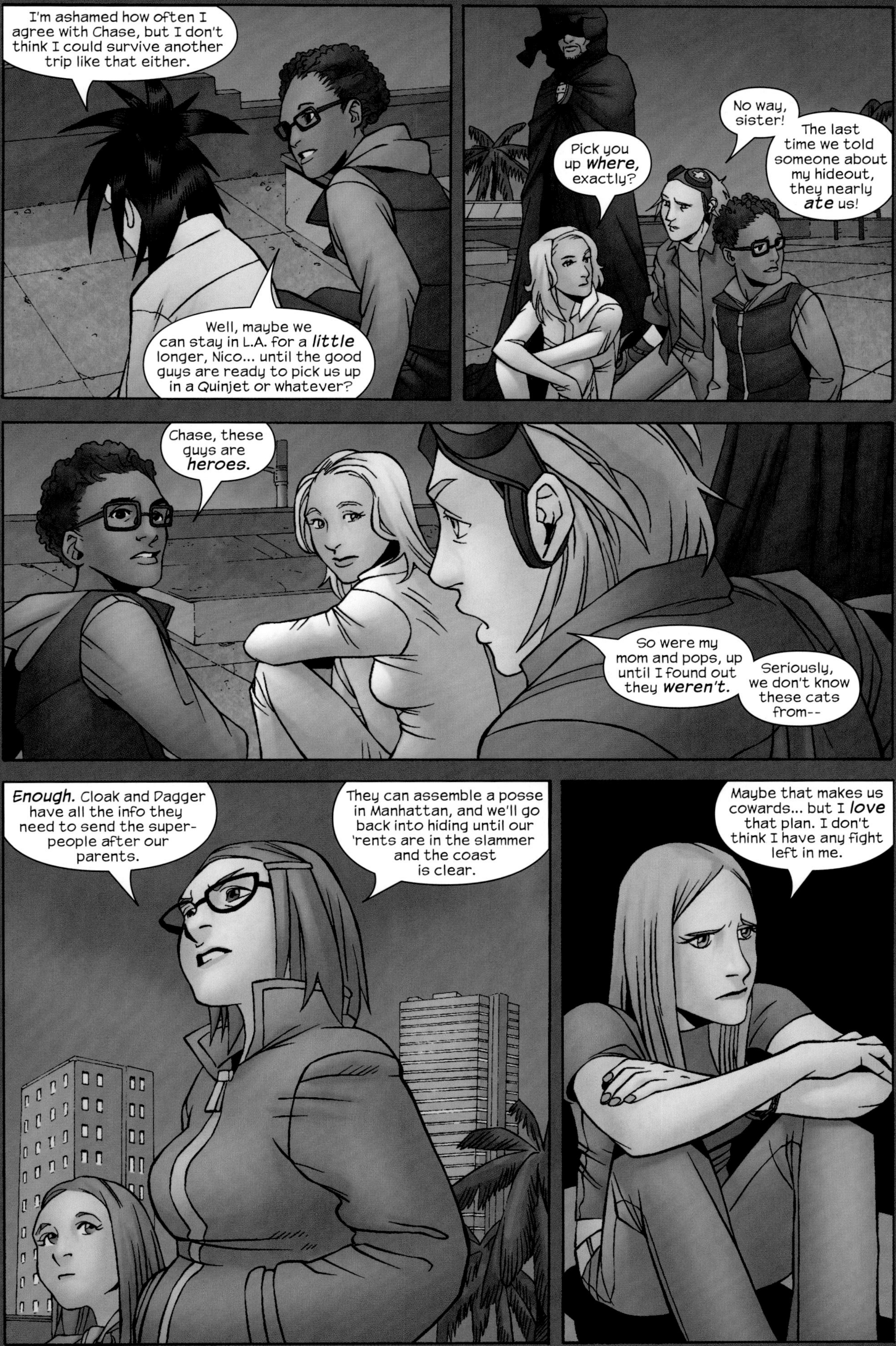
I'm ashamed how often I agree with Chase, but I don't think I could survive another trip like that either.
Well, maybe we can stay in L.A. for a *little* longer, Nico... until the good guys are ready to pick us up in a Quinjet or whatever?
Pick you up *where,* exactly?
No way, sister!
The last time we told someone about my hideout, they nearly *ate* us!
Chase, these guys are *heroes.*
So were my mom and pops, up until I found out they *weren't.*
Seriously, we don't know these cats from--
Enough. Cloak and Dagger have all the info they need to send the super-people after our parents.
They can assemble a posse in Manhattan, and we'll go back into hiding until our 'rents are in the slammer and the coast is clear.
Maybe that makes us cowards... but I *love* that plan. I don't think I have any fight left in me.

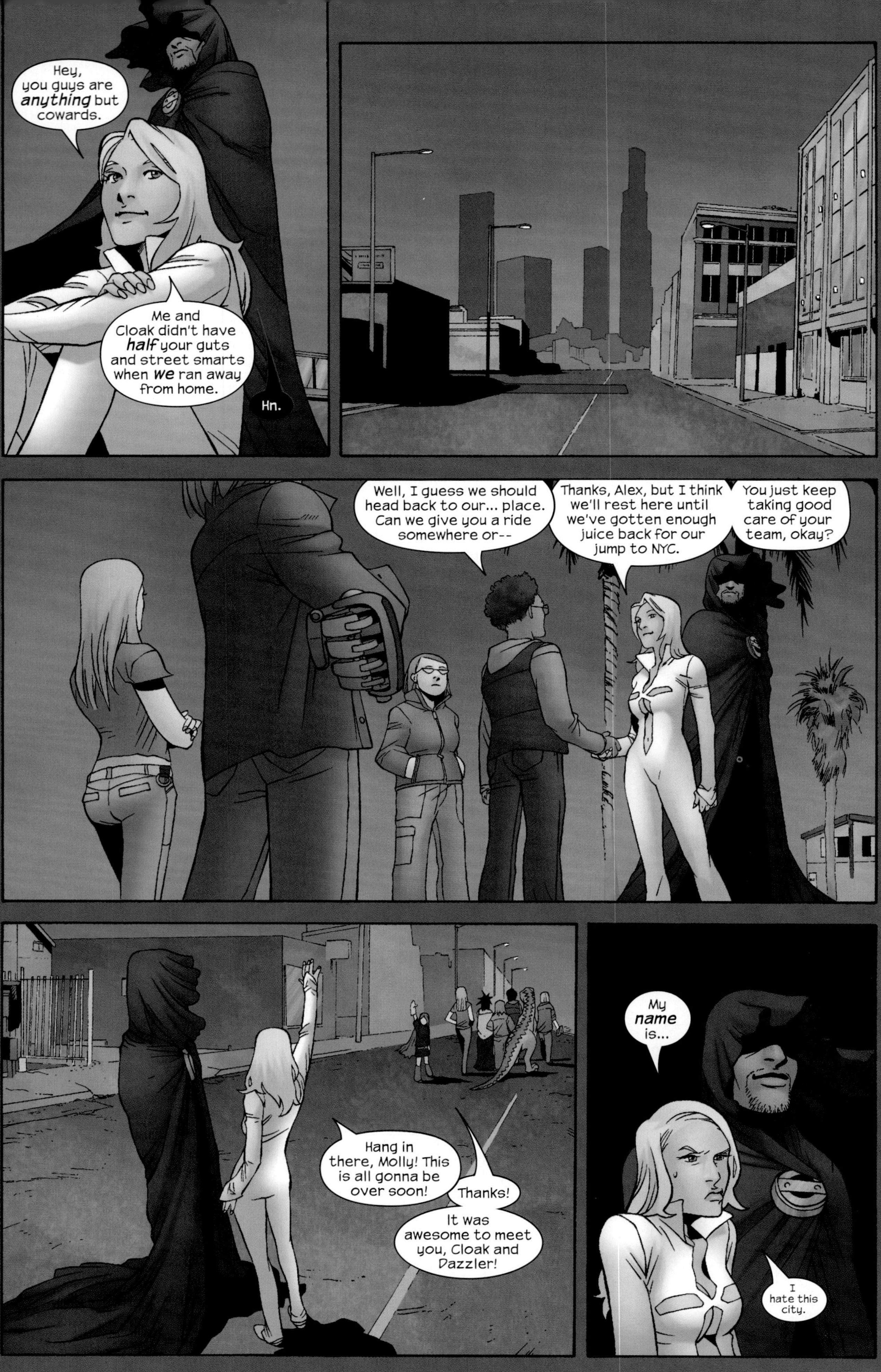
Hey, you guys are *anything* but cowards.
Me and Cloak didn't have *half* your guts and street smarts when *we* ran away from home.
Hn.
Well, I guess we should head back to our... place. Can we give you a ride somewhere or--
Thanks, Alex, but I think we'll rest here until we've gotten enough juice back for our jump to NYC.
You just keep taking good care of your team, okay?
Hang in there, Molly! This is all gonna be over soon!
Thanks!
It was awesome to meet you, Cloak and Dazzler!
My *name* is...
I hate this city.

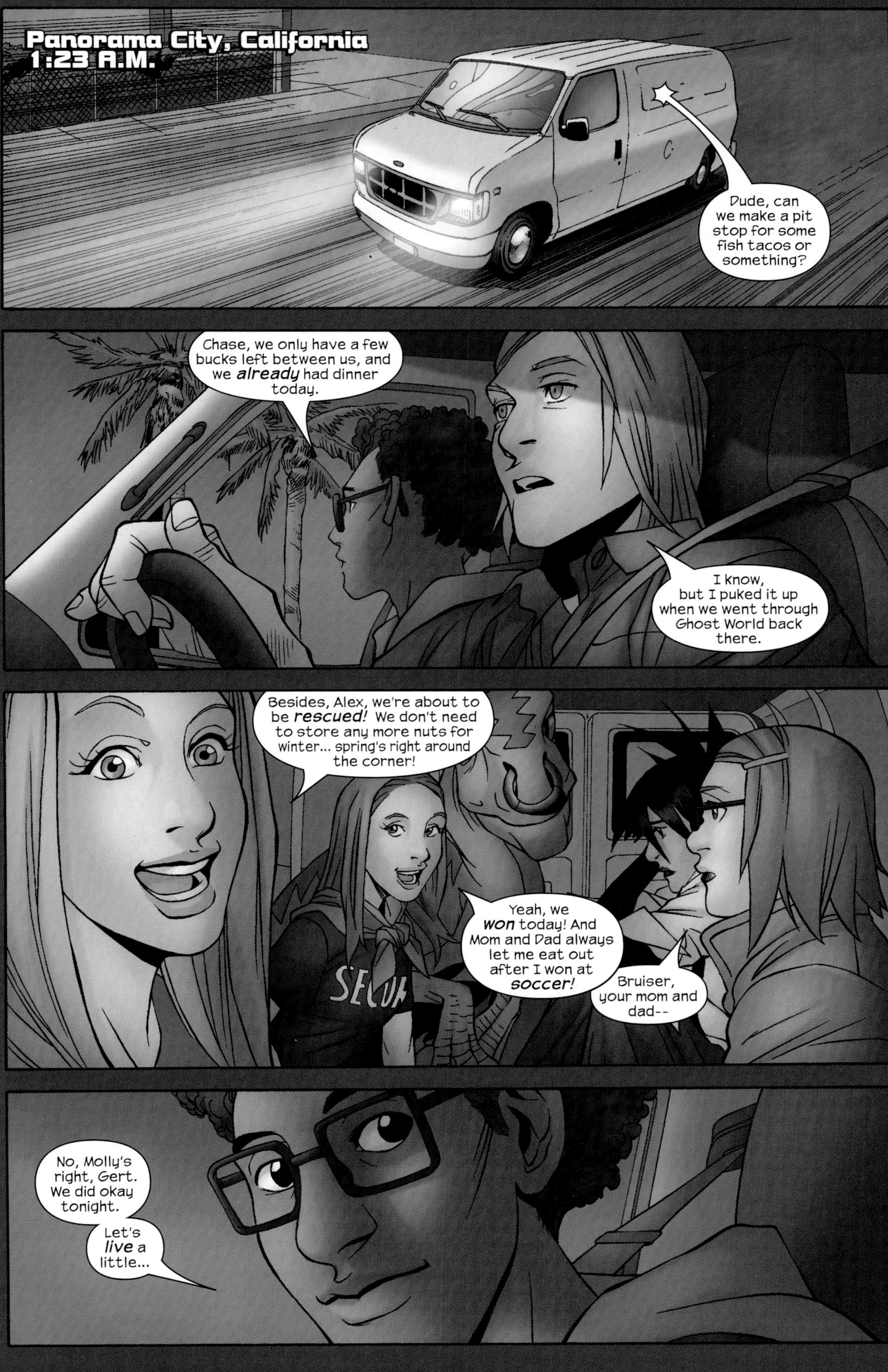
Panorama City, California
1:23 A.M.
Dude, can we make a pit stop for some fish tacos or something?
Chase, we only have a few bucks left between us, and we *already* had dinner today.
I know, but I puked it up when we went through Ghost World back there.
Besides, Alex, we're about to be *rescued!* We don't need to store any more nuts for winter... spring's right around the corner!
Yeah, we *won* today! And Mom and Dad always let me eat out after I won at *soccer!*
Bruiser, your mom and dad--
No, Molly's right, Gert. We did okay tonight.
Let's *live* a little...

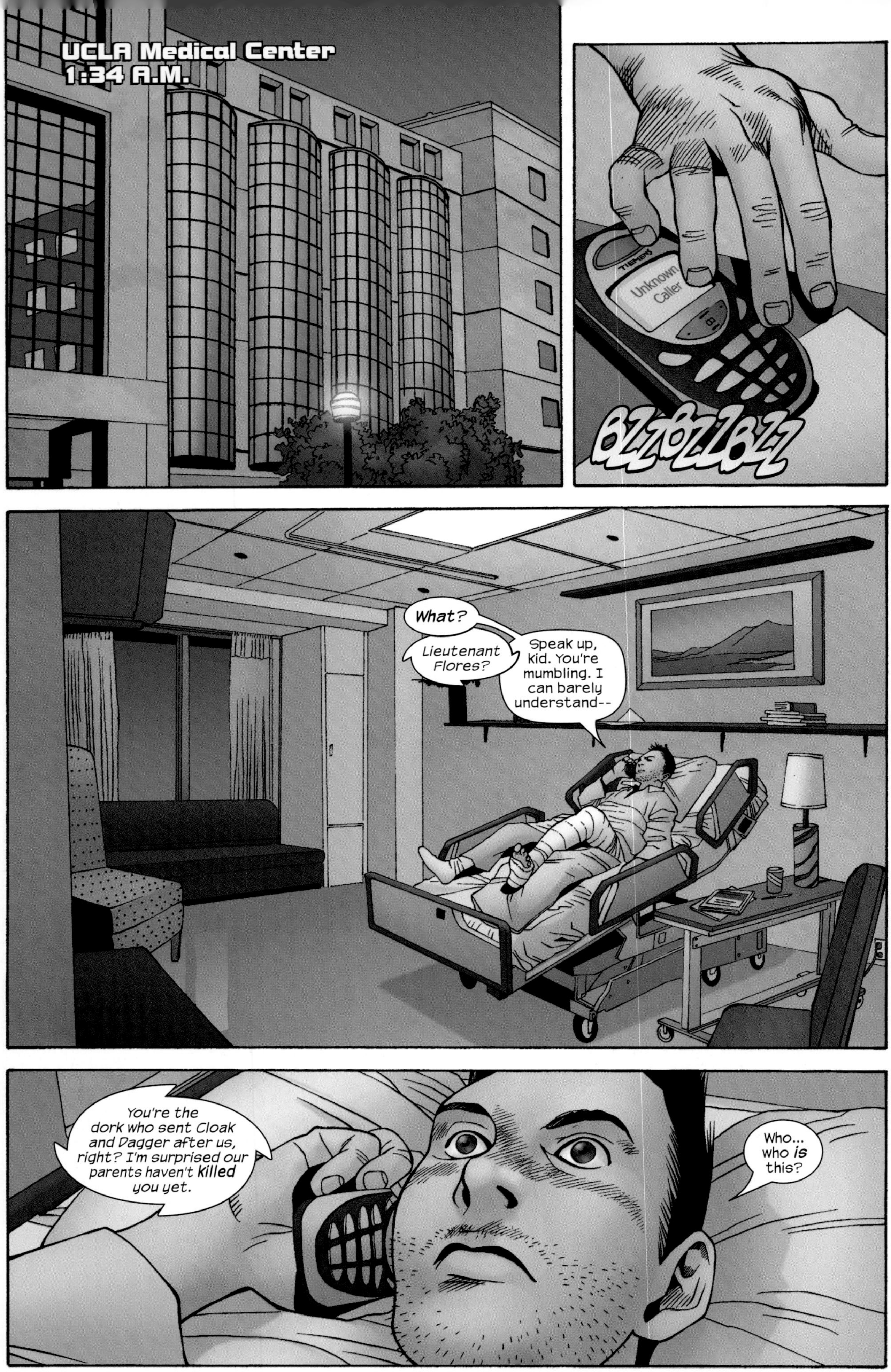
UCLA Medical Center
1:34 A.M.
Unknown Caller
BZZBZZBZZ
What?
Lieutenant Flores?
Speak up, kid. You're mumbling. I can barely understand--
You're the dork who sent Cloak and Dagger after us, right? I'm surprised our parents haven't killed you yet.
Who... who is this?

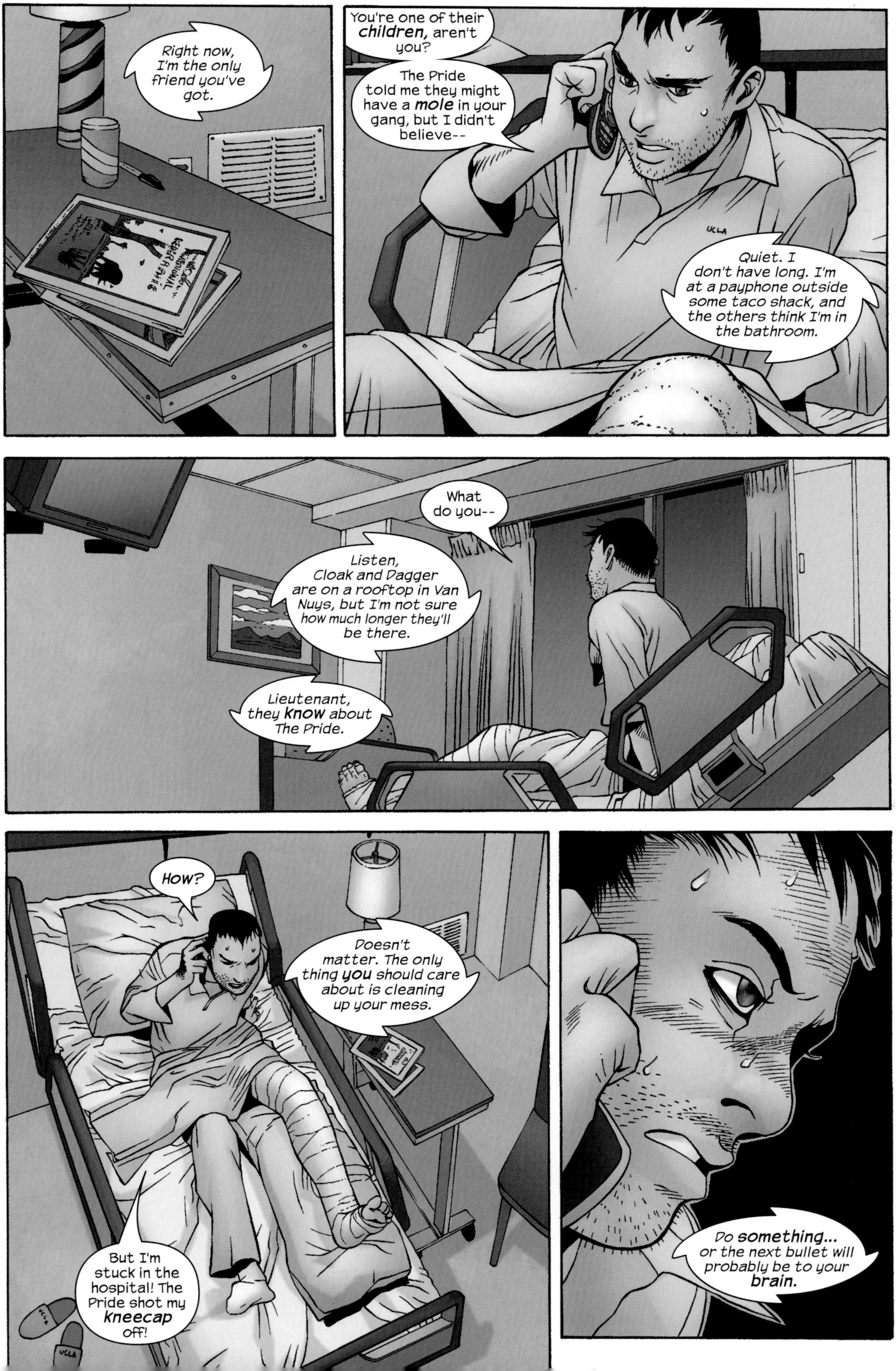

Right now, I'm the only friend you've got.
You're one of their *children,* aren't you?
The Pride told me they might have a **mole** in your gang, but I didn't believe--
Quiet. I don't have long. I'm at a payphone outside some taco shack, and the others think I'm in the bathroom.
UCLA
What do you--
Listen, Cloak and Dagger are on a rooftop in Van Nuys, but I'm not sure how much longer they'll be there.
Lieutenant, they **know** about The Pride.
HOW?
Doesn't matter. The only thing **you** should care about is cleaning up your mess.
But I'm stuck in the hospital! The Pride shot my **kneecap** off!
UCLA
Do **something...** or the next bullet will probably be to your **brain.**

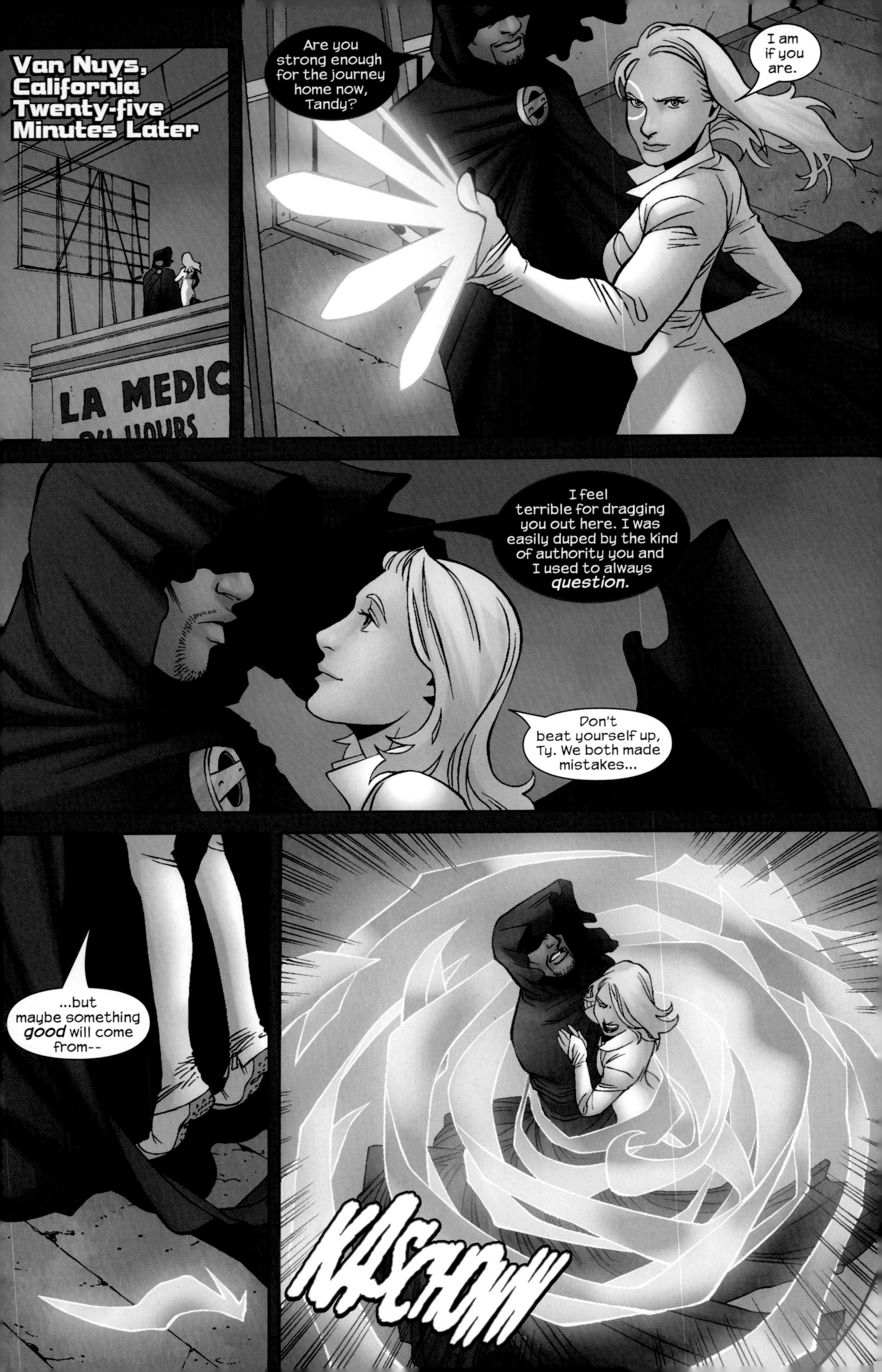
Van Nuys, California Twenty-five Minutes Later
LA MEDIC
Are you strong enough for the journey home now, Tandy?
I am if you are.
I feel terrible for dragging you out here. I was easily duped by the kind of authority you and I used to always question.
Don't beat yourself up, Ty. We both made mistakes...
...but maybe something good will come from--
KASHOWW

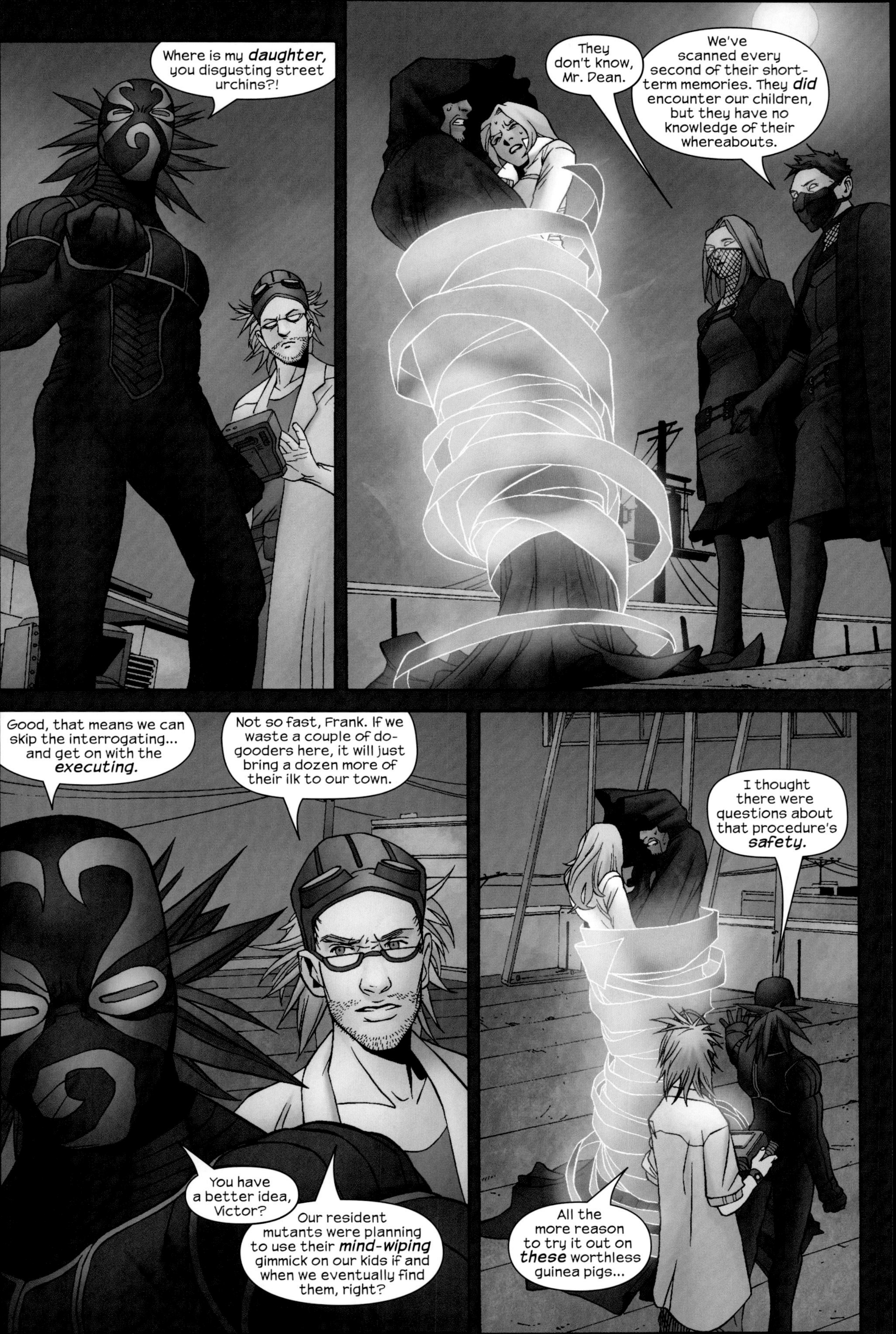

Where is my *daughter,* you disgusting street urchins?!
They don't know, Mr. Dean.
We've scanned every second of their short-term memories. They *did* encounter our children, but they have no knowledge of their whereabouts.
Good, that means we can skip the interrogating... and get on with the *executing.*
Not so fast, Frank. If we waste a couple of do-gooders here, it will just bring a dozen more of their ilk to our town.
You have a better idea, Victor?
Our resident mutants were planning to use their *mind-wiping* gimmick on our kids if and when we eventually find them, right?
I thought there were questions about that procedure's *safety.*
All the more reason to try it out on *these* worthless guinea pigs...

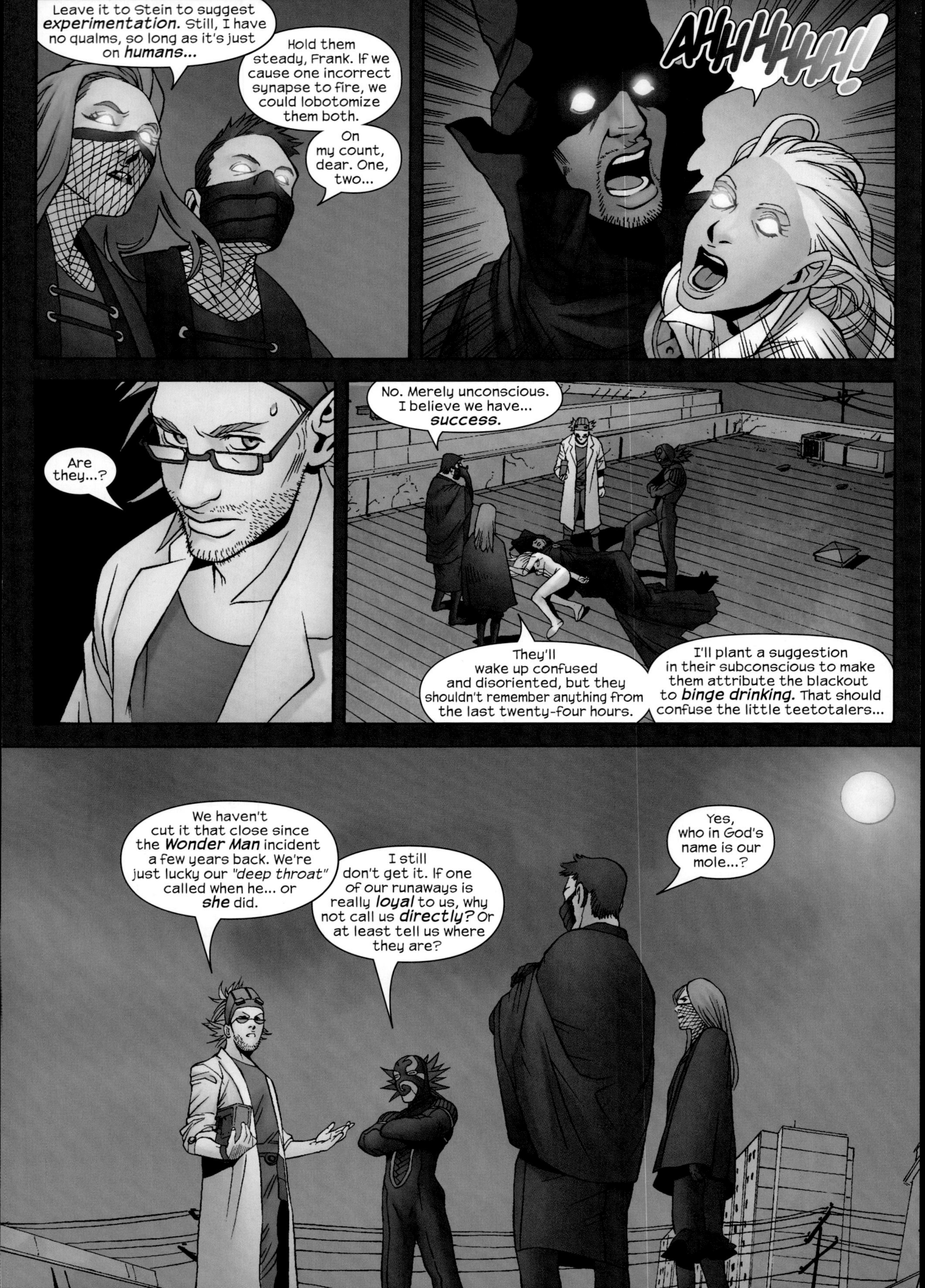
Leave it to Stein to suggest experimentation. Still, I have no qualms, so long as it's just on humans...
Hold them steady, Frank. If we cause one incorrect synapse to fire, we could lobotomize them both.
On my count, dear. One, two...
AHHHHHH!
Are they...?
No. Merely unconscious. I believe we have... success.
They'll wake up confused and disoriented, but they shouldn't remember anything from the last twenty-four hours.
I'll plant a suggestion in their subconscious to make them attribute the blackout to binge drinking. That should confuse the little teetotalers...
We haven't cut it that close since the Wonder Man incident a few years back. We're just lucky our "deep throat" called when he... or she did.
I still don't get it. If one of our runaways is really loyal to us, why not call us directly? Or at least tell us where they are?
Yes, who in God's name is our mole...?

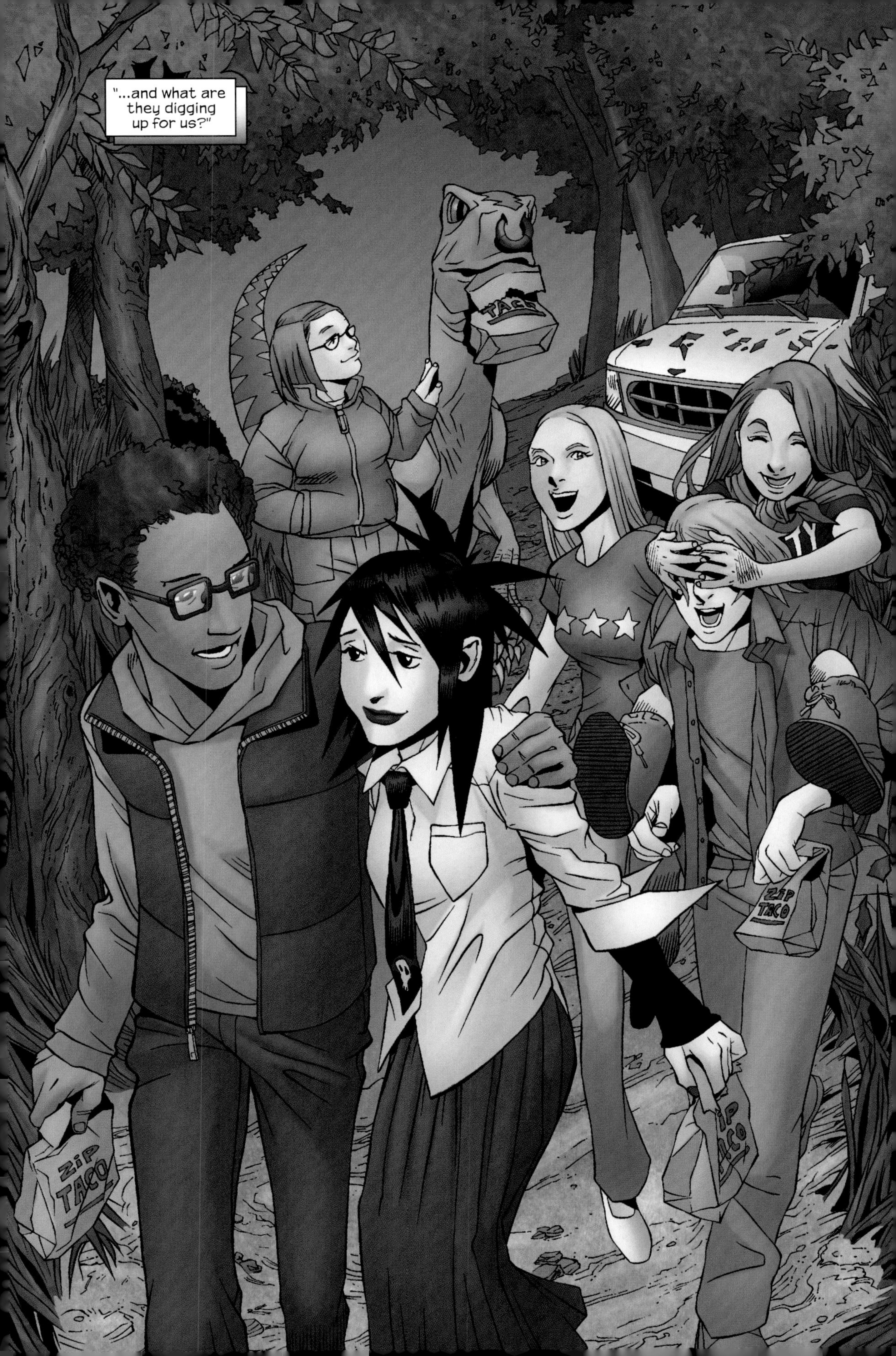
"...and what are they digging up for us?"
TACO
ZIP TACO
ZIP TACO
ZIP TACO

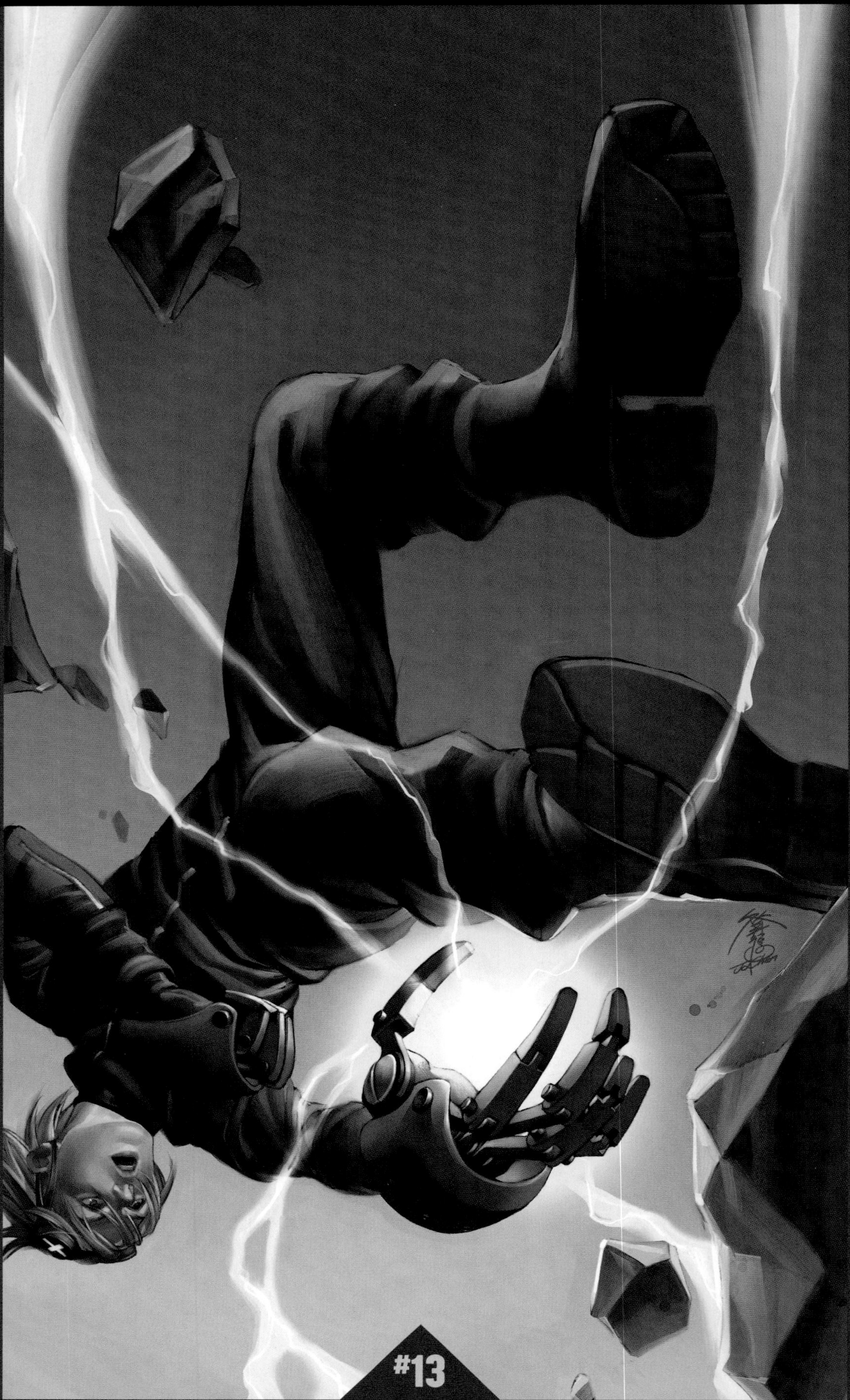
#13

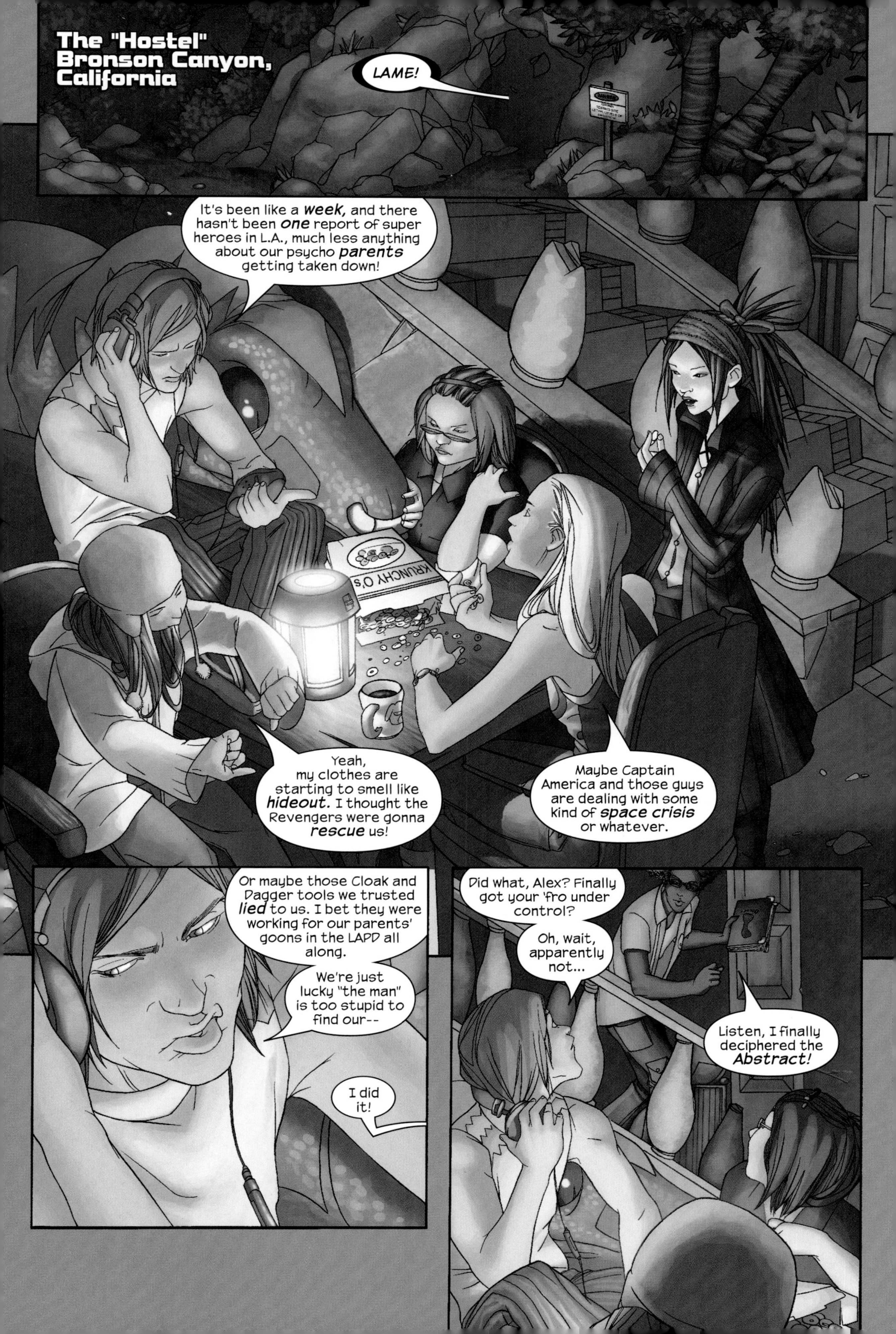
The "Hostel"
Bronson Canyon,
California
LAME!
It's been like a week, and there hasn't been one report of super heroes in L.A., much less anything about our psycho parents getting taken down!
KRUNCHY O's
Yeah, my clothes are starting to smell like hideout. I thought the Revengers were gonna rescue us!
Maybe Captain America and those guys are dealing with some kind of space crisis or whatever.
Or maybe those Cloak and Dagger tools we trusted lied to us. I bet they were working for our parents' goons in the LAPD all along.
We're just lucky "the man" is too stupid to find our--
I did it!
Did what, Alex? Finally got your 'fro under control?
Oh, wait, apparently not...
Listen, I finally deciphered the Abstract!

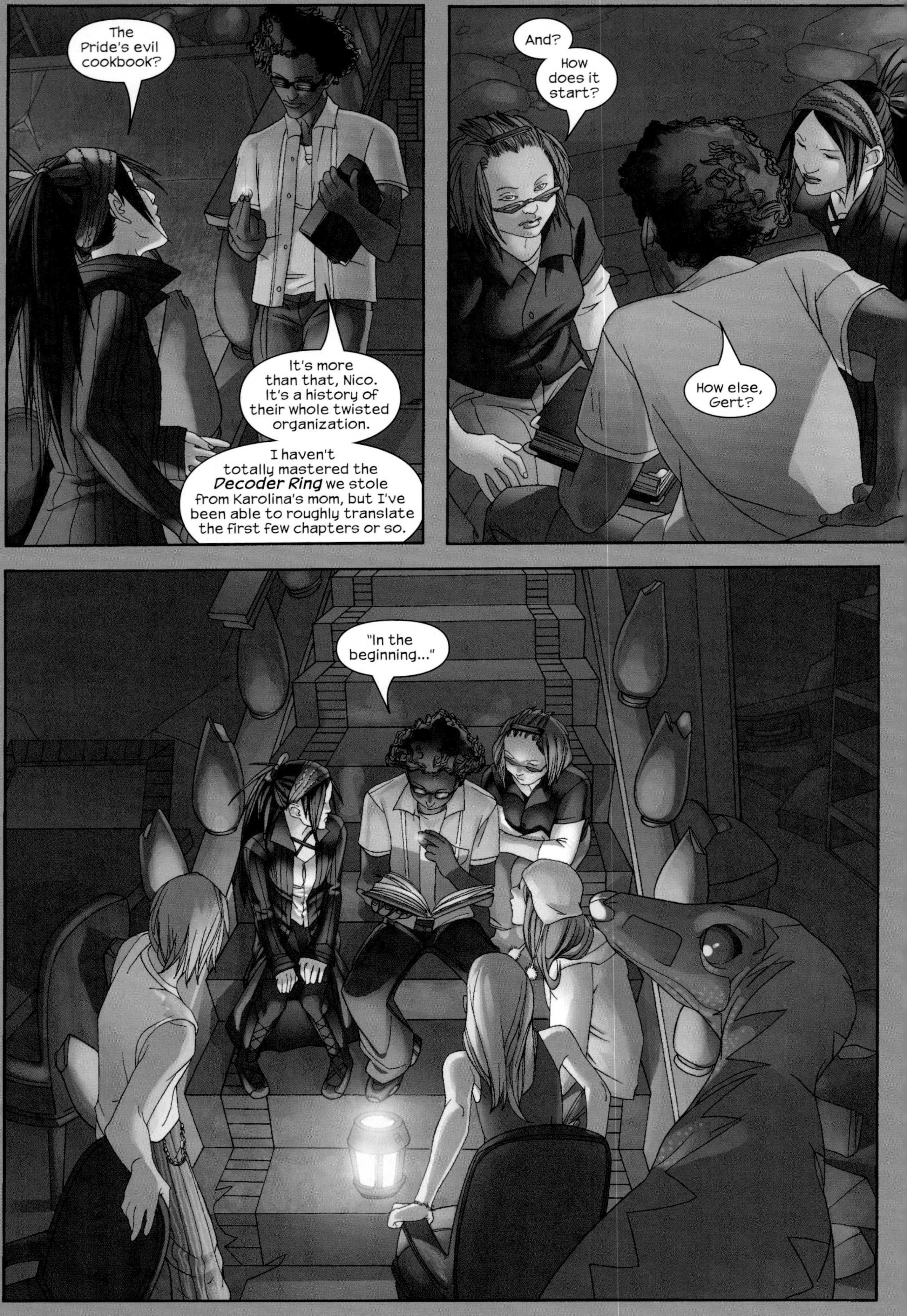
The Pride's evil cookbook?
It's more than that, Nico. It's a history of their whole twisted organization.
I haven't totally mastered the *Decoder Ring* we stole from Karolina's mom, but I've been able to roughly translate the first few chapters or so.
And?
How does it start?
How else, Gert?
"In the beginning..."

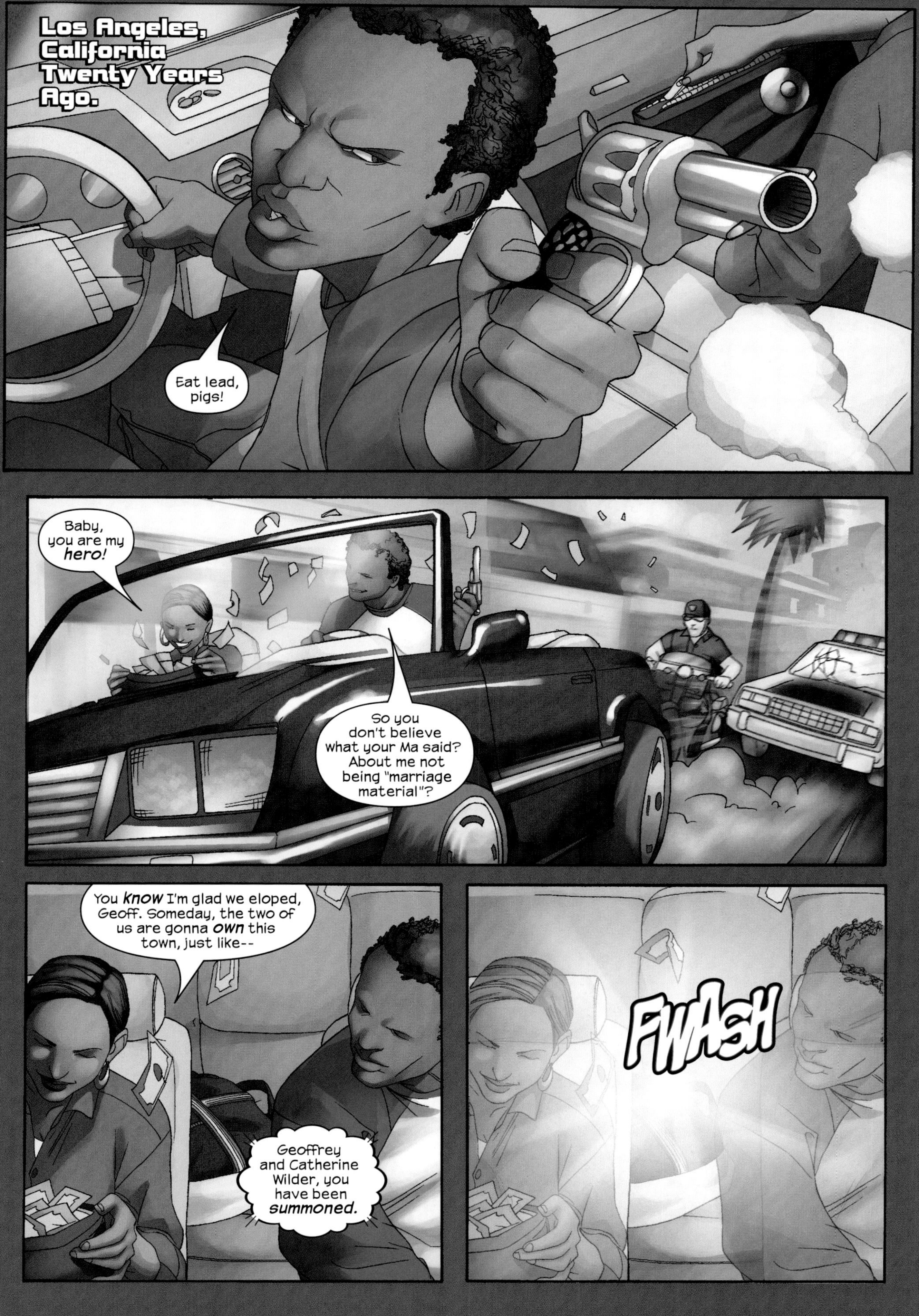
Los Angeles, California Twenty Years Ago.
Eat lead, pigs!
Baby, you are my *hero!*
So you don't believe what your Ma said? About me not being "marriage material"?
You **KNOW** I'm glad we eloped, Geoff. Someday, the two of us are gonna **OWN** this town, just like--
Geoffrey and Catherine Wilder, you have been ***summoned.***
FWASH

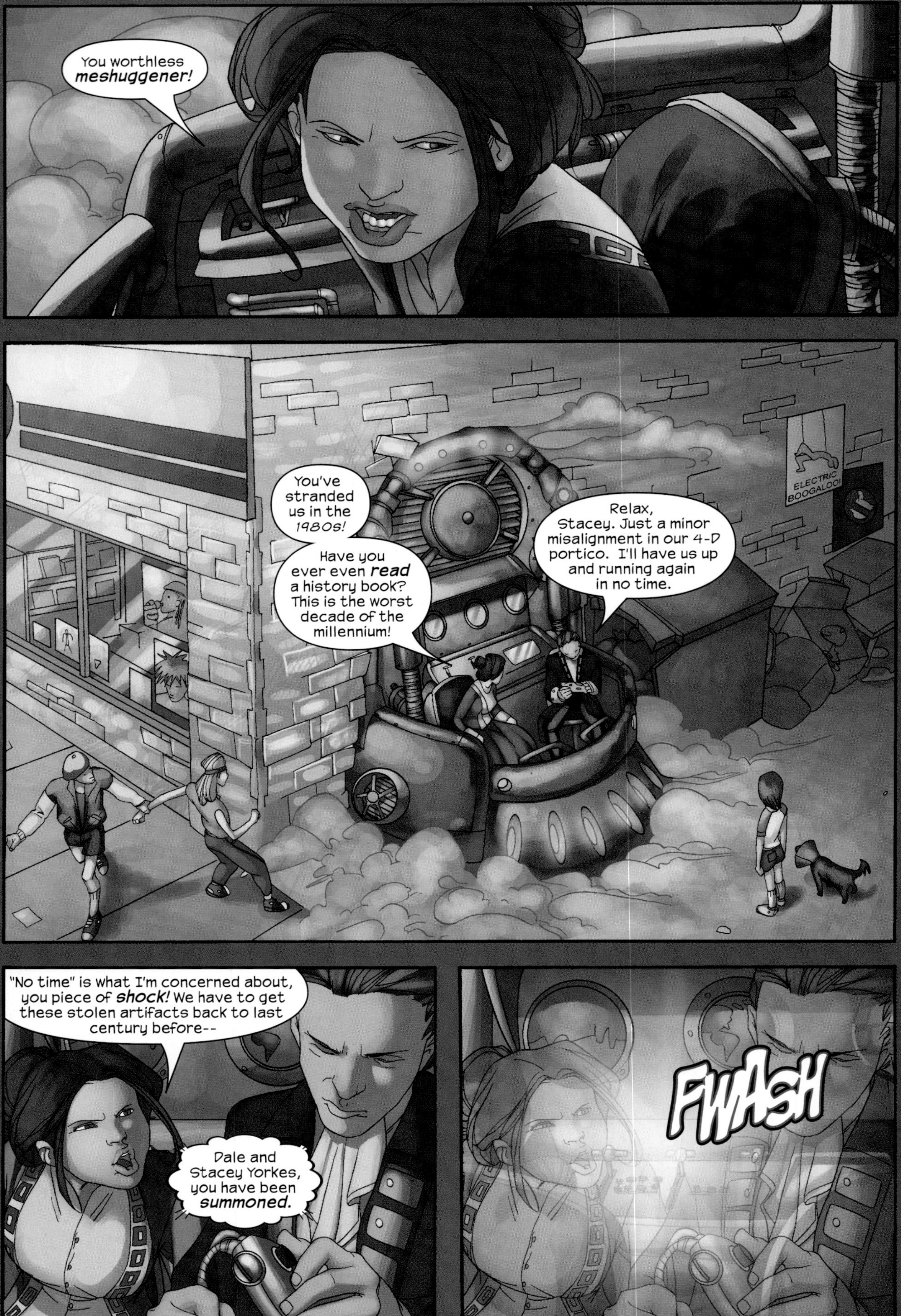
You worthless *meshuggener!*
You've stranded us in the *1980s!*
Have you ever even ***read*** a history book? This is the worst decade of the millennium!
Relax, Stacey. Just a minor misalignment in our 4-D portico. I'll have us up and running again in no time.
ELECTRIC BOOGALOO!
"No time" is what I'm concerned about, you piece of ***shock!*** We have to get these stolen artifacts back to last century before--
Dale and Stacey Yorkes, you have been ***summoned.***
FWASH

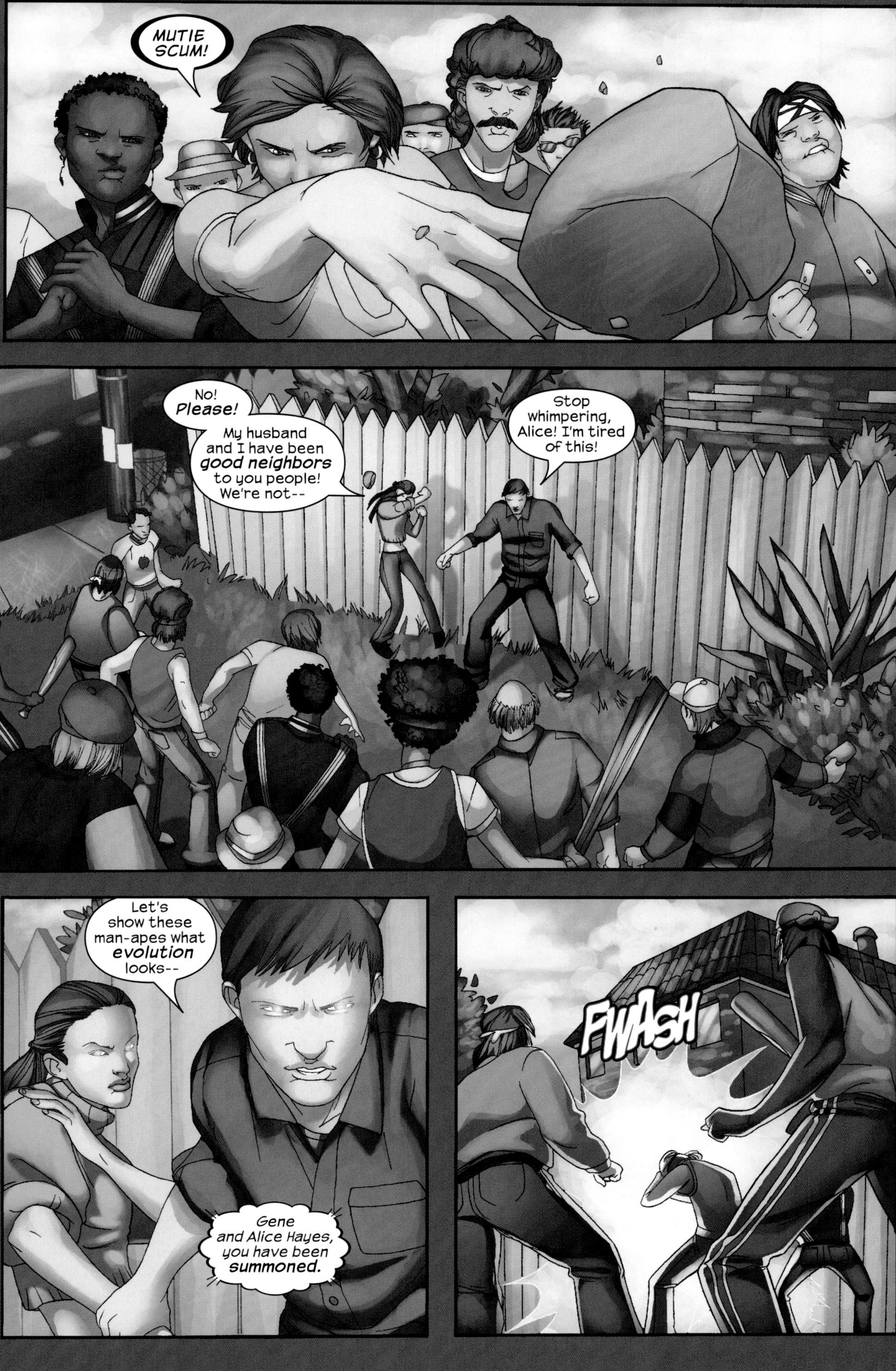
MUTIE SCUM!
No! Please!
My husband and I have been good neighbors to you people! We're not--
Stop whimpering, Alice! I'm tired of this!
Let's show these man-apes what evolution looks--
Gene and Alice Hayes, you have been summoned.
FWASH

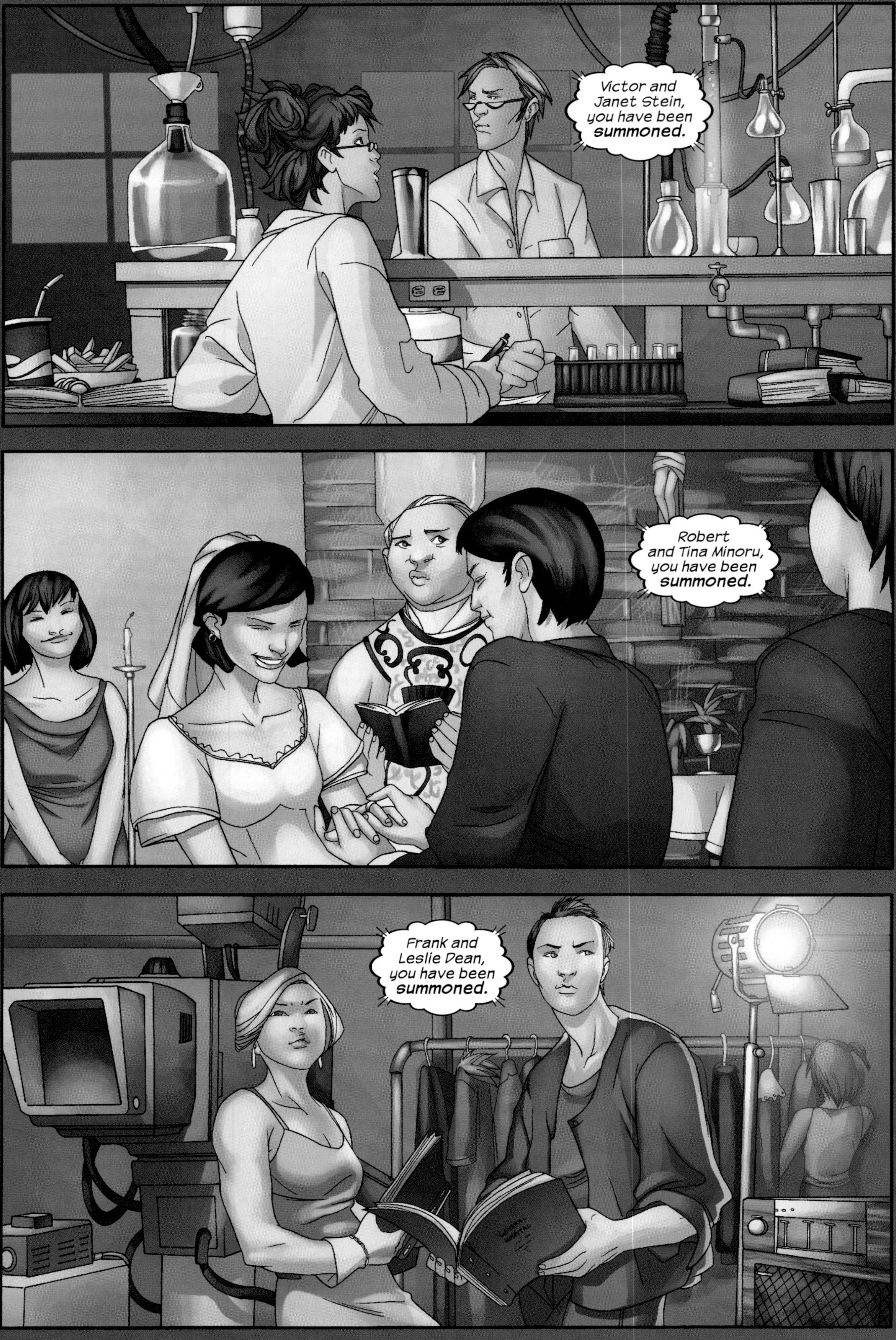
Victor and Janet Stein, you have been **summoned.**
Robert and Tina Minoru, you have been **summoned.**
Frank and Leslie Dean, you have been **summoned.**
GENERAL HOSPITAL

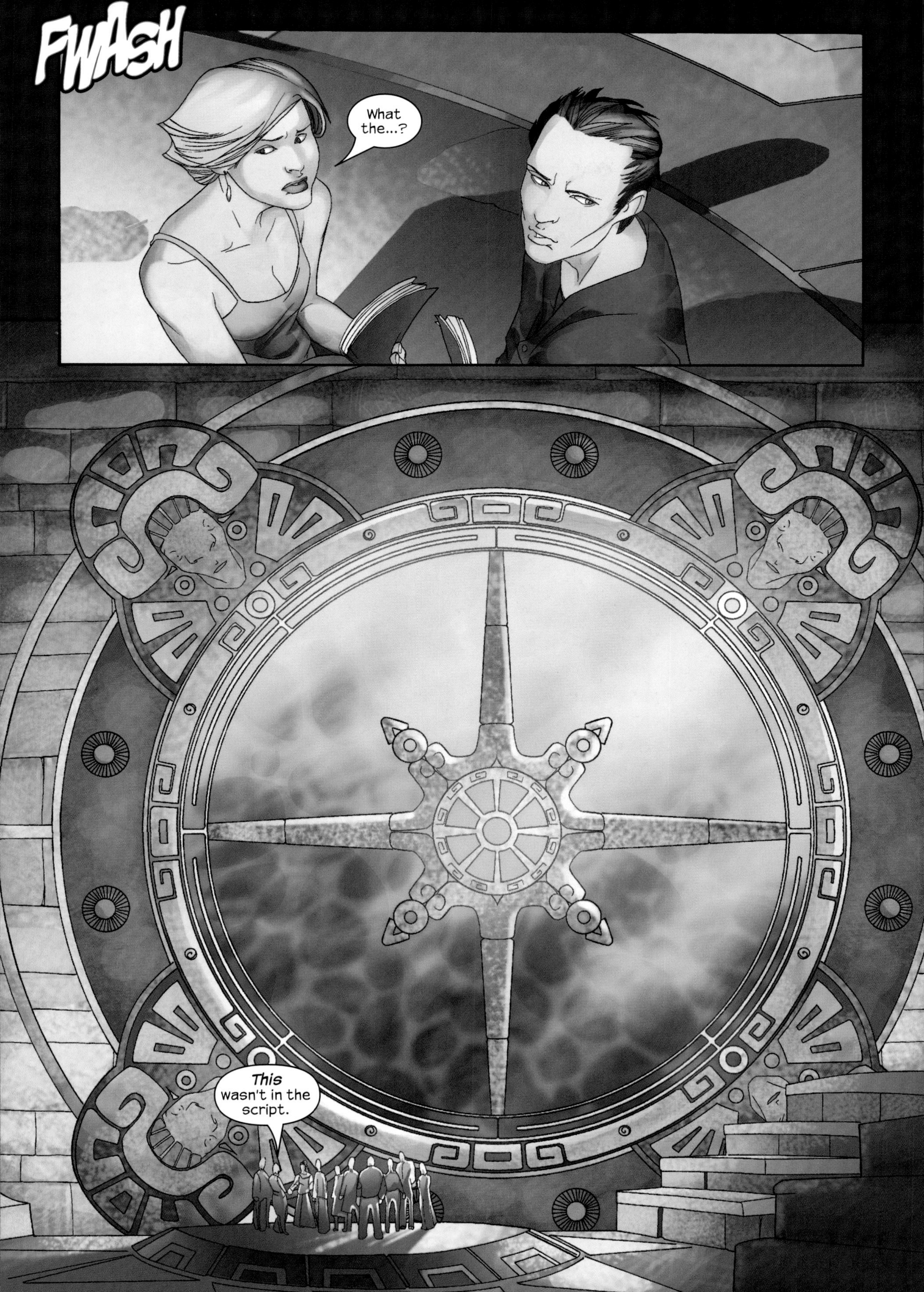
FWASH
What the...?
This wasn't in the script.

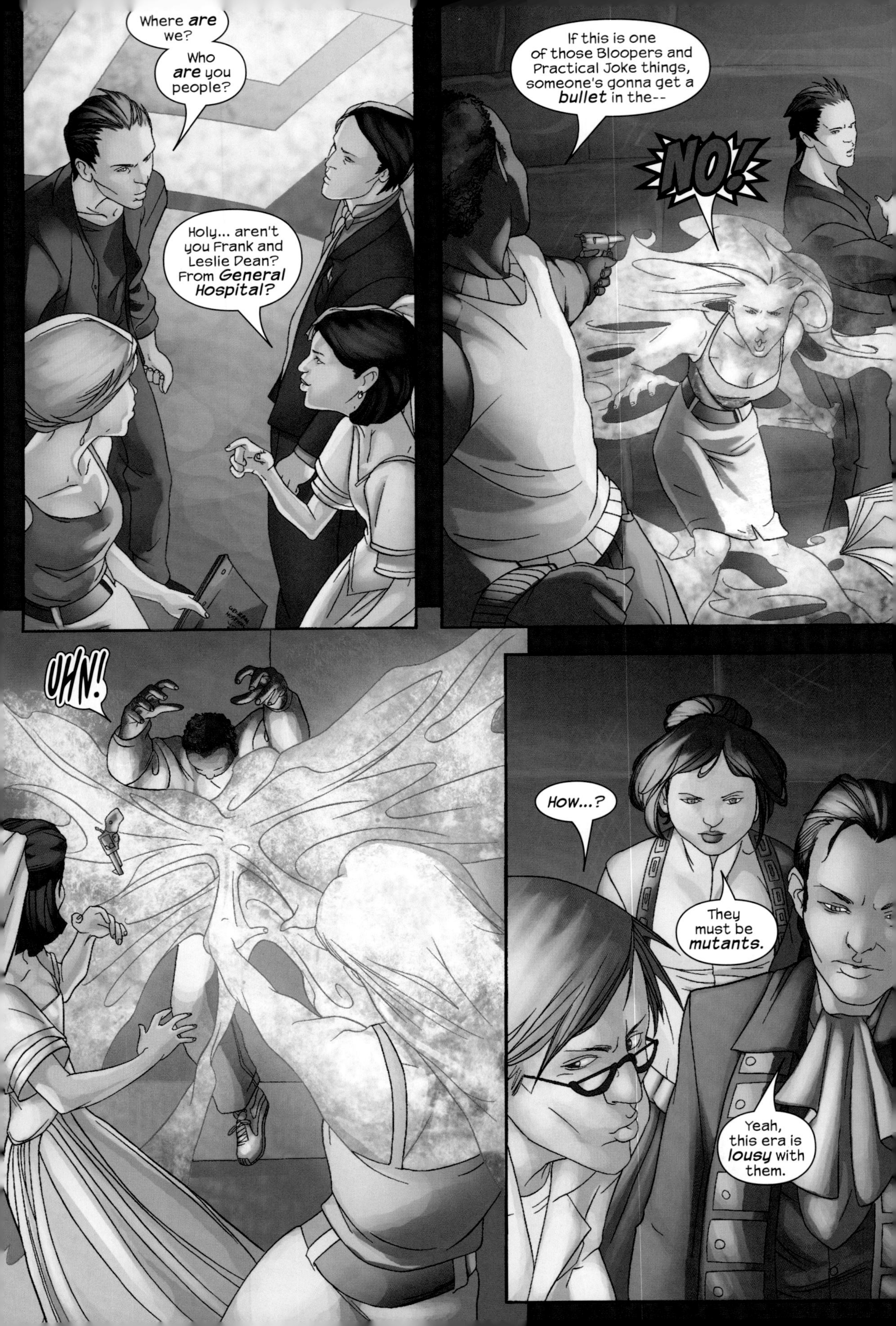
Where are we?
Who are you people?
Holy... aren't you Frank and Leslie Dean? From General Hospital?
If this is one of those Bloopers and Practical Joke things, someone's gonna get a bullet in the--
NO!
UHN!
HOW...?
They must be mutants.
Yeah, this era is lousy with them.

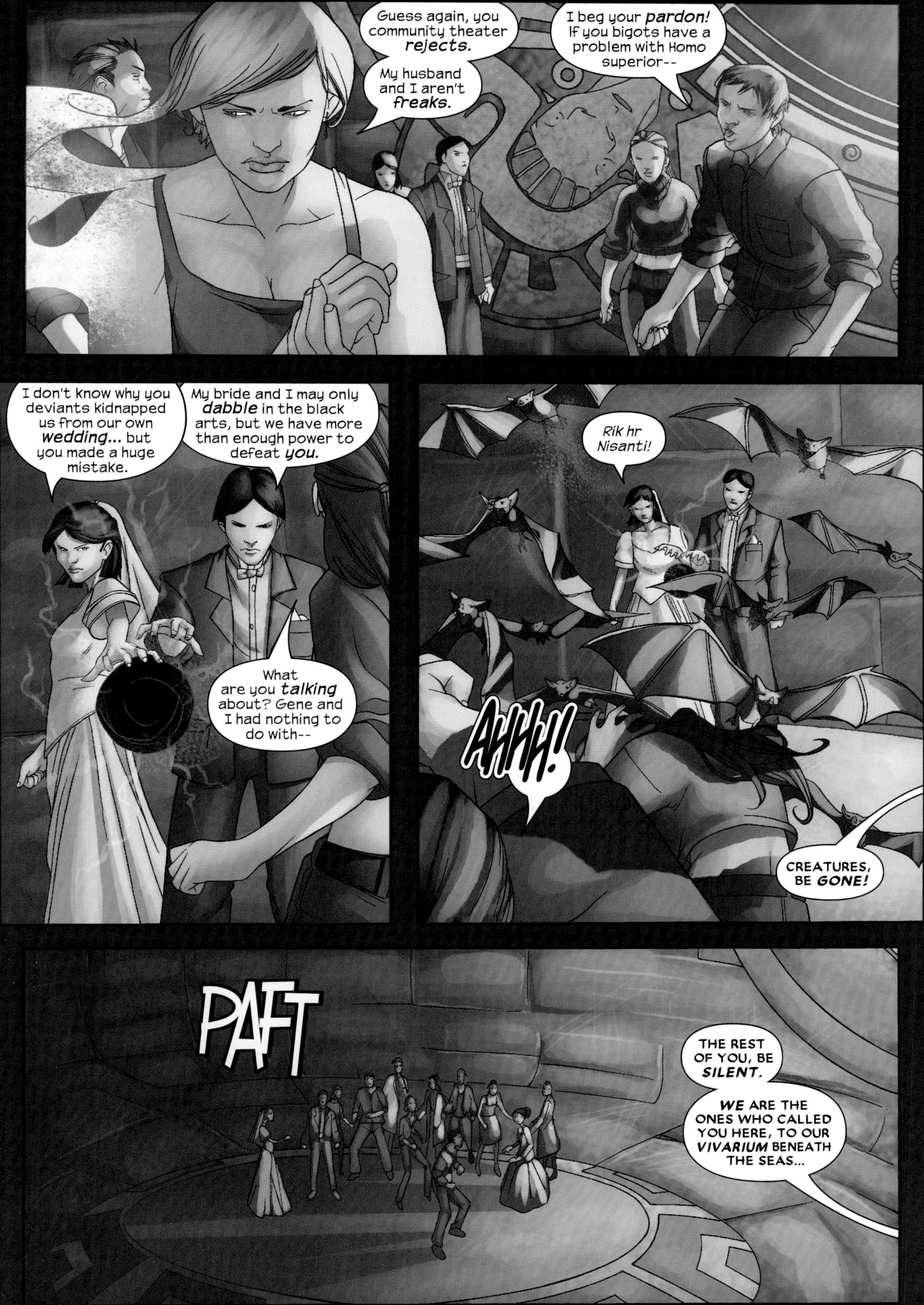
Guess again, you community theater rejects.
My husband and I aren't freaks.
I beg your pardon! If you bigots have a problem with Homo superior--
I don't know why you deviants kidnapped us from our own wedding... but you made a huge mistake.
My bride and I may only dabble in the black arts, but we have more than enough power to defeat you.
What are you talking about? Gene and I had nothing to do with--
Rik hr Nisanti!
AHHH!
CREATURES, BE GONE!
PAFT
THE REST OF YOU, BE SILENT.
WE ARE THE ONES WHO CALLED YOU HERE, TO OUR VIVARIUM BENEATH THE SEAS...

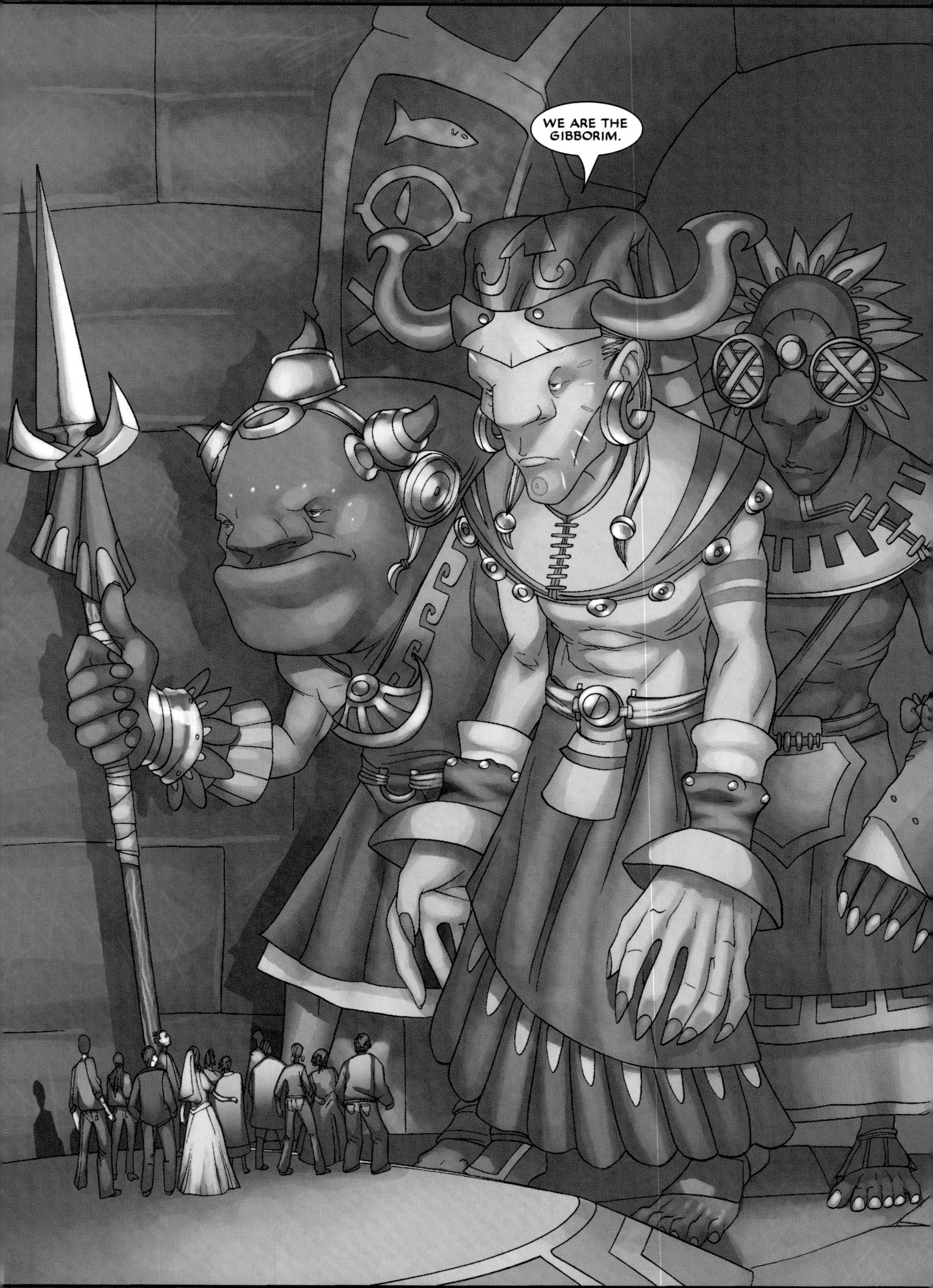
WE ARE THE GIBBORIM.

Whoa! Back up... the *whozit*?

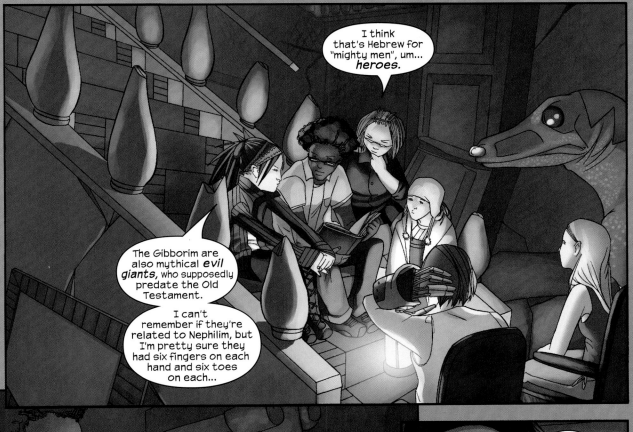

I think that's Hebrew for "mighty men", um... *heroes.*

The Gibborim are also mythical *evil giants*, who supposedly predate the Old Testament.

I can't remember if they're related to Nephilim, but I'm pretty sure they had six fingers on each hand and six toes on each...

What?

I like books about monsters. Sue me...

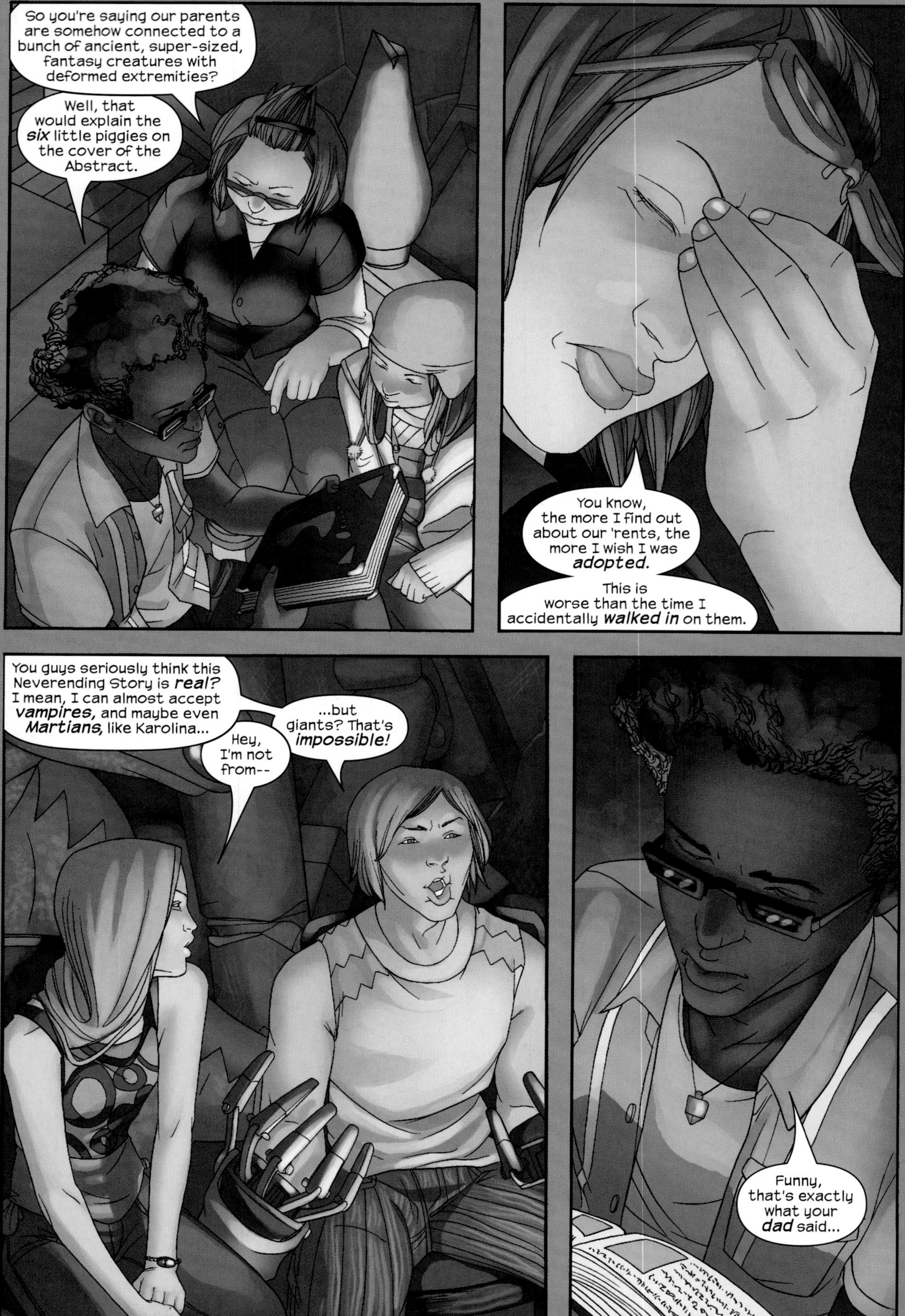
So you're saying our parents are somehow connected to a bunch of ancient, super-sized, fantasy creatures with deformed extremities?
Well, that would explain the *six* little piggies on the cover of the Abstract.
You know, the more I find out about our 'rents, the more I wish I was *adopted.*
This is worse than the time I accidentally *walked in* on them.
You guys seriously think this Neverending Story is *real?* I mean, I can almost accept *vampires,* and maybe even *Martians,* like Karolina...
Hey, I'm not from--
...but giants? That's *impossible!*
Funny, that's exactly what your *dad* said...

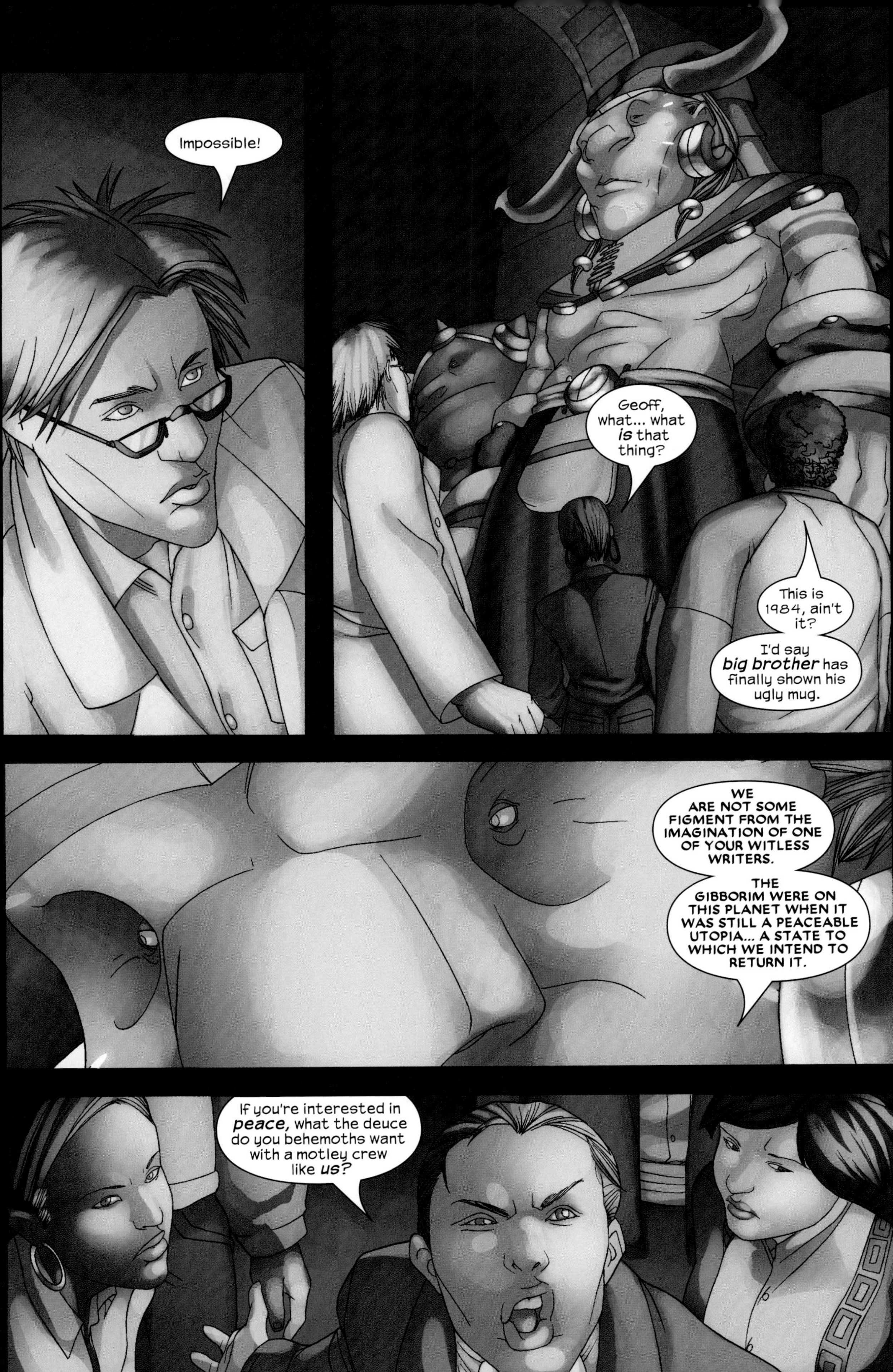
Impossible!
Geoff, what... what *is* that thing?
This is 1984, ain't it?
I'd say **big brother** has finally shown his ugly mug.
WE ARE NOT SOME FIGMENT FROM THE IMAGINATION OF ONE OF YOUR WITLESS WRITERS.
THE GIBBORIM WERE ON THIS PLANET WHEN IT WAS STILL A PEACEABLE UTOPIA... A STATE TO WHICH WE INTEND TO RETURN IT.
If you're interested in *peace,* what the deuce do you behemoths want with a motley crew like *us?*

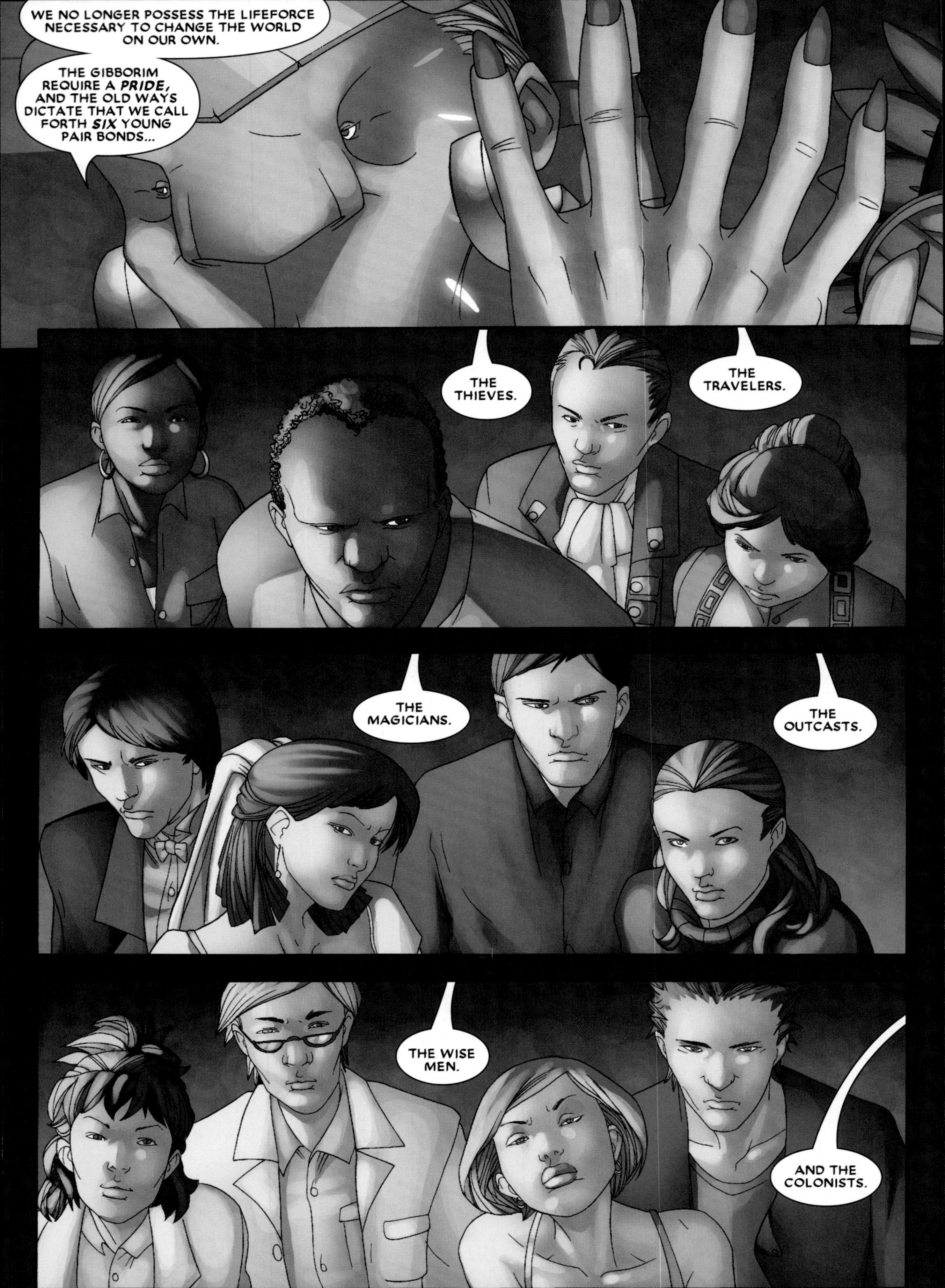
WE NO LONGER POSSESS THE LIFEFORCE NECESSARY TO CHANGE THE WORLD ON OUR OWN.
THE GIBBORIM REQUIRE A *PRIDE*, AND THE OLD WAYS DICTATE THAT WE CALL FORTH *SIX* YOUNG PAIR BONDS...
THE THIEVES.
THE TRAVELERS.
THE MAGICIANS.
THE OUTCASTS.
THE WISE MEN.
AND THE COLONISTS.

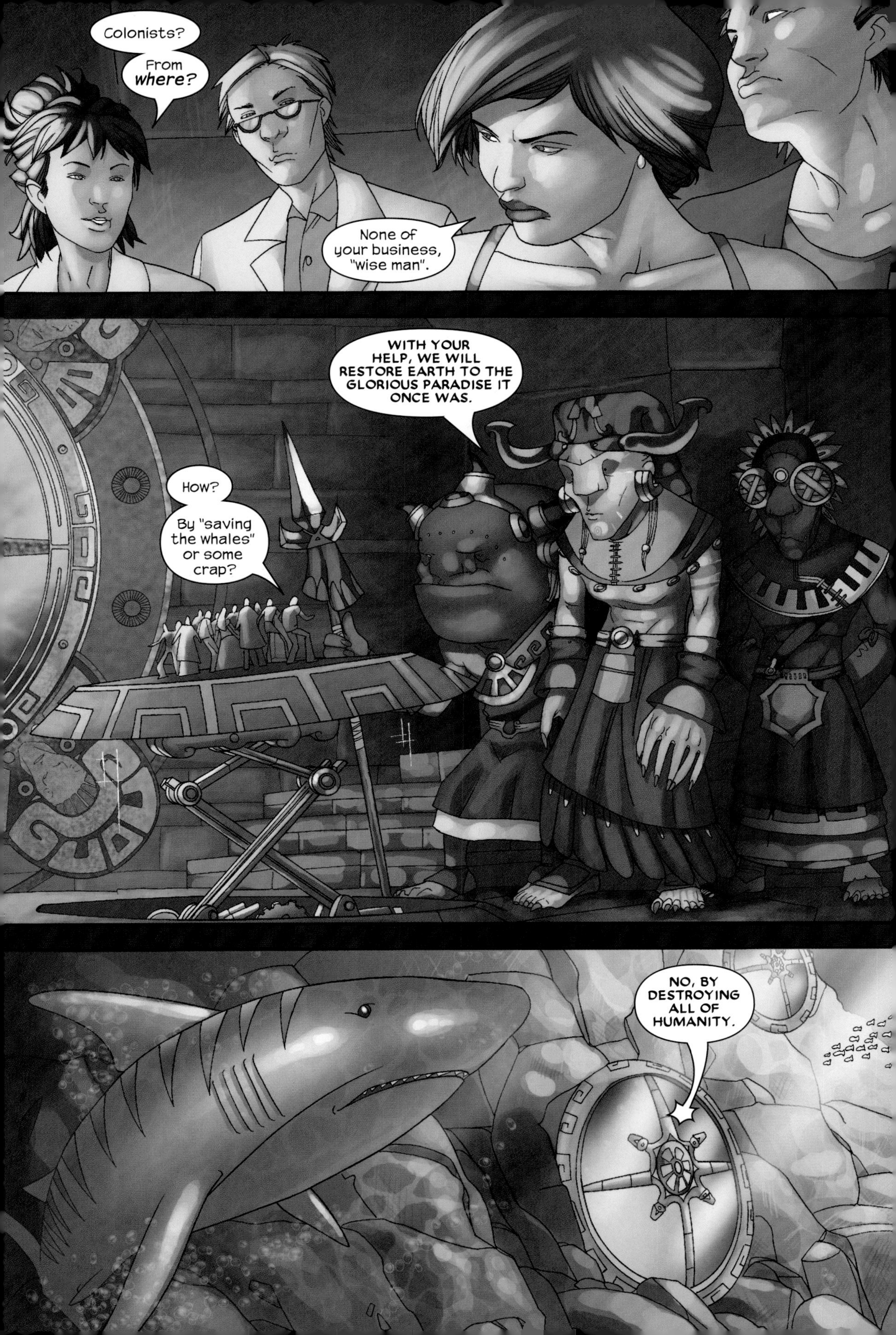
Colonists?
From where?
None of your business, "wise man".
WITH YOUR HELP, WE WILL RESTORE EARTH TO THE GLORIOUS PARADISE IT ONCE WAS.
How?
By "saving the whales" or some crap?
NO, BY DESTROYING ALL OF HUMANITY.

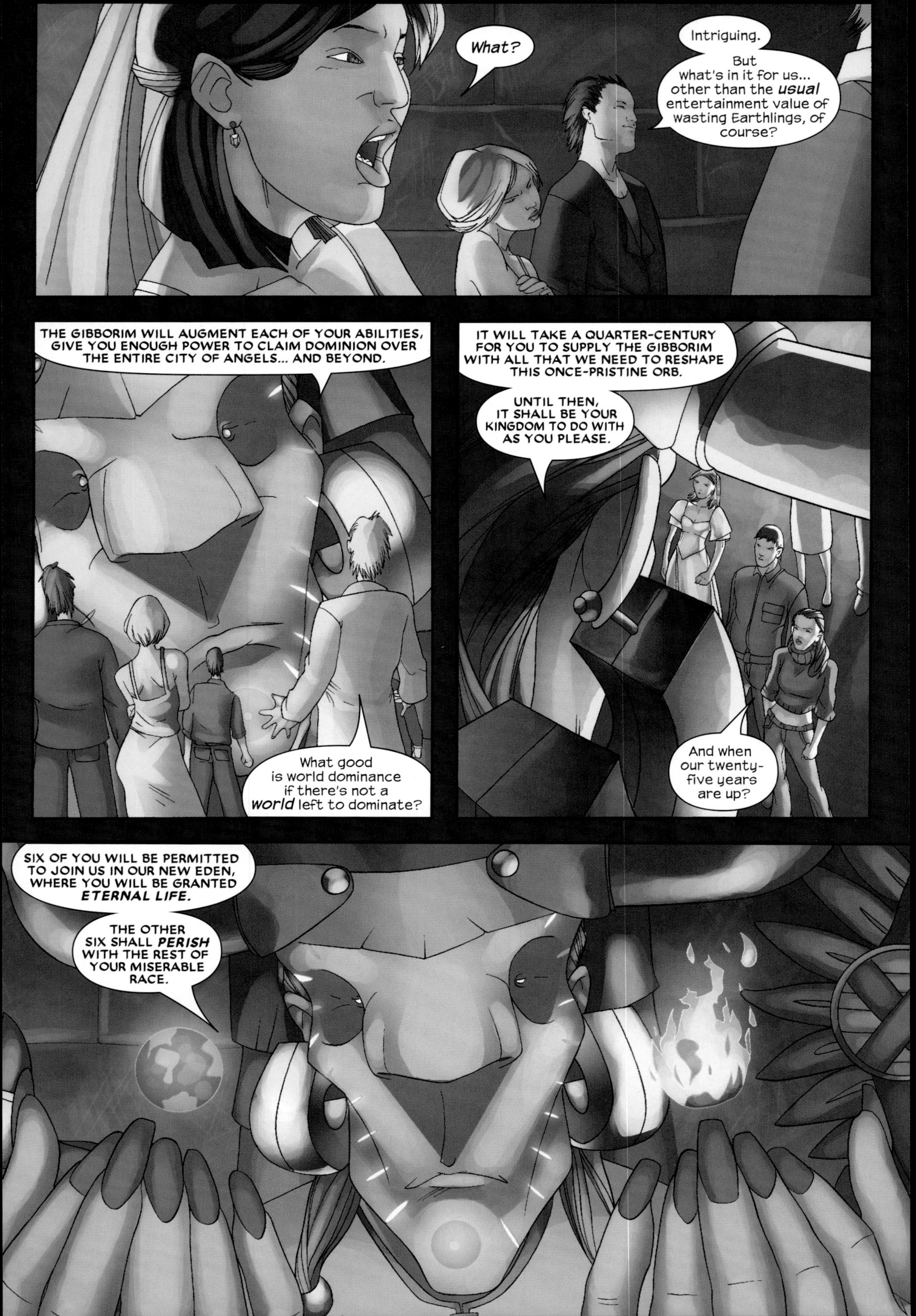
What?
Intriguing.
But what's in it for us... other than the *usual* entertainment value of wasting Earthlings, of course?
THE GIBBORIM WILL AUGMENT EACH OF YOUR ABILITIES, GIVE YOU ENOUGH POWER TO CLAIM DOMINION OVER THE ENTIRE CITY OF ANGELS... AND BEYOND.
What good is world dominance if there's not a *world* left to dominate?
IT WILL TAKE A QUARTER-CENTURY FOR YOU TO SUPPLY THE GIBBORIM WITH ALL THAT WE NEED TO RESHAPE THIS ONCE-PRISTINE ORB.
UNTIL THEN, IT SHALL BE YOUR KINGDOM TO DO WITH AS YOU PLEASE.
And when our twenty-five years are up?
SIX OF YOU WILL BE PERMITTED TO JOIN US IN OUR NEW EDEN, WHERE YOU WILL BE GRANTED *ETERNAL LIFE.*
THE OTHER SIX SHALL *PERISH* WITH THE REST OF YOUR MISERABLE RACE.

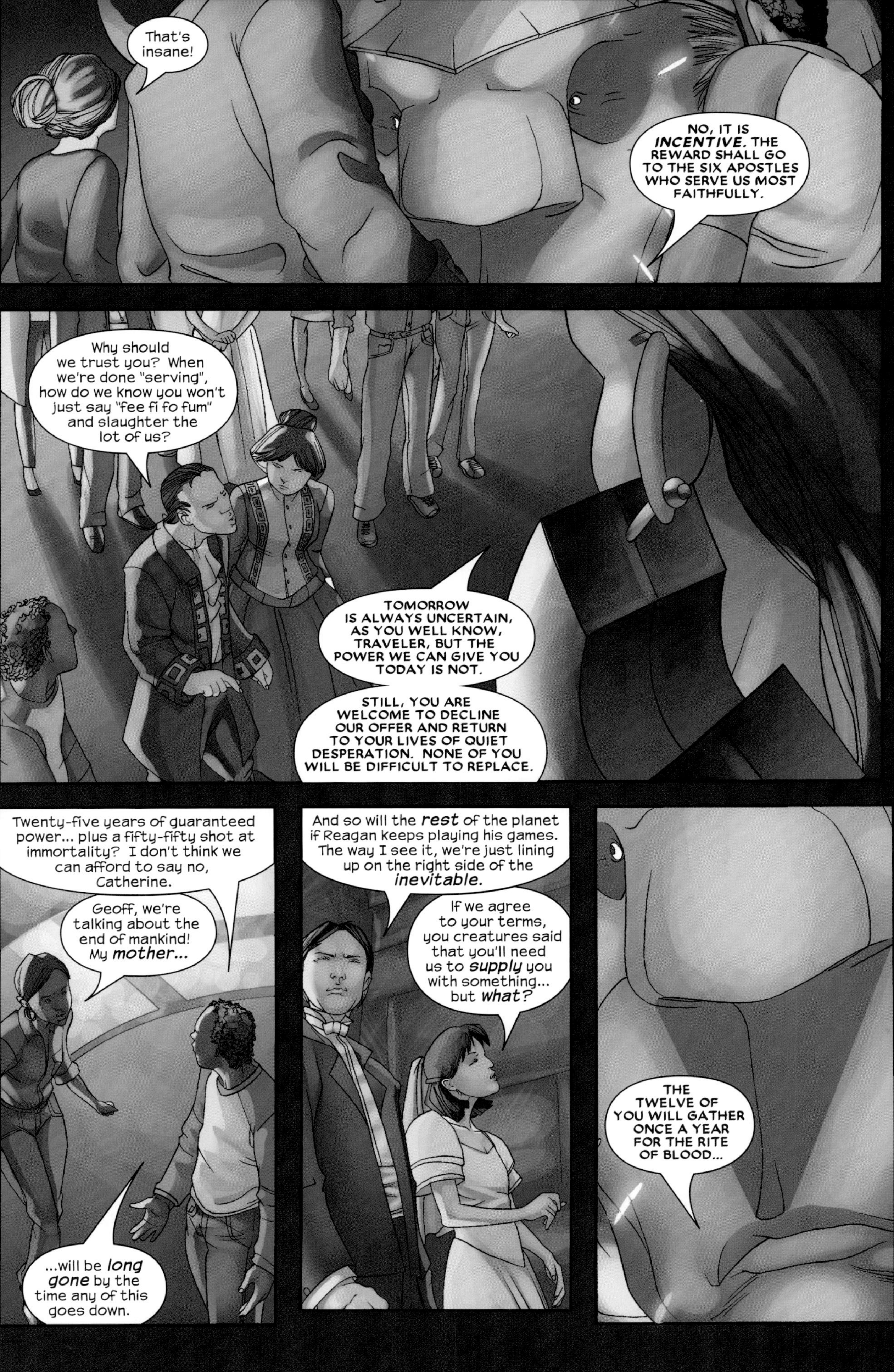
That's insane!
NO, IT IS *INCENTIVE.* THE REWARD SHALL GO TO THE SIX APOSTLES WHO SERVE US MOST FAITHFULLY.
Why should we trust you? When we're done "serving", how do we know you won't just say "fee fi fo fum" and slaughter the lot of us?
TOMORROW IS ALWAYS UNCERTAIN, AS YOU WELL KNOW, TRAVELER, BUT THE POWER WE CAN GIVE YOU TODAY IS NOT.
STILL, YOU ARE WELCOME TO DECLINE OUR OFFER AND RETURN TO YOUR LIVES OF QUIET DESPERATION. NONE OF YOU WILL BE DIFFICULT TO REPLACE.
Twenty-five years of guaranteed power... plus a fifty-fifty shot at immortality? I don't think we can afford to say no, Catherine.
Geoff, we're talking about the end of mankind! My *mother...*
...will be *long gone* by the time any of this goes down.
And so will the *rest* of the planet if Reagan keeps playing his games. The way I see it, we're just lining up on the right side of the *inevitable.*
If we agree to your terms, you creatures said that you'll need us to *supply* you with something... but *what?*
THE TWELVE OF YOU WILL GATHER ONCE A YEAR FOR THE RITE OF BLOOD...

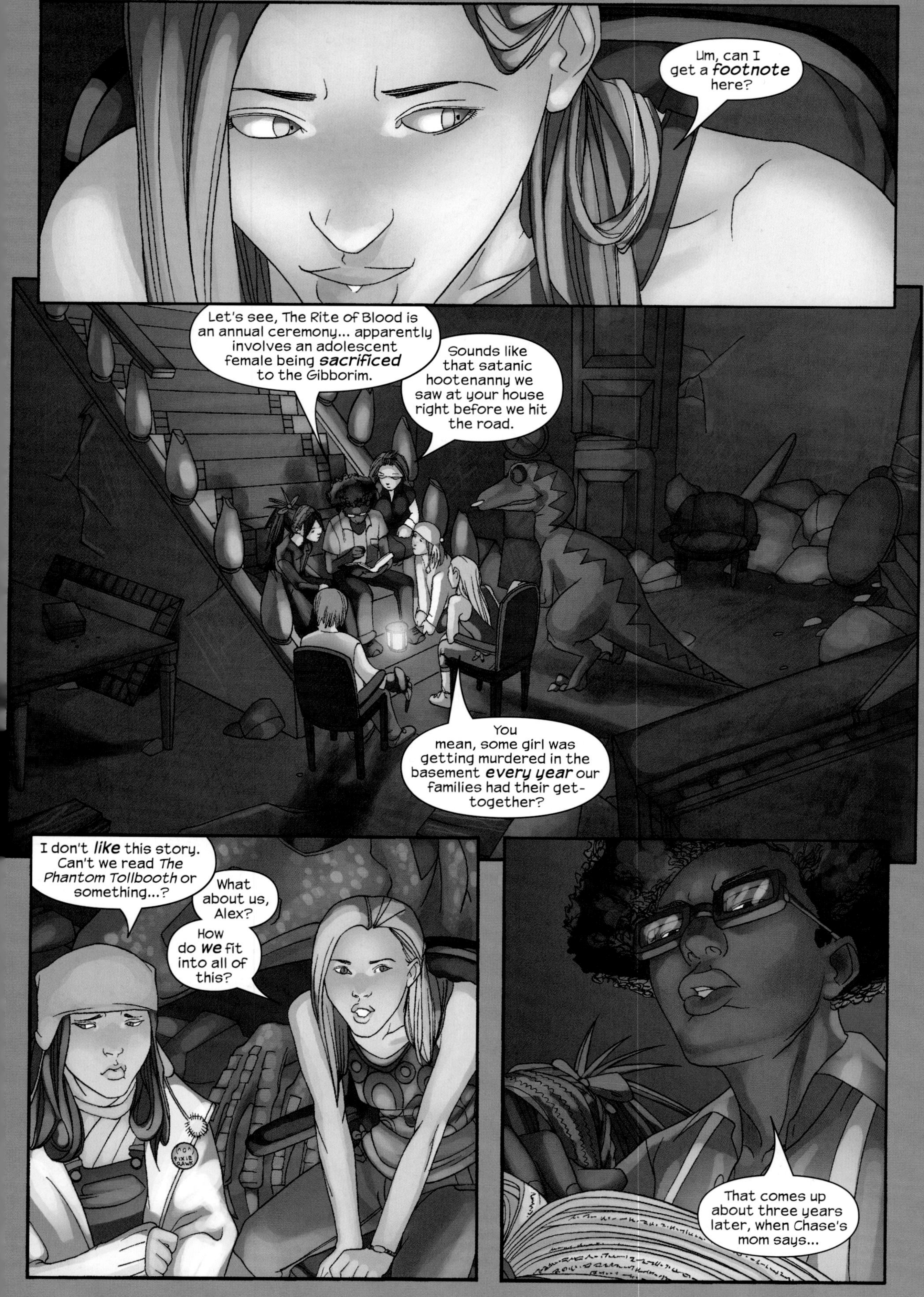
Um, can I get a *footnote* here?
Let's see, The Rite of Blood is an annual ceremony... apparently involves an adolescent female being *sacrificed* to the Gibborim.
Sounds like that satanic hootenanny we saw at your house right before we hit the road.
You mean, some girl was getting murdered in the basement *every year* our families had their get-together?
I don't *like* this story. Can't we read *The Phantom Tollbooth* or something...?
What about us, Alex?
How do *we* fit into all of this?
That comes up about three years later, when Chase's mom says...

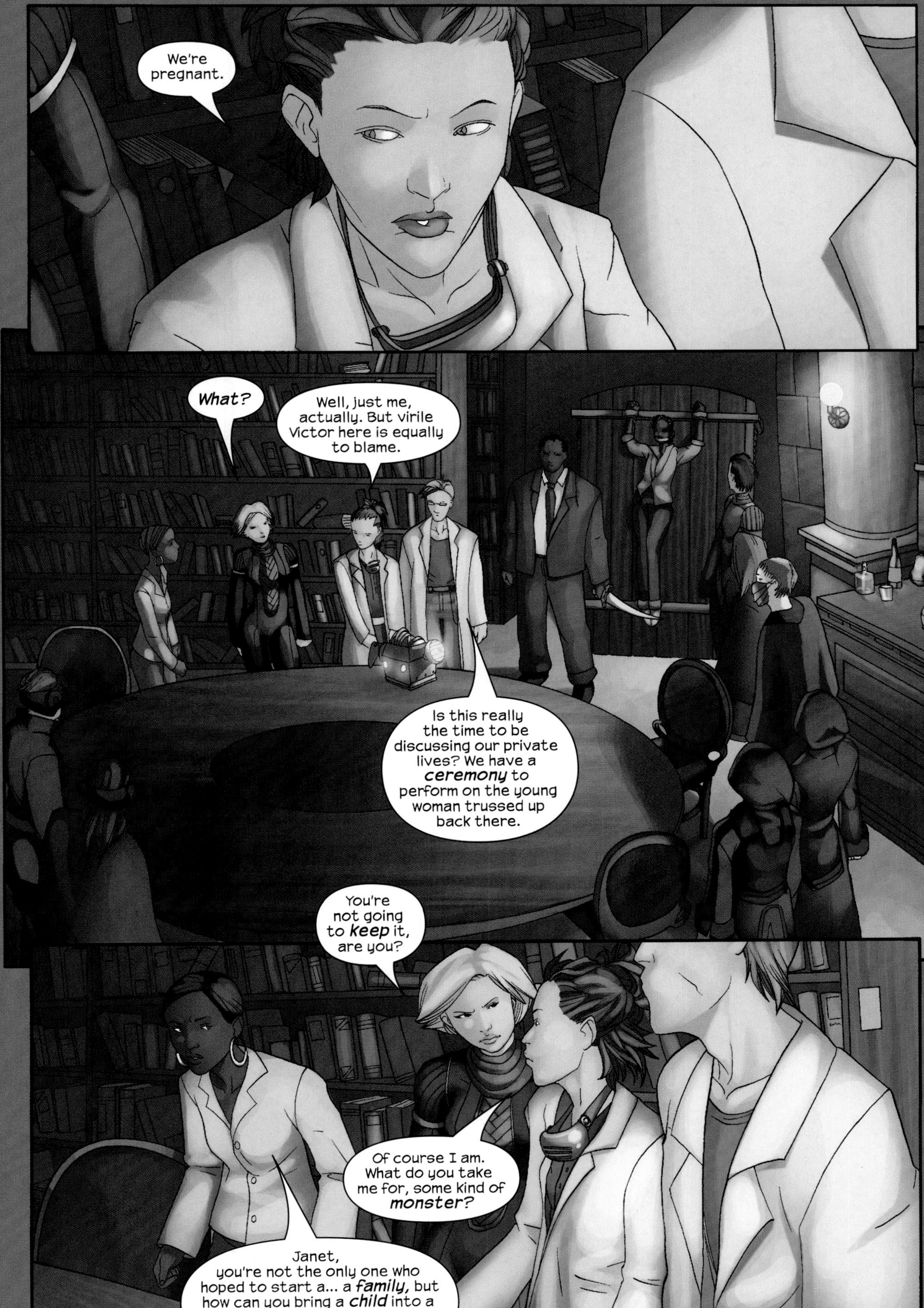
We're pregnant.
What?
Well, just me, actually. But virile Victor here is equally to blame.
Is this really the time to be discussing our private lives? We have a *ceremony* to perform on the young woman trussed up back there.
You're not going to *keep* it, are you?
Of course I am. What do you take me for, some kind of *monster*?
Janet, you're not the only one who hoped to start a... a *family,* but how can you bring a *child* into a world we're helping to *destroy?*

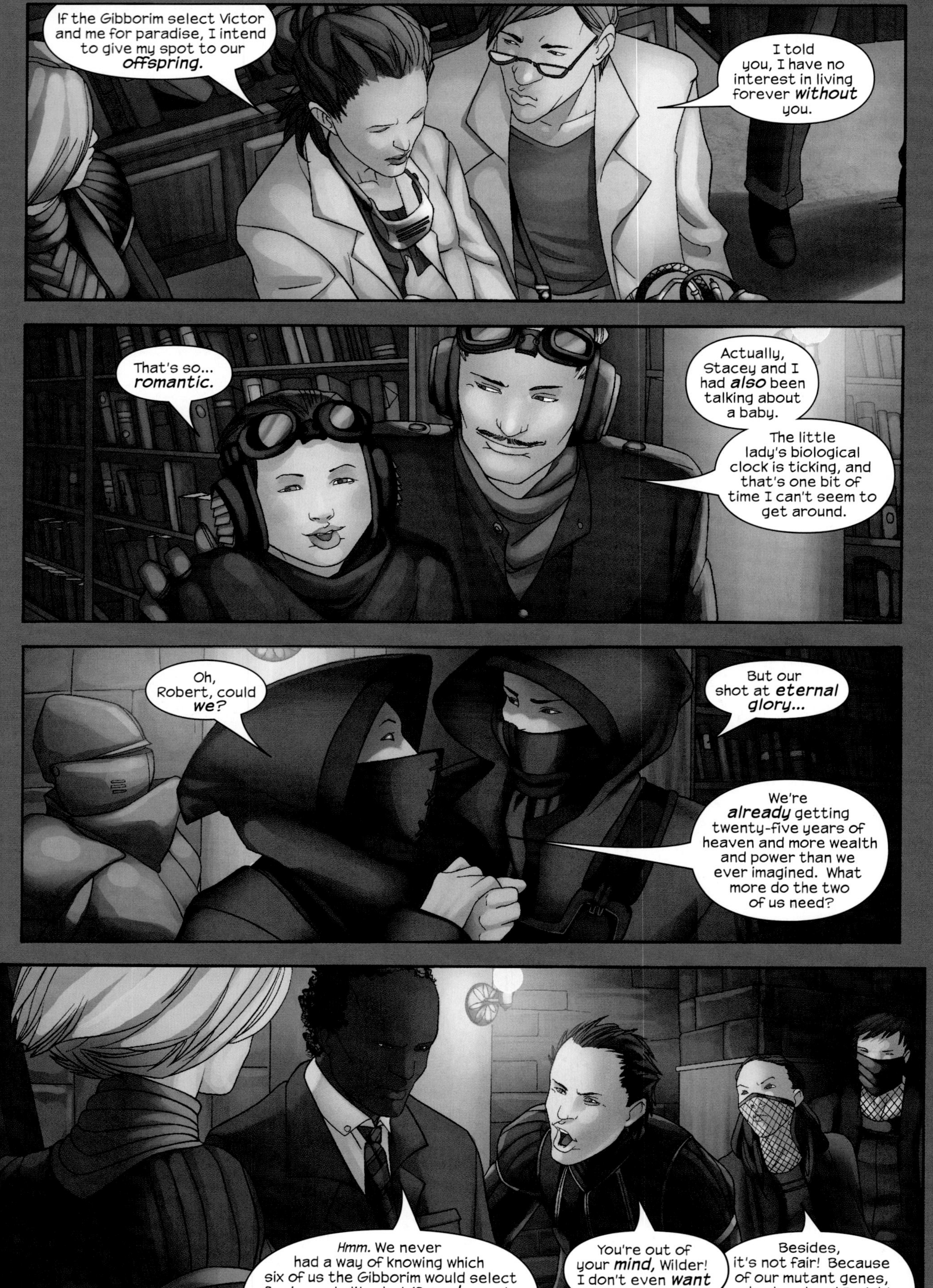

If the Gibborim select Victor and me for paradise, I intend to give my spot to our *offspring.*
I told you, I have no interest in living forever *without* you.
That's so... *romantic.*
Actually, Stacey and I had *also* been talking about a baby.
The little lady's biological clock is ticking, and that's one bit of time I can't seem to get around.
Oh, Robert, could *we?*
But our shot at *eternal glory...*
We're *already* getting twenty-five years of heaven and more wealth and power than we ever imagined. What more do the two of us need?
Hmm. We never had a way of knowing which six of us the Gibborim would select for immortality, but if *each* couple donated their place to a single child...
You're out of your *mind,* Wilder! I don't even *want* a kid!
Besides, it's not fair! Because of our mutant genes, my husband and I might not be *able* to conceive.

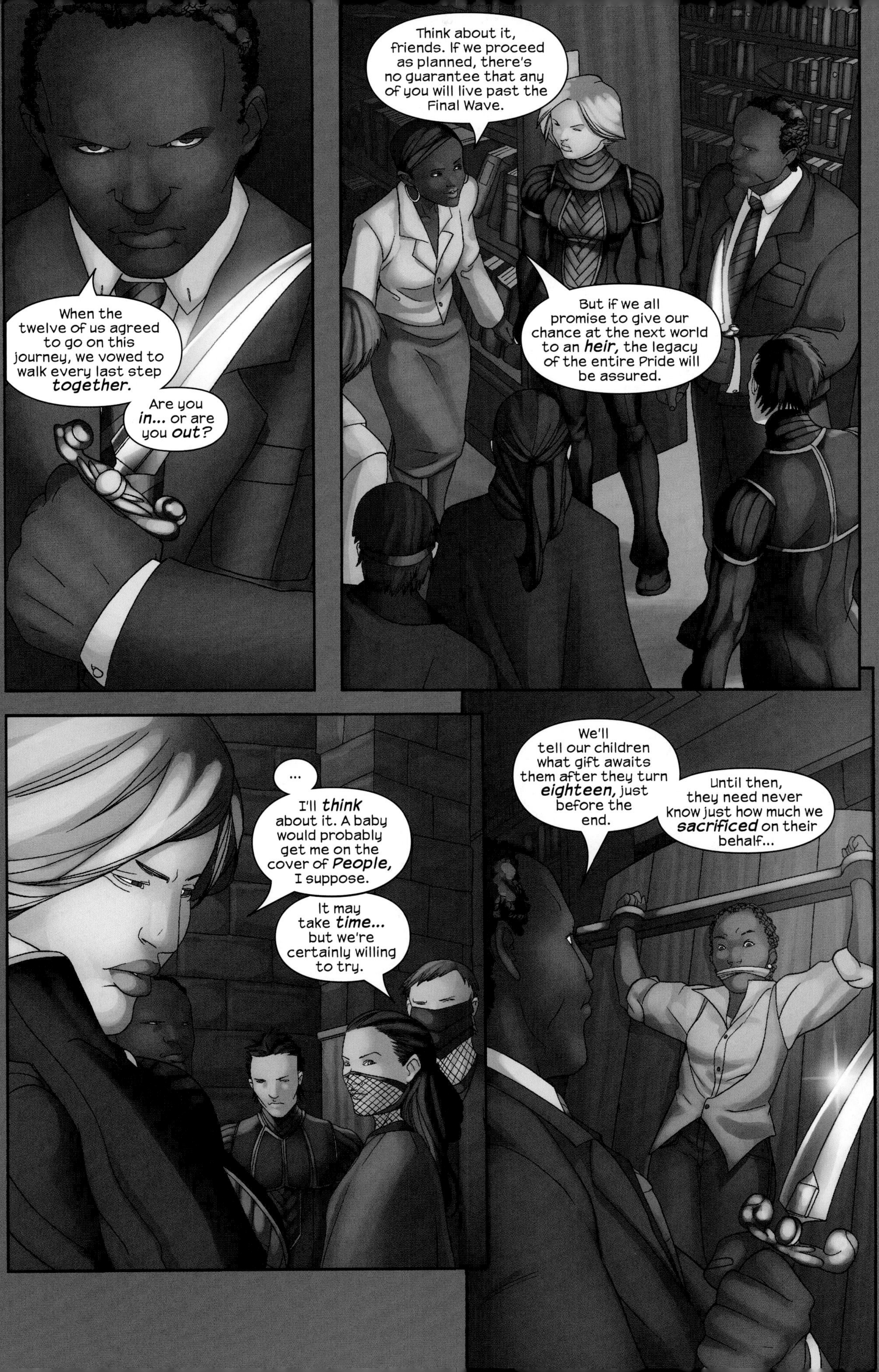
When the twelve of us agreed to go on this journey, we vowed to walk every last step *together.*
Are you *in...* or are you *out?*
Think about it, friends. If we proceed as planned, there's no guarantee that any of you will live past the Final Wave.
But if we all promise to give our chance at the next world to an *heir,* the legacy of the entire Pride will be assured.
...
I'll *think* about it. A baby would probably get me on the cover of *People,* I suppose.
It may take *time...* but we're certainly willing to try.
We'll tell our children what gift awaits them after they turn *eighteen,* just before the end.
Until then, they need never know just how much we *sacrificed* on their behalf...

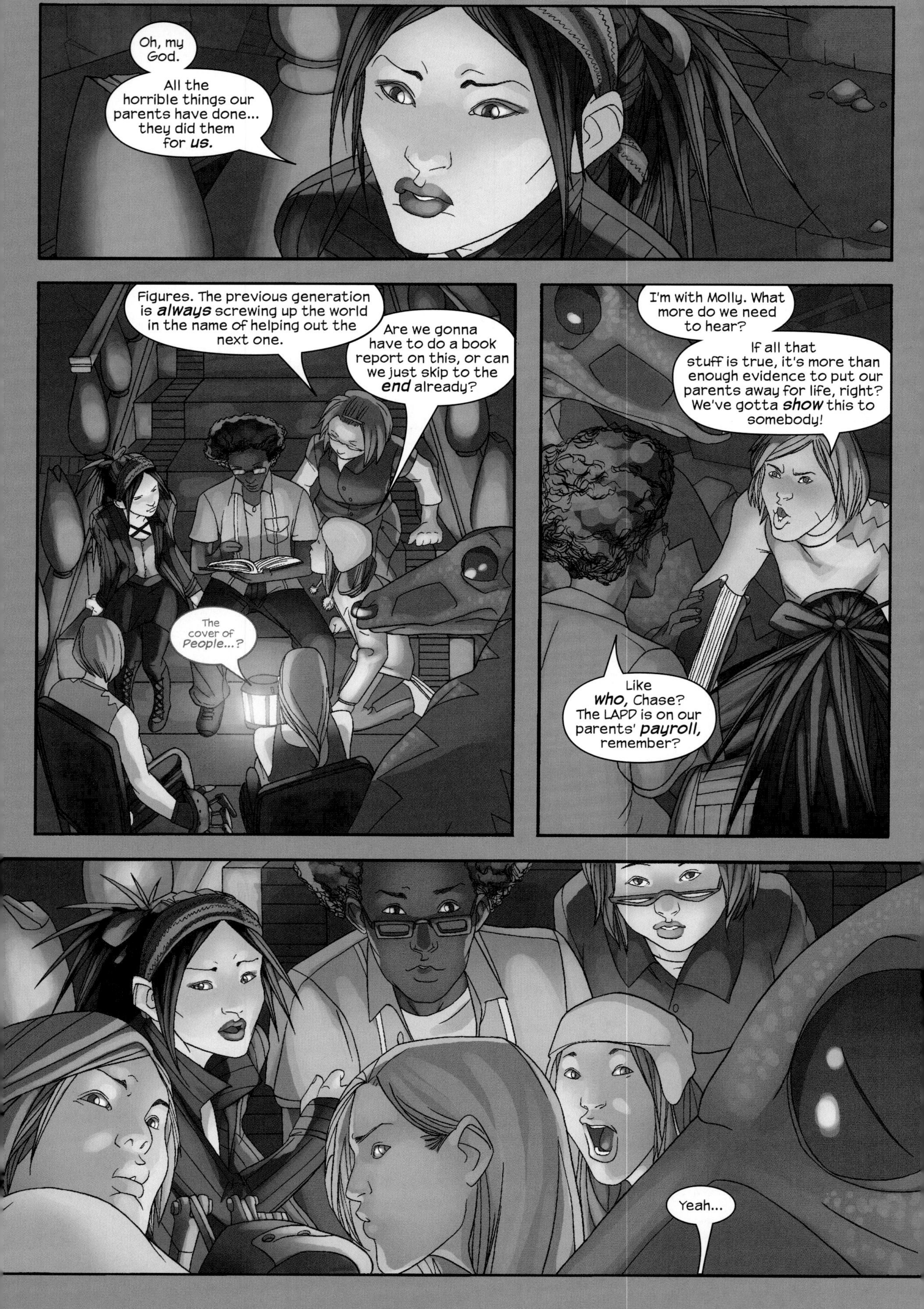

Oh, my God.
All the horrible things our parents have done... they did them for *us.*
Figures. The previous generation is ***always*** screwing up the world in the name of helping out the next one.
Are we gonna have to do a book report on this, or can we just skip to the ***end*** already?
The cover of *People...?*
I'm with Molly. What more do we need to hear?
If all that stuff is true, it's more than enough evidence to put our parents away for life, right? We've gotta ***show*** this to somebody!
Like ***who,*** Chase? The LAPD is on our parents' ***payroll,*** remember?
Yeah...

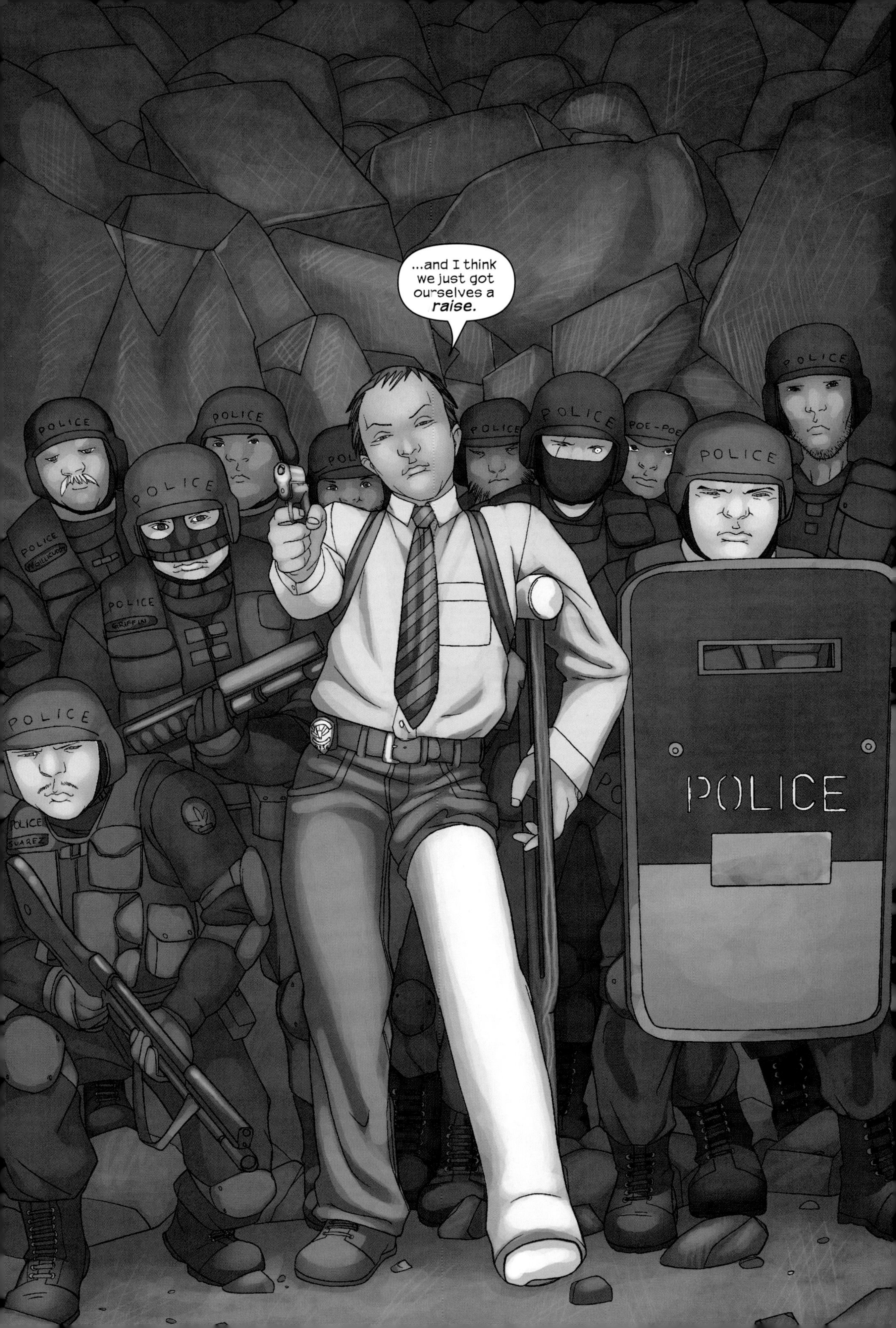
...and I think we just got ourselves a *raise.*
POLICE

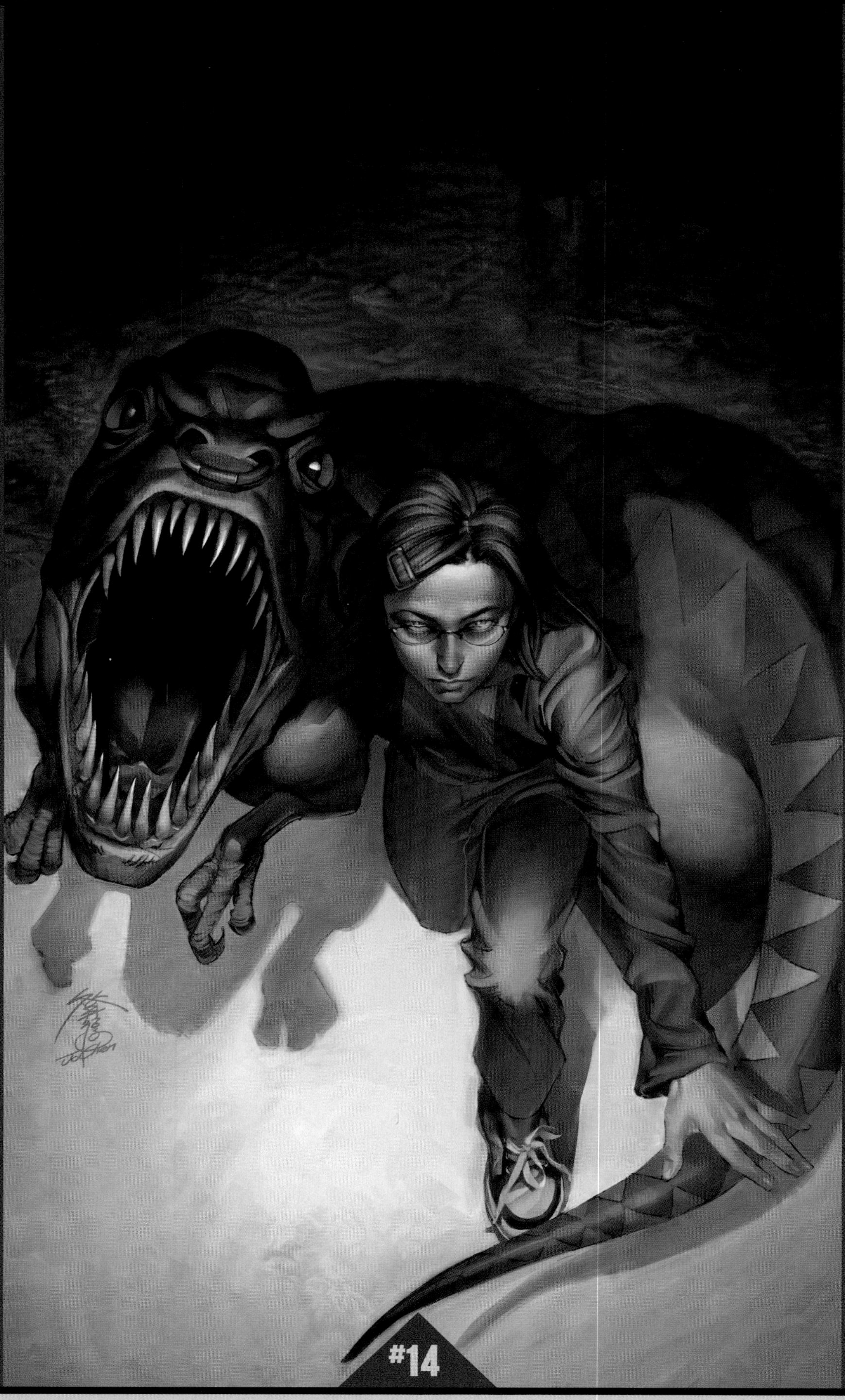
#14

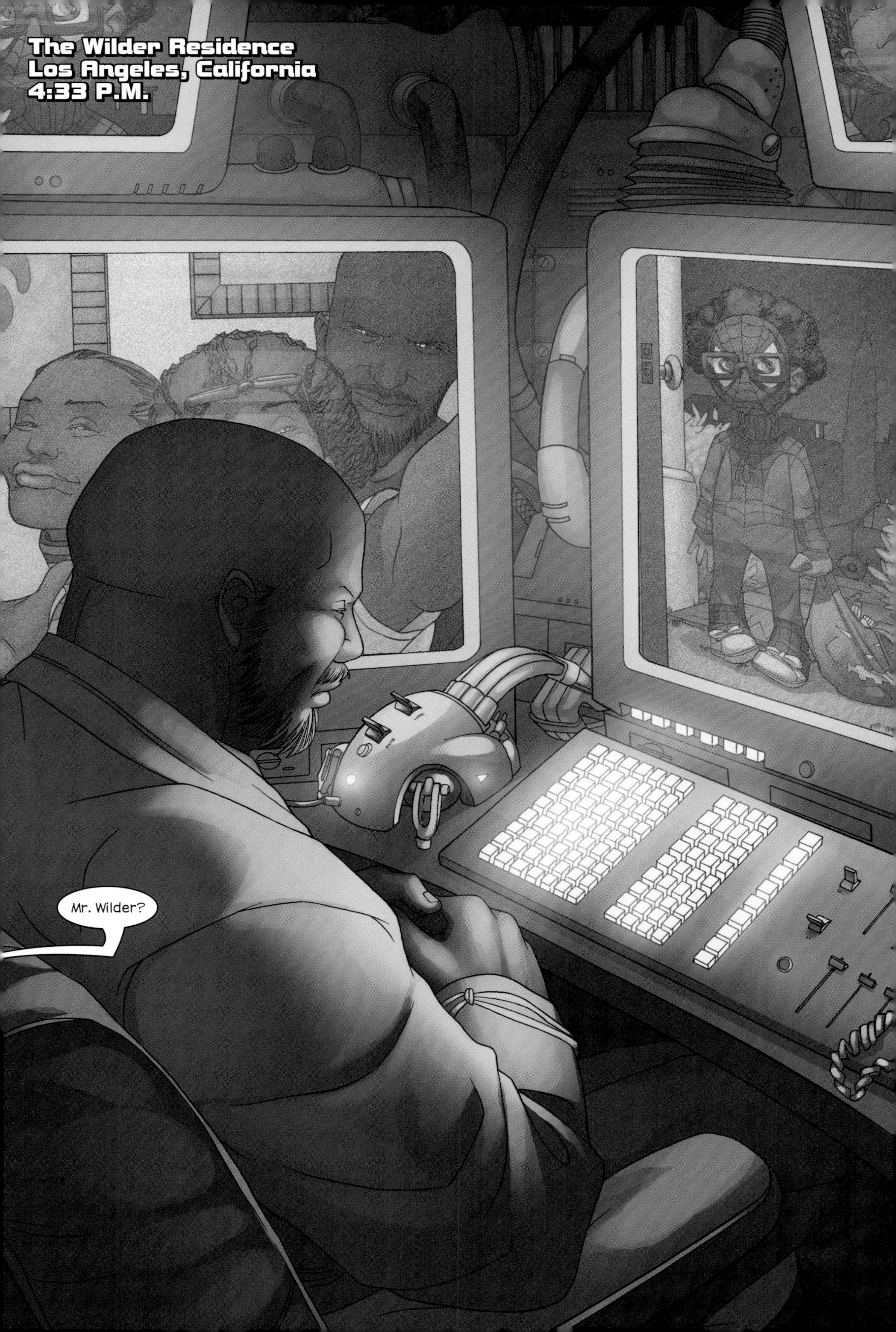
The Wilder Residence
Los Angeles, California
4:33 P.M.
Mr. Wilder?

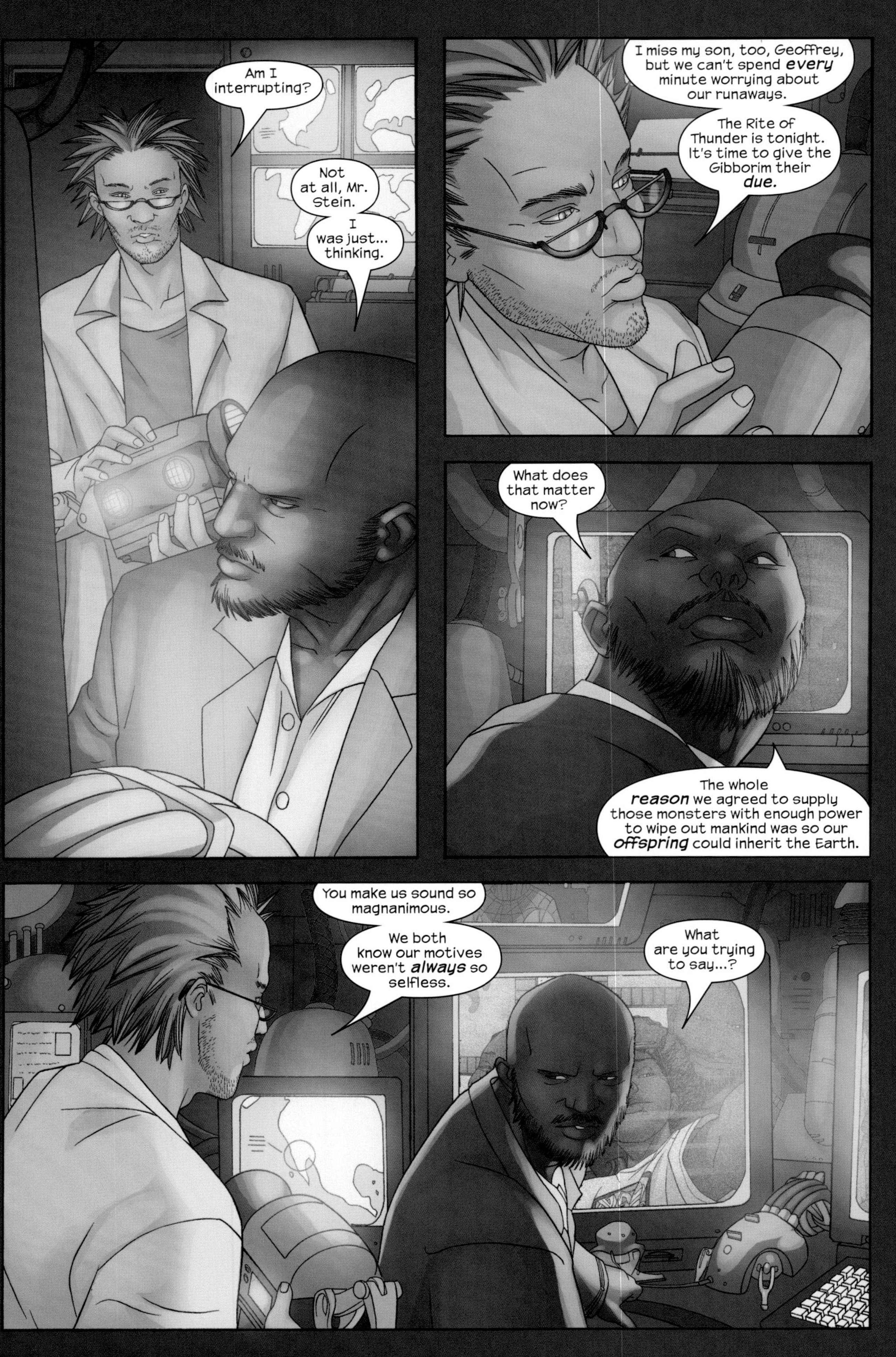
Am I interrupting?
Not at all, Mr. Stein.
I was just... thinking.
I miss my son, too, Geoffrey, but we can't spend *every* minute worrying about our runaways.
The Rite of Thunder is tonight. It's time to give the Gibborim their *due.*
What does that matter now?
The whole *reason* we agreed to supply those monsters with enough power to wipe out mankind was so our *offspring* could inherit the Earth.
You make us sound so magnanimous.
We both know our motives weren't *always* so selfless.
What are you trying to say...?

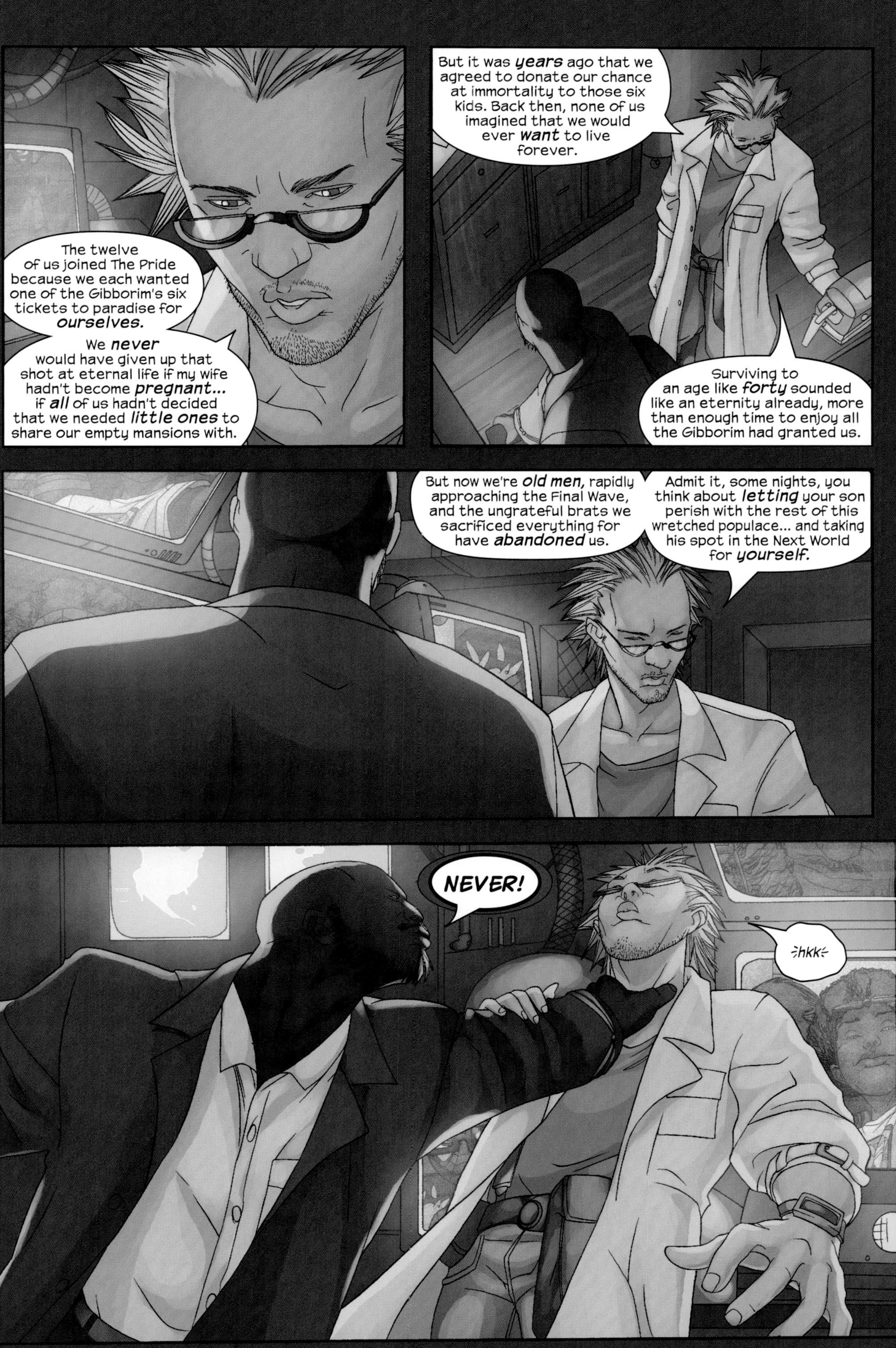
The twelve of us joined The Pride because we each wanted one of the Gibborim's six tickets to paradise for *ourselves.*
We *never* would have given up that shot at eternal life if my wife hadn't become *pregnant...* if *all* of us hadn't decided that we needed *little ones* to share our empty mansions with.
But it was *years* ago that we agreed to donate our chance at immortality to those six kids. Back then, none of us imagined that we would ever *want* to live forever.
Surviving to an age like *forty* sounded like an eternity already, more than enough time to enjoy all the Gibborim had granted us.
But now we're *old men,* rapidly approaching the Final Wave, and the ungrateful brats we sacrificed everything for have *abandoned* us.
Admit it, some nights, you think about *letting* your son perish with the rest of this wretched populace... and taking his spot in the Next World for *yourself.*
NEVER!
hkk

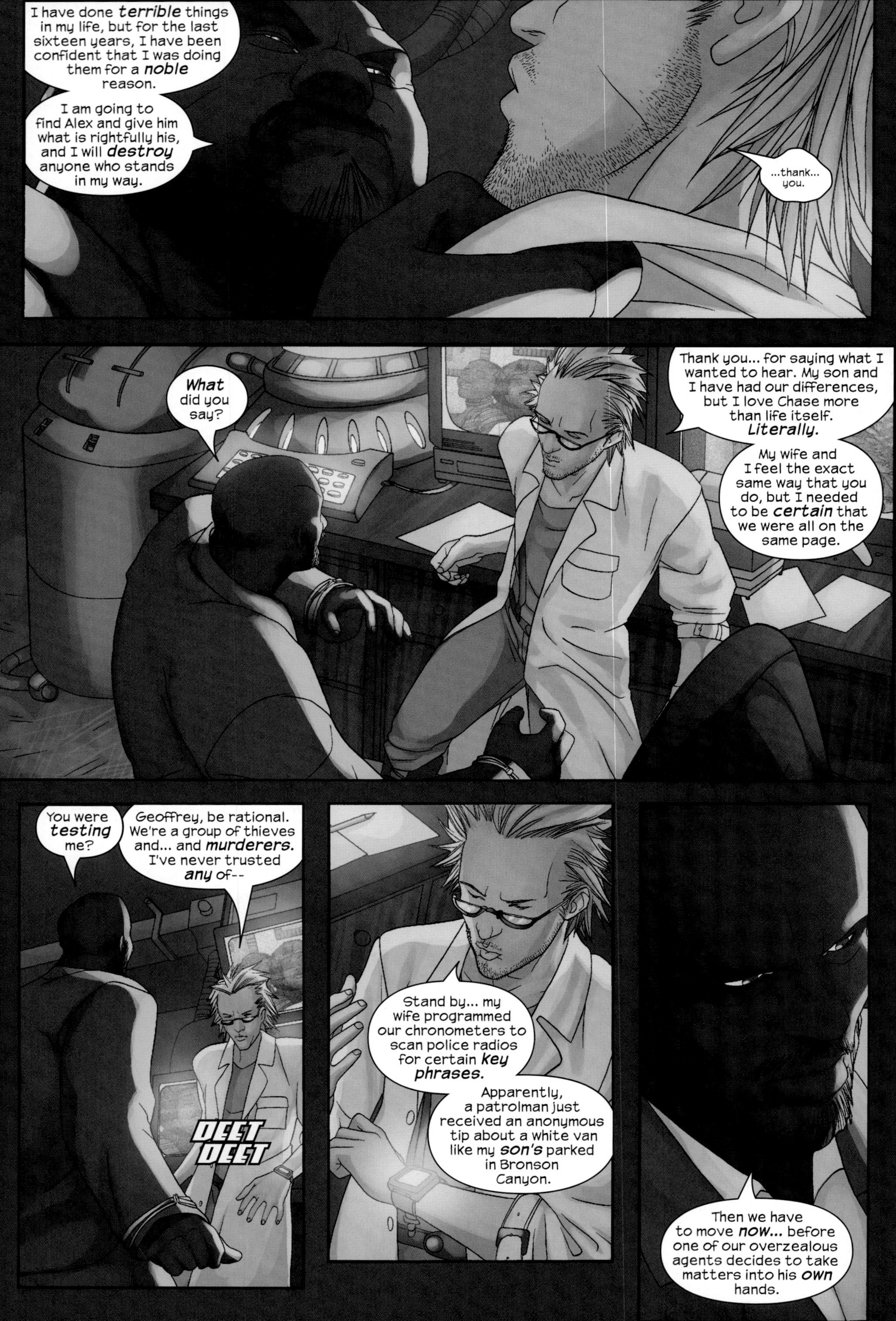

I have done terrible things in my life, but for the last sixteen years, I have been confident that I was doing them for a noble reason.
I am going to find Alex and give him what is rightfully his, and I will destroy anyone who stands in my way.
...thank... you.
What did you say?
Thank you... for saying what I wanted to hear. My son and I have had our differences, but I love Chase more than life itself. Literally.
My wife and I feel the exact same way that you do, but I needed to be certain that we were all on the same page.
You were testing me?
Geoffrey, be rational. We're a group of thieves and... and murderers. I've never trusted any of--
DEET DEET
Stand by... my wife programmed our chronometers to scan police radios for certain key phrases.
Apparently, a patrolman just received an anonymous tip about a white van like my son's parked in Bronson Canyon.
Then we have to move now... before one of our overzealous agents decides to take matters into his own hands.

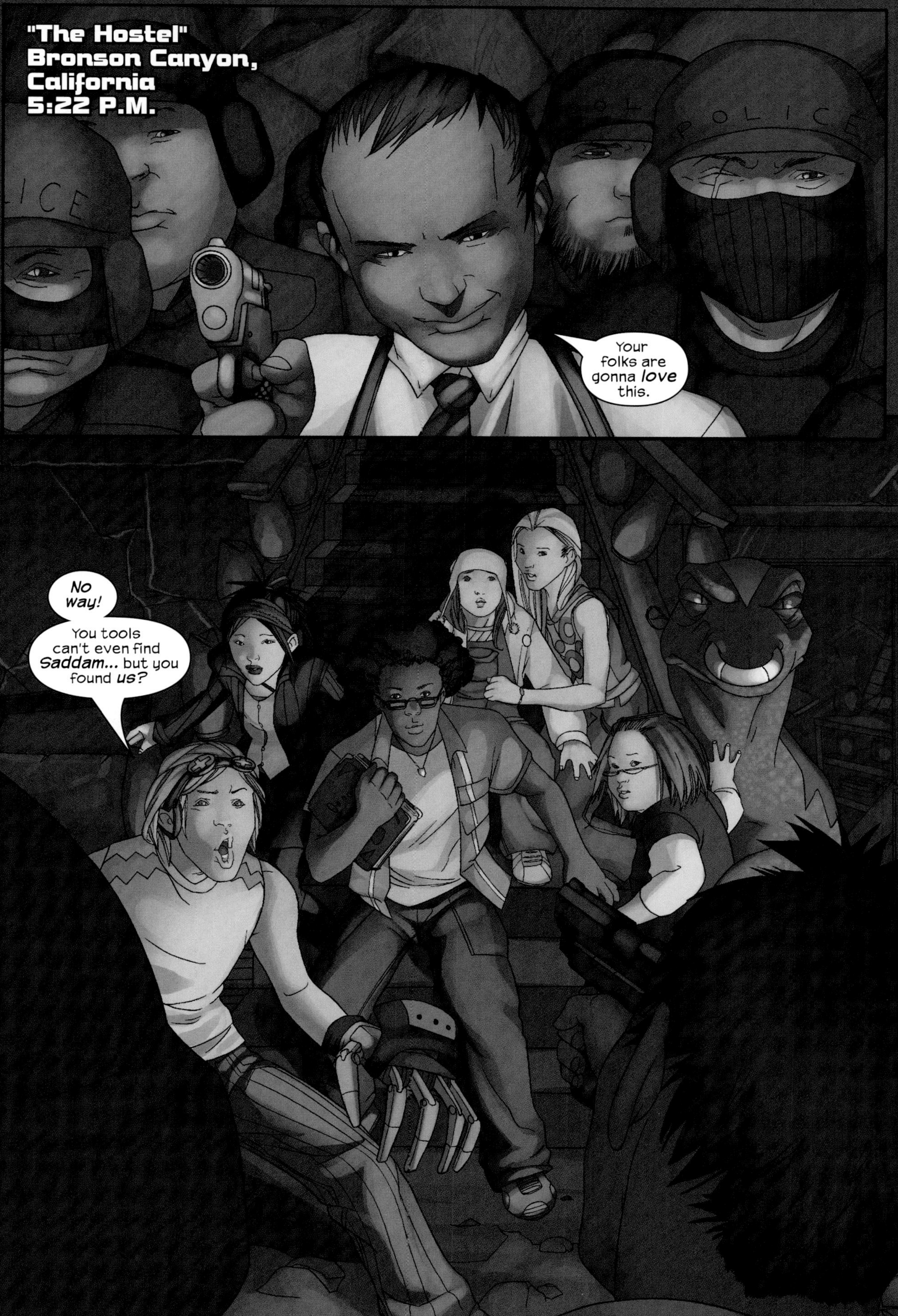
"The Hostel"
Bronson Canyon,
California
5:22 P.M.
Your folks are gonna love this.
No way!
You tools can't even find Saddam... but you found us?

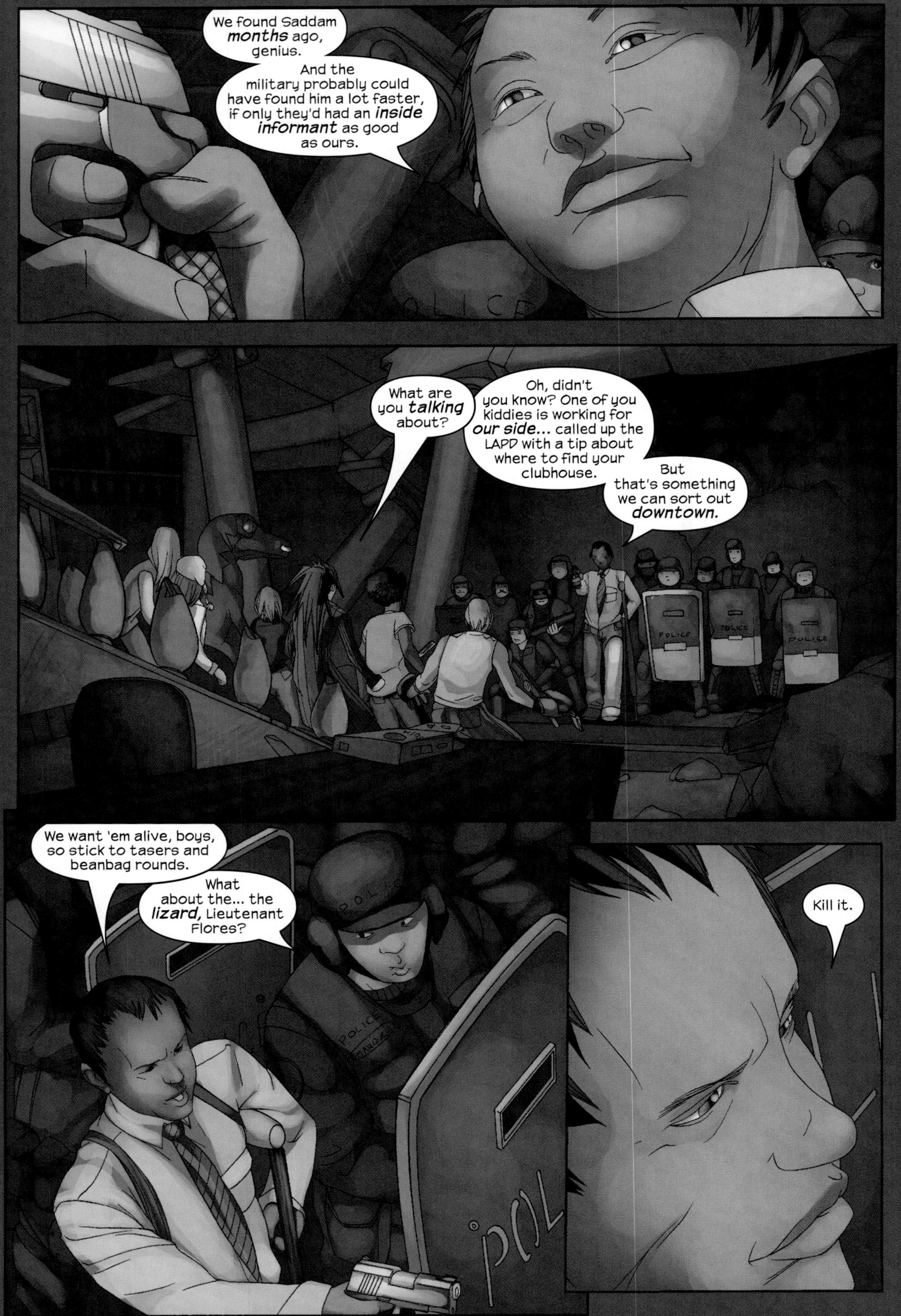
We found Saddam months ago, genius.
And the military probably could have found him a lot faster, if only they'd had an inside informant as good as ours.
What are you talking about?
Oh, didn't you know? One of you kiddies is working for our side... called up the LAPD with a tip about where to find your clubhouse.
But that's something we can sort out downtown.
POLICE
We want 'em alive, boys, so stick to tasers and beanbag rounds.
What about the... the lizard, Lieutenant Flores?
Kill it.

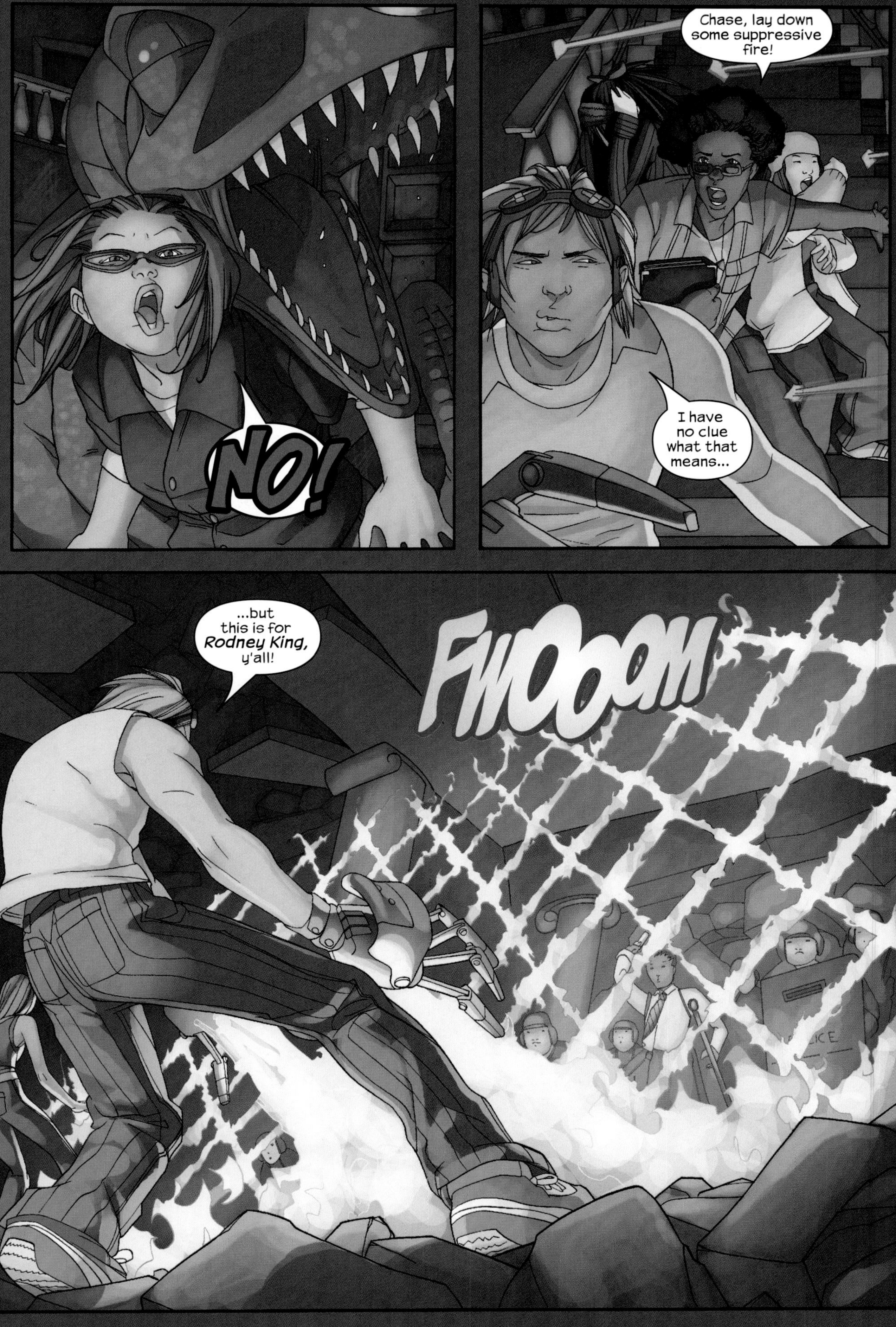
NO!
Chase, lay down some suppressive fire!
I have no clue what that means...
...but this is for *Rodney King,* y'all!
FWOOOM

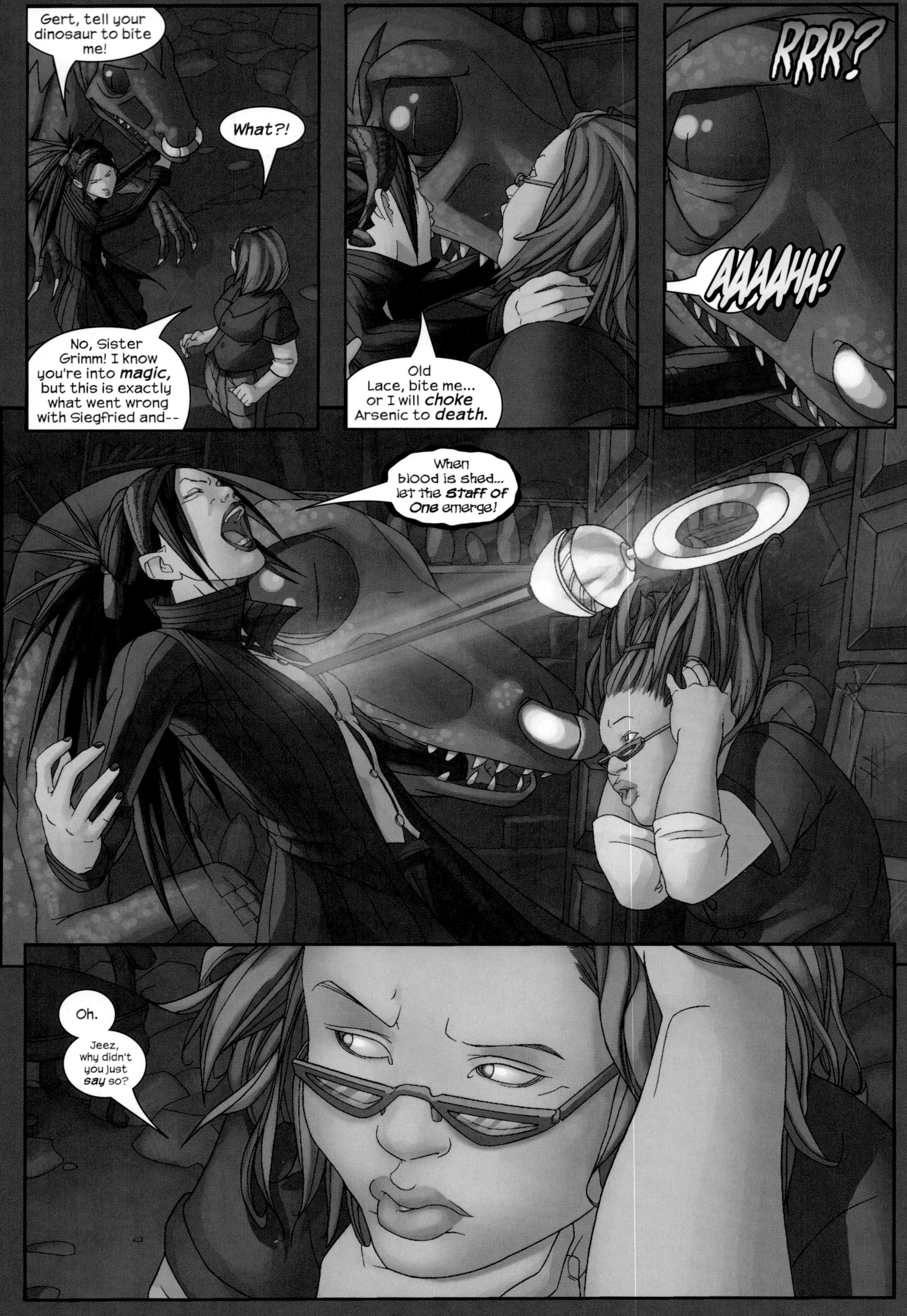
Gert, tell your dinosaur to bite me!
What?!
No, Sister Grimm! I know you're into *magic,* but this is exactly what went wrong with Siegfried and--
Old Lace, bite me... or I will *choke* Arsenic to *death.*
RRR?
AAAAHH!
When blood is shed... let the *Staff Of One* emerge!
Oh.
Jeez, why didn't you just *say* so?

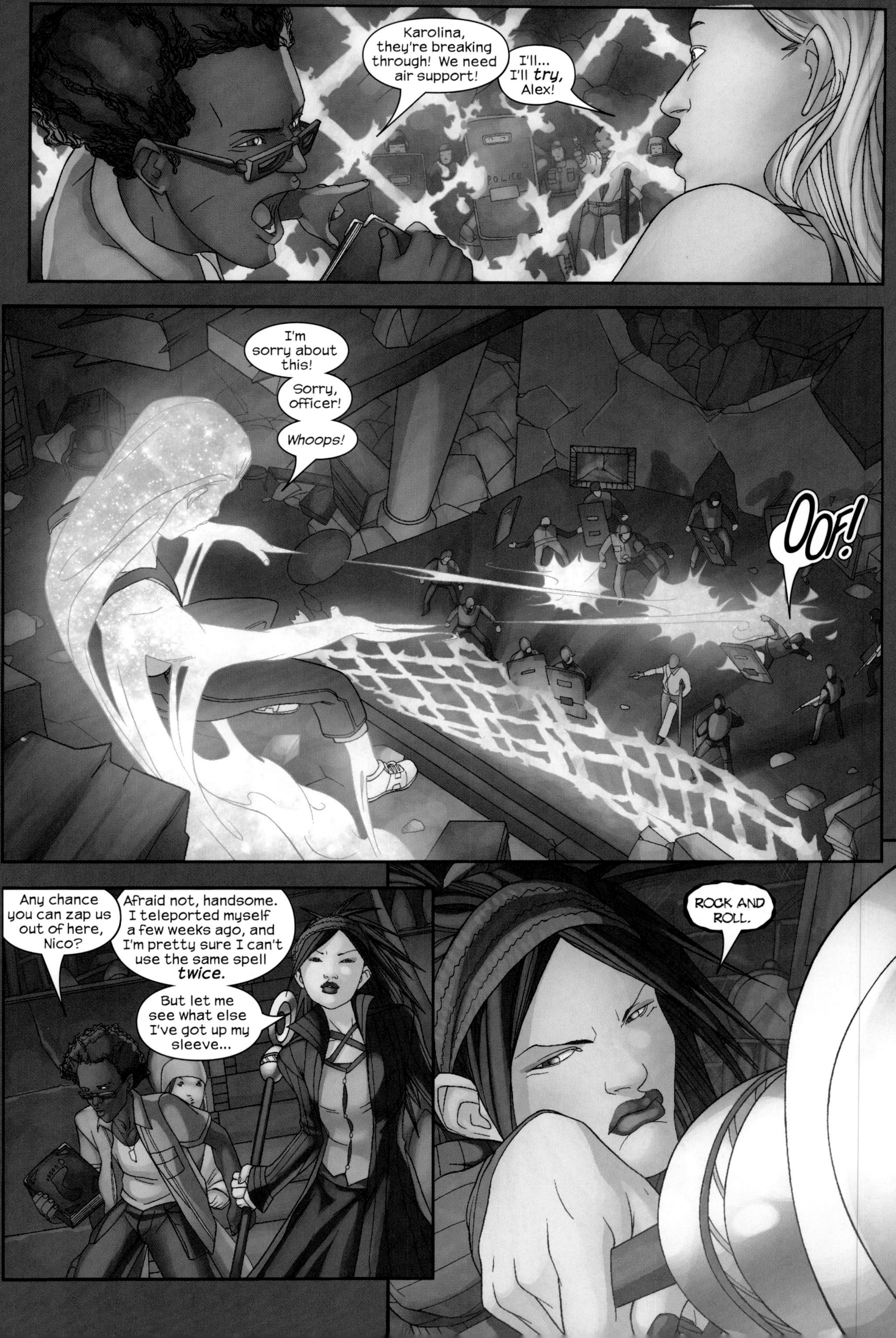
Karolina, they're breaking through! We need air support!
I'll... I'll *try*, Alex!
POLICE
I'm sorry about this!
Sorry, officer!
Whoops!
OOF!
Any chance you can zap us out of here, Nico?
Afraid not, handsome. I teleported myself a few weeks ago, and I'm pretty sure I can't use the same spell *twice*.
But let me see what else I've got up my sleeve...
ROCK AND ROLL.

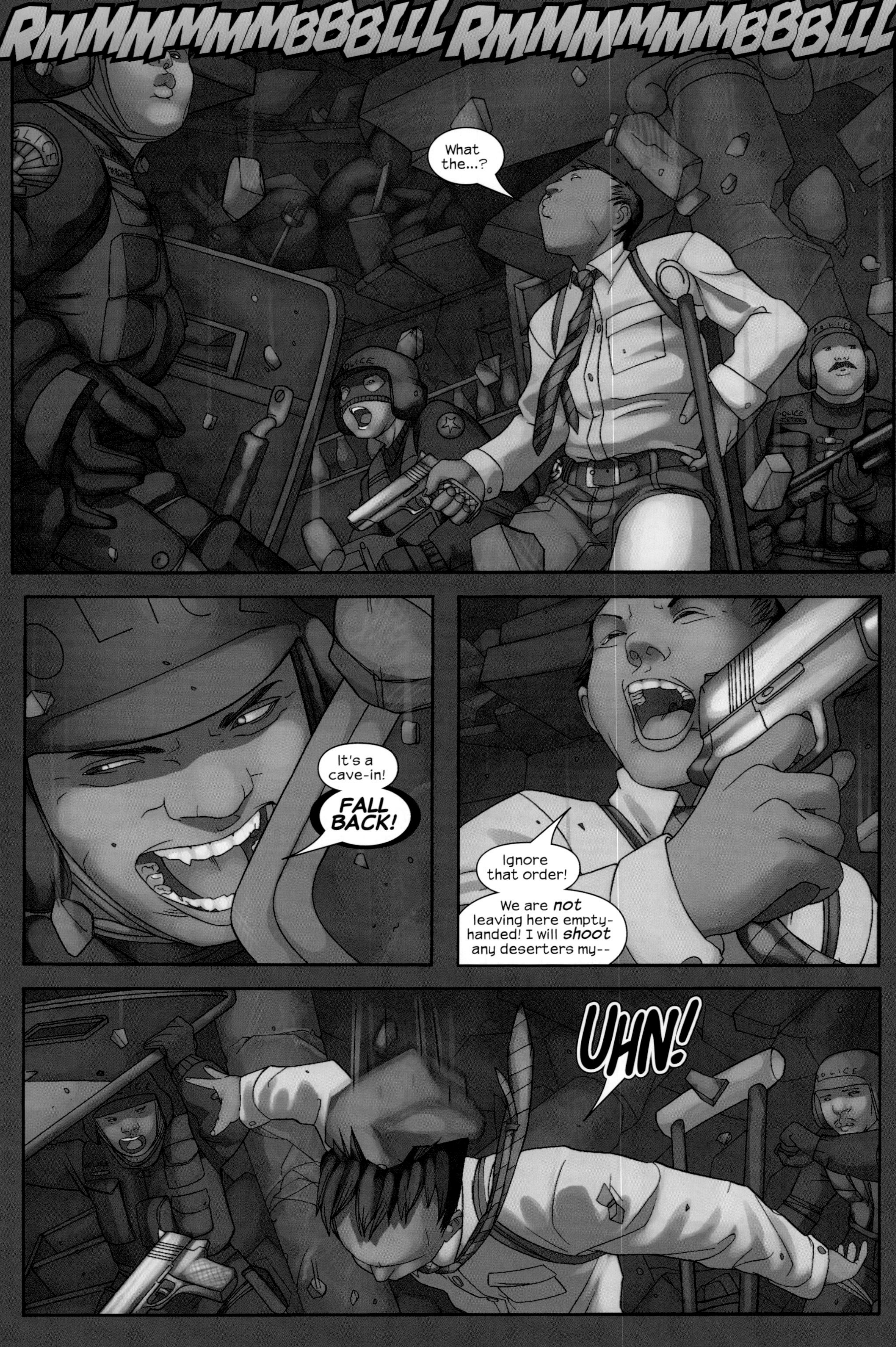
RMMMMMMMBBBLLL RMMMMMMMMBBBLLL
What the...?
It's a cave-in!
FALL BACK!
Ignore that order!
We are not leaving here empty-handed! I will shoot any deserters my--
UHN!

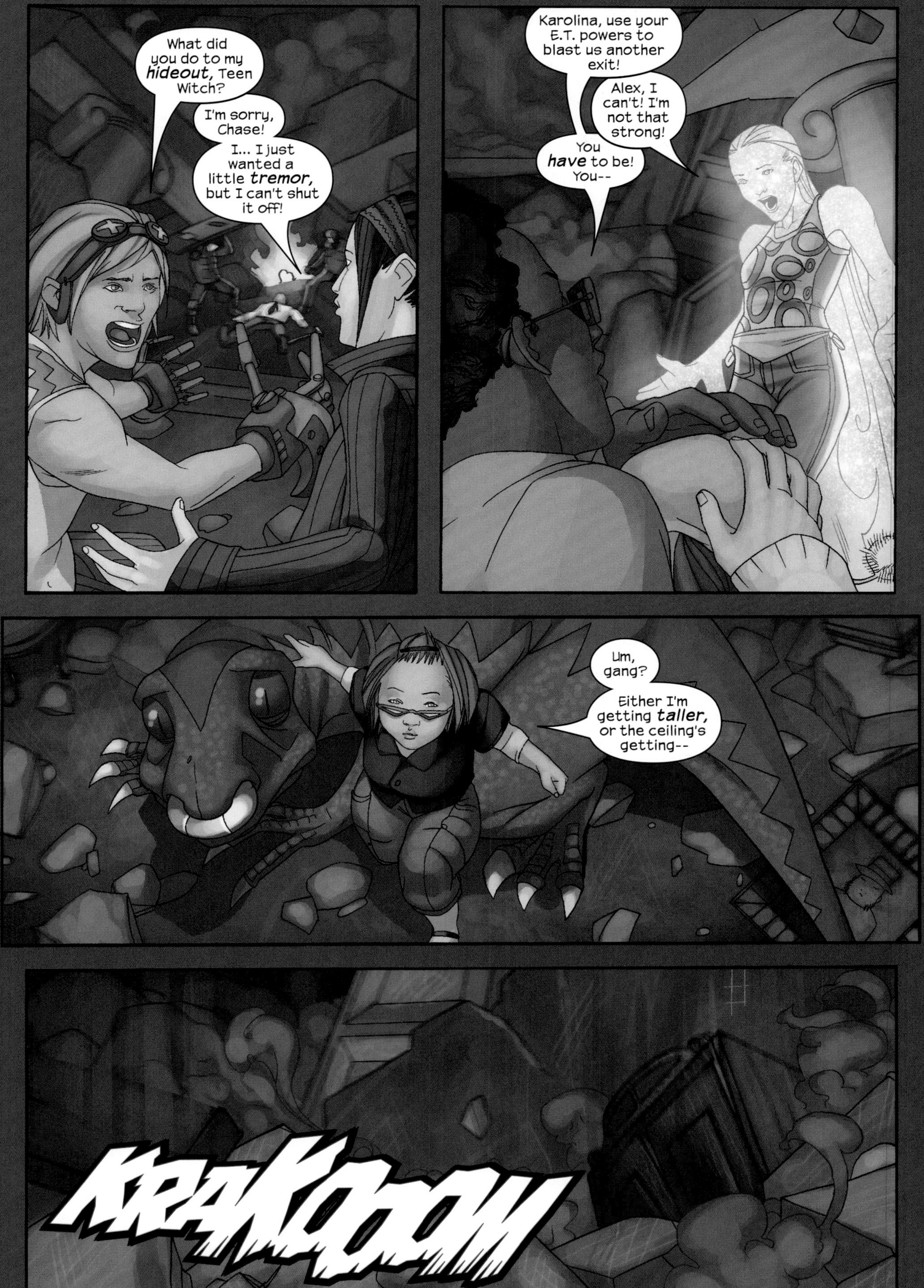

What did you do to my *hideout,* Teen Witch?
I'm sorry, Chase!
I... I just wanted a little *tremor,* but I can't shut it off!
Karolina, use your E.T. powers to blast us another exit!
Alex, I can't! I'm not that strong!
You *have* to be! You--
Um, gang?
Either I'm getting *taller,* or the ceiling's getting--
KRAKOOOM

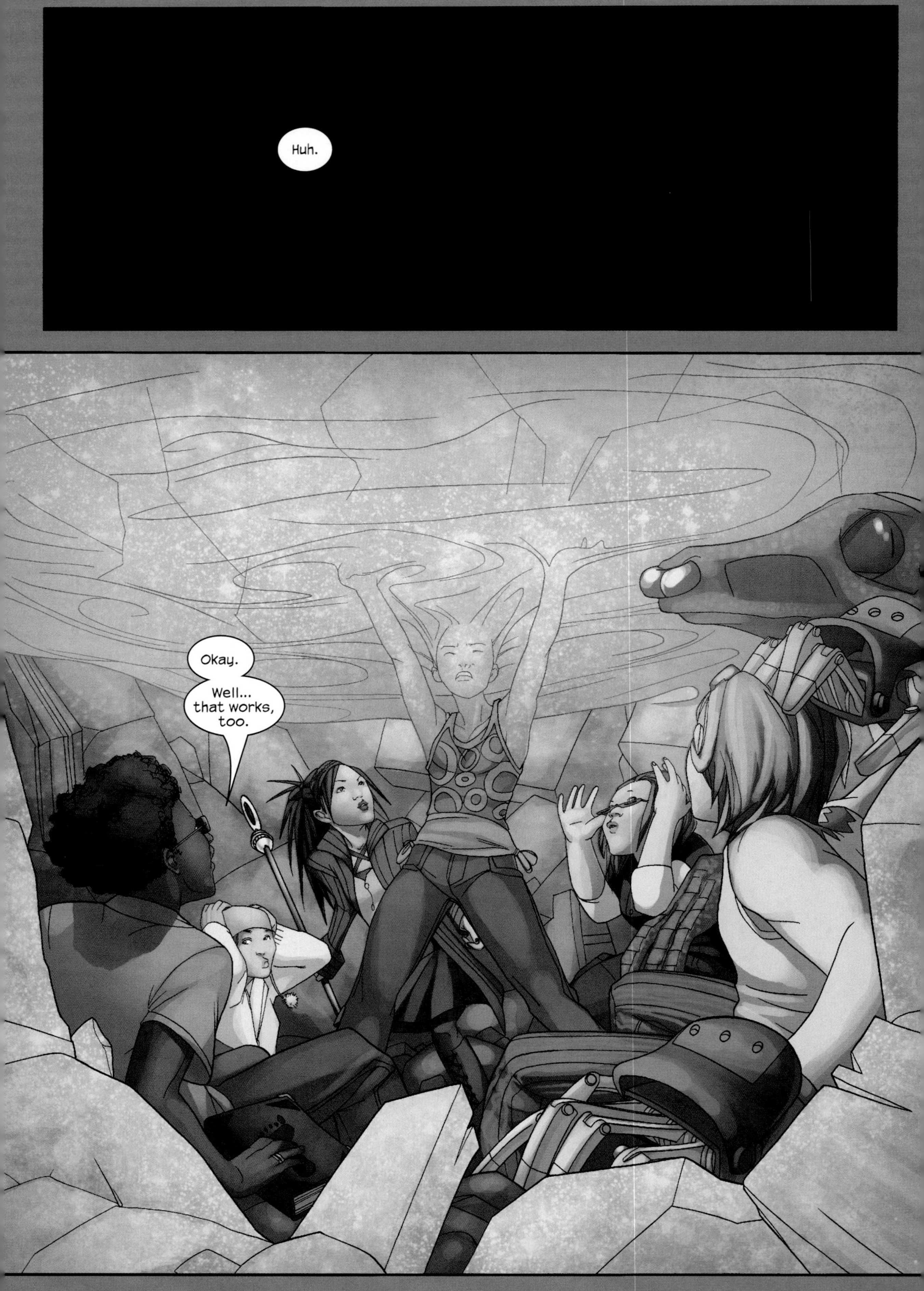
Huh.
Okay.
Well... that works, too.

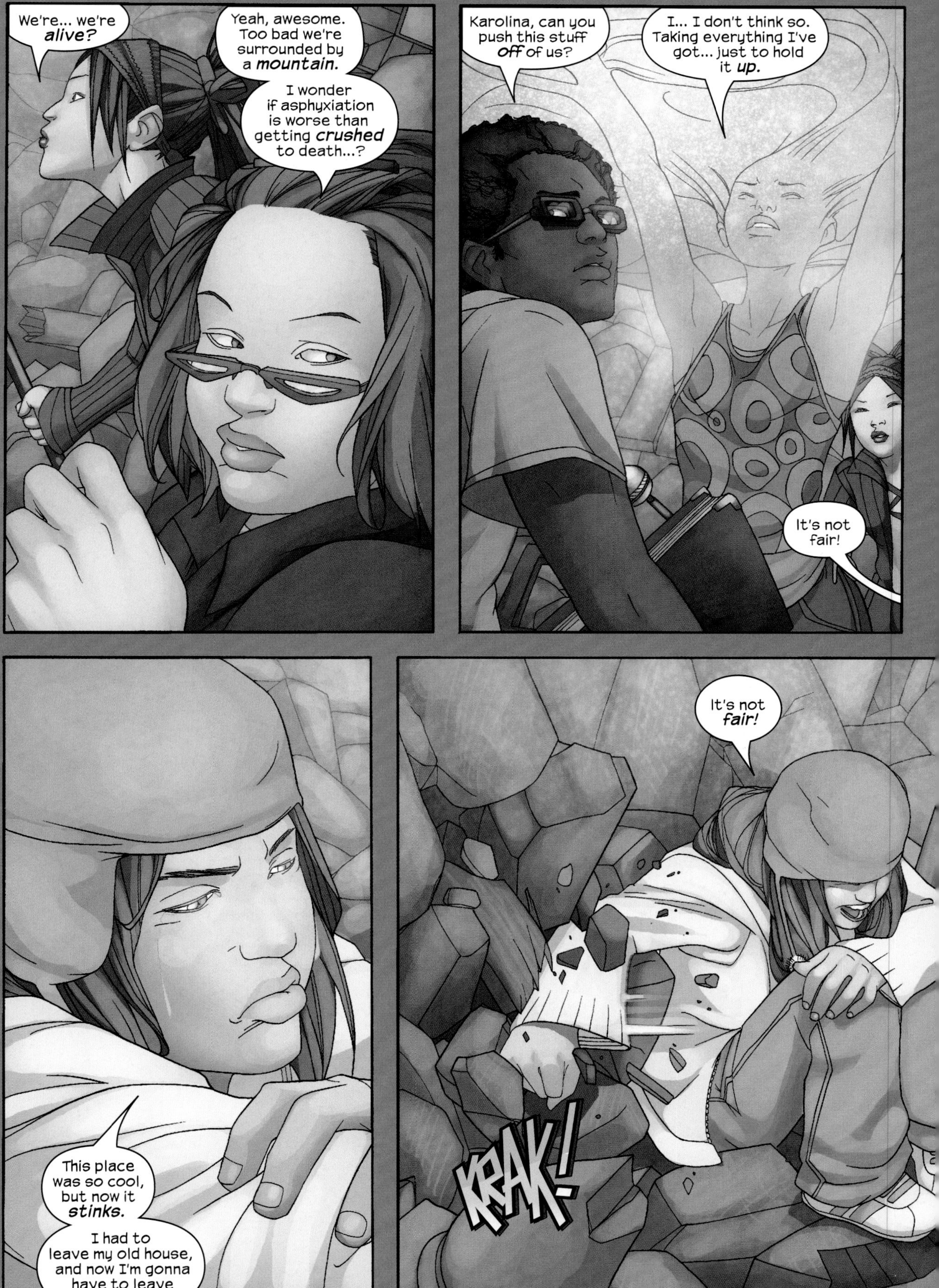
We're... we're *alive?*
Yeah, awesome. Too bad we're surrounded by a ***mountain.***
I wonder if asphyxiation is worse than getting ***crushed*** to death...?
Karolina, can you push this stuff ***off*** of us?
I... I don't think so. Taking everything I've got... just to hold it ***up.***
It's not fair!
This place was so cool, but now it ***stinks.***
I had to leave my old house, and now I'm gonna have to leave ***this*** one?
It's not ***fair!***
KRAK!

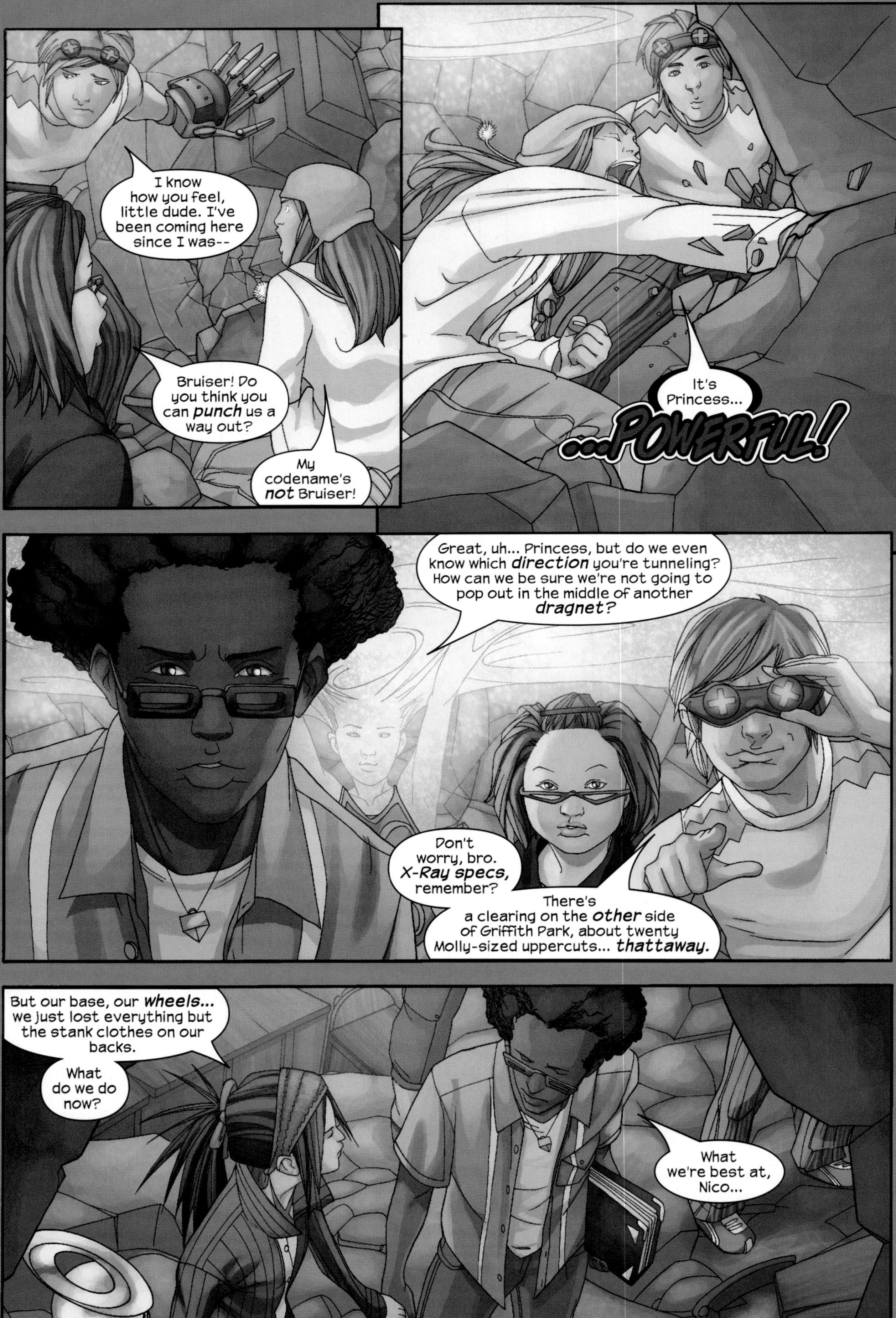
I know how you feel, little dude. I've been coming here since I was--
Bruiser! Do you think you can *punch* us a way out?
My codename's *not* Bruiser!
It's Princess...
...POWERFUL!
Great, uh... Princess, but do we even know which *direction* you're tunneling? How can we be sure we're not going to pop out in the middle of another *dragnet?*
Don't worry, bro. *X-Ray specs,* remember?
There's a clearing on the *other* side of Griffith Park, about twenty Molly-sized uppercuts... *thattaway.*
But our base, our *wheels...* we just lost everything but the stank clothes on our backs.
What do we do now?
What we're best at, Nico...

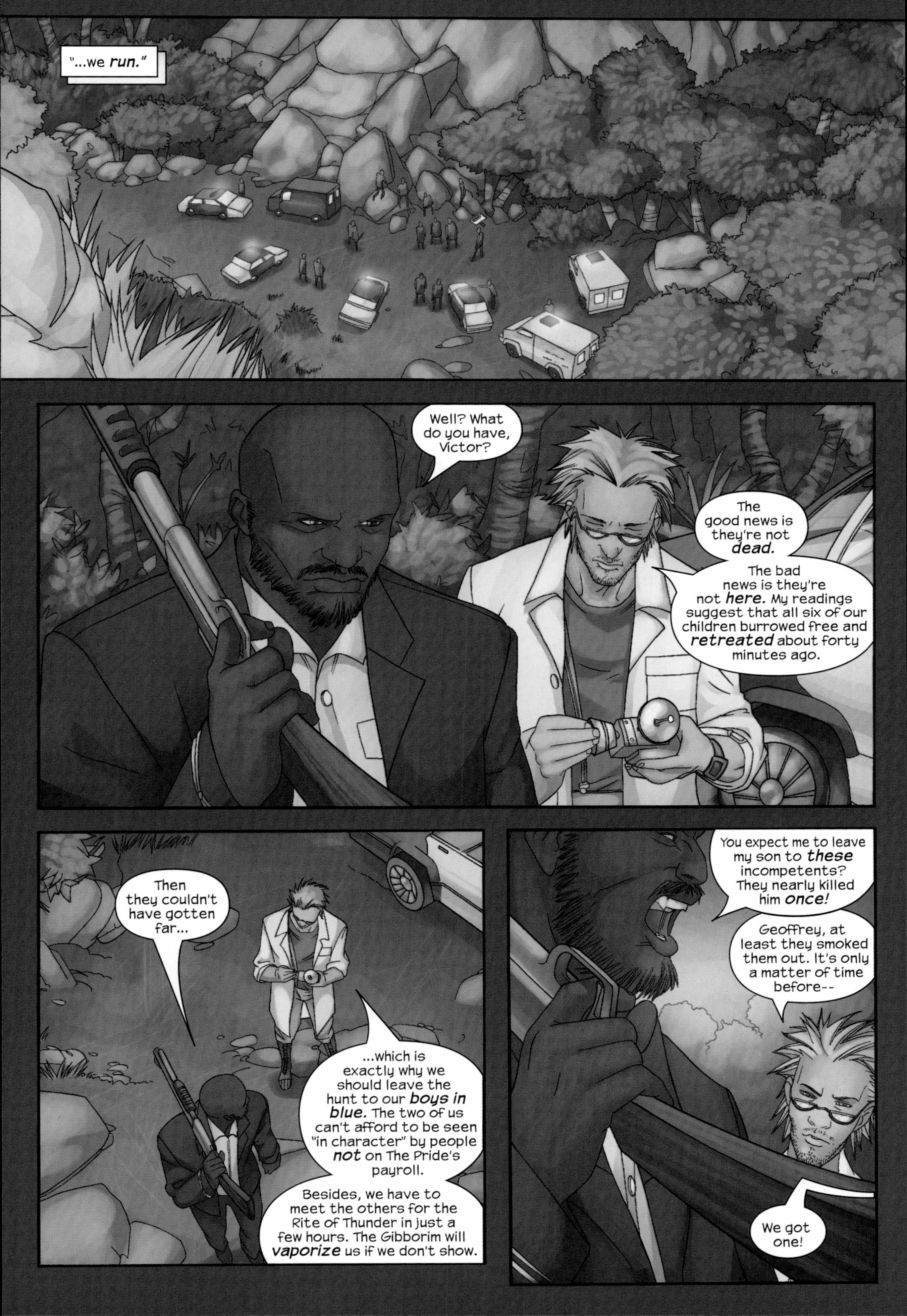
"...we run."
Well? What do you have, Victor?
The good news is they're not dead.
The bad news is they're not here. My readings suggest that all six of our children burrowed free and retreated about forty minutes ago.
Then they couldn't have gotten far...
...which is exactly why we should leave the hunt to our boys in blue. The two of us can't afford to be seen "in character" by people not on The Pride's payroll.
Besides, we have to meet the others for the Rite of Thunder in just a few hours. The Gibborim will vaporize us if we don't show.
You expect me to leave my son to these incompetents? They nearly killed him once!
Geoffrey, at least they smoked them out. It's only a matter of time before--
We got one!

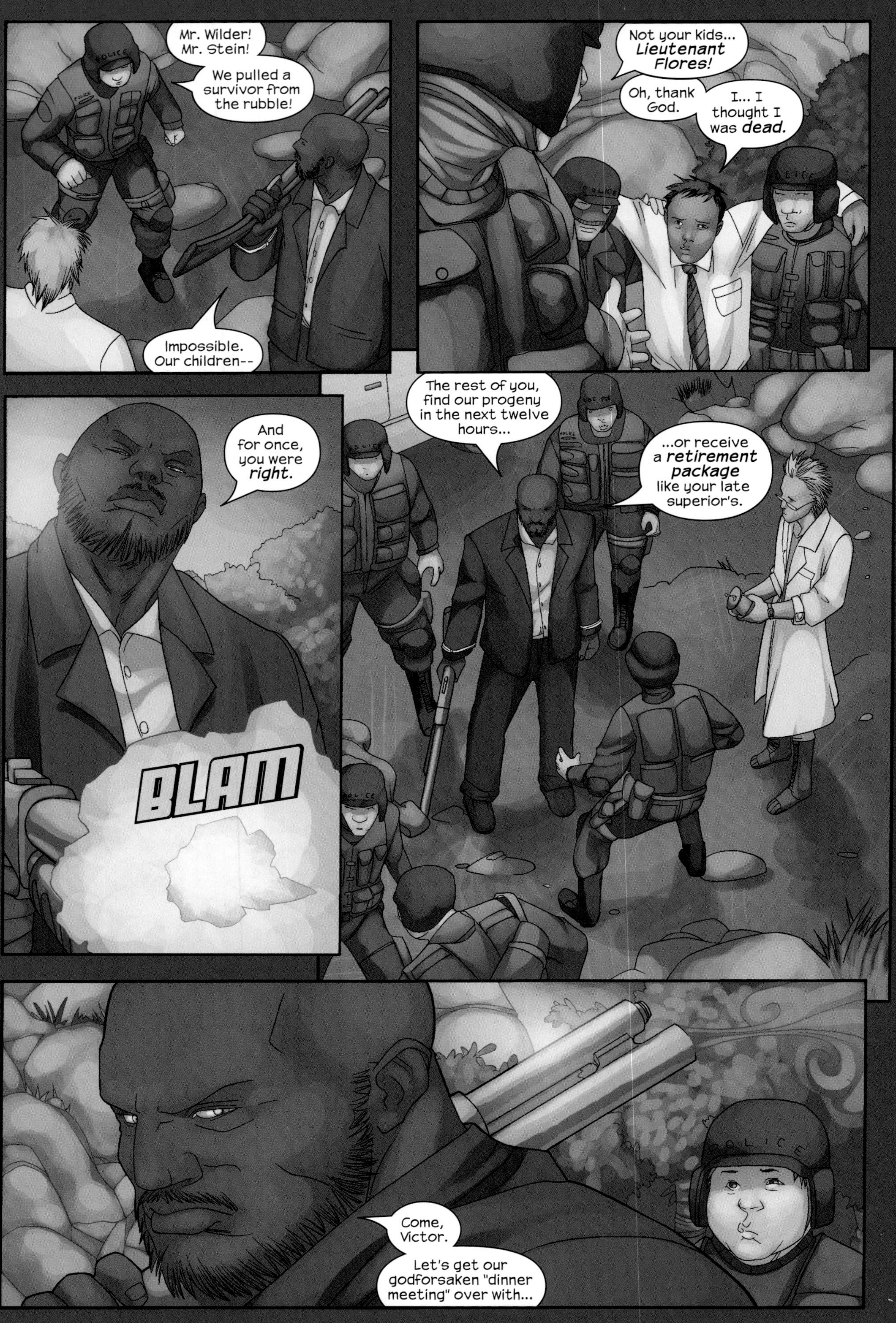
Mr. Wilder! Mr. Stein!
We pulled a survivor from the rubble!
Impossible. Our children--
Not your kids... Lieutenant Flores!
Oh, thank God.
I... I thought I was dead.
And for once, you were right.
BLAM
The rest of you, find our progeny in the next twelve hours...
...or receive a retirement package like your late superior's.
Come, Victor.
Let's get our godforsaken "dinner meeting" over with...

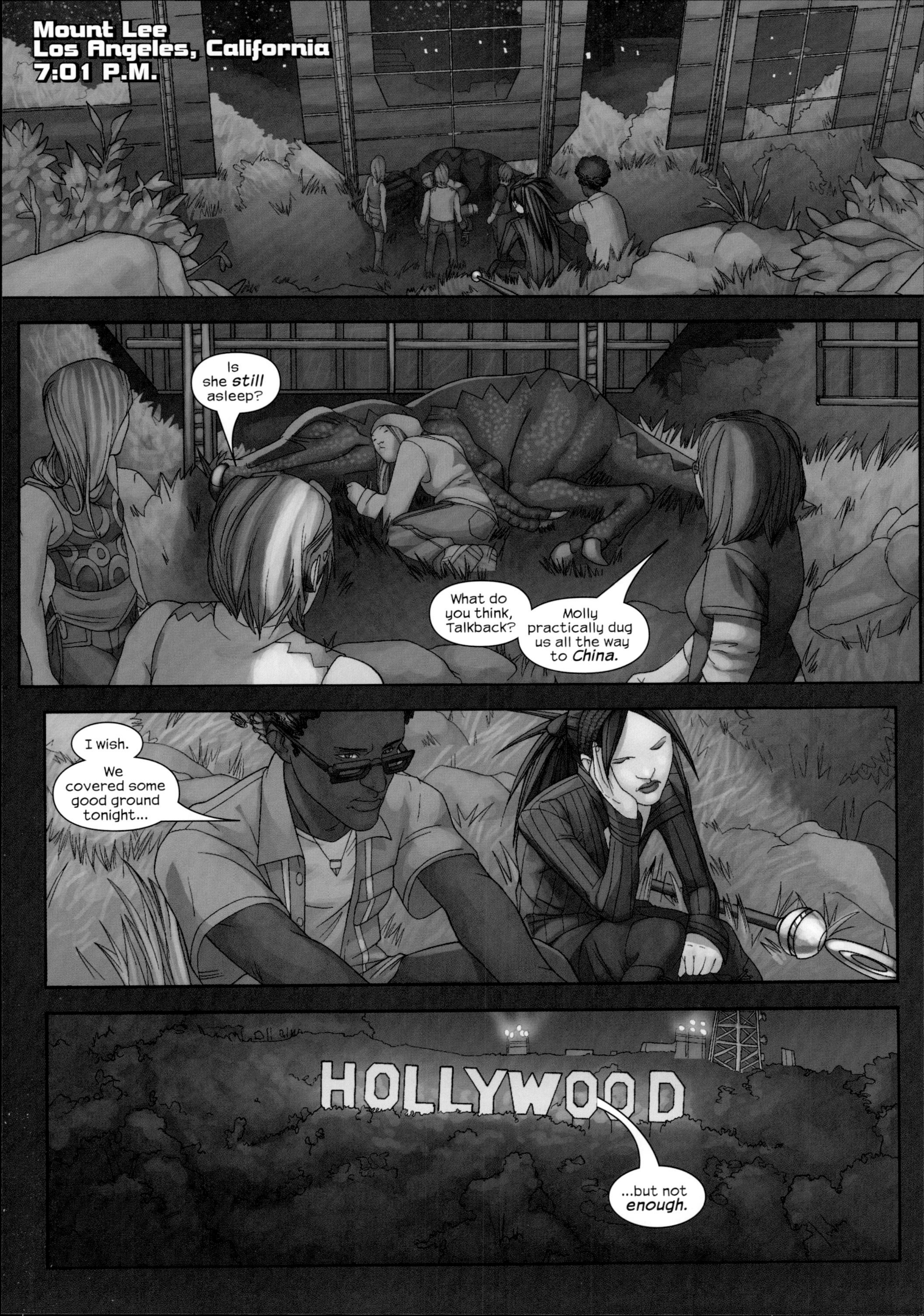
Mount Lee
Los Angeles, California
7:01 P.M.
Is she *still* asleep?
What do you think, Talkback?
Molly practically dug us all the way to *China.*
I wish.
We covered some good ground tonight...
...but not *enough.*

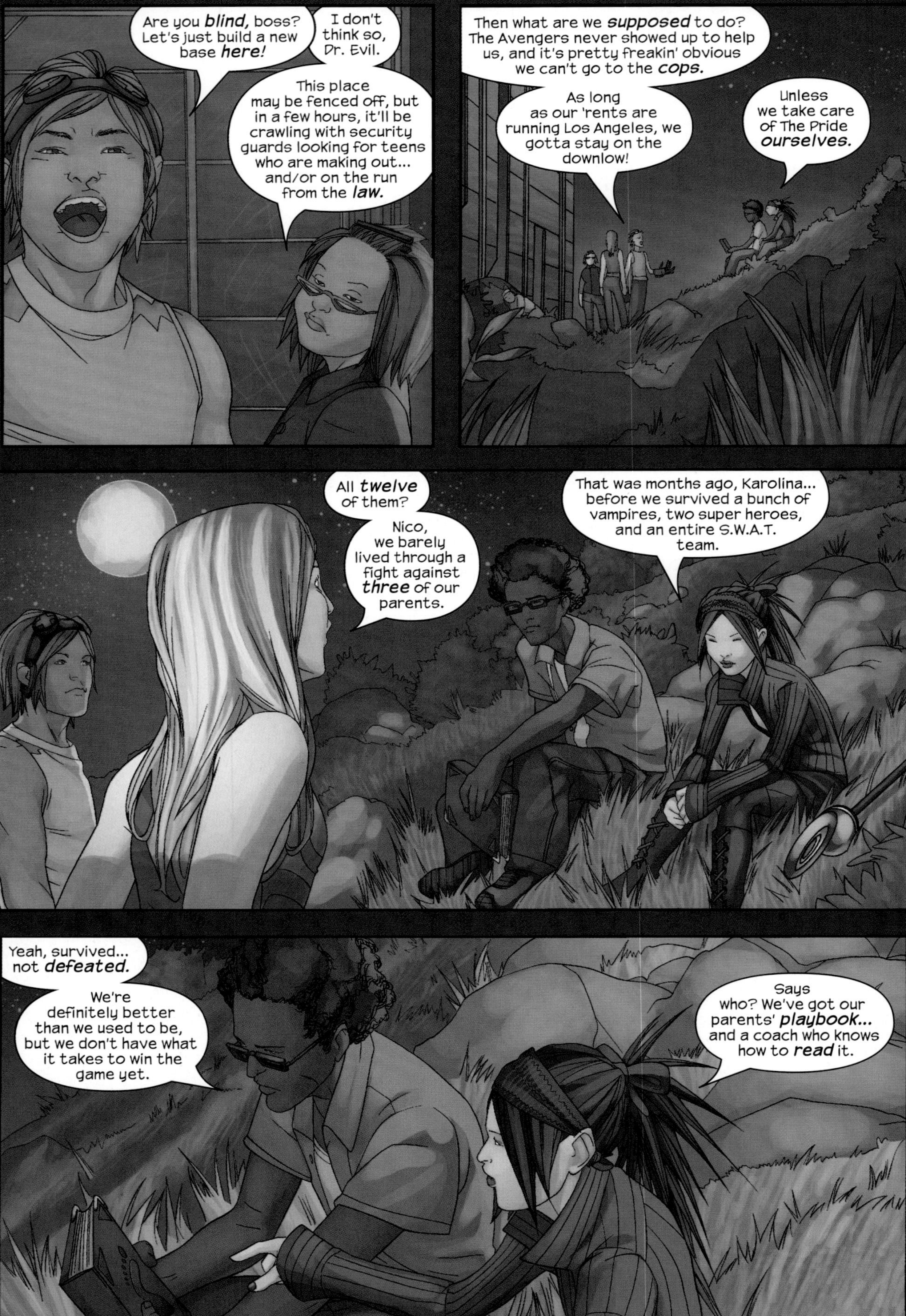
Are you *blind,* boss? Let's just build a new base *here!*
I don't think so, Dr. Evil.
This place may be fenced off, but in a few hours, it'll be crawling with security guards looking for teens who are making out... and/or on the run from the *law.*
Then what are we *supposed* to do? The Avengers never showed up to help us, and it's pretty freakin' obvious we can't go to the *cops.*
As long as our 'rents are running Los Angeles, we gotta stay on the downlow!
Unless we take care of The Pride *ourselves.*
All *twelve* of them?
Nico, we barely lived through a fight against *three* of our parents.
That was months ago, Karolina... before we survived a bunch of vampires, two super heroes, and an entire S.W.A.T. team.
Yeah, survived... not *defeated.*
We're definitely better than we used to be, but we don't have what it takes to win the game yet.
Says who? We've got our parents' *playbook...* and a coach who knows how to *read* it.

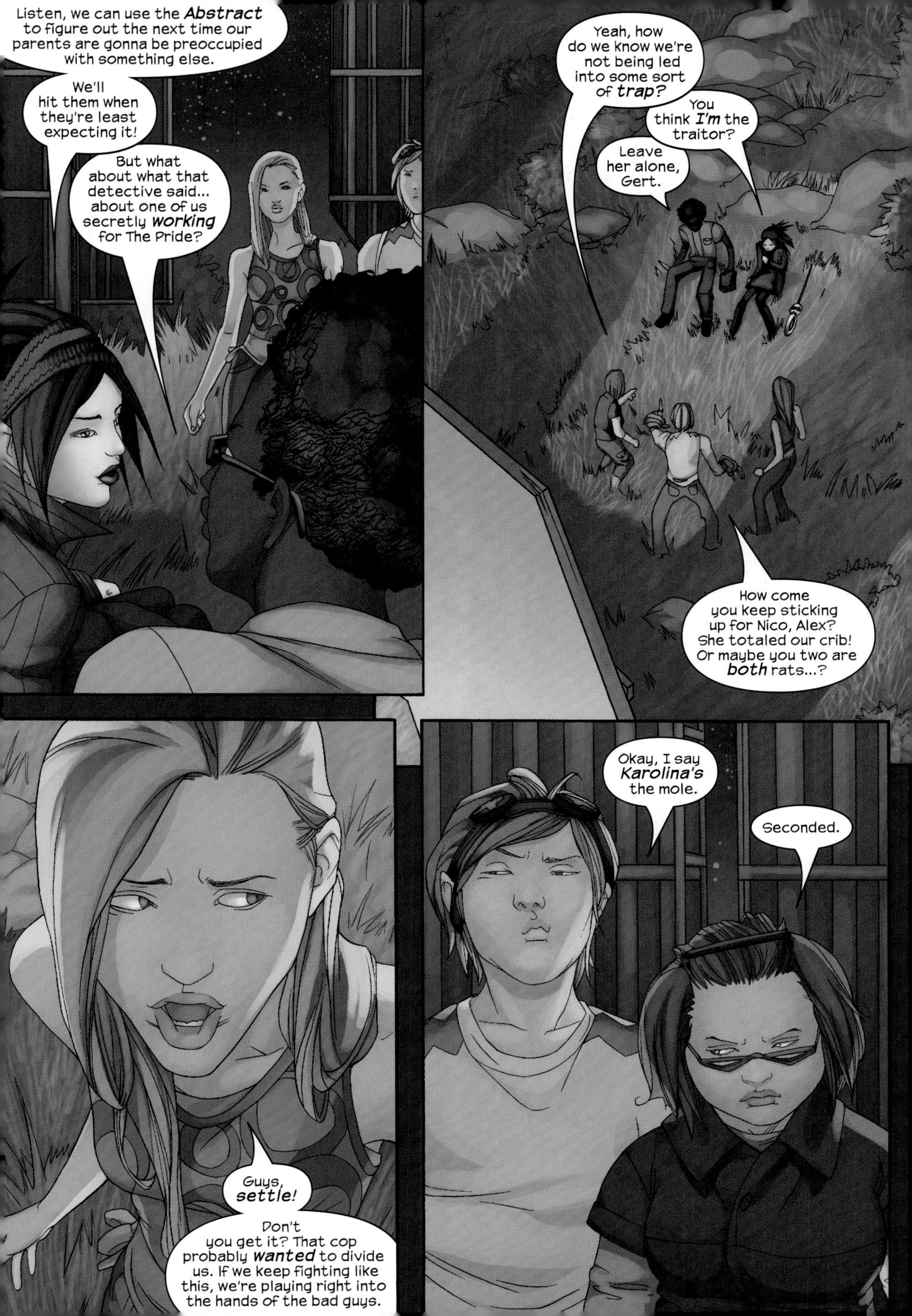
Listen, we can use the ***Abstract*** to figure out the next time our parents are gonna be preoccupied with something else.
We'll hit them when they're least expecting it!
But what about what that detective said... about one of us secretly ***working*** for The Pride?
Yeah, how do we know we're not being led into some sort of ***trap?***
You think ***I'm*** the traitor?
Leave her alone, Gert.
How come you keep sticking up for Nico, Alex? She totaled our crib! Or maybe you two are ***both*** rats...?
Guys, ***settle!***
Don't you get it? That cop probably ***wanted*** to divide us. If we keep fighting like this, we're playing right into the hands of the bad guys.
Okay, I say ***Karolina's*** the mole.
Seconded.

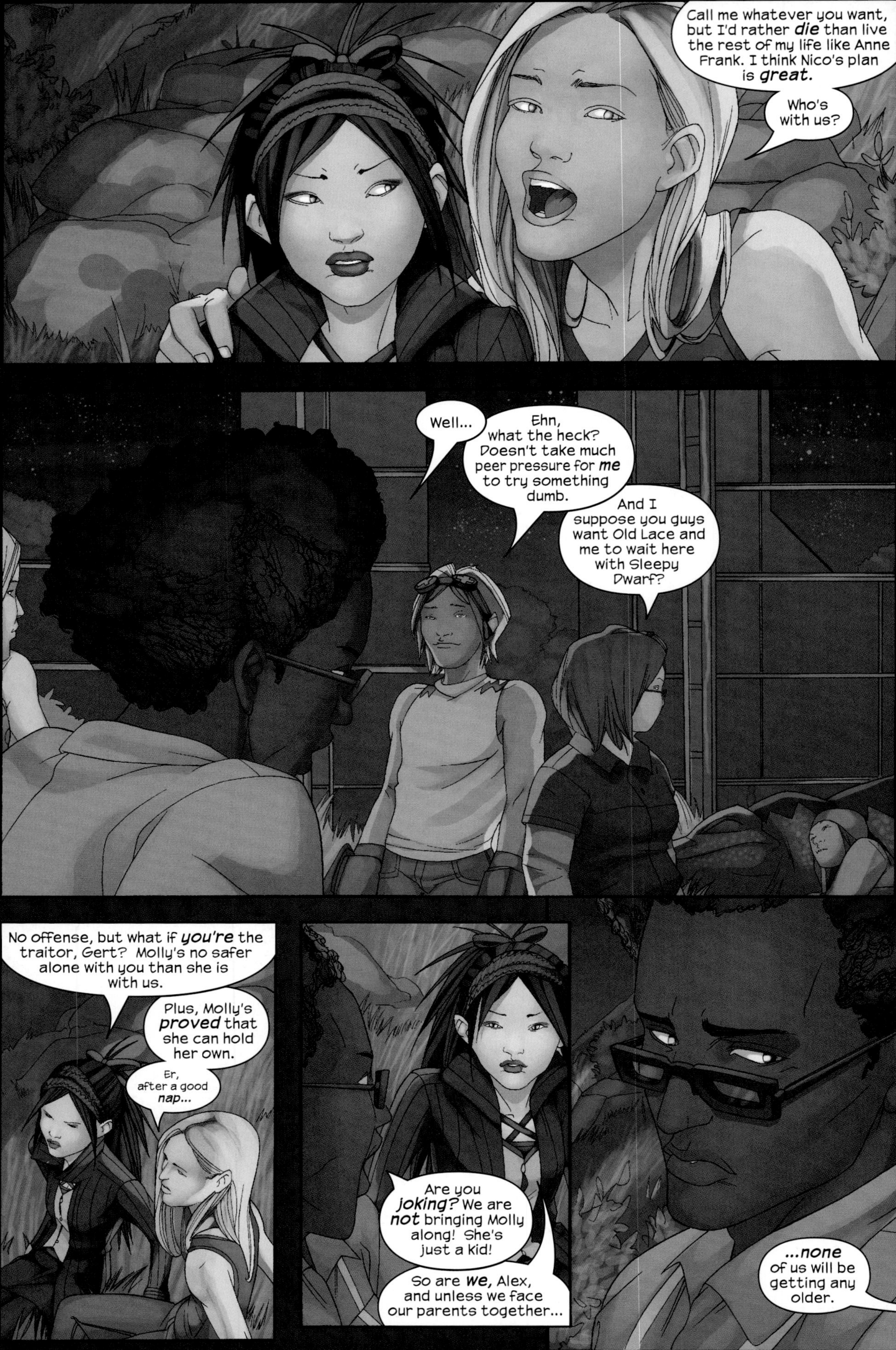
Call me whatever you want, but I'd rather die than live the rest of my life like Anne Frank. I think Nico's plan is great.
Who's with us?
Well...
Ehn, what the heck? Doesn't take much peer pressure for me to try something dumb.
And I suppose you guys want Old Lace and me to wait here with Sleepy Dwarf?
No offense, but what if you're the traitor, Gert? Molly's no safer alone with you than she is with us.
Plus, Molly's proved that she can hold her own.
Er, after a good nap...
Are you joking? We are not bringing Molly along! She's just a kid!
So are we, Alex, and unless we face our parents together...
...none of us will be getting any older.

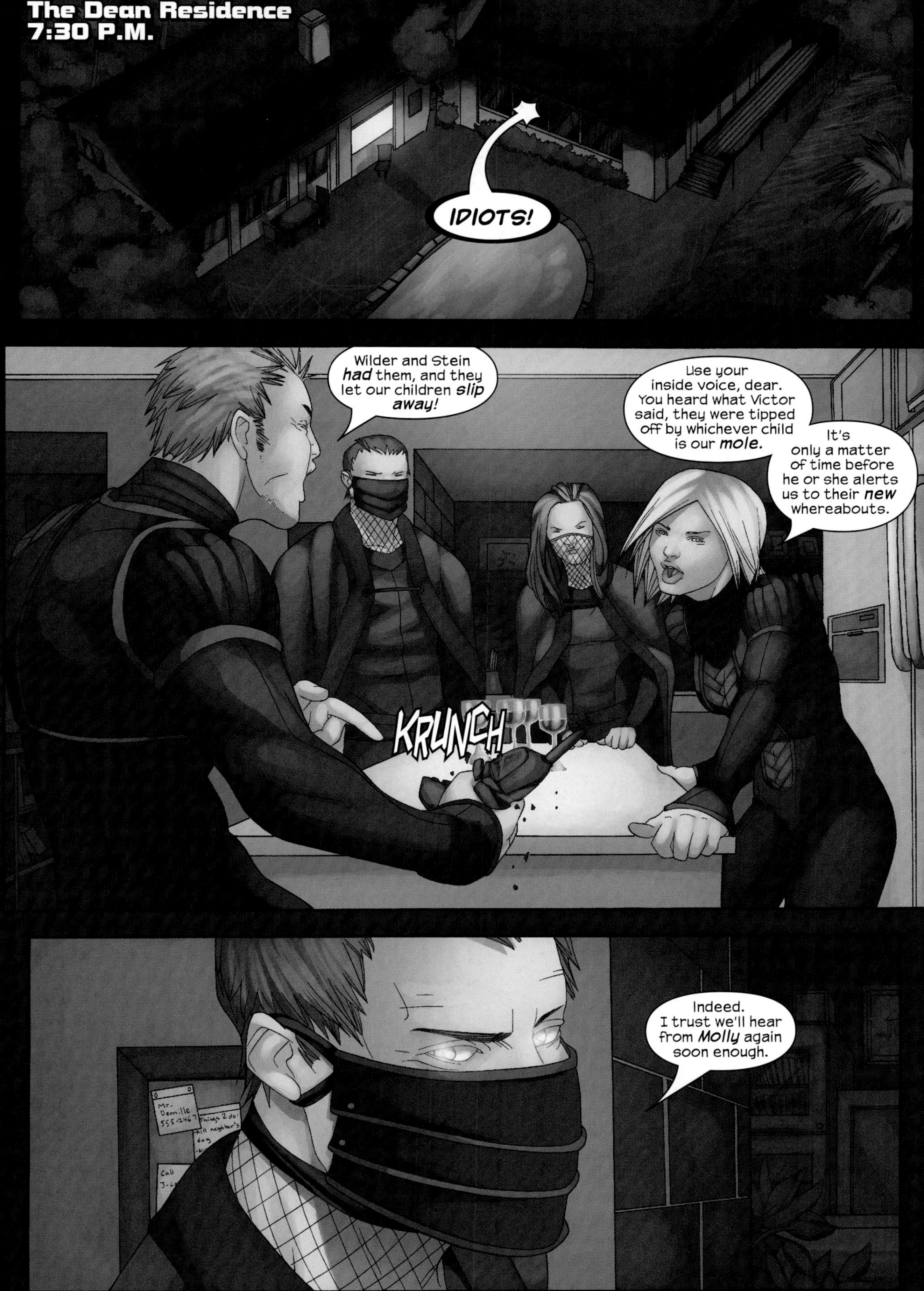
The Dean Residence
7:30 P.M.
IDIOTS!
Wilder and Stein had them, and they let our children slip away!
Use your inside voice, dear. You heard what Victor said, they were tipped off by whichever child is our mole.
It's only a matter of time before he or she alerts us to their new whereabouts.
KRUNCH
Indeed. I trust we'll hear from Molly again soon enough.

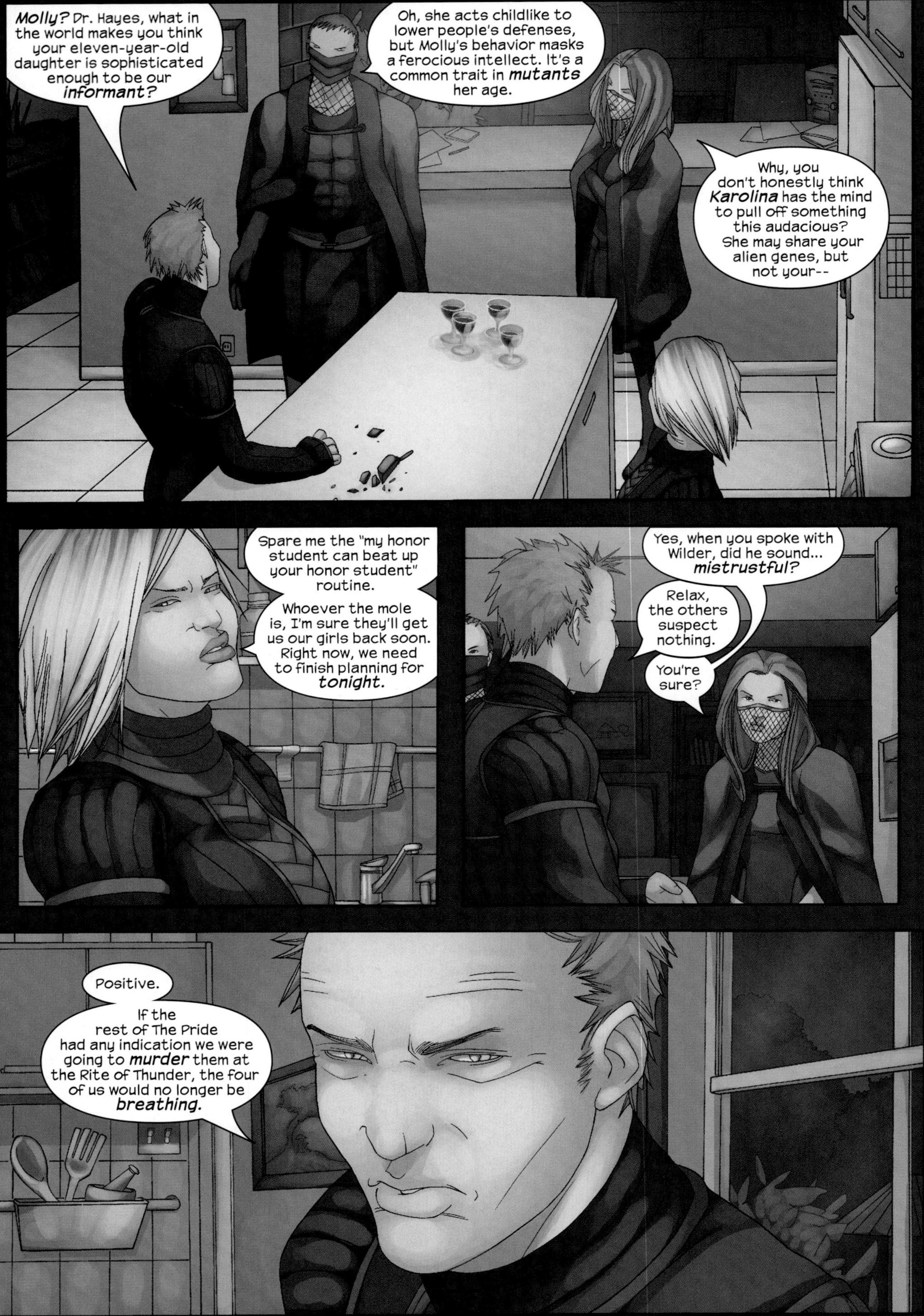
Molly? Dr. Hayes, what in the world makes you think your eleven-year-old daughter is sophisticated enough to be our informant?
Oh, she acts childlike to lower people's defenses, but Molly's behavior masks a ferocious intellect. It's a common trait in mutants her age.
Why, you don't honestly think Karolina has the mind to pull off something this audacious? She may share your alien genes, but not your--
Spare me the "my honor student can beat up your honor student" routine.
Whoever the mole is, I'm sure they'll get us our girls back soon. Right now, we need to finish planning for tonight.
Yes, when you spoke with Wilder, did he sound... mistrustful?
Relax, the others suspect nothing.
You're sure?
Positive.
If the rest of The Pride had any indication we were going to murder them at the Rite of Thunder, the four of us would no longer be breathing.

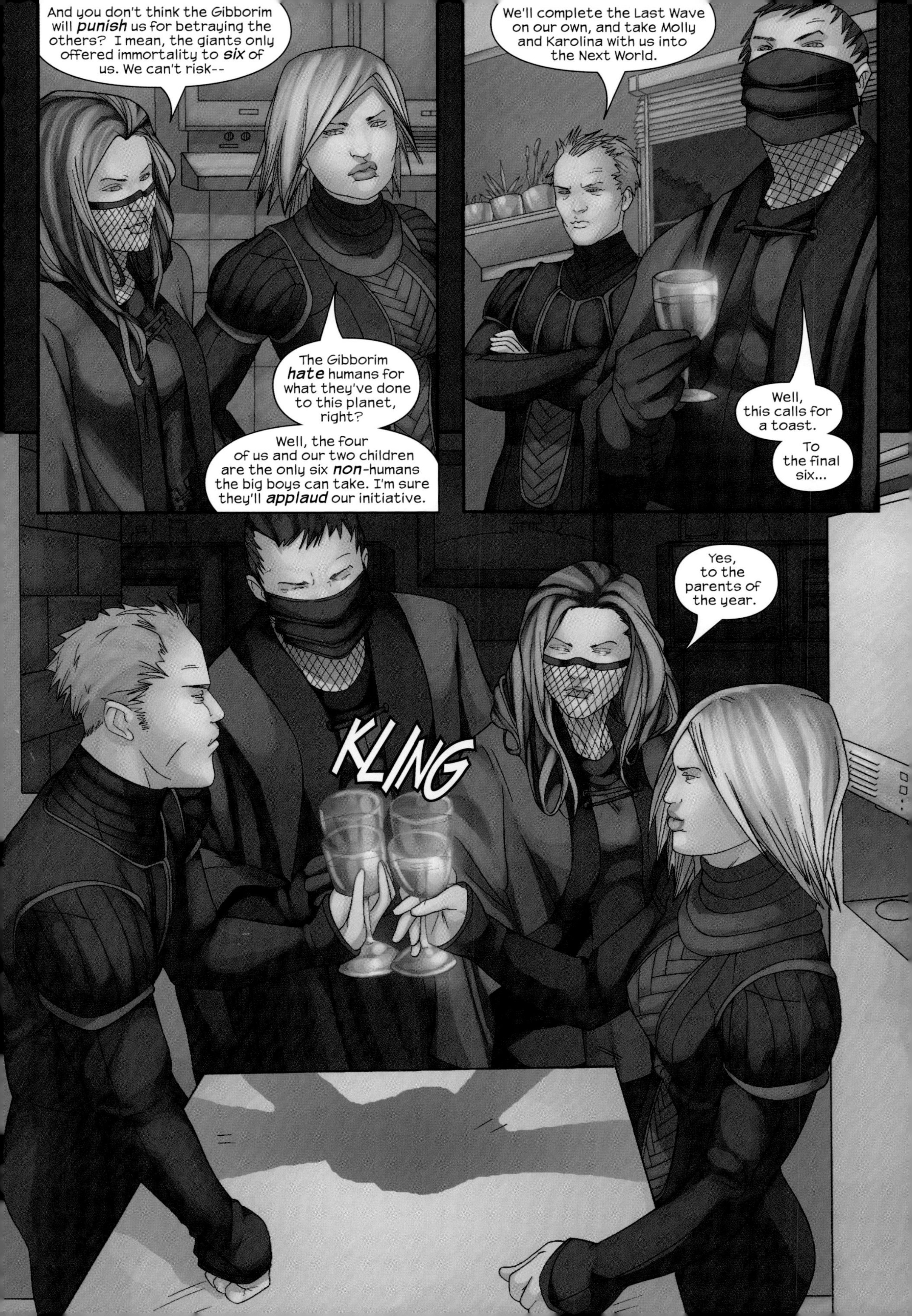

And you don't think the Gibborim will *punish* us for betraying the others? I mean, the giants only offered immortality to *six* of us. We can't risk--
The Gibborim *hate* humans for what they've done to this planet, right?
Well, the four of us and our two children are the only six *non*-humans the big boys can take. I'm sure they'll *applaud* our initiative.
We'll complete the Last Wave on our own, and take Molly and Karolina with us into the Next World.
Well, this calls for a toast.
To the final six...
Yes, to the parents of the year.
KLING

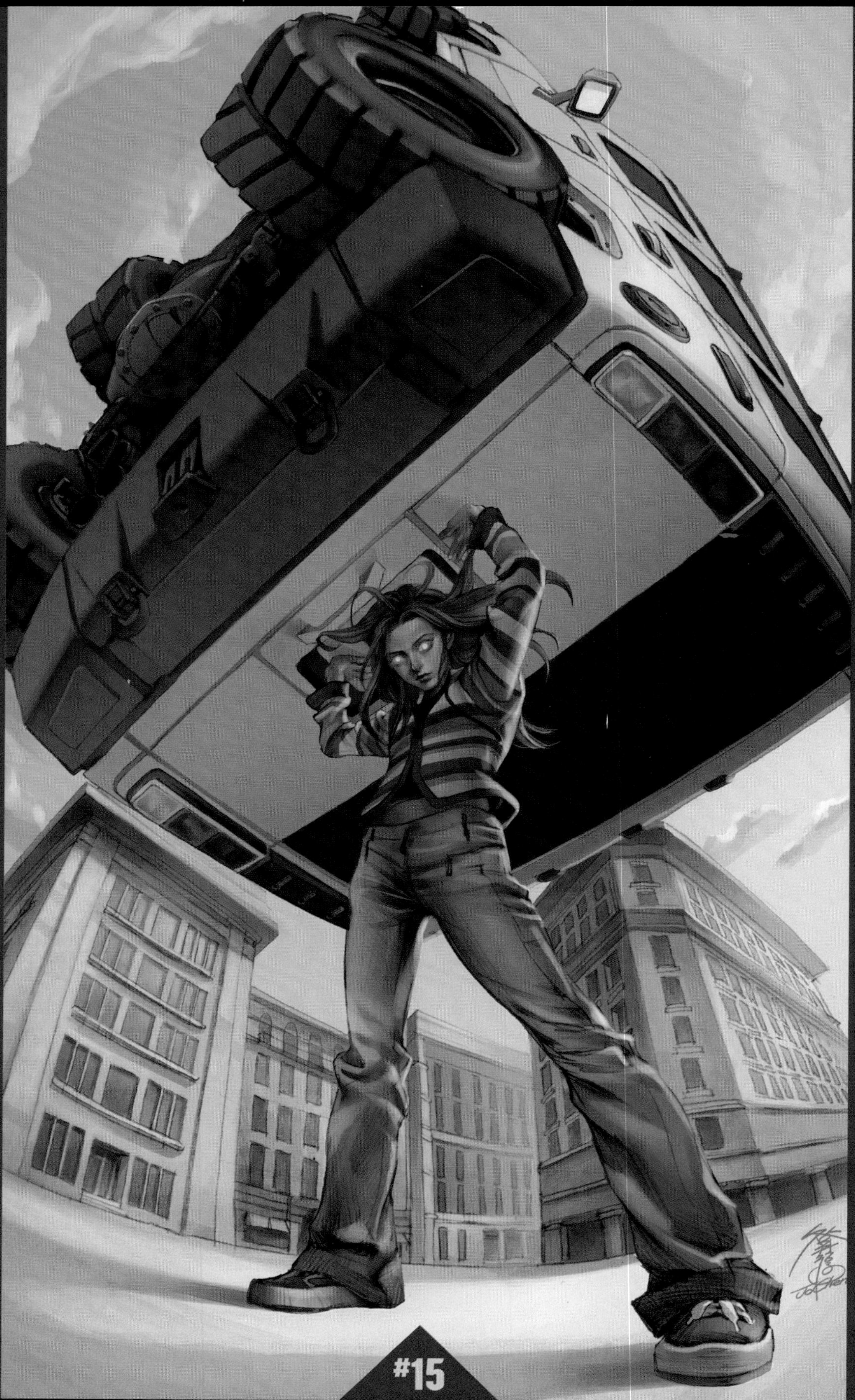
#15

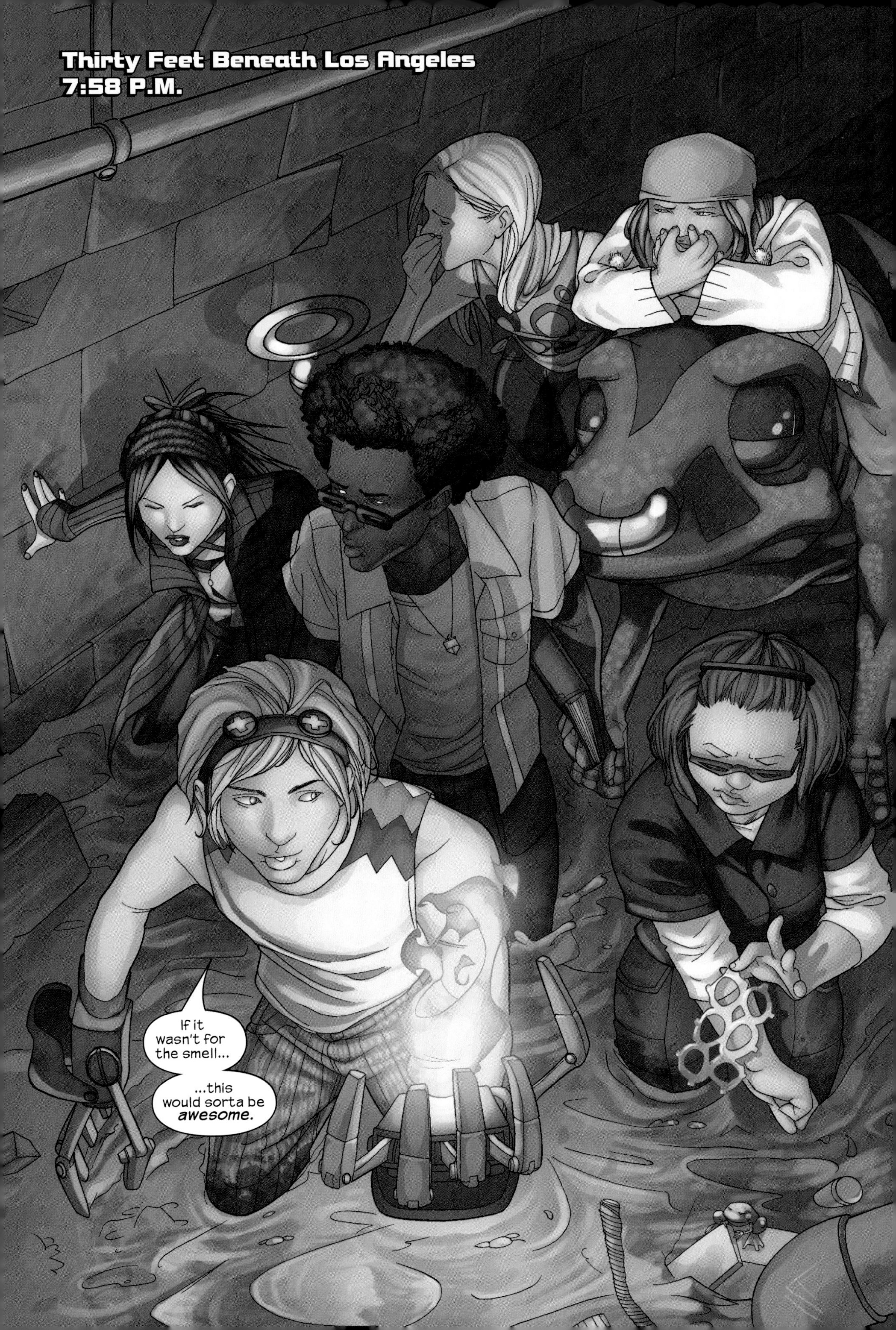
Thirty Feet Beneath Los Angeles
7:58 P.M.
If it wasn't for the smell...
...this would sorta be *awesome.*

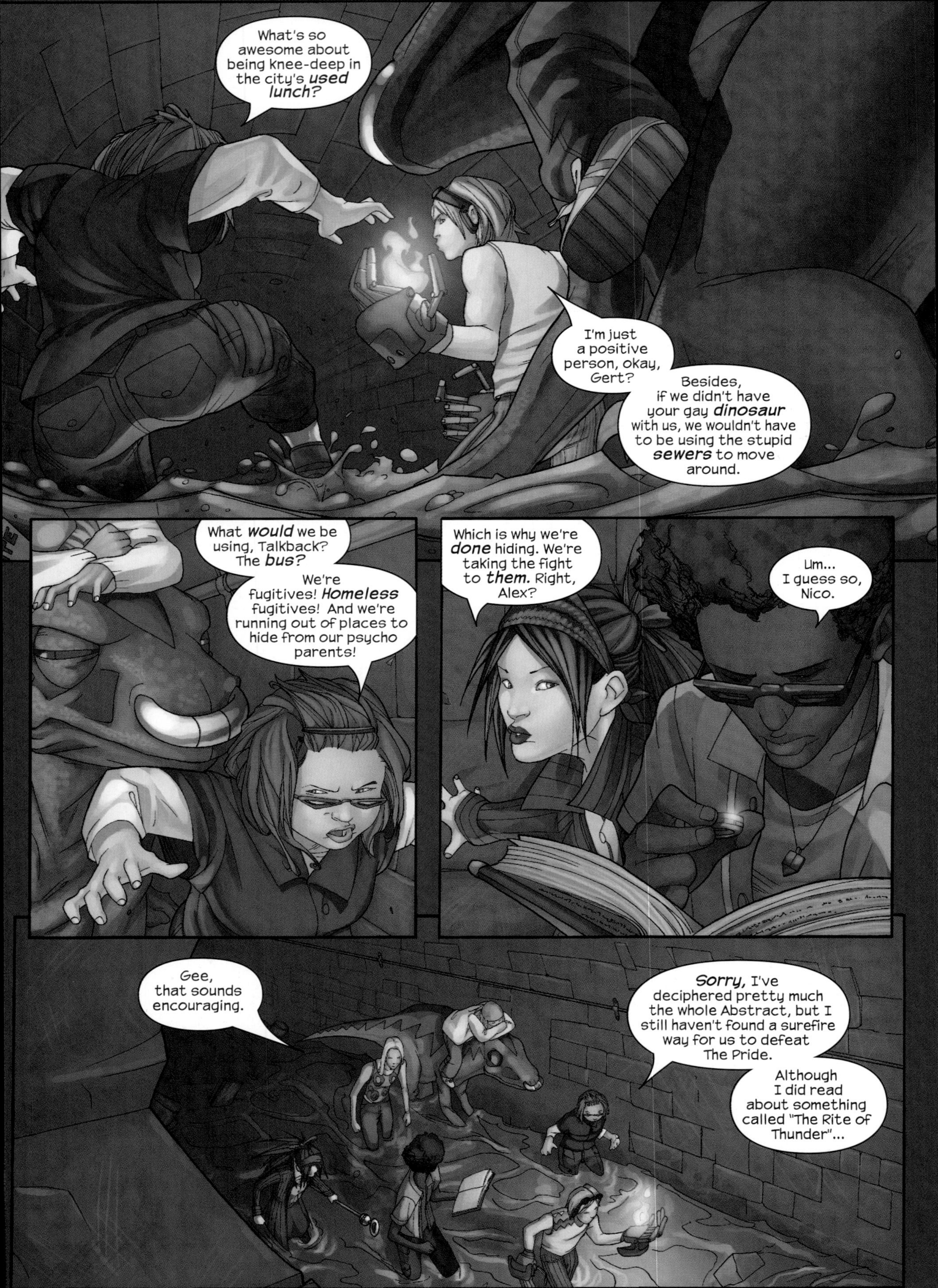
What's so awesome about being knee-deep in the city's *used lunch*?
I'm just a positive person, okay, Gert?
Besides, if we didn't have your gay *dinosaur* with us, we wouldn't have to be using the stupid *sewers* to move around.
What *would* we be using, Talkback? The *bus?*
We're fugitives! *Homeless* fugitives! And we're running out of places to hide from our psycho parents!
Which is why we're *done* hiding. We're taking the fight to *them.* Right, Alex?
Um... I guess so, Nico.
Gee, that sounds encouraging.
Sorry, I've deciphered pretty much the whole Abstract, but I still haven't found a surefire way for us to defeat The Pride.
Although I did read about something called "The Rite of Thunder"...

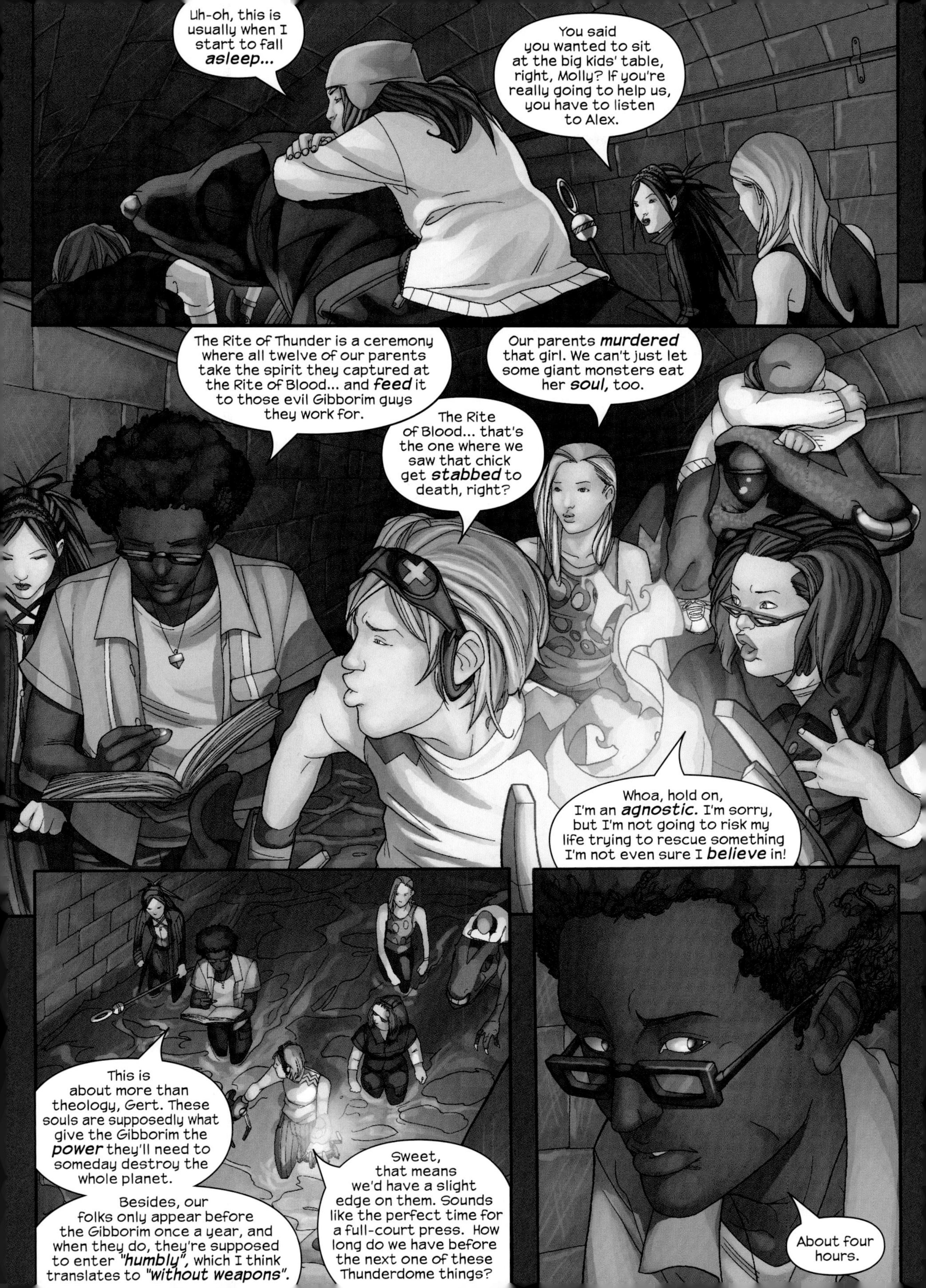
Uh-oh, this is usually when I start to fall asleep...
You said you wanted to sit at the big kids' table, right, Molly? If you're really going to help us, you have to listen to Alex.
The Rite of Thunder is a ceremony where all twelve of our parents take the spirit they captured at the Rite of Blood... and feed it to those evil Gibborim guys they work for.
Our parents murdered that girl. We can't just let some giant monsters eat her soul, too.
The Rite of Blood... that's the one where we saw that chick get stabbed to death, right?
Whoa, hold on, I'm an agnostic. I'm sorry, but I'm not going to risk my life trying to rescue something I'm not even sure I believe in!
This is about more than theology, Gert. These souls are supposedly what give the Gibborim the power they'll need to someday destroy the whole planet.
Besides, our folks only appear before the Gibborim once a year, and when they do, they're supposed to enter "humbly", which I think translates to "without weapons".
Sweet, that means we'd have a slight edge on them. Sounds like the perfect time for a full-court press. How long do we have before the next one of these Thunderdome things?
About four hours.

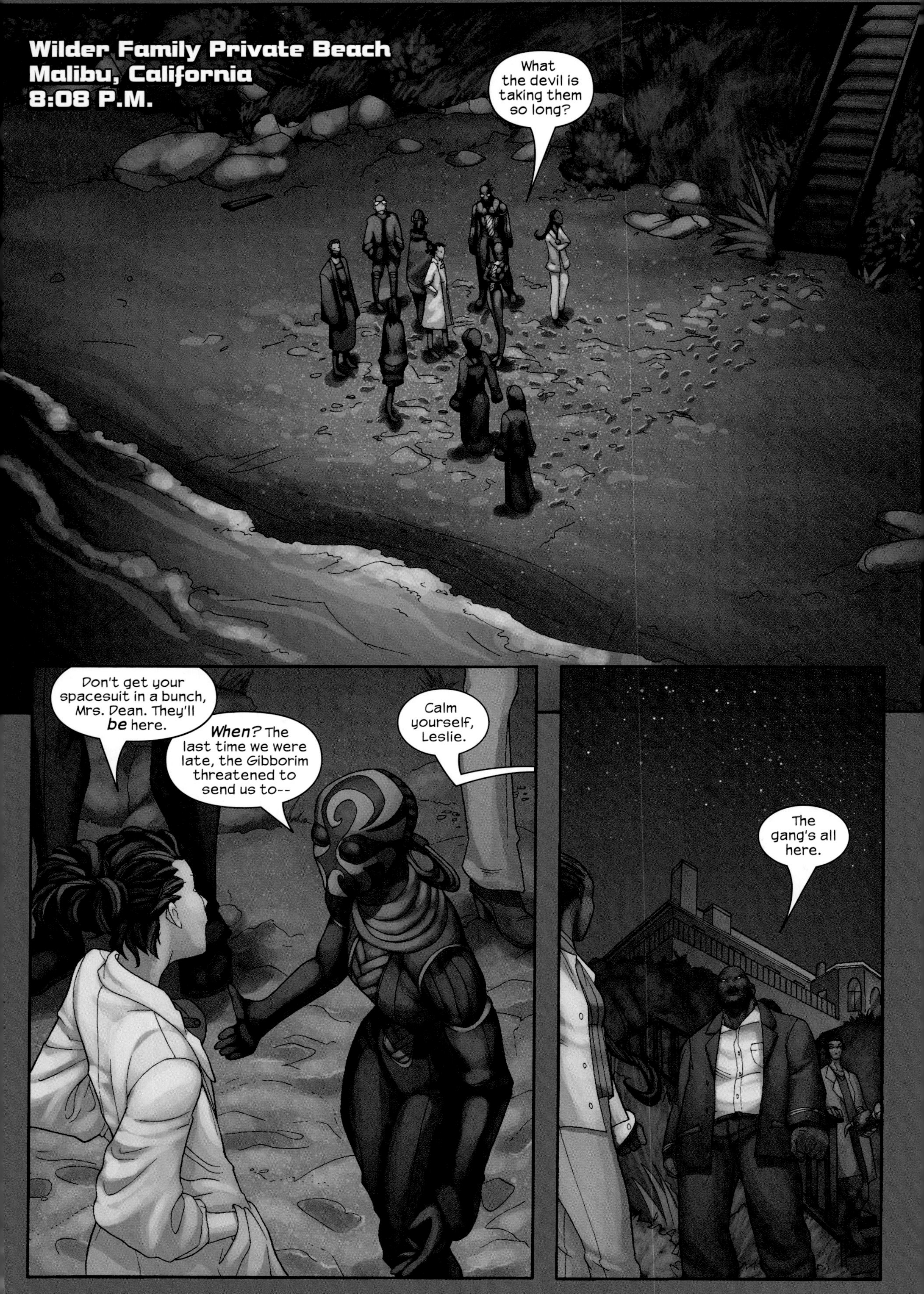
Wilder Family Private Beach
Malibu, California
8:08 P.M.
What the devil is taking them so long?
Don't get your spacesuit in a bunch, Mrs. Dean. They'll *be* here.
When? The last time we were late, the Gibborim threatened to send us to--
Calm yourself, Leslie.
The gang's all here.

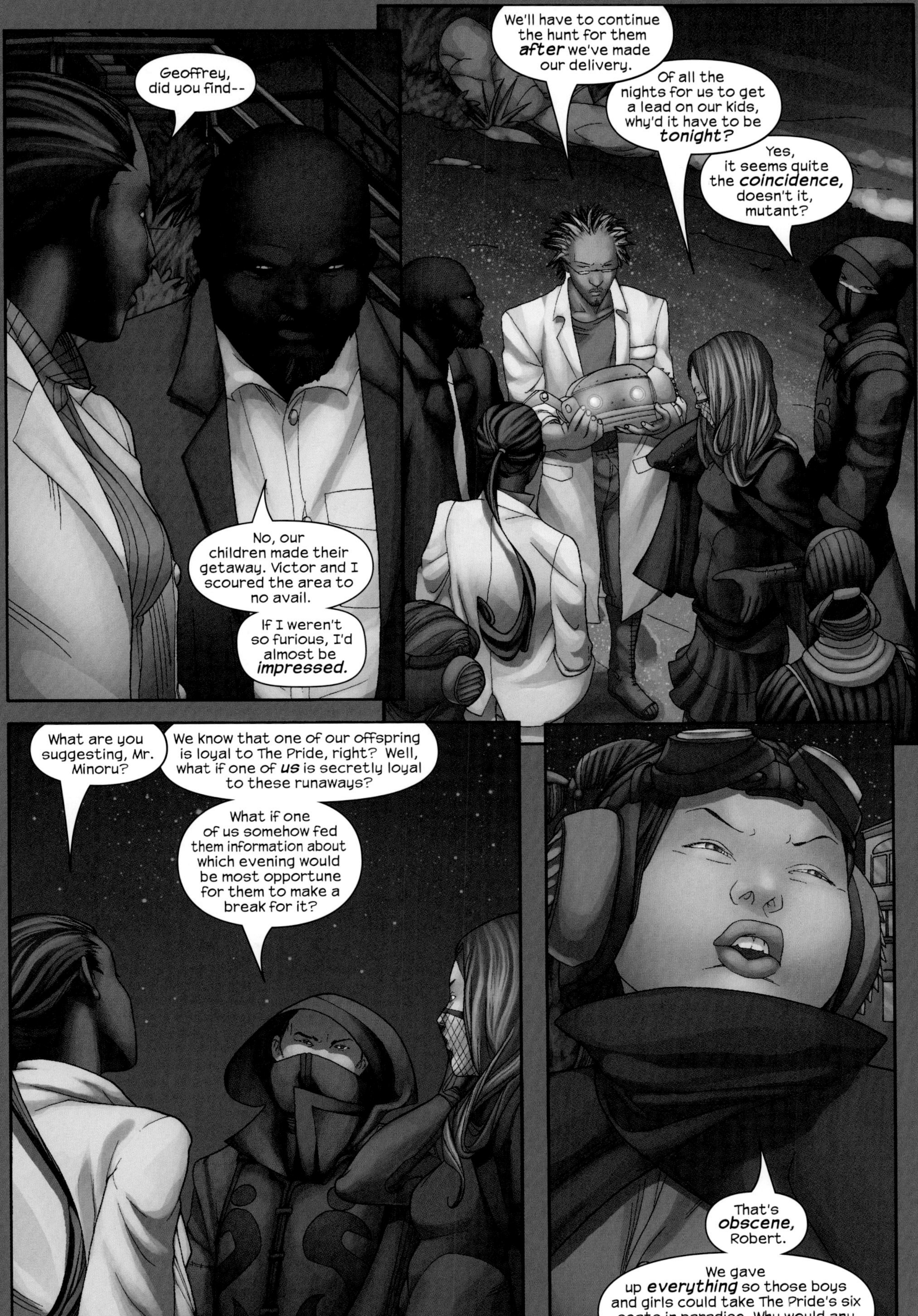
Geoffrey, did you find--
No, our children made their getaway. Victor and I scoured the area to no avail.
If I weren't so furious, I'd almost be impressed.
We'll have to continue the hunt for them after we've made our delivery.
Of all the nights for us to get a lead on our kids, why'd it have to be tonight?
Yes, it seems quite the coincidence, doesn't it, mutant?
What are you suggesting, Mr. Minoru?
We know that one of our offspring is loyal to The Pride, right? Well, what if one of us is secretly loyal to these runaways?
What if one of us somehow fed them information about which evening would be most opportune for them to make a break for it?
That's obscene, Robert.
We gave up everything so those boys and girls could take The Pride's six seats in paradise. Why would any of us help them escape that?

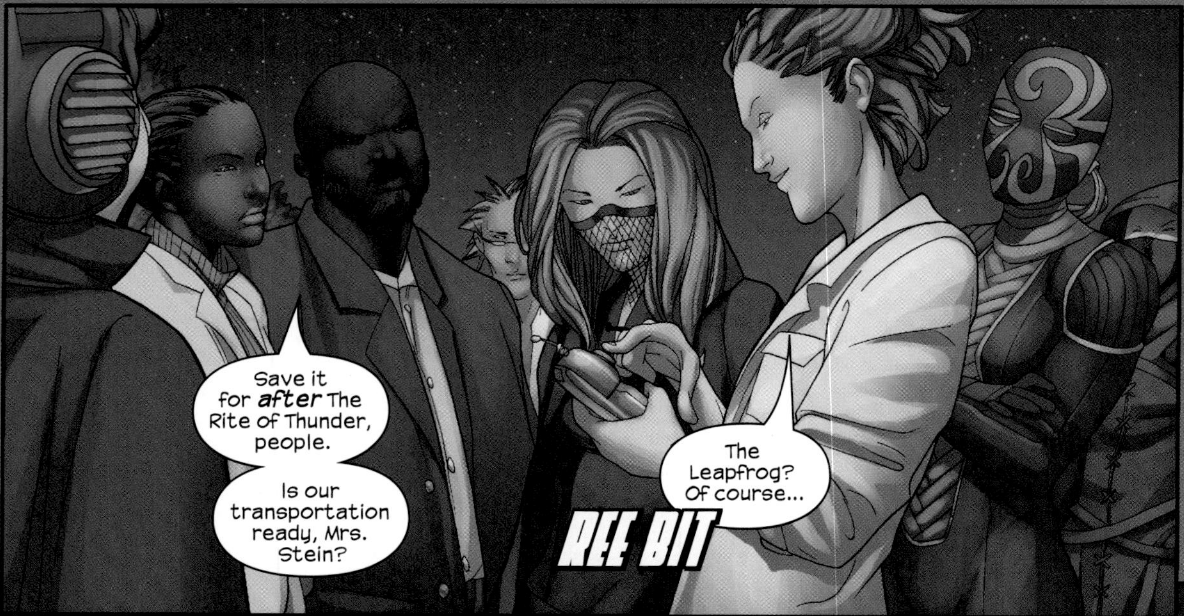
Save it for after The Rite of Thunder, people.
Is our transportation ready, Mrs. Stein?
REE BIT
The Leapfrog? Of course...

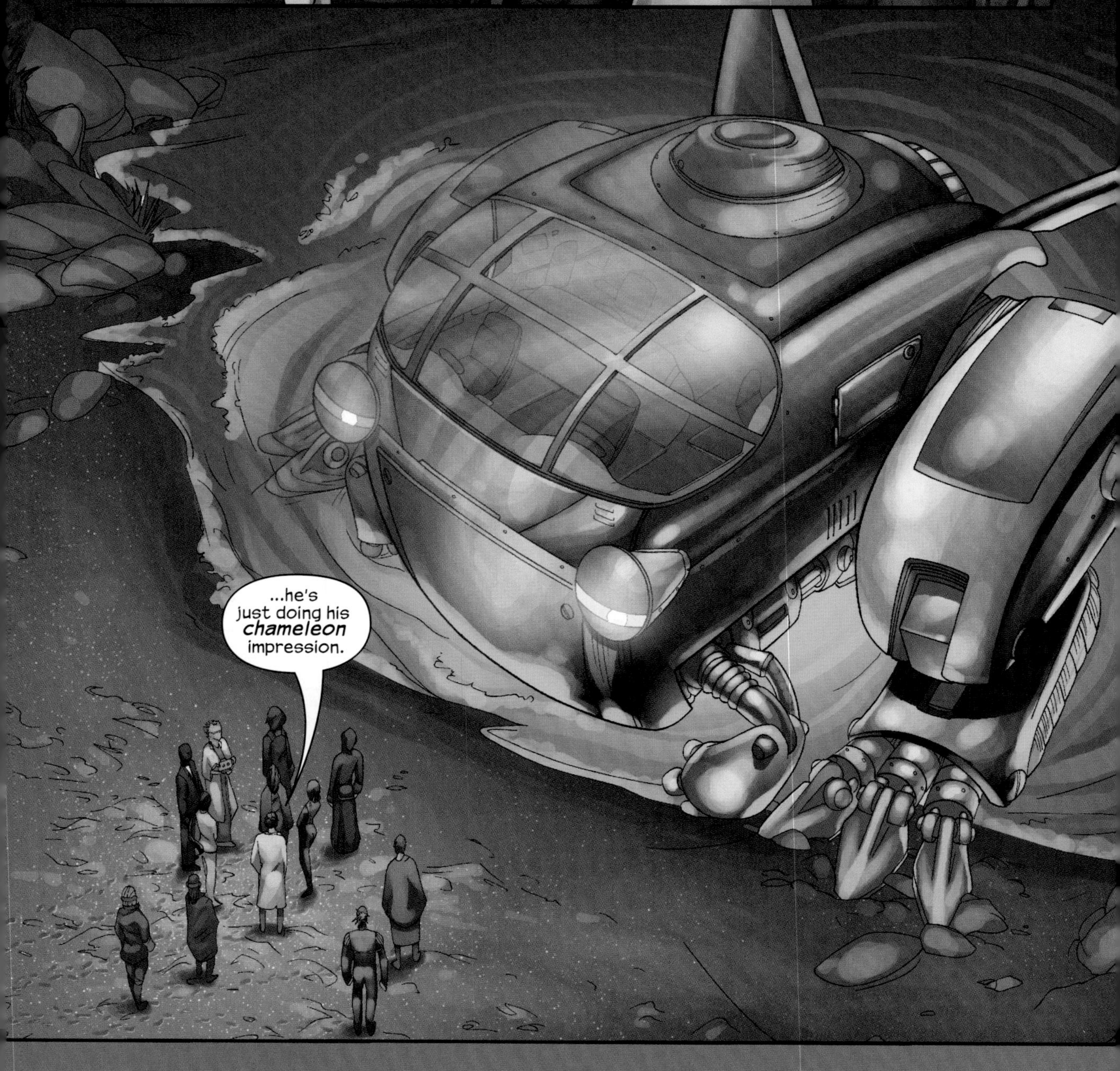
...he's just doing his chameleon impression.

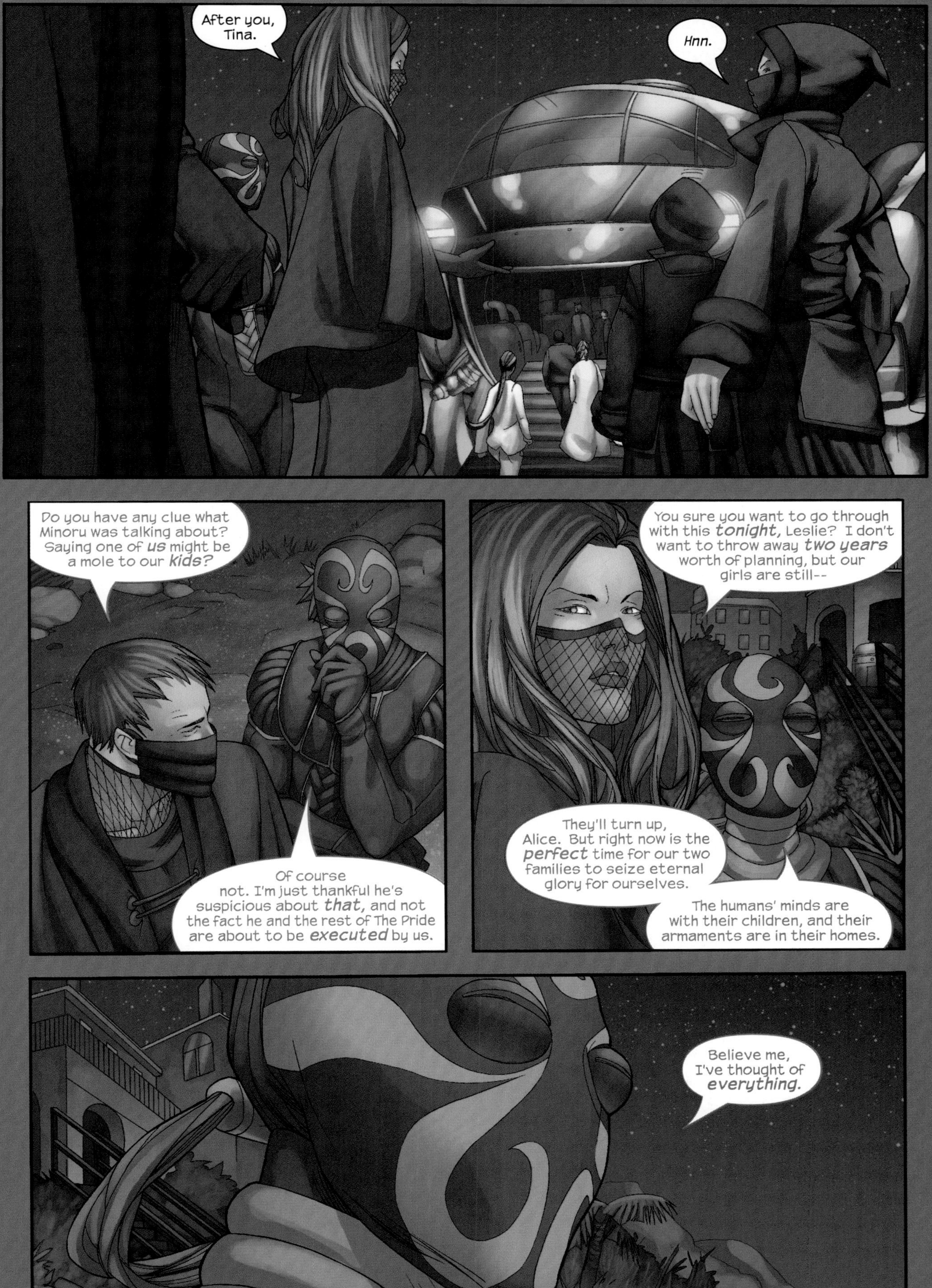
After you, Tina.
Hnn.
Do you have any clue what Minoru was talking about? Saying one of *us* might be a mole to our *kids?*
Of course not. I'm just thankful he's suspicious about *that,* and not the fact he and the rest of The Pride are about to be *executed* by us.
You sure you want to go through with this *tonight,* Leslie? I don't want to throw away *two years* worth of planning, but our girls are still--
They'll turn up, Alice. But right now is the *perfect* time for our two families to seize eternal glory for ourselves.
The humans' minds are with their children, and their armaments are in their homes.
Believe me, I've thought of *everything.*

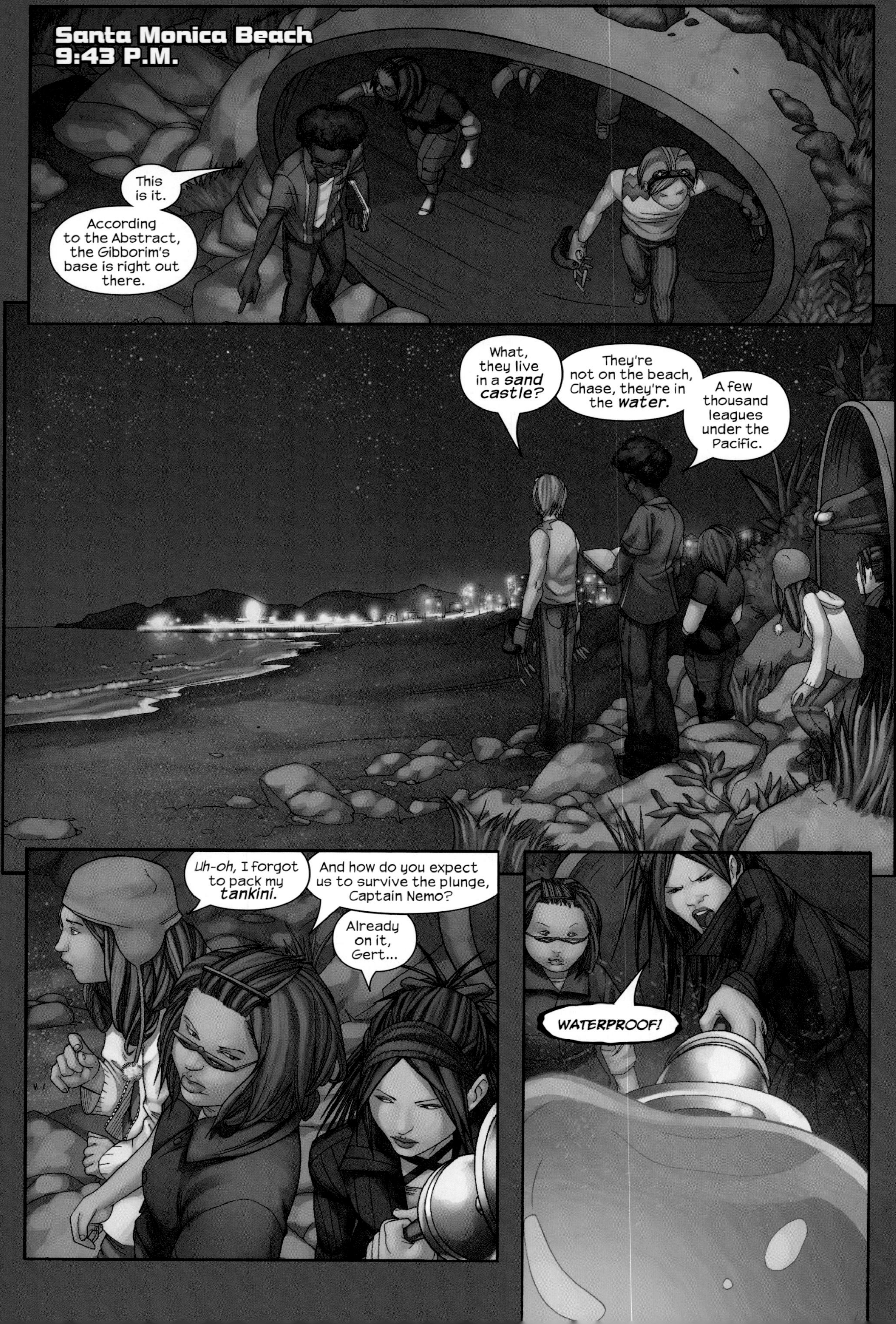
Santa Monica Beach
9:43 P.M.
This is it.
According to the Abstract, the Gibborim's base is right out there.
What, they live in a *sand castle*?
They're not on the beach, Chase, they're in the *water*.
A few thousand leagues under the Pacific.
Uh-oh, I forgot to pack my *tankini.*
And how do you expect us to survive the plunge, Captain Nemo?
Already on it, Gert...
WATERPROOF!

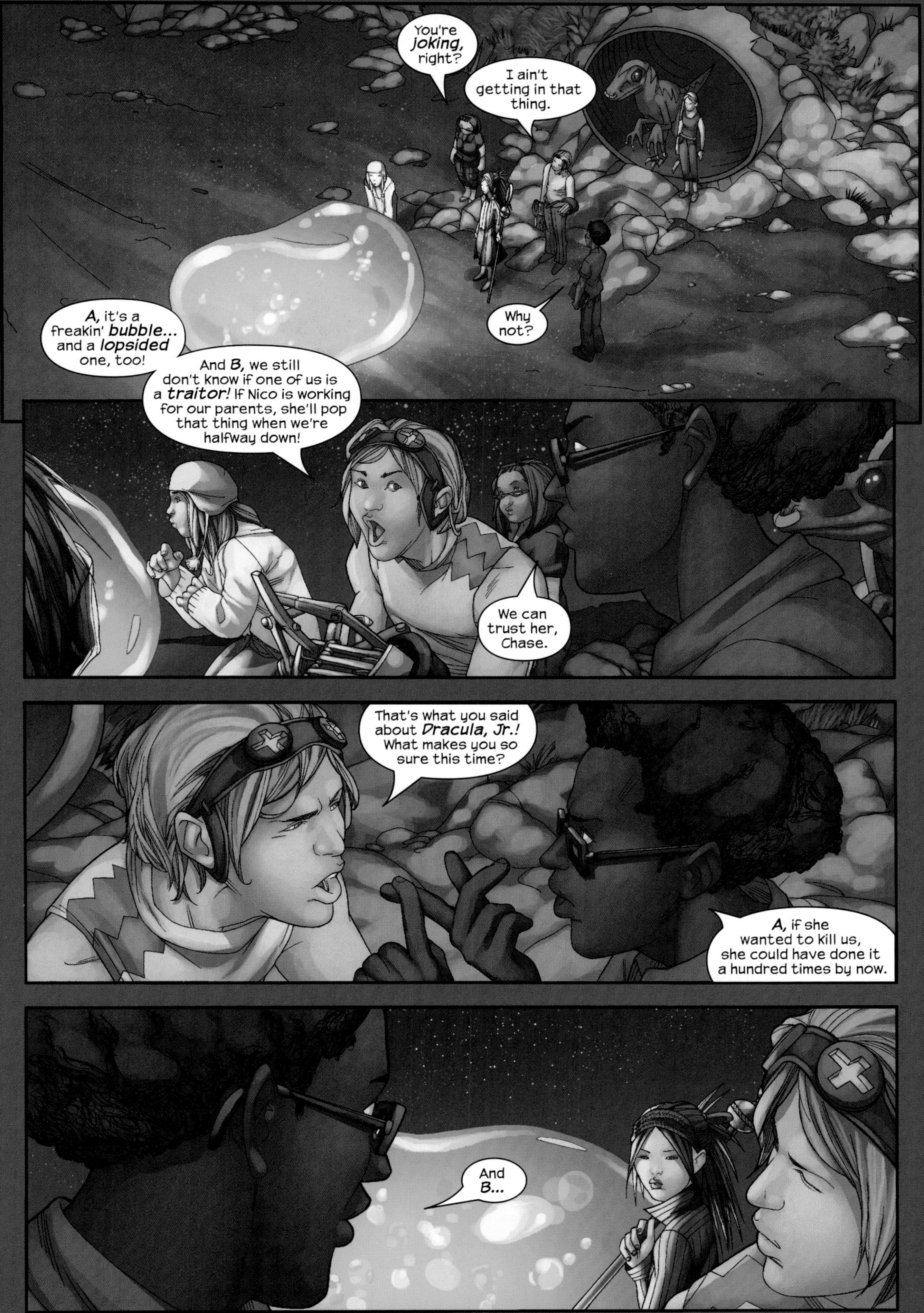
You're *joking,* right?
I ain't getting in that thing.
Why not?
A, it's a freakin' *bubble...* and a *lopsided* one, too!
And *B,* we still don't know if one of us is a *traitor!* If Nico is working for our parents, she'll pop that thing when we're halfway down!
We can trust her, Chase.
That's what you said about *Dracula, Jr.!* What makes you so sure this time?
A, if she wanted to kill us, she could have done it a hundred times by now.
And *B...*

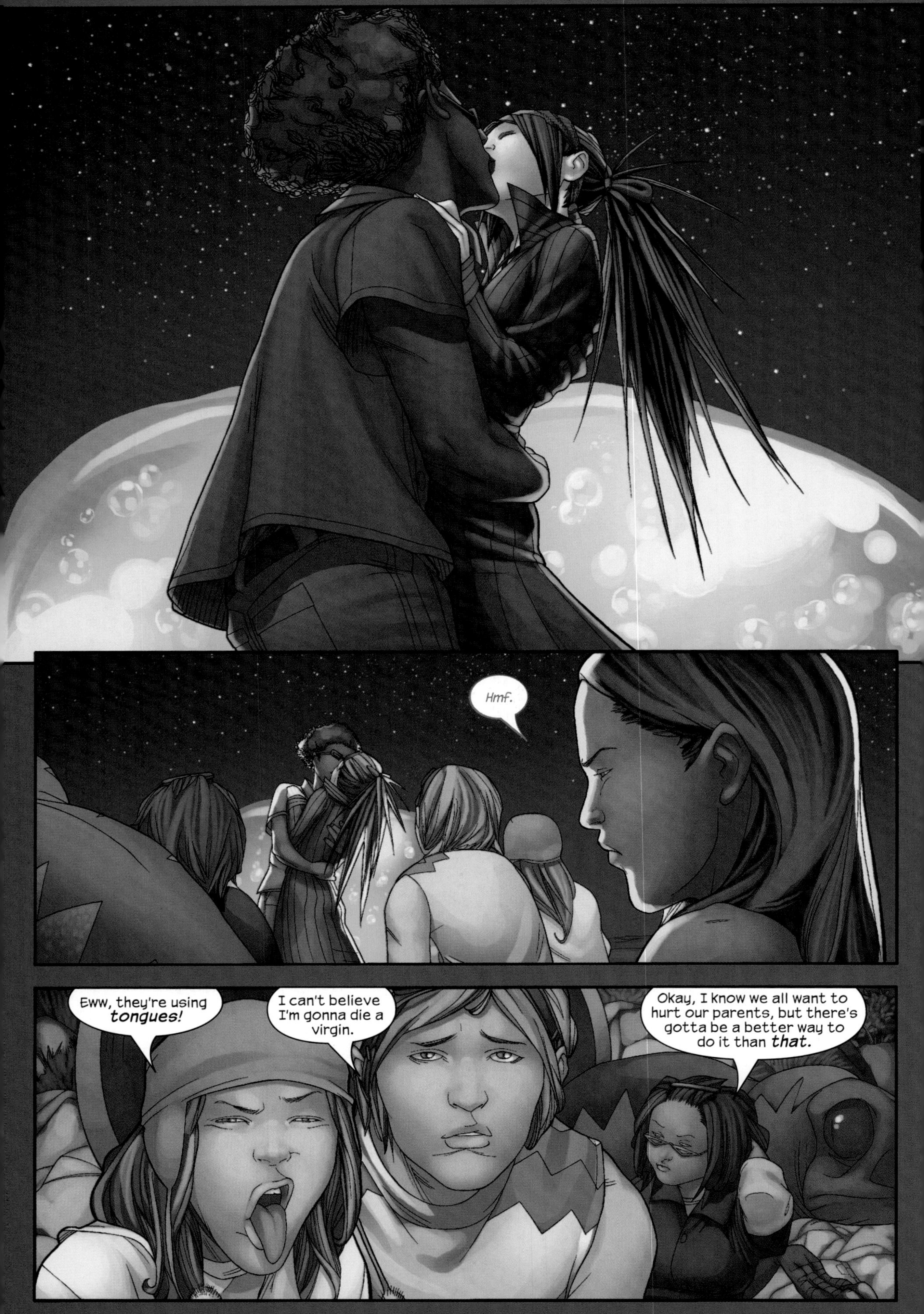
Hmf.
Eww, they're using *tongues!*
I can't believe I'm gonna die a virgin.
Okay, I know we all want to hurt our parents, but there's gotta be a better way to do it than *that.*

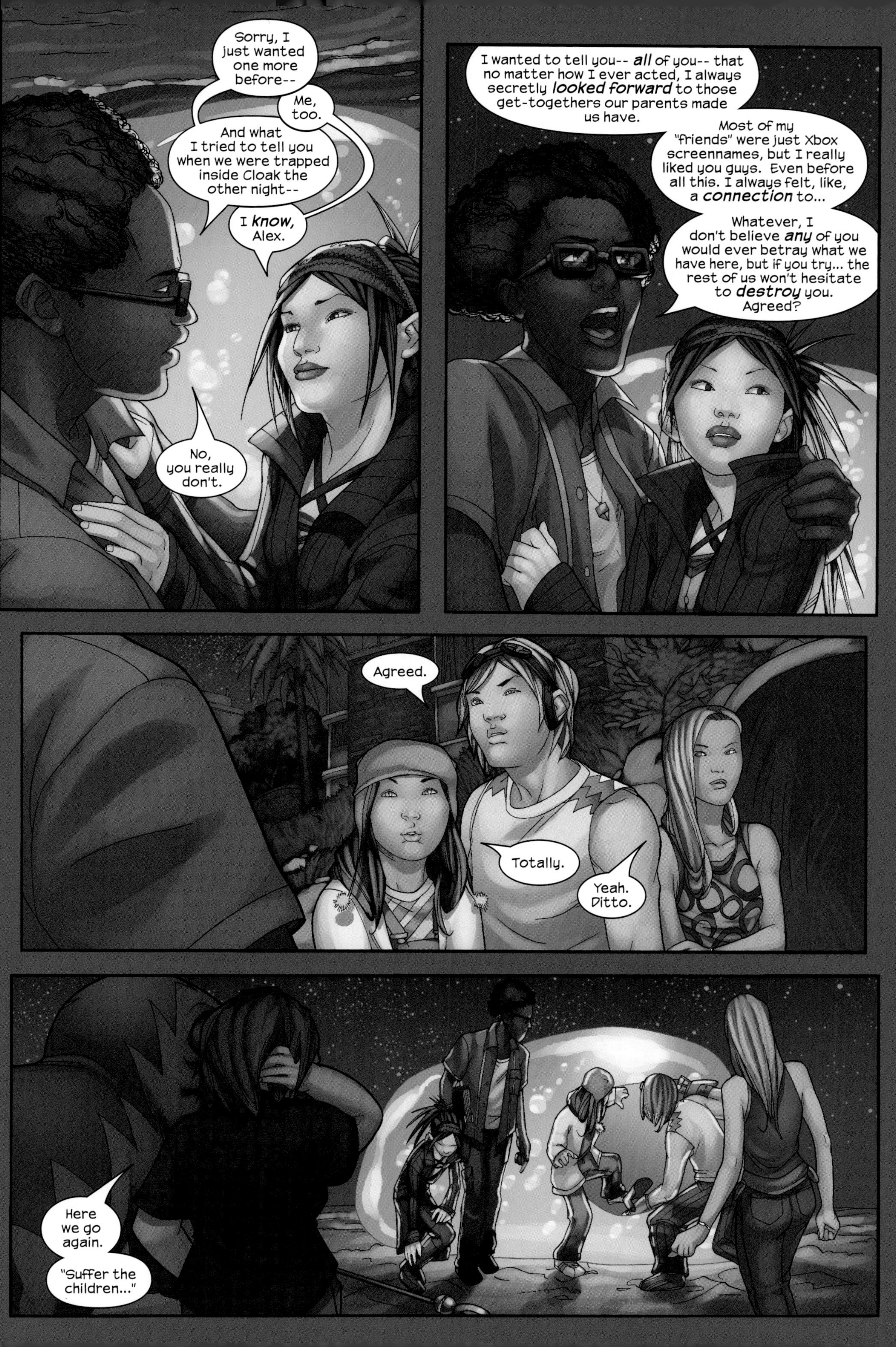
Sorry, I just wanted one more before--
Me, too.
And what I tried to tell you when we were trapped inside Cloak the other night--
I *know,* Alex.
No, you really don't.
I wanted to tell you-- *all* of you-- that no matter how I ever acted, I always secretly *looked forward* to those get-togethers our parents made us have.
Most of my "friends" were just Xbox screennames, but I really liked you guys. Even before all this. I always felt, like, a *connection* to...
Whatever, I don't believe *any* of you would ever betray what we have here, but if you try... the rest of us won't hesitate to *destroy* you. Agreed?
Agreed.
Totally.
Yeah. Ditto.
Here we go again.
"Suffer the children..."

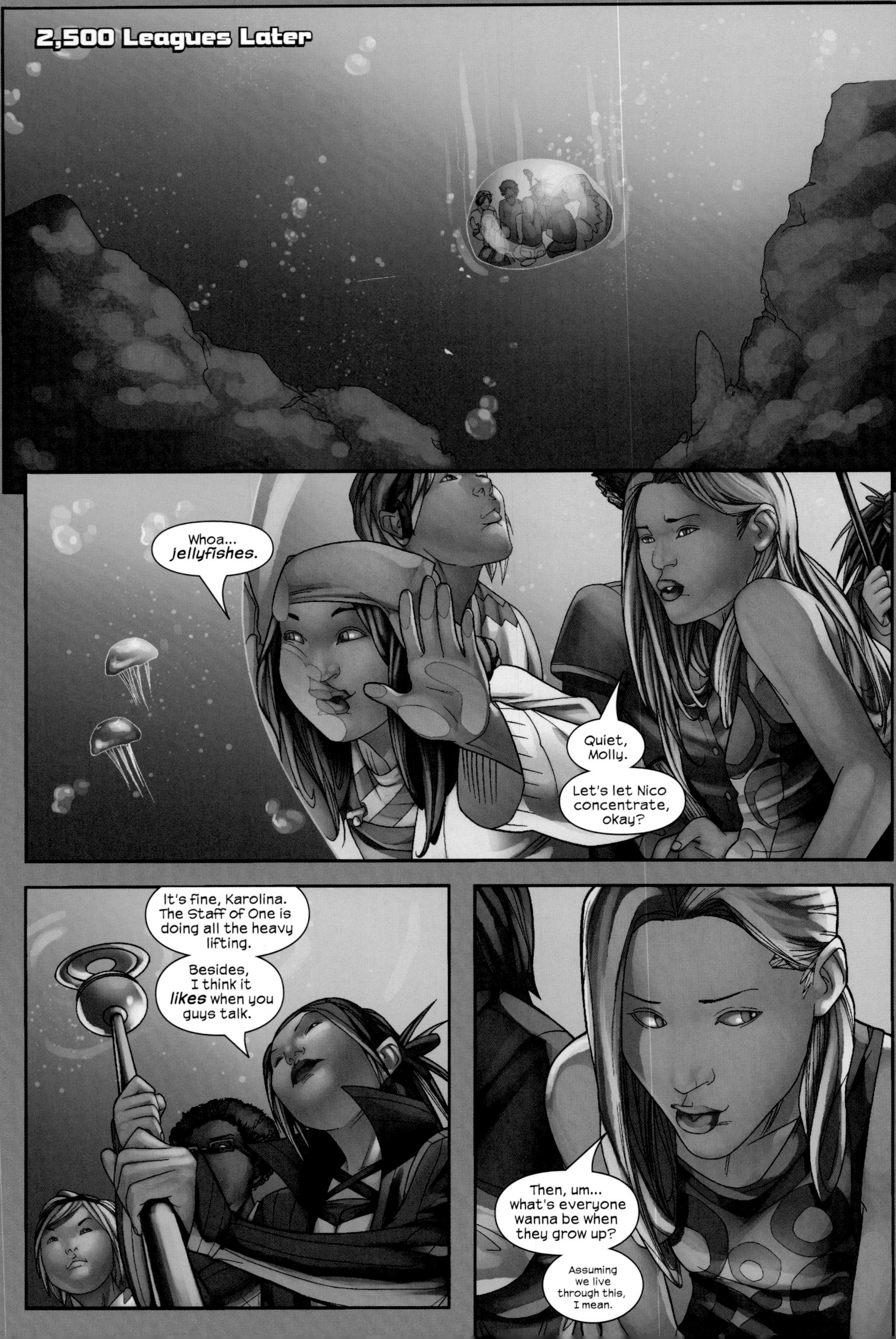
2,500 Leagues Later
Whoa... *jellyfishes.*
Quiet, Molly.
Let's let Nico concentrate, okay?
It's fine, Karolina. The Staff of One is doing all the heavy lifting.
Besides, I think it *likes* when you guys talk.
Then, um... what's everyone wanna be when they grow up?
Assuming we live through this, I mean.

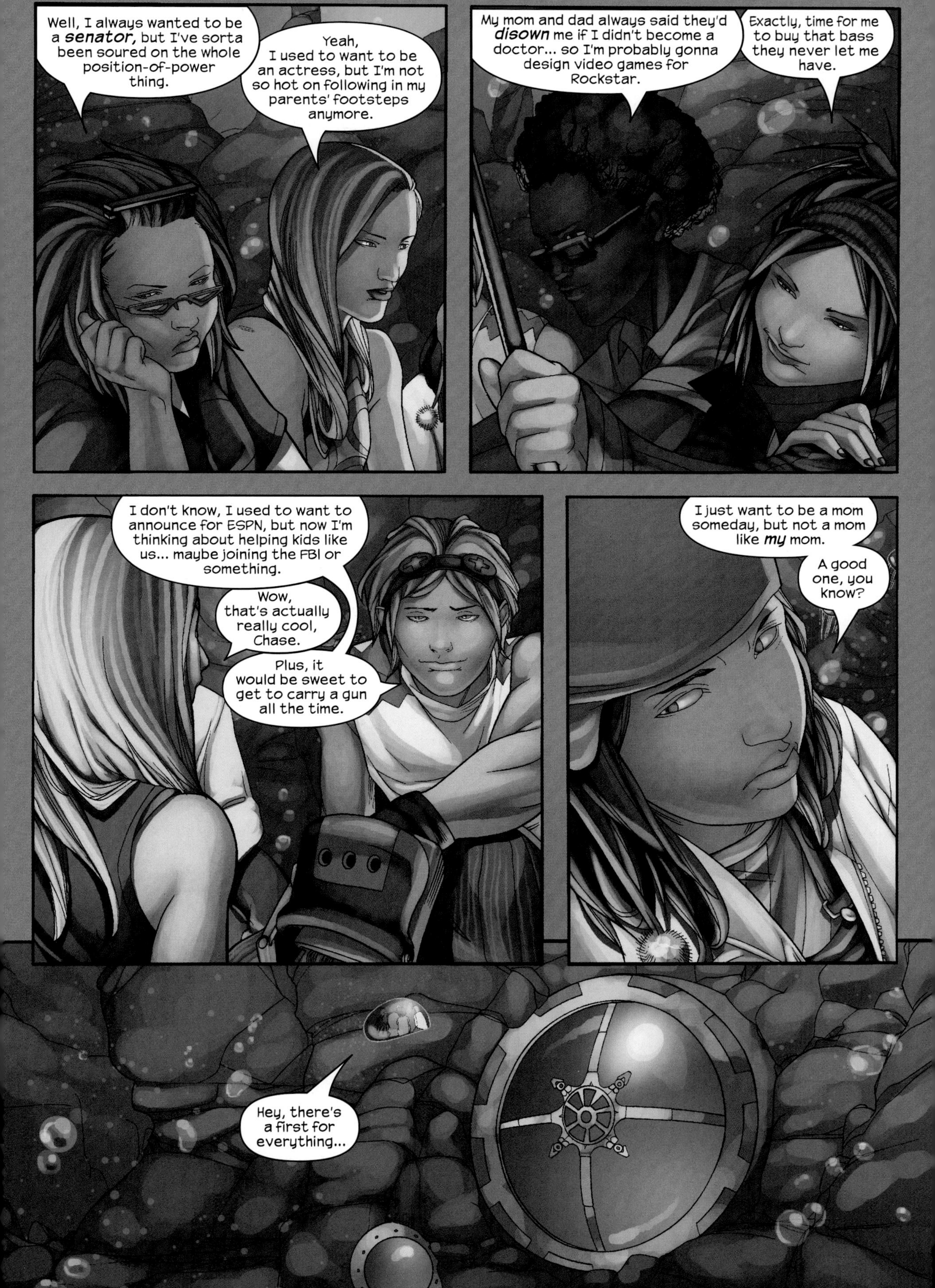

Well, I always wanted to be a senator, but I've sorta been soured on the whole position-of-power thing.
Yeah, I used to want to be an actress, but I'm not so hot on following in my parents' footsteps anymore.
My mom and dad always said they'd disown me if I didn't become a doctor... so I'm probably gonna design video games for Rockstar.
Exactly, time for me to buy that bass they never let me have.
I don't know, I used to want to announce for ESPN, but now I'm thinking about helping kids like us... maybe joining the FBI or something.
Wow, that's actually really cool, Chase.
Plus, it would be sweet to get to carry a gun all the time.
I just want to be a mom someday, but not a mom like my mom.
A good one, you know?
Hey, there's a first for everything...

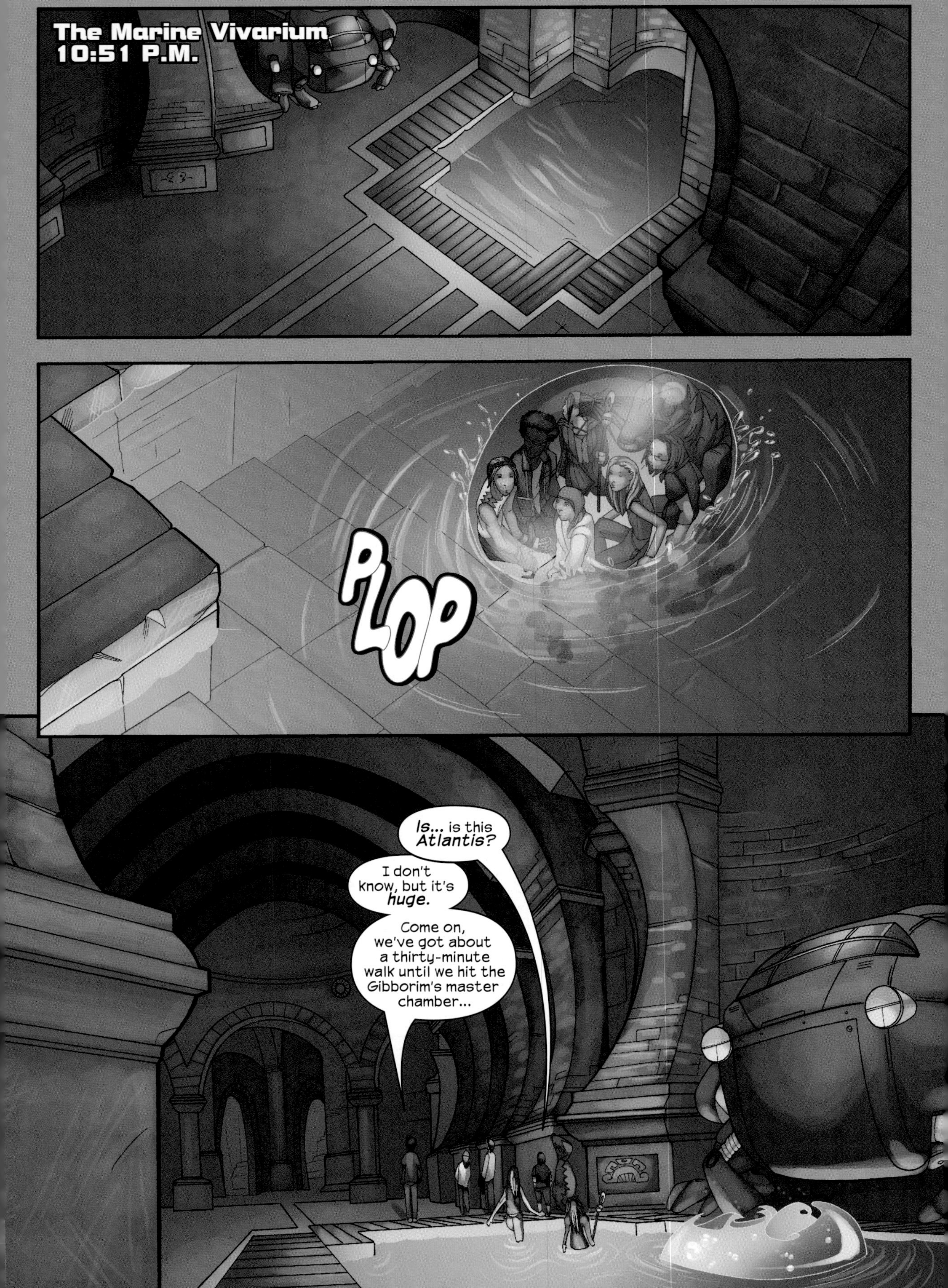

The Marine Vivarium
10:51 P.M.
PLOP
Is... is this *Atlantis?*
I don't know, but it's *huge.*
Come on, we've got about a thirty-minute walk until we hit the Gibborim's master chamber...

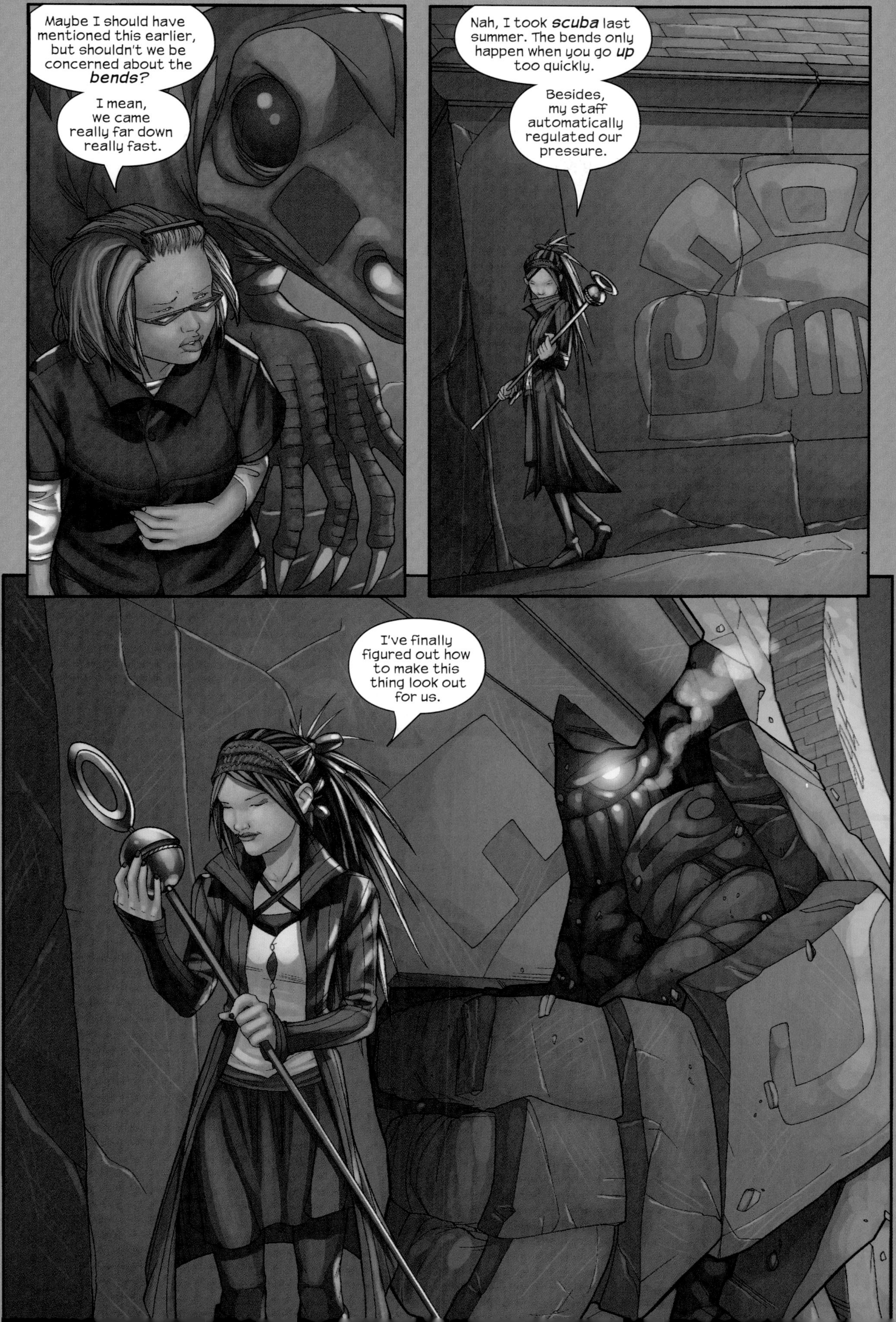
Maybe I should have mentioned this earlier, but shouldn't we be concerned about the *bends*?
I mean, we came really far down really fast.
Nah, I took *scuba* last summer. The bends only happen when you go *up* too quickly.
Besides, my staff automatically regulated our pressure.
I've finally figured out how to make this thing look out for us.

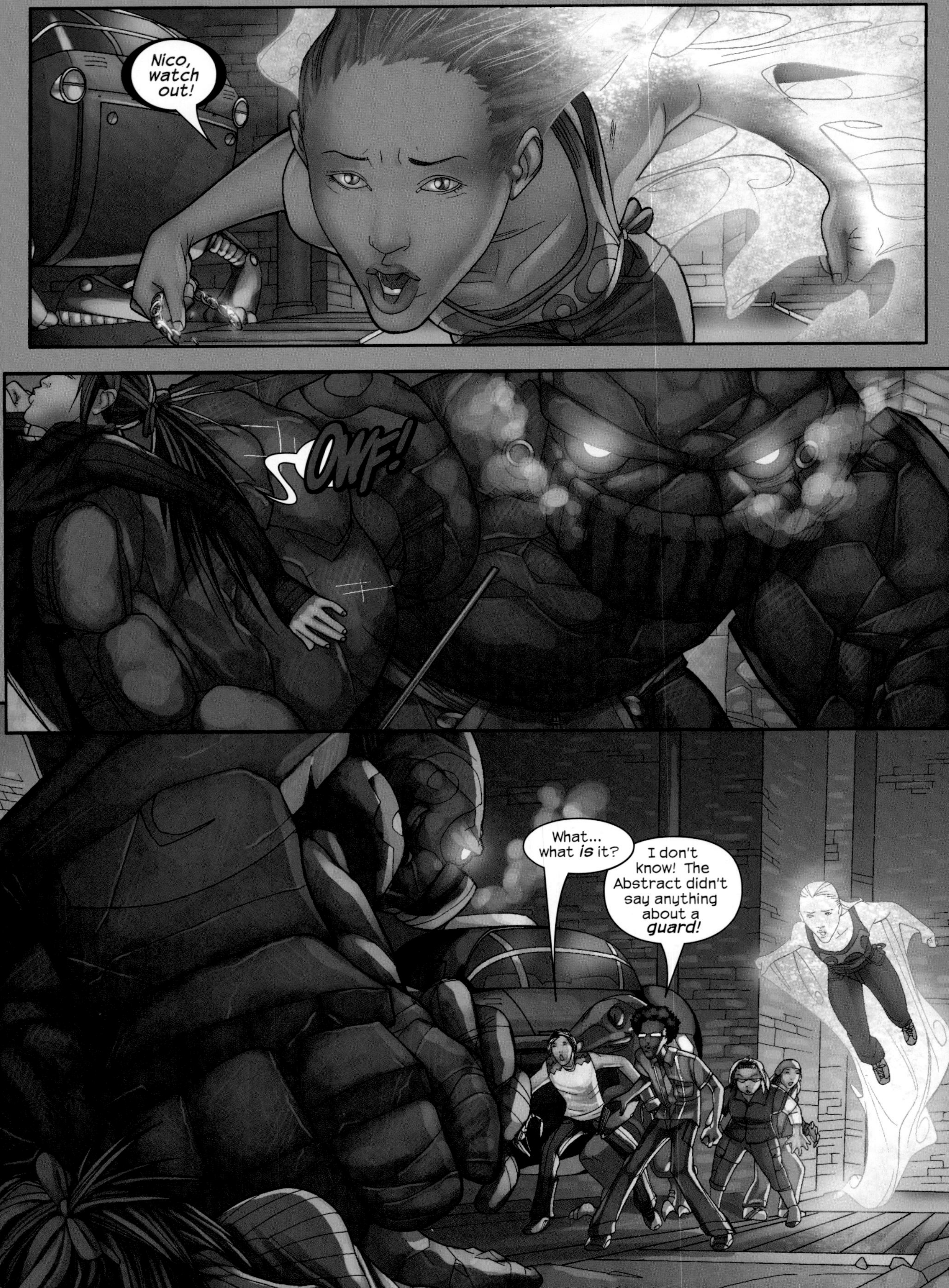
Nico, watch out!
SOMF!
What... what *is* it?
I don't know! The Abstract didn't say anything about a *guard!*

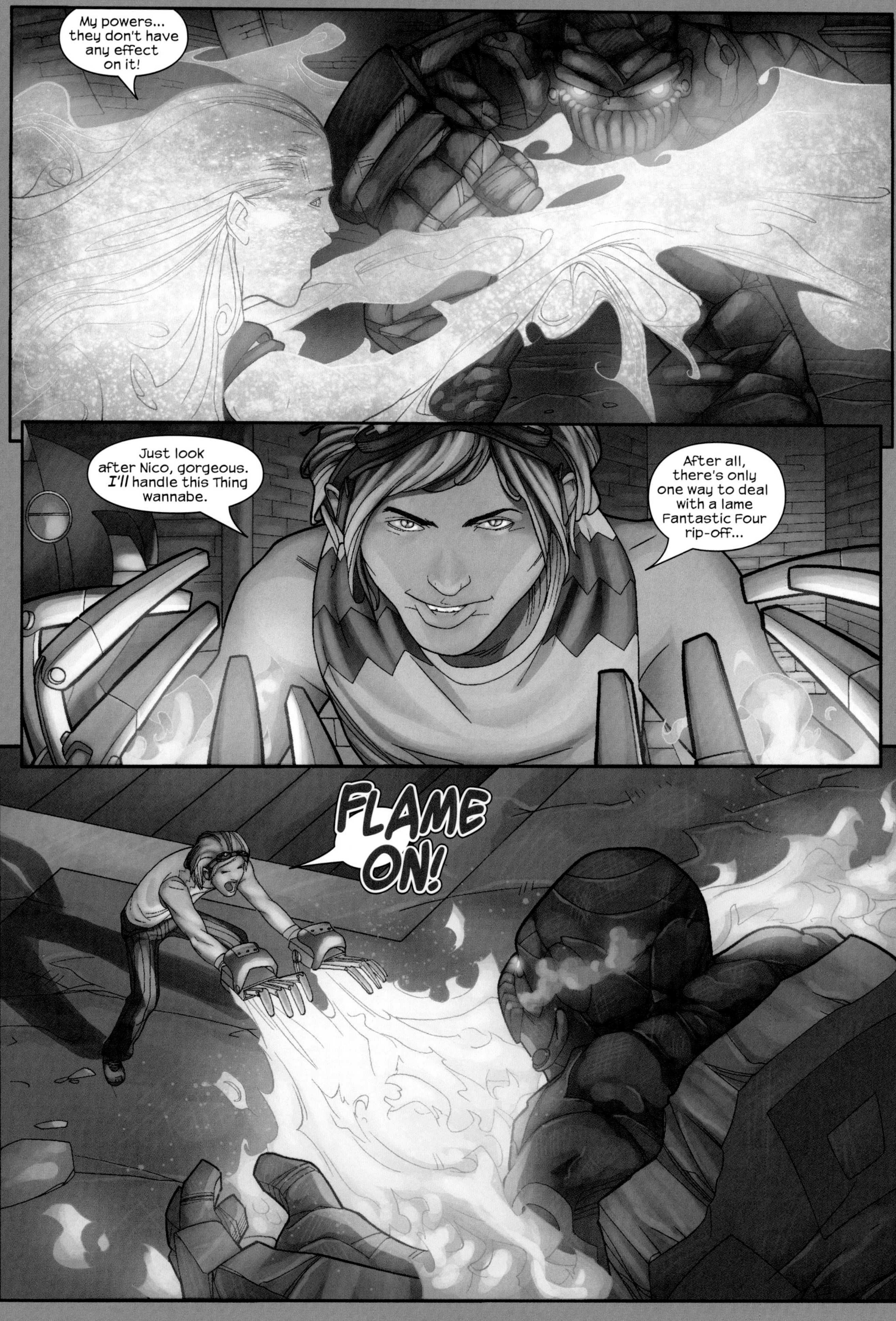
My powers... they don't have any effect on it!
Just look after Nico, gorgeous. *I'll* handle this Thing wannabe.
After all, there's only one way to deal with a lame Fantastic Four rip-off...
FLAME ON!

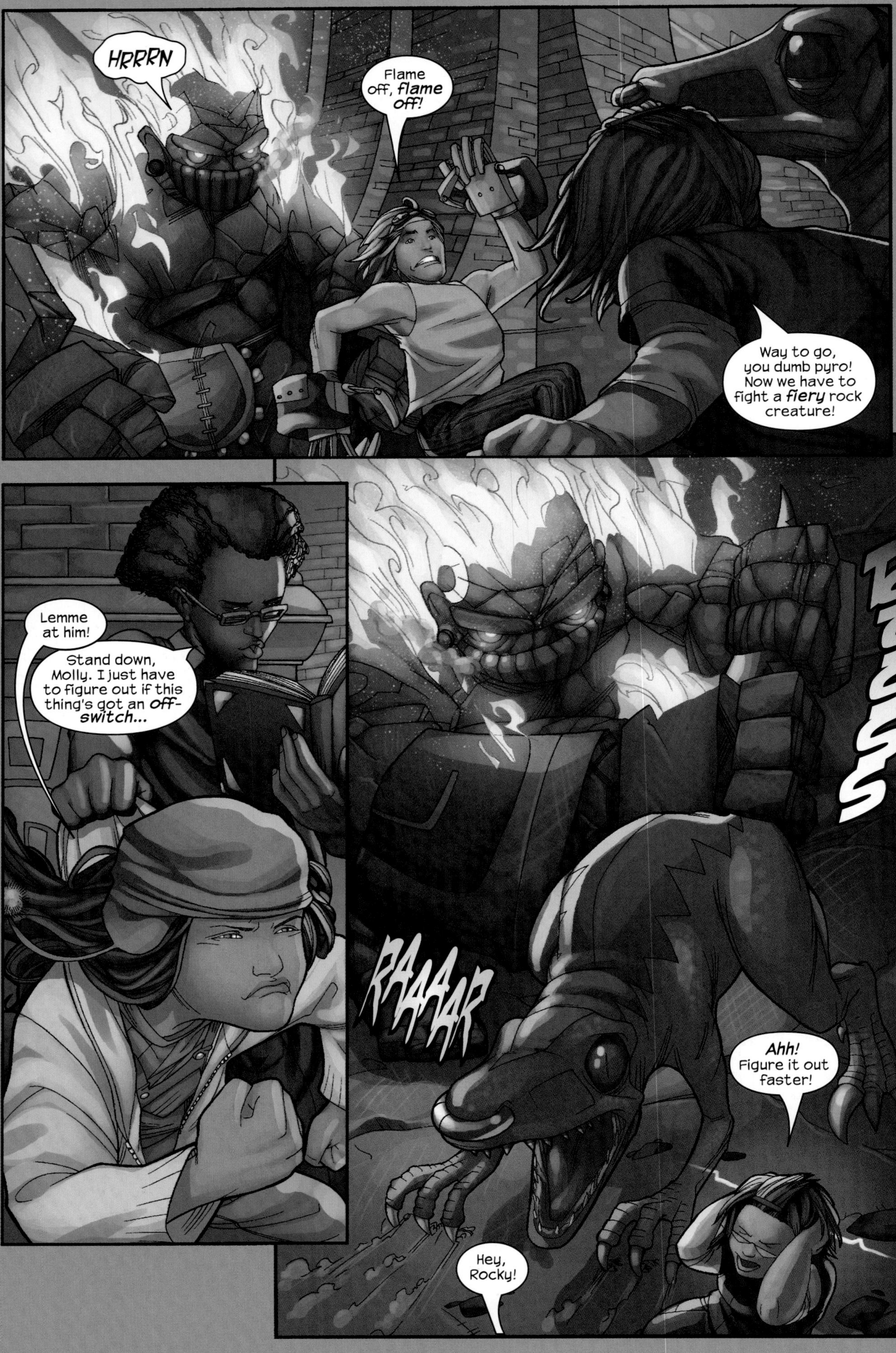
HRRRN
Flame off, *flame off!*
Way to go, you dumb pyro! Now we have to fight a *fiery* rock creature!
Lemme at him!
Stand down, Molly. I just have to figure out if this thing's got an *off-switch...*
TSSSSSS
RAAAAR
Ahh! Figure it out faster!
Hey, Rocky!

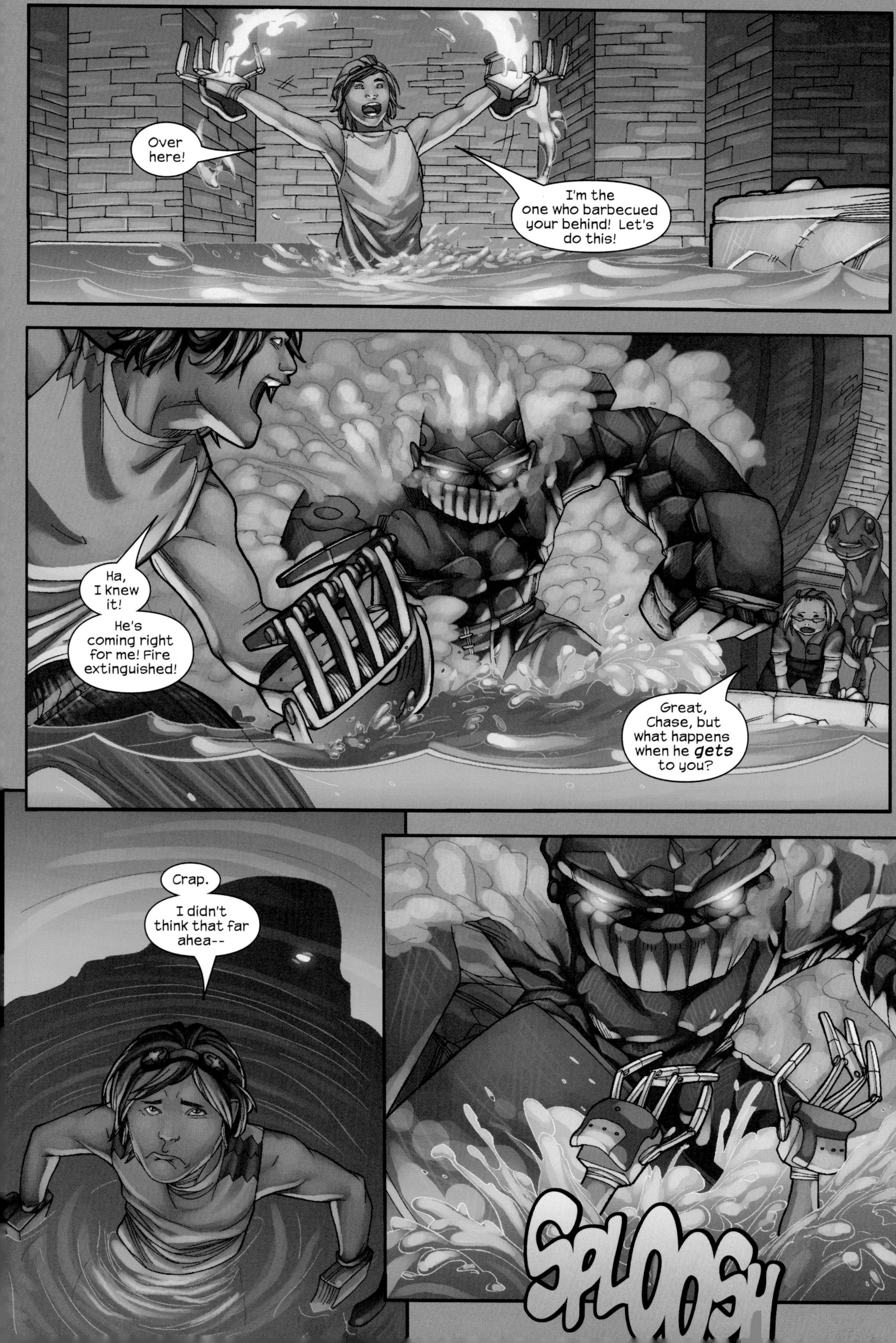
Over here!
I'm the one who barbecued your behind! Let's do this!
Ha, I knew it!
He's coming right for me! Fire extinguished!
Great, Chase, but what happens when he *gets* to you?
Crap.
I didn't think that far ahea--
SPLOOSH

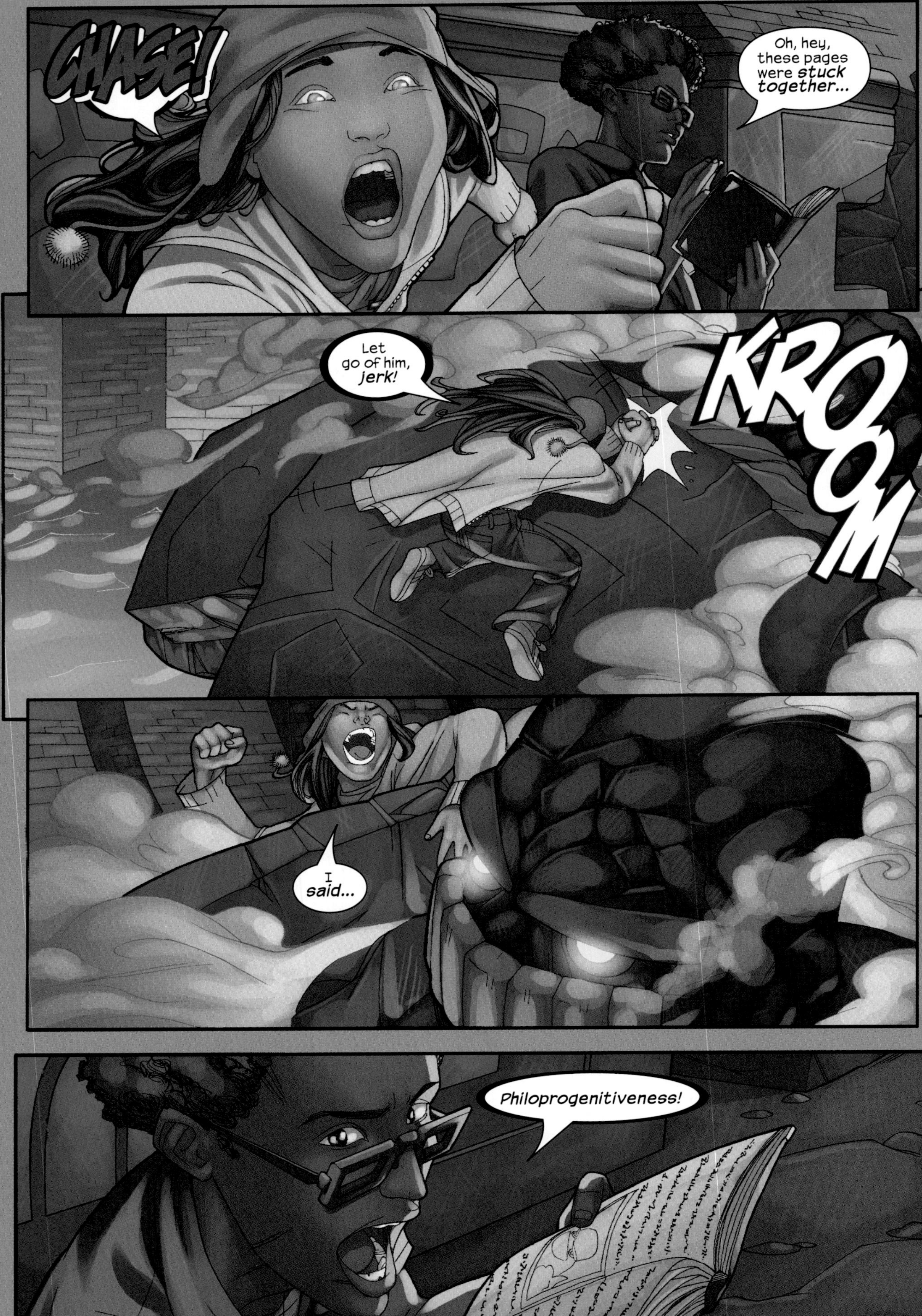
CHASE!
Oh, hey, these pages were stuck together...
Let go of him, jerk!
KROOM
I said...
Philoprogenitiveness!

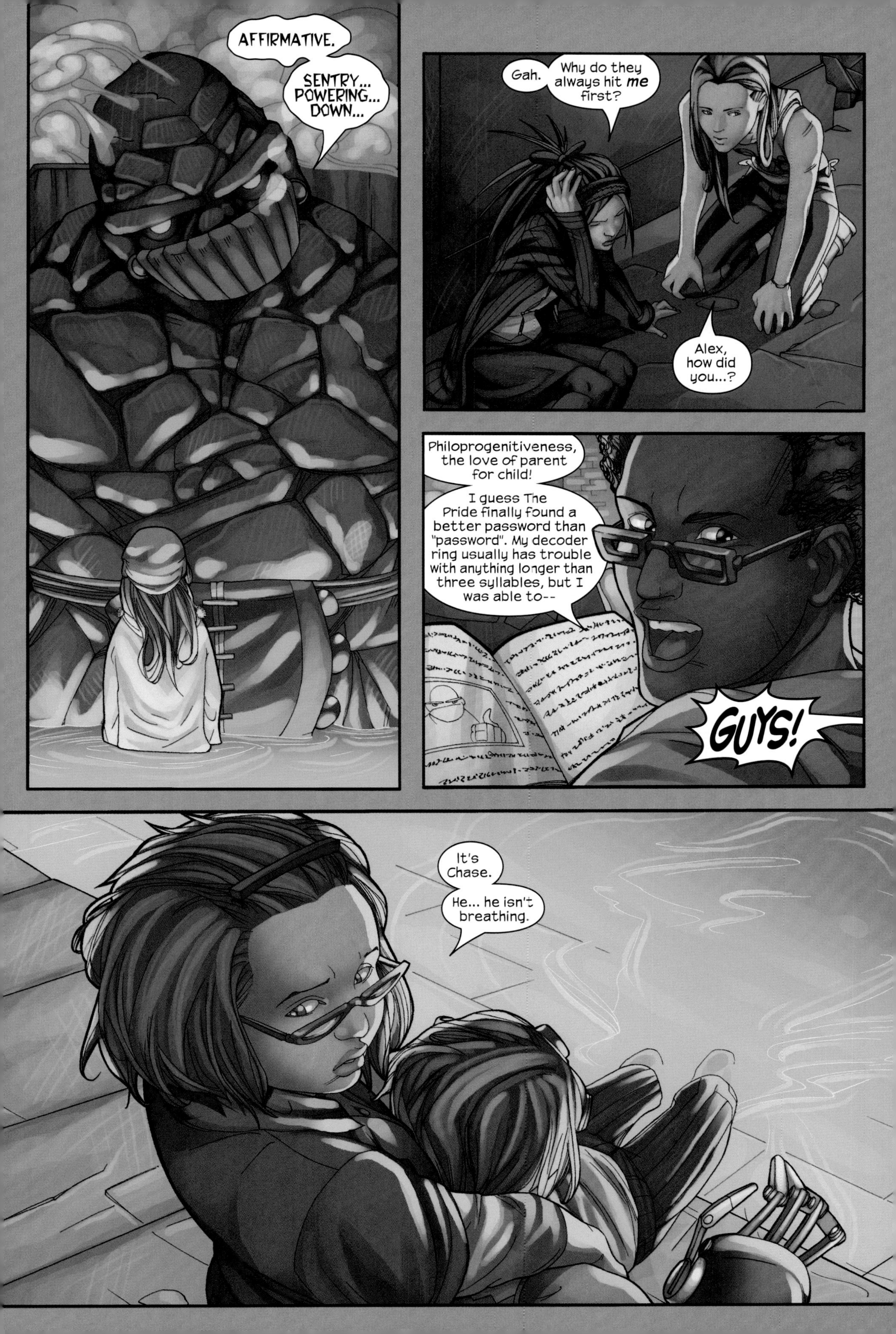
AFFIRMATIVE.
SENTRY... POWERING... DOWN...
Gah.
Why do they always hit *me* first?
Alex, how did you...?
Philoprogenitiveness, the love of parent for child!
I guess The Pride finally found a better password than "password". My decoder ring usually has trouble with anything longer than three syllables, but I was able to--
GUYS!
It's Chase.
He... he isn't breathing.

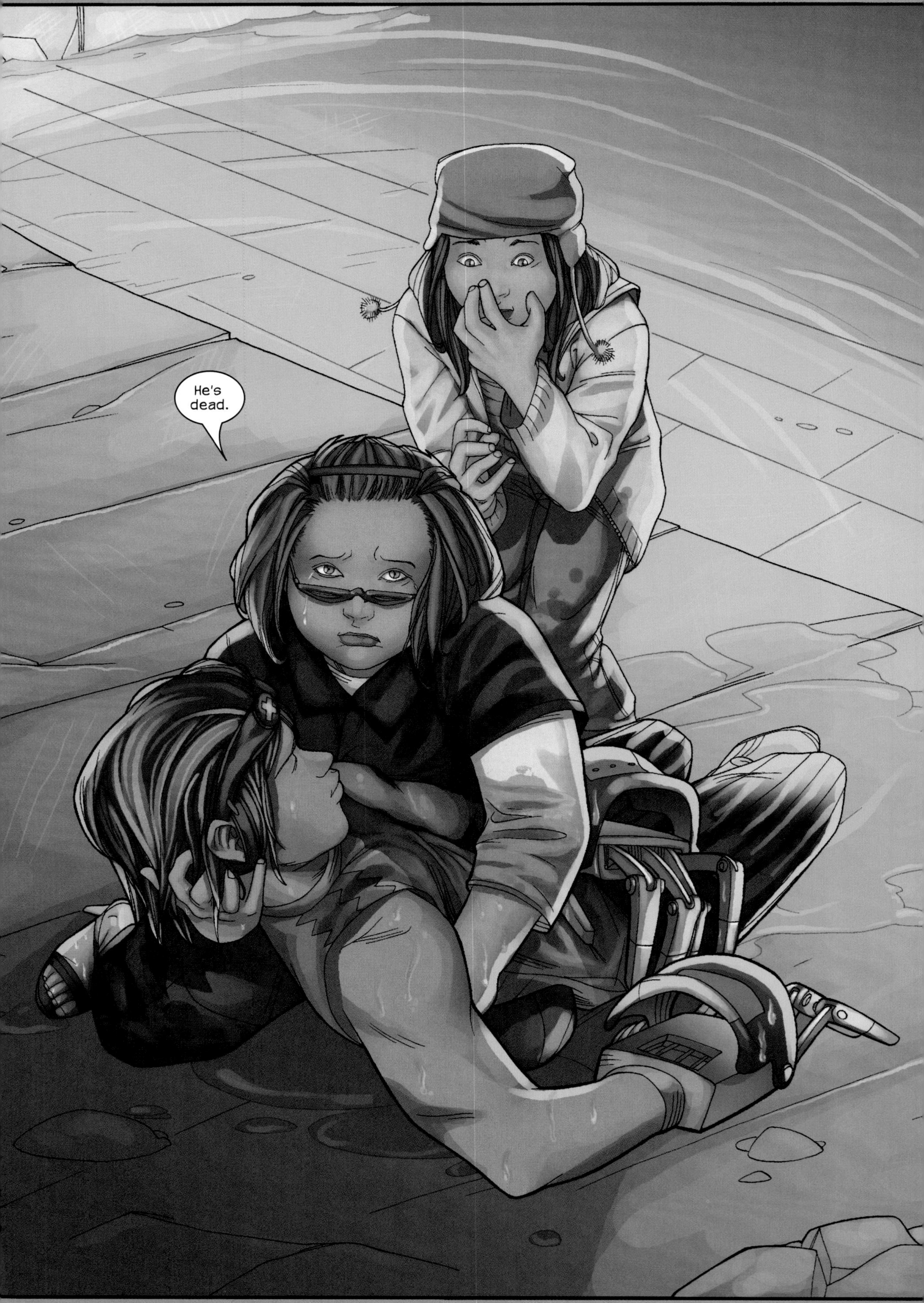
He's dead.

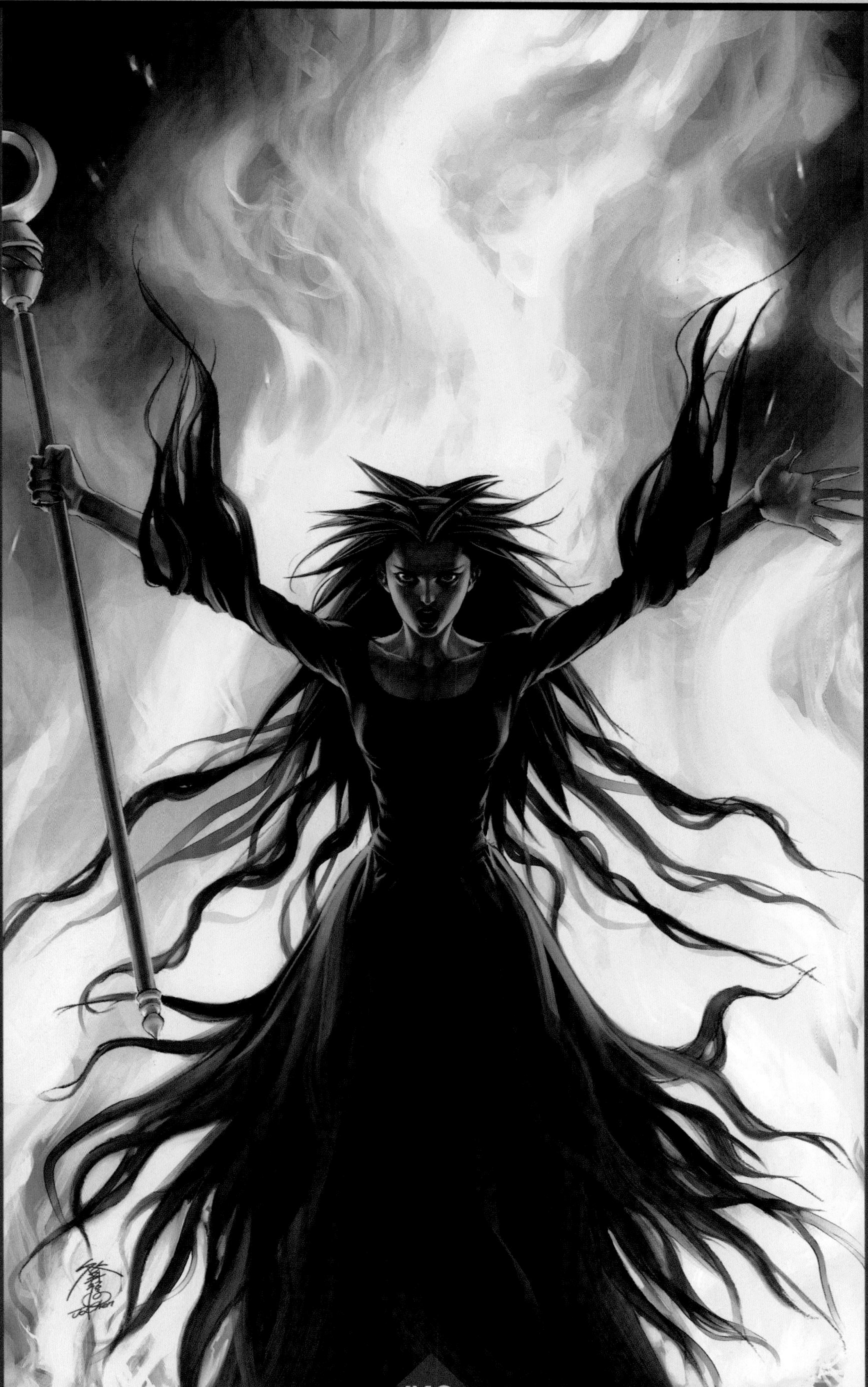
#16

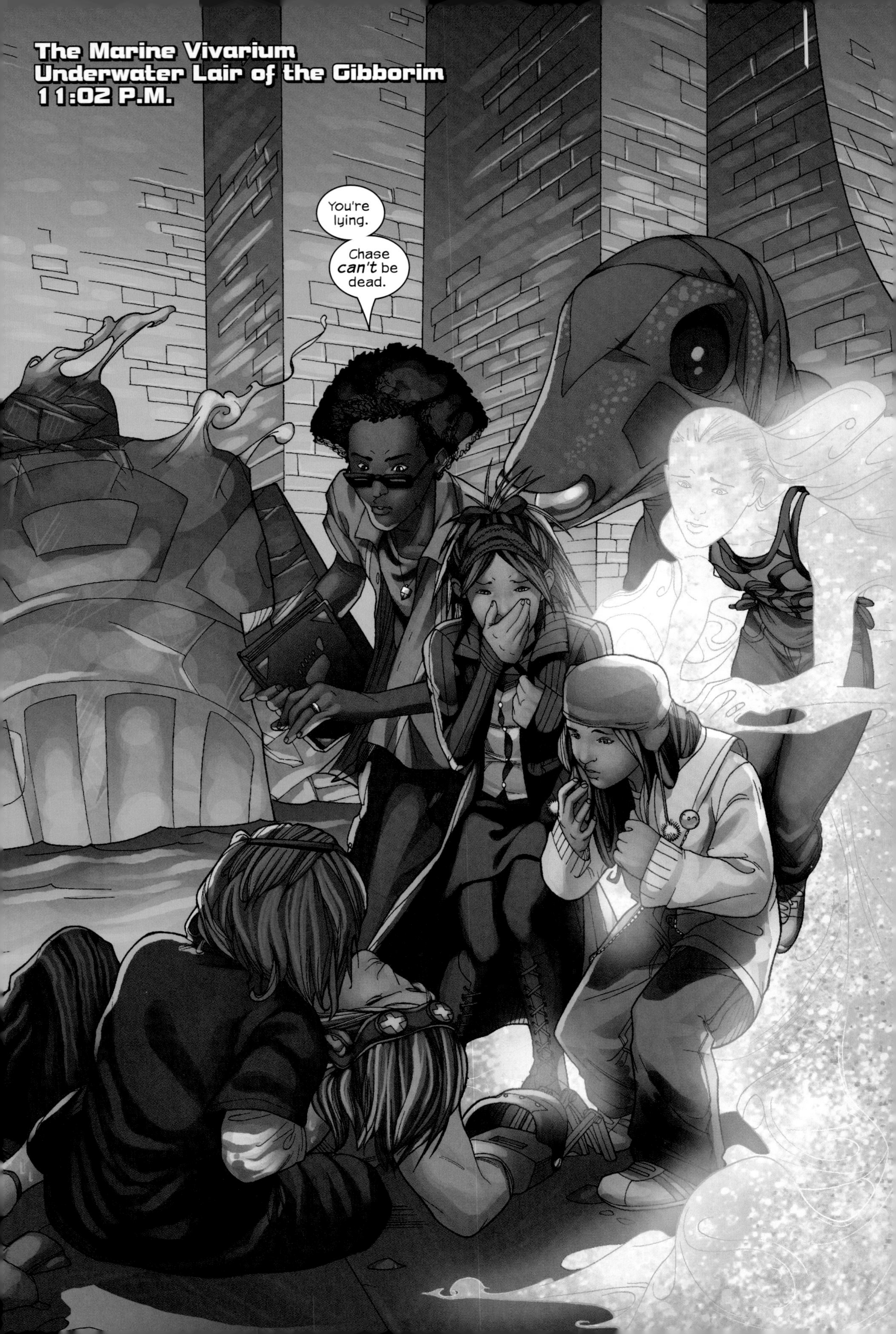
The Marine Vivarium
Underwater Lair of the Gibborim
11:02 P.M.
You're lying.
Chase can't be dead.

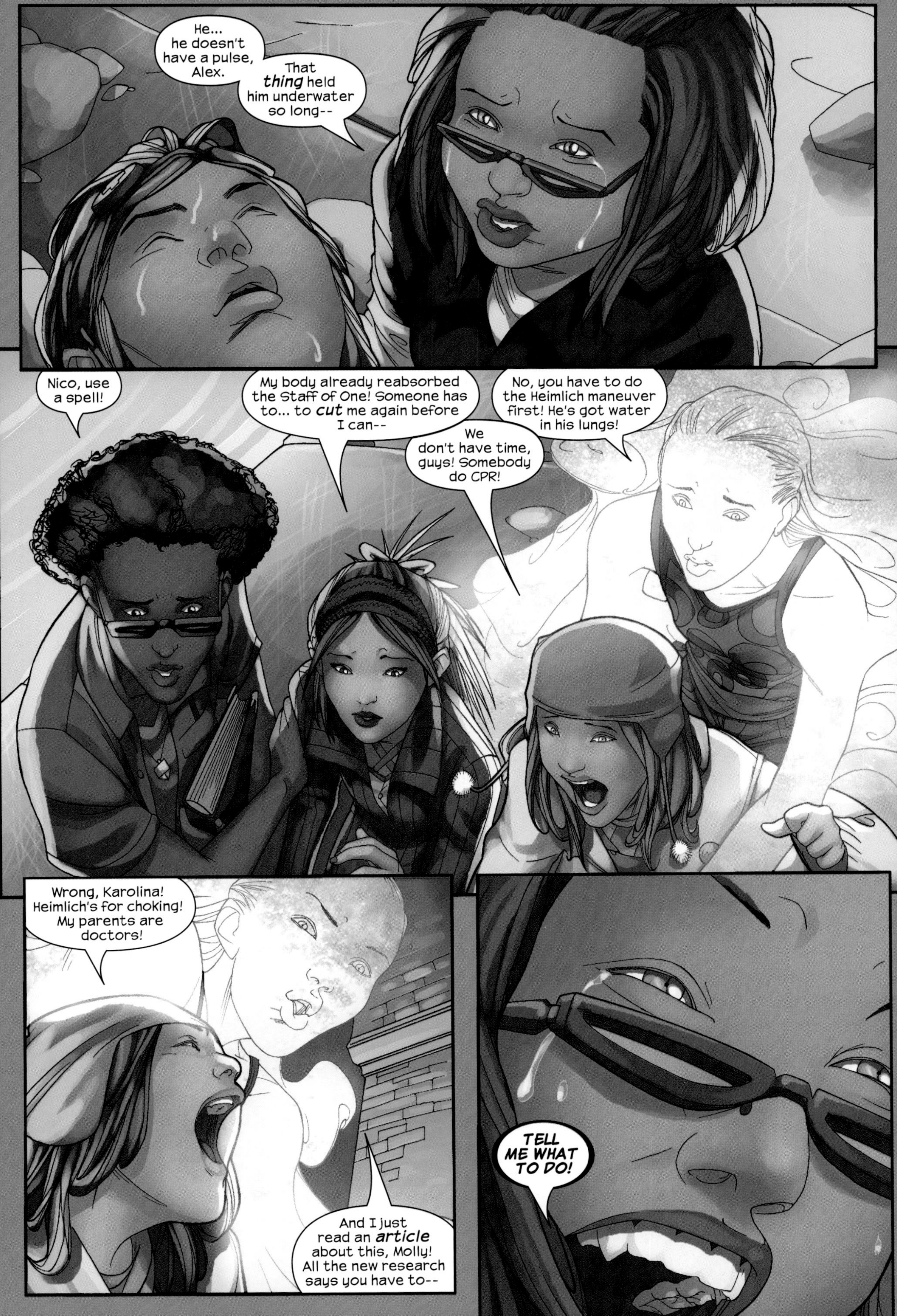
He... he doesn't have a pulse, Alex.
That *thing* held him underwater so long--
Nico, use a spell!
My body already reabsorbed the Staff of One! Someone has to... to *cut* me again before I can--
No, you have to do the Heimlich maneuver first! He's got water in his lungs!
We don't have time, guys! Somebody do CPR!
Wrong, Karolina! Heimlich's for choking! My parents are doctors!
And I just read an *article* about this, Molly! All the new research says you have to--
TELL ME WHAT TO DO!

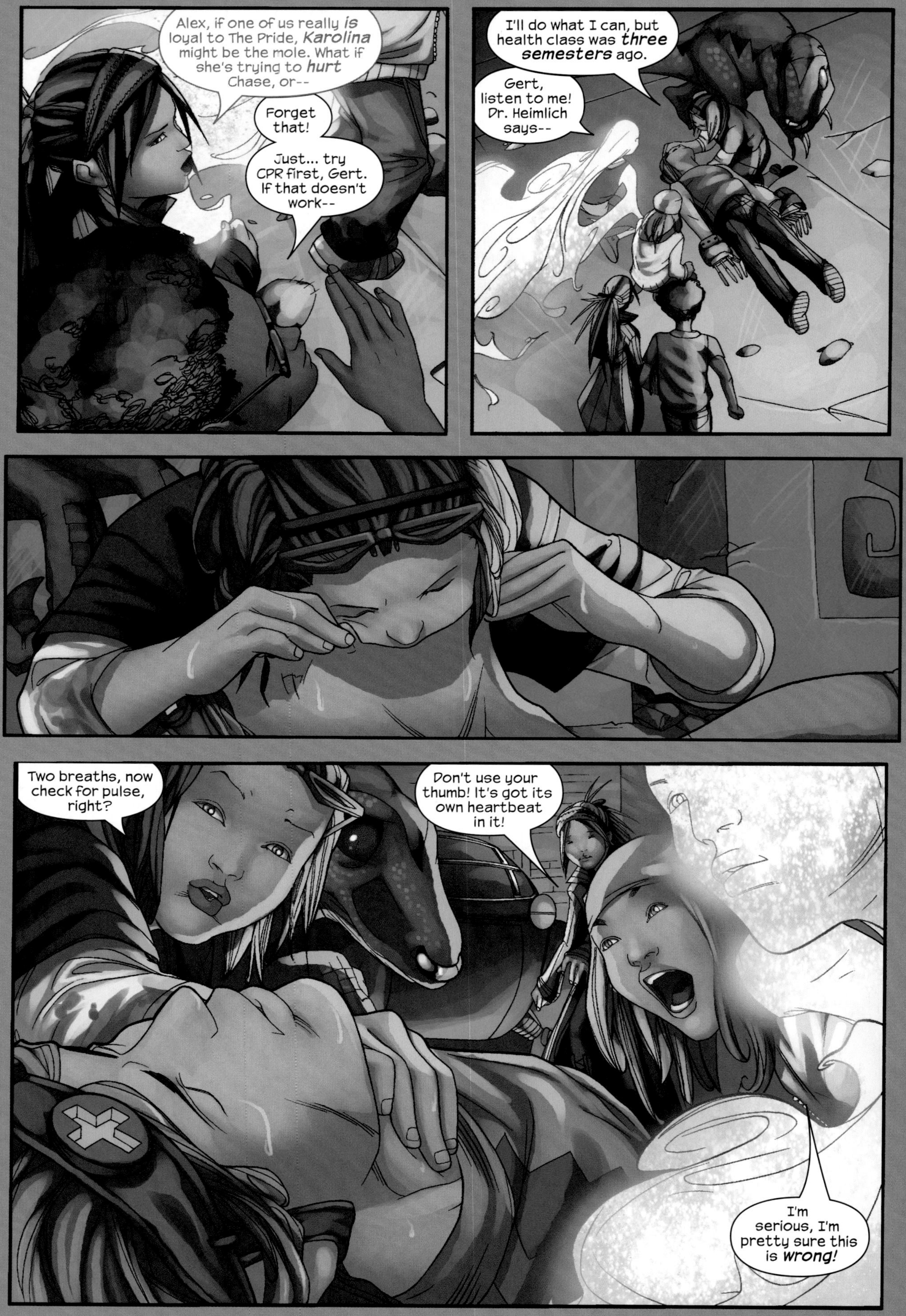
Alex, if one of us really *is* loyal to The Pride, *Karolina* might be the mole. What if she's trying to *hurt* Chase, or--
Forget that!
Just... try CPR first, Gert. If that doesn't work--
I'll do what I can, but health class was *three semesters* ago.
Gert, listen to me! Dr. Heimlich says--
Two breaths, now check for pulse, right?
Don't use your thumb! It's got its own heartbeat in it!
I'm serious, I'm pretty sure this is *wrong!*

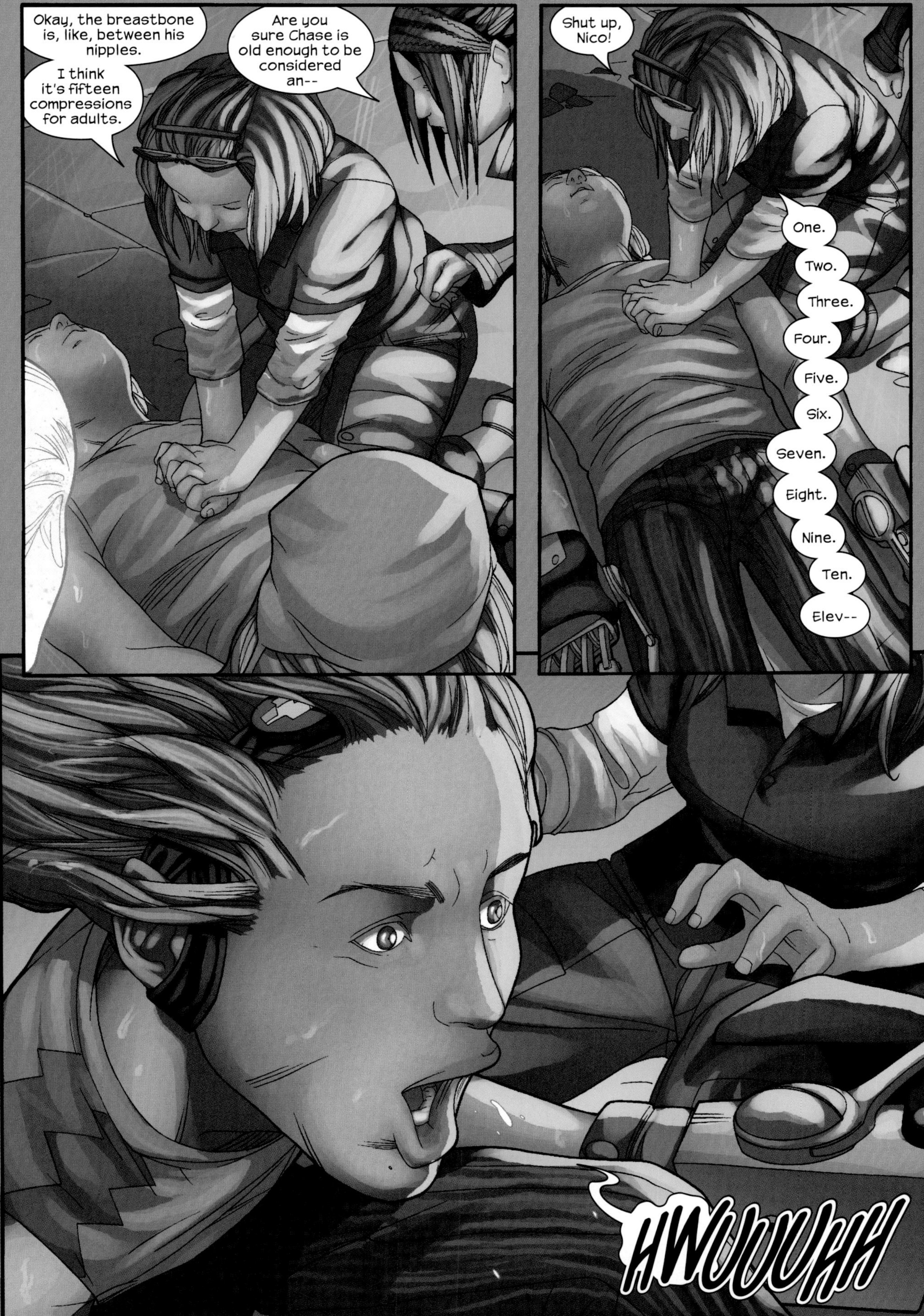
Okay, the breastbone is, like, between his nipples.
I think it's fifteen compressions for adults.
Are you sure Chase is old enough to be considered an--
Shut up, Nico!
One.
Two.
Three.
Four.
Five.
Six.
Seven.
Eight.
Nine.
Ten.
Elev--
HWUUUUHH

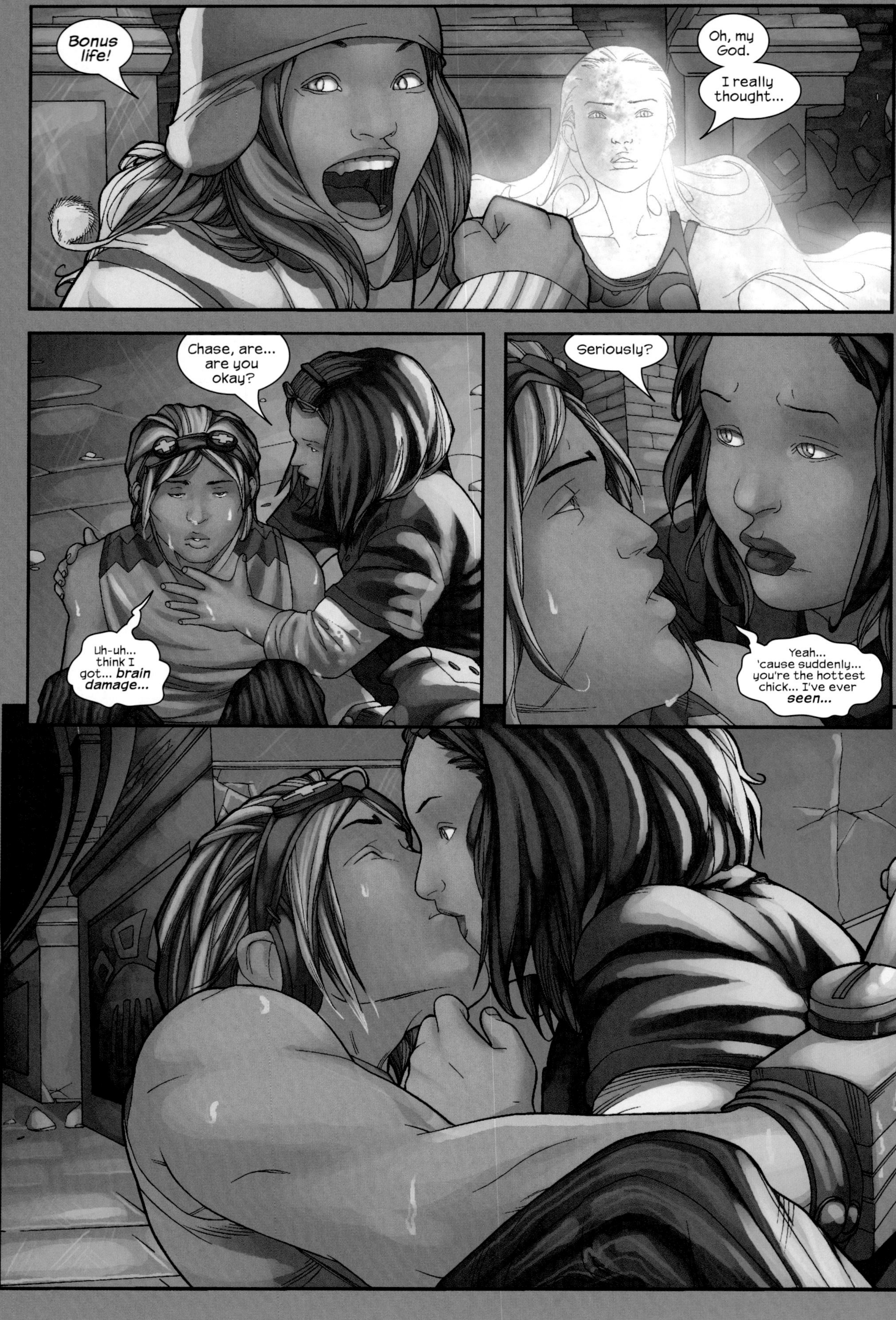
Bonus life!
Oh, my God.
I really thought...
Chase, are... are you okay?
Uh-uh... think I got... *brain damage...*
Seriously?
Yeah... 'cause suddenly... you're the hottest chick... I've ever *seen...*

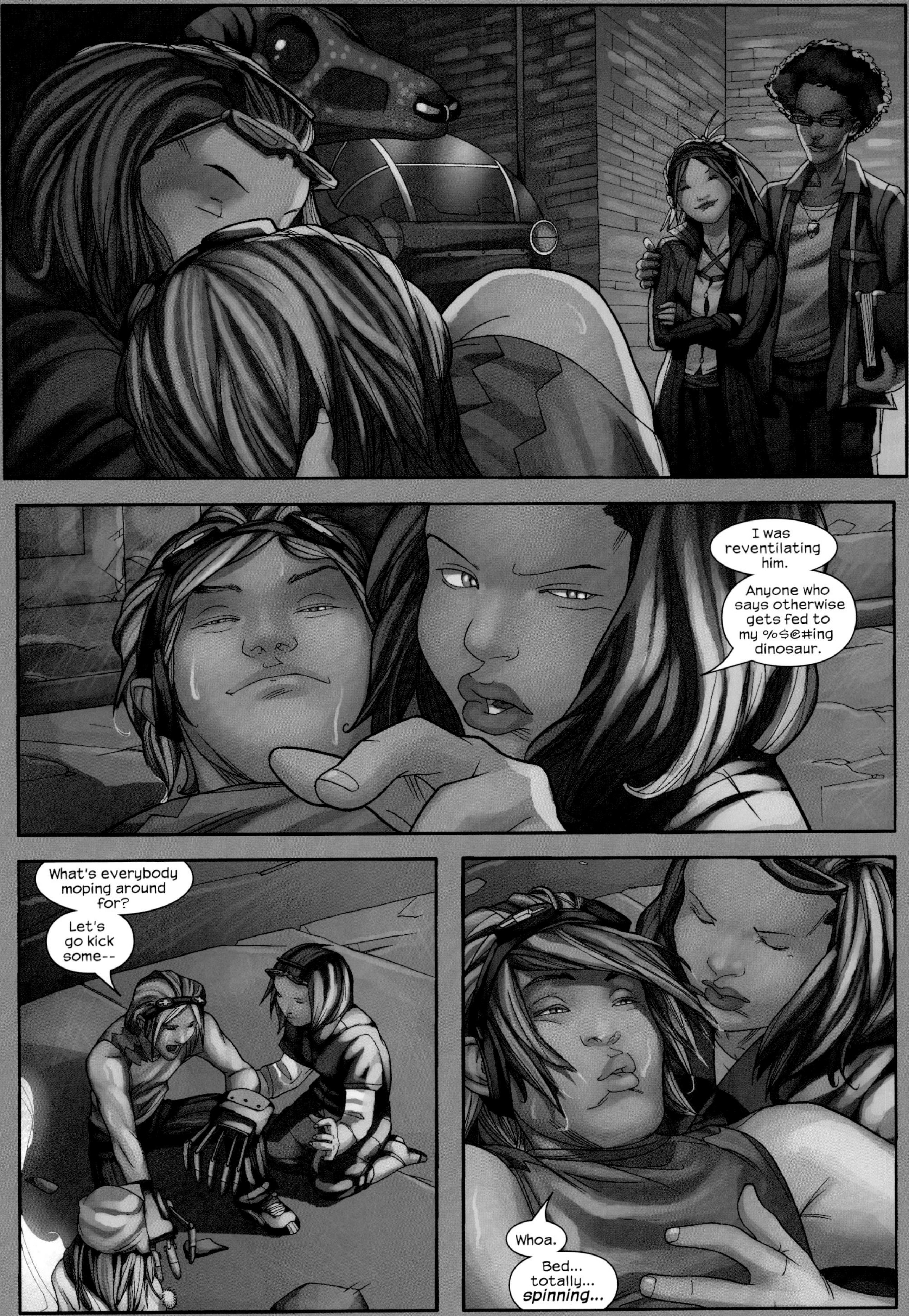
I was reventilating him.
Anyone who says otherwise gets fed to my %$@#ing dinosaur.
What's everybody moping around for?
Let's go kick some--
Whoa.
Bed... totally... *spinning...*

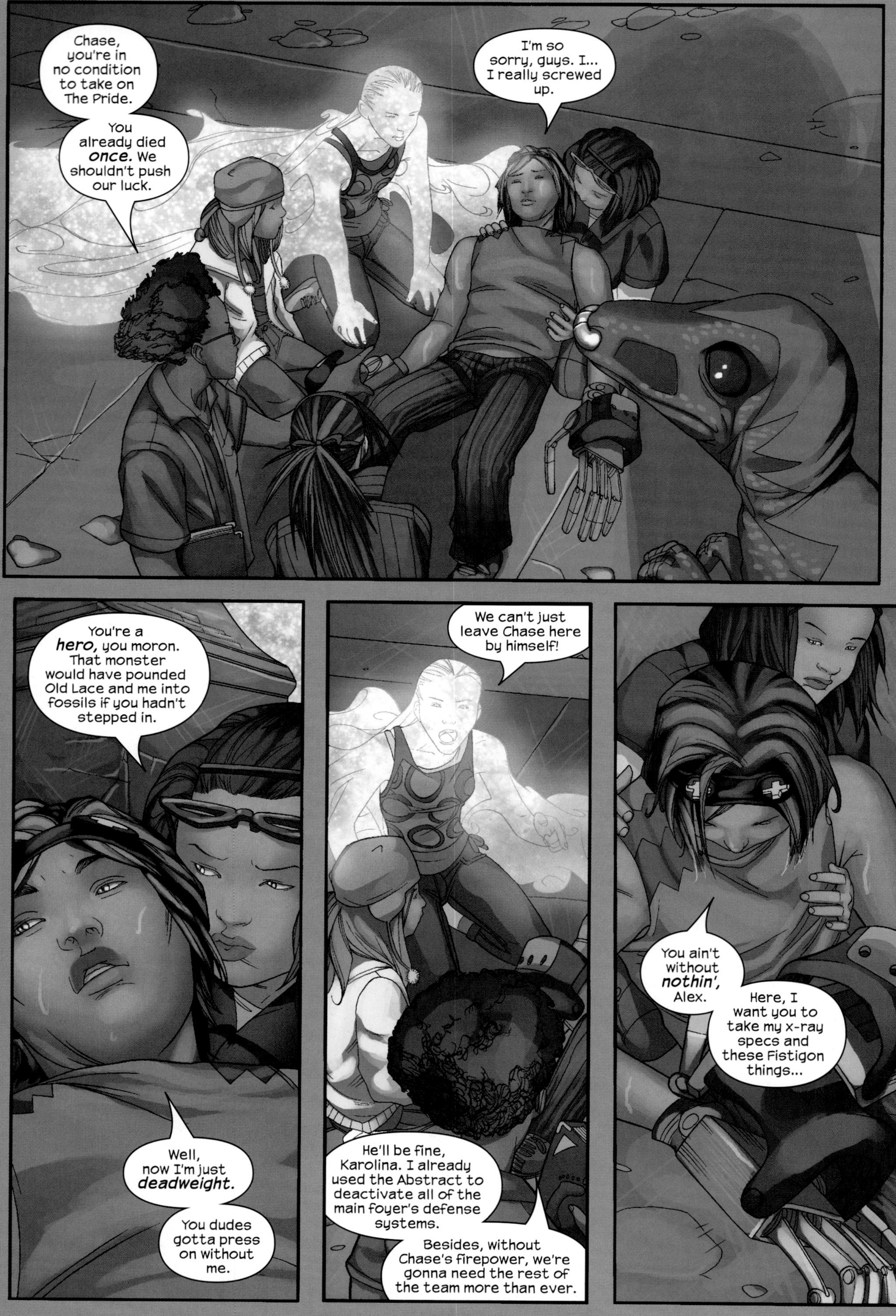
Chase, you're in no condition to take on The Pride.
You already died *once.* We shouldn't push our luck.
I'm so sorry, guys. I... I really screwed up.
You're a *hero,* you moron. That monster would have pounded Old Lace and me into fossils if you hadn't stepped in.
Well, now I'm just *deadweight.*
You dudes gotta press on without me.
We can't just leave Chase here by himself!
He'll be fine, Karolina. I already used the Abstract to deactivate all of the main foyer's defense systems.
Besides, without Chase's firepower, we're gonna need the rest of the team more than ever.
You ain't without *nothin',* Alex.
Here, I want you to take my x-ray specs and these Fistigon things...

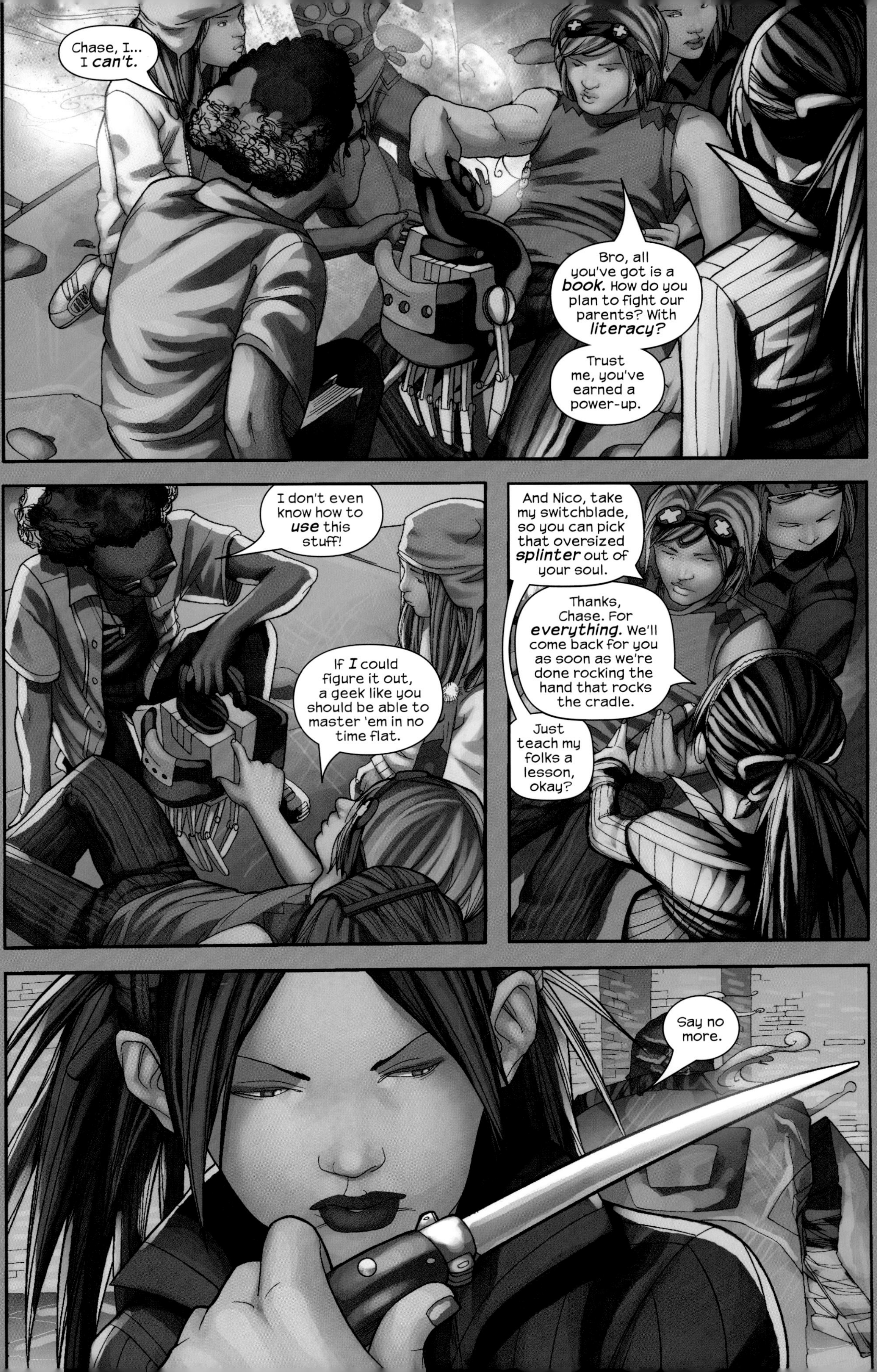
Chase, I... I *can't.*
Bro, all you've got is a **book.** How do you plan to fight our parents? With *literacy?*
Trust me, you've earned a power-up.
I don't even know how to *use* this stuff!
If *I* could figure it out, a geek like you should be able to master 'em in no time flat.
And Nico, take my switchblade, so you can pick that oversized *splinter* out of your soul.
Thanks, Chase. For *everything.* We'll come back for you as soon as we're done rocking the hand that rocks the cradle.
Just teach my folks a lesson, okay?
Say no more.

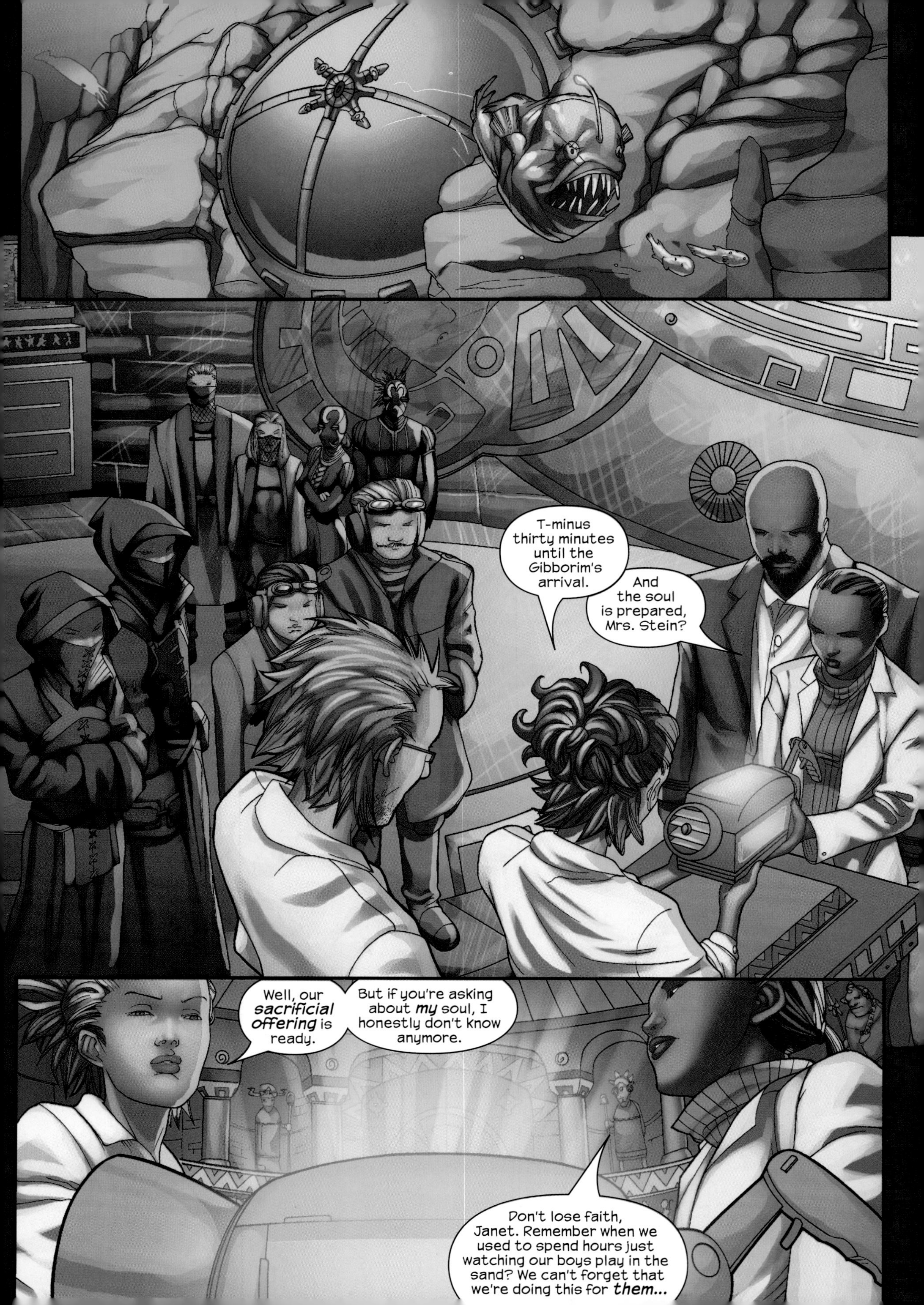

T-minus thirty minutes until the Gibborim's arrival.
And the soul is prepared, Mrs. Stein?
Well, our *sacrificial offering* is ready.
But if you're asking about *my* soul, I honestly don't know anymore.
Don't lose faith, Janet. Remember when we used to spend hours just watching our boys play in the sand? We can't forget that we're doing this for *them...*

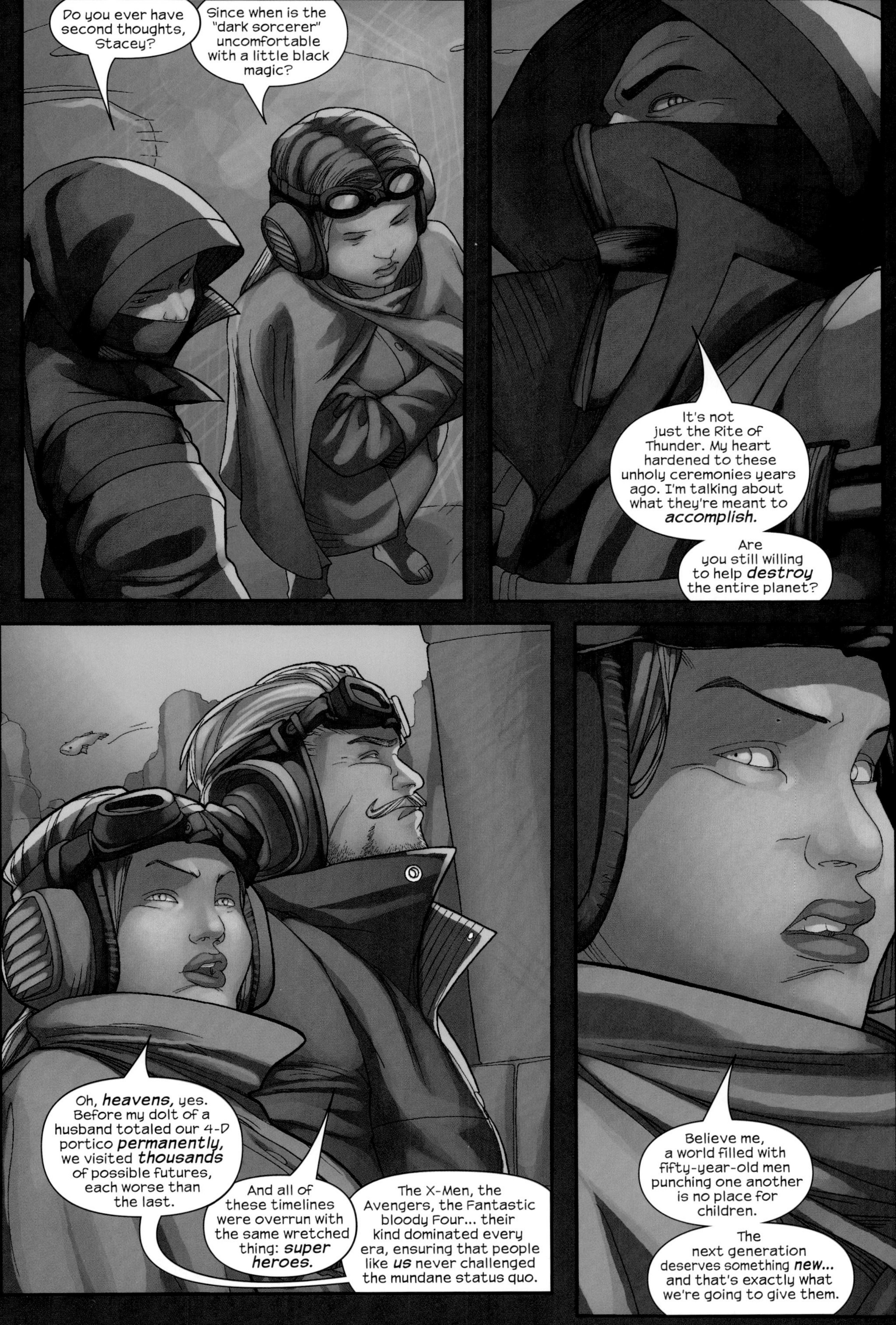
Do you ever have second thoughts, Stacey?
Since when is the "dark sorcerer" uncomfortable with a little black magic?
It's not just the Rite of Thunder. My heart hardened to these unholy ceremonies years ago. I'm talking about what they're meant to *accomplish.*
Are you still willing to help *destroy* the entire planet?
Oh, *heavens,* yes. Before my dolt of a husband totaled our 4-D portico *permanently,* we visited *thousands* of possible futures, each worse than the last.
And all of these timelines were overrun with the same wretched thing: *super heroes.*
The X-Men, the Avengers, the Fantastic bloody Four... their kind dominated every era, ensuring that people like *us* never challenged the mundane status quo.
Believe me, a world filled with fifty-year-old men punching one another is no place for children.
The next generation deserves something *new...* and that's exactly what we're going to give them.

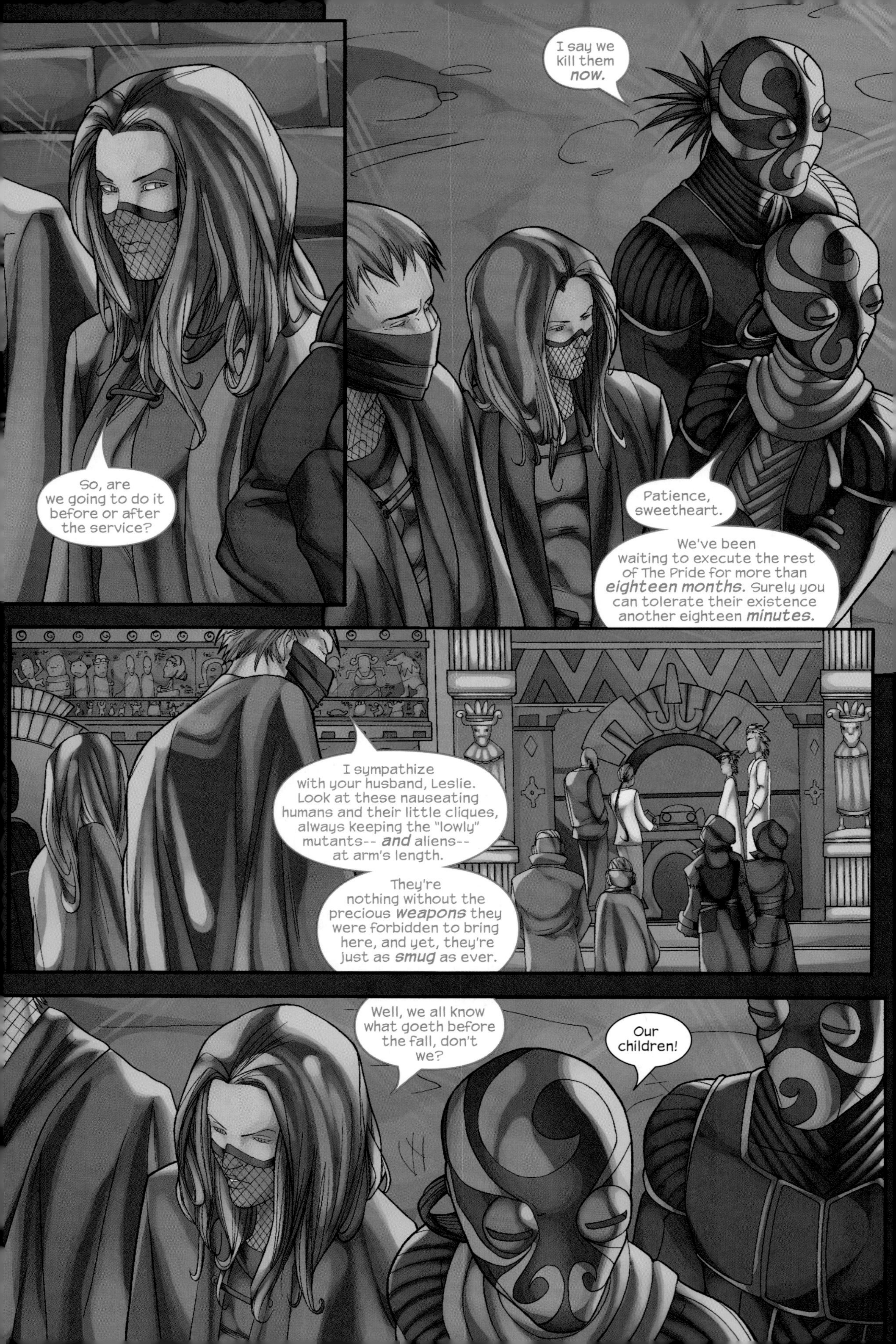
So, are we going to do it before or after the service?
I say we kill them *now.*
Patience, sweetheart.
We've been waiting to execute the rest of The Pride for more than **eighteen months.** Surely you can tolerate their existence another eighteen ***minutes.***
I sympathize with your husband, Leslie. Look at these nauseating humans and their little cliques, always keeping the "lowly" mutants-- ***and*** aliens-- at arm's length.
They're nothing without the precious ***weapons*** they were forbidden to bring here, and yet, they're just as ***smug*** as ever.
Well, we all know what goeth before the fall, don't we?
Our children!

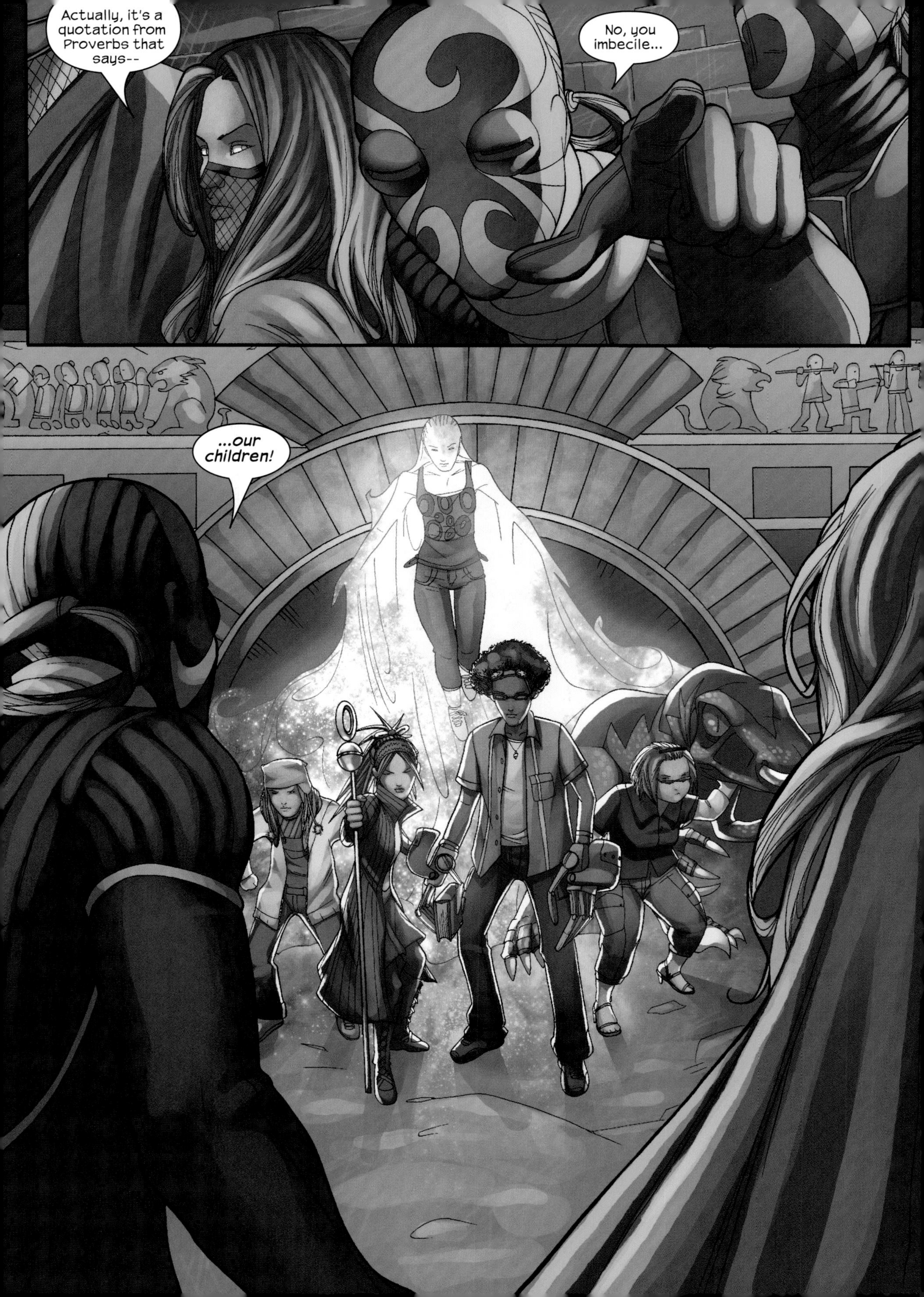

Actually, it's a quotation from Proverbs that says--
No, you imbecile...
...our children!

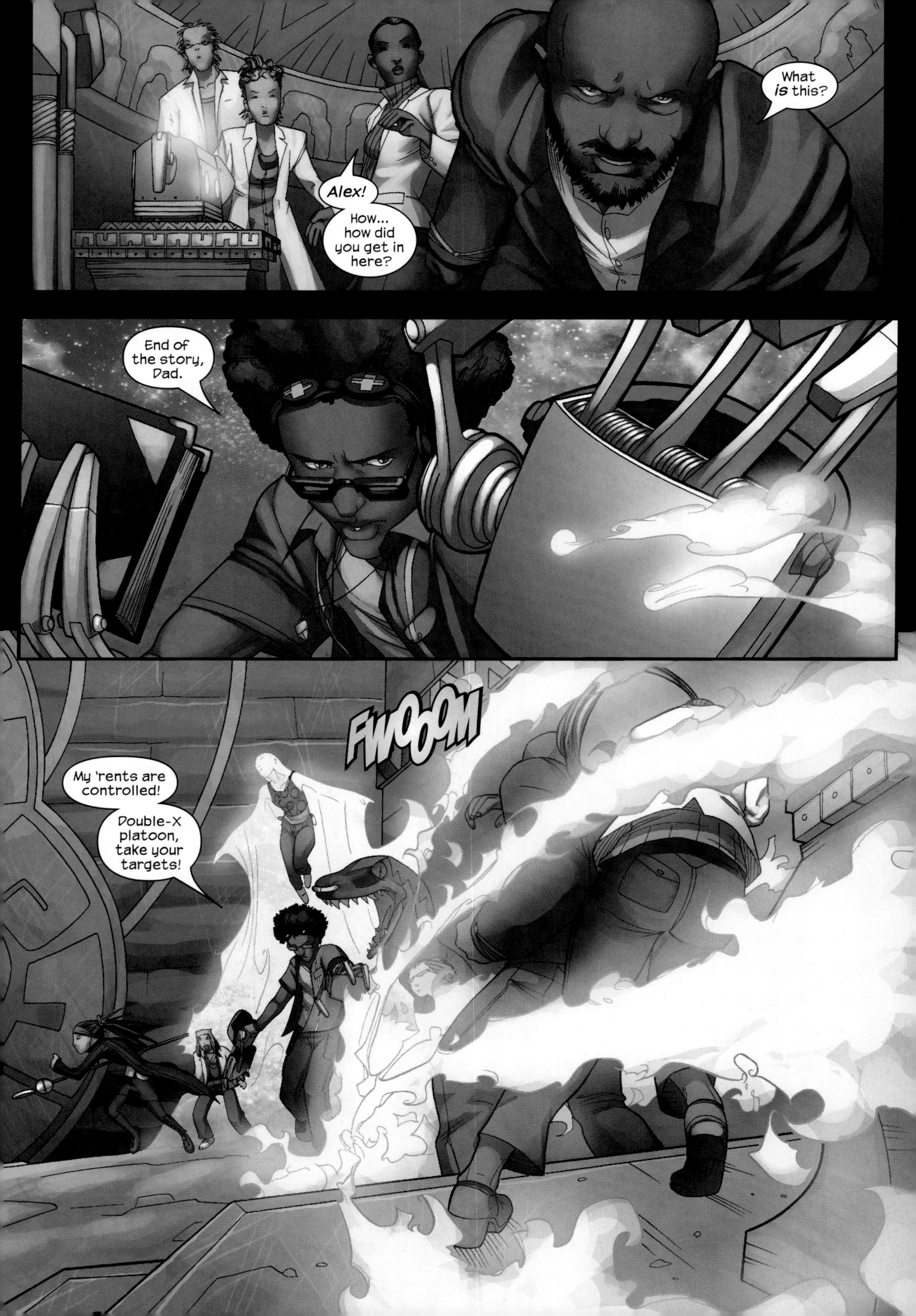
What *is* this?
Alex!
How... how did you get in here?
End of the story, Dad.
FWOOOM
My 'rents are controlled!
Double-X platoon, take your targets!

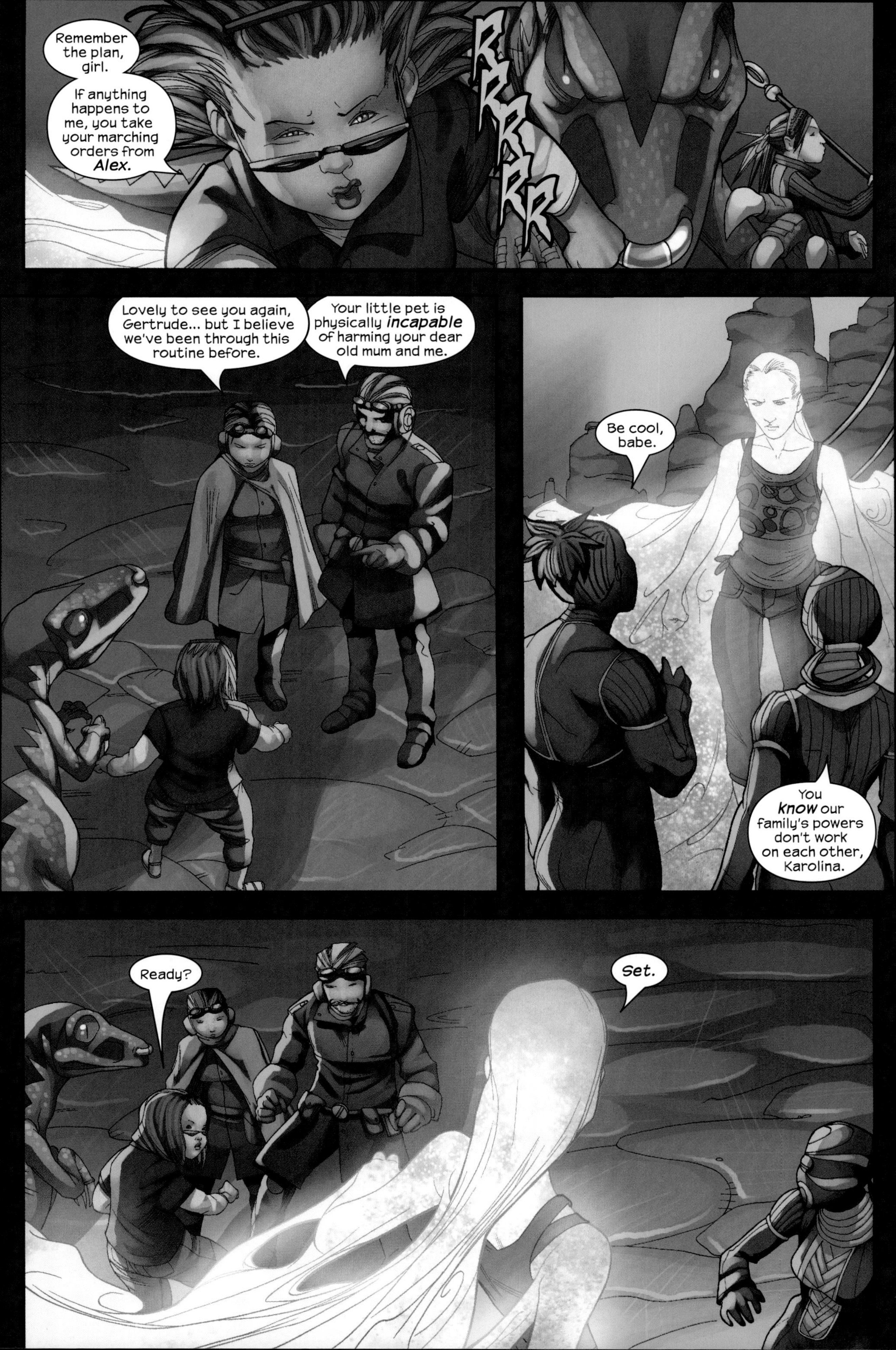

Remember the plan, girl.
If anything happens to me, you take your marching orders from *Alex.*
RRRRRRR
Lovely to see you again, Gertrude... but I believe we've been through this routine before.
Your little pet is physically *incapable* of harming your dear old mum and me.
Be cool, babe.
You *know* our family's powers don't work on each other, Karolina.
Ready?
Set.

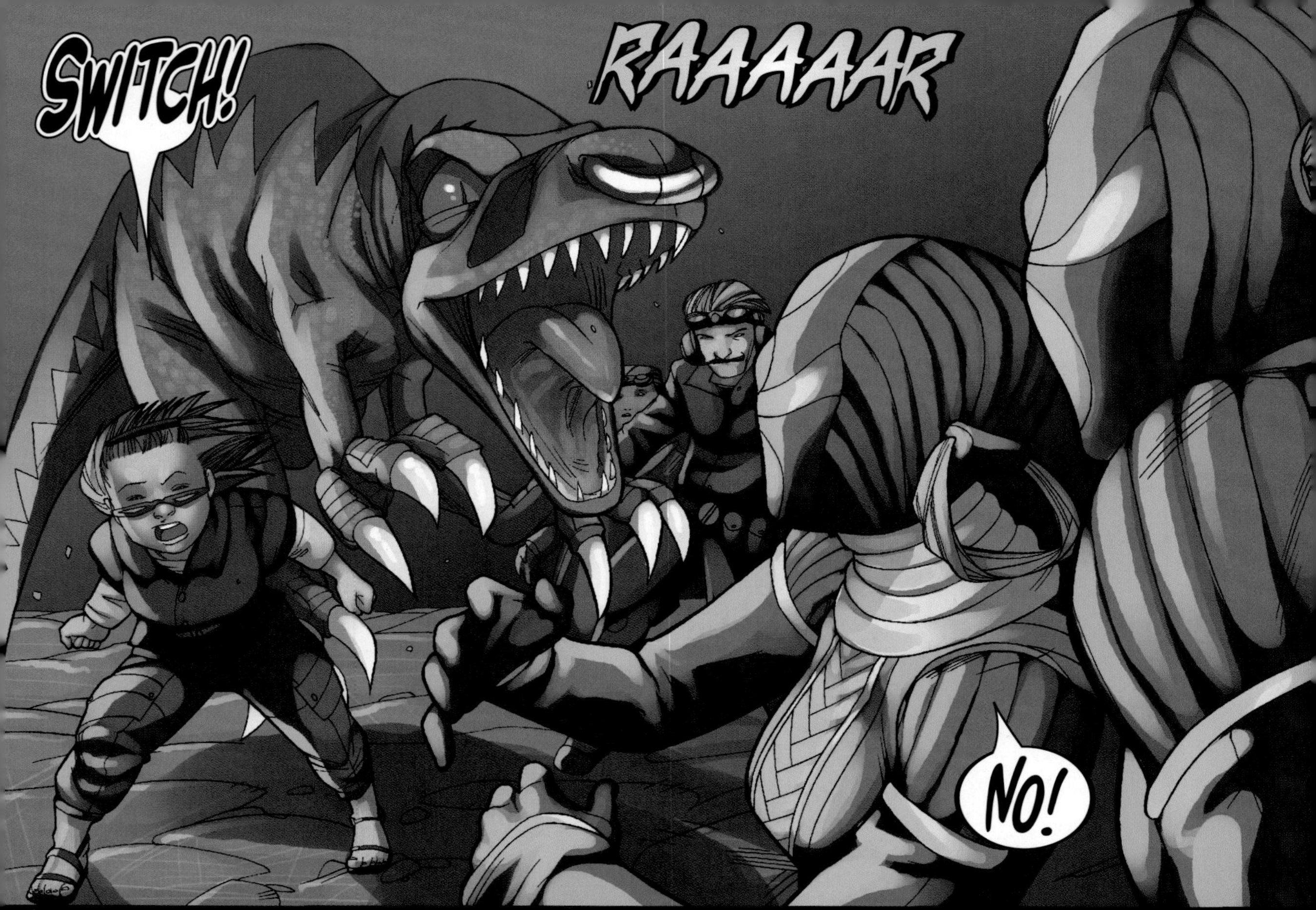
SWITCH!
RAAAAAR
NO!

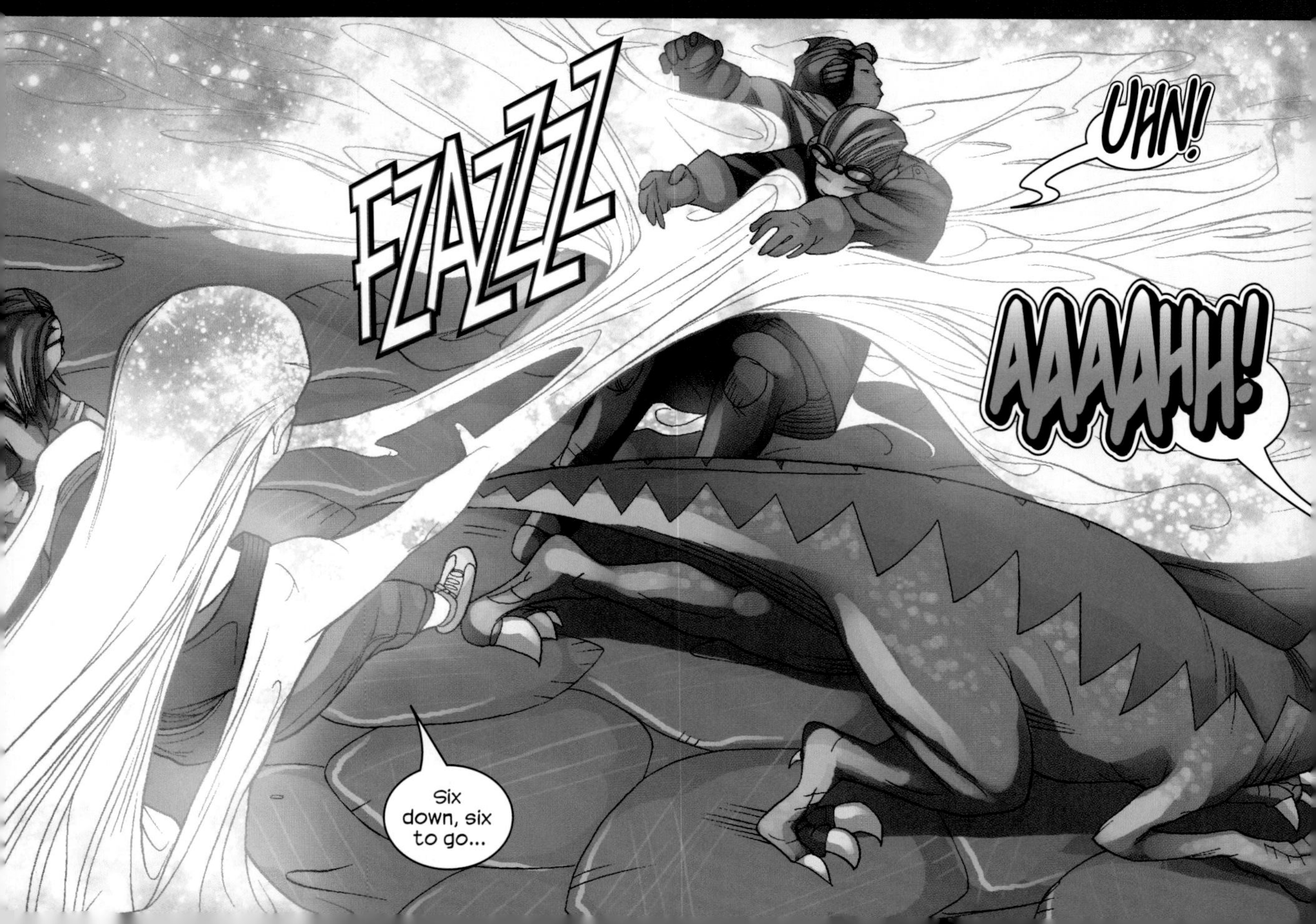
FZAZZZ
UHN!
AAAAHH!
Six down, six to go...

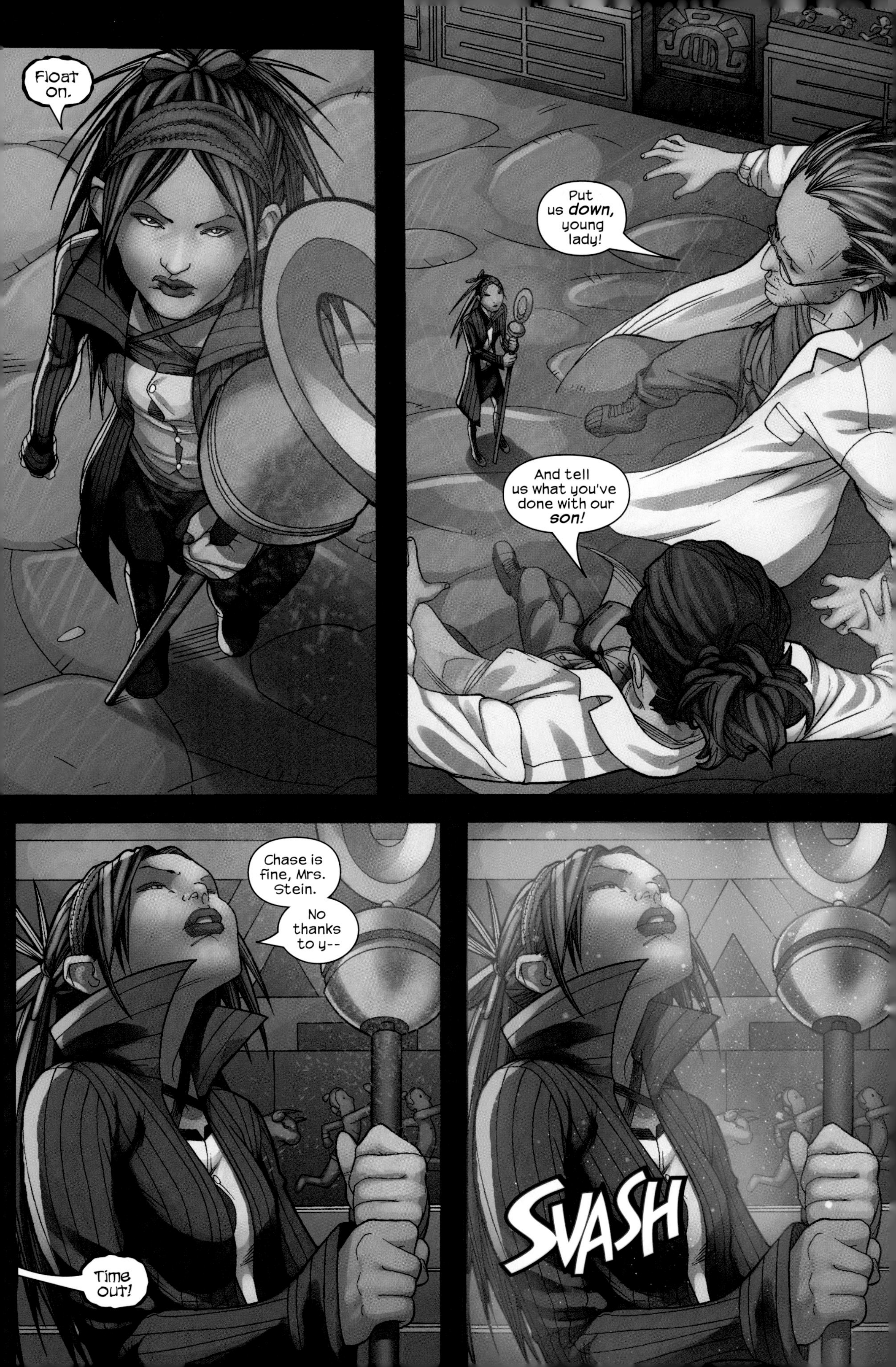

Float on.
Put us down, young lady!
And tell us what you've done with our son!
Chase is fine, Mrs. Stein.
No thanks to y--
Time out!
SVASH

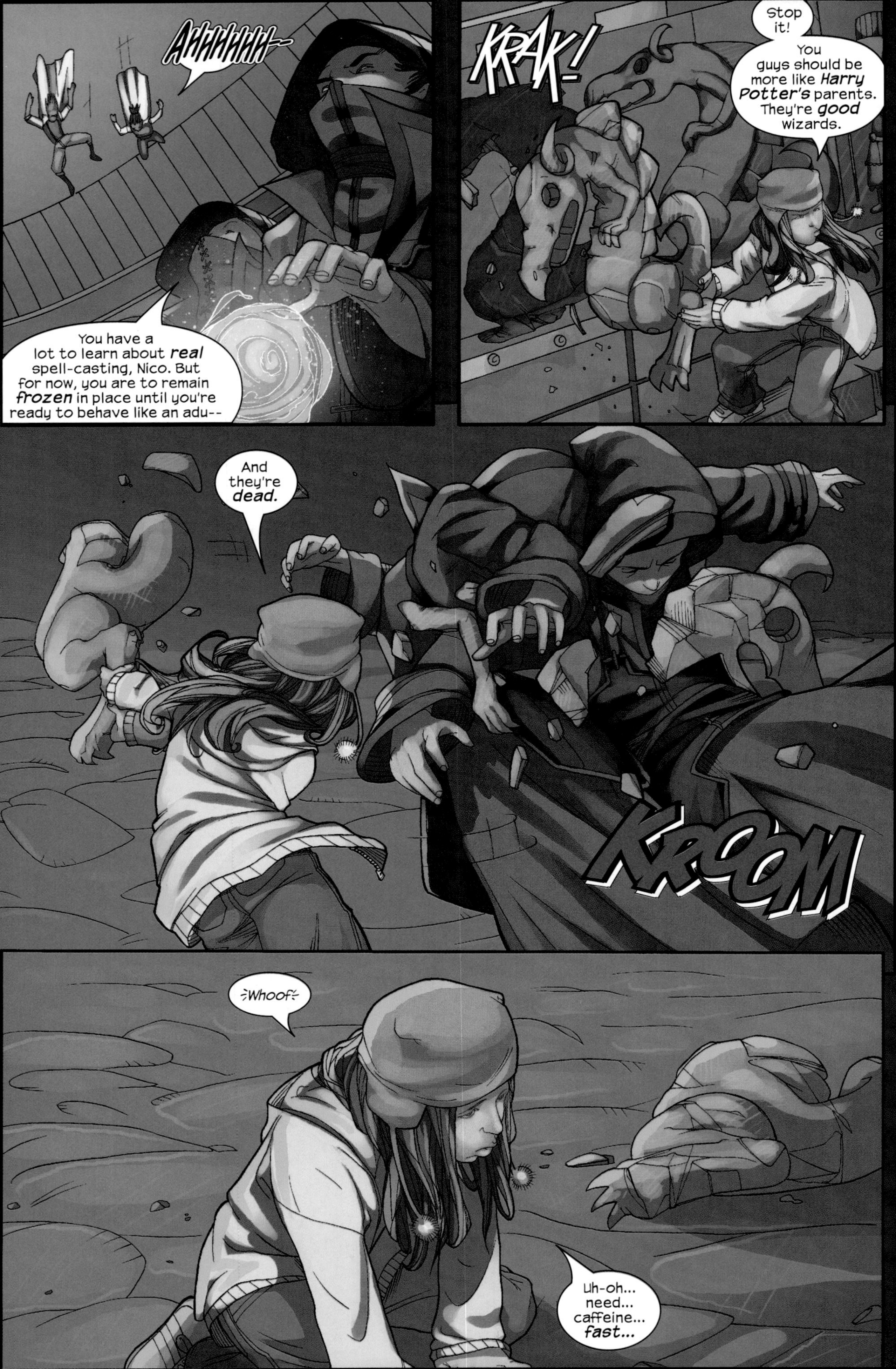

AHHHHHH--
You have a lot to learn about real spell-casting, Nico. But for now, you are to remain frozen in place until you're ready to behave like an adu--
KRAK!
Stop it!
You guys should be more like Harry Potter's parents. They're good wizards.
And they're dead.
KROOM
Whoof
Uh-oh... need... caffeine... fast...

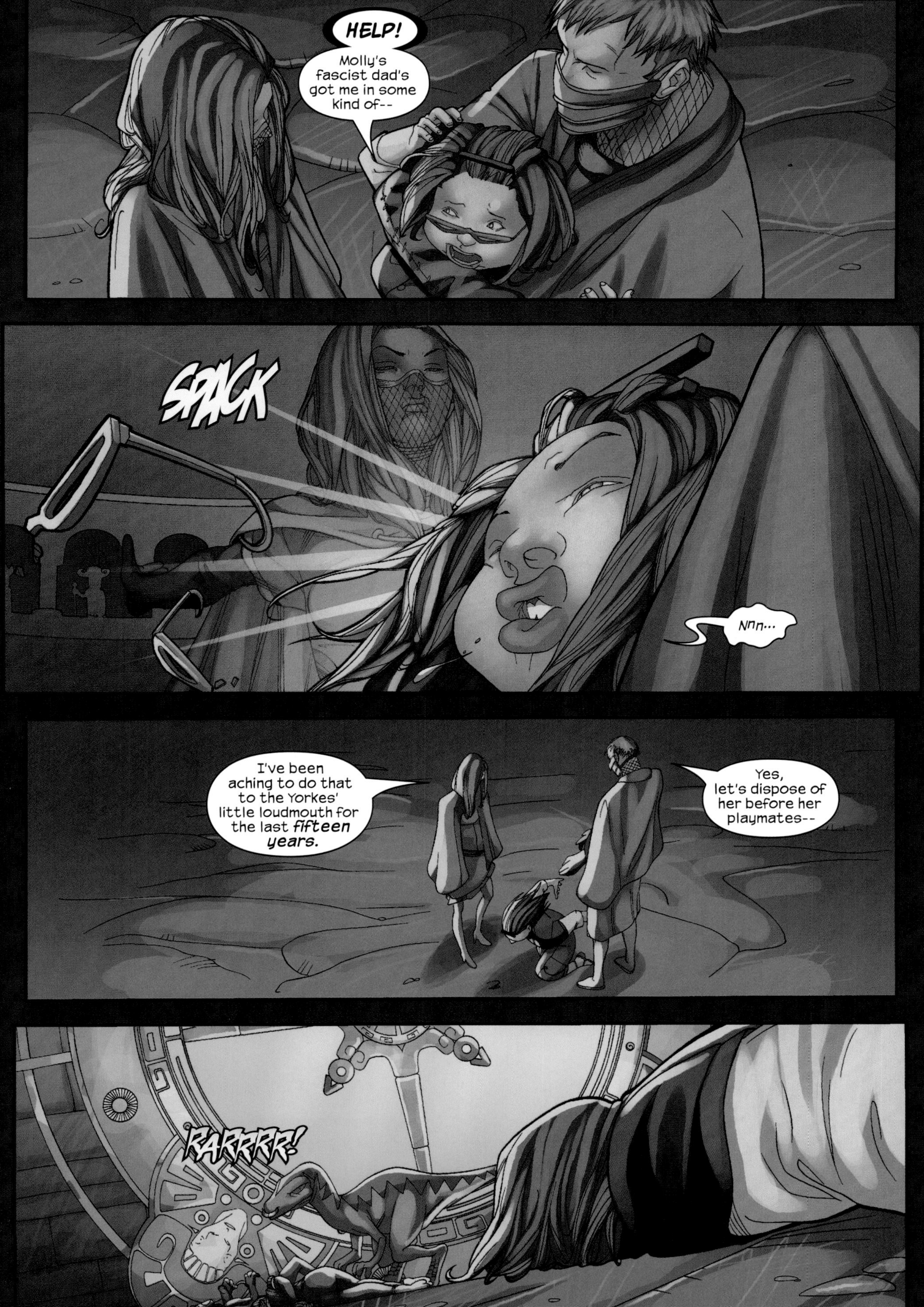
HELP!
Molly's fascist dad's got me in some kind of--
SPACK
Nnn...
I've been aching to do that to the Yorkes' little loudmouth for the last *fifteen years.*
Yes, let's dispose of her before her playmates--
RARRRR!

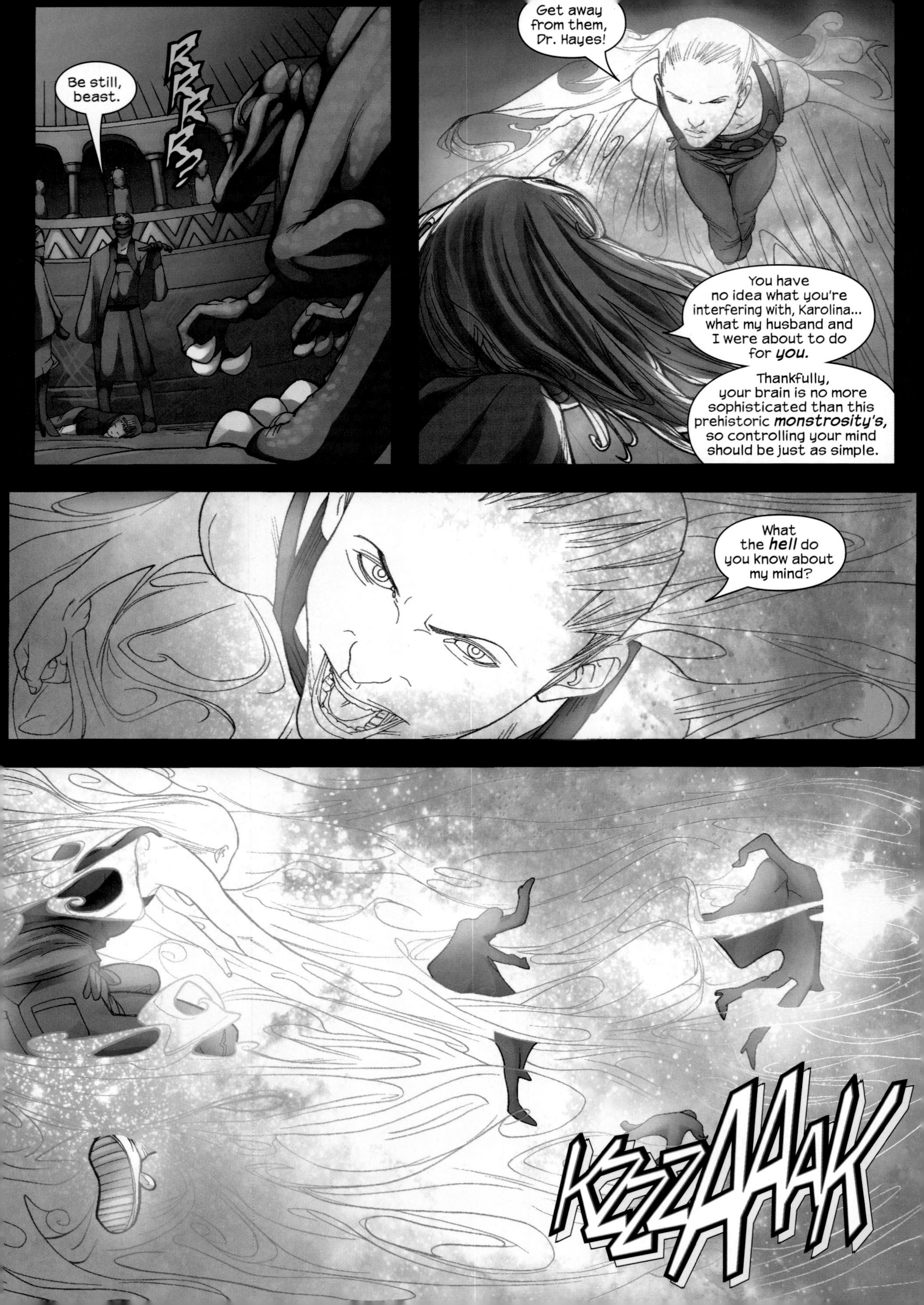

Be still, beast.
RRRR!
Get away from them, Dr. Hayes!
You have no idea what you're interfering with, Karolina... what my husband and I were about to do for *you.*
Thankfully, your brain is no more sophisticated than this prehistoric *monstrosity's,* so controlling your mind should be just as simple.
What the *hell* do you know about my mind?
KZZZAAAK

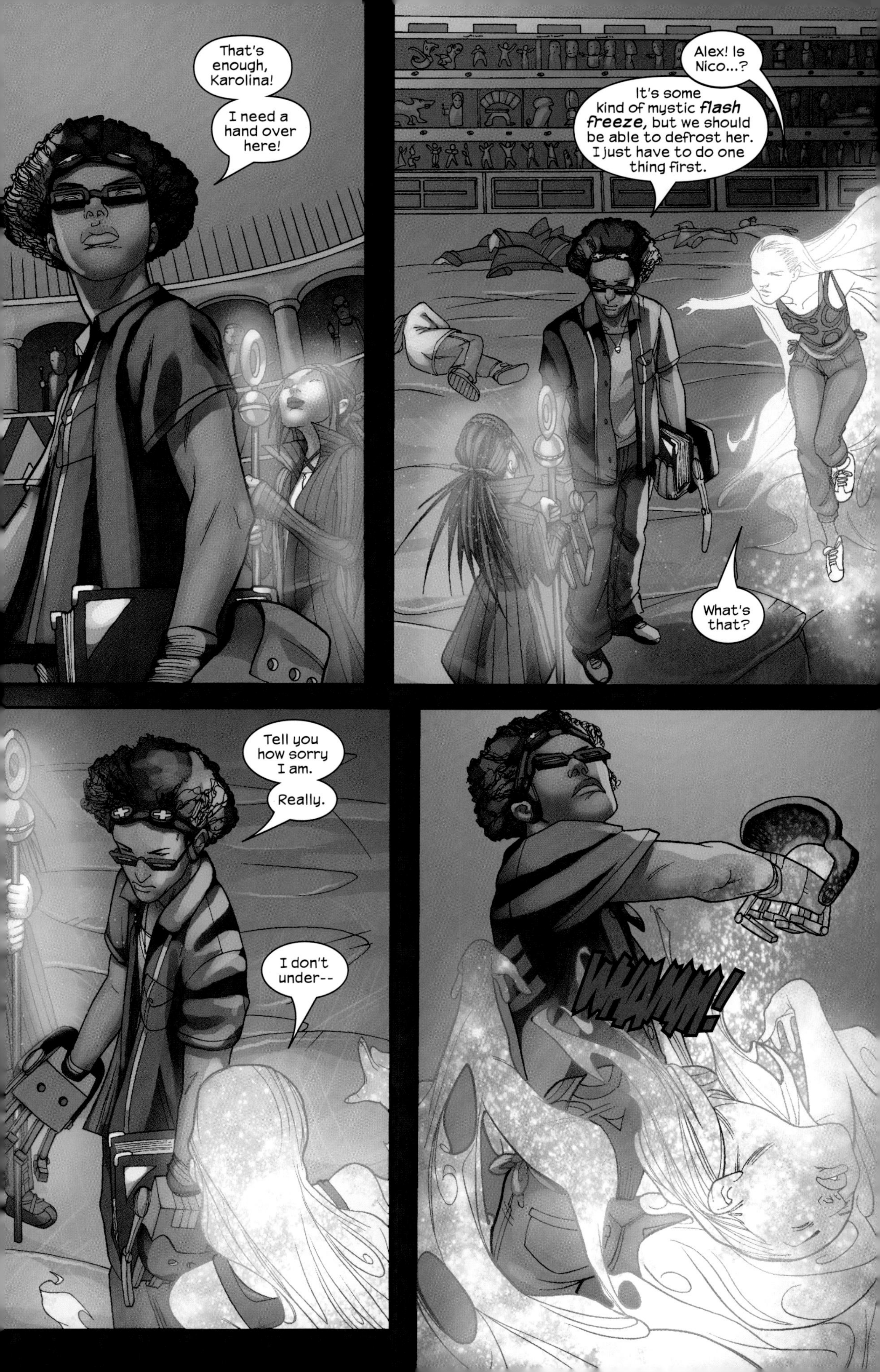
That's enough, Karolina!
I need a hand over here!
Alex! Is Nico...?
It's some kind of mystic flash freeze, but we should be able to defrost her. I just have to do one thing first.
What's that?
Tell you how sorry I am.
Really.
I don't under--
WHAMM!

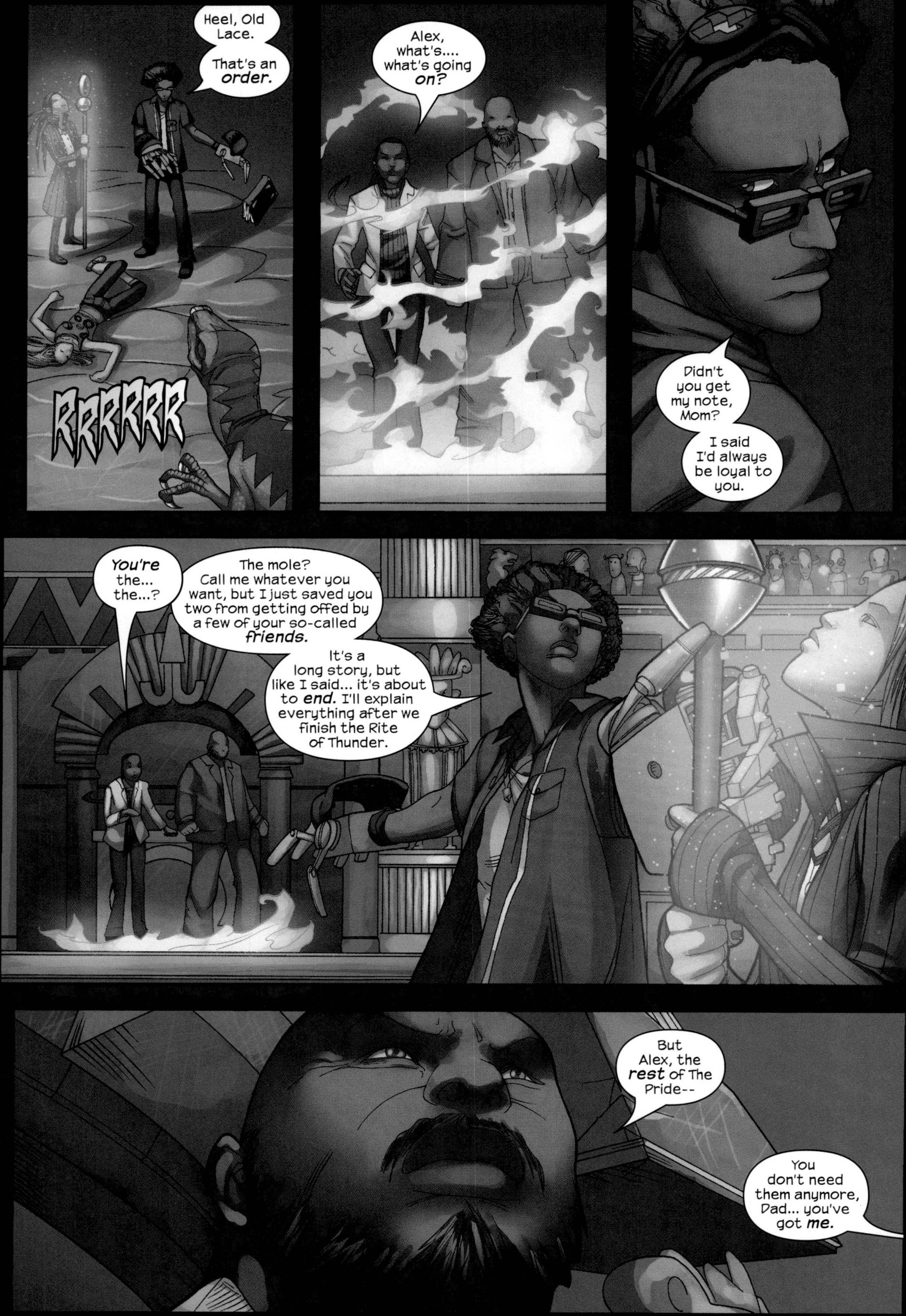
Heel, Old Lace.
That's an *order.*
RRRRRR
Alex, what's.... what's going *on?*
Didn't you get my note, Mom?
I said I'd always be loyal to you.
You're the... the...?
The mole? Call me whatever you want, but I just saved you two from getting offed by a few of your so-called *friends.*
It's a long story, but like I said... it's about to *end.* I'll explain everything after we finish the Rite of Thunder.
But Alex, the *rest* of The Pride--
You don't need them anymore, Dad... you've got *me.*

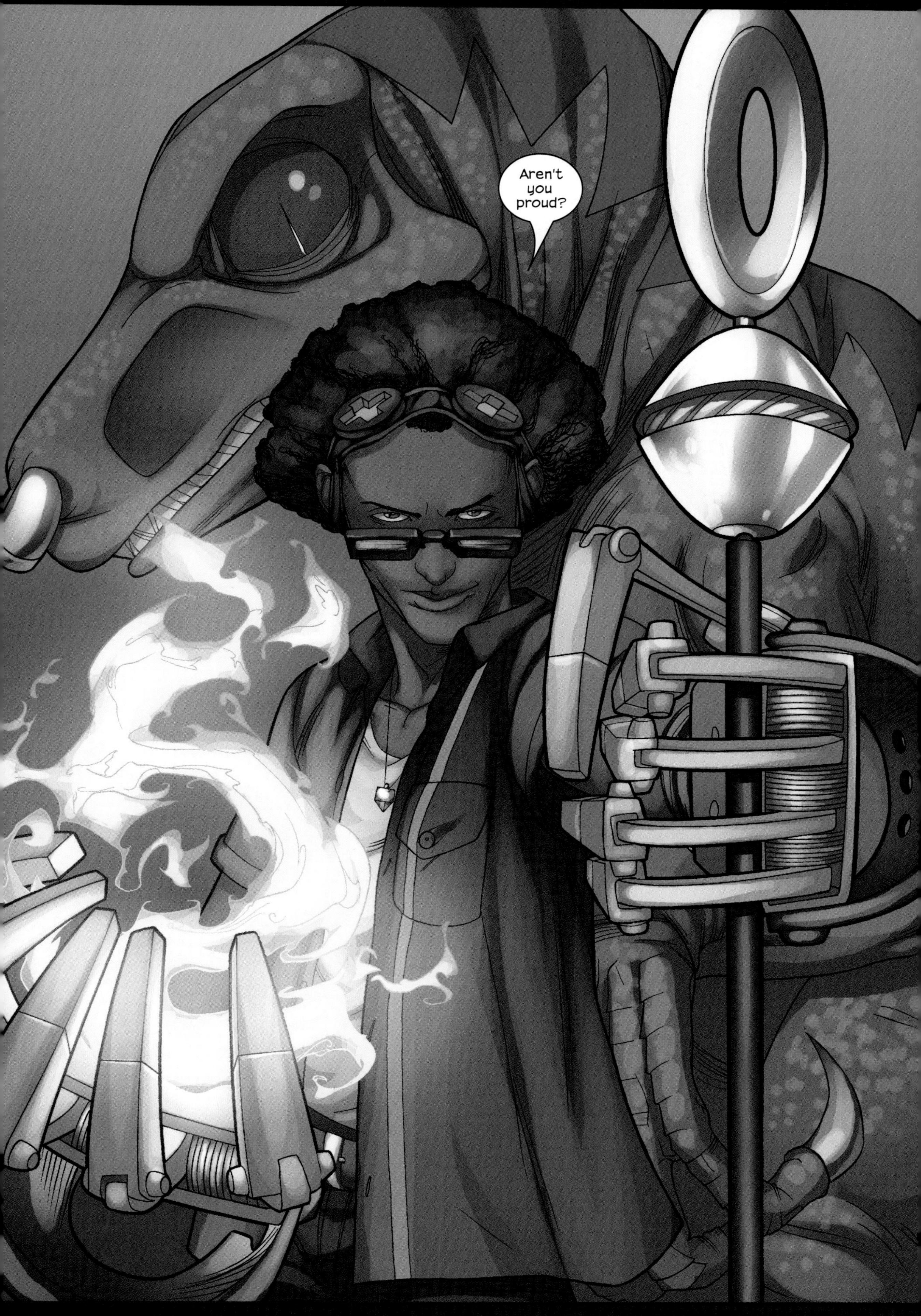
Aren't you proud?

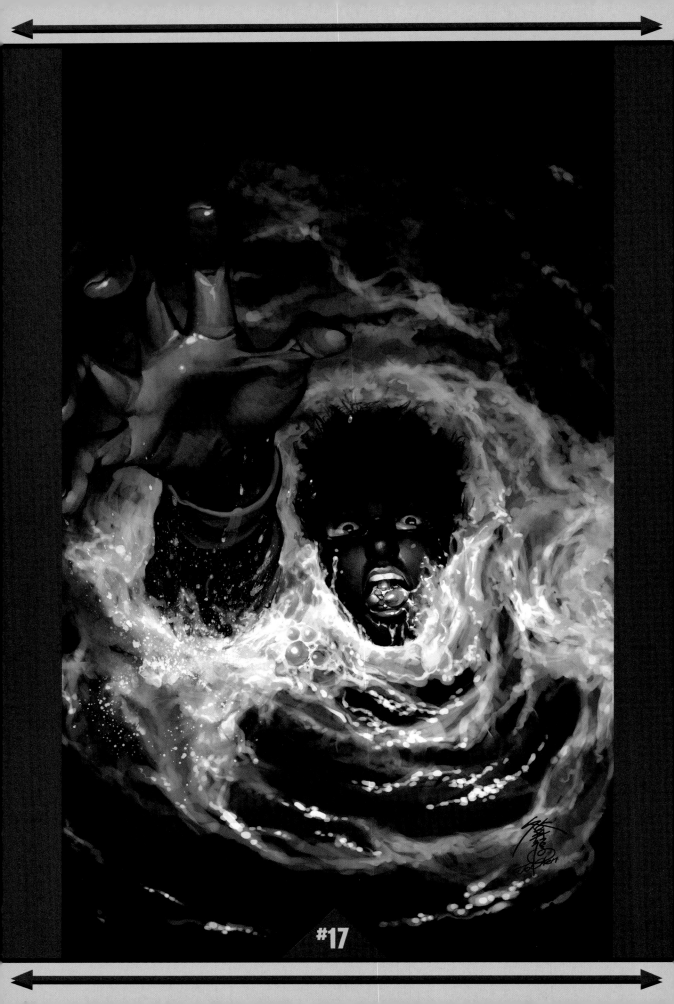

#17

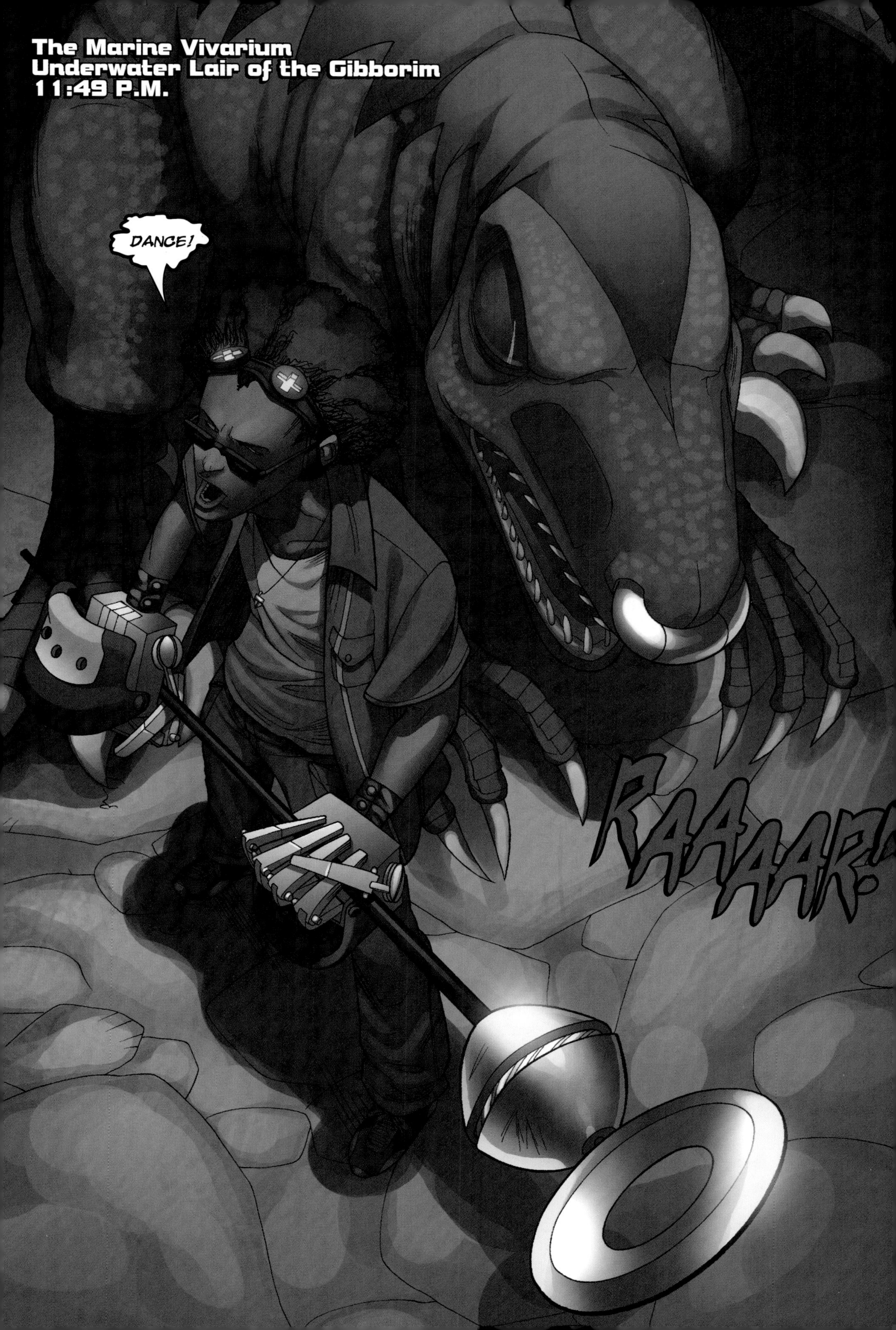
The Marine Vivarium
Underwater Lair of the Gibborim
11:49 P.M.
DANCE!
RAAAAR!

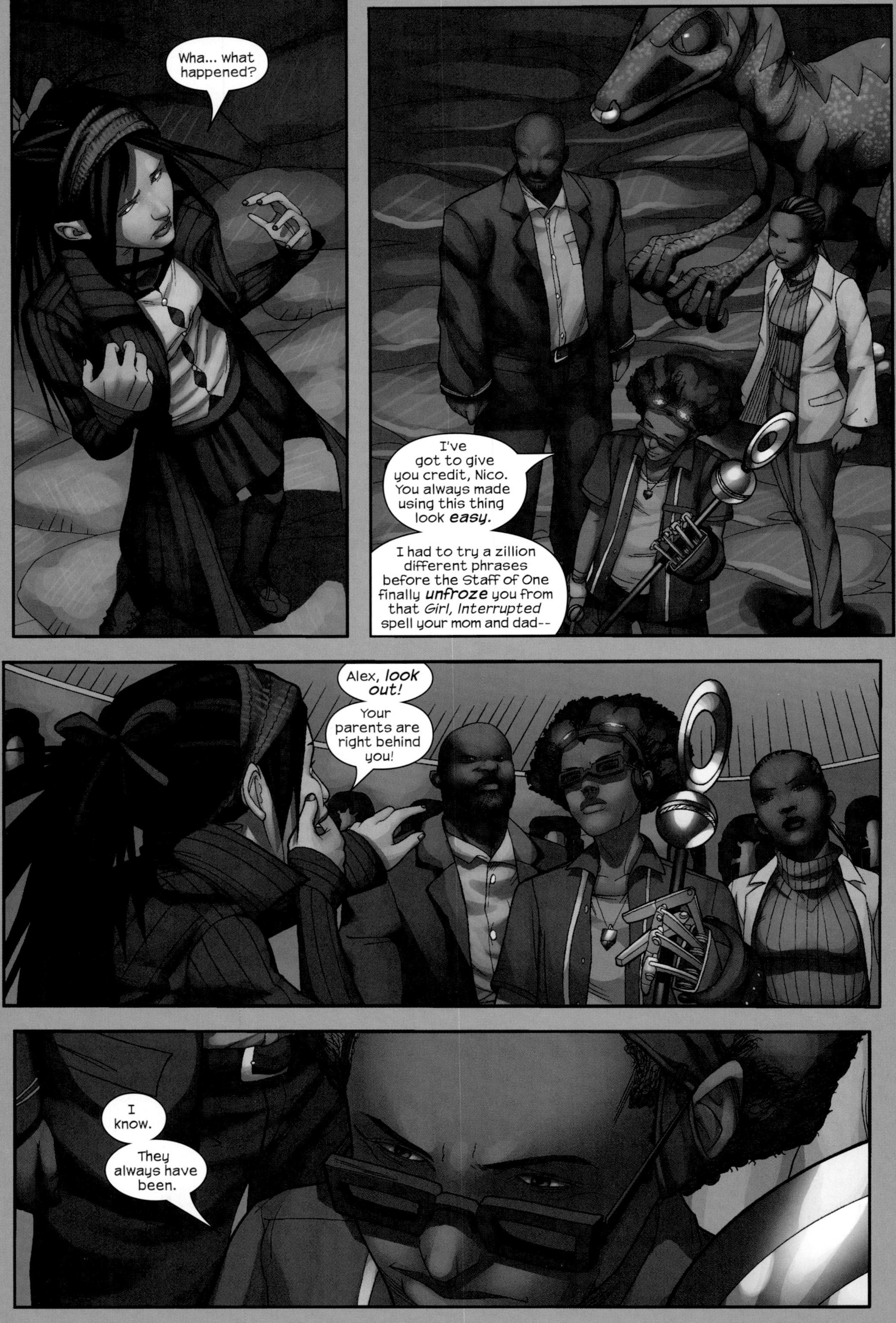
Wha... what happened?
I've got to give you credit, Nico. You always made using this thing look *easy.*
I had to try a zillion different phrases before the Staff of One finally ***unfroze*** you from that *Girl, Interrupted* spell your mom and dad--
Alex, ***look out!***
Your parents are right behind you!
I know.
They always have been.

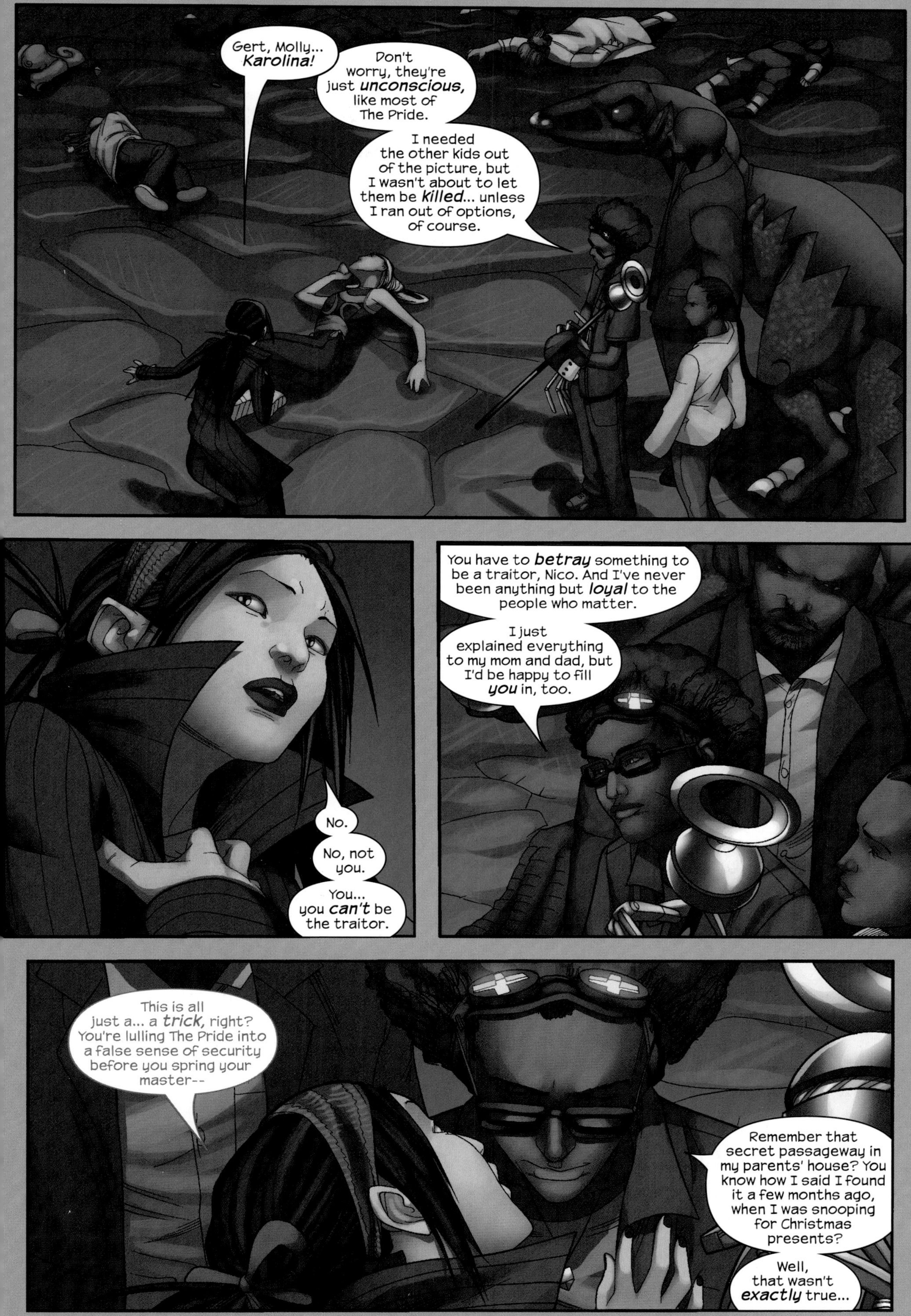

Gert, Molly... Karolina!
Don't worry, they're just unconscious, like most of The Pride.
I needed the other kids out of the picture, but I wasn't about to let them be killed... unless I ran out of options, of course.
No.
No, not you.
You... you can't be the traitor.
You have to betray something to be a traitor, Nico. And I've never been anything but loyal to the people who matter.
I just explained everything to my mom and dad, but I'd be happy to fill you in, too.
This is all just a... a trick, right? You're lulling The Pride into a false sense of security before you spring your master--
Remember that secret passageway in my parents' house? You know how I said I found it a few months ago, when I was snooping for Christmas presents?
Well, that wasn't exactly true...

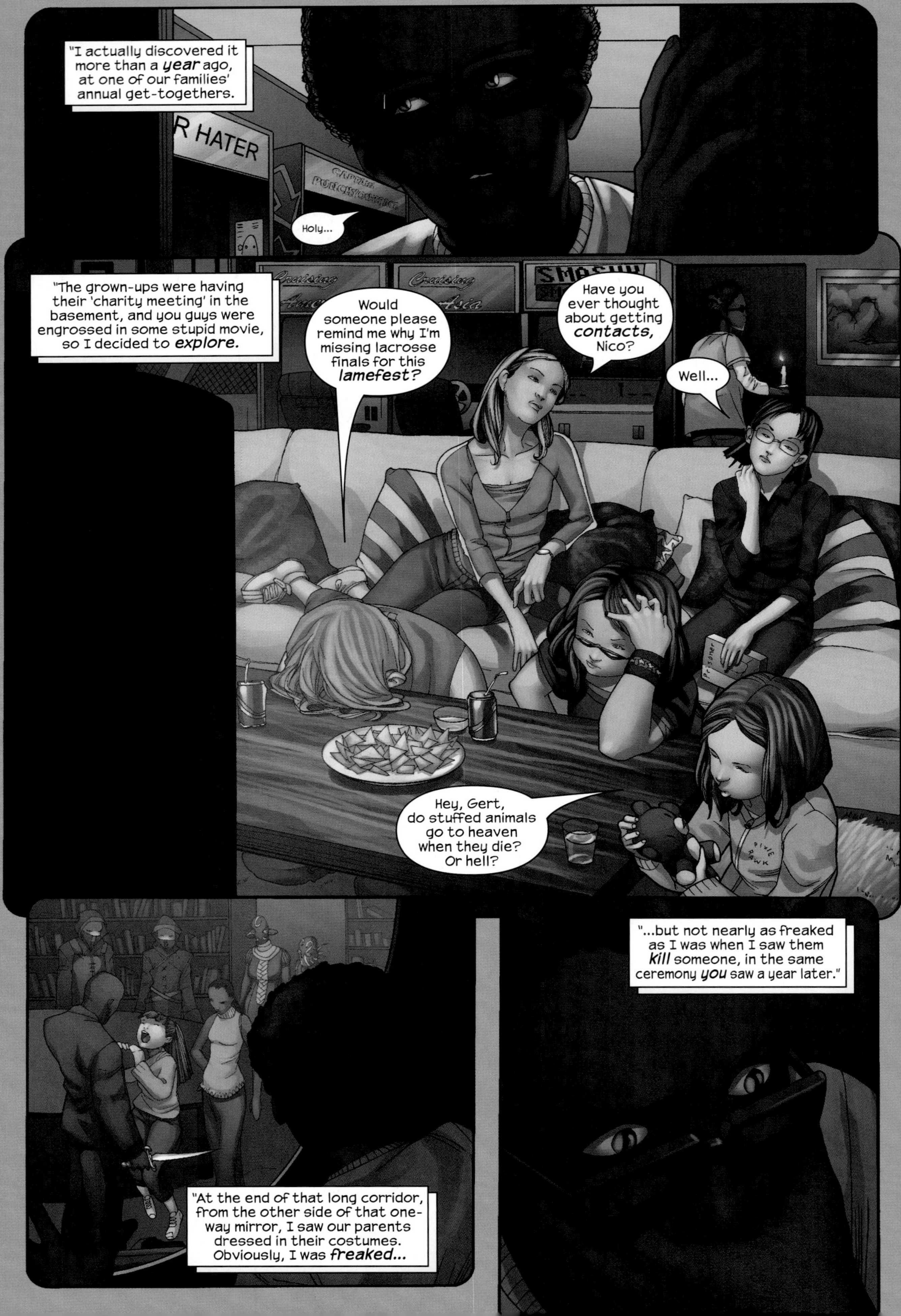

"I actually discovered it more than a *year* ago, at one of our families' annual get-togethers.
R HATER
Holy...
"The grown-ups were having their 'charity meeting' in the basement, and you guys were engrossed in some stupid movie, so I decided to *explore.*
Would someone please remind me why I'm missing lacrosse finals for this *lamefest?*
Have you ever thought about getting *contacts,* Nico?
Well...
Hey, Gert, do stuffed animals go to heaven when they die? Or hell?
"At the end of that long corridor, from the other side of that one-way mirror, I saw our parents dressed in their costumes. Obviously, I was *freaked...*
"...but not nearly as freaked as I was when I saw them *kill* someone, in the same ceremony *you* saw a year later."

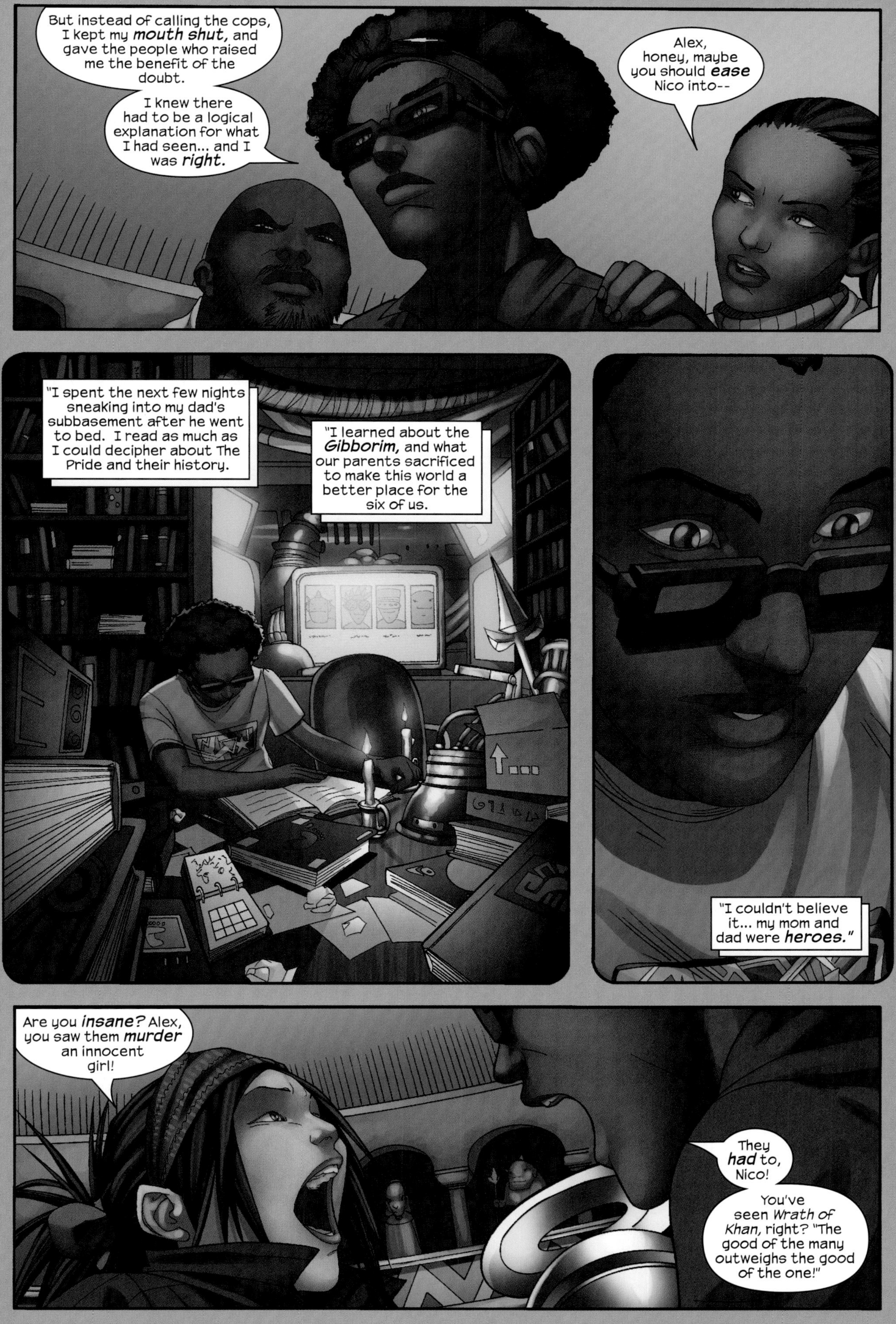

But instead of calling the cops, I kept my mouth shut, and gave the people who raised me the benefit of the doubt.
I knew there had to be a logical explanation for what I had seen... and I was right.
Alex, honey, maybe you should ease Nico into--
"I spent the next few nights sneaking into my dad's subbasement after he went to bed. I read as much as I could decipher about The Pride and their history.
"I learned about the Gibborim, and what our parents sacrificed to make this world a better place for the six of us.
"I couldn't believe it... my mom and dad were heroes."
Are you insane? Alex, you saw them murder an innocent girl!
They had to, Nico!
You've seen Wrath of Khan, right? "The good of the many outweighs the good of the one!"

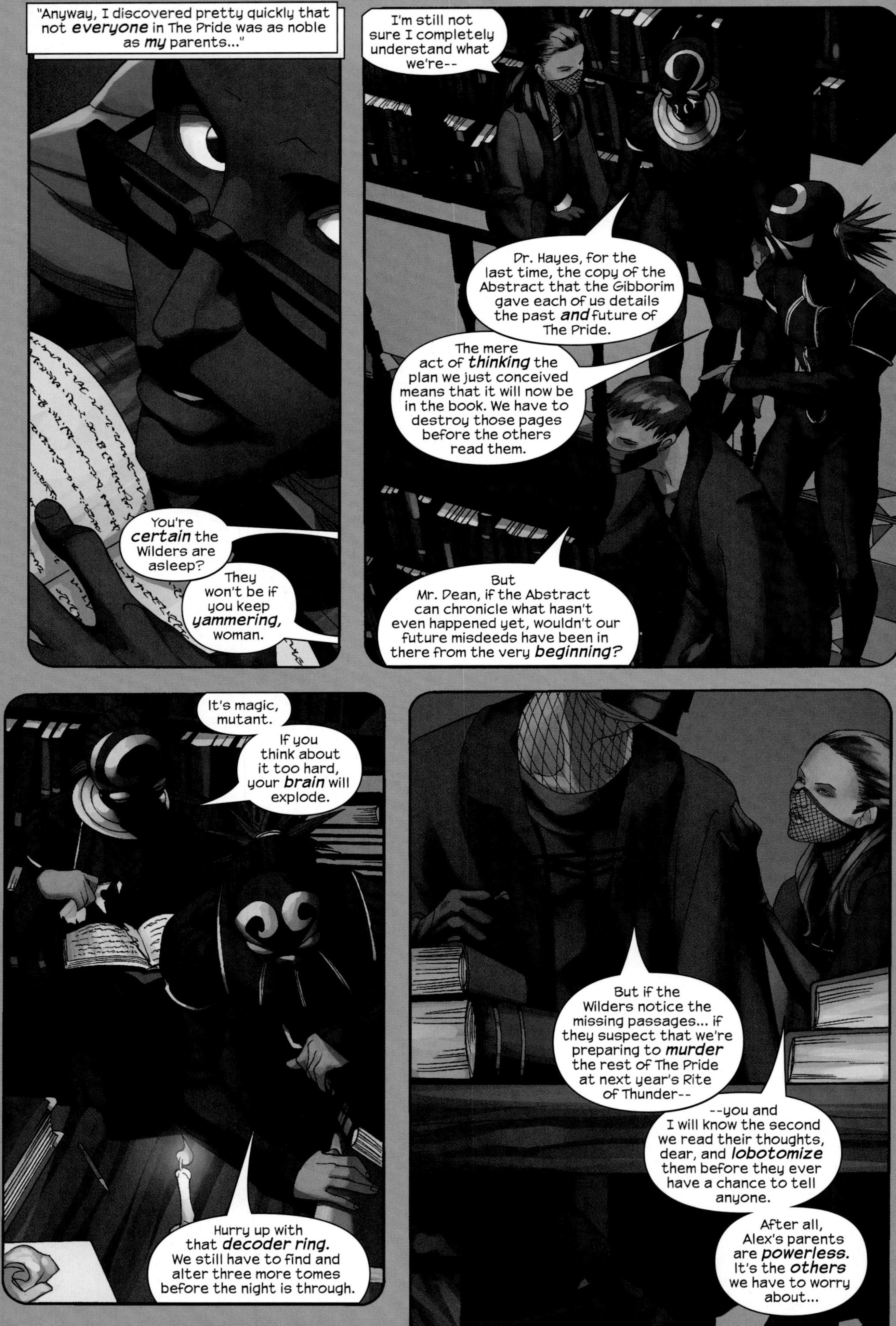
"Anyway, I discovered pretty quickly that not *everyone* in The Pride was as noble as *my* parents..."
You're *certain* the Wilders are asleep?
They won't be if you keep *yammering,* woman.
I'm still not sure I completely understand what we're--
Dr. Hayes, for the last time, the copy of the Abstract that the Gibborim gave each of us details the past *and* future of The Pride.
The mere act of *thinking* the plan we just conceived means that it will now be in the book. We have to destroy those pages before the others read them.
But Mr. Dean, if the Abstract can chronicle what hasn't even happened yet, wouldn't our future misdeeds have been in there from the very *beginning?*
It's magic, mutant.
If you think about it too hard, your *brain* will explode.
Hurry up with that *decoder ring.* We still have to find and alter three more tomes before the night is through.
But if the Wilders notice the missing passages... if they suspect that we're preparing to *murder* the rest of The Pride at next year's Rite of Thunder--
--you and I will know the second we read their thoughts, dear, and *lobotomize* them before they ever have a chance to tell anyone.
After all, Alex's parents are *powerless.* It's the *others* we have to worry about...

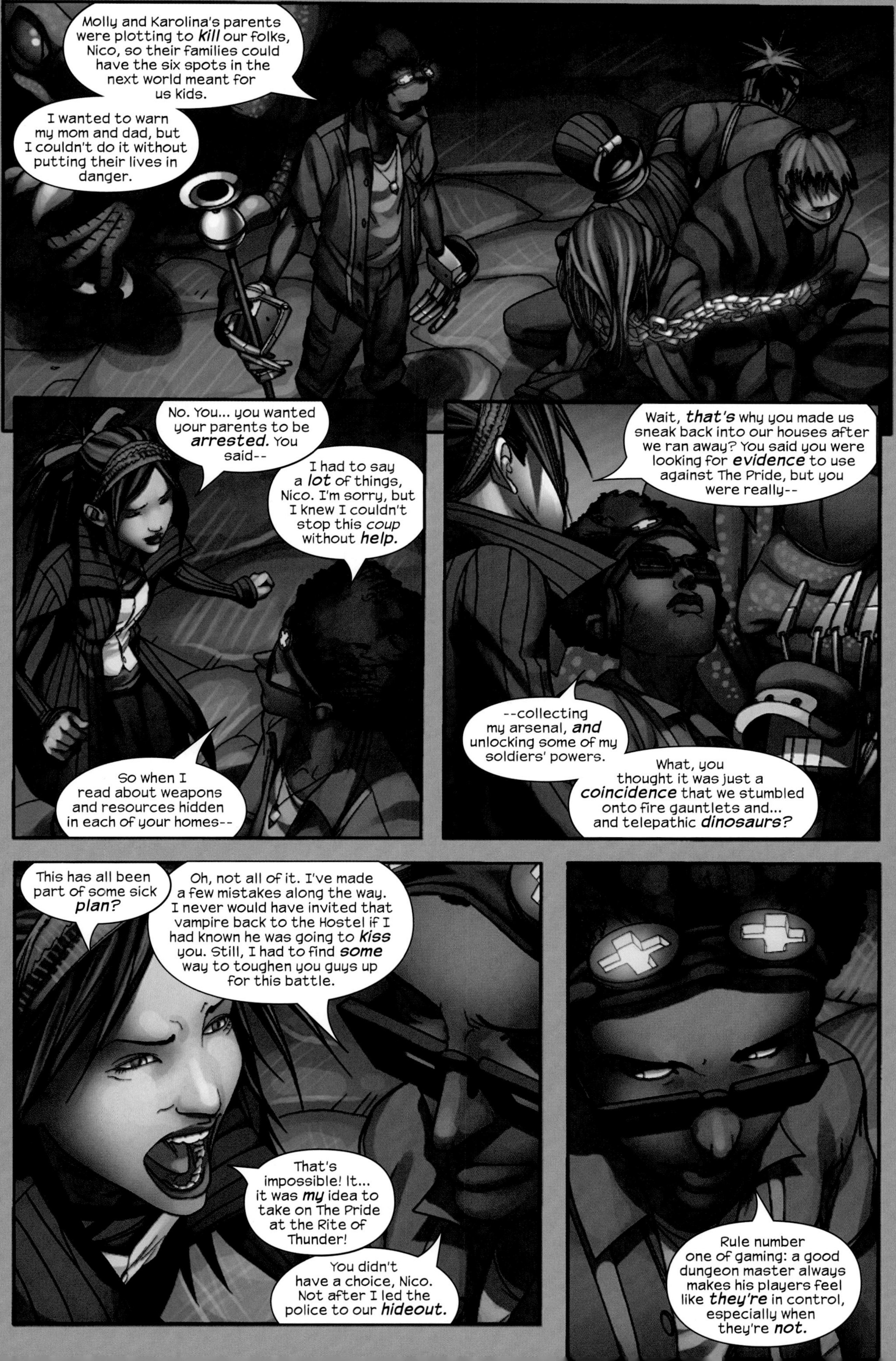
Molly and Karolina's parents were plotting to *kill* our folks, Nico, so their families could have the six spots in the next world meant for us kids.
I wanted to warn my mom and dad, but I couldn't do it without putting their lives in danger.
No. You... you wanted your parents to be *arrested.* You said--
I had to say a *lot* of things, Nico. I'm sorry, but I knew I couldn't stop this *coup* without *help.*
So when I read about weapons and resources hidden in each of your homes--
Wait, *that's* why you made us sneak back into our houses after we ran away? You said you were looking for *evidence* to use against The Pride, but you were really--
--collecting my arsenal, *and* unlocking some of my soldiers' powers.
What, you thought it was just a *coincidence* that we stumbled onto fire gauntlets and... and telepathic *dinosaurs?*
This has all been part of some sick *plan?*
Oh, not all of it. I've made a few mistakes along the way. I never would have invited that vampire back to the Hostel if I had known he was going to *kiss* you. Still, I had to find *some* way to toughen you guys up for this battle.
That's impossible! It... it was *my* idea to take on The Pride at the Rite of Thunder!
You didn't have a choice, Nico. Not after I led the police to our *hideout.*
Rule number one of gaming: a good dungeon master always makes his players feel like *they're* in control, especially when they're *not.*

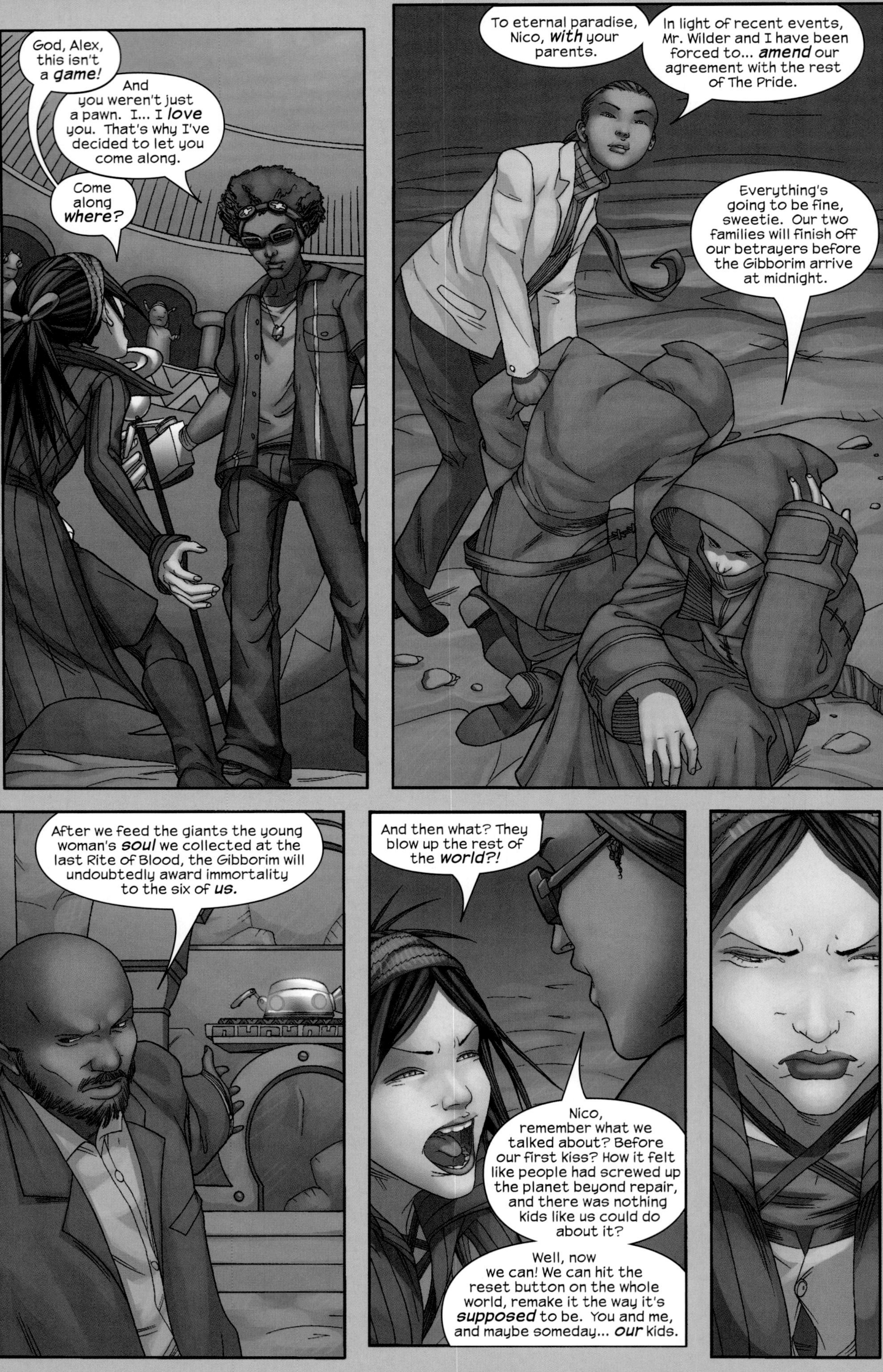
God, Alex, this isn't a game!
And you weren't just a pawn. I... I love you. That's why I've decided to let you come along.
Come along where?
To eternal paradise, Nico, with your parents.
In light of recent events, Mr. Wilder and I have been forced to... amend our agreement with the rest of The Pride.
Everything's going to be fine, sweetie. Our two families will finish off our betrayers before the Gibborim arrive at midnight.
After we feed the giants the young woman's soul we collected at the last Rite of Blood, the Gibborim will undoubtedly award immortality to the six of us.
And then what? They blow up the rest of the world?!
Nico, remember what we talked about? Before our first kiss? How it felt like people had screwed up the planet beyond repair, and there was nothing kids like us could do about it?
Well, now we can! We can hit the reset button on the whole world, remake it the way it's supposed to be. You and me, and maybe someday... our kids.

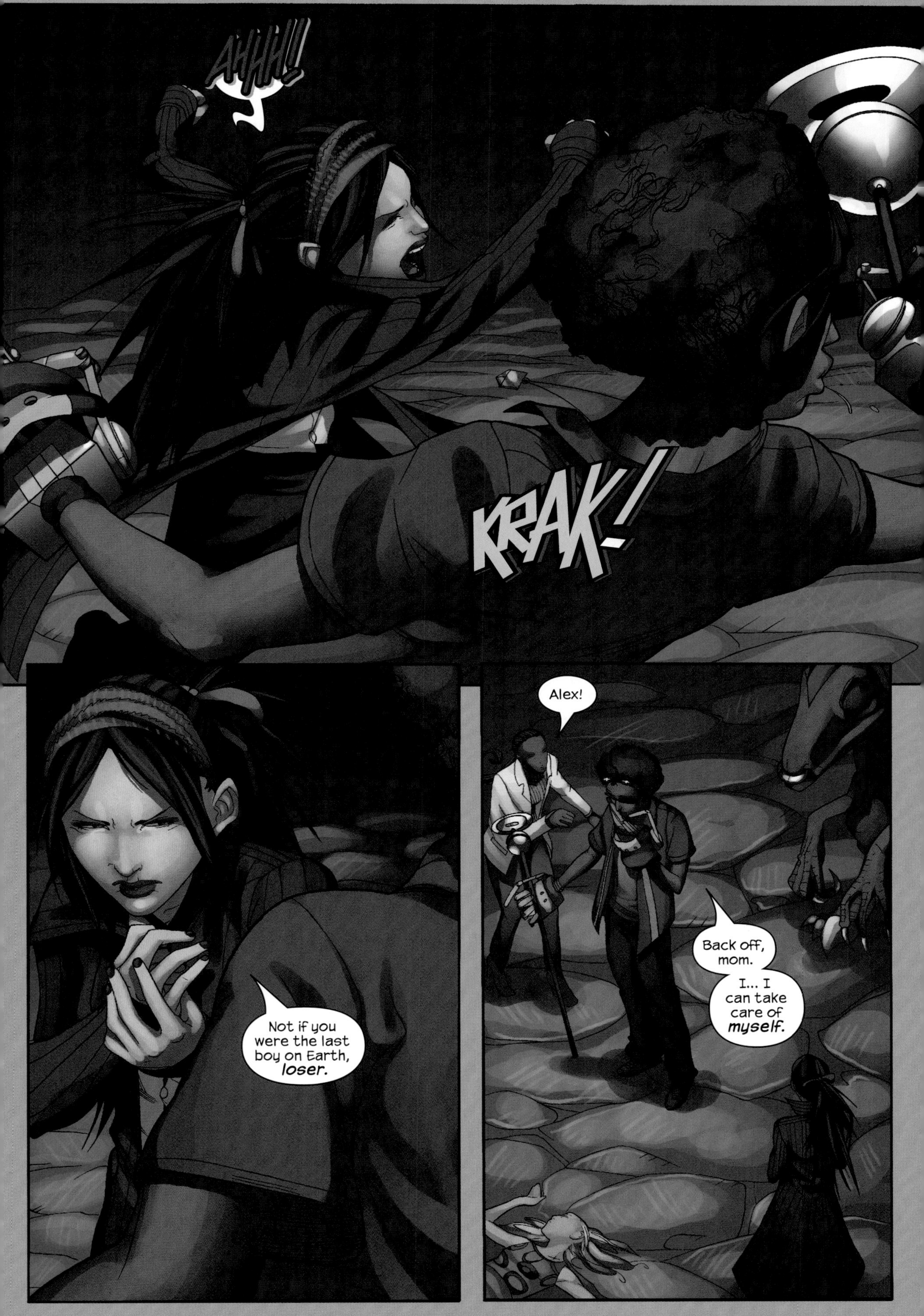
AHHH!!
KRAK!
Not if you were the last boy on Earth, *loser.*
Alex!
Back off, mom.
I... I can take care of *myself.*

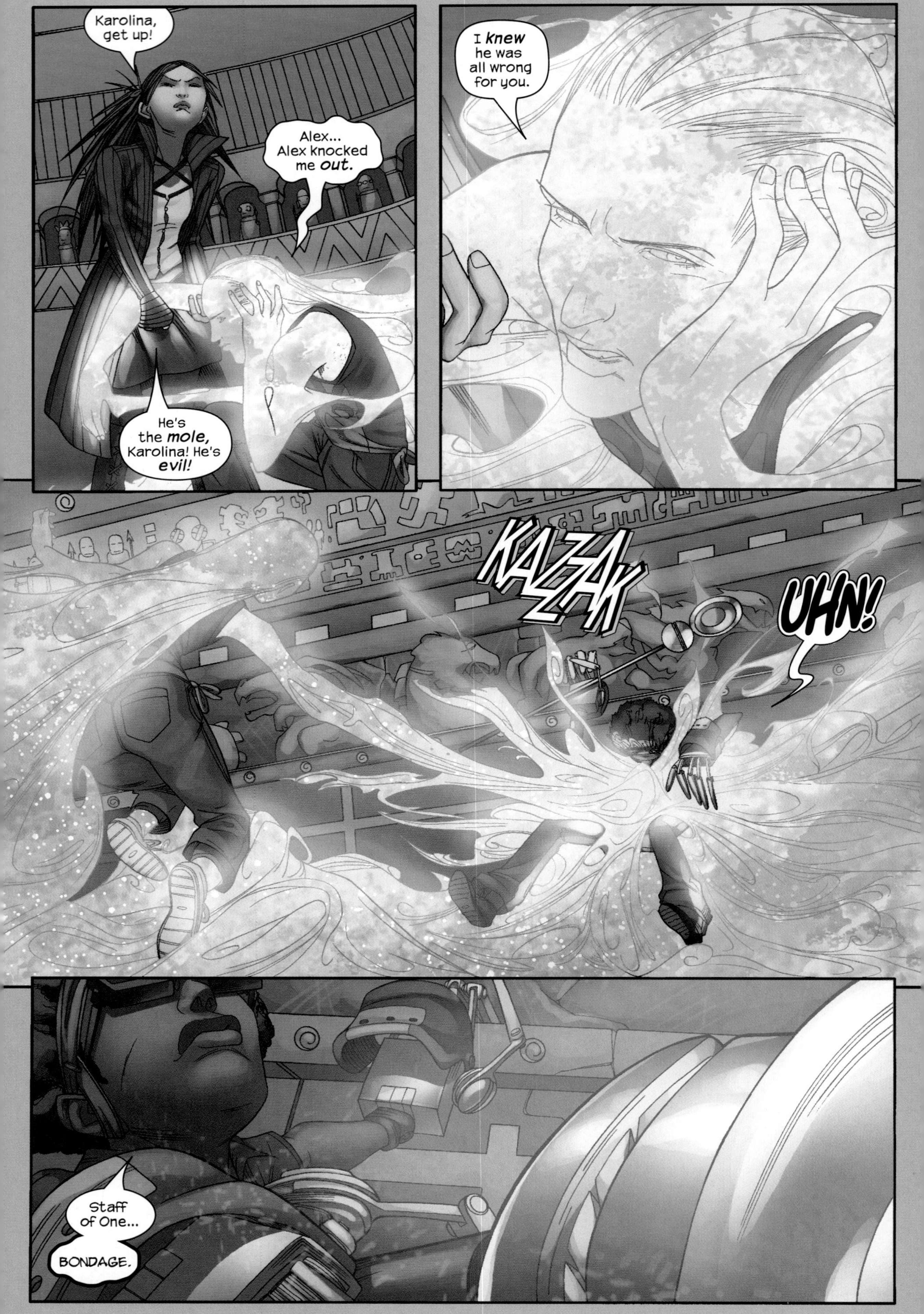
Karolina, get up!
Alex... Alex knocked me *out.*
He's the *mole,* Karolina! He's *evil!*
I *knew* he was all wrong for you.
KAZZAK
UHN!
Staff of One...
BONDAGE.

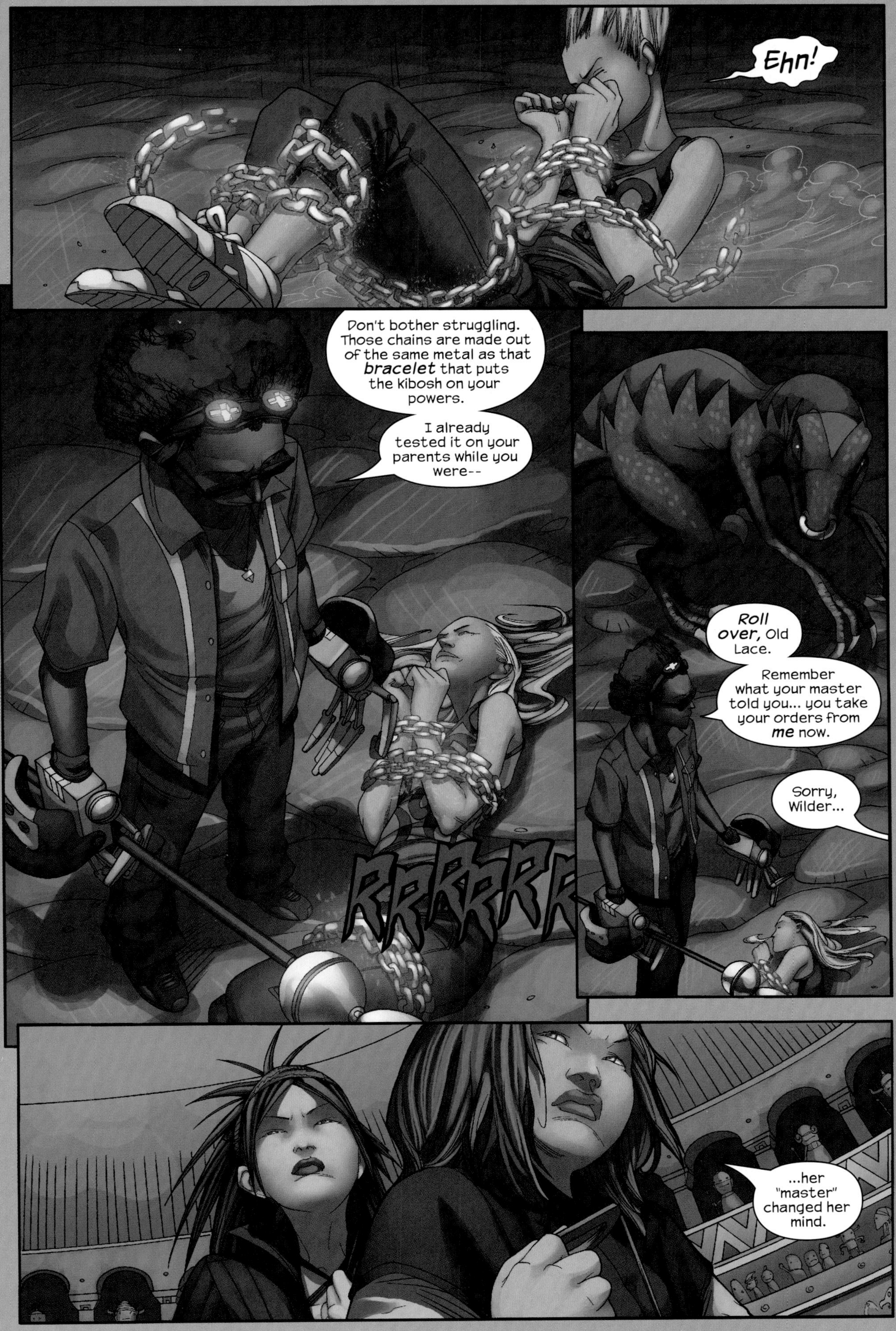
Ehn!
Don't bother struggling. Those chains are made out of the same metal as that *bracelet* that puts the kibosh on your powers.
I already tested it on your parents while you were--
RRRRRR
Roll over, Old Lace.
Remember what your master told you... you take your orders from *me* now.
Sorry, Wilder...
...her "master" changed her mind.

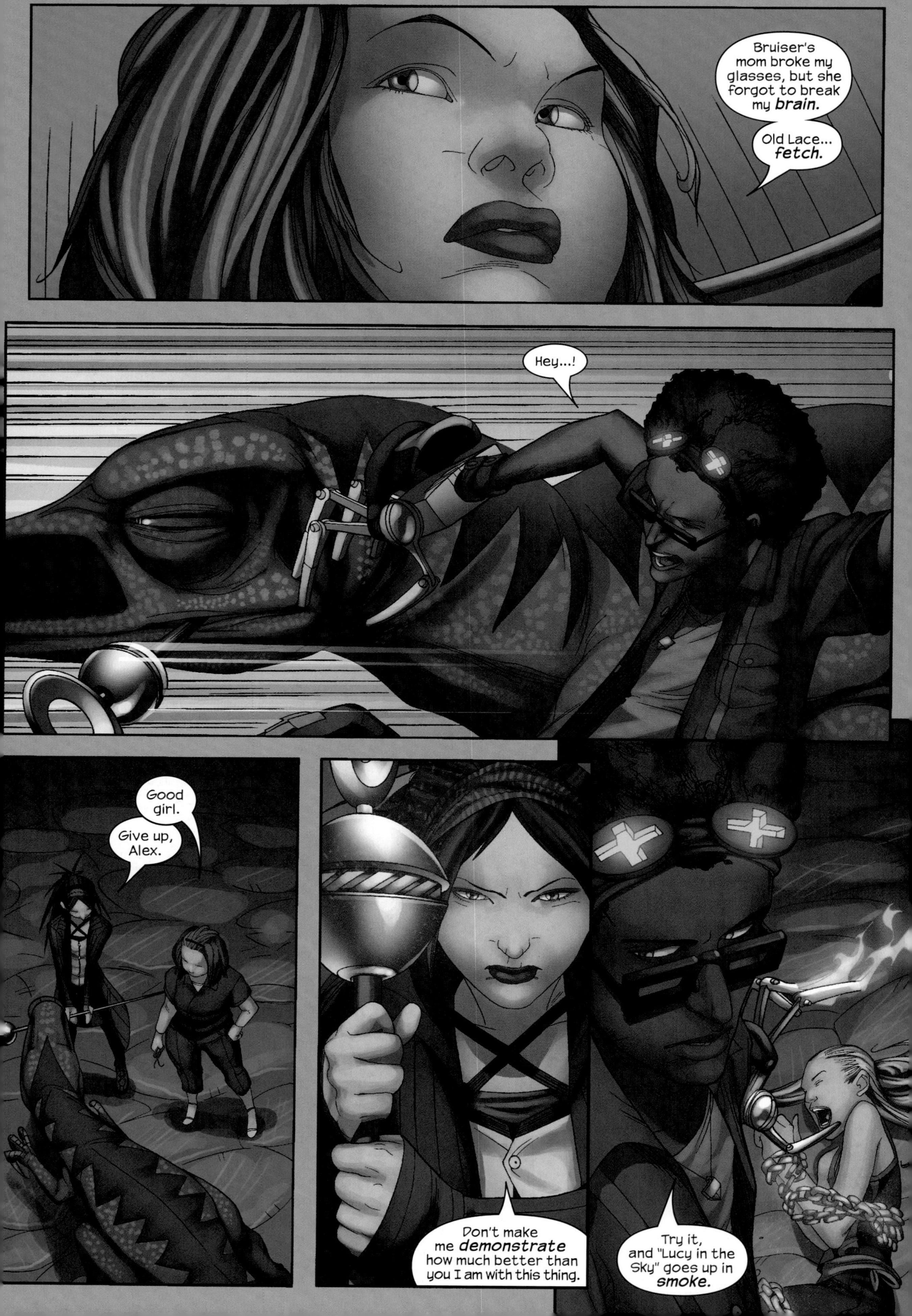

Bruiser's mom broke my glasses, but she forgot to break my *brain.*
Old Lace... *fetch.*
Hey...!
Good girl.
Give up, Alex.
Don't make me *demonstrate* how much better than you I am with this thing.
Try it, and "Lucy in the Sky" goes up in *smoke.*

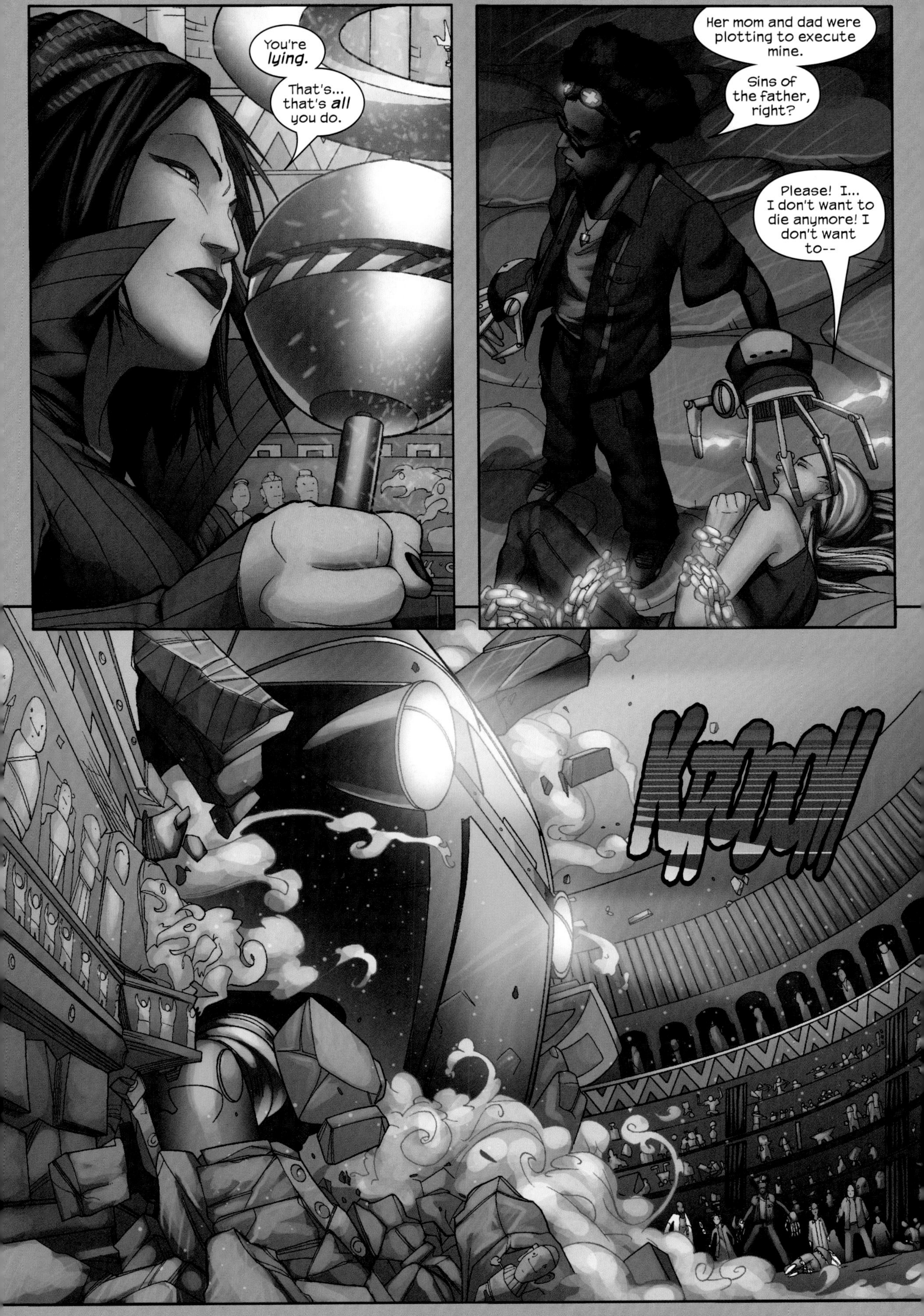
You're *lying.*
That's... that's *all* you do.
Her mom and dad were plotting to execute mine.
Sins of the father, right?
Please! I... I don't want to die anymore! I don't want to--
KRADOOM

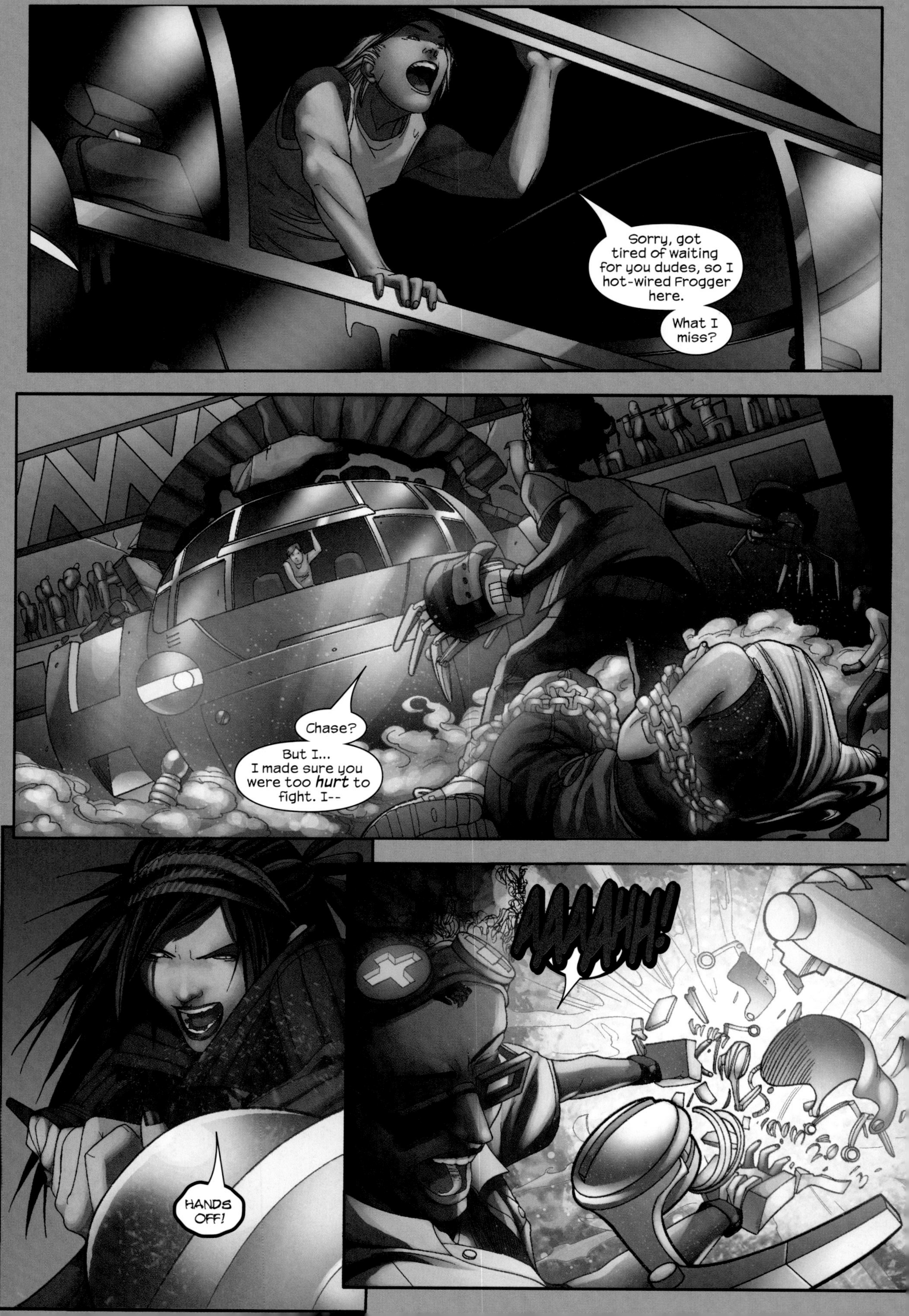

Sorry, got tired of waiting for you dudes, so I hot-wired Frogger here.
What I miss?
Chase?
But I... I made sure you were too *hurt* to fight. I--
HANDS OFF!
AAAAHH!

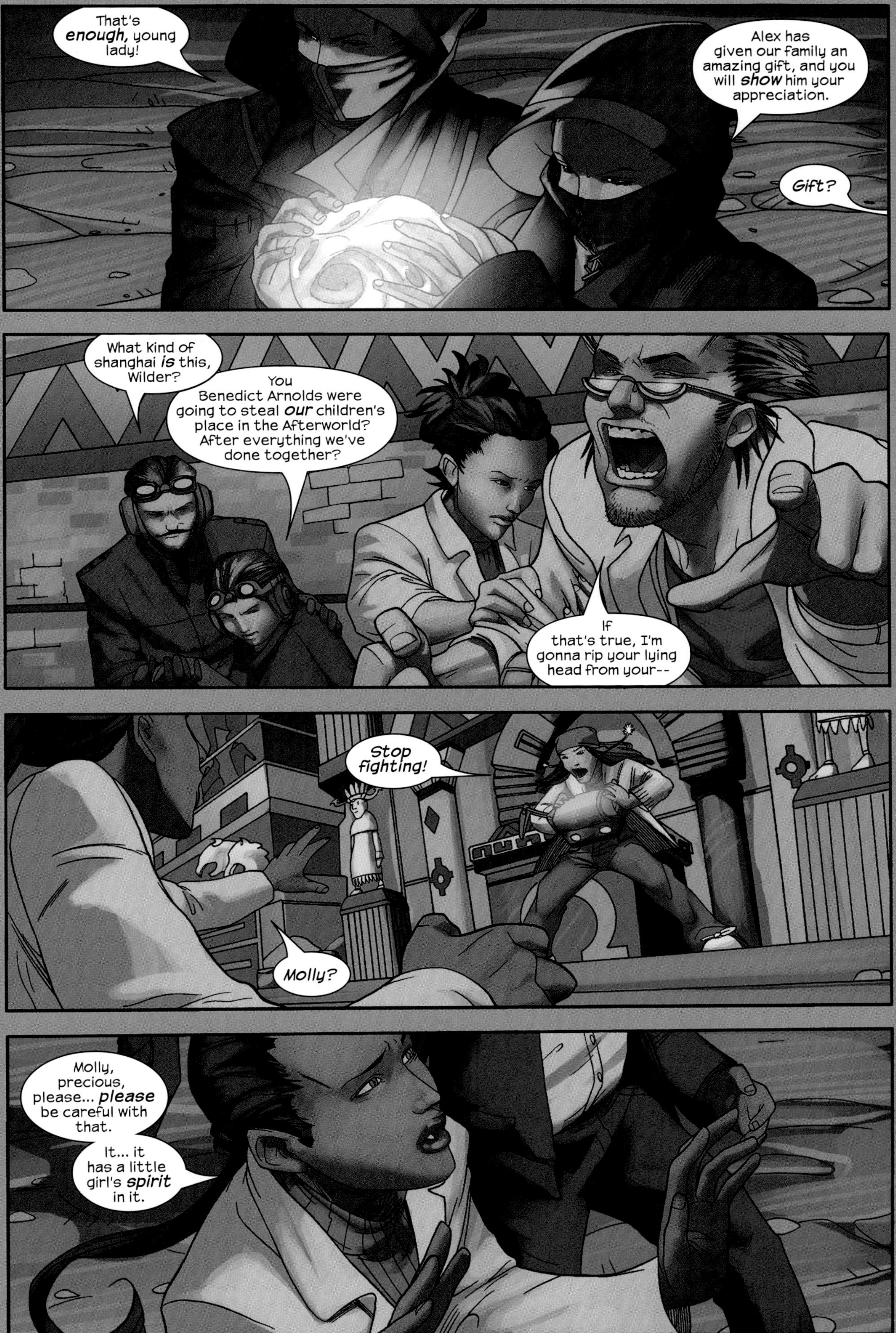

That's *enough,* young lady!
Alex has given our family an amazing gift, and you will *show* him your appreciation.
Gift?
What kind of shanghai *is* this, Wilder?
You Benedict Arnolds were going to steal *our* children's place in the Afterworld? After everything we've done together?
If that's true, I'm gonna rip your lying head from your--
Stop fighting!
Molly?
Molly, precious, please... *please* be careful with that.
It... it has a little girl's *spirit* in it.

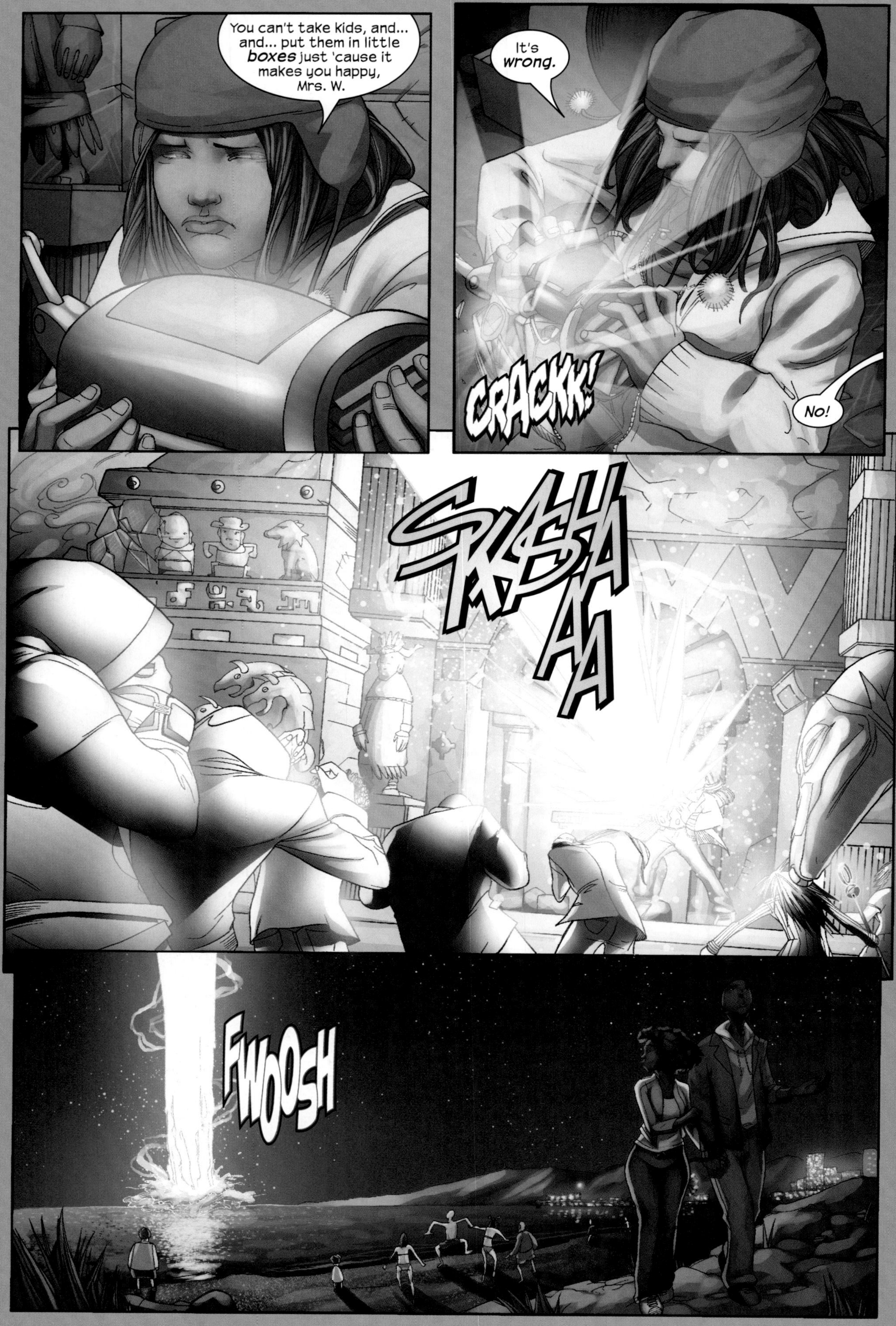
You can't take kids, and... and... put them in little *boxes* just 'cause it makes you happy, Mrs. W.
It's *wrong.*
CRACKK!
No!
SKASHAAA
FWOOSH

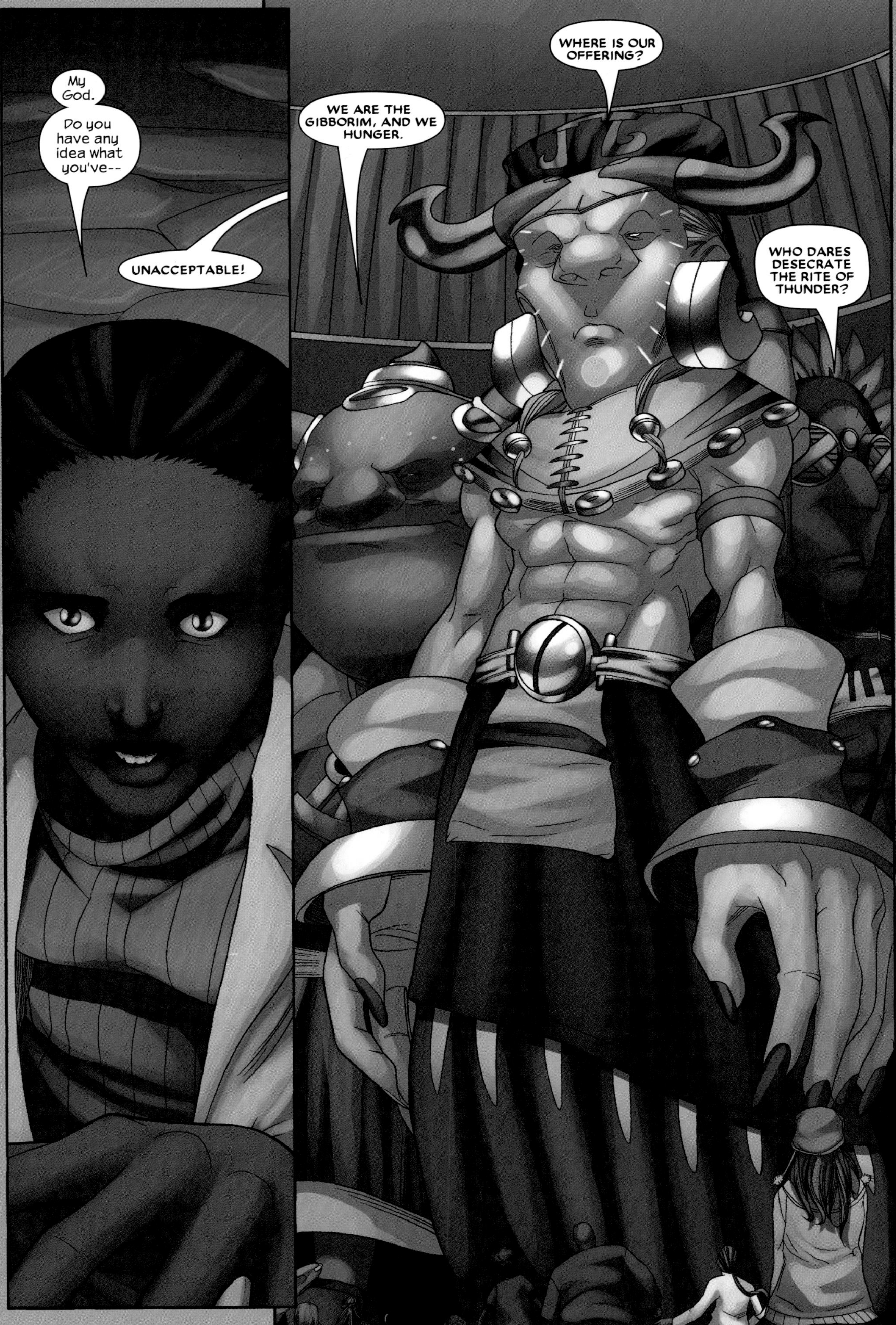
My God.
Do you have any idea what you've--
UNACCEPTABLE!
WE ARE THE GIBBORIM, AND WE HUNGER.
WHERE IS OUR OFFERING?
WHO DARES DESECRATE THE RITE OF THUNDER?

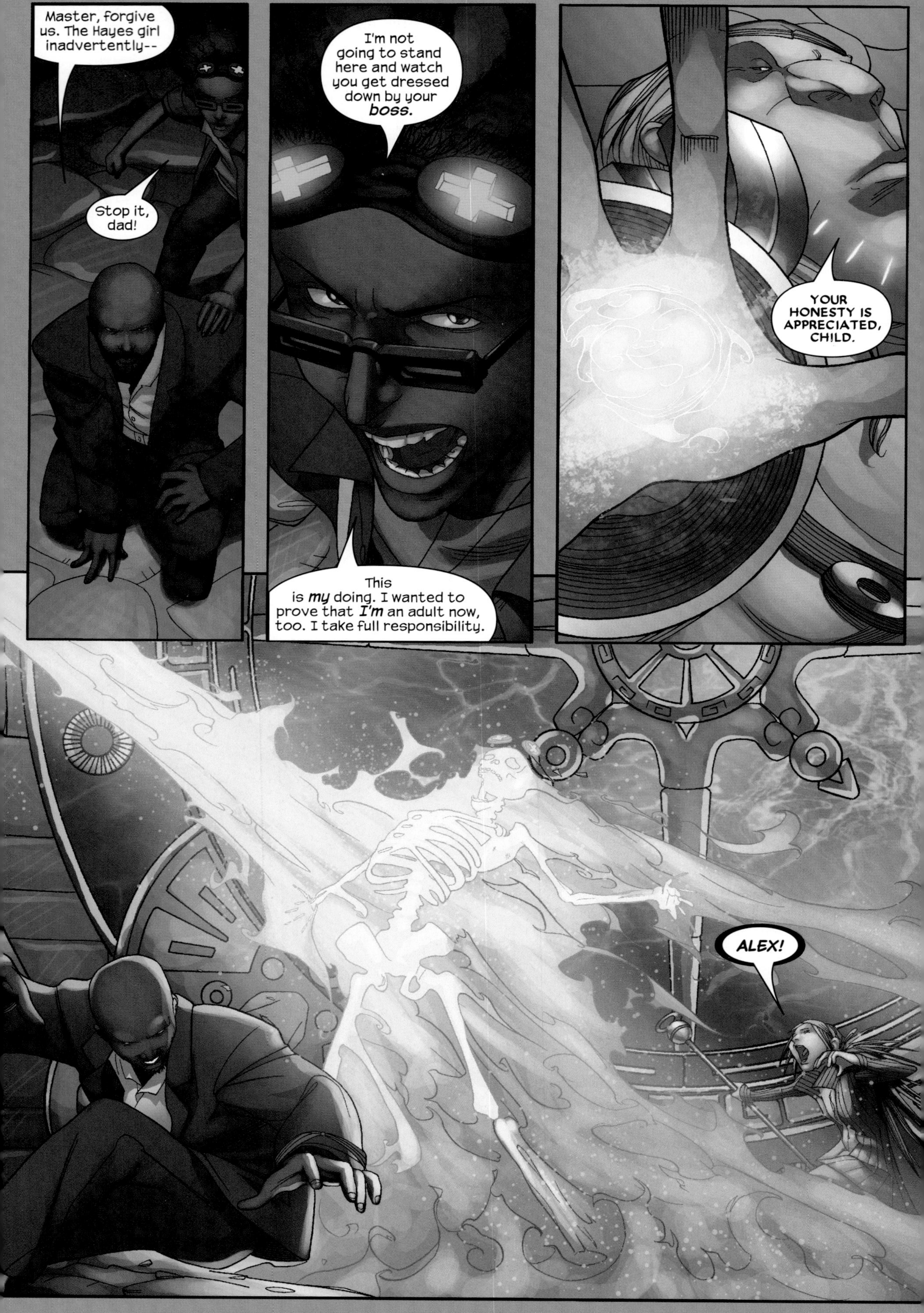
Master, forgive us. The Hayes girl inadvertently--
Stop it, dad!
I'm not going to stand here and watch you get dressed down by your *boss.*
This is *my* doing. I wanted to prove that *I'm* an adult now, too. I take full responsibility.
YOUR HONESTY IS APPRECIATED, CHILD.
ALEX!

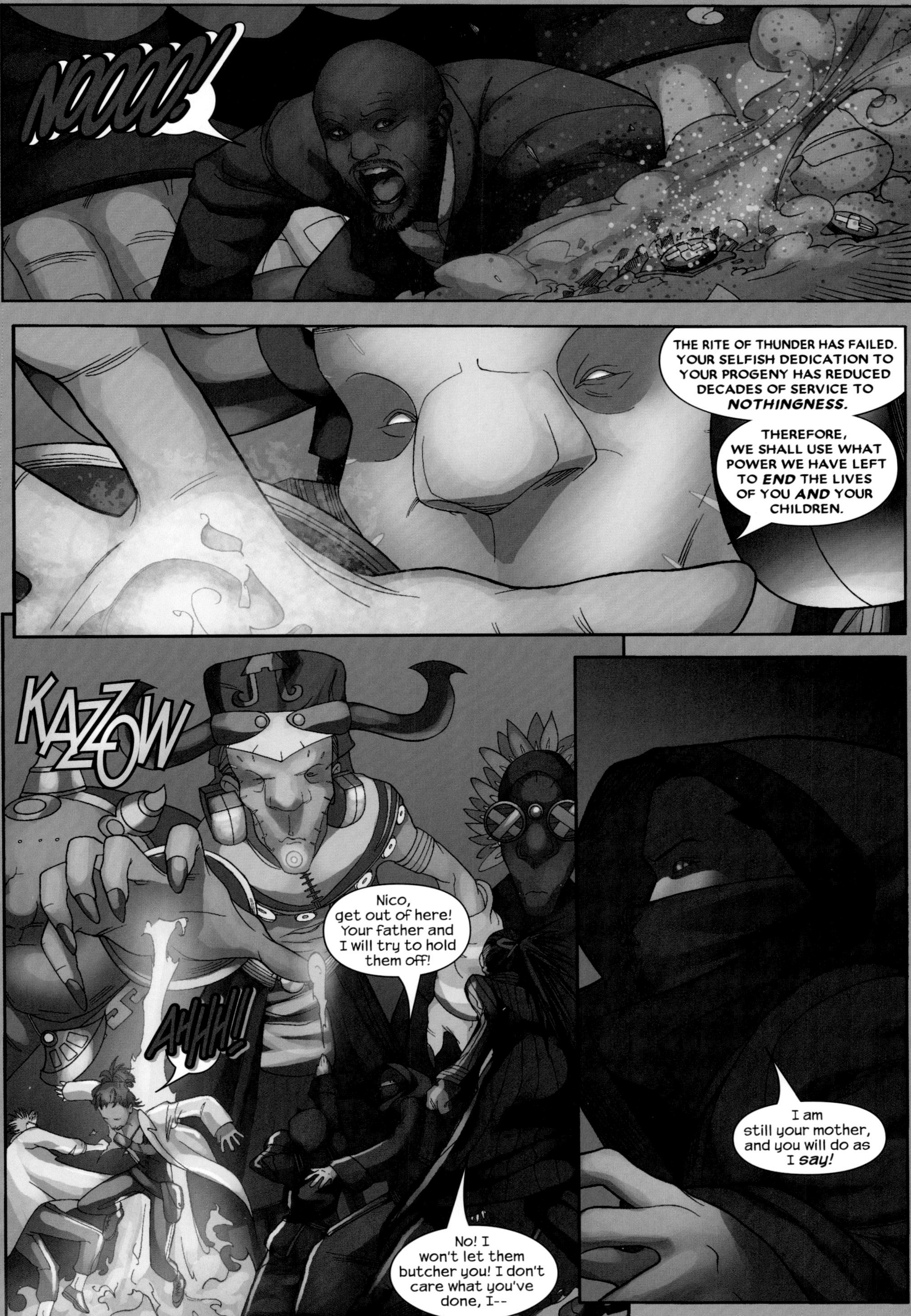
NOOOO!
THE RITE OF THUNDER HAS FAILED. YOUR SELFISH DEDICATION TO YOUR PROGENY HAS REDUCED DECADES OF SERVICE TO *NOTHINGNESS.*
THEREFORE, WE SHALL USE WHAT POWER WE HAVE LEFT TO *END* THE LIVES OF YOU *AND* YOUR CHILDREN.
KAZZOW
Nico, get out of here! Your father and I will try to hold them off!
AHHH!!
No! I won't let them butcher you! I don't care what you've done, I--
I am still your mother, and you will do as I *say!*

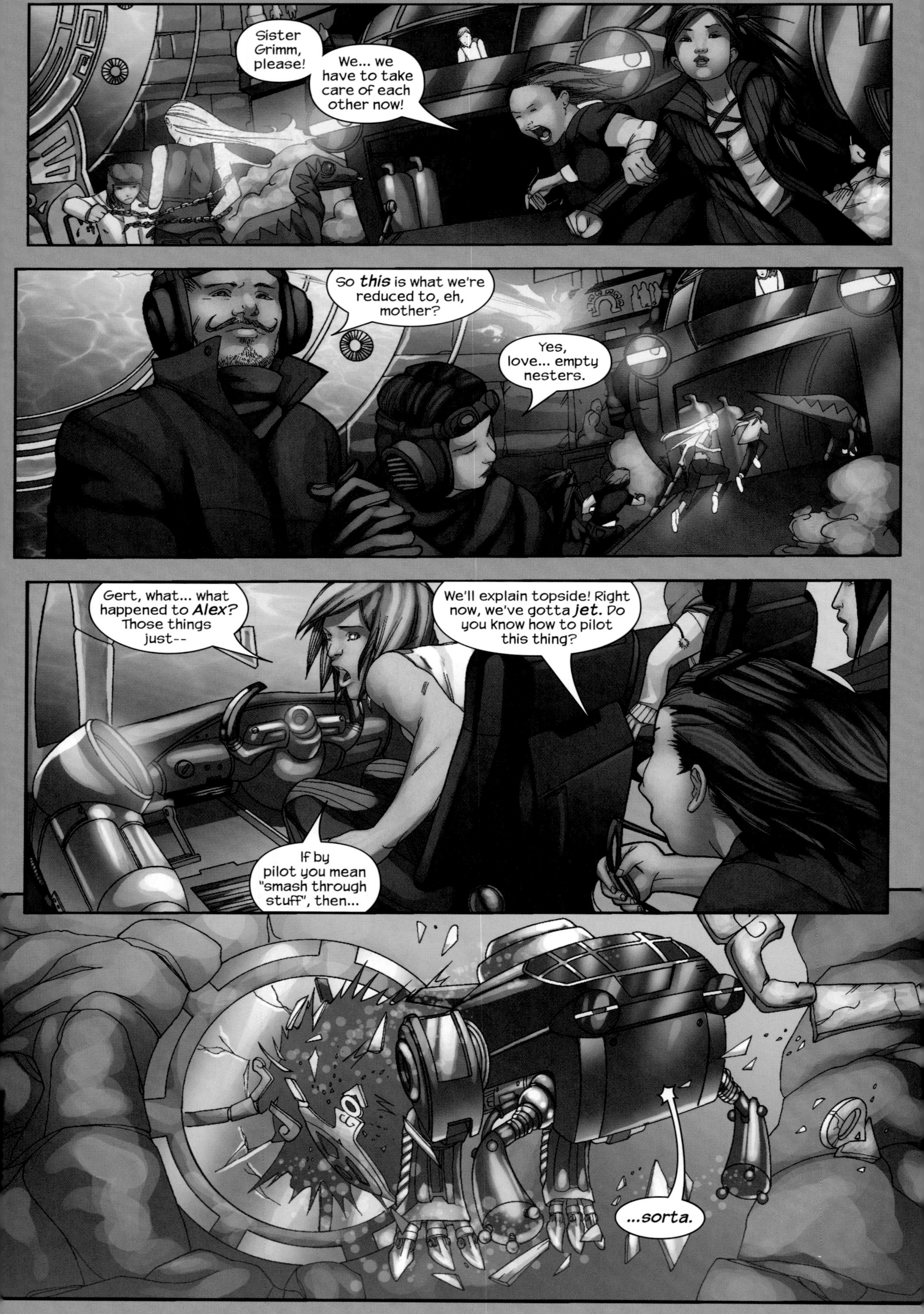
Sister Grimm, please!
We... we have to take care of each other now!
So *this* is what we're reduced to, eh, mother?
Yes, love... empty nesters.
Gert, what... what happened to *Alex*? Those things just--
We'll explain topside! Right now, we've gotta *jet.* Do you know how to pilot this thing?
If by pilot you mean "smash through stuff", then...
...sorta.

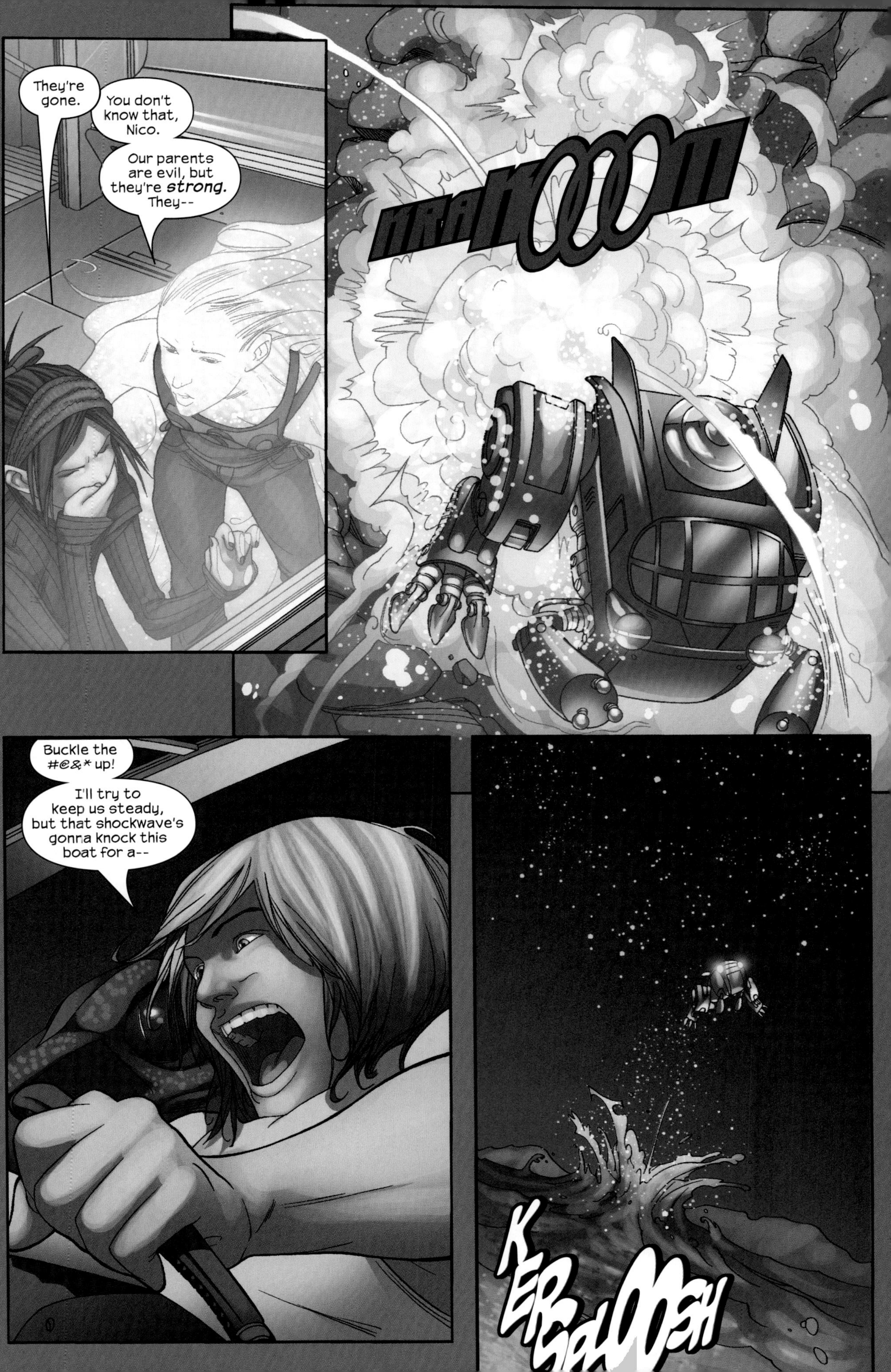
They're gone.
You don't know that, Nico.
Our parents are evil, but they're *strong.* They--
KRAKOOOM
Buckle the #@&* up!
I'll try to keep us steady, but that shockwave's gonna knock this boat for a--
KERSPLOOSH

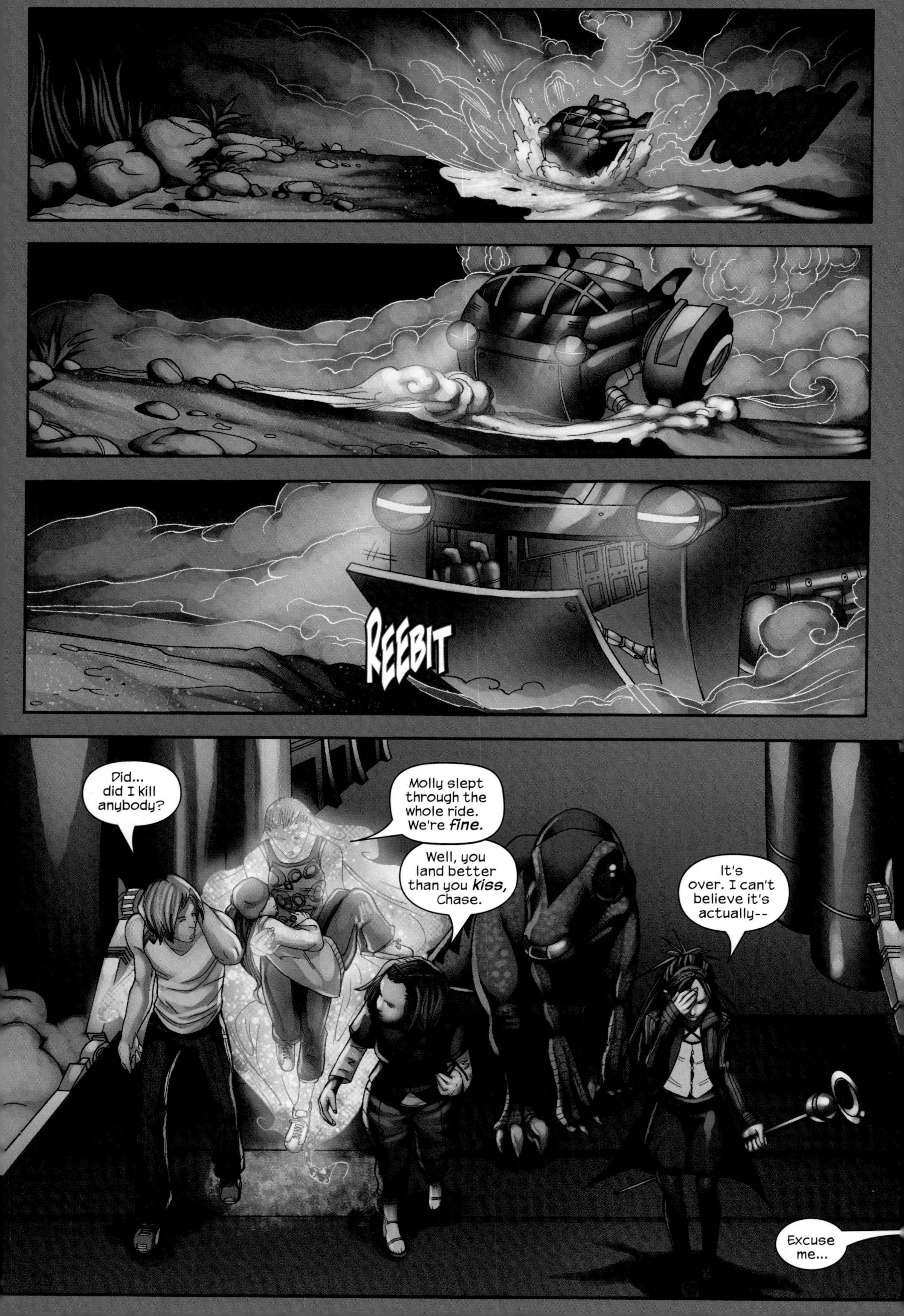
REEBIT
Did... did I kill anybody?
Molly slept through the whole ride. We're *fine.*
Well, you land better than you *kiss,* Chase.
It's over. I can't believe it's actually--
Excuse me...

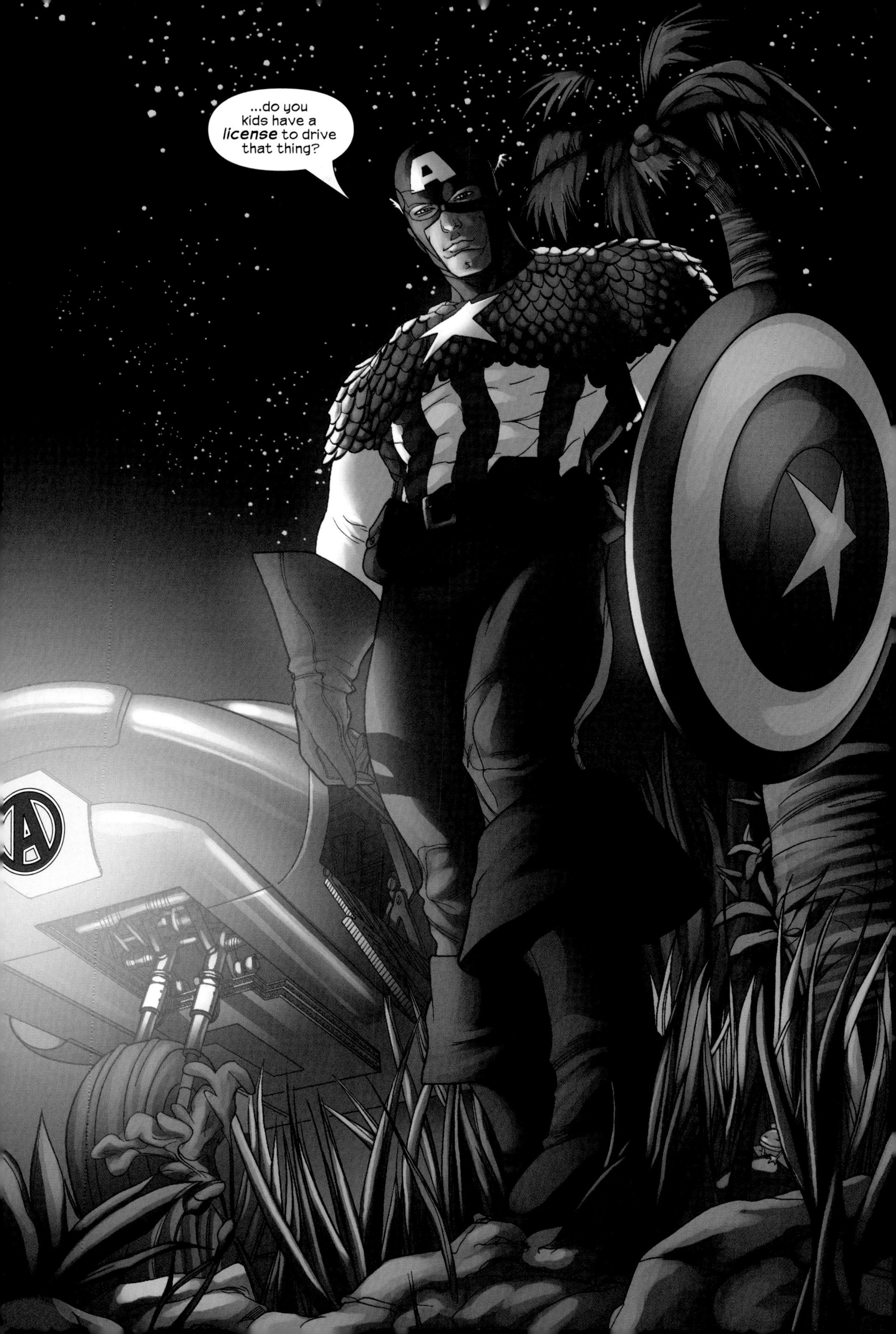
...do you kids have a *license* to drive that thing?

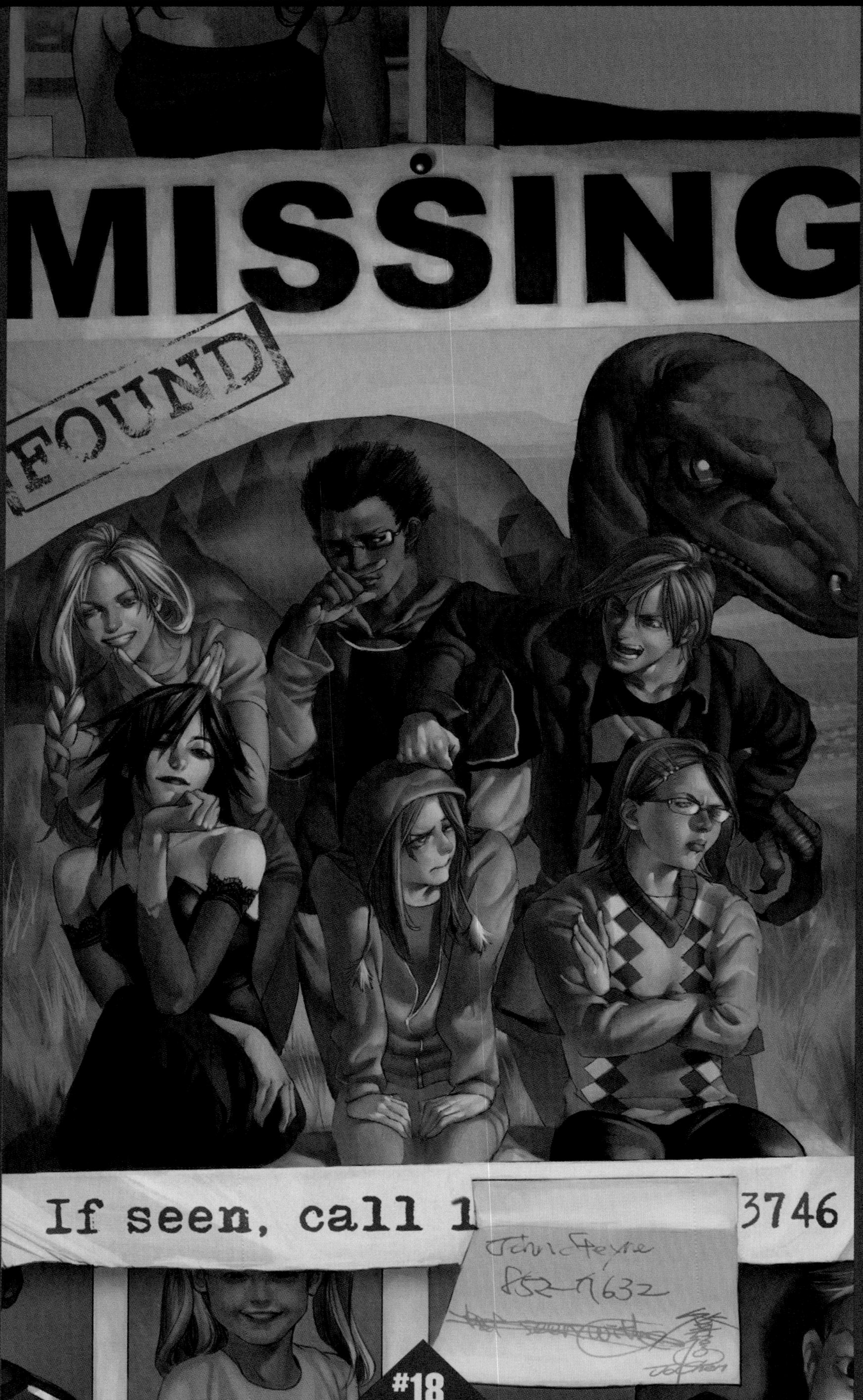
MISSING
FOUND
If seen, call 1
3746
#18

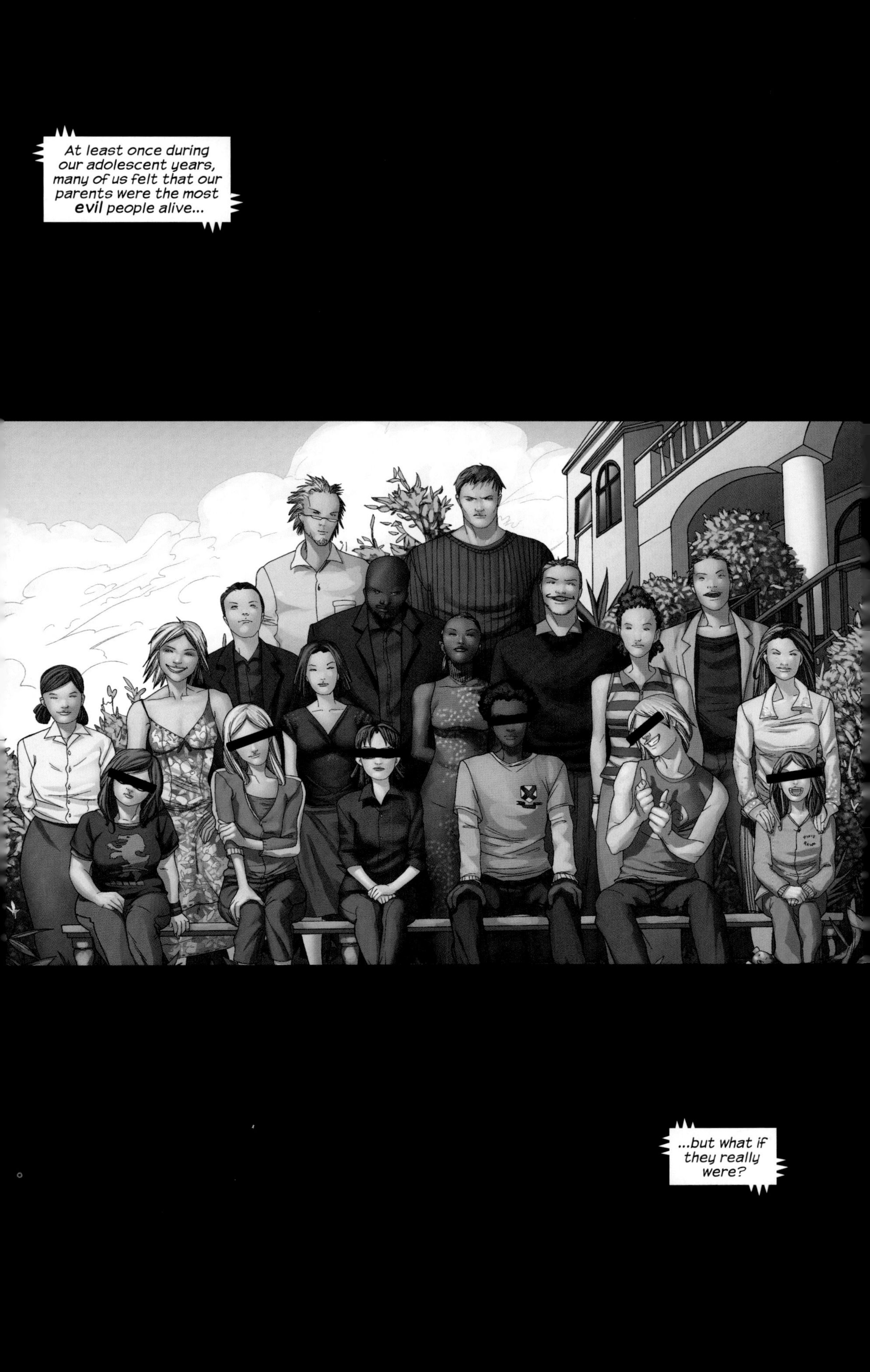
At least once during our adolescent years, many of us felt that our parents were the most **evil** people alive...
...but what if they really were?

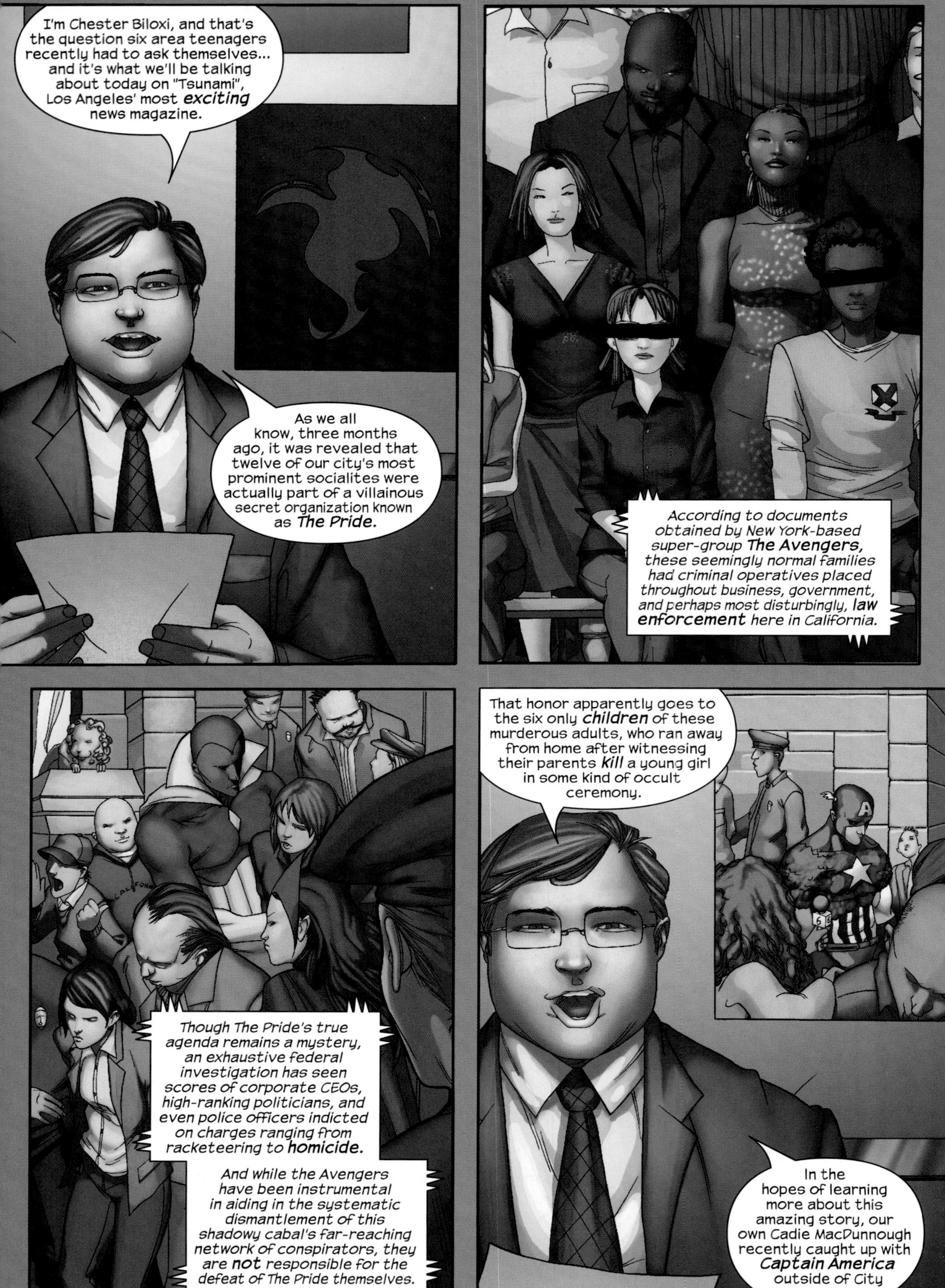
I'm Chester Biloxi, and that's the question six area teenagers recently had to ask themselves... and it's what we'll be talking about today on "Tsunami", Los Angeles' most exciting news magazine.
As we all know, three months ago, it was revealed that twelve of our city's most prominent socialites were actually part of a villainous secret organization known as The Pride.
According to documents obtained by New York-based super-group The Avengers, these seemingly normal families had criminal operatives placed throughout business, government, and perhaps most disturbingly, law enforcement here in California.
Though The Pride's true agenda remains a mystery, an exhaustive federal investigation has seen scores of corporate CEOs, high-ranking politicians, and even police officers indicted on charges ranging from racketeering to homicide.
And while the Avengers have been instrumental in aiding in the systematic dismantlement of this shadowy cabal's far-reaching network of conspirators, they are not responsible for the defeat of The Pride themselves.
That honor apparently goes to the six only children of these murderous adults, who ran away from home after witnessing their parents kill a young girl in some kind of occult ceremony.
In the hopes of learning more about this amazing story, our own Cadie MacDunnough recently caught up with Captain America outside of City Hall.

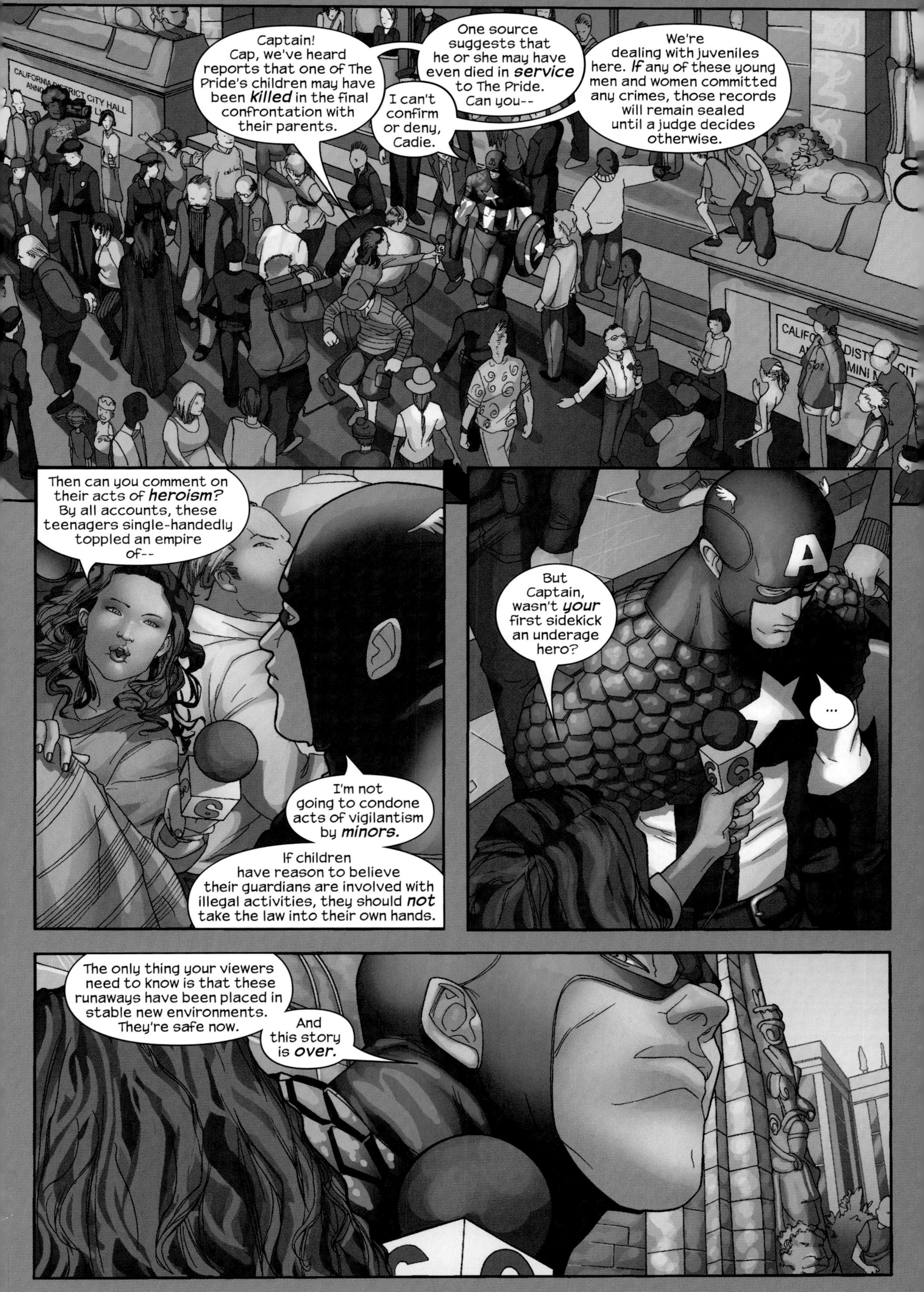
CALIFORNIA DISTRICT CITY HALL
Captain! Cap, we've heard reports that one of The Pride's children may have been *killed* in the final confrontation with their parents.
I can't confirm or deny, Cadie.
One source suggests that he or she may have even died in *service* to The Pride. Can you--
We're dealing with juveniles here. *If* any of these young men and women committed any crimes, those records will remain sealed until a judge decides otherwise.
Then can you comment on their acts of *heroism*? By all accounts, these teenagers single-handedly toppled an empire of--
I'm not going to condone acts of vigilantism by *minors.*
If children have reason to believe their guardians are involved with illegal activities, they should *not* take the law into their own hands.
But Captain, wasn't *your* first sidekick an underage hero?
...
The only thing your viewers need to know is that these runaways have been placed in stable new environments. They're safe now.
And this story is *over.*

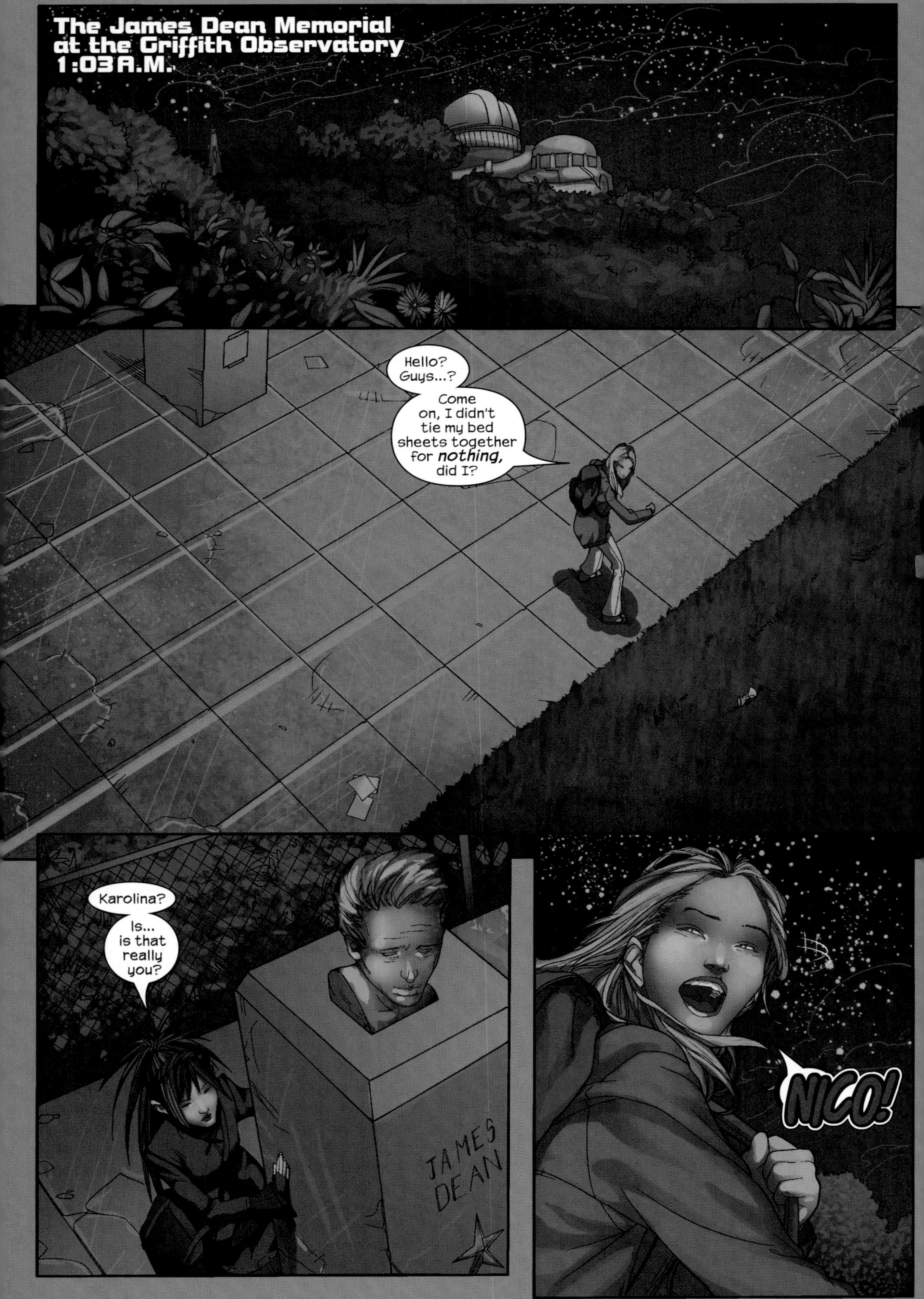
The James Dean Memorial
at the Griffith Observatory
1:03 A.M.
Hello? Guys...?
Come on, I didn't tie my bed sheets together for *nothing,* did I?
Karolina?
Is... is that really you?
JAMES DEAN
NICO!

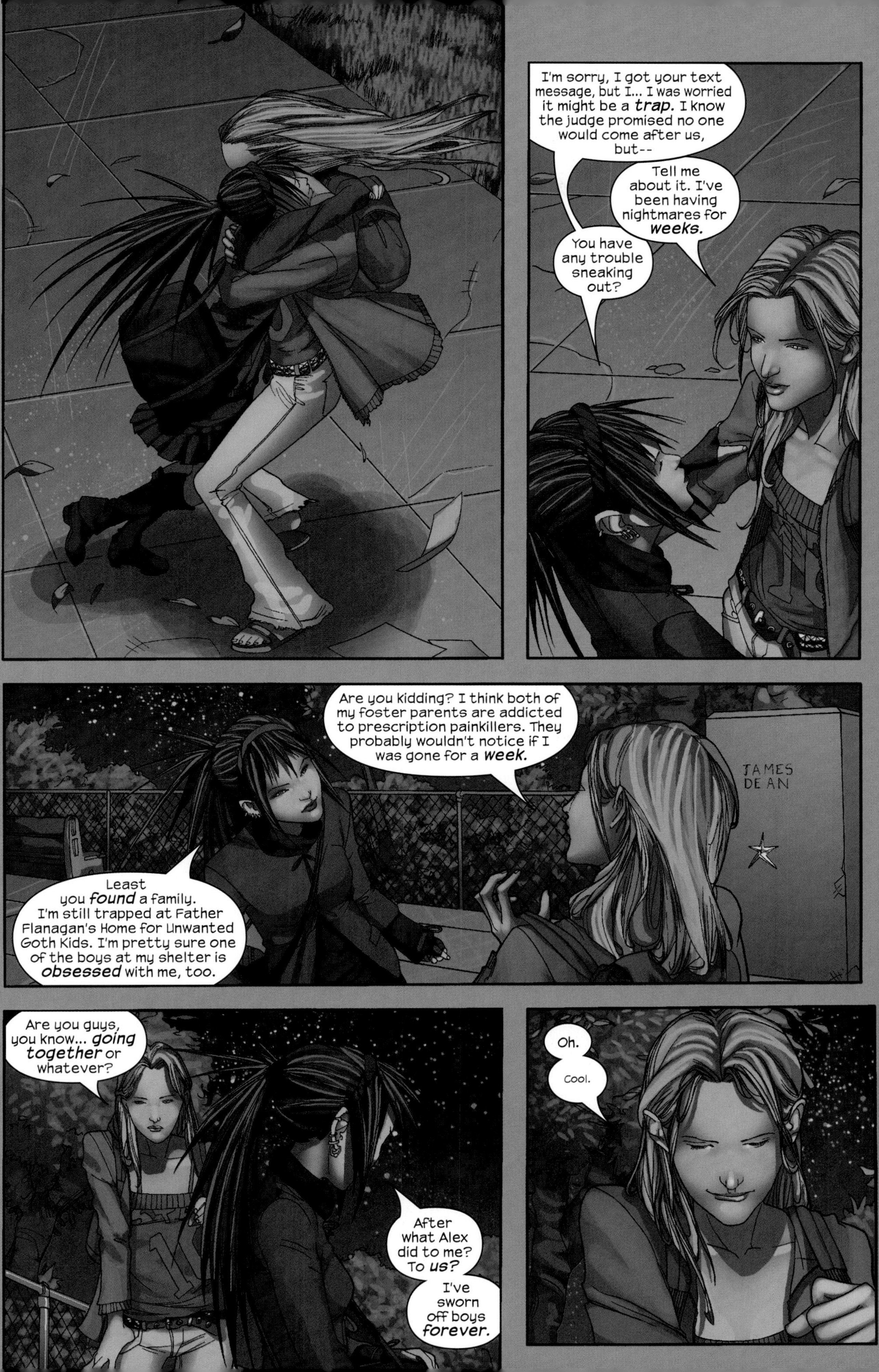
I'm sorry, I got your text message, but I... I was worried it might be a trap. I know the judge promised no one would come after us, but--
Tell me about it. I've been having nightmares for weeks.
You have any trouble sneaking out?
Are you kidding? I think both of my foster parents are addicted to prescription painkillers. They probably wouldn't notice if I was gone for a week.
JAMES DEAN
Least you found a family. I'm still trapped at Father Flanagan's Home for Unwanted Goth Kids. I'm pretty sure one of the boys at my shelter is obsessed with me, too.
Are you guys, you know... going together or whatever?
After what Alex did to me? To us?
I've sworn off boys forever.
Oh.
Cool.

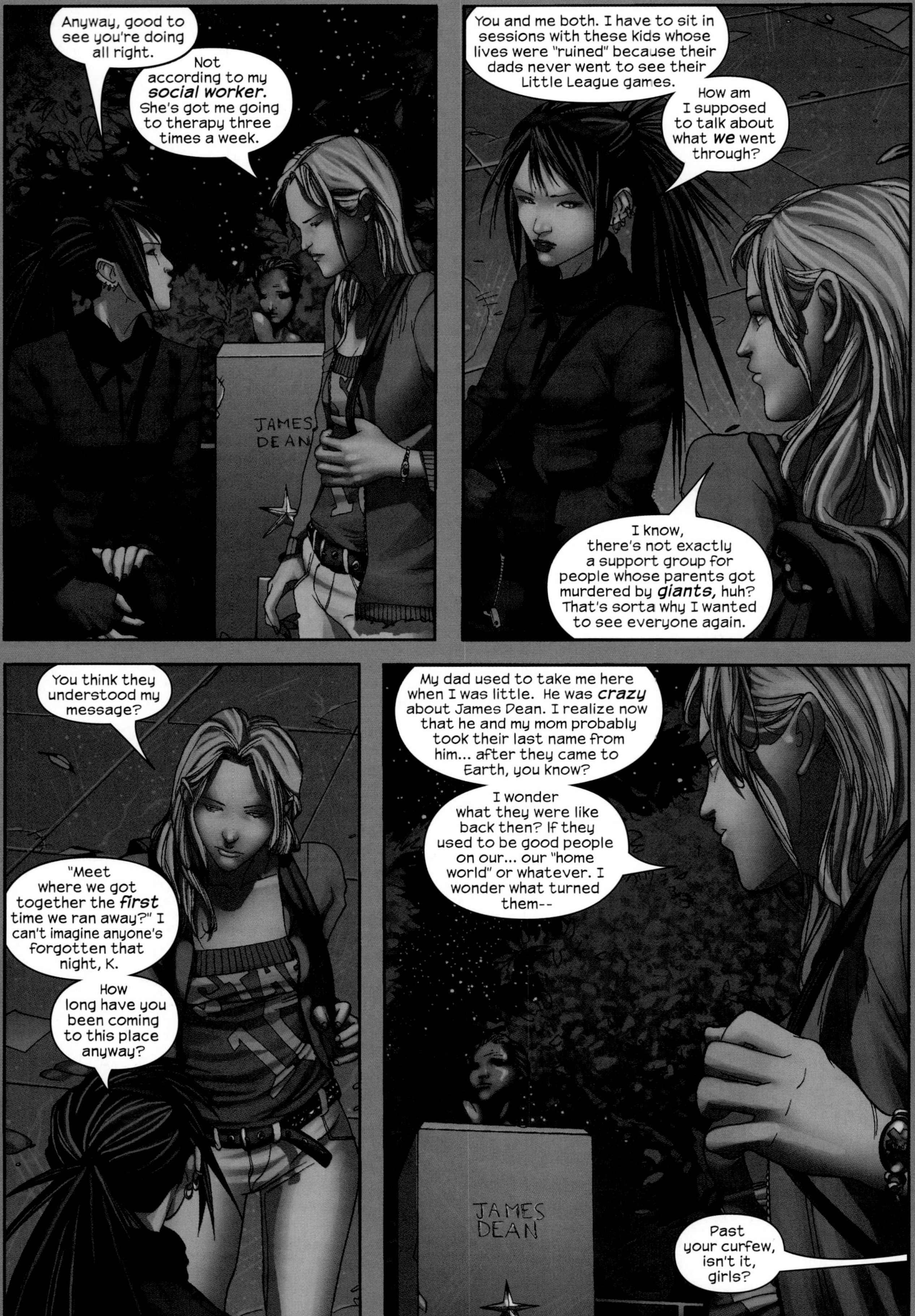
Anyway, good to see you're doing all right.
Not according to my *social worker.* She's got me going to therapy three times a week.
JAMES DEAN
You and me both. I have to sit in sessions with these kids whose lives were "ruined" because their dads never went to see their Little League games.
How am I supposed to talk about what *we* went through?
I know, there's not exactly a support group for people whose parents got murdered by *giants,* huh? That's sorta why I wanted to see everyone again.
You think they understood my message?
"Meet where we got together the *first* time we ran away?" I can't imagine anyone's forgotten that night, K.
How long have you been coming to this place anyway?
My dad used to take me here when I was little. He was *crazy* about James Dean. I realize now that he and my mom probably took their last name from him... after they came to Earth, you know?
I wonder what they were like back then? If they used to be good people on our... our "home world" or whatever. I wonder what turned them--
JAMES DEAN
Past your curfew, isn't it, girls?

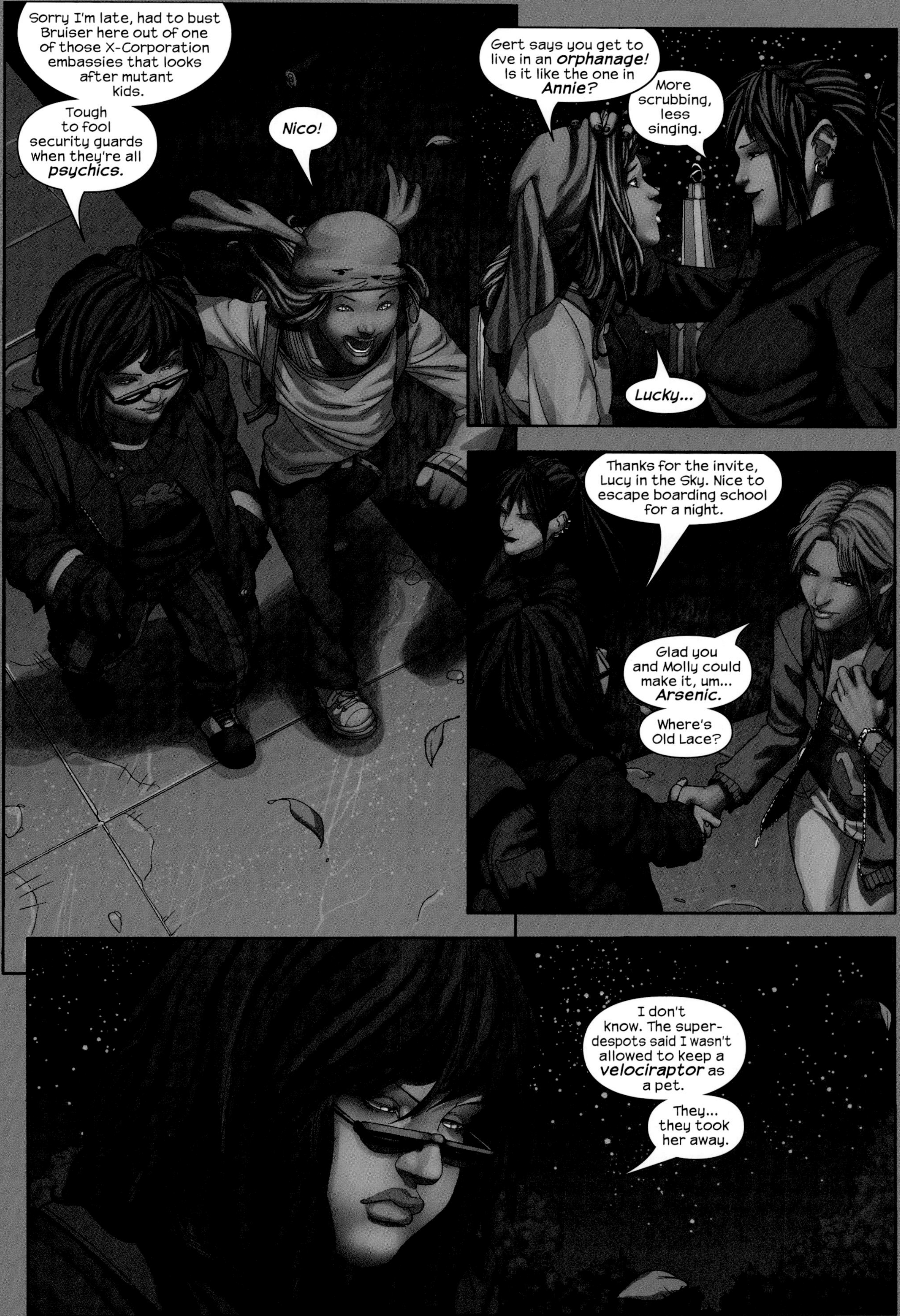
Sorry I'm late, had to bust Bruiser here out of one of those X-Corporation embassies that looks after mutant kids.
Tough to fool security guards when they're all *psychics.*
Nico!
Gert says you get to live in an *orphanage!* Is it like the one in *Annie?*
More scrubbing, less singing.
Lucky...
Thanks for the invite, Lucy in the Sky. Nice to escape boarding school for a night.
Glad you and Molly could make it, um... *Arsenic.*
Where's Old Lace?
I don't know. The super-despots said I wasn't allowed to keep a *velociraptor* as a pet.
They... they took her away.

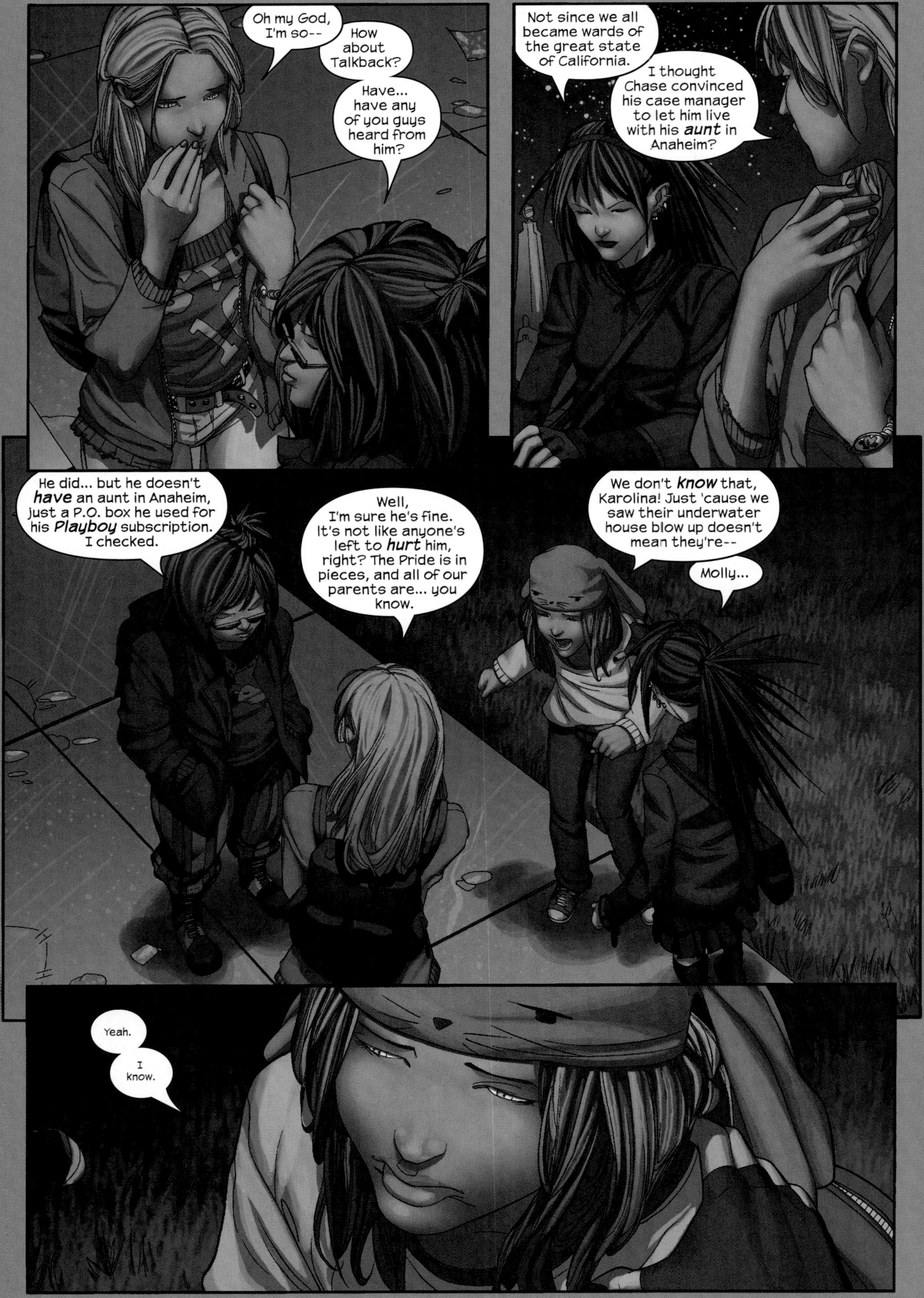
Oh my God, I'm so--
How about Talkback?
Have... have any of you guys heard from him?
Not since we all became wards of the great state of California.
I thought Chase convinced his case manager to let him live with his *aunt* in Anaheim?
He did... but he doesn't *have* an aunt in Anaheim, just a P.O. box he used for his *Playboy* subscription. I checked.
Well, I'm sure he's fine. It's not like anyone's left to *hurt* him, right? The Pride is in pieces, and all of our parents are... you know.
We don't *know* that, Karolina! Just 'cause we saw their underwater house blow up doesn't mean they're--
Molly...
Yeah.
I know.

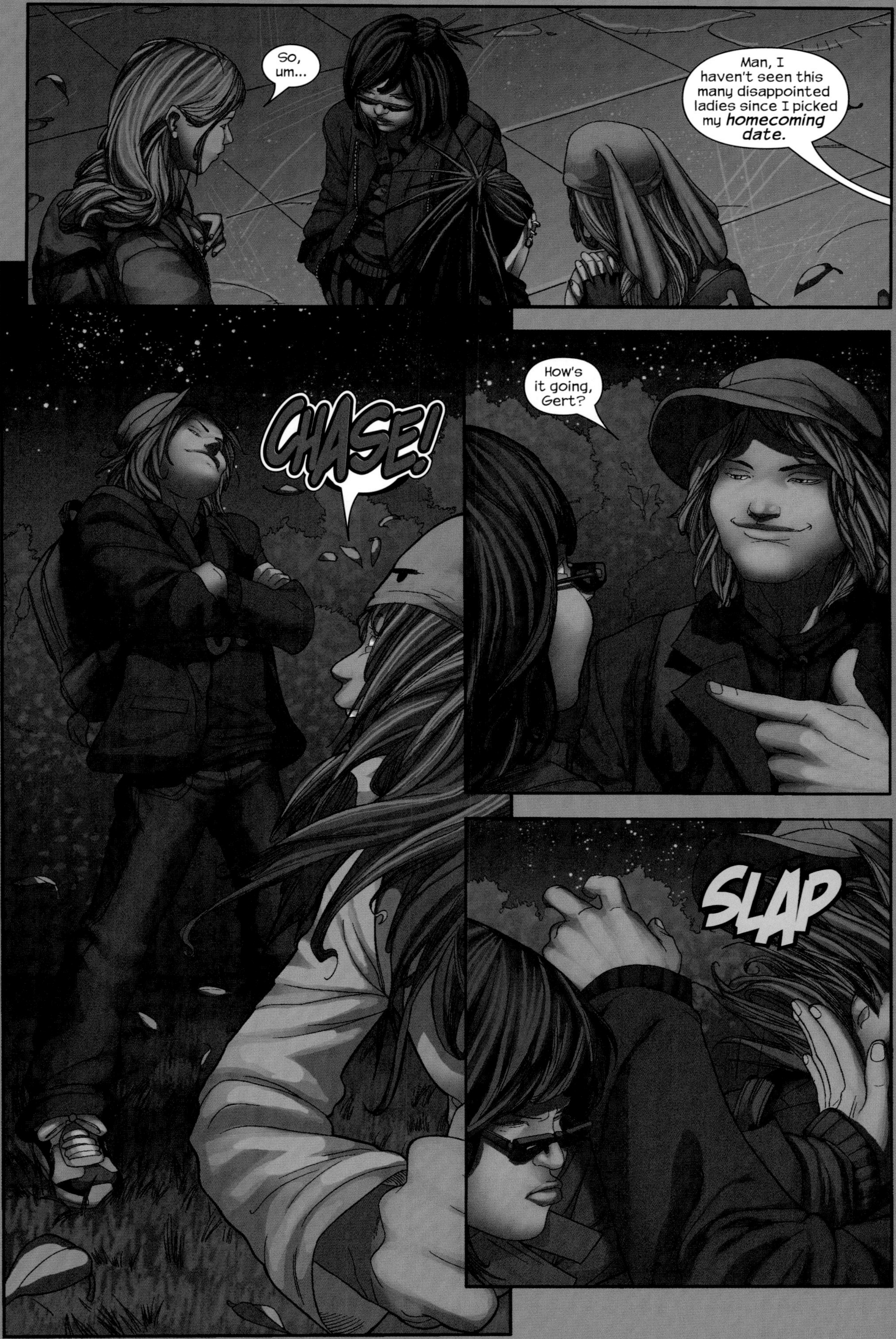
So, um...
Man, I haven't seen this many disappointed ladies since I picked my *homecoming date.*
CHASE!
How's it going, Gert?
SLAP

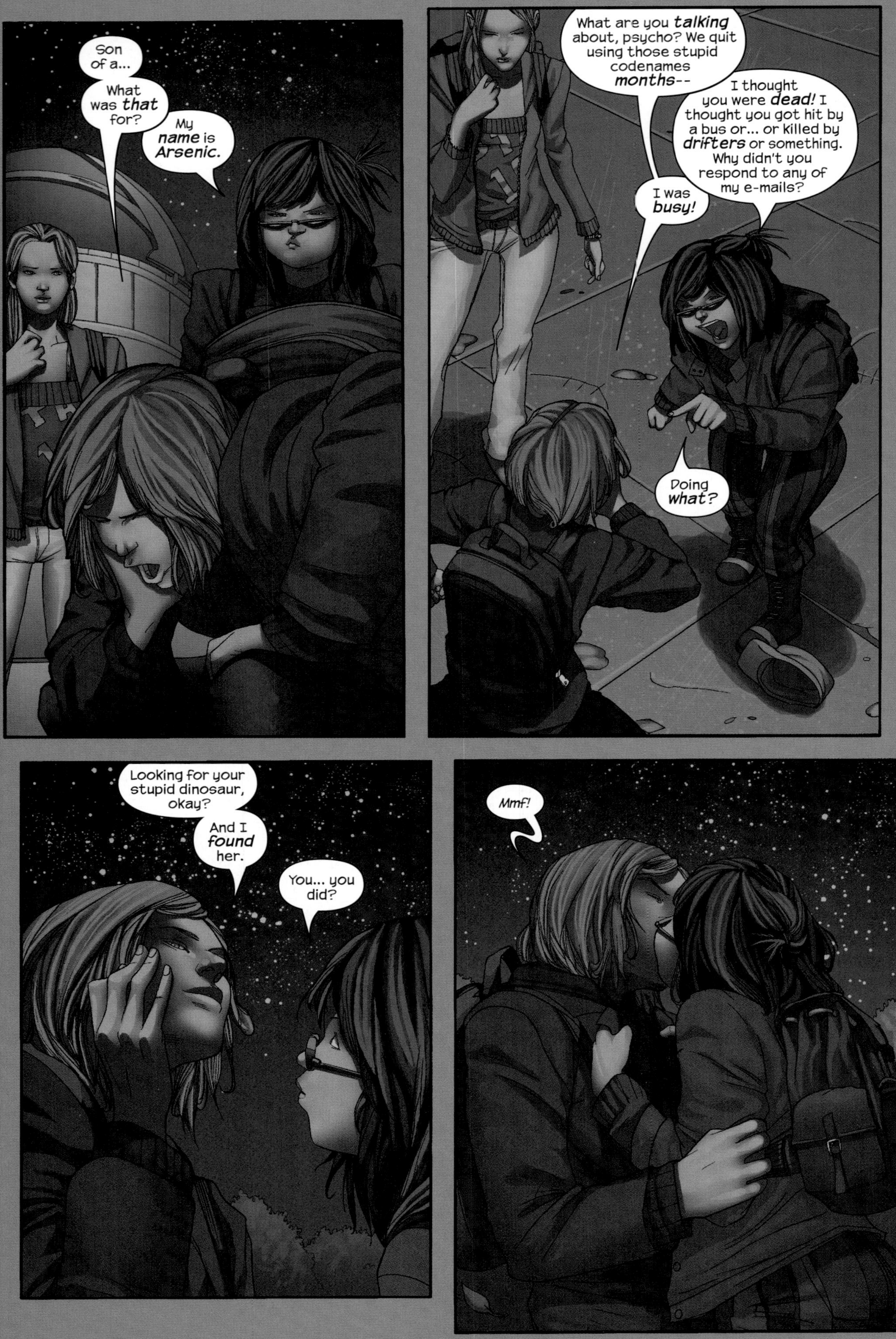
Son of a...
What was that for?
My name is Arsenic.
What are you talking about, psycho? We quit using those stupid codenames months--
I thought you were dead! I thought you got hit by a bus or... or killed by drifters or something. Why didn't you respond to any of my e-mails?
I was busy!
Doing what?
Looking for your stupid dinosaur, okay?
And I found her.
You... you did?
Mmf!

Mmmm...

Ick, I forgot about how much freakin' *snogging* you guys do.

"Snogging"? Where the heck did you pick up--

Um, Chase, if you come up for air at some point... could you tell us *where* Old Lace is?

Oh, remember when the Avengers had a West Coast team, back when we were kids? These zoning permits I, uh... *found* showed that they still have a storage facility somewhere on Palos Verdes.

Exact address is classified, but I figure Arsenic's dino-sense will start tingling when we get close.

Then what the hell are we waiting for?

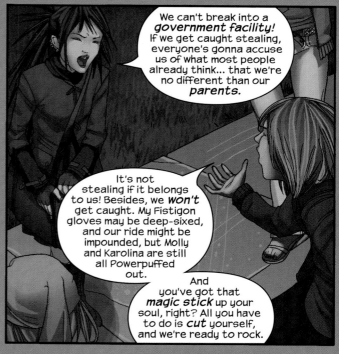

We can't break into a *government facility!* If we get caught stealing, everyone's gonna accuse us of what most people already think... that we're no different than our *parents.*

It's not stealing if it belongs to us! Besides, we *won't* get caught. My Fistigon gloves may be deep-sixed, and our ride might be impounded, but Molly and Karolina are still all Powerpuffed out.

And you've got that *magic stick* up your soul, right? All you have to do is *cut* yourself, and we're ready to rock.

Yeah, but I... I haven't used the Staff of One since--

Please, Sister Grimm. My mom and dad kept Old Lace locked away for *years.*

If we let that happen to her again, how are we any better than them?

Well...

JAMES DEAN

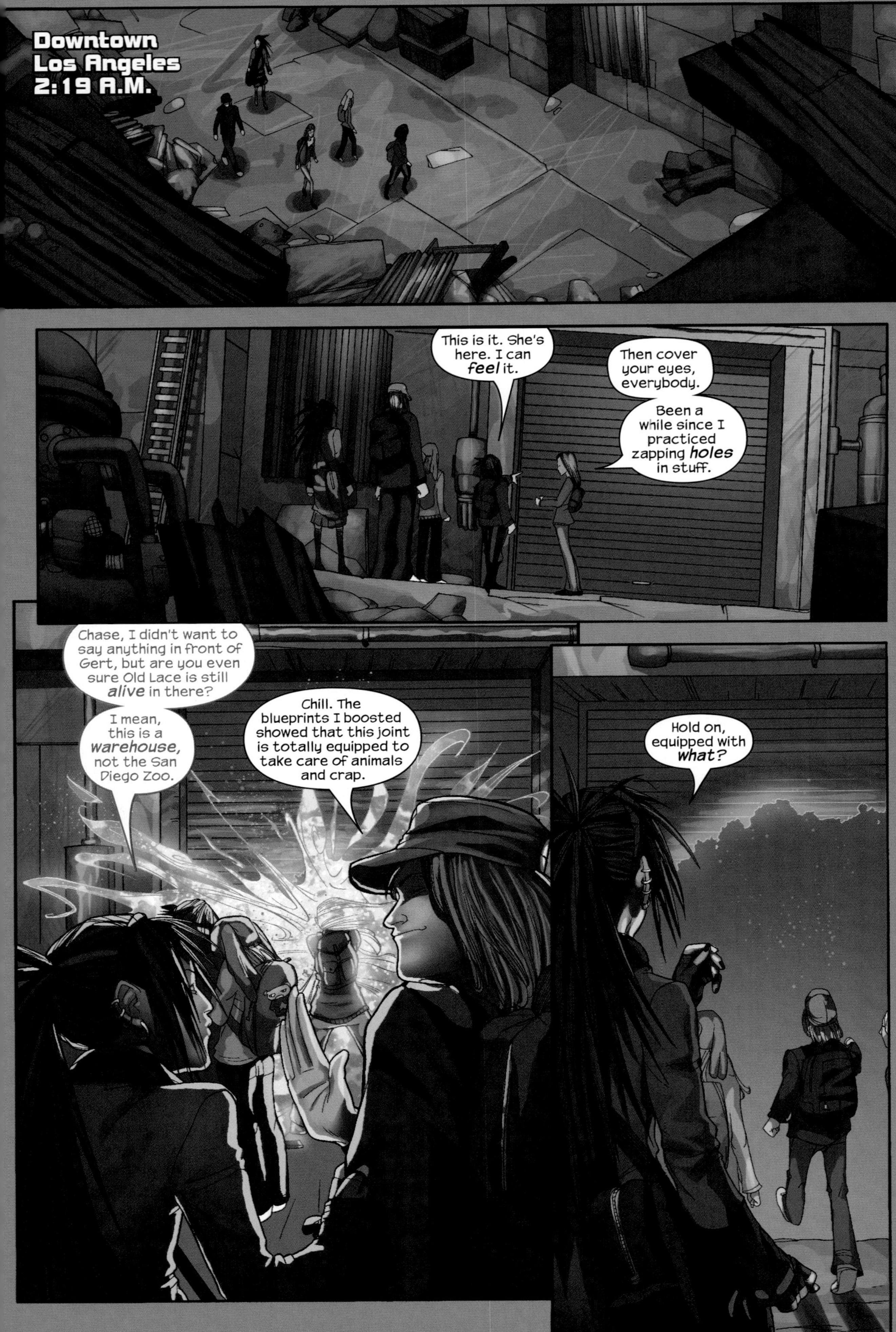
Downtown Los Angeles 2:19 A.M.
This is it. She's here. I can *feel* it.
Then cover your eyes, everybody.
Been a while since I practiced zapping *holes* in stuff.
Chase, I didn't want to say anything in front of Gert, but are you even sure Old Lace is still *alive* in there?
I mean, this is a *warehouse*, not the San Diego Zoo.
Chill. The blueprints I boosted showed that this joint is totally equipped to take care of animals and crap.
Hold on, equipped with *what?*

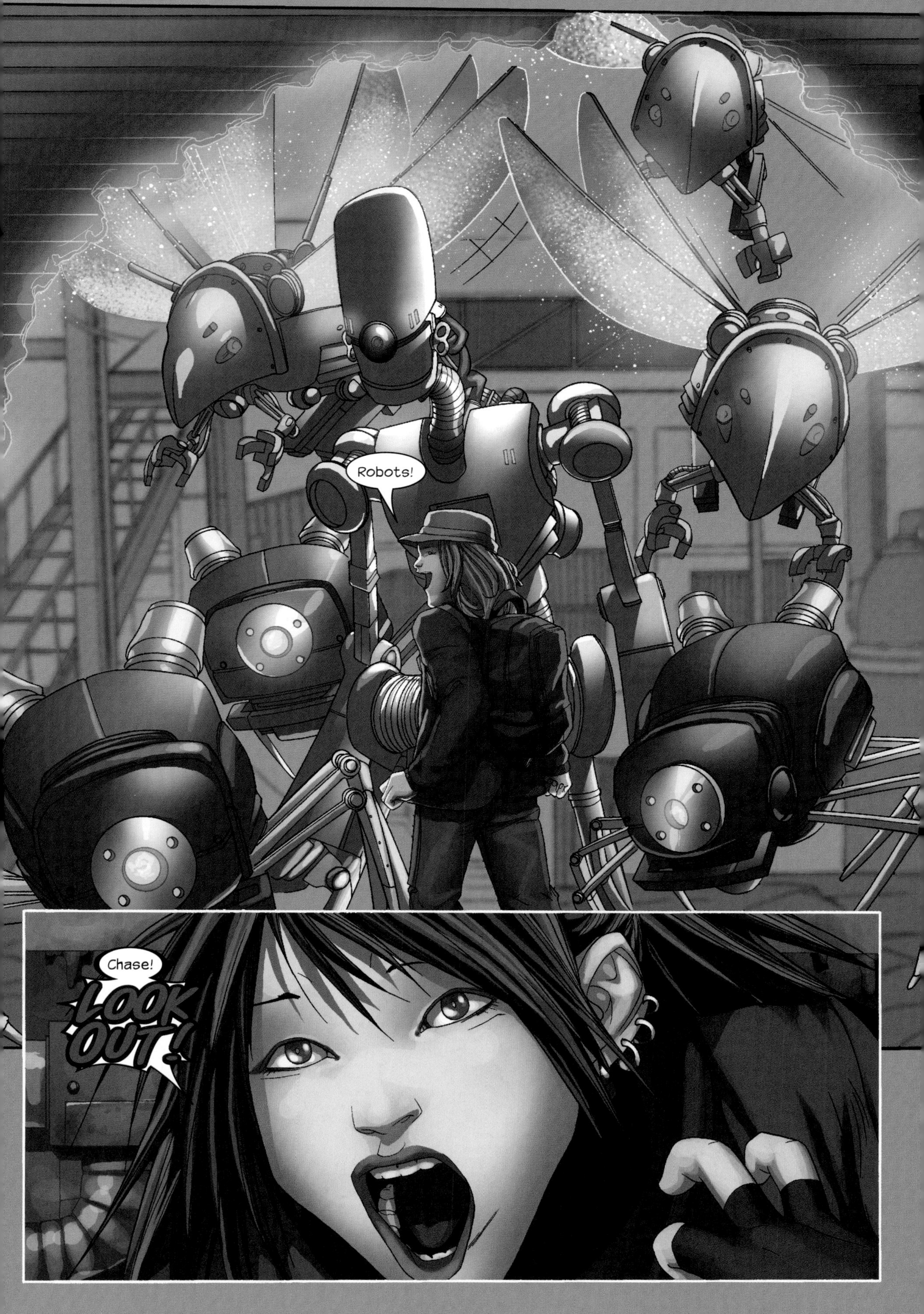
Robots!
Chase!
LOOK OUT!

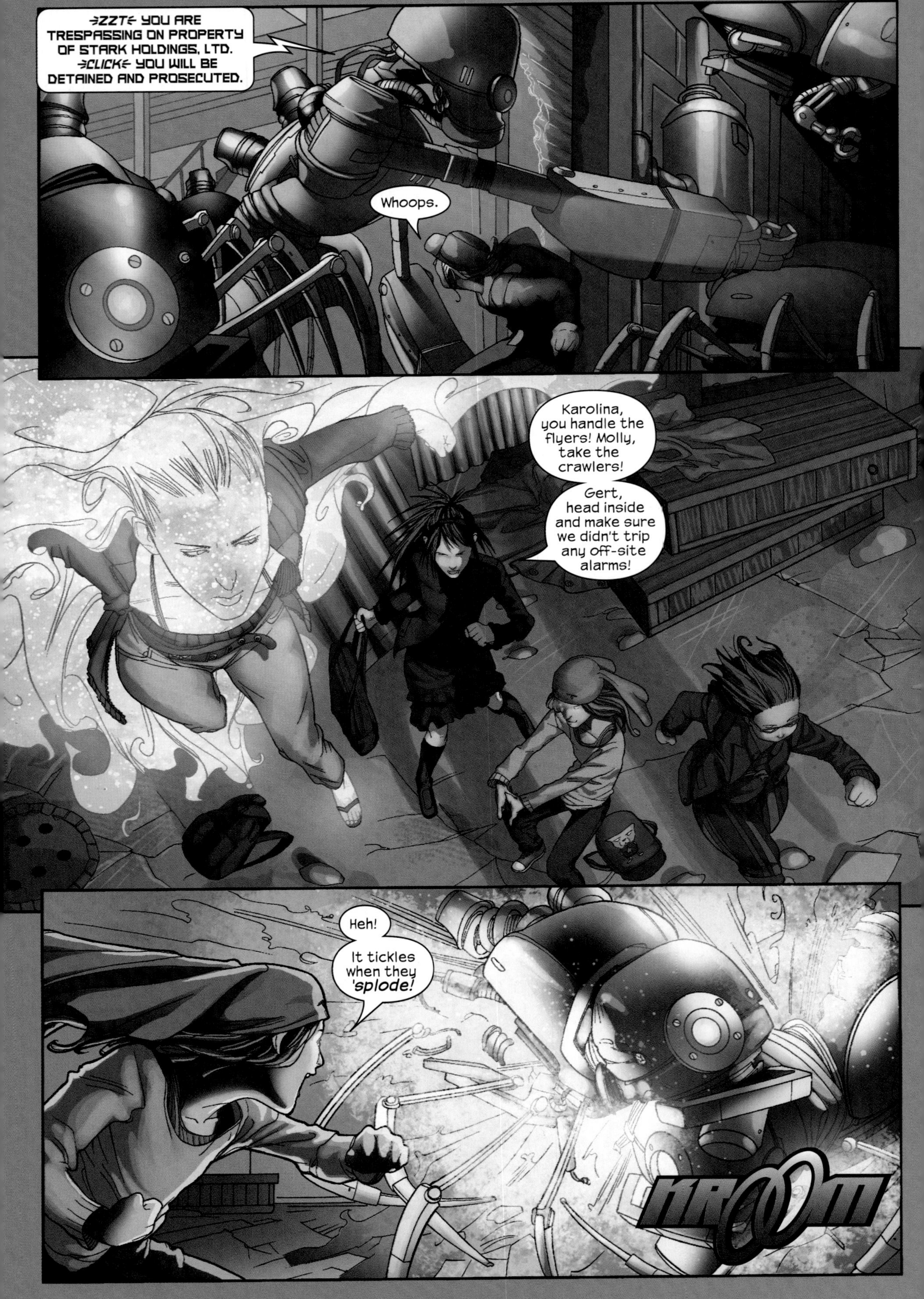

≥ZZT≤ YOU ARE TRESPASSING ON PROPERTY OF STARK HOLDINGS, LTD. ≥CLICK≤ YOU WILL BE DETAINED AND PROSECUTED.
Whoops.
Karolina, you handle the flyers! Molly, take the crawlers!
Gert, head inside and make sure we didn't trip any off-site alarms!
Heh!
It tickles when they *'splode!*
KROOM

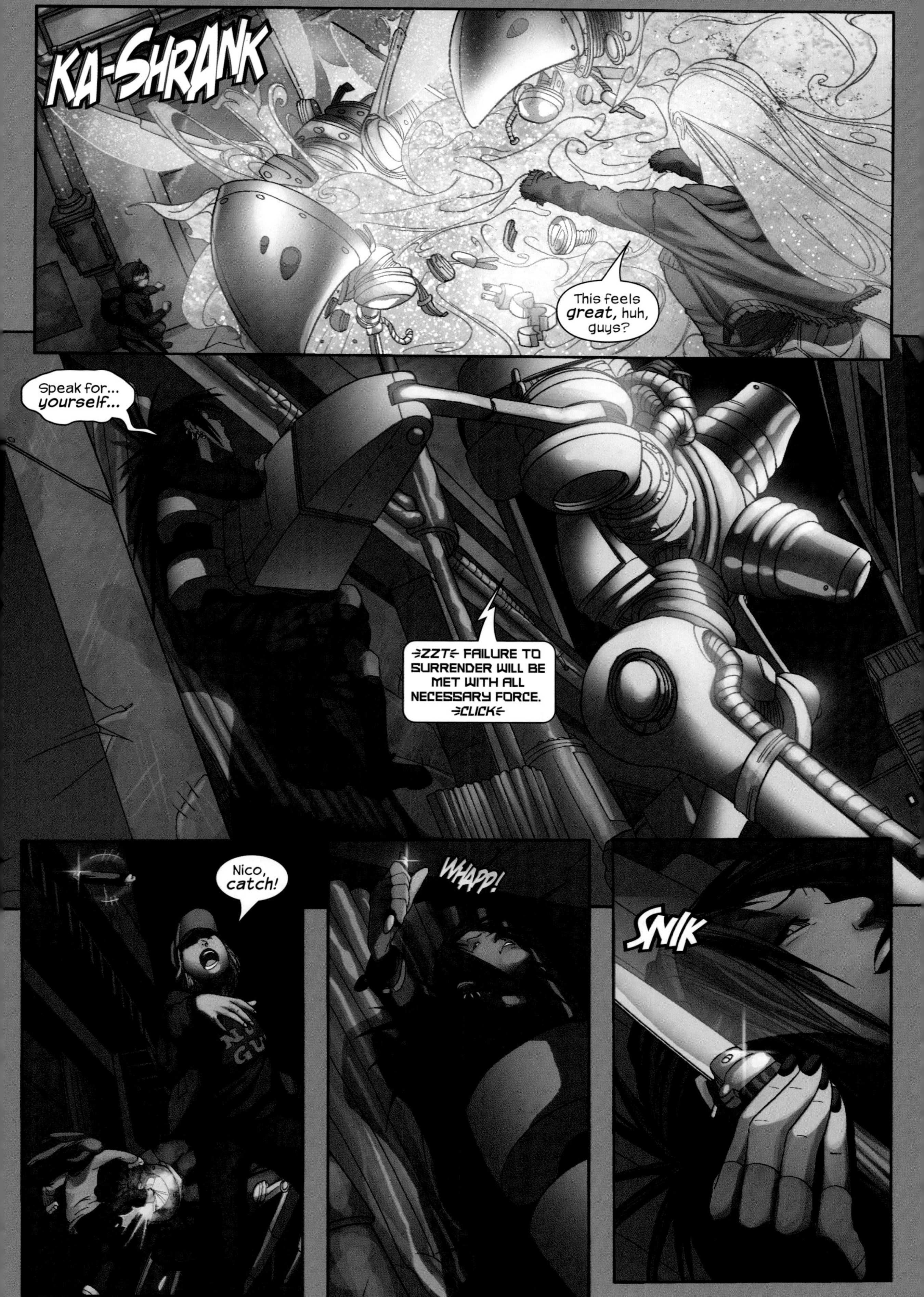
KA-SHRANK
This feels great, huh, guys?
Speak for... yourself...
ZZT FAILURE TO SURRENDER WILL BE MET WITH ALL NECESSARY FORCE. CLICK
Nico, catch!
WHAPP!
SNIK

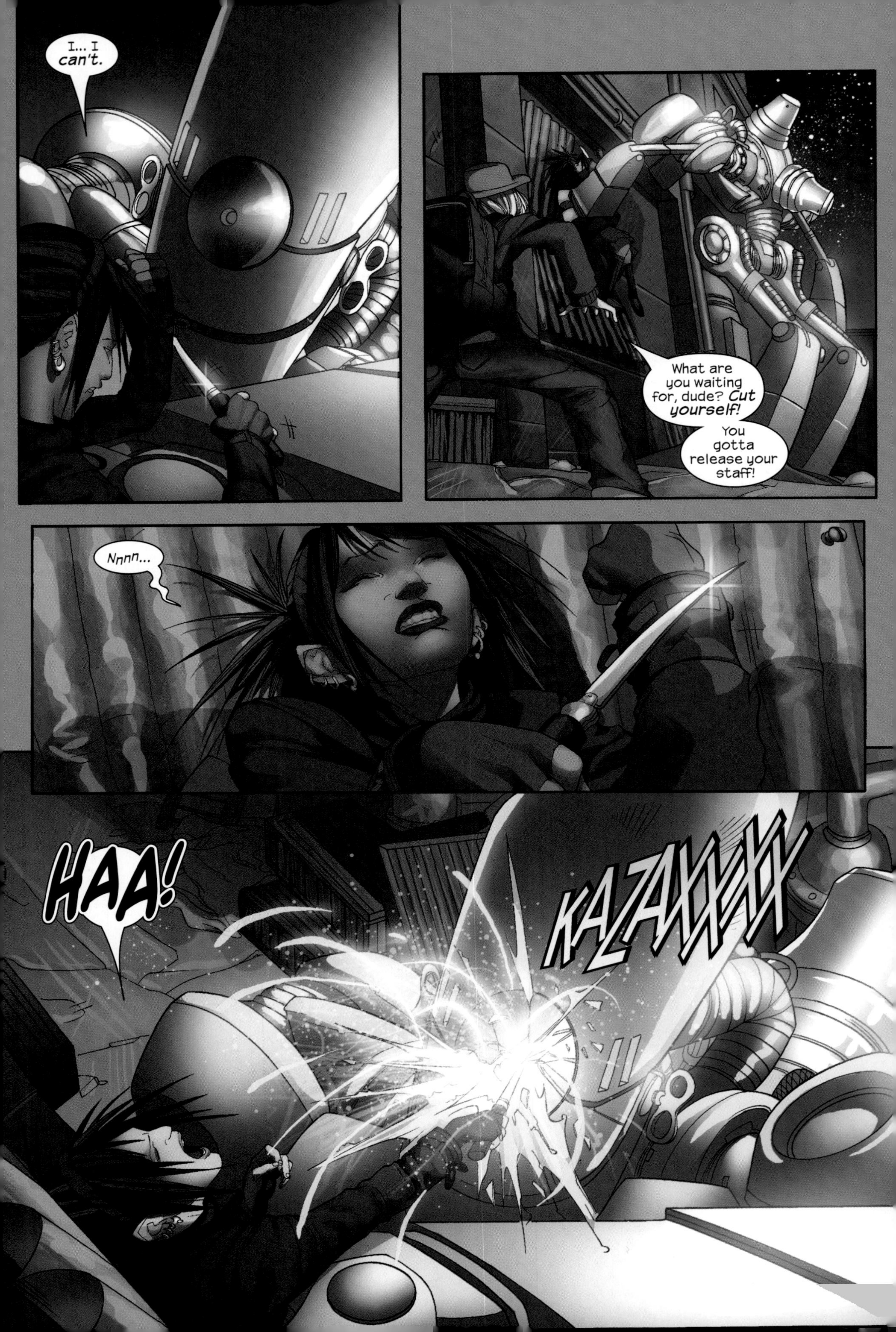
I... I can't.
What are you waiting for, dude? Cut yourself!
You gotta release your staff!
Nnnn...
HAA!
KAZAXXXX

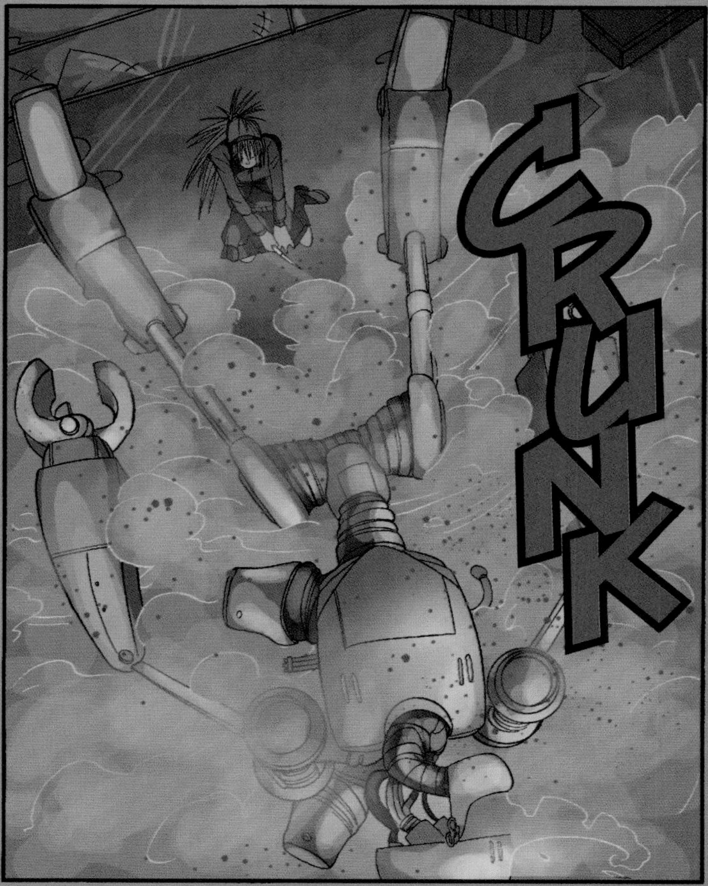
CRUNK
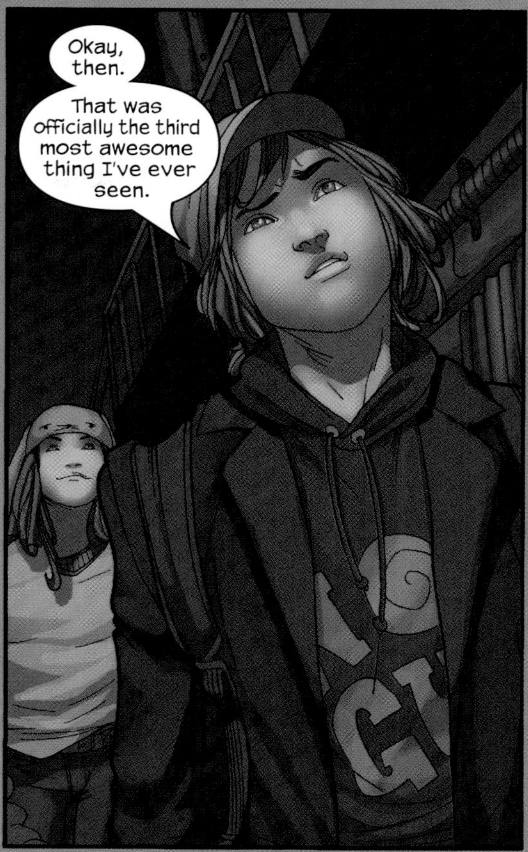
Okay, then.
That was officially the third most awesome thing I've ever seen.
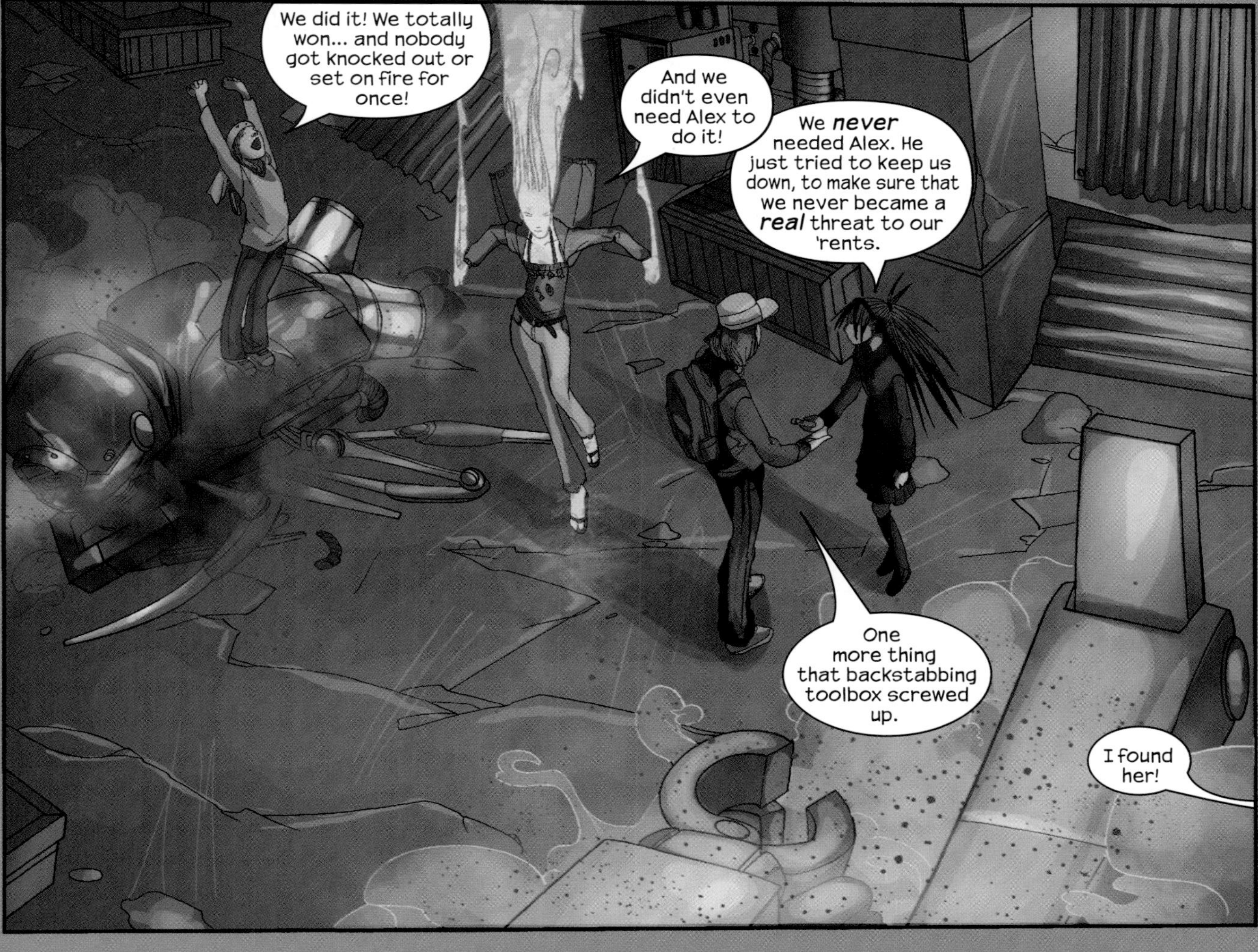
We did it! We totally won... and nobody got knocked out or set on fire for once!
And we didn't even need Alex to do it!
We *never* needed Alex. He just tried to keep us down, to make sure that we never became a ***real*** threat to our 'rents.
One more thing that backstabbing toolbox screwed up.
I found her!

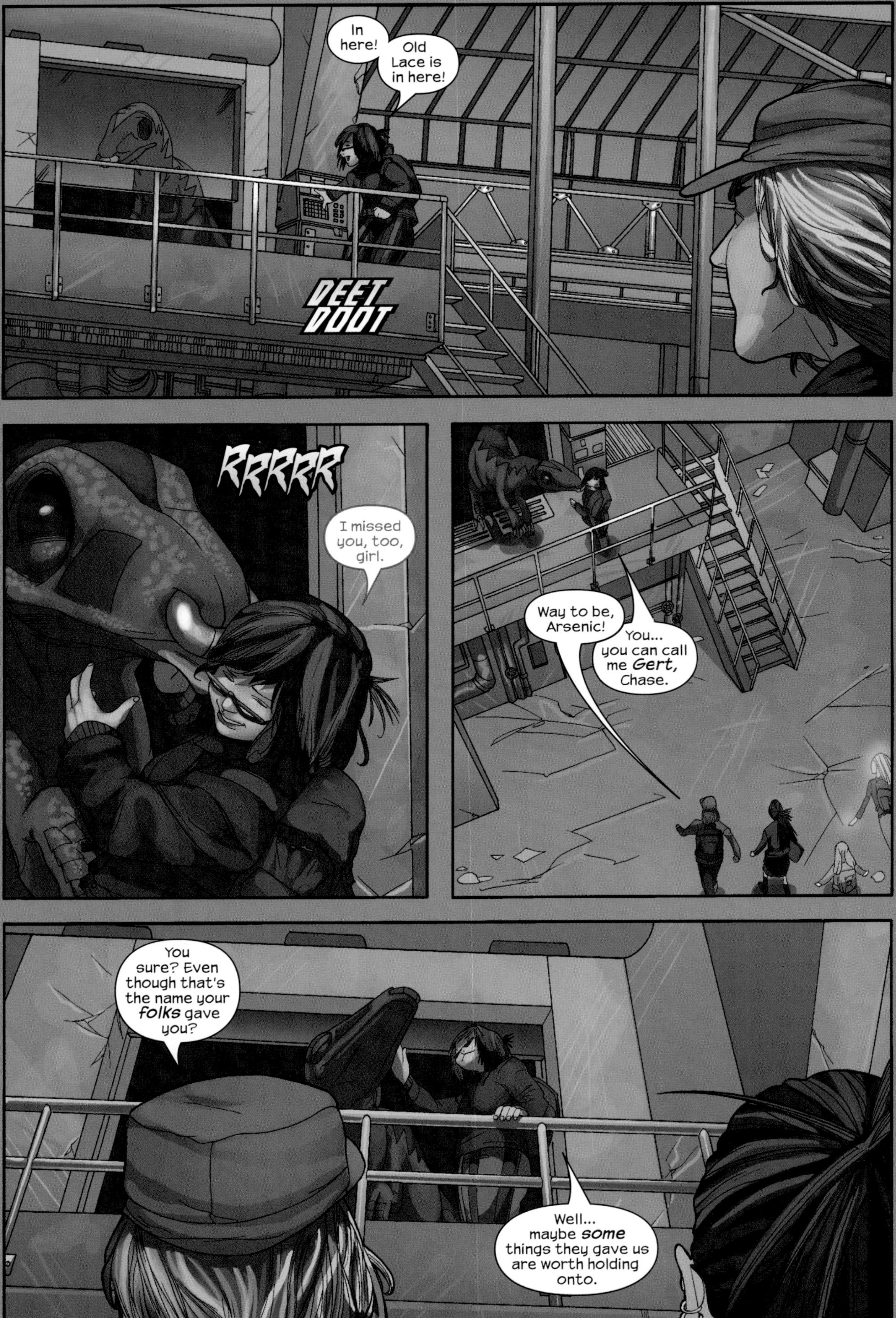

In here!
Old Lace is in here!
DEET DOOT
RRRRR
I missed you, too, girl.
Way to be, Arsenic!
You... you can call me *Gert*, Chase.
You sure? Even though that's the name your *folks* gave you?
Well... maybe *some* things they gave us are worth holding onto.

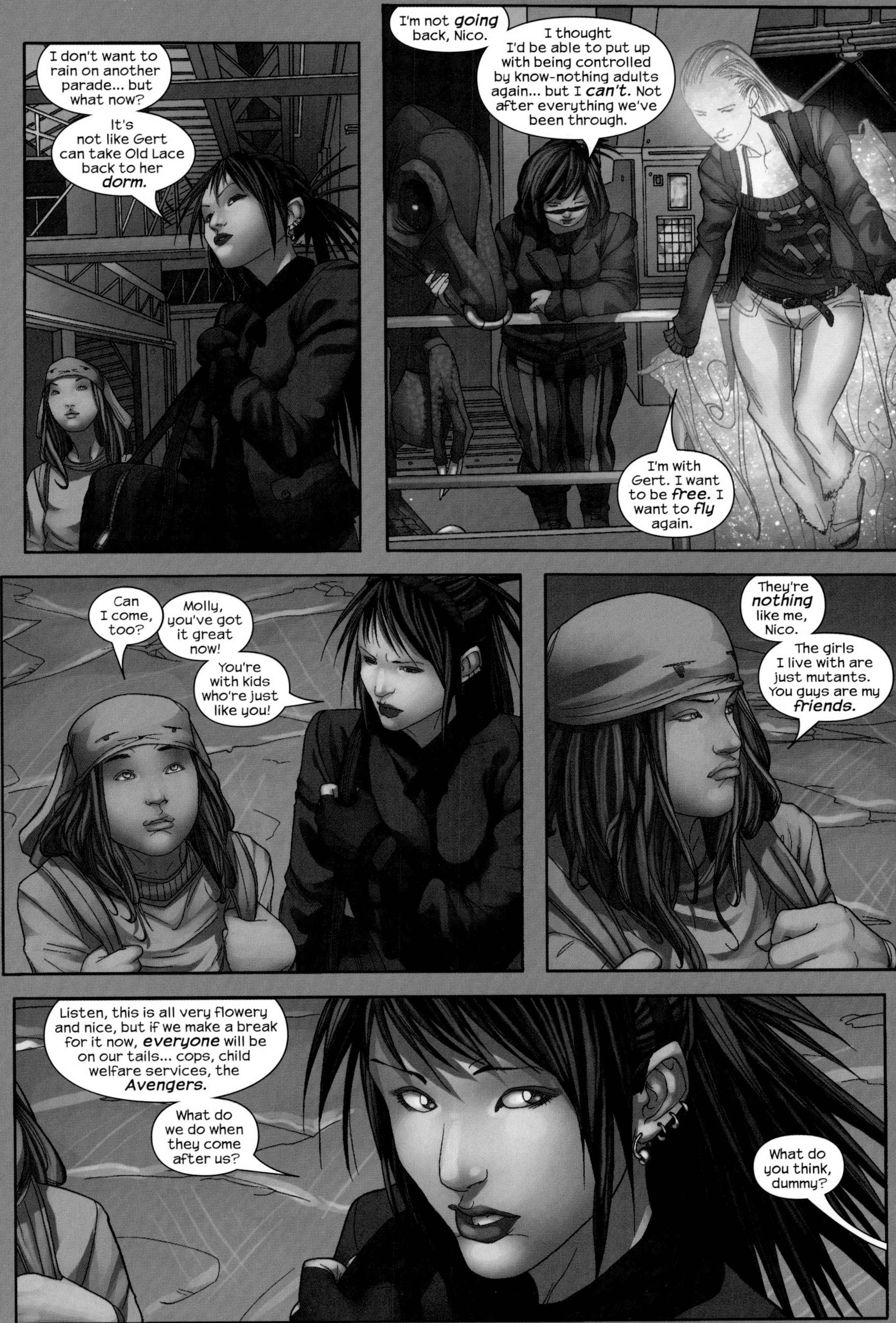
I don't want to rain on another parade... but what now?
It's not like Gert can take Old Lace back to her *dorm.*
I'm not *going* back, Nico.
I thought I'd be able to put up with being controlled by know-nothing adults again... but I *can't.* Not after everything we've been through.
I'm with Gert. I want to be *free.* I want to *fly* again.
Can I come, too?
Molly, you've got it great now!
You're with kids who're just like you!
They're *nothing* like me, Nico.
The girls I live with are just mutants. You guys are my *friends.*
Listen, this is all very flowery and nice, but if we make a break for it now, *everyone* will be on our tails... cops, child welfare services, the *Avengers.*
What do we do when they come after us?
What do you think, dummy?

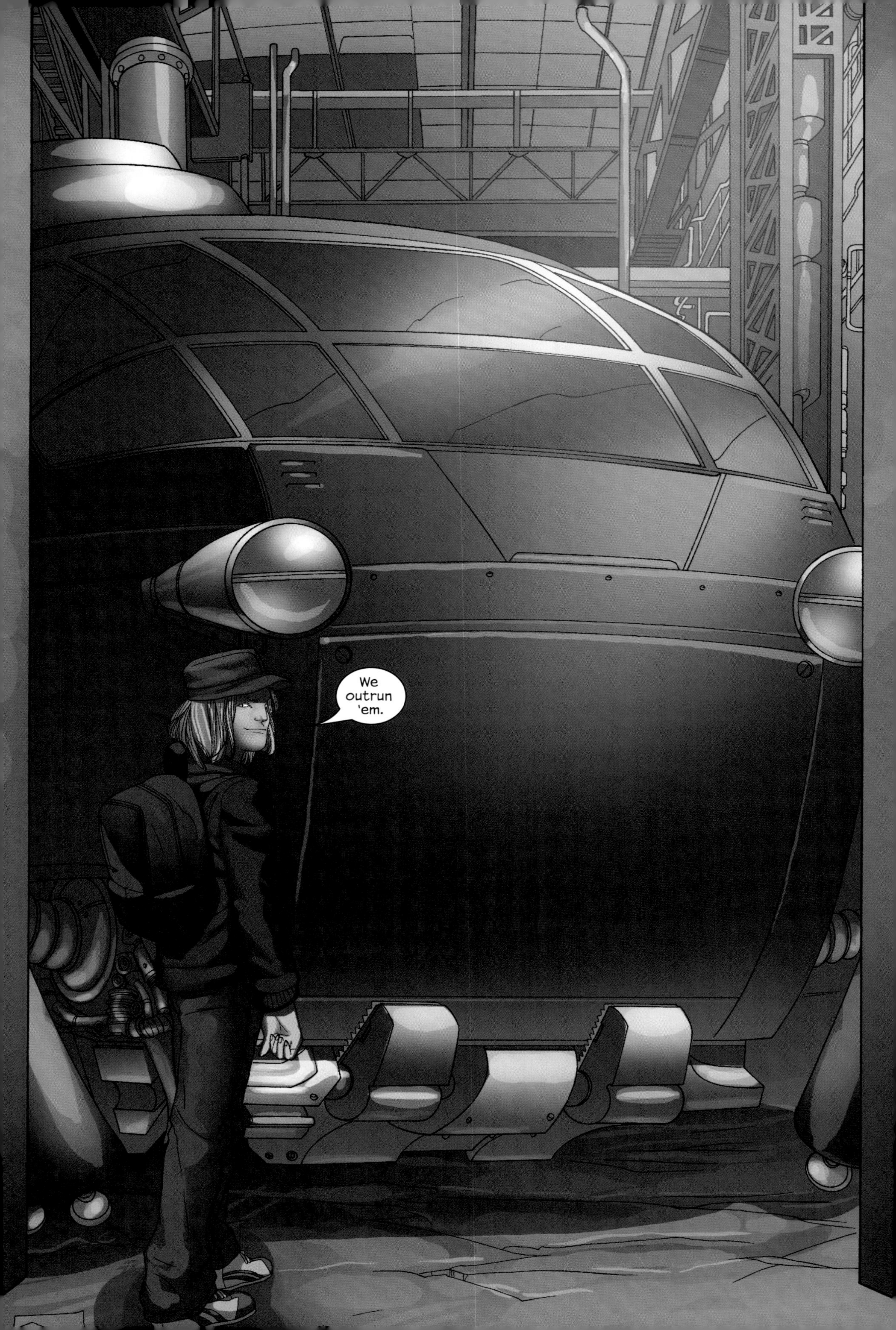
We outrun 'em.

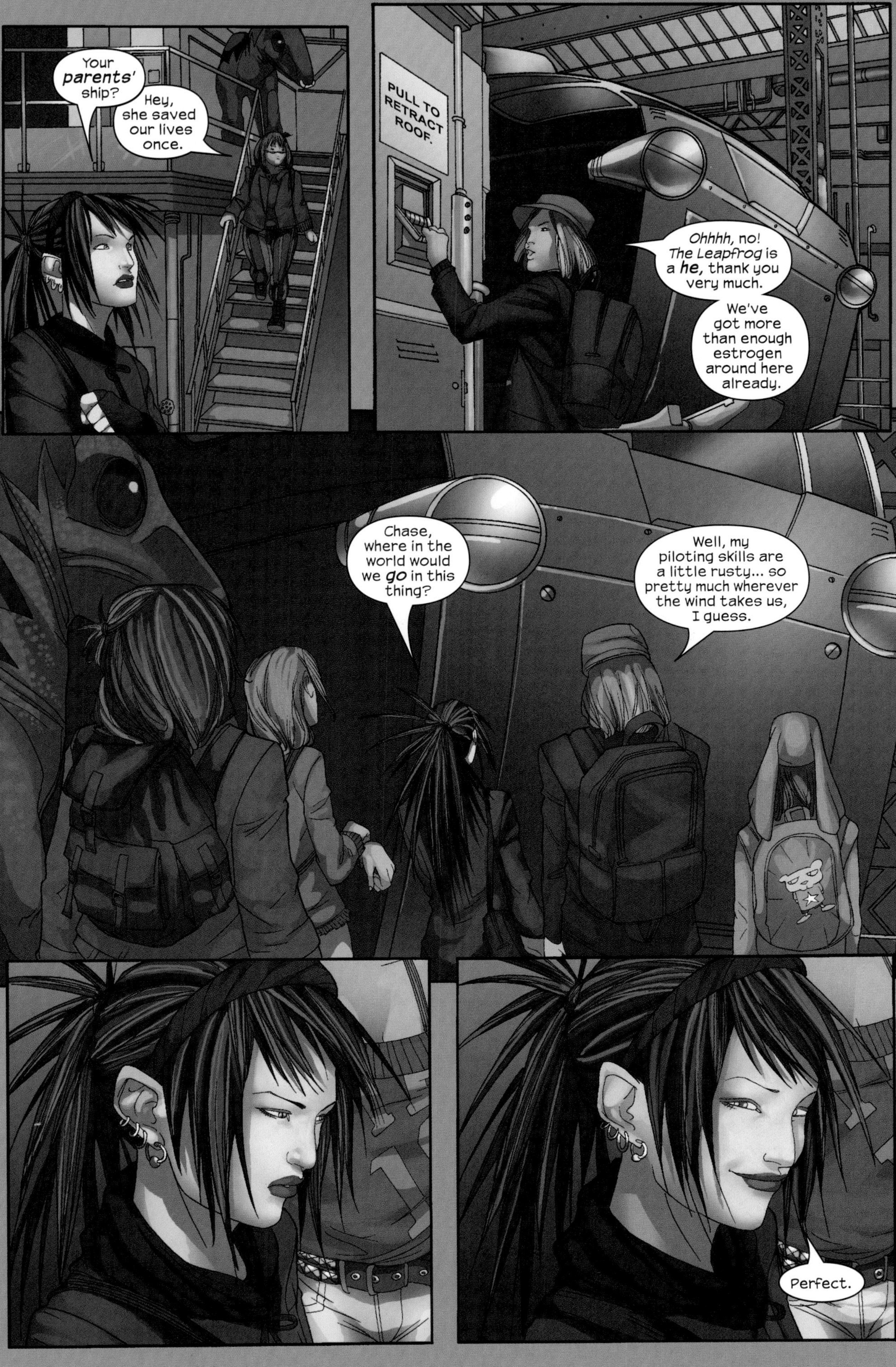

Your *parents'* ship?
Hey, she saved our lives once.
PULL TO RETRACT ROOF.
Ohhhh, no! The Leapfrog is a ***he,*** thank you very much.
We've got more than enough estrogen around here already.
Chase, where in the world would we ***go*** in this thing?
Well, my piloting skills are a little rusty... so pretty much wherever the wind takes us, I guess.
Perfect.

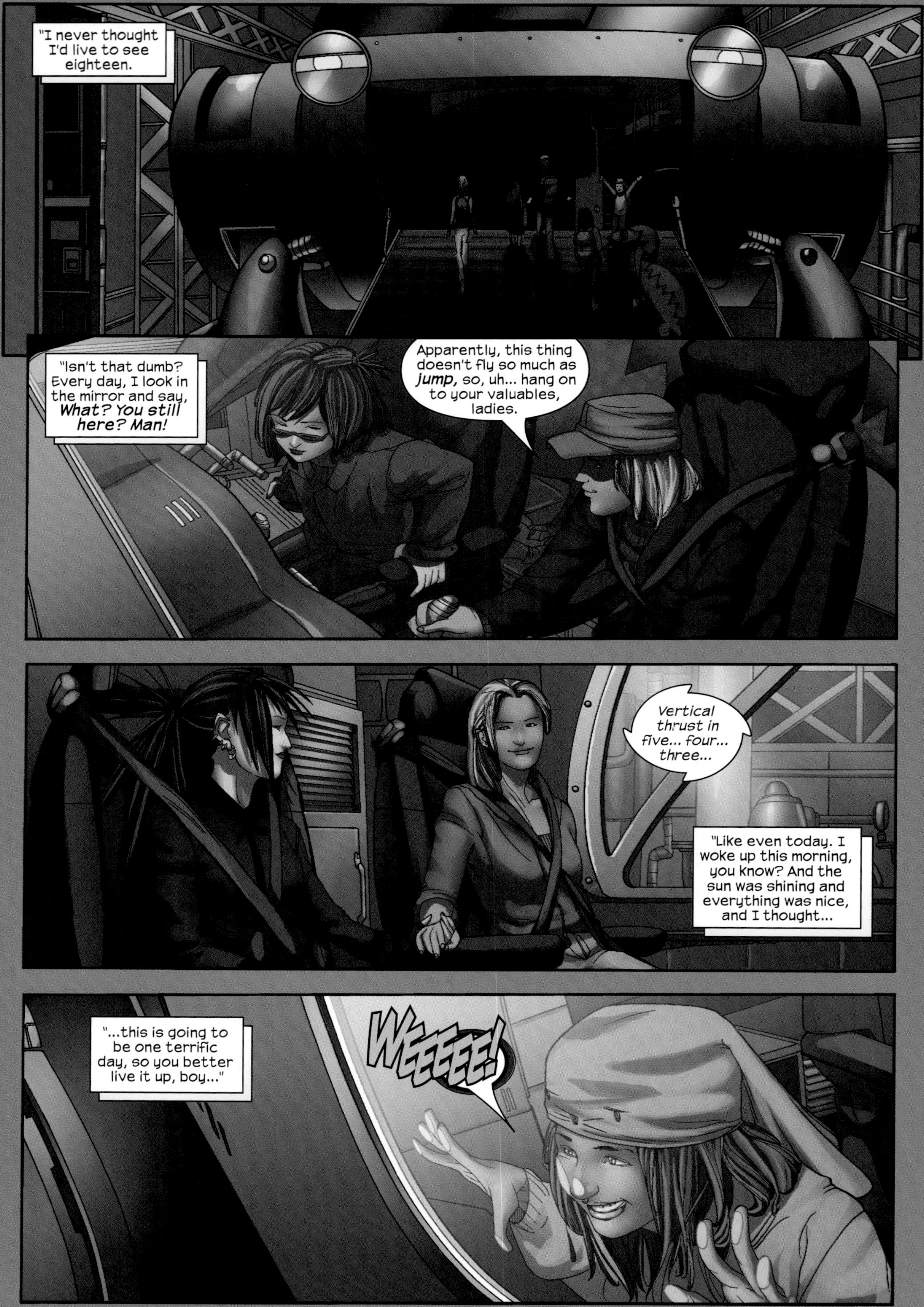
"I never thought I'd live to see eighteen.
"Isn't that dumb? Every day, I look in the mirror and say, *What? You still here? Man!*
Apparently, this thing doesn't fly so much as *jump,* so, uh... hang on to your valuables, ladies.
Vertical thrust in five... four... three...
"Like even today. I woke up this morning, you know? And the sun was shining and everything was nice, and I thought...
"...this is going to be one terrific day, so you better live it up, boy..."
WEEEEE!

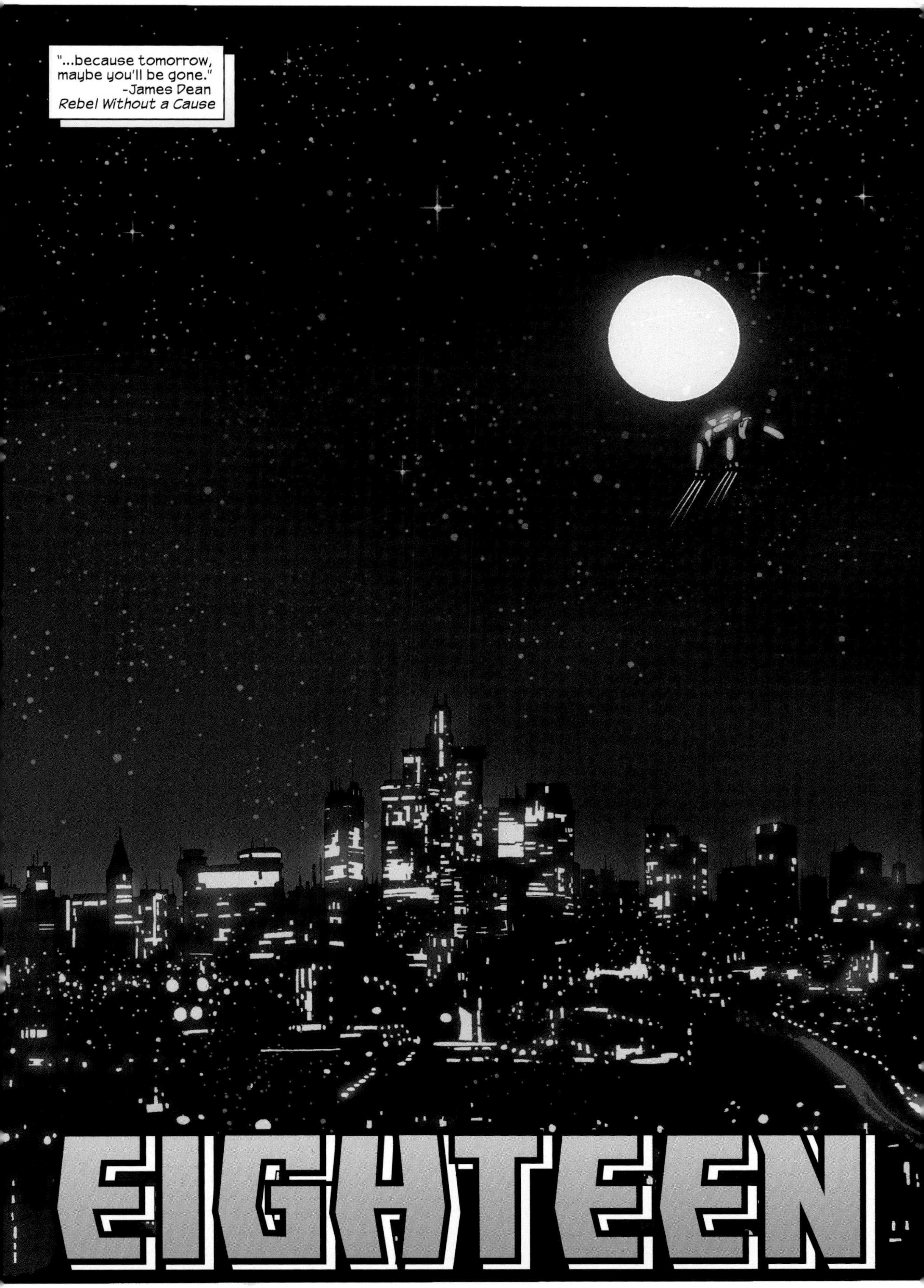
"...because tomorrow, maybe you'll be gone."
-James Dean
Rebel Without a Cause
EIGHTEEN

THIS LETTER APPEARED IN RUNAWAYS #18, FOLLOWED BY BRIAN K. VAUGHAN'S RESPONSE:

Team Runaways,

Last issue? What do you mean, LAST ISSUE? What the hell does that mean? Did you type it wrong? Were you thinking of something else, like maybe the *Sub-Mariner* or the *Smurfs*? How can there be a last issue when the story is obviously going to continue for years? You're some kind of wrong person. Have it looked into.

Your fan,
Joss Whedon

Yep, that's the real Joss Whedon, of BUFFY, ASTONISHING X-MEN and, uh, ROSEANNE fame. Cool, huh? But thanks to the vocal support of loyal readers like you (and Joss), I am thrilled to announce that this is NOT the last issue of Runaways. Our kids are going on a well-deserved vacation for a few short months, but the entire creative team will be bringing them back in early 2005 for RUNAWAYS #1! One chapter in the lives of our young heroes has ended, but an all-new, all-different one is about to begin.

THANK YOU NOTE FROM CHRISTINA STRAIN

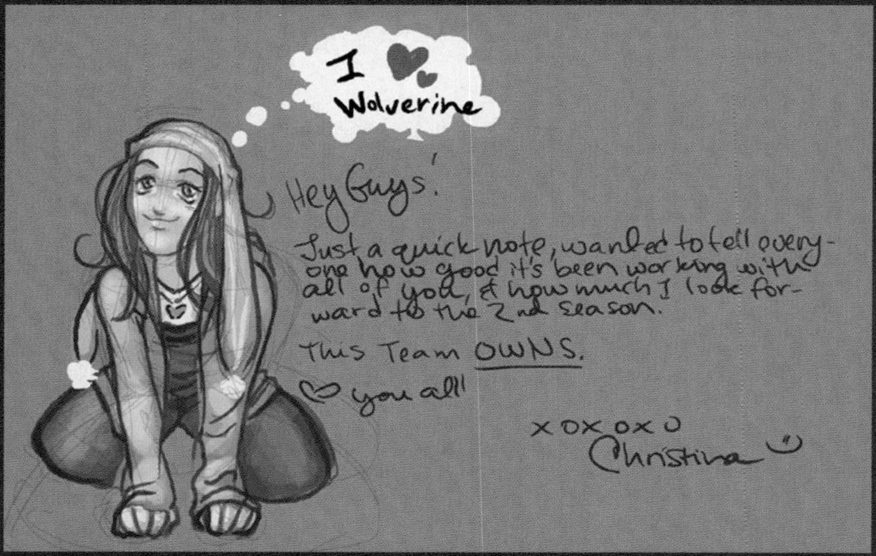

I ♥ Wolverine
Hey Guys!
Just a quick note, wanted to tell every-one how good it's been working with all of you, & how much I look for-ward to the 2nd season.
This Team OWNS.
♥ you all!
xoxoxo
Christina

RUNAWAYS
Expanded Proposal
by Brian K. Vaughn

At some point in their lives, all young people believe that their parents are the most evil people alive.

But what if they really are?

When six young friends discover that their parents are actually super-villains, the teenagers agree to run away from their respective homes. Using the unique gifts they inherited (or stole) from their immoral mothers and fathers, these fugitive heroes vow to do everything they can to atone for their parents' crimes.

Smallville meets Harry Potter in this all-ages action/adventure series.

THE PREMISE

Alex Wilder always knew that there was something strange about his parents, a happily married couple of wealthy Los Angeles socialites. Instead of family reunions, the Wilders host annual get-togethers with five other families. While the adults discuss their charity program in private, Alex has to hang out with their kids, an oddball collection of five other only children.

At one of these gatherings, the six teenagers make a horrifying discovery. They learn that their parents actually lead something called The Pride, an underworld organization of criminal kingpins, mad scientists, alien warlords, mutant terrorists, tyrannical time-travelers, and dark wizards. Working largely in secret to obtain complete world dominion, these all-new villains make Dr. Doom look like Dr. Evil.

The kids try to tell the authorities what they've learned, but the police are either disbelieving or under the far-reaching influence of the Pride. With no one else to turn to, the six teens agree to run away from their homes, but not before they pilfer strange technology and mystical devices from their corrupt parents.

Now on the run from their enraged families (some of whom want the children killed), the Runaways take up residence in the Hostel, an underground youth hotel buried during a California earthquake. In this unique, totally accessible new corner of the Marvel Universe, the would-be heroes give themselves new names, new attire, and a new purpose... to protect the community, right the wrongs of their parents, and one day bring the Pride to justice.

Still, the fruit usually doesn't fall too far from the tree, and some Runaways will have to fight the temptation to follow in their parents' footsteps. Matters will grow even more complicated when it becomes apparent that one of the Runaways may actually be a mole, loyal to the lethal Pride.

THE CHARACTERS

Wilder - The oldest of the Runaways, Alex Wilder is a seventeen-year-old African-American male. Though he has no powers, Wilder is a brilliant young strategist with a passion for directors like Hitchcock and online games like EverQuest. Now co-leader of the Runaways, Wilder is ashamed that his role-model parents are actually two criminal kingpins who fund the Pride's terrorist activities, and he intends to do whatever it takes to bring them down.

Sister Grimm - Rachel Messina is the sixteen-year-old daughter of two of the world's oldest and most powerful dark magicians (who now pose as wealthy antique dealers). Before she runs away from home, the crafty raven-haired girl grabs a dusty tome filled with spells. Now calling herself "Sister Grimm," Rachel struggles to master these black magicks (despite her religious background). The other co-leader of the Runaways, Sister Grimm is romantically attached to Wilder.

Lucy in the Sky - Leslie Dean is a stunningly beautiful, happy-go-lucky, sixteen-year-old girl who never imagined that her parents were actually alien warlords (who hide from intergalactic police under the guise of earthly real estate magnates). In some ways, Leslie has it much harder than her fellow Runaways. Not only does she discover the awful truth about her parents, but she also learns that she's really an alien. Still, this revelation becomes a lot easier to accept when she finds that her otherworldly physiology allows her to fly. Taking her codename from a favorite song, "Lucy in the Sky" will discover new and wonderful powers every day she's on the team. If only she could get _____ to fall in love with her, her life would be complete.

Talkback - The team's only other male (tradition be damned!), John Stein is the sixteen-year-old son of two "mad scientists," a couple that claims to be nothing more than successful software engineers. Inheriting little of his parents' technical know-how (he would rather play lacrosse), John is nevertheless able to obtain experimental hi-tech gauntlets before escaping from his broken home. Dubbed "Talkback" by his teammates, John hates taking orders, preferring to fly headlong into battle. Thankfully, his extensive array of hi-tech gadgets usually prevents him from getting hurt. Talkback is more than a bit obsessed with Leslie, and he's constantly vying for her attention.

Arsenic & Old Lace - Ferociously independent (if a little socially inept), Gertie Yorkes isn't the least bit surprised to hear that her retired parents are actually time-traveling despots from an apocalyptic future. Eager to leave home, she takes something from her parents hidden sub-basement before jetting, a ferocious velociraptor genetically engineered in the 87th Century to telepathically serve its master (in this case, Gertie). Calling herself "Arsenic," Gertie names her loyal dinosaur "Old Lace." Together, they're an extremely formidable, extremely odd duo.

Bruiser - The youngest member of the Runaways, Molly Hayes is the thirteen-year-old homo superior daughter of two Hollywood actors (who are actually mutant terrorists). Shortly before joining the team, Molly discovers that her genetic makeup grants her extraordinary strength. The little girl can bench a city bus without breaking a sweat... but she'd much rather watch the new Kylie Minogue video on TRL. Gertie (who acts like an overprotective older sister around Molly), jokingly nicknames her "Bruiser," a handle that seems preposterous given her sweet and innocent exterior. Molly claims that she's eager to do the right thing, but deep down, she just misses her Mommy and Daddy.

THE TONE
I started getting into comics when I was about twelve, but I had almost no interest in books like Power Pack or Teen Titans. Even though they were well crafted, they seemed like they were aimed at little kids (which no twelve-year-olds think of themselves as). I was more interested in books like X-Men, cool stories about badass outcasts (which is what most twelve-year-olds think of themselves as).

Now that Grant Morrison is writing X-Men for readers my age, Marvel could use a new all-ages series that's smart and edgy, but also PG-rated and absolutely continuity-free. I'm confident The Runaways can be that book.

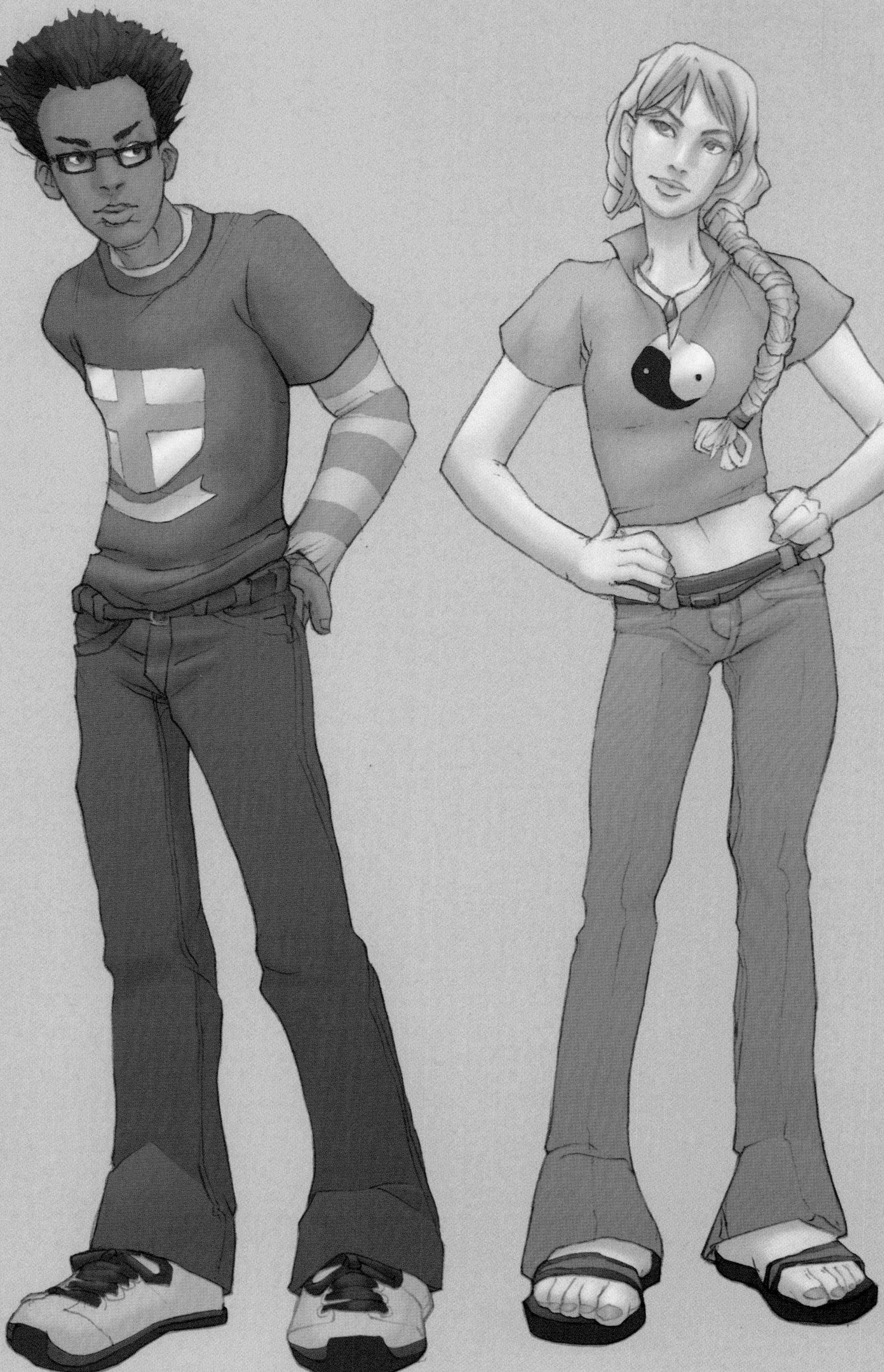

Combining action, romance, humor, and some Harry Potter-style darkness, The Runaways is a series that older readers will definitely enjoy, and a book that retailers can confidently put into the hands of younger customers (if such a thing still exists).

THE STORIES

Like the excellent first arc of Ultimate Spider-Man, we'll be starting from square one and taking time to tell a character-driven origin story. These are my tentative plans for our first six issues:

Issue #1 - We open with Spider-Man and Daredevil working together to capture the Hulk... only to reveal that this is actually teenager Alex Wilder playing an online role-playing game starring his favorite real-world superheroes. (This will quickly establish that our protagonist is a young, intelligent, contemporary aspiring hero.) Alex's parents barge in and order him off the computer. Their guests are about to arrive.

The Wilders are soon joined by five other wealthy families, each made up of two loving parents and their single child. As the grown-ups discuss their charity work in private, Alex is forced to entertain the other kids (which is almost as awkward as having to hang out with those strange second cousins you only see at Thanksgiving). Here, we quickly establish the basic relationships of the six teenagers: Alex and goth Rachel are attracted to each other, flighty Leslie has a secret crush on _____, jock John has a secret crush on Leslie, and everyone hates misfit Gertie, except for prepubescent Molly, who trusts the older girl enough to ask her about the "strange things" happening to her body.

Instead of playing Playstation like they normally do, the six teens decide to spy on their parents' private meeting. Watching from a secret passage Alex recently discovered, the kids are amazed to see the way the adults behave behind closed doors. But when Alex's father produces an orphaned infant (obtained on the black market) from inside a box, the suddenly troubled kids tell young Molly to shut her eyes. The teens watch in horror as their parents reveal their unique powers, and use them to perform some kind of dark sacrificial ritual.

After the baby is killed (off-panel!), the adults smile and toast, "To the end of the world as we know it." From their hidden vantage point behind a one-way mirror, the kids react with fear and disbelief. Suddenly, one of the adults turns to the mirror, and asks, "What was that noise?"

Issue #2 - The adults burst into the secret passageway... only to find it empty. They make sure that their children are still playing Playstation in another room, and return to their vile work. Alone again, the kids drop their calm facades and freak out. Did they really see what they thought they saw, or was it some kind of game? What the hell are they supposed to do now?

Rather than confront their apparently evil elders and possibly end up dead, the kids resolve to meet up in secret later that night (except for young Molly, who they decide to keep in the dark about this). They struggle to act natural when their parents finally exit their "meeting," and exchange terse farewells before leaving.

Escaping their homes after midnight, the kids reconvene at the parking lot of a nearby mall (minus young Molly). After much deliberation, they decide to call the Avengers and tell them about their parents' secret lives as super-villains. But when the Avengers' hotline is busy, they're forced to call a homicide detective at a local precinct. When the man laughs at their "evil parents" story, the kids realize that they're going to have to find some hard evidence before anyone will believe them. Alex found nothing when he searched his home for the infant's corpse or any of the murder weapons used in the ritual, so the group decides to pile in John's van and check out Gertie's house next.

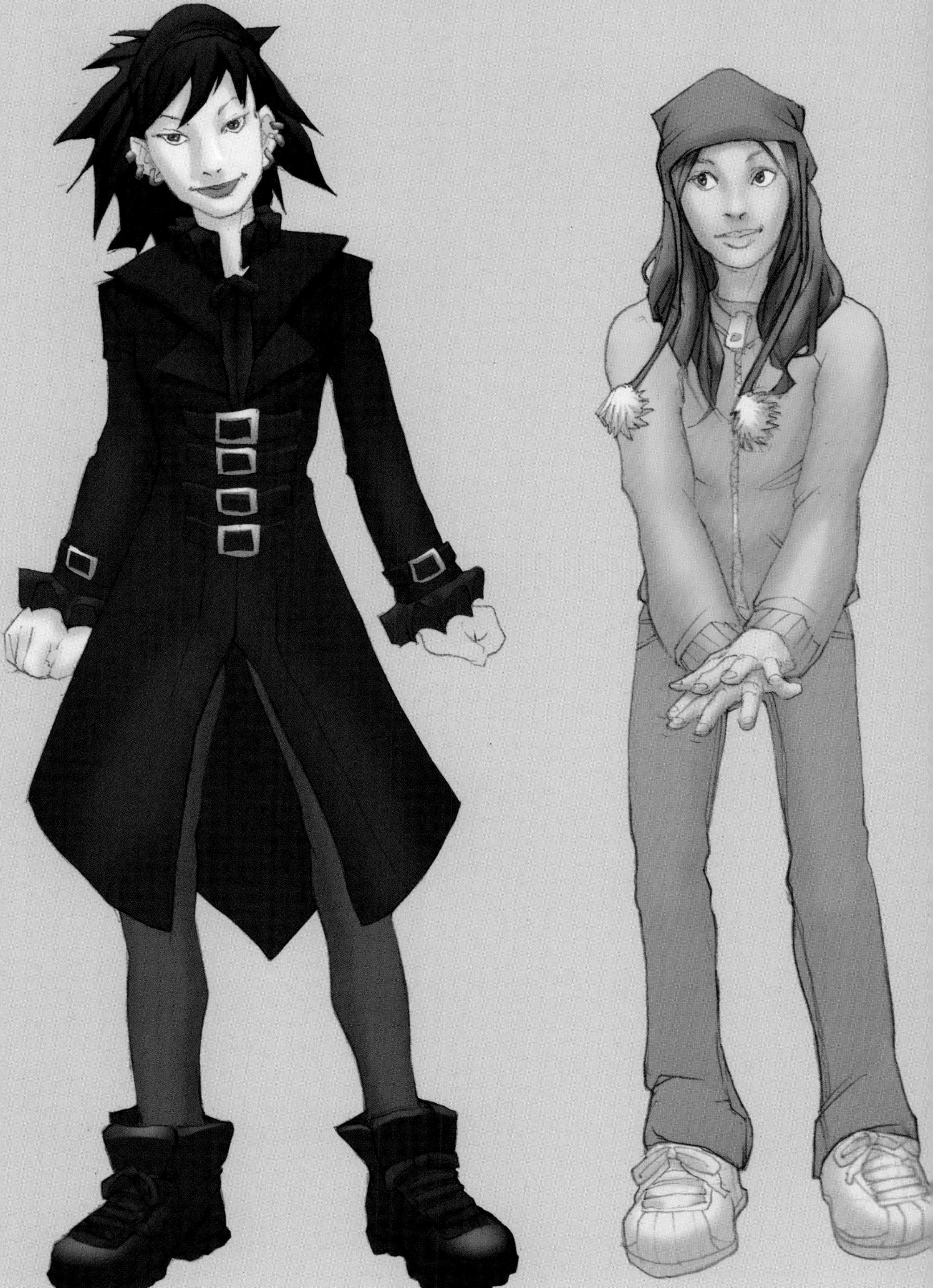

Sneaking inside (Gertie's parents are asleep), the kids soon find a secret passageway much like the one in Alex's house. Spelunking down a deep corridor, they suddenly hear something behind them. The kids turn to see a giant velociraptor baring its fangs!

Issue #3 - The group screams in terror, but the dinosaur politely bows in front of Gertie. A note around its neck explains that this beast was meant to be a gift for Gertie in the event of her time-traveling parents' death. The cyborg raptor responds only to her commands, and is trained to protect her from the countless enemies Gertie's evil mother and father have apparently made over the years. The kids scour the rest of the catacombs for evidence, but retreat after finding nothing (dinosaur in tow).

As relationships and jealousy blossom, the kids head to Rachel's home, where they eventually find a passageway in the woods behind her house. Inside, they discover the book of spells Rachel's warlock parents used during the sacrifice. But because of her Christian faith, Rachel refuses to try any of the "black spells" found inside. Desperate for more damning evidence, the group decides to press on.

Finally, the kids try the secret chamber inside Leslie's house (her parents are out of town), where the attractive young woman finds out about her alien heritage. At first, she's completely horrified, but when Leslie discovers that the "medical bracelet" she's been forced to wear her whole life is the only thing inhibiting her from using her power of flight, she perks right up. Unfortunately, the group finds nothing else of value, and so moves on to John's home.

Meanwhile, back at the police precinct the kids phoned last issue, the Captain asks one of his detectives about the strange call that came in earlier. The Captain laughs nervously when he hears the story about the kids and their "super-villain parents," but he soon retreats to his office and calls Alex's father, whispering, "My Lord, I think we may have a problem..."

Issue #4 - Inside a secret lab underneath John's house, the young athlete is shocked to learn that his parents appear to be brilliant mad scientists. How could a guy who flunked biology be the son of two scientific geniuses, the other kids wonder. John tries on a pair of hi-tech gauntlets, when he suddenly hears a voice say, "That's enough, children. I just received a troubling call from Alex's father. Your little scavenger hunt is over." The kids turn around to see John's parents, both wielding huge sci-fi weapons!

Gertie's pet raptor leaps to her defense, but is quickly neutralized. Alex leads the others in a decent fight, but they're no match for the two more experienced adults. The teenagers are almost defeated, when Rachel sacrifices her beliefs to cast a black spell that temporarily overpowers John's parents.

The kids are able to retreat, but Alex soon gets a call on his cell phone. It's his mother, who says, "Alex, you need to stop this immediately... or I'm afraid we'll have no choice but to do something terrible to your young friend Molly."

Issue #5 - Sick at the thought of anything happening to Molly, our heroes foolishly decide to rescue their youngest companion from the home of her evil mutant parents.

Naturally, when they arrive, the group is greeted by several adults, Rachel's mother, Gertie's father, and both of Molly's parents (who are using their perplexed daughter as a human shield). The teenagers use what little they've learned about their weapons/abilities, but they're once again soundly defeated by their more powerful elders.

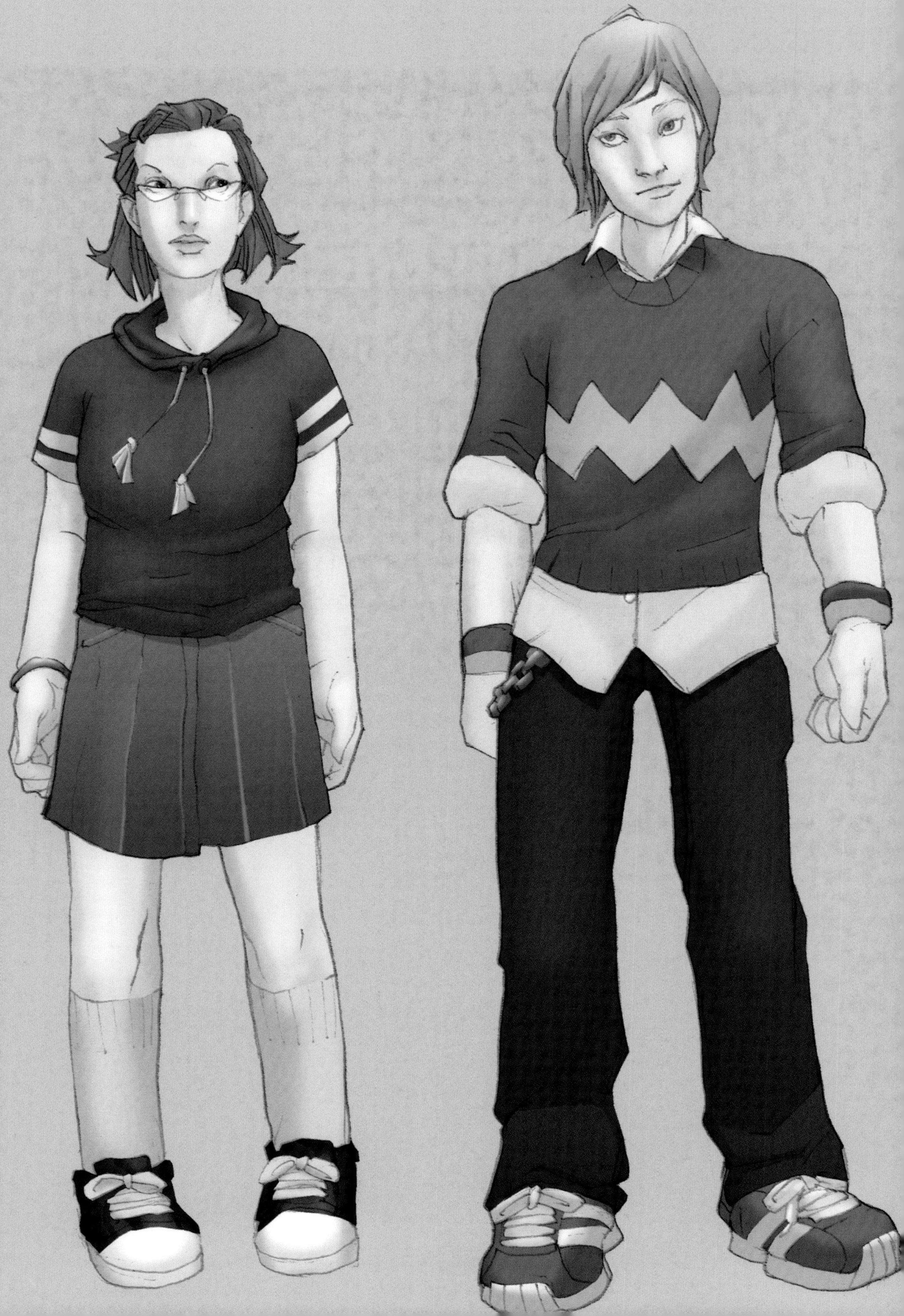

Molly's father is about to hurt her friend Gertie, when Molly suddenly breaks free of her mother's grasp and punches her father through a wall! Clearly, when Molly was telling Gertie about the changes happening to her body back in Issue #1, she didn't mean puberty... she meant the onset of her mutant powers!

This briefly turns the tide of the fight, and the kids barely escape alive. Before fleeing the house with Molly, Alex grabs something called "The Compendium," an encrypted book that appears to have information about the adults' clandestine organization, "The Pride."

Though they never found the body of the slain infant, the teenagers decide that they now have more than enough information to take to the authorities. But when one of the kids turns on the radio in John's van, they hear a startling report. The police are looking for a teenager named Alex Wilder... who apparently killed an infant in his own home. When interviewed, Alex's parents say that this murder "might have something to do with their son's involvement in violent online role-playing games," and the cops suspect that some of Alex's friends may have helped commit this heinous act.

Simultaneously, the framed kids say, "Oh, $#@*."

Issue #6 - Realizing that even the police are under the control of their parents' evil empire, our heroes are now wanted fugitives with no one to turn to. Rachel reveals that she has a secret hiding place that she's been going to since she was a little girl, and the group is forced to take shelter in this abandoned underground youth hospice.

Frightened and overwhelmed, the six formerly wealthy kids now have nothing but each other. Betrayed by their duplicitous families, the teenagers are united by their desire to do whatever it takes to destroy the Pride, and to right their parents' wrongs. Creating codenames and disguises for themselves, an unlikely new team of heroes is born.

Finally, in an intriguing epilogue to our first arc, we revisit the teenagers' assembled parents. The Pride is distraught by the evening's turn of events, but heartened by an unsigned electronic communiqué they receive. It reads, "Mom and Dad - I love you, and I know you have reasons for doing what you did. Don't worry, I will always be loyal to you."

The Next Arc - As the Runaways start to decode the Compendium they stole in our last storyline, they begin to realize just how powerful their parents really are, and how much damage their secret organization has done over the last twenty years. Accepting that they're not yet ready to take on the Pride, the masked teenagers decide to use their newfound powers to protect the community (and maybe atone for some of their parents' sins in the process). They start by attempting to capture a group of bank robbers terrorizing Los Angeles... but the Runaways soon discover that being a superhero isn't as easy as it looks on TV.

Meanwhile, romances and feuds between team members continue to develop. And elsewhere, the Pride comes up with an ambitious plan to lure their "wayward" children back home.

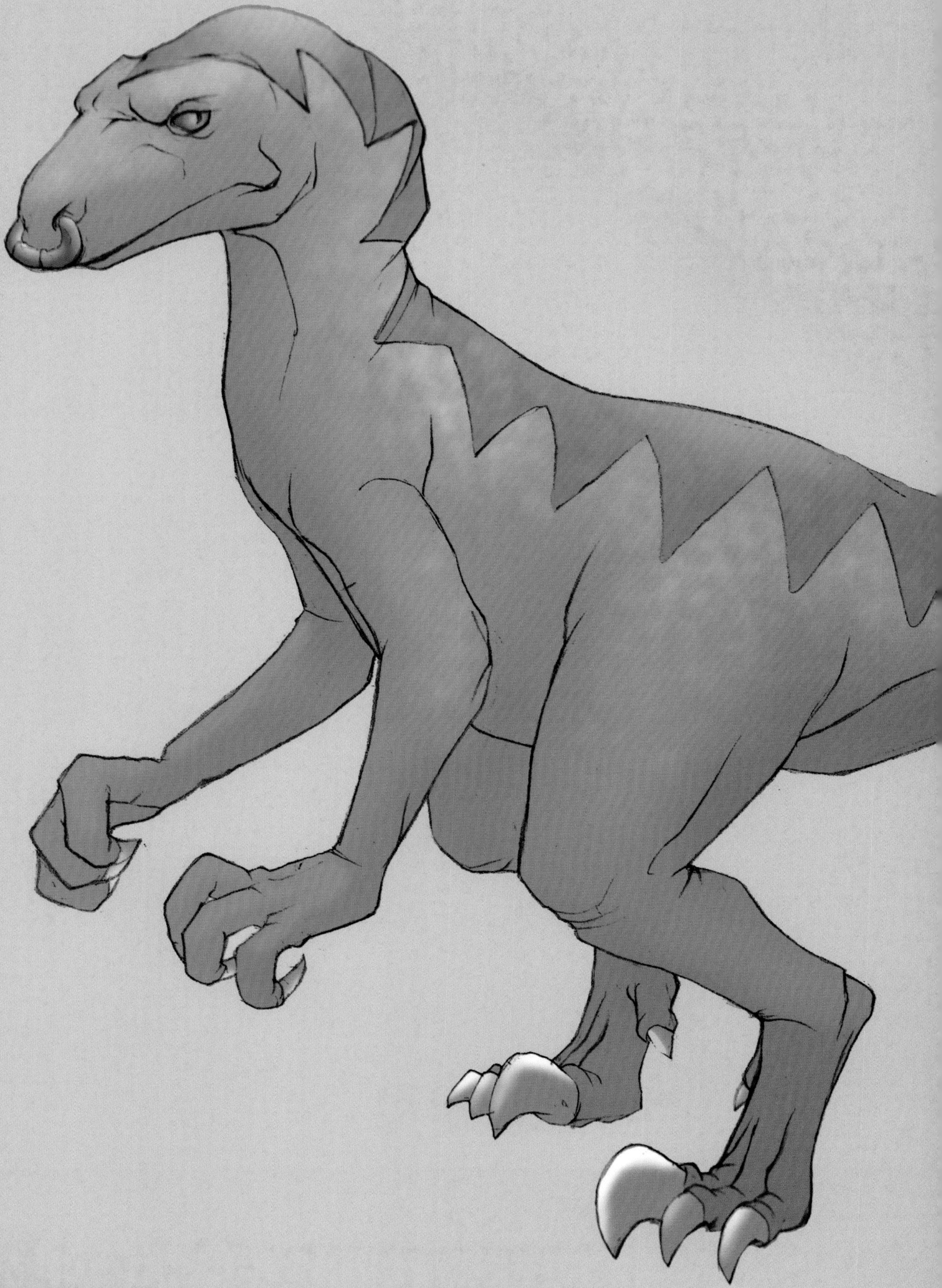

ADRIAN ALPHONA SKETCHBOOK

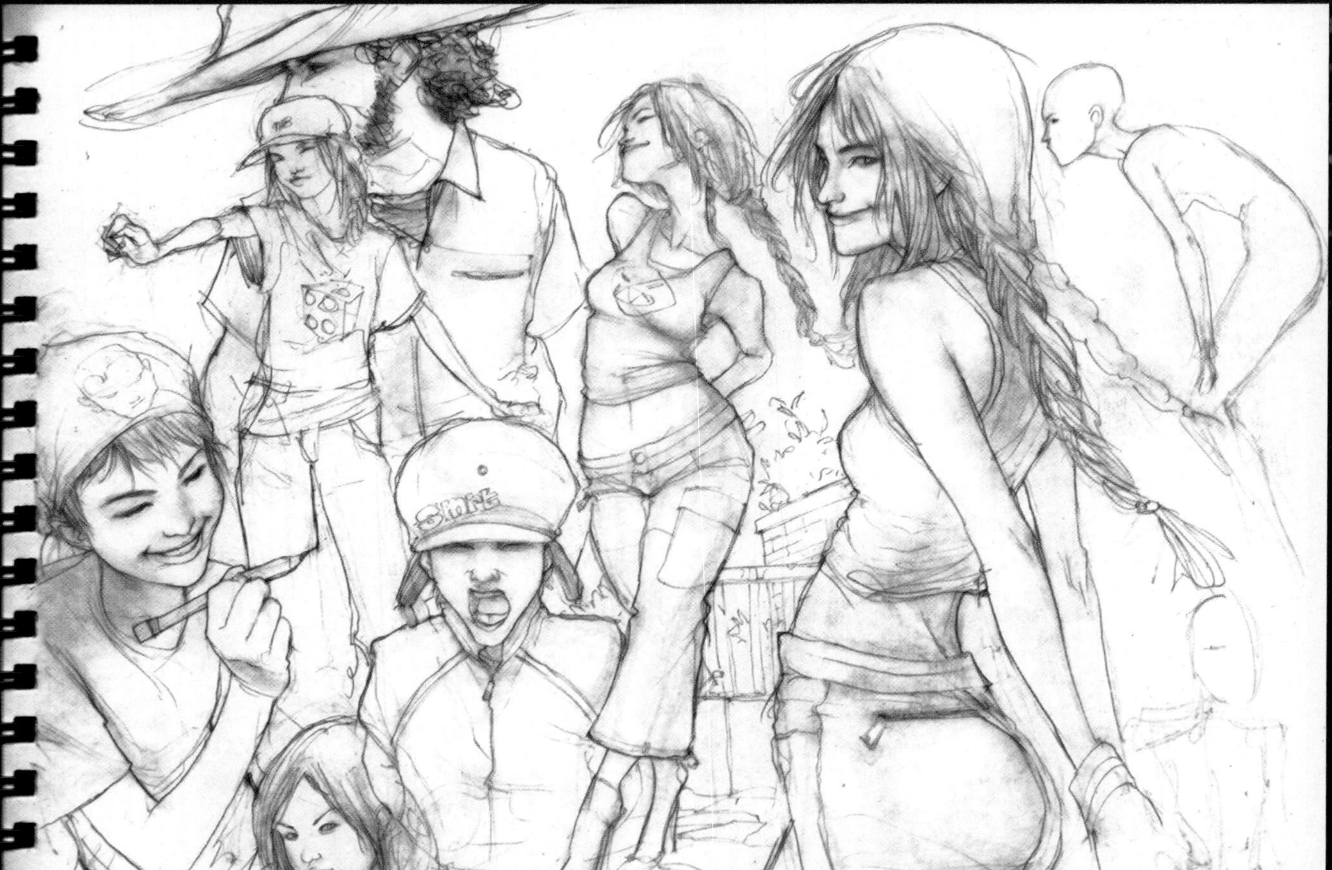
July 15
2004

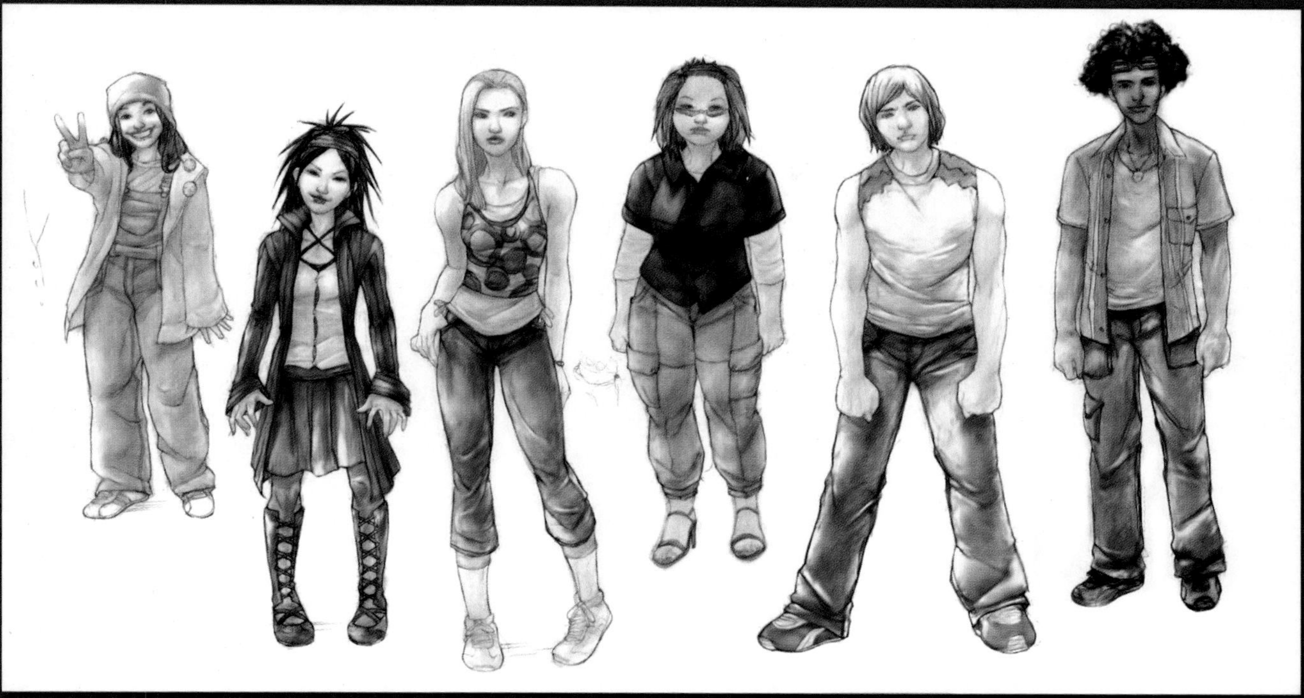

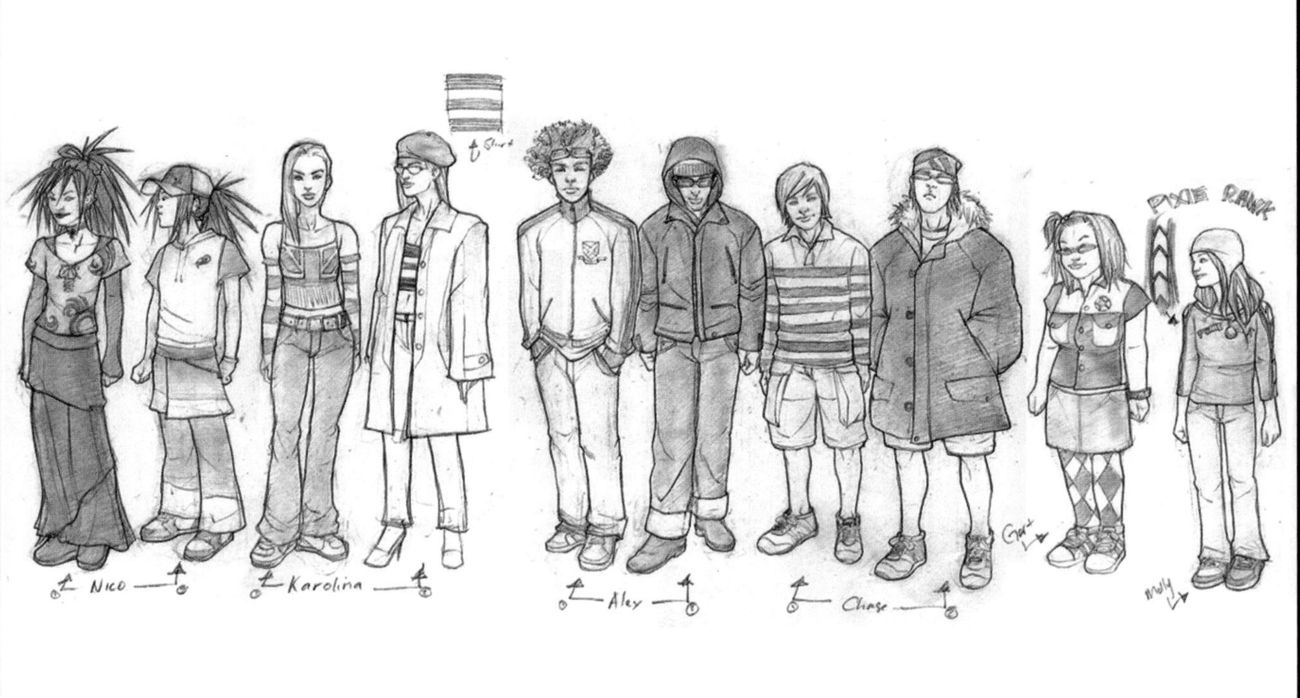

Nico
Karolina
Alex
Chase
Gert
Molly

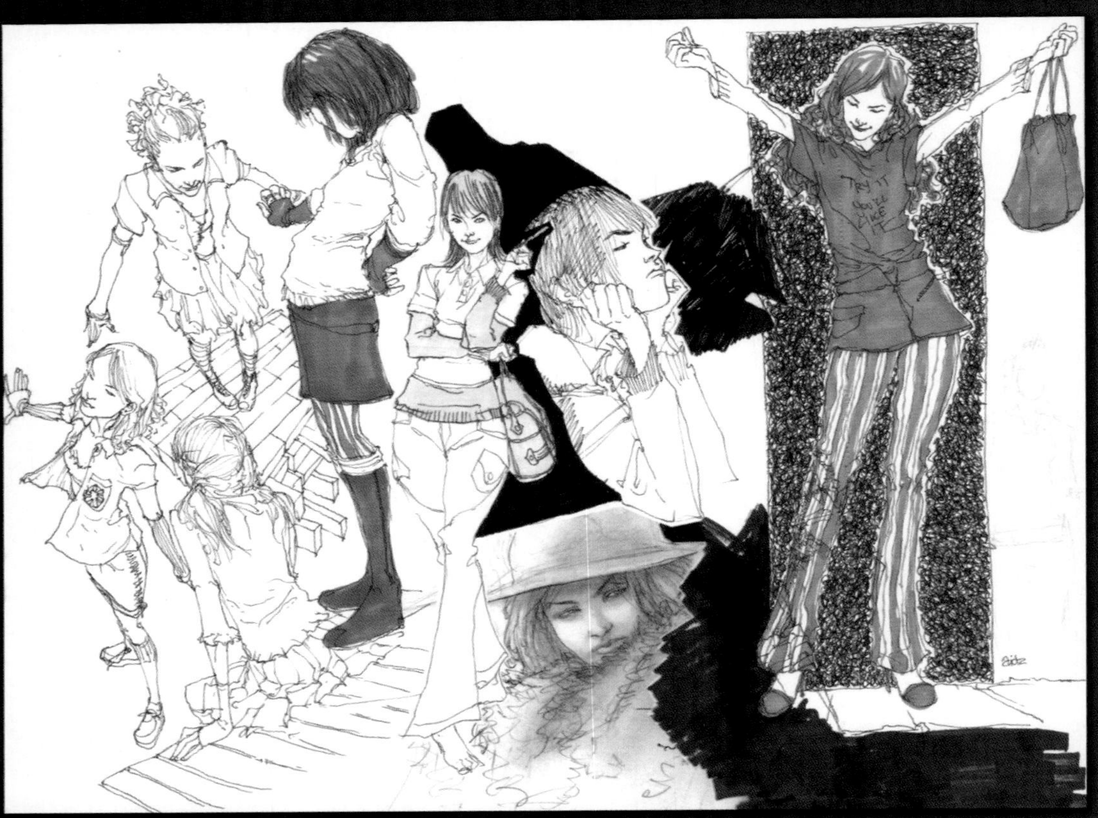
TRY IT

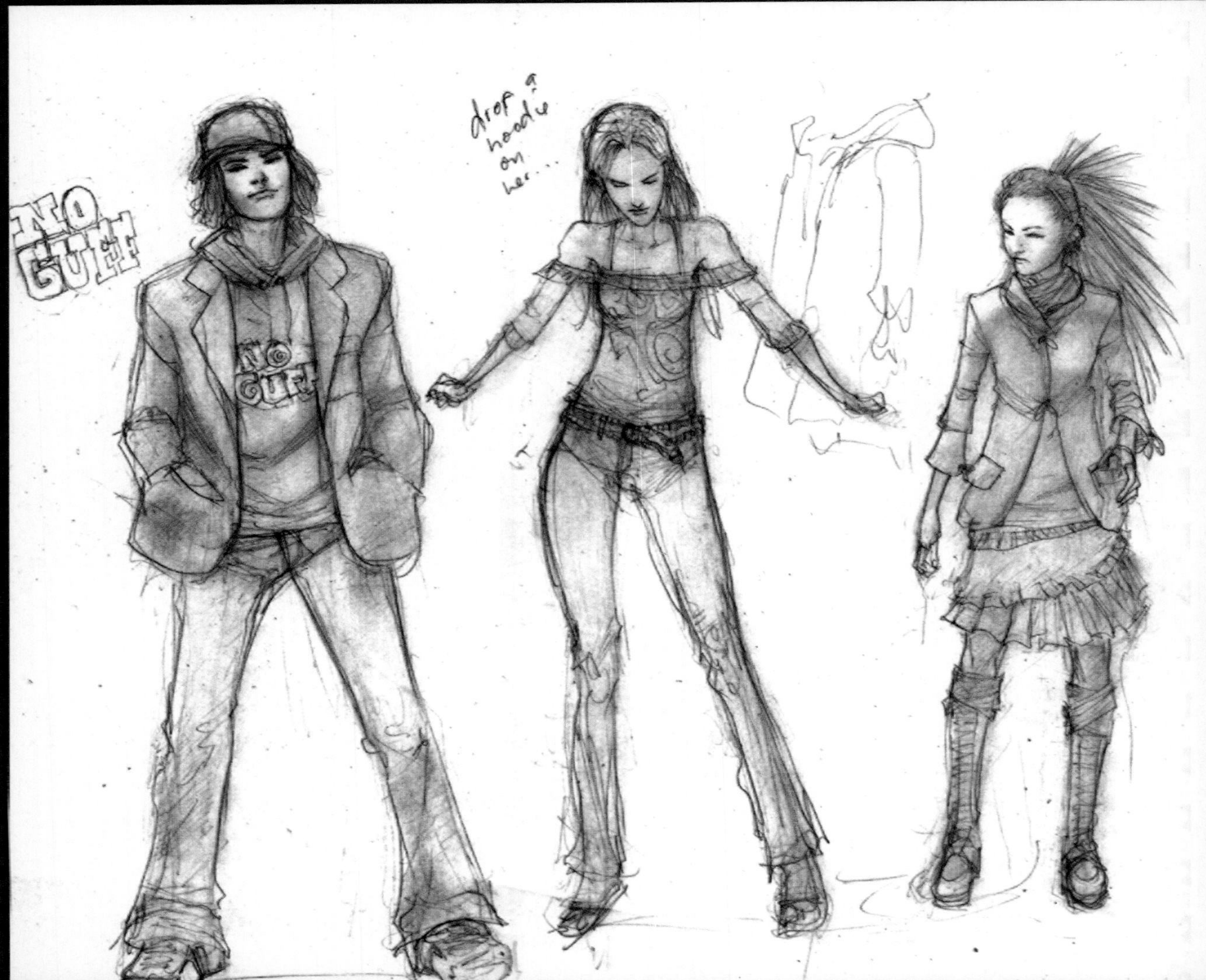
NO GUM
drop a hoodie on her...
NO GUM

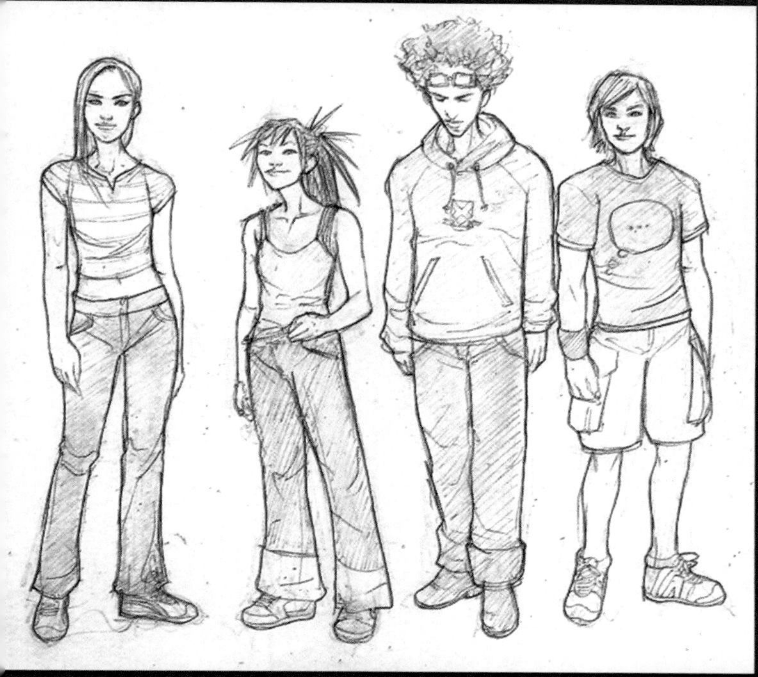

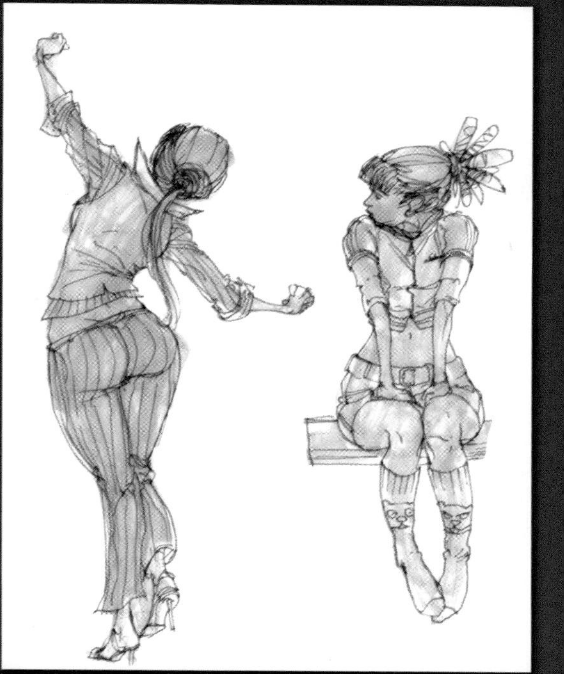

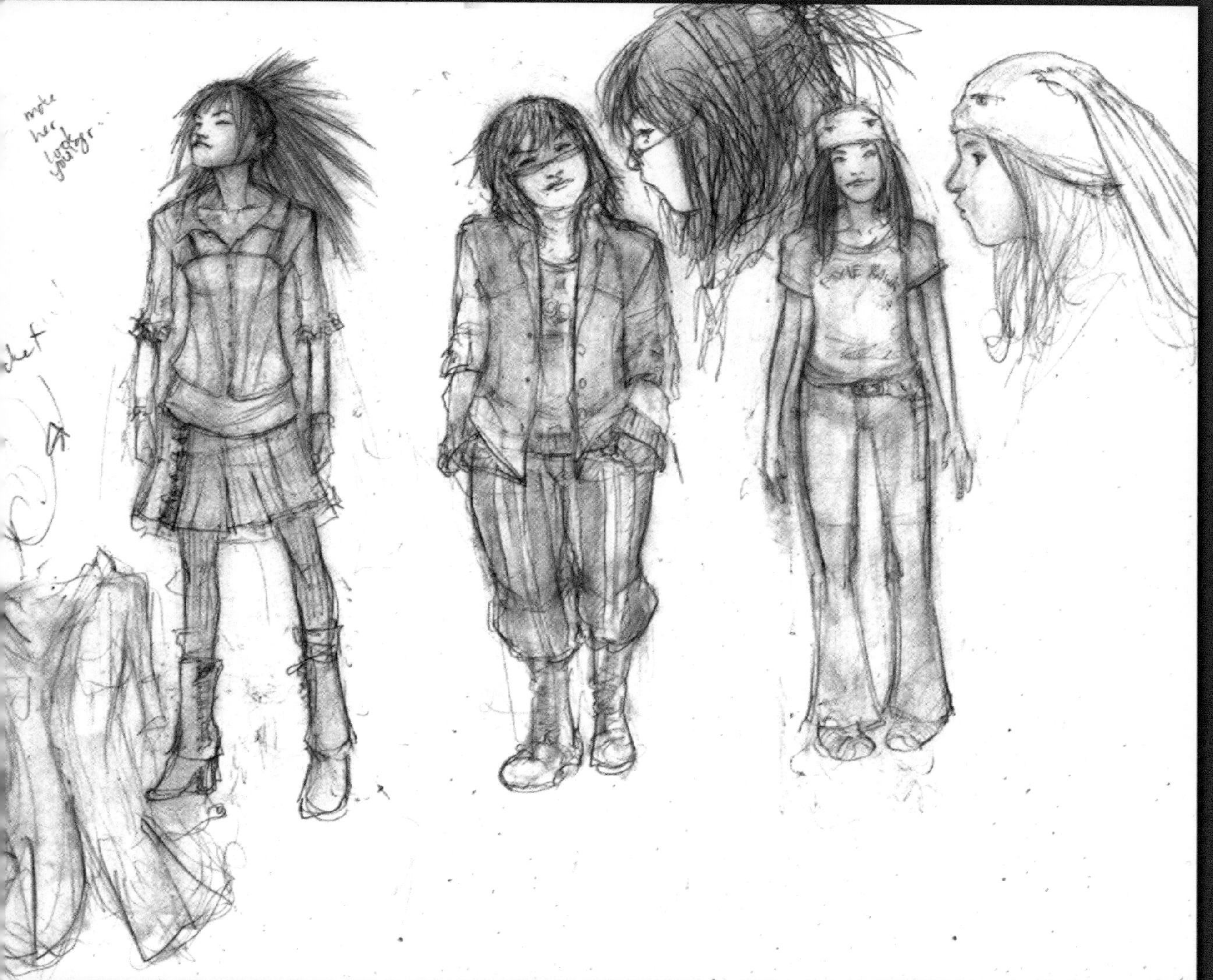

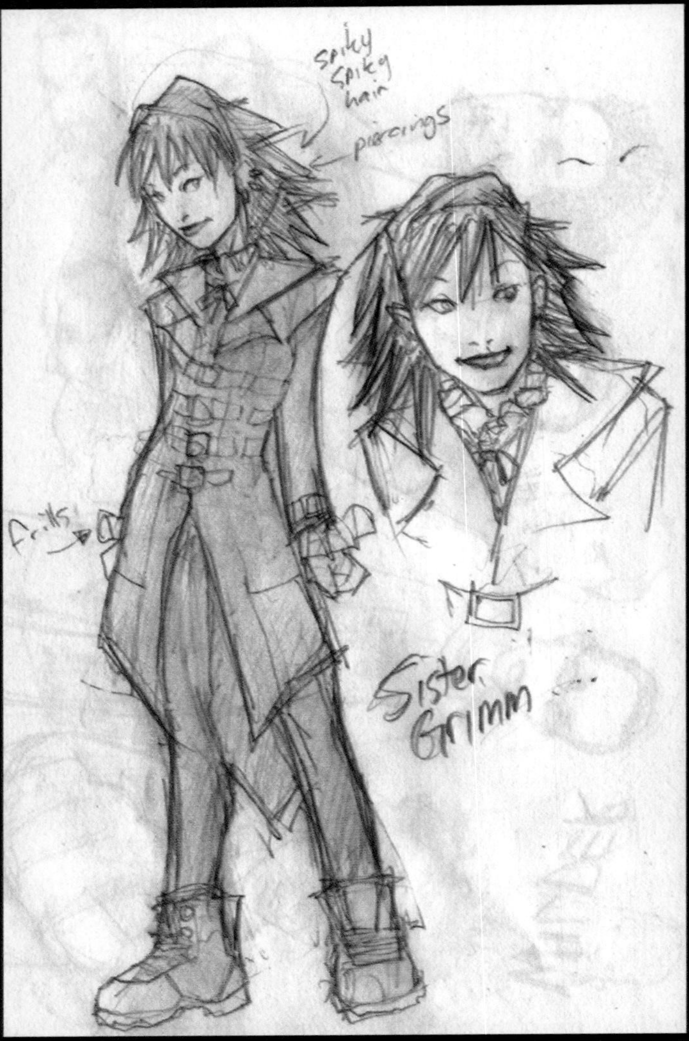
spiky
spiky
hair
piercings
frills
Sister Grimm

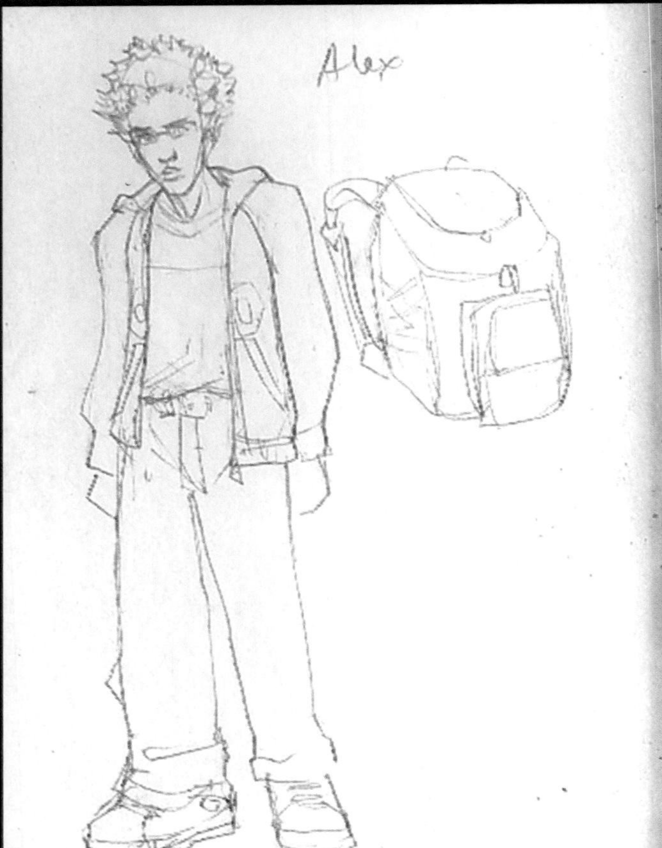
Alex

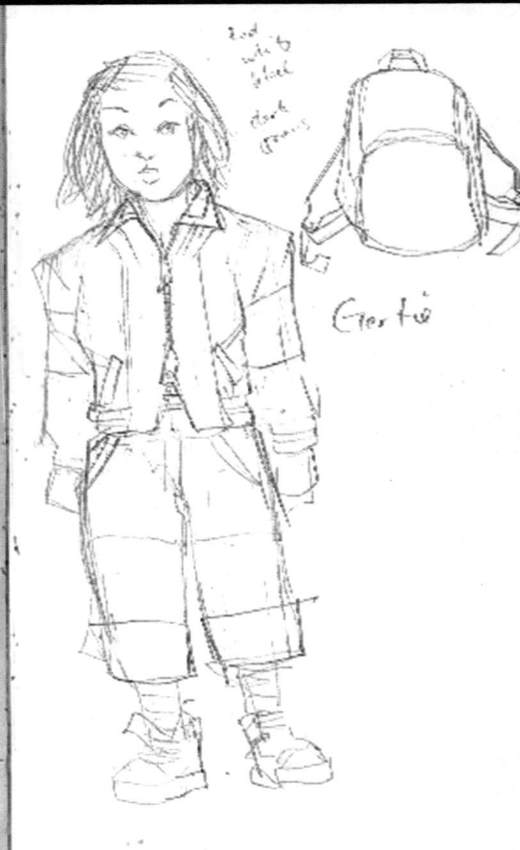
Gertie

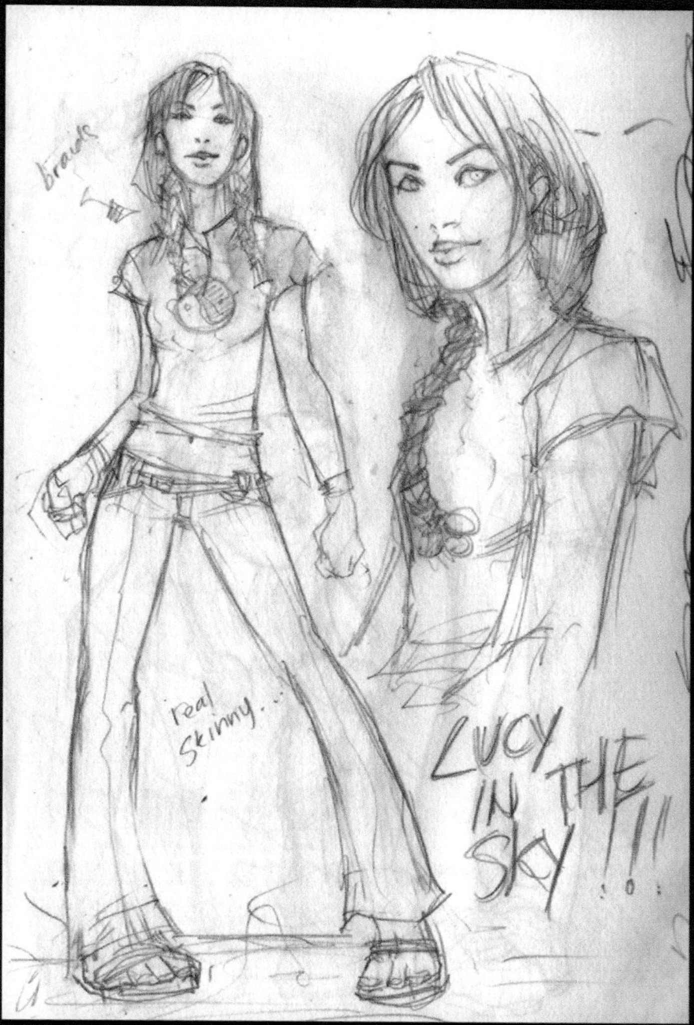
braids
real skinny...
LUCY IN THE SKY!!

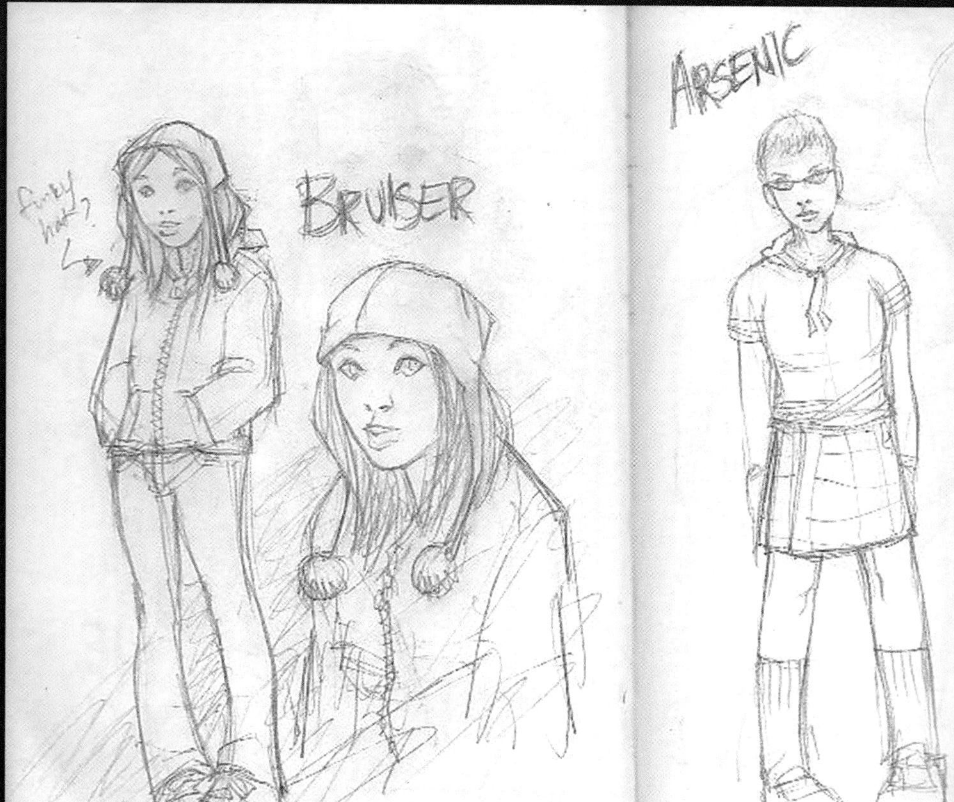
funky hat?
BRUISER
ARSENIC

PROMOTIONAL SKETCHES BY ADRIAN ALPHONA

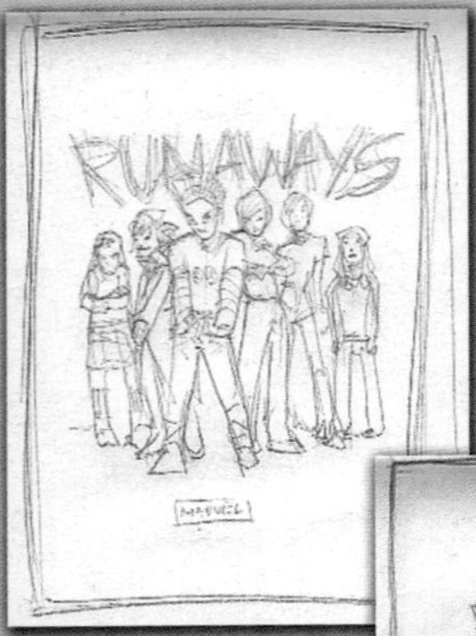
RUNAWAYS
MARVEL

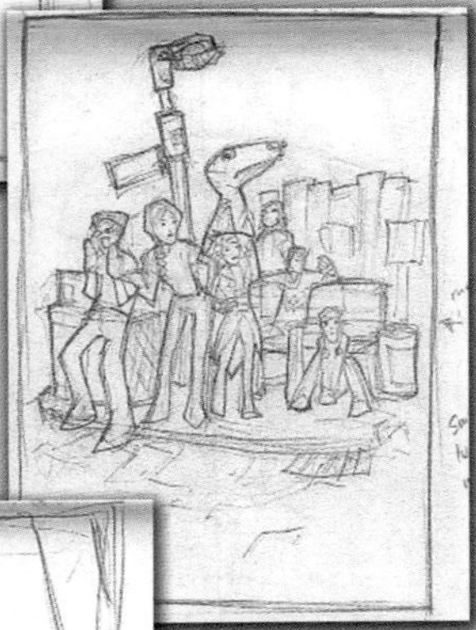

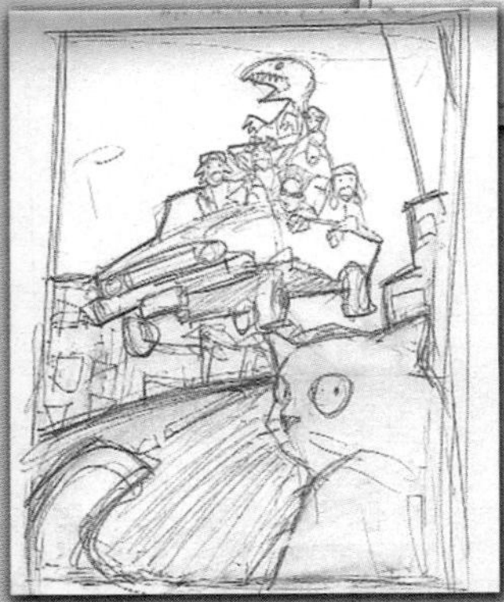

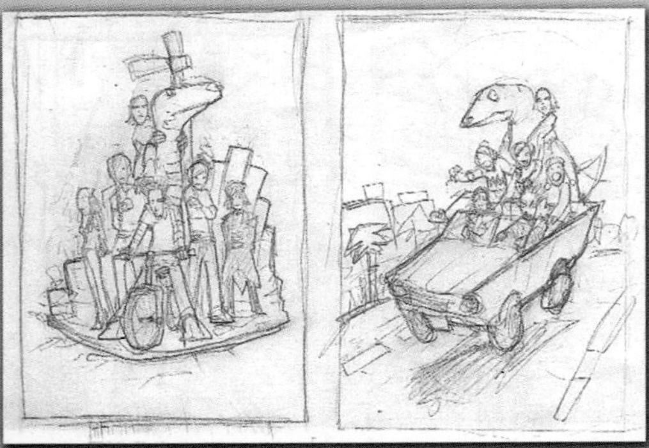

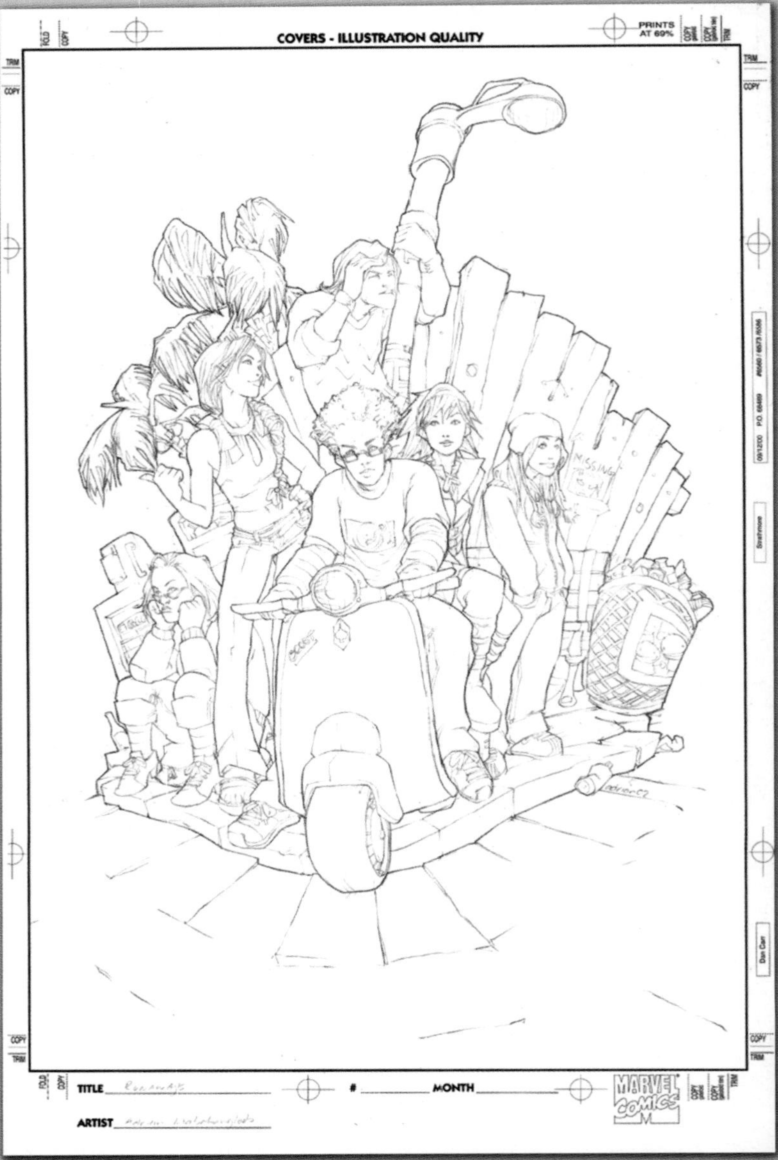
COVERS - ILLUSTRATION QUALITY
PRINTS AT 69%
TRIM
COPY
FOLD
MISSING
TITLE
#
MONTH
ARTIST
MARVEL COMICS

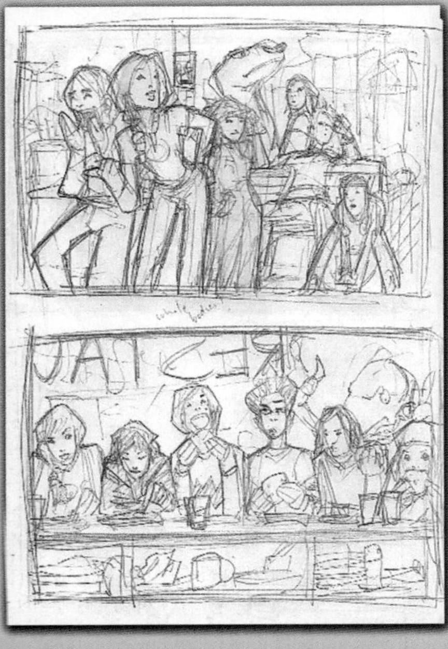

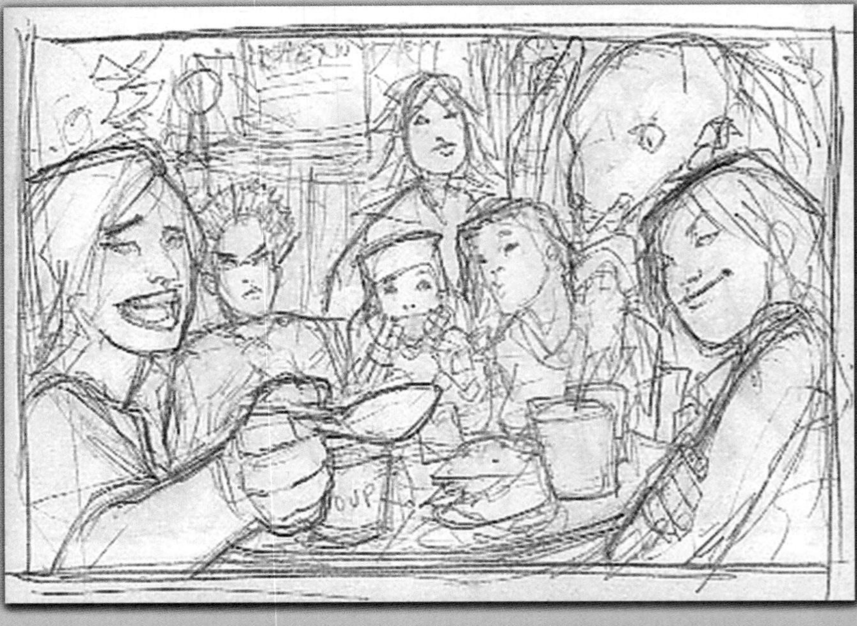

PROMOTIONAL ART BY ADRIAN ALPHONA

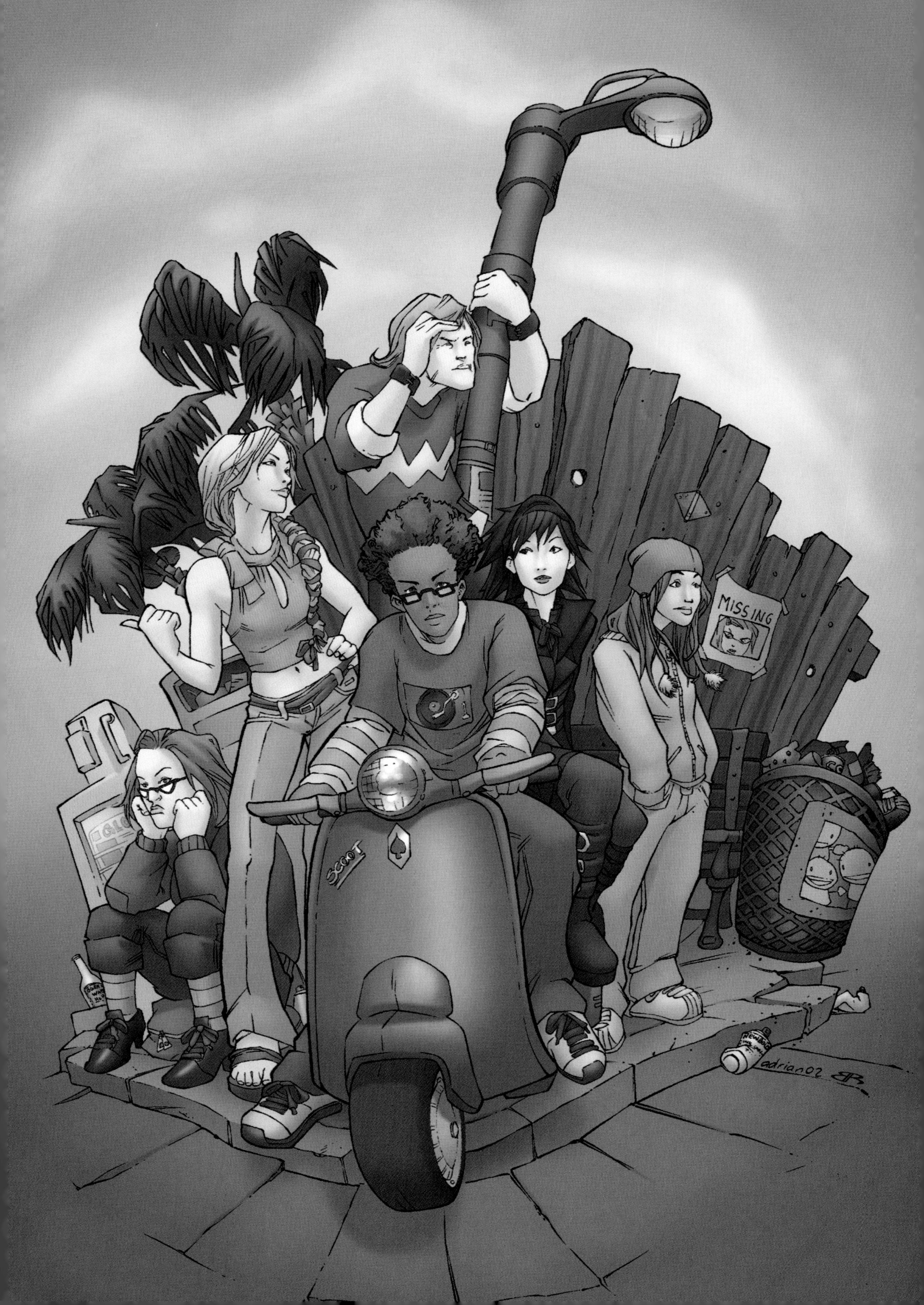
MISSING
SCOOT
adrian02

BRIAN K. VAUGHAN

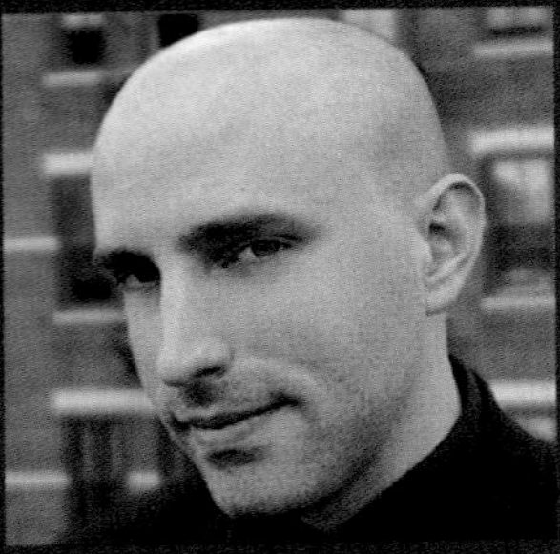

BRIAN K. VAUGHAN

Having written comics professionally since he was a film school nerd at NYU, Brian K. Vaughan is the co-creator of several critically acclaimed series, including *Y: The Last Man*, *Ex Machina*, *The Hood*, and of course, *Runaways*. Born in Cleveland in 1976, Brian currently resides in California with his playwright wife, though he looks forward to leaving the evil home of the villainous Pride soon.

Brian pretended to run away when he was seven years old, though he really just hid behind a couch and waited patiently to hear how concerned his parents would be over his disappearance. Much to his disappointment, for at least the next twelve hours, his mom and dad went about their lives as if nothing were different. That was most likely the day that *Runaways* was born. (Brian's older brother swears that this story is completely imagined, but when has Brian ever lied?)

If you'd like to know about BKV and his neuroses, please stop by his geektastic website at www.bkv.tv.

ADRIAN ALPHONA

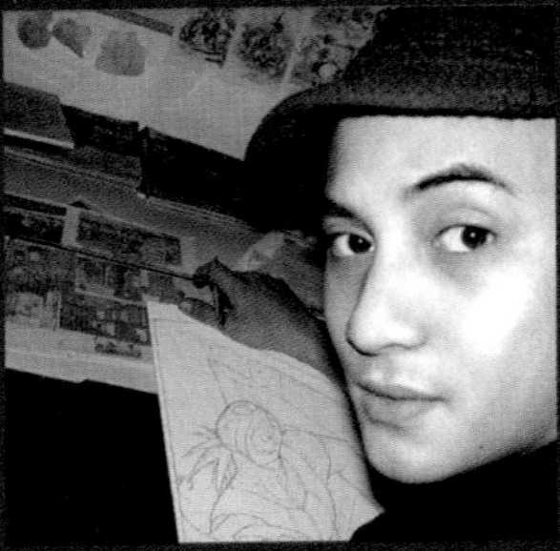

ADRIAN ALPHONA

Runaways represents Canadian artist Adrian Alphona's first comic-book assignment. Alphona, who studied graphic design at George Brown College in Toronto, has been hailed as "the smartest young artist working today" by *Runaways* collaborator Brian K. Vaughan. As a member of the Toronto-based Bright Anvil Studios, Alphona's work is featured on the art collective's website, www.brightanvil.com. Alphona is the regular artist on a new volume of *Runaways* with Vaughan, continuing the monthly adventures of this fan-favorite Marvel Comics teen team.

CRAIG YEUNG

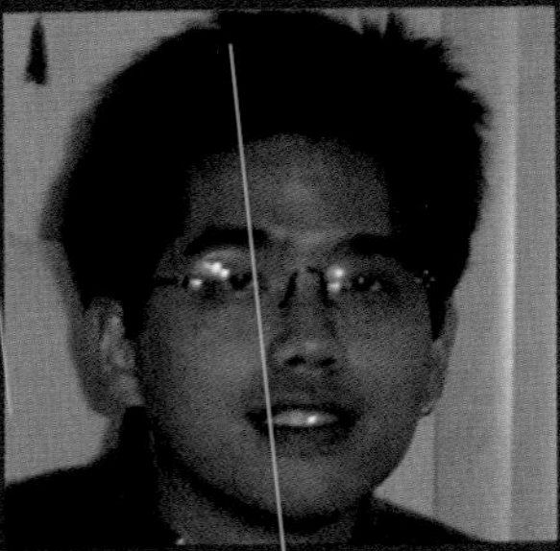

CRAIG YEUNG

Craig Yeung was born and raised in Toronto ON, Canada. After getting his Bachelor's degree, he went back to Ontario College of Art to pursue his love of comics and visual arts. His previous works include *Outlaw 7*, *Buffy the Vampire Slayer*, *Warhammer Monthly*, *Uncanny X-Men*, and *Marvel Age Spider-Man*. Craig currently works out of Bright Anvil Studios (www.brightanvil.com).

CHRISTINA STRAIN

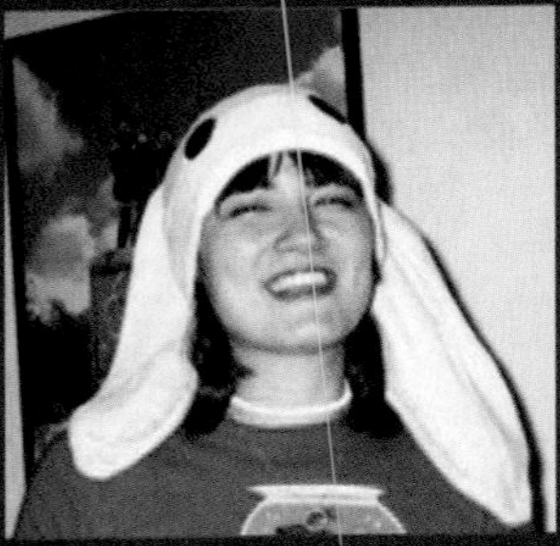

CHRISTINA STRAIN

Once upon a time, there was a princess who colored for Crossgen. Two months later, Crossgen left her with a new and expensive lease on an apartment. Then she met a stable boy named Erik Ko who introduced her to two fairy godmothers — C.B. and MacKenzie. These two kind spirits granted Christina her wish to continue coloring and provided her with a brand new sparkly pair of magical shackles called *Runaways* and *Mary Jane*. The two shackles make her expensive apartment a little less expensive and feed her and her stable of pets on occasion. She wouldn't have it any other way.

JO CHEN

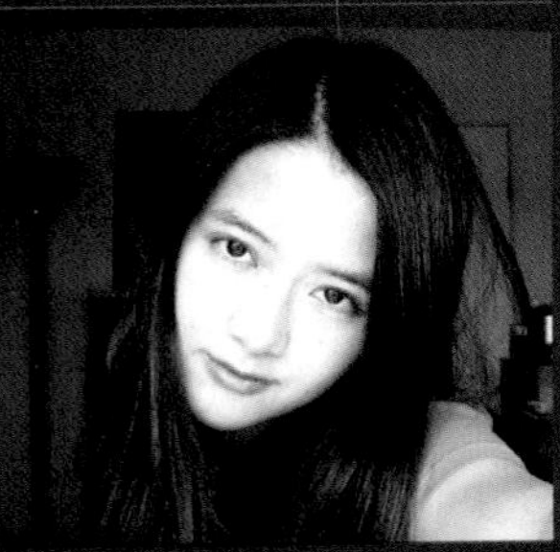

JO CHEN

Born in Taipei, Taiwan on the 4th of July, Jo Chen began working in comics professionally at age 14, when Da Ran Publishing underwrote her comic group's first volume of short stories. Since immigrating to the U.S. with her family in 1994, she has continued to work steadily in the comic book industries in both hemispheres, publishing her double volume manga *The Other Side of the Mirror* in Asia, while establishing herself in the U.S. as a commodity with the majors.

In the intervening years, Jo has produced interiors and cover art for such series as Wildstorm's *Robotech* and *Racer X*, part of its successful Speed Racer series, Dreamwave's *Darkminds Macropolis*, D.C. Comics' *Robin and The Demon*, Vertigo's *Fight For Tomorrow*, UDON's *Street Fighter*, Top Cow's *Battle of the Planets*, Marvel's *Taskmaster*, *Thor: Son of Asgard* and *Runaways*, and has most recently collaborated with Joss Whedon, the creator of *Buffy the Vampire Slayer*, and Dark Horse Comics on work for *Serenity*, as a tie-in with the release of the motion picture. She is now hard at work with writer Brian K. Vaughan and editor MacKenzie Cadenhead on the final covers for the *Runaways* second series. When Jo has a few moments to spare, she works on interiors for her doujin *Cruel to be Kind*, fleshes out character designs for her Chinese-mythological saga *The Specter King* and updates her website http://www.jo-chen.com.

TAKESHI MIYAZAWA

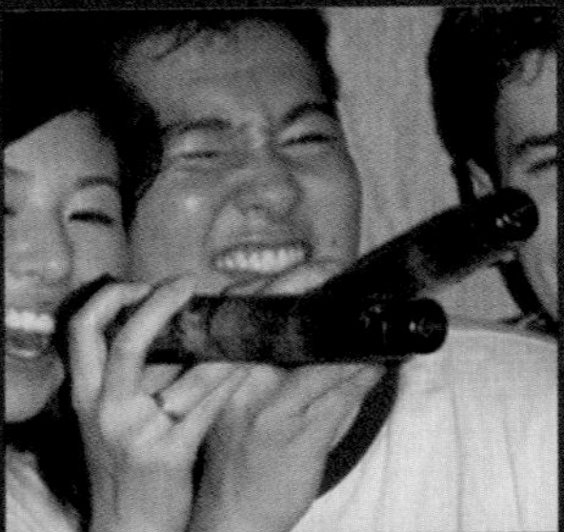

TAKESHI MIYAZAWA

Artist Takeshi Miyazawa broke into the industry after his two self-published mini-comics attracted the attention of writer J. Torres. Following his collaboration with Torres on *Sidekicks*, Miyazawa earned an assignment on *Mary Jane*, featuring Peter Parker's longtime girlfriend in her own solo series for Marvel Comics. Miyazawa has also applied his artistic talents to *Robotech: Invasion*, as well as strips for *Nylon* and *Spin* magazine. In addition to his printed work, Miyazawa is the co-creator of the web-exclusive BFX Project comic on bfxproject2.com.